Social network analysis is used widely in the social and behavioral sciences, as well as in economics, marketing, and industrial engineering. The social network perspective focuses on relationships among social entities; examples include communications among members of a group, economic transactions between corporations, and trade or treaties among nations. The focus on relationships is an important addition to standard social and behavioral research, which is primarily concerned with attributes of the social units.

Social Network Analysis: Methods and Applications reviews and discusses methods for the analysis of social networks with a focus on applications of these methods to many substantive examples. The book is organized into six parts. The introductory chapters give an overview of the social network perspective and describe different kinds of social network data. The second part discusses formal representations for social networks, including notations, graph theory, and matrix operations. The third part covers structural and locational properties of social networks, including centrality, prestige, prominence, structural balance, clusterability, cohesive subgroups, and affiliation networks. The fourth part examines methods for social network roles and positions and includes discussions of structural equivalence, blockmodels, and relational algebras. The properties of dyads and triads are covered in the fifth part of the book, and the final part discusses statistical methods for social networks.

Social Network Analysis: Methods and Applications is a reference book that can be used by those who want a comprehensive review of network methods, or by researchers who have gathered network data and want to find the most appropriate method by which to analyze them. It is also intended for use as a textbook, as it is the first book to provide comprehensive coverage of the methodology and applications of the field.

SOCIAL NETWORK ANALYSIS

Structural analysis in the social sciences

Mark Granovetter, editor

Other books in the series:

The series *Structural Analysis in the Social Sciences* presents approaches that explain social behavior and institutions by reference to *relations* among such concrete entities as persons and organizations. This contrasts with at least four other popular strategies: (a) reductionist attempts to explain by a focus on individuals alone; (b) explanations stressing the causal primacy of such abstract concepts as ideas, values, mental harmonies, and cognitive maps (thus, "structuralism" on the Continent should be distinguished from structural analysis in the present sense); (c) technological and material determinism; (d) explanations using "variables" as the main analytic concepts (as in the "structural equation" models that dominated much of the sociology of the 1970s), where structure is that connecting variables rather than actual social entities.

The social network approach is an important example of the strategy of structural analysis; the series also draws on social science theory and research that is not framed explicitly in network terms, but stresses the importance of relations rather than the atomization of reductionism or the determinism of ideas, technology, or material conditions. Though the structural perspective has become extremely popular and influential in all the social sciences, it does not have a coherent identity, and no series yet pulls together such work under a single rubric. By bringing the achievements of structurally oriented scholars to a wider public, the *Structural Analysis* series hopes to encourage the use of this very fruitful approach.

Mark Granovetter

SOCIAL NETWORK ANALYSIS: METHODS AND APPLICATIONS

STANLEY WASSERMAN
University of Illinois

KATHERINE FAUST
University of South Carolina

CAMBRIDGE
UNIVERSITY PRESS

CAMBRIDGE UNIVERSITY PRESS
Cambridge, New York, Melbourne, Madrid, Cape Town, Singapore, São Paulo

Cambridge University Press
40 West 20th Street, New York, NY 10011–4211, USA
www.cambridge.org
Information on this title:www.cambridge.org/9780521382694

First published 1994
Reprinted 1995
Reprinted with corrections 1997
13th printing 2005

Printed in the United States of America

A catalogue record for this book is available from the British Library.

ISBN-13   978-0-521-38269-4 hardback
ISBN-10   0-521-38269-6 hardback

ISBN-13   978-0-521-38707-1 paperback
ISBN-10   0-521-38707-8 paperback

To Sarah

and

To Don and Margaret Faust

Contents

List of Tables

List of Illustrations

Preface

Our goal for this book is to present a review of network analysis methods, a reference work for researchers interested in analyzing relational data, and a text for novice social networkers looking for an overview of the field. Our hope is that this book will help researchers to become aware of the very wide range of social network methods, to understand the theoretical motivations behind these approaches, to appreciate the wealth of social network applications, and to find some guidance in selecting the most appropriate methods for a given research application.

The last decade has seen the publication of several books and edited volumes dealing with aspects of social network theory, application, and method. However, none of these books presents a comprehensive discussion of social network methodology. We hope that this book will fill this gap. The theoretical basis for the network perspective has been extensively outlined in books by Berkowitz (1982) and Burt (1982). Because these provide good theoretical overviews, we will not dwell on theoretical advances in social network research, except as they pertain directly to network methods. In addition, there are several collections of papers that apply network ideas to substantive research problems (Leinhardt 1977; Holland and Leinhardt 1979; Marsden and Lin 1982; Wellman and Berkowitz 1988; Breiger 1990a; Hiramatsu 1990; Weesie and Flap 1990; Wasserman and Galaskiewicz 1994). These collections include foundational works in network analysis and examples of applications from a range of disciplines.

Finally, some books have presented collections of readings on special topics in network methods (for example, Burt and Minor 1983), papers on current methodological advances (for example, Freeman, White and Romney 1989), or elementary discussions of basic topics in network analysis (for example, Knoke and Kuklinski 1982; Scott 1992). And there are a number of monographs and articles reviewing network methodology (Northway 1952; Lindzey and Borgatta 1954; Mitchell 1974; Roistacher 1974; Freeman 1976; Burt 1978b; Feger, Hummell, Pappi, Sodeur, and Ziegler 1978; Klovdahl 1979; Niesmoller and Schijf 1980; Burt 1980; Alba 1981; Frank 1981; Wellman 1983; Rice and Richards 1985; Scott 1988; Wellman 1988a; Wellman and Berkowitz 1988; Marsden 1990b). Very recently, a number of books have begun to appear, discussing advanced methodological topics. Hage and Harary (1983) is a good example from this genre; Boyd (1990), Breiger (1991), and Pattison (1993) introduce the reader to other specialized topics.

However, the researcher seeking to understand network analysis is left with a void between the elementary discussions and sophisticated analytic presentations since none of these books provides a unified discussion of network methodology. As mentioned, we intend this book to fill that void by presenting a broad, comprehensive, and, we hope, complete discussion of network analysis methodology.

There are many people to thank for their help in making this book a reality. Mark Granovetter, the editor of this series for Cambridge University Press, was a source of encouragement throughout the many years that we spent revising the manuscript. Lin Freeman, Ron Breiger, and Peter Marsden reviewed earlier versions of the book for Cambridge, and made many, many suggestions for improvement. Alaina Michaelson deserves much gratitude for actually reading the *entire* manuscript during the 1990–1991 academic year. Sue Freeman, Joe Galaskiewicz, Nigel Hopkins, Larry Hubert, Pip Pattison, Kim Romney, and Tom Snijders read various chapters, and had many helpful comments. Colleagues at the University of South Carolina Department of Sociology (John Skvoretz, Pat Nolan, Dave Willer, Shelley Smith, Jimy Sanders, Lala Steelman, and Steve Borgatti) were a source of inspiration, as were Phipps Arabie, Frank Romo, and Harrison White. Dave Krackhardt, John Padgett, Russ Bernard, Lin Freeman, and Joe Galaskiewicz shared data with us. Our students Carolyn Anderson, Mike Walker, Diane Payne, Laura Koehly, Shannon Morrison, and Melissa Abboushi were wonderful assistants. Jill Grace provided library assistance. We also thank the authors of the computer programs we used to help analyze the data in the book — Karel Sprenger and Frans Stokman (*GRADAP*), Ron Breiger (*ROLE*), Noah Friedkin (*SNAPS*), Ron Burt (*STRUCTURE*), and Lin Freeman, Steve Borgatti, and Martin Everett (*UCINET*). And, of course, we are extremely grateful to Allison, Drew, Eliot, Keith, Ross, and Sarah for their notoriety!

Emily Loose, our first editor at Cambridge, was always helpful in finding ways to speed up the process of getting this book into print. Elizabeth Neal and Pauline Ireland at Cambridge helped us during the last stages of production. Hank Heitowit, of the Interuniversity Consortium for Political and Social Research at the University of Michigan (Ann Arbor) made it possible for us to teach a course, Social Network Analysis, for the last seven years in their Summer Program in Quantitative Methods. The students at ICPSR, as well as the many students at the University of Illinois at Urbana-Champaign, the University of South Carolina, American University, and various workshops we have given deserve special recognition. And lastly, we thank Murray Aborn, Jim Blackman, Sally Nerlove, and Cheryl Eavey at the National Science Foundation for financial support over the years (most recently, via NSF Grant #SBR93-10184 to the University of Illinois).

We dedicate this book to Sarah Wasserman, and to Don Faust and Margaret Faust, without whom it would not have been possible.

Stanley Wasserman
Grand Rivers, Kentucky

Katherine Faust
Shaver Lake, California

August, 1993

Note to Revised Printing: We thank our readers for finding the errors (both typographical and otherwise) in the original that have been corrected in this revised printing.

September, 1996

Part I
Networks, Relations, and Structure

1
Social Network Analysis in the Social and Behavioral Sciences

The notion of a *social network* and the methods of social network analysis have attracted considerable interest and curiosity from the social and behavioral science community in recent decades. Much of this interest can be attributed to the appealing focus of social network analysis on *relationships* among social entities, and on the patterns and implications of these relationships. Many researchers have realized that the network perspective allows new leverage for answering standard social and behavioral science research questions by giving precise formal definition to aspects of the political, economic, or social structural environment. From the view of social network analysis, the social environment can be expressed as patterns or regularities in relationships among interacting units. We will refer to the presence of regular patterns in relationship as *structure*. Throughout this book, we will refer to quantities that measure structure as *structural variables*. As the reader will see from the diversity of examples that we discuss, the relationships may be of many sorts: economic, political, interactional, or affective, to name but a few. The focus on relations, and the patterns of relations, requires a set of methods and analytic concepts that are distinct from the methods of traditional statistics and data analysis. The concepts, methods, and applications of social network analysis are the topic of this book.

The focus of this book is on methods and models for analyzing social network data. To an extent perhaps unequaled in most other social science disciplines, social network methods have developed over the past fifty years as an integral part of advances in social theory, empirical research, and formal mathematics and statistics. Many of the key structural measures and notions of social network analysis grew out of keen insights of researchers seeking to describe empirical phenomena and are motivated by central concepts in social theory. In addition, methods have developed to test specific hypotheses about network structural properties arising in the course of substantive research and model testing. The result of this symbiotic relationship between theory and method is a strong grounding of network analytic techniques in both application and theory. In the following sections we review the history and theory of social network analysis from the perspective of the development of methodology.

Since our goal in this book is to provide a compendium of methods and applications for both veteran social network analysts, and for naive but curious people from diverse research traditions, it is worth taking some time at the outset to lay the foundations for the social network perspective.

1.1 The Social Networks Perspective

In this section we introduce social network analysis as a distinct research perspective within the social and behavioral sciences; distinct because social network analysis is based on an assumption of the importance of relationships among interacting units. The social network perspective encompasses theories, models, and applications that are expressed in terms of relational concepts or processes. That is, relations defined by linkages among units are a fundamental component of network theories. Along with growing interest and increased use of network analysis has come a consensus about the central principles underlying the network perspective. These principles distinguish social network analysis from other research approaches (see Wellman 1988a, for example). In addition to the use of relational concepts, we note the following as being important:

- Actors and their actions are viewed as interdependent rather than independent, autonomous units
- Relational ties (linkages) between actors are channels for transfer or "flow" of resources (either material or nonmaterial)
- Network models focusing on individuals view the network structural environment as providing opportunities for or constraints on individual action
- Network models conceptualize structure (social, economic, political, and so forth) as lasting patterns of relations among actors

In this section we discuss these principles further and illustrate how the social network perspective differs from alternative perspectives in practice. Of critical importance for the development of methods for social network analysis is the fact that the unit of analysis in network analysis is not the individual, but an entity consisting of a collection of individuals and the linkages among them. Network methods focus on dyads (two actors and their ties), triads (three actors and their ties), or larger systems (subgroups of individuals, or entire networks). Therefore, special methods are necessary.

Formal Descriptions. Network analysis enters into the process of model development, specification, and testing in a number of ways: to express relationally defined theoretical concepts by providing formal definitions, measures and descriptions, to evaluate models and theories in which key concepts and propositions are expressed as relational processes or structural outcomes, or to provide statistical analyses of multirelational systems. In this first, descriptive context, network analysis provides a vocabulary and set of formal definitions for expressing theoretical concepts and properties. Examples of theoretical concepts (properties) for which network analysis provides explicit definitions will be discussed shortly.

Model and Theory Evaluation and Testing. Alternatively, network models may be used to test theories about relational processes or structures. Such theories posit specific structural outcomes which may then be evaluated against observed network data. For example, suppose one posits that tendencies toward reciprocation of support or exchange of materials between families in a community should arise frequently. Such a supposition can be tested by adopting a statistical model, and studying how frequently such tendencies arise empirically.

The key feature of social network theories or propositions is that they require concepts, definitions and processes in which social units are linked to one another by various relations. Both statistical and descriptive uses of network analysis are distinct from more standard social science analysis and require concepts and analytic procedures that are different from traditional statistics and data analysis.

Some Background and Examples. The network perspective has proved fruitful in a wide range of social and behavioral science disciplines. Many topics that have traditionally interested social scientists can be thought of in relational or social network analytic terms. Some of the topics that have been studied by network analysts are:

- Occupational mobility (Breiger 1981c, 1990a)

- The impact of urbanization on individual well-being (Fischer 1982)
- The world political and economic system (Snyder and Kick 1979; Nemeth and Smith 1985)
- Community elite decision making (Laumann, Marsden, and Galaskiewicz 1977; Laumann and Pappi 1973)
- Social support (Gottlieb 1981; Lin, Woelfel, and Light 1986; Kadushin 1966; Wellman, Carrington, and Hall 1988; Wellman and Wortley 1990)
- Community (Wellman 1979)
- Group problem solving (Bavelas 1950; Bavelas and Barrett 1951; Leavitt 1951)
- Diffusion and adoption of innovations (Coleman, Katz, and Menzel 1957, 1966; Rogers 1979)
- Corporate interlocking (Levine 1972; Mintz and Schwartz 1981a, 1981b; Mizruchi and Schwartz 1987, and references)
- Belief systems (Erickson 1988)
- Cognition or social perception (Krackhardt 1987a; Freeman, Romney, and Freeman 1987)
- Markets (Berkowitz 1988; Burt 1988b; White 1981, 1988; Leifer and White 1987)
- Sociology of science (Mullins 1973; Mullins, Hargens, Hecht, and Kick 1977; Crane 1972; Burt 1978/79a; Michaelson 1990, 1991; Doreian and Fararo 1985)
- Exchange and power (Cook and Emerson 1978; Cook, Emerson, Gillmore, and Yamagishi 1983; Cook 1987; Markovsky, Willer, and Patton 1988)
- Consensus and social influence (Friedkin 1986; Friedkin and Cook 1990; Doreian 1981; Marsden 1990a)
- Coalition formation (Kapferer 1969; Thurman 1980; Zachary 1977)

The fundamental difference between a social network explanation and a non-network explanation of a process is the inclusion of concepts and information on *relationships* among units in a study. Theoretical concepts are relational, pertinent data are relational, and critical tests use distributions of relational properties. Whether the model employed seeks to understand individual action in the context of structured relationships, or studies structures directly, network analysis operationalizes structures in terms of networks of linkages among units. Regularities or patterns in interactions give rise to *structures*. "Standard" social science perspectives usually ignore the relational information.

Let us explore a couple of examples. Suppose we are interested in corporate behavior in a large, metropolitan area, for example, the level and types of monetary support given to local non-profit and charitable organizations (see, for example, Galaskiewicz 1985). Standard social and economic science approaches would first define a population of relevant units (corporations), take a random sample of them (if the population is quite large), and then measure a variety of characteristics (such as size, industry, profitability, level of support for local charities or other non-profit organizations, and so forth).

The key assumption here is that the behavior of a specific unit does not influence any other units. However, network theorists take exception to this assumption. It does not take much insight to realize that there are many ways that corporations decide to do the things they do (such as support non-profits with donations). Corporations (and other such actors) tend to look at the behaviors of other actors, and even attempt to mimic each other. In order to get a complete description of this behavior, we must look at corporate to corporate relationships, such as membership on each others' boards of directors, acquaintanceships of corporate officers, joint business dealings, and other relational variables. In brief, one needs a network perspective to fully understand and model this phenomenon.

As another example, consider a social psychologist studying how groups make decisions and reach consensus (Hastie, Penrod, and Pennington 1983; Friedkin and Cook 1990; Davis 1973). The group might be a jury trying to reach a verdict, or a committee trying to allocate funds. Focusing just on the outcome of this decision, as many researchers do, is quite limiting. One really should look how members influence each other in order to make a decision or fail to reach consensus. A network approach to this study would look at interactions among group members in order to better understand the decision-making process. The influences a group member has on his/her fellow members are quite important to the process. Ignoring these influences gives an incomplete picture.

The network perspective differs in fundamental ways from standard social and behavioral science research and methods. Rather than focusing on attributes of autonomous individual units, the associations among these attributes, or the usefulness of one or more attributes for predicting the level of another attribute, the social network perspective views characteristics of the social units as arising out of structural or relational processes or focuses on properties of the relational systems themselves. The task is to understand properties of the social (economic or political) structural environment, and how these structural properties influence observed characteristics and associations among characteristics. As Collins (1988) has so aptly pointed out in his review of network theory,

> Social life is relational; it's only because, say, blacks and whites occupy particular kinds of patterns in networks in relation to each other that "race" becomes an important variable. (page 413)

In social network analysis the observed attributes of social actors (such as race or ethnicity of people, or size or productivity of collective bodies such as corporations or nation-states) are understood in terms of patterns or structures of ties among the units. Relational ties among actors are primary and attributes of actors are secondary.

Employing a network perspective, one can also study patterns of relational structures directly without reference to attributes of the individuals involved. For example, one could study patterns of trade among nations to see whether or not the world economic system exhibits a core-periphery structure. Or, one could study friendships among high school students to see whether or not patterns of friendships can be described as systems of relatively exclusive cliques. Such analyses focus on characteristics of the network as a whole and must be studied using social network concepts.

In the network analytic framework, the ties may be any relationship existing between units; for example, kinship, material transactions, flow of resources or support, behavioral interaction, group co-memberships, or the affective evaluation of one person by another. Clearly, some types of ties will be relevant or measurable for some sorts of social units but not for others. The relationship between a pair of units is a property of the pair and not inherently a characteristic of the individual unit. For example, the number (or dollar value) of Japanese manufactured automobiles exported from Japan to the United States is part of the trade relationship between Japan and the United States, and not an intrinsic characteristic of either one country or the other. In sum, the basic unit that these relational variables are measured on is the pair of actors, not one or the other individual actors. It is important for methods described in this book, that we assume that one has measurements on interactions between all possible pairs of units (for example, trade among all pairs of nations).

It is important to contrast approaches in which networks and structural properties are central with approaches that employ network ideas and measurements in standard individual-level analyses. A common usage of network ideas is to employ network measurements, or statistics calculated from these network measurements, as variables measured at the individual actor level. These derived variables are then incorporated into a more standard "cases by variables" analysis. For example, the range of a person's social support network may be used as an actor-level variable in an analysis predicting individual mental well-being (see Kadushin 1982), or occupational status attainment (Lin and Dumin 1986; Lin, Ensel, and Vaughn 1981; Lin, Vaughn, and Ensel 1981). We view analyses such as these as auxiliary network studies. Network theories and measurements become explanatory factors or variables in understanding individual behavior. We note that such an analysis still uses individual actors as the basic modeling unit. Such analyses do not focus on the network structure or network processes directly.

Our approach in this book is that network measurements are *central*. We do not discuss how to use network measurements, statistics, model parameter estimates, and so forth, in further modeling endeavors. These usual data analytic concerns are treated in existing standard statistics and methods texts.

The Perspective. Given a collection of actors, social network analysis can be used to study the structural variables measured on actors in the set. The relational structure of a group or larger social system consists of the pattern of relationships among the collection of actors. The concept of a network emphasizes the fact that each individual has ties to other individuals, each of whom in turn is tied to a few, some, or many others, and so on. The phrase "social network" refers to the set of actors and the ties among them. The network analyst would seek to model these relationships to depict the structure of a group. One could then study the impact of this structure on the functioning of the group and/or the influence of this structure on individuals within the group.

In the example of trade among nations, information on the imports and exports among nations in the world reflects the global economic system. Here the world economic system is evidenced in the observable transactions (for example, trade, loans, foreign investment, or, perhaps, diplomatic exchange) among nations. The social network analyst could then attempt to describe regularities or patterns in the world economic system and to understand economic features of individual nations (such as rate of economic development) in terms of the nation's location in the world economic system.

Network analysis can also be used to study the process of change within a group over time. Thus, the network perspective also extends longitudinally. For example, economic transactions between nations could certainly be measured at several points in time, thereby allowing a researcher to use the network prespective to study changes in the world economic system.

The social network perspective thus has a distinctive orientation in which structures, their impact, and their evolution become the primary focus. Since structures may be behavioral, social, political, or economic, social network analysis thus allows a flexible set of concepts and methods with broad interdisciplinary appeal.

1.2 Historical and Theoretical Foundations

Social network analysis is inherently an interdisciplinary endeavor. The concepts of social network analysis developed out of a propitious meeting of social theory and application, with formal mathematical, statistical, and computing methodology. As Freeman (1984) and Marsden and Laumann (1984) have documented, both the social sciences, and mathematics and statistics have been left richer from the collaborative efforts of researchers working across disciplines.

Further, and more importantly, the central concepts of relation, network, and structure arose almost independently in several social and behavioral science disciplines. The pioneers of social network analysis came from sociology and social psychology (for example, Moreno, Cartwright, Newcomb, Bavelas) and anthropology (Barnes, Mitchell). In fact, many people attribute the first use of the term "social network" to Barnes (1954). The notion of a network of relations linking social entities, or of webs or ties among social units emanating through society, has found wide expression throughout the social sciences. Furthermore, many of the structural principles of network analysis developed as researchers tried to solve empirical and/or theoretical research puzzles. The fact that so many researchers, from such different disciplines, almost simultaneously discovered the network perspective is not surprising. Its utility is great, and the problems that can be answered with it are numerous, spanning a broad range of disciplines.

In this section we briefly comment on the historical, empirical, and theoretical bases of social network methodology. Some authors have seen network analysis as a collection of analytic procedures that are somewhat divorced from the main theoretical and empirical concerns of social research. Perhaps a particular network method may appear to lack theoretical focus because it can be applied to such a wide range of substantive problems from many different contexts. In contrast, we argue that much network methodology arose as social scientists in a range of disciplines struggled to make sense of empirical data and grappled with theoretical issues. Therefore, network analysis, rather than being an unrelated collection of methods, is grounded in important social phenomena and theoretical concepts.

Social network analysis also provides a formal, conceptual means for thinking about the social world. As Freeman (1984) has so convincingly argued, the methods of social network analysis provide formal statements about social properties and processes. Further, these concepts must be defined in precise and consistent ways. Once these concepts have been defined precisely, one can reason logically about the social world. Freeman cites *group* and *social role* as two central ideas which, until they were given formal definitions in network terms, could only serve as "sensitizing concepts." The payoff of mathematical statements of social concepts is the development of testable process models and explanatory theories. We are in full agreement with Leinhardt's statement that "it is not possible to build effective explanatory theories using metaphors" (Leinhardt 1977, page xiv). We expand on this argument in the next section.

1.2.1 Empirical Motivations

It is rare that a methodological technique is referred to as an "invention" but that is how Moreno described his early 1930's invention, the *sociogram* (Moreno 1953). This innovation, developed by Moreno along with Jennings, marked the beginning of *sociometry* (the precursor to social network analysis and much of social psychology). Starting at this time point, this book summarizes over a half-century of work in network analysis. There is wide agreement among social scientists that Moreno was the founder of the field of sociometry — the measurement of interpersonal relations in small groups — and the inspiration for the first two decades of research into the structure of small groups. Driven by an interest in understanding human social and psychological behavior, especially group dynamics, Moreno was led to invent a means for depicting the interpersonal structure of groups: the sociogram. A sociogram is a picture in which people (or more generally, any social units) are represented as points in two-dimensional space, and relationships among pairs of people are represented by lines linking the corresponding points. Moreno claimed that "before the advent of sociometry no one knew what the interpersonal structure of a group 'precisely' looked like" (1953, page lvi). This invention was revealed to the public in April 1933 at a convention of medical scholars, and was found to be so intriguing that the story was immediately picked up by *The New York Times* (April 3, 1933, page 17), and carried in newspapers across the United States. Moreno's interest went far beyond mere depiction. It was this need to model important social phenomena that led to two of the mainstays of social network analysis: a visual display of group structure, and a probabilistic model of structural outcomes.

Visual displays including sociograms and two or higher dimensional representations continue to be widely used by network analysts (see Klovdahl 1986; Woelfel, Fink, Serota, Barnett, Holmes, Cody, Saltiel, Marlier, and Gillham 1977). Two and sometimes three-dimensional spatial representations (using multidimensional scaling) have proved quite useful for presenting structures of influence among community elites (Laumann and Pappi 1976; Laumann and Knoke 1987), corporate interlocks (Levine 1972), role structures in groups (Breiger, Boorman, and Arabie 1975; Burt 1976, 1982), and interaction patterns in small groups (Romney and Faust 1982; Freeman, Freeman, and Michaelson 1989).

Recognition that sociograms could be used to study social structure led to a rapid introduction of analytic techniques. The history of this development is nicely reviewed by Harary, Norman, and Cartwright (1965), who themselves helped pioneer this development. At the same time, methodologists discovered that matrices could be used to represent social network data. These recognitions and discoveries brought the power of mathematics to the study of social systems. Forsyth and Katz (1946), Katz (1947), Luce and Perry (1949), Bock and Husain (1950, 1952), and Harary and Norman (1953) were the first to use matrices in novel methods for the study of social networks.

Other researchers also found inspiration for network ideas in the course of empirical research. In the mid-1950's, anthropologists studying urbanization (especially British anthropologists — such as Mitchell and Barnes) found that the traditional approach of describing social organization in terms of institutions (economics, religion, politics, kinship, etc.) was not sufficient for understanding the behavior of individuals in complex societies (Barnes 1954; Bott 1957; Mitchell 1969; Boissevain 1968;

Kapferer 1969). Furthermore, as anthropologists turned their attention to "complex" societies, they found that new concepts were necessary in order to understand the fluid social interactions they observed in the course of ethnographic field work (for example, see Barnes 1954, 1969a; Boissevain 1968; also Mitchell 1969; and Boissevain and Mitchell 1973, and papers therein). Barnes (1972), Whitten and Wolfe (1973), Mitchell (1974), Wolfe (1978), Foster (1978/79), and others provide excellent reviews of the history of social network ideas in anthropology. Many of the current formal concepts in social network analysis, for example, density (Bott 1957), span (Thurman 1980), connectedness, clusterability, and multiplexity (Kapferer 1969), were introduced in the 1950's and 1960's as ways to describe properties of social structures and individual social environments. Network analysis provided both a departure in theoretical perspective and a way of talking about social phenomena which were not easily defined using then current terminology.

Many social psychologists of the 1940's and 1950's found experimental structures useful for studying group processes (Leavitt 1949, 1951; Bavelas 1948, 1950; Smith 1950; and many others; see Freeman, Roeder, and Mulholland 1980, for a review). The experimentally designed communication structures employed by these researchers lent themselves naturally to graphical representations using points to depict actors and lines to depict channels of communication. Key insights from this research program indicated that there were both important properties of group structures and properties of individual positions within these structures. The theory of the impact of structural arrangement on group problem solving and individual performance required formal statements of the structural properties of these experimental arrangements. Structural properties found by these researchers include the notions of actor *centrality* and group *centralization*.

Clearly, important empirical tendencies led to important new, network methods. Very important findings of tendencies toward reciprocity or *mutuality* of positive affect, structural balance, and transitivity, discovered early in network analysis, have had a profound impact on the study of social structure. Bronfenbenner (1943) and Moreno and Jennings (1945) were the first to study such tendencies quantitatively.

1.2.2 Theoretical Motivations

Theoretical notions have also provided impetus for development of network methods. Here, we explore some of the theoretical concepts that have motivated the development of specific network analysis methods. Among the important examples are: social group, isolate, popularity, liaison, prestige, balance, transitivity, clique, subgroup, social cohesion, social position, social role, reciprocity, mutuality, exchange, influence, dominance, conformity. We briefly introduce some of these ideas below, and discuss them all in more detail as they arise in later chapters.

Conceptions of social group have led to several related lines of methodological development. Sociologists have used the phrase "social group" in numerous and imprecise ways. Social network researchers have taken specific aspects of the theoretical idea of social group to develop more precise social network definitions. Among the more influential network group ideas are: the graph theoretic entity of a *clique* and its generalizations (Luce and Perry 1949; Alba 1973; Seidman and Foster 1978a; Mokken 1979; and Freeman 1988); the notion of an interacting community (see Sailer and Gaulin 1984); and social circles and structures of affiliation (Kadushin 1966; Feld 1981; Breiger 1974; Levine 1972; McPherson 1982). The range and number of mathematical definitions of "group" highlights the usefulness of using network concepts to specify exact properties of theoretical concepts.

Another important theoretical concept, *structural balance*, was postulated by Heider during the 1940's (Heider 1946), and later Newcomb (1953). Balanced relations were quite common in empirical work; consequently, theorists were quick to pose theories about why such things occurred so frequently. This concept led to a very active thirty-year period of empirical, theoretical, and quantitative research on triples of individuals.

Balance theory was quantified by mathematicians using graph theoretical concepts (Harary 1953, 1955b). Balance theory also influenced the development of a large number of structural theories, including *transitivity*, another theory postulated at the level of a triple of individuals.

The related notions of social *role*, social *status*, and social *position* have spawned a wide range of network analysis methods. Lorrain and White were among the first social network analysts to express in social network terms the notion of social role (Lorrain and White 1971). Their foundational work on the mathematical property of *structural equivalence* (individuals who have identical ties to and from all others in a network) expressed the social concept of role in a formal mathematical procedure. Much of the subsequent work on this topic has centered on appropriate conceptualizations of notions of position (Burt 1976; Faust 1988; Borgatti and Everett 1992a) or role (White and Reitz 1983, 1989;

Winship and Mandel 1983; Breiger and Pattison 1986) in social network terms.

1.2.3 Mathematical Motivations

Early in the theoretical development of social network analysis, researchers found use for mathematical models. Beginning in the 1940's with attempts to quantify tendencies toward *reciprocity*, social network analysts have been frequent users and strong proponents of quantitative analytical approaches. The three major mathematical foundations of network methods are graph theory, statistical and probability theory, and algebraic models. Early sociometricians discovered graph theory and distributions for random graphs (for example, the work of Moreno, Jennings, Criswell, Harary, and Cartwright). Mathematicians had long been interested in graphs and distributions for graphs (see Erdös and Renyi 1960, and references therein), and the more mathematical social network analysts were quick to pick up models and methods from the mathematicians. Graph theory provides both an appropriate representation of a social network and a set of concepts that can be used to study formal properties of social networks.

Statistical theory became quite important as people began to study reciprocity, mutuality, balance, and transitivity. Other researchers, particularly Katz and Powell (1955), proposed indices to measure tendencies toward reciprocation.

Interest in reciprocity, and pairs of interacting individuals, led to a focus on threesomes. Empirical and theoretical work on balance theory and transitivity motivated a variety of mathematicians and statisticians to formulate mathematical models for behavior of triples of actors. Cartwright and Harary (1956) were the first to quantify structural balance propositions, and along with Davis (1967), discussed which types of triads (triples of actors and all observed relational linkages among the actors) should and should not arise in empirical research. Davis, Holland, and Leinhardt, in a series of papers written in the 1970's, introduced a wide variety of random directed graph distributions into social network analysis, in order to test hypotheses about various structural tendencies.

During the 1980's, research on statistical models for social networks heightened. Models now exist for analyzing a wide variety of social network data. Simple log linear models of dyadic interactions are now commonly used in practice. These models are often based on Holland and Leinhardt's (1981) p_1 probability distribution for relational data.

This model can be extended to dyadic interactions that are measured on a nominal or an ordinal scale. Additional generalizations allow one to simultaneously model multivariate relational networks. Network interactions on different relations may be associated, and the interactions of one relation with others allow one to study how associated the relational variables are. In the mid-1970's, there was much interest in models for the study of networks over time. Mathematical models, both deterministic and stochastic, are now quite abundant for such study.

Statistical models are used to test theoretical propositions about networks. These models allow the processes (which generate the data) to show some error, or lack of fit, to proposed structural theories. One can then compare data to the predictions generated by the theories to determine whether or not the theories should be rejected.

Algebraic models have been widely used to study multirelational networks. These models use algebraic operations to study combinations of relations (for example, "is a friend of," "goes to for advice," and "is a friend of a friend") and have been used to study kinship systems (White 1963; Boyd 1969) and network role structures (Boorman and White 1976; Breiger and Pattison 1986; Boyd 1990; and Pattison 1993).

Social network analysis attempts to solve analytical problems that are non-standard. The data analyzed by network methods are quite different from the data typically encountered in social and behavioral sciences. In the traditional data analytic framework one assumes that one has a set of measurements taken on a set of independent units or cases; thus giving rise to the familiar "cases by variables" data array. The assumption of sampling independence of observations on individual units allows the considerable machinery of statistical analysis to be applied to a range of research questions. However, social network analysis is explicitly interested in the interrelatedness of social units. The dependencies among the units are measured with structural variables. Theories that incorporate network ideas are distinguished by propositions about the relations among social units. Such theories argue that units are not acting independently from one another, but rather influence each other. Focusing on such structural variables opens up a different range of possibilities for, and constraints on, data analysis and model building.

1.2.4 In Summary

The historical examination of empirical, theoretical, and mathematical developments in network research should convince the reader that social network analysis is far more than an intuitively appealing vocabulary, metaphor, or set of images for discussing social, behavioral, political, or economic relationships. Social network analysis provides a precise way to define important social concepts, a theoretical alternative to the assumption of independent social actors, and a framework for testing theories about structured social relationships.

The methods of network analysis provide explicit formal statements and measures of social structural properties that might otherwise be defined only in metaphorical terms. Such phrases as webs of relationships, closely knit networks of relations, social role, social position, group, clique, popularity, isolation, prestige, prominence, and so on are given mathematical definitions by social network analysis. Explicit mathematical statements of structural properties, with agreed upon formal definitions, force researchers to provide clear definitions of social concepts, and facilitate development of testable models. Furthermore, network analysis allows measurement of structures and systems which would be almost impossible to describe without relational concepts, and provides tests of hypotheses about these structural properties.

1.3 Fundamental Concepts in Network Analysis

There are several key concepts at the heart of network analysis that are fundamental to the discussion of social networks. These concepts are: actor, relational tie, dyad, triad, subgroup, group, relation, and network. In this section, we define some of these key concepts and discuss the different levels of analysis in social networks.

Actor. As we have stated above, social network analysis is concerned with understanding the linkages among social entities and the implications of these linkages. The social entities are referred to as *actors*. Actors are discrete individual, corporate, or collective social units. Examples of actors are people in a group, departments within a corporation, public service agencies in a city, or nation-states in the world system. Our use of the term "actor" does not imply that these entities necessarily have volition or the ability to "act." Further, most social network applications focus on collections of actors that are all of the same type (for example, people in a work group). We call such collections *one-mode networks*. However, some methods allow one to look at actors of conceptually different types or levels, or from different sets. For example, Galaskiewicz (1985) and Galaskiewicz and Wasserman (1989) analyzed monetary donations made from corporations to nonprofit agencies in the Minneapolis/St. Paul area. Doreian and Woodard (1990) and Woodard and Doreian (1990) studied community members' contacts with public service agencies.

Relational Tie. Actors are linked to one another by social *ties*. As we will see in the examples discussed throughout this book, the range and type of ties can be quite extensive. The defining feature of a tie is that it establishes a linkage between a pair of actors. Some of the more common examples of ties employed in network analysis are:

- Evaluation of one person by another (for example expressed friendship, liking, or respect)
- Transfers of material resources (for example business transactions, lending or borrowing things)
- Association or affiliation (for example jointly attending a social event, or belonging to the same social club)
- Behavioral interaction (talking together, sending messages)
- Movement between places or statuses (migration, social or physical mobility)
- Physical connection (a road, river, or bridge connecting two points)
- Formal relations (for example authority)
- Biological relationship (kinship or descent)

We will expand on these applications and provide concrete examples of different kinds of ties in the discussion of network applications and data in Chapter 2.

Dyad. At the most basic level, a linkage or relationship establishes a tie between two actors. The tie is inherently a property of the pair and therefore is not thought of as pertaining simply to an individual actor. Many kinds of network analysis are concerned with understanding ties among pairs. All of these approaches take the *dyad* as the unit of analysis. A dyad consists of a pair of actors and the (possible) tie(s) between them. Dyadic analyses focus on the properties of pairwise relationships, such as whether ties are reciprocated or not, or whether specific types of multiple relationships tend to occur together. Dyads are discussed in detail in Chapter 13, while dyadic statistical models are discussed in Chapters 15 and 16. As we will see, the dyad is frequently the basic unit for the statistical analysis of social networks.

Triad. Relationships among larger subsets of actors may also be studied. Many important social network methods and models focus on the *triad*; a subset of three actors and the (possible) tie(s) among them. The analytical shift from pairs of individuals to triads (which consist of three potential pairings) was a crucial one for the theorist Simmel, who wrote in 1908 that

> ...the fact that two elements [in a triad] are each connected not only by a straight line – the shortest – but also by a broken line, as it were, is an enrichment from a formal-sociological standpoint. (page 135)

Balance theory has informed and motivated many triadic analyses. Of particular interest are whether the triad is transitive (if actor i "likes" actor j, and actor j in turn "likes" actor k, then actor i will also "like" actor k), and whether the triad is balanced (if actors i and j like each other, then i and j should be similar in their evaluation of a third actor, k, and if i and j dislike each other, then they should differ in their evaluation of a third actor, k).

Subgroup. Dyads are pairs of actors and associated ties, triads are triples of actors and associated ties. It follows that we can define a *subgroup* of actors as any subset of actors, and all ties among them. Locating and studying subgroups using specific criteria has been an important concern in social network analysis.

Group. Network analysis is not simply concerned with collections of dyads, or triads, or subgroups. To a large extent, the power of network analysis lies in the ability to model the relationships among systems of actors. A system consists of ties among members of some (more or less bounded) group. The notion of group has been given a wide range of definitions by social scientists. For our purposes, a *group* is the collection of all actors on which ties are to be measured. One must be able to argue by theoretical, empirical, or conceptual criteria that the actors in the group belong together in a more or less bounded set. Indeed, once one decides to gather data on a group, a more concrete meaning of the term is necessary. A group, then, consists of a finite set of actors who for conceptual, theoretical, or empirical reasons are treated as a finite set of individuals on which network measurements are made.

The restriction to a *finite* set or sets of actors is an analytic requirement. Though one could conceive of ties extending among actors in a nearly infinite group of actors, one would have great difficulty analyzing data on such a network. Modeling finite groups presents some of the more problematic issues in network analysis, including the specification of network boundaries, sampling, and the definition of group. Network sampling and boundary specification are important issues.

Early network researchers clearly recognized extensive ties among individuals (de Sola Pool and Kochen 1978; see Kochen 1989 for recent work on this topic). Indeed, some early social network research looked at the "small world" phenomenon: webs and chains of connections emanating to and from an individual, extending throughout the larger society (Milgram 1967; Killworth and Bernard 1978).

However, in research applications we are usually forced to look at finite collections of actors and ties between them. This necessitates drawing some boundaries or limits for inclusion. Most network applications are limited to a single (more or less bounded) group; however, we could study two or more groups.

Throughout the book, we will refer to the entire collection of actors on which we take measurements as the *actor set*. A network can contain many groups of actors, but only one (if it is a one-mode network) actor set.

Relation. The collection of ties of a specific kind among members of a group is called a *relation*. For example, the set of friendships among pairs of children in a classroom, or the set of formal diplomatic ties maintained by pairs of nations in the world, are ties that define relations. For any group of actors, we might measure several different relations (for example, in addition to formal diplomatic ties among nations, we might also record the dollar amount of trade in a given year). It is important to note that a relation refers to the collection of ties of a given kind measured on pairs of actors from a specified actor set. The ties themselves only exist between specific pairs of actors.

Social Network. Having defined actor, group, and relation we can now give a more explicit definition of social network. A *social network* consists of a finite set or sets of actors and the relation or relations defined on them. The presence of relational information is a critical and defining feature of a social network. A much more mathematical definition of a social network, but consistent with the simple notion given here, can be found at the end of Chapter 3.

In Summary. These terms provide a core working vocabulary for discussing social networks and social network data. We can see that social network analysis not only requires a specialized vocabulary, but also deals with conceptual entities and research problems that are quite difficult to pursue using a more traditional statistical and data analytic framework.

We now turn to some of the distinctive features of network analysis.

1.4 Distinctive Features of Network Theory and Measurement

It is quite important to note the key features that distinguish network theory, and consequently network measurement, from the more usual data analytic framework common in the social and behavioral sciences. Such features provide the necessary motivation for the topics discussed in this book.

The most basic feature of network measurement, distinctive from other perspectives, is the use of structural or relational information to study or test theories. Many network analysis methods provide formal definitions and descriptions of structural properties of actors, subgroups of actors, or groups. These methods translate core concepts in social and behavioral theories into formal definitions expressed in relational terms. All of these concepts are quantified by considering the relations measured among the actors in a network.

Because network measurements give rise to data that are unlike other social and behavioral science data, an entire body of methods has been developed for their analysis. Social network data require measurements on ties among social units (or actors); however, attributes of the actors may also be collected. Such data sets need social network methods for analysis. One cannot use multiple regression, t-tests, canonical correlations, structural equation models, and so forth, to study social network data or to test network theories. This book exists to organize, present, critique, and demonstrate the large body of methods for social network analysis.

Social network analysis may be viewed as a broadening or generalization of standard data analytic techniques and applied statistics which usually focus on observational units and their characteristics. A social network analysis must consider data on ties among the units. However, attributes of the actors may also be included.

Measurements on actors will be referred to as network *composition*. Complex network data sets may contain information about the characteristics of the actors (such as the gender of people in a group, or the GNP of nations in the world), as well as structural variables. Thus, the sort of data most often analyzed in the social and behavioral sciences (cases and variables) may also be incorporated into network models. But the fact that one has not only structural, but also compositional, variables can lead to very complicated data sets that can be approached only with sophisticated graph theoretic, algebraic, and/or statistical methods.

Social network theories require specification in terms of patterns of relations, characterizing a group or social system as a whole. Given appropriate network measurements, these theories may be stated as propositions about group relational structure. Network analysis then provides a collection of descriptive procedures to determine how the system behaves, and statistical methods to test the appropriateness of the propositions. In contrast, approaches that do not include network measurements are unable to study and/or test such theories about structural properties.

Network theories can pertain to units at different levels of aggregation: individual actors, dyads, triads, subgroups, and groups. Network analysis provides methods to study structural properties and to test theories stated at all of these levels. The network perspective, the theories, and the measurements they spawn are thus quite wide-ranging. This is quite unique in the social and behavioral sciences. Rarely does a standard theory lead to theoretical statements and hence measurements at more than a single level.

1.5 Organization of the Book and How to Read It

The question now is how to make sense of the more than 700 pages sitting in front of you. First, find a comfortable chair with good reading light (shoo the cats, dogs, and children away, if necessary). Next, make sure your cup of coffee (or glass of scotch, depending on the time of day) is close at hand, put a nice jazz recording on the stereo, and have a pencil or highlighting pen available (there are *many* interesting points throughout the book, and we are *sure* you will want to make note of them).

This book is organized to highlight several themes in network analysis, and to be accessible to readers with different interests and sophistication in social network analysis. We have mentioned these themes throughout this chapter, and now describe how these themes help to organize the methods discussed in this book. These themes are:

- The complexity of the methods
- Descriptive versus statistical methods

- The theoretical motivation for the methods
- The chronological development of the methods
- The level of analysis to which the methods are appropriate

Since social network analysis is a broad, diverse, and theoretically varied field, with a long and rich history, it is impossible to reflect all of these possible thematic organizations simultaneously. However, insofar as is practical and useful, we have tried to use these themes in the organization of the book.

1.5.1 Complexity

First, the material progresses from simple to complex. The remainder of Part I reviews applications of network analysis, gives an overview of network analysis methods in a general way, and then presents notation to be used throughout the book. Part II presents graph theory, develops the vocabulary and concepts that are widely used in network analysis, and relies heavily on examples. It also discusses simple actor and group properties. Parts II, III, and IV require familiarity with algebra, and a willingness to learn some graph theory (presented in Chapter 4). Parts V and VI require some knowledge of statistical theory. Log linear models for dyadic probabilities provide the basis for many of the techniques presented later in these chapters.

1.5.2 Descriptive and Statistical Methods

Network methods can be dichotomized into those that are descriptive versus those that are based on probabilistic assumptions. This dichotomy is an important organizational categorization of the methods that we discuss. Parts II, III, and IV of the book are based on the former. The methods presented in these three parts of the book assume specific descriptive models for the structure of a network, and primarily present descriptive techniques for network analysis which translate theoretical concepts into formal measures.

Parts V and VI are primarily concerned with methods for testing network theories and with statistical models of structural properties. In contrast to a descriptive approach, we can also begin with stochastic assumptions about actor behavior. Such models assume that there is some probabilistic mechanism (even as simple as flipping a coin) that underlies observed, network data. For example, one can focus on dyadic interactions, and test whether an observed network has a specified amount of reciprocity in the ties among the actors. Such a test uses standard statistical theory, and thus one can formally propose a null hypothesis which can then be rejected or not. Much of Chapter 13 is devoted to a description of these mechanisms, which are then used throughout Chapters 14, 15, and 16.

1.5.3 Theory Driven Methods

As we have discussed here, many social network methods were developed by researchers in the course of empirical investigation and the development of theories. This categorization is one of the most important of the book.

Part III covers approaches to groups and subgroups, notably cliques and their generalizations. Sociological tendencies such as cohesion and influence, which can cause actors to be "clustered" into subgroups, are among the topics of Chapters 7 and 8. Part IV discusses approaches related to the sociological notions of social role, status and position, and the mathematical property of structural equivalence and its generalizations. The later sections of the book present statistical methods for the analysis of social networks, many of which are motivated by theoretical concerns. Part V covers models for dyadic and triadic structure, early sociometry and social psychology of affective relations (dyadic analyses of Chapter 13), and structural balance and transitivity (triadic analyses of Chapters 6 and 14).

1.5.4 Chronology

It happens that the chapters in this book are approximately chronological. The important empirical investigations of social networks began over sixty years ago, starting with the sociometry of Moreno. This research led to the introduction of graph theory (Chapter 4) to study structural properties in the late 1940's and 1950's, and methods for subgroups and cliques (Chapter 7), as well as structural balance and transitivity (Chapters 6 and 14). More recently, H. White and his collaborators, using the sociological ideas of formal role analysis (Nadel and Lorrain), introduced structural equivalence (Chapter 9), and an assortment of related methods, in the 1970's, which in the 1980's, led to a collection of algebraic network methods (Chapters 11 and 12).

As can be seen from our table of contents, we have mostly followed this chronological order. We start with graph theory in Chapter 4, and discuss descriptive methods in Parts III and IV before moving on to the more recent statistical developments covered in Parts V and VI. However, because of our interest in grouping together methods with similar substantive and theoretical concerns, a few topics are out of historical sequence (structural balance and triads in Chapters 6 and 14 for example). Thus, Part V (Dyadic and Triadic Methods) follows Part IV (Roles and Positions). This reversal was made to place dyadic and triadic methods next to the other statistical methods discussed in the book (Part VI), since the methods for studying dyads and triads were among the first statistical methods for networks.

1.5.5 Levels of Analysis

Network methods are usually appropriate for concepts at certain levels of analysis. For example, there are properties and associated methods pertaining just to the actors themselves. Examples include how "prominent" an actor is within a group, as quantified by measures such as centrality and prestige (Chapter 5), actor-level expansiveness and popularity parameters embedded in stochastic models (Chapters 15 and 16), and measures for individual roles, such as isolates, liaisons, bridges, and so forth (Chapter 12). Then there are methods applicable to pairs of actors and the ties between them, such as those from graph theory that measure actor distance and reachability (Chapter 4), structural and other notions of equivalence (Chapters 9 and 12), dyadic analyses that postulate statistical models for the various states of a dyad (Chapter 13), and stochastic tendencies toward reciprocity (Chapter 15). Triadic methods are almost always based on theoretical statements about balance and transitivity (Chapter 6), and postulate certain behaviors for triples of actors and the ties among them (Chapter 14).

Many methods allow a researcher to find and study subsets of actors that are homogeneous with respect to some network properties. Examples of such applications include: cliques and other cohesive subgroups that contain actors who are "close" to each other (Chapter 7), positions of actors that arise via positional analysis (Chapters 9 and 10), and subgroups of actors that are assumed to behave similarly with respect to certain model parameters arising from stochastic models (Chapter 16). Lastly, there are measures and methods that focus on entire groups and all ties. Graph theoretic measures such as connectedness and diameter

(Chapter 4), group-level measures of centralization, density, and prestige (Chapter 5), as well as blockmodels and role algebras (Chapters 9, 10, and 11) are examples of group-level methods.

1.5.6 Chapter Prerequisites

Finally, it is important to note that some chapters are prerequisites for others, while a number of chapters may be read without reading all intervening chapters. This ordering of chapters is presented in Figure 1.1. A line in this figure connects two chapters if the earlier chapter contains material that is necessary in order to read the later chapter. Chapters 1, 2, 3, and 4 contain the introductory material, and should be read before all other chapters. These chapters discuss social network data, notation, and graph theory.

From Chapter 4 there are five possible branches: Chapter 5 (centrality); Chapter 6 (balance, clusterability, and transitivity); Chapter 7 (cohesive subgroups); Chapter 9 (structural equivalence); or Chapter 13 (dyads). Chapter 8 (affiliation networks) follows Chapter 7; Chapters 10 (blockmodels), 11 (relational algebras), and 12 (network role and position) follow, in order, from Chapter 9; Chapter 15 (statistical analysis) follows Chapter 13. Chapter 14 requires both Chapters 13 and 6. Chapter 16 (stochastic blockmodels and goodness-of-fit) requires both Chapters 15 and 10. Lastly, Chapter 17 concludes the book (and is an epilogue to all branches).

A good overview of social network analysis (with an emphasis on descriptive approaches including graph theory, centrality, balance and clusterability, cohesive subgroups, structural equivalence, and dyadic models) could include Chapters 1 through 10 plus Chapter 13. This material could be covered in a one semester graduate course. Alternatively, one could omit Chapter 8 and include Chapters 15 and 16, for a greater emphasis on statistical approaches.

One additional comment — throughout the book, you will encounter two symbols used to label sections: $\bigcirc$ and $\bigotimes$. The symbol $\bigcirc$ implies that the text that follows is tangential to the rest of the chapter, and can be omitted (except by the curious). The symbol $\bigotimes$ implies that the text that follows requires more thought and perhaps more mathematical and/or statistical knowledge than the other parts of the chapter, and should be omitted (except by the brave).

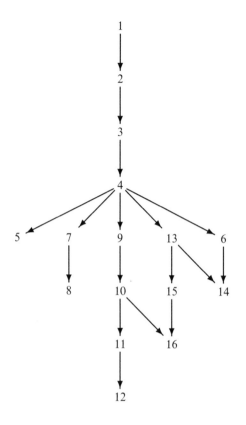

Fig. 1.1. How to read this book

1.6 Summary

We have just described the history and motivations for social network analysis. Network theories and empirical findings have been the primary reasons for the development of much of the methodology described in this book.

A complete reading of this book, beginning here and continuing on to the discussion of network data in Chapter 2, then notation in Chapter 3, and so forth, should provide the reader with a knowledge of network methods, theories, and histories. So without further ado, let us begin....

2
Social Network Data: Collection and Applications

This chapter discusses characteristics of social network data, with an emphasis on how to collect such data sets. We categorize network data in a variety of ways, and illustrate these categories with examples. We also describe the data sets that we use throughout the book. As noted in Chapter 1, the most important difference between social network data and standard social and behavioral science data is that network data include measurements on the relationships between social entities. Most of the standard data collection procedures known to every social scientist are appropriate for collecting network data (if properly applied), but there are a few techniques that are specific to the investigation of social networks. We highlight these similarities and differences in this chapter.

2.1 Introduction: What Are Network Data?

Social network data consist of at least one structural variable measured on a set of actors. The substantive concerns and theories motivating a specific network study usually determine which variables to measure, and often which techniques are most appropriate for their measurement. For example, if one is studying economic transactions between countries, one cannot (easily) rely on observational techniques; one would probably use archival records to obtain information on such transactions. On the other hand, friendships among people are most likely studied using questionnaires or interviews, rather than using archival or historical records. In addition, the nature of the study determines whether the entire set of actors can be surveyed or whether a sample of the actors must be taken.

The nature of the structural variables also determines which analytic methods are appropriate for their study. Thus, it is crucial to understand the nature of these variables. The data collection techniques described here determine, to some degree, the characteristics of the relations.

2.1.1 Structural and Composition Variables

There are two types of variables that can be included in a network data set: *structural* and *composition*. Structural variables are measured on pairs of actors (subsets of actors of size 2) and are the cornerstone of social network data sets. Structural variables measure ties of a specific kind between pairs of actors. For example, structural variables can measure business transactions between corporations, friendships between people, or trade between nations. Actors comprising these pairs usually belong to a single set of actors.

Composition variables are measurements of actor attributes. Composition variables, or *actor attribute* variables, are of the standard social and behavioral science variety, and are defined at the level of individual actors. For example, we might record gender, race, or ethnicity for people, or geographical location, after-tax profits, or number of employees for corporations. Some of the methods we discuss allow for simultaneous analyses of structural and composition variables.

2.1.2 Modes

We will use the term "mode" to refer to a distinct set of entities on which the structural variables are measured (Tucker 1963, 1964, 1966; Kroonenberg 1983; Arabie, Carroll, and DeSarbo 1987). Structural variables measured on a single set of actors (for example, friendships among residents of a neighborhood) give rise to one-mode networks. The most common type of network is a *one-mode* network, since all actors come from one set.

There are types of structural variables that are measured on two (or even more) sets of entities. For example, we might study actors from two different sets, one set consisting of corporations and a second set consisting of non-profit organizations. We could then measure the flows of financial support flows from corporations to non-profit actors. A network data set containing two sets of actors is referred to as a *two-mode* network, to reflect the fact that there are two sets of actors. A two-mode network data set contains measurements on which actors from one of the sets have ties to actors in the other set. Usually, not all actors can initiate ties. Actors in one of the sets are "senders," while those in the other are "receivers" (although the relation itself need not be directional). We will consider one-mode and two-mode, and even mention higher-mode, social networks in this book.

2.1.3 Affiliation Variables

A special type of two-mode network that arises in social network studies is an *affiliation* network. Affiliation networks are two-mode, but have only one set of actors. The second mode in an affiliation network is a set of *events* (such as clubs or voluntary organizations) to which the actors belong. Thus, in affiliation network data the two modes are the actors and the events. In such data, the events are defined not on pairs of actors, but on subsets of actors. These subsets can be of any size. A subset of actors affiliated with an affiliation variable is that collection of actors who participate in a specific event, belong to a given club, and so forth. Each affiliation variable is defined on a specific subset of actors.

For example, consider a set of actors, and three elite clubs in some city. We can define an affiliation variable for each of these three clubs. Each of these variables gives us a subset of actors — those actors belonging to one of the clubs.

The collections of individuals affiliated with the events can be found in a number of ways, depending on the substantive application. When events are clubs, boards of directors of corporations, or committees, the membership lists or rosters give the actors affiliated with each event. Often events are informal social occasions, such as parties or other gatherings, and observations or attendance or interactions among people provide the affiliations of the actors (Bernard, Killworth, and Sailer 1980, 1982; Freeman and Romney 1987). One of the earliest, and now classic, examples of an empirical application is the study of Davis, Gardner, and Gardner (1941) of the cohesive subgroups apparent in the social activities of women in a Southern city. Using newspaper records and interviews, they recorded the attendance of eighteen women at fourteen social events.

2.2 Boundary Specification and Sampling

A number of concerns arise in network studies that must be addressed prior to gathering any network data. Typically, a researcher must first identify the population to be studied, and if sampling is necessary, worry about how to sample actors and relations. These issues are considered here.

2.2.1 What Is Your Population?

A very important concern in a social network study is which actors to include. That is, who are the relevant actors? Which actors are in the population? In the case of small, closed sets of actors (such as all employees at a service station, faculty in an academic department, or corporations headquartered in a major metropolitan area), this issue is relatively easy to deal with. For other studies, the *boundary* of the set of actors may be difficult (if not impossible) to determine. The boundary of a set of actors allows a researcher to describe and identify the population under study.

Actors may come and go, may be many in number and hard to enumerate, or it may be difficult even to determine whether a specific actor belongs in a set of actors. For example, consider the study of elites in a community. The boundary of the set, including all, and only, the elites within the community, may be difficult, or impossible, to determine. However, frequently there will be a clear "external" definition of the boundary of the set which enables the researcher to determine which actors belong in it.

In some instances it is quite plausible to argue that a set of actors is relatively bounded, as for example, when there is a fairly complete membership roster. In such a case, the entire set of members can make up the actor set. However, there are other instances when drawing boundaries around a set is somewhat arbitrary. In practice, while network researchers recognize that the social world consists of many (perhaps infinite) links of connection, they also find that effective and reasonable limits can be placed on inclusion. Network researchers often define actor set boundaries based on the relative frequency of interaction, or intensity of ties among members as contrasted with non-members.

Laumann, Marsden, and Prensky (1989) describe two different approaches to boundary specification in social network studies. The first way, which they refer to as the *realist* approach, focuses on actor set boundaries and membership as perceived by the actors themselves. For example, a street-corner gang is acknowledged as a social entity by its members (it may even have a name — "Jets" or "Sharks") and the membership of the gang is the collection of people the members acknowledge as belonging to the gang. The second way of specifying network boundaries, which Laumann, Marsden, and Prensky refer to as the *nominalist* approach, is based on the theoretical concerns of the researcher. For example, a researcher might be interested in studying the flow of computer messages among researchers in a scientific specialty. In such a study, the list of actors might be the collection of people who published papers on the topic in the previous five years. This list is constructed for the analytical purposes of the researcher, even though the scientists themselves might not perceive the list of people as constituting a distinctive social entity. Both of these approaches to boundary specification have been used in social network studies.

Consider now two specific examples of how researchers have defined network boundaries. The first example illustrating the problem of identifying the relevant population of actors comes from a study of how information or new ideas diffuse through a community. Coleman, Katz, and Menzel (1957) studied how a new drug was adopted by physicians. Their solution to the problem of boundary identification is as follows:

> It was decided to include in the sample, as nearly as possible, *all* the local doctors in whose specialities the new drug was of major potential significance. This assured that the "others" named by each doctor in answer to the sociometric questions were included in the sample. (page 254)

The second example comes from the study of community leaders by Laumann and Pappi (1973). They asked community leaders to define the boundary by identifying the elite actors in the community of Altneustadt. These leaders were asked to

> ... name all persons [who] are now in general very influential in Altneustadt.

From these lists, each of which can be considered a sample of the relevant actors in the elite network, the actor set was enumerated.

Many naturally occurring groups of actors do not have well-defined boundaries. However, all methods must be applied to a specific set of data which assumes not only finite actor set size(s), but also enumerable set(s) of actors. Somehow, in order to study the network, we must enumerate a finite set of actors to study.

For our purposes, the set of actors consists of all social units on which we have measurements (either structural variables, or structural and compositional variables). Social network analysis begins with measurements on a set of actors. Researchers using methods described here must be able to make such an assumption. We assume, prior to any data gathering, that we can obtain relevant information on all substantively important actors; such actors will be included in the actor set. However, some actors may be left out unintentionally or for other reasons. Thus, the constitution of the actor set (that is, its size and composition) depends on both practical and theoretical concerns. The reason for the assumption that the actor set consists of all social units on which we have measurements is quite simple — the methods we discuss here cannot handle amorphous set boundaries. We will always start our analyses with a set (or sets) of actors, and we must be able to enumerate (or label) all members.

Many network studies focus on small collectivities, such as classrooms, offices, social clubs, villages, and even, occasionally, artificially created and manipulated laboratory groups. All of these examples have clearly defined actor set boundaries; however, recent network studies of actors such as elite business leaders in a community (Laumann and Pappi 1976), interorganizational networks in a community (Galaskiewicz 1979, 1985; Knoke 1983; Knoke and Wood 1981; Knoke and Kuklinski 1982), and interorganizational networks across an entire nation (Levine 1972) have less well-defined boundaries.

In several applications, when the boundary is unknown, special sampling techniques such as *snowball sampling* (Goodman 1949, 1961; Erickson 1978) and *random nets* (first proposed by Rapoport 1949a, 1949b, 1950, and especially 1963; recently resurrected by Fararo 1981, 1983, and Fararo and Skvoretz 1984) can be used to define actor set boundaries. Examples of social network studies using snowball sampling include: Johnson (1990) and Johnson, Boster, and Holbert (1989) on commercial fishermen; Moore (1979) and Alba and Moore (1978) on elite networks. Such sampling techniques are discussed in the next section.

2.2.2 Sampling

Sometimes, it may not be possible to take measurements on all the actors in the relevant actor set. In such situations, a sample of actors may be taken from the set, and inferences made about the "population" of actors from the sample. Typically, the sampling mechanism is known, and the sample is a good, probability sample (with known selection probabilities).

We will not assume in this book that the actors in the actor set(s) are samples from some population. Most network studies focus on well-defined, completely enumerated sets, rather than on samples of actors from larger populations. Methodology for the latter situation is considerably different from methods for the former. With a sample, one usually views the sample as representative of the larger, theoretically interesting population (which must have a well-defined boundary and hence, a known size), and uses the sampled actors and data to make inferences about the population. For example, in a study of major corporate actors in a national economy, a sample of corporations may be taken in order to keep the size of the problem manageable; that is, it might take too much time and/or too many resources actually to take a census of this quite large population.

There is a large literature on network sampling, both applied and theoretical. The primary focus of this literature is on the estimation of network properties, such as the average number of ties per actor (see Chapter 4), the degree of reciprocity present (see Chapter 13), the level of transitivity (see Chapters 6 and 14), the density of the relation under study (see Chapter 5), or the frequencies of ties between subgroups of actors (see Chapter 7) based on the sampled units.

Frank (1977a, 1977b, 1977c, 1978b, 1979a, 1979b, 1980, 1985) is the most widely known and most important researcher of sampling for social networks. His classic work (Frank 1971) and more recent review papers (Frank 1981, 1988) present the basic solutions to the problems that arise when the entire actor set is not sampled. Erickson and Nosanchuk (1983) review the problems that can arise with network sampling based on a large-scale application of the standard procedures to a network of over 700 actors. Various other sampling models are discussed by Hayashi (1958), Goodman (1961), Bloemena (1964), Proctor (1967, 1969, 1979), Capobianco (1970), Sheardon (1970), and Cabobianco and Frank (1982).

One very clever network sampling idea originated with Goodman (1961). A snowball network sample begins when the actors in a set of sampled respondents report on the actors to whom they have ties of a specific kind. All of these nominated actors constitute the "first-order" zone of the network. The researcher then will sample all the actors in this zone, and gather all the additional actors (those nominated by the actors in the first-order zone who are not among the original respondents or those in this zone). These additional actors constitute the "second-order" zone. This snowballing proceeds through several zones. Erickson (1978) and Frank (1979b) review snowball sampling, with the goal of understanding how other "chain methods" (methods designed to trace ties through a network from a source to an end; see, for example, Granovetter 1974, and Useem 1973, for applications) can be used in practice. Chain methods include snowball sampling and the small world technique discussed below. Erickson also discusses at length the differences between standard network sampling and chain methods.

In some network sampling situations, it is not clear what the relevant sampling unit should be. Should one sample actors, pairs of actors, triples of actors, or perhaps even subsets of actors? Granovetter (1977a, 1977b) and Morgan and Rytina (1977) have sensitized the network community to these issues (see also Erickson, Nosanchuk, and Lee 1981, and Erickson and Nosanchuk 1983). In other situations, one might sample actors, and have them report on their ties and the ties that might exist among the actors they choose or nominate. Such samples give rise to "ego-centered" networks (defined later in this chapter). With a sample of ego-centered networks, one usually wants to make inferences about the entire population of such networks (see for example, the epidemiological networks discussed by Klovdahl 1985; Laumann, Gagnon, Michaels, Michael, and Coleman 1989; and Morris 1989, 1990). Statistically, sampling dyads or ego-centered networks leads to sampling designs which are not simple; the sampling is actually clustered, and one must adjust the standard statistical summaries to allow for possible biases (Reitz and Dow 1989).

2.3 Types of Networks

There are many different types of social networks that can be studied. We will categorize networks by the nature of the sets of actors and the properties of the ties among them. As mentioned earlier in this chapter, we define the *mode* of a network as the number of sets of entities on which structural variables are measured. One-mode networks, the predominate type of network, study just a single set of actors, while two-mode networks focus on two sets of actors, or one set of actors and one set of events. One could even consider three- (and higher) mode networks, but rarely have social network methods been designed for such complicated data structures. Our discussion in this section is organized by the number of modes in the network. We will first discuss one-mode networks (with a single set of actors), then discuss two-mode networks, first with two sets of actors and then with one set of actors and one set of events. Applications of these three types of networks are the focus for methods presented in this book.

The number of modes in a network refers to the number of distinct kinds of social entities in the network. This usage is slightly different from the use of the term "mode" in the psychometric literature (Tucker 1964;

Carroll and Arabie 1980). In that literature, mode refers to a "particular class of entities" (Carroll and Arabie 1980, page 610). Thus, a study in which subjects respond to a set of stimuli (such as questionnaire items) gives rise to two modes: the subjects and the stimulus items. In the standard sociometric data design, a number of actors are presented with a list of the names of other people in the actor set, and asked to rate each other person in terms of how much they "like" that person. In a non-network context one could view these data as two-mode: the people as respondents are the first mode, and the names of the people as stimulus (questionnaire) items are the second mode. However, as a social network, these data contain only a single set of actors, and thus, in our terminology, it is a one-mode network in which the relation of friendship is measured on a single set of people. One might very well be interested in studying the set of respondents making evaluations of the other people, in addition to studying the people as the "stimuli" that are being evaluated. In that case one would consider respondents and stimuli as two different modes (Feger and Bien 1982; Noma 1982b; Kumbasar, Romney, and Batchelder n.d.).

We first categorize networks by how many modes the network has (one or two), and by whether affiliational variables are measured. There are, however, other kinds of relational data that are not one of these types. One example is data arising from an ego-centered network design. Data on such networks are gathered using special sampling strategies that allow the researcher to focus on a specific set of respondents, and the ties that these respondents have to particular others. We briefly describe special ego-centered networks and special dyadic designs at the end of this section.

We turn now to a discussion of one-mode, two-mode, and then affiliational, and egocentric and special networks.

2.3.1 One-Mode Networks

Suppose the network under study is one-mode, and thus involves measurements on just a single set of actors. Consider first the nature of the actors involved in such networks.

Actors. The actors themselves can be of a variety of types. Specifically, the actors may be

- People

- Subgroups
- Organizations
- Collectives/Aggregates:
  - Communities
  - Nation-states

Note that subgroups usually consist of people, organizations usually consist of subgroups of people, while communities and nation-states are larger entities, containing many organizations and subgroups. Thus, there is a natural progression of types of actors from sets of people, to collections or aggregates. Throughout this book, we will illustrate methodology with examples consisting of social network data on different types of actors.

Relations. The relations measured on the single set of actors in a one-mode network are usually viewed as representing specific substantive connections, or "relational contents" (Knoke and Kuklinski 1982). These connections, measured at the level of pairs of actors, can be of many types. Barnes (1972) distinguishes, quite generally, between attitudes, roles, and transactions. Knoke and Kuklinski (1982) give a more extensive list of general kinds of relations. Specifically, the kinds of relations that we might study include:

- Individual evaluations: friendship, liking, respect, and so forth
- Transactions or transfer of material resources: lending or borrowing; buying or selling
- Transfer of non-material resources: communications, sending/receiving information
- Interactions
- Movement: physical (migration from place-to-place), social (movement between occupations or statuses)
- Formal roles
- Kinship: marriage, descent

One or more of these types of relations might be measured for a single set of actors.

Individual evaluations are usually measurements of positive or negative affect of one person for another. Sometimes, these relations are labeled *sentiment*, and classically were the focus of the early sociometricians (see Moreno 1934; Davis 1970; Davis and Leinhardt 1972). Without question, such relations historically have been the most studied.

Transactions, or transfers of material resources, include business transactions, imports and exports of goods, specific forms of social support, such as lending and borrowing, contacts made by one actor of another in order to secure valuable resources, and transfer of goods. Such relations include exchange of gifts, borrowing or lending items, and sales or purchases (Galaskiewicz and Marsden 1978; Galaskiewicz 1979; Laumann, Galaskiewicz, and Marsden 1978). Social support ties are also examples of transactions (Wellman 1992b).

Transfers of non-material resources are frequently communications between actors, where ties represent messages transmitted or information received. These ties involve sending or receiving messages, giving or receiving advice, passing on gossip, and providing novel information (Lin 1975; Rogers and Kincaid 1981; Granovetter 1974). Information about innovations is frequently diffused over such communication channels (Coleman, Katz, and Menzel 1966; Rogers 1979; Michaelson 1990).

Interactions involve the physical interaction of actors or their presence in the same place at the same time. Examples of interactions include: sitting next to each other, attending the same party, visting a person's home, hitting, hugging, disciplining, conversing, and so on.

Movement can also be studied using network data and processes. Individuals moving between communities can be counted, as well as workers changing jobs or people changing statuses (see, for example, Breiger 1981c).

Formal roles, such as those dictated by power and authority, are also relational. Ties can represent authority of one actor over others, especially in a management setting (White 1961). Example of formal roles include boss/employee, teacher/student, doctor/patient, and so on.

Lastly, kinship relations have been studied using network methods for many years. Ties can be based on marriage or descent relationships and marriage or family relationships can be described using social network methods (for example, see White 1963; Boyd 1969).

Actor Attributes. In addition to relational information, social network data sets can contain measurements on the characteristics of the actors. Such measurements of actor attribute variables constitute the composition of the social network.

These variables have the same nature as those measured in non-network studies. People can be queried about their age, gender, race, socioeconomic status, place of residence, grade in school, and so on. For corporate actors, one can measure their profitability, revenues, geographical location, purpose of business, and so on. The "size, shape, and flavor" of the actors constituting the network can be measured in many ways.

2.3.2 Two-Mode Networks

Suppose now that the network under study is two-mode, and thus involves measurements on two sets of actors, or on a set of actors and a set of events. We will first consider the case in which relations are measured on pairs of actors from two different actor sets. We will then discuss a special kind of two-mode network in which measurements are taken on subsets of actors.

Two Sets of Actors. Relations in a two-mode network measure ties between the actors in one set and actors in a second set. We call such networks *dyadic* two-mode networks, since these relations are functions of dyads in which the first actor and the second actor in the dyad are from different sets.

With respect to the different types of actors, the types of relations, and the types of actor attribute variables, all of our discussion about one-mode networks is relevant. Note, however, that there can be multiple types of actors, and we can have a unique collection of attribute variables for each set of actors.

Actors. In a two-mode network that contains two sets of actors, these actors can be of the general types as described for one-mode networks. However, the two sets of actors may be of different types.

Relations. In a two-mode network with two sets of actors, at least one relation is measured between actors in the two sets. In a more extensive two-mode network data set, relations can also be defined on actors within a set. However, for the network to be truly two-mode with two sets of actors, at least one relation must be defined between the two sets of actors.

An example of such a network can be found in Galaskiewicz and Wasserman (1989). The data analyzed there consisted of two sets of actors: a collection of corporations headquartered in the Minneapolis/St. Paul metropolitan area, and the non-profit organizations (such as the Red Cross, United Way, public radio and television stations) which rely on contributions from the public sector for their operating budgets. The primary relation was the flow of donations from the corporations to the non-profit organizations, clearly a two-mode relation. Also, it is important to note that this relation is *unidirectional* since it flows from actors in one set to actors in the other set, but not the reverse. In addition, the analysis by Galaskiewicz and Wasserman considered a number of relations defined just for the corporations (such as shared country club memberships among the chief executive officers) and several just for the non-profits (such as interlocking boards of directors). A part of this data set will be discussed in more detail later in this chapter.

One Set of Actors and One Set of Events. The next type of two-mode social network, which we refer to as an *affiliation network*, arises when one set of actors is measured with respect to attendance at, or affiliation with, a set of events or activities. The first mode in an affiliation network is a set of actors, and the second is a set of events which affiliates the actors.

An example comes from Davis, Gardner, and Gardner (1941), as described and analyzed by Homans (1950) and Breiger (1974). A set of women attended a variety of social functions, and this attendance was recorded over a period of several months. Each social function can be viewed as a variable, and a binary measurement made as to whether a specific actor attended the specific function. These variables are termed *affiliational*. Such data and networks are called *affiliation* networks, or sometimes, *membership* networks. And since the affiliations are measured on subsets of actors, such networks are non-dyadic, two-mode networks.

Actors. In an affiliation network, we have a first set of actors, and a second set of events or activities to which the actors in the first set attend or belong. The types of actors in affiliation networks can be exactly the same as those in one-mode and two-mode networks. The only requirement is that the actors must be affiliated with one or more events.

Events. In affiliation networks, actors (the first mode) are related to each other through their joint affiliation with events (the second mode). The events are often defined on the basis of membership in clubs or voluntary organizations (McPherson 1982), attendance at social events (Davis, Gardner, and Gardner 1941), sitting on a board of directors, or socializing in a small group (Bernard, Killworth, and Sailer 1980, 1982; Wilson 1982).

The nature of the events, which affiliate the actors, depends on the type of actors involved. People may attend social functions or belong to athletic clubs, subgroups of people may attend various committee meetings (for example, departments at a major university send representatives to college committee meetings), organizations may be represented on various boards of directors in a community, or countries might belong to treaty organizations, and so on.

Attributes. We can have actor attribute variables that are of the same types as those for one-mode and two-mode networks. In addition, the events themselves may have characteristics associated with them which can be measured and included in the network data set. For example, clubs will be of a particular size or located in a specific geographical area. Events usually occur at discrete points in time, as well as in particular geographical places. Thus, there can be two sets of attribute variables in an affiliation network data set: attributes of the actors, and attributes of the events.

Methods for analyzing affiliation network data are described in Chapter 8, and are applied to a network data set giving the memberships of a set of chief executive officers of major corporations in Minneapolis/St. Paul in a set of exclusive clubs.

2.3.3 Ego-centered and Special Dyadic Networks

Not all structural data give rise to standard social network data sets. With standard network data (regardless of how many modes the network has), one enumerates not only the actors, but the relevant pairs as well. All actors (theoretically) can relate to each other in one-mode networks. In two-mode networks with two sets of actors, all actors in the first mode can (theoretically) relate to all in the second. However, some data collection designs gather structural information on some pairs but not others. An example of such data arises in studies of couples. Each partner in the couple can interact with the other but with no other person during counseling sessions. Interactions during these sessions are then recorded. When interest centers on a collection of pairs (husband-wife, father-son, and so forth), one frequently samples from a large population of such pairs. We will refer to these non-network relational data as *special dyadic* designs.

An actor may also relate to a limited number of "special" other actors. For example, one might observe mothers interacting with their own children in an experimental situation. In this case, mothers only interact with their own children, and children only interact with their own mother. Thus, the partners for one person (either mother or child) are different from the partners for another. In this situation, the design of the experiment constrains the interactions among the set of people so that all people cannot, theoretically, interact with all others.

Another related design is an *ego-centered* network. An ego-centered network consists of a focal actor, termed *ego*, as set of alters who have ties to ego, and measurements on the ties among these alters. For example, when studying people, one samples respondents, and each respondent reports on a set of alters to whom they are tied, and on the ties among these alters. Such data are often referred to as *personal network* data. Clearly these data are relational, but limited, since ties from each actor are measured only to some (usually only a few) alters. For example, in 1985 the General Social Survey conducted by the National Opinion Research Center (see Burt 1984, 1985) asked respondents:

> Looking back over the last six months — who are the people with whom you discussed matters important to you? (1984, page 119)

Respondents also reported on the ties between the people they listed. Bernard, Johnsen, Killworth, McCarty, Shelley, and Robinson (1990), Killworth, Johnsen, Bernard, Shelley, and McCarty (1990), Huang and Tausig (1990), Burt (1984, 1985), Marsden (1987, 1990b), Wellman (1993), as well as Campbell, Marsden, and Hurlbert (1986) discuss measurement of such personal, ego-centered networks.

Ego-centered networks have been widely used by anthropologists to study the social environment surrounding individuals (Boissevain 1973) or families (Bott 1957). Ego-centered networks are also used quite often in the study of social support. The term "social support" has been used to refer to social relationships that aid the health or well-being of an individual. The emphasis on relationships has allowed researchers to study support using social networks. Such networks are of great interest in clinical and community psychology, as well as in sociology. A variety of hypotheses (see Hammer 1983; Cohen and Syme 1985) have been offered to explain how personal relationships, as reflected by such ego-centered networks, can affect the emotional and physical well-being of an individual.

The methods described in this book assume that there are no theoretical limitations on interactions among actors. A social network arises when all actors can, theoretically, have ties to all relevant actors. The primary object of study for methods discussed in this book is this complete collection of actors (one or more sets) and the ties among them.

2.4 Network Data, Measurement and Collection

We now turn to issues concerning the measurement and collection of network data, the accuracy, validity, and error associated with these data, and particular design considerations that can arise in network studies.

2.4.1 Measurement

Social network data differ from standard social and behavioral science data in a number of important ways. Most importantly, social network data consist of one (or more) relations measured among a set of actors. The presence of relations has implications for a number of measurement issues, including the unit of observation (actor, pair of actors, relational tie, or event), the modeling unit (the actor, dyad, triad, subset of actors, or network), and the quantification of the relations (directional vs. nondirectional; dichotomous vs. valued). We will discuss each of these issues in turn.

Social network data can be studied at a number of different levels: the individual actor, the pair of actors or dyad, the triple of actors or triad, a subset of actors, or the network as a whole. We will refer to the level at which network data are studied as the *modeling unit*. However, social network data often are gathered at a level that is different from the level at which they are modeled. We discuss the unit of observation and the modeling unit in the next two sections.

Unit of Observation. The unit of observation is the entity on which measurements are taken. Most often social network data are collected by observing, interviewing, or questioning individual actors about the ties from these actors to other actors in the set. Thus, the unit of observation is an actor, from whom we elicit information about ties. The dyad is the unit of observation when one measures ties among pairs of actors directly. For example, one could record instances of aggression among pairs of children on a playground. When affiliation network data are collected, the unit of observation is often the event. The researcher selects events or social occasions, and for each event, records the actors who are affiliated with it.

Modeling Unit. Just as social network data can be observed at a number of levels, there are several levels at which network data can be modeled or summarized. These levels are the:

- Actor
- Dyad
- Triad
- Subgroup
- Set of actors or network

In categorizing network methods, it is useful to consider the level to which a model or network property applies. Some network properties pertain to actors (for example the number of "choices" that an individual actor receives from others in the network). Other properties pertain to pairs of actors (for example, if one person "chooses" another as a friend, is the "choice" returned by the second person?). Models at the level of the triad consider triples of actors and the ties among them. Many methods pertain to subgroups of actors; for example, one could study whether there are subsets of actors in the network who interact frequently with each other. Finally many properties pertain to the network as a whole, for example, the proportion of ties that are present in the network.

Relational Quantification. There are two properties of relations that are important for understanding their measurement, and for categorizing the methods described here: whether the relation is *directional* or *nondirectional,* and whether it is *dichotomous* or *valued.* In a directional relation, the relational tie between a pair of actors has an origin and a destination; that is, the tie is directed from one actor in the pair to the other actor in a pair. For example, one country exports manufactured goods to a second country; the first country is the source of the manufactured goods, and the second country is the destination. In a nondirectional relation the tie between a pair of actors does not have a direction. For example, we could define a tie as present between two countries if they share a border.

A second important property of a relation is whether it is dichotomous or valued. Dichotomous relations are coded as either present or absent, for each pair of actors. For example one could record whether one country sends an ambassador to a second country; thus giving rise to a dichotomous relation that can only take on two values: "send" or "not send." On the other hand, valued relations can take on a range of values, indicating the strength, intensity, or frequency of the tie between each pair of actors. For example, we could record the dollar value of manufactured goods that are exported from one country to a second country, thus giving rise to a valued relation.

2.4.2 Collection

There are a variety of ways in which social network data can be gathered. These techniques are:

* Questionnaires
* Interviews
* Observations
* Archival records
* Experiments
* Other techniques, including ego-centered, small world, and diaries

Each of these techniques will be discussed and illustrated with examples.

Questionnaire. This data collection method is the most commonly used (especially when actors are people). The questionnaire usually contains questions about the respondent's ties to the other actors. Questionnaires are most useful when the actors are people, and the relation(s) that are being studied are ones that the respondent can report on. For example, people can report on who they like, respect, or go to for advice. Questionnaires can also be used when the actor in a study is a collective entity, such as a corporation, but an individual person representing the collective reports on the collective's ties. For example, Galaskiewicz (1985) asked officers in charge of corporate giving whether or not the corporation had made a donation to a non- profit agency.

There are three different question formats that can be used in a questionnaire:

* Roster vs. free recall
* Free vs. fixed choice
* Ratings vs. complete rankings

In the following sections we will discuss each of these formats and describe examples of their use.

Roster vs. Free Recall. One issue in the design of a questionnaire to gather network data is whether each actor should be presented with a complete list, or *roster*, of the other actors in the actor set. Rosters can be constructed only when the researcher knows the members in the set prior to data gathering. For example, Krackhardt and Stern (1988) collected information on friendships among members of a university class as part of their study of "simulated" corporations. They had each person rate their friendship with every member of the class on a five point scale:

> Everyone in the class completed a questionnaire which asked them to rate every other person in the class as to how close a friend he or she was. The directions for this questionnaire included the following: "Please place a check in the space that best describes your relationship with each person on the list." The names of everyone participating in the game were listed below, with five categories from which the respondent could choose: "trust as a friend", "know well", "acquaintance", "associate name with face", and "do not know". (page 131)

For some network designs, the researcher does not present a complete list of the actors in the network to the respondent on the questionnaire. In such instances, it is common simply to ask respondents to "name those people with whom you *(fill in specific tie)*". Such a format, where respondents generate the list of names, is called *free recall*. For example, Rapoport and Horvath (1961) studied friendships in two junior high schools. Students were asked to list their best friends, but were not presented with a roster. Specifically,

> Each pupil in both schools was asked to write his name, age, grade, and home room number on a card and to fill in the blanks in the statements:
> - "My best friend in (name of school) Junior High School is ..."
> - "My second best friend is ..."
> - ...
> - "My eighth best friend is. ..." (page 281)

Note here how the network membership is known beforehand (all students in a school are the set of actors) but students listed their friends using free recall.

In some settings, the researcher might not even have a list; that is, the actors within the actor set might not even be known in advance. In this situation, sampling or enumeration techniques are necessary (as we have discussed earlier in this chapter). For example, in studies of community elites (Friedkin 1984; Moore 1979; Alba and Moore 1978), selected actors are asked to name other actors they believe to be influential in the community.

Free vs. Fixed Choice. If actors are told how many other actors to nominate on a questionnaire (for example, to name a specific number of "best friends"), then each person has a fixed number of "choices" to make. Such designs are termed *fixed choice.* In a fixed choice design each actor has a fixed maximum number of ties to the other actors in the set of actors. For example, Coleman, Katz, and Menzel (1957), in a study of diffusion of a medical innovation among physicians, interviewed all physicians in a community. Specifically,

> Each doctor interviewed was asked three sociometric questions:
> (i) "To whom did he most often turn for advice and information?"
> (ii) "With whom did he most often discuss his cases in the course of an ordinary week?"
> (iii) "Who were the friends, among his colleagues, whom he saw most often socially?"
> In response to each of these questions, the names of three doctors were requested. (page 254)

In this study, each person was constrained to have no more than three ties for each of the three relations.

On the other hand, if actors are not given any such constraints on how many nominations to make, the data are *free choice.* For example, Carley and Wendt (1988) studied the ties among people in an "invisible college" of users of a computer program at a variety of universities.

> Each individual was asked to denote for each member of the user group whether or not they:
> • Had an office next to each other
> • Attended the same school at the same time
> • Shared an office
> • Lived in the same living group or apartment
> • Were at the same school at the same time
> • Were in the same academic department at the same time

Note that there is no constraint on the number of people that an individual respondent can choose on these six relations.

The study of a university class by Krackhardt and Stern (1988) was a free choice design, since respondents were not limited in the number of friends they could choose. The Rapoport and Horvath design allowed each student to make eight choices; however, as Rapoport and Horvath note, students did not always fill in all of the 8 choices. Similarly, in a study of 384 sociograms that were collected using a fixed choice procedure, Holland and Leinhardt (1973) found that in fewer than 20 percent of the data sets did all respondents conform to the fixed number of choices.

Later in this chapter, we discuss limitations of social network data collected using fixed choice designs.

Ratings vs. Complete Ranking. In some network designs, actors are asked to rate or rank order all the other actors in the set for each measured relation. Such measurements reflect the intensity of strength of ties. Ratings require each respondent to assign a value or rating to each tie. Complete rankings require each respondent to rank their ties to all other actors.

An example of a complete rank order design is the study by Bernard, Killworth, and Sailer (1980). They asked each of forty members of a social science research office to report the amount of communication with each other member of the office using the following procedure:

> ... each participant was given the familiar deck of cards containing the names of the other participants. They arranged (that is, ranked) the cards from most to least on how often they talked to others in the office during a normal working day. (page 194)

Such data are *complete rankings* or *complete rank orders*. This questionnaire design is quite different from that employing *ratings* of the ties.

Alternatively, one can gather ratings from each actor about their ties to other members on every relation. These ratings can be dichotomous, as in the Carley and Wendt (1988) study (ties are either present or absent), or valued, as in the Krackhardt and Stern (1988) study where ratings were made by choosing one of five possible categories for the strength of each tie.

Full rank-orders and rating scales with multiple response categories produce *valued* relations. Response formats where respondents either nominate a person or not on a given relation produce *dichotomous* relations. In either case, when "choices" are directed from respondents to the people they name, the resulting relations are *directional*.

Interview. Interviews, either face-to-face or over the telephone, are occasionally used to gather network data in instances where questionnaires are not feasible. For example, Galaskiewicz (1985) interviewed the chief executive officers of the largest corporations in the Minneapolis/St. Paul metropolitan area. Chief executive officers were much more willing to participate in face-to-face interviews than via an impersonal questionnaire.

Interviews have been used to gather data from respondents in ego-centered networks, such as the 1985 NORC General Social Survey (Burt 1984, 1985), Wellman's study of social support in East York, Ontario (Wellman 1979; Wellman, Carrington, and Hall 1988; Wellman and Wortley 1990, and references therein), and Fischer's study of friendships in a community in Northern California (Fischer 1982).

Observation. Observing interactions among actors is another way to collect network data. This method has been widely used in field research to study relatively small groups of people who have face-to-face interactions (Roethlisberger and Dickson 1961; Kapferer 1969; Hammer, Polgar, and Salzinger 1969; Thurman 1980; Bernard and Killworth 1977; Killworth and Bernard 1976; Bernard, Killworth, and Sailer 1980, 1982; Freeman and Romney 1987; Freeman, Romney, and Freeman 1987; Freeman, Freeman, and Michaelson 1988, 1989). For example, Freeman, Freeman, and Michaelson (1988, 1989) observed a collection of fifty-four windsurfers on a beach in Southern California.

> Observations on the subjects' interaction patterns were made for two half-hour periods on each day of 31 consecutive days. (Freeman, Freeman, and Michaelson 1989, page 234)

The information recorded was the number of minutes of interaction between pairs of people.

Observational methods have been used extensively in the studies of Bernard, Killworth, and Sailer (Bernard and Killworth 1977; Killworth and Bernard 1976; Bernard, Killworth, and Sailer 1980, 1982). These researchers systematically observed interactions among people in a variety of social settings, such as a social science research office, faculty, staff, and graduate students in a university department, and members of a college fraternity. Their research focused on the relationship between these observed interactions and actors' recollections of their own interactions. Since data are collected by observing interactions, without requiring verbal responses from the people, this method is quite useful with people who are not able to respond to questionnaires or interviews.

Observational methods are widely used in the study of interactions among non-human primates (Dunbar and Dunbar 1975; Sade 1965). For instance, Wolfe (see MacEvoy and Freeman n.d.) observed a colony of monkeys, and recorded which monkeys visited a river together. Sailer and Gaulin (1984) present data collected on interactions among members of a colony of mantled howler monkeys.

Observational methods are also useful for collecting affiliation network data. The researcher can record who attends each of a number of social events. For example, Freeman, Romney, and Freeman (1987) recorded which faculty members and graduate students attended a weekly departmental colloquium over the course of a semester. Each colloquium is an event in this affiliation network.

In some studies, the researcher observes a set of actors for an extended period of time, and then summarizes his or her impressions of the ties among all pairs of actors in the set (Roethlisberger and Dickson 1961; Kapferer 1969; Thurman 1980). The ties are based on the researcher's impressions.

Archival Records. Some network researchers measure ties by examining measurements taken from records of interactions. Such records can take many forms, such as measurements on past political interactions among nations, previously published citations of one scholar by another, and so on. Burt and Lin (1977) discuss how social networks can be obtained from archival data, such as journal articles, newspapers, court records, minutes of executive meetings, and the like. Frequently, as noted by Burt and Lin, such data give rise to longitudinal relations and can be used to reconstruct ties that existed in the past. For example, Burt (1975, 1983) obtained information on interactions among corporate actors from the front pages of previously published issues of *The New York Times.*

Rosenthal, Fingrutd, Ethier, Karant, and McDonald (1985) used biographical records to study the organizational affiliations of women reformers in the 19th century in New York. These researchers were interested in the overlaps among the organizations. The list of women and their affiliations was compiled from biographical dictionaries which included information about organizational affiliations of 202 women, and 1015 organizations. These data are thus affiliation data compiled from archival sources.

Galaskiewicz (1985) obtained information on memberships of the chief executive officers of corporations in Minneapolis/St. Paul in elite country clubs by examining the membership rosters of the clubs. Other researchers have conducted similar elite studies by looking at volumes such as *Who's Who*, and social registers.

Another common use of archival records is for the study of sociology of science, specifically, patterns of citations among scholars. One can examine "who cites whom" in order to understand diffusion of a scientific innovation (Burt, 1978/1979a; Breiger 1976; McCann 1978; Noma 1982a, 1982b; Doreian and Fararo 1985; White and McCann 1988; Michaelson 1991; Carley and Hummon 1993). In these studies, the unit of observation is a citation, but since a given article usually contains many citations, the actor can be the article containing the citation, or the journal containing the article, or even the authors of the cited articles.

All of the data collection methods discussed above attempt to measure the ties among all the actors in the set. Many network studies employ a variety of data collection methods for recording ties, in addition to gathering actor attribute information. These data collection methods (questionnaires, observations, interviews, experiments, and so forth) are common social and behavioral science procedures.

Other. Here, we focus on other designs for collecting relational data. These include the cognitive social structure design (which is an extension of sociometric data to include actor perceptions of the network), experimental studies (in which network data are collected under controlled situations), and studies in which information is collected on ties among just some actors. Often these studies are used to estimate the size (de Sola Pool and Kochen 1978; Freeman and Thompson 1989; Bernard, Johnsen, Killworth, and Robinson 1989; Wellman 1992b) or composition (Verbrugge 1977; Wellman 1979; Marsden 1988; Wellman and Wortley 1990, and references therein) of an individual's ego-centered network. Perhaps only a few actors are chosen as respondents. Or, the actors might not even be members of a well-defined set of actors. Clearly in these instances, we are not studying a network with a boundary. We refer to such studies as special network designs.

In the next paragraphs, we discuss data collection procedures for cognitive social structure designs, experimental, ego-centered networks, and small- and reverse small-world techniques.

Cognitive Social Structure. In a standard sociometric questionnaire, one asks respondents about their own ties. A variation of this design is to ask respondents to give information on their perceptions of other actors' network ties. Such designs are called *cognitive social structures* because they measure perceived relations (Krackhardt 1987a; Kumbasar, Romney, and Batchelder n.d.).

As an example, Krackhardt and Porter (1985) studied turnover in several fast food restaurants. They were interested in the employees' perceptions of friendships among all other employees in the restaurant. Thus, they had to gather information from each person not only about their own friendships, but also about their perceptions of the friendships among all other pairs of employees. They collected network data at two points in time.

Their procedure is described as follows:

> In the first questionnaire, each person in the work group was asked to record who they perceived to be a friend of whom. While simple on the surface, this substantial task required that employees consider all possible pairs of friends in the restaurant. To accomplish this, the respondent was told to check the names of all those listed whom he or she thought would be considered a friend by employee # 1 (for example, "Henry"). Then, the same list was repeated on the next page, and the respondent was asked to check all names of those whom he or she thought would be considered a friend of employee # 2 ("Rita"). This process was repeated a total of N times (for N employees). In this way, we could assess each person's perception of everyone's friends, their own as well as their coworkers. (page 250)

Alternatively, one can ask respondents to report subgroups of people who form relatively tightly knit subgroups within the larger collection of people (Freeman, Freeman, and Michaelson 1988, 1989).

Data collected using a cognitive social structure design gives considerably more information than the usual sociometric design, since actors report not only on their own ties, but also on their perceptions of ties among all pairs of actors.

Experimental. Social network data can be collected using experimental designs. There are (at least) two basic ways to conduct such experiments. First, one can choose a set of actors and observe their interactions in an experimentally controlled situation. The researcher then records interactions or communications between pairs of actors. Ties may be observed between all pairs of actors. Second, one can not only choose actors but also specify which pairs of actors are permitted to communicate with each other during the experiment. One only records the frequency or content of communications between those pairs of actors who are permitted to interact.

Group problem-solving experiments (Bavelas 1950; Leavitt 1949, 1951) in which actors are assigned to positions within the network defined by the experimenter and allowed to communicate only with specific others are an example of the second type of experiment. The experimenter manipulates both group members and their ties. Power and exchange experiments are also of the second type (Cook, Emerson, Gilmore, and Yamagishi 1983; Bonacich 1987; Markovsky, Willer, and Patton 1988; and Friedkin and Cook 1990). The experimenter assigns actors to positions, and allows certain pairs of actors to negotiate the exchange of resources.

Ego-centered. An ego-centered, or *local,* network consists of a focal person or respondent (ego), a set of alters who have ties to ego, and measurements on the ties from ego to alters and on the ties between alters. One begins by asking a collection of respondents about their ties to other people to elicit the set of alters. In 1985 the NORC General Social Survey (see Burt 1984, 1985) asked a sample of 1531 people

> From time to time, most people discuss important matters with other people. Looking back over the past six months, who are the people with whom you discussed matters important to you? (page 119)

One also asks respondents information about the ties among the people that the respondent has named. The 1985 General Social Survey contained a question about the ties among all pairs of people named by the respondent. If we label two of the people named by a particular respondent "Alter 1" and "Alter 2," then the question can be worded

> Please think about the relations between the people you just mentioned. Some of them may be total strangers, in the sense that they would not recognize each other if they bumped into each other on the street. Others might be especially close, as close to each other as they are to you. First think about [Alter 1] and [Alter 2]. Are these people total strangers? (Burt 1985, page 120)

Such measurements give rise to ego-centered networks.

Small World. Special network designs are also used in small world and reverse small world studies. A small world study is an attempt to determine how many actors a respondent is removed from a target individual based on acquaintanceship. Of primary interest is not only how long these "chains" are, but also the characteristics of the intermediate actors in the chain. This data collection design was pioneered by Milgram (Milgram 1967; Travers and Milgram 1969). Korte and Milgram (1970) describe the typical small world study as follows:

> The small world method consists of presenting each of the persons in a "starting population" with the description of a given "target person" — his name, address, occupation, and other selected information. The task of a starter is to advance a booklet toward the target person by sending

the booklet to a personal acquaintance whom he considers more likely than himself to know the target. Each person in turn advances the booklet in this manner until the chain reaches the target. (page 101)

Often the intermediaries are asked to return a postcard to the researcher reporting some basic demographic characteristics. The researcher can then compare characteristics of successful and unsuccessful chains. Korte and Milgram (1970), Erickson and Kringas (1975), and Shotland (1976) have also used this design, as discussed by Lin (1989), and by papers in the volume edited by Kochen (1989).

A reverse small world study focuses on the ties from a specific respondent to a variety of hypothetical targets (Killworth and Bernard 1978; Cuthbert 1989). Cuthbert (1989) states:

> ... individuals are asked to imagine that they will pass something to someone who is to eventually reach a target person they do not know. They are instructed to think of someone they know, who might be a first link in a chain to the target person. ... The respondent is given a list of possible targets who are located geographically and socially in different parts of the society. In this way the reverse small world method clearly maps the outgoing network of the people who complete the questionnaire. (page 212)

White (1970) discusses the possible biases that can arise by using the small world technique. Many of these biases arise because response rates are typically much lower with this form of network data collection. Better estimation strategies of network properties are discussed by White (1970) and by Hunter and Shotland (1974).

Diary. Another way to gather social network data is to ask each respondent to keep a continuous record of the other people with whom they interact (for example, Gurevich 1961; de Sola Pool and Kochen 1978). Such methods have been used in the study of personal networks among people. For example, see Cubbitt (1973), Mitchell (1974), and Higgins, McClean, and Conrath (1985).

Social support researchers sometimes ask respondents to keep daily records of all people with whom they come into contact. In addition to generating a list of people in every respondent's personal network, these data sets frequently include information on the type of relation and characteristics of the alters in each ego-centered network (see Reis, Wheeler, Kernix, Spiegel, and Nezlek 1985; Pagel, Erdly, and Becker 1987).

2.4.3 Longitudinal Data Collection

Occasionally, a researcher is interested in how ties in a network change over time. In studies of such processes, one measures one or more relations at fixed intervals of time. Such designs allow one to study how stable ties are and whether such ties ever reach an equilibrium state. There are (usually) two research questions to be answered when studying longitudinal network data. The first is how the process has changed over time, while the second question asks how well the past, or the history of the process, can predict the future. Some comments on how to gather longitudinal social network data can be found in Wasserman (1979).

Longitudinal social network data can be collected using any of the methods described above (questionnaire, interview, observation, and so on). There have been some important longitudinal studies, primarily of sociometric relations, such as friendship. Other researchers have looked at communications throughout a network over time.

Nordlie (1958) and Newcomb (1961) studied two 1956 University of Michigan fraternities, each containing seventeen men housed together, for a period of fifteen weeks. All students were incoming transfer students who were initially unknown to each other. Each person was asked to rank each of his fellow fraternity members on the basis of positive feeling. Rankings were recorded each week, except for week 9. These data were studied in depth by Nordlie (1958), White, Boorman, and Breiger (1976), Boorman and White (1976), and Wasserman (1980).

Bernard, Killworth, and Sailer (1980, 1982) studied another fraternity over time, this one existing in the late 1970's in Morgantown, West Virginia. The fifty-eight fraternity members had been living together at least three months. Interactions among members within the fraternity were recorded by an outside observer every fifteen minutes, twenty-one hours per day, for five days. This observation process was conducted three times during the year. The observer noted every group in conversation, yielding a very rich set of longitudinal interaction ties. In addition, the researchers asked the fraternity members both about their "friendships" within the fraternity and about their recollections of their interactions with other fraternity members at the end of each of the three observation periods. To measure the interaction relation, the students were asked to give a rating of their interactions with each of the other actors on an ordinal scale of 1 (no communication) to 5 (great deal of communication). Thus, three longitudinal relations were studied: interaction (measured almost continuously for three different five-day periods), friendship, and recalled communication (measured at three points in time).

Another classic example is Freeman's *EIES* data, which consist of measurements of computer mail interactions, over the course of an eighteen month period, among a set of quantitative researchers studying social networks. These data are described at the end of this chapter. Yet another example comes from Katz and Proctor's (1959) study of ties in an eighth-grade classroom of twenty-five boys and girls. These data consist of friendship choices made four times during the school year. The data were gathered by Taba (1955), who focused on the differences and similarities between boy-boy and girl-girl choices, and "mixed gender" ties.

2.4.4 *Measurement Validity, Reliability, Accuracy, Error*

As we noted in Chapter 1, social network research is concerned with studying patterns of social structure. As Freeman and Romney (1987) note, "social structure refers to a relatively prolonged and stable pattern of interpersonal relations" (1987, pages 330–331). In their discussion of measurement error in sociometry, Holland and Leinhardt (1973) refer to this pattern as the *true structure*, in contrast to the *observed structure* contained in the measured network data, which might contain error. Important concerns in social network measurement are the validity, reliability, and measurement error in these data. In addition, since social network data are often collected by having people report on their own interactions, the accuracy of these self-report data is also a concern. Surprisingly little work has been done on the issues of validity, reliability, and measurement error in social network data. A recent paper by Marsden (1990b) reviews this work; we summarize this and other research briefly here.

"Accuracy". Often sociometric data are collected by having people report on their interactions with other people. For example, a researcher might ask each actor to report "With whom did you talk last week?", or "What other people were at the party with you last Saturday?" In either case, the respondent is asked to recall his or her interactions. An important issue is the relationship between information collected using verbal reports and information collected by observing the peoples' interactions.

Considerable research has been done on the question of *informant accuracy* in social network data. Much of this research was conducted by Bernard, Killworth, and Sailer using very clever data collection designs in which they observed interactions among people in several different communities (for example, a fraternity, a research office, and ham radio operators) and also asked the same people to report on their interactions (Bernard and Killworth 1977, 1979; Killworth and Bernard 1976, 1979; Bernard, Killworth, and Sailer 1980, 1982; Bernard, Killworth, Kronenfeld, and Sailer 1985). They concluded that about half of what people report about their own interactions is incorrect in one way or another. Thus, people are not very good at reporting on their interactions in particular situations.

However, recent studies by Freeman, Romney, and colleagues (Romney and Faust 1982; Romney and Weller 1984; Freeman and Romney 1987; Freeman, Romney, and Freeman 1987; Freeman, Freeman, and Michaelson 1988) and by Hammer (1980, 1985) argue that particular interactions are not of primary concern to social network researchers. Rather, as we noted above, the "true" structure of the network, relatively stable patterns of interaction, are of most interest. Thus it is these long-term patterns the researcher should be studying and estimating, not the particular interactions of individuals. Freeman, Romney, and Freeman (1987) argue that verbal reports (recall of interactions) should be understood using principles of memory and cognition. They found that what people report about their interactions is in fact related to the long-range social structure, rather than to particular instances.

Another issue related to the accuracy of network data occurs when the actors in the network are organizations (for example corporations) but information on ties is collected from individuals as representatives of the organization. For example, Galaskiewicz (1985) measured donations from corporations to non-profit agencies by interviewing the officer in charge of corporate giving. One must be able to assume that the individual who is interviewed in fact has knowledge of the information being sought.

Validity. A measure of a concept is *valid* to the extent that it actually measures what it is intended to measure. Often, a researcher assumes that the measurements of a concept are indeed valid. For example, one might assume that asking people "Which people in this group are your friends?" has face validity as a measure of friendship, in the sense that the answer to the question gives a set of actors who are related to the respondent through friendship ties.

However, the validity of a measure of a concept is seldom tested in a rigorous way. A more formal notion of validity, *construct validity*, arises when measures of concepts behave as expected in theoretical predictions. Thus, the construct validity of social network measures can be studied by examining how these measures behave in a range of theoretical propositions (Mouton, Blake, and Fruchter 1955b; Burt, Marsden, and Rossi 1985).

Very little research on the construct validity of measures of network concepts has been conducted. In one study of this important idea, Mouton, Blake, and Fruchter (1955b) reviewed dozens of sociometric studies and found that sociometric measures, such as number of choices received by an actor, were related to a number of actor characteristics, such as leadership and effectiveness, thus demonstrating the construct validity of those sociometric measures.

Reliability. A measure of a variable or concept is *reliable* if repeated measurements give the same estimates of the variable. In a standard psychometric test-theoretic framework (see Lord and Novick 1968; Messick 1989), the reliability of a measure can be assessed by comparing measurements taken at two points in time (test-retest reliability), or by comparing measurements based on subsets of test items (split-halves or alternative forms). For the test-retest assessment of reliability to be appropriate, one must assume that the "true" value of a variable has not changed over time. This assumption is likely to be inappropriate for social network properties, since social phenomena can not be assumed to remain in stasis over any but the shortest spans of time. Assessing reliability of social network measurements using the test-retest approach is therefore problematic. Three approaches that have been used to assess the reliability of social network data are: test-retest comparison, comparison of alternative question formats, and the reciprocity of sociometric choices (Conrath, Higgins, and McClean 1983; Hammer 1985; Laumann 1969; Tracy, Catalano, Whittaker, and Fine 1990).

Reliability of sociometric data can also be assessed at different levels. One can study the reliability of the "choices" made by individual actors, or one can study the reliability of measures aggregated over a number of individual responses (for example, the popularity of an actor measured as the total number of choices it received) (Mouton, Blake, and Fruchter 1955a; Burt, Marsden, and Rossi 1985).

Although it is difficult to draw general conclusions from the research on the reliability of social network data collected from interviews or questionnaires, several findings are noteworthy. Sociometric questions using ratings or full rank orders are more reliable (have higher test-restest reliability) than fixed choice designs in which just a few responses are allowed (Mouton, Blake, and Fruchter 1955a). Responses to sociometric questions about more intense or intimate relations have higher rates of reciprocation than sociometric questions about less intense or intimate relations (see Marsden 1990b; Hammer 1985). Lastly, the reliability of aggregate measures (such as popularity) is higher than the reliability of "choices" made by individual actors (Burt, Marsden, and Rossi 1985).

Measurement Error. Measurement error occurs when there is a discrepancy between the "true" score or value of a concept and the observed (measured) value of that concept. It is common to assume that the observations or measurements of a concept are an additive combination of the "true" score plus error (or noise). This error, the difference between the true and observed values, is referred to as *measurement error*.

Holland and Leinhardt (1973) present a thorough discussion of measurement error and its implications in social network research. As they note, in social network research the measurements are the collection of ties among actors in the network, represented in the sociomatrix or sociogram. These measurements may differ from the "true" structure of the network. Since there are several levels at which we can study social networks (for example, one can look at properties of actors, pairs of actors, subsets of actors, or the network as a whole), it is important to understand the implications of measurement error at each of these levels.

Of particular importance in the discussion presented by Holland and Leinhardt is the error that arises in fixed choice data collection designs. Recall that in a fixed choice design, the respondent is instructed to nominate or name some fixed number of others for each relation. For example, each person may be asked to "List your three best friends." This design introduces error since it is quite unlikely that all people have exactly three best friends. The restriction of the nomination process also introduces error into the measurement of other network properties, such as properties of triads (triples of actors and their ties) and of subgroups.

2.5 Data Sets Found in These Pages

We now turn our attention to the network data sets that we focus on throughout this book. Each is described in detail, with attention given to the issues mentioned earlier in the chapter. All of these data sets, including measurements on all relations and actor attributes (if included) can be found in Appendix B. As the reader will see, these data are quite diverse, coming from a variety of disciplines and theoretical concerns. There are five primary data sets we discuss below.

2.5.1 Krackhardt's High-tech Managers

This is a one-mode network, with three relations measured on a set of people. These data were gathered by Krackhardt (1987a) in a small manufacturing organization on the west coast of the U.S. This organization had been in existence for ten years and produced high-tech machinery for other companies. The firm employed approximately one hundred people, and had twenty-one managers. These twenty-one managers are the set of actors for this data set. Throughout the book, we will refer to this example as "Krackhardt's high-tech managers." Krackhardt's interest in these data focused on the managers' perceptions of the entire network of informal advice and friendship relations. Specifically, he was interested in the perceptions held by the managers of the structure of the entire network. As we note later, he gathered much more extensive data than we will use. Here, we are interested only in the reports made by each manager of his or her own advice seeking and friendships.

Each manager was given a questionnaire and asked two questions: "Who would [you] go to for advice at work?" and "Who are your friends?" Each manager was given a roster of the names of the other managers, and asked (in a free choice setting) to check the other managers to whom they would go for advice at work, and with whom they were friends. Krackhardt also gathered a third relation based on the official organizational chart. He recorded "who reports to whom" for all twenty-one managers.

Thus, this is a multirelational data set, with three relations: "advice," "friendship," and "reports to." All three are dichotomous and directional. The first two were gathered from questionnaires, and the third, from organizational records. These relations were measured for a single point in time. The friendship relation clearly is an individual evaluation, while the advice relation is a verbal report of an interaction between actors. The third relation is a measurement of the formal bureaucratic structure within the organization. So, this data set has three very different types of relations.

The network is one-mode, since we have just a single set of twenty-one actors. The actors are people. This data set also includes four actor attributes: age; length of time employed by the organization (tenure); level in the corporate hierarchy; and the department. The first two are measured in years. There are four departments in the firm. All but the president of the firm have a department attribute coded as an integer from 1 to 4. The level attribute is measured on an integer scale from 1 to 3: 1 = CEO, 2 = vice president, and 3 = manager.

Of primary interest to Krackhardt were the perceptions held by each actor of the friendships and advice seeking within the firm. Each actor was asked to evaluate all the ties between all actors, not just the ties involving the respondent. In this way, Krackhardt was able to study perceptions of network structure. For example, how were an actor's actual reported friendships perceived by all the other actors? Krackhardt (1987a) categorized actors by their importance (as measured by centrality indices) and found that more important actors had better perceptions than those less important.

2.5.2 Padgett's Florentine Families

This is a one-mode network with two relations measured among a set of families. These multirelational network data, compiled by Padgett, consist of the marriage and business ties among 16 families in 15th century Florence, Italy. These data were compiled from the history of this period given by Kent (1978). The 16 families were chosen for analysis from a much larger collection of 116 leading Florentine families because of their historical prominence. Padgett (1987), Padgett and Ansell (1989, 1993), and Breiger and Pattison (1986) have extensively analyzed these data. Throughout, we will refer to this example as "Padgett's Florentine families."

The actors in this network are families. As noted by Breiger and Pattison, the family was an important economic and political unit, so the history of 15th century Florence can be well understood by focusing on families, rather than individual people. In the early 1430's, a political battle was waged in Florence for control of the government, primarily between the Medicis and the Strozzis, two of the families included in this data set. An excellent account of this history can be found in Padgett (1987). We note that Padgett and Ansell (1989) studied seventy-one families, and were interested in how the Medici family rose to dominate Florence between 1427 and 1434. Of primary interest to them was the association between the two relations, marriage and business.

The two measured relations are marriage and business. Both are nondirectional and dichotomous, and are transactional, since the business relation as well as the marital ties were used to solidify political and economic alliances. A marital tie exists between a pair of families if a member of one family marries a member of the other. A business tie exists if, for example, a member of one family grants credits, makes a loan, or has a joint business partnership with a member of another family (Breiger and Pattison 1986).

For these data, Padgett was not able to determine how families married each other or how families did business with each other. This nondirectionality is proper for marital ties, but perhaps not for business dealings. A variety of authors (including Breiger and Pattison 1986) have remarked that the nondirectionality of the business relation is unfortunate, since loans and credits are clearly directed from one family to another. More recent research by Padgett and Ansell (1993) contains an updated coding of the marriage relation that records both the family for the bride and the family for the groom, so that a directional marital relation can be studied. Both relations reflect activities occurring during this time period, but are not longitudinal.

The actors are families, 16 in number. There are three actor attributes: net wealth in 1427 (as taken from government records); number of priors (seats on the city council) from 1282–1344; and number of business or marriage ties in the total network (consisting of all 116 families).

2.5.3 Freeman's EIES Network

This is a one-mode network with two relations measured on a set of people. These data come from a computer conference among researchers working in the emerging scientific specialty of social network research, organized by Freeman, and sponsored by the National Science Foundation. These data were collected as part of a study of the impact of the Electronic Information Exchange System (*EIES*) housed at the New Jersey Institute of Technology. Fifty researchers interested in social network research participated. We focus here on the thirty-two people who completed the study. These researchers included sociologists, anthropologists, and statisticians/mathematicians. As part of the conference, a computer network was set up and participants were given computer terminals and access to a network for sending electronic mail messages to other participants. We note that this study was done prior to the widespread use of *BITNET*, *INTERNET*, and other popular computer networks that are widely available to academics today; consequently, this study involved a novel way for researchers to communicate. For more details of this study, see S. Freeman and L. Freeman (1979), L. Freeman and S. Freeman (1980), and Freeman (1986). A more detailed description of the design of this study can be found in Bernard, Killworth, and Sailer (1982). Here, we will refer to this example as "Freeman's *EIES* network."

Of particular interest are the network data arising from this study. Two relations, messages sent and acquaintanceships, were recorded. As part of this project, the computer system recorded all message transactions, specifically the origin and destination of the message, the day and time, and the number of lines in the message. Records were kept for several months. We therefore have a record of the number of messages sent from each participant to every other participant. We restrict our attention to the total number of messages sent from one actor to another; however, this message-sending relation can be defined for any time interval, for example, the number of messages sent in a given month. A second relation is acquaintanceship, and was gathered by a questionnaire. At the beginning and at the end of the project, participants were asked to fill out a questionnaire that included, among other things, a network question. Each participant was asked to indicate, for every other participant, whether she/he: (1) did not know the other, (2) had heard of the other but had not met him/her, (3) had met the other, (4) was a friend of the other, or (5) was a close personal friend of the other. This acquaintanceship relation is longitudinal, measured at two points in time: at the beginning of the study (January 1978), and at the end (September 1978) (S. Freeman and L. Freeman 1979).

There are two attribute variables in this data set: Primary disciplinary affiliation of the person; and Number of citations of the researcher's work in the *Social Science Citation Index* for the year 1978 (when the research started). The disciplinary affiliation variable has four categories: (1) sociology, (2) anthropology, (3) mathematics or statistics, and (4) other. The citation variable is coded as the number of citations.

These data are a part of a more comprehensive data set gathered by Bernard (who, along with Freeman, supplied us with these data) to study the accuracy of informants' reports of communications (see Bernard, Killworth, and Sailer 1982). Freeman (1986) studied the impact of this newly formed computer network on the acquaintanceships and friendships among the network researchers. Wasserman and Faust (1989) used these data to demonstrate the application of correspondence and canonical analysis to social network data.

2.5.4 Countries Trade Data

This is a one-mode network with five relations measured on countries. These data were gathered by us for use in this book. The actors are countries, selected from a list of sixty-three countries given in Smith and White (1988). We chose countries representing different categories from across several developmental classifications: Snyder and Kick's (1979) core/periphery status, Nemeth and Smith's (1985) alternative world system classification and level of industrialization, and a historical economic base from Lenski (as reported in Breedlove and Nolan 1988). We also chose countries both to span the globe and to represent politically and economically interesting characteristics. Only countries for which data were reported in 1984 commodity trade statistics were eligible for inclusion. We also attempted to reduce the number of shared borders between countries; however, some politically interesting countries are included even though they share borders (Israel and Syria, for example). Because of data availability, less-developed nations (African nations in particular) are probably under-represented in this set.

The final twenty-four countries represented as actors in this network are a geographically, economically, and politically diverse set, chosen to represent a range of interesting features and to span the categories of existing world system/development typologies. We will refer to these data as the *countries trade network*. Because of the selection mechanism, we will assume that this set of actors is representative of all possible countries.

Five relations were measured. Four of them are economic and one is political. The relations are:

- Imports of food and live animals
- Imports of crude materials, excluding fuel
- Imports of mineral fuels
- Imports of basic manufactured goods
- Diplomatic exchange

The first four relations are taken from the United Nations Commodity Trade Statistics (1984). We chose these four types of commodities (with single digit section codes 0, 2, 3, and 6 from the commodity trade statistics) since these commodities were studied originally by Breiger (1981a). The last relation comes from *The Europa Year Book* (Europa Publications 1984), which lists for each country those countries that have embassies or high commissions in the host country.

All five relations are dichotomous and directional. The four economic relations were reported on a continuous US$ scale. The reported values indicate the amount of goods (of the specified type) in 100,000 US$ imported by one country from the other (the UN does not list trade amounts under 100,000 US$). In order to standardize the imports to control for the vastly different economy sizes across countries, we first standardized each value by dividing by the country's total imports on that commodity. If the realized proportion was less than 0.01%, we coded the tie as absent. Otherwise, the tie was coded as present. This standardization actually had very little impact. Most of the ties that were changed from "trade present" to "trade absent" were large countries (US, Japan, UK) importing small amounts from very small countries (Madagascar, Liberia, Ethiopia).

The diplomatic relation records a tie as present if one country has an embassy or a high commission in another country. These data are taken from the 1984 *Europa Year Book* (Europa Publications 1984).

The data set includes four attribute variables reflecting the economic and social characteristics of the countries. The first two attribute variables measure annual rates of change between 1970 and 1981. They are: Annual population growth rate between 1970 and 1981, and Annual growth rate in GNP per capita between 1970 and 1981. The second two attribute variables measure rates of education and energy consumption. These variables are: Secondary school enrollment ratio in 1980, and Energy consumption per capita in 1980 (measured in kilo coal equivalent). Researchers have argued that these variables are related either to level of national development (industrialization) or to world system status. Measurements on these four variables were taken from The World Bank (1983).

Numerous social scientists have used network methods and data to study the world political and economic system (Snyder and Kick 1979; Nemeth and Smith 1985; Breiger 1981c). These researchers are primarily interested in whether location in a network "system" affects the rates of industrialization and development.

2.5.5 Galaskiewicz's CEOs and Clubs Network

This data set is a two-mode, affiliation network. The first mode consists of twenty-six chief executive officers (and spouses) of the major corporations, banks, and insurance companies headquartered in the Minneapolis/St. Paul metropolitan area. These data were gathered by Galaskiewicz through interviews with the CEOs and records of the clubs and boards. Thus, the first mode is a set of corporate CEOs as actors. The second mode is a collection of fifteen clubs, cultural boards, and corporate boards of directors to which the CEOs belong. There are two country clubs (Woodhill Country Club and Somerset Country Club), three metroplitan clubs (Minnesota Club, Minneapolis Club, and the Womens Club), four prestigious cultural organizations (such as Guthrie Theater, Minnesota Orchestra Society, Walker Art Center, St. Paul Chamber Orchestra, Minnesota Public Radio), and the six corporate boards of the *FORTUNE* 500 manufacturing firms and *FORTUNE* 50 banks headquartered in the area. These data record which CEO belongs to each of the clubs and boards. These memberships are for 1978–1981 (as discussed by Galaskiewicz 1985). We will refer to these data as *Galaskiewicz's CEOs and clubs*.

All data are dichotomous, indicating presence or absence of a membership. The first mode is a set of people, and the second, a set of organizations. The data are affiliational, and represent memberships. There are a number of attributes that are measured for both modes. For the first mode, we can categorize the actors by the nature of the corporations they head. For the second, we can categorize the organizations by their nature (clubs or corporate boards).

2.5.6 Other Data

In addition, we analyze a hypothetical data set throughout the book. This data set is used mostly to illustrate calculations, and consists of six second-grade children. It has measurements on four relations, three measured for the first mode (a set of six children) and one for actors in the first mode choosing actors in the second mode (a set of four teachers). One of the relations is longitudinal — friendship at the beginning and end of the school year. In addition, we have a single affiliation relation (party attendance). There are also a number of attributes that are recorded for both children and teachers, which will be introduced as needed.

Part II
Mathematical Representations of Social Networks

3

Notation for Social Network Data

Social network data consist of measurements on a variety of relations for one or more sets of actors. In a network data set we may also have recorded information on attributes of the actors. We will need notation for the set of actors, the relations themselves, and the actor attributes so that we can refer to important network concepts in a unified manner.

In this chapter, we introduce notation and illustrate with examples. We start by defining notation for a single, dichotomous relation. We then move to more complicated network data sets involving more than one set of actors and/or more than one relation. We will need a notational system flexible enough to handle the wide range of network data sets that are encountered in practice. We note that the only type of structural variable discussed in this chapter is relational. Chapter 8 presents notation and methodology for affiliational networks.

For the reader who already is familiar with social networks and the ways in which social network data can be denoted, or the reader who is only interested in specific techniques, we recommend a quick reading of the material in this chapter. Specifically, such readers can glance at Section 2 and the examples used in this chapter (perhaps skipping the material on multiple relations), and return to this chapter as needed.

There are many ways to describe social network data mathematically. We will introduce three different notational schemes. These schemes can each be adapted to represent a wide range of network data. However, for some forms of data and some types of network methods, one notation scheme may be preferred to the others, because of its appropriateness, clarity, or efficiency. The notations are:

- Graph theoretic
- Sociometric

● Algebraic

Each scheme will be described and illustrated in detail. We will show how these schemes overlap, and discuss when a specific scheme is more useful than the others. Graph theoretic notation is most useful for centrality and prestige methods, cohesive subgroup ideas, as well as dyadic and triadic methods. Sociometric notation is often used for the study of structural equivalence and blockmodels. Algebraic notation is most appropriate for role and positional analyses and relational algebras. We should note that there are other ways to denote social network data, some of which are used to study specific statistical models. Such schemes will be mentioned, when needed, in later chapters.

The graph theoretic notation scheme can be viewed as an elementary way to represent actors and relations. It is the basis of the many concepts of graph theory used since the late 1940's to study social networks. The notation provides a straightforward way to refer to actors and relations, and is completely consistent with the notation from the other three schemes. Mathematicians and statisticians such as Bock, Harary, Katz, and Luce were among the first to view networks as directed and undirected graphs (see Forsyth and Katz 1946; Katz 1947; Luce and Perry 1949; Bock and Husain 1950, 1952; Harary and Norman 1953). Graph theory texts such as Flament (1963) and Harary (1969) describe social network applications. We should also direct the reader to other texts on graph theory and social networks, such as Harary, Norman, and Cartwright (1965), and Hage and Harary (1983), that present graph theoretic notation for social network data. Mathematical sociology texts, such as Coleman (1964), Fararo (1973), and Leik and Meeker (1975), contain elementary discussions of the use of graph theory in social network analysis.

The second notation scheme, sociometric notation, is by far the most common in the social network literature. One presents the data for each relation in a two-way matrix, termed a *sociomatrix*, where the rows and columns refer to the actors making up the pairs. Sociomatrices began to be used more than fifty years ago after their introduction by Moreno (1934) in his pioneering research in sociometry (see also Moreno and Jennings 1938).

Most major computer software packages for social network data analyze network information presented in sociomatrices. Further, many methods are defined for sociomatrices. This notational scheme is probably the most useful for readers interested in the methods discussed in Parts III and IV of the book. Sociomatrices are *adjacency matrices* for *graphs*, and consequently, this second notational scheme is directly related to the first.

The third notational scheme, algebraic notation, is used to study multiple relations. This notation is useful for studying network role structures and relational algebras. Such analyses use algebraic techniques to compare and contrast measured relations, and derived compound relations. A compound relation is the composition or combination of two or more relations. For example, if we have measured two relations, "is a friend of" and "is an enemy of," for a set of people, then we might be interested in the composition of these two relations: "friends' enemies." The focus of such algebraic techniques is on the associations among the relations measured on pairs of actors, across the entire set of actors. This notation is designed for one-mode networks, and was first used by White (1963) and Boyd (1969).

We now turn to each of these notations, show how they are related, discuss when each is useful, and illustrate each with examples.

3.1 Graph Theoretic Notation

A network can be viewed in several ways. One of the most useful views is as a *graph*, consisting of *nodes* joined by *lines*. Chapter 4 discusses graph theory at length. Here, we introduce some simple graph theoretic notation, and show how this notation can be used to label the actors and relations in a network data set.

Suppose we have a set of actors. We will refer to this set as $\mathcal{N}$. The set $\mathcal{N}$ contains g actors in number, which we will denote by $\mathcal{N} = \{n_1, n_2, \ldots, n_g\}$. The symbol $\mathcal{N}$ is commonly used to stand for the set, since the graph theory literature frequently refers to this set as a collection of <u>nodes</u> of a graph. For example, consider a collection of $g = 6$ second-grade children: Allison, Drew, Eliot, Keith, Ross, and Sarah. We have $\mathcal{N} = \{$Allison, Drew, Eliot, Keith, Ross, Sarah$\}$, a collection of six actors, so that we can refer to the children by their symbols: $n_1 = $ Allison, $n_2 = $ Drew, $n_3 = $ Eliot, $n_4 = $ Keith, $n_5 = $ Ross, and $n_6 = $ Sarah.

3.1.1 A Single Relation

We now assume that we have a single relation for the set of actors $\mathcal{N}$. That is, we record whether each actor in $\mathcal{N}$ relates to every other actor on this relation. To start, we will let the relation be dichotomous and directional. Thus, n_i either relates to n_j or does not. For now, we do not consider the strength of this interaction or how frequently n_i interacts with n_j.

Consider an ordered pair of actors, n_i and n_j. Either the first actor in the ordered pair relates to the second or it does not. Since the relation is directional, the pair of actors n_i and n_j is distinct from the pair n_j and n_i (that is, order matters). If a tie is present, then we say that the ordered pair is an element of a special collection of pairs, which we will refer to as $\mathscr{L}$. If an ordered pair is in $\mathscr{L}$, then the first actor in the pair relates to the second on the relation under consideration.

Note that there can be as many as $g(g-1)$ elements (the total number of ordered pairs in $\mathscr{L}$), and as few as 0.

If the ordered pair under consideration is $< n_i, n_j >$, and if there is a tie present, we will write $n_i \to n_j$. The elements, or ordered pairs, of relating actors in $\mathscr{L}$ will be denoted by the symbol l. Let us assume that there are L entries in $\mathscr{L}$, so that $\mathscr{L} = \{l_1, l_2, \dots, l_L\}$. The elements in $\mathscr{L}$ can be represented graphically by drawing a line from the first actor in the element to the second. It is customary to refer to such a graph as a *directed graph*, since the lines have a direction. Directed lines are referred to as *arcs*. We use the symbol $\mathscr{L}$ to refer to the set of directed L̲ines and the symbol l to refer to the individual directed l̲ines in the set. We will frequently refer to such ordered pairs of relating actors as *directed lines* or *arcs*.

Since a graph consists of a set of nodes $\mathscr{N}$, and a set of lines $\mathscr{L}$, it can be described mathematically by the two sets, $(\mathscr{N}, \mathscr{L})$. We will use the symbol $\mathscr{G}$ to denote a graph. It is important to note that for the graph theoretic notation scheme, these two sets (a set of actors, and a set of ordered pairs of actors, or arcs) suffice for mathematical descriptions of the crucial components in a network on which a single, dichotomous relation is measured.

On some relations, an individual actor does not usually relate to itself. When studying such relations, one does not consider *self-choices*.

There are relations that are *nondirectional*; that is, we cannot distinguish between the line from n_i to n_j and the line from n_j to n_i. For example, we may consider a set of actors, and record whether they "live near each other." Clearly, this is a nondirectional relation — if n_i lives near n_j, then n_j lives near n_i. There is only one measurement to be made for each pair, rather than two as with a directional relation. The two ordered pairs have identical relational interactions. The set $\mathscr{L}$ now contains at most $g(g-1)/2$ pairs. The order of the pair of actors in these relating pairs no longer matters, since both actors relate to each other in the same way.

Return to our example, and suppose that the single, dichotomous directional relation is "friendship," so that we consider whether each child views every other child as a friend. Suppose further that eight of the possible thirty ordered pairs are friendships (that is, eight of the thirty possible arcs are present) and that the other twenty-two are not friendships (or that there are twenty-two arcs absent). Let these $L = 8$ pairs be <Allison, Drew>, <Allison, Ross>, <Drew, Sarah>, <Drew, Eliot>, <Eliot, Drew>, <Keith, Ross>, <Ross, Sarah>, and <Sarah, Drew>. Thus, for the elements of $\mathscr{L}$, l_1 = <Allison, Drew>, l_2 = <Allison, Ross>, ... , and l_8 = <Sarah, Drew>. The data tell us that Allison views Drew as a friend, Allison also views Ross as a friend, Drew states that Sarah is his friend, and so forth. It is also interesting to note that this friendship is not reciprocal; that is, if n_i states that n_j is his friend (or $n_i \rightarrow n_j$), it is possible that this sentiment is not returned — n_j may not "choose" n_i as a friend (or $n_j \nrightarrow n_i$).

A graph can be presented as a diagram in which nodes are represented as points in a two-dimensional space and arcs are represented by directed arrows between points. Thus, these six children can be represented as points in a two-dimensional space. It is important to note that the actual location of points in this two-dimensional space is irrelevant. We can take these points, and draw in the eight arcs representing these eight ordered pairs of children who are friends. This directed graph or *sociogram* is shown in Figure 3.1.

3.1.2 ◯ *Multiple Relations*

We may have more than one relation in a social network data set. Graph theoretic notation can be generalized to multirelational networks, which could include both directional and nondirectional relations. For example, we may study whether the corporations in a metropolitan area do business with each other — does n_i sell to n_j, for example — and whether they interlock through their boards of directors — does an officer of corporation n_i sit on the board of directors of corporation n_j? Given the notation presented for the case of a single dichotomous relation, it is easy to generalize it to multiple relations.

Suppose that we are interested in more than one relation defined on pairs of actors taken from $\mathscr{N}$. Let R be the number of relations.

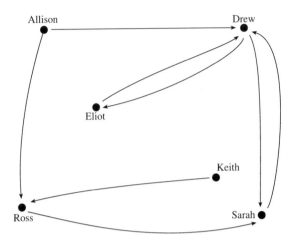

Fig. 3.1. The six actors and the directed lines between them — a sociogram

Each of these relations can be represented as a graph or directed graph; hence, each has associated with it a set of lines or arcs, specifying which (directed) lines are present in the (directed) graph for the relation (or, which (ordered) pairs are "relating"). Thus, each relation has a corresponding set of arcs, $\mathscr{L}_r$, which contains L_r ordered pairs of actors as elements. Here, the subscript r ranges from 1 to R, the total number of relations.

Each of these R sets defines a directed graph on the nodes in $\mathscr{N}$. These directed graphs can be viewed in one or more figures. So, each relation is defined on the same set of nodes, but each has a different set of arcs. Thus, we can quantify the rth relation by $(\mathscr{N}, \mathscr{L}_r)$, for $r = 1, 2, \ldots, R$.

For example, return to our second-graders, and now consider $R = 3$ relations: 1) who chooses whom as a friend, measured at the beginning of the school year; 2) who chooses whom as a friend, measured at the end of the school year; and 3) who lives near whom. The first two relations are directional, while the last is nondirectional. Suppose that $L_1 = 8$ ordered pairs of actors, $L_2 = 11$, and $L_3 = 12$. Below, we list these three sets.

Relation 1 Friendship at Beginning	Relation 2 Friendship at End	Relation 3 Lives Near
<Allison, Drew>	<Allison, Drew>	(Allison, Ross)
<Allison, Ross>	<Allison, Ross>	(Allison, Sarah)
<Drew, Sarah>	<Drew, Sarah>	(Drew, Eliot)
<Drew, Eliot>	<Drew, Eliot>	(Keith, Ross)
<Eliot, Drew>	<Drew, Ross>	(Keith, Sarah)
<Keith, Ross>	<Eliot, Ross>	(Ross, Sarah)
<Ross, Sarah>	<Keith, Drew>	
<Sarah, Drew>	<Keith, Ross>	
	<Ross, Keith>	
	<Ross, Sarah>	
	<Sarah, Drew>	

For a nondirectional relation, such as "lives near," measurements are made on unordered rather than ordered pairs. Clearly, when one actor relates to a second, the second relates to the first; therefore, since Allison lives near Ross, Ross lives near Allison. When listing the pairs of relating actors (or arcs) for a nondirectional relation, each pair can be listed no more than once. We use $(\bullet, \bullet)$ to denote pairs of actors for whom a tie is present on a nondirectional relation, and use $< \bullet, \bullet >$ to denote ties on a directional relation.

Examining such lists can be difficult. An alternative way to present the three sets $\mathscr{L}_1$, $\mathscr{L}_2$, and $\mathscr{L}_3$ is graphically. We can place the arcs for directed graphs or lines for undirected graphs on three figures (one for each relation), or on a single figure containing points representing the six actors and arcs or lines for all relations, simultaneously. We use different types of lines in Figure 3.2 for the different relations: solid, for relation 1 (friend at beginning); dashed, for relation 2 (friend at end); and dotted, for relation 3 (lives near). Since friendship is a directional relation, there are arrowheads indicating the directionality of an arc. Since "lives near" is nondirected, there are no arrowheads on these lines. This figure is an example of a *multivariate directed graph*; such graphs are described in more detail in Chapter 4.

3.1.3 Summary

To review, we have assumed that there is just one set of actors. This assumption will be relaxed in a later section of this chapter. In this simple

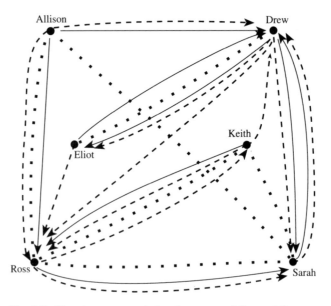

Fig. 3.2. The six actors and the three sets of directed lines — a multi-variate directed graph

situation, there is just a single kind of pair of actors, those with both actors in the single set $\mathcal{N}$. The number of actors in $\mathcal{N}$ is g. Assuming that we have R relations, we have a set of arcs associated with each relation, $\mathcal{L}_1, \mathcal{L}_2, \dots, \mathcal{L}_R$. Each set of arcs can have as many as $g(g-1)$ entries in these sets. The entries in each set are exactly those ordered pairs for which the first actor relates to the second actor on the relation in question. Thus, one needs to specify the set $\mathcal{N}$ and the R sets of arcs to describe completely the network data set.

We should mention that this notation scheme does not extend well to valued relations. Graph theory is not well designed for data sets that record the strength or frequency of the interaction for a pair of actors. One can use special graphs, such as signed graphs and valued graphs (see Chapter 4), to represent valued relations, but many of the more elegant results from graph theory do not apply to this extension. However, sociometric notation is general enough to handle valued relations.

3.2 Sociometric Notation

Sociometry is the study of positive and negative affective relations, such as liking/disliking and friends/enemies, among a set of people. A social network data set consisting of people and measured affective relations between people is often referred to as *sociometric*.

Relational data are often presented in two-way matrices termed *sociomatrices*. The two dimensions of a sociomatrix are indexed by the sending actors (the rows) and the receiving actors (the columns). Thus, if we have a one-mode network, the sociomatrix will be square.

A sociomatrix for a dichotomous relation is exactly the *adjacency matrix* for the graph (or *sociogram*) quantifying the ties between the actors for the relation in question. So, this notation can be viewed as complementary to graph theoretic notation described in the previous section. In these next paragraphs, we describe the history of sociomatrices and sociograms. We then show how social network data can be denoted by a set of sociomatrices.

Sociometry has grown and expanded over the past half century, so that such studies are now usually called simply sociological or occasionally social psychological. The first sociometricians published much of their research in the journal *Sociometry*, which was renamed first *Social Psychology* and then *Social Psychology Quarterly* in the late 1970's. Moreno was *Sociometry*'s founding editor (in 1937). Moreno and other researchers developed a very useful notation for social networks, which we will refer to as sociometric notation. We describe this classic notation in this section.

Sociograms and sociomatrices were first used by Moreno (1934), who demonstrated how they could represent the relational interactions pictured in a sociogram. The focus of Moreno's research, and much of the sociometric literature of the 1930's and 1940's, was how advantageous it was to picture interpersonal interactions using sociograms, even for sets with many actors. In fact, Moreno (see "Emotions Mapped," 1933) aspired to draw a sociometric "map" of New York City, but the best he could do was a sociogram for a community of size 435 (included as a foldout in Moreno 1934). Both Moreno (1934) and Northway (1940) proposed rules for drawing sociograms. These pioneering sociometricians looked for techniques to show the acceptability of each actor relative to the set of actors as a whole and to determine which "choices" were the most important to the group structure. Lindzey and Byrne (1968), building on Moreno's original guidelines, provide a very good discussion of the measurement of relations. Recently, because of innovations in computing, there has been renewed interest in the graphical representations of social network data (Klovdahl 1986).

Moreno actually preferred the use of sociograms to sociomatrices, and had several arguments in print with proponents of sociomatrices, such as Katz. Moreno used his position as editor of *Sociometry* frequently to interject editor's notes into articles in his journal.

Even with the growing interest in figures such as sociograms, researchers were unhappy that different investigators using the same data could produce as many different sociograms (in appearance) as there were investigators. As we have mentioned, the placement of actors and lines in the two-dimensional space is completely arbitrary. Consequently, the use of the sociomatrix to denote social network data increased in the 1940's. The literature in the 1940's presented a variety of methods for analyzing and manipulating sociomatrices (see Dodd 1940; Katz 1947; Festinger 1949; Luce and Perry 1949; and Harary, Norman, and Cartwright 1965). For example, Dodd (1940) described simple algebraic operations for square sociomatrices indexed by the set of actors. He also showed how rows and columns of such matrices could be aggregated to highlight the relationships among sets of actors, rather than the individual actors themselves. Forsyth and Katz (1946) advocated the use of sociomatrices over sociograms to standardize the quantification of social interactions and to represent network data "more objectively" (page 341). This research appears to be the first to focus on derived subgroupings of actors. Katz (1947) proposed a "canonical" decomposition of a sociomatrix to facilitate the comparison of an observed sociomatrix to a target sociomatrix, an idea first proposed by Northway (1940, 1951, 1952). He also showed how sociomatrices could be rearranged using permutation matrices to identify subgroups of actors, and how choices made by a particular actor could be viewed as a multidimensional vector. Festinger (1949) applied matrix multiplication to sociomatrices and described how products of a sociomatrix (particularly squares and cubes) can be used to find cliques or subgroups of similar actors (see also Chabot 1950). Since such powers have simple graph theoretic interpretation (see Chapter 4's discussion of 2- and 3-step walks), this research helped begin the era of graph theoretic approaches to social network analysis. Luce and Perry (1949) and Luce (1950) proposed one of the first techniques to find cliques or subgroups of actors using (for that time) rather sophisticated sociomatrix calculations backed up with an elaborate set of theorems describing the properties and uniqueness of their approach (which was termed *n-clique analysis*; see Chapter 7). Bavelas (1948, 1950) and Leavitt (1951) introduced the notion of centrality (see Chapter 5) into social network analysis. By the end of the decade, researchers had begun to think about electronic calculations for sociometric data (Beum and Criswell 1947; Katz 1950; Beum and Brundage 1950) consisting of a collection of sociomatrices. Research of Katz (1953), MacRae (1960), Wright and Evitts (1961), Coleman (1964), Hubbell (1965), and methods discussed by Mitchell (1969) rely extensively on computers to find various graph theoretic measures. The 1950's and early 1960's became the era of graph theory in sociometry.

The line between sociometric and graph theoretic approaches to social network analysis began to become blurred during the early history of the discipline, as computers began to play a bigger role in data analysis. Sociograms waned in importance as sociomatrices became more popular and as more mathematical and statistical indices were invented that used sociomatrices, much to the dismay of Moreno (1946).

History is certainly on the side of this notational scheme. In fact, most research papers and books on social network methodology begin with the definition of a sociomatrix. Readers who are interested in the topics in Parts II and III will find this notation most useful. For most social network methods, sociometric notation is probably the only notation necessary. It is also the scheme preferred by most network analysis computer programs. It is important to note, however, that sociometric notation can not easily quantify or denote actor attributes, and thus is limited. It is useful when actor attributes are not measured. The relationship between sociometric notation and the more general graph theoretic notation contributes to the popularity of this approach.

As is done throughout this chapter, we split our discussion of sociometric notation and sociomatrices into several parts. We first describe how to construct these two-dimensional sociometric arrays when only one set of actors and one relation is present, and then, when one set of actors and two (or more) relations are measured. Our discussion of two (or more) sets of actors can be found at the end of the chapter.

3.2.1 Single Relation

Let us suppose that we have a single relation measured on one set of g actors in $\mathcal{N} = \{n_1, n_2, \ldots, n_g\}$. We let $\mathcal{X}$ refer to this single valued, directional relation. This relation is measured on the ordered pairs of actors that can be formed from the actors in $\mathcal{N}$.

Consider now the measurements taken on each ordered pair of actors. Define x_{ij} as the value of the tie from the ith actor to the jth actor on the single relation. We now place these measurements into a *sociomatrix*. Rows and columns of this sociomatrix index the individual actors, arranged in identical order. Since there are g actors, the matrix is of size $g \times g$. Sociometric notation uses such matrices to denote measurements on ties.

For the relation $\mathscr{X}$, we define $\mathbf{X}$ as the associated sociomatrix. This sociomatrix has g rows and g columns. The value of the tie from n_i to n_j is placed into the (i, j)th element of $\mathbf{X}$. The entries are defined as:

$$x_{ij} \quad = \quad \text{the value of the tie from } n_i \text{ to } n_j$$
$$\text{on relation } \mathscr{X}, \tag{3.1}$$

where i and j ($i \neq j$) range over all integers from 1 to g. An example will be given shortly. One can think of the elements of $\mathbf{X}$ as the coded values of the relation $\mathscr{X}$. If the relation is dichotomous, then the values for the tie are simply 0 and 1.

Pairs listing the same actor twice, (n_i, n_i), $i = 1, 2, \ldots, g$, are called "self-choices" for a specific relation and are usually undefined. These self-choices lie along the main diagonal of the sociomatrix; consequently, the main diagonal of a sociomatrix is usually full of undefined entries. However, there are situations in which self-choices do make sense. In such cases, the entries $\{x_{ii}\}$ of the sociomatrix are defined. Usually, we will assume undefined sociomatrix diagonals since most methods ignore these elements.

Assume now that this relation is valued and discrete. We will then assume that the possible values for the relation come from the set $\{0, 1, 2, \ldots, C - 1\}$, for $C = 2, 3, \ldots$. If the relation is dichotomous, then $C = 2$ possible values. Thus, C is defined as the number of different values the tie can take on. If the relation is valued and discrete, but takes on other than integer values from 0 to $C - 1$, then we can easily transform the actual values into the values for this set. For example, if the relation can take on the values $-1, 0, 1$, then we can map -1 to 0, 0 to 1, and $+1$ to 2 (so that $C = 3$). One nice feature of sociometric notation is its ability to handle valued relations.

Since the case of a single relation is just a special case of the multirelational situation, we now turn to this more general case.

3.2.2 Multiple Relations

Suppose that we have R relations $\mathscr{X}_1$, $\mathscr{X}_2$, ..., $\mathscr{X}_R$ measured on a single set of actors. We assume that we have R relations indexed by $r = 1, 2, ..., R$. As with a single relation, these relations are valued, and the values for relation $\mathscr{X}_r$ come from the set $\{0, 1, 2, ..., C_r - 1\}$.

Consider now the measurements on each possible ordered pair of actors. We define x_{ijr} as the strength of the tie from the ith actor to the jth actor on the rth relation. We now place these measurements into a collection of sociomatrices, one for each relation. Rows and columns of each sociomatrix index the individual actors, arranged in identical order. Thus, the rows and columns of all the sociomatrices are labeled identically. Each matrix is of size $g \times g$.

Consider one of the relations, say $\mathscr{X}_r$, and define $\mathbf{X}_r$ as the sociomatrix associated with this relation. The value of the tie from n_i to n_j is placed into the (i, j)th element of $\mathbf{X}_r$. The entries are defined as:

$$x_{ijr} = \text{the value of the tie from } n_i \text{ to } n_j$$
$$\text{on relation } \mathscr{X}_r, \tag{3.2}$$

where i and j ($i \neq j$) range over all integers from 1 to g, and $r = 1, 2, ..., R$. As mentioned, x_{ijr} takes on integer values from 0 to $C_r - 1$. One can think of the elements of $\mathbf{X}_r$ as the coded values of the relation $\mathscr{X}_r$. There are R, $g \times g$ sociomatrices, one for each relation defined for the actors in $\mathscr{N}$. In fact, one can view these R sociomatrices as the layers in a three-dimensional matrix of size $g \times g \times R$. The rows of these sociomatrices index the sending actors, the columns index the receiving actors, and the layers index the relations. Sometimes, this matrix is referred to as a *super-sociomatrix*, representing the information in a multirelational network.

Consider again our example, consisting of a collection of $g = 6$ children and $R = 3$ relations: 1) Friendship at beginning of the school year; 2) Friendship at end of the school year; and 3) Lives near. All three relations are dichotomous, so that $C_1 = C_2 = C_3 = 2$. These three relations are pictured in a single multivariate or multirelational sociogram in Figure 3.2. In Table 3.1 below, we give the three 6×6 dichotomous sociomatrices for the three relations. Note how in Figure 3.2, a "1" in entry (i, j) for the rth sociomatrix indicates that $n_i \rightarrow n_j$ on relation $\mathscr{X}_r$ (or, $n_i \overset{\mathscr{X}_r}{\rightarrow} n_j$, for short).

To illustrate, look at the first relation and the first arc in $\mathscr{L}_1$. In Section 3.1, we said that this arc is $l_1 = $ <Allison, Drew>. Allison $\rightarrow$ Drew is

Table 3.1. *Sociomatrices for the six actors and three relations of Figure 3.2*

Friendship at Beginning of Year

	Allison	Drew	Eliot	Keith	Ross	Sarah
Allison	-	1	0	0	1	0
Drew	0	-	1	0	0	1
Eliot	0	1	-	0	0	0
Keith	0	0	0	-	1	0
Ross	0	0	0	0	-	1
Sarah	0	1	0	0	0	-

Friendship at End of Year

	Allison	Drew	Eliot	Keith	Ross	Sarah
Allison	-	1	0	0	1	0
Drew	0	-	1	0	1	1
Eliot	0	0	-	0	1	0
Keith	0	1	0	-	1	0
Ross	0	0	0	1	-	1
Sarah	0	1	0	0	0	-

Lives Near

	Allison	Drew	Eliot	Keith	Ross	Sarah
Allison	-	0	0	0	1	1
Drew	0	-	1	0	0	0
Eliot	0	1	-	0	0	0
Keith	0	0	0	-	1	1
Ross	1	0	0	1	-	1
Sarah	1	0	0	1	1	-

represented by the arc l_1. Thus, there is an arc from Allison to Drew in the sociogram for the first relation, indicating that Allison chooses Drew as a friend at the beginning of the school year. The first entry in $\mathcal{L}_1$ is exactly this arc. This arc is how this tie is denoted by graph theoretic notation. Consider now how this single tie is coded with sociometric notation. Consider the first sociomatrix in Table 3.1. Consider the entry which quantifies Allison (n_1) as a sender (the first row) and Drew (n_2) as a receiver (the second column) on relation $\mathcal{X}_1$. This entry is in the $(1,2)$ cell of this sociomatrix, and contains a 1 indicating that

$$x_{121} = \text{the value of the tie from } n_1 \text{ to } n_2 \text{ on relation } \mathcal{X}_1$$
$$= 1.$$

Note also that $x_{211} = 0$, indicating that Drew does not choose Allison as a friend at the beginning of the school year; that is, Drew $\nrightarrow$ Allison. This friendship is clearly one-sided, and is not reciprocated.

As one can see, sociometric notation is simple, once one gets used to reading information from two-dimensional sociomatrices. Also note how the diagonals of all three sociomatrices in Table 3.1 are undefined — by design, children are not allowed to choose themselves as friends, and we do not record whether a child lives near himself or herself.

These sociomatrices are the adjacency matrices for the two directed graphs and one undirected graph for the three dichotomous relations. The graphs and the sociomatrices represent exactly the same information. In graph theoretic notation, there are two sets of arcs and one set of lines, $\mathscr{L}_1$, $\mathscr{L}_2$, $\mathscr{L}_3$, which list the ordered pairs of children that are tied for the first two relations and the pairs of children that are tied for the third. If an ordered pair is included in the first or second $\mathscr{L}$ set, then there is an arc drawn from the first child in the pair (the sender) to the second (the receiver). And if an unordered pair of actors is included in the third line set, then there is a line between the two children in the pair. In sociometric notation, the entry in the corresponding cell of the sociomatrix is unity.

We also want to note that the third relation in this network data set is nondirectional; that is, there is a line from n_i to n_j whenever there is a line from n_j to n_i, and vice versa. Note how we were able to code this relation in the sociomatrix given in Table 3.1. Also note that the sociomatrix for a nondirectional relation is symmetric; that is, $x_{ij} = x_{ji}$. One very nice feature of sociometric notation is that it can easily handle both directional and nondirectional relations.

3.2.3 Summary

As we have stated in this section, sociometric notation is the oldest, and perhaps the easiest, way to denote the ties among a set of actors. A single two-dimensional sociomatrix is defined for each relation, and the entries of this matrix code the ties between pairs of actors. Generalizing to valued relations is also easy — the entries in a sociomatrix are the values of the ties, not simply 0's and 1's.

Sociometric notation is very common, the notation of choice for network computing, and will be our first choice of a notational scheme throughout this book. However, as we have mentioned, there are network data sets for which sociometric notation is more difficult to use — specifically, those which contain information on the attributes of the

actors. For example consider our second-graders. If we knew their ethnicity (coded on some nominal scale), it would be difficult to include this
information in the three sociomatrices (but see Frank and Harary 1982,
for an alternative representational scheme).

To conclude, we will frequently use sociomatrices to present network
data. These arrays are very convenient (and space-saving!) devices to
denote network data sets.

3.3 ○Algebraic Notation

Let us now focus on relations in multirelational networks. In order
to present algebraic methods and models for multiple relations (such
as relational algebras) in Chapters 11 and 12, it is useful to employ a
notation that is different from, though consistent with, the sociometric
and graph theoretic notations that we have just discussed. We will refer
to this scheme as *algebraic notation*. Algebraic notation is most useful
for multirelational networks since it easily denotes the "combinations"
of relations in these networks. However, it can also be used to describe
data for single relational networks.

There are two major differences between algebraic notation and sociometric notation. First, one refers to relations with distinct capital letters,
rather than with subscripted $\mathcal{X}$'s. For example, we could use F to denote
the relation "is a friend of" and E for the relation "is an enemy of."
Second, we will record the presence of a tie from actor i to actor j on
relation F as iFj. This is a shorthand for the sociometric and graph
theoretic notation. Rather than indicating ties as $i \to j$, we will replace
the $\to$ with the letter label for the relation.

In general, $x_{ijF} = 1$ if $n_i \to n_j$ on the relation labeled $\mathcal{X}_F$ (or F for
short). This tie will be denoted by $i \overset{F}{\to} j$, or shortened even further to
iFj. This latter notation, iFj, is algebraic.

Referring to our example, we label the relation "is a friend of at the
beginning of the school year" as F. We would record the tie implied by
"child i chooses child j as a friend at the beginning of the school year"
as iFj. In sociometric notation, iFj means that $x_{ijF} = 1$, and implies that
there is a "1" in the cell at row i and column j of the sociomatrix for
this relation.

Algebraic notation is especially useful for dichotomous relations, since
it codes the presence of ties on a given relation. Extensions to valued relations can be difficult. However, the limitation to dichotomous relations

presents no problem for us, since the models that use algebraic notation are specific to dichotomous relations. The advantages of this notation are that it allows us to distinguish several distinct relations using letter designations, and to record *combinations* of relations, such as "friends' enemy," or "mother's brother," or a "friend's neighbor." Unfortunately, this notational scheme can not handle valued relations or actor attributes.

3.4 ○Two Sets of Actors

A network may include two sets of actors. Such a network is a two-mode network, with each set of actors constituting one of the modes. A researcher studying such a network might focus on how the actors in one set relate to each other, how the actors in the other set relate to each other, and/or how actors in one set relate to the actors in the other set. In this situation, we need to distinguish between the two sets of actors and the different types of ties. We note that relations defined on two sets of actors often yield complicated network data sets. It is thus quite complicated to give "hard-and-fast" notation rules to apply to every and all situations. We recommend that for multirelational data sets one make an inventory of measured relations and modify the rules given below to apply to the situation at hand.

There are many social networks that involve two sets of actors. For example, we might have a collection of teachers and students who are interacting with each other. Consider the relations "is a student of" and "attends faculty meetings together." The relation "is a student of" can only exist between a student and a teacher. The relation "attends faculty meetings together" is defined only for pairs of teachers.

We will call the first actor in the pair the *sender* and the second actor the *receiver*. Other authors have called these actors *originators* and *recipient*, or simply, *actors* and *partners*. With this understanding, we can distinguish between the two actors in the pair. If the relation is defined on a single set of actors, both actors in the pair can be senders and both can be receivers. The interesting "wrinkle" that arises if there are two sets of actors is that the senders might come only from the first set and the receivers only from the second.

We will let $\mathcal{N}$ refer to the first set of actors and $\mathcal{M}$ refer to the second set. The set $\mathcal{N}$ contains g actors and the second set $\mathcal{M}$ contains h actors. The set $\mathcal{M}$ contains elements $\{m_1, m_2, \ldots, m_h\}$, so that m_i is a typical actor in the second set. Further, there are $\binom{h}{2}$ dyads that can be formed from actors in $\mathcal{M}$.

In this section, we will first discuss the two types of pairs that can arise when relations are measured on two (or even more) sets of actors. We present only sociometric notation, since it is sufficient.

To illustrate the notation, we return to our collection of six second-grade children, and now consider a second set of actors, $\mathcal{M}$, consisting of $h = 4$ adults. We define $m_1 = $ Mr. Jones, $m_2 = $ Ms. Smith, $m_3 = $ Mr. White, and $m_4 = $ Ms. Davis. In total, we have ten actors, which are grouped into these two sets. Considering just the actors in $\mathcal{M}$, there are $4(4 - 1)/2 = 6$ additional unordered pairs.

3.4.1 ⊗*Different Types of Pairs*

With two sets of actors, there can be two types of pairs — those that consist of actors from the same set and those that consist of actors from different sets. We will call the former *homogeneous* and the latter *heterogeneous*. Thus, in homogeneous pairs the senders and receivers are from the same set, while in heterogeneous pairs actors are from different sets. We discuss each of these types, beginning with homogeneous pairs.

We can further distinguish between two kinds of homogeneous pairs by noting that there are two sets from which the actors can come. The two kinds of homogeneous pairs are:

- Sender and Receiver both belong to $\mathcal{N}$
- Sender and Receiver both belong to $\mathcal{M}$

In a data set with just one set of actors, the pairs are all homogeneous. However, when there are two sets of actors, there are two kinds of homogeneous pairs.

Of more interest when there are two sets of actors are the pairs that contain one actor from each set. These heterogeneous pairs are also of two kinds, depending on the sets to which the sender and receiver belong. Assuming the relation for the heterogeneous pairs is directional, the originating actor must belong to a different set than the receiving actor. Since there are two sets of actors, we get two kinds of heterogeneous pairs:

- Sender belongs to $\mathcal{N}$ and Receiver belongs to $\mathcal{M}$
- Sender belongs to $\mathcal{M}$ and Receiver belongs to $\mathcal{N}$

It is important to distinguish between these two collections of heterogeneous pairs. Relations defined on the first collection of pairs can be quite different from those defined on the second. For example, if

$\mathcal{N}$ is a set of major corporations in a large city and $\mathcal{M}$ is a set of non-profit organizations (such as churches, arts organizations, charitable institutions, etc.), then we could study how the corporations in $\mathcal{N}$ make charitable contributions to the non-profits in $\mathcal{M}$. Such a relation would not be defined for the other collection of heterogeneous pairs, since it is virtually impossible for non-profits to contribute money to the welfare of the corporations.

3.4.2 ○ Sociometric Notation

We now turn our attention to sociometric notation and sociomatrices for the relations defined for both homogeneous *and* heterogeneous pairs. The notation will have to allow for the fact that the sending and receiving actors could come from different sets. We assume that we have a number of relations. The measurements for a specific relation can be placed into a sociomatrix, and there is one sociomatrix for each relation.

A sociomatrix is indexed by the set of originating actors (for its rows) and the set of receiving actors (for its columns) and gives the values of the ties from the row actors to the column actors. If the relation is defined for actors from different sets, then in general, its sociomatrix will not be square. Rather, it will be *rectangular*.

Let us pick one of the relations, say $\mathcal{X}_r$, and suppose that it is defined on a collection of heterogeneous pairs in which the originating actor is from $\mathcal{N}$ and the receiving actor is from $\mathcal{M}$. The sociomatrix $\mathbf{X}_r$, giving the measurements on $\mathcal{X}_r$, has dimensions $g \times h$. The (i, j)th cell of this matrix gives the measurement on this rth relation for the pair of actors (n_i, m_j). The (i, j)th entry of the sociomatrix $\mathbf{X}_r$ is defined as:

$$x_{ijr} \quad = \quad \text{the value of the tie from } n_i \text{ to } m_j$$
$$\text{on the relation } \mathcal{X}_r. \tag{3.3}$$

The actor index i ranges over all integers from 1 to g, while j ranges over all integers from 1 to h, and $r = 1, 2, \ldots , R$. As with relations defined on a single set of actors, x_{ijr} takes on integer values from 0 to $C_r - 1$.

Here, i can certainly equal j, since these two indices refer to different sets. The value of x_{iir} is meaningful.

When there are two sets of actors, there are four possible types of sociomatrices, each of which might be of a different size. The rows and columns of the sociomatrices will be labeled by the actors in the sets involved: the rows for the sending actor set and the columns for

Table 3.2. *The sociomatrix for the relation "is a student of" defined for heterogeneous pairs from* $\mathcal{N}$ *and* $\mathcal{M}$

		$\mathcal{M}$			
		Mr. Jones	Ms. Smith	Ms. Davis	Mr. White
	Allison	1	0	0	0
	Drew	0	1	0	0
$\mathcal{N}$	Eliot	0	0	1	0
	Keith	0	0	0	1
	Ross	0	0	1	0
	Sarah	0	1	0	0

the receiving actor set. We will denote the sociomatrices by using their sending and receiving actor sets, so, for example, the sociomatrix $\mathbf{X}^{\mathcal{N}\mathcal{M}}$ contains measurements on a relation defined from actors in $\mathcal{N}$ to actors in $\mathcal{M}$. These sociomatrices and their sizes are:

- $\mathbf{X}_r^{\mathcal{N}}$, dimensions $= g \times g$
- $\mathbf{X}_r^{\mathcal{M}}$, dimensions $= h \times h$
- $\mathbf{X}_r^{\mathcal{N}\mathcal{M}}$, dimensions $= g \times h$
- $\mathbf{X}_r^{\mathcal{M}\mathcal{N}}$, dimensions $= h \times g$

The second two types are, in general, rectangular. As always, in each sociomatrix, x_{ijr} is the value of the tie from actor i to actor j on the rth relation of that particular type.

Clearly, this notational scheme can accommodate multiple relations. However, since there may be a different number of relations defined for the four different types of pairs of actors, there may be different numbers of sociomatrices of each type.

To illustrate, consider an example with two sets of actors: students and teachers. Suppose there are four adults, second-grade teachers at the elementary school that is attended by six children. Define a relation, "is a student of." This relation is defined for heterogeneous pairs of actors for which the sender belongs to $\mathcal{N}$ and the receiver belongs to $\mathcal{M}$; that is, a child "is a student of" an adult teacher, but not vice versa. Table 3.2 gives the sociomatrix for the two-mode relation "is a student of" from our network of second-grade children. This relation is defined for the heterogeneous pairs consisting of a child as the sender and an adult as a receiver. This is a dichotomous relation $(C = 2)$, and is measured on the $6 \times 4 = 24$ heterogeneous pairs of children and teachers.

Note that there is only one 1 in every row of this matrix, since a child can have only one teacher. The entries in a specific column give the children that are taught by each teacher. Note how easily this array codes the information in the directional relation between two sets of actors. It is important to note that with sociometric notation all we need is one sociomatrix (with the proper dimensions) for each relation.

3.5 Putting It All Together

We conclude this chapter by pulling together all three notations into a single, more general framework. To begin, we note that the collection of actors, the relational information on pairs of actors, and possible attributes of the actors constitute a collection of data that can be referred to as a *social relational system*. Such a system is a conceptualization of the actors, pairs, relations, and attributes found in a social network.

As we have shown in this chapter, the data for a social relational system can be denoted in a variety of ways. It is important to stress that when dichotomous relations are considered, the three notational systems discussed in this chapter are capable of representing the entire data set.

We will use the symbols "$n_i \rightarrow n_j$" as shorthand notation for n_i "chooses" n_j on the single relation in question; that is, the arc from n_i to n_j is contained in the set $\mathscr{L}$, so that there is a tie present for the ordered pair $< n_i, n_j >$. If this arc is an element of $\mathscr{L}$, then there is a directed line from node i to node j in the directed graph or sociogram representing the relationships between pairs of actors on the relation. Sometimes we will replace "$n_i \rightarrow n_j$" with "$i \rightarrow j$" if no confusion could arise. With algebraic notation, if we label this relation by, say, F, we can also state that iFj. And with sociometric notation, we record this tie as $x_{ij} = 1$ in the proper sociomatrix.

As we have mentioned in our discussion of graph theoretic notation, if one has a single set of g actors, $\mathscr{N}$, then there are $g(g-1)$ ordered pairs of actors. In addition to $\mathscr{N}$, the set $\mathscr{L}$ contains the collection of ordered pairs of actors for which ties are present.

Some social network methodologists refer to the set of actors and the set of arcs as the *algebraic structure* $S = <\mathscr{N}, \mathscr{L}>$ (Freeman 1989). S is the standard representation of the simplest possible social network. For us, this is the graph theoretic representation.

One can define a graph from S by stating that the directed graph $\mathscr{G}_d$ is the ordered pair $<\mathscr{N}, \mathscr{L}>$, where the elements of $\mathscr{N}$ are nodes in the graph, and the elements of $\mathscr{L}$ are the ordered pairs of nodes for which there is a tie from n_i to n_j ($n_i \rightarrow n_j$).

Nodes and arcs are the basic building blocks for graph theoretic notation. To relate these concepts to the elements of sociometric notation, we consider again the collection of all ordered pairs of actors in $\mathcal{N}$. Sometimes this collection is denoted $\mathcal{N} \times \mathcal{N}$, a Cartesian product of sets. We define a binary quantity x_{ij} to be equal to 1 if the ordered pair $< n_i, n_j >$ is an element of $\mathcal{L}$ (that is, if there is a tie from n_i to n_j) and equal to 0 if the ordered pair is not an element of $\mathcal{L}$. This quantity is a mapping from the elements of the collection of ordered pairs to the set containing just 0 and 1. These quantities are exactly the elements of the binary $g \times g$ sociomatrix $\mathbf{X}$.

A relation is the collection of all ordered pairs for which $n_i \rightarrow n_j$. It is thus a subset of $\mathcal{N} \times \mathcal{N}$. In algebraic notation, capital letters (such as F) are used to refer to specific relations and to denote which ties are present. A relation is thus the set of all pairs of actors for which $n_i \rightarrow n_j$, or $x_{ij} = 1$, or iFj.

Thus, one can see the equivalence between the graph theoretic notation, and the sociometric notation (built on sociomatrices), and the algebraic notation (dependent on relations such as F). Freeman (1989) views the triple consisting of the algebraic structure S, the directed graph or sociogram $\mathcal{G}_d$, and the adjacency matrix or sociomatrix $\mathbf{X}$ as a social network:

$$\mathcal{S} = < S, \mathcal{G}_d, \mathbf{X} > .$$

This triple provides a nice abstract definition of the central concept of this book. And, it shows how these notational schemes are usually viewed together as providing the three essential components of the simplest form of a social network:

- A set of nodes and a set of arcs (from graph theoretic notation)
- A sociogram or graph (produced from the sets of nodes and arcs)
- A sociomatrix (from sociometric notation)

It is important to note that most of the generalizations of this simple social network $\mathcal{S}$, such as to valued relations, multiple relations, more than one set of actors, and relations measured over time, can be viewed in just the same way as the situation described here (single dichotomous relation measured on a single set of actors). The only wrinkle is that actor attributes are not easily quantified by using these concepts. The best one can do is to define a new matrix, $\mathbf{A}$, of dimensions (number of actors) × (number of attributes) to hold the measurements on the attribute variables. One could even include this information in the social network definition, so that a more complicated social network is $\mathscr{S} = \langle S, \mathscr{G}_d, \mathbf{X}, \mathbf{A} \rangle$.

Lastly, we should note that nowhere in this chapter did we discuss affiliation relations. We have introduced affiliation networks in Chapter 2, and will defer a mathematical description until Chapter 8.

4
Graphs and Matrices

by Dawn Iacobucci

This chapter presents the terminology and concepts of *graph theory*, and describes basic matrix operations that are used in social network analysis. Both graph theory and matrix operations have served as the foundations of many concepts in the analysis of social networks (Hage and Harary 1983; Harary, Norman, and Cartwright 1965). In this chapter, the notation presented in Chapter 3 is used, and more concepts and ideas from graph theory are described and illustrated with examples. The topics covered in this chapter are important for the methods discussed in the remaining chapters of the book, but they are especially important in Chapter 5 (Centrality, Prestige, and Related Actor and Group Measures), Chapter 6 (Structural Balance, Clusterability, and Transitivity), Chapter 7 (Cohesive Subgroups), and Chapter 8 (Affiliations, Co-memberships, and Overlapping Subgroups).

We start this chapter with a discussion of some reasons why graph theory and graph theoretic concepts are important for social network analysis. We then define a graph for representing a nondirectional relation. We begin with simple concepts, and progressively build on these to achieve more complicated, and more interesting, graph theoretic concepts. We then define and discuss directed graphs, for representing directional relations. Again, we begin with simple directed graph concepts and build to more complicated ideas. Following this, we discuss signed and valued graphs. We then define and discuss hypergraphs, which are used to represent affiliation networks. In the final section of this chapter we define and illustrate basic matrix operations that are used in social network analysis, and show how many of these matrix operations can be used to study the graph theoretic concepts discussed in the earlier sections of this chapter.

4.1 Why Graphs?

Graph theory has been useful in social network analysis for many reasons. Among these reasons are the following (see Harary, Norman, and Cartwright 1965, page 3). First, graph theory provides a vocabulary which can be used to label and denote many social structural properties. This vocabulary also gives us a set of primitive concepts that allows us to refer quite precisely to these properties. Second, graph theory gives us mathematical operations and ideas with which many of these properties can be quantified and measured (see Freeman 1984; Seidman and Foster 1978b). Last, given this vocabulary and these mathematics, graph theory gives us the ability to prove theorems about graphs, and hence, about representations of social structure. Like other branches of mathematics, graph theory allows researchers to prove theorems and deduce testable statements. However, as Barnes and Harary (1983) have noted, "Network analysts ... make too little use of the *theory* of graphs" (page 235). Although the representation of a graph and the vocabulary of graph theory are widely used by social network researchers, the theorems and derivations of graph theory are less widely used by network methodologists. Some notable exceptions include the work of Davis, Everett, Frank, Hage, Harary, Johnsen, Peay, Roberts, and Seidman, among others.

In addition to its utility as a mathematical system, graph theory gives us a representation of a social network as a model of a social system consisting of a set of actors and the ties between them. By *model* we mean a simplified representation of a situation that contains some, but not all, of the elements of the situation it represents (Roberts 1976; Hage and Harary 1983). When a graph is used as a model of a social network, points (called *nodes*) are used to represent actors, and lines connecting the points are used to represent the ties between the actors. In this sense, a graph is a model of a social network, in the same way that a model train set is a model of a railway system.

Graphs have been widely used in social network analysis as a means of formally representing social relations and quantifying important social structural properties, beginning with Moreno (1934), and developed further by Harary (Harary 1959a; Harary 1959b; Harary 1969; Hage and Harary 1983; Harary, Norman, and Cartwright 1965) and others (for example, Frank 1971; Seidman and Foster 1978a, 1987b; Foster and Seidman 1982, 1983, 1984). Graph theory has been used heavily in anthropology (Mitchell 1980; Hage 1973, 1976a, 1976b, 1979; Hage and Harary 1983; Abell 1970; Barnes 1969b; Barnes and Harary 1983; Zachary 1977), social psychology (Heider 1944, 1946, 1958; Davis 1967; Bavelas 1948, 1950; Leavitt 1951; Freeman 1977, 1979; Freeman, Roeder, and Mulholland 1980), communications, business, organizational research, and geography (Pitts 1965, 1979).

The visual representation of data that a graph or sociogram offers often allows researchers to uncover patterns that might otherwise go undetected (Moreno 1934; Hoaglin, Mosteller, and Tukey 1985; Tukey 1977; Velleman and Hoaglin 1981).

Matrices are an alternative way to represent and summarize network data. A matrix contains exactly the same information as a graph, but is more useful for computation and computer analysis. Matrix operations are widely used for definition and calculation in social network analysis, and are the primary representation for most computer analysis packages (*GRADAP, UCINET, STRUCTURE, SNAPS, NEGOPY*). However, only the program *GRADAP* is explicitly graph theoretic.

We will illustrate the graph theoretic concepts discussed in this chapter on small, simple social networks. Most of these examples will consist of hypothetical data created to demonstrate specific properties of graphs. We will also refer to the data collected by Padgett on the marital alliances between sixteen families in 15th century Florence, Italy.

In the following section, we describe properties of *graphs*, where a line between two nodes is *nondirectional*. Graphs are used for representing nondirectional relations. Following the discussion of graphs, we describe properties of *directed graphs*, where a line is directed from one node to another. Directed graphs, or *digraphs*, are used for representing directional relations, where the tie has an origin and a destination.

4.2 Graphs

A graph is a model for a social network with an undirected dichotomous relation; that is, a tie is either present or absent between each pair of actors. Nondirectional relations include such things as co-membership in formal organizations or informal groups, some kinship relations such as "is married to," "is a blood relative of," proximity relations such as "lives near," and interactions such as "works with." In a graph, *nodes* represent actors and *lines* represent ties between actors. In graph theory, the nodes are also referred to as *vertices* or *points*, and the lines are also known as *edges* or *arcs*.

A *graph* $\mathscr{G}$ consists of two sets of information: a set of *nodes*, $\mathscr{N} = \{n_1, n_2, \ldots, n_g\}$, and a set of lines, $\mathscr{L} = \{l_1, l_2, \ldots, l_L\}$ between pairs of nodes. There are g nodes and L lines. In a graph each line is an unordered pair of distinct nodes, $l_k = (n_i, n_j)$. Since lines are unordered pairs of nodes, the line between nodes n_i and n_j is identical to the line between nodes n_j and n_i $(l_k = (n_i, n_j) = (n_j, n_i))$. We will exclude the possible line between a node and itself, (n_i, n_i). Such lines are called *loops* or *reflexive ties*. Also, we do not allow an unordered pair of nodes to be included more than once in the set of lines. Thus, there can be no more than one line between a pair of nodes. A graph that has no loops and includes no more than one line between a pair of nodes is called a *simple graph*. Unless we note otherwise, the graphs that we consider in this chapter are simple graphs.

In a graph of a social network with a single nondirectional dichotomous relation, the nodes represent actors, and the lines represent the ties that exist between pairs of actors on the relation. A line $l_k = (n_i, n_j)$ is included in the set of lines, $\mathscr{L}$, if there is a tie present between the two actors in the network who are represented by nodes n_i and n_j in the graph.

Taken together, the two sets of information (nodes and lines) may be used to refer formally to a graph in terms of its node set and its line set. Thus we can denote a graph with node set $\mathscr{N}$ and line set $\mathscr{L}$ as $\mathscr{G}(\mathscr{N}, \mathscr{L})$. However, when there is no ambiguity about the node set and the line set, we will refer to a graph simply as $\mathscr{G}$.

Two nodes, n_i and n_j, are *adjacent* if the line $l_k = (n_i, n_j)$ is in the set of lines $\mathscr{L}$. A node is *incident* with a line, and the line is incident with the node, if the node is one of the unordered pair of nodes defining the line. For example, nodes n_1 and n_2 are incident with line $l_1 = (n_1, n_2)$. Each line is incident with the two nodes in the unordered pair that define the line.

A graph that contains only one node is *trivial*; all other graphs are nontrivial. A graph that contains g nodes and no lines $(L = 0)$ is *empty*. Trivial and empty graphs are of little substantive interest. In social networks, these graphs would correspond to a network consisting of only one actor (the trivial graph) and a network consisting of more than one actor, but no ties between the actors (the empty graph).

A graph $\mathscr{G}(\mathscr{N}, \mathscr{L})$ can also be presented as a diagram in which points depict nodes, and a line is drawn between two points if there is a line between the corresponding two nodes in the set of lines, $\mathscr{L}$. The location

	Actor	Lives near:
n_1	Allison	Ross, Sarah
n_2	Drew	Eliot
n_3	Eliot	Drew
n_4	Keith	Ross, Sarah
n_5	Ross	Allison, Keith, Sarah
n_6	Sarah	Allison, Keith, Ross

$$l_1 = (n_1, n_5)$$
$$l_2 = (n_1, n_6)$$
$$l_3 = (n_2, n_3)$$
$$l_4 = (n_4, n_5)$$
$$l_5 = (n_4, n_6)$$
$$l_6 = (n_5, n_6)$$

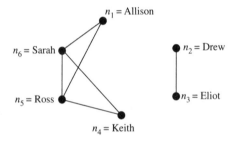

Fig. 4.1. Graph of "lives near" relation for six children

of points on the page is arbitrary, and the length of the lines between points is meaningless. The only information in the graph is the set of nodes and presence or absence of lines between pairs of nodes. In social network analysis, such a diagram is frequently referred to as a *sociogram*.

An example of a graph is given in Figure 4.1. We begin with a small graph so that all of its elements may be easily identified. The sets of nodes and lines are also listed. In this example, we can take the six nodes to represent the six children and the undirected relation "lives near," discussed in Chapter 3. In this example there are $g = 6$ nodes and $L = 6$ lines. A line between two nodes indicates that the children represented by these nodes live near each other. For example, Sarah, n_6, and Allison, n_1, live near each other so the line (n_1, n_6) is included in the set of lines. Allison and Eliot, n_3, do not live near each other, so the line (n_1, n_3) is not in the set of lines.

Social networks can be studied at several levels: the actor, pair or dyad, triple or triad, subgroup, and the group as a whole. In graph theoretic terms, these levels correspond to different *subgraphs*. Many social network methods consider subgraphs contained in a graph. For example, dyads and triads are (very small) subgraphs.

4.2.1 Subgraphs, Dyads, and Triads

Subgraphs. A graph $\mathcal{G}_s$ is a *subgraph* of $\mathcal{G}$ if the set of nodes of $\mathcal{G}_s$ is a subset of the set of nodes of $\mathcal{G}$, and the set of lines in $\mathcal{G}_s$ is a subset of the lines in the graph $\mathcal{G}$. If we denote the nodes in $\mathcal{G}_s$ as $\mathcal{N}_s$ and the lines in $\mathcal{G}_s$ as $\mathcal{L}_s$, then $\mathcal{G}_s$ is a subgraph of $\mathcal{G}$ if $\mathcal{N}_s \subseteq \mathcal{N}$ and $\mathcal{L}_s \subseteq \mathcal{L}$. All lines in $\mathcal{L}_s$ must be between pairs of nodes in $\mathcal{N}_s$. However, since $\mathcal{L}_s$ is a subset of $\mathcal{L}$, there may be lines in the graph between pairs of nodes in the subgraph that are not included in the set of lines in the subgraph.

Figure 4.2 gives an example of a graph and some of its subgraphs. In $\mathcal{G}$, the set of nodes consists of $\mathcal{N} = \{n_1, n_2, n_3, n_4, n_5\}$ and $\mathcal{L} = \{l_1, l_2, l_3, l_4\}$. In the subgraph in Figure 4.2b the set of nodes is $\mathcal{N}_s = \{n_1, n_3, n_4\}$ and the set of lines is $\mathcal{L}_s = \{l_2\}$. Notice that the subgraph does not include the line $l_4 = (n_3, n_4)$.

Any generic subgraph may not include all lines between the nodes in the subgraph. There are (at least) two special kinds of subgraphs that can be derived from a graph. One can take a subset of nodes and consider all lines that are between the nodes in the subset. Such a subgraph is *node-generated*, since the subset of nodes has produced the subgraph. Or, one can take a set of subset of lines, and consider all nodes that are incident with the lines in the subset. Such a subgraph is *line-generated*. We discuss each of these below.

Node- and Line-Generated Subgraphs. First consider node-generated subgraphs. A subgraph, $\mathcal{G}_s$, is *generated by a set of nodes*, $\mathcal{N}_s$, if $\mathcal{G}_s$ has node set $\mathcal{N}_s$, and line set $\mathcal{L}_s$, where the set of lines, $\mathcal{L}_s$, includes *all* lines from $\mathcal{L}$ that are between pairs of nodes in $\mathcal{N}_s$. Whereas a subgraph does not necessarily include all of the lines from $\mathcal{L}$ that are between nodes in $\mathcal{N}_s$, a subgraph generated by node set $\mathcal{N}_s$ must include all lines from $\mathcal{L}$ that are present between pairs of nodes in $\mathcal{N}_s$.

In social network analysis, a node-generated subgraph results if the researcher considers only a subset of the g members of the network. Some

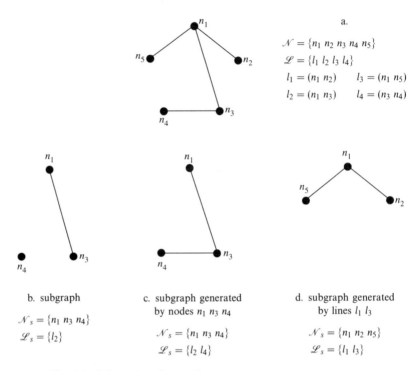

a.

$\mathcal{N} = \{n_1\ n_2\ n_3\ n_4\ n_5\}$

$\mathcal{L} = \{l_1\ l_2\ l_3\ l_4\}$

$l_1 = (n_1\ n_2)$ $l_3 = (n_1\ n_5)$

$l_2 = (n_1\ n_3)$ $l_4 = (n_3\ n_4)$

b. subgraph

$\mathcal{N}_s = \{n_1\ n_3\ n_4\}$

$\mathcal{L}_s = \{l_2\}$

c. subgraph generated
by nodes $n_1\ n_3\ n_4$

$\mathcal{N}_s = \{n_1\ n_3\ n_4\}$

$\mathcal{L}_s = \{l_2\ l_4\}$

d. subgraph generated
by lines $l_1\ l_3$

$\mathcal{N}_s = \{n_1\ n_2\ n_5\}$

$\mathcal{L}_s = \{l_1\ l_3\}$

Fig. 4.2. Subgraphs of a graph

relational data might be missing for some of the network members, and thus the researcher can only study ties among the remaining actors. In a longitudinal study in which a network is studied over time, some actor, or subset of actors, might leave the network. Analyses of the network might have to be restricted to the subset of actors for whom data are available for all time points. Node-generated subgraphs are widely used in the analysis of cohesive subgroups in networks (see Chapter 7). These methods focus on subsets of actors among whom the ties are relatively strong, numerous, or close.

Now consider line-generated subgraphs. A subgraph, $\mathcal{G}_s$, is *generated by a set of lines*, $\mathcal{L}_s$, if $\mathcal{G}_s$ has line set $\mathcal{L}_s$, and node set $\mathcal{N}_s$, where the set of nodes, $\mathcal{N}_s$, includes all nodes from $\mathcal{N}$ that are incident with lines in $\mathcal{L}_s$. Figure 4.2c shows the subgraph generated by the set of nodes $\mathcal{N}_s = \{n_1, n_3, n_4\}$. In this subgraph both lines $l_2 = (n_1, n_3)$ and $l_4 = (n_3, n_4)$ are included, since a node-generated subgraph includes all lines between the nodes in the graph. Figure 4.2d shows the subgraph generated by the set of lines $\mathscr{L}_s = \{l_1, l_3\}$. The set of nodes in this subgraph includes all nodes incident with lines l_1 and l_3, so $\mathscr{N}_s = \{n_1, n_2, n_5\}$.

So there are two special kinds of subgraphs that we will consider. Throughout the book, most of the subgraphs we consider will be node-generated subgraphs.

An important feature of a subgraph is whether it is *maximal* with respect to some property. A subgraph is maximal with respect to a given property if that property holds for the subgraph $\mathscr{G}_s$, but does not hold if any node or nodes are added to the subgraph. We will return to this property and illustrate it later in this chapter.

Dyads. A dyad, representing a pair of actors and the possible tie between them, is a (node-generated) subgraph consisting of a pair of nodes and the possible line between the nodes. In a graph an unordered pair of nodes can be in only one of two states: either two nodes are adjacent or they are not adjacent. Thus, there are only two dyadic states for an undirected relation represented as a graph; either the actors in the dyad have a tie present, or they do not.

Triads. Triadic analysis is also based on subgraphs, where the number of nodes is three. A triad is a subgraph consisting of three nodes and the possible lines among them. In a graph, a triad may be in one of four possible states, depending on whether, zero, one, two, or three lines are present among the three nodes in the triad. These four possible triadic states are shown in Figure 4.3.

There has been much theoretical research on triads. For example, Granovetter (1973) refers to the triad with two lines present and one line absent as the *forbidden triad*. He argues that if lines represent strong ties between actors, then if actor i has a strong tie with actor j, and actor j in turn has a strong tie with actor k, it is unlikely that the tie between actor i and actor k will be absent. This type of triad, with only two lines, is forbidden in Granovetter's model.

Both dyads and triads are node-generated subgraphs, since they are defined as a subset of nodes and all lines between pairs of nodes in the subset.

We now consider properties of nodes and graphs that can be defined using the concepts of adjacency and incidence for the nodes and lines in a graph.

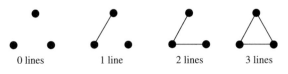

Fig. 4.3. Four possible triadic states in a graph

4.2.2 Nodal Degree

The *degree* of a node, denoted by $d(n_i)$, is the number of lines that are incident with it. Equivalently, the degree of a node is the number of nodes adjacent to it. The degree of a node is a count that ranges from a minimum of 0, if no nodes are adjacent to a given node, to a maximum of $g - 1$, if a given node is adjacent to all other nodes in the graph. A node with degree equal to 0 is called an *isolate*.

The degree of a node, $d(n_i)$, may be obtained by counting the number of lines incident with it. In the example in Figure 4.1, the degrees of the nodes are: $d(n_1) = 2, d(n_2) = 1, d(n_3) = 1, d(n_4) = 2, d(n_5) = 3$, and $d(n_6) = 3$.

Degrees are very easy to compute, and yet can be quite informative in many applications. For example, if we observe children playing together, and represent children by nodes, and instances of pairs of children playing by lines in a graph, then a node with a small degree would indicate a child who played with few others, and a node with a large degree would indicate a child who played with many others. Or, in the study of Padgett's Florentine families, and the relation of marriage, a node with a large degree represents a family that has many marital ties to other families in the network. The degree of a node is a measure of the "activity" of the actor it represents, and is the basis for one of the centrality measures that we discuss in Chapter 5.

In many applications, it is informative to summarize the degrees of all the actors in the network. The mean nodal degree is a statistic that reports the average degree of the nodes in the graph. Denoting the mean degree as $\bar{d}$, we have

$$\bar{d} = \frac{\sum_{i=1}^{g} d(n_i)}{g} = \frac{2L}{g}. \tag{4.1}$$

One might also be interested in the variability of the nodal degrees. If all the degrees of all of the nodes are equal, the graph is said to be *d-regular*, where d is the constant value for all the degrees ($d(n_i) = d$, for all i and some value d). d-regularity can be thought of as a measure of uniformity. We will discuss d-regularity in more detail below in the context of directed graphs. If a graph is not d-regular, the nodes differ in degree. The variance of the degrees, which we denote by S_D^2, is calculated as:

$$S_D^2 = \frac{\sum_{i=1}^g (d(n_i) - \bar{d})^2}{g}. \tag{4.2}$$

A graph that is d-regular has $S_D^2 = 0$. Variability in nodal degrees means that the actors represented by the nodes differ in "activity," as measured by the number of ties they have to others. The variability of nodal degrees is one measure of graph centralization that we discuss in Chapter 5.

The nodal degrees are an important property of a graph, and we will often want to control for or condition on the set of nodal degrees in a graph when we use statistical models to study tendencies toward higher-order network properties (such as reciprocity). We return to this idea in our discussion of digraphs, below. Statistics for degrees (means, variances, and so forth) and statistical distributions and inference are discussed in more detail in Chapters 5 and 13.

4.2.3 Density of Graphs and Subgraphs

Degree is a concept that considers the number of lines incident with each node in a graph. We can also consider the number and proportion of lines in the graph as a whole. A graph can only have so many lines. The maximum possible number is determined by the number of nodes. Since there are g nodes in the graph, and we exclude loops, there are $\binom{g}{2} = g(g-1)/2$ possible unordered pairs of nodes, and thus $g(g-1)/2$ possible lines that could be present in the graph. This is the maximum number of lines that can be present in a graph.

Consider now what proportion of these lines are actually present. The *density* of a graph is the proportion of possible lines that are actually present in the graph. It is the ratio of the number of lines present, L, to the maximum possible. The density of a graph, which we denote by Δ, is calculated as:

$$\Delta = \frac{L}{g(g-1)/2} = \frac{2L}{g(g-1)}. \tag{4.3}$$

The density of a graph goes from 0, if there are no lines present ($L = 0$), to 1, if all possible lines are present ($L = g(g-1)/2$).

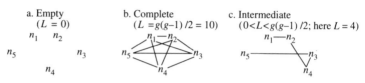

Fig. 4.4. Complete and empty graphs

If all lines are present, then all nodes are adjacent, and the graph is said to be *complete*. It is standard to denote a complete graph with g nodes as K_g. A complete graph contains all $g(g-1)/2$ possible lines, the density is equal to 1, and all nodal degrees are equal to $g - 1$.

An example of a complete graph in a social network would be a relation such as "communicates with," where all g actors communicated with all other actors.

There is a straightforward relationship between the density of a graph and the mean degree of the nodes in the graph. Noticing that the sum of the degrees is equal to $2L$ (since each line is counted twice, once for each of the two nodes incident with it — see equation (4.1)), we can combine equations (4.3) and (4.1) to get:

$$\Delta = \frac{\bar{d}}{(g - 1)}. \tag{4.4}$$

In other words, the density of a graph is the average proportion of lines incident with nodes in the graph.

Figure 4.4 shows an example of an empty graph, a complete graph, and a graph with an intermediate number of lines ($L = 4$) for $g = 5$.

We can also define the density of a subgraph, which we will denote by Δ_s. The density of subgraph $\mathcal{G}_s$ is defined as the number of lines present in the subgraph, divided by the number of lines that could be present in the subgraph. We denote the number of nodes in subgraph $\mathcal{G}_s$ as g_s, and the number of lines in the subgraph as L_s. The possible number of lines in a subgraph is equal to $g_s(g_s - 1)/2$. We calculate the density of the subgraph as:

$$\Delta_s = \frac{2L_s}{g_s(g_s - 1)}. \tag{4.5}$$

The density of a subgraph expresses the proportion of ties that are present among a subset of the actors in a network. This measure is used to evaluate the cohesiveness of subgroups (see Chapter 7) and to construct blockmodels and related simplified representations of networks (see Chapters 9 and 10).

We now turn to an example to demonstrate nodal degree and graph density.

4.2.4 Example: Padgett's Florentine Families

Padgett's Florentine families network includes a set of sixteen Italian families in the early 15th century. The relation we consider here is marriage between pairs of families. Notice that the relation of marriage is nondirectional because the statement "a member of family i is married to a member of family j" is equivalent to the statement "a member of family j is married to a member of family i." In the graph, each family is represented as a node and the presence of a marriage between a pair of families is represented as a line. We label the sixteen nodes with the families' surnames.

The graph for this example is given in Figure 4.5. There are $g = 16$ nodes in this graph, and $L = 20$ lines between the pairs of nodes. Even with as few as sixteen actors and twenty ties, the graph looks rather complicated.

Let us now consider the nodal degrees and density of this social network. Notice that the Pucci family, n_{12}, is not related to any of the other families by the marriage relation. It is thus an isolate on the marriage relation. Note that the degrees sum to $2L = 40$. The mean nodal degree is $\bar{d} = (40/16) = 2.5$, the median is 3.0, and $S_D^2 = 1.46^2$. Thus, families have (on average) between two and three marriages to other families in this group. The Guadagni and Strozzi families, n_7 and n_{15}, have slightly more than average since their degrees are 4, and the Medici family, n_9, has quite a bit more than average with a degree of 6. The density of the graph is $20/120 = 0.167$.

Substantively, we know that much of the political posturing at this time in history centered on the Medici and the Strozzi families. Figure 4.5 indicates that these families seem to be important ones with respect to marital alliances. That is, these families have large degrees, and thus many marriages with the other families in this network. However, the Guadagni's, n_7, also have a large number of marriages.

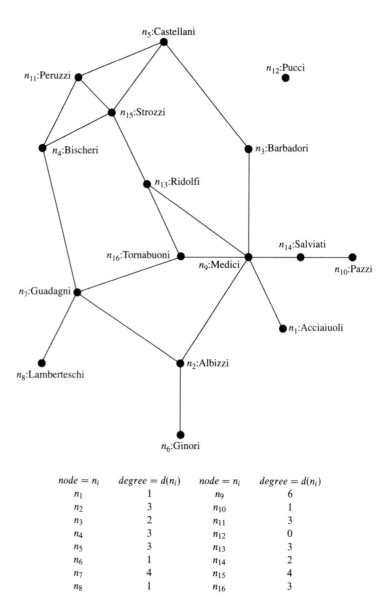

Fig. 4.5. Graph and nodal degrees for Padgett's Florentine families, marriage relation

node $= n_i$	degree $= d(n_i)$	node $= n_i$	degree $= d(n_i)$
n_1	1	n_9	6
n_2	3	n_{10}	1
n_3	2	n_{11}	3
n_4	3	n_{12}	0
n_5	3	n_{13}	3
n_6	1	n_{14}	2
n_7	4	n_{15}	4
n_8	1	n_{16}	3

4.2.5 Walks, Trails, and Paths

In the previous section we considered the tie between a pair of nodes in terms of whether the nodes were adjacent or not. In this section we consider other ways in which two nodes can be linked by "indirect" routes that pass through the other nodes in the graph. We define and illustrate properties that are used to study the connectivity of graphs, to define the distance between pairs of nodes, and to identify nodes and lines that are critical for the connectivity of the graph.

These properties are not only important in themselves, but are also building blocks for later properties. In particular, *walks* and *paths* will allow us to calculate the distance between two nodes. We will define *walks,* their *inverses,* and measurement of the *lengths* of walks. We also describe special types of walks called *trails, paths, tours,* and *cycles.* Using the definition of paths, we define *geodesic distance, diameter,* and *eccentricity.*

In social network studies it is often important to know whether it is possible to reach some node n_i from another node n_j. If it is possible, it may also be interesting to know how many ways it can be done, and which of these ways is optimal with respect to one of several criteria. For example, we might wish to understand the communication of information among employees in an organization. An important consideration is whether information originating with one employee could eventually reach all other employees, and if so, how many lines it must traverse in order to get there. One might also consider whether there are multiple routes that a message might take to go from one employee to another, and whether some of these paths are more or less "efficient."

Walks in a Graph. A *walk* is a sequence of nodes and lines, starting and ending with nodes, in which each node is incident with the lines following and preceding it in the sequence. The listing of a walk, denoted by W, is an alternating sequence of incident nodes and lines beginning and ending with nodes. The beginning and ending nodes may be different. In addition, some nodes may be included more than once, and some lines may be included more than once. The *length* of a walk is the number of occurrences of lines in it. If a line is included more than once in the walk, it is counted each time it occurs.

Because (simple) graphs have at most one line between each pair of nodes, there is no ambiguity about which line is between any two nodes, and a walk may be described by just listing the nodes involved and excluding the lines. The starting node and the ending node of a walk

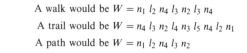

A walk would be $W = n_1\ l_2\ n_4\ l_3\ n_2\ l_3\ n_4$

A trail would be $W = n_4\ l_3\ n_2\ l_4\ n_3\ l_5\ n_4\ l_2\ n_1$

A path would be $W = n_1\ l_2\ n_4\ l_3\ n_2$

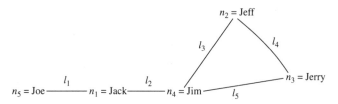

Fig. 4.6. Walks, trails, and paths in a graph

are the first and last nodes of W and are referred to as the *origin* and *terminus* of W. The *inverse* of a walk, denoted by W^{-1}, is the walk W listed in exactly the opposite order, using the same nodes and lines.

Figure 4.6 contains a hypothetical structure of communication ties among $g = 5$ employees. This structure might arise if actors Jeff, Jerry, and Jim (n_2, n_3, n_4) all communicate with each other and report through Jim (n_4) to Jack (n_1), who in turn reports to Joe (n_5). One possible walk through this network would be $W = n_1 l_2 n_4 l_3 n_2 l_3 n_4$. For example, perhaps Jack (n_1) passes a memo to Jim (n_4). Jim leaves the memo on Jeff's (n_2) desk. Jeff does not realize Jim was the one to leave the memo, and Jeff thinks he should bring the memo to Jim's attention, so he sends the memo back to Jim.

Notice several properties about this walk. First, not all nodes are involved: the message never reached Joe (n_5) or Jerry (n_3). Second, some nodes were used more than once: Jim (n_4) was included in the walk twice. Third, some lines were not used (that is, l_1, l_4, l_5), and some lines were used more than once (that is, l_3). The walk $W = n_1 l_2 n_4 l_3 n_2 l_3 n_4$ may be written more briefly as $W = n_1 n_4 n_2 n_4$. The origin and terminus in this walk are n_1 and n_4. The length of the walk is 3, since there are three lines: l_2, l_3, l_3. The length is 3 even though only two distinct lines are contained in this walk, because one of these lines is included twice. The inverse of the walk is $W^{-1} = n_4 n_2 n_4 n_1$.

A walk is the most general kind of sequence of adjacent nodes, since there are no restrictions on which nodes and lines may be included (aside from adjacency of nodes). Special kinds of walks, which we consider next, are more restrictive in that they require that nodes or lines be used no more than once.

◯**Trails and Paths.** Trails and paths are walks with special characteristics. A *trail* is a walk in which all of the lines are distinct, though some node(s) may be included more than once. In the communications example, a trail means no communication tie is used more than once. The length of a trail is the number of lines in it.

A *path* is a walk in which all nodes and all lines are distinct. For example, a path through a communication network means no actor is informed more than once. The length of a path is the number of lines in it.

Notice that every path is a trail, and every trail is a walk. So any pair of nodes connected by a path is also connected by a trail and by a walk. Thus, a walk is the most general and a path is the least general kind of "route" through a graph. Since all paths are walks (but without repeating nodes or lines) a path is likely to be shorter compared to a walk or a trail. In a path in the communications network, no employee is informed more than once, and no pair of employees discusses the matter more than once. In applications to social networks, we will often focus on paths rather than walks.

One of the trails in Figure 4.6 is $n_4 n_2 n_3 n_4$ (no line is repeated). One of the paths is $n_1 n_4 n_2$ (no line or node is repeated).

There may be more than one path between a given pair of nodes. For example, in Figure 4.6 there are two paths between n_1 and n_2: $n_1 n_4 n_2$ and $n_1 n_4 n_3 n_2$.

A very important property of a pair of nodes is whether there is a path between them, or not. If there is a path between nodes n_i and n_j, then n_i and n_j are said to be *reachable*. For example, if we consider a network of communications among people in which lines in a graph represent channels for transmission of messages between people, then if two actors are reachable, it is possible for a message to travel from one actor to the other by passing the message through intermediaries. If two actors are not reachable, then there is no path between them, and no way for a message to travel from one actor to the other.

◯**Closed Walks, Tours, and Cycles.** Some walks begin and end at the same node. A walk that begins and ends at the same node is called a *closed walk*. In Figure 4.7, a closed walk is:

$$W = n_5 n_1 n_4 n_3 n_2 n_4 n_1 n_5.$$

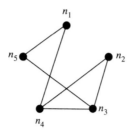

Tour n_3 n_2 n_4 n_3 n_5 n_1 n_4 n_3

Cycles n_5 n_1 n_4 n_3 n_5

n_2 n_3 n_4 n_2

n_2 n_4 n_1 n_5 n_3 n_2

Closed walk n_5 n_1 n_4 n_3 n_2 n_4 n_1 n_5

Fig. 4.7. Closed walks and cycles in a graph

A *cycle* is closed walk of at least three nodes in which all lines are distinct, and all nodes except the beginning and ending node are distinct. A graph that contains no cycles is called *acyclic*. The graph in Figure 4.6 is not acyclic, since there is the cycle $W = n_4 n_2 n_3 n_4$.

A *tour* is a closed walk in which each line in the graph is used at least once. A tour in Figure 4.7 is:

$$W = n_3 n_2 n_4 n_3 n_5 n_1 n_4 n_3.$$

Cycles are important in the study of balance and clusterability in signed graphs (a topic we return to later in this chapter, and discuss in detail in Chapter 6).

Other special closed walks are those that include each and every node, or include each and every line. *Eulerian* trails are special closed trails that include every line exactly once (see Biggs, Lloyd, and Wilson 1976). Analogous closed walks can be defined in which each node is included exactly once. A cycle is labeled *Hamiltonian* if every node in the graph is included exactly once.

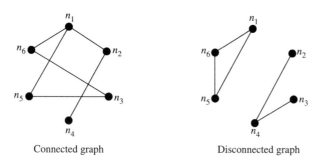

Fig. 4.8. A connected graph and a graph with components

4.2.6 Connected Graphs and Components

An important property of a graph is whether or not it is connected. A graph is *connected* if there is a path between every pair of nodes in the graph. That is, in a connected graph, all pairs of nodes are reachable. If a graph is not connected, then it is *disconnected*. Consider the example of communications among employees in an organization. If the graph representing communications among the employees is connected, then messages can travel from any employee to each and every other employee through the pairwise communication channels. However, if the graph representing this network is disconnected, then some pair of people cannot send or receive messages from each other using the communication channels.

Components. The nodes in a disconnected graph may be partitioned into two or more subsets in which there are no paths between the nodes in different subsets. The connected subgraphs in a graph are called *components*. A component of a graph is a maximal connected subgraph. Remember that a maximal entity is one that cannot be made larger and still retain its property. That is, a component is a subgraph in which there is a path between all pairs of nodes in the subgraph (all pairs of nodes in a component are reachable), and (since it is maximal) there is no path between a node in the component and any node not in the component. One cannot add another node to the subgraph and still retain the connectedness. If there is only one component in a graph, the graph is connected. If there is more than one component, the graph is disconnected.

Consider Figures 4.8a and 4.8b. The graph in Figure 4.8a is connected since there is a path between each pair of nodes. However, the graph in Figure 4.8b is not connected, since there is no path between n_1 and n_2. The graph in Figure 4.8b is *disconnected*, since there are pairs of nodes that do not have a path between them. For the graph in Figure 4.8b, the nodes can be partitioned into subsets $\mathcal{N}_1 = \{n_1, n_6, n_5\}$, $\mathcal{N}_2 = \{n_2, n_3, n_4\}$. The subgraphs generated by the different sets, $\mathcal{N}_1$ and $\mathcal{N}_2$ are the *components* of $\mathcal{G}$. In Figure 4.8b, the graph has two components.

Note that Padgett's Florentine families' marriage ties produce a disconnected graph because the Pucci family, represented by node n_{12}, is an isolate (that is, $d(n_{12}) = 0$). The two components in this graph are the subgraphs generated by the subsets:

- $\mathcal{N}_1 = \{n_1, n_2, \ldots, n_{11}, n_{13}, \ldots, n_{16}\}$
- $\mathcal{N}_2 = \{n_{12}\}$

4.2.7 Geodesics, Distance, and Diameter

Now let us consider the paths between a pair of nodes. It is likely that there are several paths between a given pair of nodes, and that these paths differ in length. A shortest path between two nodes is referred to as a *geodesic*. If there is more than one shortest path between a pair of nodes, then there are two (or more) geodesics between the pair. The *geodesic distance* or simply the *distance* between two nodes is defined as the length of a geodesic between them. We will denote the geodesic distance between nodes n_i and n_j as $d(i, j)$. The distance between two nodes is the length of any shortest path between them. If there is no path between two nodes (that is, they are not reachable), then the distance between them is infinite (or undefined). If a graph is not connected, then the distance between at least one pair of nodes is infinite (because the distance between two nodes in different components is infinite). In a graph, a geodesic between n_i and n_j is also a geodesic between n_j and n_i. Thus the distance between n_i and n_j is equal to the distance between n_j and n_i; $d(i, j) = d(j, i)$.

Consider the graph in Figure 4.9. In this graph, the path $n_3 n_4 n_5$ is of length 2, since it contains two lines. This path is also a geodesic between n_3 and n_5; hence, $d(3, 5) = 2$ (the path $n_3 n_2 n_4 n_5$ is of length 3 and is thus not a geodesic). Figure 4.9 also gives the geodesic distances between all pairs of nodes in this graph.

Geodesic distances

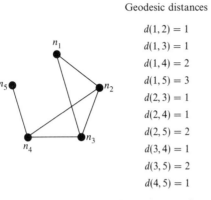

$d(1,2) = 1$

$d(1,3) = 1$

$d(1,4) = 2$

$d(1,5) = 3$

$d(2,3) = 1$

$d(2,4) = 1$

$d(2,5) = 2$

$d(3,4) = 1$

$d(3,5) = 2$

$d(4,5) = 1$

Diameter of graph $= \max d(i,j) = d(1,5) = 3$

Fig. 4.9 Graph showing geodesics and diameter

Distances are quite important in social network analyses. They quantify how far apart each pair of nodes is, and are used in two of the centrality measures (discussed in Chapter 5) and are an important consideration for constructing some kinds of cohesive subgroups (discussed in Chapter 7).

○**Eccentricity of a Node.** Consider the geodesic distances between a given node and the other $g - 1$ nodes in a connected graph. The *eccentricity* or *association number* of a node is the largest geodesic distance between that node and any other node (Harary and Norman 1953; Harary 1969). Formally, the eccentricity of node n_i in a connected graph is equal to the maximum $d(i,j)$, for all j, (or $\max_j d(i,j)$). The eccentricity of a node can range from a minimum of 1 (if a node is adjacent to all other nodes in the graph) to a maximum of $g - 1$. It summarizes how far a node is from the node most distant from it in the graph. Several measures of centrality, such as the center and the centroid of a graph, are based on the eccentricity of the nodes. We discuss these in more detail in Chapter 5.

Diameter of a Graph. Consider the largest geodesic distance between any pair of nodes in a graph, that is, the largest eccentricity of any node. The *diameter* of a connected graph is the length of the largest geodesic between any pair of nodes (equivalently, the largest nodal eccentricity). Formally, the diameter of a connected graph is equal to the maximum $d(i, j)$, for all i and j (or $\max_i \max_j d(i, j)$). The diameter of a graph can range from a minimum of 1 (if the graph is complete) to a maximum of $g - 1$. If a graph is not connected, its diameter is infinite (or undefined) since the geodesic distance between one or more pairs of nodes in a disconnected graph is infinite.

Returning to the example in Figure 4.9 we see that the largest geodesic between any pair of nodes is 3 (between nodes n_1 and n_5). Thus the diameter of this graph is equal to 3.

The diameter of a graph is important because it quantifies how far apart the farthest two nodes in the graph are. Consider a communications network in which the ties are the transmission of messages. Focus on messages sent between all pairs of actors. Then, assuming messages always take the shortest routes (that is, via geodesics), we are guaranteed that a message can travel from any actor to any other actor, over a path of length no greater than the diameter of the graph.

Diameter of a Subgraph. We can also find the diameter of a subgraph. Consider a (node-generated) subgraph with node set $\mathcal{N}_s$ and line set $\mathcal{L}_s$ containing all lines from $\mathcal{L}$ between pairs of nodes in $\mathcal{N}_s$. The distance between a pair of nodes within the subgraph is defined for paths containing nodes from $\mathcal{N}_s$ and lines from $\mathcal{L}_s$. The distance between nodes n_i and n_j in the subgraph is the length of the shortest path between the nodes *within* the subgraph. Any path, and thus any geodesic, including nodes (and thus lines) outside the subgraph, is not considered. The *diameter of a subgraph* is the length of the largest geodesic within the subgraph.

4.2.8 Connectivity of Graphs

We now use the ideas of reachability between pairs of nodes, the concept of a connected graph, and components in a disconnected graph to define nodes and lines that are critical for the connectivity of a graph. We also present measures of how connected a graph is as a whole. The connectivity of a graph is a function of whether a graph remains connected when nodes and/or lines are deleted. We discuss each of these in turn.

Cutpoints. A node, n_i, is a *cutpoint* if the number of components in the graph that contains n_i is fewer than the number of components

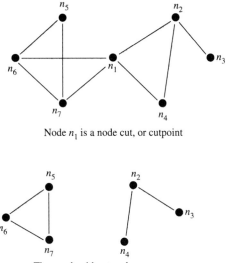

Node n_1 is a node cut, or cutpoint

The graph without node n_1

Fig. 4.10. Example of a cutpoint in a graph

in the subgraph that results from deleting n_i from the graph. That is, consider graph $\mathcal{G}$ with node set $\mathcal{N}$ which includes node n_i, and the subgraph $\mathcal{G}_s$ with node set $\mathcal{N}_s = \mathcal{N} - n_i$ that results from dropping n_i and all of its incident lines from graph $\mathcal{G}$. Node n_i is a cutpoint if the number of components in $\mathcal{G}$ is less than the number of components in $\mathcal{G}_s$.

For example, n_1 in Figure 4.10 is a cutpoint. This graph has one component, but if n_1 is removed, the graph has two components. In a communications network, an actor who is a cutpoint is critical, in the sense that if that actor is removed from the network, the remaining network has two subsets of actors, between whom no communication can travel.

The concept of a cutpoint can be extended from a single node to a *set* of nodes necessary to keep the graph connected. If a set of nodes is necessary to maintain the connectedness of a graph, these nodes are referred to as a *cutset*. If the set is of size k, then it is called a k-node cut. A cutpoint is a 1-node cut. If a set of nodes is a cutset, then the number of components in the graph that contains the set of nodes is fewer than

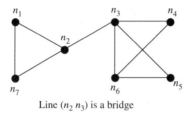

Line ($n_2 n_3$) is a bridge

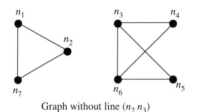

Graph without line ($n_2 n_3$)

Fig. 4.11. Example of a bridge in a graph

the number of components in the subgraph that results from deleting the set of nodes from the graph.

Bridges. A notion analogous to that of cutpoint exists for lines. A bridge is a line that is critical to the connectedness of the graph. A *bridge* is a line such that the graph containing the line has fewer components than the subgraph that is obtained after the line is removed (nodes incident with the line remain in the subgraph). The removal of a bridge leaves more components than when the bridge is included. If line l_k is a bridge, then the graph $\mathscr{G}$ with line set $\mathscr{L}$ including l_k has fewer components than the subgraph $\mathscr{G}_s$ with line set $\mathscr{L} - l_k$, the graph obtained by deleting line l_k.

The line (n_2, n_3) in Figure 4.11 is a bridge. If the line (n_2, n_3) is removed from the graph, there is no path between nodes n_1 and n_5 (for example) and the graph becomes disconnected. In Figure 4.11, if the line (n_2, n_3) were nonexistent, nodes n_1, n_2, and n_7 would not be reachable from nodes n_3, n_4, n_5, and n_6.

Similarly, an *l-line cut* is a set of l lines that, if deleted, disconnects the graph. A bridge is a 1-line cut. In graphs representing social networks, a bridge is a critical tie, or a critical interaction between two actors.

Example. For the marriage relation for Padgett's Florentine families, the Medici family, n_9, is a cutpoint. With all sixteen nodes, the graph has two components. Without n_9, there are now two more components, giving four in total. If Family Medici is removed, n_1, the Acciaiuoli family becomes an isolate, and the Salviati and Pazzi families, n_{10} and n_{14}, are not reachable from the other families. There are other cutpoints in the graph. The marriage between the Salviati and Medici families, represented by the line (n_9, n_{14}), is a bridge (since its removal isolates the Salviati and Pazzi families).

One can consider the extent of connectivity in a graph in terms of the number of nodes or the number of lines that must be removed in order to leave the graph disconnected. The connectivity of a graph is one measure of its "cohesiveness" or robustness.

⊗**Node- and Line-Connectivity.** One way to measure the cohesiveness of a graph is by its connectivity. A graph is cohesive if, for example, there are relatively frequent lines, many nodes with relatively large degrees, or relatively short or numerous paths between pairs of nodes. Cohesive graphs have many short geodesics, and small diameters, relative to their sizes. If a graph is not cohesive then it is "vulnerable" to the removal of a few nodes or lines. That is, a vulnerable graph is more likely to become disconnected if a few nodes or lines are removed.

We can use the notions of a cutset and a line cut to define two measures of the connectivity of a graph. One measure describes the connectivity of the graph based on the removal of nodes, and the other describes the connectivity of the graph based on the removal of lines (Harary 1969).

The *point-connectivity* or *node-connectivity* of a graph, $\kappa(\mathcal{G})$, is the minimum number κ for which the graph has a κ-node cut. It is the minimum number of nodes that must be removed to make the graph disconnected, or to leave a trivial graph (Harary 1969, page 43). If the graph is disconnected, then $\kappa = 0$, since no node must be removed. If the graph contains a cutpoint, then $\kappa = 1$ since the removal of the single node leaves the graph disconnected. If a graph contains no node whose removal would disconnect the graph, but it contains a pair of nodes whose removal together would disconnect the graph, then $\kappa = 2$, since two is the minimum number of nodes that must be removed to make the graph disconnected. Thus, higher values of κ indicate higher levels of connectivity of the graph.

An example of a 2-node cut is given in Figure 4.12. The 2-node cut consists of n_2 and n_4, because without them n_3 would not be connected

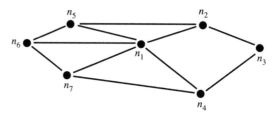

n_2 and n_4 comprise a 2-node cut

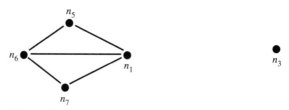

The graph without n_2 and n_4

Fig. 4.12. Connectivity in a graph

to the remainder of the graph. In Figure 4.12, $\kappa(\mathcal{G}) = 2$. The graph may be disconnected if $\kappa \geq 2$ nodes are removed, but $\kappa = 2$ is the minimum. That is, the removal of any single node ($\kappa = 1$) would not result in a disconnected graph. In Figure 4.10, $\kappa(\mathcal{G}) = 1$, since there is a node whose removal disconnects the graph (n_1 is a cutpoint).

The value κ is the minimum number of nodes that must be removed to make the graph disconnected. Thus, removing any number of nodes less than κ does not make the graph disconnected. For any value k less than κ, the graph is said to be *k-node connected*.

A complete graph has no cutpoint; all nodes are adjacent to all others, so the removal of any one node would still leave the graph connected. In order to disconnect a complete graph, one would need to remove $g - 1$ nodes, resulting in a trivial graph ($g = 1$), so $\kappa(K_g) = g - 1$.

The *line-connectivity* or *edge-connectivity* of a graph, $\lambda(\mathcal{G})$, is the minimum number λ for which the graph has a λ-line cut. The value, λ, is the minimum number of lines that must be removed to disconnect the graph or leave a trivial graph (Harary 1969, page 43). In Figure 4.10, $\lambda(\mathcal{G}) = 1$, since line l_4 is a bridge. Removing more than one line may also destroy the graph's connectedness, but the minimum number of lines whose removal disconnects the graph is 1 (specifically line l_4). If $\lambda(\mathcal{G}) \geq l$, the graph is said to be *l-line connected*, since l is the minimum number of lines that must be removed to make the graph disconnected.

The larger the node-connectivity or the line-connectivity of a graph is, the less vulnerable the graph is to becoming disconnected. We will return to ideas of connectivity in Chapter 7 and discuss how these ideas can be used to define cohesive subgroups.

4.2.9 Isomorphic Graphs and Subgraphs

Two graphs, $\mathcal{G}$ and $\mathcal{G}^*$, are *isomorphic* if there is a one-to-one mapping from the nodes of $\mathcal{G}$ to the nodes of $\mathcal{G}^*$ that preserves the adjacency of nodes.

A one-to-one mapping means that each node in $\mathcal{G}$ is mapped to one (and only one) node in $\mathcal{G}^*$, and each node in $\mathcal{G}^*$ is mapped to one (and only one) node in $\mathcal{G}$. Let us denote nodes in $\mathcal{G}$ as $\mathcal{N} = \{n_1, n_2, \ldots, n_g\}$ and nodes in $\mathcal{G}^*$ as $\mathcal{N}^* = \{n_1^*, n_2^*, \ldots, n_g^*\}$. We will use the notation $\phi(n_i) = n_k^*$ to indicate that node n_i in $\mathcal{G}$ is mapped to node n_k^* in $\mathcal{G}^*$. The inverse of this mapping, ϕ^{-1}, is the mapping that maps node n_k^* in $\mathcal{G}^*$ to node n_i in $\mathcal{G}$; $\phi^{-1}(n_k^*) = n_i$. Since the mapping is a one-to-one mapping, $\phi(n_i) = n_k^*$ if and only if $\phi^{-1}(n_k^*) = n_i$.

The mapping preserves adjacency if nodes that are adjacent in $\mathcal{G}$ are mapped to nodes that are adjacent in $\mathcal{G}^*$, and nodes that are not adjacent in $\mathcal{G}$ are mapped to nodes that are not adjacent in $\mathcal{G}^*$, and vice versa. Formally, two graphs are isomorphic if for all $n_i, n_j \in \mathcal{N}$ and $n_k^*, n_l^* \in \mathcal{N}^*$ there exists a one-to-one mapping, $\phi(n_i) = n_k^*$ and $\phi(n_j) = n_l^*$ such that $l_m = (n_i, n_j) \in \mathcal{L}$ if and only if $l_o = (n_k^*, n_l^*) \in \mathcal{L}^*$. If two nodes are adjacent in one graph, then the nodes they are mapped to must also be adjacent in the isomorphic graph.

Consider the two graphs in Figure 4.13. Each graph has $g = 6$ nodes and $L = 6$ lines, and the nodes in each graph are labeled. A *labeled graph* is a graph in which the nodes have names or labels attached to them. The labels may be the names of the actors represented by the nodes, or they may be numbers or letters distinguishing the nodes. Isomorphic graphs are indistinguishable except for the labels on the nodes. For example, Figure 4.13a contains a graph $\mathcal{G}^*$ that is isomorphic to that in Figure 4.13b, $\mathcal{G}$.

Isomorphisms between graphs are important because if two graphs are isomorphic, then they are identical on all graph theoretic properties. For

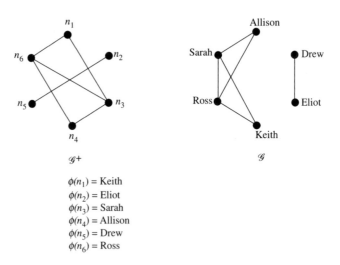

Fig. 4.13. Isomorphic graphs

example, two isomorphic graphs have the same number of nodes, the same number of lines, the same density, the same diameter, and so on. Thus, if we know that a particular graph theoretic property holds for graph $\mathscr{G}$ then we know that the property holds for any graph $\mathscr{G}^*$ that is isomorphic to $\mathscr{G}$.

It is also important to consider the nodes in isomorphic graphs. If two graphs $\mathscr{G}$ and $\mathscr{G}^*$ are isomorphic, and n_i in graph $\mathscr{G}$ is mapped to node n_k^* in $\mathscr{G}^*$, ($\phi(n_i) = n_k^*$) then n_i and n_k^* are identical with respect to all graph theoretic properties (they have the same nodal degree, the same eccentricity, and so on). This property is quite important in defining some kinds of positional equivalences that we discuss in Chapter 12.

We can also consider isomorphic subgraphs. Two subgraphs, $\mathscr{G}_s$ and $\mathscr{G}_s^*$, are *isomorphic* if there is a one-to-one mapping from the nodes of $\mathscr{G}_s$ to the nodes of $\mathscr{G}_s^*$ that preserves the adjacency of nodes (as defined above). Subgraphs that are isomorphic belong to the same *isomorphism class*. Studies of dyads (Chapter 14) and triads (Chapter 15) rely on the isomorphism of very small subgraphs.

We now consider graphs with special properties.

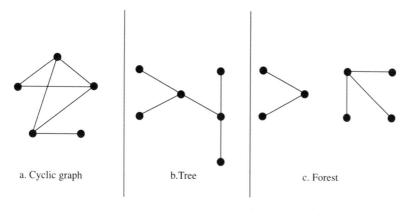

a. Cyclic graph   b.Tree   c. Forest

Fig. 4.14. Cyclic and acyclic graphs

4.2.10 ○ *Special Kinds of Graphs*

Complement. The *complement*, $\overline{\mathscr{G}}$, of a graph, $\mathscr{G}$, has the same set of nodes as $\mathscr{G}$, a line is present between an unordered pair of nodes in $\overline{\mathscr{G}}$ if the unordered pair is *not* in the set of lines in $\mathscr{G}$, and a line is not present in $\overline{\mathscr{G}}$ if it is present in $\mathscr{G}$. In other words, if nodes n_i and n_j are adjacent in $\mathscr{G}$, then n_i and n_j are not adjacent in $\overline{\mathscr{G}}$, and if nodes n_i and n_j are not adjacent in $\mathscr{G}$, then n_i and n_j are adjacent in $\overline{\mathscr{G}}$. The line sets for these two graphs have no intersection at all, and their union is the set of all possible lines (all unordered pairs of nodes).

Trees. A graph that is connected and is acyclic (contains no cycles) is called a *tree*. In some ways trees are rather simple graphs, since they contain the minimum number of lines necessary to be connected, and they do not contain cycles. Several characteristics of trees are particularly important. First, trees are minimally connected graphs since every line in the graph is a bridge (or line cut). The removal of any one line causes the graph to be disconnected. Second, the number of lines in a tree equals the number of nodes minus one ($L = g - 1$). Adding another line adds a cycle to the graph, and hence the graph is no longer a tree. Third, there is only one path between any two nodes in a tree. If this is not true, the graph contains a cycle, which by definition a tree does not contain.

A graph that is disconnected (has more than one component) and contains no cycles is called a *forest*. In a forest, each component is a tree.

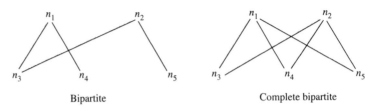

Bipartite   Complete bipartite

Fig. 4.15. Bipartite graphs

In general, the number of lines in a tree or forest equals the number of nodes minus the number of components of the graph. So, L equals g minus the number of components of $\mathscr{G}$. For a tree $L = g - 1$ since the number of components for a tree is 1.

The graph in Figure 4.14b is a tree. It is easy to verify that each pair of nodes is connected via some path, and the graph is acyclic. The graph in Figure 4.14a is not a tree, because it contains a cycle. The graph in Figure 4.14c is a forest. In the forest in Figure 4.14c, $L = 5$, or g minus 2 components.

Bipartite Graphs. If the nodes in a graph can be partitioned into two subsets, $\mathscr{N}_1$ and $\mathscr{N}_2$, so that every line in $\mathscr{L}$ is an unordered pair of nodes in which one node is in $\mathscr{N}_1$ and the other node is in $\mathscr{N}_2$, then the graph is *bipartite*. In a bipartite graph there are two subsets of nodes and all lines are between nodes belonging to different subsets. Nodes in a given subset are adjacent to nodes from the other subset, but no node is adjacent to any node in its own subset.

A *complete bipartite* graph is a bipartite graph in which every node in $\mathscr{N}_1$ is adjacent to every node in $\mathscr{N}_2$. Complete bipartite graphs are usually denoted K_{g_1,g_2}, where g_1 is the number of nodes in $\mathscr{N}_1$, and g_2 is the number of nodes in $\mathscr{N}_2$.

An example of a bipartite graph and a complete bipartite graph is given in Figure 4.15. Nodes n_1 and n_2 belong to $\mathscr{N}_1 = \{n_1, n_2\}$ and nodes n_3, n_4, n_5 belong to $\mathscr{N}_2 = \{n_3, n_4, n_5\}$.

A two-mode network with two sets of actors and a relation linking actors in one set to actors in the second set can be represented as a bipartite graph. But a bipartite graph may also exist in a one-mode network. A graph of an exogamous marriage system is bipartite, if, for example, women from clan A take husbands from clan B, and men from clan B take wives from clan A. In that case, all marriages unite partners from different clans.

The partitioning of the nodes in a graph can be generalized from two subsets $\mathcal{N}_1$ and $\mathcal{N}_2$ to s subsets $\mathcal{N}_1, \mathcal{N}_2, \ldots, \mathcal{N}_s$. An *s-partite* graph is one in which there is a partitioning of the nodes into s subsets so that all lines are between a node in $\mathcal{N}_i$ and a node in $\mathcal{N}_j$, where $i \neq j$. All lines are between nodes in different subsets and no nodes in the same subset are adjacent.

The notion of a complete bipartite graph can also be extended to a *complete s-partite graph*. A graph is a complete s-partite graph if all pairs of nodes belonging to different subsets are adjacent. All possible between-subset lines are present, and there are no lines incident with two nodes belonging to the same subset (equivalently, no nodes in the same subset are adjacent).

An example of a network that might be described by a bipartite graph is the set of monetary donations transacted between corporations in a specific geographic area, and the non-profit organizations headquartered in this area. We initially place all firms, both corporations and non-profit organizations, into a single actor set, $\mathcal{N}$. We then measure the flows of donations among these firms. Since the non-profit organizations usually have limited cash resources and thus can not support themselves financially, they must rely on the corporations for donations. We find that the only lines in this graph connect corporations to non-profit organizations. Thus, we have a bipartite graph, with the corporations residing in set $\mathcal{N}_1$ and non-profit organizations in set $\mathcal{N}_2$.

Thus far, we have focused our discussion on *graphs*, where a line between nodes is either present or absent. As we have emphasized before, graphs are useful for representing nondirectional relations. In the next section we discuss directed graphs, which are used for representing directional relations.

4.3 Directed Graphs

Many relations are *directional*. A relation is directional if the ties are oriented from one actor to another. The import/export of goods between nations is an example of a directional relation. Clearly goods go from one nation to another; one nation is the source and the other is the destination of the goods. In a social network representing trade among nations, the ties are directional and the graph representing such ties must be directed. Choices of friendships among children are another example of a directional relation. The claim of friendship is directed from one child to another child. Child i may choose child j as a friend, but that does not necessarily imply child j chooses child i as a friend.

In this section we define a directed graph and describe those definitions and concepts for directed graphs that are most useful for social network analysis. We refer the reader to Hage and Harary (1983), Harary, Norman, and Cartwright (1965), or other graph theory reference books for further discussion of directed graphs.

A directional relation can be represented by a *directed graph*, or *digraph* for short. A digraph consists of a set of nodes representing the actors in a network, and a set of arcs directed between pairs of nodes representing directed ties between actors. The difference between a graph and a directed graph is that in a directed graph the direction of the lines is specified. Directed ties between the pairs of actors are represented as lines in which the orientation of the relation is specified. These oriented lines are called *arcs*.

A *directed graph*, or *digraph*, $\mathscr{G}_d(\mathscr{N}, \mathscr{L})$, consists of two sets of information: a set of nodes $\mathscr{N} = \{n_1, n_2, \ldots, n_g\}$, and a set of arcs, $\mathscr{L} = \{l_1, l_2, \ldots, l_L\}$. Each arc is an *ordered pair* of distinct nodes, $l_k = < n_i, n_j >$. The arc $< n_i, n_j >$ is directed from n_i (the origin or sender) to n_j (the terminus or receiver). The difference between an arc (in a digraph) and a line (in a graph) is that an arc is an *ordered pair* of nodes (to reflect the direction of the tie between the two nodes) whereas a line is an unordered pair of nodes (it simply records the presence of a tie between two nodes).

We let L be the number of arcs in $\mathscr{L}$. Since each arc is an ordered pair of nodes, there are $g(g-1)$ possible arcs in $\mathscr{L}$.

As in a graph, a node is *incident* with an arc if the node is in the ordered pair of nodes defining the arc. For example, both nodes n_i and n_j are incident with the arc $l_k = < n_i, n_j >$. However, in a digraph, since an arc is an ordered pair of nodes, we can distinguish the first from the second node in the pair. Thus, the concept of adjacency of pairs of nodes in a digraph is somewhat more complicated than adjacency of pairs of nodes in a graph. We must consider whether a given node is first (sender) or second (receiver) in the ordered pair defining the arc. Specifically, node n_i is *adjacent to* node n_j if $< n_i, n_j > \in \mathscr{L}$, and node n_j is *adjacent from* node n_i if $< n_i, n_j > \in \mathscr{L}$.

When a digraph is presented as a diagram the nodes are represented as points and the arcs are represented as directed arrows. The arc $< n_i, n_j >$ is represented by an arrow from the point representing n_i to the point representing n_j. For example, if actor i nominates actor j as a friend,

	Actor	Likes at beginning of year
n_1	Allison	Drew Ross
n_2	Drew	Eliot Sarah
n_3	Eliot	Drew
n_4	Keith	Ross
n_5	Ross	Sarah
n_6	Sarah	Drew

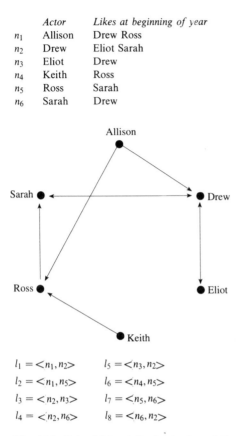

$l_1 = <n_1, n_2>$ $\quad l_5 = <n_3, n_2>$

$l_2 = <n_1, n_5>$ $\quad l_6 = <n_4, n_5>$

$l_3 = <n_2, n_3>$ $\quad l_7 = <n_5, n_6>$

$l_4 = <n_2, n_6>$ $\quad l_8 = <n_6, n_2>$

Fig. 4.16. Friendship at the beginning of the year for six children

there would be an arc originating at i and terminating at j. If actor j returned the friendship choice, there would be another arc, this one originating at j and terminating at i.

To illustrate a directed graph let us consider the choices of friendship among our six children at the beginning of the year. These choices are represented in the directed graph in Figure 4.16. The $g = 6$ nodes represent the six children, and the arcs represent friendship nominations. So, there is an arc from one node to another if the child represented by the first node chose the child represented by the second node as a friend. For example Ross, n_5, chose Sarah, n_6, as a friend, so the arc $< n_5, n_6 >$ is included in the graph.

Many concepts for graphs (such as subgraph) presented and defined earlier in this chapter are immediately applicable to directed graphs, and thus do not require special discussion. However, some concepts, such as isomorphism classes for dyads and triads, nodal degree, walks, and paths are somewhat different in directed graphs, and thus need special discussion. We now turn to these digraph topics.

4.3.1 Subgraphs − Dyads

One of the most important subgraphs in a digraph is the dyad, consisting of two nodes and the possible arcs between them. Since there may or may not be an arc in either direction for a pair of nodes, n_i and n_j, there are four possible states for each dyad. However, there are only three isomorphism classes (all dyads are identical to one of these three types).

The first isomorphism class of a dyad is the *null* dyad. Null dyads have no arcs, in either direction, between the two nodes. The dyad for nodes n_i and n_j is null if neither of the arcs $< n_i, n_j >$ nor $< n_j, n_i >$ is contained in the set of arcs, $\mathscr{L}$. The second isomorphism class is called *asymmetric*. An asymmetric dyad has an arc between the two nodes going in one direction or the other, but not both. The dyad for nodes n_i and n_j is asymmetric if either one of the arcs $< n_i, n_j >$ *or* $< n_j, n_i >$, but not both, is contained in the set of arcs, $\mathscr{L}$. Thus, there are two possible asymmetric dyads, but they are isomorphic. The third isomorphism class is called a *mutual* or *reciprocal* dyad. Mutual dyads have two arcs between the nodes, one going in one direction and the other going in the opposite direction. The dyad for nodes n_i and n_j is mutual if *both* arcs $< n_i, n_j >$ *and* $< n_j, n_i >$ are contained in the set of arcs, $\mathscr{L}$. Thus the three isomorphism classes for dyads are: null, asymmetric, and mutual.

If the directed graph represents the friendship relation, a null dyad is one in which neither person chooses the other. The asymmetric dyad occurs when one person chooses the other, without the choice being reciprocated. In a mutual dyad both actors in the pair choose each other as friends.

Figure 4.17 shows the dyads for the example of friendships at the beginning of the year among the six children (presented in Figure 4.16). Since there are $g = 6$ children, there are $6(5 − 1)/2 = 15$ dyads to consider. Figure 4.17 shows the state of each of these 15 dyads.

The arc with a double-headed arrow between n_2 and n_3 indicates a mutual dyad. Asymmetric dyads are represented by one-way arcs, such

n_1	$\longrightarrow$	n_2	(asymmetric)
n_1		n_3	(null)
n_1		n_4	(null)
n_1	$\longrightarrow$	n_5	(asymmetric)
n_1		n_6	(null)
n_2	$\longleftrightarrow$	n_3	(mutual)
n_2		n_4	(null)
n_2		n_5	(null)
n_2	$\longleftrightarrow$	n_6	(mutual)
n_3		n_4	(null)
n_3		n_5	(null)
n_3		n_6	(null)
n_4	$\longrightarrow$	n_5	(asymmetric)
n_4		n_6	(null)
n_5	$\longrightarrow$	n_6	(asymmetric)

Fig. 4.17. Dyads from the graph of friendship among six children at the beginning of the year

as from n_1 to n_2. The dyad involving Allison, n_1, and Keith, n_4, is a null dyad, since neither arc is present.

The kinds of dyads that arise in a directed graph are quite interesting and important for describing a social network. Tendencies for reciprocity (mutuality) and/or asymmetry in a digraph are often summarized by counting the number of dyads in each of the three isomorphism classes. Chapter 13 discusses these ideas and presents some models for dyads.

One could study subgraphs of any size for a digraph. Dyads are clearly subgraphs of size two. Triads, subgraphs of size three, are important for studying ideas such as balance, clusterability, and transitivity (which we describe in detail in Chapter 6). Cohesive subgroups are also studied by focusing on subgroups (see Chapter 7).

We now discuss how several of the concepts for graphs are applied to directed graphs. We will focus on the most important directed graph concepts including the nodal degrees, walks, paths, reachability, and connectivity.

4.3.2 Nodal Indegree and Outdegree

In a graph, the degree of a node is the number of nodes adjacent to it (equivalently, the number of lines incident with it). In a digraph, a node can be either *adjacent to*, or *adjacent from* another node, depending on the "direction" of the arc. Thus, it is necessary to consider these cases separately. One quantifies the tendency of actors to make "choices"; the other quantifies the tendency to receive "choices."

The *indegree* of a node, $d_I(n_i)$, is the number of nodes that are adjacent *to* n_i. The indegree of node n_i is equal to the number of arcs of the form $l_k = <n_j, n_i>$, for all $l_k \in \mathcal{L}$, and all $n_j \in \mathcal{N}$. Indegree is thus the number of arcs terminating at n_i.

The *outdegree* of a node, $d_O(n_i)$, is the number of nodes adjacent *from* n_i. The outdegree of node n_i is equal to the number of arcs of the form $l_k = <n_i, n_j>$, for all $l_k \in \mathcal{L}$, and all $n_j \in \mathcal{N}$. Outdegree is thus the number of arcs originating with node n_i.

The indegrees and outdegrees for each node may be obtained by considering the arcs in the digraph. Thus, the outdegrees for the six nodes, representing children, in Figure 4.16 are:

- $d_O(n_1) = 2$
- $d_O(n_2) = 2$
- $d_O(n_3) = 1$
- $d_O(n_4) = 1$
- $d_O(n_5) = 1$
- $d_O(n_6) = 1$

The indegrees are:

- $d_I(n_1) = 0$
- $d_I(n_2) = 3$
- $d_I(n_3) = 1$
- $d_I(n_4) = 0$
- $d_I(n_5) = 2$
- $d_I(n_6) = 2$

In social network applications, these degrees can be of great interest. The outdegrees are measures of *expansiveness* and the indegrees are measures of *receptivity*, or *popularity*. If we consider the sociometric relation of friendship, an actor with a large outdegree is one who nominates many others as friends. An actor with a small outdegree nominates fewer friends. An actor with a large indegree is one whom many others nominate as a friend, and an actor with a small indegree is chosen by few others. Outdegrees may be fixed by the data collection design, if, for example, a researcher collects data in which each respondent is instructed to "name your three closest friends." In such a setting, if all respondents in fact named three closest friends, then all outdegrees would equal 3.

Indegrees and outdegrees are useful measurements for many different types of networks and relations, although the terms "expansive" and "popular" may be somewhat inappropriate in some cases. For example, consider the countries trade network, and the relation "exports manufactured goods to" among countries. A country with high outdegree is a heavy exporter, and a country with high indegree is a heavy importer.

In many statistical models we might want to control for, or condition on, either the indegrees or the outdegrees of the nodes. For example, if we are studying the tendency for mutual choices within a network, we might control for the nodal outdegrees; that is, we would study the tendency for mutuality, given the propensity of our actors to make choices. Such statistical conditioning is used in Chapters 13–16.

It is often useful to summarize the indegrees and/or the outdegrees of all the actors in the network using the mean indegree or the mean outdegree. As we will see, these two numbers are equal, since they are considering the same set of arcs, but from different "directions." We will denote the mean indegree as $\bar{d}_I$, and the mean outdegree as $\bar{d}_O$. These are calculated as:

$$\bar{d}_I = \frac{\sum_{i=1}^{g} d_I(n_i)}{g}$$

$$\bar{d}_O = \frac{\sum_{i=1}^{g} d_O(n_i)}{g}. \tag{4.6}$$

Since the indegrees count arcs incident from the nodes, and the outdegree count arcs incident to the nodes, $\sum_{i=1}^{g} d_I(n_i) = \sum_{i=1}^{g} d_O(n_i) = L$, and thus we can see that $\bar{d}_I = \bar{d}_O$ and equations (4.6) simplify to:

$$\bar{d}_I = \bar{d}_O = \frac{L}{g}. \tag{4.7}$$

One might also be interested in the variability of the nodal indegrees and outdegrees. Unlike the mean indegree and the mean outdegree, the variance of the indegrees is not necessarily the same as the variance of the outdegrees. For example, consider a sociometric question in which each person is asked to name her three closest friends. If all people in fact make three nominations, then there is no variance in the outdegrees (all $d_O(n_i) = 3$). However, it is likely that people will receive different numbers of "choices"; thus, there will be variability in the indegrees (the $d_I(n_i)$'s will differ from each other). The variance of the indegrees, which we denote by $S_{D_I}^2$, is calculated as:

$$S_{D_I}^2 = \frac{\sum_{i=1}^{g}(d_I(n_i) - \bar{d}_I)^2}{g}.$$ (4.8)

Similarly, the variance of the outdegrees, which we denote by $S_{D_O}^2$, is calculated as:

$$S_{D_O}^2 = \frac{\sum_{i=1}^{g}(d_O(n_i) - \bar{d}_O)^2}{g}.$$ (4.9)

Both of these measures quantify how unequal the actors in a network are with respect to initiating or receiving ties. These measures are simple statistics for summarizing how "centralized" a network is. We return to this idea in Chapter 5.

Types of Nodes in a Directed Graph. The indegrees and outdegrees of the nodes in a directed graph can be used to distinguish four different kinds of nodes based on the possible ways that arcs can be incident with the node. Recall that the indegree of node n_i, denoted by $d_I(n_i)$, is equal to the number of nodes adjacent to it, and the outdegree of node n_i, denoted by $d_O(n_i)$, is equal to the number of nodes adjacent from it. In terms of the indegree and outdegree there are four possible kinds of nodes: the node is an isolate, the node only has arcs originating from it, the node only has arcs terminating at it, or the node has arcs both to and from it. Graph theorists provide a vocabulary for labeling these four kinds of nodes (Harary, Norman, and Cartwright 1965, page 18; Hage and Harary 1983). According to this classification, a node is a(n):

- *Isolate* if $d_I(n_i) = d_O(n_i) = 0$,
- *Transmitter* if $d_I(n_i) = 0$ and $d_O(n_i) > 0$,
- *Receiver* if $d_I(n_i) > 0$ and $d_O(n_i) = 0$,
- *Carrier* or *ordinary* if $d_I(n_i) > 0$ and $d_O(n_i) > 0$

The distinction between a carrier and an ordinary node is that, although both kinds have both positive indegree and positive outdegree, a carrier has both indegree and outdegree precisely equal to 1, whereas an ordinary node has indegree and/or outdegree greater than 1.

Several authors have argued that this typology, or some variant of it, is useful for describing the "roles" or "positions" of actors in social networks (Burt 1976; Marsden 1989; Richards 1989a).

4.3.3 Density of a Directed Graph

The density of a directed graph is equal to the proportion of arcs present in the digraph. It is calculated as the number of arcs, L, divided by the possible number of arcs. Since an arc is an ordered pair of nodes, there are $g(g-1)$ possible arcs. The density, Δ, is:

$$\Delta = \frac{L}{g(g-1)}. \tag{4.10}$$

The density of a digraph is a fraction that goes from a minimum of 0, if no arcs are present, to a maximum of 1, if all arcs are present. If the density is equal to 1, then all dyads are mutual.

4.3.4 An Example

Now let us illustrate nodal indegree and outdegree, and the density of a directed graph on the example of friendships among Krackhardt's high-tech managers. Clearly a directed graph is the appropriate representation for these friendship choices, since each choice of friendship is directed from one manager to another (and is not necessarily reciprocated).

Table 4.1 presents the nodal indegrees and outdegrees, the mean and variance of the indegrees and outdegrees, and the density of the graph. From these results we see that there are no isolates in this network (there are no managers with both indegree and outdegree equal to 0). However, there are two managers (managers 7 and 9) who did not make any friendship nominations. The mean number of friendship choices made (and received) is equal to 4.86. The density of the relation is equal to 0.243.

4.3.5 Directed Walks, Paths, Semipaths

Walks and related concepts in graphs can also be defined for digraphs, but one must consider the direction of the arcs. We first define directed walks, directed paths, and semipaths for directed graphs and then define closed walks (cycles and semicycles) for directed graphs.

A *directed walk* is a sequence of alternating nodes and arcs so that each arc has its origin at the previous node and its terminus at the subsequent node. More simply, in a directed walk, all arcs are "pointing" in the same direction. The length of a directed walk is the number of instances of arcs in it (an arc is counted each time it occurs in the walk).

Table 4.1. *Nodal degree and density for friendships among Krackhardt's high-tech managers*

Manager	Indegree	Outdegree
1	8	5
2	10	3
3	5	2
4	5	6
5	6	7
6	2	6
7	3	0
8	5	1
9	6	0
10	1	7
11	6	13
12	8	4
13	1	2
14	5	2
15	4	8
16	4	2
17	6	18
18	4	1
19	5	9
20	3	2
21	5	4

$L = 102$

$g = 21$

$\bar{d}_I = \bar{d}_O = 102/21 = 4.86$

possible number of arcs: $21(20) = 420$

$\Delta = 102/420 = 0.243$

$S^2_{D_I} = 2.17^2$

$S^2_{D_O} = 4.37^2$

For example, consider the digraph in Figure 4.18. One directed walk in this figure is $W = n_5 n_1 n_2 n_3 n_4 n_2 n_3$.

Recall that a trail in a graph is a walk in which no line is included more than once. A *directed trail* in a digraph is a directed walk in which no arc is included more than once. Similarly, a *directed path* or simply a *path* in a digraph is a directed walk in which no node and no arc is included more than once. A path joining nodes n_i and n_j in a directed graph is a sequence of distinct nodes, where each arc has its origin at the previous node, and its terminus at the subsequent node. Thus, a path in a directed graph consists of arcs all "pointing" in the same direction. The length of a path is the number of arcs in it.

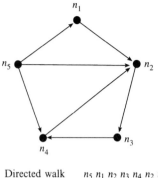

Directed walk	$n_5\ n_1\ n_2\ n_3\ n_4\ n_2\ n_3$
Directed path	$n_5\ n_4\ n_2\ n_3$
Semipath	$n_1\ n_2\ n_5\ n_4\ n_3$
Cycle	$n_2\ n_3\ n_4\ n_2$
Semicycle	$n_1\ n_2\ n_5\ n_1$

Fig. 4.18. Directed walks, paths, semipaths, and semicycles

Now, consider removing the restriction that all arcs "point" in the same direction. We will simply consider walks and paths in which the arc between previous and subsequent nodes in the sequence may go in either direction. A *semiwalk* joining nodes n_i and n_j is a sequence of nodes and arcs in which successive pairs of nodes are incident with an arc from the first to the second, or by an arc from the second to the first. That is, in a semiwalk, for all successive pairs of nodes, the arc between adjacent nodes may be either $< n_i, n_j >$ or $< n_j, n_i >$. In a semiwalk the direction of the arcs is irrelevant. The length of a semiwalk is the number of instances of arcs in it.

A *semipath* joining nodes n_i and n_j is a sequence of distinct nodes, where all successive pairs of nodes are connected by an arc from the first to the second, or by an arc from the second to the first for all successive pairs of nodes (Harary, Norman, and Cartwright 1965; Peay 1975). In a semipath the direction of the arcs is irrelevant. The length of a semipath is the number of arcs in it.

Note that every path is a semipath, but not every semipath is a path (see Harary, Norman, and Cartwright 1965, for more discussion).

Closed walks can also be defined for directed graphs. A *cycle* in a directed graph is a closed directed walk of at least three nodes in which all nodes except the first and last are distinct. A *semicycle* in a directed graph is a closed directed semiwalk of at least three nodes in which all nodes except the first and last are distinct. In a semicycle the arcs may go in either direction, whereas in a cycle the arcs must all "point" in the same direction. Semicycles are used to study structural balance and clusterability (see Chapter 6).

Figure 4.18 gives examples of a directed walk, a directed path, a semipath, a cycle, and a semicycle.

4.3.6 Reachability and Connectivity in Digraphs

Using the ideas of paths and semipaths, we can now define reachability and connectivity of pairs of nodes, and the connectedness of a directed graph.

Pairs of Nodes. In a graph a pair of nodes is reachable if there is a path between them. However, in order to define reachability in a directed graph, we must consider directed paths. Specifically, if there is a directed path from n_i to n_j, then node n_j is *reachable from* node n_i.

Consider now both paths and semipaths between pairs of nodes. We can define four different ways that two nodes can be connected by a path, or semipath (Harary, Norman, and Cartwright 1965; Frank 1971; Peay 1975, 1980). A pair of nodes, n_i, n_j, is:

(i) *Weakly connected* if they are joined by a *semipath*

(ii) *Unilaterally connected* if they are joined by a *path* from n_i to n_j, or a *path* from n_j to n_i

(iii) *Strongly connected* if there is a *path* from n_i to n_j, *and* a path from n_j to n_i; the path from n_i to n_j may contain different nodes and arcs than the path from n_j to n_i

(iv) *Recursively connected* if they are strongly connected, and the path from n_i to n_j uses the same nodes and arcs as the path from n_j to n_i, in reverse order

Notice that these forms of connectivity are increasingly strict, and that any strict form implies connectivity of any less strict form. For example, any two nodes that are recursively connected are also strongly connected, unilaterally connected, and weakly connected. Figure 4.19 illustrates these different kinds of connectivity. In each case nodes n_1 and n_4 in the graph demonstrate the different versions of connectivity.

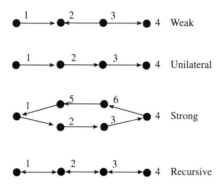

Fig. 4.19. Different kinds of connectivity in a directed graph

Digraph Connectedness. It is now possible to define four different kinds of connectivity for digraphs (Peay 1975, 1980). If a digraph is connected, then it is connected by one of these four kinds of connectivity; otherwise, it is not connected. Since there are four types of connectivity between pairs of nodes in a directed graph, there are four definitions of graph connectivity for a digraph. A directed graph is:

(i) *Weakly connected* if all pairs of nodes are weakly connected
(ii) *Unilaterally connected* if all pairs of nodes are unilaterally connected
(iii) *Strongly connected* if all pairs of nodes are strongly connected
(iv) *Recursively connected* if all pairs of nodes are recursively connected

In a weakly connected digraph, all pairs of nodes are connected by a semipath. In a unilaterally connected digraph, between each pair of nodes there is a directed path from one node to the other; in other words at least one node is reachable from the other in the pair. In a strongly connected digraph each node in each pair is reachable from the other; there is a directed path from each node to each other node. In a recursively connected digraph, each node, in each pair, is reachable from the other, and the directed paths contain the same nodes and arcs, but in reverse order. As with the definitions of connectivity for pairs of nodes, these are increasingly strict graph connectivity definitions.

From these definitions it should be clear that every strongly connected digraph is unilaterally connected, but the reverse is not true. When maximal subgraphs are derived from digraphs in which the actors are unilaterally, or strongly, connected, the subgraph is referred to as a *unilateral*, or *strong*, component in the digraph. These ideas are used to study cohesive subgroups in directed graphs (see Chapter 7).

4.3.7 Geodesics, Distance and Diameter

The (geodesic) distance between a pair of nodes in a graph is the length of a shortest path between the two nodes, and is the basis for defining the diameter of the graph. In a directed graph, the paths from node n_i to node n_j may be different from the paths from node n_j to node n_i (because paths in a directed graph consider the direction of the arcs). Thus, the definitions of distance and diameter in a directed graph are somewhat more complicated than in a graph.

Consider the paths from node n_i to node n_j. A geodesic from node n_i to node n_j is a shortest path *from* n_i to n_j. The distance from n_i to n_j, denoted by $d(i, j)$, is the length of a geodesic from n_i to n_j. It is important to note that since the paths from n_i are likely to be different from the paths from n_j to n_i (since paths require that all arcs are "pointing" in the same direction) the geodesics from n_i to n_j may be different from the geodesics from n_j to n_i. Thus, the distance, $d(i, j)$, from n_i to n_j may be different from the distance, $d(j, i)$, from n_j to n_i. For example, in Figure 4.18 $d(4, 2) = 1$ whereas $d(2, 4) = 2$. If there is no path from n_i to n_j (as might be the case when the graph is only weakly or unilaterally connected) then there is no geodesic from n_i to n_j, and the distance from n_i to n_j is undefined (or infinite).

Now, consider the diameter of a directed graph. As in a graph, the diameter of a directed graph is the length of the longest geodesic between any pair of nodes. This definition of geodesic is useful if there is a *path* from each node to each other node in the graph; that is, the graph is strongly connected or recursively connected. However, if the graph is only unilaterally or weakly connected, then, as noted above, some distances are undefined (or infinite). Thus, the diameter of a weakly or unilaterally connected directed graph is undefined.

4.3.8 ○Special Kinds of Directed Graphs

In this section we describe several kinds of digraphs with important properties. We begin by defining digraph complement and digraph converse.

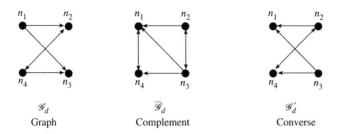

Fig. 4.20. Converse and complement of a directed graph

Complement and Converse of a Digraph. Now let us consider two kinds of digraphs that can be derived from a digraph. These derived digraphs can be used to represent the opposite and the negation of a relation.

The *complement*, $\overline{\mathcal{G}_d}$, of a directed graph, $\mathcal{G}_d$, has the same set of nodes as $\mathcal{G}_d$, but there is an arc present between an ordered pair of nodes in $\overline{\mathcal{G}_d}$ if the ordered pair is *not* in the set of arcs in $\mathcal{G}_d$, and an arc is not present in $\overline{\mathcal{G}_d}$ if it is present in $\mathcal{G}_d$. In other words, if the arc $< n_i, n_j >$ is in $\mathcal{G}_d$, then the arc $< n_i, n_j >$ is not in $\overline{\mathcal{G}_d}$, and if the arc $< n_i, n_j >$ is not in $\mathcal{G}_d$, then the arc $< n_i, n_j >$ is in $\overline{\mathcal{G}_d}$.

The *converse*, $\mathcal{G}_d'$, of a directed graph, $\mathcal{G}_d$, has the same set of nodes as $\mathcal{G}_d$, but the arc $< n_i, n_j >$ is in $\mathcal{G}_d'$ only if the arc $< n_j, n_i >$ is in $\mathcal{G}_d$ (Harary 1969). The converse, $\mathcal{G}_d'$, is obtained from $\mathcal{G}_d$ by reversing the direction of all arcs. The arcs in the converse connect the same pairs of nodes as the arcs in the digraph, but all arcs are reversed in direction. That is, an arc in the digraph from n_i to n_j becomes an arc in the converse from n_j to n_i. Figure 4.20 shows a directed graph, its converse, and its complement.

The converse of a directed graph might be helpful in thinking about relations that have "opposites." For example, the converse of a digraph representing a dominance relation (for example, n_i "wins over" n_j) would represent the submissive relation (n_j "loses to" n_i). On the other hand, the complement of a digraph might be used to represent the absence of a tie, or as *not* the relation. For example, in the digraph representing the relation of friendship the arc $< n_i, n_j >$ means i "chooses" j as a friend. In the digraph representing the complement of the relation of friendship, the arc $< n_i, n_j >$ means i "does not choose" j as a friend.

Tournaments. One other special type of a digraph is a *tournament*, which mathematically represents a set of actors competing in some event(s) and a relation indicating superior performances or "beats" in competition (see Moon 1968). If team n_i beats team n_j, an arc is directed from n_i toward n_j. Of particular interest are *round-robin* tournaments, where each team plays each other team exactly once. Such tournaments can be modeled as *round robin designs* (Kenny 1981; Kenny and LaVoie 1984; Wong 1982). These competitive records form a special type of digraph, because each pair of nodes is connected by exactly one arc. Methodology for such designs is related to the Bradley-Terry-Luce model for paired comparisons, which allows for statistical estimation of population propensities for dominance (Bradley and Terry 1952; Thurstone 1927; Coombs 1951; Mosteller 1951; Frank 1981; and David 1988).

4.3.9 Summary

Digraphs are the appropriate representation of social networks in which relations are dichotomous (ties are either present or absent) and directional. However, many relations are valued; that is, the ties indicate the strength or intensity of the tie between each pair of actors. Thus, we need to generalize both graphs and directed graphs so that we can represent the *strength* of ties between actors in a network. The graph for a valued relation must convey more information by representing the strength of an arc or a line. For example, observations of the number of interactions between pairs of people in a group require valued relations. Similarly, ratings of friendship in which people distinguish between "close personal friends," "friends," "acquaintances," and "strangers" must be represented by a graph in which the arcs also have a value indicating the strength of the tie. In the next sections we define and discuss signed graphs (in which the lines or arcs take on a positive or negative sign). In the section following that we discuss valued graphs (in which the lines or arcs can take on a values from the real numbers).

4.4 Signed Graphs and Signed Directed Graphs

Occasionally relations are measured in which the ties can be interpreted as being either positive or negative in affect, evaluation, or meaning. For example, one might measure the relations "loves" and "hates" among the people in a group, or the relations "is allied with" and "is at war with" among countries. Such relations can be represented as a signed graph, or as a signed directed graph. We begin by defining a signed graph, and then generalize to a signed directed graph. Signed graphs and signed directed graphs are important in the study of balance and clusterability (discussed in Chapter 6).

4.4.1 Signed Graph

A *signed graph* is a graph whose lines carry the additional information of a valence: a positive or negative sign. A signed graph consists of three sets of information: a set of nodes, $\mathcal{N} = \{n_1, n_2, \ldots, n_g\}$, a set of lines, $\mathcal{L} = \{l_1, l_2, \ldots, l_L\}$, and a set of valences (or signs), $\mathcal{V} = \{v_1, v_2, \ldots, v_L\}$, attached to the lines. As usual, each line is an unordered pair of distinct nodes, $l_k = (n_i, n_j)$. But now, associated with each line is a valence, v_k either "+" or "−". A line, $l_k = (n_i, n_j)$ is assigned the valence $v_k = +$ if the tie between actors i and j is positive in meaning or affect, and a valence $v_k = -$ if the tie between the actors represented by the nodes is negative. We denote a signed graph as $\mathcal{G}_+(\mathcal{N}, \mathcal{L}, \mathcal{V})$, or simply $\mathcal{G}_+$.

For example, we can represent alliances and hostilities among nations using a signed graph by letting nodes represent countries, and letting signed lines represent whether pairs of countries are at war with each other, "−", or have a treaty with each other, "+".

A *complete signed graph* is a signed graph in which all unordered pairs of nodes are included in the set of lines. Since all lines are present in a complete signed graph, and all lines have a valence either "+" or "−", each unordered pair of nodes is assigned either "+" or "−".

Dyads and Triads. In a signed graph, each dyad is in one of three states: There is a positive line between them, there is a negative line between them, or there is no line between them. In a complete signed graph each dyad is in one of two states, either "+" or "−".

In a complete signed graph, a triad may be in one of four possible states, depending on whether zero, one, two, or three positive (or negative) lines are present among the three nodes.

Cycles. Many properties of signed graphs (such as balance and clusterability) depend on cycles and properties of cycles. In this section we define the *sign* of a cycle in a signed graph. Recall that a cycle is a closed walk in which all nodes except the beginning and ending node are distinct. Notice that each line in a cycle in a signed graph is either "+" or "−". In a signed graph, the *sign* of a cycle is defined as the product of

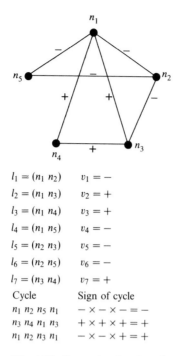

$$l_1 = (n_1\ n_2) \qquad v_1 = -$$
$$l_2 = (n_1\ n_3) \qquad v_2 = +$$
$$l_3 = (n_1\ n_4) \qquad v_3 = +$$
$$l_4 = (n_1\ n_5) \qquad v_4 = -$$
$$l_5 = (n_2\ n_3) \qquad v_5 = -$$
$$l_6 = (n_2\ n_5) \qquad v_6 = -$$
$$l_7 = (n_3\ n_4) \qquad v_7 = +$$

Cycle	Sign of cycle
$n_1\ n_2\ n_5\ n_1$	$-\times-\times-=-$
$n_3\ n_4\ n_1\ n_3$	$+\times+\times+=+$
$n_1\ n_2\ n_3\ n_1$	$-\times-\times+=+$

Fig. 4.21. Example of a signed graph

the signs of the lines included in the cycle; where the sign of the product is defined as:

- $(+)(+) = +$
- $(+)(-) = -$
- $(-)(-) = +$

In brief, if a cycle has an even number of negative, "$-$", lines, then its sign is positive. However, if a cycle has an odd number of negative lines, its sign is negative.

Figure 4.21 gives an example of a signed graph and some of its cycles.

4.4.2 Signed Directed Graphs

It is straightforward to extend the idea of a signed graph to a *signed directed graph*. A signed directed graph is a directed graph in which

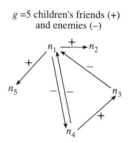

$g = 5$ children's friends (+)
and enemies (−)

Fig. 4.22. Example of a signed directed graph

the arcs have the additional information of a positive or negative sign. A signed digraph consists of three sets of information: a set of nodes, $\mathcal{N} = \{n_1, n_2, \ldots, n_g\}$, a set of arcs, $\mathcal{L} = \{l_1, l_2, \ldots, l_L\}$, and a set of valences, $\mathcal{V} = \{v_1, v_2, \ldots, v_L\}$, attached to the arcs. In a signed directed graph, each arc is an ordered pair of distinct nodes, $< n_i, n_j >$. Associated with each arc is a valence, either "+" or "−". Since the arc $l_k = < n_i, n_j >$ is distinct from the arc $l_m = < n_i, n_j >$, the sign v_k may be different from the sign v_m. We can denote a signed directed graph as $\mathcal{G}_{d\pm}(\mathcal{N}, \mathcal{L}, \mathcal{V})$, or simply $\mathcal{G}_{d\pm}$.

Claims of friendship and enmity among people can be represented as a signed directed graph. Nominations of friends might be represented by a "+" and nominations of enemies might be represented by a "−". Figure 4.22 contains an example of a signed digraph, which we can take to represent such friendship and enmity nominations among people.

Semicycles. In a signed directed graph the most general cycles are usually referred to as *semicycles*. Recall that a semicycle is a closed sequence of distinct nodes and arcs in which each node is either adjacent to or adjacent from the previous node in the sequence. Thus a semicycle is a cycle in which the arcs may point in either direction. The *sign of a semicycle* is the product of the signs of the arcs in it.

This idea is important for studying balance and clusterability in signed directed graphs (see Chapter 6).

Signed graphs and signed directed graphs generalize graphs and directed graphs by allowing the lines or arcs to have valences. Now, let us generalize even further by allowing the lines or arcs to have other (usually numerical) values.

4.5 Valued Graphs and Valued Directed Graphs

Often social network data consist of valued relations in which the strength or intensity of each tie is recorded. Examples of valued relations include the frequency of interaction among pairs of people, the dollar amount of trade between nations, or the rating of friendship between people in a group. Such relations cannot be fully represented using a graph or a directed graph, since lines or arcs in a graph or directed graph are only present or absent (dichotomous: 0 or 1). Thus, the next step in the generalization of graphs and digraphs is to add a *value* or *magnitude* to each line or arc. Valued graphs are the appropriate graph theoretic representation for valued relations. In this section we define and describe valued graphs.

There are several special valued graphs; for example, weighted graphs and integer weighted graphs (Roberts 1976), nets and networks (Harary 1969), and Markov chains. We will briefly describe each. Concepts and definitions for valued graphs are not as well developed as they are for graphs and directed graphs; thus, our discussion of valued graphs will be briefer than our discussion of graphs and directed graphs.

A *valued graph* or a *valued directed graph* is a graph (or digraph) in which each line (or arc) carries a value. A valued graph consists of three sets of information: a set of nodes, $\mathcal{N} = \{n_1, n_2, \ldots, n_g\}$, a set of lines (or arcs), $\mathcal{L} = \{l_1, l_2, \ldots, l_L\}$, and a set of values, $\mathcal{V} = \{v_1, v_2, \ldots, v_L\}$, attached to the lines (or arcs). Associated with each line (in a graph) or each arc (in a digraph) is a value from the set of real numbers (Flament 1963). We denote a valued graph by $\mathcal{G}_V(\mathcal{N}, \mathcal{L}, \mathcal{V})$, or simply $\mathcal{G}_V$. Roberts (1976) refers to a valued digraph as a *weighted digraph*.

A valued graph represents a nondirectional valued relation, such as the number of interactions observed between each pair of people in a group. The number of interactions between actor i and actor j is the same as the number of interactions between actor j and actor i. In a valued graph the line between node n_i and node n_j is identical to the line between node n_j and node n_i ($l_k = (n_i, n_j) = (n_j, n_i)$), and thus there is only a single value, v_k, for each unordered pair of nodes.

A valued directed graph represents a directional valued relation, such as the dollar amount of manufactured goods exported from each country to each other country. Country i may export a different amount of manufactured goods to country j than country j exports to country i. In a valued directed graph, the arc from node n_i to node n_j is not the same as the arc from node n_j to node n_i ($l_k = < n_i, n_j > \neq l_m = < n_j, n_i >$), and thus there are two distinct values, one for each possible arc for the ordered pair of nodes. In general, for $l_k = < n_i, n_j >$ and $l_m = < n_j, n_i >$, v_k does not necessarily equal v_m.

Some authors allow the values to be non-numerical (for example, letters or colors). Harary, Norman, and Cartwright (1965) refer to such a valued graph as a *network*.

Special cases of valued graphs and valued directed graphs place restrictions on the possible values that the lines or arcs can take. Harary (1969) refers to a valued graph in which all values are from the *positive real numbers* as a *network* (note how a variety of authors differ in their definition of the term "network"). If all values in a valued digraph are from the set of integers, then it is what Roberts (1976) refers to as an *integer weighted digraph*.

One can also consider a signed graph in which positive lines have the value $+1$ and negative lines have the value -1 as an integer-weighted graph, with integer values $+1$ and -1. A signed graph is thus a special case of a valued graph in which the values are only $+1$ and -1. Similarly, a graph is a special case of a valued graph in which each and every line has a value equal to 1.

One specific application of valued graphs that has been studied extensively is the set of graphs whose values are probabilities. These graphs are known as Markov chains, and their corresponding sociomatrices are often referred to as transition matrices or stochastic matrices (Harary 1959b). In a Markov chain the values of all arcs incident from each node are constrained to sum to 1, for all n_i, $\sum v_k = 1$ for all $l_k = < n_i, n_j >$, $j = 1, 2, \ldots, g$; further, $0 \leq v_k \leq 1$.

Often we will restrict our attention to relations that are discrete-valued, and thus can be represented as integer-weighted graphs or integer-weighted digraphs, where the values are from the non-negative integers. In this case, the value of an arc in a digraph (or a line in a graph) takes on the values $m = 1, 2, \ldots, C$.

As another example, if nominations of three best friends and three worst enemies were requested, ties might be labeled $+3$ for a best friend, $+2, +1, -1, -2$, and -3 for a worst enemy.

Figure 4.23 gives an example of a valued digraph. This figure lists the arcs and their values. For example, the arc $l_4 = < n_5, n_2 >$ has a value of 3, so $v_4 = 3$.

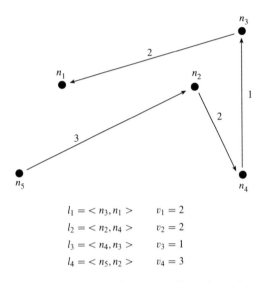

$$l_1 = \ < n_3, n_1 > \qquad v_1 = 2$$
$$l_2 = \ < n_2, n_4 > \qquad v_2 = 2$$
$$l_3 = \ < n_4, n_3 > \qquad v_3 = 1$$
$$l_4 = \ < n_5, n_2 > \qquad v_4 = 3$$

Fig. 4.23. Example of a valued directed graph

4.5.1 Nodes and Dyads

Nodes in Valued Graphs. Each node in a valued graph can have a number of lines incident with it. Similarly, each node in a valued digraph can have a number of arcs incident to it and/or from it. To each line or arc is attached a value. In a graph or digraph, nodal degree is equal to the number of lines incident with the node or the number of arcs incident to it or from it. The idea of degree does not generalize well to valued graphs, since one must consider the values attached to the lines.

One way to generalize the notion of degree to valued graphs and digraphs is to average the values over all lines incident with a node, or all arcs incident to or from a node. Such a measure reflects the average value of the lines incident with the node or of the arcs to or from the node.

Dyads in Valued Graphs. A dyad in a valued graph has a line between nodes with a specific strength. A dyad in a valued directed graph has arcs between the nodes. Each of the two arcs $< n_i, n_j >$ and $< n_j, n_i >$ has a value, which we denote by v_k and v_m. These values most likely will be different. It is of interest in such settings to compare the v_k to v_m. Models for such dyads are discussed in Chapter 15.

4.5.2 Density in a Valued Graph

In a graph or digraph, density, Δ, is defined as the ratio of the number of lines or arcs present to the maximum possible that could arise. Another way to view the density of a graph or a digraph is as the average of the values assigned to the lines/arcs. Each line or arc is given a value of 1, and pairs of nodes for which lines are absent are given a value of 0. The sum of these values is equal to the number of lines or arcs; one then divides this sum by its maximum possible value.

To generalize the notion of density to a valued graph or digraph, one can average the values attached to the lines/arcs across all lines/arcs. Thus, for a valued graph/digraph, the density is $\Delta = \sum v_k / g(g-1)$ where the sum is taken over all k. This measures the average strength of the lines/arcs in the valued graph/digraph.

4.5.3 ○ Paths in Valued Graphs

Walks and paths in valued graphs are defined the same way as they are in graphs (as an alternating sequence of nodes and lines beginning and ending with nodes). However, in a valued graph (or valued digraph) since the lines (or arcs) have values attached to them, concepts such as reachability of a pair of nodes, length of a path, and distance between a pair of nodes become more complicated. In order to define these concepts for valued graphs, we must consider the values attached to each of the lines (or arcs) in a path. As Peay (1980) has noted, there are a number of different, and reasonable, ways to define distance and values for paths in a valued graph. The choice of which definition to use depends on the interpretation of the lines (arcs) and values in the graph. As in a graph, nodes n_i and n_j are *reachable* if there is a path between them. In a valued graph we can also consider "strengths" or "values" of reachability.

Value of a Path. The *value* of a path (semipath) is equal to the smallest value attached to any line (arc) in it (Peay 1980). Formally, the value of $W = l_1, l_2, \ldots, l_k$ from n_i to n_j equals $\min(v_1, v_2, \ldots, v_k)$. The value of a path is thus the "weakest link" in the path. This idea makes most sense if larger values indicate stronger ties. For example, if the lines represent the amount of communication between each pair of people in a group, then the value of a path between two people represents the most "restricted" amount of communication between any pair of people in the path.

Now, for simplicity, consider a valued graph in which the values attached to the lines are discrete and ordinal, and take on values $1, 2, \ldots, C$ (this is a simplifying condition that is not necessary). We define a *path at level c* as a path between a pair of nodes such that each and every line in the path has a value greater than or equal to c; that is, $v_l \geq c$ for all v_l in the path (Doreian 1969, 1974). In general, paths that include only lines with large values will have higher path values, whereas paths that include lines with small values will have lower path values. Since all values in a path at level c are greater than or equal to c, a path at level c is also a path at all values less than or equal to c. This concept is used to study cohesive subgroups for valued graphs (Chapter 7).

Reachability. We can generalize reachability for a pair of nodes to strengths of reachability in a valued graph (Doreian 1974). Consider all paths between a pair of nodes. Each of these paths has a value. The higher the value, the "stronger" the lines included in the path. In a valued graph, two nodes are *reachable at level c* if there is a path at level c between them. In other words, if two nodes are reachable at level c then there is at least one path between them that includes no line with a value less than c. If two nodes are reachable at level c, then they are reachable at any value less than c.

Path Length. If the values attached to the lines (or arcs) can be thought of as "costs" associated with the tie (such as the amount of time required to go from point i to point j), then it is useful to define the length of a path as the sum of the values of the lines in it. Flament (1963) defines the *length* of a path in a valued graph as equal to the sum of the values of the lines included in the path. If all values are equal to 1, then this definition is equivalent to the definition of path length for a graph or a directed graph since the sum is simply the number of lines (arcs) in the path. One possible problem with this quantification of path length in a valued graph is that a high value for a path can result either if the values of the lines in the path are high, or if the path is long (and thus contains many lines).

Figure 4.24 gives an example of a valued graph. It also gives the lengths and values of some paths in this graph.

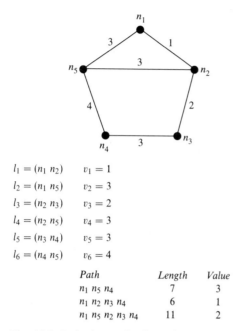

$l_1 = (n_1\ n_2)$ $v_1 = 1$
$l_2 = (n_1\ n_5)$ $v_2 = 3$
$l_3 = (n_2\ n_3)$ $v_3 = 2$
$l_4 = (n_2\ n_5)$ $v_4 = 3$
$l_5 = (n_3\ n_4)$ $v_5 = 3$
$l_6 = (n_4\ n_5)$ $v_6 = 4$

Path	Length	Value
$n_1\ n_5\ n_4$	7	3
$n_1\ n_2\ n_3\ n_4$	6	1
$n_1\ n_5\ n_2\ n_3\ n_4$	11	2

Fig. 4.24. Paths in a valued graph

In the previous sections we discussed graphs (for representing dichotomous nondirectional relations) and described graphs that generalize graphs in two different ways. Directed graphs are used for representing directional relations and generalize graphs by considering the direction of the arcs between pairs of nodes. Both graphs and directed graphs represent dichotomous relations. The second way to generalize graphs (and directed graphs) is to allow the lines (or arcs) to carry values. Signed and valued graphs and digraphs generalize graphs by removing the restriction that lines (arcs) be either present or absent. A third way to generalize graphs and digraphs is to have more than one relation measured on a pair of nodes. We consider this generalization next.

4.6 Multigraphs

So far, we have discussed simple graphs, where there is at most one line between a pair of nodes. A simple graph is the appropriate representation for a social network in which a single relation is measured. When there is more than one relation, a *multigraph* is the appropriate graph theoretic representation. A multigraph, or a *multivariate (directed) graph* is a generalization of a simple graph or digraph that allows more than one set of lines (Flament 1963).

If more than one relation is measured on the same set of actors, then the graph representing this network must allow each pair of nodes to be connected in more than one way. For example, for Krackhardt's high-tech managers, each person was asked with whom they were "friends," and from whom they sought advice on the job. That is, two relations were measured on the set of actors.

A multigraph $\mathscr{G}$ consists of a set of *nodes*, $\mathscr{N} = \{n_1, n_2, \ldots, n_g\}$, and two or more sets of lines, $\mathscr{L}^+ = \{\mathscr{L}_1, \mathscr{L}_2, \ldots, \mathscr{L}_R\}$. We let R be the number of sets of lines in the multigraph, and we subscript the lines to denote to which set it belongs. If each relation is nondirectional, each line in each of the R sets is an unordered pair of distinct nodes, $l_{kr} = (n_i, n_j)$. A pair of nodes may be included in more than one set of lines. Since there are R sets of lines, each unordered pair of nodes may have from 0 up to R lines between them.

Returning to the definition of a simple graph, a graph is called *simple* if it contains no loops (or self-choices) and if each pair of nodes is joined by 0 or 1 lines. If a graph contains loops and/or any pair of nodes is adjacent via *more than one* line the graph is *complex*. Much of graph theory concentrates on simple graphs, and most of the graph theoretic concepts network researchers use pertain to simple graphs. Accordingly, most of the methods that we discuss in later chapters focus on simple graphs.

Graphs and directed graphs consider *pairs* of nodes. Lines and arcs are defined as pairs or ordered pairs of nodes. The next generalization of graphs is to consider ties among subsets of nodes.

4.7 ⊗Hypergraphs

Some social network applications consider ties among subsets of actors in a network, such as the tie among people who belong to the same club or civic organization. Such networks, called affiliation networks, or membership networks, require considering subsets of nodes in a graph, where these subsets can be of any size. Hypergraphs are the appropriate representations for such networks.

An affiliation network is a two-mode network consisting of a set of actors and a set of events. Each event is a subset of the actors from

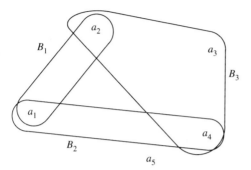

Fig. 4.25. Example of a hypergraph

$\mathcal{N}$. Thus, affiliation network data cannot be fully represented in terms of pairwise ties, since the subsets can include more than two actors. A *hypergraph*, rather than a graph, is the appropriate representation for affiliation network data.

Formally, a *hypergraph* consists of a set of objects and a collection of subsets of objects, in which each object belongs to at least one subset, and no subset is empty (Berge 1989). The objects are called *points* and the collections of objects are called *edges*. In general, for point set $\mathcal{A} = \{a_1, a_2, \ldots, a_g\}$, and edge set $\mathcal{B} = \{B_1, B_2, \ldots, B_h\}$, the hypergraph is denoted by $\mathcal{H} = (\mathcal{A}, \mathcal{B})$.

An important feature of a hypergraph is that it can also be described by the *dual hypergraph*, denoted $\mathcal{H}^{\ast}$, by reversing the roles of the points and the edges. In general, if the hypergraph $\mathcal{H} = (\mathcal{A}, \mathcal{B})$ has point set $\mathcal{A}$ and edge set $\mathcal{B}$, then the dual hypergraph $\mathcal{H}^{\ast} = (\mathcal{B}, \mathcal{A})$ has point set $\mathcal{B}$ and edge set $\mathcal{A}$.

To distinguish between points and edges, we introduce the following notation. When the elements in $\mathcal{A}$ are viewed as points and the elements in $\mathcal{B}$ are viewed as edges (as in hypergraph $\mathcal{H} = (\mathcal{A}, \mathcal{B})$) we will denote the elements of $\mathcal{A}$ using lowercase letters: $\{a_1, a_2, \ldots, a_g\}$, and the edges from set $\mathcal{B}$ using uppercase letters: $\{B_1, B_2, \ldots, B_h\}$. In the dual hypergraph, $\mathcal{H}^{\ast} = (\mathcal{B}, \mathcal{A})$ with elements in $\mathcal{B}$ as points and elements in $\mathcal{A}$ as edges, we will denote the elements in $\mathcal{A}$ using uppercase letters: $\{A_1, A_2, \ldots, A_g\}$ and the elements in $\mathcal{B}$ using lowercase letters: $\{b_1, b_2, \ldots, b_h\}$.

The hypergraph in Figure 4.25 has point set $\mathcal{A} = \{a_1, a_2, a_3, a_4\}$, and edge set $\mathscr{B} = \{B_1, B_2, B_3\}$. This hypergraph could represent four actors attending three social events.

The hypothetical example in Figure 4.25 can be described in terms of each edge in $\mathscr{B}$ and the subset of points in $\mathscr{A}$ that it includes:

$$B_1 = \{a_1, a_2\}$$
$$B_2 = \{a_1, a_4\}$$
$$B_3 = \{a_2, a_3, a_4\}$$

Alternatively, we can list each element in $\mathscr{A}$ as an edge, and the elements in $\mathscr{B}$ as the points contained in it:

$$A_1 = \{b_1, b_2\}$$
$$A_2 = \{b_1, b_3\}$$
$$A_3 = \{b_3\}$$
$$A_4 = \{b_2, b_3\}$$

Hypergraphs are more general than graphs. A graph is a special case of a hypergraph in which the number of points in each edge is exactly equal to two. Any graph can be represented as a hypergraph, by letting the nodes in the graph be the points in the hypergraph, and letting each line $l_k = (n_i, n_j)$ in the graph be an edge in the hypergraph. Each edge thus contains exactly two points.

4.8 Relations

Social networks are often described using formal mathematical notation as *mathematical relations* (Hage and Harary 1983; Fararo 1973; Pattison 1993; and others). We now describe this representation of a social network.

4.8.1 Definition

A mathematical relation focuses on the ordered pairs of actors in a network between whom a substantive tie is present. Relations are widely used in algebraic methods (Chapter 11).

Consider a set of objects, $\mathscr{N} = \{n_1, n_2, \ldots, n_g\}$. In a social network these objects are the actors. In a graph, these are the nodes. In a social network, ties link pairs of actors. Thus, we focus on ordered pairs of objects from $\mathscr{N}$.

The Cartesian product of two sets (or of a set with itself) is a useful mathematical entity for studying relations. The Cartesian product of two sets, $\mathcal{M}$ and $\mathcal{N}$, is the collection of all ordered pairs in which the first element in the pair belongs to set $\mathcal{M}$ and the second element belongs to set $\mathcal{N}$. We denote the Cartesian product of sets $\mathcal{M}$ and $\mathcal{N}$ as $\mathcal{M} \times \mathcal{N}$. If there are h elements in $\mathcal{M}$ and g elements in $\mathcal{N}$, and each of the h elements in $\mathcal{M}$ is paired with each of the g elements in $\mathcal{N}$, then there are $h \times g$ elements in the Cartesian product of $\mathcal{M}$ and $\mathcal{N}$.

Now, consider the Cartesian product of a set with itself: $\mathcal{N} \times \mathcal{N}$. This Cartesian product consists of all ordered pairs of objects from $\mathcal{N}$. If the set $\mathcal{N}$ is the set of all actors in a network, then the Cartesian product $\mathcal{N} \times \mathcal{N}$ is the set of all ordered pairs of actors. Thus, $\mathcal{N} \times \mathcal{N}$ is the collection of all ordered pairs of actors for whom substantive ties could be present. For example, if we are studying friendship among people, and the set of actors is $\mathcal{N}$, then the Cartesian product, $\mathcal{N} \times \mathcal{N}$, is the set of all possible ordered pairs of people, in which the first person could choose the second person as a friend. However, friendship ties are usually present between only some of the ordered pairs of people.

A *relation*, R, on the set $\mathcal{N}$ is defined as a subset of the Cartesian product $\mathcal{N} \times \mathcal{N}$ (Hage and Harary 1983). In substantive terms, the relation R consists of all ordered pairs $< n_i, n_j >$ for whom the substantive tie from i to j is present. Relations are conveniently expressed using algebraic notation (see Chapter 3). If the ordered pair $< n_i, n_j > \in R$ then we write iRj.

4.8.2 Properties of Relations

There are several important properties of relations: reflexivity, symmetry, and transitivity. Unlike a simple graph that excludes loops, a relation allows the possible $< n_i, n_i >$ tie to be present. A relation is *reflexive* if all possible $< n_i, n_i >$ ties are present in R; that is, iRi for all i. If *no* $< n_i, n_i >$ ties are present in R, then the relation is *irreflexive*. If a relation is neither reflexive nor irreflexive, then it is *not reflexive* (Fararo 1973; and Hage and Harary 1983). A relation that is not reflexive is one on which iRi for some but not all i.

Symmetry is another property of a relation. A relation is *symmetric* if it has the property that iRj if and only if jRi, for all i and j. That is, the ordered pair $< n_i, n_j > \in R$ if and only if $< n_j, n_i > \in R$. A symmetric relation is one in which all dyads are either mutual or null.

On some relations the presence of the $< n_i, n_j >$ tie implies the absence of the $< n_j, n_i >$ tie. Such a relation is *antisymmetric*. An antisymmetric relation is one on which iRj implies that not jRi. An example of an antisymmetric relation is the relation "beats" in a sporting tournament if each team plays each other team no more than once. If team *i* beats team *j*, then it cannot be the case that team *j* beats team *i* (if they play only once and no ties are allowed).

A relation that is neither symmetric nor antisymmetric is called *not symmetric*, *non-symmetric*, or *asymmetric*. A relation that is not symmetric is one for which iRj and jRi, for some but not all *i* and *j*.

A third important property of a relation is whether or not it is transitive. A relation is *transitive* if whenever iRj and jRk, then iRk, for all *i*, *j*, and *k*. Substantively, transitivity captures the notion that "a friend of a friend is a friend." If person *i* "chooses" person *j* as a friend, and person *j* in turn "chooses" person *k* as a friend, then, if friendship is transitive, person *i* will "choose" person *k* as a friend.

We will return to these important properties below and show how matrices can be used to study symmetry, reflexivity, and transitivity in social networks.

4.9 Matrices

The information in a graph $\mathscr{G}$ may also be expressed in a variety of ways in matrix form. There are two such matrices that are especially useful. The first is the *sociomatrix*, first introduced in Chapter 3. The second is the *incidence* matrix. We will begin by describing these matrices for a single nondirectional relation (or graph), and then generalize to matrices for directional relations (digraphs), valued relations (valued graphs), and hypergraphs.

4.9.1 Matrices for Graphs

The Sociomatrix. The primary matrix used in social network analysis is called the *adjacency* matrix, or *sociomatrix*, and is denoted by **X**. Graph theorists refer to this matrix as an *adjacency matrix* because the entries in the matrix indicate whether two nodes are adjacent or not. In the study of social networks, the adjacency matrix is usually referred to as a sociomatrix. Sociomatrix is the term we will use most often.

A sociomatrix is of size $g \times g$ (*g* rows and *g* columns) for one-mode networks. There is a row and column for each node, and the rows and columns are labeled $1, 2, \ldots, g$. The rows and columns index nodes in the graph, or actors in the network, in identical order. The entries in the sociomatrix, x_{ij}, record which pairs of nodes are adjacent. In the

Table 4.2. *Example of a sociomatrix: "lives near" relation for six children*

X

	n_1	n_2	n_3	n_4	n_5	n_6
n_1	-	0	0	0	1	1
n_2	0	-	1	0	0	0
n_3	0	1	-	0	0	0
n_4	0	0	0	-	1	1
n_5	1	0	0	1	-	1
n_6	1	0	0	1	1	-

sociomatrix, there is a 1 in the (i, j)th cell (row i, column j) if there is a line between n_i and n_j, and a 0 in the cell otherwise. In other words, if nodes n_i and n_j are adjacent, then $x_{ij} = 1$, and if nodes n_i and n_j are not adjacent, then $x_{ij} = 0$.

For the present, we are focusing on graphs where the lines are not directed and are neither signed nor valued. That is, a line between two nodes is either present or it is absent. If a line is present, it goes both from n_i to n_j and from n_j to n_i; thus, $x_{ij} = 1$, and $x_{ji} = 1$.

The sociomatrix for a graph (for a nondirectional relation) is *symmetric*. A matrix is symmetric if $x_{ij} = x_{ji}$ for all i and j; thus the entries in the upper right and lower left triangles are identical. The entries on the diagonal, values of x_{ii}, are udefined, if we do not allow loops in the graph.

The sociomatrix for a complete graph contains 1's in all off-diagonal cells. Since all nodes are adjacent, $x_{ij} = x_{ji} = 1$ for all $i \neq j$. The sociomatrix for an empty graph contains 0's everywhere, since no nodes are adjacent.

For example in Figure 4.1, nodes n_2 and n_3 are adjacent, since the line $l_1 = (n_2, n_3)$ is in the set of lines $\mathscr{L}$. Thus, $x_{23} = 1$ and $x_{32} = 1$ in the sociomatrix. Nodes n_1 and n_3 are not adjacent, since there is no line between the two, therefore $x_{13} = 0$ and $x_{31} = 0$.

The sociomatrix for the graph in Figure 4.1 is given in Table 4.2. Note that the diagonal entries are undefined, since we are focusing on simple graphs, those without loops; that is, x_{ii} is undefined if there are no loops. Also note the entries are binary, since a line is either present, $x_{ij} = 1$, or absent, $x_{ij} = 0$, between any two nodes. Thus, the sociomatrix for a graph contains only 1's and 0's, since pairs of nodes are either adjacent, or not. Finally, note the matrix is symmetric, since a line between n_i and n_j is also a line between n_j and n_i, so $x_{ij} = x_{ji}$.

Table 4.3. *Example of an incidence matrix: "lives near" relation for six children*

I

	l_1	l_2	l_3	l_4	l_5	l_6
n_1	1	1	0	0	0	0
n_2	0	0	1	0	0	0
n_3	0	0	1	0	0	0
n_4	0	0	0	1	1	0
n_5	1	0	0	1	0	1
n_6	0	1	0	0	1	1

In summary, the sociomatrix records for each pair of nodes whether the nodes are adjacent or not. The next matrix we describe records which nodes are incident with which lines.

The Incidence Matrix. The second matrix that can be used to present the information in a graph is called the *incidence matrix*, **I**, or $\mathbf{I}(\mathcal{G})$, and records which lines are incident with which nodes. The incidence matrix has nodes indexing the rows, and lines indexing the columns. Since there are g nodes and L lines, the matrix **I** is of size $g \times L$; there is a row for every node, and a column for every line. The matrix entry I_{ij} equals 1 if node n_i is incident with line l_j, and equals 0 if node n_i is not incident with line l_j. Since the line $l_k = (n_i, n_j)$ is incident with the two nodes n_i and n_j, each column in **I** has exactly two 1's in it, recording the two nodes incident with the line.

The incidence matrix is binary, since a line is either incident with a node or it is not. However, it is not necessarily square.

The incidence matrix for the graph in Figure 4.1 is given in Table 4.3. Note that since there are $g = 6$ nodes and $L = 6$ lines, **I** is 6×6.

The sociomatrix and the incidence matrix both contain all the information in a graph. The set of nodes and lines in a graph is completely described by the information in either matrix.

4.9.2 Matrices for Digraphs

The sociomatrix, **X**, of a digraph has elements x_{ij} equal to 1 if there is an arc from row node n_i to column node n_j, and 0 otherwise. The value in cell x_{ij} is equal to 1 if the arc $< n_i, n_j >$ is in $\mathcal{L}$. That is, the entry in the (i, j)th cell of **X** is equal to 1 if the actor represented by row node n_i "chooses" the actor represented by column node n_j. Since the "choice"

Table 4.4. *Example of a sociomatrix for a directed graph: friendship at the beginning of the year for six children*

X

	n_1	n_2	n_3	n_4	n_5	n_6
n_1	-	1	0	0	1	0
n_2	0	-	1	0	0	1
n_3	0	1	-	0	0	0
n_4	0	0	0	-	1	0
n_5	0	0	0	0	-	1
n_6	0	1	0	0	0	-

from i to j is substantively different from the "choice" from j to i, the entry in x_{ij} may be different from the entry in x_{ji}. For example, if actor i "chose" actor j, but j did not reciprocate, there would be a 1 in the x_{ij} cell, and a 0 in the x_{ji} cell.

The sociomatrix for the digraph in Figure 4.16 (the relation is friendship at the beginning of the school year) is given in Table 4.4. Note that, for example, the mutual choices between actors Drew (n_2) and Sarah (n_6) are represented by a 1 in both the x_{26} and x_{62} cells of this sociomatrix.

4.9.3 Matrices for Valued Graphs

A valued graph can also be represented as a sociomatrix. The entry in cell x_{ij} is the value associated with the line between node n_i and node n_j in a valued graph, or the value associated with the arc from n_i to n_j in a valued directed graph.

The sociomatrix for a valued graph (representing a valued nondirectional relation) has entries, x_{ij}, that record the value v_k associated with the line or arc l_k between n_i and n_j. For an undirected valued graph, there is a single value, v_k, associated with the line $l_k = (n_i, n_j)$, and thus the value in cell (i, j) is equal to the value in cell (j, i); $x_{ij} = x_{ji} = v_{ij}$. However, for a directed valued graph the arc $l_k =< n_i, n_j >$ with value v_k and the arc $l_m =< n_j, n_i >$ with value v_m are distinct. Thus, $x_{ij} = v_k$ and $x_{ji} = v_m$, which may differ. The entry in cell (i, j) of **X** records the strength of the tie from actor i to actor j.

4.9.4 Matrices for Two-Mode Networks

For two-mode networks the sociomatrix is of size $g \times h$, where the rows label the nodes in $\mathcal{N} = \{n_1, n_2, \ldots, n_g\}$ and the columns label the nodes in $\mathcal{M} = \{m_1, m_2, \ldots, m_h\}$.

4.9.5 ◯Matrices for Hypergraphs

The matrix for a hypergraph, denoted by **A**, is a g by h matrix that records which points are contained within which edges. For the hypergraph, $\mathcal{H}(\mathcal{N}, \mathcal{M})$, with point set $\mathcal{N} = \{n_1, n_2, \ldots, n_g\}$ and edge set $\mathcal{M} = \{M_1, M_2, \ldots, M_h\}$, the matrix $\mathbf{A} = \{a_{ij}\}$ has an entry $a_{ij} = 1$ if point n_i is in edge M_j, and 0 otherwise. The matrix **A** has been called the *incidence* matrix for the hypergraph (Berge 1989), since it codes which points are incident with which edges.

The sociomatrix is the most common form for presenting social network data. It is especially useful for computer analyses. In addition, it is a very flexible representation since graphs, directed graphs, signed graphs and digraphs, and valued graphs and digraphs can all be represented as sociomatrices.

4.9.6 Basic Matrix Operations

In this section we describe and illustrate basic matrix operations that are used in social network analysis.

Vocabulary. The *size* of a matrix (also called its *order*) is defined as the number of rows and columns in the matrix. A matrix with g rows and h columns is of size g by h, or equivalently $g \times h$. A sociomatrix for a network with a single set of actors and one relation has g rows and g columns, and is thus of size $g \times g$. If a matrix has the same number of rows and columns, it is *square*. Otherwise, it is *rectangular*. A sociomatrix for a single set of actors and a single relation is necessarily square.

Each entry in a matrix is called a *cell*, and is denoted by its row index and column index. So, cell x_{ij} is in row i and column j of the matrix.

For a square matrix, the *main diagonal* of the matrix consists of the entries for which the index of the row is equal to the index of the column, that is, $i = j$. Thus, the main diagonal contains the entries in the x_{ii} cells, for $i = 1, 2, \ldots, g$. In a sociomatrix, the entries on the main diagonal are the self-"choices" of actors in the network, or the loops in the graph. If these are undefined, as they are when we exclude loops from a graph or do not measure self-choices of actors in the network, then the entries on the main diagonal of a sociomatrix are undefined. In this instance, we will put a "−" in the (i,i)th diagonal entry of a sociomatrix.

An important property of a square matrix is whether it is *symmetric*. A matrix is symmetric if $x_{ij} = x_{ji}$, for all cells. If this is not true, then the matrix is not symmetric, that is, if there are some cells where $x_{ij} \neq x_{ji}$. The sociomatrix for a graph (representing a nondirectional relation) is symmetric, since the line (n_i, n_j) is identical to the line (n_j, n_i), and thus $x_{ij} = x_{ji}$ for all i and j. However, the sociomatrix for a digraph (representing a directional relation) is not necessarily symmetric, since the arc $< n_i, n_j >$ is not the same as the arc $< n_i, n_j >$, and thus the entry in cell x_{ij} is not necessarily the same as the entry in cell x_{ji}.

We now turn to some important matrix operations, including matrix permutation, the transpose of a matrix, matrix addition and subtraction, matrix multiplication, and Boolean matrix multiplication.

Matrix Permutation. In a graph the assignment of numbers to the nodes is arbitrary. The only information in the graph is which pairs of nodes are adjacent. Similarly, in a sociomatrix, the order of the rows and columns indexing the actors in the network or the nodes in the graph is arbitrary, so long as the rows and columns are indexed in the same order. Any rearrangement of rows, and simultaneously of columns, of the sociomatrix does not change the information about adjacency of nodes, or ties between actors. Sometimes it is useful to rearrange the rows and columns in the sociomatrix to highlight patterns in the network. For example, if the relation represented in a sociomatrix is advice-seeking among managers in several departments in a corporation, then it might be useful to place managers in the same department next to each other in the rows and columns of the sociomatrix in order to study advice-seeking within departments.

A *permutation* of a set of objects is any reordering of the objects. If a set contains g objects, then there are $g! = g \times (g-1) \times (g-2) \times \cdots \times 1$ possible permutations of these objects. For example, there are $3 \times 2 \times 1 = 6$ permutations of the integers $\{1, 2, 3\}$. Thus, there are six ways to rearrange the rows and columns of a sociomatrix for three actors, simply by relabeling (simultaneously) the rows and columns.

Matrix permutations can be used in the study of cohesive subgroups (Chapter 7), and are especially important in constructing blockmodels (Chapter 10), and in evaluating the goodness-of-fit of blockmodels (Chapter 16). Matrix permutations are also useful if the graph is bipar-

Table 4.5. *Example of matrix permutation*

X

	n_1	n_2	n_3	n_4	n_5
n_1	-	0	1	0	1
n_2	0	-	0	1	0
n_3	1	0	-	0	1
n_4	0	1	0	-	0
n_5	1	0	1	0	-

X permuted

	n_5	n_1	n_3	n_2	n_4
n_5	-	1	1	0	0
n_1	1	-	1	0	0
n_3	1	1	-	0	0
n_2	0	0	0	-	1
n_4	0	0	0	1	-

tite. Recall that the nodes in a bipartite graph can be partitioned so that all lines are between nodes in different subsets. Thus, it is helpful to permute the rows and columns of the sociomatrix so that nodes in the same subset are in rows (and columns) that are next to each other in the sociomatrix.

Sometimes the patterns of ties between actors is not clear until we permute both the rows and the columns of the matrix. For example in Table 4.5, an arbitrary labeling of nodes might have ordered the rows (and columns) n_1, n_2, n_3, n_4, n_5, as in the sociomatrix at the top of the table. However, the permutation at the bottom of the table has the nodes in the order: 5, 1, 3, 2, 4, there are now 1's in the upper left and lower right corners of the sociomatrix. With this new order of rows and columns, it is clear that ties are present among the nodes represented by rows and columns 5, 1, and 3 and among nodes represented by rows and columns 2 and 4, but there are no ties between these two subsets. This pattern of two separate subsets was difficult, if not impossible, to see in the original sociomatrix.

Transpose. The *transpose* of a matrix is constructed by interchanging the rows and columns of the original matrix. For matrix $\mathbf{X}$ we denote its transpose as $\mathbf{X}'$ with entries $\{x'_{ij}\}$. For matrix $\mathbf{X}$, the elements of its transpose $\mathbf{X}'$ are $x'_{ij} = x_{ji}$.

If a matrix, $\mathbf{X}$, is symmetric, then $\mathbf{X}$ and its transpose, $\mathbf{X}'$, are identical; $\mathbf{X} = \mathbf{X}'$. Thus, the matrix for a graph (representing a nondirectional

Table 4.6. *Transpose of a sociomatrix for a directed relation: friendship at the beginning of the year for six children*

X'

	n_1	n_2	n_3	n_4	n_5	n_6
n_1	-	0	0	0	0	0
n_2	1	-	1	0	0	1
n_3	0	1	-	0	0	0
n_4	0	0	0	-	0	0
n_5	1	0	0	1	-	0
n_6	0	1	0	0	1	-

relation) is always identical to its transpose, since $x_{ij} = x_{ji}$ for all i and j. However, the matrix for a digraph (representing a directional relation) is not necessarily identical to its transpose, since the sociomatrix for a directional relation is not, in general, symmetric.

The transpose of a sociomatrix is substantively interesting since it is analogous to reversing the direction of the ties between pairs of actors. In a sociomatrix, an entry of 1 in cell (i, j) indicates that there is a tie from row actor i to column actor j. In the transpose of the sociomatrix, a 1 in cell (i, j) indicates that row actor i *received* a tie from column actor j. For a directional relation represented as a directed graph, the transpose of the sociomatrix represents the converse of the directed graph; $x'_{ij} = 1$ if $x_{ji} = 1$.

Table 4.6 gives the transpose of the sociomatrix in Table 4.4.

Addition and Subtraction. The addition of two matrices of the same size (the same number of rows and columns) is defined as the sum of the elements in the corresponding cells of the matrices. For matrices **X** and **Y**, both of size g by h, we define $\mathbf{Z} = \mathbf{X} + \mathbf{Y}$, where $z_{ij} = x_{ij} + y_{ij}$.

Similarly we can define matrix subtraction as the difference between the elements in the corresponding cells of the matrices. For matrices **X** and **Y**, both of size g by h, we define $\mathbf{Z} = \mathbf{X} - \mathbf{Y}$, where $z_{ij} = x_{ij} - y_{ij}$.

Matrix Multiplication. Matrix multiplication is a very important operation in social network analysis. It can be used to study walks and reachability in a graph, and is the basis for compounding relations in the analysis of relational algebras (see Chapter 11).

Consider two matrices: **Y** of size $g \times h$, and **W** of size $h \times k$. The number of columns in **Y** must equal the number of rows in **W**. We define

$$\mathbf{YW} = \mathbf{Z}$$

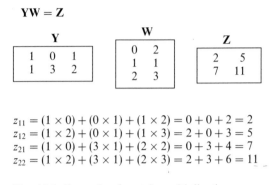

$$z_{11} = (1 \times 0) + (0 \times 1) + (1 \times 2) = 0 + 0 + 2 = 2$$
$$z_{12} = (1 \times 2) + (0 \times 1) + (1 \times 3) = 2 + 0 + 3 = 5$$
$$z_{21} = (1 \times 0) + (3 \times 1) + (2 \times 2) = 0 + 3 + 4 = 7$$
$$z_{22} = (1 \times 2) + (3 \times 1) + (2 \times 3) = 2 + 3 + 6 = 11$$

Fig. 4.26. Example of matrix multiplication

the product of two matrices as $\mathbf{Z} = \mathbf{YW}$ where the elements of $\mathbf{Z} = \{z_{ij}\}$ are equal to:

$$z_{ij} = \sum_{l=1}^{h} y_{il} w_{lj}. \tag{4.11}$$

The matrix product $\mathbf{Z}$ has g rows and k columns. The value in cell (i, j) of $\mathbf{Z}$ is equal to the sum of the products of corresponding elements in the ith row of $\mathbf{Y}$ and the jth column of $\mathbf{W}$.

Figure 4.26 gives an example of matrix multiplication. The first matrix in the product, $\mathbf{Y}$, is of size 2×3, and the second matrix, $\mathbf{W}$, is of size 3×2. Hence, the product, $\mathbf{Z}$, is of size 2×2.

Powers of a Matrix. Now, consider the sociomatrix $\mathbf{X}$ of size g by g. We denote the product of a matrix times itself, $\mathbf{XX}$ as $\mathbf{X}^2$, with entries $x_{ij}^{[2]}$. Since there are g rows and g columns in $\mathbf{X}$ there are also g rows and g columns in $\mathbf{X}^2$.

Multiplying $\mathbf{X}^2$ by the original sociomatrix, $\mathbf{X}$, yields the matrix $\mathbf{X}^3 = \mathbf{XXX}$. In general, we define $\mathbf{X}^p$ ($\mathbf{X}$ to the pth power) as the matrix product of $\mathbf{X}$ times itself, p times.

Table 4.7 shows a matrix and some of its powers.

Boolean Matrix Multiplication. The result of multiplying two matrices, say $\mathbf{X}$ and $\mathbf{Y}$, is a new matrix, $\mathbf{Z}$, with entries whose values are defined by equation (4.11). In many social network applications it is sufficient to consider only whether these entries are non-zero. Such arithmetic is usually referred to as *Boolean*. Boolean matrix multiplication yields the Boolean product of two matrices, which we denote by $\mathbf{Z}^{\otimes} =$

$\mathbf{X} \otimes \mathbf{Y}$. The entries of a Boolean product are either 0 or 1, and are defined as:

$$z_{ij}^{\otimes} = \begin{cases} 1 & \text{if } \sum_{l=1}^{h} y_{il}w_{lj} > 0 \\ 0 & \text{if } \sum_{l=1}^{h} y_{il}w_{lj} = 0. \end{cases}$$

Thus Boolean matrix multiplication results in values that are equal to 1 if regular matrix multiplication results in a non-zero entry, and equal to 0 otherwise. Boolean multiplication is the basis for constructing relational algebras (Chapter 11), and can be used to study walks and reachability in graphs.

4.9.7 Computing Simple Network Properties

Now, let us see how these matrix operations can be used to study some graph theoretic concepts. We will first describe how to use matrix multiplication to study walks and reachability in a graph and then show how properties of matrices can be used to quantify nodal degree and graph density.

Walks and Reachability. Matrix operations can be used to study walks and reachability in both graphs and directed graphs.

Graphs. first, let us consider the sociomatrix for a graph (representing a nondirectional relation). As defined in equation (4.11), the value $x_{ij}^{[2]} = \sum_{k=1}^{g} x_{ik}x_{kj}$. The product $x_{ik}x_{kj}$, one term in this sum, is equal to 1 only if both $x_{ik} = 1$ and $x_{kj} = 1$. In terms of the graph, $x_{ik}x_{kj} = 1$ only if both lines (n_i, n_k) and (n_k, n_j) are present in $\mathcal{L}$. If this is true, then the walk $n_i n_k n_j$ is present in the graph. Thus, the sum $\sum_{k=1}^{g} x_{ik}x_{kj}$ counts the number of walks of length 2 between nodes n_i and n_j, for all k. The entries of $\mathbf{X}^2 = \{x_{ij}^{[2]}\}$ give exactly the number of walks of length 2 between n_i and n_j.

Similarly, we can consider walks of any length by studying powers of the matrix $\mathbf{X}$. For example, elements of $\mathbf{X}^3$ count the number of walks of length 3 between each pair of nodes. Such multiplications can be used to find walks of longer lengths. In general, the entries of the matrix $\mathbf{X}^p$ (the matrix $\mathbf{X}$ raised to the pth power) give the total number of walks of length p from node n_i to node n_j.

Recall that two nodes are reachable if there is a path (and thus, a walk) between them. Since every path is a walk, we can study reachability of pairs of nodes by considering the powers of the matrix $\mathbf{X}$ that count walks of a given length. Also, recall that the longest possible path in a graph is equal to $g - 1$ (any path longer than $g - 1$ must include some node(s) more than once, and so is not a path). Thus, if two nodes are reachable, then there is at least one path (and thus at least one walk) of length $g - 1$ or less between them.

Consider now whether there is a walk of length k or less between two nodes, n_i and n_j. If there is a walk of length k or less, then, for some value of $p \leq k$, the element $x_{ij}^{[p]}$ will be greater than or equal to 1. One way to determine whether two nodes are reachable is to examine all matrices, $\{X^p, 1 \leq p \leq g - 1\}$. If two nodes are reachable, then there is a non-zero entry in one or more of the matrices of this set. When these product matrices are summed, for $p = 1, 2, \ldots, (g - 1)$, we obtain a matrix,

$$X^{[\Sigma]} = X + X^2 + X^3 + \ldots + X^{g-1}$$

whose entries give the total number of walks from n_i to n_j, of any length less than or equal to $g - 1$. Since any two nodes that are reachable are connected by a path (and thus a walk) of length $g - 1$ or less, non-zero entries in the matrix $X^{[\Sigma]}$ indicate pairs of nodes that are reachable. A 0 in cell (i, j) of $X^{[\Sigma]}$ means that there is no walk between nodes n_i and n_j, and thus these two nodes are not reachable.

It is useful to define a *reachability* matrix, $X^{[R]} = \{x_{ij}^{[R]}\}$, that simply codes for each pair of nodes whether they are reachable, or not. The entry in cell (i, j) of $X^{[R]}$ is equal to 1 if nodes n_i and n_j are reachable, and equal to 0 otherwise. We can calculate these values by looking at the elements of $X^{[\Sigma]}$, and noting which ones are non-zero. Non-zero elements of $X^{[\Sigma]}$ indicate reachability; hence, we define

$$x_{ij}^{[R]} = \begin{cases} 1 & \text{if } x_{ij}^{[\Sigma]} \geq 1 \\ 0 & \text{otherwise.} \end{cases} \tag{4.12}$$

The elements of $X^{[R]}$ indicate whether nodes n_i and n_j are reachable or not.

Directed Graphs. Now, consider matrix products of sociomatrices for directed graphs. These products will allow us to study directed walks and reachability for directed graphs.

First, look at the entries in X^2. If X is a sociomatrix for a directed graph, then $x_{ij} = 1$ means that the arc $< n_i, n_j >$ is in $\mathscr{L}$. As usual, the value of the product $x_{ik}x_{kj}$ is equal to 1 if both $x_{ik} = 1$ and $x_{kj} = 1$. In the directed graph, $x_{ik}x_{kj} = 1$ only if both arcs $< n_i, n_k >$ and $< n_k, n_j >$

are present in $\mathscr{L}$. If this is true, then the directed walk $n_i \to n_k \to n_j$ is present in the graph. The sum $\sum_{k=1}^{g} x_{ik}x_{kj}$ thus counts the number of directed walks of length 2 beginning at node n_i and ending at node n_j, for all k. Thus, the entries of $\mathbf{X}^2 = \{x_{ij}^{[2]}\}$ give exactly the number of directed walks of length 2 from n_i to n_j.

Similarly, we can consider directed walks of any length by studying powers of the matrix $\mathbf{X}$. In general, the entries of the matrix $\mathbf{X}^p$ (the pth power of the sociomatrix for a directed graph) give the total number of directed walks of length p beginning at row node n_i and ending at column node n_j.

As with the powers of the sociomatrix for a graph, when the product matrices, $\mathbf{X}^p$, are summed, for $p = 1, 2, \ldots, (g-1)$, we obtain a matrix, denoted by $\mathbf{X}^{[\Sigma]}$, whose entries give the total number of directed walks from row node n_i to column node n_j, of any length less than or equal to $g - 1$.

We can also define the reachability matrix for a directed graph, $\mathbf{X}^{[R]} = \{x_{ij}^{[R]}\}$, that codes for each pair of nodes whether they are reachable, or not. The entry in cell (i, j) of $\mathbf{X}^{[R]}$ is equal to 1 if there is a directed path from row node n_i to column node n_j, and equal to 0 otherwise. If $x_{ij}^{[R]} = 1$ then node n_j is reachable from node n_i. Since directed paths consist of arcs all "pointing" in the same direction, there may be a directed path from node n_i to node n_j (thus $x_{ij}^{[R]} = 1$), without there necessarily being a directed path from node n_j to node n_i (thus $x_{ji}^{[R]}$ could $= 0$). Thus, the reachability matrix for a directed graph is not, in general, symmetric.

Geodesics and Distance. The (geodesic) distance from n_i to n_j can be found by inspecting the power matrices. The distance from one node to another is the length of a shortest path between them. In a graph, this distance is the same from n_i to n_j as it is from n_j to n_i. In a digraph, these distances can be different.

These distances are sometimes arrayed in a *distance matrix*, with elements $d(i, j)$. To find these distances using matrices, focus on the (i, j) elements of the power matrices, starting with $p = 1$. When $p = 1$, the power matrix is the sociomatrix, so that if $x_{ij} = 1$, the nodes are adjacent, and the distance between the nodes equals 1. If $x_{ij} = 0$ and $x_{ij}^{[2]} > 0$, then there is a shortest path of length 2. And so forth. Consequently, the first power p for which the (i, j) element is non-zero gives the length of the shortest path and is equal to $d(i, j)$. Mathematically, $d(i, j) = \min_p x_{ij}^{[p]} > 0$.

Table 4.7. *Powers of a sociomatrix for a directed graph*

X

	n_1	n_2	n_3	n_4	n_5	n_6
n_1	-	1	0	0	1	0
n_2	0	-	1	0	0	1
n_3	0	1	-	0	0	0
n_4	0	0	0	-	1	0
n_5	0	0	0	0	-	1
n_6	0	1	0	0	0	-

X^2

	n_1	n_2	n_3	n_4	n_5	n_6
n_1	0	0	1	0	0	2
n_2	0	2	0	0	0	0
n_3	0	0	1	0	0	1
n_4	0	0	0	0	0	1
n_5	0	1	0	0	0	0
n_6	0	0	1	0	0	1

X^3

	n_1	n_2	n_3	n_4	n_5	n_6
n_1	0	3	0	0	0	0
n_2	0	0	2	0	0	2
n_3	0	2	0	0	0	0
n_4	0	1	0	0	0	0
n_5	0	0	1	0	0	1
n_6	0	2	0	0	0	0

X^4

	n_1	n_2	n_3	n_4	n_5	n_6
n_1	0	0	3	0	0	3
n_2	0	4	0	0	0	0
n_3	0	0	2	0	0	2
n_4	0	0	1	0	0	1
n_5	0	2	0	0	0	0
n_6	0	0	2	0	0	2

X^5

	n_1	n_2	n_3	n_4	n_5	n_6
n_1	0	6	0	0	0	0
n_2	0	0	4	0	0	4
n_3	0	4	0	0	0	0
n_4	0	2	0	0	0	0
n_5	0	0	2	0	0	2
n_6	0	4	0	0	0	0

The diameter of a graph or digraph is the length of the largest geodesic in the graph or digraph. If the graph is connected or if the digraph is at least strongly connected, the diameter of the graph is then the largest entry in the distance matrix; otherwise, the diameter is infinite or undefined.

Computing Nodal Degrees. In this section we describe how to calculate nodal degree from the matrices associated with graphs and directed graphs. We first describe calculations of nodal degree for a graph, and then nodal indegree and outdegree for a directed graph.

Graphs. Recall that the degree of a node, $d(n_i)$, is equal to the number of lines incident with the node in the graph. Nodal degrees may be found by summing appropriate elements in either the sociomatrix or in the incidence matrix. In the incidence matrix $\mathbf{I}$, with elements $\{I_{ij}\}$, the degrees of the nodes are equal to the row sums, since the rows correspond to nodes and the entries are 1 for every line incident with the row node. Specifically,

$$d(n_i) = \sum_{j=1}^{L} I_{ij}.$$

Each row contains as many 1's as there are lines incident with the node in that row. Thus, summing over columns (that is, lines) gives the number of lines incident with the node.

In the sociomatrix $\mathbf{X}$ for a graph (representing a nondirectional relation) the nodal degrees are equal to either the row sums or the column sums. The ith row or column total gives the degree of node n_i:

$$d(n_i) = \sum_{j=1}^{g} x_{ij} = \sum_{i=1}^{g} x_{ij} = x_{i+} = x_{+j}. \tag{4.13}$$

Directed Graphs. Now consider the indegrees and outdegrees of nodes in a directed graph. Recall that the indegree of a node is the number of nodes incident *to* the node (the number of arcs terminating at it) and the outdegree of a node is the number of arcs incident *from* the node (the number of arcs originating from it). Notice that row i of a sociomatrix contains entries $x_{ij} = 1$ if node n_j is incident from node i. The number of 1's in row i is thus the number of nodes incident *from* node n_i, and is equal to the *outdegree* of node n_i. Similarly, the entries in column i of a sociomatrix contain entries $x_{ji} = 1$ if node n_j is incident *to* node n_i. Thus, the number of 1's in column i is equal to the *indegree* of node n_i. The row totals of **X** are equal to the nodal outdegrees, and the column totals of **X** are equal to the nodal indegrees. Formally,

$$d_O(n_i) = \sum_{j=1}^{g} x_{ij} = x_{i+},$$ (4.14)

and

$$d_I(n_i) = \sum_{j=1}^{g} x_{ji} = x_{+i}.$$ (4.15)

Computing Density. The density of a graph, digraph, or valued (di)graph can be calculated as the sum of all entries in the matrix, divided by the possible number of entries:

$$\Delta = \frac{\sum_{i=1}^{g} \sum_{j=1}^{g} x_{ij}}{g(g-1)}.$$ (4.16)

4.9.8 Summary

We have showed how many of the graph theoretic properties for nodes, pairs of nodes, and the graph as a whole can be calculated using matrix representations. These representations are quite useful, as Katz (1947) first realized.

4.10 Properties of Graphs, Relations, and Matrices

In this chapter we have noted three important properties of social networks: reflexivity, symmetry, and transitivity. In this section, we show how they can be studied by examining matrices, relations, and graphs.

4.10.1 Reflexivity

In our discussion of graphs we have focused on simple graphs, which, by definition, exclude loops. Thus, a simple graph is irreflexive, since no $< n_i, n_i >$ are present. On occasion, however, one may wish to allow loops. In that case, if all loops are present, the graph represents a reflexive relation. In a sociomatrix loops are coded by the entries along the main diagonal of the matrix, x_{ii} for all i. A relation is reflexive if, in the sociomatrix, $x_{ii} = 1$ for all i. An irreflexive relation has entries on the main diagonal of the sociomatrix that are undefined. Finally, a relation that is not reflexive (also not irreflexive) has some, but not all, values of $x_{ii} = 1$. In terms of a directed graph, some, but not all, $< n_i, n_i >$ arcs are present.

4.10.2 Symmetry

A relation is symmetric if, whenever i "chooses" j, then j also "chooses" i; thus, iRj if and only if jRi. A nondirectional relation (represented by a graph) is always symmetric. In a directed graph symmetry implies that whenever the arc $l_k =< n_i, n_j >$ is in the set of lines $\mathscr{L}$, the arc $l_m =< n_j, n_i >$ is also in $\mathscr{L}$. In other words, dyads are either null or mutual. The sociomatrix for a symmetric relation is symmetric; $x_{ij} = x_{ji}$ for all distinct i and j. If the matrix $\mathbf{X}$ is symmetric, then it is identical to its transpose, $\mathbf{X}'$; $x_{ij} = x'_{ij}$ for all i and j.

4.10.3 Transitivity

Transitivity is a property that considers patterns of triples of actors in a network or triples of nodes in a graph. A relation is transitive if every time that iRj and jRk, then iRk. If the relation is "is a friend of," then the relation is transitive if whenever i "chooses" j as a friend and j "chooses" k as a friend, then i "chooses" k as a friend.

Transitivity can be studied by considering powers of a sociomatrix. Recall that $\mathbf{X}^{[2]} = \mathbf{XX}$ codes the number of walks of length 2 between each pair of nodes in a graph; thus, an entry $x_{ij}^{[2]} \geq 1$ if there is a walk $n_i \rightarrow n_k \rightarrow n_j$ for at least one node n_k. Thus, in order for the relation to be transitive, whenever $x_{ij}^{[2]} \geq 1$, then x_{ij} must equal 1.

One can check for transitivity of a relation by comparing the square of a sociomatrix with the sociomatrix. Thus, a transitive relation is noteworthy in that ties present in $\mathbf{X}^2$ are a subset of the ties present in $\mathbf{X}$.

4.11 Summary

Graph theory is a useful way to represent network data. Actors in a network are represented as nodes of a graph. Nondirectional ties between actors are represented as lines between the nodes of a graph. Directed ties between actors are represented as arcs between the nodes in a digraph. The valences of ties are represented by a "+" or "−" sign in a signed graph or digraph. The strength associated with each line or arc in a valued graph or digraph is assigned a value. Many of the concepts of graph theory have been used as the foundation of many theoretical concepts in social network analysis.

There are many, many references on graph theory. We recommend the following texts. Harary (1969) and Bondy and Murty (1976) are excellent mathematical introductions to graph theory, with coverage ranging from proofs of many of the statements we have made, to solutions to a variety of applied problems. The excellent text by Frank (1971) is more mathematically advanced and focuses on social networks. Similarly, the classic text by Harary, Norman, and Cartwright (1965) is also focused on directed graphs, and is quite accessible to beginners. Roberts (1976, 1978) and Hage and Harary (1983) provide very readable, elementary introductions to graph theory, with many concepts illustrated on anthropological network data. In their introduction to network analysis, Knoke and Kuklinski (1982) also describe some elementary ideas in graph theory. Ford and Fulkerson (1962), Lawler (1976), Tutte (1971), and others give mathematical treatments of special, advanced topics in graph theory, such as theories of matroids and optimization of network configurations. The topic of tournaments is treated in the context of paired comparisons by David (1988). A more mathematical discussion of tournaments can be found in Moon (1968). Berge (1989) discusses hypergraphs in detail.

Part III

Structural and Locational Properties

5

Centrality and Prestige

One of the primary uses of graph theory in social network analysis is the identification of the "most important" actors in a social network. In this chapter, we present and discuss a variety of measures designed to highlight the differences between important and non-important actors. Definitions of *importance*, or synonymously, *prominence*, have been offered by many writers. All such measures attempt to describe and measure properties of "actor location" in a social network. Actors who are the most important or the most prominent are usually located in strategic locations within the network. As far back as Moreno (1934), researchers have attempted to quantify the notions of sociometric "stars" and "isolates."

We will discuss the most noteworthy and substantively interesting definitions of importance or prominence along with the mathematical concepts that the various definitions have spawned. Among the definitions that we will discuss in this chapter are those based on *degree*, *closeness*, *betweenness*, *information*, and simply the *differential status* or *rank* of the actors. These definitions yield actor indices which attempt to quantify the prominence of an individual actor embedded in a network. The actor indices can also be aggregated across actors to obtain a single, group-level index which summarizes how variable or differentiated the set of actors is as a whole with respect to a given measure. We will show how to calculate both actor and group indices in this chapter.

Throughout this chapter, we will distinguish between relations that are directional (yielding directed graphs) and those that are not (yielding undirected graphs). The majority of the *centrality* concepts discussed in this chapter are designed for graphs (and thus, symmetric sociomatrices), and most of these, just for dichotomous relations. The notion of *prestige*, however, can only be quantified by using relations for which we can distinguish "choices" sent from choices received by the actors, and therefore, can only be studied with directed graphs. With directional relations, measures such as outdegree and indegree are quite likely to be different, and (as we will see in this chapter) prestigious actors are usually those with large indegrees, or "choices" received. Both centrality and prestige indices are examples of measures of the prominence or importance of the actors in a social network. We will consider definitions of prestige other than the indegree of an actor, and show that prestigious actors not only are chosen or nominated by many actors, but the actors who are doing the choosing must also be prestigious. So, the chapter will be split into two main parts: the first, presenting centrality measures for nondirectional relations, and the second, discussing both centrality and prestige measures for directional relations.

The substantive nature of the relation under study clearly determines which types of measures are appropriate for the network. Directional relations give two types of actor and group measures, based on both centrality and prestige, while nondirectional relations give just one type, based on centrality alone. We describe four well-known varieties of centrality in this chapter, illustrating and defining them first for nondirectional relations. We will then discuss directional relations, and not only show how these four centrality measures can be extended to such relations, but also define three measures of prestige, based on degree, proximity, and status or rank. This latter measure of status or rank has been shown to be quite useful in practice.

All these measures are first defined at the level of the individual actor. The measures can then be aggregated over all actors to obtain a group-level measure of either centralization or group prestige. Such aggregate measures are thus defined at the level of the entire set of actors. They attempt to measure how "centralized" or "prestigious" the set of actors is as a whole. We will present several methods for taking the individual actor indices, and combining them to arrive at a single, group-level index. These methods are as simple as variances, and as complicated as ratios of the average difference of the actor index from its maximum possible value to the maximum of this average difference. The group-level indices are usually between 0 and 1, and thus are not difficult to interpret.

Throughout the chapter, we will apply the actor and group measures to a variety of data, both real and artificial. Three artificial graphs that very nicely highlight the differences among the measures we describe are shown in Figure 5.1. These graphs, all with $g = 7$, will be labeled the star graph (Figure 5.1a), the circle (Figure 5.1b), and the line graph (Figure 5.1c; see

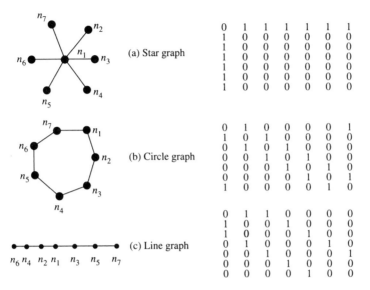

Fig. 5.1. Three illustrative networks for the study of centrality and prestige

Freeman 1980a). We will refer to these graphs or networks frequently, since the centrality of the actors in these graphs varies greatly, as does the centralization of the graphs. Just a quick glance at these figures shows that the nodes in the graphs are quite different. For example, all nodes in the circle are interchangeable, and hence should be equally central. One node in the star completely outranks the others, while the other six themselves are interchangeable. In the line graph, the nodes' centrality clearly decreases from that for n_1, to n_2 and n_3, and so on, to n_6 and n_7, who are peripheral in this graph.

Many graph theoretic centrality concepts are discussed in Hage and Harary (1983) and in the other general references given in Chapter 4. Based on our understanding of the major concepts of graph theory, as presented in Chapter 4, it should be clear that we can define (maybe even invent) many graph theoretic centrality notions, such as the "center" and "centroid" of a graph, with the goal of quantifying importance or prominence. But the major question still remains unanswered: Are the nodes in the graph center and/or in the graph centroid and/or with maximal degree the most "central" nodes in a substantive sense — that is, does the center, or centroid, of a graph contain the most important actors? In part, this is a question about the validity of the measures of centrality — do they really capture what we substantively mean be "importance" or "prominence"? Can we simply focus on the actors who are "chosen" the most to find the most important actors? Of course, unless we define what we mean by the terms "important" and "prominent," these questions are not answerable.

Thus, we first will define prominence or importance, and discuss how the terms "central" and "prestigious" quantify two important aspects of prominence. We will then answer questions about which actors are the most important, and will find that the best centrality notions are first based primarily on substantive theory, and then use graph theory to be quantified.

5.1 Prominence: Centrality and Prestige

We begin by assuming that one has measurements on a single, di-chotomous relation, although some of the measures discussed here are generalizable to other types of network data. We will not be concerned here with a signed or multirelational situation, even though such situations are very interesting (both methodologically and substantively). These types of relations have not been studied using the ideas discussed in this chapter.

We will consider an actor to be *prominent* if the ties of the actor make the actor particularly visible to the other actors in the network. This equating of prominence to visibility was made by Knoke and Burt (1983). Hubbell (1965) and Friedkin (1991) note that prominence should be measured by looking not only at direct or adjacent ties, but also at indirect paths involving intermediaries. This philosophy is maintained throughout. To determine which of the g actors in a group are prominent, one needs to examine not only all "choices" made by an actor and all "choices" received, but indirect ties as well.

If a relation is nondirectional, the ith row of the sociomatrix $\mathbf{X}$, $(X_{i1}, X_{i2}, \ldots, X_{ig})$, is identical to the ith column $(X_{1i}, X_{2i}, \ldots, X_{gi})$. Thus, actor i's prominence within a network is based on the pattern of these $g - 1$ possible ties or entries in the sociomatrix, defining the location of actor i. If the relation is directional, the ith row of the sociomatrix differs from the ith column, so that actor i's prominence is based on the $2(g - 1)$ entries in the sociomatrix involving i. Some of the specific definitions of prominence will also consider choices made through intermediaries, or third parties, but such choices will almost always be of secondary concern.

This definition of prominence is still rather vague. Are prominent actors the objects of many "choices" from followers, while non-prominent actors (or followers) are not? What properties of these "choices" make an actor more visible than the other actors or the "object of" many ties? And what shall we do about indirect choices? This definition is also relative to the nature of the "choices" made by the other actors. Prominence is difficult to quantify, since many actor indices that are functions of just the ith row and column of the sociomatrix would qualify as measures of prominence.

To allow researchers to define better the important actors as those with more visibility and to understand better the meaning of the concept, Knoke and Burt distinguish two types of visibility, or to us, two classes of prominence — centrality and prestige. Both these types are based on the relational pattern of the row and column entries of the sociomatrix associated with each actor. This dichotomy is very useful and a very important contribution to the extensive literature on prominence. Let us now define both these versions of prominence, after which we will show how they can be quantified first for nondirectional relations, and then for directional ones.

5.1.1 Actor Centrality

Prominent actors are those that are extensively involved in relationships with other actors. This involvement makes them more visible to the others. We are not particularly concerned with whether this prominence is due to the receiving (being the recipient) or the transmission (being the source) of many ties — what is important here is that the actor is simply *involved*. This focus on involvement leads us to consider first nondirectional relations, where there is no distinction between receiving and sending. Thus, for a nondirectional relation, we define a *central* actor as one involved in many ties. However, even though centrality seems most appropriate for nondirectional relations, we will, later in this chapter, show how such indices can also be calculated for directional relations.

This definition of centrality was first developed by Bavelas (1948, 1950). The idea was applied in the late 1940's and early 1950's in laboratory experiments on communication networks (rather than from observed, naturally occurring networks) directed by Bavelas and conducted by

Leavitt (1949, 1951), Smith (1950), and Bavelas and Barrett (1951). As Freeman (1979) reports, these first experiments led to many more experiments in the 1950's and 1960's (see Burgess 1968, Rogers and Agarwala-Rogers 1976, and the citations in Freeman 1979, for reviews). In recent research, Freeman (1977, 1979, 1980a) has advocated the use of centrality measures to understand group structure, by systematically defining the centrality notions we discuss below. At the same time, he introduced a new centrality measure based on betweenness (see below).

As Knoke and Burt (1983) point out, sociological and economic concepts such as access and control over resources, and brokerage of information, are well suited to measurement. These concepts naturally yield a definition of centrality since the difference between the source and the receiver is less important than just participating in many interactions. Assuming that one is studying a relevant relation (such as communication), those actors with the most access or most control or who are the most active brokers will be the most central in the network.

We will employ a simple notation for actor centrality measures, first used by Freeman (1977, 1979). We let C denote a particular centrality measure, which will be a function of a specific n_i. There will be a variety of measures introduced in this chapter, so we will subscript C with an index for the particular measure under study. If we let A be a generic measure, then one of the actor centralities defined below will be denoted by $C_A(n_i)$. We will use a variety of different values for A to distinguish among the different versions of centrality. As usual, the index i will range over the integers from 1 to g.

5.1.2 *Actor Prestige*

Suppose we can make a distinction between ties sent and ties received, as is true for directional relations. We define a *prestigious* actor as one who is the object of extensive ties, thus focusing solely on the actor as a recipient. Clearly, prestige is a more refined concept than centrality, and cannot always be measured. The prestige of an actor increases as the actor becomes the object of more ties but not necessarily when the actor itself initiates the ties. In other words, one must look at ties directed *to* an actor to study that actor's prestige. Since indegrees are only distinguishable from outdegrees for directional relations, we will not be able to quantify prestige of an actor unless the relation is directional, a point that we discuss in more detail below.

Quantification of prestige, and the separation of the concept from centrality, is somewhat analogous to the distinction frequently made between outdegrees and indegrees (which, as the reader will see, are simple measures of centrality and prestige, respectively). One must look at ties directed to an actor to study that actor's prestige. Since indegrees are only distinguishable from outdegrees for directional relations, we will not be able to quantify prestige unless the relation is directional.

We should note that the term "prestige" is perhaps not the best label for this concept (in some situations). For example, if the relation under study is one of negative affect, such as "despises" or "do not want as a friend," then actors who are prestigious on this relation are not held in very high regard by their peers. Such actors are certainly renowned, but it is for negative feelings, rather than positive. Further, if the relation is "advises," the actors considered prestigious by their peers might be those that are senders, rather than receivers. Nevertheless, the term has become established in the literature, and we will use it, keeping in mind that the substantive nature of the measured relation is quite important when interpreting the property.

Prestige has also been called *status* by authors such as Moreno (1934), Zeleny (1940a, 1940b, 1941, 1960), Proctor and Loomis (1951), Katz (1953), and Harary (1959c). We will introduce several status measures later in this chapter. But we will label these indices *rank* measures, since the term "status" has been used extensively in other network methodology (see Chapters 9 and 10). All these actor prestige measures attempt to quantify the rank that a particular actor has within a set of actors. Other synonyms include *deference*, and simply *popularity*. Recently, Bonacich (1972a, 1972b, 1987) has generalized Katz's (1953), Hubbell's (1965), and Taylor's (1969) ideas, and presented a new family of rank measures. All these rank (or status) indices are examples of prestige measures, and we will discuss them in detail later in the chapter.

We let P denote a particular prestige measure, which will be defined for a specific actor, n_i. There will be three measures introduced in this chapter, so we will subscript P with an index for the particular measure under study.

5.1.3 Group Centralization and Group Prestige

We should note that even though the focus of this chapter is on measures for actors that primarily allow us to quantify importance, one can take many of the measures and combine them across actors to get a group-level measure. These group-level measures allow us to compare different networks easily. When possible in this chapter, we will give formulas for group centralization or prestige measures, although most research on these measures is restricted to centralization.

We should first ask exactly what a group-level index of centralization is measuring. The general index that we introduce below has the property that the larger it is, the more likely it is that a single actor is quite central, with the remaining actors considerably less central. The less central actors might be viewed as residing in the periphery of a centralized system. Thus, this group-level quantity is an index of *centralization*, and measures how variable or heterogeneous the actor centralities are. It records the extent to which a single actor has high centrality, and the others, low centrality. It also can be viewed as a measure of how unequal the individual actor values are. It is (roughly) a measure of variability, dispersion, or spread. Early network researchers interested in centrality, particularly Leavitt (1951), Faucheux and Moscovici (1960), and Mackenzie (1966a), proposed that group-level indices of centralization should reflect such tendencies. Nieminen (1974) and Freeman (1977) also adopt this view, and discuss group centralization measurement.

One can view such a centralized network in Figure 5.1. The star graph is maximally central, since its one central actor has direct contact with all others, who are not in contact with each other. Examining the other two graphs in this figure should indicate that the degree of centralization can vary just by changing a few ties in the network.

Freeman (1979) adopts a convenient, general mathematical definition for a group-level index of centralization. Recall that $C_A(n_i)$ is an actor centrality index. Define $C_A(n^*)$ as the largest value of the particular index that occurs across the g actors in the network; that is, $C_A(n^*) = \max_i C_A(n_i)$.

From these quantities, $\sum_{i=1}^{g} [C_A(n^*) - C_A(n_i)]$ is the sum of the differences between this largest value and the other observed values, while $\max \sum_{i=1}^{g} [C_A(n^*) - C_A(n_i)]$ is the theoretical maximum possible sum of differences in actor centrality, where the differences are taken pairwise between actors. This latter maximum is taken over all possible graphs, with g actors. As we will see, this maximum occurs for the star graph.

The sum of differences becomes the numerator, while the theoretical maximum possible sum becomes the denominator in Freeman's index. The denominator is a theoretical quantity, and is not computed by looking at a specific graph; rather, it is calculated by considering all possible networks, with a fixed g, and then determining analytically how large the sum of differences can actually be. We have the general centralization index:

$$C_A = \frac{\sum_{i=1}^{g} [C_A(n^*) - C_A(n_i)]}{\max \sum_{i=1}^{g} [C_A(n^*) - C_A(n_i)]}. \tag{5.1}$$

The index will always be between 0 and 1. C_A equals 0 when all actors have exactly the same centrality index (that being $C_A(n^*)$), and equals 1 if one actor, "completely dominates or overshadows" the other actors.

Yet another view of graph centralization is offered by Høivik and Gleditsch (1975), who view centralization in a graph more simply than Freeman as the *dispersion* in a set of actor centrality indices. Later in this chapter, we show how such a view is related to Freeman's approach.

We note that one could also construct group-level prestigious measures, but the theoretical maximum values needed in the denominator are usually not calculable (except in special cases). Thus, we usually use something simpler (as we note later in this chapter) like a variance.

In addition to centralization measures, other researchers have proposed graph-level indices based on the *compactness* of a graph. Bavelas (1950), Flament (1963), Beauchamp (1965), and Sabidussi (1966) state that very centralized graphs are also compact, in the sense that the distances between pairs of nodes are small. These authors also proposed an index of actor centrality based on closeness (that is, small distances), as we will discuss later in this chapter.

We will illustrate the quantities defined in this chapter using two examples. First, we will continue to use Padgett's Florentine family network as an example of a network with a nondirectional relation. Second, we introduce the countries trade network as an example of a network of nations, with trade of basic manufactured goods as a directional relation.

5.2 Nondirectional Relations

Suppose that we have a single set of actors, and a single, dichotomous nondirectional relation measured on the pairs of actors. As usual, we let **X** refer to the matrix of social network data. For such data, the *i*th row of the sociomatrix is identical to the *i*th column. An example of such a matrix can be found in Appendix B, and discussed in Chapter 2. These data measure the alliances among families in 15th century Florence formed by interfamilial marriages. The corresponding sociogram is shown in Chapter 3, where it is discussed at length as an example of a graph with 16 nodes. In order to find the most important actors, we will look for measures reflecting which actors are at the "center" of the set of actors. We will introduce several definitions of this center, including actors with maximum degree, betweenness, closeness, and information.

5.2.1 Degree Centrality

The simplest definition of actor centrality is that central actors must be the most active in the sense that they have the most ties to other actors in the network or graph. Nowhere is this easier to see than by comparing a graph resembling a star to one resembling a circle, shown in Figure 5.1 for networks with $g=7$ actors. A star graph has the property that exactly one actor has ties to all $g-1$ other actors, and the remaining $g-1$ actors have only their single tie to the first actor. The first actor is clearly the most active, and one could view this high level of activity as a large amount of centrality. This very active actor should thus have a maximal centrality index. Here, we measure activity simply as degree. Contrast this star graph with the circle graph also shown in Figure 5.1. A circle has no actor more active than any other actor; indeed, all actors are interchangeable, so all actors should have exactly the same centrality index. Note also that this type of centrality focuses only on direct or adjacent choices. Prominence here is equated to "activity" or simply "degree."

Actor Degree Centrality. The degree of an actor is important; thus, a centrality measure for an individual actor should be the degree of the node, $d(n_i)$. Thus, following suggestions made by Proctor and Loomis (1951) and Shaw (1954), and then many other researchers (Glanzer and Glaser 1959; Faucheux and Moscovici 1960; Garrison 1960; Mackenzie 1964, 1966a; Pitts 1965; Nieminen 1973, 1974; Czepiel 1974; Rogers 1974; and Kajitani and Maruyama 1976; and reviewed by Freeman 1979), we define $C_D(n_i)$ as an actor-level degree centrality index. We let

$$C_D(n_i) = d(n_i) = x_{i+} = \sum_j x_{ij} = \sum_j x_{ji}. \tag{5.2}$$

We need not comment on the properties of this measure; it is discussed in detail in Chapter 4. We do note that one problem with this measure is that it depends on the group size g; indeed, its maximum value is $g-1$. Consequently, a proposed standardization of the measure

$$C'_D(n_i) = \frac{d(n_i)}{g-1} \tag{5.3}$$

is the proportion of nodes that are adjacent to n_i. $C'_D(n_i)$ is independent of g, and thus can be compared across networks of different sizes.

Donninger (1986) considers the distribution of equation (5.3), using the probabilistic graph models of Erdös and Renyi (1960). He gives an approximation to the distribution of degrees, which can then be used to place confidence intervals on both the actor- and group-level degree indices.

A related index, one for "ego density," is given by Burt (1982) and Knoke and Kuklinski (1982). An ego density for a nondirectional relation is simply the ratio of the degree of an actor to the maximum number of ties that could occur. Kapferer (1969, 1973) generalizes this, and defines another index, the "span" of an actor, as the percentage of ties in the network that involve the actor or the actors that the primary actor is adjacent to. Thus, the central actor in a star graph has a span of unity.

Refer to the three graphs of Figure 5.1. The degrees for the seven actors in the star graph are 6 (for n_1) and 1 (for $n_2 - n_7$). Thus, the denominator for the standardized actor-level indices $C'_D(n_i)$ is $g - 1 = 6$. The standardized indices have values $\{1.0, 0.167, \ldots, 0.167\}$ — clearly there is one maximally central actor, and six peripheral actors. The degrees for the circle graph are all $d(n_i) = 2$, so that the indices are all equal: $C'_D(n_i) = 0.333$, indicating a low-moderate level of centrality, constant across all actors. Lastly, contrast this network to the line graph, in which $n_1 - n_5$ all have $C'_D(n_i) = 0.333$ also, but the last two actors are less central: $C'_D(n_6) = C'_D(n_7) = 0.167$. The absence of the line between n_6 and n_7 (which is the difference between the circle graph and the line graph) has forced these two actors to be less central than the other five. These centralities and standardized centralities were calculated by hand, although the program *UCINET* calculates these quantities as standard output of its centrality subprogram.

An actor with a high centrality level, as measured by its degree, is "where the action is" in the network. Thus, this measure focuses on the most visible actors in the network (as required by Knoke and Burt's (1983) definition of prominence). An actor with a large degree is in direct contact or is adjacent to many other actors. This actor should then begin to be recognized by others as a major channel of relational information, indeed, a crucial cog in the network, occupying a central location. In contrast, and in accordance with this centrality definition, actors with low degrees are clearly peripheral in the network. Such actors are not active in the relational process. In fact, if the actor is completely isolated (so that $d(n_i) = 0$), then removing this actor from the network has no effect on the ties that are present.

Group Degree Centralization. We now present several degree-based measures of graph centralization. A centralization measure quantifies the range or variability of the individual actor indices. The set of degrees, which represents the collection of actor degree indices, can be summarized in a variety of ways. Freeman (1979) recommends use of the general index (5.1). Applying his general formula for graph centralization here we find

$$C_D = \frac{\sum_{i=1}^{g}[C_D(n^*) - C_D(n_i)]}{\max \sum_{i=1}^{g}[C_D(n^*) - C_D(n_i)]}. \tag{5.4}$$

The $\{C_D(n_i)\}$ in the numerator are the g actor degree indices, while $C_D(n^*)$ is the largest observed value. The denominator of this index can be calculated directly (see Freeman 1979), and equals $(g-1)(g-2)$. Thus,

$$C_D = \frac{\sum_{i=1}^{g}[C_D(n^*) - C_D(n_i)]}{[(g-1)(g-2)]} \tag{5.5}$$

can be used as an index to determine how centralized the degree of the set of actors is. The index is also a measure of the dispersion or range of the actor indices, since it compares each actor index to the maximum attained value.

This index reaches its maximum value of 1 when one actor chooses all other $g-1$ actors, and the other actors interact only with this one, central actor. This is exactly the situation in a star graph. The index attains its minimum value of 0 when all degrees are equal, indicating a *regular* graph (as defined in Chapter 4). This is exactly the situation realized in the circle graph. Graphs that are intermediate to these two (such as the line graph of Figure 5.1) have indices between 0 and 1, indicating varying amounts of centralization of degree. In fact, the line graph has a $C_D = 0.067$.

Another standard statistical summary of the actor degree indices is the variance of the degrees,

$$S_D^2 = \left[\sum_{i=1}^{g}(C_D(n_i) - \overline{C}_D)^2\right]/g, \tag{5.6}$$

where $\overline{C}_D$ is the mean actor degree index. The variance is recommended as a group-level index of centrality by Snijders (1981a, 1981b), reflecting the view of Høivik and Gleditsch (1975) that centralization is synonymous with the *dispersion* or heterogeneity of an actor index. This index attains its minimum value of 0 when all degrees are equal or when the graph is regular.

The maximum value of S_D^2 depends on g and the entire set of degrees. Snijders (1981a, 1981b) recommends that one normalize S_D^2 by the maximum possible variance given the set of degrees actually observed, to obtain a dimensionless index. The formulas for undirected graphs are complicated; we refer those interested to Snijders (1981a, 1981b). The formulas for directed graphs are easier to report, and we do so later in this chapter when we discuss directional relations. One can also test statistically whether a graph is more heterogeneous (with regard to its degree distribution) than expected by chance. Tests such as this one will be described in general in Chapter 13.

Coleman (1964) also recommends the use of S_D^2 as a measure of "hierarchization" (similar to centralization). In fact, Coleman goes on to suggest that one use a more general function of the degrees for this measure; in particular, he chooses the function $xlog(x)$, which yields an information- or entropy-based measure of hierarchization, not unlike those proposed by Mackenzie (1966b) or Stephenson and Zelen (1989) (see below).

There are simpler group-level degree indices. In fact, recognizing that the simplest actor-level index is the degree of the actor, one can take the average of the degrees to get the mean degree, $\overline{C}_D = \sum C_D(n_i)/g = \sum x_{i+}/g$. This quantity varies between 0 and $g - 1$, so to standardize it, one should divide by $g-1$. This average degree, divided by $g-1$, is exactly the density of the graph: $\sum C_D(n_i)/g(g - 1) = \sum C_D'(n_i)/g = \Delta$. Thus, mathematically, the density is also the average standardized degree. The densities of the three graphs in Figure 5.1 are 0.286 (star), 0.333 (circle), and 0.286 (line).

The density of a graph is perhaps the most widely used group-level index. It is a recommended measure of group cohesion (see Blau 1977), and its use can be traced back at least as far as Kephart (1950) and Proctor and Loomis (1951). Bott (1957) used densities to quantify network "knittedness," while Barnes (1969b) used them to determine how "close-knit" empirical networks were. It is very important in blockmodels and other role-algebraic techniques (see Part IV, particularly Chapter 10). Density takes on values between 0 (empty graph) and 1 (complete graph), and is the average of the standardized actor degree indices, $\{C_D'(n_i)\}$, as well as the fraction of possible ties present in the network for the relation under study. Friedkin (1981) studies the use of density as a summarization tool in network analysis, and concludes that densities can be misleading, especially if the values are small. This result is often due to the fact that as group sizes increase, network density decreases if actor degrees remain unchanged. Friedkin recommends that both density and group size be considered simultaneously, especially if the graph shows tendencies toward subgrouping (see Chapter 7).

The density of a graph is, thus, an overly simplified version of a group-level degree index, constructed by taking the actor degree indices and ignoring Freeman's two principles for group-level indices. It is also an average. As is quite common in data analysis, averages are sometimes difficult to interpret. One also needs information on how dispersed the numbers that make up the average are. So, one frequently computes the variance of these numbers, and reports it along with the average. We therefore recommend the simultaneous use of centralization measures such as S_D^2 and C_D along with average degree and graph density.

It is important to note, however, that indices such as average degree and density are not really centralization measures. As mentioned earlier, centralization should quantify the range or variability of the individual actor indices. Thus, S_D^2, and of course C_D are valid centralization measures, while the average degree or the graph density, which are quantifications of average actor tendencies rather than variability, are not.

Example. Turn now to Padgett's network of Florentine families and examine the marriage relation. The standardized actor degree centralities are shown in the first column of Table 5.1 (along with other actor-centrality and centralization indices which will be discussed later in this chapter). These centralities were calculated using *UCINET*.

One can see that the Medici family (n_9) is the most central family, with respect to degree. For this actor, $C_D'(n_9) = 0.400$, an index considerably larger than the next most central actors (Guadagni and Strozzi families), with $C_D'(n_7) = C_D'(n_{15}) = 0.267$. Six of the families have an index of 0.200; the remaining seven families have small indices. The group-level degree centralization index is $C_D = 0.267$, a rather small value, indicating that the difference between the largest and smallest actor-level indices is not very great. There is little variability. The average degree is $\overline{C}_D = 40/16 = 2.50$, quite small, but not surprising given the nature of the relation (marital ties, something not particularly common). We also note that the variance of the degrees (not the standardized actor

Table 5.1. *Centrality indices for Padgett's Florentine families (*Actor and centralization indices calculated by dropping* n_{12} = *Pucci from the actor set.*)

	With g = 16 actors		With g = 15 actors			
	$C'_D(n_i)$	$C'_B(n_i)$	$C'_D(n_i)^*$	$C'_C(n_i)^*$	$C'_B(n_i)^*$	$C'_I(n_i)^*$
Acciaiuoli	0.067	0.000	0.071	0.368	0.000	0.049
Albizzi	0.200	0.184	0.214	0.483	0.212	0.074
Barbadori	0.133	0.081	0.143	0.438	0.093	0.068
Bischeri	0.200	0.090	0.214	0.400	0.104	0.074
Castellani	0.200	0.048	0.214	0.389	0.055	0.070
Ginori	0.067	0.000	0.071	0.333	0.000	0.043
Guadagni	0.267	0.221	0.286	0.467	0.255	0.081
Lamberteschi	0.067	0.000	0.071	0.326	0.000	0.043
Medici	0.400	0.452	0.429	0.560	0.522	0.095
Pazzi	0.067	0.000	0.071	0.286	0.000	0.033
Peruzzi	0.200	0.019	0.214	0.368	0.022	0.069
Pucci	0.000	0.000	—	—	—	—
Ridolfi	0.200	0.098	0.214	0.500	0.114	0.080
Salvati	0.133	0.124	0.143	0.389	0.143	0.050
Strozzi	0.267	0.089	0.286	0.438	0.103	0.070
Tornabuoni	0.200	0.079	0.214	0.483	0.092	0.080
Centralization	0.267	0.383	0.257	0.322	0.437	—

degree centrality indices) S_D^2 = 2.125, and the density of this relation (which is the average standardized degree) is 0.167, indicating (as noted) a relatively sparse sociomatrix. The density of this relation is quite a bit less than that for the three hypothetical graphs in Figure 5.1, for instance.

5.2.2 Closeness Centrality

The second view of actor centrality is based on closeness or distance. The measure focuses on how *close* an actor is to all the other actors in the set of actors. The idea is that an actor is central if it can quickly interact with all others. In the context of a communication relation, such actors need not rely on other actors for the relaying of information, an idea put forth by Bavelas (1950) and Leavitt (1951). As noted by Beauchamp (1965), actors occupying central locations with respect to *closeness* can be very productive in communicating information to the other actors. If the actors in the set of actors are engaged in problem solving, and the focus is on communication links, efficient solutions occur when one actor has very short communication paths to the others. Thus, this *closeness* view of centrality relies heavily on economic considerations.

Hakimi (1965) and Sabidussi (1966) quantified this notion that central actors are close, by stating that central nodes in a network have "minimum steps" when relating to all other nodes; hence, the geodesics, or shortest paths, linking the central nodes to the other nodes must be as short as possible. With this explanation, researchers began equating closeness with *minimum distance*. The idea is that centrality is inversely related to distance. As a node grows farther apart in distance from other nodes, its centrality will decrease, since there will be more lines in the geodesics linking that node to the other nodes.

Examine the star network in Figure 5.1. The node at the center of this star is adjacent to all the other nodes, has the shortest possible paths to all the other actors, and hence has maximum closeness. There is exactly one actor who can reach all the other actors in a minimum number of steps. This actor need not rely on the other actors for its interactions, since it is tied to all others.

Actor Closeness Centrality. Actor centrality measures reflecting how close an actor is to the other actors in the network have been developed by Bavelas (1950), Harary (1959c), Beauchamp (1965), Sabidussi (1966), Moxley and Moxley (1974), and Rogers (1974). As reviewed by Freeman (1979), the simplest measure is that of Sabidussi (1966), who proposed that actor closeness should be measured as a function of geodesic distances. As mentioned above, as geodesics increase in length, the centrality of the actors involved should decrease; consequently, distances, which measure the length of geodesics, will have to be weighted inversely to arrive at Sabidussi's index. Note how this type of centrality depends not only on direct ties, but also on indirect ties, especially when any two actors are not adjacent.

We let $d(n_i, n_j)$ be the number of lines in the geodesic linking actors i and j; that is, as defined in Chapter 4, $d(\bullet, \bullet)$ is a distance function. The total distance that i is from all other actors is $\sum_{j=1}^{g} d(n_i, n_j)$, where the sum is taken over all $j \neq i$. Thus, Sabidussi's (1966) index of actor closeness is

$$C_C(n_i) = \left[\sum_{j=1}^{g} d(n_i, n_j) \right]^{-1}. \tag{5.7}$$

The subscript C is for "closeness." As one can see, the index is simply the inverse of the sum of the distances from actor i to all the other actors.

At a maximum, the index equals $(g-1)^{-1}$, which arises when the actor is adjacent to all other actors. At a minimum, the index attains the value of 0 in its limit, which arises whenever one or more actors are not reachable from the actor in question. A node is said to be *reachable* from another node if there is a path linking the two nodes; otherwise, the nodes are not reachable from each other. Thus, the index is only meaningful for a connected graph.

To verify this assertion, suppose that the graph is disconnected — specifically, let there be one isolated node, with degree 0. The geodesics from all the other nodes to this specific node (n_k) are infinitely long $(d(n_i, n_k) = \infty$ for all $i \neq k)$, since the node is not reachable. Hence, the distance sum for every actor is ∞, and the actor closeness indices are all 0. This is a large drawback of this index.

As we have noted, the maximum value attained by this index depends on g; thus, comparisons of values across networks of different sizes are difficult. Beauchamp (1965) made the suggestion of standardizing the indices so that the maximum value equals unity. To do this, we simply multiply $C_C(n_i)$ by $g-1$:

$$
\begin{aligned}
C'_C(n_i) &= \frac{g-1}{\left[\sum_{j=1}^{g} d(n_i, n_j)\right]} \\
&= (g-1)C_C(n_i).
\end{aligned} \tag{5.8}
$$

This standardized index ranges between 0 and 1, and can be viewed as the inverse average distance between actor i and all the other actors. It equals unity when the actor is adjacent to all other actors; that is, when the actor is maximally close to all other actors.

Graph theorists have simplified this concept of centrality, and talked about the *center* of a graph, using the graph-theoretic notion of distance (see Chapter 4). Specifically, the *Jordan center* (see Jordan 1869) of a graph is the subset of nodes that have the smallest maximum distance to all other nodes. To find such a center, one can take a $g \times g$ matrix of geodesic distances between pairs of nodes (where the entries are the lengths of the shortest paths or geodesics between all pairs of nodes), and then find the largest entry in each row. These distances (which are sometimes called *eccentricities*) are the maximum distances from every actor to their fellow actors. One then simply finds the smallest of these maximum distances. All nodes that have this smallest maximum distance are part of the center of the graph.

A related notion is the *centroid* of a graph (see Sylvester 1882), which is based on the degrees of the nodes and which is most appropriate for graphs that are trees. The idea is to consider all branches or paths emanating from each node, and define the *weight* of each branch as the number of lines in it. The weight of a node is the maximum weight of any branch at the node. The *centroid* is thus the subset of all nodes that have the smallest weight.

All the graphs in Figure 5.1 are connected, so that all geodesic distances are finite; therefore, the closeness indices can be calculated. For the star graph, $C'_C(n_1) = 1.0$, while the other actors all have indices equal to 0.545. For the circle graph, the actor indices are all equal to 0.5. For the line graph, the indices vary from $C'_C(n_1) = 0.50$ to a low of $C'_C(n_6) = C'_C(n_7) = 0.286$.

We note that there are clever algorithms for finding the geodesics in a graph, and then computing their lengths. We refer the reader to (for example) Flament (1963), and Harary, Norman, and Cartwright (1965). Such algorithms are standard in network computing programs such as *UCINET* and *SNAPS* (see Appendix A).

Group Closeness Centralization. We now consider how to measure group centralization using actor closeness centralities. We first report Freeman's (1979) index, which uses the general graph centralization index, (5.1), given above. We then will consider alternative group closeness indices.

Freeman's general group closeness index is based on the standardized actor closeness centralities, shown in equation (5.8). This index has numerator

$$\sum_{i=1}^{g} [C'_C(n^*) - C'_C(n_i)],$$

where $C'_C(n^*)$ is the largest standardized actor closeness in the set of actors. Freeman shows that the maximum possible value for the numerator is $[(g-2)(g-1)]/(2g-3)$, so that the index of group closeness is

$$C_C = \frac{\sum_{i=1}^{g} [C'_C(n^*) - C'_C(n_i)]}{[(g-2)(g-1)]/(2g-3)}. \tag{5.9}$$

This index, as with the group degree centralization index, reaches its maximum value of unity when one actor "chooses" all other $g-1$ actors (that is, has geodesics of length 1 to all the other actors), and the other actors have geodesics of length 2 to the remaining $(g-2)$ actors. This is exactly the situation realized by a star graph. The proof of this fact is rather complicated, and must be done by induction. We refer the reader to Freeman (1979). The index can attain its minimum value of 0 when the lengths of geodesics are all equal, for example in a complete graph or in a circle graph. For the line graph of Figure 5.1, the index equals 0.277, a relatively small value.

Bolland (1988) proposes a measure (for both actors and groups) that utilizes both degree and closeness of actors. His "continuing flow" centrality index is based on the number of paths (of any length) that originate with each actor. Thus, the measure considers all paths, those of length 1 (that are the focus of C_D) and those indirect (whose distances are reflected in the magnitude of C_C). We discuss this measure in more detail at the end of this chapter.

There are other group-level closeness indices. We may simply summarize the set of g actor-level closeness centralities $\{C'_C(n_i)\}$ by a single statistic, reflecting the tendency toward closeness manifested by all the actors in the set of actors. Such a statistic, to be an effective index, should reach its extremes in the cases of the circle graph (equal distances), and the star graph (one minimally distant actor).

We recommend that one calculate the variance of the standardized actor closeness indices,

$$S_C^2 = \left[\sum_{i=1}^{g}(C'_C(n_i) - \overline{C}_C)^2\right] /g, \tag{5.10}$$

which summarizes the heterogeneity among the $\{C'_C(n_i)\}$. We note that average normed closeness, $\overline{C}_C = \sum C'_C(n_i)/g$, is simply the mean of the actor-level closeness centralities. The variance attains its minimum value of 0 in a network with equal actor indices (in this case, equal distances between all nodes). Such a network need not be complete (have maximal degree). This index grows as the network becomes less homogeneous (with respect to distances), and thus more centralized. The average normed closeness, $\overline{C}_C$, together with S_C^2, provide simple summary statistics for the entire set of actor closeness indices.

The Example Again. Consider again Padgett's network data, discussed earlier. Actor n_{12} = Pucci (as can be seen from the actor degree centrality value of $C_D(n_{12}) = 0$) is an isolate. Consequently, the distances to this actor from all other actors are infinite, and thus, family Pucci is not reachable and the graph is not connected. Actor closeness centrality indices are then also infinite, and cannot be calculated.

Thus, we dropped family Pucci from the set of actors, giving us a smaller network of $g - 1 = 15$ families, but now we have (for the purpose of demonstrating the calculations of closeness centralities) a connected graph. The actor centralities and centralization indices calculated for this smaller network are shown in Table 5.1 and are indexed with asterisks to distinguish them from indices calculated for the full set of actors. The actor closeness centralities are shown in Column 4, while the actor degree centralities for the smaller set of actors (sans family Pucci) are shown in Column 3. Once again family Medici is the most central actor, but several families are almost as central: Albizzi, Guadagni, Ridolfi, and Tornabuoni.

Note that family Strozzi, which had a rather large actor degree central-ity index, has a relatively small actor closeness centrality index. Strozzi has apparently married into a moderately large number of other families, but is not particularly close to the other families; that is, there are many "steps" in the marital linkages from Strozzi to the others.

The closeness indices are much larger than the degree indices, and none of the families have small values. Families Acciaiuoli, Ginori, Lamberteschi, and Pazzi are still the least central. These indices also vary less than the degree indices (from 0.326 to 0.560, as opposed to 0.071 to 0.429 for degree centralities), indicating a much more uniform spread of closenesses. The closeness centralization index is $C_C^* = 0.322$, calculated for the smaller network, and the average closeness centrality and variance are $\overline{C}_C = 0.415$ and $S_C^2 = 0.0056$. This is a small variance, indicating once again the small range of the actor closeness centralities.

5.2.3 Betweenness Centrality

Interactions between two nonadjacent actors might depend on the other actors in the set of actors, especially the actors who lie on the paths be-tween the two. These "other actors" potentially might have some control over the interactions between the two nonadjacent actors. Consider now whether a particular actor might be able to control interactions between pairs of other actors in the network. For example, if the geodesic between actors n_2 and n_3 is $n_2 n_1 n_4 n_3$ — that is, the shortest path between these actors has to go "through" two other actors, n_1 and n_4 — then we could say that the two actors contained in the geodesic might have control over the interaction between n_2 and n_3. Glance again at our star network in Figure 5.1, and note that the most central actor lies on all fifteen geodesics linking the other six actors. This "actor in the middle," the one *between* the others, has some control over paths in the graph. A look at the line network in Figure 5.1 shows that the actors in the middle of this graph might have control over some of the paths, while those at the edge might not. Or, one could state that the "actors in the middle" have more "interpersonal influence" on the others (see Freeman 1979, or Friedkin 1991).

The important idea here is that an actor is central if it lies between other actors on their geodesics, implying that to have a large "between-ness" centrality, the actor must be *between* many of the actors via their geodesics.

Several early centrality researchers recognized the strategic importance of locations on geodesics. Both Bavelas (1948) and Shaw (1954) suggested that actors located on many geodesics are indeed central to the network, while Shimbel (1953) and Cohn and Marriott (1958) noted that such central actors play important roles in the network. None of these researchers, however, were able to quantify this notion of betweenness. It took roughly twenty years, however, until Anthonisse (1971), and later Freeman (1977) and Pitts (1979), suggested that the the locations of actors on geodesics be examined.

Actor Betweenness Centrality. Let us simply quote from Shimbel (1953), reiterated by Pitts (1979), who stated the importance of geodesics and the actors they contain for measuring betweenness and network control:

> Suppose that in order for [actor] i to contact [actor] j, [actor] k must be used as an intermediate station. [Actor] k in such a network has a certain "responsibility" to [actors] i and j. If we count all of the minimum paths which pass through [actor] k, then we have a measure of the "stress" which [actor] k must undergo during the activity of the network. (page 507)

Here, actors who have sufficient stress also possess betweenness, according to this rather political view of network flows.

Specifically, one should first count the number of geodesics linking actors j and k (all these geodesics will be of the same length, $d(n_j, n_k)$), and then determine how many of these geodesics contain actor i, for all distinct indices i, j, k. Shimbel goes on to state that

> A vector giving this [count of minimum paths] for each [actor] of the network would give us a good idea of the stress conditions *throughout the system*. (page 507; emphasis is ours)

Shaw (1954) was the first to recognize that this stress was also betweenness, noting that, in the case of a communication relation where actors could not form new lines, central actors could refuse to pass along messages. Anthonisse (1971) and Freeman (1977) first quantified this idea.

We want to consider the probability that a "communication," or simply a path, from actor j to actor k takes a particular route. We assume that lines have equal weight, and that communications will travel along the shortest route (regardless of the actors along the route). Since we are just considering shortest paths, we assume that such a communication follows one of the geodesics. When there is more than one geodesic between j and k, all geodesics are equally likely to be used. Freeman estimates this probability as follows: Let g_{jk} be the number of geodesics linking the two actors. Then, if all these geodesics are equally likely to be chosen for the path, the probability of the communication using any one of them is simply $1/g_{jk}$. We also consider the probability that a distinct actor, i, is "involved" in the communication between the two actors. We let $g_{jk}(n_i)$ be the number of geodesics linking the two actors that contain actor i. Freeman then estimates this probability by $g_{jk}(n_i)/g_{jk}$, making the critical assumption that geodesics are equally likely to be chosen for this path. (We comment on this assumption later in the chapter.)

The actor betweenness index for n_i is simply the sum of these estimated probabilities over all pairs of actors not including the ith actor:

$$C_B(n_i) = \sum_{j<k} g_{jk}(n_i)/g_{jk} \qquad (5.11)$$

for i distinct from j and k. So, this index, which counts how "between" each of the actors is, is a sum of probabilities. It has a minimum of zero, attained when n_i falls on no geodesics. Its maximum is clearly $(g-1)(g-2)/2$, which is the number of pairs of actors not including n_i. The index reaches the maximum when the ith actor falls on all geodesics. Since the index's values depend on g, we standardize it just like the other actor centrality indices:

$$C_B'(n_i) = C_B(n_i)/[(g-1)(g-2)/2]. \qquad (5.12)$$

Standardized in this way, it now takes on values between 0 and 1, and can easily be compared to the other actor indices, as well as across networks and relations. Unlike the closeness indices, these betweenness indices $\{C_B'(n_i)\}$ can be computed even if the graph is not connected. This is certainly an advantage. As with our other actor indices, algorithms for first finding the geodesics in a graph, and then counting how many of them contain each of the actors, are available, and are implemented in network computer programs such as *UCINET*.

The quantities summed on the right-hand side of equation (5.11) are discussed in more detail in Freeman (1980a). Specifically, if we sum the $g_{jk}(n_i)/g_{jk}$ estimated probabilities over k, we obtain measures of the pair-dependency of actor j on actor i. These values, which can also be viewed as indices of how much "gatekeeping" n_i does for n_j, are crucial components of both the $\{C_B(n_j)\}$ and the $\{C_C(n_j)\}$. Gatekeeping of one actor for another is simply the act of being on geodesics from the latter actor to all other actors, regardless of where the geodesics are going. Actors on whom others are "locally dependent" are central in the network. One can measure the level of gatekeeping for every pair of actors in the network, focusing on how much gatekeeping the second actor does for the first.

Returning again to the graphs of Figure 5.1, we find that for the star graph, $C'_B(n_1) = 1.0$, while $C'_B(n_2) = \cdots = C'_B(n_7) = 0$. This is an idealized situation, since only actor 1 lies on any of the geodesics. The actor betweenness indices in the circle graph are all equal to 0.2, and for the line graph, vary from $C'_B(n_1) = 0.6$ to $C'_B(n_6) = C'_B(n_7) = 0$. In this last graph, actors n_2 and n_3 are almost as central as n_1, since $C'_B(n_2) = C'_B(n_3) = 0.533$.

Group Betweenness Centralization. Group centralization indicies based on betweenness allow a researcher to compare different networks with respect to the heterogeneity of the betweenness of the members of the networks. We first report Freeman's (1979) index for quantifying the overall level of betweenness in the set of actors, which summarizes the actor betweenness indices given in equation (5.11).

Freeman's group betweenness centralization index has numerator $\sum_{i=1}^{g}[C_B(n^*) - C_B(n_i)]$, where $C_B(n^*)$ is the largest realized actor betweenness index for the set of actors. The reason for using the nonstandardized indices rather than the standardized ones (see equation (5.12)) will follow. Freeman shows that the maximum possible value for this sum is $(g-1)^2(g-2)/2$, so that the index of group betweenness is

$$C_B = \frac{2\sum_{i=1}^{g}[C_B(n^*) - C_B(n_i)]}{[(g-1)^2(g-2)]}. \tag{5.13}$$

Freeman (1979) shows that this simplifies to the index given in Freeman (1977):

$$C_B = \frac{\sum_{i=1}^{g}[C'_B(n^*) - C'_B(n_i)]}{(g-1)};$$

(5.14)

that is, the calculation can also be made equivalently with the standardized indices. Freeman (1977) also demonstrates that the index reaches its maximum value (unity) for the star graph. Its minimum value (0) occurs when all actors have exactly the same actor betweenness index — that is, in a network in which all actors are equal in betweenness. The line graph of Figure 5.1 has $C_B = 0.311$.

There are additional group-level betweenness indices, for example the variance of the actor-level betweenness indices. Such centralization indices provide additional summaries of the heterogeneity or variability of betweenness in the entire set of actors.

The Example, Once Again. Actor betweenness centralities are given for Padgett's Florentine families and the marriage relation in Table 5.1, Columns 2 and 5. The second column gives the betweenness centralities calculated for the network consisting of all actors, and the fifth column, for the network without the Pucci family. Note how many actors have 0 indices — families Acciaiuoli, Ginori, Lamberteschi, Pazzi, and of course Pucci — the same actors that had the smallest actor closeness centrality indices. The betweenness indices allow the Medici family, and, to a lesser extent, the Guadagni family, to stand out, just as with the actor degree centralities.

Clearly, families Medici and (perhaps) Guadagni are the most central families in this set of actors on this marital relation. The betweenness centralization index is $C_B = 0.437$, larger than the other centralization indices, reflecting the fact that the Medici family is much more central than any of the other families.

Note how these betweenness indices compare to the other two actor centrality indices. Some actors with moderately large closeness and degree scores have small betweenness indices — families Barbadori and especially Tornabuoni. Family Strozzi, which has a large degree index, has a small betweenness index. Such differences indicate that the betweenness indices can be quite different measures of actor centrality than degree- and closeness-based indices.

5.2.4 ⊗*Information Centrality*

Of all these indices, Freeman's centrality measure based on betweenness of actors on geodesics has found the most use, because of its generality. But, this index assumes that all geodesics are equally likely when estimating the critical probability that an actor falls on a particular geodesic. That is, if there are g_{ij} geodesics between actors i and j, then the probability that a particular geodesic is "chosen" for the "flow of information" between these two actors is simply $1/g_{ij}$. While this is a justifiable assumption for some purposes, it may not be appropriate here.

Suppose we focus on the actors "contained" in these geodesics. Freeman ignores the fact that if some actors on the geodesics have large degrees, then the geodesics containing these expansive actors are more likely to be used as shortest paths than other geodesics. That is, if an actor has a degree of, say, 10, and this actor is on a geodesic, then this actor is more likely than actors with smaller degrees to be on other geodesics, simply because of its expansiveness. Freeman's assumption is reasonable only if all actors have equal degrees. For such regular graphs, it is not unreasonable to assume that all geodesics between a pair of nodes are equally likely to be "used" for a path. Relaxing this assumption is difficult, and requires a more sophisticated statistical model that allows for unequal probabilities.

A second, more important generalization can also be considered. Freeman, in considering betweenness counts, focuses only on geodesics. That is, paths with distances greater than the minimum path length attained by the geodesics are ignored. Substantively, this might not be realistic. For example, if we consider communication relations, there may be good reasons for actors to choose paths for their communications that are longer than the geodesics. We quote:

> It is quite possible that information will take a more circuitous route either by random communication or [by being] channeled through many intermediaries in order to "hide" or "shield" information. (Stephenson and Zelen 1989, page 3)

So, it may make sense to generalize the notion of betweenness centrality so all paths between actors, with weights depending on their lengths, are considered when calculating betweenness counts.

The index of centrality developed by Stephenson and Zelen (1989) does exactly this. One considers the combined path from one actor to another, by taking all paths, including the geodesics, and assigning them weights. A weighted function of this combined path is then calculated, using as weights the inverses of the lengths of the paths being combined. The weights assigned to the paths making up the combined path are determined so that the "information" in the combined path is maximized.

Geodesics are usually given weights of unity, while paths with lengths longer than the geodesic length receive smaller weights based on the *information* that they contain. The information of a path is defined quite simply as the inverse of its length.

Mackenzie (1966b) was the first to propose the use of *information theory* for the study of centrality, particularly in commnication networks. He defined a "Total Participation Index" for actors in a network, but his rather mathematical presentation has prevented wider adoption of the idea. Bolland's (1988) index of continuing flow also considers all paths originating with each actor, but does not consider betweenness counts.

The concept of information is quite old, and has a rich tradition in statistics (Shannon and Weaver 1949; Khinchin 1957; Kullback 1959; Gokhale and Kullback 1978; see also Coleman 1964; Theil 1967; and Allison 1978, for applications in economics and sociology). It is used extensively in estimation theory and categorical data analysis. Information is usually defined as the inverse of the variance of an estimator. If an estimator has a small variance, it has large information, and thus is considered "good." The opposite is also true: poor estimators with large variances have little information. We can apply this approach to centrality by extending betweenness on geodesics to all possible paths, weighting according to the information that these paths contain. The betweenness counts are then generalized to reflect the information contained in all paths.

Stephenson and Zelen (1989) give a nice discussion of the use of information in statistical estimation as applied to the paths between nodes in a graph. In brief, the length of any path is directly related to the variance of transmitting a signal from one node to another; thus, the information contained in this path is the reciprocal of this variance. Thus, any path (and hence, each and every combined path) has an "information content." Lastly, the information of a node is the harmonic average of the information for the combined paths from the node to all other nodes.

Actor Information Centrality. This version of centrality focuses on the information contained in all paths originating with a specific actor. The information of an actor averages the information in these paths, which, in turn, is inversely related to the variance in the transmission of a signal from one actor to another.

To calculate information centrality indices, Stephenson and Zelen recognized that the information contained in an incidence matrix (see Chapter 4), which codes the nodes and the links between them, is exactly the same as the information contained in the data vector and incidence matrix for an incomplete block design with two treatments per block (see Cochran and Cox 1957). This exact equality allowed Stephenson and Zelen to adopt a statistical model, common in the statistical design of experiments (see St. John and Draper 1975; Box, Hunter, and Hunter 1978; Silvey 1981), designed for such incomplete block designs. The model focuses on all the "signals" flowing between all pairs of nodes (or pairs of rows of the incidence matrix). One estimates the strengths of these signals, and calculates their variances. If V_{jk} is the variance of the estimate of the signal for the path linking nodes n_j and n_k, then the information associated with this path is simply $1/V_{jk}$. The information for an actor is a function of all the information for paths flowing out from the actor. The chosen function is the harmonic average. We refer the reader to the appendix of Stephenson and Zelen (1989) for more mathematical details.

To apply this idea to graphs, the actor information indices are functions of a simple $g \times g$ matrix. We give the most general formulation of the index, which assumes that the relation is nondirectional, but not necessarily dichotomous. A crucial component of the formula is the sum of the strengths or values for the lines incident with a node. This sum is simply a row total (or column total) of the sociomatrix. The sum is the degree of a node when the measured relation is dichotomous, or the sum of the strengths of all ties incident to a node when the relation is valued.

The calculation begins as follows. One first creates a $g \times g$ matrix $\mathbf{A}$, which has diagonal elements

$$a_{ii} = 1 + \text{ sum of values for all lines incident to } n_i \qquad (5.15)$$

and off-diagonal elements

$$a_{ij} = \begin{cases} 1 & \text{if nodes } n_i \text{ and } n_j \text{ are not adjacent} \\ 1 - x_{ij} & \text{if nodes } n_i \text{ and } n_j \text{ are adjacent.} \end{cases} \qquad (5.16)$$

As usual, x_{ij} is the value of the tie between actors i and j, so that the elements of $\mathbf{A}$ are easily calculated from the sociomatrix. One next calculates the inverse of $\mathbf{A}$: $\mathbf{C} = \mathbf{A}^{-1}$, which has elements $\{c_{ij}\}$.

We should note that not every $\mathbf{A}$ matrix can be inverted. In fact, if the sociomatrix has one (or more) rows (and hence columns) full of zeros, the corresponding $\mathbf{C}$ is not defined. In this instance, actor information centralities cannot be computed. We recommend that the actors who are isolates be dropped from the set of actors, and indices calculated just for the non-isolates.

To get the information indices, one needs two intermediate quantities. These are sums of elements of $\mathbf{C}$: $T = \sum_{i=1}^{g} c_{ii}$ and $R = \sum_{j=1}^{g} c_{ij}$. T is simply the trace or the sum of the diagonal entries of the matrix, while R is any one of the row sums (all the row sums are equal). With these two quantities, and the elements of $\mathbf{C}$, one lastly calculates

$$C_I(n_i) = \frac{1}{c_{ii} + (T - 2R)/g} \qquad (5.17)$$

as the information centrality index for actor i.

This index measures how much information is contained in the paths that originate (and end) at a specific actor. The index has a minimum value of 0, but no maximum value; indeed, if $T = 2R$, and $c_{ii} = 0$, the index would equal ∞. Stephenson and Zelen (1989) recommend that one use relative information indices, obtained by dividing each index $C_I(n_i)$ by the total of all indices:

$$C_I'(n_i) = \frac{C_I(n_i)}{\sum_i C_I(n_i)}. \qquad (5.18)$$

The relative information indices, $\{C_I'(n_i)\}$, are bounded by 0 and 1, and sum to unity. These indices can be interpreted as the proportion of total "information" flow in a graph controlled by an individual actor. The constraint that the indices sum to unity is unique to this index, and makes comparisons with the other actor-level centrality indices difficult. Necessary calculations are not complicated, and involve manipulations of the sociomatrix, and then a single matrix inversion. One can "program" them with *SAS PROC IML* or *GAUSS*.

Return once again to the graphs of Figure 5.1. We find that for the star graph, $C_I'(n_1) = 0.2340$, while $C_I'(n_2) = \cdots = C_B'(n_7) = 0.1277$. Notice that even though only node n_1 lies on any of the geodesics, the information centralities for the other six nodes are not zero. The actor information indices in the circle graph are all equal to 0.1429, and for the line graph, vary from $C_I'(n_1) = 0.1822$ to $C_I'(n_6) = C_I'(n_7) = 0.1041$. In this last graph, nodes n_2 and n_3 are almost as central as n_1, since $C_I'(n_2) = C_I'(n_3) = 0.1682$. Remember that the actor information centralities are normed differently from the other actor centralities — they must sum to unity, so that if one actor has a large index, the other actors must have smaller indices.

Use of this information index has been limited. Stephenson (1989) and Stephenson and Zelen (1989) apply this methodology to networks of baboons, while Stephenson (1989) and Frey (1989) use this index (and others) to study a network of forty AIDS patients, linked by sexual contact (Auerbach, Darrow, Jaffe, and Curran 1984; Klovdahl 1985; see also Laumann, Gagnon, Michaels, Michael, and Coleman 1989; Morris 1989, 1990). Marsden (1990b) has used information indices in a study of the effect of random sampling on estimation of the parameters of the network effects or social process model (see Erbring and Young 1979; Doreian 1981; Friedkin 1986, 1990; Marsden 1990a; and Burt 1987).

Group Information Centralization. The summary group-level information index proposed by Stephenson and Zelen is simply the average information across actors:

$$\overline{C}_I = \sum_i C_I(n_i). \tag{5.19}$$

This index has limits that depend on g, unfortunately, and so is difficult to compare across networks. As we have mentioned throughout this chapter, averages are not centralization indices. A real group-level information centralization index is the variance of the actor information indices:

$$S_I^2 = \left[\sum_{i=1}^{g} (C_I'(n_i) - \overline{C}_I)^2 \right] / g. \tag{5.20}$$

One could also apply Freeman's (1979) general index (5.1) to information indices, although (to our knowledge) no one has calculated the denominator (the maximum possible sum of differences between the observed indices and the largest attained index) for a Freeman information centralization index.

For the graphs of Figure 5.1, the variances are 0.001614, 0.000986, and 0.0, for the star, line, and circle graphs, respectively. Thus, the star graph is most heterogeneous, and the circle, the least.

As mentioned, this information actor-level index of centrality is the only index (that we are aware of) that can be applied to valued relations. Further, as we have discussed, it generalizes Freeman's widely used index of betweenness, since it considers all paths, not just geodesics. We comment further on the differences among all the indices discussed here at the end of the chapter. Further research and application should demonstrate the usefulness of the actor information centrality index (5.18).

Last Look at Padgett's Florentine Families. As we have noted, family Pucci is not married to any other families; it is an isolate, and consequently, the actor information centralities cannot be calculated because the **C** matrix cannot be inverted. Thus, we dropped this actor from the set of actors, and calculated actor information centralities for the other fifteen actors. These indices are shown in Column 6 of Table 5.1. It is difficult to compare these indices to the others, since only the information centralities are constrained to sum to unity. They must be between 0 and 1, just like all the other types of centrality, but are forced to be smaller in magnitude because of this constraint.

The Medici family is still the most central family, although the Guadagni, Tornabuoni, and Ridolfi families have indices not much smaller than that for Medici. These four families consistently have the largest actor centrality indices. The Pazzi, Ginori, Lamberteschi, and Acciaiuoli families are the least central families; in fact, the ordering of the actors with respect to information centrality is almost identical to that for betweenness centrality. The main difference between the two sets of centralities is the range of values — the range is much smaller for information. The variance of the actor information centralities is $S_I^2 = 0.000297$, quite small, reflecting the small range of the values due to the unity summation constraint.

We now turn to indices that can be applied to social network data consisting of directional relations.

5.3 Directional Relations

In the previous section, we discussed nondirectional relations, and introduced four actor-level indices for centrality (and associated centralization indices). These indices are:

(i) Degree — equation (5.3)
(ii) Closeness — equation (5.8)
(iii) Betweenness — equation (5.12)
(iv) Information — equation (5.18)

We now discuss how these, and other kinds of indices (specifically, those designed to measure prestige), can be calculated for directional relations.

Suppose that we have a single set of actors, and a single, dichotomous directional relation. With such data, we can distinguish between "choices made" and "choices received." An example of such data that we will be analyzing in this section can be found in Chapter 2; specifically, the countries trade network data which show import and export of basic manufactured goods among a collection of $g=24$ countries. These data are discussed in some detail in Chapter 2, and will be examined at length in Chapters 9–12. Clearly for these data, imports are substantively different from exports, and it is interesting to study which actors are important importers and which are significant exporters. To identify these important actors on this relation, we will examine both aspects of prominence: centrality and prestige.

As mentioned at the beginning of the chapter, centrality indices for directional relations generally focus on choices made, while prestige indices generally examine choices received, both direct and indirect. We will discuss how to calculate centrality indices for directional relations here, but the emphasis in this section will be prestige, and in particular, three types of prestige indices.

We first discuss how the four centrality indices, degree, closeness, betweenness, and information, can be extended to directional relations. For this extension, we examine actors from the perspective of the choices or nominations that are made. Two of the centrality indices are easily applied to directional relations (degree and closeness indices), while the other two (betweenness and information), because of their reliance on nondirected paths and geodesics, are not.

One can also examine the choices received by actors. This allows us to study which actors in the set of actors are prestigious. We will present and discuss three types of prestige indices.

5.3.1 *Centrality*

To extend to directional relations the centrality indices based on degree, closeness, betweenness, and information, and the group-level indices which aggregate the actor-level indices (equations (5.5), (5.9), (5.13), (5.19)), we must consider how each is computed and how the network properties that are crucial for each are defined for directional relations.

Degree. An actor index for degree centrality can easily be calculated for directional relations. Such indices are meaningful if no restrictions, as in a fixed choice design, are placed on the choices made by the actors. Since centrality indices focus on the choices made, we take the outdegree of each actor, rather than the degree (which we used for nondirectional relations): $C'_D(n_i) = x_{i+}/(g-1)$. A group-level index of degree centralization can be calculated as suggested in equation (5.4). The denominator of this index when the measured relation is directional can be calculated to be $(g-1)^2$. These actor and group-level indices have exactly the same properties as degree indices for nondirectional relations.

Closeness. An actor index for closeness centrality can also be calculated for directional relations. Specifically, we define the distances between any two actors, as discussed in Chapter 4, as the length of the geodesic(s) from n_i to n_j. With a directed graph, the geodesic(s) from n_i to n_j may not be the same as the one(s) from n_j to n_i, so that $d(n_i, n_j)$, the length of the geodesic(s), may not equal $d(n_j, n_i)$. These $\{d(n_i, n_j)\}$ are elements of a $g \times g$ distance matrix.

Actor-level centrality indices for closeness are calculated by taking the sum of row i of the distance matrix to obtain the total distance n_i is from all the other actors, and then dividing by $g - 1$ (the minimum possible total distance). The reciprocal of this ratio gives us an actor-level index for closeness. The formula is exactly the same as for nondirectional relations. Specifically, the actor-level closeness centrality index for directional relations is

$$C'_C(n_i) = (g - 1) / \left[\sum_{j=1}^{g} d(n_i, n_j) \right]. \tag{5.21}$$

This index has exactly the same properties as discussed following equation (5.8). A group-level closeness index based on Freeman's general formula (5.1) can be obtained using the standardized indices; however, to our knowledge, no one has calculated the denominator of this index when the measured relation is directional.

One problem with this actor-level centrality index based on closeness is that it is not defined unless the digraph is strongly connected (that is, if there is a directed path from i to j, for all actors i and j); otherwise, some of the $\{d(n_i, n_j)\}$ will be ∞, and equation (5.21) will be undefined. The same problem arises with graphs based on nondirectional relations, as discussed earlier. One remedy to this problem is to consider only those actors that i can reach, ignoring those that are unreachable from i.

This simple index, $C'_C(n_i)$, can be generalized by considering the *influence range* of n_i as the set of actors who are reachable from n_i. This set contains all actors who are reachable from i in a finite number of steps. This notion is common to graph theory, and is related to an idea first used by Lin (1976) to describe the set of actors reachable *to* n_i (see below). We define J_i as the number of actors in the influence range of actor i. This count J_i equals the number of actors who are reachable from n_i. Note that this idea can also be applied to nondirectional relations.

An "improved" actor-level centrality closeness index considers how proximate n_i is to the actors in its influence range. We define closeness now by just focusing on distances from actor i *to* the actors in its influence range. We consider the average distance these actors are from n_i. This average distance, $\sum d(n_i, n_j)/J_i$, where the sum is taken over all actors j in the influence range of actor i, is a refined measure of closeness. Note that this sum ignores actors who are not reachable from n_i, so that unlike the first closeness centrality measures, it is defined even if the graph is not strongly connected. We can define

$$C_C^*(n_i) = \frac{J_i/(g-1)}{\sum d(n_i, n_j)/J_i},$$
(5.22)

where the summation again is just over those actors in the influence range of n_i.

One can see that this index is a ratio of the fraction of the actors in the group who are reachable $(J_i/(g-1))$, to the average distance that these actors are from the actor $(\sum d(n_i, n_j)/J_i)$. This index is quite similar to an index for prestige that we discuss in the next section.

Other. The other two centrality indices for nondirectional relations, based on betweenness and information, were derived using theory and algorithms designed specifically for nondirectional relations. Gould (1987) has extended the betweenness index to directional relations, by considering geodesics between any two actors. Gould shows that the algorithm to find actor betweenness indices for nondirectional relations can be applied to directional relations, since the basic algorithm automatically uses ordered (rather than unordered) pairs of actors.

The $\{C_B(n_i)\}$ indices defined in equation (5.11) are thus calculated correctly for both directional and nondirectional relations; however, the $\{C_B'(n_i)\}$ indices defined in equation (5.12) must be multiplied by 2. The maximum value for the index is $(g-1)(g-2)$, so that these standardized scores must be multiplied by a factor of two to be correct (since the maximum for nondirectional relations is $(g-1)(g-2)/2$). We note that Gould's (1987) extension is based on the assumption that a directional relation can be turned into a nondirectional relation by coding all mutual dyads as lines and ignoring asymmetric dyads. Thus, there is a line in the derived undirected graph between two actors if and only if both actors choose each other in the original digraph.

For an information index, we could consider directed geodesics and longer directed paths between actors. All these paths will be directed, given the nature of the data. However, we do not know how to generalize Stephenson and Zelen's (1989) theory for information indices to directional relations.

Thus, we recommend the use of just two centrality indices, $C'_D(n_i)$, and $C'_C(n_i)$ or $C^*_C(n_i)$, for directed graphs. In our later discussions of the countries trade network data, we calculate not only actor prestige indices, but also these two actor centrality indices. Since choices received are usually more interesting than those made, neither of these centrality indices is as useful as the measures of prestige that we discuss below. If the relation allows one to distinguish between choices made and choices received, then the latter, along with prestige indices calculated from them, can give important insights into social structure, as we will demonstrate with our example.

5.3.2 Prestige

With directional relations, choices received are quite interesting to a network analyst. Thus, measures of centrality may not be of as much concern as measures of prestige. We now discuss several prestige measures, which we will illustrate on the countries trade network data. We recommend that both centrality and prestige measures be computed for directional relations, since they do attempt to measure different structural properties.

There has been little research on group-level prestige indices. However, such measures would certainly be welcome and interesting, since they could quantify prestige heterogeneity (and possibly hierarchization or network stratification).

We also note that there has been little work done on applications of prestige measures to actual digraphs. For example, it is not known which digraphs have maximal group-level prestige indices. More research on such important issues is clearly needed.

Degree Prestige. The simplest actor-level measure of prestige is the indegree of each actor, which we denoted by $d_I(n_i)$ in Chapter 4. The idea is that actors who are prestigious tend to receive many nominations or choices (see Alexander 1963). So, we define

$$P_D(n_i) = d_I(n_i) = x_{+i}. \tag{5.23}$$

As with the comparable indices based on outdegrees, equation (5.23) is dependent upon the group size g; thus, the standardization

$$P_D'(n_i) = \frac{x_{+i}}{g-1} \tag{5.24}$$

gives us the proportion of actors who choose actor i, which is sometimes called a "relative indegree." The larger this index is, the more prestigious is the actor. Maximum prestige occurs when $P_D'(n_i) = 1$; that is, when actor i is chosen by all other actors. This index is quite simple to compute, and is usually provided as output from network analysis computer packages, such as *UCINET*.

Proximity Prestige. This simple index, $P_D'(n_i)$, counts only actors who are adjacent to actor i. One can generalize this index by defining the *influence domain* of actor i as the set of actors who are both directly *and* indirectly linked to actor j. Such actors are reachable to i, or alternatively, are those from whom i is reachable. Reachability is discussed in Chapter 4. Thus, the influence domain consists of all actors whose entries in the ith column of the distance matrix or the reachability matrix are finite. This notion was first used by Lin (1976). We define I_i as the number of actors in the influence domain of actor i. This count I_i equals the number of actors who can reach actor i. We use the idea of an influence domain in the next prestige index.

A second actor-level index of prestige considers how proximate n_i is to the actors in its influence domain. We define *proximity* as closeness that focuses on distances *to* rather than *from* each actor. In other words, what matters now is how close all the actors are to n_i. Since the relation is directional, such closeness will no doubt differ from the closeness that n_i is to the other actors. As stressed in Chapter 4, with digraphs, distance *to* a node can be quite different from distance *from*.

We consider the average distance these actors are to n_i. This average distance, $\sum d(n_j, n_i)/I_i$, where the sum is taken over all actors j in the influence domain of actor i, is a crude measure of proximity. Note that it ignores actors who cannot reach n_i, so that unlike our closeness and information centrality measures, it is defined even if the network is not connected (when some actors are not reachable from other actors). This index depends on the size of the group, and is difficult to compare across networks.

But, we can look at the ratio of the proportion of actors who can reach i to the average distance these actors are from i. Thus, a better measure of proximity takes the average distance, standardizes it, and then takes reciprocals. From a suggestion by Lin (1976), we define

$$P_P(n_i) = \frac{I_i/(g-1)}{\sum d(n_j, n_i)/I_i},$$ (5.25)

where the summation again is just over those actors in the influence domain of n_i. One can easily see that this index is a ratio of the fraction of the actors in the set of actors who can reach an actor ($I_i/(g-1)$) to the average distance that these actors are to the actor ($\sum d(n_j, n_i)/I_i$). As actors who can reach i become closer, on average, then the ratio becomes larger.

This ratio index, based on the average distance actors in an influence domain are to i, has the same properties as the centrality index for actor closeness (see equation (5.7)). The index weights prestige according to closeness or proximity. Note that if all actors are adjacent to n_i, then all the $d(n_j, n_i) = 1$, $I_i = g - 1$, and the average standardized distance is simply $1/(g-1)$. This gives $P_P(n_i) = 1$, the maximum value of the prestige actor proximity index. If an actor is unreachable, then $I_i = 0$, and $P_P(n_i) = 0$. Thus, the limits of this index are 0 and 1, and the magnitude of the index reflects how proximate an actor is from the set of actors as a whole. Similar indices were proposed by Mackenzie (1966a) and Arney (1973).

One could easily take the variance of the $\{P_P(n_i)\}$ to obtain a group-level prestige index based on proximity. In addition, the average of the actor-level indices can be used to summarize the set of actors as a whole. The average is proportional to the average of the reciprocals of the average distances to the actors. These two group-level indices are

$$\overline{P}_P = \sum_{i=1}^{g} \frac{P_P(n_i)}{g}$$ (5.26)

and

$$S_P^2 = \sum_{i=1}^{g} \frac{(P_P(n_i) - \overline{P}_P)^2}{g}.$$ (5.27)

The average will be between 0 and 1. It equals 1 in a complete directed graph, and 0 in an empty directed graph. The variance will be positive, and measures how much heterogeneity is present in the set of actors, with respect to proximity.

Another index based on proximity was proposed by Harary (1959c), who considered not only the prestige of each actor (which he referred to as *status*, defined as the total distance of actor i to all other actors) but also the *contrastatus* of an actor (defined as the total distance to

n_i of all other actors, not just those in the influence domain). In our terminology, these quantities are $\sum_j d(n_i, n_j)$ (on which the closeness indices for centrality are based) and the sum $\sum_j d(n_j, n_i)$ (which, as just mentioned, is key to the proximity indices for prestige). Using these terms, status (for Harary) is synonymous with actor-level closeness centrality, while contrastatus is similar to actor-level proximity prestige. Harary defines the *net status* of an actor as the difference between these two sums. The idea of constructing an index for prestige that is a difference of two simpler indices was first suggested by Zeleny (1940a, 1940b, 1941, 1960). Zeleny's *sociation index* is the difference of the average of the overall "intensity" of ties in the group (measured by the density of ties in the sociomatrix if the relation is dichotomous) and the number of choices made by actor i. Refinements of this idea generate both a social status index and a social adjustment index, measured at the level of the individual actor.

These actor and group-level prestige indices based on proximity or graph distances to each actor can be useful. Actors are judged to be prestigious based on how close or proximate the other actors in the set of actors are to them. However, one should simultaneously consider the prestige of the actors that are proximate to the actor under study. If many prestigious actors "choose" an actor, the actor should be judged more prestigious than an actor who is "chosen" only by peripheral actors. Thus, one should "weight" the distances used in the proximity indices by measures of the prestige of the actors in the influence domain. Seeley (1949) was the first to realize this; using children and friendship as the network actors and relation under study, he states:

> How should we represent each ... child's popularity, as shown by the choices, weighting those choices according to the "popularity" of the source-of-choice child? (page 234)

To answer this question, we turn to yet another class of prestige indices.

⊗**Status or Rank Prestige.** Let us now consider a method to measure the prestige of the actors in a set of actors based on their status or rank within the set of actors. We have described several prestige measures that look at indegrees and distance, but none of these reflects the prominence of the individual actors who are doing the "choosing." We need to combine the numbers of direct "choices" or distances to a specific actor, with the status or rank of the actors involved. If one's influence domain is full of prestigious actors, one's prestige should also be high. If, however, an actor's domain contains only peripheral, or marginally important, actors, then the rank of this actor should be low.

To quantify this idea requires some sophisticated mathematics. An actor's rank depends on the ranks of those who do the choosing; but note that the ranks of those who are choosing depend on the ranks of the actors who choose them, and so on. As Seeley (1949) goes on to state:

> ... both "source" and "target" children are the same children, [so] we seem to be, and indeed we are, involved in an "infinite regress": [*i*'s status] is a function of the [status] of those who choose him; and their [status] is a function of those who choose them, and so *ad infinitum*. (pages 234–235)

Seeley (1949) was the first to propose a solution to this problem. His idea and solution was also discussed by Katz (1953), Hubbell (1965), Taylor (1969), Bonacich (1972a, 1972b, 1987), Coleman (1973), Burt (1982), Mizruchi, Mariolis, Schwartz, and Mintz (1986), and Tam (1989). We discuss this line of research here. We first want to note that researchers usually refer to the property under study as "status" (or even "power"); however, because of the use of this term in the relational analysis of social networks using role algebras (see Part IV), we have chosen to use the term "rank" as a synonym for "status." Thus, actors will be said to be prestigious with respect to their rank within the set of actors if they have large values on the measures described below.

The simplest way to present the solution to this "infinite regress" situation is first to define $P_R(n_i)$ as the actor-level rank prestige measure for actor i within the set of actors. The theory behind prestige as rank states that an actor's rank is a function of the ranks of the actors who choose the actor. Thus, if we take the ith column of the sociomatrix, which contains entries indicating which actors choose n_i, we can multiply these entries by the ranks of the other actors in the set of actors to obtain a linear combination measuring the rank of n_i:

$$P_R(n_i) = x_{1i}P_R(n_1) + x_{2i}P_R(n_2) + \cdots + x_{gi}P_R(n_g). \qquad (5.28)$$

For example, if n_2 is chosen by n_5 and n_7, so that $x_{52} = x_{72} = 1$ and all the other $g - 2$ entries in the second row of the sociomatrix are 0, then the rank index for this actor is defined as $P_R(n_2) = P_R(n_5) + P_R(n_7)$. In this example, if actors n_5 and n_7 are of high rank, so will be n_2. An actor's rank increases if the actor receives choices from high-ranking actors.

Thus, mathematically, we have g equations (5.28), all of which depend on all the indices themselves, the $\{P_R(n_i)\}$. So, we have a system of g linear equations with g unknowns. If we take the entire sociomatrix, $\mathbf{X}$, and put the set of rank indices into a vector $\boldsymbol{p} = (P_R(n_1), P_R(n_2), \ldots, P_R(n_g))'$, we can easily write this system of equations as

$$\boldsymbol{p} = \mathbf{X}'\boldsymbol{p}. \tag{5.29}$$

Or, rearranging terms, we obtain $(\mathbf{I} - \mathbf{X}')\boldsymbol{p} = \mathbf{0}$, where $\mathbf{I}$ is the identity matrix of dimension g, and $\boldsymbol{p}$ and $\mathbf{0}$ are vectors of length g.

This equation is identical to a characteristic equation (used to find the eigensystem of a matrix), in which $\boldsymbol{p}$ is an eigenvector of $\mathbf{X}'$ corresponding to an eigenvalue of 1. One solution to this system is to force $\mathbf{X}'$ to have such an eigenvalue. Thus, to solve this equation, one must put some constraints on either $\mathbf{X}'$, or on the indices themselves; otherwise, as first noted by Katz (1953), equation (5.29) has no finite solution. In fact, many authors, as we will note shortly, have worked on this problem, and all their solutions can be categorized based on the exact constraints that they place on the sociomatrix or on the system (5.29) itself.

Katz (1953) recommends that one first standardize the sociomatrix to have column sums of unity. The effect of this standardization on the system (5.29) is that the system becomes a familiar matrix characteristic equation, with a well-known solution. We also recommend Katz's normalization. Specifically, one finds the eigenvector associated with the largest eigenvalue of the standardized $\mathbf{X}'$. The first eigenvalue of the standardized $\mathbf{X}'$ will be unity (due to the constraint that the sociomatrix have unity column sums), and the eigenvector associated with this eigenvalue will be the vector of rank indices, $\boldsymbol{p}$.

As mentioned, the largest eigenvalue will be unity (if not, one has made a computation error). Call this eigenvector associated with this eigenvalue $\boldsymbol{p}_1$. Then, the elements of this vector are the actor rank prestige indices:

$$\boldsymbol{p}_1 = (P_R(n_1), P_R(n_2), \ldots, P_R(n_g))'.$$

Large rank prestige indices imply that an actor is chosen either by a few other actors who have large rank prestige, or by many others with low to moderate rank prestige. Remember that an actor's rank is a weighted sum of the ranks of those who choose the actor.

There are refinements of this normalization which we now discuss; however, we should note that such refinements are unnecessarily complicated. Katz's simple standardization discussed above, and the extracted eigenvector, are easy to interpret; more intricate refinements give no additional explanatory information. Katz (1953) also proposed that one introduce an "attenuation parameter" a to adjust for the lower "effectiveness" of longer paths in a network. He begins with the matrix $a\mathbf{X} + a^2\mathbf{X}^2 + \ldots + a^k\mathbf{X}^k + \ldots$, which is like an "attenuated number of paths between any two nodes" matrix. The system (5.29) is then modified by considering the column sums of this matrix (as we discuss below); unfortunately, the parameter a is unknown, and must be estimated (actually guessed) for a given sociomatrix.

To solve Katz's modification of the system, we must find a vector p that solves the new system of equations (which arises from the matrix sum mentioned above)

$$\{[(1/a)\mathbf{I} - \mathbf{X}']p\} = x, \tag{5.30}$$

where x is the vector of indegrees of the unstandardized $\mathbf{X}$. The difference between this modification and the original system (5.29) is the presence of the parameter a, and the fact that the system now is equated to the indegrees, rather than the zero vector. Katz recommends that the reciprocal of the attenuation parameter should be between the largest eigenvalue of the unstandardized $\mathbf{X}$, and twice this largest eigenvalue. That is, if we define λ_1 as this largest eigenvalue, then $\lambda_1 < (1/a) < 2\lambda_1$. It clearly is advantageous from a computing standpoint to choose $(1/a)$ to be equal to an integer. Given such an a and $\mathbf{X}$, a vector of rank indices can easily be computed; one need only solve the equations of the system (5.30). We refer the reader to Katz (1953) for details and an example.

Taylor (1969) reviews Katz (1953) and Harary (1959c), and concludes that one not only needs to standardize the sociomatrix to have column sums of unity, but also to have row sums of unity, thereby adjusting not only for status but also for contrastatus, as does Harary. Taylor's combined measure is derived from an eigenvector of a matrix that has both adjustments (but not the eigenvectors associated with the eigenvalues of unity, which these matrices are forced to have because of the standardizations). Since this index considers both distance to and distance from an actor, as well as the rank of an actor, it can be viewed as a combination of rank, closeness, and proximity. It should be clear that there is a variety of ways to modify systems such as (5.29).

Hubbell (1965) and Bonacich (1972a, 1972b, 1987) proposed methods for identifying cohesive subgroups of actors (see Chapter 7), and by so doing, generalized Seeley's (1949) prestige measure further. Specifically, Hubbell, in searching for an "input-output" model for "clique" detection, derives a "status score" for each actor by taking Seeley's (1949) basic equation (5.28) and adding a constant for each actor. This constant is labeled the "exogenous contribution" of each actor to its own prestige. This assumption yields a matrix equation, which, with suitable constraints on the entries of the sociomatrix (such as unity column sums), can be solved for the vector of indices. Bonacich (1972b) suggests that the prestige vector be normed by multiplying it by a single parameter (with the best choice being the largest eigenvalue). With this normalization, the vector of indices is exactly the eigenvector associated with this largest eigenvalue.

Bonacich (1987), based on his earlier research, proposed a two-parameter family of prestige measures. In addition to the attenuation parameter of Katz (1953), which Bonacich calls a dependence parameter and denotes by β, a scale parameter, α, is introduced into the system of equations. The magnitude of β reflects the degree to which an actor's prestige is a function of the prestige of the actors to whom the actor is connected. The relationship is monotonic, and the parameter can be negative. Bonacich discusses bargaining situations in which prestige (or power, as he refers to it) arises when connections are made to those who are powerless. Bonacich gives an example of an exchange network from Cook, Emerson, Gilmore, and Yamagishi (1983) that has negative dependence. The choice of α depends on the value chosen for the dependence parameter β. Katz's (1953) single parameter prestige indices take $\alpha = 1$. Mathematical details, and examples of the use of this family can be found in Bonacich (1987).

Mizruchi, Mariolis, Schwartz, and Mintz (1986) (see also Mizruchi and Bunting 1981) focus attention on Bonacich's (1972a, 1972b) measure of prestige, and show how his index can be dichotomized as follows: one part due to the amount of prestige that an actor gets from another actor ("derived" prestige), and one due to the prestige that comes back to the original actor after being initially sent to the other actor ("reflected" prestige). This partition of prestige into derived and reflected parts was first suggested by the work of Mintz and Schwartz (1981a, 1981b). The goal of this research is to identify *hubs*, those actors adjacent to many peripheral actors, and *bridges*, those adjacent to few central or prestigious actors. We regret this usage of the term "bridge," which is usually synonymous with a graph theoretic line-cut (see Chapter 4). Hubs have large reflected prestige indices, while bridges have large derived prestige indices. This partition of prestige into derived and reflected parts was first suggested by the work of Mintz and Schwartz (1981a,

1981b). We refer the reader to Mizruchi, Mariolis, Schwartz, and Mintz (1986) for substantive interpretations of hubs and bridges. And, we refer the reader to Tam (1989) for a detailed mathematical study of the relationship between this approach and the more standard actor-level prestige indices.

To our knowledge, the only network computing package that calculates these prestige indices based on rank is *GRADAP* (Sprenger and Stokman 1989). However, the indices themselves are basically the elements of an eigenvector of a matrix based on **X**. Such eigenvectors are not difficult to find, given the available statistical computing packages. We discuss this calculation in more detail in our example. Most of the more complicated indices are elements of eigenvectors of suitably standardized sociomatrices. Thus, all can be calculated using numerical analysis packages such as that provided by *IMSL* and writing short *FORTRAN* computer programs. The *IBM*-compatible personal computer package *GAUSS* (GAUSS 1988), which contains many basic matrix manipulation features, can also do these calculations.

5.3.3 A Different Example

To best understand the use of these centrality and prestige indices, let us look at the Countries Trade Network data, and illustrate the calculation of the $\{P_P(n_i)\}$ and the $\{P_R(n_i)\}$ on these data. As mentioned, we will focus on the directional basic manufactured goods trade relation. Remember that the (i, j)th entry of the sociomatrix for this trade relation is unity if country i exports basic manufacturing goods to country j. Thus, countries are central if they export to others, and countries are prestigious if they import from other countries. In other words, prestigious actors are those with many imports (or those who import from many prestigious actors).

We first calculated actor degree and closeness centralities for the twenty-four countries in this network data set. These indices are shown in Table 5.2. The $\{C'_D(n_i)\}$ for the entire group are given in the first column. Two countries, n_{14} = Liberia, and n_{20} = Syria, export no basic manufactured goods to any of the other countries, so have zero row sums, even though they do import from some of the other countries. Since both these countries have zero outdegree, the directed graph representing this relation is not strongly or unilaterally connected (it is, however, weakly connected), and we cannot calculate closeness indices for the complete group. Thus, we dropped these two countries, and recalculated degree centralities, as well as closeness centralities for this reduced, but unilat-

Table 5.2. *Centrality indices for the countries trade network (*Actor and centralization indices calculated by dropping n_{14} = Liberia and n_{20} = Syria from the actor set.)*

	With g = 24 actors	With g = 22 actors	
	$C'_D(n_i)$	$C'_D(n_i)^*$	$C'_C(n_i)^*$
Algeria	0.174	0.190	0.553
Argentina	0.565	0.619	0.724
Brazil	0.913	0.905	0.913
China	0.913	0.905	0.913
Czechoslovakia	0.913	0.905	0.913
Ecuador	0.087	0.095	0.525
Egypt	0.391	0.429	0.636
Ethiopia	0.087	0.095	0.525
Finland	0.913	0.952	0.955
Honduras	0.043	0.048	0.512
Indonesia	0.609	0.667	0.750
Israel	0.478	0.524	0.667
Japan	1.000	1.000	1.000
Liberia	0.000	—	—
Madagascar	0.043	0.048	0.500
New Zealand	0.478	0.524	0.667
Pakistan	0.565	0.524	0.667
Spain	0.957	0.952	0.955
Switzerland	1.000	1.000	1.000
Syria	0.000	—	—
Thailand	0.609	0.619	0.724
United Kingdom	0.957	0.952	0.955
United States	1.000	1.000	1.000
Yugoslavia	0.783	0.810	0.840

erally connected digraph. These indices are shown in Columns 3 and 4 of Table 5.2.

Focus your attention on the smaller set of countries, those that export (have non-zero outdegrees). There are many "central" exporting countries. In order of decreasing degree centrality (using the smaller group), we have Japan, Switzerland, and United States (all with C'_D = 1.000), Finland, Spain, United Kingdom (these three with an index of 0.952), Brazil, China, Czechoslovakia (all tied at 0.905), Yugoslavia, Indonesia, Thailand, Israel, New Zealand, Pakistan, and so forth. The smallest exporters, and hence least central on this index, are Algeria, Ecuador, Ethiopia, Honduras, and Madagascar. We have almost exactly the same ordering at the top and at the bottom with closeness centrality as with degree centrality. The more developed countries appear to be the most central actors. It is remarkable that these two sets of actor indices agree so well.

The centralization indices for the group of 22 are $C_D^* = 0.333$, and $C_C^* = 0.495$, neither of which is particularly large, reflecting the uniform spread of the indices from the United States, Japan, and Switzerland at the top, to Madagascar at the bottom. The closeness centralities are larger than the degree centralities, and have a smaller range. The variance of the outdegrees is $S_D^2 = 71.64$, rather large (note that the outdegrees have a range of 0 to 23, with a mean of 13.1), so that the variance of the normalized actor degree centralities is 0.135. The variance of the normalized actor closeness centralities is only $S_C^2 = 0.0328$, much smaller than that for the degree indices, indicating more homogeneous actor closeness centralities. This homogeneity is probably due to the fact that the density of this relation is large (0.626) so that one can get from any country to any other country in relatively few steps, giving small distances from country to country on average. We also note that most countries trade with the "biggest" countries, so that even if the smaller countries do not trade with each other, their proximity to the big countries implies that the smaller countries are never very far away from each other (with respect to paths through the digraph).

We now turn to the calculation of the prestige indices. These indices are shown in Table 5.3. Prestige for these countries and this relation is synonymous with high involvement in the importing of basic manufactured goods from other countries. The first column contains the degree prestige indices for all twenty-four countries, and the second, the proximity prestige indices. Notice that even though Liberia and Syria do not export in this group (and hence have outdegrees of zero) we are still able to calculate the proximity prestige indices.

As can be seen from equation (5.24), the standardized degree prestige indices are simply the relative indegrees, standardized by dividing by their maximum possible value, $g - 1$. Such quantities are standard output from most network computer packages. The proximity prestige indices can be calculated by first determining the $\{I_i\}$ values, the number of actors who can reach actor i, and then dividing these values by $g - 1$. This ratio is then divided by the average distances of all actors to actor i. Note that these average distances use the columns of the sociomatrix, rather than the rows (as the actor closeness indices do). In fact, if one transposes the sociomatrix, the average distances to an actor become the average distances involving the rows. Thus, the closeness centralities, which use

Table 5.3. *Prestige indices for the countries trade network*

	$P'_D(n_i)$	$P'_P(n_i)$	$P'_R(n_i)$
Algeria	0.565	0.661	0.222
Argentina	0.435	0.599	0.805
Brazil	0.478	0.619	1.000
China	0.652	0.710	0.711
Czechoslovakia	0.565	0.661	0.818
Ecuador	0.391	0.599	0.183
Egypt	0.522	0.599	0.482
Ethiopia	0.435	0.710	0.131
Finland	0.652	0.590	0.758
Honduras	0.391	0.581	0.072
Indonesia	0.609	0.599	0.617
Israel	0.435	0.599	0.682
Japan	0.739	0.767	0.680
Liberia	0.391	0.564	0.000
Madagascar	0.261	0.532	0.106
New Zealand	0.609	0.684	0.461
Pakistan	0.609	0.684	0.525
Spain	0.739	0.767	0.673
Switzerland	0.652	0.710	0.765
Syria	0.522	0.619	0.000
Thailand	0.652	0.710	0.589
United Kingdom	0.695	0.767	0.633
United States	0.826	0.799	0.644
Yugoslavia	0.652	0.710	0.680

the average distances from an actor to all other actors, calculated on the transposed sociomatrix, are exactly the average distances needed for the actor proximity prestige indices.

For the example, we note that all countries are reachable from all countries except Liberia (n_{14}) and Syria (n_{20}). Hence, the influence domain for the countries is the reduced group, giving $I_i = 21$. From equation (5.25), note that this gives us a numerator of $21/23$ for all countries.

Examining Table 5.3 we see that the degree prestige indices cover a relatively narrow range of values, from 0.261 (for Madagascar) to 0.826 (for United States). Many countries import from almost all the other countries, and thus have large degree prestige indices: Spain, Japan, United Kingdom, China, Finland, Switzerland, Thailand, and Yugoslavia. The countries with the smallest degree prestige indices (and hence, few imports) are Argentina, Ecuador, Ethiopia, Honduras, Israel, Madagascar, and Liberia. Note that the prestigious countries are similar to the most central, except Thailand and Yugoslavia are prestigious, but not terribly central (import more but export less) and Brazil and Czechoslovakia are central but not prestigious (export more but import less). The least prestigious countries are also the least central.

Column 2 of Table 5.3 gives the actor proximity prestige indices, which have a much smaller range than those based on degree; in fact, the variance of the degree prestige indices is 0.0177, and just 0.0054 for the proximity prestige indices. We have exactly the same countries at the top and at the very bottom. Note, however, that the smallest proximity indices are 0.532 (Madagascar), indicating that even Madagascar is not terribly distant from the other countries. This is probably due to the large density for this relation; most countries do import from the countries in this group. We note that the average actor degree prestige index is 0.562, while the average actor proximity prestige index is 0.660.

Lastly, we turn to the actor status or rank prestige index. We take the sociomatrix, normalize it to have column sums of unity (by dividing by the indegrees), transpose it, and calculate its eigenvalues. Note that this sociomatrix is not symmetric; hence, the standard routines for extracting eigenvalues and eigenvectors, which are designed for symmetric matrices (such as covariance and correlation matrices), cannot be used. We used a small *FORTRAN* program, which calls the *IMSL* routine *EVCRG*. This subroutine extracts eigenvalues and eigenvectors from any real-valued matrix. Such quantities can be complex-valued, so care must be taken in interpreting the output.

As mentioned, the largest eigenvalue of the relevant matrix is unity. The elements of the eigenvector associated with this eigenvalue are the rank-prestige indices. For the countries' basic manufactured goods relation, the indices for the twenty-four countries are shown in Column 3 of Table 5.3. These indices are quite different from the other prestige indices. The ordering of the countries with respect to rank prestige is Brazil, Czechoslovakia, Argentina, Switzerland, Finland, China, Israel, Yugoslavia, and then Spain, United States, and United Kingdom. The addition of Argentina and Israel to this "prestigious subset" is somewhat surprising, since these two countries have small indegrees; but remember, what is important here is not how many countries a country is adjacent to, but the prestige of these countries. Specifically, prestigious countries are those that import goods from nations who in turn import goods. Clearly, Brazil, Czechoslovakia, and Argentina are linked directly to other prestigious countries.

5.4 Comparisons and Extensions

Several authors have compared the performance of the many centrality and prestige indices discussed in this chapter, either on real or simulated data, or both. Earlier researchers, such as Stogdill (1951), concentrated on different measures of actor degrees, thus focusing attention on only one centrality index. Most notable of recent comparative research are studies by Freeman (1979), Freeman, Roeder, and Mulholland (1980), Knoke and Burt (1983), Doreian (1986), Bolland (1988), Stephenson and Zelen (1989), and Friedkin (1991). We now review these comparisons.

The first, extensive study of centrality indices was undertaken by Freeman (1979). Freeman lists all thirty-four possible graphs with $g = 5$ nodes (itemized by Uhlenbeck and Ford 1962), and compares actor- and group-level degree, closeness, and betweenness centrality measures across the graphs. In brief, Freeman demonstrated that the betweenness indices best "captured" the essence of the important actors in the graphs. As we have mentioned throughout this chapter, closeness centrality indices could not be computed for disconnected graphs, and the star graph always attained the largest centralization score, while the circle graph attained the smallest centralization. Other, less obvious findings include:

- The three measures of centrality under review differed noticeably in their rankings of the thirty-four graphs.
- The range of variation in the actor centrality and group centralization scores is greatest for betweenness; that is, betweenness centralities generate the largest actor variances.
- The range of variation in the actor centrality and group centralization scores is least for degree; that is, degree centralities appear to generate the smallest actor variances.

Further, the more theoretical nature of the betweenness indices leads Freeman to recommend their useage over the other two.

Freeman, Roeder, and Mulholland (1980) replicated the MIT experiments, conducted by Bavelas (1950), Smith (1950), and Leavitt (1951), designed to study the effects of the structure of a network on problem solving, perception of leadership, and personal satisfaction (the three variables measured for each actor). Freeman, Roeder, and Mulholland sought to determine which of the three centrality indices (degree, closeness, and betweenness) was most relevant to the same tasks undertaken by the same kinds of networks studied in the earlier experiments. Freeman, Roeder, and Mulholland used four different graphs, all with $g = 5$, and found that betweenness indices best measured which actor in the set of actors was viewed most frequently as a leader. Both the degree and betweenness indices were important indicators of group performance (with respect to efficiency of problem solving). However, the closeness index (based on graph distance) was not even "vaguely related to experimental results" (Freeman, Roeder, and Mulholland 1980).

Knoke and Burt (1983), as part of their classic paper distinguishing between centrality and prestige, studied five centrality indices and five prestige indices. These indices were calculated for the Galesburg, Illinois, physician network studied by Coleman, Katz, and Menzel (1966) to identify diffusion of a medical innovation. Within each set of five indices, two were based on degree (see equation (5.3)), one on closeness (equation (5.8)), and one on either betweenness (for centrality — equation (5.12)) or rank (for prestige — equation (5.28)). The five centrality actor-level indices were calculated on a symmetrized version of the data (so that the graph was nondirected) and the five prestige indices, for the actual data. All these indices are output from the computer program *STRUCTURE* (Burt 1989). For the Galesburg network, the correlations among the centrality and among the prestige indices were high, as expected. In addition, the centrality and prestige indices were also associated. This strong association, which Knoke and Burt (1983) study further by using additional actor attributes (such as the date that the medical innovation was adopted) is described by these researchers as a unique feature of the network under study. It is thus difficult to extend these findings to general network data.

Doreian (1986) reviewed the work of Katz (1953), Harary (1959c), and Hubbell (1965), and focused on measures of "relative standing" of the actors in small networks. He criticized prestige indices based on degree or rank as being arbitrary (which is certainly true of Katz's and Hubbell's prestige indices, since there is not natural choice for scaling or attenuation parameters). Doreian advocated the use of an "iterated Hubbell" index, which converges to a standardized eigenvector of a function of a matrix derived from the sociomatrix. The advantage of this index is that it produces prestige measures that correspond well to the regular equivalences of the actors in the network (see White and Reitz 1983; and Chapter 12).

Bolland (1988) studied four centrality measures: degree, closeness, betweenness, and a new measure, "continuing flow," which combines degree and closeness. Bolland's continuing flow index examines all paths of (at most) a fixed length and counts how many of these paths originate with the *i*th actor. This count is then standardized, and the fixed length allowed to get as large as possible. Unlike the closeness and betweenness indices, this index considers all paths of any length, not just geodesics.

Bolland examined a network data set giving influence relationships among forty people involved in educational policy-making in Chillicothe, Ohio (see Bolland 1985). In addition to reporting extensive data analyses of this network, he conducted a Monte Carlo analysis by adding random and systematic variation to the network to obtain a number of "noisy" networks. These simulated networks were similar, but not exactly equal to, the original data. Each noisy network was replicated one hundred times to study the validity, robustness, and sensitivity of each of the four centrality indices.

Bolland's findings supported the earlier work of Freeman (1979). Specifically, degree-based measures of centrality are sensitive to small changes in network structure. Betweenness-based measures of centrality are useful and capable of capturing small changes in the network, but are error-prone. Closeness measures are much too sensitive to network change. Lastly, Bolland found the continuing flow index to be relatively insensitive to systematic variation, and useful in most circumstances. He recommends the use of both betweenness and continuing flow indices in practice.

Stephenson and Zelen (1989) compared their information centrality index to the other centrality indices using two data sets — the social network of forty AIDS patients mentioned earlier and a Gelada baboon colony of $g = 12$ animals, before and after the introduction of two additional group members. These latter data, gathered by Dunbar and Dunbar (1975), are analyzed longitudinally by Stephenson (1989). Stephenson and Zelen conducted the only comparison of the degree, closeness, and betweenness centrality measures, with the newer information index. There are several differences between information centrality indices and betweenness centrality indices. Specifically, information indices are much more "continuous" than those based on betweenness, which really are counts, rather than continuous-valued quantities. Thus, information indices can be more sensitive to slight arc changes than betweenness indices. Peripheral actors do not have much effect on the computed values of betweenness indices, since these actors rarely lie on geodesics; however, such actors can have significant effects in a network (especially in networks modeling disease transmission). Information indices are much more likely to measure the impact of these peripheral actors. Degree centrality indices have a limited ability to distinguish among actors with differing centrality. The range of possible values for a degree-based index is quite small, so that such indices are not very sensitive.

Friedkin (1991) offers a different theoretical foundation for the commonly used centrality measures based on a social influence process. He derives degree, closeness, and betweenness centrality measures by assuming that the network effects model (which basically is an application of an autoregressive model for spatially distributed actors or units) is appropriate. This model has been proposed for use in network analysis by Erbring and Young (1979), Doreian (1981), Burt (1987), and Friedkin and Johnsen (1990). The three measures are

(i) Total effects centrality — the total relative effect of an actor on the other actors in the network

(ii) Immediate effects centrality — the rapidity with which an actor's total effects are realized

(iii) Mediative effects centrality — the extent to which particular actors have a role in transmitting the total effects of other actors

Friedkin shows that these measures arise as "side effects" of the network process model of social influence. As can be seen by their definitions, they are congruent with the degree, closeness, and betweenness actor-centrality indices discussed here. Friedkin's work can be extended to directional relations, including real-valued ties, due to the measurement generality of the social process model. Such generalizations would yield new, theoretical rationales for prestige measures.

To gain a better understanding about how important a specific actor is to a network, one can take an actor with a large betweenness index, and drop it from the network (allowing this actor to serve as a "cutpoint"). Counting the number of components generated by this deletion will give an indication of how much "betweenness" this actor exerts over the network. Truly central actors will force many disconnected components to arise. Stephenson (1989) does this for the AIDS network, and finds that four of the actors in this network, which have large betweenness indices, do not "break up" the network when deleted. Betweenness is just one — of many — manifestations of the primary centrality concept. One should not utilize any single centrality measure. Each has its virtues and utility.

We should note that there is a variety of actor- and group-level degree-based indices that can be calculated and examined when more than one relation is measured. For example, one can study how likely it is that an actor chooses another actor on more than one relation. Such an index uses the quantities $x_{ij}(m) = 1$ if at least m of the ties $x_{ij1}, x_{ij2}, \ldots, x_{ijR}$ are equal to 1. An actor-level multiplex index can be calculated by averaging the quantities just over j. A group-level *multiplex index* can be calculated from these quantities, simply by averaging them over all i and j. An index based on network cohesion (for each relation) can be based on the number of dyads that are mutual.

With multirelational data, we suggest that the indices described in this chapter be calculated for *each* relation. We do not recommend (as some authors have, such as Knoke and Burt 1983) that the relations be aggregated into a single sociomatrix, unless there are strong substantive reasons for such aggregations (such as two measures of friendship combined into a single positive affect relation). Further multirelational analyses, designed to measure how similar actors are across relations and how associated the relations are, are discussed in Chapter 16.

6
Structural Balance and Transitivity

One of the most important concepts to emerge from the early days of social network analysis was *balance theory*. The early focus in balance theory was on the cognition or awareness of sociometric relations, usually positive and negative affect relations such as friendship, liking, or disliking, from the perspective of an individual.

The idea of balance arose in Fritz Heider's (1946) study of an individual's cognition or perception of social situations. Heider focused on a single individual and was concerned about how this individual's attitudes or opinions coincided with the attitudes or opinions of other "entities" or people. The entities could be not only people, but also objects or statements for which one might have opinions. He considered ties, which were signed, among a pair or a triple of entities. Specifically, Heider (1946) states:

> In the case of two entities, a balanced state exists if the [ties] between them [are] positive (or negative) in all aspects. ... In the case of three entities, a balanced state exists if all three possible [ties] are positive in all respects, or if two are negative, and one positive. (page 110)

For example, we can consider two individuals, focusing on one of them as primary, and their opinions about a statement, such as "We must protect the environment." If both actors are friends, then they should react similarly to this statement — either both should oppose the statement (and hence, both have a negative opinion about it) or both should favor it (and have positive opinions). If either of these holds, there is balance, and the primary individual perceives this. If neither result holds, there is no balance, and the primary individual perceives this cognitive dissonance. With respect to Heider's theory, the opinions are viewed as ties (linking the actor to the statement), which must be consistent (in sign) with the positive friendship tie between the two individuals.

Heider's cognitive balance was soon generalized to *structural balance*, which focuses not on the single individual, but on a set of people or a group. With a group, one must consider all people, one at a time. A group is structurally balanced, if, when two people like each other (a "+" tie in the network), then they are consistent in their evaluation of all other people. If *i* and *j* "like" each other, then they both either "like" or "dislike" the same other people, and if *i* and *j* dislike each other, then they disagree in their evaluation of all other people. As we will see, in a structurally balanced group, the people can be partitioned into two subsets in such a way that within subsets all ties are positive and between all are negative.

Graph theory was used by Harary (1953, 1955b) and Cartwright and Harary (1956; see also 1979) to mathematically formalize Heider's concepts and to quantify the character of balanced network structures. As we will discuss, the notion of a *graph cycle* (defined in Chapter 4) becomes crucial in determining how balanced a particular structure is.

Structural balance has been used in many applications, including the study of international relations among nations, where the relations measured are usually political alliances during times of warfare (Young 1971; Brown 1979). It has also been used to study politicians or community elites as actors with positive and negative cooperation as relations (Laumann and Pappi 1973; Knoke 1990). The goal in these studies is to examine the social structure, and to look for how much "tension" is present, caused by conflicting negative and positive relationships among subsets of actors. Balance theory is discussed in most substantively based graph theory texts — for example, see Harary, Norman, and Cartwright (1965), Leik and Meeker (1975), Roberts (1978), and Hage and Harary (1983, 1991). Fritz Heider (1944, 1946, 1958; see also the historical review paper of 1979), and later Newcomb (1953), Abelson and Rosenberg (1958), and Zajonc (1960, 1968), were the first theorists to consider whether various arrangements within subgroups of individuals were "balanced" with respect to positive and negative affect. Numerous authors in sociology, social psychology, and anthropology, for example, Evans-Pritchard (1929), Homans (1950), Lévi-Strauss (1949), and Radcliffe-Brown (1940), were studying similar ideas in a range of contexts. Heider, in his review paper of 1979, notes that Wertheimer (1923), as well as Spinoza were quite influential in his thinking about phenomenal causality and interpersonal relations, which allowed him to postulate the concepts of cognitive balance.

As we discuss in this chapter, this early research led to the first substantive empirical and model-based clustering methods for social network data (see Chapter 7). Structural balance (and its many generalizations, particularly transitivity) will be discussed in this chapter. These ideas have had a deep and long-lasting impact on social network methodology. Many of the topics discussed in Chapters 7, 10, and 14 were developed (at least in part) to study whether subgraphs are balanced or triads are transitive. Thus, we will return to balance and transitivity frequently throughout this book.

So, the study of structural balance in a social network, consisting of a relation measured for a set of actors, requires that the ties have a sign or a valence. As Heider stated, we must be able to distinguish positives from negatives. The network must be representable as a signed graph or signed digraph. We begin with this assumption.

6.1 Structural Balance

A signed graph allows the lines to carry either positive or negative signs. The lines can be coded with two signs: either "+" or "−". For example, if the relation under study is "liking," then a "+" implies i and j like each other, a "−" implies i and j dislike each other. The absence of a line implies neither liking nor disliking.

If one has a signed digraph, quantifying a directional relation, then the arc linking i to j is either a "+" or a "−", and is distinct from the arc linking j to i. This distinction forces us to consider balance for graphs and directed graphs separately. In Figure 4.22, we gave an example of a signed directed graph, using the directional relation of friendship among children, so that, for example, a "+" attached to an arc indicated a friend, and a "−", an enemy. Note that because the relation is directional, i's feelings toward j may differ from j's feelings toward i.

We will now describe structural balance, first for nondirectional signed relations, and then for directional signed relations. We then give a variety of theorems (actually definitions derived from the formal definition of balance) that allow us to characterize the balance properties of specific relations. This discussion will then be generalized to clusterability, and later to transitivity. The generalizations of structural balance do not necessarily have to be applied to signed relations. Fortunately, the tenets of transitivity are relevant to any relation. Thus, we will relax the restriction to signed relations later in this chapter.

Before we start, let us look at a generic *signed relation*. The relation must be capable of expressing both positive and negative attitudes or sentiments. The class of affective relations certainly has this property: like and dislike can both be measured, as can friends and enemies, praise and blame, love and hate, and so forth. A relation must be representable as a signed graph or digraph in order to be studied using ideas of balance: positive ties as well as negative ties must be possible. The negative ties are usually viewed as the antonyms of the positive ones. One can treat the positive and negative ties separately and suppose that two distinct (but certainly associated) relations are measured. The classic network data set collected by Sampson (1968) contains four pairs of positive/negative relations: esteem/disesteem, like/dislike, praise/blame, and influence/negative influence. Notice how the negative aspect of each relation is the antonym or opposite of the positive, not simply its absence.

Graph theorists (such as Harary 1957) note that a signed graph or signed digraph must satisfy a principle of *antithetical duality*: the dual (or opposite or antonym) of signed graph changes the signs of the lines from "+" to "−" or "−" to "+". When this is applied twice to a line or arc, the sign of the original line or arc is obtained. Thus, the opposite of a negative tie is a positive tie. We can express this "arithmetic" as: $(-)(-) = (+)$ and, $(+)(+) = (+)$. For now, we will assume that the relation under study satisfies this principle. This implies that relations such as "communicates with" or "interacts with," which are not signed and thus have no obvious dual, cannot be studied with balance theory.

6.1.1 Signed Nondirectional Relations

Heider theorized about the cognition of social relationships. Such cognitive perceptions and the consistency of attitudes have played an important role in early social psychological theories (see, for example, Abelson, Aronson, McGuire, Newcomb, Rosenberg, and Tannenbaum 1968). Specifically, he studied a single person, which he denoted by a P, for the *person*, and another individual, denoted by O for the *other*. He considered how the positive or negative attitude of the primary person toward an entity or object (X) was consistent with the attitude of the other person toward the object. Sometimes, a third person (denoted by Q) can be the object, rather than a non-living entity.

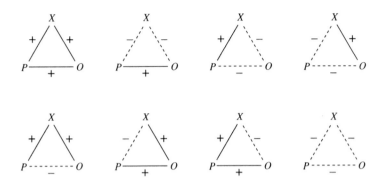

Fig. 6.1. The eight possible *P-O-X* triples

Let us assume that this attitude is captured by a signed, nondirectional relation (which will usually be affective), so that the line connecting *P* with *X*, measuring *P*'s attitude about the object, carries either a "+" if the attitude is, say, positive affect, or a "−" if the attitude is negative (note that we assume that *P* has an attitude toward the object, so that the line will not be absent). We should note that the object under consideration could be almost anything that the two people can have an opinion about: a situation, a movie, a person, a philosophy, and so forth.

Triples. For simplicity throughout this chapter, we will always refer to the third party as an object *X*, but note that this third party can indeed be another person. If the third party is an actor, *Q*, one typically ignores the attitudes of *Q* toward *P* and *O*.

To be a little more concrete, we will use the relation like/dislike throughout this chapter. Taking the two actors and the object (a *P-O-X* triple), there are eight possible mathematical representations or graphs for this triple of entities, which are shown in Figure 6.1. A solid line in the figure denotes a positive attitude (liking), while a dashed line denotes a negative attitude (disliking). The four graphs at the top of Figure 6.1 and the four graphs at the bottom of Figure 6.1 are usually referred to as *P-O-X triples*. In these figures, both actors are allowed to express their attitude toward the object, and we can also record the attitude (like or dislike for our example) toward each other, which is assumed to be common to both.

In order to characterize the graphs in Figure 6.1, we focus on the cycles present. Recall the definition of a cycle, given in Chapter 4. For a signed relation, we can define the *sign of a cycle* as the product of the signs of the lines constituting the cycle. The multiplication rules for this product are discussed in Chapter 4, as well. Thus, cycles can be either positive or negative. The sign of a cycle is a crucial concept when considering whether a graph is balanced.

Examine the four triples in the top row of the figure. These triples and the associated lines are special. Each graph is a cycle of length 3 and each has either 0 or 2 negative lines. If we consider the signs of the lines, the four graphs all have cycle sign of "+". A cycle will always have a positive sign if there is an even number of negative lines. The four graphs at the bottom of the figure also contain cycles, but not one of these four has an even number of negative lines. The products of the signs for the cycles in these four graphs are all "−": either $(+)(+)(-)$ for the first three, or $(-)(-)(-)$ for the last one. Thus, these eight graphs fall naturally into two subsets: one set containing the four graphs with positive cycles, and one set containing the four graphs with negative cycles.

The most important consideration is how to interpret any one of these graphs. First, take the graph at the upper left of Figure 6.1 which has three positive lines. Both actors P and O are positive about the object, and positive about each other. Such agreement is likely to be "pleasing" to the actors. The second graph in the top row also shows agreement among the actors: both have a negative opinion about the object, but possess positive attitudes about each other. The last two graphs in the first row display disagreement about the object: one actor is positive while the other is negative. Such conflict is likely to be uncomfortable to the actors, and consequently, one might expect negative attitudes toward each other, as indicated by the dashed line betwen P and O in these two graphs. These four graphs are to be expected if agreement about an object produces a positive feeling between the people, while a disagreement gives a negative feeling. This positive sentiment between people produces agreement. Negative sentiment leads to disagreement (see Johnsen 1985, 1986).

Compare these four graphs at the top with the four at the bottom. In all of the graphs at the bottom of the figure, the expected does not arise. Specifically in these four graphs, if the two nodes have lines with the same sign to the object, then the actors represented by the nodes have a negative attitude toward each other (the first and fourth graphs). And if the two nodes have lines with different signs to the object, the actors have a positive attitude toward each other (the second and third graphs). Clearly, these four graphs are strange. The four graphs at the top could imply that the two actors involved would work well together, without internal tension, while the four at the bottom imply the opposite. If the object is a person, rather than an object, then the four graphs at the top of Figure 6.1 represent affective relational structures which minimize tension within the triple.

Balance. If all the cycles in a graph of length 3 have positive signs, the graph is balanced. Sociologists and social psychologists have used the term "structural balance" to refer to groups of people and affective relations that substantively are "pleasing" or lack intrapersonal psychological "tension." We will formally define a triple of nodes, and the lines between them, as *balanced* if the cycle has a positive sign. Thus, the four graphs at the top of Figure 6.1 are all balanced and, hence, are permissible by structural balance, while the four at the bottom are not. To extend this definition to a graph with more than three nodes requires a statement about all possible cycles in the graph. One must also consider cycles of any size, not just triples, since structural balance applies to any subset of nodes.

The signed graph need not be complete, so that some lines may be absent. As an example, consider a signed graph with $g = 7$ nodes, as shown in Figure 6.2. This graph has five positive lines and five negative lines present. Only ten of the possible twenty-one lines are present. If we look for cycles, we find four of length 3, and two of length 4. The cycles are: $n_1 n_2 n_4 n_1$, $n_1 n_3 n_4 n_1$, $n_4 n_5 n_6 n_4$, $n_5 n_6 n_7 n_5$, and $n_1 n_2 n_4 n_3 n_1$, $n_4 n_5 n_6 n_7 n_4$. Of the six, all but one has a positive sign. The cycle $n_5 n_6 n_7 n_5$ has a negative sign, since it contains just single "−". Remember that for balance, the negative lines in a cycle must be even in number. One would conclude that because of this single negative cycle, the entire graph is not balanced. This census of all cycles in a signed graph gives us the following general definition of a balanced signed graph, directly from Cartwright and Harary (1956):

Definition 6.1 *A signed graph is balanced if and only if all cycles have positive signs.*

This definition can also be applied to valued graphs with lines valued at $+1$, -1, and 0. That is, "zero"-valued ties have no sign; one considers only the cycles in the graph involving lines with signs.

We note that it is possible for a graph (or digraph) to be neither balanced nor unbalanced. If a graph contains no cycles, it can be

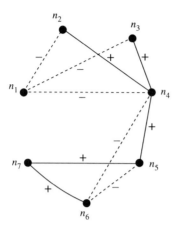

Fig. 6.2. An unbalanced signed graph

neither balanced nor unbalanced. Researchers typically use the phrase "vacuously balanced" to refer to graphs and digraphs that are neither balanced nor unbalanced — neither fish nor fowl. Later in this chapter we will discuss vacuously balanced graphs and digraphs at greater length.

A very important consequence of this definition, proved by Harary (1953, 1955b), and a result that is quite useful in classification of actors to subsets, is that if a signed graph is balanced, then one can partition the nodes into two subsets in such a way that only positive lines join nodes within subsets, and negative lines join nodes between subsets. One of these subsets may be empty (that is, contain no nodes). Another consequence (see Harary, Norman, and Cartwright 1965) is that all paths connecting any two nodes must all have the same sign (where the sign of a path is defined as the product of the signs attached to the lines in the path).

Consider the example in Figure 6.3, which is a balanced signed graph. There are four cycles — one of length 4 and three of length 3 — and all have positive signs). For this graph with six nodes, we can partition the nodes into the two subsets $\{n_2, n_3, n_4, n_5\}$ and $\{n_1, n_6\}$ so that all the positive lines in the subgraph fall among the nodes in the first subset, and all negative lines occur between nodes in different sets. This partition for balanced structures is quite important.

This evolution in thinking about structural balance from triples to entire graphs leads to the *clusterability* of actors. This highlights an

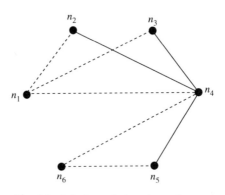

Fig. 6.3. A balanced signed graph

important generalization of this idea first mentioned by Heider: that balanced triples have actor partitions for which positive ties occur within and negative between. We will return to clusterability as a generalization of structural balance later in this chapter.

6.1.2 Signed Directional Relations

Suppose that the relation under investigation is directional, so that the relevant representation is a signed digraph. To generalize balance to such structures requires some care, since there are a number of ways to examine cycles in directed graphs. Remember from Chapter 4 that a cycle in a digraph requires all arcs to be "pointed in the same direction." We will actually relax our definition of balance so that with digraphs, we do not need cycles in order to consider the balance of a structure.

To illustrate, consider the triple shown in Figure 6.4, which has one negative arc, and two positive arcs. This digraph does not contain a cycle, since the arc from n_1 to n_2 is oriented in the wrong direction (but we can still consider whether or not it is balanced). Reversing the direction of this arc would give us a digraph with a cycle of length 3, $n_1 n_3 n_2 n_1$, with a negative sign, and hence (using the definition of balance given for nondirectional relations) the digraph appears to be an unbalanced structure.

As we define below, the digraph shown in Figure 6.4 is actually unbalanced. Note that there is clear "tension" in unbalanced structures such as this one. Person 1 "likes" person 3 as well as person 2, but this

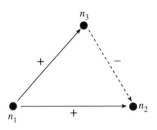

Fig. 6.4. An unbalanced signed digraph

friend n_3 "dislikes" person 2 — clearly, a tension producer for person 1, who might realize that this friendliness with person 2 is not consistent with the friend n_3's unfriendliness with person 2.

To formally define balance in signed digraphs, we consider not paths and cycles, but *semipaths* and *semicycles*. As defined in Chapter 4, we ignore the directions of the arcs, and define a semipath as a sequence of nodes and arcs, beginning and ending with nodes in such a way that a particular arc in the semipath goes from either the previous node to the next node, or vice versa. For an example, refer to Figure 6.4. The sequence $n_2 n_1 n_3$, along with the arcs between these nodes, is a semipath, but not a path, since the arc between n_2 and n_1 goes not from n_2 to n_1, but from n_1 to n_2. We do not care about the direction of the arc between any two nodes adjacent to each other in the semipath, but only that an arc exists. A semicycle is a semipath in which all nodes are distinct, and the first and last nodes are identical. A cycle is a semicycle in which the arcs connect the ith node to the $(i + 1)$st node. That is, the ith node in the semicycle is adjacent to the $(i + 1)$st. In our figure, the sequence $n_2 n_1 n_3 n_2$ is a semicycle. We define the sign of a semicycle as the product of the signs attached to the arcs making up the semicycle. Thus, the sign for the semicycle $n_2 n_1 n_3 n_2$ in Figure 6.4 is $(+)(-)(+) = (-)$.

With these definitions, we can state:

Definition 6.2 *A signed digraph is balanced if and only if all semi-cycles have positive signs.*

In a balanced signed digraph, all semicycles must have an even number of negative signs attached to the arcs. Thus, just as with balance for a signed graph, one must check the signs of all semicycles (rather than cycles). Every semicycle, regardless of its length, must be checked, and all semicycle signs must be positive. The semicycle in Figure 6.4, $n_2n_1n_3n_2$, has a sign "−", so this digraph is not balanced.

We should note that there is a very comprehensive set theoretic approach to structural balance given by Flament (1963), similar to Freeman's (1989) representation for social network data discussed at the end of Chapter 3.

6.1.3 ○Checking for Balance

A single unbalanced cycle or semicycle insures that the graph or digraph is not balanced. So, it is natural to consider how many cycles or semicycles in a graph or digraph do not have positive signs. From this consideration, one can develop graph-level indices measuring the amount of unbalance in a structure. We turn to this topic in the next few paragraphs.

Before doing so, let us think about a method to determine whether a graph or digraph is balanced. One needs to look at all cycles or semicycles of length 3, 4, and so forth to check for balance. All must have positive signs.

If we start with the sociomatrix for a graph, then one can show that if the graph is balanced, then the entries along the diagonal of the sociomatrix raised to a power p, $\mathbf{X}^p$, must all be non-negative for all powers $p = 1, 2, \ldots, g$. Cycles have a maximum length of g, so we need not raise the sociomatrix to any power greater than g.

We demonstrate this fact in Table 6.1 for the balanced graph in Figure 6.3. We note that the numbers on the diagonals of the power sociomatrices for balanced graphs are the sums of the signs of closed walks, with lengths equal to the powers of the respective matrices. Thus, for example, a diagonal entry of $\mathbf{X}^3$, $x_{ii}^{[3]}$, is the sums of signs of closed walks of length 3, starting and ending with n_i. Since the graph is balanced, this entry must be positive. As can be seen from the table, all diagonal entries of all the power matrices are positive; therefore, the graph is balanced.

Checking for balance using sociomatrix powers for a directed graph is a bit more complicated. Rather than give all the details here, we refer the reader to Harary, Norman, and Cartwright (1965), pages 352–355. Specifically, one needs to replace the entries in the sociomatrix with symbols, reflecting the signs of the arcs. If both $n_i \rightarrow n_j$ and $n_j \rightarrow n_i$ are present, then this circumstance is taken into account. A symmetric valency matrix is constructed which has entries of o, p, n, and a, depending on the sign of the sum of $x_{ij} + x_{ji}$. This valency matrix is

Table 6.1. *Powers of a sociomatrix of a signed graph, to demonstrate cycle signs, and hence, balance*

X

	n_1	n_2	n_3	n_4	n_5	n_6
n_1	0	-1	-1	-1	0	0
n_2	-1	0	0	1	0	0
n_3	-1	0	0	1	0	0
n_4	-1	1	1	0	1	-1
n_5	0	0	0	1	0	-1
n_6	0	0	0	-1	-1	0

X^2

	n_1	n_2	n_3	n_4	n_5	n_6
n_1	3	-1	-1	-2	-1	1
n_2	-1	2	2	1	1	-1
n_3	-1	2	2	1	1	-1
n_4	-2	1	1	5	1	-1
n_5	-1	1	1	1	2	-1
n_6	1	-1	-1	-1	-1	2

X^3

	n_1	n_2	n_3	n_4	n_5	n_6
n_1	4	-5	-5	-7	-3	3
n_2	-5	2	2	7	2	-2
n_3	-5	2	2	7	2	-2
n_4	-7	7	7	6	6	-6
n_5	-3	2	2	6	2	-3
n_6	3	-2	-2	-6	-3	2

X^4

	n_1	n_2	n_3	n_4	n_5	n_6
n_1	17	-11	-11	-20	-10	10
n_2	-11	12	12	13	9	-9
n_3	-11	12	12	13	9	-9
n_4	-20	13	13	33	12	-12
n_5	-10	9	9	12	9	-8
n_6	10	-9	-9	-12	-8	9

X^5

	n_1	n_2	n_3	n_4	n_5	n_6
n_1	42	-37	-37	-59	-30	30
n_2	-37	24	24	53	22	-22
n_3	-37	24	24	53	22	-22
n_4	-59	53	53	70	45	-45
n_5	-30	22	22	45	20	-21
n_6	30	-22	-22	-45	-21	20

X^6

	n_1	n_2	n_3	n_4	n_5	n_6
n_1	133	-101	-101	-176	-89	89
n_2	-101	90	90	129	75	75
n_3	-101	90	90	129	75	75
n_4	-176	129	129	255	115	-115
n_5	-89	75	75	16	66	-65
n_6	89	-75	-75	-115	-65	66

then raised to various powers, by using a special set of algebraic rules that govern the addition and multiplication of its entries. These rules are given in Harary, Norman, and Cartrwright (1965, page 354). The diagonal entries of the valency matrix raised to all powers $1, 2, \ldots, g$ must be all p or o for the graph to be balanced. Examples can be found in Harary, Norman, and Cartwright (1965).

6.1.4 An Index for Balance

To quantify how "unbalanced" an unbalanced graph or digraph is, one first must count the number of cycles (for a graph) or the number of semicycles (for a digraph) that have negative signs. An index such as this is usually referred to as a *cycle index for balance*. One can then compare this to the total number of cycles or semicycles present to construct an index. This index takes on values between 0 (completely unbalanced) to 1 (balanced).

We define PC as the number of positive (semi)cycles in a (di)graph, and TC as the total number of (semi)cycles. The index for unbalancedness is then PC/TC. Cycle indices can be calculated using matrices, as discussed by Cartwright and Gleason (1966). Variants on this index (see Harary 1959a; Henley, Horsfall, and De Soto 1969; Norman and Roberts 1972a, 1972b; Roberts 1978) involve weighting the components of this ratio index by using the length of the (semi)cycles.

Harary (1959a, 1960) considers a *line index for balance* equal to the number of signs attached to lines or arcs whose signs must be changed in order for the graph or digraph to become balanced. This number is exactly equal to the number of lines or arcs that must be removed in order for the graph or digraph to become balanced. Other measures of balance are discussed at length in Taylor (1970).

6.1.5 Summary

Structural balance has been quite important in sociology, social psychology, and anthropology. References to its use in practice and theory abound — Taylor (1970), who presents both a text for readers on balance and social interaction, and critically reviews the literature, cites nearly 200 papers and books. Hage and Harary (1983), in their chapter on signed graphs, and Hage and Harary (1991) cite many anthropological studies of balance in networks. Davis (1963, 1967, 1968b) takes a variety of very important studies and formulates a large number of propositions about social structure from the writings of these theorists. The studies are Durkheim (1947), Stouffer Suchman, DeVinney, Star, and Williams (1949), Merton and Kitt (1950), Homans (1950, 1961), Festinger (1954, 1957), Berelson, Lazarsfeld, and McPhee (1954), Lazarsfeld and Merton (1954), Katz and Lazarsfeld (1955), Lipset, Trow, and Coleman (1956), Bott (1957), Coleman (1957), Fiedler (1958), and Davis (1959). Many of these propositions make direct statements about *P-O-X* triples. Remarkably, all are consistent with the basic postulates of structural balance. But, as we note below, balance certainly has its limitations. And, structural balance, as noted by Granovetter (1979) need not apply to the behavior of actors outside of small group settings. Some ties, especially those that make (semi)cycles have negative signs, may be reinforced by a wide variety of institutional, economic, and political constraints. Triples forbidden by structural balance can exist (and indeed, be quite stable) in certain political macro-situations.

The most important aspect of structural balance is that the nodes in a balanced graph can be partitioned into two subsets or clusters. This fact follows directly from the original theorem for balance involving the signs of cycles, and allows one to consider clusters of actors among whom all ties are possible. It also allowed researchers, in the 1950's and 1960's, to consider ways to generalize structural balance, so that actors could possibly be partitioned into more than two subsets. We now turn to these generalizations.

6.2 Clusterability

Harary (1954) proved that balanced signed graphs have partitions of nodes into two clusters or subsets such that only positive lines join nodes in the same cluster and only negative lines join nodes in different clusters. Thus, actors in the same cluster have no negative ties with each other, while actors in different clusters have no positive ties between them. There can be no more than two clusters, however. If the signed graph is balanced, then two nodes who have a negative line between themselves must be in different clusters. And if the balanced signed graph has no negative lines, it has just a single cluster of nodes.

Davis (1967, 1968b) noted that actual graphs or digraphs, representing a set of actors and a signed nondirectional or directional relation, actually appear to form clusters of this sort, but that the number of clusters is often more than two. Davis (1979) notes that this was indeed an empirical finding, prompted by research on a variety of different networks.

Definition of Clusterability. This empirical finding of more than two clusters led Davis (1967) to propose a generalization of balance for signed graphs that had more than two clusters of nodes. Such graphs were said to obey the theorems of clusterability, rather than balance. Formally, for signed graphs:

Definition 6.3 *A signed graph is clusterable, or has a clustering, if one can partition the nodes of the graph into a finite number of subsets such that each positive line joins two nodes in the same subset and each negative line joins two nodes in different subsets. The subsets derived from the clustering are called clusters.*

In brief, a balanced signed graph has one or two clusters. A signed graph that is not balanced may still be clusterable, and can have more than two clusters.

Cartwright and Harary (1968) related this clusterability problem to the classic problem of the colorability of graphs (where the clusters are actually color sets) and extended Davis' research in special ways. It is interesting to note that some of the clusterable structures considered by Davis, Cartwright, and Harary were recognized earlier by Heider to be problematic, from the standpoint of balance (more on this later).

The most important clusterability research is that of Davis (1967), in which a number of theorems are presented contrasting the concept of clustering with structural balance for graphs. Davis (1967) begins by arguing that sets of actors in a network have empirical tendencies to split into three, four, or possibly more subgroups of actors, or *clusters*. He asks:

> What conditions are necessary and sufficient for the [nodes] of a graph to be separated into two *or more* subsets such that each positive line joints two [nodes] of the same subset and each negative line joins [nodes] from different subsets? (page 181)

We note that Davis first considered only complete signed graphs. In reality, signed graphs are rarely complete, and every possible line may not be present. Thus, Davis' ideas are usually relaxed to allow some ties between actors within clusters (or subsets) to be absent. We present two theorems here, one for signed graphs and one for complete signed graphs.

Theorems. These two theorems give the conditions under which a signed graph has a *clustering*; that is, under what conditions on the cycles of a graph will the graph be clusterable? The second theorem is more specific than the first, since it is appropriate only for complete signed graphs, where all nodes are adjacent. It is important since it shows that for complete signed graphs, one need only look at cycles of length 3 to determine clusterability.

6.2.1 The Clustering Theorems

We begin with the first clustering theorem. It comes directly from Davis (1967), who also gives the proof.

Theorem 6.1 *A signed graph has a clustering if and only if the graph contains no cycles which have exactly one negative line.*

An example of a signed, clusterable graph is given in Figure 6.5, which was taken from Davis (1967). The graph in this figure has $g=6$ nodes and 8 lines: 2 positive lines and 7 negative. It clearly is not complete, since six pairs of nodes do not have lines between them. One can verify that there are four cycles of length 3 in this signed graph: $n_1 n_2 n_6 n_1$, $n_2 n_3 n_6 n_2$, $n_3 n_4 n_5 n_3$, and $n_3 n_5 n_6 n_3$. In addition, there are three cycles of length 4, one cycle of length 5, and one cycle of length 6. Since two of the four cycles of length 3 have negative signs ($n_1 n_2 n_6 n_1$ and $n_2 n_3 n_6 n_2$), the graph is not balanced. Nevertheless, it is clusterable. None of these cycles contains exactly one line with a sign of "$-$", so, by the theorem, the graph is clusterable.

There are four clusters in the graph: $\{n_4, n_5, n_6\}$, $\{n_1\}$, $\{n_2\}$, and $\{n_3\}$. Three of the clusters contain just one node, while one contains three. We should note that this clustering is not unique — there is also a second way to cluster these nodes. One can combine the second and third clusters (since n_1 and n_3 are not joined by a negative line), to give three clusters: $\{n_4, n_5, n_6\}$, $\{n_1, n_3\}$, and $\{n_2\}$. This lack of uniqueness, as we will see, is due to the fact that the graph is not complete. This can be quite a drawback in applications.

If we consider triples as we did when discussing structural balance (see Figure 6.1), we recall that there were four triples not permissible under the structural balance conditions. However, with clusterability, we see that there are now only three, rather than four, triples that are not permissible. The triple with three "$-$"s is allowed under clusterability, but not balance theory. That is, the graph is still clusterable even if a cycle of length 3 has three "$-$" lines. The two cycles in Figure 6.5 mentioned

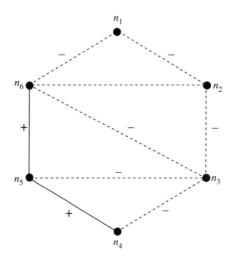

Fig. 6.5. A clusterable signed graph (with no unique clustering)

above ($n_1 n_2 n_6 n_1$ and $n_2 n_3 n_6 n_2$) are of this type, and are allowed under clustering (since they have three, not one, negative lines).

Clustering is less strict than balance. With clusterability, actors can be partitioned into more than two clusters. If there is more than one pair of actors with negative lines, then these actors are segregated into different clusters. Specifically, if there is a triple of actors in a cycle containing three negative lines, these three actors can be partitioned into three different clusters. The negative lines will be between clusters. Such a partitioning is not possible with balance, since there can be only two subsets of actors. We should note that this theorem is quite general, since it can be applied to signed graphs that are not necessarily complete. And clusterability allows the sign of a cycle of length 3 to be negative.

Consider now a complete signed graph. The following theorem extends clusterability to complete signed graphs; its last condition is *very* important. Again, it comes directly from Davis (1967).

Theorem 6.2 *The following four statements are equivalent for any complete signed graph:*

- *The graph is clusterable.*
- *The graph has a unique clustering.*

- *The graph has no cycle (of any length) with exactly one negative line.*
- *The graph has no cycle of length 3 with exactly one negative line.*

When the signed graph is complete, it is now possible to have a unique clustering. Note, also, the last condition of the theorem. The lack of some lines between nodes in a signed graph (as in Figure 6.5) makes it more difficult to check for clusterability, and if such a graph is clusterable, we have no guarantee that the clustering is unique. Lack of completeness prevents us from guaranteeing a unique clustering. A clusterable complete signed graph has a unique clustering, and this clustering can be verified by looking just at all the triples. As Davis (1979) notes, referring to the last condition concerning triples, "... 'threezies' were the key to the whole thing."

Flament (1963) proved that a complete graph is balanced if and only if all its cycles of length 3 are balanced (that is, if such cycles all have positive signs). Davis' clustering theorems, coupled with Flament's (1963) finding that the properties of triples were sufficient to assess the balance of a complete signed graph, led to nearly two decades of research on statistical and deterministic models for triples. Through these theorems, the properties of the triples of nodes in a graph tell us whether theoretically important structural properties are present. The prominent methodology for triples arising from this research will be discussed at length in Chapter 14.

We should note that these theorems and this research focus only on signed graphs. One can easily extend these theorems to signed digraphs (representing a set of actors and a signed directional relation) by looking at semicycles within the digraph. One need only replace the terms "graph," "nondirected," and "cycle" with the terms "digraph," "directed," and "semicycle" in Theorems 1 and 2 and the following discussions.

The uniqueness of the clusters is an important feature of clusterable complete signed graphs. There is only one way to form these clusters. If the graph is not complete but is clusterable, there may be more than one acceptable way to form the clusters. Complete graphs are quite rare in practice; thus, good methods for finding "good" sets of clusters from not complete graphs are very important.

If the signed graph (or digraph) under study is not complete, then (as stated by the first clusterability theorem) one has to look at all cycles, not just those of length 3. The absence of cycles of length 3 that have just one negative line is a necessary, but not a sufficient, condition for clusterability. If one can show that some of these cycles contain single negative lines or arcs, then the (di)graph is not clusterable, and one need not proceed to check cycles of longer length.

Signed graphs for which all cycles of length 3 meet the criteria of the theorem, but cycles of longer length do not, are viewed as *limited clusterable*, and are discussed by Harary, Norman, and Cartwright (1965). Cartwright and Harary (1979) refer to a signed (di)graph whose nodes can be partitioned into S subsets as an *S-clusterable* (di)graph. Balanced (di)graphs are 2-clusterable.

Consider briefly graphs and digraphs that have no cycles. Such graphs can be quite sparse and vacuous with respect to properties such as balance and clusterability. If a (di)graph does not meet any of the conditions for testing such properties, it is referred to as *vacuous*. Graphs and digraphs are called *vacuously balanced* or *vacuously clusterable* by Cartwright and Harary (1956) if they have no cycles or semicycles at all. Such structures, such as a triple of nodes with just two positive lines, are vacuous, clearly lacking the "tension" of unbalanced graphs or the "pleasantness" of balanced ones.

One can construct and calculate indices of clusterability analogous to the indices of balance discussed earlier in this chapter. There are line indices and cycle indices. There are also a variety of generalizations of clusterability, which we discuss later in this chapter. There are also extensions of these theoretical ideas to signed, valued graphs; for example, see Cartwright and Harary (1970) and Kaplan (1972).

6.2.2 Summary

Indeed, triples are key. In brief, all balanced signed (di)graphs are clusterable, but clusterable signed (di)graphs may or may not be balanced. And if the signed (di)graph is complete, one need only check cycles of length 3 for verifying balance, and hence clusterability. For balance, cycles of length 3 with three negative lines are a problem. Such cycles are allowed for clusterability, but not balance.

Note how the $(-)(-)(-)$ cycle is allowed with clusterability, but not with structural balance. The three actors must be placed into three distinct subsets (since none of them have positive ties with each other), but this is impossible with structural balance. Only two subsets are allowed, so one of them would have to contain two actors with a negative relationship.

In a partition into clusters, clusterability allows these three actors to be completely separated.

6.3 Generalizations of Clusterability

With these clusterability theorems in hand, a number of researchers embarked on empirical investigations. Questions such as how common clusterable signed (di)graphs are, and whether such signed (di)graphs were balanced needed answers. Such investigations required surveying many sociomatrices obtained from diverse sources. Further, the empirical studies had to be accompanied by statistical models that allowed those interested to study whether departures from theoretical models such as clusterability were "statistically large."

The necessary statistical techniques are beyond the scope of the current chapter. We will return to a study of triples and balance, and its successor, transitivity, in Chapter 14. But we can report here how the theorems of clusterability were generalized due to unexpected empirical evidence.

6.3.1 Empirical Evidence

Leinhardt (1968, 1973), Davis and Leinhardt (1968, 1972), and Davis (1970) gathered nearly 800 sociomatrices from many different sources, and discovered a few interesting facts. First, they found that many relations measured were directional. The recommended strategy of focusing on semicycles in such structures was difficult to implement. Secondly, asymmetric dyads, in which one actor chooses another actor, but the choice is not reciprocated, were very common. The ideas of balance and clusterability needed to be modified to take such situations into account (rather than ignoring the directionality of these arcs, which was the current practice when attention is focused on semicycles). Thirdly, they found that signed relations were rather rare. Thus, they decided to modify the theories of balance and clusterability for signed directional relations. When these new theories were later found lacking, Holland and Leinhardt (1971) revised them to unsigned directional relations.

Davis and Leinhardt also found that in some digraphs, one subset of actors chose a second, while actors in this second subset chose members of a third subset. The clusters of actors appeared to be ranked, or hierarchical in nature, with the actors "on the bottom" choosing those "at the top" (but not vice versa).

6.3.2 ○ *Ranked Clusterability*

Davis and Leinhardt (1968) consequently presented a concept of *ranked clusters*, for complete signed directed graphs. Abandoning balance and clusterability allowed them to focus on the sixteen possible triples that are possible with this type of digraph. The sixteen are shown in Figure 6.6. Notice that this idea can only be applied to complete digraphs, so that every pair of nodes has two arcs between them, both of which have a sign. Actor *i* must have either a positive or a negative tie to actor *j*, and vice versa.

Theory states that one need only examine triples when studying clusterability for complete signed graphs. The ranked clusterability model, which is discussed in detail by Davis and Leinhardt (1968), also states that for such relations, one need only check threesomes. There are sixteen possible kinds of threesomes that can arise in a complete signed digraph. These sixteen, which are shown in Figure 6.6 (adapted from a figure in Leik and Meeker 1975), are made up of only three kinds of dyads: ++ dyads, in which both arcs in the dyad have positive signs; −− dyads, in which both arcs in the dyad have negative signs; and +− dyads, in which one arc has a "+" and one has a "−".

Davis and Leinhardt (1972) state:

> Relations of the sort we have called [+−] are assumed to connect persons in different levels, while [the other dyadic] relations are assumed to connect persons in the same level. Further, we assume that in pairs connected by [+−] relations, the recipient of the positive relationship is in the higher level. (page 220)

They continue,

> [++] relations are assumed to connect persons in the same [cluster] within a level. [−−] relations are assumed to connect persons in different cliques within a level. (page 220)

These two quotes nicely summarize which types of triads are possible, and which ones are not according to the postulates of ranked clusterability for complete signed digraphs. In brief, ranked clusterability postulates that ++ dyads occur only within clusters and −− dyads only between clusters at the same level of the hierarchy or order of clusters. The interesting +− dyads also occur between clusters, but at different levels. Thus, actors in a lower cluster should have positive ties to actors in a higher-ranked cluster and negative ties to actors in a lower-ranked cluster. One can see how such a model postulates that "lower" clusters of actors choose upwardly.

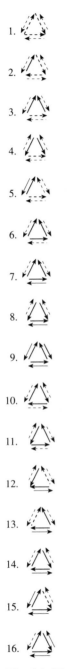

Fig. 6.6. The sixteen possible triads for ranked clusterability in a complete signed graph

Ranked clusterability, in which the positive arcs emanating to or from the nodes in [+−] dyads are postulated to "point" in the same direction, states that the triples numbered 2, 10, 11, 12, 13, 14, 15, and 16 of Figure 6.6 should not occur in practice. These "miserable" eight (Davis 1979) depart from both clusterability and ranked clusterability. The empirical study of the 800 sociomatrices in the Davis/Leinhardt sociometric data bank found that the vast majority of triples were not of these eight types (as reported in the reminiscenses of Davis 1979). Unfortunately, triple 2, which is not allowed, was quite common. Davis and Leinhardt (1972) concluded that

> ... we may say that we have had some success in showing that [+−] relationships tend toward a rank structure and some success in showing that [++] and [−−] relations tend toward clusterability, but we have had more limited success in showing how these two "structures" are integrated to make a coherent whole. (page 249)

Not only was triple 2 quite common, but so was triple 16. As Davis (1979) notes, there was strong empirical evidence for 6/8th's of a theorem. These two triples are quite common in positive affect relations which are in an "early" development stage; that is, assuming that the relation under study will change over time, these triples contain dyads which might evolve into triples which are not prohibited.

This ranked clusterability model was quite elegant, but little used. The ideas were quickly modified to account for another finding from the study of the 800 sociomatrices in the Davis/Leinhardt sociometric data bank — signed digraphs just are not very commonly collected.

The lack of signed graphs or digraphs in the 800 sociomatrices is not surprising. The common technique for measuring affective relations (see Chapter 2) is simply to pose only two alternatives to each actor about every other actor: presence or absence of the tie in question. Davis and associates clearly needed an approach that could handle non-signed, directional relations. Adaptation of the "pre-1968" ideas to non-signed relations did not come until consideration of transitivity, found first in Holland and Leinhardt (1971). The first generalizations of clusterability continued to focus on signed relations.

6.3.3 Summary

Holland and Leinhardt (1970) were the first to suggest the extension of these ideas to non-signed directional relations. To turn ranked clusterability for complete signed digraphs into an equivalent idea for digraphs without signs is quite simple. We take the idea of ranked clusters for complete signed digraphs, and do not consider arcs with negative signs. Then, any arc with a sign of "$-$" is removed from the signed digraph. We then drop the positive signs from the remaining arcs. The assumption is that the relation under study is the "positive" part of the signed relation — for example, we study only "like," "not like," and "dislike." Figure 6.7 shows the triples of Figure 6.6, without the negative arcs. The triples arising from directional relations are commonly referred to as *triads*, since we consider the threesome of nodes, and all the arcs between them.

We note that the two problematic triads from ranked clusterability found empirically to be quite common have one and five arcs. These are the triads numbered 2 and 16 in Figure 6.7. Holland and Leinhardt showed that ranked clusterability is a special case of a more general set of theorems which naturally blend balance, clusterability, and ranked clusterability. Their *partially ordered clusterability* leads naturally to a consideration of the concept of *transitivity*.

Holland and Leinhardt (1971) reviewed the postulates of balance theory, clusterability, and ranked clusterability, as well as transitive tournaments (Landau 1951a, 1951b, and 1953; Hempel 1952), and proposed the very general concept of transitivity to explain social structures. Transitivity includes all the earlier ideas as special cases. From a transitive digraph, one can obtain balanced, clusterable, and ranked clusterable graphs by making various assumptions about reciprocity and asymmetry of choices. During the past two decades, evidence has accumulated that transitivity is indeed a compelling force in the organization of social groups. We now present this idea.

6.4 Transitivity

We turn our attention to a triple of actors, i, j, and k, and the ties between them. We state:

Definition 6.4 *The triad involving actors i, j, and k is transitive if whenever $i \rightarrow j$ and $j \rightarrow k$ then $i \rightarrow k$.*

If either of the two conditions of this statement is not met (that is, if $i \not\rightarrow j$ and/or $j \not\rightarrow k$), then the triple is termed *vacuously transitive*. Vacuously transitive triples are neither transitive nor intransitive. Note how the focus has shifted from cycles in signed graphs to semicycles in signed digraphs to transitive triads in ordinary digraphs.

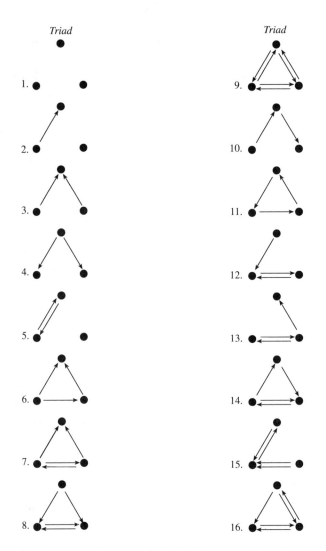

Fig. 6.7. The sixteen possible triads for transitivity in a digraph

From this definition we have the following theorem:

Theorem 6.3 *A digraph is transitive if every triad it contains is transitive.*

We note that if a transitive digraph has no asymmetric dyads — that is, if all choices are reciprocated — then it is clusterable. Clusterable digraphs require mutual dyads to be within and null dyads to be between clusters. Thus, clusterability is a special case of transitivity. Ranked clusterable digraphs are also transitive. In fact, transitivity is the most general idea of this type for graphs and digraphs.

Refer again to Figure 6.7. The following triads are transitive: 6, 7, 8, 9. Triads 1, 2, 3, 4, 5 are vacuously transitive. They do not contain enough arcs to meet the conditions of the theorem, so cannot be transitive or intransitive. Triads 10, 11, 12, 13, 14, 15, 16 are intransitive. Vacuously transitive triads can occur and the digraph itself can still be transitive. Now, rather than eight "miserable" triples from ranked clusterability, there are only seven intransitive triads.

Notice that Definition 6.4 is stated for ordered triples of actors. Thus, we must look at ordered triples rather than triads. Note also that each threesome of actors consists of six distinct ordered triples of actors. Some of these triples may have transitive choices, as defined in Definition 6.4, while others may be intransitive. Still others may be vacuously transitive. A triple must be of one of these types. For the triad itself to be labeled transitive, all ordered triples of actors present in a triad must be either transitive or vacuously transitive. If any one of the triples is intransitive, so is the triad.

For example, look at triad 16 in Figure 6.7. As is the case with all triads, triad 16 has six triples. This triad, along with its triples and their statuses, are listed in Figure 6.8. Three of the triples are transitive, while one of them (the second) is not. The other two triples are vacuously transitive (for example, the first triple, $n_i n_j n_k$, is neither transitive nor intransitive since actor i does not have a tie to actor j). The second triple, $n_i n_k n_j$, is clearly intransitive, since $n_i \rightarrow n_k$, $n_k \rightarrow n_j$, but $n_i \nrightarrow n_j$. Thus, this triad is considered intransitive because of this single intransitive triple. The number of transitive and/or intransitive triples within a particular type of triad is very important when quantitatively and statistically assessing the amount of transitivity in a digraph. We discuss this issue in much greater detail in Chapter 14.

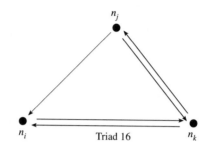

Triple #1 : n_i n_j n_k
  $n_i \not\to n_j$ $n_j \to n_k$ $n_i \to n_k$ Vacuously transitive
Triple #2 : n_i n_k n_j
  $n_i \to n_k$ $n_k \to n_j$ $n_i \not\to n_j$ Intransitive
Triple #3 : n_j n_i n_k
  $n_j \to n_i$ $n_i \to n_k$ $n_j \to n_k$ Transitive
Triple #4 : n_j n_k n_i
  $n_j \to n_k$ $n_k \to n_i$ $n_j \to n_i$ Transitive
Triple #5 : n_k n_i n_j
  $n_k \to n_i$ $n_i \not\to n_j$ $n_k \to n_j$ Vacuously transitive
Triple #6 : n_k n_j n_i
  $n_k \to n_j$ $n_j \to n_i$ $n_k \to n_i$ Transitive

Fig. 6.8. The type 16 triad, and all six triples of actors

The generality of transitivity can be seen, for example, by looking at triad 2 from Figure 6.7. This triad, which is not allowed under ranked clusterability, has just a single asymmetric dyad, so it is vacuously transitive. Vacuously transitive triples are allowed under transitivity, so type 2 triads can arise, without invalidating the idea.

The other triad that was problematic for ranked clusterability was triad 16, which we described in detail above. Davis and Leinhardt showed that this triad occurred far too frequently. But this triad is almost transitive. Only one of its six triples is intransitive. So, the presence of this 5/6th's transitive/vacuously transitive triad in a data set is not such a big deal (assuming transitivity is operating).

Holland and Leinhardt (1972) provide strong, statistical evidence that transitivity is a very important structural tendency in social networks. By relying on the Davis/Leinhardt sociometric data bank, Holland and Leinhardt present evidence of transitive social structure. Holland and Leinhardt (1975, 1978, 1979) and Johnsen (1985, 1986) show that transitivity is one of many "null hypotheses" that can be tested by examining triads and the triples they contain.

The statistical methodology for determining how many intransitivities can be present in an actual data set, before concluding that transitivity does not hold, is discussed in Chapter 14.

6.5 Conclusion

Transitive digraphs (called t-graphs by Holland and Leinhardt 1971), and the mathematical methods based on them are quite important. These structures, methods, and theorems unified over two decades of theorizing about balance, clusterability and its generalizations, and transitivity, in sociology and social psychology. Transitivity has been shown to be a key structural property in social network data. In fact, many recent methods center on finding "what else" remains in a data set after "removing" tendencies toward transitivity. The idea of a *transitivity bias* or structural tendency in social network data was discussed as early as Rapoport (1953, 1963) and Fararo and Sunshine (1964) (see also the discussion of random and biased nets in Fararo and Skvoretz 1984, 1987; Skvoretz 1985, 1990). There are, of course, other tendencies that can occur in a social network — in fact, we spend much of the remainder of this book describing and quantifying them. But after tendencies toward reciprocity were discussed in the 1940's, balance and its generalization, transitivity, were the earliest theories to play an important part in social network analysis.

As we have discussed in this chapter, Cartwright and Harary (1956) used graph theory to quantify Heider's (1946) balance theory, and proposed a theorem that implied that a set of actors, if balanced, could be partitioned into two subsets. The data, unfortunately, had to be from a signed graph in order to apply this idea. Davis (1967) recognized that the decomposition of a set of actors into just two subgroups was not empirically likely; consequently, he expanded upon structural balance by proposing theorems that showed under what conditions such partitions could arise. Davis's ranked clusterability included balance theory as a special case, and thus seemed far more appropriate for social network data. Again, the restriction to signed graphs was quite a limitation; Davis and Leinhardt's (1972) empirical searches recognized that most social network data included unsigned, rather than signed, relations.

With this empirical knowledge, Davis and Leinhardt (1968) combined the common tendency toward clustering with a second structural tendency toward ranking or differential status, to show how directional relations could generate structures resembling hierarchically arranged clusters.

Going a step further, concentrating on the very common directional, unsigned relations, Holland and Leinhardt (1970) showed how ideas about partially ordered clusters, generalizing ranked clusterability, lead naturally to transitivity. During the past two decades, research, such as Mazur (1971), Davis, Holland, and Leinhardt (1971), Holland and Leinhardt (1973, 1979), Killworth (1974), Frank (1979a), Frank and Harary (1979, 1980, 1982), and Johnsen (1985, 1986), has continued the development of transitivity, but the major efforts can be found in the work of Heider, Cartwright, Harary, Davis, Holland, and Leinhardt during the period 1945–1972.

Many researchers have studied the implications of balance theory and transitivity for social structures: to name but a few, Morrissette (1958), Rodrigues (1967, 1981), Horsfall and Henley (1969), Johnsen (1970), Wellens and Thistlethwaite (1971a, 1971b), Crano and Cooper (1973), Rodrigues and Ziviani (1974), Willis and Burgess (1974), Mower White (1977, 1979), Moore (1978), Tashakkori and Insko (1979), Newcomb (1981), Feld and Elmore (1982a), Rodrigues and Dela Coleta (1983), Chase (1982), Gupta (1985, and references therein), Mohazab and Feger (1985), especially the review of Zajonc (1968), and the work of Fararo and Skvoretz mentioned earlier. Transitivity underlies many social network methods. It will arise in Chapters 10 and especially 14, where we present statistical methods for determining the extent of transitivity in a social network. The ideas presented in Chapter 6 were important not only to network theorists, but to many methodologists.

We note in conclusion that while this small set of graph theorists, sociologists, social psychologists, and statisticians were working on mathematical models of balance, clusterability, and transitivity, other methodologists were busy studying about cliques and cohesive subgroups. This area of research is described in the next chapter.

7

Cohesive Subgroups

One of the major concerns of social network analysis is identification of cohesive subgroups of actors within a network. Cohesive subgroups are subsets of actors among whom there are relatively strong, direct, intense, frequent, or positive ties. These methods attempt, in part, to formalize the intuitive and theoretical notion of social group using social network properties. However, since the concept of social group as used by social and behavioral scientists is quite general, and there are many specific properties of a social network that are related to the cohesiveness of subgroups, there are many possible social network subgroup definitions.

In this chapter and the next we discuss methods for finding cohesive subgroups of actors within a social network. In this chapter we discuss methods for analyzing one-mode networks, with a single set of actors and a single relation. In Chapter 8 we continue the discussion of cohesive subgroups and related ideas, but focus on affiliation networks. Affiliation networks are two-mode networks consisting of a set of actors and a set of events. Cohesive subgroups in one-mode networks focus on properties of pairwise ties, whereas cohesive subgroups in two-mode affiliation networks focus on ties existing among actors through their joint membership in collectivities. Thus, one major difference between this chapter and the next is whether one-mode or two-mode data are being analyzed.

We begin with an overview of the theoretical motivation for studying cohesive subgroups in social networks and discuss general properties of cohesive subgroups that have influenced network formalizations. We then discuss how to assess the cohesiveness of network subgroups, and extend subgroup methods to directional relations and to valued relations. The final section of this chapter briefly discusses alternative approaches for studying cohesiveness in networks using multidimensional scaling and factor analysis. Most of the methods discussed in this chapter are based on graph theoretic ideas, and use graph theoretic concepts and notation. Thus, it might be useful to review Chapter 4 before reading the rest of this chapter.

7.1 Background

In this section we discuss the theoretical background for social groups, briefly outline some ways to conceptualize cohesive subgroups, and review key notation and graph theoretic concepts that are used to study cohesive subgroups.

7.1.1 Social Group and Subgroup

Many authors have discussed the role of social cohesion in social explanations and theories (Burt 1984; Collins 1988; Erickson 1988; Friedkin 1984). Friedkin examines the use of network cohesion as an explanatory variable in sociological theories, especially for studying the emergence of consensus among members of a group:

> Structural cohesion models are founded upon the causal propositions that pressures toward uniformity occur when there is a positively valued interaction between two persons; that these pressures may occur by being "transmitted" through intermediaries even when two persons are not in direct contact; and that such indirect pressures toward uniformity are associated with the number of short indirect communication channels connecting the persons. (1984, page 236)

Consequently, according to this idea, one expects greater homogeneity among persons who have relatively frequent face-to-face contact or who are connected through intermediaries, and less homogeneity among persons who have less frequent contact (Friedkin 1984). In his review of sociological theory, Collins (1988) also states the importance of cohesion in social network analysis:

> The more tightly that individuals are tied into a network, the more they are affected by group standards .... (page 416)

Collins continues, noting that

> Actually, there are two factors operating here, which we can see from network analysis: how many ties an individual has to the group and how closed the entire group is to outsiders. Isolated and tightly connected groups make up a clique; within such highly cohesive groups, individuals tend to have very homogeneous beliefs. (page 417)

Cohesive subgroups are theoretically important according to these theories because of social forces operating through direct contact among subgroup members, through indirect conduct transmitted via intermediaries, or through the relative cohesion within as compared to outside the subgroup. Such theories provide motivation for cohesive subgroup methods for one-mode social networks (in which ties are measured between pairs of actors). These ideas are all used to study cohesive subgroups in social networks.

The notions of social group, subgroup, clique, and so on are widely used in the social sciences, particularly in social psychology and sociology. Although the notion of social group has received widespread attention in the social sciences, researchers often use the word without giving it a precise formal definition. As noted by Freeman (1984, 1992a) and Borgatti, Everett, and Freeman (1991) authors often assume that since "everybody knows what it means" it can be used without precise definition. Freeman reviews the history of the concept of group in sociology with special attention to network formalizations of this concept (Freeman 1992a).

Many network researchers who have developed or reviewed methods for cohesive subgroups in social networks have noted that these methods attempt to formalize the notion of social group (Seidman and Foster 1978a, 1978b; Alba and Moore 1978; Mokken 1979; Burt 1980; Freeman 1984, 1992a; Sailer and Gaulin 1984). According to these authors, the concept of social group can be studied by looking at properties of subsets of actors within a network. In social network analysis, the notion of subgroup is formalized by the general property of *cohesion* among subgroup members based on specified properties of the ties among the members. However, since the property of cohesion of a subgroup can be quantified using several different specific network properties, cohesive subgroups can be formalized by looking at many different properties of the ties among subsets of actors.

Although the literature on cohesive subgroups in networks contains numerous ways to conceptualize the idea of subgroups, there are four general properties of cohesive subgroups that have influenced social network formalizations of this concept. Briefly, these are:

- The mutuality of ties
- The closeness or reachability of subgroup members
- The frequency of ties among members

- The relative frequency of ties among subgroup members compared to non-members

Subgroups based on mutuality of ties require that all pairs of subgroup members "choose" each other (or are adjacent); subgroups based on reachability require that all subgroup members be reachable to each other, but not necessarily adjacent; subgroups based on numerous ties require that subgroup members have ties to many others within the subgroup; and subgroups based on the relative density or frequency of ties require that subgroups be relatively cohesive when compared to the remainder of the network. Successive definitions weaken the first notion of adjacency among all subgroup members. These general subgroup ideas lead to methods that focus on different social network properties. Thus, our discussion in this chapter is divided into sections, each of which takes up methods that are primarily motivated by one of these ideas.

In contrast to these ideas that focus on ties between pairs of actors in one-mode networks, some cohesive subgroup ideas are concerned with the linkages that are established among individuals by virtue of their common membership in collectivities. These ideas motivate methods for studying affiliation networks, which we discuss in Chapter 8.

Before we present the subgroup methods for one-mode networks, let us review some basic concepts and definitions from graph theory.

7.1.2 Notation

Our presentation of notation here is intentionally brief, since these ideas were covered in detail in Chapters 3 and 4. To start, we will limit our attention to graphs, and thus, to dichotomous nondirectional relations.

We begin with a graph, $\mathscr{G}$, consisting of a set of nodes, $\mathscr{N}$, and a set of lines, $\mathscr{L}$. Each line connects a pair of nodes in $\mathscr{G}$. Two nodes that are connected by a line are said to be *adjacent*. A node generated subgraph, $\mathscr{G}_s$, of $\mathscr{G}$, consists of a subset of nodes, $\mathscr{N}_s$, where $\mathscr{N}_s \subseteq \mathscr{N}$, along with the lines from $\mathscr{L}$ that link the nodes in $\mathscr{G}_s$. We will refer to a subset of nodes as a *subgroup* or *subset*, and the nodes along with the lines among them as a *subgraph*. A graph is *complete* if all nodes are adjacent; that is, if each pair of nodes is connected by an line. Similarly, a subgraph, $\mathscr{G}_s$, is complete if all pairs of nodes in it are adjacent.

A *path* connecting two nodes is a sequence of distinct nodes and lines beginning with the first node and terminating with the last. If there is a path between two nodes then they are said to be *reachable*. The *length* of a path is the number of lines in it. A shortest path between two nodes is called a *geodesic*, and the (geodesic) distance between two nodes, denoted by $d(i, j)$, is the length of a shortest path between them. The *diameter* of a graph is the length of the longest geodesic between any pair of nodes in the graph. In other words, the diameter of a graph is the maximum geodesic distance between any pair of nodes; max($d(i, j)$), for $n_i, n_j \in \mathcal{N}$. Similarly, the *diameter of a subgraph* can be defined as the longest geodesic between two nodes within the subgraph. The diameter of a subgraph is defined on the subset of nodes and lines that are present in the subgraph.

A graph is *connected* if there is a path between each pair of nodes in the graph. A subgraph is connected if there is a path between each pair of nodes in the subgraph, and the path contains only nodes and lines within the subgraph. The *degree* of a node, $d(i)$, is the number of nodes that are adjacent to it. The degree of node i in subgraph $\mathcal{G}_s$ is denoted by $d_s(i)$, and is defined as the number of nodes within the subgraph that are adjacent to node i.

A subgraph is said to be *maximal* with respect to some property (for example, completeness) if that property holds for the subgraph, but does not hold if additional nodes and the lines incident with them are added to the subgraph. If a subgraph is maximal with respect to a property, then that property holds for the subgraph, $\mathcal{G}_s$, but not for any larger subgraph that contains $\mathcal{G}_s$ (Mokken 1979). For example, a *component* of a graph is a maximal connected subgraph (Hage and Harary 1983). The presence of two or more components in a graph indicates that the graph is *disconnected*.

We can now define some interesting subgroup ideas using these graph theoretic concepts.

7.2 Subgroups Based on Complete Mutuality

The earliest researchers interested in cohesive subgroups gathered and studied sociometric data on affective ties, such as friendship or liking in small face-to-face groups, in order to identify "cliquish" subgroups. Network data on friendship nominations often give rise to directional dichotomous relations. Festinger (1949) and Luce and Perry (1949) argued that cohesive subgroups in directional dichotomous relations would be characterized by sets of people among whom all friendship choices were mutual. Specifically, Luce and Perry and Festinger proposed that a clique for a relation of positive affect is a subset of people among whom all choices are mutual, and no other people can be added to the subset who also have mutual choices with all members of the subset. This definition of a clique is appropriate for a directional dichotomous relation.

The clique is the foundational idea for studying cohesive subgroups in social networks. Graph theory provides a precise formal definition of a clique that is appropriate for a *nondirectional* dichotomous relation.

7.2.1 Definition of a Clique

A *clique* in a graph is a maximal complete subgraph of three or more nodes. It consists of a subset of nodes, all of which are adjacent to each other, and there are no other nodes that are also adjacent to all of the members of the clique (Luce and Perry 1949; Harary, Norman, and Cartwright 1965). The restriction that the clique contain at least three nodes is included so that mutual dyads are not considered to be cliques. One can think of a clique as a collection of actors all of whom "choose" each other, and there is no other actor in the group who also "chooses" and is "chosen" by all of the members of the clique.

The clique definition is a useful starting point for specifying the formal properties that a cohesive subgroup should have. It has well-specified mathematical properties, and also captures much of the intuitive notion of cohesive subgroup; however, it has limitations, which we discuss below.

Figure 7.1 shows a graph and a listing of the cliques contained in it. The reader can verify that these subgraphs are in fact cliques, and that there are no remaining cliques in the graph.

Notice that cliques in a graph may overlap. The same node or set of nodes might belong to more than one clique. For example, in Figure 7.1 node 3 belongs in all three cliques. Also, there may be nodes that do not belong to any cliques (for example node 7 in Figure 7.1). However, no clique can be entirely contained within another clique, because if it were the smaller clique would not be maximal.

7.2.2 An Example

We will use the example of the relations of marriage and business among Padgett's Florentine families to illustrate cohesive subgroups throughout this chapter. Recall that both of these relations are dichotomous and nondirectional. We used the network analysis programs *GRADAP 2.0*

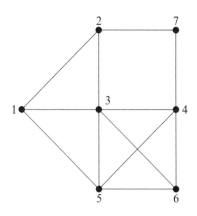

cliques: $\{1,2,3\}$, $\{1,3,5\}$, and $\{3,4,5,6\}$

Fig. 7.1. A graph and its cliques

(Sprenger and Stokman 1989) and *UCINET IV* (Borgatti, Everett, and Freeman 1991) to do the subgroup analyses described in this chapter.

First consider the relation of marriage among these families. For the marriage relation there are three cliques:

- Bischeri Peruzzi Strozzi
- Castellani Peruzzi Strozzi
- Medici Ridolfi Tornabuoni

Only seven of the sixteen families in this network belong to any clique on the marriage relation. Furthermore, the cliques are small; each clique contains only the minimum three families. By definition, there has been a marriage between all pairs of families in each clique. Notice that the first two cliques contain two members in common (Peruzzi and Strozzi), and differ only by a single member. However, the four families, Bischeri, Castellani, Peruzzi and Strozzi, do not form a clique because there is no marriage tie between Castellani and Bischeri.

For the business relation there are five cliques:

- Barbadori Castellani Peruzzi
- Barbadori Ginori Medici
- Bischeri Guadagni Lamberteschi
- Bischeri Lamberteschi Peruzzi
- Castellani Lamberteschi Peruzzi

Eight of the sixteen families belong to at least one clique on the business relation, and some families (for example Lamberteschi, Bischeri, and Peruzzi) belong to several cliques on this relation. As we saw with the marriage relation, the cliques are small (no more than three members) and there is considerable overlap among them. However, the cliques that are present in the business relation are different from the cliques that are present in the marriage relation.

7.2.3 Considerations

A clique is a *very* strict definition of cohesive subgroup. In fact, Alba (1973) calls it "stingy." The absence of a single line, or in sociometric terms, the absence of a single tie or "choice," will prevent a subgraph from being a clique. In a sparse network there may be very few cliques (as with the marriage relation among the Florentine families). In addition, the sizes of the cliques will be limited by the degree of the nodes. This can be a problem if the number of ties that an actor can have is limited by the data collection design. For example, in a sociometric study using a fixed choice design in which respondents are asked to list their three best friends, each person can be adjacent to at most three other people. Thus there can be no clique with more than four members. In general, if actors are restricted to k ties, then there can be no clique in the resulting data that has more than $k + 1$ members.

Early researchers were concerned with methods for detecting cliques in networks (Festinger 1949; Luce and Perry 1949; Luce 1950; Harary and Ross 1957). More recently, researchers have realized that cliques seldom are useful in analysis of actual data because the definition is too strict. Actual data rarely contain interesting cliques, since the absence of a single tie among subgroup members prevents the subgroup from meeting the clique definition. In addition, cliques that do occur are often quite small, and overlap one another (as we have seen in the analysis of Padgett's Florentine families).

An additional limitation of clique as a formalization of cohesive subgroup is that there is no internal differentiation among actors within a clique (Doreian 1969; Seidman and Foster 1978a, 1978b; Freeman 1992a, 1992b). Since a clique is complete, within the clique all members are graph theoretically identical. All clique members are adjacent to all other clique members, thus there are no distinctions among members based on graph theoretic properties within the clique. If we expect that the cohesive subgroups within a network should exhibit interesting internal structure, such as having some core actors who are more strongly identified with the subgroup and other peripheral actors who are less identified with it, then a clique might be an inappropriate definition of cohesive subgroup.

On the other hand, some researchers working with large network data sets (that include hundreds or even thousands of actors) have found that there may be numerous, but largely overlapping, cliques in the group (Alba and Moore 1978). In such cases, the cliques themselves might not be very informative. Instead, the researcher might study the overlap among the cliques. Studying how cliques overlap is one way to focus on the differentiation or internal structure of subgroups within the network. A recent paper by Freeman (1992b) describes how to use lattices (which we define in Chapter 8) to study the overlap among cliques in social network.

An active area of recent research is the development of methods to extend the definition of cohesive subgroup to make the resulting subgroups more substantively and theoretically interesting. These methods weaken the notion of clique so that the subgroups are less "stingy." There are obviously numerous ways to loosen the definition by removing required properties of a subgraph. These definitions describe subgraphs that are not cliques, but rather, are "clique-like" entities. The "trick" is to develop formal mathematical definitions that have known graph theoretic properties, and also capture important intuitive and theoretical aspects of cohesive subgroups. Two different structural properties have been used to relax the clique notion: first, Luce (1950), and later Alba (1973) and Mokken (1979), have used properties of reachability, path distance, and diameter to extend the clique definition; second, Seidman and Foster (1978a) and Seidman (1981b, 1983b) used nodal degree to propose alternative cohesive subgroup ideas. Both of these ideas take the clique as a starting point, and extend it by removing one or more restrictions. We will describe each of these in turn.

7.3 Subgroups Based on Reachability and Diameter

Reachability is the motivation for the first cohesive subgroup ideas that extend the notion of a clique. These alternative subgroup ideas are useful if the researcher hypothesizes that important social processes occur through intermediaries. For example, the diffusion of information has been hypothesized to occur in this way (Erickson 1988). Conceptually, there should be relatively short paths of influence or communication between all members of the subgroup. Subgroup members might not be adjacent, but if they are not adjacent, then the paths connecting them should be relatively short.

7.3.1 *n-cliques*

Recall that the geodesic distance between two nodes, denoted by $d(i, j)$, is the length of a shortest path between them. Cohesive subgroups based on reachability require that the geodesic distances among members of a subgroup be small. Thus, we can specify some cutoff value, n, as the maximum length of geodesics connecting pairs of actors within the cohesive subgroup. Restricting geodesic distance among subgroup members is the basis for the definition of an n-clique (Alba 1973; Luce 1950). An *n-clique* is a maximal subgraph in which the largest geodesic distance between any two nodes is no greater than n. Formally, an n-clique is a subgraph with node set $\mathcal{N}_s$, such that

$$d(i, j) \leq n \text{ for all } n_i, n_j \in \mathcal{N}_s \tag{7.1}$$

and there are no additional nodes that are also distance n or less from all nodes in the subgraph.

When $n = 1$, the subgraphs are cliques, since all nodes are adjacent. Increasing the value of n gives subgraphs in which longer geodesic distances between nodes are permitted. A value of $n = 2$ is often a useful cutoff value. 2-cliques are subgraphs in which all members need not be adjacent, but all members are reachable through at most one intermediary.

Let us look at an example to illustrate n-cliques. Figure 7.2, taken from Alba (1973) and Mokken (1979), contains a single clique, $\{1, 2, 3\}$, which, by definition, is a 1-clique. In this graph, there are two 2-cliques: $\{1, 2, 3, 4, 5\}$ and $\{2, 3, 4, 5, 6\}$. Notice that these two 2-cliques share four of their five members. In addition, it is important to note that even though we are using a maximum geodesic distance of $n = 2$ to find the 2-cliques, the first 2-clique ($\{1, 2, 3, 4, 5\}$) has a diameter of 3. The geodesic between nodes 4 and 5 includes node 6, which is not a member of this 2-clique. *Within* this 2-clique, the shortest path between 4 and 5 is the path 4, 2, 3, 5, which is of length 3. Thus, n-cliques can be found in which the intermediaries in a geodesic between a pair of n-clique members are not themselves n-clique members.

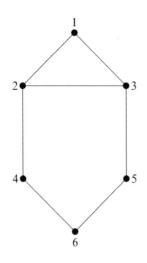

2-cliques: $\{1,2,3,4,5\}$ and $\{2,3,4,5,6\}$
2-clan: $\{2,3,4,5,6\}$
2-clubs: $\{1,2,3,4\}$, $\{1,2,3,5\}$, and $\{2,3,4,5,6\}$

Fig. 7.2. Graph illustrating *n*-cliques, *n*-clans, and *n*-clubs

7.3.2 An Example

Let us return to the example of marriage and business relations among Padgett's Florentine families to illustrate *n*-cliques. We used the program *GRADAP 2.0* (Sprenger and Stokman 1989) for this analysis. There are thirteen 2-cliques in the marriage relation:

- Acciaiuoli Albizzi Barbadori Medici Ridolfi Salviati Tornabuoni
- Albizzi Bischeri Guadagni Lamberteschi Tornabuoni
- Albizzi Bischeri Guadagni Ridolfi Tornabuoni
- Albizzi Ginori Guadagni Medici
- Albizzi Guadagni Medici Ridolfi Tornabuoni
- Barbadori Castellani Medici Ridolfi Strozzi
- Barbadori Castellani Peruzzi Ridolfi Strozzi
- Barbadori Medici Ridolfi Strozzi Tornabuoni
- Bischeri Castellani Peruzzi Ridolfi Strozzi
- Bischeri Guadagni Peruzzi Ridolfi Strozzi
- Bischeri Guadagni Ridolfi Strozzi Tornabuoni

- Guadagni Medici Ridolfi Strozzi Tornabuoni
- Medici Pazzi Salviati

There are four 2-cliques on the business relation:

- Barbadori Bischeri Castellani Lamberteschi Peruzzi
- Barbadori Castellani Ginori Medici Peruzzi
- Barbadori Ginori Medici Pazzi Salviati Tornabuoni
- Bischeri Castellani Guadagni Lamberteschi Peruzzi

Notice that the 2-cliques are both larger and more numerous than the cliques found for both the marriage and business relations. Since the definition of an n-clique is less restrictive than the definition of a clique, when n is greater than 1 it is likely that a network will contain more n-cliques than cliques. It is also likely that the n-cliques will be larger than the cliques.

7.3.3 Considerations

There are several important properties of n-cliques, some of which limit the usefulness of this cohesive subgroup definition. Since n-cliques are defined for geodesic paths that can include any nodes in the graph, two problems might arise: first, an n-clique, as a subgraph, may have a diameter greater than n, and second, an n-clique might be disconnected. The first problem arises because the requirement that nodes be connected by paths of length n or less does not require that these paths remain within the subgroup (Alba 1973; Alba and Moore 1978). Geodesics connecting a pair of nodes in an n-clique may include nodes that lie outside of the n-clique. Thus, the diameter of the *subgraph* can be larger than n. The second problem is that an n-clique may not even be connected. Two nodes may be connected by a geodesic of n or less which includes nodes outside the n-clique, and these two nodes may have no path connecting them that includes only n-clique members. These problems indicate that n-cliques are not as cohesive as we might like for studying cohesive subgroups (Alba and Moore 1978; Mokken 1979).

7.3.4 n-clans and n-clubs

One idea to "improve" n-cliques is to restrict them so that the resulting subgroups that are identified are more cohesive, and do not have the problems of n-cliques. A useful restriction is to require that the diameter of an n-clique be no greater than n. Mokken (1979) has described two logical ways to do this. The first, which he calls an *n-clan*, starts with the n-cliques that are identified in a network and excludes those n-cliques that have a diameter greater than n. The second approach, called an *n-club*, defines a new entity, a *maximal n-diameter subgraph*.

An *n-clan* is an n-clique in which the geodesic distance, $d(i, j)$, between all nodes in the subgraph is no greater than n for paths *within* the subgraph. The n-clans in a graph can be found by examining all n-cliques and excluding those that have diameter greater than n. Any n-cliques that include pairs of nodes whose geodesics require non-subgroup members are excluded from consideration. The n-clans in a graph are those n-cliques that have diameter less than or equal to n (Alba 1973; Mokken 1979). All n-clans are n-cliques.

An *n-club* is defined as a maximal subgraph of diameter n. That is, an n-club is a subgraph in which the distance between all nodes *within the subgraph* is less than or equal to n; further, no nodes can be added that also have geodesic distance n or less from all members of the subgraph. n-clubs are not necessarily n-cliques, though they are always subgraphs of n-cliques.

Although conceptually similar, n-clans and n-clubs are somewhat different, as illustrated in Figure 7.2. This example is taken from Alba (1973) and Mokken (1979), and illustrates the difference between n-cliques, n-clans, and n-clubs. For this graph, taking $n = 2$ results in the following sets:

- 2-cliques: $\{1, 2, 3, 4, 5\}$ and $\{2, 3, 4, 5, 6\}$
- 2-clan: $\{2, 3, 4, 5, 6\}$
- 2-clubs: $\{1, 2, 3, 4\}$, $\{1, 2, 3, 5\}$, and $\{2, 3, 4, 5, 6\}$

First, consider the 2-cliques and 2-clans. Since the 2-clique $\{1, 2, 3, 4, 5\}$ has diameter greater than 2 (the distance from 4 to 5 is equal to 3) it is not an 2-clan. The 2-clique $\{2, 3, 4, 5, 6\}$ is a 2-clan since its diameter is not greater than 2. Now, consider the 2-clubs. The 2-clubs $\{1, 2, 3, 4\}$ and $\{1, 2, 3, 5\}$ both have diameter equal to 2, and are maximal, since no node can be added to either subgraph without increasing its diameter. Notice that each of these 2-clubs is a subgraph of the 2-clique $\{1, 2, 3, 4, 5\}$ (whose diameter is greater than 2). Finally, the 2-club $\{2, 3, 4, 5, 6\}$ has a diameter of 2 and is maximal.

As this example illustrates, 2-clubs are either 2-cliques, or are subgraphs of 2-cliques. Mokken (1979) demonstrates that all n-clans are also n-

cliques, and all *n*-clubs are contained within *n*-cliques. Furthermore, all *n*-clans are also *n*-clubs, though there can be *n*-clubs that are not *n*-clans.

As Sprenger and Stokman (1989) have noted, "hardly anybody" has used *n*-clans and *n*-clubs, and more research is needed on these cohesive subgroup ideas. The *n*-clans in a social network are relatively easy to find by examining the *n*-cliques, and eliminating those with diameter greater than *n*. The *n*-clubs are difficult to find, and often routines for *n*-clubs are not included in standard network analysis packages. Therefore, in the following example we restrict our attention to *n*-clans.

An Example. We will use the marriage and business relations for Padgett's Florentine families to illustrate *n*-clans. For the business relation, all of the four 2-cliques have a diameter that is 2 or less, and therefore these four 2-cliques are also 2-clans. For the marriage relation, five of the 2-cliques have diameter greater than 2, so they are excluded from the list of 2-clans. This leaves eight 2-clans:

- Acciaiuoli Albizzi Barbadori Medici Ridolfi Salviati Tornabuoni
- Albizzi Bischeri Guadagni Lamberteschi Tornabuoni
- Albizzi Ginori Guadagni Medici
- Albizzi Guadagni Medici Ridolfi Tornabuoni
- Barbadori Castellani Medici Ridolfi Strozzi
- Bischeri Castellani Peruzzi Ridolfi Strozzi
- Bischeri Guadagni Ridolfi Strozzi Tornabuoni
- Medici Pazzi Salviati

The difference between the 2-cliques and the 2-clans on the marriage relation is that the five 2-cliques with diameter greater than 2 are excluded. For example, the diameter of the 2-clique {Barbadori, Medici, Ridolfi, Strozzi, Tornabuoni} is greater than 2, since the geodesic between Strozzi and Barbadori (which is of length 2) includes Castellani (who is not in this 2-clique).

7.3.5 Summary

The three definitions of cohesive subgroups discussed in this section are primarily motivated by the property of reachability among the nodes in a subgraph. An *n*-clique simply requires that there is some short path (geodesic) between subgroup members, though this short path may go outside the subgraph. An *n*-clique may be seen as too loose a definition of cohesive subgroup, and restrictions requiring geodesic paths to remain within the subgroup can be applied by requiring the subgraph to have a given maximum diameter. *n*-clubs and *n*-clans are two possible definitions that have the desired restrictions.

As Erickson (1988) has noted, cohesive subgroup definitions based on reachability are important for understanding "processes that operate through intermediaries, such as the diffusion of clear cut and widely salient information" (Erickson 1988, page 108). In studying network processes such as information diffusion that "flow" through intermediaries, cohesive subgroups based on indirect connections of relatively short paths provide a reasonable approach.

A related cohesive subgroup idea is influence among subgroup members. This idea provides the motivation for Hubbell's (1965) adaptation of economic input-output models to sociometric data. Hubbell argues that ties between actors are "channels for the transmission of influence" (1965, page 377). Influence occurs both through direct contact and through indirect chains of contact via other actors. The goal is to identify subgroups of actors among whom there is a relatively strong mutual influence, whether the influence is direct or indirect. Hubbell's approach relies on measures of influence based on a weighting of adjacencies and paths of influence, and a partitioning of actors based on the degree to which subgroup members mutually influence each other.

In contrast, if one hypothesizes that network processes require direct contact among actors, and perhaps repeated, direct, contact to several actors, then a different cohesive subgroup definition is required. We turn now to subgroup methods that study cohesive subgroups by focusing on adjacency between actors, rather than on paths and geodesics.

7.4 Subgroups Based on Nodal Degree

In this section we describe cohesive subgroup ideas that are based on the adjacency of subgroup members. These approaches are based on restrictions on the minimum number of actors adjacent to each actor in a subgroup. Since the number of actors adjacent to a given actor is quantified by the degree of the node in a graph, these subgroup methods focus on nodal degree. Subgroups based on nodal degree require actors to be adjacent to relatively numerous other subgroup members. Thus, unlike the clique definition that requires all members of a cohesive subgroup to be adjacent to *all* other subgroup members, these alternatives require that all subgroup members be adjacent to some minimum number of other subgroup members.

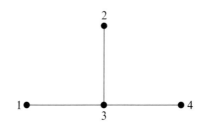

Fig. 7.3. A vulnerable 2-clique

Subgroups based on adjacency between members are useful for understanding processes that operate primarily through direct contacts among subgroup members. For example, Erickson hypothesizes that "multiple redundant channels of communication" will be related to the accuracy of information and the recognizability of subgroups (Erickson 1988, page 108).

These definitions arise in part because of the "vulnerability" of n-cliques. Seidman and Foster (1978) observed that n-cliques often are not robust. One measures robustness by considering "the degree to which the structure is vulnerable to the removal of any given individual" (Seidman and Foster 1978, page 142). Robustness is often assessed using measures of connectivity (see Chapter 4). Robust subgraphs are little affected by the removal of individual nodes. For example, consider the 2-clique in Figure 7.3 consisting of nodes 1, 2, 3, and 4. Although all pairs of nodes are within path distance 2 of each other, these paths all contain node 3. Node 3 is critical for the connections between other nodes. Furthermore, 1, 2, and 4 are not connected to each other through any paths that do not contain 3. This 2-clique is vulnerable to the removal of node 3.

The possible lack of robustness of n-cliques was one consideration that led to the proposal of an alternative subgroup definition. This alternative definition, the *k-plex*, builds on the notion that cohesive subgroups should contain sets of actors among whom there are relatively numerous adjacencies (Seidman 1978; Seidman and Foster 1978).

7.4.1 k-plexes

A *k-plex* is a maximal subgraph containing g_s nodes in which each node is adjacent to no fewer than $g_s - k$ nodes in the subgraph. In other words, each node in the subgraph may be lacking ties to no more than k subgraph members. We denote the degree of a node i in subgraph $\mathscr{G}_s$ by $d_s(i)$. A *k*-plex as a subgraph in which $d_s(i) \geq (g_s - k)$ for all $n_i \in \mathscr{N}_s$ and there are no other nodes in the subgraph that also have $d_s(i) \geq (g_s - k)$. That is, the *k*-plex is maximal.

Since there are g_s nodes in the subgraph, and we do not consider loops, the degree of a node within the subgraph cannot exceed $g_s - 1$. Thus, if $k = 1$, the subgraph is a clique (the "missing" line is the reflexive line from the node to itself). As k gets larger, each node is allowed more missing lines within the subgraph. Since nodes within a *k*-plex will be adjacent to many other members, a *k*-plex is more robust than an *n*-clique, and removal of a single node is less likely to leave the subgraph disconnected.

Seidman and Foster (1978) discuss properties of *k*-plexes. An important property of a *k*-plex is that the diameter of a *k*-plex is constrained by the value of *k*. Seidman and Foster prove that in a *k*-plex of g_s nodes, if $k < (g_s + 2)/2$, then the diameter of $\mathscr{G}_s$ is less than or equal to 2. Thus, if the value of *k* is small relative to the size of the *k*-plex, the *k*-plex will have a small diameter. They also note that if $\mathscr{G}_s$ is a *k*-plex with g_s nodes, then for any subgraph $\mathscr{G}_k$ of *k* nodes from $\mathscr{G}_s$, the set of nodes in $\mathscr{G}_k$ plus all nodes in $\mathscr{G}_s$ that are adjacent to the nodes in $\mathscr{G}_k$ constitute the node set of the *k*-plex $\mathscr{G}_s$. Thus, if you take any subset of *k* nodes in a *k*-plex, and then consider these *k* nodes along with the nodes adjacent to them, then all nodes in the *k*-plex (from which the subset is drawn) either will be in the original subset of *k* nodes or will be adjacent to one of these nodes (Seidman and Foster 1978).

An Example. Again, we return to the example of marriage and business relations for Padgett's Florentine families. We used the program *UCINET IV* (Borgatti, Everett, and Freeman 1991) for this analysis. Since 1-plexes are the same as cliques, we will examine the 2-plexes. Also, since $k=2$ means that two ties may be absent, we will restrict the size of the 2-plexes so that we only consider subgraphs with four or more members. For the marriage relation there are two 2-plexes, involving eight families:

- Albizzi Guadagni Medici Tornabuoni

- Bischeri Castellani Peruzzi Strozzi

Within each of these 2-plexes, each family is missing at most one marriage tie to one of the other families (since two ties can be missing, and one is the undefined reflexive tie). For the business relation there are three 2-plexes, involving six families:

- Barbadori Castellani Lamberteschi Peruzzi
- Bischeri Castellani Lamberteschi Peruzzi
- Bischeri Guadagni Lamberteschi Peruzzi

Notice that for both the marriage and the business relations there are relatively few 2-plexes, compared to fairly numerous 2-cliques.

Considerations. Choosing a useful value of k so that the resulting subgroups are both interesting and interpretable depends in part on the relationship between the sizes of the resulting subgroups and the chosen value of k. If the value of k is large relative to the size of a subgroup, then the k-plex can be quite sparse. For example, a 2-plex of size three might be meaningless, since all three nodes could be missing ties to $k = 2$ other nodes. A 2-plex of size four could also be quite sparse, since each node could have two lines present and two lines absent, and still meet the 2-plex requirement. Therefore, in practice the researcher should restrict the size of a k-plex so that it is not too small relative to the number of ties that are allowed to be missing.

7.4.2 k-cores

Another approach to cohesive subgroups based on nodal degree is the *k-core* (Seidman 1983b). A k-core is a subgraph in which each node is adjacent to at least a minimum number, k, of the other nodes in the subgraph. In contrast to the k-plex, which specifies the acceptable number of lines that can be *absent* from each node, the k-core specifies the required number of lines that must be *present* from each node to others within the subgraph. As before, we define the degree of node i within a subgraph, $d_s(i)$, as the number of nodes within the subgraph that are adjacent to i. We then define a k-core in terms of minimum nodal degree *within* the subgraph. A subgraph, $\mathcal{G}_s$, is a k-core if

$$d_s(i) \geq k \text{ for all } n_i \in \mathcal{N}_s.$$

A k-core is thus defined in terms of the minimum degree within a subgraph, or the minimum number of adjacencies that must be present. Seidman (1983b) notes that although k-cores themselves are not necessarily interesting cohesive subgroups, they are "areas" of a graph in which other interesting cohesive subgroups will be found.

7.5 Comparing Within to Outside Subgroup Ties

The three general cohesive subgroup approaches discussed so far in this chapter are based on properties of ties within the subgroup (adjacency, geodesic distance, or number of ties among subgroup members). However, as Seidman notes, cohesive subgroups "...in social networks have usually been seen informally as sets of individuals more closely tied to each other than to outsiders" (1983a, page 97). Thus, the intuitive notion of cohesive subgroup derives both from the relative strength, frequency, density, or closeness of ties within the subgroup, and the relative weakness, infrequency, sparseness, or distance of ties from subgroup members to nonmembers (Bock and Husain 1950; Alba 1973; Seidman 1983a; Sailer and Gaulin 1984; Freeman 1992a).

As Alba (1973) has noted, there are at least two different aspects to the concept of a cohesive subgroup: the concentration of ties within the subgroup, and a comparison of strength or frequency of ties within the subgroup to the strength or frequency of ties outside the subgroup. Alba has referred to the comparison of within to between subgroup ties as the "centripetal-centrifugal" dimension of cohesive subgroups. This idea has led to subgroup definitions that compare the prevalence of ties within the subgroup to the sparsity of ties outside the subgroup (Alba 1973; Bock and Husain 1950; Freeman n.d.; Sailer and Gaulin 1984). In this section we describe methods for analysis of subgroups based on comparison of ties within the subgroup to ties outside the subgroup.

The fourth cohesive subgroup idea is that cohesive subgroups should be relatively cohesive within compared to outside. Thus, instead of concentrating simply on properties of the ties among members within the subgroup, it is necessary to compare these to properties of ties to actors outside the subgroup.

It will be useful to define some additional graph properties before we describe these methods. Recall that a graph $\mathcal{G}$ consists of a set of nodes $\mathcal{N}$, and a set of lines $\mathcal{L}$. To start we will restrict our attention to dichotomous, undirected graphs. We will be interested in subsets of nodes $\mathcal{N}_s \subseteq \mathcal{N}$, and the subgraph $\mathcal{G}_s$ induced by node set $\mathcal{N}_s$. In addition, we can denote the subset of nodes that are in $\mathcal{N}$ but not in $\mathcal{N}_s$ as $\mathcal{N}_t = \mathcal{N} - \mathcal{N}_s$. $\mathcal{N}_t$ and $\mathcal{N}_s$ are mutually exclusive and exhaustive subsets. Now, there are three sets of lines in the graph: lines between nodes within the subset $\mathcal{N}_s$, lines between nodes in $\mathcal{N}_s$ and nodes in $\mathcal{N}_t$, and lines between nodes within $\mathcal{N}_t$. There are g nodes in $\mathcal{N}$, g_s nodes in $\mathcal{N}_s$, and $g_t = g - g_s$ nodes in $\mathcal{N}_t$. There are $g(g-1)/2$ possible lines in the entire graph, $g_s(g_s-1)/2$ possible lines within $\mathcal{N}_s$, and $g_s \times g_t$ possible lines between members of $\mathcal{N}_s$ and "outsiders" belonging to $\mathcal{N}_t$.

Let us first consider an "ideal" type of subgraph which exhibits the most extreme realization of a cohesive subgroup in which there are ties within the subgroup but not between subgroup members and outsiders (Freeman n.d.). Such an ideal subgroup would consist of ties between *all* pairs of members within the subgroup, and *no* ties from subgroup members to actors not in the subgroup. In graph theoretic terms, such a subgraph is a *complete component* of the graph. All nodes in a complete component are adjacent, and there are no nodes outside the subgraph that are adjacent to any node in the component. Freeman has called such a subgraph a *strong alliance*. A strong alliance is also a clique, since it is complete and maximal. But, a strong alliance is a stricter subgroup definition than is a clique. There are many cliques that are not strong alliances.

A strong alliance is a stricter subgroup definition than a clique and is clearly too restrictive for data analytic purposes. However, there are natural graph theoretic relaxations of the strong alliance that define useful cohesive subgroup methods. Also a strong alliance provides a formal standard against which to compare observed cohesive subgroups to assess their cohesiveness.

7.5.1 LS Sets

An *LS* set is a subgroup definition that compares ties within the subgroup to ties outside the subgroup by focusing on the greater frequency of ties among subgroup members compared to the ties from subgroup members to outsiders (Luccio and Sami 1969; Lawler 1973; Seidman 1983a; Borgatti, Everett, and Shirey 1990). Seidman defines an *LS* set as follows:

> a set of nodes S in a social network is an *LS* set if each of its proper subsets has more ties to its complement within S than to the outside of S. (Seidman 1983a, page 98)

Consider the subgraph $\mathscr{G}_s$ with node set $\mathscr{N}_s$, and the subsets of nodes that can be taken from $\mathscr{N}_s$. We will define a subset of nodes taken from $\mathscr{N}_s$ as $\mathscr{Q}$, so that $\mathscr{Q} \subset \mathscr{N}_s$. The set of nodes, $\mathscr{N}_s$, is an *LS* set if any proper subset $\mathscr{Q} \subset \mathscr{N}_s$ has more lines to the nodes in $\mathscr{N}_s - \mathscr{Q}$ (other nodes in the subset) than to $\mathscr{N} - \mathscr{N}_s$ (nodes outside the subset) (see Seidman 1983a, page 97).

The definition of an *LS* set compares the frequency of ties within and between subsets. There are three basic sets to consider: $\mathscr{Q} \subset \mathscr{N}_s \subseteq \mathscr{N}$. The set $\mathscr{Q}$ is a "wild card" that stands for any possible subset of nodes that can be selected from $\mathscr{N}_s$ (the potential *LS* set). Next there are two additional sets that consist of nodes in one of these three sets but not in another: $\mathscr{N} - \mathscr{N}_s$ and $\mathscr{N}_s - \mathscr{Q}$. There are two kinds of lines to consider: lines from $\mathscr{Q}$ to $\mathscr{N}_s - \mathscr{Q}$ and lines from $\mathscr{Q}$ to $\mathscr{N} - \mathscr{N}_s$. Lines within the *LS* set, $\mathscr{N}_s$ (that is, from any subset of the nodes in the *LS* set to remaining *LS* set members), should be more numerous than lines from a subset of nodes in an *LS* set to non-*LS* set members.

Seidman (1983a) and Borgatti, Everett, and Shirey (1990) have described several important properties of *LS* sets. First, since all subsets of the *LS* set have more ties within than outside the subset, they are relatively robust, and do not contain "splinter" groups. This leads Borgatti, Everett, and Shirey (1990) to hypothesize that *LS* sets in a network will be relatively stable through time. An important relationship between the *LS* sets in a given graph is that any two *LS* sets either are disjoint (share no members) or one *LS* set contains the other (Borgatti, Everett, and Shirey 1990). Unlike cliques, *n*-cliques, and *k*-plexes, *LS* sets cannot overlap by sharing some but not all members. The fact that *LS* sets are related by containment means that within a graph there is a hierarchical series of *LS* sets.

7.5.2 *Lambda Sets*

Recently, Borgatti, Everett, and Shirey (1990) have extended the notion of an *LS* set. Their approach, which they call a *lambda set*, is motivated by the idea that a cohesive subset should be relatively robust in terms of its *connectivity*. That is, a cohesive subset should be hard to disconnect by the removal of lines from the subgraph. The extent to which a pair of nodes remains connected by some path, even when lines are deleted from the graph, is quantified by the *edge connectivity* or *line connectivity* of the pair of nodes (see Chapter 4). The line connectivity of nodes i and j, denoted $\lambda(i, j)$, is equal to the minimum number of lines that must be removed from the graph in order to leave no path between the two nodes. The line connectivity of two nodes is also equal to the number of paths between them that contain no lines in common (the number of line-disjoint or line-independent paths). The smaller the value of $\lambda(i, j)$, the more vulnerable i and j are to being disconnected by removal of lines. The larger the value of $\lambda(i, j)$, the more lines must be removed from the graph in order to leave no path between i and j.

Using the notion of line connectivity, Borgatti, Everett, and Shirey (1990) define a *lambda set*. The logic of the definition of a lambda set is similar to the definition of an *LS* set. Consider pairs of nodes in the subgraph $\mathcal{G}_s$, with node set $\mathcal{N}_s$. The set of nodes, $\mathcal{N}_s$, is a lambda set if any pair of nodes in the lambda set has larger line connectivity than any pair of nodes consisting of one node from within the lambda set and a second node from outside the lambda set. Formally, a *lambda set* is a subset of nodes, $\mathcal{N}_s \subseteq \mathcal{N}$, such that for all $i, j, k \in \mathcal{N}_s$, and $l \in \mathcal{N} - \mathcal{N}_s$, $\lambda(i, j) > \lambda(k, l)$.

Since high values of λ require high line connectivity within the lambda set, successively increasing values of λ gives rise to a series of lambda sets in a given network. These lambda sets do not overlap unless one lambda set is contained within another. An advantage of lambda sets is that they are more general than *LS* sets. Any *LS* set in a network will be contained within a lambda set, and a given network is more likely to contain lambda sets than it is to contain *LS* sets (Borgatti, Everett, and Shirey 1990).

One important property of lambda sets is that nodes within a lambda set are not necessarily cohesive in terms of either adjacency or geodesic distance, the two properties that are the basis for other kinds of cohesive subsets that we have discussed. Members of a lambda set do not need to be adjacent, and since there is no restriction on the length of paths that connect nodes within a lambda set, members of a lambda set may be quite distant from one another in the graph (Borgatti, Everett, and Shirey 1990).

So far we have described formal definitions of cohesive subgroups. Now we turn to some measures of how cohesive a subgroup is.

7.6 Measures of Subgroup Cohesion

Several researchers have proposed measures for the extent to which ties are concentrated within a subgroup, rather than between subgroups (Bock and Husain 1950; Alba 1973; Sailer and Gaulin 1984; Freeman n.d.). These measures are primarily descriptive, although Alba presents a probability model for his measure. The problem of assessing the "goodness" of an assignment of actors to cohesive subgroups within a network is related to issues we discuss in Chapter 16, under the topic of goodness-of-fit indices. In this section we present some descriptive measures, and leave the statistical approaches for later, after we have developed the necessary background (in Chapters 13 and 15).

Bock and Husain (1950) proposed that one way to search for cohesive subgroups in a social network is iteratively to construct subgroups so that the ratio of the strength of ties within the subgroup to ties between subgroups does not decrease appreciably with the addition of new members. They note the similarity of this analytic problem to the analysis of sets of test items to identify subsets of highly correlated items. If there are g members in the whole network, and g_s members in a subgroup $\mathcal{N}_s$, then a measure of the degree to which strong ties are within rather than outside the subgroup is given by the ratio:

$$\frac{\frac{\sum_{i \in \mathcal{N}_s} \sum_{j \in \mathcal{N}_s} x_{ij}}{g_s(g_s-1)}}{\frac{\sum_{i \in \mathcal{N}_s} \sum_{j \notin \mathcal{N}_s} x_{ij}}{g_s(g-g_s)}}. \tag{7.2}$$

The numerator of this ratio is the average strength of ties within the subgroup and the denominator is the average strength of the ties that are from subgroup members to outsiders. For a dichotomous relation the numerator is the density of the subgroup. For a valued relation the numerator is the average strength of ties within the subgroup. If the ratio is equal to 1, then the strength of ties does not differ within the subgroup as compared to outside the subgroup. If the ratio is greater than 1, then the ties within the subgroup are more prevalent (or stronger) on average than are the ties outside the subgroup. Bock and Husain suggest that cohesive subgroups of actors can be constructed by successively adding members to an existing subgroup, so long as the additional members do not greatly decrease the value of this ratio.

As we mentioned above, Alba (1973) views the measure in equation (7.2) in terms of two separate components. The numerator is a measure of the cohesiveness of a subgroup, and the denominator is a measure of sparsity of ties to actors outside the subgroup. Alba calls these the "centripetal" and "centrifugal" properties, respectively. Further, he presents formulas for the probability of obtaining the density of a subgroup equal to or greater than the observed density, given the density of the graph.

Alba (1973) uses the hypergeometric probability function to calculate the probability of observing exactly L_s lines in a subgraph of g_s nodes, taken from a graph with g nodes and L lines. Equivalently, this is the probability of drawing a random sample without replacement of $g_s(g_s - 1)/2$ dyads (the number of dyads within the subgroup) and observing exactly L_s ties present, from a graph of $g(g - 1)/2$ dyads and $L = x_{++}/2$ ties. The probability that the observed number of lines in the subgraph is equal to q is given by the following hypergeometric probability (Alba 1973, page 122):

$$P(L_s = q) = \frac{\dbinom{L}{q} \dbinom{\frac{g(g-1)}{2} - L}{\frac{g_s(g_s-1)}{2} - q}}{\dbinom{\frac{g(g-1)}{2}}{\frac{g_s(g_s-1)}{2}}}. \tag{7.3}$$

Equation (7.3) is the probability of obtaining exactly q lines in the subgraph. The probability that we are interested in is the probability of q *or more* lines; that is, the probability of a subgraph that is as dense or denser than the one we observe. Thus, we must sum the probabilities from equation (7.3) for values of q from L_s, the observed number of lines in the subgraph, to its maximum possible, which is either $g_s(g_s - 1)/2$, the possible number of lines that could be present in the subgraph, or $L = x_{++}/2$, the observed number of lines in the graph, whichever is less. The formula for the probability of observing q or more lines in a subgraph of size g_s from a graph with L lines is:

$$P(L_s \geq q) = \sum_{k=q}^{\min(L, \frac{g_s(g_s-1)}{2})} \frac{\dbinom{L}{k} \dbinom{\frac{g(g-1)}{2} - L}{\frac{g_s(g_s-1)}{2} - k}}{\dbinom{\frac{g(g-1)}{2}}{\frac{g_s(g_s-1)}{2}}}. \tag{7.4}$$

If the calculated probability in equation (7.4) is small, then the observed frequency of lines within the subgraph is greater than would be expected by chance, given the frequency of lines in the graph as a whole. Thus, this probability can be interpreted as a p-value for the null hypothesis that there is no difference between the density of the subgraph and the density of the graph as a whole.

Freeman (n.d.) provides another approach to measuring the cohesiveness of a subgroup. Freeman's measure is based on his model of strict alliances (see discussion above) and the extent to which a given subgroup approaches that strictly defined property. Sailer and Gaulin (1984) discuss several alternative measures of cohesiveness of a subgroup, depending on how one conceptualizes the concentration of interactions within as opposed to outside the subgroup.

So far we have described cohesive subgroup methods for dichotomous nondirectional relations. We now discuss extensions of cohesive subgroups to relations that are valued or directional. These extensions allow the cohesive subgroup ideas discussed in the previous sections to be applied to a much wider range of social network data.

7.7 Directional Relations

Cohesive subgroup ideas can be extended to directional relations. We will continue to restrict our attention to dichotomous relations. Recall that a directional relation is one in which a tie has an origin and a destination. A directional relation can be represented as a directed graph. An arc in the directed graph is present from i to j if $i \rightarrow j$, or equivalently, if i "chooses" j. In a sociomatrix for a directional relation x_{ij} might not equal x_{ji}.

There are several ways to define cohesive subgroups for directional relations. The most straightforward way is to consider only the reciprocated ties that are present in the graph (Festinger 1949; Luce and Perry 1949; Luce 1950). More generally, it is possible to define properties of connectedness for directional relations, and then use these properties to define cohesive subgroups for directional relations. We will discuss each approach in turn.

7.7.1 Cliques Based on Reciprocated Ties

Recall that the definition of a clique originally proposed by Festinger (1949) and Luce and Perry (1949) focused on directional affective relations and required that all ties between all pairs of clique members be reciprocated. Thus, cliques can be found in a directional relation by focusing only on those ties that are reciprocated ($x_{ij} = x_{ji} = 1$). In analyzing a directional relation, this is equivalent to symmetrizing the sociomatrix by taking the minimum of the entries in corresponding off-diagonal cells. More precisely, we can define a new nondirectional relation, $\mathcal{X}^{min}$, where

$$x_{ij}^{min} = x_{ji}^{min} = \begin{cases} 1 & \text{if } x_{ij} = x_{ji} = 1, \\ 0 & \text{otherwise.} \end{cases}$$

The new relation $\mathscr{X}^{min}$ contains only ties that are reciprocated ($x_{ij} = x_{ji} = 1$) or null ($x_{ij} = x_{ji} = 0$). The sociomatrix representation for this relation is symmetric. The relation $\mathscr{X}^{min}$ can then be analyzed using methods for finding cliques or other cohesive subgroups in a nondirectional relation. However, if there are few reciprocated ties the resulting symmetric relation will be quite sparse, and might not yield many cohesive subgroups.

An Example. As an example of a clique analysis of a dichotomous directional relation we will consider the Friendship relation for Krackhardt's high-tech managers. Recall that each manager was asked, "Who are your friends?" Thus, a friendship tie is directed from one manager to another, and friendship choices need not be reciprocated. To find cliques (subsets of actors among whom all choices are reciprocated), it is necessary to analyze only those ties that are reciprocated. This is accomplished by symmetrizing the sociomatrix as described above. We analyzed the symmetrized sociomatrix for the friendship relation using *UCINET IV* (Borgatti, Everett, and Freeman 1991). There are six cliques, containing nine of the managers.

- 1 4 12
- 4 12 17
- 5 11 17
- 5 11 19
- 11 15 19
- 12 17 21

Notice that these cliques are small, containing only the minimum three members, and there is considerable overlap among them.

7.7.2 Connectivity in Directional Relations

A more flexible way to extend cohesive subgroup ideas to directional relations uses definitions of semipaths and connectivity for directed graphs. These ideas generalize the definitions of path, path distance, and connectivity from graphs to directed graphs, and were defined in Chapter 4. We will begin by briefly reviewing the two kinds of paths for digraphs and then use these kinds of paths to describe four ways to extend the notion of connectivity and n-cliques to directed graphs (Harary, Norman, and Cartwright 1965; Peay 1975a, 1980).

Recall that a *path* from node i to node j in a directed graph is a sequence of distinct nodes, where each arc has its origin at the previous node and its terminus at the subsequent node. Thus, a path in a directed graph consists of arcs all "pointing" in the same direction. The length of a path is the number of arcs in it. A *semipath* from node i to node j is a sequence of distinct nodes, where all successive pairs of nodes are connected by an arc from the first to the second, or by an arc from the second to the first. In a semipath the direction of the arcs is irrelevant. The length of a semipath is the number of arcs in it.

There are four different ways in which two nodes can be connected by a path, or semipath, of n arcs or fewer. Our definitions come from Peay (1980, pages 390–391). A pair of nodes, i, j, is:

(i) *Weakly n-connected* if they are joined by a *semipath* of length n or less

(ii) *Unilaterally n-connected* if they are joined by a *path* of length n or less from i to j, *or* a *path* of length n or less from j to i

(iii) *Strongly n-connected* if there is a *path* of length n or less from i to j, *and* a path of length n or less from j to i; the path from i to j may contain different nodes and arcs than the path from j to i

(iv) *Recursively n-connected* if they are strongly n-connected, and the path from i to j uses the same nodes and arcs as the path from j to i, in reverse order

These are increasingly strict connectivity definitions. A pair of nodes connected by a stricter kind of connectivity is also connected by weaker kinds.

7.7.3 *n-cliques in Directional Relations*

It is now possible to define four different kinds of cohesive subgroups based on the four types of connectivity (see Peay 1975, 1980). In each case, a cohesive subgroup is defined as a subgraph of three or more nodes that is maximal with respect to the specified property. The property is the kind of connectivity between the nodes in the subgraph. Since there are four kinds of connectivity in a directed graph, there are four definitions of cohesive subgroups. These are natural extensions of the definition of an *n*-clique described above.

(i) A *weakly connected n-clique* is a subgraph in which all nodes are weakly n-connected, and there are no additional nodes that are also weakly n-connected to all nodes in the subgraph.

(ii) A *unilaterally connected n-clique* is a subgraph in which all nodes are unilaterally n-connected, and there are no additional nodes that are also unilaterally n-connected to all nodes in the subgraph.

(iii) A *strongly connected n-clique* is a subgraph in which all nodes are strongly n-connected, and there are no additional nodes that are also strongly n-connected to all nodes in the subgraph.

(iv) A *recursively connected n-clique* is a subgraph in which all nodes are recursively n-connected, and there are no additional nodes that are also recursively n-connected to all nodes in the subgraph.

As with the definitions of connectivity, these are increasingly strict cohesive subgroup definitions.

Finding some kinds of n-cliques in directional dichotomous relations is straightforward. Finding weakly connected n-cliques and recursively connected n-cliques requires symmetrizing the relation using the appropriate rule, and then using a standard n-clique algorithm. Since weakly connected n-cliques require a semipath of length n or less between all members, the direction of the arcs in the semipath is irrelevant. Thus, we can construct a symmetric relation, $\mathcal{X}^{max}$, with values x_{ij}^{max}, in which a tie is present from i to j if either $i \rightarrow j$ or $j \rightarrow i$. The relation $\mathcal{X}^{max}$ is defined as:

$$x_{ij}^{max} = x_{ji}^{max} = \begin{cases} 1 & \text{if either } x_{ij} = 1 \text{ or } x_{ji} = 1, \\ 0 & \text{otherwise.} \end{cases}$$

The n-cliques in $\mathcal{X}^{max}$ are the weakly connected n-cliques in $\mathcal{X}$.

Recursively connected n-cliques require not only a path of length n or less between all pairs of members, but the paths must contain exactly the same nodes in the reverse order. Thus, one must only consider arcs in both directions. In order to find recursively connected n-cliques, one can construct a symmetric relation, $\mathcal{X}^{min}$ (as defined above), in which a tie in $\mathcal{X}^{min}$ is present only if both $x_{ij} = 1$ and $x_{ji} = 1$. The n-cliques in $\mathcal{X}^{min}$ are the recursively connected n-cliques in $\mathcal{X}$.

An Example. To illustrate n-cliques for a dichotomous directional relation we will use the friendship relation from Krackhardt's high-tech managers. We only present the recursively connected 2-cliques and the weakly connected 2-cliques, which, as we have discussed above, can be found by using an appropriately symmetrized sociomatrix, and a usual *n*-clique program (for example, in *GRADAP* or *UCINET IV*).

There are eight recursively connected 2-cliques:

- 1 2 4 12 16
- 1 2 4 12 17 21
- 1 2 18 21
- 1 4 8 12 17
- 3 5 11 15 19
- 4 5 6 11 12 17 21
- 5 11 13 15 17 19
- 11 14 15 19

Seventeen of the twenty-one managers belong to at least one of the recursively connected 2-cliques. Since managers 7 and 9 have outdegrees equal to 0 on this relation (they did not choose anyone on the friendship relation), they cannot belong to either recursively or strongly connected *n*-cliques.

There are four weakly connected 2-cliques:

- 1 2 3 4 5 8 9 10 11 12 15 17 19 20 21 16 6 14 7
- 1 2 3 4 5 8 9 10 11 12 15 17 19 20 21 16 6 18
- 1 2 3 4 5 8 9 10 11 12 15 17 19 20 21 13 18
- 1 2 3 4 5 8 9 10 11 12 15 17 19 20 21 13 14

All of the twenty-one managers belong to at least one of the four weakly connected 2-cliques, and the vast majority (fifteen of the twenty-one managers) belong to all of them. Clearly, these weakly connected 2-cliques are not very cohesive.

7.8 Valued Relations

Relations are often valued. Valued relations indicate the strength or intensity of ties between pairs of actors. For instance, social network data can be collected by having each person indicate their degree of "liking for" or "acquaintance with" each other person in a group using a five point rating scale. Or, one could record the number of social occasions at which each pair of actors were both present. Cohesive subgroups in valued relations focus on subsets of actors among whom ties are strong or frequent; thus, ties among subgroup members should have high values.

Valued relations are represented as valued graphs. A valued graph, $\mathcal{G}(\mathcal{N}, \mathcal{L}, \mathcal{V})$, consists of a set of nodes, $\mathcal{N}$, a set of lines, $\mathcal{L}$, and a set of values, $\mathcal{V}$, indicating the strength of each line. The value attached to a line codes the strength of the tie between the pair of actors. A valued relation can be represented as a sociomatrix where x_{ij} is the value of the tie from actor i to actor j. We will assume that measurements on the valued relation are at least ordinal, and take on C values, such that $0 \leq x_{ij} \leq C - 1$, for all i and j. The highest possible value indicates the strongest tie between any pair of actors. Smaller values of x_{ij} indicate weaker ties. Thus, since the relation is assumed to be at least ordinal, if $x_{ij} < x_{kl}$, the tie from i to j is weaker than the tie from k to l. For simplicity we will limit our attention to nondirectional valued relations. In a nondirectional valued relation the strength of the tie from actor i to actor j is the same as the strength of the tie from actor j to actor i. If the relation is nondirectional $x_{ij} = x_{ji}$ for all i and j, and the sociomatrix is symmetric.

In general, a cohesive subgroup of actors in a valued network is a subset of actors among whom ties have high values. Thus, if we consider the values attached to the ties among subgroup members, these values should be relatively high. Since the values of the ties range from 0 (indicating the weakest possible tie) to $C - 1$ (indicating the strongest tie), more cohesive subgroups will have ties with values close to $C - 1$ whereas less cohesive subgroups will have ties with values lower than $C - 1$. Thus, in a valued relation we can study cohesive subgroups that vary in the strength of ties among members.

In studying cohesive subgroups in valued relations we will consider a threshold value, c, for the value of ties within the subgroup. By increasing (or decreasing) the threshold value we can find more (or less) cohesive subgroups. Since the values of the ties range from 0 to $C - 1$, the threshold value c can take on values between 0 and $C - 1$.

We will now define a clique, n-clique, and k-plex for a valued relation. We then describe how valued relations can be analyzed to study these cohesive subgroups. Further discussion of cliques and related ideas for valued relations can be found in Doreian (1969) and Peay (1974, 1975a, 1980).

7.8.1 Cliques, n-cliques, and k-plexes

Let us first define a *clique at level c*. A clique at level c is a subgraph in which the ties between all pairs of actors have values of c or greater, and there is no other actor outside the clique who also has ties of strength c or greater to all actors in the clique. Formally, a subgraph $\mathscr{G}_s$ with actor set $\mathscr{N}_s$ is a clique at level c if for all actors $i, j \in \mathscr{N}_s$, $x_{ij} \geq c$, and there is no actor k, such that $x_{ki} \geq c$ for all $i \in \mathscr{N}_s$ (Peay 1975a).

We can successively increase (or decrease) the threshold value, c, through the range of values 0 to $C - 1$. By increasing the threshold value, we will be able to identify subgroups that are more and more cohesive, and by decreasing the threshold value, we will identify subgroups that are less and less cohesive. Using increasingly strict cutoff values leads to a hierarchical series of cliques. It is important to note that a clique that is present at a given cutoff value, c, will be a clique, or will be contained within a larger clique, at any less stringent cutoff value, c', where $c' < c$ (Doreian 1969; and Peay 1974).

Now, let us consider n-cliques in valued relations. In valued relations, n-cliques are based on the values of the geodesics between subgroup members. Recall that a path at level c in a valued graph is a path in which all lines have values of c or greater. Also, two nodes in a valued graph are reachable at level c if there is a path at level c between them. In a valued relation, an n-clique at level c requires that geodesics between subgroup members contain lines that have values that are all c or greater. Thus, an n-clique at level c in a valued graph contains members all of whom are reachable at level c by a path of length n or less (Peay 1975a). Since subgroup members are reachable at level c, there is a path at level c between each pair of n-clique members.

One can also define a k-plex at level c for a valued relation. A k-plex at level c in a valued relation requires that all g_s members of the k-plex have ties with values of c or greater to no fewer than $g_s - k$ of the other k-plex members.

We now describe how to find cliques, n-cliques, and k-plexes in valued relations.

Finding Cliques, n-cliques, and k-plexes. One way to study cohesive subgroups in valued relations is to define one or more derived dichotomous relations based on the strength of the ties in the original valued relation (Doreian 1969). We will then be able to use the subgroup approaches for dichotomous relations to analyze valued relations by analyzing the derived dichotomous relations.

Given a set of actors, $\mathscr{N}$, and a valued relation, $\mathscr{X}$, we define a new dichotomous relation, $\mathscr{X}^{(c)}$, such that there is a tie from actor i to j in $\mathscr{X}^{(c)}$ if the value of the tie from i to j in $\mathscr{X}$ is greater than or equal to the specified value, c. In this new dichotomous relation ties are present among all pairs of actors who have ties in $\mathscr{X}$ with values of c or greater. We denote this new, derived dichotomous relation as $\mathscr{X}^{(c)}$, with sociomatrix $\mathbf{X}^{(c)} = \{x_{ij}^{(c)}\}$, where

$$
x_{ij}^{(c)} = \begin{cases} 1 & \text{if } x_{ij} \geq c \\ 0 & \text{otherwise.} \end{cases}
$$

For any valued relation we can define an increasingly strict series of cutoff values, c, that spans the range of values $0 \leq c \leq C - 1$. Each value of c defines a dichotomous relation and its corresponding graph and sociomatrix. With larger values of c, ties are present in $\mathscr{X}^{(c)}$ only if there is a relatively strong tie between actors in $\mathscr{X}$. Thus for larger values of c, the relation $\mathscr{X}^{(c)}$ may be fairly sparse. For small values of c, a tie is present in $\mathscr{X}^{(c)}$ even if the strength of the tie in $\mathscr{X}$ is relatively low, and thus this relation can be fairly dense. In fact, a cutoff value of $c = 0$ results in a complete relation (and a complete graph) since all defined values of $\mathbf{X}^{(0)}$ will be equal to unity. Thus, in practice, there are $C - 1$ nontrivial graphs that can be defined from a valued graph with C levels. It is important to note that for two cutoff values, c and c', with $c' < c$, all of the ties present in $\mathscr{X}^{(c)}$ will also be present in $\mathscr{X}^{(c')}$; in other words, $\mathscr{X}^{(c')}$ "includes" $\mathscr{X}^{(c)}$.

We now illustrate cliques in a valued relation using a hypothetical valued graph and the dichotomous relations that can be derived from it.

An Example. Figure 7.4 presents the sociomatrix for a valued relation and the graphs that can be derived from this relation. The values of the relation range from 0 to $C - 1 = 5$. Thus, there are five possible nontrivial graphs that can be derived from this valued relation using increasingly strict cutoff values.

Consider the cliques that may be present in each derived graph, starting from the strictest cutoff value, $c = 5$. At the strictest cutoff, $c = 5$, there are no cliques. As c decreases there are more, and larger, cliques in the derived graphs. The results of a clique analysis of each of the five derived graphs are:

- $c = 5$: no cliques
- $c = 4$: $\{1, 2, 3\}$
- $c = 3$: $\{1, 2, 3\}$
- $c = 2$: $\{1, 2, 3\}$ and $\{3, 4, 5\}$
- $c = 1$: $\{1, 2, 3, 4\}$ and $\{3, 4, 5\}$

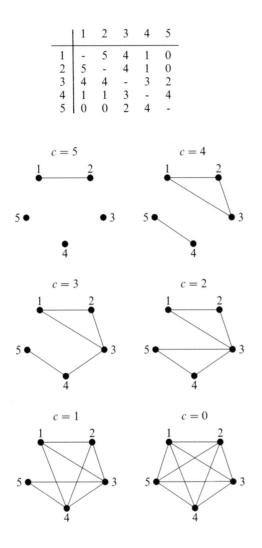

	1	2	3	4	5
1	-	5	4	1	0
2	5	-	4	1	0
3	4	4	-	3	2
4	1	1	3	-	4
5	0	0	2	4	-

Fig. 7.4. A valued relation and derived graphs

Notice that the clique containing nodes 1, 2, and 3 that occurs at $c = 4$ continues to be a clique, or is subsumed within a larger clique, at all less stringent values of c.

In general, every derived dichotomous relation defines a graph that can be analyzed using methods for finding cohesive subgroups, described above. For example, one can analyze each of the graphs derived from a valued relation and study the cliques, k-plexes, or n-cliques that may exist in each of the graphs. Each of the $C - 1$ graphs may (or may not) contain cohesive subgroups.

Actors among whom ties have large values can appear in cohesive subgroups at strict cutoff levels, whereas actors among whom ties have small values can only appear in cohesive subgroups at less strict cutoff levels. As Doreian (1969) notes, analyzing the derived graphs for increasingly stringent values of c results in a hierarchical series of cohesive subgroups. This hierarchical series allows one to study the internal structure of cohesive subgroups.

The approaches presented in this section generalize cohesive subgroup ideas that were initially developed for dichotomous relations and apply them to valued relations. Thus, the definitions of clique, n-clique, and k-plex remain the same, but are applied to dichotomous relations derived from the valued relation. An alternative approach for studying cohesive subgroups in valued relations is to define cohesive subgroup ideas specifically for valued relations (Freeman 1992a).

7.8.2 Other Approaches for Valued Relations

In a recent paper, Freeman (1992a) reviews sociological approaches to the concept of social "group" and discusses formalizations of this concept using data on frequency of interactions among people in naturally occurring communities. Data on interaction frequencies give rise to valued relations. Freeman's argument, expanding on ideas presented by Winship (1977) and Granovetter (1973), is that membership in a "group" should be characterized by relatively frequent face-to-face interactions among members. Specifically, if actors i, j, and k are members of a "group," then if i and j interact frequently, and j and k interact frequently, then i and k should have at least some amount of interaction. This idea of cohesiveness of subgroups builds on Granovetter's (1973) ideas of strong and weak ties, and extends the ideas of transitivity and clusterability to valued relations. Advantages of this approach are that the resulting cohesive subgroups form a hierarchical series, and different subgroups do not overlap unless one subgroup is fully contained within another.

7.9 Interpretation of Cohesive Subgroups

The result of a cohesive subgroup analysis is a list of subsets of actors within the network who meet the specified subgroup definition. For example, the result of a clique analysis is a list of the cliques in the network and the actors who belong to each clique. For a given analysis it might be the case that no subsets of actors meet the specified subgroup definition (for example, it might be that there are no cliques in a given network), or it might be the case that there are numerous subsets of actors that meet the specified subgroup definition (for example, the *n*-clique analysis of the marriage relation among Padgett's Florentine families resulted in thirteen 2-cliques). In any case, the researcher must interpret the results of the analysis. In this section we discuss three levels at which one might interpret the results of a cohesive subgroup analysis. These levels are the:

(i) Individual actor
(ii) Subset of actors
(iii) Whole group

In terms of individual actors, the simplest distinction is between actors who belong to one or more cohesive subset(s), and actors who do not belong to any cohesive subset. Thus, we can make a distinction between "members" and "non-members." One can then relate this distinction to other actor characteristics, for example, by studying whether subgroup "members" differ from "non-members" in theoretically important ways. It could also be the case that "non-members" occupy critical locations between groups; for example, they might have high betweenness centrality. The network analysis program *NEGOPY* (Richards 1989a) uses a similar distinction to describe types of actors in a network.

The result of a cohesive subgroup analysis can also be interpreted in terms of the characteristics of the members of the subsets. If the network data set contains information on attributes of the actors, then one can use these attributes to describe the subsets. For example, it might be the case that members of the same subgroup are more similar to each other than they are to outsiders. This method of interpretation was used by Alba and Moore (1978) to describe the composition of subgroups of elite decision makers.

Finally, the result of a cohesive subgroup analysis can be used to describe the network as a whole. Consider two quite different ways that a network might be organized. On the one hand, a network could be a single cohesive set. On the other hand, the network could be "fragmented" into two or more subgroups. In the first case, cohesive subgroups within the network would be largely overlapping, and would contain most of the actors in the network. We saw this pattern for the *n*-clique analysis of Friendship among Kackhardt's high-tech managers. In the second case, fragmentation of the network would show up as two or more cohesive subgroups that did not share members in common. Hence, the numbers of actors in the subgroups and the degree to which these subgroups overlap can be used to describe the structure of the network as a whole.

7.10 Other Approaches

All of the cohesive subgroup ideas discussed in the previous sections define specific graph theoretic properties that should be satisfied in order to identify a subset of actors as a cohesive subgroup. For all of these approaches, the analytic problem is to examine a set of social network data to see whether any subsets of actors meet the specified subgroup definition. The result is the possible assignment of actors to one or more cohesive subgroups. An alternative, and more exploratory, approach to cohesion in social networks seeks to represent the group structure in a network as a whole. Collections of actors among whom there are relatively strong ties can become more visible by displaying functions or rearrangements of the graphs or sociomatrices. We now describe these approaches.

7.10.1 *Matrix Permutation Approaches*

The earliest contributions to cohesive subgroup analysis of social networks were concerned with systematic ways for ordering rows and columns of a sociomatrix to reveal the subgroup structure of a network (Forsyth and Katz 1946; Katz 1947). The subgroup structure is seen in the relative prevalence (or sparsity) of ties among some subsets of actors. An informative sociomatrix should make this subgroup structure readily apparent. If there are subgroups of actors in a network who tend to choose each other and tend not to choose actors outside their subgroup, then it is very useful to rearrange the rows and columns of the sociomatrix so that actors in the same subgroup occupy rows (and columns) that are close to one another in the sociomatrix. Thus, there might be some "preferred ordering" of the rows and columns of the sociomatrix that would best reveal the structure of the group (Katz 1947). If one had objective criteria for this ordering, then different researchers could construct the same preferred sociomatrix. One could then inspect the rearranged sociomatrix and identify subgroups of actors among whom there are prevalent or strong ties.

An important property of a good ordering of a sociomatrix is that subsets of actors who have strong ties to each other should occupy adjacent rows (and columns), or at least should occupy rows (and columns) that are close in the sociomatrix. If actors who "choose" each other occupy rows and columns that are close in the sociomatrix, then ties that are present will be concentrated on the main diagonal of the sociomatrix, and ties that are absent will be concentrated far from the main diagonal of the sociomatrix. For a dichotomous relation, 1's will be close to the main diagonal and 0's will be in the upper right and lower left of the sociomatrix. In analyzing a valued relation, ties with larger values will be concentrated along the main diagonal and ties with smaller values will be found in cells of the matrix that are off the main diagonal.

The goal is to permute the rows (and simultaneously the columns) of the sociomatrix to concentrate "choices" along the main diagonal (Katz 1947). Subgroups of actors who "choose" one another will then be close to each other in rows (columns) of the sociomatrix, and their choices will be close to the main diagonal of the sociomatrix.

Since the mid-1940's, numerous authors have proposed objective criteria for permuting rows and columns of a matrix to concentrate "choices" along the main diagonal of a matrix (Katz 1947; Beum and Brundage 1950; Coleman and MacRae 1960; Hubert 1985, 1987; Hubert and Arabie 1989; Hubert and Schultz 1976; Arabie, Hubert, and Schleutermann 1990). Some of these methods are applicable to matrices in general, and are thus not restricted to sociomatrices.

Figure 7.5 shows a small hypothetical sociomatrix, first in original order, and then with the rows and columns permuted so that actors who have ties to each other are close to one another in the sociomatrix.

Systematic procedures for permuting rows and columns of a sociomatrix seek to minimize a function that quantifies the extent to which ties with high values are far from the main diagonal (assuming that high values code strong ties). Recall that x_{ij} is the value of the tie from actor i to actor j. Furthermore, i and j index the rows/columns of the sociomatrix (for example, $i = 2$ refers to row 2 of the sociomatrix). Therefore, we would like to have large values of x_{ij} correspond to small differences between the indices i and j. Small differences between the indices can be

X

	n_1	n_2	n_3	n_4	n_5
n_1	-	0	1	0	1
n_2	0	-	0	1	0
n_3	1	0	-	0	1
n_4	0	1	0	-	0
n_5	1	0	1	0	-

X permuted

	n_5	n_1	n_3	n_2	n_4
n_5	-	1	1	0	0
n_1	1	-	1	0	0
n_3	1	1	-	0	0
n_2	0	0	0	-	1
n_4	0	0	0	1	-

Fig. 7.5. A hypothetical example showing a permuted sociomatrix

quantified either by small values of $|i - j|$ or by small values of $(i - j)^2$. The largest values of x_{ij} should occupy cells in which the indices i and j are close. The smallest values of x_{ij} should occupy cells in which the indices i and j are far apart.

For an entire matrix a summary measure of how close large values of x_{ij} are to the main diagonal is given by:

$$\sum_{i=1}^{g}\sum_{j=1}^{g} x_{ij}(i - j)^2 \text{ for } i \neq j. \tag{7.5}$$

The quantity in equation (7.5) is relatively small when large values of x_{ij} occupy cells of the sociomatrix with small differences between the indices i and j. This quantity is relatively large when large values of x_{ij} occupy cells of the sociomatrix with large differences between the indices i and j. If the value of equation (7.5) is small, then the ordering of rows and columns in the sociomatrix places actors among whom there are relatively strong ties close to each other, as is desired. On the other hand, if the value of this quantity is relatively large, then the ordering of rows and columns in the sociomatrix probably is not the best possible ordering for revealing cohesive subgroups of actors. Katz (1947) suggests permuting rows and simultaneously columns of the sociomatrix to minimize this quantity.

Beum and Brundage (1950), Coleman and MacRae (1960), and Arabie, Hubert, and Schleutermann (1990) suggest strategies for reordering rows and columns of the sociomatrix so that i and j corresponding to large values of x_{ij} are moved closer together. This problem of *sociomatrix permutation* to optimize a given quantity is an instance of the more general analysis problem of combinatorial optimization. Finding the single best ordering of rows and columns of a data array is computationally intensive, and, short of trying all possible permutations, there may be no guarantee that the optimum has been reached. Algorithms for permuting rows and columns to minimize a given objective function can be found in Arabie, Hubert, and Schleutermann (1990 and references therein) and a more general review of this data analytic approach can be found in Arabie and Hubert (1992).

The result of a matrix permutation analysis is a reordering of the rows and columns of the sociomatrix so that actors that are close in the sociomatrix tend to have relatively strong ties. However, a matrix permutation analysis does not indicate the boundaries between, or membership in, any subgroups that might exist in the network. Therefore, matrix permutation methods do not locate discrete subgroups. These methods do provide a preferred ordering in which to present a sociomatrix. Nevertheless, it can be quite informative to present the sociomatrix with rows and columns permuted to suggest the subgroup structure.

Other approaches to subgroup identification include methods for presenting the subgroup structure of a social network using standard data analytic methods to display proximities among actors. Approaches in this tradition use multidimensional scaling, hierarchical clustering, or factor analysis to represent the proximities among network actors. We will briefly describe multidimensional scaling and factor analysis for representing proximities among actors.

7.10.2 *Multidimensional Scaling*

Often the researcher is confronted with a set of network data and simply wishes to display the proximities among actors in the group. Such representations can be quite useful for understanding the internal structure of the group, for revealing which actors are "close" to each other, and for presenting possible cleavages between subgroups. Standard clustering and multidimensional scaling techniques can be used to represent proximities among actors when appropriate network measures are used as input.

Multidimensional scaling has been used by many network analysts to represent proximities among actors. Just a few of the many substantive examples include: studies of community elites (Laumann and Pappi 1973,

1976), naturally occurring communities (Freeman, Romney, and Freeman 1987; Freeman, Freeman, and Michaelson 1988; Arabie and Carroll 1989; Doreian and Albert 1989), organizational culture (Krackhardt and Kilduff n.d.), scientific communities (Arabie 1977), and state supreme court precedents (Caldeira 1988).

Multidimensional scaling is a very general data analysis technique, and there are numerous texts and articles describing multidimensional scaling (see for example Kruskal and Wish 1978; Schiffman, Reynolds, and Young 1981; and Coxon 1982). Multidimensional scaling seeks to represent proximities (similarities or dissimilarities) among a set of entities in low-dimensional space so that entities that are more proximate to each other in the input data are closer in the space, and entities that are less proximate to each other are farther apart in the space. The usual input to multidimensional scaling is a one-mode symmetric matrix consisting of measures of similarity, dissimilarity, or proximity between pairs of entities. To study cohesive subsets of actors in a network the input to multidimensional scaling should be some measure of pairwise proximity among actors, such as the geodesic distance between each pair of actors. The output of multidimensional scaling is a set of estimated distances among pairs of entities, which can be expressed as coordinates in one-, two-, or higher-dimensional space. Results are also displayed as a diagram in which the coordinates are used to locate the entities in the resulting one-, two-, or three-dimensional space. Using multidimensional scaling to study cohesive subgroups shows which subsets of actors are relatively close to each other in a graph theoretic sense.

An Example. To illustrate multidimensional scaling for studying cohesive subgroups we use the marriage relation for Padgett's Florentine families. Recall that this relation is dichotomous and nondirectional. Analyzing the sociomatrix directly using multidimensional scaling is unwise. Since there are only 0's and 1's in this matrix the multidimensional scaling solution would be very unstable. Instead, it is useful to compute a valued measure of proximity among pairs of actors. One such measure is the geodesic distance between pairs of actors. In our example we use the matrix of the geodesic distances among pairs of families as input to multidimensional scaling. We used *GRADAP* (Sprenger and Stokman 1989) to calculate the path distances, and *SYSTAT* (Wilkinson 1987) to do the multidimensional scaling. The Pucci family is an isolate on the marriage relation and thus was omitted from the multidimensional scaling. The final multidimensional scaling solution in two dimensions

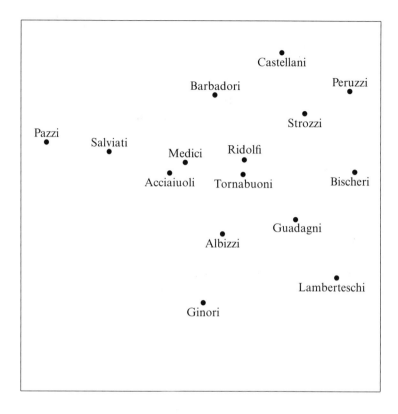

Fig. 7.6. Multidimensional scaling of path distances on the marriage relation for Padgett's Florentine families (Pucci family omitted)

has stress equal to 0.0198 (Kruskal, stress form 1). This result is presented in Figure 7.6.

Notice in Figure 7.6 that one of the most prominent families, Medici, is located in the center of the plot. It is also interesting to note that the six families (Bischeri, Castellani, Guadagni, Lamberteschi, Peruzzi, and Strozzi) identified by Kent (1978; also see Breiger and Pattison 1986) as being in the anti-Medici faction are, without exception, all on the right side of the plot.

7.10.3 ○ *Factor Analysis*

Factor analysis of sociometric data was quite widespread and influential in the early history of network analysis (Bock and Husain 1952; MacRae 1960; Wright and Evitts 1961). Both direct factor analysis (in which a sociomatrix is input directly into a factor analytic program) and factor analysis of a correlation or covariance matrix derived from the rows (or columns) of a sociomatrix have been used to reveal aspects of network structure. In studying cohesive subgroups, Bonacich (1972b) shows that if a group contains non-overlapping subsets of actors in which actors within each subset are connected by either adjacency or paths, then a factor analysis of the sociomatrix will reveal this subgroup structure. However, one should be quite cautious about using factor analysis on dichotomous data, since results can be quite unstable.

Although factor analysis can be used to study cohesive subgroups in an exploratory way, the most influential and important cohesive subgroup ideas are those (such as cliques and related ideas) that express specific formal properties of cohesive subgroups and locate such subgroups that might exist within a network data set.

7.11 Summary

In this chapter we have presented methods for studying cohesive subgroups in social networks, for dichotomous nondirectional relations, directional relations, and valued relations. These methods are motivated by theoretically important properties of cohesive subgroups, and present alternative ways of quantifying the idea of social group using social networks. We also presented methods for assessing the cohesiveness of subgroups.

8
Affiliations and Overlapping Subgroups

In this chapter we discuss methods for analyzing a special kind of two-mode social network that represents the affiliation of a set of actors with a set of social occasions (or events). We will refer to these data as *affiliation* network data, or measurements on an affiliation variable. This kind of two-mode network has also been called a *membership network* (Breiger 1974, 1990a) or *hypernetwork* (McPherson 1982), and the affiliation relation has also been referred to as an *involvement relation* (Freeman and White 1993).

8.1 Affiliation Networks

Affiliation networks differ in several important ways from the types of social networks we have discussed so far. First, affiliation networks are two-mode networks, consisting of a set of actors and a set of events. Second, affiliation networks describe collections of actors rather than simply ties between pairs of actors. Both of these features of affiliation networks make their analysis and interpretation somewhat distinct from the analysis and interpretation of one-mode networks, and lead us to the special set of methods discussed in this chapter. Among the important properties of affiliation networks that require special methods and interpretations are:

- Affiliation networks are two-mode networks
- Affiliation networks consist of subsets of actors, rather than simply pairs of actors
- Connections among members of one of the modes are based on linkages established through the second mode

- Affiliation networks allow one to study the dual perspectives of the actors and the events

We will return to these ideas throughout this chapter.

Methods for studying two-mode affiliation networks are less well developed than are methods for studying one-mode networks. As a consequence, many of the methods we discuss in this chapter are concerned with representing affiliation networks using graph theoretic and related ideas, rather than with analyzing these networks.

We begin with a review of the theoretical motivations for studying affiliation networks. We then discuss how affiliation networks establish linkages among the entities in each of the modes. We will see that we can begin with data on an affiliation network and derive arrays that are standard one-mode sociomatrices. Next, we present examples of analyses of the one-mode matrices that are derived from an affiliation network. Finally, we examine what the affiliation network implies about the association between the actors and the events, and present two approaches for analyzing the two modes simultaneously.

8.2 Background

In this section we review some of the more influential theoretical and substantive contributions to the study of affiliation networks. We will also note some of the different motivations for studying affiliation networks and introduce the basic concepts that we will use in discussing affiliation networks.

8.2.1 Theory

The importance of studying affiliation networks is grounded in the theoretical importance of individuals' memberships in collectivities. Such research has a long history in the social sciences, especially in sociology.

Simmel (1950, 1955) is widely acknowledged as being among the first social theorists to discuss the theoretical implications of individuals' affiliations with collectivities (which he called *social circles*). In quite simplified form, his argument is that multiple group affiliations (for example with family, voluntary organizations, occupational groups) are fundamental in defining the social identity of individuals. He argued that the individual "is determined sociologically in the sense that the groups 'intersect' in his person by virtue of his affiliation with them" (page 150).

Many social scientists have developed and expanded on Simmel's insights (Breiger 1974, 1990b, 1991; Foster and Seidman 1982, 1984; Kadushin 1966; McPherson 1982; McPherson and Smith-Lovin 1982).

Kadushin (1966) clarified the notion of a social circle as an important kind of social entity, one without a formal membership list, rules, or leadership. He also outlined the differences between social circles and other kinds of social groups. In his work, the social circle is seen as an unobservable entity that must be inferred from behavioral similarities among collections of individuals. One of Kadushin's important insights is that social circles provide conditions for development of interpersonal connections.

Affiliation networks are especially useful for studying urban social structures. As Foster and Seidman (1984) observe:

> ...due to their size and complexity, urban social structures are never described either by social scientists or urban residents exclusively in terms of dyadic relationships. Accordingly, most anthropologists have recognized that an important component of urban structure arises from collections of overlapping subsets such as voluntary associations, ethnic groups, action sets, and quasi-groups.... (page 177)

To be used in social network analysis, the social occasions which define events in affiliation networks must be collections of individuals whose membership is known, rather than inferred (as in Kadushin's models of social circles). We assume, as did Breiger (1974), that

> usage of the term "group" is restrictive in that I consider only those groups for which membership lists are available — through published sources, reconstruction from field observation or interviews, or by any other means. (1974, page 181)

Common to all of these views is the idea that actors are brought together through their joint participation in social events. Joint participation in events not only provides the opportunity for actors to interact, but also increases the probability that direct pairwise ties (such as acquaintanceship) will develop between actors. For example, belonging to the same club (voluntary organization, boards of directors, political party, labor union, committee, and so on) provides the opportunity for people to meet and interact, and thus constitutes a link between individuals. Similarly, when a person (or a number of people) participate in more than one event, a linkage is established between the two events. Overlap in group membership allows for the flow of information between groups, and perhaps coordination of the groups' actions. For example, the interlock among corporate boards through sharing members might facilitate coordination among companies (Sonquist and Koenig 1975). The fact that events can be described as collections of actors affiliated with them and actors can be described as collections of events with which they are affiliated is a distinctive feature of affiliation networks.

8.2.2 Concepts

Because affiliation networks are different from the social networks we have discussed so far in this book, we will need to introduce some new concepts, vocabulary, and notation. Most importantly, since affiliation networks are two-mode networks, we need to be clear about both of the modes. As usual, we have a set of actors, $\mathcal{N} = \{n_1, n_2, \ldots, n_g\}$, as the first of the two-modes. In affiliation networks we also have a second mode, the *events*, which we denote by $\mathcal{M} = \{m_1, m_2, \ldots, m_h\}$.

The events in an affiliation network can be a wide range of specific kinds of social occasions; for example, social clubs in a community, treaty organizations for countries, boards of directors of major corporations, university committees, and so on. When there is no ambiguity in meaning we will use the terms "club," "board of directors," "party," "committee," and so on to describe specific kinds of events. We do not require that an event necessarily consist of face-to-face interactions among actors at a particular physical location at a particular point in time. For example, we could record memberships in national organizations where people do not have face-to-face meetings that include all members. We do require that we have a list of the actors affiliated with each of the events.

In the most general sense, we will say that an actor is *affiliated* with an event, if, in substantive terms, the actor belongs to the club, attended the meeting, sits on the board or directors, is on the committee, went to the party, and so on. When there is no ambiguity, we might also say that the actor belongs to, was at, or is a member of an event, depending on the particular application.

As we have noted, affiliation networks consist of information about subsets of actors who participate in the same social activities. Since activities usually contain several actors, rather than simply pairs of actors, an affiliation network contains information on collections of actors that are larger than pairs. Thus, affiliation networks cannot be analyzed thoroughly by looking at pairs or dyads of actors or events.

Another important property of affiliation networks is the *duality* in the relationship between the actors and the events. In emphasizing this property, Breiger (1990a, 1990b, 1991) refers to such networks as *dual networks*. In the more general literature, the term "duality" is used in various, often imprecise, ways to refer to the complementary relationship between two kinds of entities. However, the duality in affiliation networks refers specifically to the alternative, and equally important, perspectives by which actors are linked to one another by their affiliation with events, and at the same time events are linked by the actors who are their members. Therefore, there are two complementary ways to view an affiliation network: either as actors linked by events, or as events linked by actors. A formal statement of the duality of the relationship between actors and events was given in the classic paper by Breiger (1974). We present this formal statement of the duality below.

Analytically, the duality of an affiliation network means that we can study the ties between the actors or the ties between the events, or both. For example, in one-mode analysis focusing on ties between actors, two actors have a pairwise tie if they both are affiliated with the same event. Focusing on events, two events have a pairwise tie if one or more actors is affiliated with both events. When we focus on ties between actors, we will refer to the relation between actors as one of *co-membership*, or *co-attendance*. When we focus on ties between events, we will refer to the relation between events as *overlapping* or *interlocking* events. On some occasions both forms of one-mode relations are referred to as *co-occurrence* relations (MacEvoy and Freeman n.d.).

These one-mode ties, either between actors or between events, are derived from the affiliation data and can be studied using methods for analyzing one-mode networks. However, it is often more interesting to analyze both modes simultaneously by studying the relationship between the actors and the events with which they are affiliated. Such two-mode analyses study the actors, the events, and the relationship between them at the same time. We will discuss both one-mode and two-mode analyses in this chapter.

In summary, affiliation networks are relational in three ways: first, they show how the actors and events are related to each other; second, the events create ties among actors; and third, the actors create ties among events.

8.2.3 Applications and Rationale

Numerous research applications have employed affiliation networks, either explicitly or implicitly. The following list is a small sample: membership on a corporate board of directors (Allen 1982; Bearden and Mintz 1987; Burt 1978/79b; Fennema and Schijf 1978/79; Levine 1972; Mariolis 1975; Mintz and Schwartz 1981a, 1981b; Mizruchi 1984; Mokken and Stokman 1978/79; Sonquist and Koenig 1975), records of the club memberships of a set of community decision makers or elites (Domhoff 1975; Galaskiewicz 1985), memberships in voluntary organizations (McPherson 1982), records of the academic institutions with which researchers have been affiliated (Freeman 1980b), ceremonial events attended by members of a village (Foster and Seidman 1984), committees on which university faculty sit (Atkin 1974, 1976), social events people attend (Breiger 1974; Davis, Gardner, and Gardner 1941; Homans 1950), high school clubs (Bonacich 1978), observations of collections of individuals' interactions (Bernard, Killworth, and Sailer 1980, 1982; Freeman and Romney 1987; Freeman, Romney, and Freeman 1987; Freeman, Freeman, and Michaelson 1988), trade partners of major oil exporting nations (Breiger 1990b), the overlap of subspecialties within an academic discipline (Cappell and Guterbock 1992; Ennis 1992), and the fate of Chinese political figures (Schweizer 1990).

Given this wide range of applications, it is useful to note three primary rationales for studying affiliation networks. First, some authors argue that individuals' affiliations with events provide direct linkages between the actors and/or between the events. Second, other authors argue that contact among individuals who participate in the same social events provides conditions under which pairwise ties among individuals become more likely. Third, one can view the interaction between actors and events as a social system that is important to study as a whole. Let us examine each of these perspectives in more detail, and describe what each perspective implies for the analysis of affiliation network data.

The first, and perhaps most common, motivation for studying affiliation networks is that the affiliations of actors with events constitute a direct linkage, either between the actors through memberships in events, or between the events through common members. Examples of this perspective include studies of interlocking directorates (cited above), Foster and Seidman's study of Thai households and ceremonies, and observations of interactions between people in small face-to-face communities. Studies of this sort often focus on the frequency of interactions between people compiled from observations or records of peoples' social interactions.

Second, some researchers have treated affiliations as providing conditions that facilitate the formation of pairwise ties between actors. In his discussion of the diffusion of innovations, Kadushin notes that "influence patterns flow along the lines of social circles" (page 789). Thus, the affiliation of individuals with social groups provides the opportunity for interpersonal influence. Similarly, in his discussion of voluntary organizations, McPherson (1982) states that one can "view the members of face-to-face organizations as groups with heightened probability of contact" (page 226). Common group membership increases the probability of establishing pairwise ties, such as becoming acquainted or becoming friends.

Feld (1981) is one of the key contributors to this perspective. He argues that it is important to examine the larger social context or social environment within which networks of ties arise, and the ways in which this environment influences patterns in network structures (such as transitivity, balance, or clustering). His idea is based on the organization of activities around *foci*.

> A focus is defined as a social, psychological, legal, or physical entity around which joint activities are organized (e.g., work places, voluntary organizations, hangouts, families, etc.). (page 1016)

Foci are important for understanding the emergence of dyadic ties, because, according to Feld, "individuals whose activities are organized around the same focus will tend to become interpersonally tied and form a cluster" (1981:1016). Thus, not only are pairwise ties more likely between people who share a focus, but these ties are likely to form specific kinds of network patterns, such as clusters.

In formalizing the insights of this perspective, Freeman (1980b) has borrowed concepts and terminology from algebraic topology (Atkin 1972, 1974) to express these ideas. In his analysis of the development of friendship among a set of social science researchers, Freeman argues that having been located in the same institution (university department) at the same time, or having attended conferences together, provided the opportunity for becoming acquainted and forming friendships. Atkin (1972, 1974) uses the term "backcloth" to refer to the structure of ties among the events and "traffic" to refer to the pairwise ties or acquaintanceships that take place on the backcloth.

The third reason for studying affiliation networks is to model the relationships between actors and events as a whole system. Thus, one would study the structure and properties of the social system composed of actors' affiliations with events, and events' membership, as a whole.

However, there are very few methods for studying actors and events simultaneously.

Each of these three rationales implies a slightly different approach to data analysis and modeling. The first motivation would lead one to study either the one-mode network of ties between pairs of actors implied by their affiliations with events, or the one-mode network of ties between pairs of events implied by the actors they have in common. The second motivation implies that the researcher has measured both an affiliation network and a one-mode relation of pairwise ties either between actors or between events, and that these pairwise ties would be more likely to occur along lines defined by the affiliations. The third motivation would analyze both modes simultaneously and focus on the ties between them.

In the next section we describe several ways to present affiliation networks using graph theoretic and other representations.

8.3 Representing Affiliation Networks

In this section we discuss several ways to represent affiliation networks. We start by defining a matrix that records the affiliations of a set of actors with a set of events. We then describe graph theoretic representations of affiliation networks, including a bipartite graph and a hypergraph. As we will see, all of these representations of affiliation networks contain the same information.

8.3.1 The Affiliation Network Matrix

The most straightforward presentation of an affiliation network is the matrix that records the affiliation of each actor with each event. This matrix, which we will call an *affiliation matrix*, $\mathbf{A} = \{a_{ij}\}$, codes, for each actor, the events with which the actor is affiliated. Equivalently, it records, for each event, the actors affiliated with it. The matrix, $\mathbf{A}$, is a two-mode sociomatrix in which rows index actors and columns index events. Since there are g actors and h events, $\mathbf{A}$ is a $g \times h$ matrix. There is entry of 1 in the (i, j)th cell if row actor i is affiliated with column event j, and an entry of 0 if row actor i is not affiliated with column event j. From the perspective of the events, there is an entry of 1 if the column event includes the row actor, and an entry of 0 if the column event does not include the row actor. Formally,

Actor	Event		
	Party 1	Party 2	Party 3
Allison	1	0	1
Drew	0	1	0
Eliot	0	1	1
Keith	0	0	1
Ross	1	1	1
Sarah	1	1	0

Fig. 8.1. Affiliation network matrix for the example of six children and three birthday parties

$$a_{ij} = \begin{cases} 1 \text{ if actor } i \text{ is affiliated with event } j \\ 0 \text{ otherwise.} \end{cases}$$

Each row of **A** describes an actor's affiliation with the events. Similarly, each column of **A** describes the membership of an event.

Figure 8.1 gives the affiliation matrix for a hypothetical example of six second-grade children (the example introduced in Chapter 2) and their attendance at three birthday parties. In this example the actors are the children, and the events are the birthday parties. In Figure 8.1, a 1 indicates that the row child attended the column birthday party. Looking at the first row of Figure 8.1, we see that Allison attended Parties 1 and 3 and did not attend Party 2. Similarly, looking at column 2, we see that Drew, Eliot, Ross, and Sarah attended Party 2, and that Allison and Keith did not attend that party.

Several properties of **A** are important to note. Since the 1's in a row code the events with which an actor is affiliated, the row marginal totals of **A**, $\{a_{i+}\}$, are equal to the number of events with which each actor is affiliated. If a row marginal total is equal to 0, it means that the actor did not attend any of the events, and if a row marginal total is equal to h, the total number of events, it means that the actor attended all of the events. Similarly, the column marginal totals, $\{a_{+j}\}$, are equal to the number of actors who are affiliated with each event. A column marginal total equal to 0 means that the event had no actors affiliated with it, and a column marginal total equal to g means that all actors are affiliated with that event.

8.3.2 Bipartite Graph

An affiliation network can also be represented by a *bipartite graph*. A bipartite graph is a graph in which the nodes can be partitioned into two subsets, and all lines are between pairs of nodes belonging to different subsets. An affiliation network can be represented by a bipartite graph by representing both actors and events as nodes, and assigning actors to one subset of nodes and events to the other subset. Thus, each mode of the network constitutes a separate node set in the bipartite graph. Since there are g actors and h events, there are $g + h$ nodes in the bipartite graph. The lines in the bipartite graph represent the relation "is affiliated with" (from the perspective of actors) or "has as a member" (from the perspective of events). Since actors are affiliated with events, and events have actors as members, all lines in the bipartite graph are between nodes representing actors and nodes representing events.

Figure 8.2 presents the bipartite graph for the hypothetical example of six children and three birthday parties (from Figure 8.1). Notice that, as required, all lines are between actors and events.

The bipartite graph can also be represented as a sociomatrix. The sociomatrix for the bipartite graph has $g + h$ rows and $g + h$ columns. There is an entry of 1 in the (i, j)th cell if the row actor "is affiliated with" the column event, or if the row event "has as a member" the column actor. Letting the first g rows and columns index actors, and the last h rows and columns index events, this sociomatrix has the general form:

$$\begin{bmatrix} \mathbf{0} & \mathbf{A} \\ \mathbf{A'} & \mathbf{0} \end{bmatrix}$$

The upper left $g \times g$ submatrix and the lower right $h \times h$ submatrix are filled with 0's, indicating no "affiliation" ties among the g actors (the first g rows and columns) or among the h events (the last h rows and columns). The upper right submatrix is the $g \times h$ affiliation matrix, $\mathbf{A}$, indicating "is affiliated with" ties from row actors to column events. The lower left $h \times g$ submatrix is the transpose of $\mathbf{A}$, denoted by $\mathbf{A'}$, indicating whether or not each row event includes the column actor.

Figure 8.3 gives the sociomatrix for the bipartite graph of the affiliation network of six children and three birthday parties (from Figure 8.2). Since there are $g = 6$ children and $h = 3$ parties, this sociomatrix has $6 + 3 = 9$ rows and 9 columns.

A bipartite graph highlights some important aspects of an affiliation network. As is usual in a graph, the degree of a node is the number of nodes adjacent to it. In the bipartite graph, since lines are between actors and events, the degree of a node representing an actor is equal to the number of events with which the actor is affiliated. Similarly, the degree

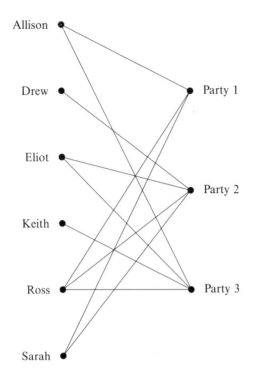

Fig. 8.2. Bipartite graph of affiliation network of six children and three parties

of a node representing an event is the number of actors who are affiliated with it. An advantage of presenting an affiliation network as a bipartite graph is that the indirect connections between events, between actors, and between actors and events are more apparent in the graph than in the affiliation matrix, **A**. Paths of length 2 or more that are obscured in the sociomatrix representation can be seen more easily in the graph. For example, in Figure 8.2 we can see that Allison and Sarah are connected to each other through their attendance at Party 1.

Bipartite graphs have been used to represent affiliation networks by Wilson (1982), and have been generalized to tripartite graphs by Fararo and Doreian (1984). We will return to the bipartite graph below when we discuss reachability and connectedness in affiliation networks.

	Allison	Drew	Eliot	Keith	Ross	Sarah	Party 1	Party 2	Party 3
Allison	-	0	0	0	0	0	1	0	1
Drew	0	-	0	0	0	0	0	1	0
Eliot	0	0	-	0	0	0	0	1	1
Keith	0	0	0	-	0	0	0	0	1
Ross	0	0	0	0	-	0	1	1	1
Sarah	0	0	0	0	0	-	1	1	0
Party 1	1	0	0	0	1	1	-	0	0
Party 2	0	1	1	0	1	1	0	-	0
Party 3	1	0	1	1	1	0	0	0	-

Fig. 8.3. Sociomatrix for the bipartite graph of six children and three parties

8.3.3 Hypergraph

Affiliation networks can also be described as collections of *subsets* of entities. The duality of affiliation networks is apparent in this approach in that each event describes the subset of actors who are affiliated with it, and each actor describes the subset of events to which it belongs. Viewing an affiliation network this way is fundamental to the *hypergraph* approach. Hypergraphs were defined in general in Chapter 4. A more extensive discussion of hypergraphs can be found in Berge (1973, 1989). In this section we show how hypergraphs can be used to represent affiliation networks.

Both actors and events can be viewed as subsets of entities. We begin with each event in an affiliation network defining a *subset* of the actors from $\mathcal{N}$. Since there are h events, there are h subsets of actors defined by the events. Similarly, each actor can be described as the subset of events from $\mathcal{M}$ with which it is affiliated. Since there are g actors, there are g subsets of events defined by the actors.

Recall that a hypergraph consists of a set of objects, called points, and a collection of subsets of objects, called edges. In a hypergraph each point belongs to at least one edge (subset) and no edge (subset) is empty. In studying an affiliation network it seems natural to start by letting the point set be the set of actors, $\mathcal{N}$, and the edge set be the set of events, $\mathcal{M}$. The hypergraph consisting of actors as the points and the events as the edges will be denoted by $\mathcal{H} = (\mathcal{N}, \mathcal{M})$. In order for a set of affiliation network data to meet the hypergraph definition, each actor must be affiliated with at least one event, and each event must include at least one actor.

An important aspect of the hypergraph representation is that the data can be described equally well by the *dual hypergraph*, denoted by $\mathcal{H}^{\star}$, by reversing the roles of the points and the edges. The dual hypergraph for an affiliation network would be $\mathcal{H}^{\star} = (\mathcal{M}, \mathcal{N})$. In the dual hypergraph for an affiliation network the events are represented as points and the actors are represented as edges.

To describe subsets defined either by actors or by events, we will introduce some notation to indicate when an event or an actor is viewed as a subset, and when an event or an actor is viewed as an element of a subset. We will use capital letters to denote subsets. Thus, when we view event j as a subset of actors we will denote it by M_j, where $M_j \subseteq \mathcal{N}$. Similarly, when we view actor i as the subset of events with which it is affiliated we will denote it by N_i, where $N_i \subseteq \mathcal{M}$.

The hypothetical example in Figure 8.1 can be described either in terms of the subsets of actors who are affiliated with each event

$$M_1 = \{n_1, n_5, n_6\}$$
$$M_2 = \{n_2, n_3, n_5, n_6\}$$
$$M_3 = \{n_1, n_3, n_4, n_5\}$$

or in terms of the subsets of events with which each actor is affiliated

$$N_1 = \{m_1, m_3\}$$
$$N_2 = \{m_2\}$$
$$N_3 = \{m_2, m_3\}$$
$$N_4 = \{m_3\}$$
$$N_5 = \{m_1, m_2, m_3\}$$
$$N_6 = \{m_1, m_2\}.$$

These subsets can also be displayed visually by representing the entities in the point set as points in space, and representing the edges as "circles" surrounding the points they include. For example, in Figure 8.4a we give the hypergraph, $\mathcal{H} = (\mathcal{N}, \mathcal{M})$, with the six children as points, and indicate the subsets of children defined by the guest lists of the parties as circles including their members. Figure 8.4b shows the dual hypergraph, $\mathcal{H}^* = (\mathcal{M}, \mathcal{N})$, obtained by reversing the roles of the children and the parties. In the dual hypergraph the parties are the points and the children define circles that contain the parties they attended.

In either the hypergraph or the dual hypergraph we say that points are incident with edges. Thus, for affiliation networks, actors are incident with the events they attend, and events are incident with the actors they include. Returning to the affiliation matrix, **A**, we see that all of the information for the hypergraph is contained in this matrix. If actors are viewed as points, and events are viewed as the edges, then **A** describes which points (actors) are incident with which edges (events). For this reason, the affiliation matrix **A** has been called an *incidence matrix* for the hypergraph (Seidman 1981a). The transpose of **A**, denoted by **A′**, presents the incidence matrix for the dual hypergraph, and shows which points (representing events) are incident with which edges (representing actors).

One of the shortcomings of a hypergraph for representing an affiliation network is that both the hypergraph and the dual hypergraph are required to show simultaneously relationships among actors and events (Freeman and White 1993).

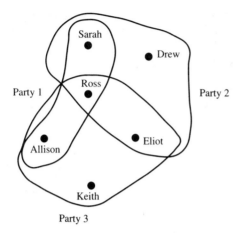

a. Hypergraph: $\mathscr{H}(\mathscr{N},\mathscr{M})$

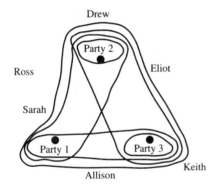

b. Dual Hypergraph: $\mathscr{H}^*(\mathscr{M},\mathscr{N})$

Fig. 8.4. Hypergraph and dual hypergraph for example of six children and three parties

Hypergraphs have been used by Seidman and Foster to study the social structure described by Thai households' attendance at ceremonial events (Foster and Seidman 1984) and to describe urban structures (Foster and Seidman 1982). McPherson (1982) has used hypergraphs to examine participation in voluntary organizations, and has discussed issues of sampling and estimation. Berge (1973, 1989) presents a mathematical discussion of graphs and hypergraphs.

8.3.4 ○*Simplices and Simplicial Complexes*

Simplices and *simplicial complexes* provide yet another way to represent affiliation networks using ideas from algebraic topology. This approach draws heavily on the work by Atkin (1972, 1974), and exploits a more geometric, or topological, interpretation of the relationship between the actors and the events.

A simplicial complex is useful for studying the overlaps among the subsets and the connectivity of the network, and can be used to define the dimensionality of the network in a precise mathematical way. Simplicial complexes can also be used to study the internal structure of the one-mode networks implied by the affiliation network by examining the degree of connectivity of entities in one mode, based on connections defined by the second mode. Although simplices and simplicial complexes are considerably more complex than hypergraphs, they share much in common with a hypergraph representation, as has been noted by Seidman (1981a) and Freeman (1980b).

Simplicial complexes have been used to study social networks by Gould and Gatrell (1979), who described a soccer match; by Freeman (1980b), who looked at the development of friendships in a scientific community against the "backcloth" of shared contacts; and by Doreian (1979a, 1980, 1981), who used this methodology to study conflict within a group, and to examine the evolution of group structure through time.

8.3.5 *Summary*

The two-mode sociomatrix, the bipartite graph, and the hypergraph are alternative representations of an affiliation network. All contain exactly the same information and thus any one can be derived from another. Each representation has some advantages. The sociomatrix is an efficient way to present the information and is most useful for data analytic purposes. Representing the affiliation network as a bipartite graph highlights the connectivity in the network, and makes the indirect chains of connection more apparent. The subset representation in a hypergraph makes it possible to examine the network from the perspective of an individual actor or an individual event, since an actor's affiliations or an event's members are listed directly. However, the hypergraph and bipartite graph can be quite unwieldy when used to depict larger affiliation networks. Since there is no loss or gain of information in one or another representation, the researcher's goals should guide selection of the best representation.

8.3.6 An example: Galaskiewicz's CEOs and Clubs

As an example of an affiliation network, we will use the data collected by Galaskiewicz on chief executive officers (CEOs) and their memberships in civic clubs and corporate boards (described in Chapter 2). The affiliation network matrix, $\mathbf{A}$, for this affiliation network is presented in the Appendix. This data set consists of a subset of twenty-six CEOs and fifteen clubs from Galaskiewicz's data. These are the fifteen largest clubs and boards and the most "active" twenty-six CEOs.

8.4 One-mode Networks

Substantive applications of affiliation networks often focus on just one of the modes, either the actors or the events. For example, research on interlocking directorates usually studies corporate boards of directors (as events) and the ways that these boards overlap by sharing members. The members are important in that they serve as links between corporate boards. In contrast, research on interactions among people focuses on the frequency with which pairs of people interact. The occasions on which people interact (the events) are only important in that they link people. Such one-mode analyses of actors or of events use matrices derived from the affiliation matrix, $\mathbf{A}$, or use graphs defined by these one-mode matrices.

One-mode analyses require "processing" the affiliation network data to give the ties between pairs of entities in one mode based on the linkages implied by the second mode. Both of these one-mode relations are nondirectional and valued.

8.4.1 Definition

First, suppose we want to consider the number of events shared by pairs of actors. Returning to the affiliation network matrix, we see that two actors who are affiliated with the same event will both have 1's in the same column of their respective rows in $\mathbf{A}$. If actors i and j are both affiliated with event, k, then $a_{ik} = a_{jk} = 1$. Thus, counting the number of times that two actors have 1's in the same columns gives the number of events the two actors have in common. The number of co-memberships for actors i and j is equal to the number of times that $a_{ik} = a_{jk} = 1$ for $k = 1, 2, \ldots, h$. Let us define $x_{ij}^{\mathcal{N}}$ as the number of events with which both actors i and j are affiliated. We use the superscript $\mathcal{N}$ to indicate that the ties on this relation are between the actors in $\mathcal{N}$. We can see that $x_{ij}^{\mathcal{N}}$ takes on values from a minimum of 0, if actors i and j are not affiliated with any of the same events, to a maximum of h, if actors i and j are both affiliated with all of the events. Furthermore, this count is symmetric; $x_{ij}^{\mathcal{N}} = x_{ji}^{\mathcal{N}}$. Formally, we can express each value of $x_{ij}^{\mathcal{N}}$ as the product of the corresponding rows in $\mathbf{A}$:

$$x_{ij}^{\mathcal{N}} = \sum_{k=1}^{h} a_{ik} a_{jk}.$$

The product, $a_{ik} a_{jk}$, is equal to 1 only if both actors i and j are affiliated with event k, and is equal to 0 if either one or both of the actors is not affiliated with event k.

We can summarize the co-membership frequencies in a $g \times g$ sociomatrix, $\mathbf{X}^{\mathcal{N}} = \{x_{ij}^{\mathcal{N}}\}$, whose entries record the number of events each pair of actors shares. The relationship between the sociomatrix for the co-membership relation, $\mathbf{X}^{\mathcal{N}}$, whose entries indicate the number of events jointly attended by each actor, and the affiliation matrix, $\mathbf{A}$, that indicates which events each actor is affiliated with, can be expressed concisely in matrix notation. Denoting the transpose of $\mathbf{A}$ as $\mathbf{A}'$, the sociomatrix $\mathbf{X}^{\mathcal{N}}$ is given by the matrix product of $\mathbf{A}$ and $\mathbf{A}'$:

$$\mathbf{X}^{\mathcal{N}} = \mathbf{A}\mathbf{A}'. \tag{8.1}$$

The matrix $\mathbf{X}^{\mathcal{N}}$ records the *co-membership* relation for actors. It is a symmetric, valued sociomatrix, indicating the number of events jointly attended by each pair of actors. In contrast to a usual sociomatrix, the values on the diagonal of $\mathbf{X}^{\mathcal{N}}$ are meaningful. These diagonal entries count the total number of events attended by each actor; $x_{ii}^{\mathcal{N}} = a_{i+}$.

Now, consider the number of actors who are affiliated with each pair of events. Studying the overlap of events requires comparing the columns of the affiliation matrix, $\mathbf{A}$. Two events that have members in common will have 1's in the same rows. Looking at the affiliations of a given actor, i, with two events, k and l, we see that if $a_{ik} = a_{il} = 1$ then events k and l both include actor i. Counting the number of times that $a_{ik} = a_{il} = 1$ for $i = 1, 2, \ldots, g$ gives the number of actors included in both events k and l. We will let $x_{kl}^{\mathcal{M}}$ be the number of actors who are affiliated with both events k and l. We use the superscript $\mathcal{M}$ to indicate ties on this relation are between events in $\mathcal{M}$. If events k and l have no actors in common then $x_{kl}^{\mathcal{M}}$ takes on its minimum value of 0. If all actors are affiliated with the two events, then $x_{kl}^{\mathcal{M}}$ will be equal to g, its maximum possible value. More formally, each value of $x_{kl}^{\mathcal{M}}$ is the product of the corresponding columns in $\mathbf{A}$:

$$x_{kl}^{\mathcal{M}} = \sum_{i=1}^{g} a_{ik} a_{il}.$$

We can now define an $h \times h$ sociomatrix, $\mathbf{X}^{\mathcal{M}} = \{x_{kl}^{\mathcal{M}}\}$, that records the number of actors each pair of events has in common. The relationship between the sociomatrix, $\mathbf{X}^{\mathcal{M}}$, and the affiliation network matrix, $\mathbf{A}$, is expressed in matrix notation by:

$$\mathbf{X}^{\mathcal{M}} = \mathbf{A}'\mathbf{A}. \tag{8.2}$$

The matrix $\mathbf{X}^{\mathcal{M}}$ is a one-mode, symmetric, valued sociomatrix indicating the number of actors that each pair of events shares. The values on the diagonal of $\mathbf{X}^{\mathcal{M}}$ are the total number of actors who are affiliated with each event; $x_{kk}^{\mathcal{M}} = a_{+k}$.

It is important to note that, together, equations (8.1) and (8.2) express the duality of actor co-memberships, $\mathbf{X}^{\mathcal{N}}$, and event overlaps, $\mathbf{X}^{\mathcal{M}}$, as functions of the affiliation matrix, $\mathbf{A}$. The affiliation matrix, $\mathbf{A}$, uniquely defines both the overlaps between events and the co-memberships of actors. Thus, the formal duality of the relationship between actors and events is expressed in the pair of equations (8.1) and (8.2) (Breiger 1974).

Co-membership matrices are quite common in social network applications, though this might not be obvious at first glance. One common form of co-membership data is the count of the number of interactions observed between each pair of actors in a network. Initially, such data consist of observations of which subsets of actors are interacting at each observational time point. These observational data are affiliation networks in which each subset of interacting actors constitutes an event. The one-mode sociomatrix, $\mathbf{X}^{\mathcal{N}}$, derived from these observations contains pairwise interaction frequencies that are essentially co-membership frequencies.

8.4.2 Examples

We now illustrate the actor co-membership matrix, $\mathbf{X}^{\mathcal{N}}$, and the event overlap matrix, $\mathbf{X}^{\mathcal{M}}$, using both the hypothetical example of six children and three birthday parties and Galaskiewicz's data on CEOs and their membership in clubs and corporate bo·,rds.

	n_1	n_2	n_3	n_4	n_5	n_6
n_1	2	0	1	1	2	1
n_2	0	1	1	0	1	1
n_3	1	1	2	1	2	1
n_4	1	0	1	1	1	0
n_5	2	1	2	1	3	2
n_6	1	1	1	0	2	2

Fig. 8.5. Actor co-membership matrix for the six children

	m_1	m_2	m_3
m_1	3	2	2
m_2	2	4	2
m_3	2	2	4

Fig. 8.6. Event overlap matrix for the three parties

First consider the six children and their attendance at three birthday parties, presented in Figure 8.1. Figure 8.5 gives the co-membership matrix, $\mathbf{X}^{\mathcal{N}}$, for this example. Since there are $g = 6$ children, $\mathbf{X}^{\mathcal{N}}$ is a square, 6×6 sociomatrix. From this matrix we see that Allison (n_1) and Drew (n_2) attended no parties together; $x_{12}^{\mathcal{N}} = 0$. However, Allison and Ross (n_5) attended two parties together. No pair of children attended more than two parties together (2 is the largest off-diagonal value in the matrix). The diagonal entries show that Ross attended the most parties ($x_{55}^{\mathcal{N}} = 3$) and Drew and Keith each attended only one party ($x_{22}^{\mathcal{N}} = x_{44}^{\mathcal{N}} = 1$). Figure 8.6 shows the event overlap matrix, $\mathbf{X}^{\mathcal{M}}$, for the example in Figure 8.1. This matrix shows that all pairs of parties shared two children. The largest parties were 2 and 3, with four children each.

Now let us illustrate the actor co-membership and event overlap matrices for Galaskiewicz's CEOs and clubs network. First, consider the co-membership matrix for actors. Figure 8.7 presents the co-membership matrix, $\mathbf{X}^{\mathcal{N}}$, for the twenty-six CEOs. This 26×26 matrix records for each pair of CEOs the number of clubs or corporate boards to which both belong. Focusing on the diagonal entries, we see that the number of memberships for the CEOs in this sample ranges from 2 to 7. CEO number 14 belongs to 7 of the fifteen clubs and boards, more than any other CEO. Considering the off-diagonal entries, we see that the number of co-memberships for pairs of CEOs ranges from 0 to 5.

We can also study the overlap among the clubs. The event overlap matrix, $\mathbf{X}^{\mathcal{M}}$, is presented in Figure 8.8. This 15×15 matrix records, for

Co-membership matrix for CEOs (rows and columns numbered 1–26):

	1	2	3	4	5	6	7	8	9	10	11	12	13	14	15	16	17	18	19	20	21	22	23	24	25	26
1	3	1	1	1	1	1	2	1	1	2	2	1	3	2	1	1	1	2	3	2	2	1	1	2	1	1
2	1	3	1	1	1	1	1	1	0	1	1	1	2	1	1	1	2	0	2	1	1	1	1	1	1	1
3	1	1	2	3	1	1	1	0	0	1	1	0	1	2	1	1	2	1	1	1	1	1	1	1	1	2
4	1	1	1	1	1	2	1	0	0	1	2	0	1	3	3	2	3	1	1	3	1	2	3	2	2	2
5	1	1	1	2	3	2	1	0	0	1	1	0	1	2	2	2	1	1	1	1	1	1	1	1	2	1
6	2	1	1	1	2	3	1	0	0	1	2	0	1	2	2	3	2	0	1	2	1	1	2	1	2	2
7	1	1	1	0	1	1	4	2	2	1	1	1	2	3	1	1	2	1	2	1	2	1	1	2	1	1
8	1	0	0	0	0	0	2	3	2	0	0	2	1	1	0	0	0	1	2	3	1	0	0	1	0	0
9	2	1	0	1	0	0	2	2	4	0	0	1	1	1	0	1	0	1	2	1	2	1	0	1	0	0
10	2	1	1	2	1	1	1	0	0	2	2	0	2	1	1	1	1	1	2	1	1	1	1	2	1	1
11	3	2	1	0	1	2	1	0	0	2	3	0	2	2	2	2	2	1	2	1	1	1	2	1	2	2
12	1	1	0	1	0	0	1	2	1	0	0	2	1	1	0	0	0	1	2	2	1	0	0	1	0	0
13	2	1	1	3	1	1	3	1	1	2	2	1	4	2	1	1	2	2	3	1	1	1	1	1	1	1
14	1	2	2	3	2	2	1	1	1	1	2	1	2	7	4	2	5	4	2	2	2	2	3	3	3	3
15	1	0	1	2	2	2	1	0	0	1	2	0	1	4	5	3	3	2	1	5	2	2	4	3	3	3
16	2	2	1	3	2	3	2	0	1	1	2	0	1	2	3	5	2	0	1	3	1	2	3	3	2	2
17	3	1	2	1	1	2	1	0	0	1	2	0	2	5	3	2	6	2	1	4	2	2	3	3	2	2
18	2	1	1	1	1	0	3	1	1	1	2	1	2	4	2	0	2	5	2	2	1	1	1	2	1	3
19	2	1	1	1	1	1	3	2	2	2	1	2	3	2	1	1	1	2	5	2	1	1	1	2	1	1
20	1	1	1	1	1	2	2	3	1	1	2	1	2	5	3	2	4	2	2	5	1	1	1	2	1	1
21	1	1	1	2	1	1	1	1	2	1	2	1	2	2	1	2	1	1	2	2	2	2	3	3	2	2
22	2	1	1	3	1	1	1	0	1	1	1	0	1	2	2	2	2	1	1	2	2	2	1	3	1	1
23	1	1	1	2	1	1	2	0	0	1	1	0	1	3	4	3	3	1	1	3	3	1	2	2	1	1
24	1	1	1	2	2	2	1	1	2	1	2	1	2	3	3	2	2	2	3	3	2	3	2	3	2	2
25	1	1	2	2	1	2	1	0	0	1	2	0	1	3	3	2	2	1	1	2	1	2	3	5	3	1
26	1	1	2	2	1	2	1	0	0	1	2	0	1	3	3	2	3	1	1	2	2	1	2	1	2	3

Fig. 8.7. Co-membership matrix for CEOs from Galaskiewicz's CEOs and clubs network

each pair of clubs, the number of CEOs in this sample of twenty-six who belong to both clubs. The diagonal entries in the event overlap matrix record the number of CEOs in this sample who belong to each club or board. We can see that Club 3 is the largest with 22 CEOs, and there are three clubs or boards with only 3 CEOs. Looking at the off-diagonal entries, the number of overlaps in club memberships ranges from a low of 0 to a high of 11 (for Clubs 2 and 3). It is interesting to note that Club 2 has 11 members ($x_{22}^{\mathscr{N}} = 11$) all of whom are also members of Club 3 ($x_{23}^{\mathscr{N}} = 11$). Thus, for this sample of CEOs, the membership of Club 2 is completely contained within the membership of Club 3. There are other inclusion relationships among clubs in this example.

We next discuss properties of affiliation networks, including properties of the one-mode networks of actors and of events, and of the two-mode affiliation network.

8.5 Properties of Affiliation Networks

In this section we define and describe several properties of affiliation networks and show how these properties can be calculated from the affiliation matrix, **A**, or from the one-mode sociomatrices, $\mathbf{X}^{\mathscr{N}}$ and $\mathbf{X}^{\mathscr{M}}$. We first consider properties of individual actors or events (including rates of participation for actors and the size of events) and then discuss properties of networks of actors and/or of events (including the density of ties among actors or among events and the connectedness of the affiliation network).

8.5.1 Properties of Actors and Events

Some simple properties of actors and events can be calculated directly from the affiliation matrix or from the one-mode sociomatrices. In this section we consider rates of participation by actors and the size of events.

Rates of Participation. One property of interest is the number of events with which each actor is affiliated. These quantities are given either by the row totals of **A** or the entries on the main diagonal of $\mathbf{X}^{\mathscr{N}}$. Thus, the number of events with which actor i is affiliated is given by $a_{i+} = \sum_{j=1}^{h} a_{ij} = x_{ii}^{\mathscr{N}}$. The number of events with which an actor is affiliated is also equal to the degree of the node representing the actor in the bipartite graph.

	1	2	3	4	5	6	7	8	9	10	11	12	13	14	15
1	3	0	2	3	0	1	1	1	1	1	0	0	0	0	1
2	0	11	11	2	1	3	0	1	1	0	3	3	3	2	6
3	2	11	22	8	3	4	2	3	5	1	4	4	4	3	8
4	3	2	8	12	1	1	3	2	4	3	3	2	2	0	4
5	0	1	3	1	3	0	1	0	1	0	1	1	0	0	1
6	1	3	4	1	0	4	0	1	0	0	0	0	1	1	3
7	1	0	2	3	1	0	4	0	1	1	0	0	0	0	0
8	1	1	3	2	0	1	0	4	0	1	0	0	0	1	1
9	1	1	5	4	1	0	1	0	6	0	0	1	1	0	1
10	1	0	1	3	0	0	1	1	0	3	1	0	0	0	0
11	0	3	4	3	1	0	0	0	0	1	4	2	1	0	3
12	0	3	4	2	1	0	0	0	1	0	2	5	2	0	3
13	0	3	4	2	0	1	0	0	1	0	1	2	5	1	3
14	0	2	3	0	0	1	0	1	0	0	0	0	1	3	0
15	1	6	8	4	1	3	0	1	1	0	3	3	3	0	9

Fig. 8.8. Event overlap matrix for clubs from Galaskiewicz's CEOs and clubs data

As McPherson (1982) has noted, this quantity is used quite frequently by researchers who are interested in people's rates of participation in social activities. For example if one were studying memberships in voluntary organizations, these totals would give the number of voluntary organizations to which each person belongs.

One can also consider the *average* number of events with which actors are affiliated. The mean number of memberships for actors is calculated as:

$$\bar{a}_{i+} = \frac{\sum_{i=1}^{g} \sum_{j=1}^{h} a_{ij}}{g} = \frac{a_{++}}{g} = \frac{\sum_{i=1}^{g} x_{ii}^{\mathcal{N}}}{g}$$

This quantity gives the mean rate of affiliation for actors, or the mean degree of actors in the bipartite graph. It could be used to compare people's rates of participation in voluntary organizations between communities.

Size of Events. One might also be interested in the size of events. The size of each event is given by either the column totals of **A** or the entries on the main diagonal of $\mathbf{X}^{\mathcal{M}}$. Thus, $a_{+j} = \sum_{i=1}^{g} a_{ij} = x_{jj}^{\mathcal{M}}$ gives the number of actors affiliated with event j. The size of an event is equal to the degree of the node representing the event in the bipartite graph.

One can also consider the average size of the events. The mean number of actors in each event is calculated as:

$$\bar{a}_{+j} = \frac{\sum_{i=1}^{g} \sum_{j=1}^{h} a_{ij}}{h} = \frac{a_{++}}{h} = \frac{\sum_{j=1}^{h} x_{jj}^{\mathcal{M}}}{h}$$

This quantity gives the average number of actors in each event, or the mean degree of nodes representing events in the bipartite graph. It could be used to study the average sizes of clubs or voluntary organizations in different communities. Sometimes the size of the events is constrained by the data collection design or by external factors. For example, a corporation may require that its board of directors be made up of a fixed number of people.

An Example. To illustrate rates of participation for actors and the size of events, consider Galaskiewicz's CEOs and clubs data. The mean number of club memberships for CEOs in this sample is equal to $\sum_{i=1}^{g} x_{ii}^{\mathcal{N}} / g = 98/26 = 3.769$. Thus, on average, each CEO belongs to 3.769 of the fifteen clubs in this sample. The mean size of clubs is equal to $\sum_{j=1}^{h} x_{jj}^{\mathcal{M}} / h = 98/15 = 6.533$. Thus, on average each club has a membership of 6.533 CEOs from this sample.

These measures of the rates of participation for actors or the size of events are appropriate for describing affiliation networks when we assume that all actors and events of interest are included in the data set. However, if the g actors are considered as a sample from a larger population (as in the subset of Galaskiewicz's CEOs and clubs data that we analyze here) then other measures are necessary in order to estimate the mean size of the events in the population. Similarly, if the h events are a sample from a population of events, then one must estimate the rates of affiliation for actors. Issues of sampling and estimation for affiliation networks are discussed in McPherson (1982) and Wasserman and Galaskiewicz (1984).

We now turn to properties of the one-mode networks and of the affiliation network.

8.5.2 Properties of One-mode Networks

In this section we describe properties of one-mode networks. We first consider the density of ties among actors and among events. We then discuss the reachability and connectedness of the affiliation network.

Density. Since the density of a one-mode network is a function of the pairwise ties between actors or between events, we will first consider these pairwise ties before defining and discussing the density of the one-mode networks derived from an affiliation network.

In studying overlaps between events it is important to note that the number of overlap ties between events is, in part, a function of the number of events to which actors belong. Similarly, the number of co-membership ties between actors is, in part, a function of the size of the events (McPherson 1982). Since an actor only creates a tie between a pair of events if it belongs to both events, an actor who belongs to only one event creates no overlap ties between events. An actor who belongs to exactly two events creates a single tie (between those two events), an actor who belongs to three events creates three ties (between all pairs of events from among the collection of three events to which it belongs), and so on. In general, an actor who belongs to a_{i+} events creates $a_{i+}(a_{i+} - 1)/2$ pairwise ties between events. Similarly, events create ties among the actors who are their members. An event with a single member creates no co-membership ties between actors. In general, an event with a_{+j} members creates $a_{+j}(a_{+j} - 1)/2$ ties between pairs of actors. Thus, the rates of membership for actors influence the number of ties between events, and the sizes of the events influence the number of ties between actors.

In a substantive context, McPherson and Smith-Lovin (1982) discuss how differences in the sizes of men's and women's voluntary organizations influence differences between men and women in the potential for establishing useful network contacts. Larger organizations provide more potential contacts for their members, and men typically belong to larger organizations than do women.

Now let us consider the density of ties in the one-mode networks of actor co-memberships and event overlaps. Density was defined and discussed in Chapter 4. Here we will focus on calculation and interpretations of density for affiliation networks. Since both the co-membership and overlap relations are initially valued, we will consider both the density of the valued relation and the density of the dichotomous relation that can be derived by considering simply whether ties are present or absent. In either case, the density of a relation is the mean of the values of the pairwise ties. For a dichotomous relation, density is interpreted as the proportion of ties that are present. For a valued relation, density is interpreted as the average value of the ties. To begin, let us consider the valued relations.

The density of a valued graph is the average value attached to the lines in the graph. For the co-membership relation defined on actors, the density, denoted by $\Delta_{(\mathcal{N})}$ (with the subscript $\mathcal{N}$ indicating that it is the density of ties among the actors in $\mathcal{N}$), is calculated by:

$$\Delta_{(\mathcal{N})} = \frac{\sum_{i=1}^{g} \sum_{j=1}^{g} x_{ij}^{\mathcal{N}}}{g(g-1)}, \qquad (8.3)$$

where $i \neq j$. The value of $\Delta_{(\mathcal{N})}$ for the co-membership relation can be interpreted as the mean number of events to which pairs of actors belong. Values of $\Delta_{(\mathcal{N})}$ range from 0 to h.

For the overlap relation among events the density $\Delta_{(\mathcal{M})}$ (where the subscript indicates that the density is among events in $\mathcal{M}$) is defined as:

$$\Delta_{(\mathcal{M})} = \frac{\sum_{k=1}^{h} \sum_{l=1}^{h} x_{kl}^{\mathcal{M}}}{h(h-1)}, \qquad (8.4)$$

where $k \neq l$. The value of $\Delta_{(\mathcal{M})}$ for the overlap relation can be interpreted as the mean number of actors who belong to each pair of events. $\Delta_{(\mathcal{M})}$ takes on values from 0 to g.

It is often useful to consider simply whether a tie is present or absent between a pair of actors or between a pair of events. For example, we might be interested in whether each pair of actors was affiliated with one or more of the same events, or whether each pair of events shared at least one actor. These relations can be studied by dichotomizing the valued relation of co-membership or of event overlap. In the dichotomous relation a tie is coded as present if the original value of the tie is greater than or equal to 1, and absent if the original value of the tie is equal to 0. We can then consider the density of each new dichotomous relation. The density of the dichotomous actor co-membership relation is interpreted as the proportion of actors who share membership in any event. The density of the dichotomous event overlap relation is interpreted as the proportion of events that share one or more members in common. These densities can be calculated using the formulas given above or in Chapter 4.

Density for both valued and dichotomous relations has been used to study affiliation networks. (For the first see Breiger 1990b, and for the second see McPherson 1982). McPherson (1982) discusses estimation and interpretation of the density of memberships in voluntary organizations collected using surveys. Breiger (1990b) discusses the relationship between the density of ties between actors and the density of ties between events. Interestingly, he demonstrates that, for the dichotomous relation in which ties are coded as present or absent, the co-membership relation can have a density equal to 1, while, for the same affiliation network, the density of the dichotomous event overlap relation can be less than 1. To illustrate, consider a simple affiliation network in which the events consist of all possible subsets of two actors. Thus, each pair of actors shares exactly one event in common, and the density of the dichotomous co-membership relation is equal to 1. However, if there are more than three actors, then the density of the dichotomous event overlap relation must be less than 1, since there are some events that do not share any members.

An Example: Galaskiewicz's CEOs and Clubs. We will use Galaskiewicz's data on CEOs and their memberships in clubs and boards to illustrate the density of ties among actors and among events. We will use both the valued and dichotomous relations of actor co-memberships and event overlaps. First consider the co-membership ties among the CEOs. The sociomatrix for the valued co-membership relation is presented in Figure 8.7. The density of this valued relation is $\Delta_{(\mathcal{N})} = 1.412$. This means that on average, pairs of CEOs share memberships in 1.412 clubs. The dichotomous co-membership relation among the CEOs records whether or not each pair of CEOs both belong to any of the same clubs (coded 1) or not (coded 0). The density of this relation is $\Delta_{(\mathcal{N})} = 0.874$. This means that 87.4% of the pairs of CEOs were co-members of one or more of the clubs in the sample.

For the valued relation of overlap between clubs (presented in Figure 8.8), the density is $\Delta_{(\mathcal{M})} = 1.486$. Thus, on average, each pair of clubs shares 1.486 CEOs (from this sample of CEOs). For the dichotomous relation, coding whether or not each pair of clubs shares one or more members, the density is $\Delta_{(\mathcal{M})} = 0.629$. Thus, 62.9% of the pairs of clubs share at least one member in common (from the CEOs in this sample).

Reachability, Connectedness, and Diameter. As noted above, one of the key reasons for studying affiliation networks is that affiliations create connections both between actors through membership in events, and between events through shared members. Common membership in organizations creates a linkage between people, and sharing members creates a linkage between groups that have one or more members in common. If we consider ties between actors or between events as potential conduits of information, then the connectedness of the affiliation network is important because information originating at any event (or with any actor) can potentially reach any other event (or other actor). Thus it becomes important to study the connectedness and reachability between actors and events in an affiliation network.

We can study both whether an affiliation network is connected (that is, whether each pair of actors and/or events is joined by some path) and the diameter of the affiliation network. If we consider the valued relations, we can also study cohesive subgroups of actors or of events.

A useful way to study reachability in an affiliation network is to consider the bipartite graph, with both actors and events represented as nodes. There are $g + h$ nodes in the bipartite graph, and there is a line between two nodes if one node representing an actor "is affiliated with" another node representing an event (or a node representing an event "has as a member" a node representing an actor). Thus all lines are between nodes representing actors and nodes representing events.

Recall that two nodes in a graph are adjacent if there is a line between them, and they are reachable if there is a path between them. In a bipartite graph representing an affiliation network, since actors are adjacent to events (and vice versa) no pair of actors is adjacent and no pair of events is adjacent. If pairs of actors are reachable, it is only via paths containing one or more events. Similarly, if pairs of events are reachable, it is only via paths containing one or more actors.

Clearly, there can be no path of length 1 between actors, since all affiliation ties are between actors and events. Similarly, there are no paths of length 1 between events. However, we can consider whether two actors are reachable through some longer path. If two actors attended the same event, then they are reachable by a path of length 2. For example, if actors represented by nodes n_i and n_j both are affiliated with the event represented by node m_k, then the path n_i, m_k, n_j exists between nodes n_i and n_j. Similarly, two events that both contain the same actor are reachable by a path of length 3. We can also consider reachability via longer paths. Actors who are not affiliated with the same event may also be reachable, but through a path with length greater than 2.

One can study reachability among pairs of nodes (including actors and events) by analyzing the bipartite graph using ideas discussed in Chapter 4. In studying affiliation networks one could analyze the $(g + h) \times (g + h)$ sociomatrix representing the bipartite graph to see whether all pairs of nodes (both actors and events) are reachable. If so, the affiliation network is connected. One can also study the diameter of the affiliation network. The diameter of an affiliation network is the length of the longest path between any pair of actors and/or events.

One can also consider connectedness and reachability by focusing on the affiliation matrix, $\mathbf{A}$, and the sociomatrices, $\mathbf{X}^{\mathcal{N}}$ and $\mathbf{X}^{\mathcal{M}}$. Breiger (1974) demonstrates that any affiliation network that is connected in the graph of co-memberships among actors is necessarily connected in the graph of overlaps among events (if no event is empty). Similarly, any affiliation network that is connected in the graph of overlaps among events is connected in the graph of co-memberships among actors (if each actor belongs to at least one event).

Examples. To illustrate connectedness and diameter in affiliation networks, we will consider both the hypothetical example of six second-grade children and their attendance at three birthday parties, and Galaskiewicz's CEOs and clubs network.

The affiliation network for the six children and three birthday parties is connected; that is, there exist paths between all pairs of children, all pairs of parties, and all pairs of children and parties. One way to see the connectedness of this affiliation network is to see that all children attended at least one party, all parties contained at least one child, and furthermore, all children attended at least one party with Ross (the fifth row/column of $\mathbf{X}^{\mathcal{N}}$ has entries that are all greater than or equal to 1). Thus, all children are reachable to/from Ross and all parties are reachable to/from Ross (Ross is included in all three parties). Although paths between pairs of children and/or parties do not need to contain Ross, it is possible to reach any child or party through paths that do include Ross. It is important to note that a connected affiliation network need not contain an actor who is affiliated with all events.

Although all pairs of parties in this network are reachable through paths of length 2 or less, this is not true for all pairs of actors. To illustrate, a shortest path (geodesic) from Drew to Keith is: Drew, Party 2, Ross, Party 3, Keith. This shortest path contains four lines. Since the longest geodesic in this network is of length 4, the diameter of this affiliation network is equal to 4.

We can also consider the connectedness of Galaskiewicz's CEOs and clubs affiliation network. This affiliation network is connected. Notice that there are several CEOs who belonged to some club with every other CEO (consider the rows/columns in $\mathbf{X}^{\mathcal{N}}$ that have no 0 entries). Thus, each member of the network can reach one of these CEOs. Since the network is connected in the ties among actors, and each event contains at least one actor, the affiliation network as a whole is connected. The longest geodesic in the network is of length 5, thus the diameter of this affiliation network is equal to 5.

In studying the connectedness of affiliation networks, we have considered whether or not paths exist between pairs of actors and/or events. We can also consider the value or strength of the paths by studying the number of shared memberships (for actors) or the number of shared members (for events). Looking at the valued relations of co-membership and/or overlap will allow us to consider cohesive subgroups within the one-mode networks and to study parts of the affiliation network that are more strongly connected.

Cohesive Subsets of Actors or Events. In Chapter 7 we discussed cliques for valued graphs. Recall that a clique is a maximal complete subgraph of three or more nodes. In a valued graph we can define a *clique at level* c as a maximal complete subgraph of three or more nodes, all of which are adjacent at level c. That is, all pairs of nodes have lines between them with values that are greater than or equal to c. By successively increasing the value of c we can locate more cohesive subgroups.

For the co-membership relation for actors, a clique at level c is a subgraph in which all *pairs* of actors share memberships in no fewer than c events. For the overlap relation for events, a clique at level c is a subgraph in which all *pairs* of events share at least c members. It is important to emphasize that although a clique in a co-membership relation for actors (or an overlap relation for events) consists of a *subset* of actors (or events) the interpretation of such cliques is limited to properties of *pairs* of actors (or events). We return to issues of interpretation below, after we illustrate cohesive subgroups for the one-mode networks.

An Example, Galaskiewicz's CEOs and Clubs. To illustrate cliques in the one-mode valued networks of co-memberships and overlaps, we will use Galaskiewicz's CEOs and clubs data. We first consider the co-membership relation for actors. We used the program *UCINET IV* (Borgatti, Everett, and Freeman 1991) to do this analysis. Recall that the largest value in the $\mathbf{X}^{\mathcal{N}}$ sociomatrix is equal to 5. For $c = 5$ there is only a single pair of CEOs who share that many memberships, thus there can be no cliques (with three or more members). Reducing the value of c to 4, we see that there is a single clique with three members. Reducing c to 3 gives seven cliques. The members of the cliques for $c = 3$ and $c = 4$ are presented in Table 8.1. Notice that the clique defined at $c = 4$ is contained within the first clique for $c = 3$. A clique at a given value of c must be a clique or be contained within a clique at any smaller value of c. Reducing c to 2 for this example gives eighteen cliques.

For the overlap relation among clubs the largest value in $\mathbf{X}^{\mathcal{M}}$ is equal to 8 (for a single pair of clubs). The largest value of c that yields any cliques (with three or more members) is $c = 6$, with a single clique of

Table 8.1. *Cliques in the actor co-membership relation for Galaskiewicz's CEOs and clubs network*

$c = 4$	$c = 3$
14, 17, 20	4, 14, 15, 17, 20, 23
	14, 15, 20, 23, 24
	1, 13, 19
	7, 14, 20
	14, 15, 25
	14, 17, 26
	15, 16, 23

Table 8.2. *Cliques in the event overlap relation for Galaskiewicz's CEOs and clubs network*

$c = 6$	$c = 5$	$c = 4$	$c = 3$	$c = 2$
2, 3, 15	2, 3, 15	2, 3, 15	2, 3, 6, 15	2, 3, 6, 15
			2, 3, 11, 15	2, 3, 4, 11, 12, 15
			2, 3, 13, 15	2, 3, 4, 12, 13, 15
		3, 4, 15	3, 4, 11, 15	
			2, 3, 12, 15	
		3, 4, 9	3, 4, 9	3, 4, 9
				1, 3, 4
				2, 3, 14
				3, 4, 7
				3, 4, 8

three members. This is also the only clique for $c = 5$. For $c = 4$ there are three cliques. Reducing c to 3 gives seven cliques, and for $c = 2$ there are eight cliques. The members of these cliques are presented in Table 8.2. We have listed the cliques and their members to facilitate comparison of subgroups between values of c.

For the co-membership relation among actors, CEOs 14, 15, 17, and 20 belong to many cliques (these are also active CEOs who belong to many clubs). For the overlap relation among clubs, Club 3 (a metropolitan club), is included in every clique (at all values of c). Clubs 2 (a country club), 4 (a metropolitan club), and 15 (a board of a cultural organization) are also included in many cliques.

Although we have used cliques to study the co-membership and overlap relations, one could also use other cohesive subgroup ideas, such as *n*-cliques or *k*-plexes for valued graphs, to study these relations.

Reachability for Pairs of Actors. An alternative way to study cohesive subgroups in valued graphs is to use ideas of connectedness for valued graphs. The goal is to describe the subsets of actors all of whom are connected at some minimum level, c. Recall that the value of a path in a valued graph as the smallest value of any line included in the path. We can use this idea to study cohesive subgroups based on levels of *reachability* either among actors in the co-membership relation or among events in the overlap relation. Thus we focus on the one-mode valued relation of co-membership for actors or the one-mode valued relation of overlap for events. In the valued graph nodes represent the actors and the values attached to the lines are the number of events shared by adjacent actors (or nodes represent events and the values are the number of actors shared between adjacent events). One can use the definitions for the *value of a path* (see Chapter 4) to define connectedness for pairs of actors in the valued graph. Two nodes are *c-connected* (or reachable at level c) if there is a path between them in which all lines have a value of no less than c. One can then locate subsets of actors all of whom are reachable at level c.

In a similar context, but using the idea of simplicial complexes, Doreian defines a set of actors *connected at level q* as a subset such that all pairs of actors in the path were co-members of at least $q + 1$ events. Computationally, finding pairs of actors who are q-connected is equivalent to finding paths of level q in the valued graph (Doreian 1969). A *q-analysis* consists of finding subsets of actors all of whom are connected at level q.

8.5.3 *Taking Account of Subgroup Size*

An important issue to consider when analyzing the one-mode networks that are derived from an affiliation network is that both the co-membership relation for actors and the overlap relation for events are valued relations based on frequency counts. The frequency of co-memberships for a pair of actors can be large if both actors are affiliated with many events, apart from whether these actors are "attracted" to each other. Similarly, the overlap between two events can be large because both include many members, apart from whether these two events "appeal to" the same kinds of actors. Several authors have argued that it is important to "standardize" or "normalize" the frequencies in order to study the pattern of interactions, apart from the marginal propensity of actors to be affiliated with many events, or for events to contain many actors (Bonacich 1972a; Faust and Romney 1985a).

In focusing on event overlap, one idea is to construct a measure of overlap that is "logically independent of group size" (Bonacich 1972, page 178). One possible pairwise measure of overlap uses odds-ratios to study the association between pairs of events, based on the number of actors common to both events, the number of actors who belong to neither event, and the numbers of actors who belong to one event but not the other. Recall that $x_{kl}^{\mathcal{M}}$ is the number of actors who are affiliated with both events k and l. We will denote the number of actors who are affiliated with neither event as $x_{\overline{kl}}^{\mathcal{M}}$, the number affiliated with k but not l as $x_{k\overline{l}}^{\mathcal{M}}$, and the number affiliated with l but not k as $x_{\overline{k}l}^{\mathcal{M}}$. For a given pair of events, m_k and m_l, each of the g actors must be either in event k or not, and either in event l or not, thus:

$$x_{kl}^{\mathcal{M}} + x_{\overline{k}l}^{\mathcal{M}} + x_{k\overline{l}}^{\mathcal{M}} + x_{\overline{kl}}^{\mathcal{M}} = g.$$

For each pair of events, one can arrange these frequencies in a two-by-two contingency table that classifies the g actors in $\mathcal{N}$ by their membership or lack of membership in the two events.

	Member of m_l	Not member of m_l
Member of m_k	$x_{kl}^{\mathcal{M}}$	$x_{k\overline{l}}^{\mathcal{M}}$
Not member of m_k	$x_{\overline{k}l}^{\mathcal{M}}$	$x_{\overline{kl}}^{\mathcal{M}}$

One measure of overlap between events that is independent of the size of the events is the odds ratio, denoted by θ_{kl}. For events k and l, θ_{kl} is calculated as:

$$\theta_{kl} = \frac{x_{kl}^{\mathcal{M}} / x_{\overline{k}l}^{\mathcal{M}}}{x_{k\overline{l}}^{\mathcal{M}} / x_{\overline{kl}}^{\mathcal{M}}} = \frac{x_{kl}^{\mathcal{M}} x_{\overline{kl}}^{\mathcal{M}}}{x_{\overline{k}l}^{\mathcal{M}} x_{k\overline{l}}^{\mathcal{M}}}. \tag{8.5}$$

The odds ratio, θ_{kl}, is equal to 1 if the odds of being in event k to not being in event k is the same for actors in event l as for actors not in event l. In other words, θ_{kl} is equal to 1 if membership in event l (or not in l) does not influence the likelihood of membership in event k (or not in k); the memberships of the two events are independent. If θ_{kl} is greater than 1, then the odds of being in event k to not being in event k is greater for actors who are in event l than for actors who are not in event l (and the odds of being in event l to not being in event l is greater for actors in event k than for actors not in event k). In other words, if θ_{kl} is greater than 1, then actors in one event tend to also be in the other, and vice versa. If θ_{kl} is less than 1, then actors in one event tend not to be in the other, and vice versa. As desired, θ_{kl} is independent of the size of the events. One could also take the natural logarithm of equation (8.5), as is common with odds ratios (Fienberg 1980; Agresti 1990):

$$\log \theta_{kl} = \log \left(\frac{x_{kl}^{\mathcal{M}} x_{\overline{kl}}^{\mathcal{M}}}{x_{\overline{k}l}^{\mathcal{M}} x_{k\overline{l}}^{\mathcal{M}}} \right). \tag{8.6}$$

One drawback of logs of odds ratios is that they are undefined if a cell of the two-by-two table is equal to 0, and so are not recommended if g is small.

Bonacich (1972) has proposed a measure of subgroup overlap which is also independent of the size of the events. His measure is analogous to the number of actors who would belong to both events, if all events had the same number of members and non-members. Bonacich analyzes these overlap measures by treating them as analogous to correlation coefficients, and calculating the centrality of the events based on their overlap. An alternative way to deal with different levels of participation of actors, or different sizes of events, is to "normalize" the $\mathbf{X}^{\mathcal{N}}$ matrix (for actors) or the $\mathbf{X}^{\mathcal{M}}$ matrix (for events) so that all row and column totals are equal. This strategy is equivalent to allowing all actors to have the same number of co-memberships or all events to have the same number of overlaps (Faust and Romney 1985a).

We now turn to some important issues to consider when studying the one-mode networks that are derived from an affiliation network.

8.5.4 Interpretation

A one-mode analysis of an affiliation network studies a single mode of the network, either the co-membership relation for actors or the overlap relation for events. Both of these are nondirectional, valued relations, measured on *pairs* of actors or events, and can be analyzed using standard social network analysis procedures for valued relations. Interpreting the results, however, requires remembering that the fundamental information that generated the one-mode networks is, in fact, two-mode affiliation network data measured on *subsets* of actors and events. In this section we discuss some important issues in interpreting the results of one-mode analyses of affiliation networks.

In constructing either the co-membership matrix, $\mathbf{X}^{\mathcal{N}}$, or the event overlap matrix, $\mathbf{X}^{\mathcal{M}}$, from the affiliation network matrix, $\mathbf{A}$, one loses information that is present in the original affiliation network. In the actor co-membership matrix, one loses the identity of the events that link the actors. In the event overlap matrix, one loses information about the identity of the actors who link the events. One only has information on how many events each pair of actors has in common, or about how many actors are both affiliated with each pair of events. Thus, although the co-membership matrix has information about the frequency of co-memberships for each pair of actors, there is no information about which events were attended, or about the characteristics of the events (such as their size), or about the identities of the other actors (if any) who attended the events. Some caution is therefore required in interpreting the information in either the co-membership matrix or the overlap matrix.

Although the affiliation matrix $\mathbf{A}$ uniquely determines both the matrix of co-memberships for actors, $\mathbf{X}^{\mathcal{N}}$, and the matrix of overlaps for events, $\mathbf{X}^{\mathcal{M}}$, the reverse is not true. In general, a given set of ties in $\mathbf{X}^{\mathcal{N}}$ (or in $\mathbf{X}^{\mathcal{M}}$) can be generated by a number of different affiliation matrices (Breiger 1990b, 1991). Thus, the specific affiliations of actors with events cannot be retrieved from either the pairwise records of co-memberships of actors or the pairwise records of event overlaps. In general, therefore, it is not possible to reconstruct the original affiliation network data from the one-mode matrices.

Another important issue arises in the interpretation of cohesive sub-groups that result from analysis of one-mode networks of actor co-memberships or event overlaps. For example, one might be tempted to infer the existence of cliques based on a cohesive subgroup analysis of the pairwise ties in the co-membership matrix, $\mathbf{X}^{\mathcal{N}}$. However, cliques (that is, maximal complete subgraphs) identified in $\mathbf{X}^{\mathcal{N}}$ need not be events in $\mathbf{A}$. As an illustration, note the clear difference between a single conversation involving three people and three separate conversations between pairs of individuals (Seidman 1981a; Wilson 1982).

To illustrate, consider the actor co-membership matrix, $\mathbf{X}^{\mathcal{N}}$, in Figure 8.5, which records the number of parties each pair of children attended together, and focus on Allison, Eliot, Ross, and Sarah (1, 3, 5, and 6). These four children form a maximal complete subgraph (clique) in the co-membership relation. Within this subset of four children, all *pairs* of children attended some party together (as seen by the non-zero entries for all pairs in the $\mathbf{X}^{\mathcal{N}}$ matrix). However, if we return to the affiliation matrix, $\mathbf{A}$, we see that Allison and Eliot attended Party 3, Allison and Sarah attended Party 1, and Eliot and Sarah attended Party 2, and although Ross was at all parties, Allison, Eliot, Ross, and Sarah were never all four present at any party. In his application of hypergraphs to social networks, Seidman (1981a) uses the term "pseudo-event" to refer to a subset of actors that form a "clique" in the one-mode co-membership relation but are not together in any event in the affiliation network.

Even though the original affiliation network consists of information about subsets of actors rather than pairs, the entries in the co-membership matrix, $\mathbf{X}^{\mathcal{N}}$, pertain to pairs of actors, and entries in the overlap matrix, $\mathbf{X}^{\mathcal{M}}$, pertain to pairs of events. Thus, usually one cannot infer any properties of subgroups larger than pairs from the entries in $\mathbf{X}^{\mathcal{N}}$ or $\mathbf{X}^{\mathcal{M}}$ (Breiger 1991).

8.6 ⊗Simultaneous Analysis of Actors and Events

By far the most interesting, yet least developed, methods for affiliation networks study the actors and the events at the same time. A complete two-mode analysis should show both the relationships among the entities within each mode, and also how the two modes are associated with each other. A two-mode analysis of an affiliation network does this by looking at how the actors are linked to the events they attend and how the events are related to the actors who attend them. In this section we describe two approaches for studying the actors and the events simultaneously.

8.6.1 ⊗*Galois Lattices*

Two important features of affiliation networks are the focus on *subsets* and the *duality* of the relationship between actors and events. The idea of subsets refers both to subsets of actors contained in events and subsets of events that actors attend. The idea of duality refers to the complementary perspectives of relations between actors as participants in events, and between events as collections of actors. The formal representation of a *Galois lattice* incorporates both of these ideas, and can be used to study both modes of an affiliation network and the relationship between them at the same time. Although Galois lattices have a fairly long history in mathematics (they were first introduced by Birkhoff in 1940), they have only recently been used to study social networks (Wille 1984, 1990; Duquenne 1991; Freeman 1992b; Freeman and White 1993).

A Lattice. We first define a lattice, and then define a special kind of lattice, called a Galois lattice, that can be used to study affiliation networks. Our description parallels Freeman and White (1993), and the reader is encouraged to consult their paper and the references cited there for more applications of Galois lattices to social networks.

Consider a set of elements $\mathcal{N} = \{n_1, n_2, \ldots, n_g\}$, and a binary relation "≤" that is reflexive, antisymmetric and transitive. Formally,

- $n_i \leq n_i$
- $n_i \leq n_j$ and $n_j \leq n_i$ if and only if $n_i = n_j$
- $n_i \leq n_j$ and $n_j \leq n_k$ implies $n_i \leq n_k$

Such a system (a relation that is reflexive, antisymmetric, and transitive) defines a *partial order* on the set $\mathcal{N}$.

For any pair of elements, n_i, n_j, we define their *lower bound* as that element n_k such that $n_k \leq n_i$ and $n_k \leq n_j$. A pair of elements may have several lower bounds. A lower bound n_k is called a *greatest lower bound* or *meet* of elements n_i and n_j if $n_l \leq n_k$ for all lower bounds, n_l, of n_i and n_j. For any pair of elements, n_i, n_j, we define their *upper bound* as that element n_k such that $n_i \leq n_k$ and $n_j \leq n_k$. An upper bound n_k is called a *least upper bound* or *join* of elements n_i and n_j if $n_k \leq n_l$ for all upper bounds n_l of n_i and n_j.

A *lattice* consists of a set of elements, $\mathcal{N}$, a binary relation, "≤," that is reflexive, antisymmetric, and transitive, and each pair of elements, n_i, n_j, has both a least upper bound and a greatest lower bound (Birkhoff 1940). A lattice is thus a partially ordered set in which each pair of elements has both a meet and a join.

An example of a lattice is the collection of all subsets from a set of elements $\mathcal{N}$ and the relation "is a subset of" $\subseteq$. Each pair of subsets has a smallest subset that is their union or join (there may be several subsets that contain all of the elements from both subsets, but the smallest of these is their join) and a largest subset that is their intersection or meet (there may be several subsets that contain only elements that are found in both subsets, but the largest of these is their meet). Thus the collection of all subsets from a given set along with the relation $\subseteq$ form a lattice.

A lattice can be represented as a diagram in which entities are presented as points, and there is a line or sequence of lines descending from point j to point i if $i \leq j$.

We can also use a lattice to represent a *collection* of subsets from a set of elements along with the null set ($\emptyset$), the universal set, and the relation $\subseteq$. Thus the collection does not include all possible subsets. This is important for representing an affiliation network using a lattice, since an affiliation network only includes some subsets, and does not, in general, contain all possible subsets of actors (defined by the events) or subsets of events (defined by the actors).

An Example. We can use a lattice to represent subsets defined by either one of the modes in an affiliation network. For example, consider the set of actors, $\mathcal{N}$, and the collection of subsets of actors defined by the membership lists of the events. This collection of subsets of actors, along with the null set, the universal set, and the relation $\subseteq$, can be represented as a lattice. We can also represent the collection of subsets of events defined by the actors' memberships, along with the null set, the universal set, and the relation $\subseteq$ as a lattice.

To illustrate, let us consider the hypothetical example of six children and three birthday parties. We will begin with the subsets of children defined by the guest lists of the parties. We include a subset of children if there is some party that consisted of exactly that collection of children. There are three parties, and thus three subsets of children plus $\emptyset$ and the universal set. Figure 8.9 shows these subsets as a lattice. In this diagram each point represents a subset of children — a subset defined by attendance at a party, the null set ($\emptyset$), or the complete set of children ($\mathcal{N}$) — and the labels on the points are the names of the parties. Each party, m_j, defines a subset of children $\mathcal{N}_{s_j} \subseteq \mathcal{N}$ by its guest list, where $n_i \in \mathcal{N}_{s_j}$ if party j included child i. There is a line in the diagram descending from one point, labeled by m_j, to another point, labeled by m_k, if $\mathcal{N}_{s_k} \subseteq \mathcal{N}_{s_j}$. In this example, since no parties are contained in each other, there are no subset or inclusion relationships among these parties, though each party is a subset of the set of all children, and has the null set as one of its subsets.

We can also represent subsets of parties as a lattice. In this lattice a subset of parties is included in the collection of subsets if there is some child who attended exactly that subset of parties. In this example there are six children, and thus six subsets of parties (we also include $\emptyset$). Figure 8.10 shows these subsets of parties along with the relation $\subseteq$ as a lattice. In this diagram each point represents a subset of parties. Since children define subsets of parties by their attendance, the labels on this diagram are the names of the children. Each child, n_i, defines a subset of parties $\mathcal{M}_{s_i} \subseteq \mathcal{M}$, where $m_j \in \mathcal{M}_{s_i}$ if child i attended party j. There is a line in the diagram descending from one point, labeled by n_i, to another point, labeled by n_l, if $\mathcal{M}_{s_l} \subseteq \mathcal{M}_{s_i}$. For example, there is a line going down from Ross to Allison since the collection of parties that Allison

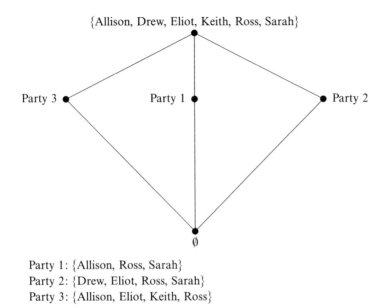

Party 1: {Allison, Ross, Sarah}
Party 2: {Drew, Eliot, Ross, Sarah}
Party 3: {Allison, Eliot, Keith, Ross}

Fig. 8.9. Relationships among birthday parties as subsets of children

attended (Parties 1 and 3) is a subset of the parties that Ross attended (Parties 1, 2, and 3).

Notice that in both Figure 8.10 and Figure 8.9 the points are identified by a single label (in other words, a single subset). Thus, it takes two separate lattices to represent both the actors and the events in the affiliation network. In a Galois lattice each point is identified by two labels (two subsets), and thus a Galois lattice can represent both actors and events simultaneously.

A Galois Lattice. A Galois lattice focuses on the relation between *two* sets. First, consider two sets of elements $\mathcal{N} = \{n_1, n_2, \ldots, n_g\}$ and $\mathcal{M} = \{m_1, m_2, \ldots, m_g\}$, and a relation λ. In general, the relation λ is defined on pairs from the Cartesian product $\mathcal{N} \times \mathcal{M}$. Thus the relation is between elements of $\mathcal{N}$ and elements of $\mathcal{M}$. In studying an affiliation network we let the sets $\mathcal{N}$ and $\mathcal{M}$ be the set of actors and the set of events, and let λ be the relation of affiliation. Thus, $n_i \lambda m_j$ if actor i is affiliated with event j. We also have the relation λ^{-1} where $m_j \lambda^{-1} n_i$ if event j contains actor i. Again, we focus on subsets, but now we will use subsets from both $\mathcal{N}$ and $\mathcal{M}$.

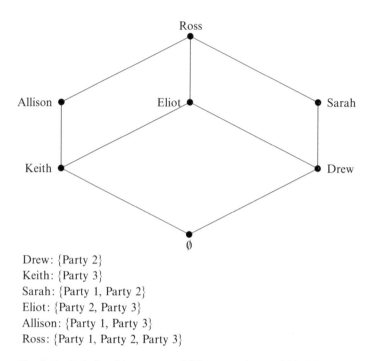

Drew: {Party 2}
Keith: {Party 3}
Sarah: {Party 1, Party 2}
Eliot: {Party 2, Party 3}
Allison: {Party 1, Party 3}
Ross: {Party 1, Party 2, Party 3}

Fig. 8.10. Relationships among children as subsets of birthday parties

Just as we have considered an *individual* actor and the subset of events with which it is affiliated, we can also consider a *subset* of actors and the *subset* of events with which all of these actors are affiliated. Similarly, we can consider a *subset* of events and the *subset* of actors who are affiliated with all of these events.

Let us define a mapping $\uparrow\colon \mathscr{N}_s \to \mathscr{M}_s$ from a subset of actors $\mathscr{N}_s \subseteq \mathscr{N}$ to a subset of events $\mathscr{M}_s \subseteq \mathscr{M}$ such that $\uparrow (\mathscr{N}_s) = \mathscr{M}_s$ if and only if $n_i \lambda m_j$ for all $n_i \in \mathscr{N}_s$ and all $m_j \in \mathscr{M}_s$. In terms of an affiliation network, the $\uparrow$ mapping goes from a subset of actors to that subset of events with which all of the actors in the subset are affiliated. The subset of events might be empty ($\mathscr{M}_s = \emptyset$). For example, if there is no event with which all actors in subset $\mathscr{N}_s$ are affiliated, then $\uparrow (\mathscr{N}_s) = \emptyset$.

We can also define a dual mapping $\downarrow\colon \mathscr{M}_s \to \mathscr{N}_s$ from a subset of events $\mathscr{M}_s$ to a subset of actors $\mathscr{N}_s$ such that $\downarrow (\mathscr{M}_s) = \mathscr{N}_s$ if and only if $m_j \lambda^{-1} n_i$ for all $m_j \in \mathscr{M}_s$ and all $n_i \in \mathscr{N}_s$. In terms of an affiliation network, the $\downarrow$ mapping goes from a subset of events to that subset of actors who are affiliated with all of the events in the subset. If there is no actor who is affiliated with all of the events in subset $\mathcal{M}_s$ then $\downarrow (\mathcal{M}_s) = \emptyset$.

To illustrate the $\uparrow$ and $\downarrow$ mappings, let us look at the hypothetical example of six children and three birthday parties. Consider the subset of children: {Allison (n_1), Sarah (n_6)}. Thus $\mathcal{N}_s = \{n_1, n_6\}$. Since Allison attended Parties 1 and 3 and Sarah attended Parties 1 and 2, the subset of parties that both attended is $\mathcal{M}_s = \{m_1\}$. The mapping $\uparrow (\mathcal{N}_s)$ for this subset of children consists of the subset of parties that both Allison and Sarah attended; thus $\uparrow (\mathcal{N}_s) = \mathcal{M}_s = \{m_1\}$. We can also consider a subset of parties and the subset of children who attended all parties in the subset. Consider the subset parties: {Party 1 (m_1), Party 2 (m_2)}. Thus $\mathcal{M}_s = \{m_1, m_2\}$. The $\downarrow$ mapping maps this subset of parties to the subset of children who attended both parties. Since only Ross (n_5) and Sarah (n_6) attended both Parties 1 and 2, for this subset of parties, $\downarrow (\mathcal{M}_s) = \mathcal{N}_s = \{n_5, n_6\}$.

Now, we can define a special kind of lattice, called a *Galois lattice*. In a Galois lattice, each point is labeled by a *pair* of entities (n_i, m_j). The binary relation "≤" is defined as (n_k, m_l) ≤ (n_i, m_j) if $n_k \subseteq n_i$ and $m_j \subseteq m_l$. A Galois lattice can be presented in a diagram where each point is a pair of entities (n_i, m_j) and there is a line or sequence of lines descending from the point representing (n_i, m_j) to the point representing (n_k, m_l) if (n_k, m_l) ≤ (n_i, m_j); equivalently: $n_k \subseteq n_i$ and $m_j \subseteq m_l$.

We can use a Galois lattice to represent an affiliation network by considering the sets $\mathcal{N}$ and $\mathcal{M}$, the affiliation relation, and the mappings $\uparrow$ and $\downarrow$. In a Galois lattice for an affiliation network, each point represents both a subset of actors and a subset of events.

In the diagram for a Galois lattice the labeling of points is simplified so that labels for entities that are implied by the relation of inclusion are not presented. Thus, in a Galois lattice for an affiliation network an actor's name is given as a label at the lowest point in the diagram such that the actor is included in all subsets of actors implied by lines ascending from that labeled point. An event is given as a label for the highest point in the diagram, such that the event is included in subsets of events implied by lines descending from the labeled point.

An Example. Figure 8.11 shows the hypothetical example of six children and three birthday parties as a Galois lattice. We used the program *DIAGRAM* (Vogt and Bliegener 1990) to construct this diagram from the affiliation network in Figure 8.1. Each point in this diagram represents both a subset of children and a subset of parties. The labels on the points are simplified as described above so that labels for children or parties that can be inferred from the inclusion relations are not presented. The top point in the diagram indicates the pair consisting of the set of all children and the empty set of parties. The point at the bottom represents Ross and the set of all parties (because Ross attended all parties, his name is associated with that collection of parties). Reading from bottom to top in the diagram, there is a line or sequence of lines ascending from a child to a party if that child attended the party. For example, there are lines ascending from Sarah to Party 1 and to Party 2 since Sarah attended Parties 1 and 2. There are sequences of lines ascending from Ross to all three parties since Ross attended all three parties. Keith and Party 3 label the same point; Keith attended only that party. Reading the diagram from top to bottom, there is a line or sequence of lines descending from a party to all children who attended the party. For example, Party 2 included Drew, Sarah, Eliot, and Ross, but not Keith and Allison. These relationships show which children attended which parties.

We can also consider relationships among the children and among the parties. In the Galois lattice we can see which children attended any of the same parties, or whether they were never at parties together. Since lines going up from each child lead to the parties they attended, if we consider two children we can see whether or not they attended any of the same parties by considering whether any lines ascending from them join at any parties. For example, Allison and Sarah both have lines going up to Party 1, so both were present at that party. However, lines ascending from Keith and Drew only intersect at the top point, indicating the empty set of parties. Thus Keith and Drew were never at the same party. The relationship of inclusion between subsets is also visible in the diagram. If a line goes up from one child to another, the upper child was never present at a party unless the lower child was also there. Thus, the set parties for the higher child is contained in the set of parties attended by the lower child. In this sense, the children at the bottom of the diagram are more toward the center of the group, and the children toward the top are more likely to be outliers.

Summary. The advantages of a Galois lattice for representing an affiliation network are the focus on subsets, and the complementary relationships between the actors and the events that are displayed in the diagram. The focus on subsets is especially appropriate for representing affiliation networks. In addition patterns in the relationships between

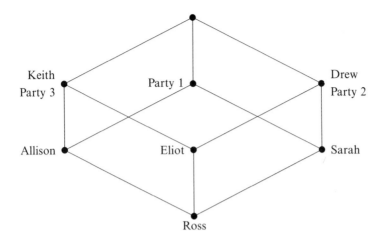

Fig. 8.11. Galois lattice of children and birthday parties

actors and events may be more apparent in the Galois lattice than in other representations. Thus, a Galois lattice serves much the same function as a graph or sociogram as a representation of a one-mode network.

There are a number of shortcomings of Galois lattices. First, the visual display of a Galois lattice can become quite complex as the number of actors and/or the number of events becomes large. This is also true for graphs and directed graphs. Second, there is no unique "best" visual representation for a Galois lattice. Although the vertical dimension represents degrees of subset inclusion relationships among points, the horizontal dimension is arbitrary. As Wille (1990) has pointed out, constructing "good" pictures for Galois lattices is somewhat of an art, since there is a great degree of arbitrariness about placement of the elements in the diagram. Finally, unlike a graph as a representation of a network, which allows the properties and concepts from graph theory to be used to *analyze* the network, such properties and further analyses of Galois lattices are not at all well developed. Thus, a Galois lattice is primarily a representation of an affiliation network, from which one might be able to see patterns in the data.

8.6.2 ⊗*Correspondence Analysis*

We now turn to another method for analyzing affiliation networks that allows one to study the actors and the events simultaneously. This method has the advantage that it provides an objective criterion for placing both actors and events in a spatial arrangement to show optimally the relationships among the two sets of entities. The method we describe in this section is *correspondence analysis*. Correspondence analysis is a widely used data analytic technique for studying the correlations among two or more sets of variables. The technique has been presented many times, under several different names including dual scaling, optimal scaling, reciprocal averaging, and so on. The history of correspondence analysis is discussed in several places; among the most accessible general treatments are Nishisato (1980), Greenacre (1984), and Weller and Romney (1990). Since our treatment of the topic is brief, we encourage the interested reader to consult these sources for more detailed discussions. Correspondence analysis and closely related approaches have been used by several researchers to study social networks (Faust and Wasserman 1993; Kumbasar, Romney, and Batchelder n.d.; Levine 1972; Noma and Smith 1985b; Romney 1993; Schweizer 1990; Wasserman and Faust 1989; Wasserman, Faust, and Galaskiewicz 1990).

Even a brief perusal of the literature reveals that there are many possible ways to motivate, derive, and interpret a correspondence analysis. In this section we will describe only one such motivation, the reciprocal averaging interpretation, since it is one of the most natural interpretations for an affiliation network. This approach is used widely in ecology to describe the distribution of species across a number of locations (Hill 1974, 1982). In that field, the goal is to describe locations (sites) in terms of the distribution of plant or animal species that are present, and simultaneously, to describe the plant or animal species in terms of their distribution across locations. (See, for example, Greenacre's 1981 analysis of the kinds of antelopes found at different game reserves.) The derivation of correspondence analysis that is appropriate for this task is the *weighted centroid* interpretation, or the *method of reciprocal averaging* (Hill 1974, 1982).

We begin with a two-way, two-mode matrix that records the incidence of entities in one mode at the locations indicated by the other mode. The affiliation network matrix, **A**, is such a table since it records the presence of actors at events. The goal of correspondence analysis is to assign a score to each of the entities in each of the modes, to describe optimally (in a way we specify below) the correlation between the two modes. One can then study these scores to see the similarities among the entities in one mode, and the location of an entity in one mode in relation to *all* entities of the other mode. One can also study the dimensionality of the data by looking at how many sets of scores are necessary to reproduce the original data. Also, we will see that these scores have nice geometric properties that will allow us to display graphically the correlations among the entities in the two-modes.

More specifically, correspondence analysis of affiliation network data will result in the assignment of scores to each of the g actors in $\mathcal{N}$ and to each of the h events in $\mathcal{M}$, and a *principal inertia* η^2 summarizing the degree of correlation between the actor scores and the event scores. We will then be able to use these scores to display each actor in terms of the events with which it is affiliated, or to display each event in terms of the actors who are affiliated with it. Following the weighted centroid (or reciprocal averaging) interpretation, the score that is assigned to an actor is proportional to the weighted average of the scores assigned to the events with which the actor is affiliated, or the scores assigned to the events are proportional to the weighted averages of the scores of the actors who are affiliated with the event. This allows us to locate each actor in a space defined by the events with which it is affiliated, or to locate each event in a space defined by the actors it includes.

Definition. In this section we describe the mathematics of correspondence analysis of the affiliation network matrix, **A**. Our treatment is descriptive, rather than statistical, and emphasizes interpretations that are appropriate for affiliation network data. One of the advantages of correspondence analysis is that it allows the researcher to study the correlation between the scores for the rows and the scores for the columns of the data array. In this section we show how these two sets of scores are related to each other via *reciprocal averaging*. The score for a given row is the weighted average of the scores for the columns, where the weights are the relative frequencies of the cells.

In fact, correspondence analysis results in a number of sets of scores (or dimensions) where the number of dimensions depends on the number of rows and columns in the matrix being analyzed. We will let $W = \min\{(g-1), (h-1)\}$. The number of dimensions resulting from a correspondence analysis is less than or equal to W.

Recall that the affiliation network matrix, $\mathbf{A} = \{a_{ij}\}$, is a $g \times h$ matrix that records the affiliation of each actor with each event. Correspondence analysis of $\mathbf{A}$ results in three sets of information:

- a set of g row scores on each of W dimensions $\{u_{ik}\}$, for $i = 1, 2, \ldots, g$, and $k = 1, 2, \ldots, W$, pertaining to the actors,
- a set of h column scores on each of W dimensions $\{v_{jk}\}$, for $j = 1, 2, \ldots, h$, and $k = 1, 2, \ldots, W$, pertaining to the events, and
- a set of W principal inertias $\{\eta_k^2\}$, for $k = 1, 2, \ldots, W$ that measure the correlation between the rows and the columns.

As we mentioned above, the scores assigned to an actor, the u's, are a weighted average of the scores for the events that the actor is affiliated with, and the scores assigned to an event, the v's, are a weighted average of the scores of the actors included in the event. By definition,

$$u_{ik} \quad \text{is proportional to} \quad \sum_{j=1}^{h} \frac{a_{ij}}{a_{i+}} v_{jk}$$

$$v_{jk} \quad \text{is proportional to} \quad \sum_{i=1}^{g} \frac{a_{ij}}{a_{+j}} u_{ik}. \tag{8.7}$$

It is customary to describe the solution to this problem as the triple $(\eta, \mathbf{u}, \mathbf{v})$, where η is the proportionality constant from equation (8.7), and $\mathbf{u}$ and $\mathbf{v}$ are the vectors of row and column scores, respectively. Substituting η_k into equation (8.7), we get the following equations, relating the row and column scores:

$$\eta_k u_{ik} = \sum_{j=1}^{h} \frac{a_{ij}}{a_{i+}} v_{jk}$$

$$\eta_k v_{jk} = \sum_{i=1}^{g} \frac{a_{ij}}{a_{+j}} u_{ik}. \tag{8.8}$$

The scores that satisfy these equations have the desired property that the row scores will be proportional to the weighted averages of the column scores and the column scores will be proportional to the weighted averages of the row scores.

Equation (8.8) shows why correspondence analysis is sometimes referred to as reciprocal averaging; the scores for one set of variables are the weighted averages of the scores for the other set, and vice versa.

Solution of these equations requires a singular value decomposition of an appropriately scaled **A** matrix, and can be accomplished with standard correspondence analysis programs, such as Greenacre's *SIMCA* (Greenacre 1986).

The **u**'s and **v**'s are commonly scaled so that, within each of the *W* sets, the weighted mean is 0 and the weighted variance is equal to η_k^2:

$$\sum_{i=1}^{g} u_{ik} \frac{a_{i+}}{a_{++}} = \sum_{j=1}^{h} v_{jk} \frac{a_{+j}}{a_{++}} = 0$$

$$\sum_{i=1}^{g} u_{ik}^2 \frac{a_{i+}}{a_{++}} = \sum_{j=1}^{h} v_{jk}^2 \frac{a_{+j}}{a_{++}} = \eta_k^2 \tag{8.9}$$

for each set $k = 1, 2, \ldots, W$. When u and v are scaled as in equation (8.9) they are referred to as the *principal coordinates* (Greenacre 1984). The advantage of this scaling is that the variance of each set of scores, within each dimension, is equal to the principal inertia, η_k^2, for that dimension.

Interpreting results of correspondence analysis requires a bit of care. Let us first distinguish between two different kinds of interpretations that we might make. First we might want to examine the relationships among the entities in each of the modes, either all of the actors or all of the events. Second, we might want to examine how the two modes are related to each other. Clearly since our concern is in studying the relationship between the two modes, we are interested in the second kind of interpretation.

The geometry of the correspondence analysis allows one to relate the score for a *single* entity of one mode to the *entire set* of scores from the other mode. In other words, we can relate a single actor score, one value of u_{ik}, to the entire set of event scores, the collection of h v_{jk}'s. Or, we can relate a single event score, a v_{jk}, to the entire set of g actor scores, the u_{ik}'s. However, as Carroll, Green, and Schaffer (1986) have pointed out, this requires careful scaling of the row and column scores. If we return to equation (8.8) we can see that the relationship between the u's and the v's depends on the proportionality constant, η_k. It is therefore useful to rescale one set of scores (either the row scores or the column scores) by dividing each by the corresponding value of η_k. Therefore, we define a new scaling of the scores, denoted by $\tilde{u}$ and $\tilde{v}$, as follows:

$$\tilde{u}_{ik} = u_{ik}/\eta_k$$
$$\tilde{v}_{jk} = v_{jk}/\eta_k. \qquad (8.10)$$

These scores have weighted mean equal to 0, and weighted variance equal to 1:

$$\sum_{i=1}^{g} \tilde{u}_{ik} \frac{a_{i+}}{a_{++}} = \sum_{j=1}^{h} \tilde{v}_{jk} \frac{a_{+j}}{a_{++}} = 0$$

$$\sum_{i=1}^{g} \tilde{u}_{ik}^{2} \frac{a_{i+}}{a_{++}} = \sum_{j=1}^{h} \tilde{v}_{jk}^{2} \frac{a_{+j}}{a_{++}} = 1 \qquad (8.11)$$

for all k. When scaled this way, the $\tilde{u}$ and $\tilde{v}$ are referred to as *standard coordinates* (Greenacre 1984, 1986).

With this rescaling, we can express a given row score u_{ik} scaled in principal coordinates in terms of the collection of column scores $\tilde{v}_{jk}$'s, scaled in standard coordinates. Combining equations (8.8) and (8.10) we see that:

$$u_{ik} = \sum_{j=1}^{h} \frac{a_{ij}}{a_{i+}} \tilde{v}_{jk}. \qquad (8.12)$$

In words, the score assigned to a given actor, a u_{ik}, is the weighted average of the scores assigned to the events, the $\tilde{v}_{jk}$'s, that the actor is affiliated with, where the weights are the cell frequencies of the affiliation matrix, a_{ij}, divided by the appropriate row total, a_{i+}. We can use these scores to locate each individual actor in a space defined by the events. Similarly, we can express a given column score scaled in principal coordinates in terms of the collection of row scores scaled in standard coordinates:

$$v_{jk} = \sum_{i=1}^{g} \frac{a_{ij}}{a_{+j}} \tilde{u}_{ik}. \qquad (8.13)$$

Using this scaling, the score assigned to a given event is the weighted average of the scores assigned to the actors who are affiliated with the event.

We can translate (rescale) from one scaling of the row and/or the column scores into the other scaling using the following equations:

$$u_{ik} = \tilde{u}_{ik}\eta_k$$
$$v_{jk} = \tilde{v}_{jk}\eta_k. \tag{8.14}$$

It is common to use the scores from a correspondence analysis to display graphically the entities represented by the row points and the column points. To study the two modes together using the reciprocal averaging interpretation we will plot points for entities in one of the modes using standard coordinates and points for entities in the other mode using principal coordinates. Thus, we will either use standard coordinates for actors (the $\tilde{u}$'s) and principal coordinates for events (the v's) or we will use standard coordinates for events (the $\tilde{v}$'s) and principal coordinates for actors (the u's).

An Example. As an example of correspondence analysis of an affiliation network, consider Galaskiewicz's CEOs and clubs network. Table 8.3 presents the first two sets of correspondence analysis scores for rows (actors) and columns (events) for this example. We used Greenacre's program *SIMCA* to do this analysis (Greenacre 1986). For these data $\eta_1^2 = 0.5756$ and $\eta_2^2 = 0.4074$. These two dimensions account for 19.79% and 14.01% of the data, respectively. The first two sets of scores are displayed in Figure 8.12. We have displayed the scores for the CEOs (n_i's) in principal coordinates and the scores for the clubs (m_j's) in standard coordinates. Thus, we can interpret the location of a point for a CEO on a given dimension as the weighted mean of the locations of the clubs with which that CEO is affiliated.

There are a couple of interesting features of the plot in Figure 8.12. First, notice that the points for the clubs (the m_j's) are more widely dispersed throughout the figure than are the points for the CEOs (the n_i's). This is a function of the scaling that we have chosen for the row and column scores. Since scores for the column points (for the clubs) are in standard coordinates, they have larger variance than do the scores for the row points (for the CEOs) and thus have greater variability on each of the dimensions. If we had used the alternative scaling (row points in standard coordinates and column points in principal coordinates) the n_i's would have greater dispersion than the m_j's. Second, notice the fairly dense collection of points toward the upper right of the figure. This collection contains the CEOs and

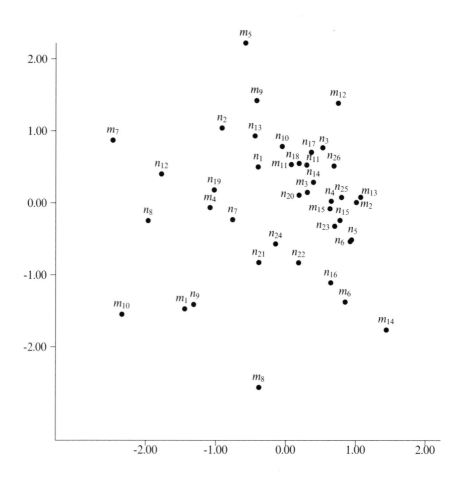

Fig. 8.12. Plot of correspondence analysis scores for CEOs and clubs example — CEOs in principal coordinates clubs in standard coordinates

clubs that we had identified as belonging to "cliques" at high levels in the valued relations of actor co-memberships and event overlaps (notice CEOs numbered 14, 17, and 20, and Clubs 2, 3, and 15). CEO 14 belongs to more clubs than any other CEO (a total of seven) and CEO 17 belongs to the second most clubs (a total of six). Club 3 is the largest club (with twenty-two members) and Club 2 is the second largest (with eleven members). Thus, this analysis in part identifies a "core" of active CEOs and clubs with large memberships.

Table 8.3. *Correspondence analysis scores for CEOs and clubs*

	Row Score			
	u_{i1}	u_{i2}	$\tilde{u}_{i1}$	$\tilde{u}_{i2}$
n_1	-0.404	0.502	-0.533	0.787
n_2	-0.920	1.079	-1.213	1.692
n_3	0.518	0.767	0.683	1.203
n_4	0.641	0.027	0.844	0.043
n_5	0.933	-0.510	1.229	-0.799
n_6	0.913	-0.534	1.203	-0.836
n_7	-0.766	-0.232	-1.009	-0.363
n_8	-1.968	-0.247	-2.593	-0.387
n_9	-1.315	-1.409	-1.733	-2.209
n_{10}	-0.063	0.785	-0.083	1.231
n_{11}	0.291	0.527	0.384	0.826
n_{12}	-1.780	0.402	-2.345	0.630
n_{13}	-0.450	0.932	-0.593	1.461
n_{14}	0.386	0.288	0.509	0.452
n_{15}	0.766	-0.242	1.009	-0.380
n_{16}	0.639	-1.107	0.842	-1.735
n_{17}	0.357	0.704	0.470	1.103
n_{18}	0.182	0.550	0.240	0.862
n_{19}	-1.026	0.181	-1.352	0.284
n_{20}	0.181	0.110	0.239	0.173
n_{21}	-0.391	-0.825	-0.515	-1.293
n_{22}	0.179	-0.829	0.236	-1.300
n_{23}	0.692	-0.323	0.911	-0.507
n_{24}	-0.153	-0.567	-0.201	-0.889
n_{25}	0.787	0.080	1.037	0.125
n_{26}	0.679	0.515	0.894	0.807

	Column Score			
	v_{j1}	v_{j2}	$\tilde{v}_{j1}$	$\tilde{v}_{j2}$
m_1	-1.096	-0.938	-1.444	-1.470
m_2	0.759	0.007	1.000	0.010
m_3	0.227	0.095	0.299	0.148
m_4	-0.824	-0.041	-1.086	-0.065
m_5	-0.445	1.418	-0.587	2.222
m_6	0.641	-0.877	0.844	-1.375
m_7	-1.876	0.554	-2.472	0.869
m_8	-0.293	-1.634	-0.385	-2.561
m_9	-0.323	0.908	-0.426	1.423
m_{10}	-1.779	-0.986	-2.344	-1.546
m_{11}	0.052	0.341	0.069	0.535
m_{12}	0.559	0.885	0.737	1.387
m_{13}	0.805	0.052	1.061	0.082
m_{14}	1.092	-1.123	1.439	-1.760
m_{15}	0.473	-0.049	0.623	-0.077

Correspondence analysis of an affiliation network formally represents two important theoretical aspects of these data. First, recall Simmel's observation that an individual's social identity is defined by the collectivities to which the individual belongs. In correspondence analysis, this insight is translated formally, and quite literally, in the reciprocal averaging interpretation expressed in equations (8.12) and (8.13). Geometrically, an actor's location in space is determined by the location of the events with which that actor is affiliated. The second theoretically important feature of affiliation networks is the duality of relationship between actors and events. This duality is captured in the fact that one can either view actors located within a space defined by the events, or one can view the events located within a space defined by the actors, and can plot scores for entities in both modes simultaneously.

To illustrate these ideas, consider the score for CEO 2 in the analysis of Galaskiewicz's CEOs and clubs data, presented in Table 8.3 and Figure 8.12. CEO 2 belongs to three clubs (Clubs 3, 5, and 7), thus its score on the first dimension, $u_{21} = -0.920$, must be the weighted average of the scores for these three clubs on this dimension (the $\tilde{v}_{j1}$'s). Notice that the score for an actor is only a function of the scores for the events to which it belongs. Following equation (8.12) we see that

$$u_{21} = \sum_{j=1}^{15} \frac{a_{2j}}{a_{2+}} \tilde{v}_{j1}$$

$$-0.920 = \frac{1}{3}(0.299) + \frac{1}{3}(-0.587) + \frac{1}{3}(-2.472). \qquad (8.15)$$

In Figure 8.12 we see that n_2 is the weighted average (or weighted centroid) of the points m_3, m_5, and m_7.

In Figure 8.12 CEOs are located at the weighted averages (weighted centroids) of the clubs to which they belong, since scores for CEOs are presented in principal coordinates and scores for clubs are in standard coordinates. Locating clubs at the weighted averages of their members would require the alternative scaling (scores for clubs in principal coordinates and scores for CEOs in standard coordinates).

8.7 Summary

In conclusion, let us reiterate some of the important features of affiliation networks that make them distinctive from the one-mode networks that we have discussed prior to this chapter, and briefly review some of the important issues to consider when analyzing affiliation networks. First, affiliation networks are two-mode networks that focus on the affiliation of a set of actors with a set of events. Since each event consists of a subset of actors, and each actor is affiliated with a subset of events, affiliation network data cannot be studied completely by looking at pairs of actors and/or pairs of events. Next, there is an important duality in the relationships among the actors and the events; actors create linkages among the events, and simultaneously the events create linkages among the actors. Although affiliation networks are two-mode networks, and the most comprehensive analyses would study both actors and events simultaneously, it is also possible to study the one-mode networks, of actors or of events. However, since affiliation networks are defined on subsets (not pairs) of actors and events there is loss of information and potential for misinterpretation when studying only the one-mode networks.

For the most part the analyses that we have described in this chapter assume that one has a complete affiliation network. That is, that all actors and all events constituting the network are included. If, on the other hand, the actors in $\mathcal{N}$ are a sample of actors from a larger population, or if the events in $\mathcal{M}$ are a sample from a larger population of events, then one must consider issues of sampling and estimation of the relevant network quantities. McPherson (1982) discusses how to estimate key network affiliation measures (including the average size of events, and average rates of affiliation).

Part IV
Roles and Positions

9

Structural Equivalence

Many methods for the description of network structural properties are concerned with the dual notions of *social position* and *social role*. In social network terms these translate into procedures for analyzing actors' structural similarities and patterns of relations in multirelational networks. These methods, which have been referred to as positional, role, or relational approaches, are the topic of Part IV. Although these methods are mathematically and formally diverse, they share a common goal of representing patterns in complex social network data in simplified form to reveal subsets of actors who are similarly embedded in networks of relations and to describe the associations among relations in multirelational networks.

The diversity of methods and potential complexity of mathematics has influenced our organization of topics in the following chapters. We begin this chapter with an overview of the theoretical and historical background for network role and positional analysis. We then discuss the basics of positional analysis. These basics will occupy Chapter 9 and the first part of Chapter 10. Chapters 9 and 10 discuss how to perform basic positional analysis using measures based on the mathematical notion of structural equivalence. In Chapters 11 and 12 we take up more advanced approaches to the notions of role and position and explore alternative formal definitions of these concepts. These chapters are concerned with the algebraic analysis of role systems using relational algebras (Chapter 11) and more general definitions of equivalence (Chapter 12).

This chapter introduces the theoretical background for studying social network roles and positions and presents an overview of positional analysis of social networks. It also defines and illustrates structural equivalence as an approach for studying network positions.

9.1 Background

In this section we review the theoretical definition of social role and social position, present a brief history of the development of these ideas, and give an overview of how ideas of role and position are used to study social networks.

9.1.1 Social Roles and Positions

The related notions of social position and social role provide the theoretical motivation for most of the methods we discuss in this part of the book. Although historically these notions have been most widely used by sociologists (for example, Merton 1957), anthropologists (Linton 1936; Nadel 1957), and social psychologists (Newcomb 1965), the formal definition of these theoretical concepts using network methods has encouraged their use to study social networks in many fields, for example political science (Snyder and Kick 1979) and management (Krackhardt and Porter 1986).

It is important to note that there is considerable disagreement among social scientists about the definitions of the related concepts of social position, social status, and social role. Among the most straightforward definitions of social role and social status are those given by Linton, who uses the term "status" in a way that is identical to our use of the term "position." Linton defines a status as "the polar position in ... patterns of reciprocal behavior." When a person "puts the rights and duties which constitute the status into effect, he is performing a role" (1936, pages 113–114). There are two important and related concepts here: *position* and *role*. In social network analysis *position* refers to a collection of individuals who are similarly embedded in networks of relations, while *role* refers to the patterns of relations which obtain between actors or between positions. The notion of position thus refers to a collection of actors who are similar in social activity, ties, or interactions, with respect to actors in other positions.

Since position is based on the similarity of ties among subsets of actors, rather than their adjacency, proximity, or reachability, this theoretical concept, and its formalization network terms, are quite different from the notion of cohesive subgroup. Actors occupying the same position need not be in direct, or even indirect, contact with one another. For example, nurses in different hospitals occupy the position of "nurse" by virtue of similar kinds of relationships with doctors and patients, though individual nurses may not know each other, work with the same doctors, or see the same patients.

The notion of social role is conceptually, theoretically, and formally dependent on the notion of social position. Whereas network position refers to a collection of actors, network role refers to associations among relations that link social positions. Thus, role is defined in terms of collections of relations and the associations among relations. In contrast to most social network methods that focus on properties of actors or subsets of actors, network role analysis focuses on associations among relations. For example, kinship roles can be defined in terms of combinations of the relations of marriage and descent. Roles within a corporate organization might be defined in terms of levels in a chain of command or authority. It is also important to note that roles are defined not simply on the linkages between *two* positions, but on how relations link the entire collection of actors and positions throughout the network. Thus, roles in social networks can be modeled at three different levels: actors, subsets of actors, and the network as a whole.

As Nadel (1957) and Lorrain and White (1971) have observed, role is not just a theoretical construct invented by social scientists, but also can be expressed in our everyday language. People recognize and label roles; even roles based on the combination of several relations. For example, some roles that can be defined by combinations of relations include: a boss's boss, a brother's friend, or an ally's enemy. In addition, some kinship roles based on combinations of relations have simple linguistic labels: brother-in-law, grandmother, uncle, aunt, and so on. However, not all network roles have simple linguistic labels, and we will also be interested in studying such roles.

As these examples show, social roles are usually based on multiple relations and the combinations of these relations. Historically, the study of network role systems began with models for kinship systems based on combinations of relations (Boyd 1969; White 1963). In studying kinship one must both consider marriage and descent. Another example where multiple relations are important is the study of roles and positions within the world economic system. One might argue that roles of countries in the world system must be understood in terms of the associations among several types of economic exchanges that occur between countries. For example, the association among the relations of "exports raw materials to" and "imports manufactured goods from" might be critical for understanding patterns of economic dependence among nations. What is important in these examples is the association among two or more relations. In their foundational paper, White, Boorman, and Breiger (1976) observe that the most informative role or positional analyses require many types of relations. Thus, the most interesting and detailed role and positional analyses will probably involve multirelational networks. However, more limited conclusions and results are possible for single relational social networks.

Positional analysis of a social network rests on the assumption that the role structure of the group and positions of individuals in the group are apparent in the measured relations present in a set of network data. This assumption appears early in the history of role and positional analysis of social networks. In their pathbreaking work, Lorrain and White comment,

> the total role of an individual in a social system has often been described as consisting of sets of relations of various types linking this person as ego to sets of others. (1971, page 50)

In this quote by Lorrain and White we see that role becomes identified with the "sets of relations," where relations are the measured ties in a social network, and position becomes identified with the "sets of others," the subsets of actors who are similarly tied to others in the network.

The use of the word position to refer to a subset of actors is clearly stated in White, Boorman, and Breiger's discussion of blockmodeling:

> each of the sets into which the population is partitioned is a position. (1976, page 769)

We note that our use of the term "network position" to refer to a collection of equivalent actors differs somewhat from Burt's usage. Burt (1976) states:

> a position in a network [is] the specified set of relations to and from each actor in a system. (1976, page 93)

Burt's approach conceptualizes a position as a collection of ties in which an actor is involved. These ties can be summarized as a "vector" of ties to and from the actor. This usage of position is the same as White, Boorman, and Breiger's *role set* (1976, page 770), and is perhaps closer to our use of the term "role," especially in the context of individual roles (which we discuss in Chapter 12).

The tasks of role and positional analysis of a social network are to provide explicit definitions of important social concepts and to identify and describe roles and positions in social networks. These two theoretical motivations can be used to give an overview of the different, though related, tasks in positional and role analysis of social networks.

9.1.2 An Overview of Positional and Role Analysis

There are two key aspects to the positional and role analysis of social networks: identifying social positions as collections of actors who are similar in their ties with others, and modeling social roles as systems of ties between actors or between positions. These two aspects are apparent in the foundational works by White, Boorman, and Breiger (1976), who focused on methods for partitioning actors, and Boorman and White (1976), who focused on models for collections of relations. In practice, many applications of these methods to substantive problems emphasize one or the other of these tasks. In fact, most analyses emphasize the similarity of actors (that is, the identification of positions) with considerably less attention to the relations among the positions.

Schematically, one can present the task of a full positional and role analysis of a social network as in Figure 9.1 (see Sailer 1978; Pattison 1982). Beginning with a set of network data consisting of a collection of relations (a multirelational data set), the ultimate goals are to "group" actors into positions based on their relational similarity, and simultaneously to describe the association among relations based on how they combine to link actors or positions (White, Boorman, and Breiger 1976; Boorman and White 1976; Sailer 1978; Breiger and Pattison 1986; Pattison 1982, 1988). As shown in this figure, the alternative paths involve (from top to bottom) grouping actors, the standard positional analysis, and (from left to right) studying the associations among relations, the usual role analysis. A complete positional and role analysis would result in both an assignment of actors to positions and a model of the system of relations that link these positions.

Let us think about the tasks of analyzing network positions and analyzing network roles separately for the moment. We will start with a one-mode network and a collection of relations. First consider the positional analysis problem (the left path from top to bottom in Figure 9.1). The major task here is to locate subsets of actors who are similar across the collection of relations. Similarity will be defined in terms of the equivalence of actors with respect to some formal mathematical property. The formal mathematical property specifies which actors will be "grouped" together in a network position. We can think of a positional analysis,

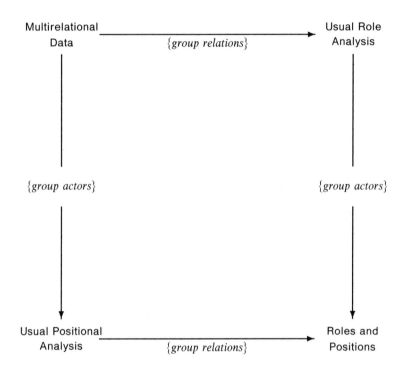

Fig. 9.1. An overview of positional and role analysis

the vertical path on the left side of the diagram, as mapping actors into equivalence classes, where (ideally) an equivalence class consists of all actors who are identical on the specified mathematical property. Structural equivalence, which we discuss in this chapter, is one such formal mathematical property for defining equivalence classes. We discuss other properties in Chapter 12.

In practice a positional analysis involves several steps. We will describe these steps in detail in the remainder of this chapter, and illustrate them with examples.

Now, let us consider the usual role analysis. A role analysis is concerned with the associations among relations. Schematically, a role analysis will traverse the horizontal paths in Figure 9.1, either along the top or along the bottom of this diagram. The distinction between the top path and the bottom path is related to the distinction between "global" roles, which describe associations among relations for an entire group, and "individual" or "local" roles, which describe associations among relations from the perspectives of individual actors or subsets of actors. We will discuss "global" roles in Chapter 11, and take up the topic of "individual" roles in Chapter 12.

Once equivalence classes (or positions) of actors have been identified, the ties between these positions must be described. Modeling ties between positions is the task represented by the horizontal arrow on the bottom of the figure. The task here is to describe the system of relations between the positions. Image matrices and density tables (which we discuss in this chapter) and blockmodels (which we discuss in Chapter 10) are common ways to model ties between positions.

The horizontal path along the top of the diagram outlines another approach to role analysis. Starting with a collection of relations the task is to describe the association among the relations. For example, in an analysis of kinship relations, one might note that the combination of relations "mother of" and "sister of" gives rise to a meaningful compound relation — "mother's sister," which (in standard American English kinship terms) is labeled "aunt." Or, to give a non-kinship example, consider the relations "friend of" and "enemy of." We would expect that the combination of these two relations might lead to other meaningful relations: "friend of a friend is a friend," "enemy of a friend is an enemy," and so on. Modeling the association among relations is the basis for the network role system.

The final step moving from top to bottom along the right side of the diagram requires grouping actors into equivalence classes based on the description of the role system resulting from the previous step. Here, as on the left side of the diagram, the critical decision is how to measure similarity among actors. The result is both a model of associations among relations (the network roles) and a partition of actors into equivalence classes that relate similarly to one another according to the roles.

In this brief overview we have described these alternative routes through a positional and role analysis as different analytic sequences, requiring grouping actors and then describing associations among relations, or describing the associations among relations and then grouping actors — with one of the two tasks coming before the other in the analysis. The most desirable strategy would accomplish these simultaneously. A simultaneous model of actors and relations would be indicated by a direct arrow from the upper left to the bottom right of Figure 9.1.

Intuitively this would require defining equivalence classes of actors and relational systems at the same time. An important question (see Sailer 1978; Pattison 1982; Breiger and Pattison 1986, 1993) is whether alternative paths through this diagram give comparable results. The approach described by Breiger and Pattison (1986) is designed to model actor relational systems and network role structure at the same time.

The scheme in Figure 9.1 can be used to organize the topics we discuss in the next four chapters. Chapter 9 is concerned with the vertical path on the left side of the diagram; methods for locating subsets of equivalent actors. Chapter 16 discusses statistical models for locating subsets of stochastically equivalent actors. Chapters 10 and 11 are concerned with the horizontal paths; describing role systems, either based on a prior aggregation of actors (blockmodels along the lower path) or from the perspective of individuals (along the upper horizontal path). Chapter 12 expands on methods for aggregating actors (using different equivalence definitions) and describing relations among these subsets, and so is concerned with the vertical paths.

Although a complete analysis would study both network positions, and the ways in which the positions are tied to each other (network roles), in practice much can be learned about the structure of a network from analyzing the similarities among actors. Most applications of positional analysis to substantive problems focus on identifying subsets of equivalent actors in a network.

9.1.3 A Brief History

The earliest and foundational formal statements of roles and positions in social networks arose in the anthropological study of kinship systems (White 1963; Boyd 1969). Using relational concepts, rules for marriage and descent could be stated in formal terms, and complex kinship systems could be described as mathematical structures. These algebraic statements give elegant descriptions of prescriptive and preferential marriage systems (as described by ethnographers), but the algebraic tools were initially less useful for analyzing social networks of measured ties between individuals (rather than between marriage classes or clans). In addition, White (1963) drew the analogy between the algebra of kinship systems and the structure of formal organizations. The use of formal role and positional analysis to study social networks with a wider variety of relations started in the 1970's, with the publication of Lorrain and White's (1971) paper on structural equivalence. Their goal was to bring algebraic techniques to the formal study of social roles in a wide variety of settings.

The mathematical concept of structural equivalence, or some generalization of it, is fundamental to virtually all positional and role analyses. The concept of structural equivalence allowed rapid development of this area in the mid-1970's, and subsequent work on measurement of structural equivalence and representation of positional and relational structures by numerous researchers brought attention and popularity to this approach. Notable contributions here include the procedures for finding subsets of structurally equivalent actors (Breiger, Boorman, and Arabie 1975; Burt 1976), methods for representing ties between positions as blockmodels (White, Boorman, and Breiger 1976; Arabie, Boorman, and Levitt 1978; Arabie and Boorman 1979), algebraic approaches for modeling relational systems (Boorman and White 1976; Pattison 1982, 1993; Boyd 1990), and clarification of the notions of structural equivalence and social position (Burt 1976; Sailer 1978; White and Reitz 1983, 1989).

Since the late 1970's attention has turned to developing alternative approaches to positional and role analysis. Extensive attention has been devoted to developing other equivalence definitions (besides structural equivalence) that are more faithful to the original theoretical concepts of social position and social role (Borgatti, Boyd, and Everett 1989; Borgatti and Everett 1989; Borgatti 1988; Breiger and Pattison 1986; Everett, Boyd, and Borgatti 1990; Mandel 1983; Pattison 1982, 1988, 1993; Sailer 1978; White and Reitz 1983, 1985, 1989; Winship and Mandel 1983; Wu 1983). In addition, some researchers have extended these initially descriptive methods using probabilistic approaches (Anderson, Wasserman, and Faust 1992; Holland, Laskey, and Leinhardt 1983; Wang and Wong 1987; Wasserman and Anderson 1987; Wong 1987).

There is a growing consensus in the social network community that structural similarity of actors (formally translated into network position) is one of the key structural properties in network analysis (Borgatti and Everett 1992a; Burt 1976, 1978a, 1980, 1982). One of the consequences of the importance of this property is a proliferation of methods and formal approaches for the positional analysis of social networks. Methods for positional and role analysis of social networks developed rapidly in the 1970's, and this continues to be an active area of investigation in network analysis (Boorman and White 1976; Borgatti 1988; Borgatti, Boyd, and Everett 1989; Borgatti and Everett 1989; Boyd 1983, 1991; Breiger, Boorman and Arabie 1975; Breiger and Pattison 1986; Burt 1976, 1990;

Everett, Boyd, and Borgatti 1990; Lorrain and White 1971; Mandel 1983; Marsden 1989; Pattison 1993; Sailer 1978; White, Boorman, and Breiger 1976; White and Reitz 1983, 1989; Winship and Mandel 1983; Wu 1983). Although methods in this area employ some of the most sophisticated mathematics used to study social networks, simple positional analysis techniques can be quite straightforward, and can provide relatively clearcut insights into the structure of a social network. Perhaps this simplicity and the widespread availability of positional analysis procedures (for example in the computer programs *STRUCTURE* (Burt 1989) and *UCINET*) (Borgatti, Everett, and Freeman 1991) have contributed to the fact that positional analysis techniques are among the most widely used descriptive methods for social network analysis.

Positional and role analyses are areas of network analysis where the power of mathematics has served well in the development of theoretical ideas and substantive applications. In particular, most of the advances in positional analysis derive in one way or another from the mathematical property of structural equivalence or its generalizations.

9.2 Definition of Structural Equivalence

Structural equivalence, introduced and defined in the now classic paper by Lorrain and White (1971), is a mathematical property of subsets of actors in a network (or nodes in a graph). Briefly, two actors are structurally equivalent if they have identical ties to and from all other actors in the network.

9.2.1 Definition

We begin with a collection of R dichotomous relations $(\mathscr{X}_1, \mathscr{X}_2, \ldots, \mathscr{X}_R)$. We will denote the presence of a tie between actors i and j on relation $\mathscr{X}_r$ as $i \xrightarrow{\mathscr{X}_r} j$. This notation generalizes our standard notation, which denotes a tie from i to j as $i \rightarrow j$, or as $x_{ijr} = 1$. Here we have further specified that the tie is on relation $\mathscr{X}_r$.

We have the following definition of structural equivalence: Actors i and j are *structurally equivalent* if, for all actors, $k = 1, 2, \ldots, g$ $(k \neq i, j)$, and all relations $r = 1, 2, \ldots, R$, actor i has a tie to k, if and only if j also has a tie to k, and i has a tie from k if and only if j also has a tie from k. More formally, i and j are structurally equivalent if $i \xrightarrow{\mathscr{X}_r} k$ if and only if $j \xrightarrow{\mathscr{X}_r} k$, and $k \xrightarrow{\mathscr{X}_r} i$ if and only if $k \xrightarrow{\mathscr{X}_r} j$, for all actors, $k = 1, 2, \ldots, g$ ($k \neq i, j$), and relations, $r = 1, 2, \ldots, R$.

Alternatively, the definition may be expressed using the more usual sociometric notation. Letting x_{ijr} indicate the presence or absence of a tie from actor i to actor j on relation $\mathscr{X}_r$, then actors i and j are structurally equivalent if $x_{ikr} = x_{jkr}$ and $x_{kir} = x_{kjr}$ for $k = 1, 2, \ldots, g$, and $r = 1, 2, \ldots, R$. If actors i and j are structurally equivalent, then ties from i terminate at exactly the same actors as ties from j, and ties to i originate from the same actors as the ties to j. We will use the notation $i \equiv j$ to denote the equivalence of actors i and j.

The definition of structural equivalence specifies the precise formal conditions that must hold for actors to be equivalent. Structurally equivalent actors have *identical* ties to and from *identical* actors, on all R relations.

We will use the term "equivalence class" or "position" to refer to a collection of equivalent (or approximately equivalent) actors. We will denote a position by $\mathscr{B}_k$ and let B be the number of positions in the network. In addition, we will use the notation $\phi(i) = \mathscr{B}_k$ to denote the assignment of actor i to position $\mathscr{B}_k$. If actors i and j are structurally equivalent, $i \equiv j$, then they are assigned to the same position; thus, if $i \equiv j$ then $\phi(i) = \phi(j) = \mathscr{B}_k$.

9.2.2 An Example

Consider the example in Figure 9.2. In this graph actors 3 and 4 are structurally equivalent since both have ties to actor 5 and both have ties from both actors 1 and 2. In addition, actors 1 and 2 are structurally equivalent because both have ties to actors 3 and 4. Looking at the sociomatrix for this example, we see that structurally equivalent actors 1 and 2 have identical rows and columns in the sociomatrix (as do actors 3 and 4). In this example, there are $B = 3$ subsets of structurally equivalent actors: $\mathscr{B}_1 = \{1, 2\}$, $\mathscr{B}_2 = \{3, 4\}$, and $\mathscr{B}_3 = \{5\}$.

Notice that if two actors are structurally equivalent then their respective rows and columns in the sociomatrix will be identical. Rows in a sociomatrix, containing their choices made, will contain 1's and 0's in exactly the same columns, and the columns, containing choices received, will contain 1's and 0's in exactly the same rows. If there is more than one relation, then the two structurally equivalent actors will have identical entries in their respective rows and columns in *all* sociomatrices.

Sociomatrix

	1	2	3	4	5
1	-	0	1	1	0
2	0	-	1	1	0
3	0	0	-	0	1
4	0	0	0	-	1
5	0	0	0	0	-

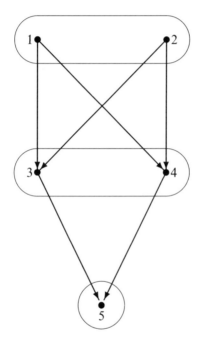

Fig. 9.2. Sociomatrix and directed graph illustrating structural equiva-lence

In terms of the structural information in a network, if two (or more) actors are structurally equivalent, then there is no structural (that is, network or graph theoretic) information pertaining to one actor and not to the other. If actors i and j are structurally equivalent, then the ties from i are identical to those from j and the ties to i are identical to those to j. Thus, i and j are adjacent to and from identical other actors. If actors i and j are structurally equivalent then they are *substitutable* (Lorrain and

White 1971; Sailer 1978). There is no loss of structural information by combining the two (or more) structurally equivalent actors into a single subset and representing them together as a single structural entity called an equivalence class or position.

9.2.3 Some Issues in Defining Structural Equivalence

In defining structural equivalence, it is important to note exactly how the definition applies to the different kinds of relations that can arise in a social network study. Specifically, we must first note whether the data set is single or multirelational. Then, for each relation, we must consider whether it is:

(i) Dichotomous or valued
(ii) Directional or nondirectional
(iii) A relation on which self-ties (the diagonal elements of the sociomatrix) are substantively meaningful

Multiple Relations. The definition of structural equivalence applies quite naturally to multirelational networks. For two actors to be structurally equivalent in a multirelational network, they must have identical ties to and from all other actors, on *all* relations. Actors i and j are structurally equivalent in a multirelational network if and only if $x_{ikr} = x_{jkr}$ and $x_{kir} = x_{kjr}$ for $k = 1, 2, \ldots, g$, $(k \neq i, j)$ and $r = 1, 2, \ldots, R$.

Valued Relations. Structural equivalence is defined easily for dichotomous relations, since a tie between a pair of actors is either present or absent. However, when relations are valued the question of whether two actors are structurally equivalent is less clear-cut. This is especially true when one has to measure how closely two actors come to being perfectly structurally equivalent (a topic we discuss below). For example, consider the valued relation of acquaintanceship in Freeman's *EIES* network. This quantity is measured as each person's reported friendship with each other member of the group on a five-point scale: 1) "unknown," 2) "person I've heard of," 3) "person I've met," 4) "friend," or 5) "close personal friend." In the strictest sense, two actors are structurally equivalent if they name and are named by exactly the same close personal friends, exactly the same friends, had met and been met by exactly the same others, and so on. For two actors to be structurally equivalent on a valued relation they must have ties with identical *values* to and from identical other actors.

Some authors have argued that actors are approximately structurally equivalent if they have the same *pattern* of ties to and from other actors (Burt 1980). If we consider a relation measuring the frequency of interactions observed among members of a group, then two actors would have the same pattern of ties if they interacted frequently with exactly the same others and interacted infrequently with exactly the same others, but the exact number of frequent or infrequent interactions would not have to be the same for the two actors. The similarity of pattern of ties is an important property when we consider how to measure structural equivalence.

Nondirectional Relations. For nondirectional relations there is no distinction between the origin and destination of a tie. Since there is no direction to the ties on a nondirectional relation there is no distinction between ties sent and ties received. Thus, the sociomatrix for a nondirectional relation is symmetric, $x_{ikr} = x_{kir}$, and one only needs to consider either the rows or the columns of the sociomatrix, but not both.

Self-ties and Graph Equivalence. Often it is the case that self-ties in a network are undefined. For example, in the relation "seeks advice from" self-ties would probably be meaningless. In such cases the diagonal entries in a sociomatrix are treated as undefined and are ignored in computations. In analyzing the structural equivalence of pairs of actors on such relations the calculation of structural equivalence would exclude self-ties.

On the other hand, sometimes reflexive ties are substantively important and should be considered. For example, consider recording the number of memos sent between and within departments in a corporation. In this example, the actors are departments in the corporation and the relation is the number of memos sent between or within departments. The values on the diagonal of the sociomatrix for this relation count the number of memos sent within each department. When a relation is reflexive ($i \rightarrow i$ for all i) and self-ties are considered substantively meaningful, then diagonal entries in the sociomatrix should be included in calculation of structural equivalence.

In the special case of a single reflexive nondirectional relation, or a single reflexive directional relation on which $x_{ij} = x_{ji}$ for all i, j, Guttman (1977) has defined a property called *graph equivalence*. Graph equivalence is closely related to structural equivalence, though since its definition is confined to a single relation with special properties, it is less general than structural equivalence. Actors i and j are *graph equivalent* if $x_{ik} = x_{jk}$ for all actors, $k = 1, 2, \ldots g$. An interesting property of graph equivalence (that is not true of structural equivalence) is that since the relation is reflexive ($i \leftrightarrow i$ and $j \leftrightarrow j$), if i and j are graph equivalent then both the $i \rightarrow j$ and the $j \rightarrow i$ ties must be present. Since i "chooses" i, j must also "choose" i in order for i and j to be graph equivalent. This has interesting implications for interpretation of equivalences. Specifically, collections of actors who are graph equivalent form complete subgraphs, and thus these subsets are in some ways similar to cohesive subgroups. Graph equivalence is a more restrictive equivalence definition than structural equivalence since actors who are graph equivalent are also structurally equivalent, but actors may be structurally equivalent without being graph equivalent.

Up to this point, we have described structural equivalence as an ideal mathematical property of pairs or subsets of actors in a social network. However, a positional analysis of a social network is more involved than simply identifying subsets of equivalent actors. Before moving on to more technical details, we will give an overview of positional analysis of a social network, and outline the specific steps that are involved.

9.3 Positional Analysis

One of the major objectives of a positional analysis is to simplify the information in a network data set. This simplification consists of a representation of the network in terms of the positions identified by an equivalence definition and a statement of how these positions are related to each other. In this section we do two things. First, we describe an ideal positional analysis using structural equivalence to illustrate the steps involved. Second, we present a list of the steps that are required for a complete positional analysis.

9.3.1 Simplification of Multirelational Networks

Consider the network represented by the sociomatrix and digraph in Figures 9.3a and b. In this form it is difficult, if not impossible, to see any regularities or patterns that might exist in this network. However, if we were to permute both the rows and the columns of the sociomatrix, in the same way, and present them in the order shown in Figure 9.3c, then we would see considerable regularity in the ties among subsets of actors. We can also partition the actors into subsets, $\mathcal{B}_k$. Specifically, we see that the rows and columns may be divided into three subsets: $\mathcal{B}_1 = \{6,3,8\}$, $\mathcal{B}_2 = \{2,5,7\}$, and $\mathcal{B}_3 = \{4,1,9\}$. Within each subset actors are structurally equivalent. These three subsets of equivalent actors are the equivalence classes, or positions in the network. Recall that $\phi(i) = \mathcal{B}_k$ denotes the assignment of actor i to position $\mathcal{B}_k$. For example, in Figure 9.3 $\phi(6) = \mathcal{B}_1$ since actor 6 is in position $\mathcal{B}_1$. These equivalence classes define a partition of the actors; each actor belongs to one, and only one, of these classes.

If all actors within each subset are structurally equivalent, then when the rows and columns of the original sociomatrix are permuted so that actors who are assigned to the same equivalence class occupy rows and columns that are adjacent, the submatrices corresponding to the ties between and within positions are filled with either all 0's or all 1's.

Once we have permuted the rows (and simultaneously the columns) of the sociomatrix so that actors in the same position are adjacent in the sociomatrix, we can further simplify the sociomatrix by collapsing the rows and columns that contain equivalent actors and present the matrix in a reduced form called an *image matrix*. In the image matrix rows and columns refer to positions, rather than individual actors. Since B is the number of positions in the network, the image matrix is of size $B \times B$. A "1" in row k, column l, of this matrix indicates that position $\mathcal{B}_k$ has a tie to position $\mathcal{B}_l$. When the model is perfect (as in Figure 9.3) so that all submatrices are either filled with 1's or filled with 0's, then there is no ambiguity about whether a tie exists between positions. Figure 9.3c shows the image matrix for this example.

The image matrix describes the ties between positions, and can be presented in a *reduced* graph. In the reduced graph, nodes represent positions and lines or arcs represent ties between positions. The reduced graph therefore has fewer nodes and fewer lines than the original graph. We use the following rule to construct the reduced graph. If there is a tie from actor i to actor j in the original graph, then there will be a tie between their respective positions in the reduced graph. More specifically, if actor i is assigned to position $\mathcal{B}_k$ and actor j is assigned to position $\mathcal{B}_l$, then $i \rightarrow j$ implies $\mathcal{B}_k \rightarrow \mathcal{B}_l$; $i \rightarrow j$ implies $\phi(i) \rightarrow \phi(j)$. This is also the definition of a *graph homomorphism*, which is important in the discussions of blockmodels and relational algebras (in Chapters 10 and 11). This rule for constructing a reduced graph includes both a rule for assigning actors to positions and a rule for assigning ties between positions based on the presence or absence of ties between actors.

In Figure 9.3 there are the following ties between positions: $\mathscr{B}_1 \leftrightarrow \mathscr{B}_1$, $\mathscr{B}_2 \leftrightarrow \mathscr{B}_2$, $\mathscr{B}_3 \leftrightarrow \mathscr{B}_3$ (reflexive ties), and $\mathscr{B}_1 \rightarrow \mathscr{B}_3$. These ties are present between positions because all actors in one position have ties to all actors in another position. For example, all actors in $\mathscr{B}_1$ have ties to all actors in position $\mathscr{B}_3$. The reduced graph for this example is shown in Figure 9.3e.

The reduced graph, along with the assignment of actors to positions, contains all of the structural information in the original graph, since all actors within a position are perfectly structurally equivalent. However, the reduced graph is clearly much simpler. An image matrix (for a single relation) or a collection of image matrices (one for each relation in a multirelational network) along with a description of which actors are assigned to which positions is called a *blockmodel*.

If the actors within the positions are not perfectly structurally equivalent, then submatrices contain both 0's and 1's, and not all actors in the position have ties to all actors in the other positions. In that case, the description of how positions are related to each other is not straightforward. We discuss this situation briefly at the end of this chapter and in detail in Chapter 10.

This example illustrates some of the results of positional analysis methods: a partition of the actors into discrete subsets (called positions) and a simplified description of the original social network data presenting the ties between positions rather than among individual actors. In practice a complete positional analysis requires four steps, which we will now describe.

9.3.2 Tasks in a Positional Analysis

Specifying the equivalence definition by which actors will be assigned to the same equivalence class is only the first step in a positional analysis. As we saw in the previous examples, there are several steps, resulting in a simplified representation of the original network data. In addition, we also need an assessment of how good the representation is. These steps are:

  (i) A formal definition of equivalence
 (ii) A measure of the degree to which subsets of actors approach that definition in a given set of network data
(iii) A representation of the equivalences
 (iv) An assessment of the adequacy of the representation

a. Sociomatrix

	1	2	3	4	5	6	7	8	9
1	-	0	0	1	0	0	0	0	1
2	0	-	0	0	1	0	1	0	0
3	0	1	-	0	1	1	1	1	0
4	1	0	0	-	0	0	0	0	1
5	0	1	0	0	-	0	1	0	0
6	0	1	1	0	1	-	1	1	0
7	0	1	0	0	1	0	-	0	0
8	0	1	1	0	1	1	1	-	0
9	1	0	0	1	0	0	0	0	-

b. Graph

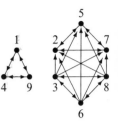

c. Permuted and partitioned sociomatrix

	6	3	8	4	1	9	2	5	7
6	-	1	1	0	0	0	1	1	1
3	1	-	1	0	0	0	1	1	1
8	1	1	-	0	0	0	1	1	1
4	0	0	0	-	1	1	0	0	0
1	0	0	0	1	-	1	0	0	0
9	0	0	0	1	1	-	0	0	0
2	0	0	0	0	0	0	-	1	1
5	0	0	0	0	0	0	1	-	1
7	0	0	0	0	0	0	1	1	-

d. Image matrix

	$\mathscr{B}_1$	$\mathscr{B}_2$	$\mathscr{B}_3$
$\mathscr{B}_1$	1	0	1
$\mathscr{B}_2$	0	1	0
$\mathscr{B}_3$	0	0	1

e. Reduced graph

Fig. 9.3. Example simplifying a network using structural equivalence

Equivalence Definition. In the first step, the *equivalence definition* specifies the formal mathematical conditions under which we will consider actors in a network to be equivalent. Structural equivalence is one such equivalence definition, but there are many others (which we discuss in

Chapter 12). In all cases the equivalence definition is stated in terms of properties of ties among actors in a network.

In actual network data, it is unlikely that any actors will be exactly equivalent. Therefore the second step requires a *measure* of the extent to which actors are equivalent, for a given definition. Doreian (1988a) makes the useful distinction between the equivalence definition and the procedure for detecting the property of equivalence (a "detector"). Pattison (1988) makes a similar distinction between the model and the algorithm for fitting the model to data. We will refer to the detector as a *measure of equivalence*. A good measure of equivalence should be based on the mathematical properties that define the relevant equivalence.

Measure of Equivalence. The second step is a *measure* of equivalence. This measure is a quantity that allows us to decide, for any given equivalence definition, whether or not (and perhaps to what extent) subsets of actors in a network are equivalent according to the given definition. An important consideration here is that the measure of equivalence in fact measures what it is supposed to measure.

Representation. The third step in a positional analysis is *representation* of the assignments of actors to equivalence classes, and a statement of the relationships between and within the classes (Pattison 1988). In the model actors are assigned to classes so that, ideally, actors within each class are equivalent to each other on the specified equivalence definition. The most common kind of representation is a *discrete* model that provides a partition of the actors in the network into a collection of equivalence classes. It is also sometimes useful to present equivalences among actors in a continuous (spatial) model.

Another important aspect of the representation is a statement of how the positions relate to each other. The reduced graph, image matrix, and blockmodel are examples of representations. A complete representation thus consists of a partition of the actors into equivalence classes and a statement of the presence or absence of ties between and within positions.

Assessment of Adequacy. The fourth step in a positional analysis is *assessment of the adequacy* of the representation. Since assessment of adequacy (sometimes called *goodness-of-fit*) usually requires probability models, we defer the discussion of this topic until later in the book. Even without this assessment, we will see that we can learn much about the structure of a set of network data and positions within the network using descriptive methods in an exploratory way.

We have already discussed the definition of structural equivalence. We now examine the measurement and representation of structural equivalence in detail.

9.4 Measuring Structural Equivalence

Structural equivalence is a mathematical property which is seldom actually realized in a set of social network data. For various reasons, including measurement error, variability in respondents' answers, restrictions on answer formats, changing relational systems, or the use of static models for representing dynamic systems, it is unlikely that two actors will be exactly structurally equivalent in a set of network data. Positional analysis methods based on structural equivalence, therefore, seek to locate and identify subsets of actors who are *approximately* structurally equivalent. Measurement of equivalence is the second task in a positional analysis. We will use the same formal definition of equivalence, specifically, structural equivalence, but will also have a measure of the degree to which subsets of actors approach this definition.

We first assume that we have a single dichotomous relation, and describe alternative approaches for measuring the degree of structural equivalence among actors based on this single relation. We then discuss various generalizations, for example, to multiple relations and to valued relations.

If we assume that self-ties are undefined, then diagonal elements in the sociomatrix, x_{ii}, will be treated as undefined and will not be included in the calculations. On the other hand, if the relation is reflexive, or if meaningful self-ties are present, the researcher may wish to include diagonal elements.

Since structural equivalence is defined as the presence of identical ties *to and from* subsets of actors, for a directional relation we examine both the rows and columns of the sociomatrix in order to determine whether subsets of actors are structurally equivalent. For directional relations, structurally equivalent actors have identical entries in their corresponding rows and columns of the sociomatrix. To the extent that two actors are not perfectly structurally equivalent, the entries in their respective rows and columns in the sociomatrix will be different. Thus, we can think about a continuum along which structural equivalence between pairs (and subsets) of actors can be measured. For example, actors i and j may have a large number (or proportion) of identical ties but still have a few ties that they do not share. In contrast, actors k and l may have very few identical ties, and thus a large number of unique others to whom they are tied. So, i and j would be more nearly structurally equivalent than would k and l.

The first measure we discuss is based on the Euclidean distance calculated between the values of the ties to and from pairs of actors.

9.4.1 Euclidean Distance as a Measure of Structural Equivalence

The use of Euclidean distance as a measure of structural equivalence was developed by Burt (Burt 1976, 1978a, 1980, 1987; Burt and Bittner 1981) and has been applied to a wide range of substantive and theoretical problems.

Let x_{ik} be the value of the tie from actor i to actor k on a single relation. We define a distance measure of structural equivalence for actors i and j as the Euclidean distance between the ties to and from these actors. For actors i and j, this is the distance between rows i and j and columns i and j of the sociomatrix:

$$d_{ij} = \sqrt{\sum_{k=1}^{g} [(x_{ik} - x_{jk})^2 + (x_{ki} - x_{kj})^2]} \qquad (9.1)$$

for $i \neq k$, $j \neq k$.

If actors i and j are structurally equivalent, then the entries in their respective rows and columns of the sociomatrix will be identical, and thus the Euclidean distance between them will be equal to 0. To the extent that two actors are not structurally equivalent, the Euclidean distance between them will be large. Euclidean distance has the properties of a distance metric: the distance from an object to itself is 0 ($d_{ii} = 0$), it is symmetric ($d_{ij} = d_{ji}$), and all distances are greater than or equal to 0 ($d_{ij} \geq 0$). For a single directional dichotomous relation on which diagonal entries are undefined, the maximum possible value of d_{ij} is $\sqrt{2(g-2)}$.

Euclidean distances are computed between all pairs of actors in a network. These pairwise distance measures are then the entries in a $g \times g$ matrix, which we denote by $\mathbf{D} = \{d_{ij}\}$. Each entry in $\mathbf{D}$ measures the structural equivalence of the row actor and the column actor.

Multiple Relations. Now, suppose that we have more than one relation. We can generalize equation (9.1) to measure structural equivalence across the collection of several relations. As usual, there are R relations, and x_{ikr} is the value of the tie from actor i to actor k on relation

$\mathcal{X}_r$. We define the distance measure of structural equivalence for actors i and j as the Euclidean distance between the ties to and from actors i and j across the collection of R relations:

$$d_{ij} = \sqrt{\sum_{r=1}^{R} \sum_{k=1}^{g} [(x_{ikr} - x_{jkr})^2 + (x_{kir} - x_{kjr})^2]} \tag{9.2}$$

for $i \neq k$, $j \neq k$. The quantity in equation (9.2) will be 0 if two actors are structurally equivalent, and will be larger if actors are not structurally equivalent. For R dichotomous directional relations on which diagonal entries are undefined, the maximum possible value of d_{ij} is $\sqrt{2R(g-2)}$.

An Example. We now illustrate measurement of structural equivalence using Euclidean distance. The example we will use is the advice relation for Krackhardt's high-tech managers. Recall that this relation was measured by asking managers: "To whom do you go for help and advice on the job?" We used the program *UCINET IV* (Borgatti, Everett, and Freeman 1991) to calculate the Euclidean distances.

Calculations include values in both rows and columns of the sociomatrix, since the relation is directional, and exclude diagonal entries. These distances are presented in Figure 9.4, as the lower left triangle of the matrix **D**. Each entry in this matrix is a measure of the extent to which the row actor and the column actor are structurally equivalent on the advice relation. Notice that no pairs of actors are structurally equivalent, since none of the off-diagonal distances is equal to 0.

9.4.2 Correlation as a Measure of Structural Equivalence

A second widely used measure of structural equivalence is the correlation coefficient. Using correlation to measure structural equivalence is quite similar to using Euclidean distance. The correlation between actor i and actor j is the usual "Pearson product-moment" correlation coefficient, computed on both the rows and columns of the sociomatrix (if the relation is directional). We denote the mean of the values in row i of the sociomatrix as $\bar{x}_{i\bullet}$, and similarly denote the mean of the values in column i as $\bar{x}_{\bullet i}$, where the calculation excludes diagonal elements. We will begin by defining correlation as a measure of structural equivalence for a single relation. We then have:

$$r_{ij} = \frac{\sum (x_{ki} - \bar{x}_{\bullet i})(x_{kj} - \bar{x}_{\bullet j}) + \sum (x_{ik} - \bar{x}_{i\bullet})(x_{jk} - \bar{x}_{j\bullet})}{\sqrt{\sum (x_{ki} - \bar{x}_{\bullet i})^2 + \sum (x_{ik} - \bar{x}_{i\bullet})^2} \sqrt{\sum (x_{kj} - \bar{x}_{\bullet j})^2 + \sum (x_{jk} - \bar{x}_{j\bullet})^2}} \tag{9.3}$$

where all the sums are over k, and $i \neq k$, $j \neq k$. These correlations are arranged in a $g \times g$ correlation matrix, which we denote by $\mathbf{C}_1$. The (i, j)th element of $\mathbf{C}_1$ is the Pearson product-moment correlation coefficient, r_{ij}, between the ith row and column and the jth row and column of the sociomatrix. Diagonal elements of the sociomatrix are excluded from calculation of the correlation. The elements of $\mathbf{C}_1$ measure the extent of structural equivalence of pairs of actors. If two actors are structurally equivalent, then the correlation between their respective rows and columns of the sociomatrix will be equal to $+1$.

Multiple Relations. Calculating correlations on multirelational networks is straightforward. We generalize equation (9.3) to include multiple relations, $r = 1, 2, \ldots, R$. However, the equation is somewhat simpler if the collection of matrices on which we calculate correlations includes both the sociomatrices, $\mathbf{X}_r$, and their transposes, $\mathbf{X}_r'$. Since the columns of the original matrix become the rows in its transpose, including the transposes in the calculation allows us to compare ties both to and from the actors. Since there are R relations, there are R sociomatrices and R transposed matrices, and thus $2R$ matrices when we consider both sociomatrices and their transposes.

Denoting the value of the tie from actor i to actor k on relation $\mathscr{X}_r$ as x_{ikr}, and assuming that we include the transposes of relations in our collection, we generalize equation (9.3) to:

$$r_{ij} = \frac{\sum_{r=1}^{2R} \sum_{k=1}^{g} (x_{ikr} - \bar{x}_{i\bullet})(x_{jkr} - \bar{x}_{j\bullet})}{\sqrt{\sum_{r=1}^{2R} \sum_{k=1}^{g} (x_{ikr} - \bar{x}_{i\bullet})^2} \sqrt{\sum_{r=1}^{2R} \sum_{k=1}^{g} (x_{jkr} - \bar{x}_{j\bullet})^2}} \qquad (9.4)$$

for $i \neq k$, $j \neq k$. As with correlations calculated on a single relation, these correlations are arranged in a $g \times g$ correlation matrix, denoted by $\mathbf{C}_1$.

An Example. We now illustrate the use of correlation as a measure of structural equivalence using the advice relation for Krackhardt's high-tech managers. Figure 9.5 presents the lower left triangle of the correlation matrix $\mathbf{C}_1$, calculated on the ties sent and received on this relation. Diagonal entries were excluded from calculations. These correlations were computed using *UCINET IV* (Borgatti, Everett, and Freeman 1991), but a standard statistical package, such as *SYSTAT* (Wilkinson 1987), will give identical results (so long as diagonal entries are treated as missing data and both the sociomatrix and its transpose are included).

In Figure 9.5, since there are no off-diagonal entries of $+1.0$, there are no actors who are structurally equivalent on the advice relation. This is the same conclusion that we reached using Euclidean distance as a measure of structural equivalence.

9.4.3 Some Considerations in Measuring Structural Equivalence

We now turn to some considerations in the measurement of structural equivalence. Our comments focus on selecting a good measure for a given relation and a comparison of the two measures (Euclidean distance, and Pearson product-moment correlation coefficient).

Other Measures of Structural Equivalence. Any measure of structural equivalence quantifies the extent to which pairs of actors meet the definition of structural equivalence. Euclidean distance and correlation are only two of a number of possible measures that could be used to measure structural equivalence. They are the most commonly used measures, perhaps because they are both part of more comprehensive positional analysis procedures (Euclidean distance in *STRUCTURE* Burt (1989), and correlation in *CONCOR*), and both are widely available in network analysis computer programs as well as in standard statistical analysis packages. However, since measuring structural equivalence fundamentally involves comparing "profiles" of two actors' rows and columns in a sociomatrix, the researcher could consider alternative similarity (or dissimilarity) measures. Two natural candidates for alternative measures are a simple match coefficient that counts the number or proportion of ties that are identical between two actors (for a dichotomous relation), or a measure of ordinal association (for a relation measured as an ordered scale).

Multiple Relations and Multiple Sociomatrices. Calculating a measure of structural equivalence usually involves calculations across two or more sociomatrices. Since structural equivalence is defined as identity of ties both to and from actors, one must calculate measures using both the sociomatrix and its transpose (unless the relation is nondirectional). Also, if the network data set is multirelational, then there are R sociomatrices, to start, and an additional R transposed matrices (for a total of $2R$ matrices). When using standard statistical packages (such as *SYSTAT*, *SPSS*, or *SAS*) rather than network analysis programs (such as *STRUCTURE*, or *UCINET*) to calculate a measure of structural equivalence, it is useful to construct a data array that includes all sociomatrices (and transposes) that are to be analyzed. The idea is to "stack" the sociomatrices by appending one sociomatrix to the bottom of another, to form a single rectangular data array. If there are R relations, each of size $g \times g$, then the "stacked" array has g columns and $2R \times g$ rows. The "stacked" data array can be treated as a "cases by variables" array, with $2R \times g$ rows as "cases," and g columns as "variables." Correlations or distances are then calculated between variables (columns). The main "trick" is to code diagonal entries in each sociomatrix and its transpose as missing data, if self-ties are undefined.

Comparison of Some Measures of Structural Equivalence. As we have noted, actors in a social network are almost never structurally equivalent. This has led to the common practice of using a measure of the degree to which pairs or subsets of actors approach structural equivalence. Measures such as correlation or Euclidean distance, which are commonly used to measure structural equivalence, do not always give the same results. The correlation between two actors may be equal to $+1$, indicating perfect structural equivalence by that measure, while the Euclidean distance between the same two actors on the same relation(s) may be non-zero, indicating that the actors are not perfectly structurally equivalent, if means and variances differ. Therefore, as "detectors" of structural equivalence, correlation and Euclidean distance differ in how two actors in a social network may fail to have identical ties, and therefore not be structurally equivalent. It is important to understand the formal properties of these measures in order to choose the appropriate measure for a given application.

The problem of measuring degree of structural equivalence is the problem of measuring the similarity (or dissimilarity) of the ties to and from pairs of actors on a given set of network data. Thus, it is a specific instance of a more general question of measurement of the similarity (or dissimilarity) of two data "profiles." In analyzing network data, the "profiles" are the rows and columns in the sociomatrices corresponding to two actors' ties. Numerous authors, both inside and outside the network community, have examined the relationships among alternative measures of similarity and dissimilarity. We will restrict our attention here to correlation and Euclidean distance, and the formal relationship between them.

	1	2	3	4	5	6	7	8	9	10	11
1	0.000										
2	3.162	0.000									
3	4.359	4.796	0.000								
4	3.873	4.359	2.828	0.000							
5	4.123	4.796	2.828	3.464	0.000						
6	4.000	3.162	4.796	4.359	5.000	0.000					
7	4.243	3.464	3.873	3.873	4.359	3.742	0.000				
8	3.317	3.317	3.464	3.162	4.000	3.317	3.873	0.000			
9	4.000	4.690	2.646	3.000	2.646	4.472	3.742	3.606	0.000		
10	3.742	4.899	4.123	3.873	3.606	4.690	4.690	4.123	4.243	0.000	
11	3.317	3.000	4.243	4.243	4.243	3.000	3.873	3.162	4.123	3.873	0.000
12	4.000	3.464	4.359	4.359	4.796	2.000	4.000	3.317	4.000	4.899	3.000
13	3.873	4.583	3.742	4.243	3.464	4.123	4.359	4.000	3.606	4.123	3.464
14	3.317	3.000	4.000	4.472	4.000	3.000	3.317	3.162	3.606	4.583	2.828
15	4.583	5.385	2.449	3.742	2.449	5.385	4.796	4.243	3.317	3.606	4.690
16	3.000	3.873	4.243	3.742	4.000	3.606	4.583	2.828	3.873	3.873	2.828
17	3.317	3.317	4.243	4.000	4.472	2.646	4.123	2.828	4.123	4.359	2.449
18	4.123	4.123	4.243	4.472	4.000	4.796	5.000	4.000	4.583	3.317	4.243
19	4.472	4.899	3.317	4.123	3.000	4.690	4.472	3.873	3.742	3.464	3.606
20	3.606	4.359	2.828	2.828	3.162	4.123	3.606	3.464	3.000	3.606	3.742
21	4.359	3.873	4.243	4.000	4.899	3.873	3.317	3.742	4.359	4.583	4.243

(continued)

	12	13	14	15	16	17	18	19	20	21
12	0.000									
13	4.123	0.000								
14	2.646	3.464	0.000							
15	5.000	4.000	4.690	0.000						
16	3.606	2.828	3.464	4.472	0.000					
17	2.236	3.742	2.828	4.690	3.162	0.000				
18	4.796	4.690	4.243	3.742	4.472	4.243	0.000			
19	4.472	2.646	3.873	3.317	3.317	4.123	4.123	0.000		
20	4.123	3.742	3.742	3.464	3.742	3.742	4.243	3.606	0.000	
21	4.123	4.899	4.000	4.690	4.472	4.000	4.472	4.796	4.243	0.000

Fig. 9.4. Euclidean distances computed on advice relation for Krackhardt's high-tech managers

	1	2	3	4	5	6	7	8	9	10	11
1	1.000										
2	0.478	1.000									
3	-0.000	-0.211	1.000								
4	0.206	-0.000	0.579	1.000							
5	0.105	-0.211	0.578	0.367	1.000						
6	0.174	0.567	-0.239	-0.000	-0.359	1.000					
7	0.053	0.368	0.211	0.206	0.000	0.328	1.000				
8	0.418	0.430	0.370	0.472	0.159	0.424	0.218	1.000			
9	0.152	-0.152	0.640	0.536	0.642	-0.147	0.275	0.305	1.000		
10	0.275	-0.275	0.112	0.218	0.324	-0.078	-0.185	0.124	0.080	1.000	
11	0.427	0.573	0.055	0.055	0.055	0.475	0.226	0.467	0.059	0.278	1.000
12	0.186	0.501	-0.000	-0.000	-0.215	0.736	0.204	0.463	0.083	-0.183	0.473
13	0.215	-0.091	0.328	0.088	0.415	-0.118	0.057	0.151	0.277	0.224	0.287
14	0.436	0.573	0.166	-0.040	0.166	0.475	0.453	0.477	0.284	-0.053	0.548
15	-0.096	-0.550	0.700	0.269	0.700	-0.495	-0.227	0.077	0.471	0.305	-0.099
16	0.544	0.257	0.078	0.290	0.174	0.191	-0.072	0.603	0.161	0.297	0.537
17	0.427	0.462	0.166	0.149	-0.055	0.595	0.113	0.587	0.059	0.053	0.661
18	0.205	0.093	0.102	-0.027	0.231	0.117	-0.387	0.310	0.021	0.444	0.343
19	-0.069	-0.259	0.436	0.119	0.538	-0.278	-0.040	0.204	0.248	0.426	0.254
20	0.316	-0.000	0.579	0.579	0.474	0.120	0.312	0.370	0.536	0.320	0.277
21	0.018	0.218	0.069	0.178	-0.277	0.425	0.436	0.320	0.053	-0.201	0.167

(continued)

	12	13	14	15	16	17	18	19	20	21
12	1.000									
13	-0.192	1.000								
14	0.601	0.251	1.000							
15	-0.243	0.323	-0.099	1.000						
16	0.154	0.494	0.303	0.041	1.000					
17	0.729	0.163	0.548	-0.099	0.420	1.000				
18	0.241	0.267	0.351	0.213	0.309	0.331	1.000			
19	-0.197	0.618	0.139	0.503	0.378	0.053	0.372	1.000		
20	0.129	0.328	0.277	0.382	0.290	0.277	0.102	0.327	1.000	
21	0.363	-0.108	0.284	-0.242	0.096	0.284	-0.261	-0.146	0.069	1.000

Fig. 9.5. Correlations calculated on the advice relation for Krackhardt's high-tech managers

The formal relationship between correlation and Euclidean distance is well known (Cronbach and Gleser 1953; Coxon 1982; Fox 1982; Rohlf and Sokal 1965; Sneath and Sokal 1973; Sokal and Sneath 1963). We will present this relationship in terms of the distance and correlation between two rows of a sociomatrix on a single relation. The relationship can be generalized to rows, columns, and layers of a multirelational sociomatrix. We will denote the means of the values in rows i and j of the sociomatrix as $\bar{x}_{i\bullet}$ and $\bar{x}_{j\bullet}$, and similarly denote the variances of rows i and j as $s_{i\bullet}^2$ and $s_{j\bullet}^2$. Calculations exclude diagonal elements and the elements x_{ij} and x_{ji}, because these values are also excluded in the calculation of distance and/or correlation between rows i and j. We can then express the relationship between the Euclidean distance, d_{ij} (equation (9.1)), and the correlation, r_{ij} (equation (9.3)), between rows i and j of a sociomatrix as:

$$d_{ij}^2 = (g - 2)[(\bar{x}_{i\bullet} - \bar{x}_{j\bullet})^2 + s_{i\bullet}^2 + s_{j\bullet}^2 - 2r_{ij}s_{i\bullet}s_{j\bullet}]. \qquad (9.5)$$

One can see from equation (9.5) that for a given correlation, r_{ij}, the Euclidean distance, d_{ij}, between two rows increases as the difference between the means of the rows increases and as the difference between the variances increases. Thus, Euclidean distance reflects a smaller amount of structural equivalence than does a correlation coefficient if the actors differ in the mean and variance of their ties. To illustrate, consider the single relation of acquaintanceship for Freeman's *EIES* network. Suppose two actors differed only in their use of the response rating scale, one consistently giving higher and the other consistently giving lower ratings, but otherwise had exactly the same acquaintances and friends. The two actors would then be measured as less equivalent by Euclidean distance than by correlation.

Some authors have described structural equivalence as the similarity in *pattern* of ties between two actors. If the researcher wants to measure similarity in pattern, then the correlation coefficient is the preferred measure. However, if one desires a measure of the identity of ties, then Euclidean distance may be preferable. The difference between Euclidean distance and correlation is especially acute when relations are valued, and when there are large differences among actors in the mean level (overall strength) of their ties. For dichotomous relations, large differences in actor degree would lead to different results using correlation or Euclidean distance. In sociometric data collected using rating scales, differences among people in their use of response categories (for example, variability across people in the tendency to over- or underestimate degrees of friendship, or to name few or many friends) would lead to different results. In records of interaction frequencies, differential rates of participation among actors would lead to different levels of structural equivalence when equivalence is measured using Euclidean distance. This problem has been debated in the literature (see Faust and Romney 1985a, 1986; Burt 1986).

One approach to this problem is to standardize relational data to remove differences in means and variances among actors before computing structural equivalence. If relations are standardized, so that all actors' rows and columns have equal mean and variance, then both correlation and Euclidean distance will give identical results; both are identical to correlations on the unstandardized data. Many network analysis computer programs (*UCINET IV* and *STRUCTURE* for example) have procedures for standardizing network data prior to analysis.

In summary, measures of structural equivalence are used to assess how close pairs of actors are to perfect structural equivalence. Further, these measures may be used to study structural equivalence for all of the kinds of relations we have discussed: single or multiple relations, dichotomous or valued relations, and directional or nondirectional relations.

9.5 Representation of Network Positions

The third step in a positional analysis includes representation of the positions and a statement of how the positions are related to each other. The major goals of a representation are to present the information in a network data set in simplified form and provide an interpretation for the results. Our discussion of representing network positions is divided into two parts. We first describe methods for partitioning actors into subsets so that actors within each subset are closer to being equivalent than are actors in different subsets. There are many informative ways to do this, including hierarchical clustering and *CONCOR*. We then discuss methods for representing how the subsets relate to each other, including density tables, image matrices, and blockmodels. Since blockmodels and their interpretation are discussed in detail in Chapter 10, these topics receive less attention in this chapter.

9.5.1 Partitioning Actors

In this section we continue to analyze the advice relation for Krackhardt's high-tech managers that we have been using throughout this chapter.

One reason to study the positional structure of this corporation is to see which subsets of managers give and receive advice from the same other managers. Also, representing the equivalences among actors based on the advice relation can help us understand the informal organization of the company, and actors' positions in the advice giving and seeking network.

If we look at a matrix of distances or correlations that measure structural equivalence (for example in Figures 9.5 and 9.4) it is virtually impossible to see any pattern in the values. Therefore it is necessary to use some method to represent the similarities (or dissimilarities) among the actors based on their degree of structural equivalence. In general, we seek a partition of the actors into subsets (positions) so that actors within each subset are more nearly equivalent, according to the equivalence definition, and actors in different subsets are less equivalent. Actors who are more nearly structurally equivalent will be placed in the same subset, and actors who are far from being structurally equivalent will be placed in different subsets.

Partitioning Actors Using *CONCOR.* Historically, one of the earliest approaches to partitioning actors into positions based on structural equivalence is the procedure commonly known as *CONCOR* (for *CON*vergence of iterated *COR*relations). This method was first used for analyzing social networks by H. White and others (Breiger, Boorman, Arabie, and Schwartz, among others) in the course of their research on the application of social networks to the algebraic study of roles (Breiger, Boorman, and Arabie 1975, White, Boorman, and Breiger 1976), and has been used extensively in network research in many fields (Anderson and Jay 1985; Breiger 1979; Breiger and Ennis 1979; Friedkin 1984; Knoke and Rogers 1979; Mitchell 1989; Mullins, Hargens, Hecht, and Kick 1977).

CONCOR is a procedure based on the *convergence of iterated correlations.* This refers to the observation that repeated calculation of correlations between rows (or columns) of a matrix (when this matrix contains correlations from the previous calculation) will eventually result in a correlation matrix consisting only of $+1$'s and -1's. Furthermore, these correlations of $+1$ and -1 occur in a pattern such that the items that are being correlated may be partitioned into two subsets where all correlations between items assigned to the same subset are equal to $+1$ and all correlations between items in different subsets will be equal to -1. This phenomenon was discovered both by the group working on social network analysis with H. White (Boorman and White 1976;

Breiger, Boorman, and Arabie 1975; Schwartz 1977; White, Boorman, and Breiger 1976) and by McQuitty and Clark, working on a completely different problem, in educational psychology (McQuitty 1968; McQuitty and Clark 1968; Clark and McQuitty 1970).

The *CONCOR* procedure starts with a sociomatrix (or a collection of sociomatrices) and first computes correlations among the rows and/or the columns of the matrix (or matrices). As we saw in the previous section, these correlations, which are arranged in a correlation matrix C_1, are one possible measure of structural equivalence. The distinctive part about the *CONCOR* procedure is that it then uses this correlation matrix, C_1, as input, and calculates correlations on the rows or columns of this matrix. In this second step, correlations are computed between all rows (or between all columns) of the first correlation matrix C_1. These "correlations of correlations" are then arranged in a second correlation matrix, which we label C_2. The entries in C_2 are correlations calculated on the first correlations. Now, C_2 is taken as input, and correlations are computed between all rows (or columns) of this matrix. These "correlations of correlations of correlations" are then the entries in a new correlation matrix, C_3. Now, suppose we continue this procedure, using the correlation matrix resulting from a given round as "input" to the correlation calculations on the next round. So finally we have "correlations of correlations of correlations of correlations of.... "

At first glance, it seems as though this process might go on forever, each round resulting in a new, and different, correlation matrix. However, it turns out that after several iterations of this procedure, the values of all correlations in the matrix are equal to either $+1$ or -1 (except in some quite unusual circumstances). Let us denote the final correlation matrix (after t iterations) as C_t. This matrix contains only $+1$'s and -1's. In addition, it is possible to permute the rows, and simultaneously, the columns of the matrix C_t, so that it can be partitioned and simplified (blocked) to have the following form:

$+1$	-1
-1	$+1$

The entities corresponding to the rows and columns of the correlation matrix may be partitioned into two subsets where the correlations (in the final correlation matrix C_t) between pairs of entities within each subset are equal to $+1$ and the correlations between pairs of entities belonging to different subsets are equal to -1.

Since the entities in this correlation matrix are the actors in the network, this partition gives a partition of the original set of actors. Each of these subsets contains actors who have similar ties to and from other actors in the network. These two subsets can be used to define positions within the network.

Certainly there may be more than two positions within a network; thus *CONCOR* may be repeated on the submatrices defined by an earlier partition to produce finer partitions. For example, one of the positions arising from the initial split into two positions may be split further by applying iterated correlations to the submatrix of the sociomatrix containing members of the subset of actors and the ties of those actors to and from the members of the whole network. Repeated application of iterated correlations to subsets of the data will produce a series of finer and finer partitions, each time splitting a prior subset into two smaller subsets. In this sense *CONCOR* may be thought of as a (divisive) hierarchical clustering method. Beginning with the entire set of actors in the network, the first application of iterated correlations divides the actors into two groups. Further applications to these subsets produce finer splits, and so on.

An important decision in an analysis using *CONCOR* is how fine the partition should be; in other words, when should one stop splitting positions? Theory and the interpretability of the solution are the primary considerations in deciding how many positions to produce. In practice, since correlations computed on small numbers of elements (here the few correlations in the matrix) are quite unstable, it is probably unwise to split positions that have three or fewer actors in them.

One way to display the results of a series of partitions from *CONCOR* is to construct a *tree-diagram* or a *dendrogram* indicating the degree of structural equivalence among the positions and identifying their members. Each level of the diagram indicates the division resulting from a split of the previous subset. A dendrogram thus represents a clustering of the actors based on the results of *CONCOR*. The labels for the actors are given along the bottom of the diagram. Interpretation of the dendrogram is straightforward. Those actors who are connected by branches low in the diagram are closer to being perfectly structurally equivalent, whereas subsets of actors who are joined only through paths high up the diagram are less structurally equivalent (or are not equivalent at all).

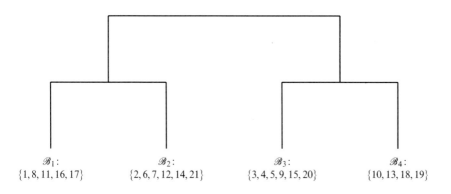

$\mathscr{B}_1$:
$\{1, 8, 11, 16, 17\}$ $\mathscr{B}_2$:
$\{2, 6, 7, 12, 14, 21\}$ $\mathscr{B}_3$:
$\{3, 4, 5, 9, 15, 20\}$ $\mathscr{B}_4$:
$\{10, 13, 18, 19\}$

Fig. 9.6. Dendrogram of positions from *CONCOR* of the advice relation for Krackhardt's high-tech managers

Now let us illustrate *CONCOR* using the advice relation for Krackhardt's high-tech managers.

An Example Using CONCOR. We will use the single relation of advice for Krackhardt's high-tech managers including both the ties given and received by the managers, but excluding diagonal entries in the sociomatrix. We used the program *UCINET 3* (MacEvoy and Freeman n.d.) to do this analysis.

Applying *CONCOR* leads first to a split into two subsets: the first subset contains actors 1, 2, 6, 7, 8, 11, 12, 14, 16, 17, and 21; the second subset contains actors 3, 4, 5, 9, 10, 13, 15, 18, 19, and 20. This split required 9 iterations before converging to a matrix containing only correlations of +1's and −1's. Each of the two subsets may be split further to give a partition of the actors into four positions:

- $\mathscr{B}_1$: 1, 8, 11, 16, 17
- $\mathscr{B}_2$: 2, 6, 7, 12, 14, 21
- $\mathscr{B}_3$: 3, 4, 5, 9, 15, 20
- $\mathscr{B}_4$: 10, 13, 18, 19

This set of positions is displayed as a dendrogram in Figure 9.6. The "branches" in this diagram indicate the partition of actors based on the series of splits from repeated applications of *CONCOR*.

Extensions. Generalizing $CONCOR$ to multirelational networks and to valued relations is straightforward once we realize that the primary matrix that $CONCOR$ analyzes is the correlation matrix, $\mathbf{C}_1$, containing the Pearson product-moment correlation coefficients as measures of similarity among pairs of actors. After the first step of computing $\mathbf{C}_1$ the procedure of iterating correlations is identical regardless of the types of relations that were included in the calculation of $\mathbf{C}_1$.

Some Comments. There are several problems with $CONCOR$ as a method for finding positions of approximately structurally equivalent actors. We comment on these issues in this section.

First, $CONCOR$'s procedure of always splitting a set into *exactly two* subsets imposes a particular form on the resulting positional structure in the network. At the end of each round of iterated correlations the result is a split of the actors into exactly two subsets. Repeated application of iterated correlations in turn splits the subset into exactly two smaller subsets. Thus, the form of the result is a series of bi-partitions, or a binary tree. This form is defined by the procedure, not by the structure of the network.

Second, in practice, the resulting partition from $CONCOR$ often has little resemblance to what are intuitively and formally understood to be social positions in the network (as discussed at the beginning of this chapter). Several authors have applied $CONCOR$ to hypothetical networks with known positional structure, and results consistently show that the partition from $CONCOR$ does not find subsets of actors who intuitively occupy social positions (Doreian 1988c; Faust 1988; Sim and Schwartz 1979).

The third problem is that the formal properties of the procedure are not well understood. Schwartz (1977) discusses in detail the mathematical properties of iterated covariances and iterated correlations on a sociomatrix, and the relationship between both of these procedures and principal component analysis. He shows that the first split of actors produced by $CONCOR$ is virtually identical to the pattern of signs ("+" and "−") on the first principal component from a principal component analysis of an appropriately scaled correlation matrix. Given the close resemblance of $CONCOR$ to principal component analysis, the fact that principal component analysis results in more detailed information (a number of components rather than simply a split of actors), and the fact that the exact mathematical properties of $CONCOR$ remain obscure (it is not clear what, if anything, it is optimizing), it is advisable to use *CONCOR* with a great deal of caution.

The next approach we describe uses clearly specifiable criteria to partition actors into positions. We turn now to a discussion and illustration of hierarchical clustering to illustrate partitioning actors.

Partitioning Actors Using Hierarchical Clustering. Hierarchical clustering is a data analysis technique that is ideally suited for partitioning actors into positions. Hierarchical clustering groups entities into subsets, so that entities within a subset are relatively similar to each other. There are many texts and articles on hierarchical clustering as a general data analysis approach (for example, Aldenderfer and Blashfield 1984; Johnson 1967; Lance and Williams 1967).

Consider the task of constructing subsets of actors so that within each subset actors are relatively more structurally equivalent. Specifically, if d_{ij} is a distance measure of structural equivalence of actors i and j, then the researcher must decide on some threshold value, α, such that pairs (or subsets) of actors i and j are considered nearly structurally equivalent if $d_{ij} \leq \alpha$. If the measure of structural equivalence is the correlation coefficient, r_{ij}, then the subsets should contain actors among whom the correlations are high; $r_{ij} \geq \alpha$. The task is to find collections of actors such that each collection contains actors who are approximately structurally equivalent at level α.

There are numerous hierarchical clustering criteria (for example, complete link, single link, average link, and so on). Complete link (also called diameter method) hierarchical clustering produces collections of entities in which *all pairs* are no less similar (no more dissimilar) than the criterion value. In practice, complete link clustering gives more homogeneous and stable clusters than alternative methods (such as single link clustering) and is less subject to problematic results (for example "chaining," where a large cluster is constructed by adding a single object at a time) (Lance and Williams 1967). The procedure is hierarchical because it uses successively less restrictive values of α to define clusters of entities. The clusters form a hierarchical series that can be displayed in a dendrogram.

Computer routines for hierarchical clustering are widely available, both in standard statistical analysis packages, and in network analysis packages. Both *STRUCTURE* and *UCINET* include hierarchical clustering programs. The input to a clustering program is (usually) a one-mode symmetric matrix in which the entries measure the similarity (or dissimilarity) of pairs of entities. A positional analysis using hierarchical clustering would use a matrix with measures of structural equivalence as input (for example, the correlation matrix C_1, or the matrix of Euclidean distances D).

Examples Using Hierarchical Clustering. Now, let us return to the example of the advice relation for Krackhardt's high-tech managers to illustrate hierarchical clustering. To compare Euclidean distance and correlation as measures of structural equivalence, we present hierarchical clusterings of both. We used the complete link hierarchical clustering program in *SYSTAT* (Wilkinson 1987) to do this analysis.

The results of the hierarchical clustering of Euclidean distances (from Figure 9.4) are presented in Figure 9.7. The least stringent criterion separates the actors into two subsets: position 1: 6, 12, 11, 17, 14, 8, 16, 1, 2, 7, and 21; and position 2: 19, 13, 5, 9, 3, 15, 4, 20, 18, and 10. A further division into four positions (dividing each of the previous subsets) gives:

- $\mathcal{B}_1$: 1, 2, 6, 8, 11, 12, 14, 16, 17
- $\mathcal{B}_2$: 7, 21
- $\mathcal{B}_3$: 3, 4, 5, 9, 13, 15, 19, 20
- $\mathcal{B}_4$: 10, 18

The results of the hierarchical clustering of correlations (from Figure 9.5) are presented in Figure 9.8. The least stringent criterion separates the actors into two subsets: position 1: 5, 9, 3, 15, 4, 20, 13, 19, 10, and 18; and position 2: 11, 17, 6, 12, 14, 2, 1, 16, 8, 21, and 7. A further division into four positions (dividing each of the previous subsets) gives:

- $\mathcal{B}_1$: 3, 4, 5, 9, 15, 20
- $\mathcal{B}_2$: 10, 13, 18, 19
- $\mathcal{B}_3$: 1, 2, 6, 8, 11, 12, 14, 16, 17
- $\mathcal{B}_4$: 7, 21

At the two-position level, the results of hierarchical clustering of Euclidean distances are *identical* to the results of hierarchical clustering of correlations and both are identical to the two-position split from *CONCOR*. Even at the four-position level the results are quite similar.

Notice that the result of a hierarchical clustering is a series of partitions of the set of entities that are being clustered (here the entities are the actors in the network). The dendrogram gives this series of partitions in the form of a tree diagram (see Figures 9.7 and 9.8). In defining positions

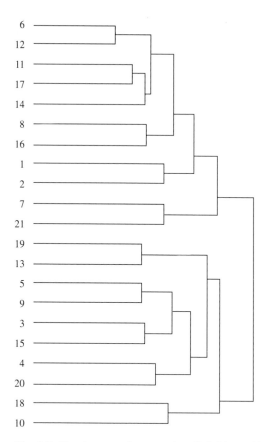

Fig. 9.7. Dendrogram for complete link hierarchical clustering of Euclidean distances on the advice relation for Krackhardt's high-tech managers

of actors, the "trick" is to choose the point along the series that gives a useful and interpretable partition of the actors into equivalence classes. Theory is the best guide. If the theory posits a specific number of classes of actors, then the researcher should use the partition with that number of classes.

Extensions. Although we have illustrated hierarchical clustering on a single, dichotomous, directional relation, hierarchical clustering can also be used to find subsets of approximately structurally equivalent actors in multirelational networks, and in networks where relations are

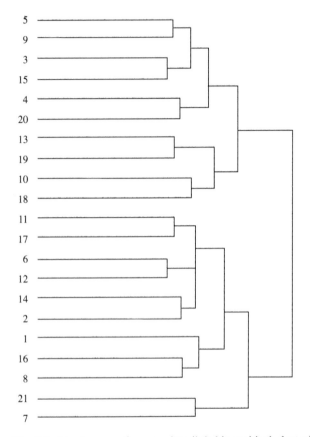

Fig. 9.8. Dendrogram for complete link hierarchical clustering of correlation coefficients on the advice relation for Krackhardt's high-tech managers

valued and/or nondirectional. The important thing to realize is that the input to a hierarchical clustering program is the matrix containing measures of structural equivalence between all pairs of actors; for example, the matrix of Euclidean distances, $\mathbf{D}$, or the matrix of correlations, $\mathbf{C}_1$. As we described in the previous section, these measures can be computed for multiple relations and/or valued relations. Therefore, once the measure of structural equivalence is computed, hierarchical clustering can be used to analyze it. When actors are assigned to positions in a multirelational network the actor assignments are consistent across all R relations.

Some Comments. Hierarchical clustering is a useful way to represent positions in social network data. Its main advantages are that it is a discrete method that gives a partition of the actors into subsets, the procedure is explicit, the interpretation is clear, and computer programs for hierarchical clustering are widely available. The disadvantages of hierarchical clustering are that the decision of how many subsets to use is often arbitrary, there are many different hierarchical clustering criteria (for example, complete link, single link, and so on), and some procedures do not give unique solutions.

A more important drawback of both *CONCOR* and hierarchical clustering is that a "grouping" (in hierarchical clustering) or a split (in *CONCOR*) that is made at one of the early stages in the analysis cannot be undone at a later stage. For example, if two actors are put into two different positions in the first split of *CONCOR*, they remain in separate positions through all further rounds. Similarly, if two actors are placed in the same cluster at an early stage of hierarchical clustering, then they remain together in all later, less restrictive, clusters.

9.5.2 Spatial Representations of Actor Equivalences

Hierarchical clustering and *CONCOR* are *discrete* models of social network positions. That is, they result in a partition of actors into mutually exclusive and exhaustive subsets. Alternatively, one can study equivalences among actors using a continuous (or spatial) model. Multidimensional scaling (MDS) is one such model. We briefly describe and illustrate multidimensional scaling in this section. Multidimensional scaling is a very general data analysis technique, and there are numerous texts and articles describing multidimensional scaling (for example, Kruskal and Wish 1978; Schiffman, Reynolds, and Young 1981; and Coxon 1982).

Although multidimensional scaling is a general data analysis technique, it has been used in social network analysis for the more specific task of representing equivalences among actors. Some of the earliest work on network positions used multidimensional scaling (Breiger, Boorman, and Arabie 1975; Burt 1976; Ennis 1982) and multidimensional scaling continues to be widely used in positional analyses of social networks (for example, Breiger and Pattison 1986; Burt 1976 1988b; Doreian 1987, 1988c; Faust 1988; Faust and Romney 1985a; Johnson 1986).

Multidimensional scaling is a data analytic technique that seeks to represent similarities (or dissimilarities) among a set of entities in low-dimensional space so that entities that are more similar to each other are closer in the space, and entities that are less similar to each other are farther apart in the space. The usual input to multidimensional scaling is a one-mode symmetric matrix consisting of pairwise measures of similarity, dissimilarity, or proximity. To study equivalences among actors in a network, the input to multidimensional scaling is some measure of pairwise equivalence among actors, such as the Pearson product-moment correlation matrix, C_1, or the matrix of Euclidean distances, D. The output of multidimensional scaling is a set of estimated distances among pairs of entities, which can be expressed as coordinates in one-, two-, or higher-dimensional space. These coordinates can then be used to display the points in space. When multidimensional scaling is used to study network positions using measures of structural equivalence as input, the results show which subsets of actors are more, and which are less, structurally equivalent.

To illustrate multidimensional scaling we use the Pearson product-moment correlation coefficients calculated on the advice relation for Krackhardt's high-tech managers. We used *SYSTAT* (Wilkinson 1987) to do the multidimensional scaling with the correlation matrix, C_1, as input. The final solution in two dimensions has stress equal to 0.12954 (Kruskal, stress form 1). This result is presented in Figure 9.9.

In this figure, actors who are closer to each other in the space are relatively more structurally equivalent, whereas actors who are farther apart are relatively less structurally equivalent. One way to study this figure is to note the attributes of managers in different regions of the figure. The president (7) and one vice president (21) are in the lower right corner; the other vice presidents (2, 14, and 18) are in the middle to upper right. All members from department 1 (managers 6, 8, 12, 17 and 21) are on the right half of the figure, whereas managers from department 2 (3, 5, 9, 13, 14, 15, 19, 20) are, with the exception of 14, on the left half of the figure. Managers from department 3 (10, 11, 18) tend to be toward the top of the figure.

Another way to study the figure is to compare the proximity of actors in the multidimensional scaling figure with the partition that resulted from *CONCOR* or from hierarchical clustering of either the Pearson product-moment correlations or of the Euclidean distances. Recall that these three methods gave the same partition at the level of two positions. Looking at the multidimensional scaling figure we can see that this split is essentially the right half versus the left half of the diagram. Further if we examine the four-position result from the hierarchical clustering of the Pearson product-moment correlations, we see a very close correspondence

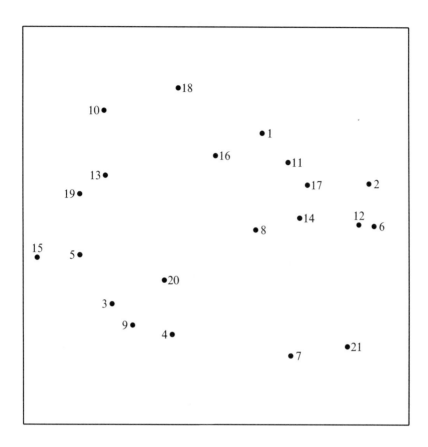

Fig. 9.9. Multidimensional scaling of correlation coefficients on the advice relation for Krackhardt's high-tech managers

with the multidimensional scaling: members of position $\mathcal{B}_1$ (3, 4, 5, 9, 15, 20) are all in the lower left corner, members of position $\mathcal{B}_2$ (10, 13, 18, 19) are in the upper left, members of position $\mathcal{B}_3$ (1, 2, 6, 8, 11, 12, 14, 16, 17) are in the upper right, and finally, members of $\mathcal{B}_4$ (7, 21) are in the lower right. Clearly these methods give quite similar results for this example.

Several authors have studied the relationship between positional analyses using multidimensional scaling, *CONCOR*, and hierarchical clustering (Breiger, Boorman, and Arabie 1975; Ennis 1982). Often researchers use multidimensional scaling in conjunction with some method for partitioning actors (such as hierarchical clustering) to study positions in networks (for example, Burt 1976; Breiger, Boorman, and Arabie 1975; Breiger 1981a; Ennis 1982). Comparisons of multidimensional scaling with *CONCOR* and hierarchical clustering have shown the results to be quite complementary.

9.5.3 Ties Between and Within Positions

The task of representing positions in a network has two parts: assigning actors to positions, and describing how the positions relate to each other. In this section we discuss the second part: describing ties between and within positions. There are three common ways to represent the ties between and within positions: a density table, an image matrix, and a reduced graph. We discuss and illustrate each of these in this section. In all cases we assume that we have a partition of the actors into equivalence classes or positions to start with. These positions could result from a clustering of some measure of equivalence (such as Euclidean distance, or correlation) or from *CONCOR*.

The starting point for all representations of positions is to permute the rows and columns of the original sociomatrix so that actors who are assigned to the same position are adjacent in the permuted sociomatrix. We use the positions defined by the partition to rearrange the rows and columns of the original sociomatrix so that the first rows and columns of the permuted sociomatrix contain the members of one position, and the next rows and columns of the sociomatrix contain the actors in the second position, and so on. Within each position, the order of actors is arbitrary. If some of the actors are nearly structurally equivalent, then the permuted sociomatrix should reveal regularities in the data that are not apparent in the unpermuted sociomatrix.

Figure 9.10 shows the advice sociomatrix for Krackhardt's high-tech managers permuted according to the positions from the hierarchical clustering of the correlations. We have also indicated the submatrices corresponding to the ties between and within positions. Notice that there is only one submatrix that is filled completely with 1's or completely with 0's (all ties among members of $\mathcal{B}_4$ are present). Also, there are several submatrices which are quite dense (for example the submatrices of ties from $\mathcal{B}_1$ to $\mathcal{B}_3$ and from $\mathcal{B}_1$ to $\mathcal{B}_4$) and there are several submatrices that are quite sparse (for example the submatrices of ties from $\mathcal{B}_3$ to $\mathcal{B}_1$, from $\mathcal{B}_3$ to $\mathcal{B}_2$, and from $\mathcal{B}_3$ to itself).

		$\mathcal{B}_1$	$\mathcal{B}_2$	$\mathcal{B}_3$	$\mathcal{B}_4$
		1 2 5 9 3 5 4 0	1 1 1 1 3 9 0 8	1 1 1 1 1 1 7 6 2 4 2 1 6 8	2 1 7
$\mathcal{B}_1$	5	- 0 0 0 0 1	1 1 1 1	1 1 1 0 1 1 1 1 1	1 1
	9	0 - 0 0 0 0	0 0 1 1	1 1 1 1 1 1 1 1 1	1 1
	3	0 1 - 0 1 1	0 0 1 1	1 1 1 1 1 1 1 0 1	1 1
	15	1 1 1 - 1 1	1 1 1 1	1 1 1 1 1 1 1 1 1	1 1
	4	0 0 0 0 - 1	0 0 1 1	1 1 1 1 0 1 1 1 1	1 0
	20	0 0 0 1 0 -	0 0 0 1	1 1 1 1 1 1 1 1 1	1 0
$\mathcal{B}_2$	13	1 1 0 0 0 0	- 0 0 1	0 0 0 0 1 1 1 0 0	0 0
	19	1 0 1 1 0 1	0 - 1 1	1 0 0 0 1 1 1 0 0	0 1
	10	1 0 1 1 1 1	1 1 - 1	1 1 0 0 0 1 1 1 1	0 0
	18	1 1 1 1 1 1	1 1 1 -	1 0 0 0 1 1 1 1 1	1 1
$\mathcal{B}_3$	11	0 0 0 0 0 0	0 0 0 0	- 0 0 0 0 1 1 0 0	0 1
	17	0 0 0 0 1 0	0 0 0 0	0 - 0 0 0 1 1 0 0	1 1
	6	0 0 0 0 0 0	0 0 0 0	0 0 - 0 0 0 0 0 0	1 0
	12	0 0 0 0 0 0	0 0 0 0	0 0 0 - 0 0 0 0 0	1 1
	14	0 0 0 0 0 0	0 0 0 1	0 0 0 0 - 1 0 0 0	1 1
	2	0 0 0 0 0 0	0 0 0 0	0 0 1 0 0 - 0 0 0	1 1
	1	0 0 0 0 1 0	0 0 0 1	0 0 0 0 0 1 - 1 1	1 0
	16	0 0 0 0 0 0	0 0 1 1	0 0 0 0 0 1 1 - 0	0 0
	8	0 0 0 0 1 0	0 0 1 1	1 0 1 0 0 1 0 0 -	1 1
$\mathcal{B}_4$	21	0 0 1 0 1 1	0 0 0 1	0 1 1 1 1 1 0 0 1	- 1
	7	0 0 0 0 0 0	0 0 0 1	1 1 1 1 1 1 0 0 0	1 -

Fig. 9.10. Advice sociomatrix for Krackhardt's high-tech managers permuted according to positions from hierarchical clustering of correlations

Density Tables. A useful way to summarize the ties between positions is in a *density table*, or *density matrix*. A density table is a matrix that has positions rather than individual actors as its rows and columns, and the values in the matrix are the proportion of ties that are present from the actors in the row position to the actors in column position. That is, the entries in the density table are Δ's. For the densities within positions, diagonal elements (x_{ii}) are excluded from calculations if self-ties are undefined.

We will continue to use the example of the positions identified by a hierarchical clustering of the correlations on the advice relation for Krackhardt's high-tech managers. Consider the ties from members of $\mathcal{B}_1$ to members of $\mathcal{B}_2$. Since there are six people in $\mathcal{B}_1$, and four people in $\mathcal{B}_2$ there are $6 \times 4 = 24$ possible ties that could be present from members

	$\mathcal{B}_1$	$\mathcal{B}_2$	$\mathcal{B}_3$	$\mathcal{B}_4$
$\mathcal{B}_1$	0.367	0.625	0.944	0.833
$\mathcal{B}_2$	0.708	0.750	0.528	0.375
$\mathcal{B}_3$	0.056	0.167	0.194	0.722
$\mathcal{B}_4$	0.250	0.250	0.667	1.000

Fig. 9.11. Density table for the advice relation from Krackhardt's high-tech managers, positions identified by hierarchical clustering of correlations

	$\mathcal{B}_1$	$\mathcal{B}_2$	$\mathcal{B}_3$	$\mathcal{B}_4$
$\mathcal{B}_1$	0	1	1	1
$\mathcal{B}_2$	1	1	1	0
$\mathcal{B}_3$	0	0	0	1
$\mathcal{B}_4$	0	0	1	1

Fig. 9.12. Image matrix for the advice relation from Krackhardt's high-tech managers, positions identified by hierarchical clustering of correlations

of $\mathcal{B}_1$ to $\mathcal{B}_2$. In Figure 9.10 we see that 15 of these 24 possible choices are present, so the density of this submatrix is equal to 0.625. This is the entry in row 1, column 2 of the density table. Figure 9.11 shows the density table for this example. These densities were calculated using *UCINET 3* (MacEvoy and Freeman n.d.).

Image Matrices. Often we would like to summarize the ties between positions in a more parsimonious way. An *image matrix* is a summary of the ties between and within positions, so that each tie is coded as either present or absent between each pair of positions. If submatrices are filled completely with 1's (oneblocks) or completely with 0's (zeroblocks) then the decision concerning whether a tie exists between positions is straightforward. However, since actual network data are seldom so perfect, we need a guideline for deciding whether a tie exists between positions.

There are several rules for constructing an image matrix from a density table, and we discuss these in detail in Chapter 10. For now, let us illustrate with one rule, the α density rule. This rule specifies a tie as present between two positions if the density of ties from actors in one position to actors in another position is greater than or equal to the density of the matrix as a whole. Letting Δ be the density of ties for the relation, we define a tie as present from position $\mathcal{B}_k$ to position $\mathcal{B}_l$ if the density of ties from members of position $\mathscr{B}_k$ to members of position $\mathscr{B}_l$ is greater than or equal to Δ.

Using this rule on the four-position model of the advice relation for Krackhardt's high-tech managers found using hierarchical clustering of correlations gives the image matrix in Figure 9.12. The density of the entire sociomatrix is 0.452. Consider the choices from members of position $\mathscr{B}_1$ to members of position $\mathscr{B}_3$. The proportion of ties from actors in position $\mathscr{B}_1$ to actors in $\mathscr{B}_3$ is 0.944. Since this is larger than the density for the whole sociomatrix, we code a tie as present from $\mathscr{B}_1$ to $\mathscr{B}_3$ in the image matrix. However, the proportion of ties that are present from members of position $\mathscr{B}_3$ to members of position $\mathscr{B}_1$ is equal to 0.056. Since this is less than the density of the sociomatrix, we code a tie as absent from position $\mathscr{B}_3$ to position $\mathscr{B}_1$. Notice the sharp gap between densities coded as present (the *smallest* of which is 0.528) and those coded as absent (the *largest* of which is 0.375).

Image matrices are fundamental to blockmodels, and since we devote all of Chapter 10 to blockmodels, we will defer further discussion of this topic until then.

Reduced Graphs. A third useful way to present the ties between and within positions is in a *reduced graph*. In a reduced graph positions are represented as nodes and ties between positions in the image matrix define the arcs between nodes. It is easy to construct the reduced graph from the image matrix. A "1" in the image matrix indicates that there is an arc from the node representing the row position to the node representing the column position in the reduced graph. In the reduced graph, there is an arc from the node representing position $\mathscr{B}_k$ to the node representing position $\mathscr{B}_l$ if there is a tie from $\mathscr{B}_k$ to $\mathscr{B}_l$ in the image matrix.

Figure 9.13 shows the reduced graph for the image matrix in Figure 9.12 of the advice relation for Krackhardt's high-tech managers. Each of the four positions is represented by a node in the graph, and the arcs represent ties present in the image matrix. Notice that $\mathscr{B}_3$ (containing the president and one of the vice presidents) and $\mathscr{B}_4$ (containing two vice presidents) primarily receive ties, whereas $\mathscr{B}_1$ and $\mathscr{B}_2$ primarily send ties.

9.6 Summary

In conclusion, let us consider some general issues in positional analysis, especially positional analysis based on structural equivalence. Although

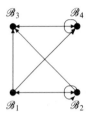

Fig. 9.13. Reduced graph for the advice relation from Krackhardt's high-tech managers, positions identified by hierarchical clustering of correlations

structural equivalence is a widely used and informative approach to the analysis of social networks, it does have some limitations, which we note here.

Recall that positional analysis of a social network, as summarized in Figure 9.1 and described in the early sections of this chapter, is motivated by the theoretical notion of social position as a collection of actors all of whom are similarly related to actors in other positions. However, structural equivalence requires that equivalent actors have *identical* ties to and from *identical* others. This leads to some potential problems, which we comment on here.

Comparison Between Populations. First, structural equivalence is a mathematical property that can only be met by actors who belong to the same population (since equivalent actors must have ties to and from identical others). This severely limits the generality of applications and conclusions that can arise from an analysis using structural equivalence. Theoretically, one would like to be able to find actors who are in the same general position – for example, all are "uncles"– even if they appear in separate data sets collected in Cincinnati and Santa Fe. However, since structural equivalence requires identical ties to and from identical other actors, comparisons across populations are precluded. The actors that belong to one population are almost always different from the actors that belong to another population.

Structural Equivalence and Cohesive Subgroups. Another important consideration in using structural equivalence is understanding exactly what structural property is specified by a particular equivalence definition. That is, what property do members of an equivalence class have in common? Using structural equivalence as the definition, members of an equivalence class are *adjacent to and from* identical other actors. Consider how this property relates to the cohesive subgroup ideas discussed in Chapter 7. All pairs of actors within a perfect structural equivalence class are connected by semipaths of length 2. In other words, actors who are structurally equivalent must be close to each other in a graph theoretic sense.

These problems with structural equivalence have motivated some researchers to develop other equivalence definitions that allow comparisons across populations and are not "confounded" with closeness or cohesion. We examine these alternative equivalences in Chapter 12.

10

Blockmodels

In the previous chapter we discussed how the formal property of structural equivalence could be used to define a partition of actors in a social network into equivalence classes, called *positions*. Each position contains actors who relate in similar ways to and from other actors in the network. In this chapter we examine how to model the relationships among these positions. Our emphasis is on how to interpret the results of a positional analysis when the results are presented as a blockmodel. The methods in this chapter are primarily descriptive and focus on properties of subsets of actors. Stochastic blockmodels are discussed in Chapter 16 along with statistical methods for assessing the goodness-of-fit of a given blockmodel. Related methods that focus on associations among relations rather than on subsets of actors are presented in Chapter 11.

We begin by defining and illustrating the concept of a *blockmodel*. We then show how blockmodels can be used to model network positional systems. The most interesting and useful features of blockmodels are their theoretical interpretations, their potential for validating structural theories, and their usefulness for comparing structural patterns across populations.

Blockmodels were introduced by White, Boorman, and Breiger (1976) for the descriptive algebraic analysis of social roles. Since then there have been many articles describing blockmodels from a methodological standpoint (Breiger, Boorman, and Arabie 1975; Arabie and Boorman 1982; Arabie, Boorman, and Levitt 1978; Light and Mullins 1979; Baker 1986), comparing blockmodels with alternative data analytic methods (Breiger, Boorman, and Arabie 1975; Schwartz 1977; Ennis 1982), and discussing alternative methods for constructing blockmodels (White, Boorman, and Breiger 1976; Breiger, Boorman, and Arabie 1975; Heil and White 1976; Panning 1982a, 1982b; Arabie, Hubert, and Schleutermann 1990). Burt has developed a complementary methodology for accomplishing many of the same goals as blockmodeling, using the concept of structural equivalence in conjunction with hierarchical clustering (Burt 1976). Recently several authors have generalized blockmodels by describing stochastic blockmodels (Holland, Laskey, and Leinhardt 1983; Wasserman and Anderson 1987; Wang and Wong 1987; Wong 1987). There have also been many applications of blockmodels and related methods to substantive problems throughout the social sciences, including studies of community elites (Breiger 1979; Breiger and Pattison 1978), scientific communities (Anderson and Jay 1985; Breiger 1976; Burt 1978/79a; Doreian and Fararo 1985; Mullins, Hargens, Hecht, and Kick 1977), the world economic system (Breiger 1981a; Nemeth and Smith 1985; Snyder and Kick 1979), interorganizational networks (Galaskiewicz and Krohn 1984; Knoke and Rogers 1979), and numerous studies of small group structure (Arabie 1984; Breiger, Boorman, and Arabie 1975; Breiger and Ennis 1979; White and Breiger 1975).

We first define a blockmodel. We then discuss different rules for constructing the image matrices that represent a blockmodel. Finally, we discuss several ways to interpret blockmodels.

10.1 Definition

We begin with a set of R dichotomous relations defined on a one-mode network of g actors. A *blockmodel* consists of two things:

(i) A partition of actors in the network into discrete subsets called positions

(ii) For each pair of positions a statement of the presence or absence of a tie within or between the positions on each of the relations

A blockmodel is thus a *model*, or a *hypothesis* about a multirelational network. It presents general features of the network, such as the ties between positions, rather than information about individual actors (White, Boorman, and Breiger 1976).

We can define a blockmodel more precisely in terms of a mapping of the actors in the network onto the positions in the blockmodel. A *blockmodel* is a partition of the actors in $\mathcal{N}$ into B positions, $\mathcal{B}_1, \mathcal{B}_2, \ldots, \mathcal{B}_B$, and onto mapping, ϕ, from $\mathcal{N}$ onto the collection of positions, where $\phi(i) = \mathcal{B}_k$ if actor i is in position $\mathcal{B}_k$. A blockmodel also specifies the ties between and within the B positions. We let b_{klr} indicate the presence or absence of a tie from position $\mathcal{B}_k$ to position $\mathcal{B}_l$ on relation $\mathcal{X}_r$, where $b_{klr} = 1$ if there is a tie from position $\mathcal{B}_k$ to position $\mathcal{B}_l$ on relation $\mathcal{X}_r$, and $b_{klr} = 0$ otherwise.

A blockmodel is also represented by an image matrix, $\mathbf{B} = \{b_{klr}\}$. The image matrix is a $B \times B \times R$ array, with entries b_{klr} indicating the presence or absence of a tie from position $\mathcal{B}_k$ to $\mathcal{B}_l$ on relation $\mathcal{X}_r$. Each layer of $\mathbf{B}$ describes the hypothesized ties between and within positions on the specific relation. The matrix $\mathbf{B}$ has also been referred to as a blockmodel, since it specifies the presence or absence of ties between positions. Whereas the original relational data are presented in the usual $g \times g \times R$ multirelational sociomatrix, a blockmodel is a simplification in that it consists of a smaller $B \times B \times R$ array, $\mathbf{B}$, that presents ties between positions.

A blockmodel thus has two components: the mapping, ϕ, that describes the assignment of actors to positions, and the matrix, $\mathbf{B}$, that specifies the presence or absence of ties between and within positions on each relation. Each actor is assigned to one and only one of the positions, and the assignment is the same across relations.

Each of the entries in the $B \times B \times R$ matrix $\mathbf{B}$ is called a *block*. Each block, b_{klr}, in the blockmodel corresponds to a submatrix of the original sociomatrix that contains the relevant interposition or intraposition ties. A block containing a 1 is called a *oneblock*, and indicates the presence of a tie from the row position to the column position. A oneblock may also be referred to as a *bond* (White, Boorman, and Breiger 1976). A block containing a 0 is called a *zeroblock*, and indicates the absence of a tie from the row position to the column position. More formally, if there is a hypothesized tie from position $\mathcal{B}_k$ to position $\mathcal{B}_l$ on relation $\mathcal{X}_r$ then $b_{klr} = 1$ in the blockmodel; b_{klr} is a oneblock. If there is no hypothesized tie from position $\mathcal{B}_k$ to position $\mathcal{B}_l$ then $b_{klr} = 0$ in the blockmodel; b_{klr} is a zeroblock.

A blockmodel is a simplified representation of multirelational network that captures some of the general features of a network's structure. Specifically, positions in a blockmodel contain actors who are approximately structurally equivalent. Actors in the same position have identical or similar ties to and from all actors in other positions. For example all actors in position $\mathcal{B}_k$ have similar ties to actors in positions $\mathcal{B}_l$, $\mathcal{B}_m$, and so on. Thus, the blockmodel is stated at the level of the positions, not individual actors.

The first step in a blockmodel analysis is the assignment of actors to positions. As we saw in Chapter 9, there are a number of ways to do this, including *CONCOR*, and hierarchical clustering of a measure of structural equivalence. However, assigning actors to positions is only one part of constructing a blockmodel. One must also determine whether or not ties exist between and within positions.

10.2 Building Blocks

Suppose that we start with a partition of actors into B positions, and have permuted the rows and the columns of the sociomatrix for each relation so that actors who are assigned to the same position occupy adjacent rows and columns in the permuted sociomatrix. In the permuted sociomatrix, all entries, x_{ij}, are the observed values of the ties between actors in the positions and all ties pertaining to ties between or within positions will be contained in submatrices of the sociomatrix. For example, see Figure 9.10 in Chapter 9 of the permuted advice sociomatrix for Krackhardt's high-tech managers. If all actors within each position are *perfectly* structurally equivalent, then all submatrices corresponding to ties within and between positions, for all relations, will be filled either completely with 0's or completely with 1's. However, in real network data, pairs (or collections) of actors are seldom structurally equivalent. In the permuted sociomatrix the submatrices corresponding to inter- and intraposition ties will usually contain both 1's and 0's. Therefore, determining whether a block in a blockmodel is a oneblock or a zeroblock is not straightforward. Constructing a blockmodel requires a rule which governs the assignment of a 0 or 1 to the tie between positions in the model.

There are several criteria which have proved useful for deciding whether a block should be coded as a zeroblock or a oneblock. These include:

- Perfect fit (fat fit)
- Zeroblock (lean fit)
- Oneblock
- α density criterion
- Maximum value — for valued data
- Mean value — for valued data

We first define each of these rules and then discuss when each one might be appropriate.

In a blockmodel, each of the $B \times B \times R$ elements of **B** contains the hypothesized value of the tie from the row position to the column position on the layer relation. As described above, b_{klr} denotes the value of the hypothesized tie from position $\mathscr{B}_k$ to position $\mathscr{B}_l$ on relation r.

If the block is a oneblock then $b_{klr} = 1$, and if the block is a zeroblock then $b_{klr} = 0$. The decision about whether a tie exists or not in each block of **B** depends on the observed values of the ties between actors in the positions. That is, b_{klr} depends on the values of x_{ijr} for $i \in \mathscr{B}_k$ and $j \in \mathscr{B}_l$. We will let g_k be the number of actors in position $\mathscr{B}_k$ and g_l be the number of actors in position $\mathscr{B}_l$. For distinct $\mathscr{B}_k$ and $\mathscr{B}_l$, there will be $g_k \times g_l$ ties from members of position $\mathscr{B}_k$ to members of position $\mathscr{B}_l$. For ties among members of the same position, there will be $g_k \times (g_k - 1)$ ties among actors in position $\mathscr{B}_k$. Note that in a blockmodel, ties from a position to itself are meaningful, and often quite important theoretically, in contrast to reflexive ties for actors and diagonal entries in a sociomatrix, which are often undefined.

The most common criteria for defining oneblocks and zeroblocks are based on the density of ties within a block. The density of ties in block b_{klr} will be denoted by Δ_{klr} and (for a dichotomous relation) is defined as the proportion of ties that are present. For $k \neq l$ this proportion is:

$$\Delta_{klr} = \frac{\sum_{i \in \mathscr{B}_k} \sum_{j \in \mathscr{B}_l} x_{ijr}}{g_k g_l}. \tag{10.1}$$

The density of ties within a position, for example block b_{kkr}, is equal to:

$$\Delta_{kkr} = \frac{\sum_{i \in \mathscr{B}_k} \sum_{j \in \mathscr{B}_k} x_{ijr}}{g_k(g_k - 1)} \tag{10.2}$$

for $i \neq j$.

We can now specify more formally some useful criteria for defining zeroblocks and oneblocks in a blockmodel.

10.2.1 Perfect Fit (Fat Fit)

The perfect fit (or fat fit) blockmodel occurs if all actors in each position are structurally equivalent. This ideal situation results in submatrices in the permuted sociomatrix filled with all 1's or with all 0's. The criterion for a perfect fit blockmodel requires that the tie between two positions on a given relation is equal to 1 only if all actors in the row position have ties to all actors in the column position, and a tie between positions is equal to 0 only if there are no ties from actors in the row position to actors in the column position (Breiger, Boorman, and Arabie 1975; Carrington, Heil, and Berkowitz 1979/80):

$$b_{klr} = \begin{cases} 0 & \text{if } x_{ijr} = 0, \text{ for all } i \in \mathscr{B}_k, j \in \mathscr{B}_l, \text{ and} \\ 1 & \text{if } x_{ijr} = 1, \text{ for all } i \in \mathscr{B}_k, j \in \mathscr{B}_l. \end{cases}$$

The only way that this criterion can be met for all blocks is if all actors in all positions are structurally equivalent. Thus, it is quite unlikely that this criterion will be useful in practice. However, as an ideal, the perfect fit criterion can provide a baseline for assessing the goodness-of-fit of a blockmodel, a topic that we discuss in detail in Chapter 16.

10.2.2 Zeroblock (Lean Fit) Criterion

The zeroblock criterion states that the tie between two positions on a given relation is 0 only if there are *no* ties from actors in the row position to actors in the column position on the specified relation, otherwise the block is a oneblock:

$$b_{klr} = \begin{cases} 0 & \text{if } x_{ijr} = 0, \text{ for all } i \in \mathcal{B}_k, j \in \mathcal{B}_l \\ 1 & \text{otherwise.} \end{cases}$$

This criterion was first proposed by White, Boorman, and Breiger (1976) (see also Arabie, Boorman, and Levitt 1978). The focus on zeroblocks as structurally important phenomena arises because of the expectation that while oneblocks might not be completely filled with 1's, blocks that contain *no* observed ties indicate important structural patterns. Substantively, if we expect that effort is required to maintain a tie, then a single observed "1" in a submatrix should be taken as an important tie in the blockmodel. For example if we recorded the incidence of military interventions by countries during a given year, these rare events would nevertheless indicate an important political tie, not only between individual countries, but also between positions. The zeroblock criterion is reasonable if ties are scarce and/or if the density of the sociomatrix is small. The fact that although zeroblocks should contain only 0's, oneblocks might contain both 1's and 0's gives rise to the alternative label *lean fit*. The oneblocks might be "lean" rather than "fat."

In practice perfect zeroblocks seem to be quite rare. When ties on a given relation are common, and thus the sociomatrix for the relation is dense, zeroblocks are unlikely. Also, for some relations zeroblocks are substantively uninteresting. For example, relations such as "has ever met" are not that effortful for actors to maintain, and therefore the presence of a single tie between two actors would not indicate an important interposition tie. This contrasts with the argument presented by White, Boorman, and Breiger (1976) that the presence of *any* tie between positions should be seen as important. The researcher should consider the substance of the relation and its density when choosing the lean fit criterion. In some cases it might be more appropriate to focus on dense rather than sparse blocks.

10.2.3 Oneblock Criterion

The oneblock criterion focuses on oneblocks rather than on zeroblocks. This criterion requires that the submatrix of the sociomatrix corresponding to the intra- or interposition ties be completely filled with 1's. All possible ties from actors in the row position to actors in the column position need to be present in order to define a oneblock, otherwise it is a zeroblock:

$$b_{klr} = \begin{cases} 1 & \text{if } x_{ijr} = 1, \text{ for all } i \in \mathscr{B}_k, \, j \in \mathscr{B}_l \\ 0 & \text{otherwise.} \end{cases}$$

The oneblock criterion might be most appropriate when the relation is dense, rather than sparse. However, in practice, oneblocks seem to be quite rare.

10.2.4 α Density Criterion

Since real social network data rarely contain (perfectly) structurally equivalent actors, blockmodels that are based on the property of structural equivalence are unlikely to contain blocks all of which are either perfect oneblocks or perfect zeroblocks. For various reasons we expect that oneblocks might contain some 0's and zeroblocks might contain some 1's. Therefore it is reasonable to define a threshold density, α, such that if the observed block density, Δ_{klr}, is greater than or equal to α then the block will be coded as oneblock, and if the observed block density is less than α then the block is coded as a zeroblock (Arabie, Boorman, and Levitt 1978). We define the α criterion as:

$$b_{klr} = \begin{cases} 0 & \text{if } \Delta_{klr} < \alpha \\ 1 & \text{if } \Delta_{klr} \geq \alpha. \end{cases}$$

One guideline for choosing a value of α is that it should depend on the density of the relations in the analysis. Two commonly used values are the overall (grand) density computed across all relations, or, since all relations are unlikely to have the same density, there could be R separate α's, one for each relation ($\alpha_r = \Delta_r$). The literature contains examples of both usages: Arabie (1984) uses a single α as a criterion in his study of positions in a prison, whereas Ennis (1982), Mullins, Hargens, Hecht, and Kick (1977), and Breiger and Ennis (1979) use α's that vary across relations. Alternatively, α could vary across rows of the blockmodel. For example, Ennis (1982) uses α equal to the mean value in the row. This would emphasize the importance of ties sent from members of row positions to members of column positions. Research has shown that global interpretations of blockmodels are quite robust under reasonable changes in values of α used to define oneblocks (Breiger, Boorman, and Arabie 1975; White, Boorman, and Breiger 1976; Breiger and Pattison 1978).

10.2.5 Comparison of Criteria

Criteria for defining oneblocks and zeroblocks depend on the *density* of ties in submatrices of the sociomatrices. The zeroblock, α density, and oneblock criteria can be viewed as different points on a continuum of cutoff values for defining oneblocks in the blockmodel. Each of these three criteria sets a value, call it $\alpha_{(1)}$, such that a block in a blockmodel is designated a oneblock if the density in the corresponding submatrix of the sociomatrix is greater than or equal to $\alpha_{(1)}$. The zeroblock criterion has the least stringent value for defining a oneblock; any block with a density greater than 0 is a oneblock. Thus the oneblock criterion specifies $\alpha_{(1)} = \epsilon$ (an arbitrarily small value). Thus, $b_{klr} = 1$ if $\Delta_{klr} \geq \epsilon$. The α density criterion is more stringent than the zeroblock criterion. The α criterion specifies cutoff values that depend on the density of the relations; $\alpha_{(1)r} = \Delta_r$, the density of relation r. Thus, for the α criterion, $b_{klr} = 1$ if $\Delta_{klr} \geq \Delta_r$. The oneblock criterion is the most stringent and specifies $\alpha_{(1)}$ equal to 1. Thus, $b_{klr} = 1$ if $\Delta_{klr} = 1$.

10.2.6 Examples

We will examine two examples in detail to illustrate these criteria for constructing image matrices. First we will look at a blockmodel for the two relations, advice and friendship, for Krackhardt's high-tech managers. We will then present a blockmodel of the multirelational network of the countries trade network using three relations: manufactured goods, raw materials, and diplomatic ties.

Krackhardt's High-Tech Managers. The high-tech managers network contains two relations, advice and friendship. We will use both of these relations to construct a blockmodel of this network. It is important to realize that since this analysis uses both relations at the same time, the results are likely to be different from the single relational analysis of these data that we presented in Chapter 9. The first step in constructing a blockmodel of these two relations is to partition the actors into subsets such that actors within each subset are approximately structurally equivalent. We used a complete link clustering of Pearson product-moment correlations (including both relations and their transposes, and excluding diagonal elements). Both the correlations and the hierarchical clustering were done in *SYSTAT* (Wilkinson 1987). The dendrogram from the hierarchical clustering gave an interesting split at the level of three clusters. These three clusters define the following three positions:

- $\mathscr{B}_1$: 3, 5, 9, 13, 15, 19, 20
- $\mathscr{B}_2$: 1, 4, 7, 8, 10, 16, 18, 21
- $\mathscr{B}_3$: 2, 6, 11, 12, 14, 17

These subsets show the mapping, $\phi(i) = \mathscr{B}_k$, for each of the twenty-one managers.

The second step in the blockmodel analysis is to describe the ties between and within positions. The starting point for defining these ties is the density table. The density tables for the advice and friendship relations are presented in Figure 10.1. These density tables contain all of the information that is necessary to construct the image matrices for the blockmodel. Let us consider the four criteria for constructing image matrices. Notice that since the densities in the submatrices are not *all* equal to either 0 or 1, the perfect fit criterion will not yield a blockmodel for this partition of actors. Similarly, since there are no submatrices with density equal to 1, the oneblock criterion would give an uninteresting blockmodel, one filled completely with 0's. The zeroblock criterion also gives an uninteresting blockmodel. Only the single block containing the ties from position $\mathscr{B}_3$ to position $\mathscr{B}_1$ on the advice relation has a density of 0. Thus, we will use the α criterion, with α_r for each relation equal to the density of the relation, Δ_r. The density of the advice relation is equal to 0.452, so any submatrix with a density greater than or equal to $\alpha_1 = \Delta_1 = 0.452$ will be coded as a oneblock in the advice image matrix. The density of the friendship relation is equal to $\alpha_2 = \Delta_2 = 0.243$, so any submatrix with a density greater than or equal to 0.243 will be coded as a oneblock in the friendship image matrix.

The image matrices for this blockmodel are presented in Figure 10.2. Each image matrix can also be presented as a reduced graph, in which nodes represent positions, and the arcs show the ties between positions.

Advice

	$\mathscr{B}_1$	$\mathscr{B}_2$	$\mathscr{B}_3$
$\mathscr{B}_1$	0.429	0.714	0.810
$\mathscr{B}_2$	0.286	0.661	0.562
$\mathscr{B}_3$	0.000	0.292	0.133

Friendship

	$\mathscr{B}_1$	$\mathscr{B}_2$	$\mathscr{B}_3$
$\mathscr{B}_1$	0.286	0.071	0.333
$\mathscr{B}_2$	0.071	0.196	0.229
$\mathscr{B}_3$	0.333	0.417	0.400

Fig. 10.1. Density tables for advice and friendship relations for Krackhardt's high-tech managers

Advice
$$\begin{bmatrix} 0 & 1 & 1 \\ 0 & 1 & 1 \\ 0 & 0 & 0 \end{bmatrix}$$

Friendship
$$\begin{bmatrix} 1 & 0 & 1 \\ 0 & 0 & 0 \\ 1 & 1 & 1 \end{bmatrix}$$

Fig. 10.2. Blockmodel image matrices for advice and friendship relations for Krackhardt's high-tech managers

Figure 10.3 gives these graphs. For the moment, simply notice that the image matrices and graphs for the two relations are quite different. We will examine these differences in more detail in the remainder of this chapter.

The Countries Trade Network Example. The countries trade network consists of a set of five dichotomous relations, four trade relations coded as imports by the column country from the row country, and a diplomatic relation, indicating that the row country has an embassy in the column country. These data were described in Chapter 2. For the blockmodel analysis we will use three relations: manufactured goods, raw materials, and diplomatic ties. All three of these relations are directional and dichotomous.

For this analysis we measured structural equivalence using the Pearson product-moment correlation coefficient, calculated on the rows and

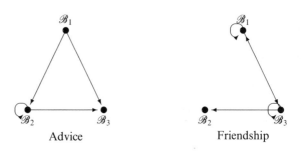

Advice   Friendship

Fig. 10.3. Reduced graphs for advice and friendship relations for Krack-hardt's high-tech managers

columns of the three sociomatrices, excluding diagonal entries. We used *UCINET* to calculate the correlations. Positions were identified using complete link hierarchical clustering in *SYSTAT* (Wilkinson 1987). To study the positions in detail, we will use a six position model. These six positions and their members are:

- $\mathscr{B}_1$: Japan, United Kingdom, United States
- $\mathscr{B}_2$: China, Czechoslovakia, Indonesia, Spain, Yugoslavia
- $\mathscr{B}_3$: Argentina, Brazil, Finland, New Zealand, Pakistan, Switzerland, Thailand
- $\mathscr{B}_4$: Algeria, Egypt, Syria
- $\mathscr{B}_5$: Ecuador, Honduras, Israel
- $\mathscr{B}_6$: Ethiopia, Liberia, Madagascar

The density tables for the three relations are presented in Figure 10.4. These tables show the proportion of ties that are present from countries in the row position to countries in the column position. Density tables and image matrices were constructed using *UCINET 3* (MacEvoy and Freeman n.d.).

Notice that these density tables have some values that are equal to 1.00 or 0.00, indicating that some submatrices corresponding to intraposition or interposition ties are either completely filled with 1's, or completely filled with 0's. Therefore, it is possible to consider using either the zeroblock or the oneblock criterion to construct the image matrices for this blockmodel. However, using the oneblock criterion gives a very sparse blockmodel, since only twenty-one of the $36 \times 3 = 108$ submatrices

Manufactured Goods

	$\mathscr{B}_1$	$\mathscr{B}_2$	$\mathscr{B}_3$	$\mathscr{B}_4$	$\mathscr{B}_5$	$\mathscr{B}_6$
$\mathscr{B}_1$	1.000	1.000	0.952	1.000	1.000	1.000
$\mathscr{B}_2$	1.000	1.000	0.914	0.933	0.467	0.533
$\mathscr{B}_3$	0.952	0.857	0.810	0.667	0.571	0.286
$\mathscr{B}_4$	0.444	0.400	0.095	0.000	0.000	0.111
$\mathscr{B}_5$	0.556	0.133	0.286	0.000	0.000	0.111
$\mathscr{B}_6$	0.222	0.067	0.000	0.000	0.000	0.000

Raw Materials

	$\mathscr{B}_1$	$\mathscr{B}_2$	$\mathscr{B}_3$	$\mathscr{B}_4$	$\mathscr{B}_5$	$\mathscr{B}_6$
$\mathscr{B}_1$	1.000	1.000	0.952	1.000	0.778	0.667
$\mathscr{B}_2$	0.867	0.800	0.657	0.600	0.267	0.133
$\mathscr{B}_3$	0.952	0.917	0.762	0.571	0.476	0.048
$\mathscr{B}_4$	0.556	0.867	0.238	0.333	0.111	0.000
$\mathscr{B}_5$	0.778	0.333	0.238	0.000	0.167	0.000
$\mathscr{B}_6$	1.000	0.333	0.143	0.556	0.222	0.000

Diplomatic Ties

	$\mathscr{B}_1$	$\mathscr{B}_2$	$\mathscr{B}_3$	$\mathscr{B}_4$	$\mathscr{B}_5$	$\mathscr{B}_6$
$\mathscr{B}_1$	1.000	1.000	0.952	1.000	1.000	1.000
$\mathscr{B}_2$	1.000	0.900	0.943	1.000	0.400	0.600
$\mathscr{B}_3$	0.952	0.857	0.714	0.714	0.429	0.238
$\mathscr{B}_4$	1.000	1.000	0.667	0.333	0.111	0.667
$\mathscr{B}_5$	1.000	0.333	0.476	0.222	0.833	0.111
$\mathscr{B}_6$	0.889	0.267	0.000	0.333	0.000	0.333

Fig. 10.4. Density tables for manufactured goods, raw materials, and diplomatic ties

have densities equal to 1, and would thus be coded as oneblocks in the blockmodel. The zeroblock criterion gives a very dense blockmodel, since only fourteen of the submatrices have densities equal to 0, and would be coded as zeroblocks. Therefore, it seems reasonable to use the α density criterion to construct the blockmodel image matrices. The densities of the three relations are:

- Exports manufactured goods, density = .562
- Exports raw materials, density = .556
- Diplomat resides in, density = .668

Since there is some variation in the densities of these relations, it is reasonable to choose α density cutoff values that are specific to the

Manufactured Goods

$$\begin{bmatrix} 1 & 1 & 1 & 1 & 1 & 1 \\ 1 & 1 & 1 & 1 & 0 & 0 \\ 1 & 1 & 1 & 1 & 1 & 0 \\ 0 & 0 & 0 & 0 & 0 & 0 \\ 0 & 0 & 0 & 0 & 0 & 0 \\ 0 & 0 & 0 & 0 & 0 & 0 \end{bmatrix}$$

Raw Materials

$$\begin{bmatrix} 1 & 1 & 1 & 1 & 1 & 1 \\ 1 & 1 & 1 & 1 & 0 & 0 \\ 1 & 1 & 1 & 1 & 0 & 0 \\ 0 & 1 & 0 & 0 & 0 & 0 \\ 1 & 0 & 0 & 0 & 0 & 0 \\ 1 & 0 & 0 & 0 & 0 & 0 \end{bmatrix}$$

Diplomatic Ties

$$\begin{bmatrix} 1 & 1 & 1 & 1 & 1 & 1 \\ 1 & 1 & 1 & 1 & 0 & 0 \\ 1 & 1 & 1 & 1 & 0 & 0 \\ 1 & 1 & 0 & 0 & 0 & 0 \\ 1 & 0 & 0 & 0 & 1 & 0 \\ 1 & 0 & 0 & 0 & 0 & 0 \end{bmatrix}$$

Fig. 10.5. Image matrices for three relations in the countries trade example

relations. Using the α density rule with relation specific α's gives the set of three image matrices, in Figure 10.5.

The collection of three image matrices, along with the assignment of countries to positions, constitutes the blockmodel for these data. For the moment, notice that no two relations have the identical image matrices, though there are features common to all three image matrices. In all image matrices all positions have ties *to* block $\mathcal{B}_1$, and overall, positions $\mathcal{B}_1$ and $\mathcal{B}_2$ are involved in more ties than are the remaining positions.

All of these rules for assigning oneblocks and zeroblocks have assumed dichotomous relations. In the next section we discuss how to construct blockmodels for valued relations.

10.2.7 Valued Relations

Blockmodels can also be constructed for valued relations. Although the relations are valued, the ties within and between positions in the image matrix **B** may be either valued or dichotomous.

For a valued relation, each submatrix of the sociomatrix corresponding to ties within or between positions may contain a range of values. Criteria for defining oneblocks and zeroblocks are more complicated than the rules used for dichotomous relations. The *maximum value* criterion for valued relations is analogous to the zeroblock criterion for dichotomous relations. Blocks that contain *only* small values are defined as zeroblocks, and blocks that contain any large values are defined as oneblocks in the blockmodel. Using this rule for valued relation, where a high number indicated a stronger tie, White, Boorman, and Breiger (1976) argued that only the two highest values "were strong enough to invalidate a zeroblock" (1976, page 750). Therefore, they defined a zeroblock as a block in which all values in the corresponding submatrix of the sociomatrix contained only small values. If we define ϵ as the highest acceptable value for a zeroblock, then the rule can be stated as:

$$b_{klr} = \begin{cases} 0 & \text{if } x_{ijr} \leq \epsilon \text{ for all } i \in \mathcal{B}_k, j \in \mathcal{B}_l \\ 1 & \text{otherwise.} \end{cases}$$

Another possible criterion is the *mean value* criterion. This criterion is based on the mean value of each relation, $\bar{x}_r$:

$$\bar{x}_r = \frac{\sum_{i=1}^{g} \sum_{j=1}^{g} x_{ijr}}{g(g-1)} \tag{10.3}$$

for $i \neq j$. When relation $\mathcal{X}_r$ is dichotomous, $\bar{x}_r = \Delta_r$, the density of the relation. If the mean value in the submatrix of a sociomatrix corresponding to ties from actors in position $\mathcal{B}_k$ to actors in position $\mathcal{B}_l$ is greater than or equal to the mean of the relation, then the block is defined as a oneblock, otherwise the block is defined as a zeroblock. This is analogous to the α density rule for a dichotomous relation. More precisely we denote the mean value of the tie from actors in position $\mathcal{B}_k$ to actors in position $\mathcal{B}_l$ on relation $\mathcal{X}_r$ by $\bar{x}_{klr}$. We can then state the mean value criterion as:

$$b_{klr} = \begin{cases} 0 & \text{if } \bar{x}_{klr} < \bar{x}_r \\ 1 & \text{if } \bar{x}_{klr} \geq \bar{x}_r. \end{cases}$$

One can also create valued blockmodels in which each block is assigned a value from within the range of values on the original relation; $0, 1, \ldots, C-1$. Using the mean value within the block as the value assigned to each block in the model ($b_{klr} = \bar{x}_{klr}$) is analogous to constructing a density table for a dichotomous relation. The value for a block would be the mean level of ties within the block.

One must consider quite carefully how the relation is measured before applying the mean value criterion. If the relation is measured on a continuum (such as a rating scale) where small values indicate a substantively negative tie, and large values indicate a substantively positive tie, then the mean value, $\bar{x}_{klr}$, could be a combination of both substantively positive and substantively negative ties within a submatrix (Arabie, Boorman, and Levitt 1978; and Arabie and Boorman 1982). In that case the researcher may prefer to use the maximum value criterion.

10.3 Interpretation

Blockmodels are hypotheses about the structure of relations in a social network. These hypotheses refer to positions of actors rather than to individuals, and they summarize features of the entire network in a multirelational system. Although blockmodels may appear deceptively simple, since they usually consist of rather small arrays of 0's and 1's, the patterns of ties between positions can present theoretically important structural properties. In the following sections we discuss three different ways to interpret a blockmodel:

(i)   Validation of a blockmodel using actor attributes
(ii) Descriptions of individual positions
(iii) Descriptions of the overall blockmodel

The first way to interpret a blockmodel uses exogenous actor attribute variables to describe the positions in the blockmodel. The latter two ways provide statements about the form of the blockmodel, **B**, without reference to the attributes of the actors.

10.3.1 Actor Attributes

One of the most straightforward ways to interpret a blockmodel is to use attributes of actors to describe the positions. If there are systematic differences between positions in the characteristics of their members, then we have some external validation of the blockmodel. A relationship between the actor attributes and the positions in the blockmodel might also indicate an association between the attribute and the structural form presented in the blockmodel.

There are many examples of network analyses that have used actor attributes to help interpret blockmodels. Investigations of positions in the world economic and political system have used growth in GNP per capita measured on countries to help understand the positional structure (Snyder and Kick 1979). Researchers studying scientific communities have used the date of a scientist's professional degree, the number of articles each has published, the number of citations made to their published work, and the dollar amount of grant money they have received to help understand the structure of scientific networks (Mullins, Hargens, Hecht, and Kick 1977; Breiger 1976). In his investigation of the social structure among prison inmates, Arabie (1984) used ethnicity, level of education, and drinking habits to validate a blockmodel. Arabie used discriminant analysis to study whether positional assignments could be predicted from the actor attributes.

Depending on one's theoretical orientation, one might argue either that the characteristics of the actors are an important determinant of their network relations that led to the observed positional structure, or, on the other hand, that the structural positions and network processes were influential in determining the characteristics of the actors. For example, world system theory argues that the position of a country in the world system influences the rate of development of the country. On the other hand, social psychologists argue that similarity between people in their characteristics leads to mutual attraction and the formation of friendships, and thus influences the structure of the group. In either case, the actor attributes are related to the network structure.

Examples. We will first examine the three-position model for Krackhardt's high-tech managers, and then look at the six-position model of the countries trade network. In each case we will present the average value of each attribute, calculated within each of the positions in the blockmodel.

Krackhardt's High-tech Managers. In addition to relations, Krackhardt recorded the following information about the characteristics of the managers in the corporation: their department, level in the official organizational chart, the number of years the manager had been with the company (tenure), and their age. One might reasonably expect that patterns of advice seeking would be related to the experience of the managers, and that experience would be reflected in the age of the managers and/or in their length of service (tenure) with the company. For all managers the mean age is 39.71 years, and the mean length of service is 11.75 years. To examine whether age and tenure vary across positions we computed the mean and standard deviation of age and

Table 10.1. *Mean age and tenure of actors in positions for Krackhardt's high-tech managers (standard deviations in parentheses)*

	Position		
	$\mathscr{B}_1$	$\mathscr{B}_2$	$\mathscr{B}_3$
Age	41.71	36.00	42.33
	(10.48)	(8.23)	(10.13)
Tenure	6.67	11.71	17.72
	(4.52)	(7.76)	(8.42)

tenure for the managers within each of the positions. These statistics are reported in Table 10.1.

Notice that members of position $\mathscr{B}_3$ are oldest on average (42.33 years) and have the longest tenure in the company (17.72 years). Position $\mathscr{B}_2$ has, on average, the youngest members (36 years), and members of intermediate tenure (11.71 years). The president and two of the three vice presidents are in position $\mathscr{B}_2$.

The Countries Trade Network. Let now consider the countries trade example, and examine the characteristics of the countries in each of the positions. Considerable research has focused on whether, and how, the position of a country in the world system affects its social and economic development. One prediction is that dependency status within the world political and economic system affects the rate of economic development of countries. Researchers using network data have constructed blockmodels of positions in the world system using data on trade, diplomatic ties, and military interventions (Snyder and Kick 1979, Nemeth and Smith 1985; Kick n.d.) or for samples of developed nations (Breiger 1981a). In addition, numerous researchers have attempted to validate these blockmodels using characteristics of countries and to compare the positions of countries resulting from blockmodels with alternative ways of classifying countries (Snyder and Kick 1979; Kick n.d.; Nolan 1983, 1987, 1988; Lenski and Nolan 1984). Among the variables that have been used to study positions of countries are four that we will use:

- Population, annual growth rate from 1970 to 1981
- GNP per capita, annual growth rate from 1970 to 1981
- Secondary school enrollment ratio in 1980

• Energy consumption per capita (in kilo coal equivalents) in 1980

At the outset, we expect that GNP per capita growth rate, secondary school enrollment ratio, and energy consumption per capita will be higher in industrialized nations than in developing nations. In contrast, population growth rate is expected to be higher in developing nations than in industrialized nations. If level of industrialization of countries is related to their position in the world trade network (as depicted in the blockmodel) then the distributions of these variables should differ systematically across the positions in the model. Table 10.2 shows the means and standard deviations of these variables within each of the six positions. Notice that there is a tendency for the means to be ordered across positions. Positions $\mathscr{B}_1$, $\mathscr{B}_2$, and $\mathscr{B}_3$ have the lowest annual growth rate in population, the highest secondary school enrollment ratio, and the highest energy consumption. Positions $\mathscr{B}_4$, $\mathscr{B}_5$, and $\mathscr{B}_6$ have the highest annual growth rate in population, the lowest secondary school enrollment ratio, and the lowest energy consumption. Annual growth rate in GNP per capita varies, but less systematically, across the positions, from a high of 4.3 for position $\mathscr{B}_2$ to a low of -0.57 for position $\mathscr{B}_6$.

These examples demonstrate that the attributes of the actors differ among the positions in these blockmodels. However, a more complete interpretation of the blockmodel requires examining how the positions are related to each other.

10.3.2 Describing Individual Positions

A second way to interpret a blockmodel is to describe how the individual positions relate to each other. This requires examining how positions send and receives ties in the blockmodel. One useful and informative strategy relies simply on the ties to and from the positions in the model (Burt 1976; Marsden 1989). Descriptive typologies of positions are useful for summarizing tendencies for positions to send and receive ties within or outside the position.

Recall that when we describe nodes in a directed graph, we can use nodal indegrees and outdegrees to distinguish four different types of nodes: *isolates* (nodes with neither indegree nor outdegree), *transmitters* (nodes with only outdegree), *receivers* (nodes with only indegree), and *carriers* or *ordinary points* (nodes with both indegree and outdegree) (see Harary, Norman, and Cartwright 1965 and Marsden 1989). As Marsden

Table 10.2. *Means of variables within positions for countries trade example*

	Position					
	$\mathscr{B}_1$	$\mathscr{B}_2$	$\mathscr{B}_3$	$\mathscr{B}_4$	$\mathscr{B}_5$	$\mathscr{B}_6$
Population annual growth rate	0.73 (.55)	1.30 (0.63)	1.60 (1.06)	3.17 (0.61)	3.13 (0.46)	2.70 (0.76)
GNP per capita annual growth rate	2.33 (0.94)	4.30 (1.83)	2.21 (1.97)	4.70 (1.47)	2.20 (2.18)	-0.57 (1.260)
Secondary school enrollment ratio	90.00 (7.55)	57.00 (26.37)	51.14 (27.70)	43.67 (9.71)	47.33 (21.94)	14.33 (4.93)
Energy consumption per capita	7217.67 (3838.70)	2615.40 (2625.32)	2892.29 (2527.21)	791.00 (185.57)	1265.67 (1354.87)	200.00 (262.73)

(1989) has noted, this classification is also useful for describing positions in networks. Thus the same labels may be used to describe how positions relate to each other.

These rather neutral labels refer simply to the presence or absence of ties to and from positions. If we also take into account the prevalence of ties among actors that are made within a position, then the description can be more informative. Burt (1976) provides a typology of positions that is useful for positively valued, affective interpersonal ties, such as respect, liking, or esteem. His typology takes into account both whether ties occur primarily within a position, and whether ties are directed to members of the position from others. First he distinguishes between positions whose members receive ties and positions whose members do not receive ties. Second, he distinguishes between positions in which less than half of their total ties to their own members, and positions whose members have half or more of their ties to their own members. By making these two distinctions one can determine whether each position receives ties or not, and whether each position has more ties within rather than outside the position. These two distinctions result in a classification into four types of positions. Isolate positions neither give many ties nor direct many ties to other positions. Sycophants have more ties to members of other positions than to themselves, and do not receive many ties. Brokers both receive ties and send ties to members of other positions. The Primary position receives ties both from members of other positions, and from its own members.

It is useful to consider the relative size of the position when examining the tendency for position members to have ties within the position. If a position is large relative to the size of the entire group, then one would expect many of the ties made by position members to be to other members of the position, simply because of their prevalence in the group, even if there were no ingroup bias in ties. Similarly, a small position would be expected to have a low proportion of ties within the position, simply because there are relatively fewer actors in the position. Thus we must consider the proportion of the total ties that are made within the position, compared to the proportion of within-position ties that would be expected if there were no within- or outside-position bias in ties.

Consider the ties from members of position $\mathscr{B}_k$. If there are g_k actors in position $\mathscr{B}_k$ then there are $g_k \times (g_k - 1)$ possible ties within the position. In the whole group, there are g actors, so there are $g_k \times (g - 1)$ possible ties in total from actors in position $\mathscr{B}_k$ (recall that self-ties are undefined). If there were no bias toward (or away) from ties within the position,

Table 10.3. *Typology of positions (adapted from Burt (1976))*

Proportion of ties within position	Proportion of ties received by position	
	~ 0	> 0
$\geq \frac{g_k-1}{g-1}$	Isolate	Primary
$\leq \frac{g_k-1}{g-1}$	Sycophant	Broker

then we would expect the proportion of a position's total ties within the position to be:

$$\frac{g_k \times (g_k - 1)}{g_k \times (g - 1)} = \frac{g_k - 1}{g - 1}. \tag{10.4}$$

One can use this proportion as a baseline for evaluating the tendency for within-position ties. Since this proportion depends on the number of actors in the position it will probably differ across positions.

Table 10.3 summarizes the typology of positions based on ties within and between positions. The columns refer to the first distinction (receiving ties or not), and the rows refer to the second distinction (proportion of ties within the position).

The labels Isolate, Sycophant, Broker, and Primary depend on the content of the relation. If the relation is negatively valued (blame, dislike, and so on) then the primary position would be more appropriately interpreted as a scapegoat, or pariah. If the relation involved the flow of material goods (such as trade among nations, or buying and selling among corporations) then a position with a high ratio of ties made to ties received (in other words, a relatively high ratio of goods sent) would be interpreted as a supplier or source, and a position with a relatively high ratio of ties received (in other words, a relatively high ratio of goods bought) would be a consumer or end-user, and the brokers would be middlemen in the transaction (Galaskiewicz and Krohn 1984).

These descriptions of kinds of network positions do not allow the researcher to test whether the tendencies are statistically large. Stochastic blockmodels (which we discuss in Chapter 16), related methods for statistical analysis of single relational networks (Chapter 15), and multiple relational networks (Chapter 16) provide statistical tests of dyadic choice probabilities, and some models provide tests of actor attribute parameters. We recommend that the researcher include such tests when appropriate.

For communication networks, where the relation is often the transmission of a message or information, Richards (1989a) has presented a typology that is also based on indegree and outdegree conditions, and makes a similar distinction among positions. Since communication is often symmetric, it is likely to be represented as a graph. Richards distinguishes first between participant and nonparticipant positions. Nonparticipants are either isolates (neither indegree nor outdegree) or "tree nodes" (have a tie to only one other node); participants are either liaisons (they link two or more others) or group members. This typology is a fundamental part of the network analysis program *NEGOPY* (Richards 1989a). Since this typology is most useful for classifying individual actors, we discuss it in more detail in Chapter 12.

Marsden (1989) has extended Burt's (1976) typology by distinguishing between the level of ties *made* by a position, the level of ties *received* by a position, and the position's *ingroup preference*. His typology combines features of the graph theoretic classification with the distinctions made in Burt's typology. Making a dichotomous (high versus low) distinction on each of these three dimensions gives a typology with eight different kinds of positions. Marsden proposes log linear models for examining these three properties.

Focusing on the indegree, outdegree, and within-position ties gives an interesting and useful description of the positions that relies simply on the ties to and from each position. However, since a blockmodel is likely to contain several relations (with quite different substantive meanings or contents) arriving at a consistent description of a given position might be difficult. The "label" for a position might not be the same across the different relations.

Now, let us look at an example to illustrate the typology of positions in Table 10.3.

Example. We will use the three-position blockmodel of advice and friendship for Krackhardt's high-tech managers. To classify the positions, it is necessary to count the number of ties from members of each position to other actors, both within and outside the position. These counts can be made by examining the sociomatrix with rows and columns permuted so that actors in the same position are adjacent in the permuted sociomatrix. Figure 10.6 gives the frequency of ties within each block, and the total number of ties given and received by each position.

First, notice that all positions receive at least some ties, on both relations. Therefore on neither relation is there an Isolate or a Sycophant

Advice

	$\mathscr{B}_1$	$\mathscr{B}_2$	$\mathscr{B}_3$	Total
$\mathscr{B}_1$	18	40	34	92
$\mathscr{B}_2$	16	37	27	80
$\mathscr{B}_3$	0	14	4	18
Total	34	91	65	190

Friendship

	$\mathscr{B}_1$	$\mathscr{B}_2$	$\mathscr{B}_3$	Total
$\mathscr{B}_1$	12	4	14	30
$\mathscr{B}_2$	4	11	11	26
$\mathscr{B}_3$	14	20	12	46
Total	30	35	37	102

Fig. 10.6. Frequency of ties within and between positions for advice and friendship

Table 10.4. *Typology of positions for Krackhardt's high-tech managers*

Position	Advice	Friendship
$\mathscr{B}_1$	Broker	Primary
$\mathscr{B}_2$	Primary	Primary
$\mathscr{B}_3$	Broker	Primary

position. Now, consider position $\mathscr{B}_2$, and its ties on the advice relation. There are $g_2 = 8$ actors in this position, so we would expect that the proportion of their ties that would be within the position would be equal to $(8 - 1)/(21 - 1) = 0.350$. In fact, members of position $\mathscr{B}_2$ have thirty-seven out of their total eighty advice ties to their own members, for a proportion of $37/80 = 0.462$. Since this proportion is higher than we would expect, this position is a Primary position on the advice relation. In contrast, consider the advice ties from members of position $\mathscr{B}_1$. We would expect that since there are $g_1 = 7$ actors in this position, that they would have $6/20 = 0.300$ of their ties to their own members. However, since only eighteen of their ninety-two advice ties (a proportion of 0.196) are to their own members, position $\mathscr{B}_1$ is Broker on the advice relation. Table 10.4 gives the classification of the three positions on each of the two relations, using the typology in Table 10.3.

Since all three positions have a greater than expected frequency of ties within their position on the friendship relation, all three positions are

Primary positions on this relation. In addition, position $\mathcal{B}_2$ is a Primary position on the advice relation. Referring to Table 10.1, we see that position $\mathcal{B}_2$ has the youngest managers, and managers with intermediate tenure. Also, the president and two of the vice presidents are in position $\mathcal{B}_2$.

For the most, part descriptions of single positions do not take into account the properties of the positions to which a given position is related. A Broker position gives and receives ties rather than having ties within the position, but the kind of positions to which it is tied are unimportant. Similarly, a "transmitter" (a position with both in- and outdegree) could be either at the bottom of a very long chain of command or pecking order, or toward the top. Thus, intermediate levels in a hierarchy would be indistinguishable (since they would have both indegree and outdegree). Although labels for kinds of positions described in this section are quite useful as a starting point for interpreting a blockmodel, they capture only a limited amount of information about the structure of the network as a whole.

10.3.3 Image Matrices

The third way to study a blockmodel is to consider the entire configuration of ties between positions that is expressed in the image matrix or matrices. Many structural theories posit patterns of ties among aggregates of actors. For example, the properties of balance and transitivity, a network system with a center and a periphery (such as has been proposed for the world economic and political system; Snyder and Kick 1979), systems characterized by a hierarchy, the domination of one or more positions over others, and cohesive subgroups can be represented by blockmodels. We describe and illustrate these patterns in this section. Theories that are expressed in terms of such patterns may be evaluated by examining the blockmodel image matrices to see whether the observed blockmodel is consistent or inconsistent with the predicted pattern. We begin by describing the images for two-position blockmodels, and then discuss some more complicated theoretical patterns that can occur in blockmodels with more than two positions.

Image Matrices for Two-position Blockmodels. Some of the simplest possible blockmodels can give quite powerful representations of theoretical statements. For example, even a two-position model, presented in a 2×2 image matrix, can represent quite important theoretical properties. In their introduction of blockmodels, White, Boorman, and Breiger (1976) present the sixteen possible arrangements that can arise in a two-position blockmodel. Since there are two positions, the image matrix for this blockmodel has $2 \times 2 = 4$ cells, each of which may be either a zeroblock or a oneblock. Thus, there are $2^4 = 16$ possible arrangements of 0's and 1's. Since the order of the positions is arbitrary, there are in fact only ten distinct images (the others are isomorphic to one of these images).

Figure 10.7 shows the sixteen possible image matrices for a two-position model. Some of these patterns have clear interpretations in terms of structural theories. A theoretical prediction about the arrangement of ties between positions gives rise to a posited image matrix. White, Boorman, and Breiger (1976) provide useful descriptions for many of these images. Image B in Figure 10.7 has a single cohesive subgroup and an isolate position (assuming a positive affective relation). Image C could indicate deference directed from members of one position to members of the other. In terms of individual position labels described in the previous section, the position initiating the tie would be a Sycophant position. Image D is "pure" reflexivity, and for a positive relation would indicate two cohesive subgroups. Image D could also represent an endogamous system in which all ties exist within subsets, or homophily where all friendship choices are between actors with similar characteristics. In the context of world trade systems, Breiger (1981) described this pattern as representing separate trading areas. Image E is "pure" symmetry. For a negative relation it would indicate opposition or hostility. Image E could also represent an exogamous system in which all ties are directed to members of another group (for example, "seeks a spouse from" in an exogamous system where marriages are between rather than within clans or villages). The combination of image D (for a positive relation) and E (for a negative relation) would be consistent with balance theory, which predicts that actors in a balanced system can be clustered so that all positive "choices" are within subsets and negative "choices" are between subsets. Image F distinguishes between an "active" position and a "passive" position, in terms of "choices" made. Image G combines aspects of a cohesive subgroup (image B) and a deference structure (C), and resembles a core-periphery system (with a Primary position and a Sycophant position). This pattern can also be interpreted as a hierarchy (Breiger 1981a). Image H is complete except for one reflexive tie. White, Boorman, and Breiger (1976) describe this as a center-periphery or hanger-on pattern. Image H is somewhat similar to image E, which has ties only between positions. Image I is complete except for the absence of one tie from one position to the other. White, Boorman, and Breiger (1976) describe this form as a hierarchy, with deferential ties within each of the two levels of the hierarchy in addition to deferential ties from one level to the other. Finally, image J is complete, and therefore shows no differentiation among positions.

Image Matrices with More than Two Positions. Certainly not all blockmodels have only two positions. More interesting, but also more complex, systems arise when there are more positions. For a three-position model there are $2^9 = 512$ possible 3×3 arrangements for a single relation, and 104 distinct image matrices (isomorphism classes). As the number of positions increases, the number of distinct image matrices increases rapidly. Instead of enumerating all of the possible images for larger blockmodels, let us examine a few "ideal" images that display theoretically important structural properties. In particular we will illustrate images that display the properties of cohesive subgroups, a center-periphery structure, a centralized system, a hierarchy, and a transitive system. Figure 10.8 shows these ideal patterns.

One of the most straightforward patterns is a system composed of *cohesive subgroups*. Such a system has an image matrix (for a single positively valued relation) that consists primarily of intraposition ties. The image matrix for this pattern has oneblocks on the main diagonal, and is reflexive at the position level (even though at the level of individual actor ties, self-ties may be undefined). However, the positions in the blockmodel may not be graph theoretic cliques. Oneblocks may contain some 0's (they may not be complete subgraphs), and an actor from one position may be connected to all of the actors in another position (the positions may not be maximal).

Another important pattern is a *center-periphery* structure. This consists of a core position which is internally cohesive, and one or more other positions with ties to the core position, but not to each other (Mullins, Hargens, Hecht, and Kick 1977). The peripheral positions may or may not be internally cohesive. Examples of core-periphery systems include an elite position and hangers-on in a social group, or the proposed three "levels" in the world system consisting of the core, periphery, and semiperiphery. In general, a center-periphery pattern is apparent in a blockmodel if the blocks in the image matrix can be permuted so that the oneblocks are primarily in the upper left triangle of the image matrix, and the zeroblocks are primarily in the lower right triangle. The center periphery pattern has been found in the trade relations in the world economic and political system (Snyder and Kick 1979; Breiger 1981a).

A related pattern is a *centralized* system. In a centralized system all ties are pointed toward (or away) from a single position. In the image matrix, all oneblocks are in the same column (if all ties are to the same position), or in the same row (if all ties are from the same position). Reflexive ties may also be present. A centralized pattern was found by Doreian and Fararo (1985) in their study of citations among major journals in sociology. The most prestigious journals were in the central position, and were cited by journals in all other positions. This pattern has also been found by Knoke and Rogers (1979) in their study of an interorganizational network.

Another possible pattern is a *hierarchy*. A hierarchy appears as unre-ciprocated ties directed from each position to the position immediately "above" it. This pattern could represent a chain of command in an organization.

A system that is *transitive* at the level of the positions is similar to a hierarchy, but all interposition ties that are implied by the property of transitivity are also present. If there is a tie from position $\mathscr{B}_k$ to position $\mathscr{B}_l$ and there is a tie from $\mathscr{B}_l$ to $\mathscr{B}_m$, then there is a tie from $\mathscr{B}_k$ to $\mathscr{B}_m$. In a fully transitive model, the rows and columns of the image matrix can be permuted so that all oneblocks are in the lower left triangle (or in the upper right triangle) of the image matrix. Depending on the substance of the relation, a transitive image could indicate dominance or deference between positions.

These patterns are useful for describing patterns as theoretically pure or ideal structures. It is likely that blockmodels for actual social network data will show some variation around these patterns, or might com-bine features of two or more patterns. Stochastic blockmodels (which we discuss in Chapter 16) are more appropriate for *testing* theoretical statements.

We now illustrate these descriptions of image matrices using both the example of Krackhardt's high-tech managers and the countries trade network.

Examples. Let us first examine the image matrices for the three relations in the countries trade example. These images are displayed

A. Null

$$\begin{bmatrix} 0 & 0 \\ 0 & 0 \end{bmatrix}$$

B. One reflexive arc

$$\begin{bmatrix} 1 & 0 \\ 0 & 0 \end{bmatrix} \text{ or } \begin{bmatrix} 0 & 0 \\ 0 & 1 \end{bmatrix}$$

C. One arc between positions

$$\begin{bmatrix} 0 & 1 \\ 0 & 0 \end{bmatrix} \text{ or } \begin{bmatrix} 0 & 0 \\ 1 & 0 \end{bmatrix}$$

D. Two arcs, reflexive

$$\begin{bmatrix} 1 & 0 \\ 0 & 1 \end{bmatrix}$$

E. Two arcs, symmetric

$$\begin{bmatrix} 0 & 1 \\ 1 & 0 \end{bmatrix}$$

F. Two arcs, reflexive and "out"

$$\begin{bmatrix} 1 & 1 \\ 0 & 0 \end{bmatrix} \text{ or } \begin{bmatrix} 0 & 0 \\ 1 & 1 \end{bmatrix}$$

G. Two arcs, reflexive and "in"

$$\begin{bmatrix} 1 & 0 \\ 1 & 0 \end{bmatrix} \text{ or } \begin{bmatrix} 0 & 1 \\ 0 & 1 \end{bmatrix}$$

H. Three arcs, 2 between positions

$$\begin{bmatrix} 0 & 1 \\ 1 & 1 \end{bmatrix} \text{ or } \begin{bmatrix} 1 & 1 \\ 1 & 0 \end{bmatrix}$$

I. Three arcs, 2 reflexive

$$\begin{bmatrix} 1 & 0 \\ 1 & 1 \end{bmatrix} \text{ or } \begin{bmatrix} 1 & 1 \\ 0 & 1 \end{bmatrix}$$

J. Complete

$$\begin{bmatrix} 1 & 1 \\ 1 & 1 \end{bmatrix}$$

Fig. 10.7. Ten possible image matrices for a two-position blockmodel

in Figure 10.5, and appear to show two different patterns. The image matrix for the manufactured goods relation shows that positions $\mathcal{B}_1$, $\mathcal{B}_2$, and $\mathcal{B}_3$ are the source of manufactured goods imported by all positions, whereas positions $\mathcal{B}_4$, $\mathcal{B}_5$, and $\mathcal{B}_6$ only import, but do not export, goods. This is similar to a centralized system, with three positions in the center. The image matrices for raw materials and diplomatic ties look similar to each other, and different from the image matrix for manufactured goods. Although neither of these two images perfectly matches one of the ideal types, both matrices are arranged so that the oneblocks are concentrated primarily in the upper left triangle of the matrix, and the zeroblocks are primarily in the lower right triangle. This pattern indicates a center-periphery system. In the countries trade example, position $\mathcal{B}_1$ is in the center, positions $\mathcal{B}_5$ and $\mathcal{B}_6$ are on the periphery, and the other positions are intermediate.

In the blockmodel for Krackhardt's high-tech managers, presented in Figures 10.2 and 10.3, the two relations, advice and friendship, have different patterns. The advice image is transitive at the level of the positions. If we think of positions seeking advice from other positions that are more prominent in the organization, then positions $\mathcal{B}_2$ and $\mathcal{B}_3$ are at the top and $\mathcal{B}_1$ is at the bottom. The pattern for friendship is not as clear. Although positions $\mathcal{B}_1$ and $\mathcal{B}_3$ have intra-position friendship ties, the system as a whole does not appear to be completely characterized by cohesive subgroups (at least for this blockmodel).

Image Matrices for Multiple Relations. Interpreting blockmodels with multiple relations can be tedious. The researcher could propose separate interpretations for each image, but in the absence of a theoretical foundation, this seems ad hoc. One possible way to interpret multirelational blockmodels is to study pairs of image matrices to see whether they exhibit common kinds of multirelational patterns, such as multiplexity or exchange. Multiplexity of relations is the tendency for two or more relations to occur together. For example, "is a friend of" and "spends time with" are two relations that might tend to occur together if people are free to choose the people they spend time with. Multiplexity in a blockmodel would be apparent if two or more image matrices were identical (or nearly identical). Exchange occurs when one relation "flows" one way, and the second relation "flows" back. For example, "pays money to" and "delivers goods to" are two relations that form an exchange in an economic transaction. The property of exchange would be apparent in a blockmodel if one image matrix were the transpose

A. Cohesive subgroups

$$\begin{bmatrix} 1 & 0 & 0 & 0 \\ 0 & 1 & 0 & 0 \\ 0 & 0 & 1 & 0 \\ 0 & 0 & 0 & 1 \end{bmatrix}$$

B. Center-periphery

$$\begin{bmatrix} 1 & 1 & 1 & 1 \\ 1 & 0 & 0 & 0 \\ 1 & 0 & 0 & 0 \\ 1 & 0 & 0 & 0 \end{bmatrix}$$

C. Centralized

$$\begin{bmatrix} 1 & 1 & 1 & 1 \\ 0 & 0 & 0 & 0 \\ 0 & 0 & 0 & 0 \\ 0 & 0 & 0 & 0 \end{bmatrix} \text{ or } \begin{bmatrix} 1 & 0 & 0 & 0 \\ 1 & 0 & 0 & 0 \\ 1 & 0 & 0 & 0 \\ 1 & 0 & 0 & 0 \end{bmatrix}$$

D. Hierarchy

$$\begin{bmatrix} 0 & 1 & 0 & 0 \\ 0 & 0 & 1 & 0 \\ 0 & 0 & 0 & 1 \\ 0 & 0 & 0 & 0 \end{bmatrix}$$

E. Transitivity

$$\begin{bmatrix} 0 & 1 & 1 & 1 \\ 0 & 0 & 1 & 1 \\ 0 & 0 & 0 & 1 \\ 0 & 0 & 0 & 0 \end{bmatrix} \text{ or } \begin{bmatrix} 0 & 0 & 0 & 0 \\ 1 & 0 & 0 & 0 \\ 1 & 1 & 0 & 0 \\ 1 & 1 & 1 & 0 \end{bmatrix}$$

Fig. 10.8. Ideal images for blockmodels with more than two positions

of the other. Thus whenever one kind of tie is present from the row position to the column position, the second kind of tie is present from the column position to the row position. As we mentioned above, the property of structural balance can also be represented as a combination of two image matrices. To show structural balance, one image matrix for a relation of positive affect has ties within positions and another image matrix of negative affect has ties between positions.

10.4 Summary

When interpreting a blockmodel, the researcher should be able to use the several approaches described in this chapter to arrive at a consistent and theoretically meaningful statement about the positions in a network, the characteristics of actors in the positions, and how the positions are related to each other. That is, the interpretations from the different approaches should support, rather than contradict, each other.

In this chapter we have discussed the interpretation of blockmodels by examining the relations separately. However, in multirelational systems we need to be able to describe systematically the associations among relations. This leads us to the next chapter, which is on relational algebras.

11

Relational Algebras

In this chapter we turn from methods for analyzing properties of actors and social positions to methods for analyzing properties of relations and the associations among relations. The methods we discuss in this chapter are concerned with the theoretical notion of *social role*, where social role is conceptualized as regular patterns in the relations between social positions. Our focus is on formalization of social role in network terms. Following the scheme that we presented in Chapter 9 (Figure 9.1) as an overview of positional and role analysis, this chapter considers methods for "grouping" relations. We will be traversing the horizontal paths, both on the top and bottom of the figure. The methods in this chapter depend on the notions of social position and the mathematical property of structural equivalence that we discussed in Chapters 9 and 10. However, they take a different perspective by focusing on relations, rather than on actors or subsets of actors.

As we saw in the previous chapter, interpreting the results of a positional analysis can be quite complicated when the analysis includes more than one relation. Distinct interpretations for separate relations become tedious and at times ad hoc. It is useful to have a unified and consistent approach for describing and modeling multiple relations and the associations among these relations. Association among relations means that some relations tend to link the same actors, or that the presence of one relation implies the presence of a second relation.

In this chapter we discuss methods for describing the *role structure* of an entire group. These methods have been referred to as *global* role analyses (Boorman and White 1976) because they describe the associations among relations that hold for the entire group. Since these methods employ algebraic approaches, they are sometimes referred to as *role algebras* or *relational algebras*.

Network relational structures or relational algebras may be used to study structural theories that are stated in terms of relations and to compare network role structures across populations, or through time. Examples of studies that have used relational algebras include models of kinship systems (Boyd 1969; White 1963), studies of naturally occurring social groups (Boorman and White 1976; Boyd 1990), interactions in a scientific community (Light and Mullins 1979), and comparisons of elites in two different communities (Breiger 1979; Breiger and Pattison 1978).

The reader should be aware at the outset that this chapter contains some of the most sophisticated mathematics in this book. The models we discuss are quite abstract, in that they capture very general features of relational structures. They are also quite formal, and interpretation often requires a great leap of faith, some simplifying assumptions, and complicated mathematics. We have attempted to present these methods in as straightforward a manner as possible, without doing too much injustice to the underlying mathematics. The interested reader is encouraged to consult the references cited throughout the chapter for further elaboration of these ideas. The payoff of these methods is the ability to compare role structures across seemingly quite different populations or contexts.

11.1 Background

The theoretical notion of social role provides the motivation for the methods in this chapter. In Chapter 9 we discussed the distinction between network positions (as collections of actors who are involved in relations in similar ways) and network roles (as the patterns or associations among relations that link actors or positions). Thus, in network terms, social role refers to the associations among relations that link social positions.

The notion of social role has generated considerable theoretical attention, especially in sociology, social psychology, and anthropology (Linton 1936; Merton 1957; Nadel 1957). Although many theorists have attempted to bring some precision to the definition of social role, the theoretical work by Nadel and Merton has had the greatest influence on methods for the analysis of social network roles. Two aspects of Nadel's (1957) formulation of the role concept have been especially important for social network role methods. First, his derivation is explicitly *relational*, in that it is based on the regularities or patterns in the relationships among individuals. Second, Nadel attempts to formalize the notion of role using a set theoretic framework to describe the "internal structure of roles" as collections of "role attributes." Although this framework does not have the analytic precision necessary for formal network analysis, it does point toward a focus on the "interrelatedness or interlocking of the relationships" (page 17), a key feature of formal network role models.

Merton's (1957) discussion of role sets as "the complement of role relationships which persons have by virtue of occupying a particular social status" (1957, page 423) has also influenced the development of network role analysis (see also Boorman and White 1976). However, because of the focus on roles at the individual level, Merton's ideas are more important for understanding individual roles (which we discuss in detail in Chapter 12).

The generality of the role concept and the focus on associations among multiple relations can be seen in the earliest formal work on network roles. For example, White (1963) draws the analogy between a formal organization and certain kinship structures, and lays the groundwork for a program of research on formal role analysis. He notes "Primary roles can be cumulated into chains defining compound roles" (page 1), thus pointing toward a focus on associations among relations. He continues to outline the theoretical framework for the formal analysis, noting that in order for a society to operate, there must be some agreement on role obligations and

> ... there must be constraints on what set of primary roles can generate the structure of compound roles. (page 1)

White also notes the complementarity of roles and the collections of individuals who occupy similar social positions, which he calls "offices."

Kinship studies were the first substantive area for development of formal network role models (White 1963; Boyd 1969). In these studies, ties of marriage and descent were used to model marriage systems. However, as Boorman and White (1976) note, these kinship systems often "are less descriptions than brilliant ideologies of social structure evolved by aboriginal civilizations" (1976, page 388). In contrast, models of network role structures explicitly study concrete social structure.

Studying associations among relations in concrete social systems is the clear goal of network role studies. Lorrain and White (1971) state as their goal:

> ... to understand the interrelations among relations within concrete social groups. ... By interrelations among relations is meant the way in which relations among the members of a social system occur in characteristic bundles and how these bundles of relations interlock and determine one another. (page 49)

Formalizing the ideas of interrelatedness, interlocking, or bundles of relations is one goal of formal network role analysis. Thus, these methods are different from methods for network positions that focus on properties of subsets of actors. Network methods for social roles focus on relations and on the associations among these relations, rather than on network properties of actors or subsets of actors. These methods use algebraic systems for representing associations among relations in multirelational networks, and employ formal properties of these algebraic representations to quantify specific features of role structures.

In this chapter and the next we present formal network definitions for the notion of social role and show how this concept applies to the different levels of analysis of networks. In this chapter we explore descriptions of network role structures; that is, models for the role structure of the entire group or network. In Chapter 12 we discuss how this formal algebraic approach can be used to describe roles of individual actors.

We begin with a description of the algebraic concepts and operations that are used to build network role structures. We then discuss methods for simplifying network role structures to reveal simpler patterns. Finally we describe methods for comparing network role structures across populations.

11.2 Notation and Algebraic Operations

Relational algebras are most appropriate and most interesting for studying multirelational networks. In order to present methods and models for multiple relations, it is useful to employ *algebraic notation* rather than the sociometric and graph theoretic notations. Algebraic notation was introduced in Chapter 3.

The are two major differences between algebraic notation and sociometric notation. First we will refer to relations with distinct capital letters rather than subscripted $\mathscr{X}$'s. For example, we could use F to denote the relation "is a friend of" and E for the relation "is an enemy of." Second, we will record the presence of a tie from actor i to actor j on relation F as iFj. This is a simple translation of the notation we have been using to indicate "choices" as $i \rightarrow j$, except that here we are replacing the $\rightarrow$ with the letter label for the relation. We can think of this as $i \rightarrow j$ on the relation labeled F becoming $i \xrightarrow{F} j$, and then shortening this to iFj. For example, if we have the relation "is a friend of" labeled F, then we would record the tie implied by "i chooses j as a friend" as iFj.

In sociometric notation, iFj means that $x_{ij} = 1$ on the relation F, and implies that there is a "1" in row i column j of the sociomatrix for this relation. Algebraic notation is useful for dichotomous relations since it codes the presence of a tie. This limitation presents no problem for the models we describe in this chapter, since these models are defined only for dichotomous relations.

The advantages of this notation are that it allows us to distinguish several distinct relations using letter designations, and to record combinations of relations.

11.2.1 Composition and Compound Relations

Given the focus on multiple relations, it is important to define the combination of relations and the associations among them in formal terms. The building blocks for the combination of relations are *primitive relations* (or *generator relations*) and the operation of *composition* of relations.

A compound relation is the result of the combination of two (or more) relations defined by the operation of composition. Using algebraic notation for two dichotomous relations, U and T, we denote the compound relation as TU. We denote the operation of composition by $\circ$. The *compound relation* TU is the result of the operation of *composition* of relations, where the tie $i(T \circ U)j$ is present if there exists some actor k such that iTk and kUj. We will use a shorthand notation for the compound relation by dropping the "$\circ$", so that the result of $T \circ U$ will be denoted by TU. The relation TU is a dichotomous relation in which there is a tie from actor i to actor j if there is a tie from actor i to some actor k on relation T, and a tie from actor k to actor j on relation U. Equivalently, $i \xrightarrow{T} k \xrightarrow{U} j$ implies $i \xrightarrow{TU} j$, which we denote by $i(TU)j$.

Compound relations may be formed either from distinct relations (for example T and U) or from the composition of a relation with itself (for example UU). The compound relation resulting from the composition of relations is also a relation, and may be displayed either as a graph with arcs indicating ties that are present on the compound relation, or as a sociomatrix, where the (i, j)th element is equal to 1 if $i(TU)j$.

One can construct the sociomatrix for a compound relation using Boolean matrix multiplication, denoted by $\otimes$. This is ordinary matrix multiplication for binary matrices, with the condition that the (i, j)th element is equal to 1 if the result of ordinary matrix multiplication is greater than 0. To illustrate, let $\mathbf{X}_T$, $\mathbf{X}_U$, and $\mathbf{X}_{TU}$ be the sociomatrices for relations T, U, and the compound relation TU, respectively. We can express the sociomatrix for $\mathbf{X}_{TU}$ as the Boolean matrix product of $\mathbf{X}_U$ and $\mathbf{X}_T$:

$$\mathbf{X}_{UT} = \mathbf{X}_U \otimes \mathbf{X}_T.$$

In the sociomatrix $\mathbf{X}_{UT}$, the ijth entry $x_{ij(TU)} = 1$ if and only if

$$\sum_k x_{ikT} x_{kjU} > 0.$$

For given actors i and j, this sum is greater than 0 only if there is some actor k such that $x_{ikT} = 1$ and $x_{kjU} = 1$. In brief, ordinary matrix multiplication records in cell (i, j) of the sociomatrix for the matrix product the *number* of intermediary actors between i and j, whereas Boolean matrix multiplication records in cell (i, j) *whether or not* there are any intermediaries between i and j.

The composition of a relation with itself, for example $U \circ U$, results in the compound relation UU, in which $i(UU)j$ means that there is a sequence of actors and ties, starting with actor i and ending with actor j, and containing two ties; $i \xrightarrow{U} k \xrightarrow{U} j$. More generally, if we denote the composition of a relation U with itself c times by U^c ($U \circ U \circ \cdots \circ U$ for c U's) then $i(U^c)j$ means there exists some sequence of c ties connecting i to j. The sequence may include the same actor more than once (for example $i \xrightarrow{U} j \xrightarrow{U} k \xrightarrow{U} j \xrightarrow{U} i$) or may include the same tie more than once. Thus, the sequence is a walk but not necessarily a path (see Chapter 4). In many ways the operation of composition of relations builds on ideas such as connectivity, paths, walks, and reachability. However, the presence of a compound tie connecting two actors only indicates that there is a sequence of ties between them, not that the sequence has any special graph theoretic properties (such as being a path or a geodesic).

Let us look at an example of compound relations in terms of their graphs. Figure 11.1 presents graphs for two directional dichotomous relations and some compound relations that can be formed from them. Relation T contains ties aTb, aTc, and cTb, with d an isolate. Relation U has ties bUc and bUd, with a an isolate. The compound relation TU, defined by the composition of relations $T \circ U$, consists of ties between pairs of actors where the first actor in the pair has a tie on relation T to some intermediary, who has a tie to the second actor on relation U. For example, since aTb and bUd, the tie $a(TU)d$ is present on the compound relation TU. Similarly, since cTb and bUd, the tie $c(TU)d$ is

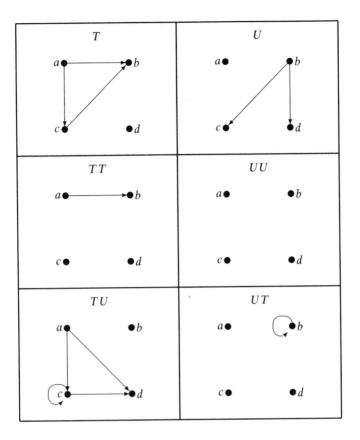

Fig. 11.1. Example of compound relations

present. Also the presence of the ties cTb and bUc implies a reflexive tie $c(TU)c$. Figure 11.1 also shows the compound relation UT, consisting of a single reflexive tie, $b(UT)b$. Notice that the relation UT is not the same as TU, illustrating the fact that composition of relations is not commutative.

Let us comment on a few important properties of compound relations. It is important to note that reflexive ties in compound relations can be quite important. For example, if we were studying the two relations, "gives money to" denoted by B, and "gives merchandise to" denoted by S, then the presence of a reflexive tie $i(BS)i$ on the compound relation BS would indicate that actor i gave money to some actor k who in turn gave merchandise back to actor i. This reflexive tie would indicate an exchange relation, in which actor i completed the exchange of money for merchandise.

Transitivity is an important property of some relations. A relation is *transitive* if whenever iTj and jTk, the tie iTk is present. Since we can express the compound relation iTj and jTk as $iTTk$, transitivity of a relation implies that all ties present in TT must be present in T. We will denote the inclusion operation by $\subseteq$. Thus if T includes all ties in TT, we write $TT \subseteq T$. To illustrate, consider the compound relation TT in Figure 11.1. TT consists of the single tie $a(TT)b$ implied by the ties aTc and cTb. This tie from a to b is also present in the relation T. Also, there are no ties in TT that are not present in T. Thus, the relation TT is fully contained in the relation T ($TT \subseteq T$) indicating that the relation T is transitive.

Other important structural properties, such as structural balance and the strength of weak ties hypothesis, can also be examined using composition of relations and compound relations.

We next describe some properties of the operation of composition of relations.

11.2.2 Properties of Composition and Compound Relations

There are several important things to note about the operation of composition of relations. We comment on these in this section.

First, the operation of composition of relations may be defined for sequences longer than two relations. These are constructed either with distinct relations (such as $TUVW$), or by "reusing" relations (for example, UUU). Examples of compound relations of long strings that might be socially meaningful include relations such as "a friend of a friend of a friend," or "a boss of a friend of a friend," or "mother's mother's mother." Each string of relations (letters) that forms a compound relation is referred to as a *word*, and the *length* of a word is the number of primitive relations in it. Analytically these long compound relations are computed through a series of operations of composition of two relations, for example, $(U \circ U) \circ U$, or through a series of Boolean matrix products.

Next, it may be the case that for a given network no ordered pairs of actors have ties on a particular compound relation. For example, the relation TU is empty or undefined in a given group if there are *no* actors i, j, and k such that iTk and kUj. In the example in Figure 11.1 the compound relation UU is empty. Sometimes it will be useful to denote an empty relation as $\emptyset$. For our hypothetical example, we could write $UU = \emptyset$. As a substantive example, in most kinship systems the compound relation "mother's wife" would be undefined. Empty compound relations may be transitory (for example, at a given point in time the relation "boss's friend" might be empty in a given corporation if the boss were a particularly foul-natured person). However, if a given compound relation were empty over a long period of time, it could indicate an important undefined social relation.

It is important to note that the operation of composition is not commutative. That is, it is not generally true that TU is equivalent (identical) to UT. If composition of relations was commutative, one would be able to say that a "mother's brother" is the same as a "brother's mother," or that a "boss's husband" is the same as a "husband's boss." It is probably the exceptional case in which these relations would be identical, and if they were identical, it would indicate a very interesting and important property of that relational structure.

Finally, the composition of relations in a given sequence or word with fixed order does not depend on the order in which the composition operations are carried out: $(T \circ U) \circ T = T \circ (U \circ T)$. In other words, the operation of composition is *associative*. This is an important mathematical property of the operation of composition that allows us to use powerful mathematical theories to model social relational structures.

The general idea of relational algebras is that we can start with a few primitive relations and generate compound relations. The collection of relations (including both primitive and compound relations) contains important features of a network role structure. The analytic problem is to simplify the information in this collection in order to present the basic patterns or regularities in the associations among relations as a description of the role structure of the network. In the next section we describe how to present relational algebras. We then discuss some ways to simplify the information in a role structure.

11.3 Multiplication Tables for Relations

We start with R *primitive* or *generator* relations. From these primitive relations we can create compound relations consisting of longer and longer strings of relations; that is, words with more and more letters. Each compound relation can also be presented as a graph or sociomatrix. Since we can continue to create words that are longer and longer, the strings of letters and thus the words could be infinite in length. However, since the number of actors, g, is finite, there are only a finite number of distinct graphs or sociomatrices that we could construct. Some of the compound relations must give rise to identical graphs. We will refer to a distinct graph as an *image* (see Boorman and White 1976; Pattison 1982). Lorrain and White (1971) refer to a distinct graph as a *morphism*.

Since there are g actors, there are g^2 possible ties for a directional dichotomous relation (if we assume that reflexive ties may be present). A tie may or may not be present for each of the g^2 ordered pairs of actors. Since there are two possible states for each tie (present or absent) there are 2^{g^2} possible images that can be created through the composition of relations. This is the same as the number of distinct labeled reflexive directed graphs or sociomatrices of size $g \times g$. Although this might certainly be a large number (for $g = 3$ there are $2^9 = 512$ possible images, for $g = 10$ there are $2^{100} = 1.2677 \times 10^{30}$) for finite g, there will be a finite number of images and thus a finite number of distinct compound relations. So, although we can construct words of infinite length, they will not give rise to an infinite number of images. Most compound relations will be identical to other compound relations or to the primitive relations.

Two compound relations that have the same images are said to be *equivalent*. They have exactly the same graph and sociomatrix, and contain exactly the same ties. Following Boorman and White's (1976) *axiom of quality*, compound relations that have the same image are *equated* and treated as a single entity in a relational analysis. For example, if we have the two relations, "is a friend of" and "is an enemy of" denoted F and E respectively, then if it were always the case that the compound relation FE (in words "is a friend's enemy") contained exactly the same ties as the relation E ("is an enemy of"), then the relation E and the compound relation FE would be equivalent, $FE = E$. Substantively we would say that all "friend's enemies" are "enemies," and all "enemies" are "friend's enemies." In a relational analysis, the primitive relation E and the compound relation FE would be treated as a single image.

Now, let us consider two possible collections of graphs (images). The first collection contains *all* words that could be constructed from a given set of primitive relations, regardless of whether the words give rise to equivalent images. We will refer to this collection as $\mathscr{S}^*$, and note that it contains an infinite number of primitive and compound relations. The second collection, which we will refer to as $\mathscr{S}$, contains only graphs that have distinct images. $\mathscr{S}$ contains all distinct primitive relations, plus those compound relations that can be formed from the primitive relations, and that produce images that are distinct from the primitive relations and distinct from other compound relations. To get the set $\mathscr{S}$ from the set $\mathscr{S}^*$ all graphs that are identical are equated, and are represented by a single image. We will denote the number of primitive and compound relations contained in $\mathscr{S}$ as R_S. Each image in the collection $\mathscr{S}$ "stands for" a number of primitive or compound relations (words) with identical images. Thus, each of the elements of $\mathscr{S}$ is an *equivalence class*, containing a collection of words that generate equivalent images. The collection $\mathscr{S}$ therefore has fewer elements than the collection $\mathscr{S}^*$. A useful way to think of the relationship between $\mathscr{S}$ and $\mathscr{S}^*$ is that $\mathscr{S}$ is a *partition* of $\mathscr{S}^*$ into R_S equivalence classes. Each equivalence class contains all words (primitive or compound relations) that have identical images.

The collection of relations $\mathscr{S}$ along with the operation of composition, $\circ$, is a *semigroup* (Boyd 1990; Pattison 1982, 1993). In general, a semigroup is a mathematical entity consisting of a set of objects and a binary operation that satisfies two important properties: it is closed under the operation, and the operation is associative. Thus, the set of relations, $\mathscr{S}$, and the operation of composition, $\circ$, form a semigroup. The result of the composition of any relations in the set is also in the set, and the operation is associative. For any relations (say T and U) in $\mathscr{S}$, the result of the composition of T and U, $T \circ U$, is also in $\mathscr{S}$. Also, for a given sequence of relations, the order in which the operation of composition is carried out does not matter: $U \circ (T \circ U) = (U \circ T) \circ U$.

11.3.1 Multiplication Tables and Relational Structures

One way to display the result of composition of relations for a given network is in a multiplication table. One reads this table like an ordinary multiplication table, though here the operation is composition ($\circ$), rather than the usual multiplication ($\times$). The elements of the set $\mathscr{S}$ are the labels for the rows and columns of the table, and each element in the body of this table is the result of the composition of the relation in the row followed by the relation in the column.

Figures 11.2 and 11.3 give an example for a hypothetical network. In Figure 11.2 we have expressed the images as graphs so that the results are more visible. Figure 11.3 contains the same table with letter designations for the relations. We begin with two primitive relations, H and L. The relation H resembles a three-level hierarchy. One could think of this as

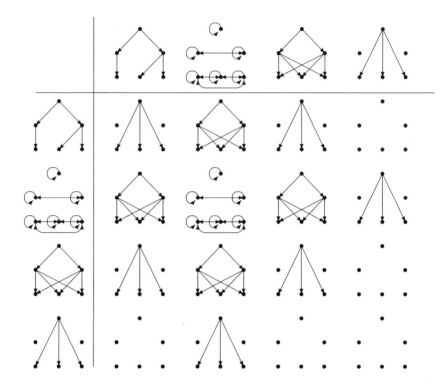

Fig. 11.2. Composition graph table for a hypothetical network

the relation "oversees the work of" in a three-level corporate hierarchy, or as the relation "is the parent of" in a three-generation family tree. The second relation, L, is a symmetric and reflexive relation with ties within levels of the hierarchy, or within generations of the family tree. One could think of this relation as "is at the same level as" or "could trade jobs with" in a corporation, or as "is the same generation as" in a family tree.

The first row and the first column in the table in Figure 11.2 list the R_S primitive and compound relations in $\mathscr{S}$ as graphs. In this example there are $R_S = 5$ distinct images: the primitive relations H and L, and three additional distinct compound relations HL, HH, and $\emptyset$. Thus, for this example, $\mathscr{S} = \{H, L, HL, HH, \emptyset\}$. For simplicity, we exclude $\emptyset$ from the multiplication table in Figure 11.2. The other four distinct images are represented by their graphs in the first row and column of the table. For example, the graph for the relation H is listed first followed by the graph for the relation L, and so on.

The entries in the body of this table are the result of composition of the relation in the row followed by the relation in the column. The entry in the first row and first column in the body of the table contains the result of the composition of H and H; $H \circ H = HH$. The compound relation HH has ties from the top (grandparent) generation to the bottom (grandchild) generation. This compound relation could be interpreted as "parent of a parent" or "boss of a boss." The entry in the second row and second column of the body of the table shows the compound relation LL. Notice that this is equivalent (identical) to the relation L, and so adds no new image to the table, or new entry to $\mathscr{S}$.

The compound relation HL (in the first row, second column of the body of the table) might be interpreted as "is the boss of a colleague of." The relation HL contains directed arrows from nodes in a given generation (level) to *all* nodes at the generation (level) immediately below. Notice that the relation HL is identical to the relation LH (though as we noted above, the operation of composition is not in general commutative). Relations HL and LH contain exactly the same ties, and thus have the same image. Also, notice the similarity between the relation HL (and LH) and the primitive relation H. All of the ties in H are also in HL. In other words, the relation H is a subset of the relation HL; $H \subset HL$. The major difference between the two relations is that H contains only some of the "intergenerational" or "interlevel" ties, whereas HL (and LH) contains *all* ties between successive generations. If H is viewed as a corporate hierarchy with two departments, and authority residing within departments, then HL (and LH) could be seen as generalized authority between adjacent levels, regardless of department. In terms of kinship, HL would represent a generalized parentage, for example in a kinship system in which all father's brothers are also called father (White 1963, page 13).

A relational structure is most commonly presented using the letters or numbers as labels for the images, rather than presenting the graphs. Figure 11.3 shows the relational structure from Figure 11.2 in terms of the letter labels for the five distinct images.

If the multiplication table contains all possible images that can result from the operation of composition on the primitive relations, then it is *closed* under the operation of composition. Thus, the relational structure

∘	H	L	HL	HH	∅
H	HH	HL	HH	∅	∅
L	HL	L	HL	HH	∅
HL	HH	HL	HH	∅	∅
HH	∅	HH	∅	∅	∅
∅	∅	∅	∅	∅	∅

Fig. 11.3. Multiplication table for a hypothetical network

$$S_1 = \{H\}$$
$$S_2 = \{L, LL, \ldots\}$$
$$S_3 = \{HL, LH, LHL, HLL, \ldots\}$$
$$S_4 = \{HH, HHL, LHH, HLH, HLHL, \ldots\}$$
$$S_5 = \{\emptyset, HHH, HLHH, HHHL, HHHH, \ldots\}$$

Fig. 11.4. Equivalence classes for a hypothetical multiplication table

in Figure 11.3 is closed, since all of the $R_S = 5$ distinct images (including the null image) that can be constructed from the primitive relations H and L are contained in the table. Such a table contains all of the information about the compound relations, since all possible compound relations that can be created will have images identical to one of the images in the table.

The information in the multiplication table also describes the set of equivalences among the relations; that is, the results of composition tell us which primitive or compound relations produce identical images. In Figure 11.3 there are $R_S = 5$ distinct images: H, L, HL, HH, and $\emptyset$. Any relation constructed from the composition of the relations H and L, in any combination and of any length, will be equivalent to one of these five images. Thus, the five images represent five equivalence classes, which we will denote by S_k for $k = 1, 2, \ldots, R_S$. Each equivalence class contains the collection of compound relations that generate identical images. These equivalences are shown in Figure 11.4. Each equivalence class includes the shortest word that generates the image, along with some, but not all, of the other words that generate the same image.

Boorman and White (1976) define the *role structure* of a network as the set of equations in the multiplication table. Since the equations in the multiplication table describe the equivalences among relations for the entire network, it is a description of the network level role structure.

It is important to note that relational algebras can be used to study either ties among actors in a sociomatrix (Boyd 1990) or ties among positions in a blockmodel (Boorman and White 1976). For simplicity,

∘	A	F	AF	FA	FF
A	A	AF	AF	A	AF
F	FA	FF	FF	FA	FF
AF	A	AF	AF	A	AF
FA	FA	FF	FF	FA	FF
FF	FA	FF	FF	FA	FF

Fig. 11.5. Multiplication table for advice and friendship, expressed as compound relations

we will illustrate relational algebras using image matrices for ties among positions. Since image matrices have fewer elements than the networks they represent, in general, relational algebras derived from image matrices are simpler than the relational algebras for entire networks.

We will now illustrate a multiplication table using two image matrices (from the blockmodel of the advice and friendship relations for Krackhardt's high-tech managers).

11.3.2 An Example

Now let us look at the role structure generated by the image matrices for the relations of advice and friendship for Krackhardt's high-tech managers. We will use the image matrices from the three-position blockmodel of advice, denoted by A, and friendship, denoted by F. This blockmodel was first described in Chapter 10. The images for advice and friendship in the three-position blockmodel are:

$$\begin{bmatrix} 0 & 1 & 1 \\ 0 & 1 & 1 \\ 0 & 0 & 0 \end{bmatrix} \text{ and } \begin{bmatrix} 1 & 0 & 1 \\ 0 & 0 & 0 \\ 1 & 1 & 1 \end{bmatrix}$$

labeled A and F respectively.

Figure 11.5 shows the multiplication table, and thus the role structure, generated by the images advice, A, and friendship, F. This multiplication table was adapted from an analysis using *UCINET IV* (Borgatti, Everett, and Freeman 1991). Composition of the relations A and F, in any combination, results in an additional three distinct images; so, there are $R_S = 2 + 3 = 5$ distinct images: $\mathscr{S} = \{A, F, AF, FA, FF\}$. We use shorthand labels to denote these images. Figure 11.6 shows these images.

$$
\begin{array}{c}
A \\
\begin{array}{ccc}
0 & 1 & 1 \\
0 & 1 & 1 \\
0 & 0 & 0
\end{array}
\end{array}
\qquad\qquad
\begin{array}{c}
F \\
\begin{array}{ccc}
1 & 0 & 1 \\
0 & 0 & 0 \\
1 & 1 & 1
\end{array}
\end{array}
$$

$$
\begin{array}{c}
AF \\
\begin{array}{ccc}
1 & 1 & 1 \\
1 & 1 & 1 \\
0 & 0 & 0
\end{array}
\end{array}
\qquad
\begin{array}{c}
FA \\
\begin{array}{ccc}
0 & 1 & 1 \\
0 & 0 & 0 \\
0 & 1 & 1
\end{array}
\end{array}
\qquad
\begin{array}{c}
FF \\
\begin{array}{ccc}
1 & 1 & 1 \\
0 & 0 & 0 \\
1 & 1 & 1
\end{array}
\end{array}
$$

Fig. 11.6. Image matrices for five distinct words formed from advice and friendship images

$$
\begin{aligned}
S_1 &= \{A, AA, AAA, AFA, AAAA, AAFA, AFAA, AFFA, \ldots\} \\
S_2 &= \{F\} \\
S_3 &= \{AF, AAF, AFF, AAAF, AAFF, AFAF, AFFF, \ldots\} \\
S_4 &= \{FA, FFA, FAA, FAAA, FAFA, FFAA, FFFA, \ldots\} \\
S_5 &= \{FF, FAF, FFF, FAAF, FFAF, FAFF, FFFF, \ldots\}
\end{aligned}
$$

Fig. 11.7. Equivalence classes for multiplication role table of advice and friendship

The multiplication table in Figure 11.5 is closed under the operation of composition. Any relation constructed from the relations A and F, in any combination and of any length, will be equivalent to one of these five images. The five images thus represent five equivalence classes. These equivalence classes are given in Figure 11.7, along with some of the words that also generate the same image. This set of equations expresses the fact that the role structure describes a partition of the set of all possible words (compound relations) that could be constructed from the primitive relations. We will often refer to the class by the shortest word that generates its image. For example, we refer to S_3 as AF since the compound relation AF is the shortest word that generates the image to which all members of this class are equivalent.

Let us note some interesting features of this role structure. First notice that the equation $AA = A$ implies that advice is transitive in this network since $AA \subseteq A$. It is also true that $A \subseteq AA$. In addition, this equation implies that $A^c = A$ for all c. The equation $FF = F$ does not hold. Also, since $FF \not\subseteq F$ friendship is not transitive. However, the equation $FFF = FF$ implies that $F^c = F^2$ for $c \geq 2$. So, composition of any

∘	1	2	3	4	5
1	1	3	3	1	3
2	4	5	5	4	5
3	1	3	3	1	3
4	4	5	5	4	5
5	4	5	5	4	5

Fig. 11.8. Multiplication table for advice and friendship

sequence of A's generates an image identical to A, and composition of any sequence of two or more F's generates an image identical to FF. The set of equivalence classes also reveals another interesting property of this role structure. If we examine the list of equivalence classes in Figure 11.7 we see that within each equivalence class all words both begin with the same letter and end with the same letter. These properties will be helpful in simplifying and interpreting role structures.

Although the multiplication table in Figure 11.5 is informative, since it expresses the equations among compound relations, it is often useful to display this information using more abstract labels (such as numbers rather than words) for the compound relations.

Figure 11.8 shows the same role table as in Figure 11.5, but with the compound relations labeled with the numbers 1 to 5 (the subscripts for the equivalence classes, S_k). Thus, we have used the indices for the equivalence classes from Figure 11.7 to represent the images in the table. The role table is especially useful for displaying the general features of the role structure, for simplifying role tables, and for comparing tables across groups (a topic we discuss below).

Looking at the rows of Figure 11.8 one can see that there are two sets of rows that contain identical entries: rows 1 and 3 are identical, as are rows 2, 4, and 5. This shows that there are two subsets of images that operate similarly when they are the first element in a compound relation. Now, looking at columns, we see that there are also two subsets of columns that are identical: 1 and 4 are identical, as are 2, 3, and 5. Notice that these subsets of similar columns are not the same as the subsets of similar rows. When we discuss the simplification of role tables the fact that certain images operate in the same way will be helpful for constructing simplified tables.

In practice, if we were to include all distinct primitive and compound relations that could be formed through the operation of composition most tables would be quite large and complicated. The problem then is to "extract" the essence of the structure and simplify this table into some reduced or simpler form that preserves the main patterns in the original table. This is a *simplification* or *reduction* of the table. How we go about simplifying a role table is the topic of the next section.

11.4 Simplification of Role Tables

In Lorrain and White's (1971) words, one of the goals of formal role and positional analysis is to

> ... understand the interrelations among relations within concrete social groups ... [where] by understanding is meant distilling simpler patterns at a higher level of abstraction — simpler not only in having fewer constituents but also in exhibiting interrelations which are more regular or transparent. (1971, page 49)

This approach is also found in the work of Boorman and White (1976) and Pattison (1981, 1982, 1993). In this section we describe strategies for simplifying role structures. We will first describe strategies based on the similarity of the individual images in the role table. We then describe strategies for simplifying a role table as a whole. The reader should consult Boorman and White (1976), Boyd (1969, 1990), Lorrain and White (1971), Pattison (1981, 1982, 1993), and others for further elaboration of the ideas discussed in this section.

The key to simplifying a role structure is to reduce the number of distinct elements (words or images) that it contains while preserving important properties of the structure. The simplified role structure thus has fewer elements than the original role structure, but contains patterns that "tend" to hold in the original structure (Pattison 1993). Since the role structure of the group is expressed in the multiplication table, a simplification of a role structure will also be a simplification of the multiplication table. The basic strategy for simplifying a role structure is to propose *equations* among words or elements of the original structure. This simplification gives rise to a reduced table in which elements that were distinct in the original table are represented by a single new entity in the reduced table. The simpler role structure can be expressed in a new, simpler table.

Any simplification of a role table that equates images involves the assignment of each of the images, $\mathscr{S} = \{S_1, S_2, \dots S_{R_S}\}$, in the original table, to one of a set of classes of images $\mathscr{Q} = \{Q_1, Q_2, \dots Q_{R_Q}\}$ in the reduced table where R_S is the number of images in the original structure and R_Q is the number of images in the simplified structure, and $R_Q < R_S$. The simplification of the table is an onto mapping from $\mathscr{S}$ to $\mathscr{Q}$. Each image in $\mathscr{S}$ is assigned to a class of images in $\mathscr{Q}$, and every class in $\mathscr{Q}$ has at least one image from $\mathscr{S}$ assigned to it. We will denote this mapping by ψ, where $\psi : \mathscr{S} \rightarrow \mathscr{Q}$, and $\psi(S_i) = Q_k$ means that image S_i is assigned to class Q_k. The set of classes in the simplification $\mathscr{Q}$ thus defines a *partition* of the images in $\mathscr{S}$.

The role table and its set of equivalences, $\mathscr{S}$, is a partition and simplification of the entire collection of words that could be constructed from the composition of relations, $\mathscr{S}^*$. For example the equivalence classes in Figure 11.7 express a mapping of some of the elements of $\mathscr{S}^*$ to $\mathscr{S}$ for the example of advice and friendship. Now, suppose we wish to reduce further the set $\mathscr{S}$ by equating more images. The reduction of the role table is a partition of the distinct images, $\mathscr{S}$, into a smaller collection of classes, $\mathscr{Q}$. Several different strategies have been proposed for simplifying role structures. It turns out, however, that for a given table there may be many different possible reductions and there may be no "best" reduction. In the following sections we discuss two general strategies for simplifying role structures. The first strategy focuses on the substantive or sociometric similarity of images in the role structure. The second strategy is based on simplifying the multiplication table that expresses the composition of relations.

11.4.1 Simplification by Comparing Images

One goal of simplification and reduction of a multiplication table is to add further equations among pairs or collections of images (or words) to reduce the total number of distinct elements in the table. In this section we discuss two strategies for deciding which words (or images) to equate based on the similarity of the images. The first strategy focuses on the meaning or substance of the relations that generate the images. The second strategy focuses on the similarity of images based on the ties they share or the ways in which the images form compound relations. Lorrain and White (1971) refer to these as the *substantive* and the *sociometric* approaches, respectively.

The substantive strategy focuses on the content, substance, or meaning of the relations included in the structure. If the researcher expects that certain primitive and/or compound relations are the same in meaning, or should operate similarly in a given population, then one might equate these relations, even if they do not contain exactly the same ties. For example, if one were studying affective relations in a small group, it might be reasonable to expect that the compound relation "friend of a friend" would be quite similar to the simple relation "friend" (friends' friends are also friends). In practice, however, the equation might not be perfect, since some friends' friends might not also be friends.

On the other hand, the sociometric approach equates images if they contain similar ties even though they might be quite different in substance or meaning (Boorman and White 1976). Following this approach, images are viewed as similar if the ties contained in them connect the same individuals (or the same sets of individuals). There are at least two approaches to assessing sociometric similarity. One approach is to use a correlation coefficient to measure the association among the relations (see Boyd 1989, 1990). Images that are strongly correlated are equated. This is the strategy used by Boyd (1989, 1990) to simplify a role structure based on sociomatrices rather than on blockmodel images.

A second way to assess similarity is to equate images if one image is a subset of the other. If all the ties in one relation are also present in the second, then the second image *contains* or *includes* the first image. A useful way to study inclusions is to use an *inclusion ordering* of relations (Boorman and White 1976; Light and Mullins 1979; Bonacich and McConaghy 1979; Pattison 1993). An inclusion ordering expresses the associations among relations in terms of the property of containment. One image, say U, is *contained in* a second image, say V, if all ties that are present in U are also present in V (though V may have ties that U does not have). If U is contained in V we write $U \subseteq V$, indicating that the ties in U are a subset of the ties in V. The inclusions among the images can be expressed in a diagram in which there is a vertical line or sequence of lines descending from one image to another image if the higher image *contains* the lower images. The relation $\subseteq$ is reflexive, antisymmetric, and transitive, and thus defines a partial order on the set of images (see Chapter 8).

To illustrate, consider five images for the role structure generated by the images advice and friendship for Krackhardt's high-tech managers. These images were presented in Figure 11.6. Figure 11.9 displays all of the inclusions that are present among these five images. In this figure there is a vertical line down from AF to A, indicating that the image for A is contained in the image for AF. Similarly, both FA and F are contained in FF.

Inclusion orderings can be used to simplify role structures by suggesting which subsets of images might be treated similarly (and thus equated).

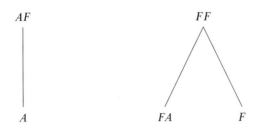

Fig. 11.9. Inclusion ordering for the images from role structure of advice and friendship

In the example of advice and friendship for Krackhardt's high-tech managers, the inclusion ordering in Figure 11.9 suggests that A is similar to AF and both FA and F are similar to FF.

The sociometric and the substantive strategies for simplifying role structures are based on an image by image comparison. However, as Boorman and White (1976) comment, there

> ... are strong grounds for rejecting a case-by-case approach to equations ... and instead developing ways of treating entire tables as integrated structures. (pages 1399–1400)

In the next section we describe a method for simplifying a role table as whole.

11.4.2 ⊗*Homomorphic Reduction*

Since a role structure might be quite complex, including many images that are associated in ways that are difficult to perceive and difficult to interpret substantively, it is important to be able to simplify the structure so that, in the words of Light and Mullins, "... the essential structural properties [become] apparent" (1979, page 104). We start by defining a condition that should hold for any "good" simplification, and then work through some examples. The mathematical notion that we employ is a *homomorphic reduction*, which we define below. The simplification of a role table involves reducing the number images by assigning subsets of images to the same class in the reduced table, and then studying the table to see whether or not any theoretically important patterns are present in the reduced table.

$\circ$	1	3	2	4	5
1	1	3	3	1	3
3	1	3	3	1	3
2	4	5	5	4	5
4	4	5	5	4	5
5	4	5	5	4	5

Fig. 11.10. Permuted and partitioned multiplication table for advice and friendship

The criterion for simplification of a role table is that the simplified table should preserve the operation of composition of relations. More formally the simplification should be a *homomorphic image* or *homomorphic reduction* of the original role table (Bonacich 1989; Boorman and White 1976; Lorrain and White 1971; Kim and Roush 1984; Pattison 1993).

Definition. A *homomorphic reduction* of a role table is an onto mapping, $\psi : \mathcal{S} \to \mathcal{Q}$, from the collection $\mathcal{S} = \{S_1, S_2, \ldots S_{R_S}\}$ to classes $\mathcal{Q} = \{Q_1, Q_2, \ldots Q_{R_Q}\}$ that preserves the operation of composition. We use the notation $\psi(S_r) = Q_q$ to indicate that S_r is assigned to class Q_q. A mapping, ψ, is a homomorphism if $\psi(S_r) \circ \psi(S_s) = \psi(S_r \circ S_s)$. Thus, the operation of composition is preserved.

Examples. We now return to the role table of advice and friendship in Figure 11.5 and examine some homomorphic reductions of the table. In the previous section we examined the multiplication table for the relations of advice and friendship in Figure 11.8 and noticed that the elements in some rows, and the elements in some columns, produced similar compound relations. We can now use these similarities in simplifying the role table.

First let us group the rows (and simultaneously the columns) of the table so that rows that produce nearly identical results are adjacent to each other. Figure 11.10 contains the same multiplication table as Figure 11.8, but with the rows, and simultaneously the columns, permuted so that images that operate similarly as the first element in a compound relation are adjacent. This table is expressed using number labels for the images, as in Figure 11.8, and shows one way that the five images may be partitioned into two classes. In terms of the original equivalence classes in Figure 11.7 and the images they include, this reduction proposes the following equations:

∘	(1)	(2)
(1)	(1)	(1)
(2)	(2)	(2)

Fig. 11.11. Homomorphic reduction of the role table for advice and friendship

$$Q_1 = \{S_1, S_3\} = \{A, AF\}$$
$$Q_2 = \{S_2, S_4, S_5\} = \{F, FA, FF\}$$

We can now present a new multiplication table using these two equivalence classes. We use the subscripts for the Q's as the labels. Also, we put these labels in parentheses to indicate that they are not the same entities as in the original multiplication table, but rather indicate classes of entities. This further reduced role table for advice and friendship is presented in Figure 11.11. This reduction can be displayed in a multiplication table that is identical in form to the usual multiplication table, but which has the equivalence classes, Q's, as elements.

This reduction is in fact a homomorphic reduction, since it satisfies the conditions of the definition; $\psi(S_r) \circ \psi(S_s) = \psi(S_r \circ S_s)$. To illustrate, consider images S_1 (A) and S_2 (F) in the original table. If the reduction is a homomorphic reduction, it must be the case that $\psi(S_1 \circ S_2) = \psi(S_1) \circ \psi(S_2)$. To check we see that $S_1 \circ S_2 = S_3$ and $\psi(S_3) = Q_1$. This is the same as $\psi(S_1) \circ \psi(S_2)$, since $\psi(S_1) = Q_1$, $\psi(S_2) = Q_2$, and $Q_1 \circ Q_2 = Q_1$. In order for the reduction to be a homomorphic reduction, this property must hold for all S_r, S_s.

Returning to the role table for the homomorphic reduction, presented in Figure 11.11, we see that the pattern in this table is quite simple. The composition of any two elements always results in an element that is in the same class as the first element of the composition. This table expresses the *first letter law* (Boorman and White 1976).

As we mentioned above, there may be more than one homomorphic reduction of a given role table. For the example of advice and friendship, if we focus on similarities among columns in the table in Figure 11.8, we are led to a different simplification than if we focus on rows. This second set of equations, which is also a homomorphic reduction, is:

$$Q_1 = \{S_1, S_4\} = \{A, FA\}$$
$$Q_2 = \{S_2, S_3, S_5\} = \{F, AF, FF\}$$

We present the permuted and partitioned multiplication table in Fig-

∘	1	4	2	3	5
1	1	1	3	3	3
4	4	4	5	5	5
2	4	4	5	5	5
3	1	1	3	3	3
5	4	4	5	5	5

Fig. 11.12. A second permuted and partitioned multiplication table for advice and friendship

∘	(1)	(2)
(1)	(1)	(2)
(2)	(1)	(2)

Fig. 11.13. A second homomorphic reduction of the role table for advice and friendship

ure 11.12 and the reduced multiplication table for this simplification in Figure 11.13. In this reduced table the composition of any two elements results in an element that is in the same class as the second element in the composition. This table satisfies the *last letter law* (Boorman and White 1976).

A few comments about these reductions are in order. In the first reduction notice that each class contains words that begin with the same letter: Q_1 contains words beginning with A, and Q_2 contains words beginning with F. This is consistent with the observation that the role table for this reduction satisfies the first letter law. In contrast, in the second reduction, each of these equivalence classes contains words that have the same last letter. Q_1 contains words ending in A whereas Q_3 contains words ending in F. This is consistent with the last letter law.

Interpretation. Role structures that are expressed in reduced tables, such as the two class models in Figures 11.11 and 11.13, can have theoretically important interpretations that can be expressed in *target tables*. Boorman and White (1976) describe several such target tables. The first letter and last letter tables (that we mentioned above) are examples of target tables. These patterns might result from the reduction of a rather complex role structure, even when the relations are quite different in substance from the relations of advice and friendship that we have been studying. Boorman and White give the following interpretations for the first letter table:

By the First Letter table, any compound word of whatever length is equated to the generator which occurs first in the word (that is, leftmost). A substantive interpretation is that any type of indirect bond [tie] takes on the quality of the direct tie to the first intermediary. ... The First Letter table, or a refinement of it, is often found when one primitive is for an objective, though positive, sort of tie (e.g., similar policy), whereas the other denotes positive affect: thus one's tie to any kind of contact of one's business associate takes on the color of a business association, whereas one views in affective terms any kind of contact through a friend. (1976, pages 1413–1414)

In the example of advice and friendship for Krackhardt's high-tech managers, the first letter law shows that compound relations with advice as the first relation operate like advice relations, and compound relations with friendship as the first relation operate like friendship relations. On the other hand, the last letter table indicates that the compound relation takes on the quality of the final letter in the word, or the final relation in the sequence.

Other target tables can represent different structural properties, such as Granovetter's (1973, 1982) *strength of weak ties* hypothesis. In terms of the composition of relations, this hypothesis states that the combination of two substantively strong ties should be a strong tie ($S \circ S = S$), whereas the combination of two weak ties, or a weak and a strong tie, will be a weak tie ($S \circ W = W \circ S = W \circ W = W$). Breiger and Pattison (1978) use this idea to evaluate the role structures for two communities' elites.

In the next section we discuss how relational algebras can be used to compare role structures across populations.

11.5 ⊗Comparing Role Structures

A role structure is a quite general description of how relations are associated in a network, independent of the particular individuals involved. Since the role structure is stated in terms of relations, if the same relations are measured on two or more different networks we can compare the role structures by comparing their role tables, even though the actors in the two groups are different. Networks in which relations are associated in similar ways will have similar role structures. In this section we discuss how to compare role structures.

The goals in comparing role structures are:

(i) To describe the similar features of the structures
(ii) To measure the degree of similarity between the structures

It is important to note that we can only compare role structures from different networks if the same, or at least comparable, relations generate both of the role structures. That is, the substantive meaning of the primitive relations in both networks must be the same. As a first step in our comparison we must establish a correspondence between the relations. For example, friendship can be measured in two networks. However, even if the relations in the two networks are not identical, it may be possible to argue that they are the same in meaning or content. For example, one might have the relation "is a friend of" measured in one network, and the relation "likes" in the other.

The first goal in comparing role structures is to describe formally the patterns or features that are shared by the two role structures. These similar features of the role structures are expressed in the multiplication tables and their semigroups.

Recall that a role structure is defined as the set of equations among relations as expressed in a role table. The role structure $\mathscr{S}$ consists of a set of distinct images, and a description of which words give rise to the same image. Whereas the collection $\mathscr{S}^*$ is the set of all possible words that could be formed from the primitive relations, the collection $\mathscr{S}$ for a particular network describes all words that give rise to identical images in that network. If two networks have the same set of primitive relations, then they will have the same collection $\mathscr{S}^*$ (the set of all possible images). However, the words (compound relations) that give rise to identical images and the role structures (expressed in the multiplication tables) may be different in the two networks.

For two distinct networks, with actor sets $\mathscr{N}$ and $\mathscr{M}$, let us denote the set of equations that hold in each network as $\mathscr{S}_{\mathscr{N}}$ and $\mathscr{S}_{\mathscr{M}}$, respectively. To compare role structures, we will compare the equations expressed in $\mathscr{S}_{\mathscr{N}}$ and $\mathscr{S}_{\mathscr{M}}$. For example, if the relation "is a friend of," denoted by F, is measured in both networks, and if the equation $F = FF$ holds in both networks, then the two networks share part of their role structure. On the other hand, if the equation $F = FF$ holds in one network but not in the other, then the two role structures differ to some extent. To compare role structures we must examine and compare entire sets of equations in a systematic way. Comparing role structures thus involves comparing the multiplication tables and the partitions of $\mathscr{S}^*$ induced by the two role structures, $\mathscr{S}_{\mathscr{N}}$ and $\mathscr{S}_{\mathscr{M}}$.

There are two alternative notions of what is meant by "shared" structure. On the one hand, some researchers argue that what is shared by two role structures is the set of associations among relations that hold in either one group *or* the other; that is, patterns that tend to hold in general in the two role structures. The joint homomorphic reduction of a role table (which we define below) studies the structure that is shared using this idea (Boorman and White 1976; Breiger and Pattison 1978; Breiger 1979; and Pattison 1981, 1982; 1993). On the other hand, some researchers argue that what is shared between two role structures is only those associations among relations that hold in *both* groups. The common structure semigroup studies the structure that is shared by two role structures using this second idea (Bonacich and McConaghy 1979; McConaghy 1981a, 1981b). We will describe each of these strategies and then illustrate both of them with an example.

11.5.1 Joint Homomorphic Reduction

In their foundational paper on role algebras, Boorman and White (1976) proposed the joint homomorphic reduction of two role structures as a way to compare two role structures and to summarize the features that they share. More recently authors have used this approach for comparing role structures from different groups (Breiger and Pattison 1978), from the same group at different times (Breiger 1979), or for comparing individual roles (Breiger and Pattison 1986) (see Chapter 12).

As defined above, $\mathscr{S}_{\mathscr{N}}$ is the role structure of the group with actor set $\mathscr{N}$ and $\mathscr{Q}_{\mathscr{N}}$ is a homomorphic reduction of $\mathscr{S}_{\mathscr{N}}$. We will let $R_{S_{\mathscr{N}}}$ and $R_{Q_{\mathscr{N}}}$ be the number of images in $\mathscr{S}_{\mathscr{N}}$ and $\mathscr{Q}_{\mathscr{N}}$, respectively. Similarly, $\mathscr{S}_{\mathscr{M}}$ is the role structure of the group with actor set $\mathscr{M}$ and $\mathscr{Q}_{\mathscr{M}}$ is a homomorphic reduction of $\mathscr{S}_{\mathscr{M}}$, with $R_{S_{\mathscr{M}}}$ and $R_{Q_{\mathscr{M}}}$ images, respectively.

The joint homomorphic reduction of two role structures is the most refined (least coarse) role structure that is a homomorphic reduction of both. More formally, we define the *joint homomorphic reduction* of $\mathscr{S}_{\mathscr{N}}$ and $\mathscr{S}_{\mathscr{M}}$ as the role structure $\mathscr{Q}_{\mathscr{N}\mathscr{M}}^{\mathrm{JNT}}$ that is a simultaneously homomorphic reduction of both $\mathscr{S}_{\mathscr{N}}$ and $\mathscr{S}_{\mathscr{M}}$, and is the most refined such role structure. We will denote the number of classes in $\mathscr{Q}_{\mathscr{N}\mathscr{M}}^{\mathrm{JNT}}$ by $R_{\mathscr{N}\mathscr{M}}^{\mathrm{JNT}}$. By most "refined" role structure, we mean that structure containing the largest number of distinct elements. In other words, since there may be more than one homomorphic reduction of a given role structure, there may also be more than one role structure that is a homomorphic reduction of two role structures. The joint homomorphic reduction, $\mathscr{Q}_{\mathscr{N}\mathscr{M}}^{\mathrm{JNT}}$, is that role structure that is a homomorphic reduction of both $\mathscr{S}_{\mathscr{N}}$ and $\mathscr{S}_{\mathscr{M}}$, and contains the largest number of classes.

The joint homomorphic reduction specifies two mappings, $\psi_{\mathscr{N}}$: $\mathscr{S}_{\mathscr{N}} \to \mathscr{Q}^{\text{JNT}}_{\mathscr{N}\mathscr{M}}$ and $\psi_{\mathscr{M}}$: $\mathscr{S}_{\mathscr{M}} \to \mathscr{Q}^{\text{JNT}}_{\mathscr{N}\mathscr{M}}$. Each of these mappings is a homomorphism as defined above, and thus preserves the operation of composition. The joint homomorphic reduction specifies both a partition of the images in each of the original role structures, and a new multiplication table that is a reduction of each of the original multiplication tables.

Since the joint homomorphic reduction is a reduction of each role structure, it will (probably) be a coarser partition of $\mathscr{S}^*$ (the collection of all possible compound relations) than either $\mathscr{S}_{\mathscr{N}}$ or $\mathscr{S}_{\mathscr{M}}$. $\mathscr{Q}^{\text{JNT}}_{\mathscr{N}\mathscr{M}}$ will (probably) have fewer classes than either $\mathscr{S}_{\mathscr{N}}$ or $\mathscr{S}_{\mathscr{M}}$. However, $\mathscr{Q}^{\text{JNT}}_{\mathscr{N}\mathscr{M}}$ has more classes than any other homomorphic reduction of both role structures.

As Boorman and White (1976) observe, the joint homomorphic reduction of two role structures is "... the result of imposing the union of all equations implied by each of the multiplication tables ..." (1976, page 1421). It contains all equations among words that hold in either one group or the other. It is therefore a simplification of both role structures, and it probably has fewer elements than either of the original role structures. Since the joint homomorphic reduction is based on the union of the role structures, it may contain equations among images that hold in only one group, or perhaps hold in neither group.

The joint homomorphic reduction, as originally defined by Boorman and White (1976) and as presented here, is a reduction of the role tables that preserves the operation of composition. More recently, Pattison (1993) has developed a complementary approach to homomorphic reduction of relational algebras that preserves the property of inclusions among images in the network. Both of these approaches have the goal of representing the essential features that are shared between role structures.

An alternative approach to comparing role structures is presented by Bonacich and McConaghy.

11.5.2 The Common Structure Semigroup

Bonacich and McConaghy argue that what is "shared" between two role structures is the set of equations among compound relations (words) that hold in *both* role structures (Bonacich 1979; Bonacich and McConaghy 1979; McConaghy 1981a, 1981b).

The *common structure semigroup* of two role structures is the least refined role structure of which both original role structures are homomorphic reductions. The common structure semigroup of $\mathscr{S}_{\mathcal{N}}$ and $\mathscr{S}_{\mathcal{M}}$ is denoted by $\mathscr{Q}_{\mathcal{N}\mathcal{M}}^{\mathrm{CSS}}$ and has $R_{\mathcal{N}\mathcal{M}}^{\mathrm{CSS}}$ classes. We have two homomorphic reductions (or mappings): $\psi_{\mathcal{N}} : \mathscr{Q}_{\mathcal{N}\mathcal{M}}^{\mathrm{CSS}} \rightarrow \mathscr{S}_{\mathcal{N}}$ from the common structure semigroup, $\mathscr{Q}_{\mathcal{N}\mathcal{M}}^{\mathrm{CSS}}$, to role structure $\mathscr{S}_{\mathcal{N}}$, and $\psi_{\mathcal{M}} : \mathscr{Q}_{\mathcal{N}\mathcal{M}}^{\mathrm{CSS}} \rightarrow \mathscr{S}_{\mathcal{M}}$ from $\mathscr{Q}_{\mathcal{N}\mathcal{M}}^{\mathrm{CSS}}$ to $\mathscr{S}_{\mathcal{M}}$. Both of the role structures $\mathscr{S}_{\mathcal{N}}$ and $\mathscr{S}_{\mathcal{M}}$ are homomorphic reductions of the common structure semigroup, and the common structure semigroup is the least refined such structure (it has the fewest number of classes) for which both $\mathscr{S}_{\mathcal{N}}$ and $\mathscr{S}_{\mathcal{N}}$ are homomorphic reductions.

In the common structure semigroup, elements are in the same class if and only if they are in the same class in both partitions. The common structure semigroup contains only those equations which hold in both groups, so it is therefore (probably) a more refined partition of $\mathscr{S}^*$ than either $\mathscr{S}_{\mathcal{N}}$ or $\mathscr{S}_{\mathcal{M}}$.

Both the joint homomorphic reduction and the common structure semigroup are ways to compare role structures from different groups. Researchers have argued the merits of both approaches. The debate is contained in the series of papers by Boorman and White (1976), Arabie and Boorman (1979), Breiger and Pattison (1978), Pattison (1981, 1982), on the one hand, and Bonacich (1979), Bonacich and McConaghy (1979), and McConaghy (1981a, 1981b), on the other. The major points of contrast in these two sets of papers are the meaning of "shared" structure and the meaning of "simplified" representation of a role structure.

11.5.3 An Example

Let us now look at an example to illustrate comparison of role structures between two groups. We will continue to consider the role structure of advice and friendship for Krackhardt's high-tech managers (see Figures 11.5 and 11.8). For comparison we will use a role structure for a classic social network data set: Roethlisberger and Dickson's Bank Wiring room (Roethlisberger and Dickson 1961). These data were collected through an extensive observational study of an electrical bank wiring department in the Western Electric Company, Hawthorne Works. We will refer to these data as the *Bank Wiring room network*. A department of fourteen workers, including wiremen, solderers, and inspectors, was observed for a period of one year. Researchers recorded the presence of six relations among the fourteen men: participation in games, arguments about opening/closing windows in the room, trading jobs, helping another person with a job, friendship, and antagonism. Each relation was recorded as a sociogram indicating the observers' judgments about the presence or absence of ties between pairs of men on each of the six relations. In their paper on blockmodels, White, Boorman, and Breiger (1976) analyzed five relations from these data (excluding the relation of trading jobs), and produced a six-position blockmodel. We will use image matrices from this blockmodel to construct the role structure for the Bank Wiring room.

To compare the role structure of the Bank Wiring room with Krackhardt's high-tech managers, we first must select two relations that correspond to the advice and friendship relations for Krackhardt's high-tech managers. To start, we will use the friendship relation for the Bank Wiring room as comparable to the friendship relation for Krackhardt's high-tech managers. Next, we will use the helping relation in the Bank Wiring room as comparable to the advice relation among the high-tech managers. In both the helping and advice relations, work-related aid is being given from one worker to another.

As images of the relations of friendship and helping for the Bank Wiring room, we use the blockmodel image matrices from White, Boorman, and Breiger's (1976, page 755) blockmodel analysis of this network. These images are:

$$
\begin{bmatrix}
1 & 1 & 1 & 0 & 1 & 1 \\
1 & 0 & 0 & 0 & 0 & 0 \\
1 & 0 & 0 & 0 & 0 & 0 \\
0 & 1 & 0 & 1 & 1 & 1 \\
1 & 0 & 0 & 1 & 1 & 1 \\
1 & 0 & 0 & 1 & 0 & 1
\end{bmatrix}
\text{ and }
\begin{bmatrix}
1 & 1 & 0 & 0 & 1 & 0 \\
1 & 0 & 0 & 0 & 0 & 0 \\
0 & 0 & 0 & 0 & 0 & 0 \\
0 & 0 & 0 & 1 & 1 & 0 \\
1 & 0 & 0 & 1 & 0 & 0 \\
0 & 0 & 0 & 0 & 0 & 0
\end{bmatrix}
$$

for helping and friendship, respectively. We have transposed the image matrix for helping presented in White, Boorman, and Breiger, since the direction of the original relation went from row positions to column positions. For comparability with advice for Krackhardt's high-tech managers, we need to have job-related aid going from column positions to row positions.

The multiplication table for helping and friendship is presented in Figure 11.14. We used *UCINET IV* (Borgatti, Everett, and Freeman 1991) to generate this multiplication table. We present this table with number labels for the images: helping is A, labeled 1, and friendship is F, labeled 2. Composition of helping and friendship resulted in an additional eight images, for a role structure with $R_{S_{\mathcal{A}}} = 10$ total images. We will compare this role structure with the role structure for

∘	1	2	3	4	5	6	7	8	9	10
A	1	3	4	7	8	7	8	7	8	7	8
F	2	5	6	9	10	9	10	9	10	9	10
AA	3	7	8	7	8	7	8	7	8	7	8
AF	4	7	8	7	8	7	8	7	8	7	8
FA	5	9	10	9	10	9	10	9	10	9	10
FF	6	9	10	9	10	9	10	9	10	9	10
AAA	7	7	8	7	8	7	8	7	8	7	8
AAF	8	7	8	7	8	7	8	7	8	7	8
FAA	9	9	10	9	10	9	10	9	10	9	10
FAF	10	9	10	9	10	9	10	9	10	9	10

Fig. 11.14. Multiplication table for helping (A) and friendship (F) for the Bank Wiring room network

Krackhardt's high-tech managers, presented in the multiplication table in Figure 11.8.

Now let us consider the joint homomorphic reduction of these two role structures. First, the joint homomorphic reduction will impose all equations among images that hold in either role structure. Then, we must check to see that the resulting reduction is in fact a homomorphic reduction of each original role structure.

Notice that the role structure for the Bank Wiring room has more elements than the role structure for Krackhardt's high-tech managers. Some images that are distinct in the Bank Wiring room role structure are equated in the role structure for Krackhardt's high-tech managers. However, there are no equations among images in the Bank Wiring room role structure that are not also present in the role structure for Krackhardt's high-tech managers. The role structure for Krackhardt's high-tech managers is a reduction of the role structure for the Bank Wiring room. But is it a homomorphic reduction?

Consider imposing the equations among images that hold for Krackhardt's high-tech managers on the role table for the Bank Wiring room. We will denote these new classes by $Q_1^{\text{JNT}}, Q_2^{\text{JNT}}, \ldots, Q_5^{\text{JNT}}$. This implies the following equations among images for the Bank Wiring room:

$$
\begin{aligned}
Q_2^{\text{JNT}} &= \{A, AA, AAA\} \\
Q_1^{\text{JNT}} &= \{F\} \\
Q_5^{\text{JNT}} &= \{AF, AAF\} \\
Q_4^{\text{JNT}} &= \{FA, FAA\} \\
Q_3^{\text{JNT}} &= \{FF, FAF\}
\end{aligned}
$$

∘	1	3	7	2	4	8	5	9	6	10
1	3	7	7	4	8	8	7	7	8	8
3	7	7	7	8	8	8	7	7	8	8
7	7	7	7	8	8	8	7	7	8	8
2	5	9	9	6	10	10	9	9	10	10
4	7	7	7	8	8	8	7	7	8	8
8	7	7	7	8	8	8	7	7	8	8
5	9	9	9	10	10	10	9	9	10	10
9	9	9	9	10	10	10	9	9	10	10
6	9	9	9	10	10	10	9	9	10	10
10	9	9	9	10	10	10	9	9	10	10

Fig. 11.15. Permuted and partitioned multiplication table for helping and friendship for the Bank Wiring room network

We can use these equations to permute the rows and simultaneously the columns of the multiplication table for the Bank Wiring room role structure. This will also allow us to check whether or not this reduction is in fact a homomorphic reduction. Figure 11.15 presents the permuted and partitioned multiplication table for the Bank Wiring room. Examining this figure, we see that within each submatrix, the labels for images are all in the same equivalence class, and this simplification preserves the operation of composition.

This reduction of the role structure for the Bank Wiring room is in fact a homomorphic reduction. It is also identical to the role structure for Krackhardt's high-tech managers. Thus, it is the joint homomorphic reduction of the two role structures. This joint role structure has $R^{JNT}_{\mathcal{N M}} = 5$ elements. The role structure for Krackhardt's managers is in fact a homomorphic reduction of the role structure for helping and friendship for the Bank Wiring room. The multiplication table for the joint homomorphic reduction is identical to the multiplication table for Krackhardt's high-tech managers, presented in Figure 11.8.

Now, consider the common structure semigroup. Recall that the common structure semigroup imposes no equations among images that do not hold in *both* role structures. Both role structures are homomorphic reductions of the common structure semigroup. As we have noted above, the role structure for Krackhardt's high-tech managers is a homomorphic reduction of the role structure for the Bank Wiring room. Thus, the role structure for the Bank Wiring room, with $R^{CSS}_{\mathcal{N M}} = 10$ elements, is the common structure semigroup for the two role structures.

So far we have described how to compare role structures. We next discuss how to measure the similarity of two role structures.

11.5.4 Measuring the Similarity of Role Structures

In this section we describe two measures of the similarity of two role structures. The first measure, denoted by $\delta_{\mathscr{S}_\mathscr{N}\mathscr{S}_\mathscr{M}}$, is based on a general measure of the dissimilarity of two partitions, proposed by Boorman and Oliver (1973) and Arabie and Boorman (1979) and adapted by Boorman and White (1976) for the comparison of role structures. The measure is based on the coarseness of the partition induced by the joint homomorphic reduction, $\mathscr{Q}^{\text{JNT}}_{\mathscr{N}\mathscr{M}}$ with $R^{\text{JNT}}_{\mathscr{N}\mathscr{M}}$ classes, as compared with the coarseness of the two role structures, $\mathscr{S}_\mathscr{N}$ with $R_{S_\mathscr{N}}$ classes and $\mathscr{S}_\mathscr{M}$ with $R_{S_\mathscr{M}}$ classes. The second measure, $r_{\mathscr{S}_\mathscr{N}\mathscr{S}_\mathscr{M}}$, is a measure of similarity that compares the two role structures to the joint homomorphic reduction and to the common structure semigroup (Pattison and Bartlett 1982).

Recall that each role structure ($\mathscr{S}_\mathscr{N}$ and $\mathscr{S}_\mathscr{M}$) consists of a set of equations that describes which compound relations produce identical images. Each equation, thus, defines an equivalence class of identical images from $\mathscr{S}^*$, the set of all possible images. $R_{S_\mathscr{N}}$ and $R_{S_\mathscr{M}}$ denote the number of equivalence classes in role structures $\mathscr{S}_\mathscr{N}$ and $\mathscr{S}_\mathscr{M}$ respectively, and $R^{\text{JNT}}_{\mathscr{N}\mathscr{M}}$ is the number of classes in the joint homomorphic reduction of $\mathscr{S}_\mathscr{N}$ and $\mathscr{S}_\mathscr{M}$. We will let c_i be the size of class i, for $i = 1, 2, \ldots, R^{\text{JNT}}_{\mathscr{N}\mathscr{M}}$. We define the coarseness of $\mathscr{Q}^{\text{JNT}}_{\mathscr{N}\mathscr{M}}$, the joint homomorphic reduction, in relation to one role structure, say $\mathscr{S}_\mathscr{N}$, as:

$$h(\mathscr{Q}^{\text{JNT}}_{\mathscr{N}\mathscr{M}|\mathscr{N}}) = \frac{\sum_{i=1}^{R^{\text{JNT}}_{\mathscr{N}\mathscr{M}}} \binom{c_i}{2}}{\binom{R_{S_\mathscr{N}}}{2}}. \tag{11.1}$$

Similarly we have $h(\mathscr{Q}^{\text{JNT}}_{\mathscr{N}\mathscr{M}|\mathscr{M}})$ as the coarseness of $\mathscr{Q}^{\text{JNT}}_{\mathscr{N}\mathscr{M}}$ in relation to role structure $\mathscr{S}_\mathscr{M}$. The quantity $h(\mathscr{Q}^{\text{JNT}}_{\mathscr{N}\mathscr{M}|\mathscr{N}})$ takes on values between 0 and 1.

Boorman and White interpret the quantity in equation (11.1) as the distance of a role structure from the joint homomorphic reduction, noting that

> ... it makes sense to treat the coarseness of these partitions as a measure of the extent of aggregation in passing from [$\mathscr{S}_\mathscr{N}$] or [$\mathscr{S}_\mathscr{M}$] to the joint reduction, in other words, as a measure of distance to the joint reduction. (1976, page 1422)

We can then measure the distance of two role structures from each other by summing the distance each is from their joint homomorphic reduction. Thus, the distance between $\mathscr{S}_{\mathcal{N}}$ and $\mathscr{S}_{\mathcal{M}}$, in relation to their joint homomorphic reduction, is:

$$\delta_{\mathscr{S}_{\mathcal{N}}\mathscr{S}_{\mathcal{M}}} = h(\mathcal{Q}^{\mathrm{JNT}}_{\mathcal{N}\mathcal{M}|\mathcal{N}}) + h(\mathcal{Q}^{\mathrm{JNT}}_{\mathcal{N}\mathcal{M}|\mathcal{M}}). \tag{11.2}$$

This quantity is a dissimilarity measure that takes on values between 0 (when $\mathscr{S}_{\mathcal{N}}$ and $\mathscr{S}_{\mathcal{M}}$ are identical, and so $\mathcal{Q}^{\mathrm{JNT}}_{\mathcal{N}\mathcal{M}}$ is identical to both) and 2 (when the only joint homomorphic reduction is trivial and equates all compound relations).

Pattison and Bartlett (1982) have proposed an alternative measure, $r_{\mathscr{S}_{\mathcal{N}}\mathscr{S}_{\mathcal{M}}}$, that can be used to quantify the similarity of role structures. Their measure has the advantage of taking into account the size of the common structure semigroup in addition to the size of the joint homomorphic reduction. Recall that $\mathscr{S}_{\mathcal{N}}$ and $\mathscr{S}_{\mathcal{M}}$ have $R_{S_{\mathcal{N}}}$ and $R_{S_{\mathcal{M}}}$ elements in each, the joint homomorphic reduction $\mathcal{Q}^{\mathrm{JNT}}_{\mathcal{N}\mathcal{M}}$ has $R^{\mathrm{JNT}}_{\mathcal{N}\mathcal{M}}$ classes, and the common structure semigroup $\mathcal{Q}^{\mathrm{CSS}}_{\mathcal{N}\mathcal{M}}$ has $R^{\mathrm{CSS}}_{\mathcal{N}\mathcal{M}}$ classes. The measure of similarity $r_{\mathscr{S}_{\mathcal{N}}\mathscr{S}_{\mathcal{M}}}$ is calculated as:

$$r_{\mathscr{S}_{\mathcal{N}}\mathscr{S}_{\mathcal{M}}} = \frac{R_{S_{\mathcal{N}}}R_{S_{\mathcal{M}}} - R^{\mathrm{CSS}}_{\mathcal{N}\mathcal{M}}}{R_{S_{\mathcal{N}}}R_{S_{\mathcal{M}}} - R^{\mathrm{JNT}}_{\mathcal{N}\mathcal{M}}} \tag{11.3}$$

(Pattison and Bartlett 1982, page 67). This measure takes on its maximum of 1 when role structures $\mathscr{S}_{\mathcal{N}}$ and $\mathscr{S}_{\mathcal{M}}$ are identical, and takes on its minimum of 0 when the common structure semigroup is equal to the direct product of $\mathscr{S}_{\mathcal{N}}$ and $\mathscr{S}_{\mathcal{M}}$ (Pattison and Bartlett 1982).

An Example. We now illustrate these two measures for the two role structures: helping and friendship for the Bank Wiring room, and advice and friendship for Krackhardt's high-tech managers. Recall that $R_{\mathscr{S}_{\mathcal{N}}} = 5$, $R_{\mathscr{S}_{\mathcal{M}}} = 10$, $R^{\mathrm{JNT}}_{\mathcal{N}\mathcal{M}} = 5$, and $R^{\mathrm{CSS}}_{\mathcal{N}\mathcal{M}} = 10$.

First consider the measure $\delta_{\mathscr{S}_{\mathcal{N}}\mathscr{S}_{\mathcal{M}}}$ and its components $h(\mathcal{Q}^{\mathrm{JNT}}_{\mathcal{N}\mathcal{M}|\mathcal{N}})$ and $h(\mathcal{Q}^{\mathrm{JNT}}_{\mathcal{N}\mathcal{M}|\mathcal{M}})$. The quantity $h(\mathcal{Q}^{\mathrm{JNT}}_{\mathcal{N}\mathcal{M}|\mathcal{M}})$ measures the coarseness of the partition in the joint homomorphic reduction compared to the role structure $\mathscr{S}_{\mathcal{M}}$. For our example, the joint homomorphic reduction has five classes whereas the role structure $\mathscr{S}_{\mathcal{M}}$ has ten elements. The assignment of elements in $\mathscr{S}_{\mathcal{N}}$ to classes in $\mathcal{Q}^{\mathrm{JNT}}_{\mathcal{N}\mathcal{M}}$ was listed above. Three elements from $\mathscr{S}_{\mathcal{M}}$ were assigned to the first class in $\mathcal{Q}^{\mathrm{JNT}}_{\mathcal{N}\mathcal{M}}$, one was assigned to the second class, and two were assigned to each of the third, fourth, and fifth classes. Thus, $c_1 = 3$, $c_2 = 1$, $c_3 = 2$, $c_4 = 2$, and $c_5 = 2$. Returning to equation (11.1) we see that:

$$h(\mathcal{Q}^{\text{JNT}}_{\mathscr{NM}|\mathscr{M}}) = \frac{\binom{3}{2} + \binom{1}{2} + \binom{2}{2} + \binom{2}{2} + \binom{2}{2}}{\binom{10}{2}}$$

$$= \frac{3 + 0 + 1 + 1 + 1}{45}$$

$$= 0.1333.$$

This is the distance of the role structure for help and friendship in the Bank Wiring room from the joint homomorphic reduction. The role structure for Krackhardt's high-tech managers is identical to the joint homomorphic reduction (each element in $\mathcal{Q}_{\mathscr{NM}}$ has exactly one element from $\mathscr{S}_{\mathscr{N}}$ assigned to it), thus:

$$h(\mathcal{Q}^{\text{JNT}}_{\mathscr{NM}|\mathscr{N}}) = \frac{0 + 0 + 0 + 0 + 0}{45}$$

$$= 0.0000.$$

Now, we calculate the dissimilarity of the two role structures as:

$$\delta_{\mathscr{S}_{\mathscr{N}}\mathscr{S}_{\mathscr{M}}} = 0.1333 + 0.0000 = 0.1333.$$

Since small values of this quantity (which takes on values between 0 and 2) indicate more similar structures, the value of 0.1333 indicates considerable similarity between the role structures for advice and friendship for Krackhardt's high-tech managers and helping and friendship in the Bank Wiring room.

Now let us illustrate the measure $r_{\mathscr{S}_{\mathscr{N}}\mathscr{S}_{\mathscr{M}}}$. This measure compares the two role structures to the size of the joint homomorphic reduction and to the size of the common structure semigroup. For our example, this quantity is equal to:

$$r_{\mathscr{S}_{\mathscr{N}}\mathscr{S}_{\mathscr{M}}} = \frac{(5)(10) - 10}{(5)(10) - 5} = \frac{40}{45} = 0.889.$$

Since this measure takes on values between 0 and 1, the value of 0.889 indicates a high degree of similarity between the two role structures.

In summary, the role structures for advice and friendship for Krackhardt's high-tech managers and for helping and friendship for the Bank Wiring room are quite similar. Substantively, we see that the relations of providing work-related aid and being friends operate similarly in these two work groups. If we consider the equations among compound relations that are expressed in the set of equivalence classes of images for the joint homomorphic reduction of these two role structures, we see that there are five kinds of compound relations operating in these groups. The first class of images includes all images (words) that contain only sequences of A's (advice); the second class includes only the primitive relation F (friendship); the third class includes images that begin with A and end with F; the fourth class includes images that both begin with F and end with A; and the fifth class includes images that both begin and end with F.

11.6 Summary

In this chapter we have focused on the analysis of multiple relations, specifically on ways to describe and model the associations among a collection of primitive and compound relations as summarized in a multiplication table. We have defined the role structure as the equations (identities) that exist among relations in this collection, and have described simplifications for role structures and ways to compare role structures across groups. The methods in this chapter are concerned with describing the role structure of the entire group. These methods are referred to as global role analyses, relational algebras, role structures, or relational structures. In the next chapter we discuss methods for individual roles and positions.

12
Network Positions and Roles

In this chapter we continue our discussion of methods for studying social network positions and roles. Referring to Figure 9.1, which presented an overview of positional and role analysis in terms of whether the major task was "grouping" relations or "grouping" actors, the methods in this chapter primarily have the goal of "grouping" actors. Such a classification gives rise to a partition of actors into positions. However, several of the methods that we discuss at the end of this chapter consider similarities among relations as a way to determine which actors should be grouped together. Specifically, these methods present alternative ways to classify actors based on their sharing of patterns or types of ties. Since positions of actors are defined in terms of patterns or types of ties, we will also consider associations among relations, and thus network roles.

We can also use the list of four tasks in a positional analysis that we presented in Chapter 9 to organize the topics in this chapter. This chapter is primarily concerned with the first and second tasks: defining equivalences and measuring how closely subsets of actors adhere to these definitions.

The methods we discuss in this chapter focus on roles for *individual* actors. Individual roles are descriptions of the network, including similarities among actors, and associations among relations, from the perspectives of individual actors. In Chapter 11 we presented methods for describing the role structure of an entire group and for comparing the role structures from different groups, without reference to the individual actors. Methods for analyzing group level role structure are sometimes called *global* role methods. In contrast, the methods presented in this chapter study roles from the perspectives of individual actors, or from the perspectives of subsets of actors. These methods are often referred to as *local* or *individual* role methods.

461

We begin with a review of the theoretical background for positions and roles in social networks, and discuss different levels of role analysis of social networks. Following that, we describe and illustrate different approaches for defining equivalence of actors, and as appropriate, for measuring the degree of equivalence. We conclude this chapter with a comparison of the different approaches.

12.1 Background

Several authors, including Homans, Merton, Goodenough, and Nadel have discussed social roles and social positions in ways that are quite useful for social network analysis. In this section we review these authors' ideas and discuss how these theoretical notions can be used to study roles and positions in social networks.

12.1.1 Theoretical Definitions of Roles and Positions

Theoretical definitions of social role often are stated as properties of individuals or sets of individuals. This usage is apparent in a statement such as, "a person takes on the role of leader in a group." A theoretical statement is provided by Homans (1967), who defines *role* as

> ... the behavior expected of a [person] occupying a particular social position. (page 11)

In contrast to social position, which refers to a collection of actors, the concept of social role refers to the ways in which occupants of a position relate to occupants of other positions. In translating these theoretical ideas into formal network analysis methods, it is useful to keep in mind the distinction between a collection of actors (a social position), and the ways that these actors relate to each other (a social role). Goodenough (1969) makes the important distinctions between *status, position,* and *role.* He argues that the fact that many authors have not carefully distinguished between status and position has led to unfortunate confusions.

> All alike treat a social category together with its attached rights and duties as an indivisible unit of analysis, which they label a "status" or "position" in a social relationship. This lumping together of independent phenomena, each with organizations of their own, accounts, I think, for our apparent inability to exploit the status-role concepts to our satisfaction in social and cultural analysis. For example, my brother is my brother, whether he honors his obligations as such or not.... I shall

consistently treat statuses as combinations of right and duty only. I shall emphasize their conceptual autonomy from social "positions" in a categorical sense by referring to the latter as *social identities*. (page 312)

Goodenough then defines the role for a social identity:

> The aggregate of its composite statuses may be said to constitute the identity's *role* in a sense a little less comprehensive than but otherwise close to Nadel's (1957) use of the term. It would be equivalent to a comprehensive "role set" in Merton's (1957:369) terms. (page 324)

Merton notes that "a particular social status involves, not a single associated role, but an array of associated roles" (1957, page 423). This collection of role relationships that an individual has with others, by virtue of occupying a particular social status, constitutes their *role set*. For example, he observes

> the status of medical student entails not only the role student, *vis-a-vis* his teacher, but also an array of other roles relating him diversely to other students, physicians, nurses, social workers, medical technicians, and the like. (1957, page 423)

The idea of a role set is quite useful for defining individual roles in social networks and we will return to it later in this chapter.

To translate theoretical notions of role and position into empirical social network methods, one assumes that the measured relations in a set of social network data are indicators of the roles of actors in different social positions. The regularities in patterns of relations among actors thus indicate regularities in roles of actors in the social positions (Faust 1988). Role analysis therefore focuses on the ties among actors, or among sets of actors.

Lorrain and White (1971) provide a clear statement of the assumptions underlying a network analysis of individual roles:

> the total role of an individual in a social system has often been described as consisting of sets of relations of various types linking this person as ego to sets of others. (page 50)

The goal of an individual role analysis is to describe the regularities in the ties that link an actor (ego) to other actors (alters). These regularities constitute the role of an individual actor in the network. Thus, social network methods for studying individual roles focus on patterns or "types" of ties among actors or subsets of actors as a way to formalize the notion of social role. We can then use these regularities in ties to define subsets of actors who have the same types of ties with others, and thus who occupy the same social position. Actors in the same position are (ideally) equivalent in that they have the same types of ties to actors in other positions. Since there are numerous ways to formalize the idea of types of ties, there are numerous ways to formalize the ideas of network role and network position. This chapter discusses several of these formalizations.

12.1.2 Levels of Role Analysis in Social Networks

In network analysis, the notion of role has been used at three conceptual levels: the entire group, a subset of actors, and an individual actor. These three levels are referred to as:

- Global role structures (Boorman and White)
- Local roles (Wu)
- Individual or ego roles (Winship and Mandel; Breiger and Pattison)

These levels differ in the level of social unit to which the description applies: the entire group, collections of individuals, or the individual.

Global role structures describe an entire group. For example, multiplication tables and role structures, that we discussed in Chapter 11, are global role procedures, since they describe the entire group. Global roles are often defined quite abstractly in terms of algebraic properties of the relations within the entire group. For example, Boorman and White (1976) define the role structure of a group:

> A *role structure* is the set of all identifications among words [compound relations] obtained by applying the Axiom of Quality to the compound images formed by multiplying generators. Mathematically, a role structure is therefore simply the Boolean matrix semigroup formed by taking Boolean matrix products of the specified generators. (page 1395)

Whereas role structures pertain to an entire group, local roles pertain to *subsets* of actors within a group. The subsets can be positions of equivalent actors (for example subsets of approximately structurally equivalent actors). A local role for a given position consists of the ways in which the position is tied to other positions in the network. Wu (1983) makes the distinction between local and global role structures:

> Thus, the role structure describes how relations interlock from a global perspective of the entire network. Local blockmodel algebras equate relations [if and only if] the corresponding blockmodel matrices are *locally identical*, that is, identical from the perspective of one or more of

the blocks [positions]. They thus describe how relations interlock from the perspective of one or more of the blocks [positions]. (page 291)

Local roles, defined for positions of actors, are similar to the descriptions of positions in blockmodel analysis presented by Marsden (1989) and Burt (1976). For a single relation, positions can be characterized as sycophant, broker, primary, and so on, depending on the patterns of ties that members of one position have with members of other positions. For multiple relations, there are many more possibilities for types of positions.

At the most specific level of analysis, roles can pertain to individual actors. These are referred to as individual or ego roles. Analyses at this level study the patterns and regularities in ties from the perspective of individual actors. Mandel (1983) makes explicit the distinction between individual roles and global role structures.

> The term *individual role definition* is therefore proposed for any procedure which associates a role with each actor strictly on the basis of patterns and regularities in his or her "personal" network. A *global role definition*, on the other hand, involves the assignment of roles to all members of the population simultaneously. (page 376)

According to Mandel (1983) properties such as the density, span, or range of an individual actor's network are individual role properties since they are defined for individual actors.

Related individual and local role ideas have been developed by Mandel (1983), Winship and Mandel (1983), Wu (1983), Everett (1985), Breiger and Pattison (1986), and Winship (1974, 1988). Closely related ideas are presented in White and Reitz (1983, 1985). Substantive examples using these methods include Krackhardt and Porter's (1986) study of turnover in a small fast-food establishment, Breiger and Pattison's (1986) analysis of Padgett's data on Florentine families, White and Reitz's (1989) analysis of a scientific discipline, Doreian's analysis of prominent political actors (Doreian 1988c; Batagelj, Doreian and Ferligoj 1992), and Faust's (1988) reanalysis of Sampson's monastery data.

We can use the patterns of ties between individual actors to describe individual roles and to identify subsets of actors who are involved in the same roles within a network. Subsets of actors with similar roles are equivalent, and occupy the same network position.

12.1.3 Equivalences in Networks

Each approach to network roles or positions specifies the graph theoretic or network properties that sets of actors must have in order to be considered equivalent in terms of the roles they play and thus the positions they occupy. Actors who are equivalent are assigned to the same equivalence class or *position*. *Structural equivalence* is one possible equivalence definition, but there are many others.

Each equivalence definition specifies an *equivalence relation*, which we denote by $\equiv$. An equivalence relation has three important properties: it is symmetric ($i \equiv j$ if and only if $j \equiv i$), reflexive ($i \equiv i$), and transitive (if $i \equiv j$ and $j \equiv k$ then $i \equiv k$). An equivalence relation defines a *partition* of a set of entities into mutually exclusive and exhaustive equivalence classes, such that all entities within a class are equivalent, and entities from different classes are not equivalent. An equivalence relation on a set of actors, $\mathcal{N}$, defines a partition of this set into B equivalence classes, $\mathcal{B}_1, \mathcal{B}_2, \ldots, \mathcal{B}_B$, such that actors who are equivalent are assigned to the same equivalence class.

Each of the positional approaches that we describe in this chapter specifies the conditions under which actors should be assigned to the same equivalence class. Each method is thus a *mapping* from the set of actors to a set of equivalence classes, where the rule for mapping actors to the same equivalence class is described by the particular equivalence definition. This idea of assigning actors to equivalence classes is the same as the idea in the first part of a blockmodel analysis, where actors are assigned to positions so that all actors in a position are (ideally) structurally equivalent. Now, we want to consider a number of different mapping rules, each based on a different kind of equivalence definition. As in a blockmodel analysis, we will denote the mapping of actor i to position $\mathcal{B}_k$ as $\phi(i) = \mathcal{B}_k$, but since we now have several different equivalence definitions, we will subscript ϕ and $\mathcal{B}_k$ to denote the relevant definition. In general, we will denote the mapping by equivalence definition "$\bullet$" as $\phi_\bullet(i)$, and we will denote an equivalence class resulting from definition "$\bullet$" by $\mathcal{B}_{(\bullet)k}$. For example, we will let $\mathcal{B}_{(SE)k}$ denote the kth class of actors who are structurally equivalent (SE). Since the mapping function assigns an actor to a class, the notation $\phi_{SE}(i) = \mathcal{B}_{(SE)k}$ denotes the assignment of actor i to class $\mathcal{B}_{(SE)k}$ by structural equivalence; all actors in class $\mathcal{B}_{(SE)k}$ are (ideally) structurally equivalent.

If two actors are equivalent then they are assigned to the same equivalence class (or network position). We will denote the equivalence of actors *i* and *j* according to definition "$\bullet$", as $i \overset{\bullet}{\equiv} j$. Since equivalent actors are assigned to the same equivalence class, $i \overset{\bullet}{\equiv} j$ implies $\phi_\bullet(i) = \phi_\bullet(j) = \mathcal{B}_{(\bullet)k}$. For example, if actors *i* and *j* are structurally equivalent (*SE*), then $i \overset{SE}{\equiv} j$, and $\phi_{SE}(i) = \phi_{SE}(j) = \mathcal{B}_{(SE)k}$.

To develop methods that are good formalizations of the theoretical notions of social position and social role, it is necessary to conceptualize the structural location of an actor (and sets of actors) in a network in rather general and abstract ways. We also need flexible ways to describe the patterns or types of the ties in which an actor is involved.

Many researchers have proposed that structural equivalence is too restrictive for studying network roles and positions, and have proposed equivalences based on more abstract properties of relational patterns (see, for example, Borgatti and Everett 1992a; Breiger and Pattison 1986; Burt 1990; Doreian 1987, 1988b; Everett 1985; Everett, Boyd, and Borgatti 1990; Faust 1988; Mandel 1983; Pattison 1988, 1993; Sailer 1978; White and Reitz 1983, 1985, 1989; Winship 1974, 1988; Winship and Mandel 1983; Wu 1983; Yamagishi 1987). In this chapter we discuss several of these more general approaches, including:

- Automorphic and isomorphic equivalence
- Regular equivalence
- Local role equivalence
- Ego algebras

These approaches are more theoretically and formally abstract than the approaches based on structural equivalence, and often require more sophisticated mathematics.

In the next sections we describe alternative equivalence definitions and discuss how to measure degrees of equivalence for each of these definitions. The order of presentation begins with the most specific approaches and then proceeds to more general and abstract approaches. We conclude with a comparison of these methods.

We begin with a hypothetical example that we will use to illustrate several of the equivalence definitions. Consider the graph in Figure 12.1. This graph might represent the relation "supervises the work of" measured on the managers and employees in a company. In terms of the network roles in this example, some people supervise the work of others, some people have their work supervised by others, and some people both supervise others and are themselves supervised. We will use this example

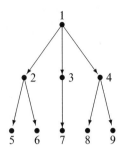

Fig. 12.1. Graph to illustrate equivalences

to illustrate structural equivalence, automorphic equivalence, and regular equivalence.

12.2 Structural Equivalence, Revisited

Recall that two actors are structurally equivalent if and only if they have identical ties to and from identical other actors. Formally, $i \stackrel{SE}{=} j$ implies $i \stackrel{\mathcal{X}_r}{\rightarrow} k$ if and only if $j \stackrel{\mathcal{X}_r}{\rightarrow} k$ and $k \stackrel{\mathcal{X}_r}{\rightarrow} i$ if and only if $k \stackrel{\mathcal{X}_r}{\rightarrow} j$ for all $\mathcal{X}_r$ and $k \neq i, j$.

Referring to Figure 12.1, there are seven subsets of structurally equivalent actors:

- $\mathcal{B}_{(SE)1} : \{1\}$
- $\mathcal{B}_{(SE)2} : \{2\}$
- $\mathcal{B}_{(SE)3} : \{3\}$
- $\mathcal{B}_{(SE)4} : \{4\}$
- $\mathcal{B}_{(SE)5} : \{5, 6\}$
- $\mathcal{B}_{(SE)6} : \{7\}$
- $\mathcal{B}_{(SE)7} : \{8, 9\}$

Since structural equivalence requires identical ties to and from identical other actors, in this example people can only be structurally equivalent if they supervise exactly the same other people, and are supervised by exactly the same others.

There are obvious limitations to structural equivalence for identifying network positions. The fact that structurally equivalent actors must have *identical* ties to and from *identical* other actors is a severe limitation. In our example, two actors can be assigned to the same "manager" position only if they supervise exactly the same employees. Managers from two different companies, or even managers in charge of two different departments, cannot be structurally equivalent. The restriction to identical ties and identical actors, as required by structural equivalence, thus does not provide a general formalization of the theoretical notion of social position (Faust 1988; Borgatti and Everett 1992a). Furthermore, structural equivalence does not allow comparison of positions and roles between populations.

Structural equivalence is the oldest and currently the most widely used definition of equivalence for positional analysis of social networks. Recently, however, numerous authors have argued that more general equivalence definitions might be more appropriate, especially if a researcher's goal is to formalize the theoretical notion of social position or to compare populations (Sailer 1978; Faust 1988; Borgatti and Everett 1992a; Winship 1988). We now discuss alternative equivalences.

As an introduction to these more general equivalences, let us consider what it means for two actors to have the same role in a social network. Since role is a general construct, independent of the identities of the particular individuals involved, we need to be able to describe and compare the general or abstract features of actors' ties, without reference to the identities of the particular alters to whom the actors are tied. For example, the supervisors from two different companies have the same role because they oversee the work of other people, though the particular individuals they supervise are different. In a set of social network data we would see that people who are "supervisors" have "oversees the work of" ties to people who are "employees." To compare roles and positions of actors in this more general sense, we need to be able to describe individual roles in terms of the patterns or types of ties that are defined for any actor who performs a given role, and thus occupies a particular position, regardless of the identity of the alters involved.

12.3 Automorphic and Isomorphic Equivalence

Several authors have proposed that the concept of *automorphic equivalence* is useful for studying positions in social networks (Borgatti and Everett 1992a; Everett, Boyd, and Borgatti 1990; Pattison 1982, 1988; Winship 1974, 1988; Winship and Mandel 1983). Automorphic equivalence is based on the idea that equivalent actors occupy indistinguishable structural locations in a network. Structural location is defined quite precisely in terms of graph isomorphism.

12.3.1 Definition

Recall that two graphs or directed graphs are *isomorphic* if there is a one-to-one mapping of the nodes in one graph to the nodes in the other graph that preserves the property of adjacency (see Chapter 4). Formally, graphs (or directed graphs) $\mathscr{G}(\mathscr{N}, \mathscr{L})$ and $\mathscr{G}'(\mathscr{N}', \mathscr{L}')$ are isomorphic if there is a one-to-one mapping of the nodes in $\mathscr{N}$ to the nodes in $\mathscr{N}'$ such that nodes that are adjacent in $\mathscr{G}$ are mapped to nodes that are adjacent in $\mathscr{G}'$. If we denote the mapping of node i as $\tau(i)$, then graphs (or directed graphs) $\mathscr{G}$ and $\mathscr{G}'$ are isomorphic if $< i, j > \in \mathscr{L}$ if and only if $< \tau(i), \tau(j) > \in \mathscr{L}'$. The property of isomorphism maps one graph (or directed graph) to another graph (or directed graph).

An analogous idea, called an *automorphism*, is defined for a single graph (or directed graph). If the mapping, τ, is from the nodes in a graph (or directed graph) back to themselves (rather than from one graph to another), then the mapping is called an automorphism. Formally, an automorphism is a one-to-one mapping, τ from $\mathscr{N}$ to $\mathscr{N}$ such that $< i, j > \in \mathscr{L}$ if and only if $< \tau(i), \tau(j) > \in \mathscr{L}$. In terms of a single relation $\mathscr{X}$, an automorphism is a one-to-one mapping from $\mathscr{N}$ to $\mathscr{N}$ such that $i \overset{\mathscr{X}}{\to} j$ if and only if $\tau(i) \overset{\mathscr{X}}{\to} \tau(j)$.

As an illustration of an automorphism consider the example in Figure 12.1. In this directed graph one possible mapping of nodes that is an automorphism is: $\tau(1) = 1$, $\tau(2) = 4$, $\tau(3) = 3$, $\tau(4) = 2$, $\tau(5) = 9$, $\tau(6) = 8$, $\tau(7) = 7$, $\tau(8) = 5$, $\tau(9) = 6$. There are also other possible automorphic mappings for this graph.

We can also define an automorphism for a multirelational network (Pattison 1988). An automorphism on a multirelational network is a one-to-one mapping, τ, such that $i \overset{\mathscr{X}_r}{\to} j$ if and only if $\tau(i) \overset{\mathscr{X}_r}{\to} \tau(j)$ for all i, j, and all $\mathscr{X}_r$.

Now, using the idea of an automorphism, we can define *automorphic equivalence*. Two actors are *automorphically equivalent* if and only if there is some automorphism, τ, that maps one of the actors to the other. Formally, i and j are automorphically equivalent, $i \overset{AE}{\equiv} j$, if and only if there exists some mapping, τ, such that $\tau(i) = j$, and the mapping, τ, is an automorphism. Since $i \overset{AE}{\equiv} j$ means that $\tau(i) = j$ (where τ is an automorphism) if actors i and j are automorphically equivalent, then $i \overset{\mathscr{X}_r}{\to} k$ implies $j \overset{\mathscr{X}_r}{\to} \tau(k)$ and $k \overset{\mathscr{X}_r}{\to} i$ implies $\tau(k) \overset{\mathscr{X}_r}{\to} j$, for all k and all $\mathscr{X}_r$.

12.3.2 Example

Returning to the example in Figure 12.1, we see that there are five subsets of automorphically equivalent (*AE*) actors. We denote these equivalence classes as $\mathscr{B}_{(AE)k}$. These classes are:

- $\mathscr{B}_{(AE)1} : \{1\}$
- $\mathscr{B}_{(AE)2} : \{2, 4\}$
- $\mathscr{B}_{(AE)3} : \{3\}$
- $\mathscr{B}_{(AE)4} : \{5, 6, 8, 9\}$
- $\mathscr{B}_{(AE)5} : \{7\}$

If we think of the relation in the directed graph in Figure 12.1 as "supervises the work of," then we see that actors 2 and 4 are automorphically equivalent, even though they supervise different people. However, actor 3 is not automorphically equivalent to actors 2 and 4. In general, to be automorphically equivalent, nodes in a graph (or directed graph) must have the same indegree and the same outdegree. Thus, in our example, to be automorphically equivalent two actors must "supervise," and be "supervised," by the same number of others. Notice that automorphic equivalence is more general than structural equivalence. Actors that are structurally equivalent are also automorphically equivalent, but the reverse is not necessarily true (for example, actors 2 and 4 in Figure 12.1 are automorphically equivalent but not structurally equivalent).

The term "automorphism" refers to a mapping of a graph (or directed graph) onto itself, whereas the term "isomorphism" refers to the mapping of one graph (or directed graph) onto another. We can define *isomorphic equivalence* in terms of a one-to-one mapping of nodes in one graph (or directed graph) to nodes in another graph (or directed graph). Nodes $i \in \mathcal{N}$ and $j \in \mathcal{N}'$ are *isomorphically equivalent* if and only if there is some mapping, τ, such that $\tau(i) = j$ and τ is an isomorphism.

In practice, the term "automorphic equivalence" is more widely used than the term "isomorphic equivalence." However, the term "isomorphic equivalence" would be more in keeping with the spirit of this line of research on social network positions, and the goal that one ought to be able to compare positions across populations.

An important property of isomorphic equivalence is that nodes from different graphs can be isomorphically equivalent. Thus, isomorphic equivalence can be used to study equivalence of actors from *different* groups. This is an important feature of any method for studying social positions and social roles since people from different populations can occupy the same social position.

The graph theoretic concept of an *orbit* refers to a subset of nodes in a graph (or directed graph) that can be mapped to one another in some automorphism (or isomorphism) (Pattison 1982; Everett, Boyd, and Borgatti 1990). Nodes i and j belong to the same orbit if $\tau(i) = j$ for some automorphism, τ. Nodes that belong to the same orbit are automorphically equivalent and are assigned to the same automorphic equivalence class, since, by definition, there is some automorphism that maps one to the other. Thus, if nodes i and j belong to the same orbit, $\phi_{(AE)}(i) = \phi_{(AE)}(j) = \mathcal{B}_{(AE)k}$. Nodes in the same orbit belong to the same automorphic equivalence position.

Automorphically equivalent nodes are identical with respect to all graph theoretic properties (Borgatti and Everett 1992a). For example, two nodes that are automorphically equivalent have the same indegree, the same outdegree, the same centrality on every possible measure (for example, betweenness, closeness, etc.), belong to the same number and size of cliques, and so on. The only thing that can differ between automorphically (or isomorphically) equivalent nodes is the "names" or "labels" attached to them (and to other nodes in the graph). Nodes that are automorphically equivalent are structurally indistinguishable when labels are removed from the graph. To illustrate, suppose that labels were removed from the nodes (and lines) in a graph or directed graph. If we now wanted to replace the node labels, there might be uncertainty about where some labels should be placed, because, without the labels, some subsets of nodes are indistinguishable. For example, consider removing the labels from the nodes in the graph in Figure 12.1. If labels were then to be replaced, the label "5" could go with any of four nodes in the graph (the nodes previously labeled "5", "6", "8", and "9"), because without the labels these four nodes are indistinguishable. These four nodes are automorphically equivalent; they belong to the same orbit.

12.3.3 Measuring Automorphic Equivalence

One of the limitations of automorphic and isomorphic equivalence as an approach for analyzing social networks is that there is no known fast algorithm that guarantees identification of automorphically equivalent nodes in *all* graphs (Everett, Boyd, and Borgatti 1990). Pattison (1988) presents a family of measures for equivalences, including automorphic equivalence, but it is quite difficult to compute. One approach to identifying subsets of *potentially* automorphically (or isomorphically) equivalent nodes in a graph is to use the insight that if two nodes are automorphically equivalent then they are identical on all possible graph theoretic properties (though the reverse is not true, nodes may be identical on any number of graph theoretic properties, and not necessarily be automorphically equivalent). Subsets of automorphically (or isomorphically) equivalent nodes must be contained within subsets of nodes that have identical values on all graph theoretic measures. For example, one can consider a number of different centrality measures (for example, degree centrality, closeness centrality, and betweenness centrality). Two nodes that do not have identical centrality scores on all possible measures of centrality cannot be automorphically equivalent. A strategy of this kind is used in the program *UCINET IV* to identify potentially automorphically equivalent nodes (Borgatti, Everett, and Freeman 1991). The problem remains, though, of how to measure the degree of automorphic equivalence between pairs of nodes in a way that is not arbitrary, and that is not difficult to compute.

For two actors to be automorphically equivalent in a social network they must have identical kinds and numbers of ties to actors who are themselves automorphically equivalent. Thus, automorphically equivalent actors must have the same indegree and outdegree. This restriction might, in some applications, be too restrictive. For example, in a corporation managers of different size departments would not be automorphically equivalent. In Figure 12.1, actors 2 and 4 are automorphically equivalent (they both "supervise" two subordinates), however, actor 3 is not automorphically equivalent to actors 2 and 4 because actor 3 "supervises" only one subordinate.

The restriction of equal number of ties is relaxed by the notion of regular equivalence.

12.4 Regular Equivalence

The notion of regular equivalence formalizes the observation that actors who occupy the same social position relate in the same ways with other actors who are themselves in the same positions (Borgatti and Everett 1992a; Faust 1988; Sailer 1978). Regular equivalence does not require actors to have identical ties to identical other actors (as required by structural equivalence) or to be structurally indistinguishable (as required by automorphic or isomorphic equivalence).

The idea of regular equivalence arose out of discussions among Boyd and Lorrain and then White and Sailer, and was first introduced by Sailer (1978), and then was developed by White and Reitz (1983, 1985, 1989), Everett and Borgatti (Borgatti and Everett 1989, 1992a, 1992b; Everett and Borgatti 1990; Borgatti 1988), and Doreian (1987), among others. Applications of regular equivalence can be found in Doreian (1988a, 1988c), Faust (1988), Krackhardt and Porter (1986), and White and Reitz (1989).

12.4.1 Definition of Regular Equivalence

Briefly, actors who are regularly equivalent have identical ties to and from *equivalent* actors. For example, neighborhood bullies occupy the same social position, though in different neighborhoods, because they beat up some kid(s) and are scolded by some irate parent(s), but they do not necessarily beat up the same kid(s) nor are they scolded by the same parent(s).

More generally, if actors i and j are regularly equivalent, and actor i has a tie to/from some actor, k, then actor j must have the same kind of tie to/from some actor, l, and actors k and l must be regularly equivalent. Formally, if actors i and j are *regularly equivalent*, $i \overset{RE}{\equiv} j$, then for all relations, $\mathcal{X}_r$, $r = 1, 2, \ldots, R$, and for all actors, $k = 1, 2, \ldots, g$, if $i \overset{\mathcal{X}_r}{\to} k$ then there exists some actor l such that $j \overset{\mathcal{X}_r}{\to} l$ and $k \overset{RE}{\equiv} l$, and if $k \overset{\mathcal{X}_r}{\to} i$ then there exists some actor l such that $l \overset{\mathcal{X}_r}{\to} j$ and $k \overset{RE}{\equiv} l$. We will denote subsets of regularly equivalent actors by $\mathcal{B}_{(RE)k}$.

Returning to the example in Figure 12.1 of a single directional relation, a partition of actors that satisfies the definition of regular equivalence is:

- $\mathcal{B}_{(RE)1} : \{1\}$
- $\mathcal{B}_{(RE)2} : \{2, 3, 4\}$
- $\mathcal{B}_{(RE)3} : \{5, 6, 7, 8, 9\}$

Notice that these equivalence classes are exactly the three "levels" in the hierarchy, and might correspond to the CEO, managers, and employees in this hypothetical company. Furthermore, managers are equivalent regardless of the size of the department they supervise, and employees are equivalent regardless of the size of the department they work in.

An important feature of regular equivalence is that a given social network (or graph) may have several partitions of actors that satisfy the definition of regular equivalence. That is, there may be several ways to assign actors to equivalence classes so that within each equivalence class actors have identical ties to and from actors in other equivalence classes. For example, the partition of actors into structural equivalence classes is a regular equivalence (structurally equivalent actors are also regularly equivalent), and the partition of actors into automorphic (or isomorphic) equivalence classes is also a regular equivalence. But, there may be other regular equivalence partitions in a given network that are neither structural equivalences nor automorphic equivalences (for instance, the partition with three equivalence classes for the example above). The coarsest partition (the partition with the fewest equivalence classes) that is consistent with the definition of regular equivalence is called the *maximal regular equivalence*. The maximal regular equivalence for the example in Figure 12.1 is the one with three equivalence classes, described above. However, the partition

- $\mathscr{B}_{(RE)1} : \{1\}$
- $\mathscr{B}_{(RE)2} : \{2, 3\}$
- $\mathscr{B}_{(RE)3} : \{4\}$
- $\mathscr{B}_{(RE)4} : \{5, 6, 7\}$
- $\mathscr{B}_{(RE)5} : \{8, 9\}$

is also a regular equivalence, but it is not the maximal regular equivalence (neither is it a structural equivalence or an automorphic equivalence partition).

Now let us consider some issues that arise in defining regular equivalence for nondirectional relations.

12.4.2 Regular Equivalence for Nondirectional Relations

As many authors have noted, in a graph (for an nondirectional relation) in which there are no isolates, the maximal regular equivalence consists of a single equivalence class containing all nodes (Faust 1985; Doreian 1987, 1988b; Borgatti 1988). For a nondirectional relation with no isolates, all actors in the single maximal regular equivalence class are adjacent to some other actor, who is also in the equivalence class. A partition consisting of a single equivalence class is trivial, and probably uninteresting. However, a nondirectional relation may also contain other regular equivalence partitions.

To illustrate, consider the graph in Figure 12.2. The maximal regular equivalence partition for this graph is $\{1, 2, 3, 4\}$. However, this graph also contains the following regular equivalence partition: $\mathscr{B}_{(RE)1} : \{1, 3, 4\}$,

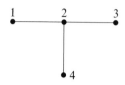

Fig. 12.2. Graph to demonstrate regular equivalence

$\mathcal{B}_{(RE)2}$: {2}. Each node in $\mathcal{B}_{(RE)1}$ is adjacent to some node in $\mathcal{B}_{(RE)2}$, and each node in $\mathcal{B}_{(RE)2}$ is adjacent to some node in $\mathcal{B}_{(RE)1}$.

One useful approach for studying regular equivalence in graphs (for nondirectional relations) is the graph theoretic concept of *neighborhood* (Everett, Boyd, and Borgatti 1990). The neighborhood of a node *i* in a graph consists of all nodes adjacent to node *i*. Recall that if nodes *i* and *j* are regularly equivalent, then for any node *k* adjacent to node *i*, there must be some node *l* adjacent to node *j*, and *k* and *l* must be regularly equivalent. Since the neighborhood of a node consists of all nodes adjacent to that node, nodes that are regularly equivalent must have the same equivalence classes of nodes in their neighborhoods across all relations. Briefly, in order to be regularly equivalent, actors must be adjacent to the same kinds (equivalence classes) of other actors. This approach to defining regular equivalence is especially useful for studying regular equivalence in nondirectional relations.

As can be seen by the definition, regular equivalence is applicable to both single and multirelational networks. Regular equivalence can also be generalized to valued relations and to two-mode networks (Borgatti and Everett 1992b).

Before we discuss measures of regular equivalence, let us consider how to represent regular equivalence partitions using a regular equivalence blockmodel.

12.4.3 Regular Equivalence Blockmodels

Recall that a blockmodel consists of a mapping of actors into equivalence classes (or positions) according to the particular equivalence definition, and for each pair of positions, a statement of whether or not there is a tie present from one position to another position.

Blockmodels can be constructed for regular equivalence classes, just as they are for structural equivalence classes (Borgatti and Everett 1992b; Batagelj, Doreian, and Ferligoj 1992). The difference between structural equivalence blockmodels and regular equivalence blockmodels is the rule for determining which blocks are oneblocks and which blocks are zeroblocks, and consequently, what oneblocks and zeroblocks imply about the corresponding entries in the submatrices of the sociomatrix. In our discussion, we will limit our attention to perfect regular equivalence blockmodels.

First consider the oneblocks in a regular equivalence blockmodel. Following the definition of regular equivalence, if actors i and j are in the same equivalence class, $\mathcal{B}_{(RE)m}$, and actor i has a tie to some actor k in equivalence class $\mathcal{B}_{(RE)p}$, then actor j (who is equivalent to i) must also have a tie to some actor l who is in $\mathcal{B}_{(RE)p}$ (actors k and l must be equivalent, though they may be different actors). Consider the image matrix for a regular equivalence blockmodel. In the image matrix, a oneblock indicating the presence of a tie from position $\mathcal{B}_{(RE)m}$ to position $\mathcal{B}_{(RE)p}$ implies that for *all* actors $i \in \mathcal{B}_{(RE)m}$, there exists *some* actor $k \in \mathcal{B}_{(RE)p}$ such that $i \rightarrow k$, and for *all* actors $l \in \mathcal{B}_{(RE)p}$ there exists *some* actor $j \in \mathcal{B}_{(RE)m}$ such that $j \rightarrow l$. In terms of the permuted and blocked sociomatrix, if the regular equivalence blockmodel includes a tie from $\mathcal{B}_{(RE)m}$ to $\mathcal{B}_{(RE)p}$, then the submatrix that contains the ties from actors in $\mathcal{B}_{(RE)m}$ to actors in $\mathcal{B}_{(RE)p}$ must have a 1 in each row and in each column. This pattern indicates ties from all actors in $\mathcal{B}_{(RE)m}$ to some actor in $\mathcal{B}_{(RE)p}$, and to all actors in $\mathcal{B}_{(RE)p}$ from some actor in $\mathcal{B}_{(RE)m}$. Perfect zeroblocks in regular equivalence blockmodels require that the corresponding submatrix in the sociomatrix be filled completely with 0's.

Let us now look at the regular equivalence blockmodel for the example in Figure 12.1 to illustrate these ideas. We present the regular equivalence blockmodel for the maximal regular equivalence consisting of three equivalence classes (described above). Figure 12.3 shows both the sociomatrix for this relation with rows and columns permuted and partitioned according to the regular equivalence classes, and the image matrix for this regular equivalence blockmodel. Since there are three equivalence classes, the image matrix is of size 3×3.

Consider the submatrix of the sociomatrix corresponding to the ties from members of position $\mathcal{B}_{(RE)2}$ to members of position $\mathcal{B}_{(RE)3}$. Since each member of $\mathcal{B}_{(RE)2}$ has a tie to at least one member of $\mathcal{B}_{(RE)3}$ this submatrix has a 1 in each row. Also, since each member of $\mathcal{B}_{(RE)3}$ has a tie from at least one member of $\mathcal{B}_{(RE)2}$, so this submatrix has

Blocked sociomatrix

	1	2	3	4	5	6	7	8	9
1	-	1	1	1	0	0	0	0	0
2	0	-	0	0	1	1	0	0	0
3	0	0	-	0	0	0	1	0	0
4	0	0	0	-	0	0	0	1	1
5	0	0	0	0	-	0	0	0	0
6	0	0	0	0	0	-	0	0	0
7	0	0	0	0	0	0	-	0	0
8	0	0	0	0	0	0	0	-	0
9	0	0	0	0	0	0	0	0	-

Image matrix for regular equivalence blockmodel

	$\mathcal{B}_{(RE)1}$	$\mathcal{B}_{(RE)2}$	$\mathcal{B}_{(RE)3}$
$\mathcal{B}_{(RE)1}$	-	1	0
$\mathcal{B}_{(RE)2}$	0	0	1
$\mathcal{B}_{(RE)3}$	0	0	0

Fig. 12.3. Blocked sociomatrix and image matrix for regular equivalence blockmodel

a 1 in each column. Thus, in the blockmodel there is a tie from $\mathcal{B}_{(RE)2}$ to $\mathcal{B}_{(RE)3}$, and in the image matrix there is a "1" indicating that $\mathcal{B}_{(RE)2} \rightarrow \mathcal{B}_{(RE)3}$. It is important to note that the submatrix of the sociomatrix corresponding to ties from members of $\mathcal{B}_{(RE)2}$ to $\mathcal{B}_{(RE)3}$ is not completely filled with 1's, as would be required for a (perfect) structural equivalence blockmodel. Figure 12.3 shows the image matrix for this regular equivalence blockmodel.

Regular equivalence blockmodels are a relatively recent development, and have received considerably less attention than structural equivalence blockmodels. As a consequence, they are less widely used. Batagelj, Doreian, and Ferligoj (1992) use the idea of a perfect (or optimal) regular equivalence blockmodel as a standard for optimally partitioning actors into regular equivalence classes. Borgatti and Everett (1992b) discuss how to extend regular equivalence blockmodels to two-mode networks.

12.4.4 ○*A Measure of Regular Equivalence*

As with structural and automorphic equivalence, a network data set may not contain any pairs or subsets of actors who are perfectly regularly equivalent. The earliest approaches to regular equivalence (Sailer 1978; White and Reitz 1985) presented measures of the degree of regular equivalence for pairs of actors in a network. More recently, authors have focused on methods for assigning actors to subsets such that the partition of actors is optimal in the sense that actors in the same subset are nearly regularly equivalent (Batagelj, Doreian, and Ferligoj 1992).

Finding subsets of regularly equivalent actors in a network data set requires simultaneously deciding whether or not the alters to whom potentially regularly equivalent actors are tied are themselves regularly equivalent. If the partition of actors into regular equivalence classes is perfect, then for any two actors, i and j, in the same equivalence class, the presence of a tie from actor i to any actor k in any equivalence class implies that actor j in the same equivalence class as i must also have a tie to some actor, l, in the same equivalence class as k. Thus, for all pairs of actors in the same regular equivalence class, their ties to and from the members of all equivalence classes must "match." One way to measure how close pairs or subsets of actors are to being regularly equivalent is to consider how well the ties to and from pairs of actors "match" each other, in the sense just described.

One of the earliest and most widely used measures of regular equivalence is embodied in the algorithm *REGE* proposed by White and Reitz (1985). This algorithm uses an iterative procedure in which estimates of the degree of regular equivalence between pairs of actors are adjusted in light of the equivalences of the alters adjacent to and from members of the pair. This procedure is described in detail in White and Reitz (1985) and Faust (1988).

We now describe this measure of regular equivalence. We will let M_{ij}^{t+1} be the estimate of the degree of regular equivalence for actors i and j at iteration $t + 1$. This quantity is a function of how well i's ties to and from all actors can be "matched" by j's ties to and from all actors, and vice versa. How well i's ties to and from a specific actor k, can be "matched" by j's ties to and from some actor m on relation $\mathscr{X}_r$ is quantified by $_{ijr}M_{kmr} = \min(x_{ikr}, x_{jmr}) + \min(x_{kir}, x_{mjr})$. Since k and m may not be perfectly regularly equivalent, the quantity $_{ijr}M_{kmr}$ is then weighted by the estimated regular equivalence of k and m from the previous iteration (M_{km}^t), and summed across relations. To locate the best matching m for i's ties to k we need to find the maximum value of $_{ijr}M_{kmr}$ for $m = 1, 2, \ldots, g$. In equation (12.1) the numerator "picks out" the best matching counterparts for all actors k and m adjacent to/from actors i and j.

The denominator of equation (12.1) is the maximum possible value of the numerator, which would be realized if all of actor i's ties to and from its alters and all of actor j's ties to and from its alters could be "matched" perfectly, and all of their alters were regularly equivalent. The maximum possible match on a relation $\mathcal{X}_r$ is given by $_{ijr}\text{Max}_{kmr} = \max(x_{ikr}, x_{jmr}) + \max(x_{kir}, x_{mjr})$. Since this quantity pertains to the particular m in the numerator, we must use the same m in the denominator; this is specified by $\max_m^*$. This measure of regular equivalence, used in the routine *REGE*, is summarized in the following equation:

$$M_{ij}^{t+1} = \frac{\sum_{k=1}^{g} \max_{m=1}^{g} \sum_{r=1}^{R} M_{km}^{t}(_{ijr}M_{kmr}^{t} + _{jir} M_{kmr}^{t})}{\sum_{k=1}^{g} \max_m^* \sum_{r=1}^{R} (_{ijr}\text{Max}_{kmr} + _{jir} \text{Max}_{kmr})}. \qquad (12.1)$$

This quantity ranges from 0 to 1 (if i and j are perfectly regularly equivalent). In the computation of M_{ij}, the equivalence of each pair of actors is revised at each iteration, t, in light of the equivalence of other pairs of actors in the network.

In practice one must decide how many iterations of the *REGE* procedure to run before accepting an estimate of pairwise regular equivalence. As a guideline, let us examine roughly what this measure "captures" at each iteration. Suppose that we have a single directional relation. In this case, the first iteration of the *REGE* algorithm distinguishes between four kinds of actors: actors who have both positive indegree and positive outdegree, actors who have zero indegree and positive outdegree, actors who have zero outdegree and positive indegree, and actors who are isolates. Actors in each of these four classes will be equivalent after the first iteration. In the second iteration, the procedure distinguishes (roughly) among actors in each of the four classes depending on whether or not they have ties to and from actors in the other four classes. The third iteration takes the chain of connections one step further. Some authors have suggested that three iterations of the procedure might be sufficient (Faust 1988). However, substantive and theoretical concerns should be most important in choosing the number of iterations.

Although the description of this algorithm seems to follow closely from the definition of regular equivalence, in practice measuring regular equivalence using this algorithm is problematic in many situations. First, it is important to note that this equivalence measure counts *ties* matched between two actors, not the number of alters matched. Also, when relations are nondirectional (and there are no isolates), when relations are reflexive ($i \rightarrow i$ for all i), or when each actor is involved in at least one reciprocated tie (so that for each i there exists some k such that $i \leftrightarrow k$), then maximizing this measure finds the maximal regular equivalence in which all actors are perfectly regularly equivalent. This happens because a reflexive or a reciprocated tie can perfectly "match" any other tie. In these cases the maximal regular equivalence is trivial and uninteresting. In addition, since the algorithm counts ties matched (rather than actors matched), the indegree and outdegree of each actor influence the measure of equivalence. Finally, since a given network may contain several regular equivalence partitions, other regular equivalences may exist in the network that are not found by the above algorithm (Doreian 1987; Borgatti 1988; Borgatti and Everett 1989).

12.4.5 An Example

Now let us illustrate regular equivalence using the two relations, advice and friendship, for Krackhardt's high-tech managers. We used the program *REGE* in *UCINET 3* (MacEvoy and Freeman n.d.) to do the calculations (identical values result from the *REGE* algorithm in *UCINET IV*). We used three iterations, and included both relations and their transposes in the calculation. The result is a 21×21 symmetric matrix of similarities (the M_{ij}'s). This matrix is presented in Figure 12.4. Notice that overall these values are all fairly large (they range from 0.654 to 0.990) but no pair of managers is perfectly regularly equivalent. Managers 7 (the president) and 9 are notable in that neither of these managers made any friendship choices. Thus, their degree of regular equivalence with other managers appears to be somewhat lower than the degree of regular equivalence among the other managers. To study these equivalences further, we could represent them using either multidimensional scaling or hierarchical clustering. Figure 12.5 shows the dendrogram from a complete link hierarchical clustering of the regular equivalences. We used the program *SYSTAT* (Wilkinson 1987) to do the hierarchical clustering.

We can use the dendrogram in Figure 12.5 to define positions containing approximately regularly equivalent managers. If we examine the dendrogram from top to bottom, we can use a cutoff where there are three clusters. These three clusters define the following positions:

	1	2	3	4	5	6	7	8	9	10	11
1	1.000										
2	0.990	1.000									
3	0.924	0.952	1.000								
4	0.986	0.978	0.915	1.000							
5	0.974	0.963	0.938	0.980	1.000						
6	0.919	0.904	0.847	0.878	0.863	1.000					
7	0.890	0.923	0.924	0.873	0.844	0.772	1.000				
8	0.986	0.978	0.968	0.988	0.977	0.901	0.952	1.000			
9	0.853	0.906	0.930	0.815	0.814	0.738	0.927	0.922	1.000		
10	0.857	0.836	0.854	0.920	0.879	0.917	0.822	0.920	0.827	1.000	
11	0.934	0.948	0.914	0.896	0.896	0.906	0.685	0.919	0.682	0.801	1.000
12	0.983	0.982	0.949	0.976	0.963	0.928	0.885	0.980	0.860	0.891	0.957
13	0.829	0.766	0.828	0.865	0.841	0.920	0.837	0.867	0.788	0.926	0.859
14	0.928	0.945	0.893	0.878	0.865	0.946	0.865	0.913	0.847	0.869	0.951
15	0.975	0.960	0.930	0.982	0.981	0.877	0.839	0.966	0.829	0.929	0.903
16	0.987	0.979	0.959	0.984	0.980	0.921	0.928	0.991	0.885	0.915	0.934
17	0.978	0.972	0.913	0.976	0.957	0.928	0.691	0.960	0.654	0.894	0.943
18	0.948	0.929	0.943	0.940	0.958	0.828	0.956	0.964	0.915	0.865	0.780
19	0.977	0.963	0.910	0.983	0.980	0.875	0.797	0.971	0.769	0.913	0.906
20	0.907	0.921	0.932	0.902	0.897	0.922	0.901	0.941	0.940	0.942	0.851
21	0.982	0.976	0.911	0.984	0.969	0.898	0.918	0.977	0.841	0.904	0.896

(continued)

	12	13	14	15	16	17	18	19	20	21
12	1.000									
13	0.903	1.000								
14	0.954	0.837	1.000							
15	0.959	0.888	0.877	1.000						
16	0.982	0.878	0.926	0.973	1.000					
17	0.974	0.902	0.935	0.956	0.965	1.000				
18	0.936	0.869	0.871	0.960	0.959	0.856	1.000			
19	0.964	0.880	0.878	0.984	0.975	0.963	0.943	1.000		
20	0.884	0.878	0.924	0.926	0.934	0.872	0.911	0.902	1.000	
21	0.975	0.864	0.904	0.971	0.979	0.970	0.929	0.967	0.904	1.000

Fig. 12.4. Regular equivalences computed using *REGE* on advice and friendship relations for Krackhardt's high-tech managers

- $\mathcal{B}_{(RE)1}$: $\{3, 7, 9, 18\}$
- $\mathcal{B}_{(RE)2}$: $\{6, 10, 13, 20\}$
- $\mathcal{B}_{(RE)3}$: $\{1, 2, 4, 5, 8, 11, 12, 14, 15, 16, 17, 19, 21\}$

Position $\mathcal{B}_{(RE)1}$ contains the president (7) and one of the vice presidents (18). The remaining vice presidents are in position $\mathcal{B}_{(RE)3}$. A more useful clustering might use a more stringent cutoff, and have five positions (dividing positions $\mathcal{B}_{(RE)2}$ and $\mathcal{B}_{(RE)3}$ each into two new positions). However,

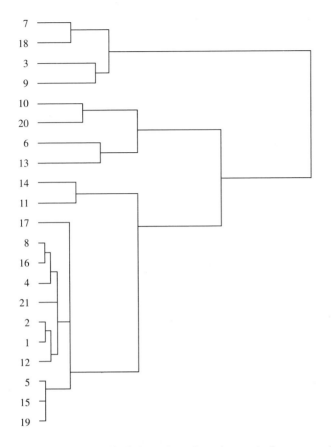

Fig. 12.5. Hierarchical clustering of regular equivalences on advice and friendship for Krackhardt's high-tech managers

the large position, $\mathscr{B}_{(RE)3}$, in the original partition appears to contain managers who are quite nearly regularly equivalent, and probably should not be split further.

12.5 "Types" of Ties

Now, let us consider two definitions of equivalence that focus on the types of ties in which each actor is involved. These two approaches, Winship and Mandel's local role equivalence and Breiger and Pattison's ego algebras, consider associations among relations from the perspectives of individual actors (Mandel 1983; Breiger and Pattison 1986; Winship

1974, 1988; Winship and Mandel 1983). Recall that the role structure for a network consists of the associations among primitive and compound relations that hold for the network as a whole. To study individual roles, we will consider the associations among relations from the perspectives of individual actors.

To describe these approaches it will be useful to return to Merton's (1957) ideas of *role relation* and *role set*, which we discussed at the beginning of this chapter. We will show how these ideas relate to social network properties for actors and pairs of actors, and then show how they can be used to define network roles and positions for individual actors.

Merton observed that people occupying a social position (which he called a social status) are involved in a number of social roles vis-à-vis occupants of other social positions. For a *pair* of positions, the *role relation* is the collection of ways in which members of that pair of positions relate to each other. For a *single* position, the collection of all of the ways in which an occupant of a particular position relates to others in other positions is called the *role set* of the position. In a social network, the role set for a position is the collection of types of ties between members of a given position and members of other positions.

To use the idea of a role set to study social networks, we need to formalize the idea of types of ties from the perspective of an individual actor, and then to evaluate whether pairs or subsets of actors have the same types of ties. If actors are involved in the same types of ties, then they perform the same network role, and are assigned to the same position. The idea is to describe the collection of primitive and compound relations in which each *individual* actor is involved, and to compare these collections of relations between actors.

Recall that social roles involve extended chains of connection among people, and thus require compound relations in addition to primitive relations. Associations among relations can be studied by focusing on the composition of relations. Just as we can study the operation of composition of relations for a group, we can also study composition of relations from the perspective of individual actors and pairs of actors.

In general we will refer to the set of relations (including primitive and compound relations) as $\mathscr{S}^+$, and let R_+ be the number of primitive and compound relations in the set. The collection of relations included in the set, and thus the number of relations in it, are different for the two approaches that we will discuss below. Each relation (primitive and compound) can be presented in a sociomatrix. If there are R_+ relations in total, we summarize these relations in a $g \times g \times R_+$ super-sociomatrix. Each layer of the super-sociomatrix is the sociomatrix for one of the relations. Winship and Mandel (1983) refer to this super-sociomatrix as a *relation box*. The number of relations included in the set, and thus the number of layers in the super-sociomatrix varies across methods.

Now, let us examine a network from two different perspectives, an individual actor and a pair of actors, and see how these perspectives relate to the ideas of role set and role relation. First, consider the collection of ties that exist between a pair of actors, i and j; that is, focus on those relations $\mathscr{X}_r$ on which $x_{ijr} = 1$. We define the *role relation* for a pair of actors, i, j, as the collection of distinct relations on which i has a tie to j. We denote this collection as $\mathscr{S}_{ij}$, where $\mathscr{S}_{ij}$ is a subset of the set of primitive and compound relations, $\mathscr{S}^+$; $\mathscr{S}_{ij} \subseteq \mathscr{S}^+$, and $\mathscr{X}_r \in \mathscr{S}_{ij}$ if $x_{ijr} = 1$. In the super-sociomatrix, information about the role relation for actors i and j is contained in the vector $\mathbf{x}_{ij} = (x_{ij1}, x_{ij2}, \ldots, x_{ijR_+})$.

Now consider an individual actor. Each actor has g possible role relations (including one with itself). The role set for an actor is the collection of all of its distinct role relations. Thus, the role set for actor i, which we will denote by $\mathscr{S}_i^*$, is the collection of all of the distinct ways that actor i relates to other actors. The role set can be studied by focusing on all of the distinct role relations; that is, we consider the distinct role relations, $\mathscr{S}_{ij}$ for $j = 1, 2, \ldots, g$. Since role relations are coded in the vectors $\mathbf{x}_{ij}$ in the super-sociomatrix, information about the role set of an actor is contained in the collection of distinct vectors $\mathbf{x}_{ij}$ for $j = 1, 2, \ldots, g$. For actor i, these vectors are in the ith (horizontal) row of the sociomatrix, across the g columns (indexing actors) and the R_+ layers, indexing relations. Winship and Mandel (1983) use the term *relation plane* to refer to this "slice" of the super-sociomatrix containing information about an actor's role set.

12.5.1 An Example

We now illustrate both role relations and role sets using the hypothetical example from Chapter 11. Consider the example of two directional relations that we used to illustrate relational algebras in Chapter 11. The graphs for these two relations are presented in Figure 12.6. Recall that the example consisted of two primitive relations, labeled H and L, and an additional three compound relations (including the null relation). In Figure 12.6 we have labeled the nodes in this graph so that we can keep track of the individual actors in this network.

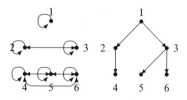

Fig. 12.6. A hypothetical graph for two relations

For this example we will consider the set of all distinct primitive and compound relations. Let us focus on one actor's "view" of this network. Start with actor 1. We see that actor 1 has the following ties with the other actors (including itself):

- $1 \xrightarrow{L} 1: \mathscr{S}_{1,1} = \{L\}$
- $1 \xrightarrow{H} 2, 1 \xrightarrow{HL} 2: \mathscr{S}_{1,2} = \{H, HL\}$
- $1 \xrightarrow{H} 3, 1 \xrightarrow{HL} 3: \mathscr{S}_{1,3} = \{H, HL\}$
- $1 \xrightarrow{HH} 4: \mathscr{S}_{1,4} = \{HH\}$
- $1 \xrightarrow{HH} 5: \mathscr{S}_{1,5} = \{HH\}$
- $1 \xrightarrow{HH} 6: \mathscr{S}_{1,6} = \{HH\}$

This list describes the types of ties that are defined for actor 1. Each type is a role relation, and the collection of different role relations constitutes actor 1's role set.

In this example actor 1 has ties to actor 2 on relations H, and HL, so the role relation $\mathscr{S}_{1,2} = \{H, HL\}$ characterizes how 1 is tied to 2. Actor 1 also has ties to actor 3 on H and HL, so these two role relations are the same; $\mathscr{S}_{1,2} = \mathscr{S}_{1,3} = \{H, HL\}$. However there is a different role relation linking actor 1 to actors 4, 5, and 6; $(\mathscr{S}_{1,4} = \mathscr{S}_{1,5} = \mathscr{S}_{1,6} = \{HH\})$ and to itself $(\mathscr{S}_{1,1} = \{L\})$. Thus, actor 1 has three distinct role relations that constitute its role set: $\mathscr{S}_{1,2} = \mathscr{S}_{1,3} = \{H, HL\}$, linking 1 to 2 and 3, $\mathscr{S}_{1,1} = \{L\}$ linking 1 to itself, and $\mathscr{S}_{1,4} = \mathscr{S}_{1,5} = \mathscr{S}_{1,6} = \{HH\}$ linking 1 to 4, 5, and 6. Also, notice that from 1's perspective relations H and HL are indistinguishable since they tie 1 to exactly the same other actors.

Now, let us look at the role sets for all actors and the role relations for all pairs of actors in this example. Figure 12.7 shows the collection of ties for each actor (as ego) to each other actor (as alter) on the five distinct primitive and compound relations. For each pair of actors the

Role relations:
Actor 1: $\mathcal{S}_{1,1} = \{L\}$, $\mathcal{S}_{1,2} = \mathcal{S}_{1,3} = \{H, HL\}$, $\mathcal{S}_{1,4} = \mathcal{S}_{1,5} = \mathcal{S}_{1,6} = \{HH\}$
Actor 2: $\mathcal{S}_{2,1} = \{HH, \emptyset\}$, $\mathcal{S}_{2,2} = \mathcal{S}_{2,3} = \{L\}$, $\mathcal{S}_{2,4} = \{H\}$, $\mathcal{S}_{2,5} = \mathcal{S}_{2,6} = \{HL\}$
Actor 3: $\mathcal{S}_{3,1} = \{HH, \emptyset\}$, $\mathcal{S}_{3,2} = \mathcal{S}_{3,3} = \{L\}$, $\mathcal{S}_{3,4} = \{HL\}$, $\mathcal{S}_{3,5} = \mathcal{S}_{3,6} = \{H\}$
Actor 4: $\mathcal{S}_{4,1} = \mathcal{S}_{4,2} = \mathcal{S}_{4,3} = \{H, HL, HH, \emptyset\}$, $\mathcal{S}_{4,4} = \mathcal{S}_{4,5} = \mathcal{S}_{4,6} = \{L\}$
Actor 5: $\mathcal{S}_{5,1} = \mathcal{S}_{5,2} = \mathcal{S}_{5,3} = \{H, HL, HH, \emptyset\}$, $\mathcal{S}_{5,4} = \mathcal{S}_{5,5} = \mathcal{S}_{5,6} = \{L\}$
Actor 6: $\mathcal{S}_{6,1} = \mathcal{S}_{6,2} = \mathcal{S}_{6,3} = \{H, HL, HH, \emptyset\}$, $\mathcal{S}_{6,4} = \mathcal{S}_{6,5} = \mathcal{S}_{6,6} = \{L\}$
Role sets:
$\mathcal{S}_1^* = \{\{L\}, \{H, HL\}, \{HH\}, \{\emptyset\}\}$
$\mathcal{S}_2^* = \mathcal{S}_3^* = \{\{L\}, \{H\}, \{HL\}, \{HH, \emptyset\}\}$
$\mathcal{S}_4^* = \mathcal{S}_5^* = \mathcal{S}_6^* = \{\{L\}, \{H, HL, HH, \emptyset\}\}$.

Fig. 12.7. Local roles

collection is the role relation, and for each actor the collection of distinct role relations is its role set.

This example has illustrated the idea of types of ties using the operation of composition of relations, and the concepts of role relation for a pair of actors and of role set of an actor. We can now use these ideas to define and compare individual roles. In the next two sections we present two different definitions and measures of equivalence for individual roles. These two methods, local role equivalence (Winship and Mandel 1983, and Mandel 1983) and ego algebras (Breiger and Pattison 1986) focus on sets of primitive and compound relations, but they differ in terms of which relations are included in the set, how individual roles are defined, and how similarity (or dissimilarity) of individual roles is calculated.

12.6 Local Role Equivalence

Winship and Mandel (1983) use the role set of each actor to define *local role equivalence*, or simply *role equivalence*. Two actors are *role equivalent* (*LRE*) if they have identical role sets. That is, actors i and j are role equivalent if the collection of ways in which actor i relates to other actors is the same as the collection of ways in which actor j relates to other actors. Recall that we denote the role set for actor i by $\mathcal{S}_i^*$. Actors i and j are role equivalent, $i \overset{LRE}{\equiv} j$, if and only if $\mathcal{S}_i^* = \mathcal{S}_j^*$. Formally, i and j are role equivalent if and only if, for every role relation $\mathcal{S}_{ik} \in \mathcal{S}_i^*$, there exists a role relation $\mathcal{S}_{jl} \in \mathcal{S}_j^*$, such that $\mathcal{S}_{ik} = \mathcal{S}_{jl}$, and for every role relation $\mathcal{S}_{jl} \in \mathcal{S}_j^*$, there exists a role relation $\mathcal{S}_{ik} \in \mathcal{S}_i^*$, such that $\mathcal{S}_{jl} = \mathcal{S}_{ik}$.

Returning to the example in Figure 12.6 and the role sets for these six actors, described in Figure 12.7, we see that the role set for actor 2 is identical to that for actor 3; $\mathscr{S}_2^* = \mathscr{S}_3^* = \{\{H\},\{HL\},\{L\},\{HH,\emptyset\}\}$. Similarly, the role sets for actors 4, 5, and 6 are identical; $\mathscr{S}_4^* = \mathscr{S}_5^* = \mathscr{S}_6^* = \{\{L\},\{H,HL,HH,\emptyset\}\}$. No other actor has a role set that is the same as actor 1's, thus there are three subsets of role equivalent actors.

12.6.1 Measuring Local Role Dissimilarity

In actual social network data, it is unlikely that two actors will be perfectly role equivalent. Just as we have measures of structural equivalence and of regular equivalence, we also have a measure of role equivalence. The measure of role equivalence between actors focuses on how well the role relations in two actors' role sets "match" each other. Following Winship and Mandel (1983), the degree of role equivalence between i and j depends on the extent to which role relations can be found in j's role set to "match" the role relations in i's role set, and vice versa.

Recall that the role set for an actor, $\mathscr{S}_i^*$ is the collection of all role relations, $\mathscr{S}_{ij}$, that this actor has with others actors, including itself. If actors i and j are role equivalent, then all of the distinct role relations in i's role set must be present in the collection of role relations in j's role set, and vice versa. The alters, k and l, for the role relations need not be the same, and there need not be the same number of role relations of a given type. Since information about the contents of the role relation for a pair of actors, say i and k, is coded in the vector $\mathbf{x}_{ik}$, one can compare role relations $\mathscr{S}_{ik}$ and $\mathscr{S}_{jl}$ by comparing the vectors $\mathbf{x}_{ik}$ and $\mathbf{x}_{jl}$. In the super-sociomatrix, the vector $\mathbf{x}_{ik} = (x_{ik1}, x_{ik2}, \ldots, x_{ikR_+})$ codes the presence and absence of ties from actor i to actor k on the R_+ relations. This vector thus contains information about the role relation for actors i and k. Similarly, the vector $\mathbf{x}_{jl}$ contains information about the role relation for actors j and l. To determine whether actors i and j are role equivalent, we compare the vectors $\mathbf{x}_{ik}$ and $\mathbf{x}_{jl}$, for $l = 1, 2, \ldots, g$. If i and j are role equivalent, then the entries in the vectors $\mathbf{x}_{ik}$ and $\mathbf{x}_{jl}$ must "match."

For actors i and j to be role equivalent, every binary vector indicating a role relation for actor i to some actor k must be identical to some vector indicating a role relation for actor j with an actor l, and vice versa. This strategy of matching vectors in a super-sociomatrix is used to decide whether identical role relations exist between a pair of actors.

Now, let us consider one measure of local role equivalence. If we begin with R relations, and then include these R relations plus all compound relations up to word length p, then the number of relations in the set is: $R_+ = R + R^2 + R^3 + \cdots + R^p$. For this approach, the relevant set of relations includes all relations and compound relations up to a given word length, and includes relations regardless of whether they are distinct or not.

A measure of the dissimilarity of two role relations is the city block distance between the vectors that code the role relations in the super-sociomatrix (which is equal to the sum of the absolute value of the differences between corresponding entries). The dissimilarity between the role relations $\mathscr{S}_{ik}$ for actors i and k (coded in the vector $\mathbf{x}_{ik}$) and $\mathscr{S}_{jl}$ for actors j and l (coded in the vector $\mathbf{x}_{jl}$) is:

$$d(\mathscr{S}_{ik}, \mathscr{S}_{jl}) = \sum_{r=1}^{R_+} |x_{ikr} - x_{jlr}|. \tag{12.2}$$

This sum is a count of the number of relations (out of R_+) on which i's tie to alter k is different from j's tie to alter l. If the sum is 0, then the role relations are identical, that is, i relates to k in exactly the same ways that j relates to l. If the sum is large, then the role relation between i and k is different from the role relation between j and l. The maximum possible value of $d(\mathscr{S}_{ik}, \mathscr{S}_{jl})$ is R_+.

Now, calculating the dissimilarity between two actors' role sets requires finding the best "match" for the role relations contained in each actor's role set among the role relations contained in the other actor's role set. Consider the similarity of the role sets for actors i and j. Since there are g actors, each of whom is related to i (we include i's role relation with itself), from i's perspective, matches must be found for each of these g actors among those actors who are related to j. Similarly, since j is related to g actors, matches must be found in i's ties for each of these g actors. From i's perspective, the best match for a given role relation, $\mathscr{S}_{ik}$, in j's set of role relations is j's role relation with alter l for whom equation (12.2) is smallest. From i's perspective this is $\min_l d(\mathscr{S}_{ik}, \mathscr{S}_{jl})$. From j's perspective the best match is $\min_k d(\mathscr{S}_{jl}, \mathscr{S}_{ik})$.

The degree of role equivalence of actors i and j compares all role relations in the role sets of the two actors; $\mathscr{S}_i^*$ and $\mathscr{S}_j^*$. The measure, $D(\mathscr{S}_i^*, \mathscr{S}_j^*)$, is defined as the sum of the minimum distances from actor i's role relations to actor j's role relations, plus the sum of the minimum distances from actor j's role relations to actor i's role relations. This quantity (Winship and Mandel 1983) is given by the following equation:

$$D(\mathscr{S}_i^*, \mathscr{S}_j^*) = \sum_{k=1}^{g} \min_l d(\mathscr{S}_{ik}, \mathscr{S}_{jl}) + \sum_{l=1}^{g} \min_k d(\mathscr{S}_{jl}, \mathscr{S}_{ik}). \tag{12.3}$$

The minimum possible value of $D(\mathscr{S}_i^*, \mathscr{S}_j^*)$ is 0, if actors i and j are perfectly role equivalent (their role sets contain identical role relations). The maximum possible is $2gR_+$.

A couple of comments are in order. First, as Winship and Mandel (1983) point out, role equivalence is based on the similarity of the vectors $\mathbf{x}_{ik}$ and $\mathbf{x}_{jl}$ for the collection of all primitive and compound relations up to a given word length. This is not exactly the same as comparing the two actors' role sets, since the role sets contain only the *distinct* role relations, whereas the set of all primitive and compound relations to a given word length may contain duplicate role relations. A given actor may have identical role relations with more than one actor, and these are counted each time they occur, not as a single role relation. In addition, since the relevant collection of relations for this approach includes primitive and compound relations up to a given word length, it does not necessarily include all possible relations that could be formed using the operation of composition. Relations that result from words that are longer than the specified word length are not included in this calculation.

An important feature of role equivalence is that it can be generalized to measure the role equivalence of actors from different networks, so long as the same relations are measured in both networks. For example if the relations "is a friend of" and "goes to for help and advice" are measured on the managers in two different corporations, then one can study the similarity of actors' roles between the two corporations. A slight modification in equation (12.3) to allow for different group sizes is all that is required. Letting $g_\mathscr{N}$ be the size of the network containing actor i, and $g_\mathscr{M}$ be the size of the network containing actor j, we can revise equation (12.3) as follows:

$$D(\mathscr{S}_i^*, \mathscr{S}_j^*) = \sum_{k=1}^{g_\mathscr{N}} \min_l d(\mathscr{S}_{ik}, \mathscr{S}_{jl}) + \sum_{l=1}^{g_\mathscr{M}} \min_k d(\mathscr{S}_{jl}, \mathscr{S}_{ik}). \qquad (12.4)$$

The approach of Winship and Mandel compares individual roles by comparing the actors' role sets. Actors are role equivalent if their role sets contain the same collections of role relations. That is, two actors are role equivalent if their "repertoires" of ways of relating with alters are the same. However, unlike regular equivalence, role equivalence does not require that role equivalent actors be tied by the same role relations to actors who are themselves role equivalent. Thus, role equivalence is more general than regular equivalence (Pattison 1988; White and Reitz 1983). Actors may be role equivalent without being regularly equivalent. White and Reitz (1983) discuss the relationship between regular equivalence

	1	2	3	4	5	6
1	0	3	3	11	11	11
2	3	0	0	5	5	5
3	3	0	0	5	5	5
4	11	5	5	0	0	0
5	11	5	5	0	0	0
6	11	5	5	0	0	0

Fig. 12.8. Role equivalences for hypothetical example of two relations

and local role equivalence. They note that local role equivalence is comparable to using the collection of relations as input to the *REGE* algorithm and calculating regular equivalence for a single iteration.

12.6.2 Examples

We will illustrate local role equivalence using both the example of two hypothetical relations in Figure 12.6 and the relations of advice and friendship for Krackhardt's high-tech managers. In both examples we used the routine *WINMAN* in the program *ROLE* (Breiger 1986).

First consider the relations H and L for the example in Figure 12.6. For this analysis we used all simple and compound relations up to length two and excluded transposes. Thus, there $R_+ = 2 + 2^2 = 6$ relations in total in this analysis (recall that identical relations are included so there are more than the five distinct relations presented in Chapter 11). The measures of local role equivalence for pairs of actors are given in Figure 12.8. Since values of 0 on this measure indicate perfect role equivalence, there are three subsets of role equivalent (*LRE*) actors:

- $\mathscr{B}_{(LRE)1} : \{1\}$
- $\mathscr{B}_{(LRE)2} : \{2, 3\}$
- $\mathscr{B}_{(LRE)3} : \{4, 5, 6\}$

Now, let us consider local role equivalence for the advice and friendship relations for Krackhardt's high-tech managers. We used the program *ROLE* (Breiger 1986) and the subroutine *WINMAN* to do these calculations. In this example we included words up to length three but did not include the transposes of the two relations. Thus, there are $R_+ = 2 + 2^2 + 2^3 = 14$ primitive and compound relations. The distances measuring the local role equivalence are given in Figure 12.9.

We clustered the distances shown in Figure 12.9 using complete link hierarchical clustering (using the program *SYSTAT*, Wilkinson 1987).

	1	2	3	4	5	6	7	8	9	10	11
1	0										
2	15	0									
3	31	30	0								
4	23	14	13	0							
5	29	42	12	27	0						
6	45	37	31	23	45	0					
7	36	29	35	23	49	21	0				
8	22	12	20	5	33	19	23	0			
9	35	41	23	25	16	46	46	30	0		
10	45	49	42	43	52	27	31	39	59	0	
11	27	22	23	18	37	19	32	13	41	29	0
12	33	24	40	25	42	42	36	24	32	61	35
13	51	65	34	43	42	44	41	41	46	41	46
14	32	26	19	20	33	26	31	18	36	36	11
15	26	37	18	30	11	43	37	34	18	39	35
16	17	16	28	16	31	28	23	12	30	30	19
17	24	17	30	20	36	33	27	19	30	55	29
18	24	14	36	22	50	38	29	20	44	50	31
19	23	36	16	26	9	44	44	30	17	47	30
20	42	44	18	25	37	24	26	23	41	29	23
21	18	7	37	24	47	35	22	19	44	49	28

(continued)

	12	13	14	15	16	17	18	19	20	21
12	0									
13	54	0								
14	40	41	0							
15	41	35	29	0						
16	25	39	26	27	0					
17	13	46	25	34	22	0				
18	11	56	31	36	21	19	0			
19	36	37	25	7	27	31	36	0		
20	41	30	28	37	28	38	44	36	0	
21	32	62	28	37	19	25	16	40	43	0

Fig. 12.9. Role equivalences for advice and friendship relations for Krackhardt's high-tech managers

The dendrogram for this clustering is in Figure 12.10. If we consider the dendrogram for this example, and the level at which there are five clusters, we have the following five subsets of approximately role equivalent managers:

- $\mathscr{B}_{(LRE)1}$: $\{13\}$
- $\mathscr{B}_{(LRE)2}$: $\{6, 7, 10, 20\}$
- $\mathscr{B}_{(LRE)3}$: $\{12, 17, 18\}$

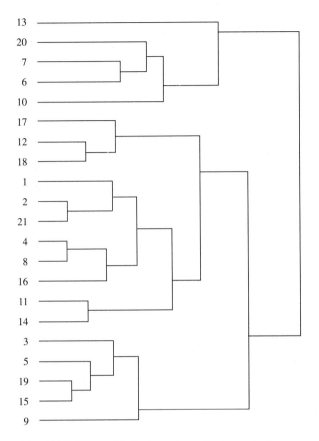

Fig. 12.10. Hierarchical clustering of role equivalences on advice and friendship relations for Krackhardt's high-tech managers

- $\mathcal{B}_{(LRE)4}$: $\{1, 2, 4, 8, 11, 14, 16, 21\}$
- $\mathcal{B}_{(LRE)5}$: $\{3, 5, 9, 15, 19\}$

$\mathcal{B}_{(LRE)4}$ contains all of the members of department 4 (1, 2, 4, 16) and three of the four vice presidents (2, 14, 21). Position $\mathcal{B}_{(LRE)5}$ contains only managers from department 2.

A related approach for studying individual roles is ego algebras (Breiger and Pattison 1986). We discuss this approach next.

12.7 ⊗Ego Algebras

Breiger and Pattison (1986) present a comprehensive scheme for modeling individual actors' roles and group role structure simultaneously. Their approach, which they refer to as *ego algebras*, builds on the algebra of relational structures. Pattison (1993) elaborates on these ideas in the context of algebraic models. Much of the mathematics of this approach is related to the mathematics used to model role structures, and was presented in Chapter 11. We recommend that the reader review the discussion in Chapter 11 before proceeding with this section.

The scheme presented by Breiger and Pattison has two major parts: the first describes the perspectives of the individual actors in order to study which actors have similar roles or positions in a network, and the second summarizes the relational features that are common to all members of the network. Since our focus in this chapter is the equivalence of individual actors, we will concentrate on the first part of Breiger and Pattison's approach. The second part of their approach has much in common with relational algebras though in general the results will be different.

The idea of ego algebras is that an individual's view of the network is based, in part, on which sets of relations "go together" by always occurring together for that actor. Now, we will use compound relations and the identity of relations from the perspectives of individual actors. We will first define composition and identity of relations for individual actors, and then show how to represent individual (or ego) algebras in a right multiplication table. Following that we describe how to compare ego algebras for different actors.

Recall that a compound relation is the combination of two relations, for example "a friend of a friend." The operation of composition of relations from the perspective of an individual actor focuses on ties emanating from the actor. From actor i's perspective, the compound relation ST is defined as $i(ST)j$ if there exists some actor k such that iSk and kTj. We can study composition of relations from the perspective of individual actors using Boolean matrix multiplication. Consider the ties from actor i to other actors on the compound relation ST. In matrix terms, these ties are the Boolean product of the $1 \times g$ vector of ties emanating from actor i on relation S times the $g \times g$ sociomatrix for relation T. The result is a $1 \times g$ vector of ties from actor i on the compound relation ST.

Compound relations and matrix multiplication for an individual actor can be represented in a right multiplication table. This table differs from the multiplication table for a network in that the elements in the rows of the table are *vectors* of ties from the actor on each relation, and the elements in the columns are the *sociomatrices* for the primitive relations. Such a multiplication table is called a *right multiplication* table. We will present examples of right multiplication tables for individual actors below.

Now, consider whether two relations are identical. For a whole group, two relations are identical if they have ties between exactly the same pairs of actors. For example the relations "is a friend of" and "goes to for help and advice" are identical in some network if whenever a person nominates another as a friend, they also name the other person as someone they go to for help and advice, and vice versa. In that case, the two relations are "globally" identical; from the perspective of the whole group, and from the perspective of any individual in the group, the relations tie exactly the same other people. In contrast, from an actor's ego-centered view, two relations are identical if ties on one relation tie this actor to exactly the same other actors as do ties on a second relation. Formally, from the perspective of actor i, relations $\mathcal{X}_r$ and $\mathcal{X}_s$ are identical if $i \overset{\mathcal{X}_r}{\to} j$ if and only if $i \overset{\mathcal{X}_s}{\to} j$ and $j \overset{\mathcal{X}_r}{\to} i$ if and only if $j \overset{\mathcal{X}_s}{\to} i$ for $j = 1, 2, \ldots, g$. Two relations may be identical from the perspective of an individual actor without being identical for the entire group. We can use these ideas to study individual roles.

Suppose that we have a multirelational network, and from it construct the semigroup, $\mathcal{S}$, containing the distinct primitive relations plus all possible distinct compound relations formed using the operation of composition. As usual, we let R_S be the total number of relations in $\mathcal{S}$. Since the semigroup is closed under the operation of composition, it contains all of the possible ways that actors in the network can be tied by the primitive relations and the compound relations that can be constructed from them.

Although we could form an infinite number of compound relations from the set of primitive relations, in fact the number of distinct relations that can be formed is finite. Some relations tie exactly the same pairs of actors, and are thus (globally) identical. The semigroup thus defines a partition of the set of all possible relations into a collection of subsets of identical relations. Now, let us take this idea of partitioning a set by identifying identical elements, and use it to analyze individual roles.

Consider an individual actor, say i, and its perspective on the relations in the semigroup $\mathcal{S}$. From i's perspective some relations tie i to exactly the same other actors. To actor i, these relations are identical. Thus, from actor i's perspective the elements of $\mathscr{S}$ can be partitioned into classes such that all relations that are identical from its perspective are assigned to the same class. Let us denote the partition of $\mathscr{S}$, based on the identity of relations from the perspective of actor i, by $\mathscr{S}_i$. We let R_{S_i} be the number of elements in $\mathscr{S}_i$ (the number of distinct relations from i's perspective), where $R_{S_i} \leq R_S$.

12.7.1 Definition of Ego Algebras

The *ego algebra* for actor i consists of a partition of relations in $\mathscr{S}$ into a set of equivalence classes, $\mathscr{S}_i$, such that relations that are identical from i's perspective are assigned to the same equivalence class, and the right multiplication table describing composition of relations from i's perspective (Breiger and Pattison 1986). An ego algebra preserves the operation of composition for right multiplication. Composition of relations is defined for ties emanating from an actor (Pattison 1993).

To illustrate, consider the two hypothetical relations H and L in Figure 12.6. As we saw in Chapter 11, the semigroup constructed from these relations contains $R_S = 5$ distinct images, including the null image. Thus, $\mathscr{S} = \{H, L, HL, HH, \emptyset\}$, and is also represented by a multiplication table, showing the composition of relations (see Figure 11.3). From the perspective of the whole group there are five distinct ways that actors can be related to each other.

Now, consider the perspectives of individual actors in this example. For each actor we present both the equations among relations (the subsets of relations that are equivalent for that actor) and the right multiplication table expressing the composition of relations from that actor's perspective. Figure 12.11 presents both the equations among relations and the right multiplication tables for the six actors.

For each actor, relations within the same subset are indistinguishable. For the entire group there are five elements in the semigroup, $R_S = 5$, however, in this example, individual actors "see" fewer distinctions among primitive and compound relations: $R_{S_1} = 4$, $R_{S_2} = R_{S_3} = 4$, and $R_{S_4} = R_{S_5} = R_{S_6} = 2$. Notice that actors 2 and 3 have identical equations among relations and identical right multiplication tables, as do actors 4, 5, and 6.

actor 1: $\{H, HL\}\{L\}\{HH\}\{\emptyset\}$

		$1 = H$	$2 = L$
1	H	3	1
2	L	1	2
3	HH	4	3
4	$\emptyset$	4	4

actors 2 and 3: $\{H\}\{L\}\{HL\}\{HH, \emptyset\}$

		$1 = H$	$2 = L$
1	H	4	3
2	L	3	2
3	HL	4	3
4	HH	4	4

actors 4, 5, and 6: $\{L\}\{H, HL, HH, \emptyset\}$

		$1 = H$	$2 = L$
1	H	1	1
2	L	1	2

Fig. 12.11. Ego algebras for the example of two relations

12.7.2 Equivalence of Ego Algebras

We can now define *ego algebra equivalence*. Two actors have identical ego algebras, and are thus ego-algebraically equivalent (EA), if the equivalences among relations and the composition of relations are the same from each actor's perspective. Formally, actors i and j are equivalent, $i \overset{EA}{\equiv} j$, if $\mathscr{S}_i$, the partition of $\mathscr{S}$ for actor i, is identical to $\mathscr{S}_j$, the partition of $\mathscr{S}$ for actor j, and their right multiplication tables are identical.

We turn now to measuring the similarity of ego algebras.

12.7.3 Measuring Ego Algebra Similarity

To measure the similarity of ego algebras we use the same approach that we used to compare the role algebras for two groups. Since each ego algebra imposes a partition on the set of relations, $\mathscr{S}$, the measure of ego algebra similarity for actors i and j compares the partitions $\mathscr{S}_i$ and $\mathscr{S}_j$ defined by the two ego algebras. We can adapt equations 11.1 and 11.2 from Chapter 11 to measure the similarity of two ego algebras (Breiger and Pattison 1986, Boorman and White 1976). For a more detailed discussion of local role algebras and comparison of role algebras see Pattison (1993).

Recall that the joint homomorphic reduction of two role structures is the most refined role structure that is a homomorphic reduction of both. Breiger and Pattison (1986) compare ego algebras by the *joint right homomorphism* of two ego algebras (see also, Pattison 1993). We use the right homomorphic reduction since ego algebras are defined for right multiplication. As with the joint homomorphic reduction of two role structures, the joint right homomorphic reduction of two ego algebras is a simplification in which equations in either ego algebra are included in the joint homomorphic reduction of the two (Breiger and Pattison 1986).

We will denote the joint right homomorphic reduction of the ego algebras for actors i and j by $\mathcal{Q}_{ij}^{\text{JNT}}$. The joint right homomorphic reduction of two ego algebras is that algebra which is a right homomorphic image of both ego algebras (Pattison, personal communication). The joint right homomorphic reduction, $\mathcal{Q}_{ij}^{\text{JNT}}$, specifies two mappings: $\psi_i : \mathcal{S}_i \to \mathcal{Q}_{ij}^{\text{JNT}}$ for actor i, and $\psi_j : \mathcal{S}_j \to \mathcal{Q}_{ij}^{\text{JNT}}$ for actor j. Each of these mappings is a right homomorphism and preserves the operation of right multiplication. Each mapping defines a partition of the relations in the ego algebra into classes so that within a class relations are equivalent for either one actor or the other. The joint right homomorphic reduction is (usually) a coarser partition of the set $\mathcal{S}$, since it equates relations that are identical from the perspective of either individual actor. A measure of the degree of equivalence of two ego algebras is a measure of how much "coarser" the partition described by their joint right homomorphic reduction is, compared to the partitions of the two ego algebras.

Let $R_{\mathcal{S}_i}$ and $R_{\mathcal{S}_j}$ be the number of equivalence classes in $\mathcal{S}_i$ and $\mathcal{S}_j$, respectively, and let R_{ij}^{JNT} be the number of classes in $\mathcal{Q}_{ij}^{\text{JNT}}$, the joint right homomorphic reduction of $\mathcal{S}_i$ and $\mathcal{S}_j$. If $R_{ij}^{\text{JNT}} < R_{\mathcal{S}_i}$, then some elements in $\mathcal{S}_i$ will be in the same class in $\mathcal{Q}_{ij}^{\text{JNT}}$. We will let c_{ik} be the number of elements from $\mathcal{S}_i$ that are in the kth class of $\mathcal{Q}_{ij}^{\text{JNT}}$, where $k = 1, 2, \ldots, R_{ij}^{\text{JNT}}$. The coarseness of $\mathcal{Q}_{ij}^{\text{JNT}}$ compared to ego algebra $\mathcal{S}_i$ is calculated as:

$$h(\mathcal{Q}_{ij|i}^{\text{JNT}}) = \frac{\sum_{k=1}^{R_{ij}^{\text{JNT}}} \binom{c_{ik}}{2}}{\binom{R_{\mathcal{S}_i}}{2}}. \tag{12.5}$$

We also have $h(\mathcal{Q}_{ij|j}^{\text{JNT}})$ the coarseness of $\mathcal{Q}_{ij}^{\text{JNT}}$ compared to ego algebra $\mathcal{S}_j$.

	1	2	3	4	5	6
1	0.00	0.33	0.33	0.50	0.50	0.50
2	0.33	0.00	0.00	0.50	0.50	0.50
3	0.33	0.00	0.00	0.50	0.50	0.50
4	0.50	0.50	0.50	0.00	0.00	0.00
5	0.50	0.50	0.50	0.00	0.00	0.00
6	0.50	0.50	0.50	0.00	0.00	0.00

Fig. 12.12. Distances between ego algebras for a hypothetical example of two relations

We can then measure the distance between two ego algebras by summing the distance each is from their joint right homomorphic reduction. The distance between the ego algebras for actors i and j, using the measure δ, is:

$$\delta_{ij} = h(\mathscr{Q}_{ij|i}^{\text{JNT}}) + h(\mathscr{Q}_{ij|j}^{\text{JNT}}). \tag{12.6}$$

This distance ranges from 0 (when $\mathscr{S}_i$ and $\mathscr{S}_j$ are identical), to 2 (when the only joint homomorphic reduction is trivial and equates all compound relations).

12.7.4 Examples

We will illustrate ego algebras using both the example of two hypothetical relations in Figure 12.6 and the relations of advice and friendship for Krackhardt's high-tech managers. In both examples we used the routine *JNTHOM* in the program *ROLE* (Breiger 1986).

First consider the example ego algebras for the two relations H and L in Figure 12.6. The distances between the ego algebras for the six actors (presented in Figure 12.11) are given in Figure 12.12. As we noted above, for this example there are three subsets of actors who are ego-algebraically equivalent (EA). These subsets are:

- $\mathscr{B}_{(EA)1} : \{1\}$
- $\mathscr{B}_{(EA)2} : \{2,3\}$
- $\mathscr{B}_{(EA)3} : \{4,5,6\}$

Now, consider the relations of advice and friendship for Krackhardt's high-tech managers. The distances between the ego algebras for the twenty-one managers in this network are presented in Figure 12.13. We can represent these distances between ego algebras using complete link hierarchical clustering (we used the program *SYSTAT*; Wilkinson 1987).

	1	2	3	4	5	6	7	8	9	10	11
1	0.000										
2	0.162	0.000									
3	0.486	0.571	0.000								
4	0.400	0.876	0.209	0.000							
5	0.200	0.643	0.286	0.200	0.000						
6	0.617	0.421	0.702	0.617	0.417	0.000					
7	1.000	1.048	1.048	1.000	0.833	1.111	0.000				
8	0.557	0.643	0.357	0.557	0.357	0.774	1.083	0.000			
9	1.000	1.048	1.048	1.000	0.833	1.111	0.000	1.083	0.000		
10	0.300	0.386	0.143	0.300	0.100	0.517	0.933	0.214	0.933	0.000	
11	0.876	0.286	0.952	0.876	0.643	0.421	1.048	1.012	1.048	0.776	0.000
12	0.617	0.421	0.702	0.617	0.417	0.056	1.111	0.774	1.111	0.517	0.421
13	0.133	0.209	0.209	0.400	0.200	0.344	1.000	0.281	1.000	0.067	0.486
14	0.071	0.119	0.155	0.557	0.357	0.492	1.083	0.429	1.083	0.214	0.357
15	0.567	0.286	0.286	0.567	0.333	0.750	0.833	0.357	0.833	0.100	0.643
16	0.146	0.127	0.182	0.449	0.509	0.439	1.151	0.596	1.151	0.382	0.320
17	0.391	0.095	0.571	0.876	0.643	0.421	1.048	0.643	1.048	0.386	0.095
18	0.311	0.476	0.133	0.400	0.467	0.611	1.133	0.548	1.133	0.333	0.752
19	0.300	0.143	0.386	0.700	0.467	0.517	0.933	0.457	0.933	0.200	0.386
20	0.486	0.571	0.000	0.209	0.286	0.702	1.048	0.357	1.048	0.143	0.952
21	0.133	0.391	0.209	0.133	0.200	0.617	1.000	0.557	1.000	0.300	0.876

(continued)

	12	13	14	15	16	17	18	19	20	21
12	0.000									
13	0.344	0.000								
14	0.238	0.107	0.000							
15	0.750	0.200	0.357	0.000						
16	0.211	0.273	0.109	0.509	0.000					
17	0.214	0.209	0.155	0.286	0.182	0.000				
18	0.611	0.222	0.169	0.467	0.077	0.476	0.000			
19	0.517	0.067	0.214	0.100	0.382	0.143	0.333	0.000		
20	0.702	0.209	0.155	0.286	0.182	0.571	0.133	0.386	0.000	
21	0.617	0.133	0.209	0.567	0.200	0.391	0.156	0.300	0.209	0.000

Fig. 12.13. Distances between ego algebras computed on advice and friendship relations for Krackhardt's high-tech managers

Figure 12.14 presents the dendrogram for the hierarchical clustering. Considering this figure, we could partition the twenty-one managers into four positions of approximately ego-algebraically equivalent positions:

- $\mathscr{B}_{(EA)1}$: $\{5, 8, 10, 13, 15, 19\}$
- $\mathscr{B}_{(EA)2}$: $\{1, 3, 4, 14, 16, 18, 20, 21\}$
- $\mathscr{B}_{(EA)3}$: $\{2, 6, 11, 12, 17\}$
- $\mathscr{B}_{(EA)4}$: $\{7, 9\}$

Position $\mathscr{B}_{EA(1)}$ contains four of the eight members of department 2 (5,

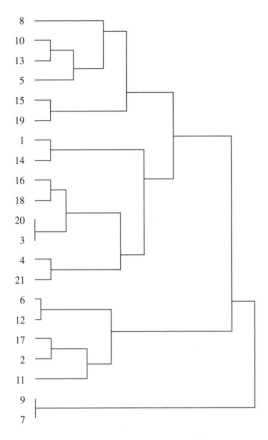

Fig. 12.14. Hierarchical clustering of distances between ego algebras on the two relations for Krackhardt's high-tech managers

13, 15, and 19). Position $\mathscr{B}_{EA(3)}$ contains three of the five members of department 1 (6, 12, and 17). Position $\mathscr{B}_{EA(2)}$ contains three of the four members of department 4 (1, 4, and 16), along with three of the four vice presidents (14, 18, and 21). Notice that there are two pairs of managers (managers 3 and 20, and managers 7 and 9) who are perfectly equivalent using the ego algebra definition.

Ego algebras can be used for single or multirelational networks, and for relations that are directional or nondirectional. One of the strengths of this approach is that ego algebras can be compared across networks, if the same relations are measured on both groups. Ego algebras have been used by Breiger and Pattison (1986) to study the marriage and business relations for Padgett's Florentine families, and by Faust (1988) to study Sampson's (1968) monastery network.

12.8 Discussion

In this section we discuss the relationships among the approaches described in this chapter. Pattison (1988) has an excellent summary of some of the approaches, and the relationships among them.

All of the methods that we have described in this chapter propose definitions under which actors in a network are to be considered equivalent. All approaches, except structural equivalence, are motivated, in part, by the idea of social position as a collection of actors all of whom are *similarly* involved in ties with other actors or sets of actors. The methods differ in terms of which specific properties are relevant to the equivalence. One of the most important differences is the generality or abstractness of the concepts.

Perhaps the most important distinction among the equivalence definitions presented here is their relative restrictiveness. By restrictive we mean that if one equivalence definition is more restrictive than another, then any actors who are equivalent by the first definition are also equivalent by the second definition, though actors who are equivalent by the second may not be equivalent by the first. Usually the more restrictive equivalence definition contains conditions that are not required by the less restrictive definition. For example, two actors who are structurally equivalent (have identical ties to and from *all* other actors) are also regularly equivalent (have identical ties to/from equivalent actors).

The five definitions can be ordered from most restrictive to least restrictive as follows:

- Structural equivalence
- Automorphic or isomorphic equivalence
- Regular equivalence
- Local role equivalence
- Ego algebra equivalence

Because the more abstract approaches are newer, computer programs for them are less widely available (though, there are individually available computer routines, and *UCINET IV* includes many of these methods). As a consequence, there are also fewer examples of applications of these methods to substantive problems.

Part V
Dyadic and Triadic Methods

13

Dyads

We now begin the second portion of the book, which, as mentioned in Chapter 1, focuses on the statistical analysis of social network data. Most of the methods discussed in Chapters 13 through 16 (Parts V and VI) are based on stochastic assumptions about the relational data contained in a social network data set. There are a variety of such stochastic assumptions, and we will introduce and describe each in depth as they arise in the next four chapters.

The statistical methods that we will present in the next six chapters are organized into two parts (Parts V and VI) to separate earlier models for subgraphs from more recent models for entire graphs and digraphs. The statistical ideas, methods, and concepts presented in these chapters are quite diverse, and were developed over a period of forty years. We will begin with Part V – Dyadic and Triadic Methods for the analysis of social network data. Statistical analyses of network data can be quite important, and can nicely complement analyses based on methods described in the first portion of the book.

These methods are different from the structural analyses discussed earlier in the book, where a theory was translated into a set of graph theoretic statements about a network. These statements were studied in a descriptive or deterministic manner. Since the methods described in Chapters 5–12 were predominantly descriptive or even exploratory, we did not need distributional assumptions about particular structural properties.

To test statistically propositions about a theory, one needs a probabilistic viewpoint; that is, one should use models based on probability distributions. Such models allow the data to show some error, or lack of fit to structural theories, but still support the theories under study. Adoption of this probabilistic approach implies that we can allow a given social network to exhibit, say, a "little bit" of intransitivity, and still be able to conclude that, overall, the network adheres to a theory of transitive triads. We can ask how much intransitivity a network can have before concluding that it is not really a transitive network.

Deterministic models can be contrasted with the statistical models discussed in Parts V and VI. Statistical models, based on some probabilistic assumptions, can cope easily with some lack-of-fit of a model to data; deterministic models cannot be relaxed in this way. Deterministic models usually force the aspect of social structure of interest (such as reciprocity, or complete transitivity or structural equivalence) to be present in the model, while statistical models assume these aspects to be absent.

13.1 An Overview

The statistical approach to network analysis has been in use since the beginnings of social network analysis. However, it was not widely used until the research of Holland and Leinhardt (1970, 1971). This research relies on empirical verification of probabilistic versions of deterministic network structural theories, which use graph theory to make predictions about network structure (for example, see Cartwright and Harary 1956; Davis 1967; and Chapter 6). We will demonstrate several of these in Chapters 13–15. This probabilistic approach to theory testing should be a useful data analytic strategy; indeed, some existing models can be interpreted with a probabilistic view. For example, as blockmodelers have noted (and as we discuss in Chapters 9 and 10), perfect or fat fits of blockmodels are indeed quite rare; consequently, α-density fits are usually used, with the understanding that some "1"'s are allowed in zeroblocks, and some "0"'s in oneblocks, up to some predetermined threshold. The use of this threshold is analogous to the use of a probability governing whether or not a given theory is supported by a significance test (as we discuss in Chapter 16).

Historically, the methods designed for subgraph analyses have been referred to as "local" methods. Local methods look at subgraphs embedded within the graph for the entire network. These methods look at subsets of the actors in $\mathcal{N}$ separately, rather than the properties of the entire collection of g actors simultaneously. Global analyses, by comparison, focus on properties of complete sets or graphs.

In brief, *local structure* is usually defined to be the regularities in a social system of actors and relations that can be studied at the level of subgraphs, rather than the entire graph or directed graph itself. The basic unit in these local analyses remains the subgraph, a smaller (usually, quite a bit smaller) unit than the entire directed graph or network. Another definition of "local" focuses on the level of the network for which substantive theories are proposed. A property, such as reciprocity as discussed here, may be a function of just a pair of actors; however, examining these two actors within the context of the entire network is required for the full study of the property. Such properties are local in scope since their level is the subgraph.

In Part V, the level of analysis is local: dyads (subgraphs of size 2 consisting of a pair of actors and all ties between them) and triads (subgraphs of size 3 consisting of a triple of actors and all ties among them). These local structures give a local view of the entire network. The next two chapters describe dyadic and triadic analyses. Dyadic methods operate at the analytic level of the dyad, and triadic methods, at the analytic level of the triad.

A very important theoretical idea, reciprocity, was studied and evaluated from the beginnings of social network analysis in the 1930's. The question, first asked about relations such as affect, is, How strong is the tendency for one actor to "choose" another, if the second actor chooses the first? Reciprocity, and the many indices of mutuality that it gave rise to, are important topics in Chapter 13. A second important theoretical concept, *structural balance*, was postulated at the beginning of the forty-year period of research on subgraph methods. We have described this concept, tracing its history and the mathematical notions (primarily centered around triads) that it spawned, in Chapter 6. Balance theory, and its successors (particularly transitivity) are important theoretical motivators for the methods for triadic analysis, described in Chapter 14.

We begin our study of statistical methods for social network data at the simplest level of analysis unique to such data — the dyad. We will start this chapter with a quick review of graph theoretic notation (from Chapter 3) and the most relevant concepts from graph theory (from Chapter 4). We will then introduce the most widely used subgraph analytic level — the dyad. We give one classic and one recent measure for the degree of reciprocity in a network, and illustrate with several examples.

We will then turn our attention to the collection of dyads that exist among a set of actors and the relations defined on the pairs of actors. An important part of this chapter is a discussion of the *dyad census*, the counts of the different types of dyads that can occur, the expected value of the numbers of these different types of dyads (assuming that specific distributions are appropriate), and tests for hypotheses about the number of choices and the number of mutual choices on a specific relation.

Much of this chapter is devoted to a discussion of random directed graph probability distributions. These distributions give us the stochastic mechanism that allows us to study subgraphs statistically. Statistical methods usually begin with an assumption that the data under investigation are realizations or observations on a collection of random variables. The first question that an analyst must answer is: "What is the stochastic nature of the random variables?" In other words: "What distribution do my random variables follow?" These distributions allow a researcher to test hypotheses about various properties of a directed graph under study, such as the number of mutual dyads (pairs of actors in which n_i "chooses" n_j and n_j "chooses" n_i). These properties will be described at length in this chapter.

Graph theorists and network probabilists have written much about random graphs. We will review some of this literature and present a set of distributions that have proven to be most useful to social network researchers. We simultaneously show how these rather mathematical devices can be used to aid network analysts.

13.2 An Example and Some Definitions

The primary question that we will address in this chapter is, How associated are the two choices that can be present in a typical dyad? Specifically, how true is it that actor i's "choice" of actor j is always reciprocated by actor j's "choice" of actor i? That is, how frequently do mutual relationships arise in a social network? Further, if the ith actor does not "choose" the jth actor, then is this non-choice reciprocated? That is, how frequently do null relationships arise? The answers to these (and related) questions depend on the states of the dyads, or pairs of actors and the relational ties that exist between the two actors in the pair.

Consider Krackhardt's high-tech managers. The twenty-one managers were asked who, among the other managers, are your "friends." The managers were also asked who they went to for advice on the job. We will contrast these two relations in this chapter. The sociomatrices under study are binary and of size 21×21. Referring to our example, if the ith manager is a friend of the jth manager, then how likely is it that the jth manager is a friend of the ith manager?

We assume that there is one set of actors or nodes, $\mathcal{N}$, and one set of arcs, $\mathcal{L}$, connecting these actors to each other. We will not consider valued relations, or even signed relations in this chapter, primarily because all of the previous research in social network analysis on dyads has focused only on dichotomous relations. We can utilize our sociometric notation and define a sociomatrix $\mathbf{X}$ to represent the data.

We will use the symbols "$i \rightarrow j$" as shorthand for i "chooses" or "relates to" j on the relation in question — that is, the arc from i to j is contained in the set $\mathcal{L}$. We should note that we will always use capital letters to represent graph properties when these properties are not assumed to be random variables. If we do introduce a stochastic mechanism, then lowercase letters will refer to realizations of the properties, or possible states or values that can arise, and uppercase will refer to the random variables themselves. For example, we will use the symbol x to denote a possible value of the random variable X — either 0 or 1. Thus, the random sociomatrix $\mathbf{X}$ contains $g(g-1)$ entries, all 0's and 1's.

From the sociomatrix $\mathbf{X}$, one can consider many interesting properties. All of these properties were introduced in Chapter 4; here, we will very quickly review them so that they can be used in the probability distributions to be described in this chapter.

First, consider the number of arcs in a directed graph. We define L to be the number of arcs (the number of 1's in the sociomatrix associated with the directed graph). L can take on any integer value from 0 (implying a digraph completely devoid of arcs, termed an *empty* digraph) to $g(g-1)$ (implying that everyone relates to everyone else, or that the digraph is *complete*). The larger that L is, for a given g, the denser the network is. In Chapter 4, we defined the density of a relation as $L/g(g-1)$, the fraction of the number of possible arcs that are present in the directed graph.

One can take this total, L, and ask how many of these arcs originate or end with each of the individual actors. The row totals of the sociomatrix are the *outdegrees* of the nodes. The outdegrees take on integer values between 0 and $g-1$ and sum to L. The column totals of the sociomatrix give the indegrees. The indegreee can be any integer between 0 and $g-1$, and sum to L.

Krackhardt's high-tech managers have $g = 21$ actors in the set $\mathcal{N}$, and $\binom{21}{2} = 210$ dyads. An introductory analysis of the sociomatrix shows that there are 102 arcs in the digraph (simply counting the number of 1's in the sociomatrix). This implies that there are $21(20) - 102 = 318$ 0's, since there can be as many as $21(20)=420$ arcs in a digraph with 21 nodes.

The density of this relation for this set of actors is $102/420 = 0.243$, implying that the digraph is slightly less than a quarter-full with arcs. The outdegrees and indegrees of the nodes were discussed in Chapter 4 — these quantities, along with some other digraph information, are shown in Table 4.1.

13.3 Dyads

In a study of dyadic relationships, the most important aspect of a social network is the collection of dyads. A *dyad* is an *unordered pair of actors* and the *arcs that exist* between the two actors in the pair. The dyad consisting of actors i and j will be denoted by $D_{ij} = (X_{ij}, X_{ji})$, for $i \neq j$. Dyads are defined for unordered pairs, where the first actor index is less than the second, so that $i < j$. Every pair of actors is then just considered once. There are exactly $\binom{g}{2} = g(g-1)/2$ dyads. However, there are $g(g-1)$ ordered pairs of actors.

Let us now consider the possible states or isomorphism classes (see Chapter 4) for dyads. There are three states. A mutual relationship between node i and node j exists when $i \rightarrow j$ *and* $j \rightarrow i$ in the dyad. We will denote this mutual state by $i \leftrightarrow j$. A mutual relationship is apparent in a sociomatrix when both the (i, j) and (j, i) cells (located symmetrically about the diagonal of $\mathbf{X}$) are unity; that is, $X_{ij} = 1$ and $X_{ji} = 1$, so that the dyad $D_{ij} = (1, 1)$. Directional relations yield mutual dyads only if both actors in a pair of actors "choose" the other on the relation.

The second state is the asymmetric dyad, which can occur in two ways. Either $i \rightarrow j$ *or* $j \rightarrow i$, but not both. Specifically, $D_{i,j} = (1, 0)$ or $(0, 1)$. If one looks at two cells in a sociomatrix $\mathbf{X}$, X_{ij} and X_{ji}, symmetrically located off the diagonal, then one and only one of these cells will contain a 1. Note that there are two kinds of asymmetric dyads — (1) $i \rightarrow j$; and (2) $i \leftarrow j$. But since the labeling in the sociomatrix is arbitrary, we really cannot distinguish the first kind from the second. All we can see is that the relationship is not reciprocated. That is the important thing to note about asymmetric dyads — the single choice is not reciprocated.

Some theorists (primarily early social psychologists such as Heider 1946, 1958, but also Price, Harburg, and Newcomb 1966; Rodrigues 1967; Gerard and Fleischer 1967; Whitney 1971; Miller and Geller 1972) view such asymmetric dyads as intermediate states of relationships that are striving for a more stable equilibrium of reciprocity or mutuality, or complete nullity (devoid of either arc). This interpretation is of course conditional on the relations under study, and is most appropriate when

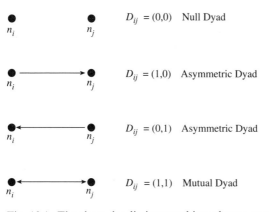

$D_{ij} = (0,0)$ Null Dyad

$D_{ij} = (1,0)$ Asymmetric Dyad

$D_{ij} = (0,1)$ Asymmetric Dyad

$D_{ij} = (1,1)$ Mutual Dyad

Fig. 13.1. The three dyadic isomorphism classes or states

the actors are individuals and the relations are positive affect. Other, more recent research views asymmetric dyads not as intermediate states, but of direct interest, since such asymmetries indicate unequal resources exist within the dyad (see Wellman 1988a).

This brings us to the third type of dyad, the null dyad, in which neither actor has a tie to the other. By default, a dyad that is not asymmetric or mutual must be null. The (i, j) and (j, i) symmetrically placed off-diagonal cells of **X** are both 0; that is, $X_{ij} = X_{ji} = 0$, implying that $D_{ij} = (0,0)$. These types of dyads are pictured in Figure 13.1.

We should note that in the latter sections of this chapter, the entries in the sociomatrix **X** will be viewed as random variables. This will imply that our $\binom{g}{2}$ dyads are also random variables. If the entries in **X** are binary (that is, if the relation under study is dichotomous), the dyads have associated with them the *bivariate* random quantity (X_{ij}, X_{ji}) specifying the value of the relational variables linking i to j and vice versa. This pair of binary random variables has four states or realizations, depending on the arcs that are present or absent in the dyad, D_{ij}. Even though there are four states, there are just three isomorphism classes for a dyad.

Lastly, we should also note that the assumption that the relation under study is dichotomous will be relaxed in Chapter 15 to allow us to model discrete, valued relations. In this case, there is still a bivariate random variable representing the state of each dyad, but this variable has considerably more states than four. Thus the terms "null," "asymmetric," and "mutual," are relevant only for dichotomous relations.

13.3.1 The Dyad Census

A dyad is an example of a *subgraph* – a subset of nodes taken from $\mathcal{N}$, and all the arcs between them. Dyads are *2-subgraphs*. There are $\binom{g}{2} = g(g-1)/2$ of these 2-subgraphs in a directed graph with g nodes. As we have noted above, each of these dyads must be mutual, asymmetric, or null. Mathematically, one says that each of these $g(g-1)/2$ pairs of nodes, and the lines existing between the nodes in the pair, is *isomorphic* to one of the three possibilities. By definition, two subgraphs are isomorphic if they are identical, except for possibly different labelings of the nodes (see Chapter 4 for a discussion of isomorphic subgraphs and graphs). That is, two isomorphic subgraphs look exactly like each other, except for a rearrangement of the labels. The three states for dyads (mutuals, asymmetrics, and nulls) are called the dyadic *isomorphism classes*.

We define M, A, and N as the numbers of mutual, asymmetric, and null dyads in a collection of $\binom{g}{2}$ dyads. These three counts sum to $\binom{g}{2}$, since these three classes provide a complete partition of the collection of dyads. The triple $< M, A, N >$ is called the *dyad census*. This triple is called a *census* because it is derived from an examination of *all* dyads in the network. Note that we look at *all* dyads in the digraph, and categorize each into its appropriate "state." The census gives an aggregate/overall view of all the dyads in the network.

One can calculate the frequencies M, A, and N directly from the elements of the sociomatrix $\mathbf{X}$ representing the digraph in question:

$$M = \sum_{i<j} X_{ij} X_{ji} \tag{13.1}$$

$$A = X_{++} - 2M \tag{13.2}$$

$$N = \binom{g}{2} - A - M, \tag{13.3}$$

where, $X_{++} = L$, the number of arcs in the digraph. One can also calculate M, A, and N using matrix operations on $\mathbf{X}$:

$$M = (1/2)\mathrm{trace}(\mathbf{XX}) \tag{13.4}$$

$$A = \mathrm{trace}(\mathbf{XX'}) - \mathrm{trace}(\mathbf{XX}) \tag{13.5}$$

$$N = \binom{g}{2} - \mathrm{trace}(\mathbf{XX'}) + (1/2)\mathrm{trace}(\mathbf{XX}). \tag{13.6}$$

In these equations, $\mathbf{X'}$ is the transpose of the matrix $\mathbf{X}$. The transpose of the (i, j)th element of $\mathbf{X}$ is x_{ji}. The trace of a matrix is the sum of its diagonal entries. Since we regard g as fixed, one can determine N from g, M, and A.

13.3.2 The Example and Its Dyad Census

Consider the three isomorphism classes for dyads (mutuals, asymmetrics, and nulls), and the frequencies with which the dyads fall into these classes (M, A, and N), in our example. These classes are pictured in Figure 13.1. The first step in a dyadic analysis is to consider every one of the dyads (there are 210 in Krackhardt's high-tech managers). For example, take the dyad consisting of actors 1 and 2, D_{12}. For Krackhardt's high-tech managers, this dyad is a mutual dyad, since actor 1 stated that he was a friend of actor 2, and vice versa. Consequently, $D_{12} = (1, 1)$. The dyad consisting of actors 1 and 8 is an asymmetric dyad, since actor 1 chose actor 8 as a friend, but actor 8 did not reciprocate the choice. That is, $D_{18} = (1, 0)$. Lastly, consider actors 1 and 21. Both of these entries are zero, indicating that this dyad is null (so $D_{1,21} = (0, 0)$).

The next step in a dyadic subgraph analysis is to study the frequencies of the dyads given by the dyad census. For our example, going over all 210 dyads, we find that $M = 23$, $A = 56$, and $N = 131$. We should note how we arrived at the three values of the dyad census. We first counted the number of mutual dyads, as shown in equation (13.4), and arrived at a count of 23. Next, we counted the number of arcs in the digraph, which we already know is 102 arcs. Since each mutual dyad involves two arcs, there are $2M = 2(23) = 46$ arcs in these mutuals. Following equation (13.5), subtracting this number from 102 gives $102 - 46 = 56$ arcs not involved in mutuals dyads; that is, there must be 56 asymmetric dyads in the network. This count is substantiated simply by going though the remaining $210 - 23 = 187$ dyads in the network, and verifying that 56 of these dyads involve one and only one arc. Since there are 210 dyads present with $g = 21$ actors, the remaining $210 - 23 - 56 = 131$ dyads must be null dyads (as stated by equation (13.6)).

A dyadic analysis seeks to answer several questions about these three values. The dyad census can be studied to see how much reciprocity of choice occurs. For example, one can ask if the observed level of mutuality (such as the 23 mutual dyads in our example) is a lot or a little. A small fraction of the dyads ($23/210 = 0.1095$) are mutuals, but how does this compare to theoretical predictions, or to comparable groups of high-tech managers? Are mutual dyads statistically more prevalent than other kinds of dyads in this organization? Are dyadic relationships more mutual (and less asymmetric) than in other, comparable groups? How does the number of null dyads (for our example, 131 nulls, or as a fraction, $131/210 = 0.624$, rather large) compare to the numbers of such dyads in other, comparable groups? What we need is an index of mutuality designed to answer these questions; two possible indices are discussed in the next section.

A statistical dyadic analysis is only possible if we allow the counts of the dyad census to be random variables; that is, if we consider the sociomatrix under study to represent a random directed graph. To do this, we will soon introduce a special class of probability models for directed graphs that will give us probability distributions for the frequencies in a k-subgraph census. These probability distributions yield (at the very least) the expected value (or average) of the frequencies in the census, and the covariance matrix of the frequencies, which will allow us to test various hypotheses about the network under study. We will show how such distributions arise in the next section.

13.3.3 An Index for Mutuality

Katz and Powell (1955) proposed an index, which we will label ρ_{KP}, to measure the tendency for actors in a group to reciprocate choices more frequently than would occur simply by chance. Such an index refines the examination of the counts in the dyad census, since the index can be used to compare groups and relations with unequal numbers of actors. The index, like many widely used indices in statistics, is dimensionless, and easy to interpret since it uses the values of 0 and 1 as benchmarks — if the reciprocity index equals 0, then there is no tendency to reciprocate; if it equals 1, the tendency is maximal (that is, all choices are reciprocated). If it is less than zero (which is possible), there is a less than chance tendency for choices to be reciprocated; that is, one observes too few mutual dyads. Thus, ρ_{KP} can be used to index the strength of the tendency toward reciprocation of choice. In brief, $-\infty < \rho_{KP} \leq 1$, where 0 indicates no tendency for reciprocation, 1, maximal tendency, and negative values, tendencies away from mutual dyads, toward asymmetrics and nulls.

We note that the index is more than just a descriptive measure. It is based on the expectation of the number of mutual dyads, assuming that choices are made by actors in some random manner.

We present the index for two particular network data collection designs. Social network data may be collected under either a *fixed choice* or a *free choice* procedure (see Chapter 2). In a fixed choice design, the investigator gathers data or instructs each respondent to name a *fixed* number of others that the actor relates to on the relation under study. In a free choice design, no restrictions are placed on the number of actors each actor can relate to. Persons may be told simply to "List all your best friends."

First consider the case of *fixed choice* data, where actors in fact make a fixed number of choices. We assume that each actor makes d choices from the $g-1$ actors available to be chosen. Following this, we will show how to calculate ρ_{KP} in the free choice situation.

Fixed Choice. One of the first calculations of the probability of a mutual choice was made by Paul Lazarsfeld, and reported by Moreno and Jennings (1938). If d is the fixed number of choices made by each of the g actors, then the probability of a mutual choice between any arbitrary pair of actors is $d^2/(g-1)^2$, assuming that choices are made completely at random and the actors in the pair are responding independently.

This calculation uses the fact that if each actor makes d choices at random from the other $g-1$ actors, then the probability that a particular actor is chosen is $(d/(g-1))$. Since actors are operating independently, the probability that a given dyad (which involves choices made by two actors independently) is mutual is $(d/(g-1))^2$.

Since there are $g(g-1)/2$ dyads, the average number of mutual dyads must be the number of dyads times the probability that any one of them is a mutual. Thus, the expected number of mutual dyads is

$$E(M) = \frac{g(g-1)}{2} \frac{d^2}{(g-1)^2} = \frac{gd^2}{2(g-1)}, \tag{13.7}$$

assuming that each actor chooses d other actors, completely at random. Here, the notation $E(M)$ implies that we are calculating the expected value of M, assuming that choices are made at random.

Consider the probability that a generic dyad, involving actors i and j, is a mutual dyad. One can calculate this probability as a product of two other probabilities

$$P(i \rightarrow j \text{ and } j \rightarrow i) = P(i \rightarrow j)P(j \rightarrow i|i \rightarrow j) \tag{13.8}$$

using the standard definition of a conditional probability. The last term above is the conditional probability of a reciprocated choice, and is of primary importance here. Katz and Powell take this conditional probability, and introduce an unknown quantity, ρ_{KP}, as follows:

$$P(j \rightarrow i|i \rightarrow j) = P(j \rightarrow i) + \rho_{KP}\, P(j \not\rightarrow i). \tag{13.9}$$

If ρ_{KP} is 0, then the conditional probability equals the unconditional probability, and choices are independent; that is, there is no tendency toward reciprocity. If $\rho_{KP} = 1$, then the right-hand side of the above equation is also 1. This arises when the choice $i \rightarrow j$ forces the choice $j \rightarrow i$; that is, these two "reciprocating" choices are completely dependent. If we substitute equation (13.9) into equation (13.8), and substitute the probabilities for choices (assuming d choices made at random), we obtain

$$
\begin{aligned}
P(i \rightarrow j \text{ and } j \rightarrow i) &= P(i \rightarrow j)P(j \rightarrow i|i \rightarrow j) \\
&= P(i \rightarrow j)[P(j \rightarrow i) + \rho_{KP}P(j \nrightarrow i)] \\
&= \frac{d}{g-1}\left[\frac{d}{g-1} + \rho_{KP}\frac{g-1-d}{g-1}\right].
\end{aligned}
$$

Using this probability, the expected value of the number of mutual dyads, conditional on the unknown value of ρ_{KP}, is $\binom{g}{2}$ times this probability; that is, rearranging terms slightly, we have

$$
E(M|\rho) = \frac{gd^2}{2(g-1)}(1 - \rho_{KP}) + \frac{gd}{2}\rho_{KP}. \tag{13.10}
$$

To estimate ρ_{KP}, Katz and Powell used a method-of-moments estimator. Specifically, we estimate the expected value of the number of mutuals, given in equation (13.10) using the number of mutuals, M, actually observed in a network. If we equate the right-hand side of (13.10) to M, we can then solve the resulting equation to obtain an estimate of ρ_{KP}:

$$
\hat{\rho}_{KP} = \frac{2(g-1)M - gd^2}{gd(g-1-d)}. \tag{13.11}
$$

Katz and Powell report that this estimate is consistent (that is, it has a variance that goes to zero as g increases) and is unbiased (that is, it has an expected value equal to ρ_{KP}). One nice feature of the estimate is that it is a linear function of M. As the number of mutual dyads increases from 0 (its minimum) to $\binom{g}{2}$ (its maximum), the estimate increases linearly.

Note that when $M = 0$, the estimate is negative, a possibly undesirable characteristic of the index. One should never see so few mutuals if choices are made at random. Katz and Powell refer to this as "anti-reciprocation," and state that this may be due to values of d taken to be too small. In fact, if $d > (g-1)/2$, then the minimum value of $\hat{\rho}_{KP}$ cannot be negative since there must be a non-zero number of mutual dyads — as we will see below. The estimated index reaches its maximum value of 1 when $M = gd/2$ (which can arise trivially when $d = (g-1)$). Katz and Powell give no distributional properties of $\hat{\rho}_{KP}$, and as far as we can determine, this is still an open area for research.

To demonstrate use of this index, consider again Krackhardt's data, and suppose (hypothetically) that each actor chooses *exactly* five other managers as friends. (The actual average outdegree is 4.9 so, just for demonstration purposes, we suppose a fixed outdegree of 5. However, this clearly ignores the variability of actor choices. We make this simplifying assumption to show how to calculate Katz and Powell's mutuality index in the fixed choice situation.) We have $g = 21$, $m = 23$, and $d = 5$, so from equation (13.11)

$$\hat{\rho}_{KP} = \frac{2(20)(23) - (21)(5)^2}{21(5)(15)} = \frac{395}{1575} = 0.2508,$$

a small value, indicating that such a network shows some indication of independence of choices made and received in a dyad (given the constant value of an outdegree of 5). Conditioning on d shows that there is just a small tendency for choices to be reciprocated.

Free Choice. We now suppose that the ith actor chooses $d_O(n_i) = x_{i+}$ other actors, and that these outdegrees are not necessarily equal. We let $L = \sum x_{i+}$ be the total number of choices, and $L_2 = \sum x_{i+}^2$ be the sum of squares of the choices made by each actor. As in the fixed choice situation, the probability that actors i and j have a mutual relationship is $x_{i+}x_{j+}/(g-1)^2$, if choices are made completely at random. Since this probability depends on the pair of actors considered, the expected value of the number of mutuals is more complicated than above. Katz and Powell calculate

$$E(M) = \frac{L^2 - L_2}{2(g-1)^2}. \tag{13.12}$$

The derivation of this expected value is rather complicated; hence we refer the reader to Katz and Powell (1955) for details. Using (13.12) and (13.10), we introduce ρ'_{KP} as the analog of ρ_{KP} in the free choice case, and obtain

$$E(M|\rho') = \frac{L^2 - L_2}{2(g-1)}(1 - \rho'_{KP}) + \frac{L}{2}\rho'_{KP}. \tag{13.13}$$

As before, we estimate ρ'_{KP} with a method-of-moments estimator $\hat{\rho}'_{KP}$, by solving equation (13.13) set equal to M:

$$\hat{\rho}'_{KP} = \frac{2(g-1)^2 M - L^2 + L_2}{L(g-1)^2 - L^2 + L_2}. \tag{13.14}$$

To illustrate, examine the outdegrees of Krackhardt's friendship relation, and calculate $L = 102$, the number of arcs, and $L_2 = 880$, the sum of squares of the outdegrees. From these values, and remembering that there are $g = 21$ actors and $M = 23$ dyads, we have

$$\hat{\rho}'_{KP} = \frac{2(20)^2(23) - 102^2 + 880}{102(20)^2 - 102^2 + 880} = \frac{8876}{31276} = 0.2838,$$

a fairly low mutuality index. This value is surprisingly large, however, given that only slightly more than 10 percent of the dyads are mutuals. There are few mutual dyads, but the tendency toward reciprocation is not negligible.

13.3.4 $\otimes$*A Second Index for Mutuality*

Achuthan, Rao, and Rao (1982) consider the range of the number of mutual dyads that can arise in a directed graph with specified outdegrees (either free choice or fixed choice designs). The value of M depends on the numbers of choices made, and its range of possible values is restricted by the outdegrees, which we assume are known. Using an unpublished 1982 suggestion of Bandyopadhyay (see Rao and Bandyopadhyay 1987), these authors proposed an index for mutuality based on the maximum and minimum values of the number of mutual dyads, M, that could occur for a given set of outdegrees. We will define M_{min} and M_{max} as the maximum and minimum numbers of mutuals, respectively, so that $M_{min} \leq M \leq M_{max}$. These values depend on the outdegrees of the digraph under consideration. Achutan, Rao, and Rao propose the index

$$\rho_B = \frac{M - M_{min}}{M_{max} - M_{min}} \tag{13.15}$$

as a standardized measure of the level of mutuality in a social network.

The maximum and minimum numbers of mutuals are defined as follows. First, consider the two functions, defined for $t = 1, 2, \ldots, g$,

$$f(t) = \sum_{i=1}^{t} x_{i+} - t(g-1) - \binom{t}{2}$$

and

$$g(t) = \sum_{i=1}^{t} x_{i+} - t(t-1) - \sum_{i=t+1}^{g} \min(t, x_{i+}).$$

Then,

$$M_{min} = \max_{0 \leq t \leq g} f(t), \tag{13.16}$$

as given in Theorem 2.2 of Achuthan, Rao, and Rao (1982), and

$$M_{max} = \left\lfloor 1/2 \left\{ \sum_{i=1}^{g} x_{i+} - \max_{0 \leq t \leq g} g(t) \right\} \right\rfloor \tag{13.17}$$

as given in the authors' Theorem 3.1, where $\lfloor \bullet \rfloor$ denotes the largest integer not exceeding $\bullet$. These theorems, and the theorem that proves the existence of a directed graph with M mutuals, where M lies between M_{min} and M_{max}, have long and somewhat tedious proofs; nevertheless, the application of the authors' results is not difficult. Neither (13.16) nor (13.17) requires complicated or extensive calculations (as we will demonstrate below).

An interesting sidelight of this research is a condition under which the minimum number of mutuals can be equal to 0; that is, when is it the case that for a specified set of outdegrees, it is possible to have no mutual dyads? The authors show that, if we let $x_{min} = min_i d_O(n_i)$ be the smallest outdegree in the digraph, then $M_{min} = 0$ if $x_{min} \leq \lfloor (g - 1)/2 \rfloor$. So, unless every actor chooses at least half of the other actors, it is possible to have no mutual dyads in the digraph. The authors also give conditions under which the maximum number of mutual dyads is equal to $L/2$, one-half the number of arcs present in the digraph. Note that M_{max} cannot exceed $L/2$, since a digraph with L choices can have no more than $L/2$ mutuals.

Let us illustrate these calculations. Consider again our example from Krackhardt. We calculate $M_{min} = 0$ and $M_{max} = 51$ (using the program *DYADS* of Walker and Wasserman 1987). Since, $M = 23$, we find $\hat{\rho}_B = (23 - 0)/(51 - 0) = 0.451$, a fairly large value, even larger in fact than $\hat{\rho}_{KP}$. In general, we have found that the $\hat{\rho}_B$ indices tend to be larger than the corresponding $\hat{\rho}_{KP}$ values.

Krackhardt's data set also contains a second relation, advice, measured for the twenty-one managers. The density of choices for this second relation is $190/420 = 0.452$, and there are 45 mutual dyads. Both of these values are larger than for the friendship relation. Clearly, it is more common for the managers to seek advice from, than be friends with, each other. This may be due to the fact that the work setting, rather than a social environment, has brought them together. For this relation, $\hat{\rho}_B = (45 - 0)/(95 - 0) = 0.474$, only a little larger than the same reciprocity index for the friendship relation. So, even though there are twice as many mutual dyads for the advice relation, the tendencies toward reciprocation are about the same since there are simply more advice relational ties.

13.3.5 ○*Subgraph Analysis, in General*

We have discussed the initial steps in a dyadic analysis, focusing on the collection of 2-subgraphs in a digraph. We will return to this discussion after the introduction of several classes of distributions for random directed graphs which will make the statistical analysis of digraphs possible. But first, let us note that in general, one can consider subgraphs of order k, or k-*subgraphs*, for $k = 0, 1, \ldots, g$.

For a given value of k, we can calculate the number of k-subgraphs as the number of ways one can choose k objects from a pool of g objects. There are

$$\binom{g}{k} = \frac{\left[g(g-1)(g-2)\cdots(g-k+1)\right]}{\left[k(k-1)(k-2)\cdots(1)\right]}$$

k-subgraphs in a directed graph with g nodes. Thus, for a network with $g = 10$ actors, there are 10 actors, 45 dyads, 120 triads, 210 tetrads, etc. Clearly, enumerating all k-subgraphs even for small k can be a time-consuming process, even for a computer.

The number of isomorphism classes for k-subgraphs grows quickly for a directional relation as k increases: there are 3 classes for $k = 2$ (dyads), 16 classes for $k = 3$ (triads), 218 classes for $k = 4$ (tetrads), 9608 for $k = 5$ (pentads), and up to several million for $k = 10$ (decads; see Harary 1955a). Davis (1953, 1954) considers how many classes exist for k-subgraphs, and gives bounds for this number, as well as for numbers of particular kinds of subgraphs (reflexive, symmetric, and so forth).

Studying subgraphs can therefore be difficult if one focuses on k-subgraphs with $k > 3$. In fact, analyses with large k may not even be parsimonious, in the sense that there may be no great reduction in complexity of a network data set if one simply translates a sociomatrix to a set of frequencies of k-subgraphs in isomorphism classes. It might be better just to use graph theoretic methods to study a network with, say, $g = 10$ actors, than to look at 8-subgraphs or 9-subgraphs. Further, the statistical properties of k-subgraphs with large k are not well-understood. But, perhaps the most important reason for keeping k small is that there are clear, theoretical motivations for the study of dyads (tendencies toward and away from reciprocity) and triads (structural balance, transitivity, and so forth). Such subgraphs allow us to study important structural properties. Very few (if any) formal structural properties have been proposed for $k > 3$. For these reasons, we will restrict our attention to just dyads and triads ($k \leq 3$).

The principles behind an analysis of k-subgraphs are the same regardless of the magnitude of k. One must:

(i) Determine the number of isomorphism classes (that is, the number of different states that the k-subgraphs can take on) and label them appropriately.

(ii) Consider every possible subset of k actors (the k-subgraphs) in the directed graph with g nodes.

(iii) Place each k-subgraph into the correct isomorphism class, and count how many k-subgraphs fall into each class. These counts give the *k-subgraph census*.

(iv) Study, with either statistical or descriptive methods, the frequencies of the k-subgraphs in the isomorphism classes. These frequencies may be compared with frequencies predicted by some formal substantive or statistical model.

We will return to dyadic analyses shortly. What follows is the beginning of a discussion of several classes of probability distributions for random digraphs.

You, the reader, might be wondering why we are spending so many pages discussing such an esoteric topic. The answer is that this topic will allow us to conduct and understand statistical tests for the components of the dyad census. As an analogy, one cannot test that a population mean is equal to zero without first adopting, and understanding, some probabilistic mechanism which generates the data under study. Such is the case here. In order to test hypotheses about the level of mutuality present in a network, we first must make some statistical assumptions about the underlying network process.

As mentioned in the introduction to this chapter, we would like to consider how much reciprocity or mutuality is present in the network under study, and to determine whether the observed level of this important structural property differs from an a priori, supposed level. The distributions discussed in the next section of this chapter will allow us to conduct such statistical analyses. These analyses are sprinkled throughout the next section; after presenting each set of these distributions, we will illustrate their use by presenting methods for statistical analysis of dyads using the distributions.

13.4 Simple Distributions

The basic family of probability distributions for directed graphs is the class of *uniform distributions*. These distributions range from the simplest possible distribution for a directed graph with g nodes to *conditional distributions* which fix, or condition on, a number of graph characteristics. We will first review uniform distributions in general, and then will show how these and other distributions can be applied to the problem considered here. We will introduce the distributions in several parts: simple distributions, conditional uniform distributions, and then other uniform distributions. After each part, we will describe the statistical methods for the dyad census that can be used, once the distributions, described in the preceding part, are assumed. These statistical methods focus on the number of arcs present in a digraph (inferences using the simple distributions), and the number of mutual dyads present in a digraph (which require conditional uniform distributions).

An important concept that we will use repeatedly throughout this section is *statistical conditioning* — that is, taking a random variable, and then deriving the distribution of that random variable *conditional* on specific (graph) properties. This conditioning implies that we restrict attention to only those random graphs that have the specific properties that are conditioned upon. For example, we will discuss a directed graph distribution that is conditional on the graph having equal outdegrees.

The distributions described here will be used extensively throughout the remainder of this book. As we discuss in Chapter 15, p_1, Holland and Leinhardt's (1981) statistical model, which forms the basis of much of the methodology of Part VI, is equivalent to one of the more complex conditional random digraph distributions presented later in this chapter.

Armed with the random directed graph distributions discussed here, we will be able to study the dyad census statistically. The first statistical analysis of social network data came from Moreno and Jennings (1938), who simulated a random network process by randomly assigning choices to individual actors. This process was the first simulation of the random digraph distribution that conditions or fixes the actor outdegrees. The simulated sociomatrices were then compared to the actual, observed matrix. Johnson (1939) employed a similar procedure to study change in social relationships. Bronfenbrenner (1943, 1944) further developed the notion of a chance model in sociometry, focusing on the binomial distribution. He estimated the probability that an individual actor, constrained to make a fixed number of choices, chooses any other actor. With this estimated probability, he simulated the Bernoulli random digraph distribution, which we discuss in this section. Actors who received significantly more or less choices than expected (based on the model) were easily identified by his approach. Bronfenbrenner also studied the distribution of the number of mutuals, although his application of statistical models here was faulty (as we discuss later in this section). Criswell (1939, 1943, 1947) also proposed a method to study the statistical significance between observed and theoretical distributions. Loomis and Pepinsky (1948) give a thorough, critical review of the first decade (1937–1947) of social network analysis, including comments on the early methodology, as does Criswell (1946a), in a review of Moreno and Jennings (1945) and Bronfenbrenner (1945).

The early sociometricians were keen to develop a reference frame, or a constant benchmark, for their analyses which could be used to determine how "structured" a particular network was, or how far the network departed from the benchmark. Moreno and Jennings (1938), Brofenbrenner (1945), Criswell (1946a), Edwards (1948), and Criswell (1950) (see also the recent comments by Glazer 1981) all had this in mind when proposing innovative statistical methods for network data. Some of these researchers actually simulated networks based on the distributions we have described here; others used probability models to determine distributions of graph properties of interest (such as the number of mutual dyads). This *constant frame of reference problem*, or the development of a benchmark to which observed data could be referred, and the many proposed solutions showed that even early network analysts desired good and proper statistical methods for their analyses.

Tagiuri (1952) and Tagiuri, Bruner, and Kogan (1955) also studied dyads, but from a multirelational viewpoint. They assumed that the researchers recorded not only positive and negative choices (which was common in early sociometry), but also data on perceptions of choices made by others. The theory of actual versus perceived choices is described in Tagiuri, Blake, and Bruner (1953), and the mathematical models for their analyses can be found in Luce, Macy, and Tagiuri (1955).

A number of researchers have reviewed the early developments of statistical methodology for social network data. Good surveys include Proctor and Loomis (1951), Lindzey and Borgatta (1954), Nehnevajsa (1955b), and Glanzer and Glaser (1959).

The tests discussed in this section should provide the reader with a good introduction to the types of significance tests that are common in subgraph analyses of social networks, while showing how to determine whether specific hypotheses about a digraph are statistically sound. For example, one can test whether actors make choices independently and with specified probabilities. Such hypotheses and associated tests can be viewed as statistical benchmarks, designed to learn more about the underlying network process generating the data.

We first focus on tests about the number of arcs in a digraph. After describing analyses for L, we will turn to the dyad census itself, and focus on one of its components, M, the number of mutual dyads. We describe a number of approaches to the statistical analysis of M (again assuming that various digraph distributions are appropriate) that have appeared in the literature over the past thirty years.

13.4.1 The Uniform Distribution – A Review

The uniform distribution arises frequently as a probability model for random variables. Consider the simple random variable giving the outcome of a single toss of a fair coin. There are two outcomes here, a head (H), and a tail (T), which we will put into a set, labeled (as it usually is in statistics) the *sample space* — $S = \{H, T\}$. Since the coin is fair, these two outcomes have equal probabilities of occurring, so that

$$P(H) = P(T) = \frac{1}{2}, \tag{13.18}$$

where P($\bullet$) refers to the *probability* that the event "$\bullet$" occurs. Note that there are two things of importance here: (1) there are a finite number of outcomes in this "statistical experiment" (two, to be exact); and (2) each outcome is equally likely.

When the realizations of a random variable can only assume a countable number of values, then the random variable is called a *discrete random variable*. We will work solely with discrete random variables for directed graphs, since the graph properties that we will measure will always have a finite number of possible values. In other words, the types of variables that are usually measured in social network studies are discrete-valued, as opposed to continuous. We are not assuming that most social network concepts are discrete-valued. However, the measurement of these concepts is usually done with discrete scales.

Each random variable that we will study has a probability distribution, which specifies the probabilities that the variable equals each of the possible realizations. The probabilities must be between 0 and 1, and must sum to unity (when summed over all realizations). The realizations will be placed into a set, which we will call the *sample space* and denote by S.

Another very simple example will help us illustrate. Consider just a single pair of actors, i and j, and the relational variable that indicates whether i chooses j, or whether there is a tie from i to j. If the relation is dichotomous, then this variable has only two possibilities: 0 and 1. Thus, the sample space for this simple variable is S $= \{0, 1\}$. To these two outcomes or realizations, we must assign probabilities.

If the realizations are equally likely to occur then the probability distribution of the random variable is *uniform* — that is, the distribution distributes the total probability mass (equal to 1) *uniformly* or equally over all possible outcomes (which we have listed in S). For our example, if $P(i \rightarrow j) = P(i \not\rightarrow j) = 1/2$, then the two events are equally likely, so that the random variable representing this single choice is a uniform random variable.

The distribution of the coin tossing variable, discussed above, is sometimes called the *Bernoulli distribution* with probability of "success" $= 1/2$. The Bernoulli distribution is characterized by independent trials (the coin tosses) and only two outcomes on each trial (head and tail), with the probability of a given outcome constant from trial to trial. The distribution of a single toss is also *uniform*, with two outcomes.

To quantify this in more general terms, take a discrete random variable, which we will call U and which has n realizations, and place the realizations in a sample space: S $= \{u_1, u_2, \ldots, u_n\}$. The statistical experiment generating the random variable has n possible outcomes so that the sample space set has n elements, which we are denoting by u's. Since U is discrete, n is finite. The random variable U is a *uniform random variable* if

$$P(u_1) = P(u_2) = \cdots = P(u_n) = \frac{1}{n}. \tag{13.19}$$

Note that all of these probabilities are equal, between 0 and 1, and the sum of the probabilites (or total mass) is unity.

The uniform distribution is sometimes called the discrete uniform distribution. The uniform distribution arises frequently in statistical experiments. It applies whenever the outcome of an experiment is "chosen at random" from all possible outcomes.

Our focus here is on the collection of directed graphs that exist for a set of g nodes. For a specific distribution, we will consider which directed graphs can occur, which ones cannot, and what are the probabilities of the possible outcomes that we might see in actual network data. The distributions that we will use to model such realizations are either uniform distributions or related to uniform distributions.

13.4.2 Simple Distributions on Digraphs

We begin by defining $\mathscr{G}_d$ as a particular directed graph (or digraph) with g nodes. The set of all possible labeled and irreflexive (or loopless — since $i \not\to i$) directed graphs with g nodes will be denoted by $G_d(\mathscr{N})$. The labeling is important, since we want to consider all possible digraphs that have various characteristics, such as all digraphs with five nodes and nine arcs. Without labels assigned to the nodes, we can only consider the number of isomorphism classes. That is, we cannot distinguish between two digraphs that are isomorphic, but have different labels attached to the nodes.

An adjacency matrix or sociomatrix $\mathbf{X}$, with elements X_{ij}, can be used to record the arcs between the nodes in $\mathscr{G}_d$. Most of the distributions discussed here will be described in terms of the sociomatrices, but as we know, there is a one-to-one correspondence between digraphs and sociomatrices, so that this discussion will not result in any loss or gain in generality. We will sometimes talk about the elements in $\mathbf{X}$ interchangeably with the arcs present in the digraph. The digraphs that we consider here are random, so that $\mathbf{X}$ itself is a random sociomatrix. A single realization, or one of the possible values of this random sociomatrix, will be denoted by $\mathbf{x}$, with elements x_{ij}.

The simple distributions for random directed graphs that we will discuss in this section are the Uniform and Bernoulli. Following this discussion, we show how these distributions can be used to study the number of arcs present in a digraph. We note that readers interested in learning more about random directed graph distributions should consult Katz and Powell (1957), Holland and Leinhardt (1975), Wasserman (1977), Fershtman (1985), Snijders and Stokman (1987), and Snijders (1989, 1991a, 1991b).

Uniform Distribution. Consider first how many digraphs are contained in $G_d(\mathscr{N})$, the set of all possible directed graphs with g nodes. Since we have restricted our attention to a single, dichotomous relation, each possible arc in the digraph is either present or absent, or each element in the sociomatrix is either a 0 or a 1 — two possibilities. Since there are g actors, each of whom may have ties to the $g - 1$ other actors, there are $g(g-1)$ possible arcs in a digraph. Consequently, there must be $2^{g(g-1)}$ different labeled sociograms or sociomatrices. For example, with $g = 3$, there are $2^6 = 64$ different labeled sociograms. The number of elements in $G_d(\mathcal{N})$ grows exponentially with g; even with only $g = 10$ actors, there are $2^{90} = 1.2379 \times 10^{27}$ possibilities. Clearly, the number of possible realizations of a random directed graph is very, very large, even for small g.

The simplest distribution on $G_d(\mathcal{N})$ is the uniform distribution. We will denote this distribution by U, and use the symbol $\sim$ simply as statistical shorthand for "is distributed as." Thus, we could say $\mathbf{X} \sim U$ to imply that a sociomatrix representing a particular digraph is distributed as a uniform random variable. Every realization is equally likely (as is always the case with uniform distributions). The sample space is exactly $G_d(\mathcal{N})$, which contains $2^{g(g-1)}$ labeled digraphs, so the uniform probability function is

$$P(\mathbf{X} = \mathbf{x}) = \frac{1}{2^{g(g-1)}}. \tag{13.20}$$

In other words, the probability that a (labeled) directed graph with g actors equals a specific "configuration" of choices is $1 \Big/ \left[2^{g(g-1)}\right]$. Thus, each of the elements of the sample space has an equal probability of $1 \Big/ \left[2^{g(g-1)}\right]$ of occurring. It is perhaps simpler to describe the arcs of the digraph under this distribution as statistically independent, Bernoulli random variables with probabilities of choices (or probabilities of arcs being present) all equal to $1/2$:

$$P(X_{ij} = 1) = \begin{cases} 1/2, & i \neq j \\ 0, & i = j. \end{cases} \tag{13.21}$$

Sometimes we will let P_{ij} be shorthand notation for $P(X_{ij} = 1)$, the probability that a specific arc is present in the digraph.

This distribution has the least "structure" of all digraph distributions. All elements of the sociomatrix are independent of all other elements, and the probability distribution of any one of the elements is the simplest possible distribution – the Bernoulli distribution with equal probabilities, which is the same as the uniform distribution on a sample space with two elements, governed by probabilities (13.18). This distribution assumes that all actors "choose" about one-half of the other actors, so that the expected degree is $(g-1)/2$ for all actors and the expected density is 0.5.

Bernoulli Distribution. The uniform distribution can be general-ized to a family of Bernoulli distributions by altering the probability that any element of the random sociomatrix equals unity. These distributions have been used extensively in the important work of Frank (see Capo-bianco 1970; Frank 1977c, 1980, 1981, 1989; and Bollobás 1985, and Karoński 1982, for reviews). These models, as we discuss in Chapter 15, can also generate parametric classes of distributions.

The general Bernoulli distribution begins with equation (13.21) and allows the $\{P_{ij}\}$ to differ and not necessarily equal $1/2$. The Bernoulli distribution, which we will denote by B, assumes that the elements of $\mathbf{X}$ are statistically independent. Thus, one can view the Uniform distribution discussed above as a special case of the Bernoulli distribution, in which the $\{P_{ij}\}$ all equal $1/2$. The arcs of the digraph are assumed to be Bernoulli random variables with probabilities

$$P(X_{ij} = 1) = \left\{ \begin{array}{ll} P_{ij}, & i \neq j \\ 0, & i = j \end{array} \right. \tag{13.22}$$

where $0 \leq P_{ij} \leq 1$. The $\{P_{ij}\}$ may differ from element to element to allow some actors to choose other actors with different probabilistic tendencies. Thus, this distribution permits some of the arcs in a random digraph to have greater probabilities of being present than other arcs. If a random digraph follows the B distribution and $P_{ij} = 1/2$ for all $i \neq j$, then the random digraph is uniformly distributed. If the $\{P_{ij}\}$ are all equal, but not equal to $1/2$, the distribution is not uniform.

The Bernoulli family of distributions will be used in Chapter 15, where we introduce a related family of distributions for digraphs. This family uses a variety of additive parameters for the logarithms of the probabilities $\{P_{ij}\}$, which reflect important, substantive tendencies.

13.5 Statistical Analysis of the Number of Arcs

This section begins with a description of statistical methods for the study of a graph property even simpler (or at a lower level) than the dyad census — L, the number of lines or arcs present in a directed graph. We start with statistical analyses of L for both historical and pedagogical reasons. Statistical studies of counts of the number of arcs preceded studies of the dyad census; in addition, it is easier to understand these earlier methods. If we assume that the random variables representing the $g(g-1)$ possible arcs in the digraph follow either the uniform or Bernoulli distribution, we can test particular hypotheses about L. Readers who are statistical novices might find this section slightly rough going. Most of the statistical theory here uses the binomial distribution and normal approximations to it, as discussed in many statistical textbooks, such as Mosteller, Fienberg, and Rourke (1983), and Weinberg and Goldberg (1990).

If the digraph is assumed to be a random digraph, governed by some probability distribution which does not condition on L, then L is a random variable. It counts how many entries in the random sociomatrix $\mathbf{X}$ are unity or how many arcs are present in the random digraph. The quantity L can take on any value from 0 to $g(g-1)$. We want to use statistical assumptions to do a significance test; specifically, is the uniform distribution a realistic assumption for $\mathbf{X}$?

13.5.1 Testing

Let us first assume that the digraph is distributed as a uniform random digraph; that is $\mathbf{X} \sim U$. This assumption implies that the elements of $\mathbf{X}$ are independent, and have a constant probability of $1/2$ of being unity; that is, each element is a Bernoulli random variable, with $P = 1/2$ of being unity. L is just equal to the count of how many of these Bernoulli random variables are unity. The sum of independent Bernoulli random variables, with constant probability P of being unity, is a Binomial random variable, with parameters equal to the number of Bernoulli random variables being summed $(g(g-1))$ and the probability that any one of the variables is unity (P). We will denote this binomial distribution and its two parameters as $\mathrm{Bin}(g(g-1), P)$, where the two distribution parameters are the two arguments. Thus, assuming that the uniform distribution is appropriate, L is a binomial random variable with parameters $g(g-1)$ and $P = 1/2$; that is, $L \sim \mathrm{Bin}(g(g-1), 1/2)$. Its probability distribution function is

$$P(L = l) = \binom{g(g-1)}{l} \left(\frac{1}{2}\right)^{g(g-1)}, \qquad (13.23)$$

where $l = 0, 1, \ldots, g(g-1)$. The expected value of L (or the number of 1's that should be present in $\mathbf{X}$, on average), $E(L)$, is $(1/2)g(g-1)$, and the variance of L is $Var(L) = (1/4)g(g-1)$. These results follow directly from the mean and variance of a binomial random variable.

So, the observed value of L for a particular digraph can be viewed as a binomial random variable, with a mean of $(1/2)g(g-1)$ and a variance of $(1/4)g(g-1)$, *if* we assume that the digraph is uniform. Consider the null hypothesis

$$H_0 : L \sim \text{Bin}(g(g-1), 1/2), \tag{13.24}$$

which follows from the distributional assumption for **X**. Clearly, if one rejects this hypothesis, then the uniform distribution is not appropriate. So, the significance test that we now outline can be used as an indicator of the validity of an assumption of the simple U distribution. If this hypothesis is rejected, one cannot, unfortunately, determine the reason. It might be because the entries in **X**, the arcs themselves, are not independent, or that the probabilities of arcs being present are not equal to $1/2$, or that these probabilities are not even constant.

To test hypothesis (13.24), we use a large sample approximation to the distribution of L. Statistical theory shows that for large values of g (about ten actors), L should be approximately Gaussian (or normally distributed). Thus, if our null hypothesis is correct, the statistic

$$z_l = \frac{l - E(L)}{\sqrt{Var(L)}} = \frac{l - g(g-1)/2}{\sqrt{g(g-1)/4}} \tag{13.25}$$

is approximately standard normal with a mean of 0 and a variance and standard deviation of 1. Here, $l = \sum_{i=1}^{g} \sum_{j=1}^{g} x_{ij}$, the number of arcs actually observed in the digraph under study.

Example. For Krackhardt's network of high-tech managers and the relation based on friendship, we have $l = 102$ arcs. If the choices made by the actors followed a binomial distribution, so that any one of the choices was a Bernoulli random variable with a probability of $1/2$ of being present, we should see $21(20)/2 = 210$ arcs in our random digraph, more than twice as many as actually observed.

Our null hypothesis for this digraph is

$$H_0 : L \sim \text{Bin}(420, 1/2)$$

since there can be as many as 420 arcs in the digraph. The test statistic for this hypothesis, equation (13.25), is $z_l = (102 - 210)/10.25 = -10.54$. Refer this statistic to its (approximate) standard normal distribution and one finds that the probability that a standard normal variable is less than -10.54 is exceedingly small. Thus, the p-value for our test is nearly 0. Such a value certainly does lead to rejection of a null hypothesis, so it is quite unlikely that these data could have been generated by such a Bernoulli process.

The advice relation from Krackhardt's network is more interesting. For the same null hypothesis, noting that $l = 190$, the test statistic is $z_l = (190 - 210)/10.25 = -1.952$. The probability that a standard normal variable is less than -1.952 is roughly 0.0255. Thus, the p-value for this test (which has a two-sided alternative hypothesis) is $2(0.0255) = 0.0510$. One would conclude that the Advice choices could have been generated by a Bernoulli process with $P = 1/2$.

So, given a social network data set and a desire to test the assumption that the uniform random digraph distribution is a valid model for the data, one can calculate a p-value for the null hypothesis given in equation (13.24) by referring the value of z_l calculated in equation (13.25) to the standard normal distribution. Specifically, one can calculate the probability that a standard normal random variable exceeds the calculated value of z_l. Since this is a two-tailed significance test, the p-value for the hypothesis is twice this probability. If this p-value is sufficiently small (sometimes less than 0.05, or occasionally, 0.01), one can conclude that the hypothesis is not tenable; that is, the network and the choices present do not allow a validation of this special hypothesis. The data do not appear to have been generated by a simple set of independent, Bernoulli random variables, with probabilities of $1/2$, that yield the entries in **X**.

Inference for Unknown P. There is a second hypothesis that can be tested using the number of arcs in a digraph. Suppose that a researcher believes that the digraph is distributed as a Bernoulli digraph, as described in the previous section, with a constant, either known or unknown, probability governing the presence of arcs. If the probability is known or can be postulated, one can modify the above test statistic to test the validity of this distribution assumption. First, assume that the elements of **X** are independent, and have a constant probability of P of being unity. These assumptions yield exactly the Bernoulli random digraph distribution discussed in the previous section, with a set of $\{P_{ij}\}$ equal to a constant value. The researcher may or may not wish to specify this constant value beforehand. If specified, the mean and variance of L are known exactly, and one can test whether the distributional assumption is reasonable; if not, one must estimate P, and hence the mean and variance of L from the data.

Assume that P is equal to P_0. As we have mentioned, if P_0 is equal to $1/2$, then this special case of the Bernoulli distribution is identical to the uniform distribution, and the test of the hypothesis can be conducted as outlined above. The distribution discussed below assumes that all the $\{P_{ij}\}$, the probabilities that $i \rightarrow j$, are equal to P_0, an unknown parameter. This one-parameter Bernoulli digraph distribution generalizes the uniform distribution by allowing P_0 to not equal $1/2$.

Specifically, we assume that $\mathbf{X} \sim B$ with a constant probability P_0. Once again, L, the number of arcs, is a random variable, with a binomial distribution with parameters $g(g-1)$ and P_0; that is, $L \sim \text{Bin}(g(g-1), P_0)$. Its probability distribution function is more general than (13.23):

$$P(L = l) = \binom{g(g-1)}{l} P_0{}^l (1 - P_0)^{g(g-1)-l}. \tag{13.26}$$

The number of arcs observed takes on values $l = 0, 1, \ldots, g(g-1)$. It follows that $E(L) = P_0 g(g-1)$ and the $Var(L)$ is $P_0(1-P_0)g(g-1)$.

We wish to test the hypothesis

$$H_0 : L \sim \text{Bin}(g(g-1), P_0) \tag{13.27}$$

where the value for P_0 is known and specified. As mentioned, if we fail to reject this hypothesis, we can statistically conclude that there is not sufficient evidence to reject the conjecture that the digraph under study could be distributed as a Bernoulli random digraph, with known, constant probability of P_0 governing the presence/absence of the arcs. The test statistic for this hypothesis is quite similar to the statistic for (13.24). Again, we assume that g is large enough to support the large sample theory for the binomial distribution; thus,

$$z_l = \frac{l - P_0 g(g-1)}{\sqrt{P_0(1-P_0)g(g-1)}} \tag{13.28}$$

is approximately standard normal with a mean of 0 and a variance and standard deviation of 1. The p-value for the significance test of hypothesis (13.27) can be found by determining the probability that a standard normal random variable exceeds the value of z_l calculated in (13.28). Since this is a two-tailed significance test, the p-value for the hypothesis is twice this probability. If this p-value is sufficiently small, one can conclude that the hypothesis (13.27) is not tenable; that is, the network and the choices present do not support this special hypothesis.

To demonstrate how to calculate test statistics (13.28) for general hypotheses (13.28) concerning the Bernoulli distribution, we return to the Krackhardt data, and the friendship relation. Suppose that a researcher had an a priori reason to suppose that a Bernoulli process was operating with the probability of an arc equal to $1/4$. So, we desire to test the hypothesis

$H_0 : L \sim \text{Bin}(g(g-1), (1/4))$.

For these data, we calculate $l = 102$ for this network with $g = 21$ actors, and note that the expected number of arcs, with $P_0 = 1/4$, is $21(20)/4 = 105$, only slightly more than actually observed. To demonstrate how to conduct this test, we calculate

$$z_l = \frac{(102 - 105)}{\sqrt{(1/4)(3/4)21(20)}},$$

which equals $-3/8.874 = 0.338$, a small value which yields a large p-value, if the null hypothesis were actually true. We would not reject the null hypothesis here, and conclude that there is evidence that a Bernoulli process with an arc probability of $1/4$ could have generated the friendship choices made by this collection of managers.

13.5.2 Estimation

If P is unknown, one can estimate this parameter from the available data and then construct a confidence interval for the unknown P. We assume that $\mathbf{X} \sim B$ with an unknown probability P. Once again, L, the number of arcs, is a random variable, with a binomial distribution and parameters $g(g-1)$ and P; that is, $L \sim \text{Bin}(g(g-1), P)$. Its probability distribution function is identical to that given in (13.26), except that we use the unknown probability P in place of the known value P_0.

The expected number of arcs is $E(L) = Pg(g-1)$ and $Var(L) = P(1-P)g(g-1)$, both of which depend on the unknown P, and hence, are unknown. The maximum likelihood estimate of this unknown probability of arcs being present is simply the empirical fraction of arcs that are present in the data set: $l/(g(g-1))$. We will denote this (and all) maximum likelihood estimates with the symbol "^" affixed to the parameter being estimated. Thus,

$$\hat{P} = \frac{\sum_{i=1}^{g} \sum_{j=1}^{g} x_{ij}}{g(g-1)} = \frac{l}{g(g-1)}$$

is the maximum likelihood estimate of P. With this estimate, we can also estimate the mean and variance of L. The maximum likelihood estimate of $E(L)$ is $\hat{P}g(g-1) = l$ and the maximum likelihood estimate of the $Var(L)$ is $\hat{P}(1-\hat{P})g(g-1)$.

One can also calculate a confidence interval for the unknown value of P. We use the large sample distribution of $\hat{P}$. Again, we assume that g is large enough to support the large sample theory for the maximum likelihood estimate of the probability parameter of the binomial distribution; thus,

$$z_1 = \frac{(P - \hat{P})}{\sqrt{P(1 - P)/g(g - 1)}} \qquad (13.29)$$

is approximately standard normal with a mean of 0, and a variance and standard deviation of 1. The denominator of (13.29) is unknown, since it depends on P, but it can be estimated using $\hat{P}$. Rearranging (13.29) and using this estimated standard deviation yields a confidence interval of P:

$$\hat{P}_{lower} \leq P \leq \hat{P}_{upper},$$

where

$$\hat{P}_{lower} = \hat{P} - z_{\alpha/2}\sqrt{\hat{P}(1 - \hat{P})/g(g - 1)}$$

and

$$\hat{P}_{upper} = \hat{P} + z_{\alpha/2}\sqrt{\hat{P}(1 - \hat{P})/g(g - 1)}.$$

Here, z_α is the upper $\alpha \times 100$ percentage point of the standard normal distribution.

Again consider the friendship relation measured on Krackhardt's high-tech managers. We obtain the estimated probability of an arc,

$$\hat{P} = \frac{102}{21(20)},$$

which is equal to 0.243, and of course, is exactly the density of choices made in the network. The endpoints for a 95 percent confidence interval (using $z_{0.025} = 1.96$) for the unknown P for this network are

$$\hat{P}_{lower} = 0.243 - 1.96\sqrt{0.243(1 - 0.243)/21(20)}$$

and

$$\hat{P}_{upper} = 0.243 + 1.96\sqrt{0.243(1 - 0.243)/21(20)},$$

giving us the interval $0.243 \pm 1.96(0.0209)$, or $(0.202, 0.284)$. This confidence interval certainly contains $1/4$, and is rather tight around its midpoint (since the standard error of $\hat{P}$ is just 0.0209). Clearly, the interval does not contain $1/2$. For the Advice relation, we calculate $\hat{P} = 0.452$, and a 95 percent confidence interval $(0.405, 0.500)$, which just barely contains $P = 1/2$.

We should note that we are not able to study the variability of L assuming the more complicated conditional uniform distributions, such as those discussed in the next section. This restriction of the statistical analysis of L to simple distributions is because the more complicated distributions condition on L; consequently, L does not vary. To study L we must work with distributions that do not fix this graph property by statistical conditioning.

13.6 ⊗Conditional Uniform Distributions

Several families of uniform distributions on digraphs can be formed by considering *conditional* uniform distributions. Earlier in this section, we defined statistical conditioning as a restriction of the possible random digraphs that can arise to only those random digraphs that have the specific properties that are conditioned upon, or fixed. Another way to view this is to first take all the possible digraphs with g nodes (the elements of $G_d(\mathcal{N})$). To obtain the sample space of a conditional uniform distribution, one then restricts attention to just some of these digraphs, those with certain characteristics. One removes from $G_d(\mathcal{N})$ all those digraphs that do not have the specific characteristics to obtain the sample space for the conditional distribution under study.

We might focus on just those digraphs with a fixed number of arcs, or outdegrees equal to some constant, or a certain number of mutual dyads. For example, if we have fixed choice data, outdegrees are usually all equal to a constant, say d. Other digraphs with varying outdegrees are simply not possible from this network data design if actors do indeed make exactly d choices. Thus, all digraphs with all outdegrees equal to d are included in the sample space, S.

In general, one determines which characteristic(s) to fix and then removes from $G_d(\mathcal{N})$ all those digraphs that do not have the specific characteristic. The remaining digraphs constitute the revised sample space, and, under a conditional uniform distribution, are equally likely to occur.

After describing the two conditional distributions

(i) Uniform distribution, conditional on the number of arcs
(ii) Uniform distribution, conditional on the outdegrees

we will show how they can be used to study statistically the number of mutual dyads present in a digraph.

13.6.1 Uniform Distribution, Conditional on the Number of Arcs

The simplest conditional uniform distribution that we consider here fixes the digraph characteristic of the number of arcs in the digraph, or unity elements in **x** (see Katz and Powell 1957). Thus, the simplest conditional uniform random digraph distribution conditions on the graph property L. Such a distribution is useful when studying the randomness of choices made by each individual actor.

We term this *conditional distribution* $U|L = x_{++}$. It is the conditional uniform distribution which gives equal probability to all digraphs with L arcs, and zero probability to all elements of $G_d(\mathcal{N})$ that do not have x_{++} arcs. The sample space for this distribution includes only those digraphs with L arcs. Each of the digraphs in the sample space is equally likely to arise. An important question is how many random digraphs satisfy the constraints placed on $G_d(\mathcal{N})$ by the conditioning.

For $U|L = x_{++}$, note that the random digraphs in the sample space S can have their x_{++} arcs in any of $g(g-1)$ "locations." In fact, one way to characterize this distribution is to note that we first place one of the x_{++} arcs at random into one of the $g(g-1)$ locations. After this randomization, we then have $x_{++} - 1$ arcs which can fall into any of the remaining $g(g-1)-1$ locations. One of these locations is then chosen at random. Thus, there are $g(g-1)$ locations for the first arc, $g(g-1)-1$ for the second, and so forth until there are $g(g-1)-l+1$ locations for the lth arc. This "sampling from **x** without replacement" continues until all $l = x_{++}$ arcs are placed at random in the digraph.

There are $\binom{g(g-1)}{l}$ ways to distribute l arcs to the $g(g-1)$ possible arc "locations." These assignments are made completely at random, so that we have

$$\frac{\{[g(g-1)][g(g-1)-1]\cdots[g(g-1)-l+1]\}}{[l(l-1)\cdots(1)]} = \binom{g(g-1)}{l}$$

different elements of S. Since this conditional distribution is a uniform distribution over this sample space, it follows that the $U|L = x_{++}$ conditional uniform distribution has probability mass function

$$P(\mathbf{X} = \mathbf{x}) = \begin{cases} \frac{1}{\binom{g(g-1)}{l}}, & \text{if } x_{++} = l \\ 0, & \text{otherwise.} \end{cases} \tag{13.30}$$

The number of random digraphs that have exactly l arcs is usually quite a bit smaller than the total number of possible digraphs — the elements of $G_d(\mathcal{N})$. There are $2^{g(g-1)}$ digraphs in $G_d(\mathcal{N})$ and $\binom{g(g-1)}{l}$ digraphs in the S for $U|L$. For example, we have already stated that there are more than 10^{27} digraphs that exist for an actor set with only $g = 10$ actors. Such a digraph can have as many as $10(9) = 90$ arcs. If we consider only random digraphs on ten nodes that have, say, thirty arcs, we find that there are "just" $\binom{90}{30} = 6.7313 \times 10^{23}$ possible digraphs, considerably fewer than the total number of digraphs (roughly, $\frac{1}{5000}$th of the total), but still quite a few. (In general, if one sums the numbers of random digraphs on g nodes with 0, 1, 2, up to $g(g-1)$ arcs, then the total number of digraphs with g nodes, exactly the number of elements in $G_d(\mathcal{N})$, $2^{g(g-1)}$, is obtained.)

It is certainly hard to think about 10^{27} or even 10^{23} directed graphs, so consider random digraphs with just $g = 4$ nodes. The set of all possible digraphs with 4 nodes, $G_d(\mathcal{N})$, with $\mathcal{N} = \{n_1, n_2, n_3, n_4\}$, has $2^{12} = 4096$ elements. There are $4 \times 3 = 12$ ordered pairs of nodes. Each of these twelve pairs is such that the first actor can relate to or choose the second actor. Thus, there can be as many as 12 arcs present in the digraph. Suppose that we consider the $U|L = 6$ distribution; that is, let us statistically condition on the presence of exactly 6 arcs. The number of digraphs with 4 nodes and 6 arcs is $\binom{12}{6} = 924$, so the sample space for the $U|C = L$ digraph distribution contains just 924 digraphs. This set is roughly one-fourth the size of $G_d(\{n_1, n_2, n_3, n_4\})$, but is still too large to enumerate easily all possibilities even though there are only 4 nodes!

13.6.2 Uniform Distribution, Conditional on the Outdegrees

Another very useful conditional uniform distribution, described by Katz and Powell (1957), is the uniform distribution which conditions on the outdegrees of the nodes in the digraph. The outdegrees for a random digraph are $\{X_{1+}, X_{2+}, \ldots, X_{g+}\}$, and we will let lowercase letters refer to the realizations for these g random variables; specifically, x_{i+} is one possible value for X_{i+}. Each x_{i+} can take on all integer values between 0 and $g-1$. One could also condition on the indegrees, or both the indegrees and outdegrees. We discuss these conditional uniform distributions later in this chapter.

$U|\{X_{i+}\}$ is a conditional uniform distribution for random directed graphs that conditions on a fixed set of outdegrees. Every directed graph with the specified outdegrees, $X_{1+} = x_{1+}, X_{2+} = x_{2+}, \ldots, X_{g+} = x_{g+}$, has equal probability of occurring. The sample space contains all digraphs with exactly the specified outdegrees. Digraphs with outdegrees not equal to the collection of specified outdegrees have zero probabilities of occurring, since such digraphs are not in the sample space. Since this distribution conditions on g quantities, there may be few digraphs with the specified outdegrees; thus, the size of this sample space S could be quite small.

This is a very useful conditional distribution since it allows a researcher to "control for" the outdegree of each node. These outdegrees are occasionally fixed by the experimental design that generated the data, such as with fixed choice designs. Good statistical practice dictates that such aspects of the design should be taken into account in any statistical analyses of the data. A good way of "controlling for" possibly fixed outdegrees is to use the uniform distribution that conditions on the outdegrees of each actor — $U|\{X_{i+}\}$. This conditioning on outdegrees does not completely remove the effects of the procedures used to gather the data. That is, if a bad data collection design was used (such as fixed choice data with a very small or very large number of nominations), nothing can improve the quality of the data. However, the use of this conditional distribution will allow the researcher to conduct a credible statistical analysis, since the search for departures from structural patterns in the data focuses only on similar networks — those networks with the same outdegrees.

Before we give the probability function for $U|\{X_{i+}\}$, let us consider how many digraphs exist with a specified set of outdegrees. It is easiest to work directly with the sociomatrix here. We need to think about how we can allocate a fixed number of 1's for the ith row of the sociomatrix. We place this fixed number of 1's in certain positions at random, while the remaining entries in the row remain 0's. We then do this allocation for all rows, allowing for different row sums in the sociomatrix.

With the row sums of a sociomatrix fixed, the rows themselves are independent. Thus, we treat each row separately, and consider how many ways there are to distribute a fixed number of 1's to the $g - 1$ positions in each row. This allocation is just a combinatorial problem, similar to that for the $U|L$ distribution. If there are $g - 1$ positions that can be filled with x_{i+} ones, then there are $(g - 1)(g - 2) \cdots (g - x_{i+} + 1)$ ways to distribute the 1's. Since there are $x_{i+}(x_{i+} - 1) \cdots (2)(1)$ ways to order the ones themselves, then we have

$$\frac{(g - 1)(g - 2) \cdots (g - x_{i+} + 1)}{x_{i+}(x_{i+} - 1) \cdots (2)(1)} = \binom{g - 1}{x_{i+}}$$

ways to place the correct number of 1's in the ith row of the sociomatrix.

Since all the rows are independent, the allocation of ones to "locations" is done separately for each row. We can multiply the number of ways to allocate the 1's to each row across all rows to obtain $\prod_{i=1}^{g} \binom{g-1}{x_{i+}}$ as the total number of digraphs that have the specified set of outdegrees. Thus, the number of elements in the sample space is $\prod_{i=1}^{g} \binom{g-1}{x_{i+}}$, a number that depends not only on the number of actors, g, but also on the outdegrees that we restrict the random digraphs to have. Each of these random digraphs is equally likely under the uniform distribution, conditional on a fixed set of outdegrees. Consequently, the $U|\{X_{i+} = x_{i+}\}$ probability distribution function is

$$P(\mathbf{X} = \mathbf{x}) = \begin{cases} \prod_{i=1}^{g} \frac{1}{\binom{g-1}{x_{i+}}}, & \text{if } X_{i+} = x_{i+} \text{ for all } i, \\ 0, & \text{otherwise.} \end{cases} \qquad (13.31)$$

If the experimental design that generated the social network data is fixed choice, then all of the $\{x_{i+}\}$ are equal to a constant, say d. Then, (13.31) simplifies somewhat to

$$P(\mathbf{X} = \mathbf{x}) = \begin{cases} \binom{g-1}{d}^{-g}, & \text{if } X_{i+} = d \text{ for all } i, \\ 0, & \text{otherwise.} \end{cases} \qquad (13.32)$$

13.7 Statistical Analysis of the Number of Mutuals

We now return to the dyad census, and particularly, one of its three components: M, the frequency of mutual dyads. We can now statistically study the dyad census and M at length.

We first introduced the dyad census in earlier sections of this chapter, and described two useful measures for the level of mutuality in a network. Random digraph distributions allow us to test hypotheses about particular graph properties. For example, as we illustrate in this section, we will assume that an observed digraph is random, distributed following the $U|\{X_{i+}\}$ distribution. From this assumption, we will be able to test hypotheses about the number of mutual dyads in a digraph.

Recall that even though the dyad census contains three counts (M, A, N), one of the three is determined by the other two and g. Thus, from a mathematical viewpoint, we need only consider two of the three components. We view the dyad census statistically as consisting of just two random graph properties, M and A. The dyad census is therefore a *bivariate* random variable, and will have a mean with two components, and a 2×2 covariance matrix. This covariance matrix has two rows and two columns, is symmetric, and contains the two variances (of M and A

on the diagonal) and the covariance of the random counts M and A off the diagonal.

Unfortunately, this bivariate focus on the dyad census is missing from the literature. Theorists and methodologists have stressed just the first of the two components, M, and have ignored the number of asymmetric dyads. One approach to a bivariate analysis of the dyad census is through the use of triads. We will return to this approach in Chapter 14. The emphasis in early sociometric studies was on the relative frequency of the number of mutual choices, and hence, excluded A. It is this literature on the statistical analysis of M that we now review.

13.7.1 *Estimation*

For a social network data set containing a single, dichotomous relation, we have used M to denote the number of mutual dyads in the network, so that $0 \leq M \leq \binom{g}{2}$. Bronfenbrenner (1943) and Moreno and Jennings (1945) were the first to study this directed graph property.

Criswell (1946b) and Edwards (1948) (see the critique by Loomis and Pepinsky 1948) calculated the correct expected value of M, assuming that each actor has a fixed outdegree equal to d. Specifically, if one assumes that $\mathbf{X} \sim U|\{X_{i+} = d\}$ (so that we only focus on digraphs with the correct outdegrees), then, as we gave earlier in equation (13.7),

$$E(M|\{X_{i+} = d\}) = \frac{gd^2}{2(g-1)}.$$

Here, the notation $E(M|\bullet)$ implies that we are calculating the expected value of M, assuming that the distribution $U|\bullet$ is operating. This calculation uses the fact that if each actor makes d choices at random from the other $g - 1$ actors, then the probability that a given dyad is mutual is $(d/(g-1))^2$. Since there are $g(g-1)/2$ dyads, the average number of mutual dyads must be the number of dyads times the probability that any one of them is a mutual. But no one seemed to know how to calculate the variance of M, Var(M).

As reviewed by Katz, Tagiuri, and Wilson (1958), Bronfenbrenner (1943), and Proctor and Loomis (1951) proposed one variance, and Criswell (1946b), another. This discrepancy arose because of the incorrect presumption that, if the random digraph has a $U|\{X_{i+} = d\}$ distribution, then M is a binomial random variable. Katz and Wilson (1956) carefully showed that the correct variance is

$$\text{Var}(M|\{X_{i+} = d\}) = E(M|\{X_{i+} = d\})\left(1 - \frac{d}{g-1}\right)^2 \qquad (13.33)$$

rather than the variance that arises from the binomial distribution (see Katz and Wilson 1956, equation 3). The correct variance, equation (13.33), differs from the binomial variance because the former includes the possible covariance that exists between dyads with one actor in common.

If one allows for differing numbers of choices among the actors, so that the more general conditional distribution $U|\{X_{i+} = x_{i+}\}$ is operating, then the mean and variance of M are considerably more complicated. Katz and Wilson (1956), and Katz and Powell (1955), show that

$$E(M|\{X_{i+} = x_{i+}\}) = \frac{1}{2(g-1)^2}\left[\left(\sum_{i=1}^{g} x_{i+}\right)^2 - \sum_{i=1}^{g} x_{i+}^2\right],$$

a formula we gave earlier in equation (13.12). If all the $\{x_{i+}\}$ are equal to d, (13.12) simplifies to $E(M|\{X_{i+} = d\})$ given in (13.7).

The expression for $\text{Var}(M|\{X_{i+} = x_{i+}\})$ involves the power sums $s_m = \sum x_{i+}^m$, for $m = 1, 2, 3, 4$. Define

$$v_1 = \frac{1}{2(g-1)^4}(-2s_1^2 s_2 + s_2^2 + 4s_1 s_3 - 3s_4)$$

$$v_2 = \frac{1}{(g-1)^3(g-2)}(s_1^2 s_2 - s_2^2 - 2s_1 s_3 + 2s_4 - s_1^3 + 3s_1 s_2 - 2s_3)$$

and

$$v_3 = \frac{1}{2(g-1)^2}(s_1^2 - s_2).$$

Katz and Wilson obtained

$$\text{Var}(M|\{X_{i+} = x_{i+}\}) = v_1 + v_2 + v_3. \qquad (13.34)$$

And, as expected, equation (13.34) simplifies to equation (13.33) if all the outdegrees are equal.

Some examples should be illustrative. Let $g = 10$, and suppose that each actor in the network is instructed to choose four other actors. With $d = 4$, we calculate from (13.7) that the expected number of mutuals is $10(4^2)/(2)(9) = 160/18 = 8.89$ out of a possible forty-five dyads. Thus, we expect that $(8.89/45) = 0.1976$ of the dyads will be mutuals. If we see many more than this number, we can conclude that on this relation, the actors reciprocate more than we would expect. The variance of M, from equation (13.33), is $8.89(1 - 4/9)^2 = 8.89(0.3086) = 2.743$. The standard deviation of M, expressed as a fraction of the number of dyads, is ($\sqrt{2.743}/45$) =0.0368.

Now suppose that the actors have unequal outdegrees. The mean and variance of M can be calculated, if we assume that $\mathbf{X} \sim U|\{X_{i+} = x_{i+}\}$. Suppose that the distribution of outdegrees is as follows: two actors have outdegrees of 2, five actors have outdegrees of 3, and three have outdegrees of 4. With these values, Katz and Wilson (1956) calculate the power sums $s_1 = 31$, $s_2 = 101$, $s_3 = 343$, and $s_4 = 1205$. Equation (13.12) gives $E(M|\{X_{i+} = x_{i+}\}) = 5.34$ and equation (13.34) gives $\text{Var}(M|\{X_{i+} = x_{i+}\}) = 2.29$. If the outdegrees are more variable, such as five actors with outdegrees of 1 and five actors with outdegrees of 7, one obtains $E(M|\{X_{i+} = x_{i+}\}) = 8.33$ and $\text{Var}(M|\{X_{i+} = x_{i+}\}) = 2.33$.

We should note that as the outdegrees become more equal, that is, as the $\{x_{i+}\}$ become more constant, one can approximate the mean and variance of M by finding the average outdegree and using it in place of d in equations (13.7) and (13.33). For the first example given in the previous paragraph, the average outdegree is 3.1, which yields an approximate expected M of 5.34 and variance of 2.30. These values are remarkably close to the exact values given above. However, if the outdegrees are quite different, this approximation is not very good (note that the average outdegree is 4, so that the calculations given for the fixed outdegree example can be used).

13.7.2 Testing

Lastly, consider the distribution of M, and tests of hypotheses about the number of mutual dyads. The exact distribution of M is known only for the very special case of $d = 1$. Katz, Tagiuri, and Wilson (1958) give cumulative probabilities of this distribution for $g = 4, 5, 6, \ldots, 11$. Katz and Wilson (1956) conjecture that the distribution is asymptotically Poisson since $E(M|\{X_{i+} = d\})$ and $\text{Var}(M|\{X_{i+} = d\})$ are asymptotically equal. Katz, Tagiuri, and Wilson (1958) state that when $g > 20d$, the Poisson distribution with parameter equal to $E(M)$ gives a sufficiently accurate approximation to the exact distribution. These authors indicate that research by Katz (which, to our knowledge, was unfortunately never published) indicates that the Poisson approximation is accurate when $g > 10d$, but when $g < 10$ and $d \geq 2$, a normal approximation is better. Even though earlier authors suggested that significance tests could be carried out for M, these findings and conjectures indicate otherwise.

However, recent research by Achuthan, Rao, and Rao (1982) gives a range of possible values for M assuming that the outdegrees are known; that is, we can determine M_{min} and M_{max} such that $M_{min} \leq M \leq M_{max}$, assuming the $U|\{X_{i+}\}$ distribution is operating. If one considers every possible integer value in the interval (M_{min}, M_{max}), then one can be assured that there is at least one digraph, with the assumed outdegrees, that has exactly that number of mutuals. As we mentioned earlier in this chapter, one can define an index for mutuality, similar to the index proposed by Katz and Powell (1955), by using the maximum and minimum numbers of possible mutuals, for a specific set of outdegrees. Unfortunately, the distribution of this index based on M_{min} and M_{max} is not known.

One can use the standard large sample testing approximations to test hypotheses about M. If g is sufficiently large (probably around 20, although the size needed depends on the true number of mutual dyads), then one can test a hypothesis about M by first dividing the difference between the observed M and the hypothesized M by the standard deviation (square root of the variance of M), and then assuming that this standardized statistic has an approximate normal distribution. A good, early application of this approach can be found in Maucorps' (1949) study of friendship, work preference, and praise among an elite group of thirty-five French army officers. The recent research of Snijders (1991a) demonstrates that nonparametric tests can be used to test hypotheses about M. Computer software for such tests (which is needed to enumerate all possible values for M) is also available (see Snijders 1991a).

We note in passing that there has been some research on the expected frequencies of different kinds of choice patterns, and the number of mutual choices, when actors fall into two (or more) subgroups. Criswell (1943) first worked on this problem, as did Seeman (1946) and Edwards (1948). Nehnevajsa (1955a) reviews this research, and discusses more probability calculations that involve actors in different groups. Glazer (1981) also proposes a solution to this problem.

13.7.3 Examples

Krackhardt's friendship relation has $M = 23$ mutual dyads. From the digraph distribution that statistically conditions on the outdegrees, we find that the expected number of mutuals is $E(M|\{X_{i+}\}) = 11.90$, and the variance is $\text{Var}(M|\{X_{i+}\}) = 3.784^2$.

Suppose we wish to test the alternative hypothesis that we have observed too many mutuals to support this null distribution assumption.

Then, a test statistic to test this hypothesis about M is $(23-11.90)/3.784 = 2.933$, which has a p-value for a one-tailed test of 0.0017. Such a value indicates that the null hypothesis may indeed be false, and that the number of mutual dyads observed may be too large, given the null distribution. We conclude that friendship has more reciprocity than one would expect by chance, given the numbers of choices made by the actors.

The advice relation has an M closer to the average. We observe 45 mutuals, and the expected number is 42.38. Since the standard deviation of the number of mutuals is 9.23, this difference $(45-42.38)$ is quite small, and there is no significant difference for the advice relation between the numbers of mutual dyads expected and observed. The tendency for advice to be reciprocated does not appear as strong as for friendship.

Thus, one can see how inference about M can lead to statements about the level of reciprocity for a relation. Unlike the indices for mutuality discussed earlier in this chapter, we can now make definitive, statistical conclusions about reciprocity, thanks to the adoption of a proper probability distribution.

13.8 ⊗Other Conditional Uniform Distributions

There are several very important conditional uniform distributions that are straightforward generalizations of the distributions that we have just discussed. Some of them are so complex that (until very recently) no simple ways existed to simulate random digraphs with these distributions. The first two are relatively easy to understand, and will be used in Chapters 14–16. The last three are more complicated. The five distributions are:

   (i) Uniform distribution conditional on indegrees
  (ii) Uniform distribution conditional on the numbers of mutual, asymmetric, and null dyads
 (iii) Uniform distribution conditional on outdegrees and indegrees simultaneously
 (iv) Uniform distribution conditional on outdegrees and number of mutuals
  (v) Uniform distribution conditional on outdegrees, indegrees, and number of mutuals

The first two distributions will be described in some detail. The first is quite similar to the conditional uniform distribution that conditions on the outdegrees, discussed earlier in the chapter. The second is quite important, fixing the three counts of the dyad census, and will be used to study the triad census in Chapter 14.

The latter three distributions are combinations of the simpler conditional distributions discussed earlier in this chapter. Of these three, the first is a combination of the conditional distribution that conditions on the outdegrees ($U|\{X_{i+}\}$) and the conditional distribution that conditions on the indegrees ($U|\{X_{+j}\}$). It will be of interest substantively to condition simultaneously on both of these sets of graph properties. The second distribution combines conditioning on the outdegrees ($U|\{X_{i+}\}$) and conditioning on specific values of the dyad census ($U|MAN$). Such a distribution is important because it controls for the outdegrees of a digraph, which are frequently fixed by experimental design, and the dyad census, which is the simplest, yet important, collection of subgraphs. As we will show, even though it appears that we only condition on M, this distribution indirectly fixes A and N. The third distribution is a combination of the first two.

A simple situation will help illustrate why these distributions are important. Suppose that a relation is measured on actors using a fixed choice design, so that all outdegrees are fixed, say, at $x_{i+} = 5$. If an examination of the dyad census reveals that mutual dyads are quite rare, so that most relationships are asymmetric, then statistical investigations concerning this network should be made by conditioning not only on the fixed outdegrees, but also on the number of mutual dyads actually observed among the data. One could assume that the sociomatrix was distributed as a uniform random matrix, conditional on the outdegrees and number of mutuals. This allows all statistical inferences to be made only among those sociomatrices with the same outdegrees and M value as observed in the data set. In this way, we fix two important aspects of this relation — the fixed outdegrees and the low level of reciprocity — in order to study if any additional structure exists in the network.

13.8.1 *Uniform Distribution, Conditional on the Indegrees*

We now examine a distribution very similar to $U|\{X_{i+}\}$. Rather than conditioning on the row totals of a sociomatrix or the outdegrees of a sociogram, this distribution conditions on the column totals or *indegrees*. We will let $\{X_{+1}, X_{+2}, \ldots, X_{+g}\}$ refer to the set of indegrees of a random digraph. Lowercase letters will refer to the realizations for these g random variables; specifically, x_{+j} is one possible value for X_{+j}. Each x_{+j} can take on all integer values between 0 and $g - 1$.

Since the column totals of a sociomatrix (the indegrees) are usually not fixed by experimental design, the $U|\{X_{+j}\}$ distribution is not used for inferential purposes as frequently as $U|\{X_{i+}\}$. However, from a structural viewpoint, it is indeed interesting to study aspects of the digraph by fixing the indegrees at the observed values. For example, is the level of reciprocity (as reflected by the magnitude of M) more than what one would expect by chance, given, say, that all indegrees are constant (that is, all actors are, roughly, equally prestigious)?

The $U|\{X_{+j}\}$ random digraph distribution is a conditional uniform distribution that conditions on a fixed set of indegrees. Every directed graph with the specified indegrees, $X_{+1} = x_{+1}, X_{+2} = x_{+2}, \ldots, X_{+g} = x_{+g}$, has equal probability of occurring. The sample space contains all digraphs with exactly the specified indegrees. Digraphs with indegrees not equal to the collection of specified indegrees have zero probabilities of occurring, since such digraphs are not in the sample space. As pointed out by Katz and Powell (1957), if one fixes the row totals of a sociomatrix, and then transposes the matrix (so that the (j, i)th element of the transposed matrix is the (i, j)th element of the original matrix), one obtains the $U|\{X_{+j}\}$ distribution, where the conditioning indegrees are the original, fixed row totals. So, fixing row sums to be equal to the specified indegrees, and then transposing, gives a random digraph distributed as a $U|\{X_{+j}\}$ random digraph.

It follows from the relationship between $U|\{X_{i+}\}$ and $U|\{X_{+j}\}$ that there are $\binom{g-1}{x_{+j}}$ ways to place the correct number of 1's in the jth column of the sociomatrix. As with the rows in a $U|\{X_{i+}\}$-distributed digraph, the columns in a $U|\{X_{+j}\}$-distributed digraph are statistically independent. We multiply the number of ways to allocate the 1's in each column across all columns to obtain $\prod_{j=1}^{g} \binom{g-1}{x_{+j}}$ as the total number of digraphs that have the specified indegrees. Each of these random digraphs is equally likely under the uniform distribution, conditional on a fixed set of indegrees. This number is the size of the sample space of digraphs under this distribution.

The $U|\{X_{+j} = x_{+j}\}$ random directed graph distribution has probability mass function

$$P(\mathbf{X} = \mathbf{x}) = \begin{cases} \prod_{j=1}^{g} \frac{1}{\binom{g-1}{x_{+j}}}, & \text{if } X_{+j} = x_{+j} \text{ for all } j, \\ 0, & \text{otherwise.} \end{cases} \tag{13.35}$$

A random digraph distributed according to this distribution can be simulated just as a random $U|\{X_{i+}\}$ digraph is simulated. One uses the fixed set of indegrees as row totals for the sociomatrix associated with the digraph, allocates x_{+j} 1's at random to the jth row, for each of the g rows, and then transposes the sociomatrix.

13.8.2 The U|MAN Distribution

We now turn to a more interesting conditional uniform distribution. Consider the numbers of the different types of dyads. The distribution discussed in these next paragraphs is one of the most frequently used random directed graph distributions in social network analysis. It is a uniform distribution which conditions on the numbers of mutual, asymmetric, and null dyads in the digraph — that is, the dyad census itself. Using our symbols for the numbers of these dyads (M, A, and N, respectively), we can refer to this distribution as $U|M = m, A = a, N = n$, where m, a, and n are the actual frequencies of the three types of dyads observed for a particular digraph. This conditional distribution was used quite extensively by Holland and Leinhardt (1975, and references therein). Snijders and Stokman (1987) extend $U|MAN$ to networks with actors partitioned into distinct subsets (such as school-children into a subset of boys and a subset of girls).

The $U|MAN$ distribution is the conditional uniform distribution which puts equal probability on all digraphs in $G_d(\mathcal{N})$ which have $M = m, A = a$, and $N = n$ dyads. We should note that the sum $m + a + n$ is exactly $\binom{g}{2}$, since every dyad must be one of the three types; consequently, a given M, A, and N must satisfy this equality for the observed value of g. This implies that one only need condition on two of these three counts, since the third will automatically be fixed.

Note that if one just pulls values for m, a, and n "out of the air," then the constraint that these three counts sum to $\binom{g}{2}$ may not be satisfied. In that case, the subset of $G_d(\mathcal{N})$ with the given values of M, A, and N may be empty. Holland and Leinhardt's preference for $U|MAN$ is due primarily to the fact that it provides a lot of conditioning while still allowing easy calculations. In fact, it is quite useful in social network analysis, when working with a specific set of graph properties (such as the triad census) to fix or condition on all "lower-level" graph properties (such as the dyad census). This is exactly the approach that we take in Chapter 14, where the $U|MAN$ distribution will be used extensively when studying triads — that is, we fix the dyad census to study triadic frequencies. In this chapter, we have also showed how one can use the

$U|L$ distribution to study dyad counts — that is, fixing the number of arcs, L, to study the numbers of the different dyad types.

We first consider how many random digraphs have exactly the specified numbers of m, a, and n dyads. That is, we want to construct a sample space consisting of only the digraphs with g nodes which have m mutual dyads, a asymmetric dyads, and n null dyads. In total, there are $\binom{g}{2} = g(g-1)/2$ dyads in the digraph. To consider the size of the sample space, we must answer the question: "How many ways can we take the dyads and divide them so that the first group has m dyads, the second a, and the third, the remainder of the dyads, will be null?"

This is a combinatorial problem, not unlike the one we considered for the $U|L$ distribution. There are $\binom{g}{2}$! ways to order all the dyads. The first m then become mutuals, the next a, asymmetrics, and the remainder $(\binom{g}{2} - m - a = n)$ become nulls. There are also $m!$, $a!$, and $n!$ ways, respectively, to order the dyads within the three sets. Lastly, each of the asymmetric dyads can go in one of two directions, and the direction for a specific asymmetric can be determined by a toss of a fair coin. Thus, there are 2^a ways of ordering the a asymmetrics. Putting this all together gives us $(2^a)[\binom{g}{2}!] \big/ [m!\, a!\, n!]$ different digraphs with m mutual, a asymmetric, and n null dyads (where $m + a + n = \binom{g}{2}$).

Thus, this statistical conditioning on the numbers of the three different kinds of dyads reduces the number of possible random digraphs from $2^{g(g-1)}$ to $(2^a)[\binom{g}{2}!] \big/ [m!\, a!\, n!]$. This conditioning can reduce the size of the sample space, S, to a number quite a bit smaller than the total number of digraphs in $G_d(\mathcal{N})$.

For example, if $g = 10$, we have $\binom{10}{2} = 45$ dyads. Assume that we are interested just in digraphs with a dyad census of $m = 10$ mutual dyads, $a = 10$ asymmetric dyads, and $n = 25$ null dyads. From the counting described in the above paragraph, we find that there are

$$\frac{(2^{10})[45!]}{[10!\,10!\,25!]} = \frac{[(1024)(1.1962 \times 10^{56})]}{[(3.6288 \times 10^6)(3.6288 \times 10^6)(1.5511 \times 10^{25})]},$$

which equals 5.9971×10^{20} possible random digraphs. Notice that this is much smaller than the entire collection of digraphs in $\mathcal{G}_d(10)$, of size approximately 10^{27}. Note also that with ten asymmetrics and ten mutuals, there are thirty arcs in the digraph. If we only condition on digraphs that have $c = 30$ arcs, we have roughly 7×10^{23} possible digraphs; consequently, specifying that these arcs are placed in a configuration that has ten asymmetrics and ten mutuals reduces the number of possible digraphs substantially.

As earlier, these numbers are much too large to comprehend. So, let us return to our little digraph, with just four nodes, and thus, six dyads. Assume that we still have six arcs, which are arranged in the digraph to yield $m = 2$ mutuals, $a = 2$ asymmetrics, and $n = 2$ nulls. One can calculate that there are

$$\frac{(2^2)6!}{2!2!2!} = \frac{2880}{64} = 45$$

digraphs with the specified values for M, A, and N. We have reduced the total possible number of digraphs with 4 nodes from 4096 to 924 by conditioning on the presence of 6 arcs, and then to 45 by requiring that these arcs exist in 2 mutuals, 2 asymmetrics, and 2 nulls. So, one can see that even though the dyad census is a simple digraph property, conditioning on it greatly reduces the size of the sample space.

In general, the more complicated the conditional distribution (that is, the more graph properties that we condition on), the fewer elements will be present in the conditional sample space. We can restrict the types of directed graphs that are of interest to us by insisting that the graphs have specific properties, namely that $M = m$, $A = a$, and $N = n$, for whatever m, a, and n we are interested in. The $U|M,A,N$ distribution conditions on two digraph properties (M and A, since N is determined by g, M, and A). Compare this to the uniform distribution conditional on the number of arcs — a distribution conditional on just one quantity. The extra conditioning provided by the second quantity greatly reduces the size of the sample space. But, at the same time, the number of possible values to condition on increases, so that there are many more $U|MAN$ distributions than $U|L$ distributions.

To find the probability mass function of a uniform or conditional uniform distribution, we need to count the number of elements in the sample space. Each of these elements is equally likely to occur, so that the probability of any one of them is simply the reciprocal of the number of elements in S. Therefore, the $U|MAN$ conditional uniform distribution has probability mass function

$$P(\mathbf{X} = \mathbf{x}) = \begin{cases} \frac{[m!\ a!\ n!]}{(2^a)\binom{g}{2}!}, & \text{if } M = m, A = a, N = n \\ 0, & \text{otherwise,} \end{cases} \tag{13.36}$$

where $m + a + n = \binom{g}{2}$.

13.8.3 More Complex Distributions

The $U|\{X_{i+}\},\{X_{+j}\}$ **Distribution.** The distribution that combines the conditioning of $U|\{X_{i+}\}$ and $U|\{X_{+j}\}$ is the $U|\{X_{i+}\},\{X_{+j}\}$ distribution. This conditional uniform distribution simultaneously conditions on both the indegrees and the outdegrees of the digraph. All digraphs with the specified values of the $\{X_{i+}\}$ and the $\{X_{+j}\}$ are equally likely. That is, the sample space includes all digraphs with $X_{i+} = x_{i+}$, $i = 1,2,\ldots,g$, and $X_{+j} = x_{+j}$, $j = 1,2,\ldots,g$. Digraphs that do not satisfy these constraints are absent from the sample space, and thus, cannot occur. This distribution is extremely important in social network analysis, since it can be used to control statistically for both choices made by each actor (frequently fixed by the experimental design) and choices received. Its relation to the simpler conditional uniform distributions is discussed by Katz and Powell (1957).

Suppose that one has a set of both indegrees and outdegrees. An interesting question is whether a sociomatrix could have arisen from a random digraph distribution with indegrees and outdegrees corresponding to the two sets. Fulkerson (1960) and Ford and Fulkerson (1962) give necessary and sufficient conditions for the existence of at least one element in the sample space. Their results, which consist of a series of inequality constraints on the $\{x_{i+}\}$ and the $\{x_{+j}\}$, can be used to determine if a set of outdegrees and a set of indegrees could have arisen from a single sociomatrix. Clearly, one necessary condition is that the row totals and column totals must sum to the same quantity: L, the total number of 1's in the sociomatrix.

Unfortunately, little is known about the $U|\{X_{i+}\},\{X_{+j}\}$ distribution. For example, one cannot write down its probability mass function.

Snijders (1991a) has developed a method, however, for enumerating all digraphs that have fixed indegrees and outdegrees. Once all the digraphs with given margins or degrees have been enumerated, this method can then be used to conduct permutation tests of simpler graph properties, such as the number of mutual dyads. Graph theorists have developed complicated, recursive formulas which give the number of digraphs that exist with specified outdegrees and indegrees. Katz and Powell (1954 and 1957) give such formulas (see also Sukhatme 1938; Gale 1957; Ryser 1957; Harary and Palmer 1966; Bekessy, Bekessy, and Komlos 1972; and Majcher 1985, who considered digraphs that can have self-choices). For example, let $g = 4$, and specify a set of outdegrees of $\{3, 2, 1, 1\}$, and indegrees of $\{2, 2, 1, 2\}$. One can calculate that there are exactly

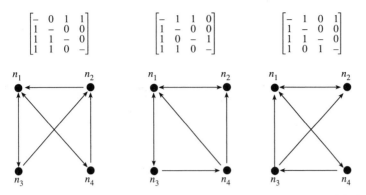

Fig. 13.2. The digraphs with the specified sets of outdegrees and indegrees

3 digraphs with these outdegrees and indegrees; they are shown, along with their sociomatrices, in Figure 13.2. Obviously, in this example, it is not difficult to write down these three digraphs directly, obviating the need for complicated formulas. But, now consider a second example, with $g = 8$ nodes, and outdegrees of $\{1, 1, 1, 1, 1, 1, 1, 1\}$ — that is, all ones — and indegrees of $\{3, 2, 1, 1, 1, 0, 0, 0\}$. Calculations are certainly needed here, and Katz and Powell's formulas give us 1143 possible digraphs with this set of indegrees, and outdegrees fixed at unity. Clearly, enumerating them all would be an enormous task.

We used Snijders' (1991a) method to calculate the expected number of mutual dyads assuming that all digraphs with specified indegrees and outdegrees are equally likely. Working once again with Krackhardt's network of high-tech managers, we assumed that the $U|\{X_{i+}\}, \{X_{+j}\}$ distribution was operating. Recall that for the friendship relation, there are twenty-three mutual dyads, while for the advice relation, there are forty-five.

First, for the friendship relation, Snijders' algorithm calculates only 13.90 expected mutual dyads, compared to the 23 observed. Since the standard deviation of M is 2.21, the difference between observed and expected here is quite large, implying that even when controlling for choices made and choices received, the level of reciprocity for this relation is quite apparent. For the advice relation, the expected number of mutual dyads is 37.05, so that we observe only about 8 more mutuals than expected. But even this small relative difference is statistically large, since the standard deviation of M is 2.00. (It is interesting to compare these expectations to those discussed earlier in the chapter, calculated by conditioning on just the outdegrees.)

The $U|M, \{X_{i+}\}$ Distribution. Another complex conditional uniform distribution worth mentioning is the uniform distribution which conditions on both the number of mutual dyads and the outdegrees. We note that such conditioning also fixes the numbers of asymmetric and null dyads. The counts A and N are fixed because the sum of the outdegrees equals L, the total number of arcs, and A (the number of asymmetric dyads) $= L - 2M$. Since the number of null dyads (N) is fixed once we condition on the number of actors (g) and M and A (because $N = \binom{g}{2} - M - A$), the $U|M, \{X_{i+}\}$ distribution actually is a combination of $U|MAN$, and $U|\{X_{i+}\}$. Little is known about this distribution, but because of the importance of the two distributions that form it, $U|M, \{X_{i+}\}$ could be quite useful in practice.

The $U|M, \{X_{i+}\}, \{X_{i+}\}$ Distribution. A very important distribution in social network analysis is the uniform distribution that conditions on the dyad census, the outdegrees, and the indegrees. This distribution, referred to as $U|M, \{X_{i+}\}, \{X_{i+}\}$, controls for choices made, choices received, and the types of dyads. This distribution combines the three conditional distributions that we have emphasized in this section. It is so complex, that it is not clear that a specified value for M is at all consistent with the specified indegrees and outdegrees. Snijders (1991b) has begun to work with this very important distribution.

13.9 Other Research

A good review of measures of reciprocity in social network data, assuming a dichotomous relation, is given by Rao and Bandyopadhyay (1987). These authors recommend use of several measures based on standardizations of ρ_B. Included in their review are a number of probabilistic-based measures of reciprocity, including a model-based parameter of tendencies toward reciprocity, which we describe in detail in Chapter 15. We should note that this reciprocity measure, which we will simply call ρ, is easily generalizable to valued relations.

There are other measures of reciprocity available, to be used in dyadic analyses. Rao and Rao (1988) extend ρ_B to valued relational variables by considering the smaller of X_{ij} and X_{ji} (which will be integer-valued) as a measure of the mutuality between actors i and j. Unfortunately, there is no easy or straightforward way to standardize such a measure.

We have presented a number of distributions that can be placed on the set of all digraphs on g nodes, $G_d(\mathcal{N})$. Several of them do not have simple probability mass functions, so that we have no idea how large their sample spaces are. Fortunately, there are many that are well understood and are easy to work with. As we have mentioned, one has to be careful when choosing values for the conditioning graph properties, since these values must be consistent. Otherwise, the sample space could very well be empty, implying no digraphs exist with the specified values for the conditioning graph properties. Usually, however, we condition using values actually observed for a digraph so that we know that the sample space has at least one element!

We should note that conditional uniform distributions for random digraphs can play an important theoretical role in social network analyses. One first must assume that the network under study is random, and that the actual data in hand is but one of many possible realizations of the random digraph. Assuming one of these random digraph distributions described here as a reference distribution allows the researcher to focus attention only on those possible digraph realizations that have certain characteristics which match those in the empirical data. With this strategy, a search for structural patterns in the data can be conducted with the knowledge that these patterns are not artifacts; that is, any interesting data features will not be due to the graph properties that have been fixed or conditioned upon.

Holland and Leinhardt (1970) chose to work with the $U|MAN$ conditional uniform distribution, stating that it approximates the more important, but too complicated $U|M, \{X_{i+}\}, \{X_{i+}\}$ conditional uniform distribution. However, this is only a weak approximation; clearly, the distribution does not control for either the set of indegrees or the set of outdegrees (which actually may be fixed by design). Katz and Powell (1957) and Wasserman (1977) proposed the use of the $U|\{X_{i+}\}$ and $U|\{X_{+j}\}$ distributions, since the former does control for the outdegrees and the latter, for a very important structural property (tendencies toward differential popularity). Our philosophy is that the more digraph distributions that are understood and can be worked with, the better that social network analysis will be.

Frequently in subgraph analyses it is useful to ask if a particular structural property (such as a tendency toward particular triads or threesomes) is due to simpler structural properties, such as dyad counts or indegrees.

One way of answering this question is to calculate the expected value of a quantity, measuring the property, using a digraph distribution that statistically conditions on the simpler properties. Since the indegrees are crude measures of popularity, and since popularity is such an important, yet simple, structural property, the $U|\{X_{+j}\}$ distribution is a useful conditional distribution for us.

For example, suppose we are interested in the number of isolated actors in a network, and choose to define an *isolated actor* as an actor with an indegree equal to $0 — x_{+j} = 0$ if actor j is an isolate. But, the data that we have gathered are fixed choice, with outdegrees fixed at 3 — $x_{i+} = 3$ by design. To study the indegrees observed, and particularly the number of actors with indegrees equal to 0, it is essential that we statistically control for the fixed outdegrees. So, we could determine the expected number of actors with indegrees of 0 by using the $U|\{X_{i+}\}$ distribution. We refer the reader to Katz (1952) for this methodology.

We note that the distributions described here are primarily used by researchers to study the statistical properties of various digraph properties. One frequently tries to determine how a random graph property, such as the number of mutual dyads, varies under specific probability distributions, such as the conditional uniform distribution that controls for the outdegrees. Some researchers (such as Holland and Leinhardt, 1975) have pioneered methods to approximate these calculations under distributions that are too hard to work with directly. Such approximations are quite valuable (for example, they allow us to work with the $U|M, \{X_{i+}\}, \{X_{i+}\}$ distribution).

Let us close this section by briefly discussing how random digraphs can be simulated, assuming that one of the distributions discussed in this chapter is appropriate. First, a digraph distributed as a uniform random variable is easily simulated using (13.21). Note that the arcs of the sociogram or the elements of the sociomatrix are all independent of one another; thus, one can simulate each arc/element one at a time, without worrying about the values assigned to the other arcs/elements. The probability that any one of the elements is unity is exactly $1/2$. So, given a fair coin, one can "toss" it $g(g-1)$ times to determine which elements of $\mathbf{X}$ are 1's or which lines between ordered pairs of actors are present. This coin, of course, can be simulated with a uniform pseudo-random number generator.

The Bernoulli distribution is simulated by taking a set of "hypothetical coins" with probabilities of heads matching the $\{P_{ij}\}$. The entries of $\mathbf{X}$ are still independent, so the coin tosses are all independent of each other.

One must toss the correct coin for each entry; that is, for the (i, j)th entry, the probability of a head must equal the probability that this entry is unity. If all these probabilities differ (and there are $g(g - 1)$ of them), then we will need $g(g - 1)$ coins. In practice, this distribution is usually simulated by taking a set of $g(g - 1)$ uniform pseudo-random numbers. Such numbers are found in volumes of statistical tables (such as Beyer 1968), or are easily generated by computer languages or by statistical computing packages (such as $SPSS^X$ or $SYSTAT$). A good discussion of simulating random digraph distributions can be found in Wasserman (1977).

We emphasize that research on the statistical analysis of M is quite limited. We have results only for the $U|\{X_{i+}\}$ distribution. The popular $U|MAN$ distribution is not relevant here, since it conditions on M, the graph property of interest. Katz, Tagiuri, and Wilson (1958, page 102) state:

> ... mutuality should not be interpreted without considering the arrays of both given and received choices.

That is, what we really need is continued research (following the pioneering work of Snijders 1991a) on the sampling distribution of M when $\mathbf{X} \sim U|\{X_{i+}\}, \{X_{+j}\}$. A large level of mutuality in a network with very unequal indegrees is much more important than in a network which is more equitable in the choices received. Interpreting M without controlling for the outdegrees *and* indegrees can be very misleading.

13.10 Conclusion

The techniques discovered and used by the early sociometricians are still some of the best ever developed, and the concerns of these methodologists about the quality of a sociometric analysis still hold today. In this chapter we have presented some of their techniques; other ideas, based on the research of these scholars, can be found in Chapters 14–16. A good social network analysis should begin with these methods. We have described a wide range of digraph distributions in this chapter, and will use them to get better insights into social structure. We now continue with applications of digraph distributions to triads.

14

Triads

Many researchers have shown, using empirical studies, that social network data possess strong deviations from randomness. That is, when one analyzes such data using baseline or null models that assume various types of randomness and specific tendencies that should arise in such data (such as equal popularity, lack of transitivity, or no reciprocity), the data often fail to agree with predictions from the models. Other researchers have reasoned that these deviations from randomness in social network data are caused by the presence of special structural patterns (such as differential popularity, transitivity, or tendencies toward reciprocity of relations) that have been studied for years by social network theorists. In Chapter 6 we described a few of these theories; in this chapter, we show how some of these theories can be tested by studying triads using the triad census (the counts of the various types of triads).

For example, consider transitivity, as defined in Chapter 6. This theory states that various triads are not possible, or at least should not occur, if actor behaviors are transitive. Certain triads should occur if behavior is indeed transitive. Suppose that a researcher has a network under investigation, and wishes to study whether this proposition is viable. We can take the triads that actually arise in the network, and compare these observed frequencies to the frequencies that are to be expected. The details of this comparison will be given in this chapter. For such comparisons, we will need some of the random directed graph distributions described in Chapter 13.

Much of the work on theories such as balance and transitivity has used the triad census and has been empirical. Holland and Leinhardt (1972, 1979) (as reviewed by Davis 1979) analyzed data from many sociometric studies. Their sociometric data bank (see Davis 1970; Leinhardt 1972; and Davis and Leinhardt 1972) contains almost 800 sociomatrices from several hundred sociometric studies. A variety of analyses of these data have verified the presence of several important structural properties, such as balance, clustering, ranked clusters, and transitivity. An important research agenda of these early researchers was to link structural patterns found in triads (microstructural tendencies) to macrostructural patterns, such as ranked clusters, partial orderings, and so on (see the work on this micro-macro linkage of Johnsen 1985, 1986). This research on triad counts is nicely summarized by Leik and Meeker (1975). We will show how statistical analyses of the triad census can test these theories, and will present the necessary statistical methods, demonstrating them on several examples.

Throughout this chapter, we will assume that we are studying a single, directional, dichotomous relation. This assumption is primarily for historical reasons; nearly all of the research on triadic methods begins with such a statement. Extensions of the triad methodologies to valued relations are quite interesting, but because of the complex mathematical structures that result, such research has not been undertaken.

At the heart of triadic analyses is the *triad census*, a set of counts of the different kinds of triads that arise in an observed network. We will show how one can examine special sums (actually, linear combinations) of these counts in order to study many important theories. The triad census does not condense the original data as much as the dyad census, since it has sixteen components rather than just three. Therefore, there is considerably more that we can learn from the triad census. Triads themselves can manifest many interesting structural properties, such as tendencies toward clustering, transitivity, and ranked clusterings. Examination of the counts contained in the triad census help the researcher determine whether any of these properties are present at the network level, and if so, to what degree.

Triads are also important in laboratory studies of social psychology that involve coalition formation (see Caplow 1956; Festinger 1957; Vinacke and Arkoff 1957; Cartwright 1959; Thibaut and Kelley 1959, pages 196–197; Kelley and Arrowood 1960; Gamson 1964; Newcomb 1968; and Henley, Horsfall, and De Soto 1969), and attitude change (see Osgood and Tannenbaum 1955; Rosenberg and Abelson 1960; and Anderson 1971, 1977). However, despite the recognition of the relevance of higher-order subgroups, most studies continue to use the dyad as the basic experimental unit (Weick and Penner 1966).

The methodology described in this chapter is statistical, and uses the random directed distributions described in Chapter 13. We introduce the triad census, and describe its components and features in detail. Many important graph features can be calculated directly from the triad census; such calculations all use linear combinations of the census, as we will see.

We present additional statistical theory for the triad census, and then apply it to the testing of substantive structural hypotheses. This theory is quite mathematical, and may be skipped by statistical novices (particularly the section concerning the mean and variance of a k-subgraph census). A triple of actors gives rise to sixty-four possible configurations of choices and non-choices. To test a theory, one must determine which of the configurations are possible (according to that theory), and then study their empirical frequencies.

14.1 Random Models and Substantive Hypotheses

The first question is what statistical model(s) should be used to study and test for non-randomness in social network data. In Chapter 13, we described a number of distributions for random directed graphs, and stated that such distributions are frequently used as null models in social network analysis. One compares the data to one of these "models" to determine how poorly the model fits the data. We argued that several nodal and dyad properties, such as

(i) Nodal outdegrees — to control for possible experimental constraints (such as fixed choice data)

(ii) Nodal indegrees — to control for differential popularity

(iii) Dyadic mutuality — to control for tendencies toward reciprocation of choices

are perhaps the important directed graph properties. One should consider the use of digraph distributions that condition on all of these properties. In this chapter, we show how this can be done approximately, so that a researcher can test whether a social network data set possesses important structural, substantive tendencies beyond the simpler tendencies that one conditions on. That is, if one uses a conditional distribution to study some data set that conditions on, say, the indegrees, then if the data do not adhere to this distributional model, one can conclude that this lack-of-fit must be due to something other than differential popularity among the actors.

We should stress that theories such as structural balance and transitivity are deterministic. They arose in the 1950's and 1960's primarily from the use of the mathematical axioms of graph theory. It became easy to state the implications of a particular theory using notions of nodes and arcs. In general, these theories state that specific subgraphs contained in the graph theoretic representation of a social network should not occur. For example, transitivity states that the certain triads, which display intransitivity because the first actor of a triple does not "choose" the third even though the first chooses the second and the second chooses the third, should not arise in a network data set. The determinism is readily apparent; certain triads should (or should not) exist. But when these theories are placed in a statistical framework, one can study the degree to which they hold for the entire network. Holland and Leinhardt (1970) summarized this approach to triadic studies quite well:

> It still remains for empirical verification to help us distinguish formal theory from formal nonsense; in this instance, [traditional network use of] graph theory, because of its deterministic nature, has limited use. For example, a statement which implies that a group cannot be balanced if a line between two points links two otherwise disconnected components may follow logically from the axioms of graph theory; it does not make much sense in the logic of empirical sociology. (page 412)

We will focus on two examples in this chapter, both of which we have discussed in Chapter 2 and have analyzed in earlier chapters in this book. We study Krackhardt's high-tech managers and the friendship relation measured on them, and Freeman's *EIES* network of researchers.

14.2 Triads

Consider a triple of actors, and assume that this triple involves n_i, n_j, and n_k, where $i \neq j \neq k$. The three actors themselves without the ties that may exist between them will be called a *triple*; when we also consider the ties that may link these three actors we have a *triad*. We define T_{ijk} as the triad, or 3-subgraph (as defined in Chapter 13) involving n_i, n_j, and n_k. In a triad, the actual order of the actors matters, so that we will always let $i < j < k$. There are six possible *ordered triples* associated with each triad, since there are six ways that we can permute three actors. Recall that we used these triples when defining transitivity in Chapter 6. So when considering ordered triples, each threesome of actors can occur six different ways. But as mentioned, it is conventional when listing triads to let $i < j < k$.

For a set of g actors, there are $\binom{g}{3}$ triads — the number of ways that we can take g items or actors, three at a time. We will let $\mathcal{T}$ denote the

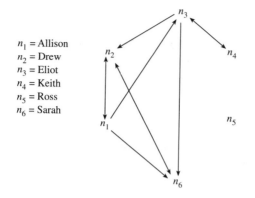

n_1 = Allison
n_2 = Drew
n_3 = Eliot
n_4 = Keith
n_5 = Ross
n_6 = Sarah

Fig. 14.1. Sociogram of friendship at the beginning of the school year for the hypothetical children network

set of all triads: $\mathscr{T} = \{T_{123},\ T_{124},\ \ldots,\ T_{(g-2),(g-1),g}\}$. This set is of size $\binom{g}{3} = (1/6)g(g-1)(g-2)$.

As an example, we take a set of six actors. Specifically, we will look at the six children that we have used as a hypothetical example throughout the book. The six children are indexed by $i = 1, 2, \ldots, 6$, and we measure a new relation: a directional dichotomous relation recording friendship at the beginning of the third grade, one full year after the beginning of the study. We have an arc from node i to node j in our directed graph representing this friendship relation if child i reports that child j is a friend at the beginning of third grade. The sociogram for this hypothetical relation and this set of actors is given in Figure 14.1. There are $\binom{6}{3} = 20$ triads that can be considered here; thus $\mathscr{T} = \{T_{123},\ T_{124},\ \ldots,\ T_{456}\}$.

Consider now how many ties can be present in a triad. There are three actors in a triad, and each actor can relate to two other actors. This gives six possible ties. In the mathematical representation of this triad, each of the six arcs can be present or absent, so that there are 2^6 = 64 realizations, "states," or possible values for a triad, if we record the node labels. If we ignore the labels, then some of these states will be isomorphic. That is, they will be structurally indistinguishable from one another. All triads that are indistinguishable form one of the isomorphism classes for triads. Remember (as discussed in Chapter 13) that a dyad has just four states and three unique, isomorphism classes: Mutual, Asymmetric (which contains two states), and Null. The question here is how many isomorphism classes exist for triads?

To answer this, let us examine some of the triadic realizations. A few of these realizations are easy to understand. The triad with no arcs present arises when the relationships between all pairs of nodes are null. Clearly, this is one very special isomorphism class for triads, which we will call the *completely null* triad. And the triad with all arcs present arises when the relationships between all pairs of nodes are mutual. This is a second isomorphism class, called the *completely mutual* triad. Only one of the sixty-four triad states occupies each of these isomorphism classes. But most of the other sixty-two states are harder to label and characterize.

For example, look at our simple example in Figure 14.1, and the triad involving children 1, 2, and 3 — Allison, Drew, and Eliot, T_{123}. In this triad, Allison is friendly toward Drew, and vice versa (so that n_1 and n_2 relate to each other), Allison chooses Eliot as a friend (n_1 relates to n_3), and lastly, Eliot chooses Drew as a friend (n_3 relates to n_2); that is, $n_1 \rightarrow n_2$; $n_2 \rightarrow n_1$; $n_1 \rightarrow n_3$; $n_3 \nrightarrow n_1$; $n_2 \nrightarrow n_3$; and $n_3 \rightarrow n_2$. This particular triad state is shown in Figure 14.2. Note that it has four of the six possible ties present. Missing are the ties from n_3 to n_1 and from n_2 to n_3. Also note that it is not particularly easy to understand this triad. We have a single mutual relationship, a two-way exchange of friendship involving Allison and Drew, and an apparent cyclic relationship involving all children in the triple: Allison "chooses" Eliot, Eliot "chooses" Drew, and Drew "chooses" Allison. We can call this particular triad a "mutual/cyclic asymmetrics" triad. Note that this triad displays transitivity (see Chapter 6); that is, $n_1 \rightarrow n_3$, $n_3 \rightarrow n_2$, and $n_1 \rightarrow n_2$. In words, Allison chooses Eliot as a friend, Eliot chooses Drew as a friend, so Allison chooses Drew as a friend as well. The triad also has two intransitivities: $n_2 \rightarrow n_1$, $n_1 \rightarrow n_3$, but $n_2 \nrightarrow n_3$, and $n_3 \rightarrow n_2$, $n_2 \rightarrow n_1$, but $n_3 \nrightarrow n_1$. The actions taken by the actors in this triad are rather complicated, so that the triad is quite interesting. This mutual/cyclic asymmetrics triad will play a crucial role in the statistical analyses of triads discussed later in this chapter.

A very important question is whether there any other triad states that are isomorphic to this mutual/cyclic asymmetrics triad. And how many different triad isomorphism classes, or *triad types* are there? Let us consider these questions by referring to the mutual/cyclic asymmetrics triad. This triad has the following arcs: $i \rightarrow j$; $j \rightarrow i$; $i \rightarrow k$; $k \nrightarrow i$; $j \nrightarrow k$; and $k \rightarrow j$, where the three actors, i, j, and k, are any three generic nodes; that is, we ignore the labels attached to the nodes. Consider now a triad state where $i \rightarrow j$; $j \nrightarrow i$; $i \nrightarrow k$; $k \rightarrow i$; $j \rightarrow k$; and $k \rightarrow j$. Drawing both of these triads will demonstrate that the first triad is isormorphic

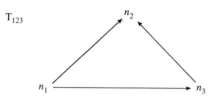

Fig. 14.2. Mutual/cyclic asymmetric triad involving children Allison (n_1), Drew (n_2), and Eliot (n_3)

to the second. The second is obtained simply by relabeling the nodes of the first.

To determine how many triad states are isomorphic to a particular state is an onerous task. One must list all sixty-four triad states and categorize them into their triad isormorphism classes. As another example, consider the simple triad that contains a single arc: one asymmetric dyad, and two null dyads. We can call this triad a "single arc" triad. There are six triad states that are isomorphic to this triad, which are shown in Figure 14.3. They are:

(i) $i \rightarrow j$; $j \nrightarrow i$; $i \nrightarrow k$; $k \nrightarrow i$; $j \nrightarrow k$; $k \nrightarrow j$.

(ii) $i \nrightarrow j$; $j \rightarrow i$; $i \nrightarrow k$; $k \nrightarrow i$; $j \nrightarrow k$; $k \nrightarrow j$.

(iii) $i \nrightarrow j$; $j \nrightarrow i$; $i \rightarrow k$; $k \nrightarrow i$; $j \nrightarrow k$; $k \nrightarrow j$.

(iv) $i \nrightarrow j$; $j \nrightarrow i$; $i \nrightarrow k$; $k \rightarrow i$; $j \nrightarrow k$; $k \nrightarrow j$.

(v) $i \nrightarrow j$; $j \nrightarrow i$; $i \nrightarrow k$; $k \nrightarrow i$; $j \rightarrow k$; $k \nrightarrow j$.

(vi) $i \nrightarrow j$; $j \nrightarrow i$; $i \nrightarrow k$; $k \nrightarrow i$; $j \nrightarrow k$; $k \rightarrow j$.

If we erase all the labels on these six triads, we would not be able to distinguish among them. Consequently, they are all isomorphic, and can all be referred to as single arc triads.

Before we list and discuss the triad isomorphism classes (there are sixteen), let us think how to determine how many exist. The answer to the triad isomorphism question is found by considering an important fact. A triad is a 3-subgraph. A 3-subgraph is an example of the general idea of a k-subgraph. To get a k-subgraph from a directed graph with g nodes, we simply delete all but k of the nodes, and the arcs involving those nodes, in the digraph. Viewed in this way, it is clear that a k-subgraph is itself a directed graph, but just with k nodes. Its sociomatrix is just a submatrix of the sociomatrix associated with the original digraph. So, one can write down the sixty-four 3×3 sociomatrices

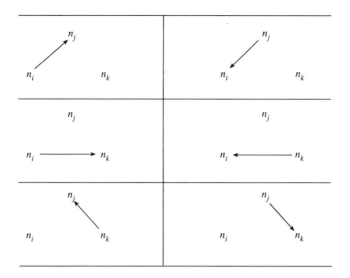

Fig. 14.3. The six realizations of the single arc triad

associated with the sixty-four triad states. Four of these sociomatrices
are listed in Table 14.1. These are the triad states considered in earlier
paragraphs: completely null triad, completely mutual triad, and the two
mutual/cyclic asymmetrics triads, which are isomorphic.

Given any two sociomatrices (here, of size 3×3), if the rows and
columns of one can be permuted to obtain the second, then the triad
states represented by the sociomatrices are isomorphic. The total number of triad types is found by considering all sixty-four triad states, and
permuting the associated sociomatrices to see how many "unique" sociomatrices exist. For the four sociomatrices given in Table 14.1, there are
three unique ones. From this enumeration of all sixty-four triad states,
one will find that there are six states isomorphic to our mutual/cyclic
asymmetrics triad. We consider two of them in Table 14.1; there are
four more (which we will not list here, but which are not hard to write
down).

There are six sociomatrices associated with the six triad states isomorphic to the single arc triad studied earlier. These sociomatrices have just
a single entry of 1. The remaining five, off-diagonal entries are all 0. This
single 1 can occur in any one of the six off-diagonal entries of a 3×3
sociomatrix. There are exactly six states isomorphic to each other, and

Table 14.1. *Some sociomatrices for three triad isomorphism classes*

Completely
Null Triad

	n_i	n_j	n_k
n_i	-	0	0
n_j	0	-	0
n_k	0	0	-

Completely
Mutual Triad

	n_i	n_j	n_k
n_i	-	1	1
n_j	1	-	1
n_k	1	1	-

Two Mutual/Cyclic
Asymmetric Triads

	n_i	n_j	n_k
n_i	-	1	1
n_j	1	-	0
n_k	0	1	-

	n_i	n_j	n_k
n_i	-	1	0
n_j	1	-	1
n_k	1	0	-

any one of the six sociomatrices can be "mapped into" any of the others simply by moving the single 1 into one of the other five locations, or by relabeling the rows and columns.

14.2.1 The Triad Census

There are sixteen isomorphism classes for the sixty-four different triad states. These classes are pictured in Figure 14.4. There are indeed several ways that these classes can be labeled. We need descriptions of the classes more accurate than the rather vague "mutual/cyclic asymmetrics" label used earlier for one of the classes. A simple labeling scheme comes from Holland and Leinhardt (1970) and Davis and Leinhardt (1972). Each type has a label with as many as four characters. The characters are:

(i) The first character gives the number of mutual dyads in the triad.

(ii) The second character gives the number of asymmetric dyads in the triad.

(iii) The third character gives the number of null dyads in the triad.

(iv) And lastly, the fourth character, if present, is used to distinguish further among the types.

This labeling scheme (which we will use here) is sometimes referred to as $M - A - N$ labeling, since it highlights the dyadic states contained within the triad.

To attach a fourth character to a label (if necessary), we use additional features of the triad. For example, there are two 030 triads, containing three asymmetric dyads, to which are attached the additional characters "T" and "C" (since the first one contains a *t*ransitivity, and the second, a *c*ycle). Two other labeling schemes, proposed by Wasserman (1977), use the numbers of actors with outdegrees (or indegrees) equal to 0, 1, or 2, within the triad.

Note that the sixteen types in Figure 14.4 are organized in a special way. The types are presented in seven rows. Within a row, the types have the same number of arcs present, from 0 (first row) to 6 (last row). The first row has just one type, the 003 triad (0 mutuals, 0 asymmetrics, and 3 nulls), containing no arcs, while the last row also has just one type, the 300 triad (3 mutuals, 0 asymmetrics, and 0 nulls, which we previously called completely mutual). Under this $M - A - N$ labeling scheme of Holland and Leinhardt, the mutual/cyclic asymmetrics triad mentioned earlier is properly termed the 120C triad, since it has 1 mutual, 2 asymmetrics, 0 nulls, and appears cyclical. Note that the fourth character, if present, is "D" (for down), "U" (for up), "T" (for transitive), or "C" (for cyclic).

Because of the nature of the triad types, every one of the $\binom{g}{3}$ triads in a directed graph with g nodes must be isomorphic to one of the sixteen classes. Thus, with some patience, one could examine each of the triads in a directed graph, and count how many of these triads belong to each of the classes. We will let T_u denote the number of these triads that belong to isomorphism class u (where u ranges over the sixteen classes listed in Figure 14.4). Thus, T_{003} is the number of 003 triads (those that are completely null) in the digraph, T_{012}, the number of 012 triads (those with just one asymmetric dyad, that we called the single arc or arc triad), and so forth. We will find it convenient to record all sixteen of these frequencies in a vector of length 16, which we will call $\mathbf{T}$. Specifically,

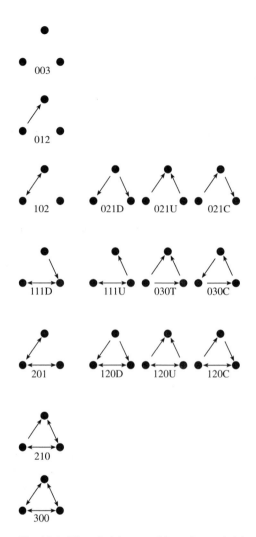

Fig. 14.4. The triad isomorphism classes (with standard *MAN* labeling)

$$\mathbf{T} = (T_{003}, T_{012}, \ldots, T_{300})', \tag{14.1}$$

where the order of the elements of $\mathbf{T}$ matches the ordering of the classes in the figure: 003, 012, 102, 021D, 021U, 021C, 111D, 111U, 030T, 030C, 201, 120D, 120U, 120C, 210, 300. $\mathbf{T}$ is a column vector, so it has dimensions 16×1. The vector $\mathbf{T}$ is referred to as the *triad census*, since the sum of the sixteen frequencies contained in it is $\binom{g}{3}$, and it gives a complete classification of all triads in a directed graph. The triad census was introduced into social network research by Davis and Leinhardt (1968 1972).

Unlike the three frequencies in the dyad census, the 16 components of **T** are difficult to calculate. There are no simple formulas. In fact, one must examine all $\binom{g}{3}$ triads, and place each into its proper category or ismorphism class. It is easy to write a computer program to do such a calculation. One such program, written in *FORTRAN*, called *TRIADS*, is discussed by Walker and Wasserman (1987).

There are twenty triads in the directed graph shown in Figure 14.1. We have already described the first triad, T_{123}. This triad has the following arcs: $n_1 \rightarrow n_2$; $n_2 \rightarrow n_1$; $n_1 \rightarrow n_3$; $n_3 \nrightarrow n_1$; $n_2 \nrightarrow n_3$; and $n_3 \rightarrow n_2$. This triad is a type 120C triad. One can see that there are many null dyads in the entire digraph; in fact, the dyad census is ($M = 3$, $A = 4$, $N = 8$), so that more than one-half of the dyads are null. This sparseness in the digraph (the density is only $(10/30) = 0.333$) gives us several 003, completely null triads. A close examination of the 20 triads shows that three of them are 003 triads, and five of them are 012 triads. The three 003 triads are T_{145}, T_{245}, and T_{456}, while the five 012 triads are T_{135}, T_{146}, T_{156}, T_{235}, and T_{356}. Of the other 12 triads that contain at least one arc, we have five 102 triads that contain a single mutual relationship (T_{124}, T_{125}, T_{246}, T_{256}, and T_{345}), two 111U triads (T_{234}, T_{346}), and one each of the 111D (T_{134}), 030T (T_{136}), 120D (T_{236}), 120C (T_{123}), and 210 (T_{126}) triads. Thus, the triad census vector is

$$\mathbf{T} = (3, 5, 5, 0, 0, 0, 1, 2, 1, 0, 0, 1, 0, 1, 1, 0)'.$$

We should note that the 111D and 111U triads are intransitive, as defined in Chapter 6, since both are missing one arc to complete the transitivity, while the 030T and 120D triads have transitivities.

The triad census is a convenient way to reduce the entire sociomatrix **X** to a smaller set of, in this case, sixteen summary statistics. The larger that g is, the more of a reduction that occurs. For a set of ten actors, the sociomatrix is of size 10×10 with ninety entries; consequently, summarizing it with just sixteen statistics is a substantial "condensation" of the information in **X**.

For specific random directed graph distributions, one can calculate the mean and variance of the triad census. Such calculations are similar to those for the mean and variance of the components of the dyad census (particularly the number of mutual dyads). The mean and variance of the triad census are multivariate quantities, and the calculations described in this chapter can be complicated. We will illustrate them in detail later in the chapter.

○**Stability of a Triad Census.** We should note an interesting fact about triads. If one changes a single arc in a directed graph (suppose the arc from i to j), only a single dyad (D_{ij}) is affected, but ($g - 2$) triads will change (all the triads that involve i and j and include the dyad D_{ij}; there are ($g - 2$) such triads, since we can complement the nodes i and j with ($g - 2$) other nodes). So, the triads are clearly not independent of each other. If the arc from i to j is deleted, many triads will change. Holland and Leinhardt (1975) note that since the triad census itself is an aggregation over all triads in a digraph,

> ... the information it contains is relatively stable and is not significantly affected by a few changes in the lines of the digraph. (page 7)

This appears contradictory to us, since we know that changing a single arc results in many triad changes. But since the triad census is a categorization of all triads, a change of a count here and there is minor. After all, there are $\binom{g}{3}$ triads, and $g - 2$ of them, which will change after a single arc change, is a small fraction of the total.

To demonstrate the effect of a single arc change on the triad census, let us take our example, and make such a change. Suppose that Allison really does not choose Drew as a friend; the earlier information was erroneous. Thus, $x_{12} = 0$, rather than the entry of unity first reported. Now, since this set $\mathcal{N}$ has $g = 6$ nodes, this single arc change will affect ($g - 2$) = 4 triads: T_{123}, T_{124}, T_{125}, T_{126}; that is, all triads that include the dyad D_{12}. These four triads will be re-assigned to different isormorphic classes. Specifically, T_{123} loses one arc, and becomes a $030C$ triad, exhibiting a single, transitive relationship. The triads T_{124} and T_{125} lose one arc from the mutual relationship between Allison and Drew, and become 012 triads, with just a single arc (from Drew to Allison). Lastly, T_{126}, the only triad with five arcs, now has just four, and becomes a 120C triad. The triad census becomes

$$\mathbf{T}_{new} = (3, 7, 3, 0, 0, 0, 1, 2, 1, 1, 0, 1, 0, 1, 0, 0)'.$$

There are now more triads with just a single arc, but the overall conclusion about this census is not that different from the conclusion about the original **T**. Most triads are either completely null or include just a single arc or single mutual, and there are a non-negligible number of intransitive triads.

Holland and Leinhardt (1973) have shown that because of this stability in the triad census, the vector **T** is relatively unaffected by measurement error (such as loss of arcs due to a fixed choice design) that can arise in social network data. This statement must be conditioned on the actual outdegrees. If the outdegrees are limited too much by the data collection design (such as fixed choice designs, perhaps requesting just two nominations, when the actors may really interact with ten other actors), no analytic technique will be able to salvage the data. Such "measurement errors" caused by fixed choice designs can have large effects on the triad counts. Analyses will be difficult, and any structure uncovered will likely be artifactual. If, however, the measurement error is not too severe, Holland and Leinhardt argue that because of its stability, **T** is an ideal statistic for network analysis. Social network data, as noted by Holland and Leinhardt, as well as Hallinan (1972), Killworth (1974), and Killworth and Bernard (1979), can be quite "buggy"; hence, triadic analyses are usually recommended.

There are disadvantages to the triad census. If interest is in a small number of nodes or arcs in the digraph, focusing on **T** will not allow the researcher to study the necessary quantities. If one is primarily interested in the number of isolated nodes in the graph, then such information will not be available from **T**. Our attitude is that the triad census is one of a number of digraph properties that should be included in a thorough network analysis since it captures and then summarizes several important structural properties (such as transitivity) in a parsimonious way.

Information from a Triad Census. There are many graph properties that can be calculated from the sixteen frequencies of the triad census. Since each of the triads is categorized into one of the sixteen classes, the sum of the counts of the triads in the various classes must be $\binom{g}{3}$. Thus, from the triad census, $\mathbf{T} = \{T_u\}$, we have an identity involving $\binom{g}{3}$:

$$\binom{g}{3} = \sum_u T_u. \tag{14.2}$$

For example, from the first triad census analyzed in the previous paragraphs, the sum of the sixteen counts is $(3+5+5+\cdots+1+0) = 20$; such a value for $\binom{g}{3}$ can only arise with $g = 6$; that is, $g = 6$ is the solution to the equation $g(g-1)(g-2)/6 = 20$. Thus, the triad census can tell us the number of nodes in the digraph. The triad census can also give us counts of the number of arcs, and the counts in the dyad census, as we discuss in the succeeding paragraphs.

Suppose we consider the number of arcs present in each of the 16 triad types. Each of the types has between 0 and 6 arcs. If we multiply the number of triads of each type by the number of arcs in the triad, and divide by $(g - 2)$, we obtain the number of arcs, L, in the directed graph. The reasoning behind the dividing by $(g - 2)$ is that each arc is contained in $(g - 2)$ triads, and so is counted $(g - 2)$ times in the triad census. The number of arcs in the sixteen triad types, listed in the same order as the types in $\mathbf{T}$, are : 0, 1, 2, 2, 2, 2, 3, 3, 3, 3, 4, 4, 4, 4, 5, 6. Let us call these sixteen numbers or coefficients c_u, for $u = 1, 2, \ldots, 16$; that is, $c_1=0$, $c_2=1$, $c_3=2$, ..., $c_{16}=6$; in general, $c_u =$ the number of arcs in the uth triad type. Then,

$$L = (1/(g - 2)) \sum_u c_u T_u \tag{14.3}$$

gives us the total number of arcs in the digraph. To demonstrate with our simple example, we find

$$l = (1/4)(0 \times 3 + 1 \times 5 + \cdots + 6 \times 0) = (40/4) = 10 \text{ arcs},$$

as can be verified by counting the number of non-zero entries in the sociomatrix.

Note how $\binom{g}{3}$, g, and L are all obtained from the triad census. The first quantity is calculated by summing all the counts in the triad census, or by multiplying each count by 1 and then summing. The second quantity is calculated by multiplying all the counts by special coefficients (in this case, the numbers of arcs in each triad type) and then summing. This process of multiplying the counts by coefficients and then summing is defined mathematically as a *linear combination* of the triad census; in general, it is equal to $\sum_u l_u T_u$, where the l_u are the coefficients of the linear combination and are specified in advance. The index u ranges over the sixteen triad types: $u = 1, 2, \ldots, 16$. The notion of a linear combination of the triad census is quite important in this chapter. It is simply the sixteen counts in the census, multiplied by specified coefficients, and then summed.

We have already seen one use of such a linear combination. As noted in equation (14.2), if these coefficients are all equal to 1, then the combination gives the sum of the triad counts, or just the total number of triads $(\binom{g}{3})$. One can use this calculation to verify that all triads have been counted during a triad census. If the sum of counts in the triad census is not $\binom{g}{3}$, then an error has been made.

We can also calculate the mean (and even the variance) of the indegrees and outdegrees. Unfortunately, the indegree and outdegree of a particular node cannot be calculated as a linear combination of the triad counts, since such statistics are properties of individual nodes and not of the directed graph as a whole. Only digraph properties can be calculated from the triad census, which is a digraph statistic itself.

For the calculation of the mean and variance of the indegrees and outdegrees, we note that the total number of ties is exactly L, a graph property that can be calculated as a linear combination of the triad census using equation (14.3). Consequently, the mean outdegree, which equals the mean indegree, is $\bar{X} = L/g$; that is, the means of these nodal properties can be found using a linear combination of the triad census:

$$\bar{X} = \frac{1}{(g(g-2))} \sum_u c_u T_u. \tag{14.4}$$

The variance of the outdegrees and variance of the indegrees can also be calculated using the triad census. We denote the variance of the outdegrees, the $\{X_{i+}\}$, by

$$S_{out}^2 = \frac{1}{g} \sum_i (X_{i+} - \bar{X})^2$$

and the variance of the indegrees, the $\{X_{+j}\}$, by

$$S_{in}^2 = \frac{1}{g} \sum_j (X_{+j} - \bar{X})^2.$$

To calculate these statistics using the triad census, we use two results, proven by Holland and Leinhardt (1975), which rely on two weighting vectors, the first with coefficients $\{b_{out,u}\}$ and the second with coefficients $\{b_{in,u}\}$. These weighting vectors are given in Table 14.2, under the two columns headed $b_{in,u}$ and $b_{out,u}$. The coefficients in these vectors are determined by studying how the variances of the degrees depend on the counts in the triad census. Using the coefficients from these two weighting vectors, we first calculate two intermediate quantities:

$$B_{out} = \sum_u b_{out,u} T_u \tag{14.5}$$

and

$$B_{in} = \sum_u b_{in,u} T_u. \tag{14.6}$$

Holland and Leinhardt (1975) show that with B_{out} from equation (14.5) and B_{in} from equation (14.6), one can then calculate the two variances. The variances depend on these two intermediate quantities, and the mean outdegree (equation 14.4):

$$S^2_{out} = (2/g)B_{out} - \bar{X}(\bar{X} - 1) \tag{14.7}$$

$$S^2_{in} = (2/g)B_{in} - \bar{X}(\bar{X} - 1). \tag{14.8}$$

Thus, one can compute these two important variances just using linear combinations of the triad census, rather than the outdegrees and indegrees themselves. The entire sociomatrix is not needed here, just the triad census.

Using our simple example of six children, whose triad census was given earlier in this chapter, we note that the outdegrees are 3, 2, 3, 1, 0, 1, and the indegrees are 1, 3, 2, 1, 0, 3. These two sets of numbers are identical; thus, the variances are $S^2_{out} = S^2_{in} = 1.222$, calculated directly from this set of six numbers.

We can also calculate the variances from the triad census. First, we use the linear combination with components $\{c_u\}$, given in Column 6 of Table 14.2, to calculate the mean number of choices. From equation (14.4), we calculate $\bar{x} = 40/[6(4)] = 1.6667$. Next, we calculate the intermediate quantities discussed above using the triad census and Columns 2 and 3 of Table 14.2: $B_{out} = (0 \times 3) + (0 \times 5) + \cdots + (3 \times 0) = 7$ and $B_{in} = (0 \times 3) + (0 \times 5) + \cdots + (3 \times 0) = 7$. From the above equations, we find that $S^2_{out} = S^2_{in} = (2/6)(7) - (1.667)(0.667) = 1.222$, verifying the direct calculation.

One can calculate several other graph properties using linear combinations of the triad census. Three important properties easily obtained in this way are the counts in the dyad census, M, A, and N. Let us define m_u as the number of mutual dyads in the uth triad type, a_u as the number of asymmetric dyads in the uth triad type, and n_u as the number of null dyads in the uth triad type. These three sets of sixteen coefficients are shown in Columns 3, 4, and 5 of Table 14.2. Using these coefficients, and remembering that each dyad in a digraph is contained in $(g - 2)$ triads, we can calculate the counts in the dyad census:

$$M = (1/(g - 2))\sum_u m_u T_u \tag{14.9}$$

Table 14.2. *Weighting vectors for statistics and hypothesis concerning the triad census*

Triad type	$b_{in,u}$	$b_{out,u}$	m_u	a_u	n_u	c_u	Trans.	Intrans.	Close friends disagreeing
003	0	0	0	0	3	0	0	0	0
012	0	0	0	1	2	1	0	0	0
102	0	0	1	0	2	2	0	0	0
021D	0	1	0	2	1	2	0	0	0
021U	1	0	0	2	1	2	0	0	0
021C	0	0	0	2	1	2	0	1	0
111D	1	0	1	1	1	3	0	1	0
111U	0	1	1	1	1	3	0	1	1
030T	1	1	0	3	0	3	1	0	0
030C	0	0	0	3	0	3	0	3	0
201	1	1	2	0	1	4	0	2	2
120D	2	1	1	2	0	4	2	0	0
120U	1	2	1	2	0	4	2	0	0
120C	1	1	1	2	0	4	1	2	1
210	2	2	2	1	0	5	3	1	1
300	3	3	3	0	0	6	6	0	0

$$A = (1/(g-2))\sum_u a_u T_u \qquad (14.10)$$

and

$$N = (1/(g-2))\sum_u n_u T_u. \qquad (14.11)$$

Thus, if we regard g as given, or simply find it from the triad census, the counts in the dyad census, M, A, and N, can be written as linear combinations of the frequencies in the triad census, using the weights $m_u/(g-2)$, $a_u/(g-2)$, and $n_u/(g-2)$.

Again demonstrating on our simple example, we find that $(0 \times 3) + (0 \times 5) + (1 \times 5) + \cdots + (3 \times 0) = 12$, so that $m = 12/4 = 3$, since $(g-2) = 4$. Similarly, using the weighting vector coefficients for the number of asymmetric dyads, $(0 \times 3) + (1 \times 5) + (0 \times 5) + \cdots + (0 \times 0) = 16$, so that $a = 16/4 = 4$. Lastly, for the number of null dyads, $(3 \times 3) + (2 \times 5) + (2 \times 5) + \cdots + (0 \times 0) = 32$, so that $n = 32/4 = 8$. Thus, the dyad census is $(3, 4, 8)$, calculated directly from the triad census (with the help of the appropriate weighting vectors given in Table 14.2. We should note that the coefficients, shown in the columns of Table 14.2, were termed *weighting vector coefficients* by Holland and Leinhardt (1975).

There are many digraph properties that can be calculated from **T**, many of which may not be obvious from the triad census itself. Further, while some of these quantities might be straightforward and relatively simple to calculate by hand, others can be quite time consuming; thus, use of **T** can simplify and speed up calculations.

We can think abstractly about all possible linear combinations of the triad census. Such a collection of graph statistics is quite important. There is much information that it contains, as we have discussed in this chapter. We will examine the collection in general in later sections of this chapter. But, the most important reason for focusing on linear combinations of **T** arises because many important structural properties, such as tendencies toward balance and transitivity, can be studied using such linear combinations. We will return to this use of the triad census after a continued examination of our example.

14.2.2 The Example and Its Triad Census

Let us turn to Krackhardt's high-tech managers, and the friendship relation. The triad census for this relation, measured on the twenty-one managers, is

$$\mathbf{T}_{friends} = (376, 366, 143, 114, 34, 35, 39, 101,$$
$$23, 0, 20, 16, 25, 9, 23, 6)'.$$

There are $\binom{21}{3} = 1330$ triads (which is the sum of these sixteen numbers). More than half of the triads are of types 003 and 012, the completely null and single arc triads. There is a surprisingly large number of $021D$ triads (114; almost 9 percent of the total), perhaps indicating some sort of hierarchical structure for this relation. Note also that there are no $030C$ triads, which of course are prohibited under the theory of transitivity.

Making sense out of sixteen numbers is difficult. In this chapter, we will first rely on linear combinations of the sixteen to make comprehension easier, and then study the entire set of sixteen counts. For example, it is easy to calculate $m = 23$, $a = 56$, and $n = 131$, directly from the triad census using the appropriate weighting vectors. And we find that $l = 102$, using the census, and Column 6 of Table 14.2. Interested readers can calculate the variances of the indegrees and outdegrees using Columns 7 and 8.

Krackhardt's advice relation is more interesting. Its triad census is

$$\mathbf{T}_{advice} = (74, 153, 90, 160, 86, 49, 59,$$
$$101, 190, 2, 72, 62, 78, 17, 107, 30)'.$$

Note that there are considerably more triads with more than 2 arcs than for the friendship relation. There are 107 210 triads, and even 30 300 triads. There are also 190 transitive 030*T* triads (roughly 14 percent of the total), a very large number, indicating an apparent large tendency toward transitivity. We will return to these data, and their tendencies, later in this chapter.

14.3 Distribution of a Triad Census

We now show how statistical analyses of the triad census can be used to test the theories of Chapter 6. We will present the necessary statistical methods, and demonstrate them on our examples. We first give some statistical results, calculations, and properties of the triad census, as a prelude to tests of structural theories such as balance and transitivity. We note first, however, that this section requires some statistical sophistication. Those readers without such background can skip to the end of this section, where we review its major points.

Random directed graph distributions can be used to study the triad census, assuming that the census has been drawn from a random directed graph. The distributional assumptions are similar to those made in Chapter 13, although we can now consider distributions that condition on the dyad census (which was not possible in Chapter 13 since we were making inferences about that census itself). We discuss the formulas which calculate the average counts of the triad census; that is, what we should expect for triad frequencies if the digraph were truly random. Such expected frequencies provide a convenient baseline to compare with observed frequencies from a digraph under study, and consequently, lead to statistical tests of the significance of various substantive hypotheses such as tendencies toward transitivity.

We should note that the distribution of the triad census, except for its mean and covariance matrix, is too complicated to calculate. (A covariance matrix is a square, symmetric array that gives the variances of the components down the diagonal, and the covariances between all pairs of components off the diagonal.) We have noted that **T** has sixteen components, and hence has a covariance matrix which has dimensions 16×16 and a multivariate distribution which is 16-dimensional.

Because of the complicated nature of the distribution, there have been approximations to it. There is good evidence (see Holland and Leinhardt 1970, 1975, 1979) that the distribution of **T** can be well-approximated by the multivariate normal distribution. Thus, we need only discuss calculations for the mean and covariance matrix of the triad census, since the multivariate normal depends only on these two parameters. Most multivariate statistical inference relies on assumptions of approximate multivariate normality. Fortunately, we will also be able to make such assumptions.

14.3.1 ⊗*Mean and Variance of a k-subgraph Census*

We begin by briefly discussing the mean and variance of a general k-subgraph census; that is, we first figure out how to calculate these two statistics for a general k-subgraph census, and then demonstrate these calculations for 3-subgraphs, or triads. The mean and variance of a k-subgraph census contain expected counts or frequencies of the isomorphism classes, and measures of how these counts vary. We note that the use of these general results is usually limited to dyads and triads, since k-subgraphs for $k \geq 4$ are far too numerous; for $k=4$, there are 120 isomorphism classes (see Chapter 4). Some results are given, however, in Moon (1968).

As stated, we start with general formulas for the expected number of k-subgraphs in each of the isomorphism classes for such subgraphs. We start with a directed graph with g nodes, and imagine that we have calculated from it a k-subgraph census with a specific number of isomorphism classes (3 for dyads, 16 for triads, 120 for tetrads, and so forth). We will let u and v be two distinct isomorphism classes for our k-subgraphs. In the case of the dyads, there are three possibilities for u and v. For triads, there are sixteen classes.

We will also let K and L be two of the $\binom{g}{k}$ distinct k-subgraphs that can be examined for a particular directed graph (for example, the $\binom{g}{2}$ dyads that must be examined for a dyadic analysis, or the $\binom{g}{3}$ triads necessary for a triadic analysis). We will therefore talk about K belonging to isomorphism class u (and/or L belonging to class v). These two subgraphs K and L will be distinct. Keep in mind the distinction here between K and L, and u and v — the former are symbols that reference subgraphs, while the latter reference isomorphism classes for those subgraphs. And, k will always be fixed at the subgraph size.

We assume that the digraph in question is random, so that we will need a notation for the various probabilities that arise with our k-subgraphs. We define the probability that any one of the k-subgraphs (K) falls into one of the isomorphism classes (u), and the probability that any pair of the k-subgraphs fall into two particular classes as follows:

$$p_K(u) = P(K \text{ is in class } u) \tag{14.12}$$

and

$$p_{K,L}(u,v) = P(K \text{ is in class } u \text{ and } L \text{ is in class } v). \tag{14.13}$$

These probabilities will be theoretically determined (as we note below) by assuming some underlying stochastic mechanism for the digraph.

The general equations for the expected frequencies of the counts in the k-subgraph census depend on averages of the $\{p_K(u)\}$. Specifically, to find the expected number of k-subgraphs falling into each of the isomorphism classes, we must average these probabilities over all k-subgraphs derived from the complete digraph:

$$\bar{p}(u) = \frac{1}{\binom{g}{k}} \sum_K p_K(u). \tag{14.14}$$

From equation (14.14), we can state the first part of Theorem 14.1 from Holland and Leinhardt (1975):

Theorem 14.1 *Using the notation given above and assuming that a random digraph is generated by some stochastic mechanism, then the expected number of k-subgraphs in class u, which we will call H_u, is*

$$E(H_u) = \binom{g}{k} \bar{p}(u). \tag{14.15}$$

This equation is quite simple. It says that the average number of k-subgraphs of a particular type is exactly equal to the total number of these k-subgraphs times the average probability that a k-subgraph is of type u.

Thus, the expected number of k-subgraphs that fall into the uth isomorphism class is computed by averaging the probabilities that the Kth k-subgraph is of type u, over all possible k-subgraphs. Further, there is one of these expectations for each of the isomorphism classes, and the expectations sum to the total number of k-subgraphs ($\binom{g}{k}$ — like they should). One determines the individual subgraph probabilities by referring to the underlying probability model for the digraph (a step that we will describe in detail below for triads and the conditional uniform distribution that conditions on the dyad census, $U|MAN$).

To evaluate how large these expected numbers really are, we need to determine the variances (and simultaneously, the square roots of the variances, the standard deviations) of the expected counts. At the same time, if interest is on linear combinations of the k-subgraph census, then we must also have formulas for the covariances of the frequency of type u k-subgraphs, and type v k-subgraphs.

In order to calculate the variances of the frequencies, and covariances between the frequencies for two different classes, we must consider how similar our pair of k-subgraphs, K and L, is. We note that these two subgraphs can have some nodes in common; in fact, the possible numbers of nodes that these two can have in common are from 0 (completely disjoint subgraphs) to k (identical subgraphs). In general, there are

$$\binom{g}{k}\binom{g-k}{k-j}\binom{k}{j}$$

pairs of k-subgraphs of a digraph with g nodes for which there are j nodes in common. We now define the average probability that any two k-subgraphs, K and L, with j nodes in common, belong to classes u and v, as

$$\bar{p}_j(u,v) = \frac{1}{\binom{g}{k}\binom{g-k}{k-j}\binom{k}{j}} \sum p_{K,L}(u,v), \tag{14.16}$$

where the sum is taken over all pairs of k-subgraphs with j nodes in common. From such average probabilities, we can give the second part of Holland and Leinhardt's first theorem:

Theorem 14.2 *Using the notation given above and assuming that a random digraph is generated by some stochastic mechanism, then the variance of the number of k-subgraphs in class u, is*

$$\begin{aligned}
Var(H_u) &= \binom{g}{k}\left\{ \bar{p}(u)(1-\bar{p}(u)) \right.\\
&+ \left. \sum_{j=0}^{k-1}\binom{g-k}{k-j}\binom{k}{j}[\bar{p}_j(u,u)-(\bar{p}(u))^2] \right\}.
\end{aligned} \tag{14.17}$$

Further, the covariance of the number of k-subgraphs in class u and the number in class v is

$$\begin{aligned}
Cov(H_u, H_v) &= \binom{g}{k}\left\{ -\bar{p}(u)\bar{p}(v) \right.\\
&+ \left. \sum_{j=0}^{k-1}\binom{g-k}{k-j}\binom{k}{j}[\bar{p}_j(u,u)-(\bar{p}(u))^2] \right\}.
\end{aligned} \tag{14.18}$$

This is no doubt a difficult theorem to comprehend (which is why this section receives a $\otimes$). We give it here just for the mathematically advanced and/or curious reader. The proofs of these theorems can be found in Holland and Leinhardt (1975). Clearly, the quantities needed to find all variances and covariances are complicated. We will turn shortly to the triad census to illustrate the calculations.

But before we do, we should note that the results in these theorems apply to any k, including $k = 2$ (dyads). Consequently, we could (although we do not here) calculate the mean and variance of the number of asymmetric dyads in a dyad census, as well as the covariance between the numbers of mutual and asymmetric dyads. We noted in Chapter 13 that the focus in the literature has been only statistics for M; with these results, however, we can consider the entire dyad census, and conduct a more complete analysis.

14.3.2 Mean and Variance of a Triad Census

We now take the two theorems given above, equations (14.15), (14.17), and (14.18), and apply them to triads. These applications can be found in Holland and Leinhardt (1970, 1975), Wasserman (1977), and Fershtman (1985).

Under the assumptions of the theorems given above, the mean, variances, and covariances of the counts in a triad census $\mathbf{T}$ are

$$E(T_u) = \binom{g}{3} \bar{p}(u) \tag{14.19}$$

$$\begin{aligned} \text{Var}(T_u) &= \binom{g}{3} \bar{p}(u)(1 - \bar{p}(u)) \\ &+ \binom{g}{3} \sum_{j=0}^{2} \binom{g-3}{3-j} \binom{3}{j} [\bar{p}_j(u,u) - (\bar{p}(u))^2] \end{aligned} \tag{14.20}$$

and

$$\begin{aligned} \text{Cov}(T_u, T_v) &= \binom{g}{3} \left\{ -\bar{p}(u)\bar{p}(v) \right. \\ &+ \left. \sum_{j=0}^{2} \binom{g-3}{3-j} \binom{3}{j} [\bar{p}_j(u,u) - (\bar{p}(u))^2] \right\}. \end{aligned} \tag{14.21}$$

Here, T_u is one of the sixteen counts of the triad census, and replaces H_u in Theorems 14.1 and 14.2. So, to calculate the average counts of the triad census, along with their variances, and the covariances between any pair of counts, we need to calculate seven sets of probabilities: $\{\bar{p}(u)\}$, the average probabilities (across all triads) that any one of the triads is of type u; $\{\bar{p}_0(u,u)\}$, $\{\bar{p}_1(u,u)\}$, $\{\bar{p}_2(u,u)\}$, the average probabilities (across all triads) that a pair of triads, with 0, 1, or 2, respectively, nodes in common, are both of the same type u; and lastly, $\{\bar{p}_0(u,v)\}$, $\{\bar{p}_1(u,v)\}$, $\{\bar{p}_2(u,v)\}$, the average probabilities (across all triads) that a pair of triads, with 0, 1, or 2, respectively, nodes in common, are of different types u and v (where $u \neq v$). It is clear that these covariances can be time-consuming to calculate (and maybe even difficult to comprehend). Fortunately, the calculations have been programmed (Walker and Wasserman 1987).

These seven sets of probabilities depend on which stochastic mechanism we assume for the directed graph itself. The most popular distribution in use for the statistical analysis of the triad census is the $U|MAN$ distribution. This distribution, popularized by Holland and Leinhardt, "fixes" the values of the dyad census at $M = m$, $A = a$, and $N = n$, and considers all digraphs with these values for the dyad census to be equally likely. It is the uniform distribution, defined on the set of all labeled digraphs with given values of M, A, and N.

Another distribution, studied by Wasserman (1977) and Fershtman (1985), that has been used to study the triad census is the $U|\{X_{i+}\}$ distribution. This distribution "fixes" the values of the outdegrees of the nodes at $X_{1+} = x_{1+}$, $X_{2+} = x_{2+}$, ..., $X_{g+} = x_{g+}$, and considers all digraphs with these values for the outdegrees to be equally likely. It is the uniform distribution, defined on the set of all labeled digraphs with given values of X_{1+}, X_{2+}, ..., X_{g+}. Researchers have stated the importance of these distributions (Feld and Elmore 1982a, 1982b; Hallinan 1982), arguing that the inequality of popularity (unequal indegrees) may cause disproportionate frequencies of particular types of triads, but were unaware of prior research on these distributions.

Additional distributions, which can be used to calculate the necessary probabilities for the means, variances, and covariances of the triad census counts, are discussed by Wasserman (1977). We also refer the interested reader to Snijders and Stokman (1987) and Snijders (1987), who extend the class of distributions for the triad census to include those where the actors have been partitioned into subsets using actor attribute variables.

Holland and Leinhardt (1975), using results from Davis and Leinhardt (1972) and Holland and Leinhardt (1970), give expressions for the seven sets of probabilities assuming that the $U|MAN$ random digraph distribution is operating. The advantage gained by using this distribution is that tendencies toward reciprocity are removed (via statistical conditioning) prior to the analysis. Thus, any triadic effects (such as transitivity) are not due to any "lower-order" tendencies.

Wasserman (1977) and Fershtman (1985) give the seven sets of probabilities assuming that either the $U|\{X_{i+}\}$ distribution or the $U|\{X_{+j}\}$ distribution is in effect. Snijders and Stokman (1987) give the probabilities necessary to calculate equations (14.19), (14.20), and (14.21), assuming variations on these three distributions which arise when nodes have been classified into distinct subsets. And, we should also mention the very important research of Snijders (1991a, 1991b) on the $U|\{X_{i+}\}, \{X_{+j}\}$ distribution. Snijders used Verbeek and Kroonenberg's (1985) "enumeration tree," designed for counting all two-way contingency tables with given marginals, to count all sociomatrices with fixed indegrees and outdegrees. This distribution has yet to be applied to the components of the triad census.

Fortunately, we need not give these sets of probabilities here, since they have been computerized. Originally, only *SOCPAC* (Leinhardt 1971) performed the calculations for the $U|MAN$ distribution (see also Appendix C to Holland and Leinhardt 1975). Recently, however, several more widely available computer packages have automated the necessary calculations, particularly a program by Noma and Smith (1978) and *TRIADS* (Walker and Wasserman 1987). Either of these programs will give the means, variances, and covariances of the counts in the triad census, assuming a variety of random digraph distributions. We note, however, because of Holland and Leinhardt's influence on triadic methods, the most commonly used distribution is $U|MAN$.

14.3.3 Return to the Example

The triad census for the friendship relation from Krackhardt's high-tech managers network was given earlier in this chapter. In Table 14.3, we give the mean vector (with all sixteen components), and in Table 14.4, the 16×16 covariance matrix for this triad census, calculated under the $U|MAN$ distribution. Table 14.3 gives the counts of the triad census (the **T** vector, which is given in the second column), the expected counts, assuming that $U|MAN$ distribution is operating (the mean vector), and the standard deviations of these counts (the square roots of the diagonal elements of the covariance matrix).

Table 14.3. *Triadic analysis of Krackhardt's friendship relation*

Triad type	Triad census	Expected value	Standard deviation
003	376	320.06	9.39
012	366	416.82	14.56
102	143	171.19	9.43
021D	114	44.09	6.22
021U	34	44.09	6.22
021C	35	88.17	8.17
111D	39	73.74	7.78
111U	101	73.74	7.78
030T	23	18.17	3.86
030C	0	6.06	2.39
201	20	28.97	4.52
120D	16	7.74	2.71
120U	25	7.74	2.71
120C	9	15.48	3.74
210	23	12.38	3.25
300	6	1.55	1.20

Table 14.4 gives the covariance matrix, again calculated under the assumption that the $U|MAN$ distribution is operating.

These quantities are standard output of the computer programs mentioned above. Note how the triad counts compare to their expectations, relative to their standard deviations (one could subtract the expectations from each count, and divide these deviations by their standard deviations, to obtain a set of standardized scores). The expected counts are what we would expect (on average) from a random directed graph, with the dyad census $M = 23$, $A = 56$, and $N = 131$. For example, we see far too many 003 triads $((376 - 320.06)/9.39 = 6$ standard deviations), and far too few 012 triads ($\approx$ 3 standard deviations). The number of 021 D triads (as noted earlier) is many more than expected. We note that the quantities in Table 14.3 are the only statistics needed to test structural hypotheses about the relation under study. Such hypotheses are usually tested by examining not the entire triad census and its expectation, but linear combinations of it, which we now discuss.

14.3.4 Mean and Variance of Linear Combinations of a Triad Census

As we have mentioned and demonstrated, linear combinations of the triad census, defined as $\sum_u l_u T_u$ where the l_u are the coefficients of the

Table 14.4. *Covariance matrix for triadic analysis of Krackhardt's friendship relation*

	003	012	102	021D	021U	021C	111D	111U
003	88.2							
012	-107.0	212.0						
102	-44.0	-3.24	88.9					
021D	4.71	-21.4	4.55	38.7				
021U	4.71	-21.4	4.55	-5.35	38.7			
021C	9.42	-42.9	9.11	-10.7	-10.7	66.8		
111D	7.87	-8.65	-19.6	-2.09	-2.09	-4.18	60.5	
111U	7.87	-8.65	-19.6	-2.09	-2.09	-4.18	-13.3	60.5
030T	6.65	-5.68	3.56	-3.57	-3.57	-7.14	-1.01	- 1.01
030C	2.22	-1.89	1.19	-1.19	-1.19	-2.38	-0.34	- 0.34
201	3.09	7.29	-18.4	1.12	1.12	2.23	-6.02	-6.02
120D	2.83	-0.38	-0.52	-0.68	-0.68	-1.35	-1.77	- 1.77
120U	2.83	-0.38	-0.52	-0.68	-0.68	-1.35	-1.77	- 1.77
120C	5.66	-0.77	-1.04	-1.35	-1.35	-2.71	-3.54	- 3.54
210	4.53	2.64	-4.09	-0.06	-0.06	-0.13	-3.66	- 3.66
300	0.57	0.74	-0.92	0.08	0.08	0.16	-0.40	-0.40

(continued)

	030T	030C	201	120D	120U	120C	210	300
030T	14.9							
030C	-1.09	5.69						
201	0.60	0.20	20.5					
120D	-0.63	-0.21	-0.43	7.36				
120U	-0.63	-0.21	-0.43	-0.38	7.36			
120C	-1.25	-0.42	-0.86	-0.76	-0.76	14.0		
210	-0.17	-0.06	-3.11	-0.58	-0.58	-1.17	10.5	
300	-0.03	-0.01	-0.86	-0.04	-0.04	-0.08	-0.37	1. 44

linear combination and are specified in advance, are very useful. Such combinations yield many graph statistics. To more fully utilize these linear combinations, we now consider how to calculate the mean and variance of general combinations.

We first need some more notation for the mean and variance of **T**. The triad census **T** contains sixteen counts, one for each of the isomorphism classes. Consequently, there is an expected count for each of the isomorphism classes, as defined in equation (14.19), for each u. We will array these components into a single vector, μ_T which is the vector of expected values of the T_u. We also have sixteen variances, and $\binom{16}{2}$ covariances, which we place into a 16 × 16 covariance matrix, Σ_T, which has the sixteen variances along the diagonal, and the covariances off the diagonal. The (u,v)th entry of $\mathbf{\Sigma}_T$ is the covariance of T_u and T_v. These variances and covariances are given in equations (14.20) and (14.21).

We remarked earlier that linear combinations of the triad census can be quite important. Besides giving us a variety of directed graph properties, they can also be used to test substantive hypotheses. In an earlier section of this chapter, we defined $\sum_u l_u T_u$ as a general linear combination, where the l_u are the coefficients of the linear combination, for the sixteen possible components of $\mathbf{T}$, indexed by u. Sometimes it will be convenient to arrange the sixteen coefficients of the linear combination into a vector $\mathbf{l}$. Vector algebra and statistical calculations give formulas for the mean and variance of any linear combination of the triad census counts. Specifically,

$$
\begin{aligned}
E\left(\sum_u l_u T_u\right) &= \sum_u l_u E(T_u) \\
&= \mathbf{l}' \boldsymbol{\mu}_T
\end{aligned}
\tag{14.22}
$$

and

$$
\mathrm{Var}\left(\sum_u l_u T_u\right) = \mathbf{l}' \mathbf{\Sigma}_T \mathbf{l}.
\tag{14.23}
$$

Formulas such as these may appear daunting, but will be very useful to test substantive hypotheses. They certainly provide a compact, shorthand notation for the mean and variance of a general linear combination of the triad census, a scalar quantity since the linear combination itself is just a single count. The operation $\mathbf{l}'\mathbf{T}$ is simply the transpose of a 16×1 vector ($\mathbf{l}$) multiplied by another vector ($\mathbf{T}$), so that the result is a scalar quantity. Applying the same principles to the variance equation (14.23), one can see that the variance is also a scalar.

14.3.5 A Brief Review

Let us summarize briefly. First, we postulated that the relation under study was random, and assumed that some random directed graph distribution governed this randomness. We then discussed (and showed in a couple of theorems) how one could compute the mean and covariance matrix for a general k-subgraph census assuming that some random directed graph distribution was indeed operating.

We next demonstrated this theory for the 3–subgraph or triad census. The theorems giving the means, variances, and covariances have been

implemented by a variety of computer programs. Most of these pro-
grams work with the $U|MAN$ random directed graph distribution, the
uniform distribution conditional on the dyad census. We then turned
to Krackhardt's network, and the measured friendship or acquaintanceship relation, and discussed the mean vector and covariance matrix
of the triad census (which was generated as output of the *TRIADS*
computer program of Walker and Wasserman 1987). To study structural hypotheses, all one needs are the mean vector and covariance
matrix.

14.4 Testing Structural Hypotheses

Consider now the various structural hypotheses, such as balance and
transitivity. The first step in the testing process is to consider how these
hypotheses can be "operationalized" in terms of triads; that is, what
predictions these theories make about the various triadic configurations
that occur (or should not occur) in a data set.

14.4.1 Configurations

The best way to proceed is to consider the configurations implied by
a theory. A *configuration* is simply a subset of the nodes and some
of the arcs that may be contained in a triad. A configuration is more
general than a subgraph since it does not have to include all the lines
that exist between the chosen nodes. Since we are only focusing on 3-
subgraphs here, the nodes must be a triple. Thus, a configuration involves
a subset of the arcs that can exist between the nodes in the triple. In
general, however, we could study theories which make propositions about
configurations involving k nodes.

It is best to think of a configuration using an example. Consider
transitivity. We take the triple of nodes i, j, and k, and assume that
$i \rightarrow j$ and $j \rightarrow k$. For this triple to be transitive, then i must also $\rightarrow k$.
These three nodes, and the three arcs, constitute a configuration. There
really are only three arcs of interest here: the arcs from i to j and from
j to k (which we assume are present) and the arc from i to k (whose
presence completes this transitive triple). Consequently, of the six arcs
which could be present in the triad involving these three nodes, we are
interested in only three of the arcs in this configuration. We will first
consider configurations of nodes and arcs, and then determine how many
of these configurations are present in the sixteen triad types.

First look at the nodes and arcs that are part of a triad. Recall that there are sixty-four possible states for each triple of nodes (since there are six possible arcs, each of which can be present or absent — 2^6), and each has a unique 3×3 sociomatrix. The general form of this sociomatrix, which contains all the data for a triple, is

$$
\begin{pmatrix}
- - - & X_{ij} & X_{ik} \\
X_{ji} & - - - & X_{jk} \\
X_{ki} & X_{kj} & - - -
\end{pmatrix},
$$

where the distinct nodes i, j, and k index both the rows and columns. Our theories will make predictions about the patterns of some of the 0's and 1's that should occur in this matrix.

An example of a configuration (that we will use below in a discussion of transitivity) is the set containing the (1,2), (2,3), and (1,3) entries from the triad sociomatrix, where the lines $i \rightarrow j$, $j \rightarrow k$, and $i \rightarrow k$ are present. It is common to picture a configuration by dropping from the triad sociomatrix those cells not of interest. For a transitivity configuration, this implies that we list only three cells (which Holland and Leinhardt referred to as a *transitive triple*). The specific configuration just mentioned can be recorded as the array

$$
\begin{pmatrix}
ij & jk & ik \\
1 & 1 & 1
\end{pmatrix},
$$

which we can recognize immediately as a transitive configuration of nodes and arcs. We note that sometimes, it may be instructive to picture these configurations with a digraph, rather than with arrays.

Configurations are used to translate substantive theories into mathematical statements about triads. These statements are then interpreted using the triad census. Configurations are useful because most theories are manifested as characteristics of triples, subsets of nodes, and arcs which are then contained in triads. As an example consider some of the triad isomorphism classes and transitivity (see Figure 14.5). The 300 triad contains six configurations involving threesomes of actors. These six are all transitive configurations. This triad type is transitive from the perspective of each of the members of the triple. In general for transitivity, each triad contains six configurations. Only those configurations which are transitive or intransitive are of interest.

The 120C triad has one transitive configuration, and two intransitive configurations. Examining Figure 14.5, and naming the actors i, j, and k (starting from the southwest vertex, and going clockwise), we can see these three configurations. We have $i \to j$, $j \to k$, and $i \to k$, the transitive configuration. But we also have two intransitive configurations: $k \to i$, $i \to j$, but $k \not\to j$, and $j \to k$, $k \to i$, but $j \not\to i$. So, a triad contains many configurations. These configurations, which consist of some subset of the entries in the generic 3×3 triadic sociomatrix, may be quite different substantively. And all must be taken into account when testing substantive hypotheses.

We can characterize each triad isomorphism class according to the numbers and nature of the configurations it contains. Such a characterization tells us about the overall presence of the configurations (and hence, a substantive theory) in the data set under study.

Let us consider a different hypothesis, and examine some configurations in more detail. We take as an example the theoretical statement by Mazur (1971), based on the standard theory from psychology detailing the close relationship between similarity and attraction:

> Friends are likely to agree, and unlikely to disagree; close friends are very likely to agree, and very unlikely to disagree. (page 308)

Holland and Leinhardt (1975) interpret "friends" as asymmetric dyads, and "close friends" as mutual dyads. To study this statement further, we assume that agreements and disagreements are made about third parties (whose own choices are irrelevant to the theory). Consequently, this statement (about friends or close friends agreeing) is about particular configurations, focusing on how the actors in either asymmetric dyads or mutual dyads relate to a third actor.

The configuration for this similarity/attraction theory has the standard structure for configurations. It can be quantified by constructing a two-row array, where the first row lists the *reading rule* for the configuration (the cells of the 3×3 array that are involved in the theory), and the second, the configuration *type* (the values of the cells that satisfy or are implied by theory). The reading rule is simply the pairs of nodes that are involved in the configuration, and the type is the list of which of these arcs are present and which are absent (that is, which of the pairs are such that the first actor relates to the second). We take actors i and j as close friends, so that the reading rule contains both ij and ji, both of which have 1's in the configuration type row. If these actors agree (as predicted by the similarity/attraction hypothesis), then they both should relate to a third actor, k. Putting all of this together gives us the "close friends agreeing" configuration, which can be quantified using the

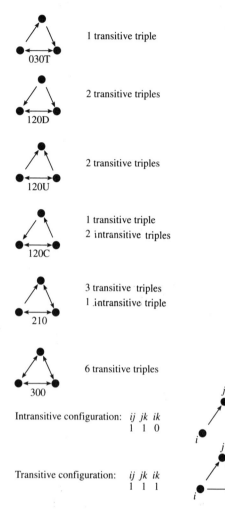

1 transitive triple

030T

2 transitive triples

120D

2 transitive triples

120U

1 transitive triple
2 intransitive triples

120C

3 transitive triples
1 intransitive triple

210

6 transitive triples

300

Intransitive configuration: ij jk ik
                              1 1 0

Transitive configuration: ij jk ik
                            1 1 1

Fig. 14.5. Transitive configurations

configuration matrix

$$\begin{pmatrix} ij & ji & ik & jk \\ 1 & 1 & 1 & 1 \end{pmatrix},$$

where the close friends agree on their choices. These close friends could also agree on their non-choices, so the theory also predicts that the configuration matrix

$$\left(\begin{array}{cccc} ij & ji & ik & jk \\ 1 & 1 & 0 & 0 \end{array}\right)$$

is likely to arise. The "close friends disagreeing" configuration matrices are

$$\left(\begin{array}{cccc} ij & ji & ik & jk \\ 1 & 1 & 0 & 1 \end{array}\right)$$

and

$$\left(\begin{array}{cccc} ij & ji & ik & jk \\ 1 & 1 & 1 & 0 \end{array}\right),$$

which, according to the theory, are equivalent. These are the four predictive configurations for close friends.

There are eight more predictive configurations, for pairs of actors who are just "friends" rather than close friends. These eight fall into four pairs, and have the same reading rule as those for close friends; that is, they all involve exactly the same ties: ij, ji, ik, jk. Their types (the second rows of the configuration matrices — the predicted values for the ties) are: 1011 and 0111 (which are equivalent); 1000 and 0100 (which are equivalent); 1010 and 0101 (which are equivalent); and 1001 and 0110 (which are equivalent). The first four are the agreements between friends, and the last four, the disagreements.

Thus, there are twelve total configurations for this theory — four involving close friends, and eight involving friends. The theory predicts that the four "friends agreeing" configurations are more likely to occur than the four "friends disagreeing." Theory also says that the two "close friends agreeing" configurations are much more likely to occur than the two "close friends disagreeing." We should note that since this hypothesis does not consider the "choices" made by the third party, it involves configurations rather than triads. Such is frequently the case with substantive theories.

The primary reason for considering configurations is that it makes the step from theoretical statement to statistical test somewhat simpler. Configurations are easier to deal with, and are more refined than triads, since the actors involved in the configuration are exactly those that play important substantive roles in the triad according to some specific theory. A triad contains many configurations. Further, many sociological and psychological theories make predictions about configurations and not triads, as we have shown for transitivity and for the similarity/attraction hypothesis. However, even though these theories must be quantified at the level of the configuration, they are all tested at the level of the triad, using the triad census. We now turn to this most important step in theory testing.

14.4.2 From Configurations to Weighting Vectors

Consider a specific substantive hypothesis, and the collection of configurations which should and/or should not occur if the hypothesis is correct. The hypothesis itself is actually a set of predictions about actor and "choice" behavior on the relation under study. Each of the configurations associated with a hypothesis to be studied will be examined, and the hypothesis judged by how frequently the configurations occur. This study can be conducted statistically using the data and the frequencies of the sixteen components of the triad census since each configuration is present in at least one of the triad types. By comparing the actual frequencies to those predicted by the configurations, we can conduct a statistical test of the hypothesis.

The first step in this procedure has already been outlined — determine which configurations are predicted or not predicted by the substantive hypothesis. For example, we have discussed the similarity/attraction hypothesis, and showed that there are six configurations that should occur (the configurations that show agreement: 1111, 1100, 1011/0111, 1000/0100) and six that should not occur (the configurations that show disagreement: 1101/1110, 1010/0101, 1001/0110). The four arcs making up the reading rule for these configurations are all *ij, ji, ik,* and *jk.*

The similarity/attraction hypothesis predicts that the first six configurations should occur much more frequently than chance, and the last six, much less. By "chance," we mean the expected numbers of these configurations that would arise as given by a random directed graph distribution, assuming that the hypothesis is true. Note that this comparison strategy is identical to the standard approach to significance testing in statistics: let the data give the empirical frequencies or value of the relevant statistic, and then compare the empirical value(s) with the value(s) to be expected based on some null model (assuming that the hypothesis is correct). We will always assume (as a null hypothesis) that the substantive theory is *not* correct; that is, the network does not display similarity of attraction, transitivity, and so on. Hence, we want to *reject* this null hypothesis, so that we will be able to state that the data give evidence in favor of the hypothesis.

We will take the configurations, and determine the triads in which they are embedded. This step requires that the researcher consider each of the relevant configurations, and find all the triads in which they occur. This determination tells us which triads should occur (assuming that the particular configuration is true) and which ones should not. We then count the number of configurations of a given kind which arise in each of the triad types. The best way to understand this step is to consider some examples. We will look at the similarity/attraction hypothesis here and, later in the chapter, will focus on transitivity.

For the similarity/attraction hypothesis, consider each of the twelve configurations. The simplest of the twelve configurations, 1111, should occur if the similarity/attraction hypothesis is true, since it implies that two close friends agree in their choice about a third party. This configuration occurs in three triads: $120U$, 210, and 300. The configuration 1111 occurs just once in triad $120U$, once in triad 210, while it occurs six times in 300. So, to enumerate the frequency with which this configuration arises in a data set, we should: (1) count the number of times $120U$ occurs; (2) count the number of times 210 occurs; (3) count the frequency of 300 triads, and multiply by 6; and then (4), sum these counts. We do this enumeration for each of the twelve configurations, and then aggregate the numbers of predicted triads across all configurations.

The steps in this process constitute the construction of a linear combination of the sixteen triad counts, or a *weighting vector*, that gives us the frequency of a configuration. If we apply the vector to the triad census, we get the empirical frequency of the configuration, while if we apply it to the mean of the triad census, calculated by assuming some random digraph distribution, we get the expected frequency of the same configuration. The weighting vector for the 1111 configuration is (0 0 0 0 0 0 0 0 0 0 1 0 1 3).

Applying this weighting vector to Krackhardt's high-tech managers and the friendship relation, we find that there are 25 $120U$ triads, 23 210 triads, and 6 300 triads. So, the linear combination of the triad census (ignoring all the triad census components which get 0 weights) equals $(1 \times 25) + (1 \times 23) + (3 \times 6) = 66$ of the 1111 configuration. From the expected values of the triad counts (see Table 14.3), we see that this configuration should occur with a frequency of $(1 \times 7.74) + (1 \times 12.38) + (3 \times 1.55) = 24.77$, considerably less than actually arose. To judge the "statistical significance" of this difference (66 versus 24.77), we need to use the covariance matrix for the triad census, and equation (14.23). This calculation is easy to do with the program *TRIADS*, and is discussed at length in the next section of the chapter.

Another interesting weighting vector is that associated with the configuration types 1101 and 1110. These types imply that close friends disagree. This configuration occurs in triads $111U$, 201 (twice), $120C$, and 210. Thus, its weighting vector is (0 0 0 0 0 0 0 1 0 0 2 0 0 1 1 0), and is given in the last column of Table 14.2. For Krackhardt's managers and the friendship relation, these triads occur with frequencies 101, 20, 9, and 23, respectively, so that the "close friends disagreeing" configuration occurs with a frequency of $(1 \times 101) + (2 \times 20) + (1 \times 9) + (1 \times 23)$, again ignoring the triads that have 0 weights. This empirical frequency of 173 should be compared to an expected frequency of 159.54, indicating that this "bad" configuration occurs less frequently than predicted.

To summarize this stage in the test statistic construction process, we form a weighting vector for each of the configurations that are predicted to occur more or less frequently than chance if the hypothesis in question is true. For Mazur's similarity/attraction theory, there are twelve configurations, and seven weighting vectors (since ten of the configurations are "paired up" into five equivalent configurations). All seven vectors are given in Table 14.5. The first four (concerned with agreements among friends or close friends) should occur more frequently than expected, if the substantive hypothesis about similarity and attraction is true for this network, while the remaining three (concerned with disagreements) should occur less frequently. If a particular triad type has a zero for a specific vector, then it does not contain the configuration(s) that represent the theory.

Once all the vectors are constructed, we can turn to the statistical theory outlined above for linear combinations of triad counts to test the relevant hypothesis. We simply take the frequencies for the collection of configurations and compare them statistically to the expected frequencies, weighting by appropriate standard errors. We now outline this final step in substantive hypothesis testing.

14.4.3 From Weighting Vectors to Test Statistics

As described above, a substantive hypothesis is first "operationalized" by determining which configurations should occur or not occur if the hypothesis is correct (for the network and relation in question). The configurations are contained in one or more triad types, so weighting vectors can be constructed to count the configuration frequencies across

Table 14.5. *Configuration types for Mazur's proposition*

Triad type	1111	1100	1011 0111	1000 0100	1101 1110	1010 0101	1001 0110
003	0	0	0	1	0	0	0
012	0	0	0	0	0	0	0
102	0	1	0	0	0	0	0
021D	0	0	0	0	0	2	0
021U	0	0	0	2	0	0	0
021C	0	0	0	1	0	0	1
111D	0	1	0	0	0	0	1
111U	0	0	0	0	1	1	0
030T	0	0	1	1	0	1	0
030C	0	0	0	0	0	0	3
201	0	0	0	0	2	0	0
120D	0	1	2	0	0	0	0
120U	1	0	0	0	0	2	0
120C	0	0	1	0	1	0	1
210	1	0	1	0	1	0	0
300	3	0	0	0	0	0	0

all triad types. These weighting vectors are simply the weights for linear combinations of the triad census components that give us the configuration frequencies.

Mathematically, we let l be one of these weighting vectors, which always has sixteen coefficients, one for each of the triad types. As usual, we let $\mathbf{T}$ denote the triad census vector. As we noted previously, $l'\mathbf{T}$ is a linear combination of the triad census, using one of the weighting vectors derived from the substantive hypothesis under study, written using linear algebra notation. This linear combination can also be written as a sum: $\sum_u l_u T_u = l'\mathbf{T}$. This linear combination is the number of times that the specific configuration, associated with the chosen weighting vector, occurs in the observed sociomatrix. Under one of the random directed graph distributions, we can calculate the expected value and covariance matrix of $\mathbf{T}$, and hence the expected number for this configuration (equation (14.22)) and its variance (equation (14.23)). This expected number is $l'\boldsymbol{\mu}_T$, and the standard error is $\sqrt{l'\Sigma_T l}$, where $\boldsymbol{\mu}_T$, the mean triad census vector, is given by the components of equation (14.19). We note that Σ_T is the 16×16 covariance matrix of the counts of the triad census, whose variances are given by equation (14.20) and covariances by equation (14.21). We comment on where to obtain these statistical quantities ($\boldsymbol{\mu}_T$

and Σ_T) — that is, which statistical package to use — later in this section.

The test statistic that we construct to study the specific configuration associated with the weighting vector compares the observed count of the frequency of this configuration, $l'T$, to its expected frequency, $l'\mu_T$. This difference must be standardized by the standard error of the configuration frequency to give us an interpretable statistic. The recommended test statistic is

$$\tau(l) = (l'T - l'\mu_T)/\sqrt{l'\Sigma_T l} \qquad (14.24)$$

and is usually assumed to have an approximate normal distribution with mean 0 and variance 1, when the hypothesis under study is true. Holland and Leinhardt (1970, 1979) lend evidence that this assumption is quite adequate. However, the accuracy of the assumption is certainly affected by the sample size, which for the triad census is $\binom{g}{3}$. We have more confidence in this assumption for social networks with larger sets of actors (say, $g > 15$). We note that this approach to hypothesis testing is identical to calculating a t-statistic to test a hypothesis about an unknown population mean. Davis and Leinhardt (1972) advocate the use of an "index" different from equation (14.24), which, unfortunately, could not be standardized, so comparisons were difficult to make. Both this index, and the tau statistic, are generalizations of an index of intransitivity proposed by Kendall and Smith (1939).

To review, a hypothesis generates a collection of configurations about actors' choices or nominations, which are predicted (by the theory) to occur or not occur. This theory can then be stated as a statistical alternative hypothesis, and tested using the available data gathered from the set of actors. The null hypothesis states that the theory is not true. The configurations associated with the theory yield a set of weighting vectors, to be applied to the counts of the triad census, since the triad types contain the various predicted (or not predicted) configurations. The weighting vectors for the theory (for example, the similarity/attraction hypothesis has seven of these vectors) are then used to calculate tau statistics (equation (14.24)) to test the hypothesis. There will be one τ for each weighting vector, and all must be evaluated simultaneously to reach a decision about the validity of the hypothesis.

The only question that remains is how to calculate the mean and variance of the triad census, and hence, the mean and variance of a linear combination of the triad census. These two quantities are needed to calculate a test statistic. The examples that we discuss here use both the $U|MAN$ distribution, which conditions on the components of the dyad census, and the $U|\{X_{i+}\}$ and $U|\{X_{+j}\}$ distributions, which condition on the outdegrees and indegrees, respectively. Comprehension of the statistical theory for these quantities is not really necessary for the typical user, since computer programs exist to calculate the mean and covariance matrix of the triad census under these three distributions.

14.4.4 An Example

To illustrate the use of the τ test statistic defined in equation (14.24), let us again take Krackhardt's managers and the measured friendship relation, and the similarity/attraction hypothesis that we have been describing. The mean and covariance of the triad census (which we discussed earlier in this chapter) are given in Table 14.3 and Table 14.4. The hypothesis makes statements about twelve configurations, and seven linear combinations of the triad census. These linear combinations are given in Table 14.5. Four of these linear combinations (see the first four weighting vectors in Table 14.5 associated with the "agreement" part of the hypothesis) are predicted by the alternative hypothesis to have empirical frequencies greater than expected; hence, the numerator of their τ statistics should be large, and positive. The other three (those associated with the "disagreement" part of the hypothesis) should be negative, since the empirical frequencies for the triads involved should be less than expected. The last three τ statistics should be large, but negative.

Consider the weighting vector for the 1111 configuration. As mentioned, only 66 triads contain this configuration. The expected frequency for this configuration, assuming that the $U|MAN$ random digraph distribution is operating, is 24.77, using the same linear combination just applied for the empirical frequency. The standard deviation of this frequency can be computed (using equation (14.23)) easily, and equals 5.20. Therefore, the τ statistic for this configuration is 7.8|99 positive (and quite large) as predicted. It clearly has a very small p-value, less than 0.0001 (which is computed simply by using the tail areas of the standard normal distribution), so that we can safely reject this part of the null hypothesis. It certainly appears that close friends agree about third parties (when both actors choose the third party) far more than predicted by chance alone.

The entire set of τ statistics, along with their configurations, are:

- Configuration 1111: $\tau = 7.90$
- Configuration 1100: $\tau = -5.14$
- Configuration 1011/0111: $\tau = 3.41$
- Configuration 1000/0100: $\tau = -0.72$
- Configuration 1101/1110: $\tau = 1.28$
- Configuration 1010/0101: $\tau = 13.91$
- Configuration 1001/0110: $\tau = -9.10$

The signs of the statistics are not all as predicted by the close friends agreeing hypothesis. The first statistic (1111) is large and positive, indicating that close friends agree about the presence of a choice to a third party. However, the second statistic (1100) is negative, indicating that close friends do not agree about non-choice of a third party. The fifth statistic (1101, 1110) is about as expected by chance, indicating that close friends are neither more nor less likely to disagree about a choice to a third party.

Holland and Leinhardt (1975) studied the similarity/attraction hypotheses carefully using 408 randomly selected sociomatrices contained in Davis and Leinhardt's (1972) sociometric data bank. All of these social networks had people as actors. The median values of τ for the 7 statistics associated with the hypotheses are:

- Configuration 1111: 3.48
- Configuration 1100: 1.73
- Configuration 1011/0111: 2.36
- Configuration 1000/0100: 1.82
- Configuration 1101/1110: −3.81
- Configuration 1010/0101: −1.73
- Configuration 1001/0110: −1.49

These results support the hypotheses. All statistics have the predicted sign. Note how similar these are to those calculated for Krackhardt's friendship relation. It appears that there is solid evidence that "close friends" agree more strongly about third parties than do just "plain" friends, especially when both friends choose the third party.

14.4.5 Another Example — Testing for Transitivity

As a second example, we consider Freeman's *EIES* data, and the acquaintanceship relation measured for the researchers. Here, we want to test the structural hypothesis about transitivity. We wish to study the proposition stated formally by Davis, Holland, and Leinhardt (1971):

> Interpersonal choices tend to be transitive — that is, if actor P chooses actor O, and actor O chooses actor X, then P is likely to choose X. (page 309)

There are two configurations relevant to the theory of transitivity. Both involve just three ordered pairs: ij, jk, and ik. The first configuration, which we will label the *intransitive configuration*, is

$$\left(\begin{array}{ccc} ij & jk & ik \\ 1 & 1 & 0 \end{array} \right) ;$$

that is, to use the classical terminology, actor P chooses actor O, actor O chooses actor X, but there is no choice of X by P. Clearly, this threesome displays an intransitive structure. The second configuration, which we will label the *transitive configuration*, is

$$\left(\begin{array}{ccc} ij & jk & ik \\ 1 & 1 & 1 \end{array} \right) .$$

These two configurations are pictured at the bottom of Figure 14.5.

There are many triads that contain these two configurations: seven triads contain as many as three intransitive configurations, while six contain as many as six (see triad 300) transitivities! The six triads containing at least one transitive triple are also shown in Figure 14.5. For simplicity, we give the two weighting vectors for these configurations on the right of Table 14.2. One could also determine the weighting vectors for theories of balance, clustering, and ranked clustering. We note there that every triad type not allowed by the transitivity hypothesis (those that have a non-zero coefficient in the intransitivity weighting vectors) are also not allowed by these other theories. This demonstrates (quantitatively) the generality of this substantive hypothesis; it contains the other hypotheses as "special cases."

Consider now Freeman's *EIES* researchers. We looked at the acquaintanceship relation, which is valued on an integer scale from 0 to 4, and measured at two points in time. We dichotomized the valued relation (just to apply this methodology) by making scores of 0 (unknown), 1 (person I've heard of, but not met), and 2 (person I've met) equal to 0, and scores of 3 (friend) and 4 (close personal friend) equal to 1. Since there are two weighting vectors, one for each configuration, there will be two τ statistics: τ_i, which measures how many intransitivities the network exhibits, and τ_t, which measures transitivities. If the actors make choices transitively, then τ_t should be large and *positive*, while τ_i should be large and *negative*. For the first time point, we calculated $\tau_t = 13.44$, and for the second, $\tau_t = 14.142$. Both are extremely large, and positive. Transitive triads occur far more than expected. There is even a bit of evidence that transitivity is increasing over time. For intransitivity, $\tau_i = -7.104$ for the first time point, and for the second, $\tau_i = -8.575$, again showing that intransitivities are decreasing over time. Clearly, intransitive triads are very rare.

We note that Holland and Leinhardt (1975) tested this transitivity hypothesis on 408 matrices chosen at random from their sociometric data bank. Using the $U|MAN$ random digraph distribution, the median value of τ_t was 5.18 (quite large!) and the median value of τ_i was -3.89. Remember that these are approximately standard normal deviates (assuming that the null hypothesis of no transitivity is true), and thus, have very small p-values.

These results are very supportive of the proposition that interpersonal choices tend to be transitive. The majority of the relations measured in the data bank are measures of positive affect, such as friendship, work with, play with, and so forth. In a study of positive affect relations measured in classrooms and other groups of schoolchildren, Leinhardt (1972, 1973) shows that transitivity tends to increase with the age of the actors (see also related research by Hallinan and Hutchins 1980). The evidence strongly supports the transitivity of such relational variables. Transitivity forces actors to interact in ways that concentrate "choices" within subgroups; consequently, there are also tendencies in sets of actors toward partitioned actor sets.

However, we note that not all relations for all sets of actors have transitive tendencies. In fact, economic relations among firms, and political relations among individuals in a large bureaucracy, can certainly be intransitive, rather than transitive. Relational ties that are expensive to maintain (that is, those using scarce resources) also are unlikely to yield transitive triples. Thus, the same configurations can be used to test a hypothesized theory, but depending on the actors and the relation, one would expect rather different p-values for the hypothesis.

14.5 Generalizations and Conclusions

Most statistical triadic analyses use the $U|MAN$ distribution; however, computer programs exist for distributions which condition on either the indegrees or outdegrees. It is possible to get approximations to the mean and variance of the triad census (and hence approximate τ statistics) using the ideas described in Appendix B of Holland and Leinhardt (1975) and applied in Holland and Leinhardt (1979). The approximation assumes that **T** is multivariate normal, and thus, standard formulas exist for the mean and variance of conditional distributions of **T**. The conditional distributions used by Holland and Leinhardt fix linear combinations of the triad census, and thus condition on the number of mutuals, the variance of the outdegrees (using B_{out} defined in equation (14.5)), and the variance of the indegrees (using B_{in} defined in equation (14.5)). We refer the interested reader to this research, but note that the strong empirical tendency toward transitivity remains even when conditioning on more lower-level graph properties.

An interesting question that arises is whether one can find a weighting vector that gives the largest possible τ test statistic. Holland and Leinhardt (1978) show how to calculate this maximal τ, whose formula is a simple function of the inverse of the covariance matrix for the triad census. Another question addressed by Holland and Leinhardt concerns whether one needs to look at higher-level subgraphs (such as tetrads) to study network intransitivities. Holland and Leinhardt (1976) (as well as Hallinan and McFarland 1975) discuss the effect that a change in the elements of the sociomatrix has on the transitivity present in the set of actors. Holland and Leinhardt show that it is not necessary to consider tetrads when examining the effect of arc changes on the number of intransitive triads.

There are other substantive theories that can be tested using the triad census. Cartwright and Harary (1977) discuss *quasi-transitivity*, which is a weakened transitivity condition allowing for *partially* ordered clusters of actors. Killworth and Bernard (1979) study a variety of hypotheses related to balance theory and transitivity. Winship (1977) considers a model for balance theory for a *continuous*, rather than dichotomous, relation, based on the triangle inequality. Hallinan (1974a, 1974b) used a weighting vector different from the one given here for testing transitivity, arguing that the 210 triad is permissible under a "weighted transitivity" hypothesis. Feld (1981) presents a theory of the social organization of friendship relations, based on, but more general than, Heider's (1946) balance theory. Triads are important to Feld's theory, but so are local bridges between actors, which can exist (much like Granovetter's (1973) weak ties) when transitive relationships are unlikely. Such bridges lead naturally to distinct subgroups of actors. More mathematical treatments of triad counts and alternative statistical models can be found in Davis (1977), Frank (1978a, 1979a), and Frank and Harary (1979, 1980).

One can also focus on individual actors, and ask how many transitive and intransitive triads each is involved in. Cartwright and Harary (1956) were the first to look at this notion of *local balance*, by considering nodal transitivity and intransitivity. Several important structural properties can be studied in this way. For example, actors involved in many intransitive and transitive triads could be important brokers or cutpoints linking almost disconnected subgroups. Killworth (1974) also discusses nodal transitivity and intransitivity, and finds that actors with high node transitivity also have high intransitivity. Peripheral actors in subgroups (that is, those actors not very central or prestigious) are likely to be involved in many 300 triads, and thus have high node transitivity. Such actors, since they are on the periphery, are also likely to be have ties to actors outside their own subgroup, and thus be involved in many 201 triads, thereby having high node intransitivity. Actors in subgroups are likely to be involved in many 300 triads, and thus have high node transitivity. Peripheral actors are also likely to have ties to actors outside theit own subgroup, and thus be involved in many 201 triads, thereby having high node intransitivity.

Hallinan and Kubitschek (1988, 1990), in one of the few studies of triads and intransitivities in recent years, examined data from elementary school classrooms (for other analyses of these same data, see Eder and Hallinan 1978; Hallinan and Smith 1985; Hallinan and Teixeria 1987a, 1987b; and Hallinan and Williams 1987). They used logistic regression, with the states of the many intransitive triads extracted from these groups of children as the response variable, and a variety of explanatory variables measured on the actors involved as predictors. They argued that intransitivity must be studied at the individual actor level, and sought an answer to the question, "Why are some actors involved in more intransitive triads than others?" The predictor variables used included the gender of the actors in the triple, the race of the actors, the number of mutual and/or asymmetric ties in the triad, grade of the children, and the point in time the triad was measured (several time periods were studied here).

Such analyses, using dyads or triads as basic modeling units, are quite interesting, but potentially flawed, since the triples are not independent of each other. The change of one "choice" can affect many triads (as we pointed out earlier in this chapter), so that the triples arising from one of the classrooms should not be interpreted as independent sampling units. This problem also arises in the log linear models of Davis (1977) and the stochastic models of Sørensen and Hallinan (1975), who view triads as independent units. Hallinan and Kubitschek recognize this, and state that this lack of independence has no effect on this analysis, but no evidence is presented to back up this assertion. Researchers using such methods should be cautioned that the basic assumptions of the logistic regression model do not hold for dependent units. An alternative way to model these basic units will be described in the next chapter.

The two chapters in Part V have focused on dyads and triads. There has been a bit of research on statistical analyses of general, k-subgraph censuses, and on other types of subgraphs. For example, there has been some interest in isomorphism classes for tetrads (4-subgraphs), but the number of such classes (over 100) is so daunting, that (to our knowledge) few statistical models exist for such subgraphs (although recent research of Frank and Strauss (1986) focuses on models that can include substantive effects, such as sociometric stars, which are functions of higher-order subgraphs).

Less-formidable structures include the rows and columns of the sociomatrix, or the ego-centered networks "beginning" or "ending" with particular actors. From the latter, one can study how likely it is that such structures are completely empty; that is, whether a particular actor receives no nominations, or is an isolate. Katz (1952) presents statistical theory for the study of isolates.

14.6 Summary

All things considered, the research program of Davis, Holland, and Leinhardt has had a tremendous impact on triadic analysis. (A detailed, rather humorous, history of this collaboration can be found in Davis 1979). Their research was also the first social network methodology to use sophisticated statistical models. Research on triads and the theories that can be tested using the triad census seems to have peaked in the mid-1970's (a special issue of the *Journal of Mathematical Sociology*, edited by Samuel Leinhardt, was devoted to this research in 1977). This date is not at all surprising, since the mid-1970's saw the introduction of structural equivalence, and the first of many methods that this important theoretical notion spawned. By 1980, structural equivalence had replaced balance and transitivity as the "hot" substantive theory in social network analysis.

There have been few papers in the 1980's in methodological and substantive journals discussing triads and related substantive theories. We have found that researchers frequently forget to study lower-order structures in their data. We feel that such analyses are quite important in social network analyses, and we hope that the methods described in this chapter will help researchers conduct additional, and important tests of substantive hypotheses.

As we have mentioned, there are many substantive questions about structure that cannot be answered by focusing on triads. Questions about connectivity, centrality and prestige, and algebraic properties of measured relations are among the issues that cannot be addressed by looking at configurations of triads. At the same time, a remarkable amount of network information can be gathered by examining configurations defined on two or three nodes. If information necessary to answer important substantive questions can be obtained from the simple subgraphs of sizes 2 and 3 (remember that one can learn all about the dyad census from the triad census), then there is no need to examine higher-order structures (tetrads, pentads, ... , subgroups).

The methods described in this chapter can be quite complementary to the subgroup methods and the role and position methods discussed in Parts III and IV. As mentioned, one logical outcome of a transitive relation is that actors can be partitioned into subgroups; however, triadic analyses cannot tell the researcher about the nature of these subgroups. Are they completely disconnected, or is there a hierarchy among the subgroups (with subgroups "choosing" upward to a top-most subgroup)? Are there more complicated relationships among the subgroups? All of these structural patterns are possible with transitivity. A researcher should consider complementing a triadic analysis with methods designed to study actor subgroupings. A complete social network analysis begins by using methods from Parts III, IV, *and* V of this book.

Part VI
Statistical Dyadic Interaction Models

15

Statistical Analysis of Single Relational Networks

by Dawn Iacobucci

We now turn our attention to stochastic models for social network data. The methodology described here continues the development of statistical methods for network data begun in Chapter 13. We begin in Chapter 15 by considering a (very special) class of statistical distributions for random directed graphs, which, as we will show, is a special case of the uniform random directed graph distributions presented in Chapter 13. This class is more interesting than the distributions of Chapter 13, and contains substantively meaningful parameters which reflect a wide variety of graph properties. Further, the parameters can actually be estimated from data. The basic model has many generalizations and extensions, some of which are described in Chapter 16.

In Chapter 16 we turn to the last question raised in Chapter 9 concerning methodology for studying a positional analysis. We want to measure the adequacy of a representation of a positional analysis. We stated that there are four tasks that have to be undertaken in a positional analysis:

(i) Define equivalence
(ii) Measure how closely the actors adhere to this definition
(iii) Represent the equivalences of the actors
(iv) Measure the adequacy of this representation

Two of the necessary tasks are measurement-oriented. These tasks are the second and fourth. The second task requires the analyst to determine how equivalent the actors are, for a given set of relations; that is, one must find which actors are equivalent, and which ones are not, using some measurement device(s). After such an examination, one then turns to the

605

third task in order to represent the discovered equivalences (and non-equivalences) mathematically. In Chapter 16, we focus on the adequacy of this mathematical model.

The statistical models described in Chapter 15 allow a researcher to perform significance tests — a formal evaluation of the statistical significance of various substantive effects based on null hypotheses. For example, an outdegree used as a descriptive measure of an actor's expansiveness cannot be evaluated as absolutely large or as significantly larger than other outdegrees, but such inferences can be made with statistical models. Furthermore, parameters that quantify the "structural effects" present in a network, such as reciprocity and tendencies toward differential indegrees, can be estimated simultaneously; for example, we can model actor expansiveness while controlling for differential actor popularity. The models described here are *dyadic interaction* models, which use the (natural) log of probabilities as their basic modeling unit. The models posit a structural form for the (natural) logarithm of the probability that actor i "chooses" actor j at one strength while actor j "chooses" actor i at a possibly different strength.

Chapter 16 first describes goodness-of-fit indices for positional analyses not based on statistical models. Next, it presents methods that assume that a statistical model is actually operating, so that the index considered arises naturally from the underlying model. We call both types of indices goodness-of-fit indices, because both attempt to measure the fit of a model to a data set, but note that there is this fundamental distinction between them. And the last section in the chapter describes generalizations and extensions of the models presented in Part VI.

Statistical network analyses allow the researcher to assess a model by measuring the fit of the model to data. In addition, statistical approaches yield flexible probabilistic models that can be generalized by using random directed distributions based on network characteristics. These distributions allow comparisons of the observed effects to hypothesized effects, as well as significance tests to determine whether an effect is due to sampling variability.

We begin this chapter by presenting models for a network with measurements on a single, directional relation for one set of actors. We then describe and demonstrate the interpretation and fitting of a basic statistical network model. Attribute variables measured on the actors can also be incorporated into the models, so that we have the flexibility to model network structure among individual actors or among subsets of actors in situations in which the subsets are defined a priori based on actor attributes. We also describe models that focus entirely on the relation, to the exclusion of the individual actors or the subsets to which they belong. Modifications of the basic statistical model are also described that allow for ordinal, rather than just nominal or dichotomous, relations. Lastly, we briefly discuss recent research on related statistical models for single relations.

Toward the end of the chapter, we present models for networks with two sets of actors in which a single relation is measured. We describe models for one set of actors in greater detail, but we also hope to encourage researchers to consider more applications to networks with two sets of actors.

This chapter does require the reader to have some background in categorical data analysis. Specifically, a knowledge of log linear models, and the methods for fitting such models to three- and four-dimensional contingency tables is needed. Those desiring more background in log linear models should study the excellent texts of Fienberg (1980), Kennedy (1983), Wickens (1989), or Agresti (1990).

The end of this chapter gives the "commands" needed to fit these models to network data using several computer packages. We give specific details on how to fit the models described in this chapter using the standard packages. Some of the computations for the basic models presented in this chapter are included in the latest release of *UCINET IV*.

More statistically knowledgeable readers may find sections of this chapter rather elementary, and possibly boring — we suggest to such readers that the elementary, discursive parts of the chapter, which explain likelihood functions and maximum likelihood estimation of the parameters in log linear models, can be skipped.

15.1 Single Directional Relations

In this section, we first describe the construction and modeling of the **Y**-*array*, a contingency table basic to our models which is derived from the relational data in **X**. This array focuses on dyads, and is descriptive of individual actors' ties to other actors.

We demonstrate these methods in detail on the hypothetical set of second-grade children. We use this fabricated social network as an illustrative example because of its small size, which makes the analyses easier to follow. We also present the application of these methods to Krackhardt's friendship relation measured on managers in a high-tech organization, and Padgett's Florentine marital and business relations. Analyses of these data display different aspects of the methodology discussed in this chapter.

15.1.1 The Y-array

The models for single relational networks are not easily fit to the X matrix, so we reorganize the network data into a different contingency table, to which the models are more easily fit. We first illustrate the construction of this new table using the small hypothetical social network of second-grade children.

Data Review and the Definition of Y. We begin by describing a model for a single, directional relation measured for a single set of actors, $\mathcal{N}$. Recall that a dyad with measurements on a directional relation consists of two actors, i and j, and the possible ties between these two actors.

The ties between the actors may be viewed from the perspective of either actor i or actor j. First, take the perspective of n_i. The relational variable X_{ij} records the possible "choice" of n_j by n_i, while the relational variable X_{ji} records the possible "choice" received by n_i from n_j. Now, take the perspective of actor j. The relational variable X_{ji} records the possible "choice" of actor i by actor j, while the relational variable X_{ij} records the possible "choice" received by actor j from actor i. Both of these perspectives are incorporated into our modeling.

Recall that a social network consisting of g actors contains $\binom{g}{2}$ dyads. In a statistical model, each dyad consists of information represented by two random variables, X_{ij} and X_{ji}. We will let D_{ij} denote the dyadic variable. With g actors and a single relation, we have $g(g-1) = 2\binom{g}{2}$ dyadic random variables to consider. We wish to model all the dyadic ties in a network simultaneously and as parsimoniously as possible.

Consider a pair of actors, a single dichotomous relation, and the dyad D_{ij}. The ties in the dyad, for both actors, can be presented in a 2×2 array. The two variables of this array, both of which have just two levels, are rather novel. The first, with two levels, which we index with a k and which can be either 0 or 1, codes the value of the tie sent by the row actor i to the column actor j. The second, also with just two levels and which we index with an l, codes the value of the tie sent by the column actor j to the row actor i. So, the ties for each and every dyad can be presented in one of these 2×2 arrays. The new indices k and l equal either 0 or 1, depending on the state of the dyad.

Consider now all dyads and this single, dichotomous relation. If we take the original $g \times g$ **X** binary matrix, and replace each entry with the appropriate 2×2 table, we obtain a new contingency table. Since there are $\binom{g}{2}$ dyads, which can be indexed by the $g \times g$ pairs of actors involved, the new contingency table will be of size $g \times g \times 2 \times 2$.

We can consider valued, as well as dichotomous, relations. The restriction to dichotomous relations common to the statistical methods presented in Chapters 13 and 14 is relaxed here. To model all dyads on a single, valued relation simultaneously, we create a four-dimensional contingency table of size $g \times g \times C \times C$. The first two dimensions of this table are indexed by the actors in $\mathcal{N}$. The size of the third and fourth dimensions is C, the number of integer values the measured relation can take on. For dichotomous data that are coded $k, l = 0$ or 1, C equals 2. For relational data coded as $k = 0, 1, 2$ and $l = 0, 1, 2$, C equals 3.

We call the $g \times g \times C \times C$ matrix **Y**, and define its entries as follows:

$$
\begin{aligned}
Y_{ijkl} \quad &= \quad 1 \text{ if the dyad } D_{ij} \text{ takes on the values} \\
&\qquad (X_{ij} = k, \ X_{ji} = l) \\
&= \quad 0 \text{ otherwise.}
\end{aligned}
\tag{15.1}
$$

The **Y**-array is a cross-classification of four variables and thus, its entries have four subscripts: The actors as senders (i), the actors as receivers (j), and the relational variables X_{ij} (indexed by the third subscript, k) and X_{ji} (indexed by the fourth subscript, l). The structure of **Y** is similar to a sociomatrix, where rows represent sending actors and columns represent receiving actors. The entry in the (i, j)th cell of a sociomatrix is x_{ij}. The (i, j)th cell of **Y** is not a single quantity, but rather a $C \times C$ submatrix. In this $C \times C$ submatrix, there will be a single 1 found in the (k, l)th cell. The remaining $C^2 - 1$ elements will be 0. Thus, one can view these submatrices as simply indicator matrices, giving the "state" of each dyad. The **Y**-array has a special symmetry, $Y_{ijkl} = Y_{jilk}$ for all (i, j) and (k, l) pairs, due to the fact that the dyad may be viewed from either the perspective of actor i or the perspective of actor j. The **Y**-array was created so that the models we are about to describe could be fit to discrete-valued relations using standard log linear modeling procedures that exist in the widely available statistical computing packages.

An Example of Y. As an example, refer to the small fabricated social network of second-grade children first introduced in Chapter 3.

Table 15.1. *Sociomatrix for the second-grade children*

Friendship at Beginning of Year

	Allison	Drew	Eliot	Keith	Ross	Sarah
n_1 Allison	-	1	0	0	1	0
n_2 Drew	0	-	1	0	0	1
n_3 Eliot	0	1	-	0	0	0
n_4 Keith	0	0	0	-	1	0
n_5 Ross	0	0	0	0	-	1
n_6 Sarah	0	1	0	0	0	-

In this network, the actors are labeled as follows: n_1 = Allison, n_2 = Drew, n_3 = Eliot, n_4 = Keith, n_5 = Ross, and n_6 = Sarah. To focus on one dyad in particular, we might observe the data for n_1 = Allison and n_5 = Ross on the relation of friendship at the beginning of the school year. The data show that Ross does not name Allison as a child he likes, but Allison nominates Ross. From Allison's perspective, the relational variable sent is $x_{15} = 1$, implying that Allison likes Ross as a friend, and the relation received is $x_{51} = 0$, implying that Allison is not liked as a friend by Ross. From Ross's perspective, the relation sent is $x_{51} = 0$, Ross does not choose Allison, and the relation received is $x_{15} = 1$, Ross is chosen by Allison. The recorded data for actors 1 and 5 in this pair $< n_1, n_5 >$ would be $D_{15} = (x_{15}, x_{51}) = (1, 0)$, so that $y_{1510} = 1$, while $y_{1500} = y_{1501} = y_{1511} = 0$.

We can build the **Y** that corresponds to the network describing friendship choices among these six children at the beginning of a school year. We first present these data as a sociomatrix in Table 15.1.

Remember that it is common statistical practice to use capital, bold-faced letters (such as **Y**) to denote random variables, while actual realizations (such as the **y** given here) have lowercase, boldfaced letters.

In Table 15.2, we present the **y**-array for these data. The size of this array is $6 \times 6 \times 2 \times 2$ because the contingency table is actors ($i = 1, 2, \ldots, 6$) by partners ($j = 1, 2, \ldots, 6$) by strength of choices sent ($x_{ij} = 0, 1$) by strength of choices received ($x_{ji} = 0, 1$), where $C = 2$.

Note the other stated properties of **y** hold in the example: In each 2×2 submatrix, there is one 1 and $(C^2 - 1) = 3$ 0's. The submatrices along the main diagonal are filled entirely with —'s, because no reflexive ties ("self-choices") are measured for this relation. Finally, note that **y** is symmetric as described earlier ($y_{ijkl} = y_{jilk}$).

Table 15.2. **y** *for the second-grade children*

		Allison		Drew		Eliot		Keith		Ross		Sarah	
i	k	$l = x_{ji}$											
		0	1	0	1	0	1	0	1	0	1	0	1
n_1 Allison	$x_{ij} = 0$	-	-	0	0	1	0	1	0	0	0	1	0
	$x_{ij} = 1$	-	-	1	0	0	0	0	0	1	0	0	0
n_2 Drew	$x_{ij} = 0$	0	1	-	-	0	0	1	0	1	0	0	0
	$x_{ij} = 1$	0	0	-	-	0	1	0	0	0	0	0	1
n_3 Eliot	$x_{ij} = 0$	1	0	0	0	-	-	1	0	1	0	1	0
	$x_{ij} = 1$	0	0	0	1	-	-	0	0	0	0	0	0
n_4 Keith	$x_{ij} = 0$	1	0	1	0	1	0	-	-	0	0	1	0
	$x_{ij} = 1$	0	0	0	0	0	0	-	-	1	0	0	0
n_5 Ross	$x_{ij} = 0$	0	1	1	0	1	0	0	1	-	-	0	0
	$x_{ij} = 1$	0	0	0	0	0	0	0	0	-	-	1	0
n_6 Sarah	$x_{ij} = 0$	1	0	0	0	1	0	1	0	0	1	-	-
	$x_{ij} = 1$	0	0	0	1	0	0	0	0	0	0	-	-

The margins of the **y**-array are quite important to the estimation of parameters for various models. These margins are sums over the elements of **y**, and are denoted with subscripts including "+" signs. A + used as a subscript on various y terms indicates that one sums over the subscripts replaced by the +'s. For example, y_{++k+} denotes the sum of the entries of **y** over i, j, and l, for each k. These sums form a one-way table with one cell for each level of k. This margin, $\{y_{++k+}\}$ gives the number of ties on the relation at the various strengths $k = 0, 1, \ldots, C - 1$. It is aggregated over actors (i), their partners (j), and the choices received (l).

For the example of the fabricated network of second-grade children (the **y**-array appears in Table 15.2), the $\{y_{++k+}\}$ margin is:

$$y_{++0+} = 22$$
$$y_{++1+} = 8$$

These numbers tell us that 22 ties have strength $k = 0$ (that is, 22 possible ties are absent), and 8 have strength $k = 1$ (that is, 8 ties are present). Another example is the y_{i+k+} margin, which gives the numbers of ties that are present ($k = 1$) and ties that are absent ($k = 0$) for each actor:

$$y_{1+0+} = 3$$
$$y_{1+1+} = 2$$

$$y_{2+0+} = 3$$
$$y_{2+1+} = 2$$
$$y_{3+0+} = 4$$
$$y_{3+1+} = 1$$
$$y_{4+0+} = 4$$
$$y_{4+1+} = 1$$
$$y_{5+0+} = 4$$
$$y_{5+1+} = 1$$
$$y_{6+0+} = 4$$
$$y_{6+1+} = 1$$

For example, n_3, n_4, n_5, and n_6, all have one tie — these four children choose just one child as a friend.

15.1.2 Modeling the Y-array

We now present statistical models for the analysis of a single, directional relation, whose data we represent by a 4-dimensional **Y**-array. Before presenting the mathematical model statement itself, we will motivate the model and describe its utility by explaining the substantive effects that the parameters of the model are designed to reflect. For a single, directional relation, we focus on effects that represent the "expansiveness" of actors, the "popularity" of their partners, and the "reciprocation" of the ties within the dyads.

Description of the Key Model Parameters. The basic model consists primarily of three sets of parameters: one set of parameters describes the actors' sending behavior, one set describes the actors' receiving behavior, and one set describes the interactions between pairs of actors within a dyad. The first set of parameters are called *expansiveness* effects. In a children's friendship network, these effects reflect the propensity of each child to nominate others as friends. The second set of parameters are called *popularity* effects. In the children's friendship example, popularity reflects the tendency for a child to be nominated by others as a friend.

Patterns of friendship choices among children are described in terms of the expansiveness and popularity of the individual children. While these terms, "expansiveness" and "popularity," might apply equally well to other network data sets, particularly when actors are people and relations measure positive affect or evaluation (for example, the expansiveness and popularity of employees as measured on a communication relation), they apply less well in other applications. For example, if the network is one describing children taking toys from other children, one would not necessarily describe as "popular" a child whose toys are frequently taken. Nevertheless, the terms "expansiveness" and "popularity" have become commonplace in the literature. We use these terms in this context to mean precisely this: parameters representing the propensities for actors to have ties to and from the other actors. Positive values of the parameters increase the probability of having ties.

The final set of parameters are those that reflect the reciprocation, or mutuality, between two actors, independent of the expansiveness or popularity of either actor. This set is not all that different from the measures of reciprocity described in Chapter 13. However, the parameters described here are not limited to dichotomous data, and are probabilistic in nature. Further, these reciprocity effects describe interactive behaviors unique to the dyad, above and beyond the probabilistic tendencies for expansiveness and popularity of the actors who comprise the dyad.

Reciprocity is the extent to which a dyad exhibits mutual, as opposed to asymmetric, ties. With respect to the statistical models discussed here, positive reciprocity parameters increase the likelihood that the dyad is mutual. The model we present for a single relation includes parameters to measure the probabilistic tendencies of all of these substantive effects: expansiveness, popularity, and reciprocity.

We estimate these parameters using log linear modeling techniques. Log linear models are the standard statistical method for studying discrete-valued data organized as counts in multi-way contingency tables (see Agresti 1984, 1990; Bishop, Fienberg, and Holland 1975; Fienberg 1980; Goodman 1979; Haberman 1978, 1979; Kennedy 1983; Wickens 1989). The vast majority of social network data are discrete, and almost always C is small. Social network data that are not discrete can often be categorized without losing important information in the data. For example, we might take a continuous measure of *time spent talking* and code it as *high, medium,* or *low*. Thus, our concentration on network models that can be fit to discrete-valued relations using log linear models seems appropriate.

The Basic Model for Dichotomous Relations. We begin by discussing the modeling of a dichotomous relation. After presenting the models for dichotomous relations, we extend the model to the more general case of discrete relations ($C > 2$).

The basic model, introduced and termed "p_1" by Holland and Leinhardt (1977, 1981), is expressed in four statements. Each of the four statements represents one of the four possible states of any given dyad: the null dyad ($X_{ij} = X_{ji} = 0$, or $Y_{ij00} = 1$), the mutual dyad ($X_{ij} = X_{ji} = 1$, or $Y_{ij11} = 1$), and two cases of asymmetric dyads ($X_{ij} = 1, X_{ji} = 0$, or $Y_{ij10} = 1$, and $X_{ij} = 0, X_{ji} = 1$, or $Y_{ij01} = 1$). We represent the (natural) log of the probabilities of each of these four dyadic states as a function of several parameters, in order to specify p_1:

$$
\begin{aligned}
\log P(Y_{ij00} = 1) &= \lambda_{ij} \\
\log P(Y_{ij10} = 1) &= \lambda_{ij} + \theta + \alpha_i + \beta_j \\
\log P(Y_{ij01} = 1) &= \lambda_{ij} + \theta + \alpha_j + \beta_i \\
\log P(Y_{ij11} = 1) &= \lambda_{ij} + 2\theta + \alpha_i + \alpha_j + \beta_j + \beta_i + (\alpha\beta).
\end{aligned}
\tag{15.2}
$$

This model is log linear. It can be viewed as an analogue of the linear models arising in analysis of variance. Log-linear models begin multiplicatively, but once the log of the response variable is taken, the model is additive, or linear, in the parameters. Thus, p_1 begins with a probability of a dyadic state as a response variable, equated to an expansiveness parameter (actually, e raised to the power of the expansiveness parameter) multiplied by a popularity parameter. When the model and response "probabilities" are transformed to the log scale, p_1 shows an expansiveness parameter *added* to a popularity parameter. The log-linear form of the model is simple to fit and to understand. The log of the probability that n_i has ties to and from n_j becomes an additive function of terms that include the expansiveness of n_i and n_j, the popularity of both actors, *and* the reciprocal effects between the two. When a parameter is positive, it contributes to (or increases) the (log) probability that n_i has a tie to n_j, and if it is negative, the probability decreases.

The $\{\lambda_{ij}\}$ parameters are mathematical necessities included in the model to insure these four probabilities sum to one for each dyad. Thus, these parameters appear in all four statements, regardless of the state of the dyad. The θ parameter is interpreted as an overall choice effect (analogous to a grand mean), reflecting the overall volume of choices sent and received. If one tie is present in the dyad, one θ appears in the statement; when the tie is reciprocated, two θ's appear.

Note that θ does not appear in the model statement when ties are not present, and $(\alpha\beta)$ is present only when the dyad is mutual. No substantive parameters appear in the first statement of the model which represents a null dyad. For asymmetric dyads, the log probabilities depend on parameters reflecting only one of the two possible ties in the dyad: dyads in which actor i chooses actor j without reciprocation (so an α_i but not an α_j is relevant, and a β_j but not a β_i is included) and dyads in which actor j chooses actor i with no reciprocated choice (so the relevant parameters are α_j and β_i, but not α_i or β_j or $(\alpha\beta)$). All the parameters appear together only for mutual dyads (the last statement of the model).

The $(\alpha\beta)$ (sometimes denoted by ρ in the literature), is also called a *mutuality* parameter. When choices on some relation, such as friendship, tend to be mutual in some network, the parameter will be positive and large. In this sense, the parameter is a measure of association between ties sent and received (analogous to a correlation coefficient for continuous data). For some relations like friendship, one would expect reciprocity to be present. However, we might not expect reciprocation for other relations, such as "assigns work to" or "asks for advice." Although a superior might ask a subordinate for advice, we might expect this to occur less frequently than the subordinate asking the superior for advise. With dichotomous data, such patterns on these relations would be modeled with a large negative, $(\alpha\beta)$ parameter indicating that actors who choose others tend not to be those chosen by those others. When reciprocation is not an important factor in a network, the reciprocity parameter would equal 0. We can view $(\alpha\beta)$ as a model-based measure of reciprocity, so that it can be compared and contrasted to the indices for reciprocity discussed in Chapter 13.

Constraints are necessary to estimate the parameters in this model. We use the standard analysis of variance-like constraints in which the parameters and their estimates sum to 0 across their subscripts. We have $\sum_i \alpha_i = 0$, and $\sum_j \beta_j = 0$.

These constraints determine the degrees of freedom (df) associated with each set of parameters. The df associated with any set of parameters is the number of parameters that are independent and free to vary. The expansiveness parameters $\{\alpha_i\}$ have a subscript of i, which ranges from 1 to g, the number of actors. There are g α_i parameters, but they are constrained to sum to 0. Thus, the df for this set of parameters is $(g-1)$ because we can calculate α_g from the other $(g-1)$ parameters. Similarly, the popularity parameters $\{\beta_i\}$ also require $(g-1)$ degrees of freedom. Lastly, the reciprocity parameter $(\alpha\beta)$ requires a single degree of freedom. Estimation of the parameters of this model is discussed in detail by Fienberg and Wasserman (1981a) and Wasserman and Weaver (1985); we also describe how to estimate these parameters shortly.

We now consider the more general form of the p_1 model, which allows us to study single relational variables that are discrete and not necessarily dichotomous (Wasserman and Iacobucci 1986). We assume that the relational variable can take on values $0, 1, \ldots, C - 1$, and that $Y_{ijkl} = 1$, when $X_{ij} = k$ and $X_{ji} = l$. The following model statement generalizes the four statements of p_1:

$$\log P(Y_{ijkl} = 1) = \lambda_{ij} + \theta_k + \theta_l + \alpha_{i(k)} + \alpha_{j(l)}$$
$$+\beta_{j(k)} + \beta_{i(l)} + (\alpha\beta)_{kl}. \tag{15.3}$$

Note the actor-level parameters in this model. The parameter $\alpha_{i(k)}$ measures the tendency for actor i to send ties at strength k, while $\beta_{j(l)}$ measures the tendency for actor j to receive ties at strength l. We will sometimes refer to such parameters as *actor-level*, because of their dependence on the individual actors.

The parameters are subject to the following constraints:

$$\theta_0 = 0$$
$$\alpha_{i(0)} = 0, \text{ for all } i$$
$$\sum_i \alpha_{i(k)} = 0, \text{ for all } k$$
$$\beta_{j(0)} = 0, \text{ for all } j$$
$$\sum_j \beta_{j(l)} = 0, \text{ for all } l$$
$$(\alpha\beta)_{k0} = 0, \text{ for all } k$$
$$(\alpha\beta)_{0l} = 0, \text{ for all } l$$
$$(\alpha\beta)_{kl} = (\alpha\beta)_{lk}$$

In words, we constrain the parameters to equal zero when a choice is made at the lowest strength ($k = 0$ or $l = 0$). This generalization of the p_1 model thus becomes equivalent to p_1 when $C = 2$. In p_1, α_i is defined only when a choice is sent ($k = 1$). Here, $\alpha_{i(k)} = 0$ when $k = 0$, but $\alpha_{i(k)}$ can be non-zero (and usually is) when choices are made at any strength ($k = 1, 2, \ldots, C - 1$). For every $k > 0$, the $\alpha_{i(k)}$ sum to 0 across actors. Because the estimates sum to zero across actors, relative comparisons among actors (at each strength) are easily made. The constraints on the

Table 15.3. *Constraints on the $\{\alpha_{i(k)}\}$ parameters in model (15.3)*

	$k = 0$	$k = 1$	$\cdots$	$k = C - 1$
$i = 1$	0	$\alpha_{1(1)}$	$\cdots$	$\alpha_{1(C-1)}$
$i = 2$	0	$\alpha_{2(1)}$	$\cdots$	$\alpha_{2(C-1)}$
$i = 3$	0	$\alpha_{3(1)}$	$\cdots$	$\alpha_{3(C-1)}$
.	.	.	.	.
.	.	.	.	.
.	.	.	.	.
$i = g$	0	$\alpha_{g(1)}$	$\cdots$	$\alpha_{g(C-1)}$
Total	0	0	$\cdots$	0

α parameters are depicted in Table 15.3. The constraints stated above are consistent with the fact that the $\{\theta_k\}$, $\{\alpha_{i(k)}\}$, $\{\beta_{j(l)}\}$, and $\{(\alpha\beta)_{kl}\}$ require $(C-1)$, $(g-1)(C-1)$, $(g-1)(C-1)$, and $C(C-1)/2$ degrees of freedom, respectively.

As before, the $\{\alpha_{i(k)}\}$ parameters are the expansiveness parameters, and the $\{\beta_{j(l)}\}$ are the popularity parameters. The $\alpha_{i(k)}$ represents the tendency (or the additive effect on the logarithm of the probability) of actor i to send ties at strength k. Similarly, $\beta_{j(l)}$ represents the tendency (or the additive effect on the logarithm of the probability) of actor j to receive ties at strength l. Actor i's expansiveness is reflected by $\alpha_{i(k)}$ and actor i's popularity by $\beta_{i(l)}$. Actor j's expansiveness is reflected by $\alpha_{j(l)}$ and actor j's popularity by $\beta_{j(k)}$.

The $\{(\alpha\beta)_{kl}\}$ parameters are the reciprocity effects. Note that these parameters do not depend on the specific actors being modeled (there is no i or j subscript). The model assumes these effects are constant across all pairs of actors. The reciprocity parameters are symmetric in their indices, $(\alpha\beta)_{kl} = (\alpha\beta)_{lk}$, so there is $C(C - 1)/2$ degrees of freedom.

The model for dichotomous data contains just a single reciprocity parameter (because $C(C-1)/2 = 2(2-1)/2 = 1$), as specified by p_1. The single $(\alpha\beta)$ parameter for modeling dichotomous relations is analogous to a measure of association. When $C > 2$, the $C \times C$ matrix of $(\alpha\beta)_{kl}$ parameters is analogous to an entire matrix of such measures. For example, $(\alpha\beta)_{15} = (\alpha\beta)_{51}$ measures the positive or negative association between ties sent at the weak strength of $k = 1$ and ties received at the much greater strength of $l = 5$.

It is important to note that when ties are valued, the α and β estimates (derived from (15.3), not (15.2)) depend on the number of possible values. For every level $k = 1,\ldots,(C - 1)$, there are g alpha's and g beta's. For a

Table 15.4. p_1 *parameter estimates for the second-graders*

Node label	Actor	$\hat{\alpha}_i$	$\hat{\beta}_i$
n_1	Allison	1.414	$-\infty$
n_2	Drew	0.817	0.867
n_3	Eliot	−0.474	−1.223
n_4	Keith	0.197	$-\infty$
n_5	Ross	−0.977	0.178
n_6	Sarah	−0.977	0.178

$$(\hat{\alpha\beta}) = 3.077$$
$$\hat{\theta} = -1.437$$

fixed k, these parameters measure how likely it is that an actor has ties (sent or received) at that particular strength.

An Example — Fitting p_1 to the Fabricated Network. To illustrate, we fit the model to the fabricated network of second-grade children and study its parameters. The parameter estimates resulting from fitting model (15.2) to the **y**-array based on the friendship choices among the 6 children are presented in Table 15.4.

Note that these parameters are on a logarithmic scale. Thus, if an α increases by 1 unit, say, from 1 to 2, the logarithm of the probability of a choice increases by 1 unit. Or, the actual probability increases by $\exp(1) = 2.718$.

The alpha estimates tell the following story: Actor 1 (Allison) has the largest expansiveness parameter. She was far more likely to have friends (at the beginning of the school year) than were any of the other children. Actor 2 (Drew) was next most likely, and actors 5 and 6 (Ross and Sarah) were least likely.

The beta estimates quantify the tendencies with which each of these children is chosen as a friend by the other children in the network. And these estimates are quite different from the alphas; specifically, two of the parameter estimates are infinite. We will discuss this situation technically later in the chapter, but for now, we note that Allison and Keith are not chosen by any other children as friends; hence, they have 0 indegrees. This forces the beta parameters to be $-\infty$ for these two children.

Whereas child 1 (Allison) was most likely to choose others, she was least likely to be chosen by others, since her $\hat{\beta}$ is the smallest (in fact, she was not chosen so her $\hat{\beta}$ is infinite). Child 4 (Keith) is similar. The other children (n_2, n_5, n_6, and n_3) can be chosen as friends, with Drew, Ross, and Sarah exhibiting positive tendencies.

The reciprocity parameter gives additional information about this relation. With dichotomous data, the analogy between the ($\alpha\beta$) parameter and a measure of association is especially easy to see. Here, the estimate is positive and large, indicating tendencies for positive association or mutual friendships — if child i nominates another j as a friend, that friend j in turn tends to reciprocate the friendship. Similarly, if n_i does not nominate n_j, n_j also tends to not nominate n_i. If this parameter estimate were negative, it would indicate a relation for which there are many non-reciprocated friendships (or asymmetric dyads).

15.1.3 Parameters

We now discuss theoretical issues and the practical means for calculating the parameter estimates of model (15.3). We also describe how to test the statistical significance of each set of parameters to see which effects in the network are statistically large.

Parameter Estimation — Theory and Practice. In this section, we discuss several issues regarding the estimation of the parameters in model (15.3). We begin with some theoretical issues (such as maximum likelihood estimation and the likelihood-ratio goodness-of-fit statistic), and then explain how to analyze network data using these methods (including significance testing of the parameters). Finally, we describe the statistical analyses of several social network data sets.

⊗*Distributions and Maximum Likelihood Estimation.* In this section, we discuss the statistical theory underlying model (15.3), including the form of the likelihood function, the statistical function from which the maximum likelihood parameter estimates are derived. Alternative estimation techniques are described later in this chapter.

Holland and Leinhardt (1981) describe model (15.3) as belonging to an *exponential family of distributions*, which means parameters can be estimated via the *maximum likelihood* estimation procedure. With maximum likelihood, estimated parameters are those that give the best fit to the data. By "fitting the data the best," we mean that the best-fitting parameters maximize the joint probability distribution of the data. It is as if many estimates of each parameter, say $\hat{\beta}_{1(1)} = 0.05$, or 0.12, or 0.73, were tried out in the model, and the value that "fits" the data the best is chosen as the "best" estimate. In practice, several values are not actually tried out; the optimal estimates for parameters are usually computed numerically through various exact (or, if necessary, approximate) mathematical procedures. These procedures are used in statistical computing packages to maximize the likelihood function (or really, the logarithm of this function, which is easier computationally).

For p_1, the goal of maximum likelihood estimation is, "Find the best (maximum likelihood) estimates of all the parameters in the model (the λ's, θ's, α's, β's, and $(\alpha\beta)$'s) that could have produced the given dyadic interaction data, represented by our y-array." The likelihood function is the joint probability distribution of the data. Maximum likelihood estimation strives to find parameters that maximize this function. The log likelihood function explicitly tells which functions of the data — which "margins" of the y-array — are needed to estimate the parameters. These margins must be specified when using a statistical computing package. We will discuss these margins at length shortly.

The log likelihood function for model (15.3) assumes independence of dyads (an assumption we discuss at the end of this chapter) and is as follows (Wasserman and Iacobucci 1986):

$$\sum_{i<j} \lambda_{ij} + \frac{1}{2}\sum_k \theta_k y_{++k+} + \frac{1}{2}\sum_l \theta_l y_{+++l}$$

$$+\frac{1}{2}\sum_i \sum_k \alpha_{i(k)} y_{i+k+} + \frac{1}{2}\sum_j \sum_l \alpha_{j(l)} y_{+j+l} \quad \cdot$$

$$+\frac{1}{2}\sum_j \sum_k \beta_{j(k)} y_{+jk+} + \frac{1}{2}\sum_i \sum_l \beta_{i(l)} y_{i++l}$$

$$+\sum_k \sum_l (\alpha\beta)_{kl} \sum_{i<j} y_{ijkl}. \tag{15.4}$$

The terms in the log likelihood function that depend on the data **y** have subscripts which include "+"s.

The margins of **y** which are needed to estimate the parameters are those arising in the log likelihood function (15.4). These margins are *sufficient statistics* for the parameters in the model. These are the only summaries of the data (**y**) that are needed to maximize the likelihood and obtain the parameter estimates. We later describe these margins at length.

Maximum likelihood estimation not only yields estimates of the parameters of a model (such as p_1), but also estimates of the random variables being modeled. In this instance, we are modeling the elements of the **Y**-array; and we will denote the maximum likelihood estimates of these quantities using "$\wedge$" 's: $\{\hat{Y}_{ijkl}\}$. These maximum likelihood estimates, which are often referred to as *fitted values*, usually do not have a simple equation to calculate them. They are calculated iteratively by the algorithm chosen to solve the likelihood equations arising from the maximum likelihood problem.

Goodness-of-Fit Statistic. Once we have fit model (15.3) to the data and obtained maximum likelihood estimates of the parameters, we need to be able to evaluate how well the model fits and which of the parameters are statistically large (that is, statistically different from 0). The statistic used in maximum likelihood estimation for these purposes is usually the *likelihood-ratio statistic*. For the log-linear models discussed here, this statistic is G^2, which, for our application, is:

$$G^2 = 2 \sum_{i<j} \sum_{k,l} y_{ijkl} \log (y_{ijkl}/\hat{y}_{ijkl}). \qquad (15.5)$$

This statistic is well-known in categorical data analysis; further. The likelihood-ratio statistic is a function of the observed data, y_{ijkl}, and the calculated model predictions (fitted values), $\hat{y}_{ijkl}$, which are standard output from log-linear model computing packages. These fitted values are the predictions for the network data arising from the model p_1. The parameter estimates can also be combined, as stated by the model, to give us the fitted values (the $\hat{y}$'s). The statistic is calculated as the sum over all cells in a contingency table of quantities that compare the observed values to the fitted values.

The fitted values, $\hat{y}_{ijkl}$, for the friendship relation for the fabricated network of second-graders are given in Table 15.5.

The goodness-of-fit statistic for our statistical models for social network data (in 15.5) has a similar interpretation. The only difference is that the sum is not taken over all cells of the **y**-array, but over all dyads ($i < j$), since the basic unit in these models is the dyad. We want to compare each dyad to its fitted value only once, so we sum over one-half of the **y**-array (remember that **y** is symmetric).

The statistic G^2, defined in equation (15.5), has the property that as we add parameters to a model and make the model more complicated, it will stay the same or go down, indicating better fit, or closer agreement of the y's and $\hat{y}$'s. This property is especially important when we compare two hierarchically nested models. For example, a model with parameters λ, θ, α, and β is hierarchically nested in a model with parameters $\lambda, \theta, \alpha, \beta$, and $(\alpha\beta)$. The models are identical except that one model contains one more set of parameters (the $\{(\alpha\beta)_{kl}\}$). The "larger" model has all the parameters of the first, plus an additional set. All of the models we consider here will be *hierarchical* — if one model can be obtained from a second model by setting some of the parameters to zero, then we say that the first model is hierarchically nested within the second.

In general, we can test hypotheses about the model parameters by comparing the test statistics for hierarchically nested models. The difference between the G^2 statistics for two hierarchically nested models is approximately asymptotically distributed as a χ^2 random variable. Thus, this difference can be compared to tabled values of χ^2 (with certain degrees of freedom) to establish whether the model with more parameters fits significantly better than the simpler model. If it does, the extra parameters are statistically important. We can compare the fit of model (15.3) to the fit of a model that is similar except that it contains no α parameters, for example. The difference between the two G^2's would be tested on $(g-1)(C-1)$ degrees of freedom in order to evaluate the statistical significance of the $\{\alpha_{i(k)}\}$.

UCINET IV can fit p_1. One can also use a standard statistical computing package, such as *GLIM, SPSS^X*, or *SYSTAT*, to fit the model and to calculate the fitted values, $\{\hat{y}_{ijkl}\}$, which are used to compute the goodness-of-fit statistic G^2. It is important to note that the G^2 and degrees of freedom obtained directly from such standard packages are incorrect, and need modifications that we describe shortly. The fitted values and the residuals (the differences between the observed table entries and the fitted table entries $\{y_{ijkl} - \hat{y}_{ijkl}\}$) can also be diagnostic of cells that are fit particularly well or particularly badly. Holland and Leinhardt (1981) discuss how to use the residuals from fitting p_1 to network data. Particularly poorly fit cells or dyads may be of special concern to a researcher. One should investigate possible reasons for the large discrepancies. When models do not fit data well, one means of improving the fit is to add parameters to the model. For example, some more complicated models have been investigated by Wasserman and Galaskiewicz (1984), Wasserman and Anderson (1987), and Wang and Wong (1987), who add terms that depend on the blocks or positions into which actors can be classified (more on this in Chapter 16).

Table 15.5. y fitted values for p_1 fit to the second-grade children

n_j

n_i	x_{ij}	Allison		Drew		Eliot		Keith		Ross		Sarah	
	x_{ji}:	0	1	0	1	0	1	0	1	0	1	0	1
Allison	0	—	—	0.30	0.00	0.78	0.00	1.00	0.00	0.46	0.00	0.46	0.00
	1	—	—	0.70	0.00	0.22	0.00	0.00	0.00	0.54	0.00	0.54	0.00
Drew	0	0.30	0.70	—	—	0.37	0.13	0.59	0.41	0.21	0.04	0.21	0.04
	1	0.00	0.00	—	—	0.06	0.45	0.00	0.00	0.13	0.62	0.13	0.62
Eliot	0	0.78	0.22	0.37	0.06	—	—	0.92	0.08	0.77	0.02	0.77	0.02
	1	0.00	0.00	0.13	0.45	—	—	0.00	0.00	0.14	0.07	0.14	0.08
Keith	0	1.00	0.00	0.59	0.00	0.92	0.00	—	—	0.74	0.00	0.74	0.00
	1	0.00	0.00	0.41	0.00	0.08	0.00	—	—	0.26	0.00	0.26	0.00
Ross	0	0.46	0.54	0.21	0.13	0.77	0.14	0.74	0.26	—	—	0.68	0.07
	1	0.00	0.00	0.04	0.62	0.02	0.07	0.00	0.00	—	—	0.07	0.17
Sarah	0	0.46	0.54	0.21	0.13	0.77	0.14	0.74	0.26	0.68	0.07	—	—
	1	0.00	0.00	0.04	0.62	0.02	0.08	0.00	0.00	0.07	0.17	—	—

Practical Guide to Fitting These Models to Data. Once the data are arranged into a **y**-array, model (15.3) can be fit (and parameters estimated) using the log-linear modeling procedures that are contained in any of the major statistical computing packages.

Comments on parameter estimation and model fitting using several of the major packages, including $SPSS^X$, *BMDP, GLIM*, and others can be found in the literature (Fienberg and Wasserman 1981b; Wasserman and Weaver 1985; Wasserman and Iacobucci 1986).

Fitting the Models. Maximum likelihood estimation of the parameters of log linear models for categorical data is discussed at length in Appendix II of Fienberg (1980). Specifically, each set of parameters has associated with it sufficient statistics, which are margins of the data array being modeled. The maximum likelihood equations, which must be solved to obtain the maximum likelihood estimates of the expected values of the cell counts (or the "fitted" values), all have the form: observed margin = fitted margin. Thus, the appropriate model parameters will be estimated, and the fitted values obtained, when we constrain the fitted margins to be equal to the observed margins. Philosophically, this is like saying, if forty men and sixty women responded to a sample survey, any modeling of the data that includes the variable gender must still reproduce the given figures of 40 and 60. Or, referring to network data, if we include β's in our model, and if actor 1 is chosen by four of the eight actors, then fitted probabilities that n_1 is chosen must sum to $(4/8) = 0.50$. This equating is the critical computation that will produce maximum likelihood estimates of cell expected values, and parameters.

Our models for single relational network data can be fit by following the theory discussed above; specifically, one focuses on the model parameters, and their sufficient statistics, which are margins of the **Y**-array. All six of the two-dimensional margins of the four-dimensional **Y**-array are the sufficient statistics for the parameters in (15.3). The same is true for p_1, since it is equivalent to the basic model when $C = 2$.

The four variables that define **Y** comprise the four dimensions of the contingency table to be modeled. We have been referring to these variables and their subscripts as:

(i) Sending actor (i)
(ii) Receiving actor (j)
(iii) Strength of choice made ($k = X_{ij}$)
(iv) Strength of choice received ($l = X_{ji}$)

We label these variables as $1, 2, 3, 4$, respectively. In order to fit model (15.3), we fit the following log-linear model to a **Y**-array:

$$[12][13][24][23][14][34]. \qquad (15.6)$$

The numbers in brackets in (15.6) are the margins of **Y**, which are sufficient statistics for the parameters in the basic model. This notation is common for log-linear models, and was first introduced by Fienberg (1980), based on the notation in Bishop, Fienberg, and Holland (1975). We will call it *Fienberg* notation.

A collection of variable numbers in brackets implies that we have included the parameter associated with the sufficient statistics given by the variable numbers in a model. Because the log-linear models considered here are hierarchical, all lower-order terms (for example, main effects) are also necessarily fit. For example, [12] is the interaction between variables 1 and 2 (that index initiating and receiving actors) and corresponds to the margin $\{Y_{ij++}\}$. This margin includes the 1-dimensional margins for these two variables ($\{Y_{i+++}\}$ and $\{Y_{+j++}\}$).

The correspondence between the margins and the parameter sufficient statistics is as follows. The [12] margin is fit in order to include the $\{\lambda_{ij}\}$ parameters in the model. Because the λ parameters must be included in all our models in order to constrain the probabilities properly, the margin [12] must always be included.

Margins [13] and [24] are sufficient statistics for the $\{\alpha_{i(k)}\}$ parameters. There is only one set of $(g-1)(C-1)$ $\{\alpha_{i(k)}\}$ expansiveness parameters, but there are two sets of margins, [13] and [24]. These margins are actually equal, due to the symmetry of the **Y**-array, and thus do not produce superfluous parameters. *Both* margins [13] and [24] must be included in any model for which we desire estimates of the alpha's.

Similarly, margins [23] and [14] are sufficient statistics for the $\{\beta_{j(l)}\}$ parameters. The margin [23] is equal to the margin [14], because of the symmetry of the **Y**-array. Both must be included in any model for which we desire estimates of the beta's.

The final margin, [34], is the sufficient statistic for the reciprocity parameters, $\{(\alpha\beta)_{kl}\}$. The only remaining parameters given in model (15.3) are the elements of the set of $\{\theta\}$'s. The sufficient statistics for these parameters are the margins [3] and [4], but since our models are hierarchical, these are automatically "fit" whenever higher-order margins [13] and [24], or [23] and [14], or [34], are fit.

Infinite Parameters. One problem in this modeling and computation process can arise when an actor has an indegree or outdegree equal to either 0 or $(g - 1)$. In the first instance, the actor neither sends nor receives any ties; while in the second, the actor either has ties to or from every other actor. We discuss each of these situations in turn. When a relation is valued, the problem also arises when all ties sent (or received) by a particular actor have exactly the same strength.

Let us focus just on dichotomous relations. Suppose first that an actor has an indegree equal to 0. Statistically, this actor has no tendency to receive ties. Thus, the fitted probabilities that this actor receives ties must all be 0's. If an actor has an outdegree equal to 0, this actor has no tendency to send ties. Thus, the fitted probabilities that this actor makes choices must all be 0's.

If a fitted probability is to be 0, then the logarithm of this probability is $-\infty$. And to make this logarithm $-\infty$, the appropriate parameter must also be $-\infty$. A 0 row sum in the sociomatrix forces the associated alpha for this actor to be $-\infty$. A zero column sum in the sociomatrix forces the associated beta for this actor to be $-\infty$. For example, two children in the fabricated second-grader network received no friendship nominations; hence, there are two betas fitted with p_1 equal to $-\infty$.

Now suppose that an actor has an indegree equal to $(g-1)$. Statistically, this actor is certain to receive ties from all other actors. Thus, the fitted probabilities that this actor receives any ties must all be 1's. If an actor has an outdegree equal to $(g - 1)$, this actor is certain to send ties to all other actors. Thus, the fitted probabilities that this actor sends ties must all be 1's.

If a fitted probability is to be unity, then the logarithm of this probability is ∞. And to make this logarithm infinity, the appropriate parameter must also be ∞. A row sum in the sociomatrix equal to $(g - 1)$ forces the associated alpha for this actor to be ∞. A column sum equal to $(g - 1)$ forces the associated beta for this actor to be ∞.

Lastly, we note that these infinite parameters are not counted when tallying up degrees of freedom. For the second-graders, we have a full set of alphas, and hence 5 degrees of freedom for these parameters, but only estimate four betas. Hence, there is only 3 degrees of freedom for the betas. Further, the infinite parameters are not considered when centering the finite parameters to sum to 0. Note once again from the second-graders that the four finite estimated betas sum to 0.

Model Comparisons and Statistical Tests for Parameters. We have presented (15.3) with three sets of meaningful parameters — representing effects of expansiveness, popularity, and reciprocity. We can conduct hypothesis tests to determine whether the actors demonstrate any or all of these effects on a relation. We can postulate and subsequently fit alternative, simpler models that might be able to reproduce the network data just as well, or almost as well, as the more complicated model (15.3). Comparing the fit of (15.3) to simpler versions of the model allows us to determine whether each set of parameters is statistically different from 0.

We use likelihood-ratio hypothesis tests to study each of the sets of parameters. The test statistic for these hypotheses compares the goodness-of-fit statistic of model (15.3) to the goodness-of-fit statistics of the simpler models. These statistics are all likelihood-ratio statistics, where the $\{\hat{y}_{ijkl}\}$ fitted values are computed from different competing models.

To be more concrete, there are seven models, shown below, that are simpler than (15.3), derived by dropping one or more sets of the parameters $\{\alpha_{i(k)}\}$, $\{\beta_{j(l)}\}$, or $\{(\alpha\beta)_{kl}\}$ from the model. A model is more *parsimonious* than (15.3) if it contains fewer parameters. Model (15.3) is listed again, and then the seven simpler models follow:

$$
\begin{aligned}
(15.3)\ \log P(Y_{ijkl} = 1) &= \lambda_{ij} + \theta_k + \theta_l + \alpha_{i(k)} + \alpha_{j(l)} \\
&\quad + \beta_{j(k)} + \beta_{i(l)} + (\alpha\beta)_{kl} \\
a)\ \log P(Y_{ijkl} = 1) &= \lambda_{ij} + \theta_k + \theta_l + \beta_{j(k)} + \beta_{i(l)} \\
&\quad + (\alpha\beta)_{kl} \\
b)\ \log P(Y_{ijkl} = 1) &= \lambda_{ij} + \theta_k + \theta_l + \alpha_{i(k)} + \alpha_{j(l)} \\
&\quad + (\alpha\beta)_{kl} \\
c)\ \log P(Y_{ijkl} = 1) &= \lambda_{ij} + \theta_k + \theta_l + \alpha_{i(k)} + \alpha_{j(l)} \\
&\quad + \beta_{j(k)} + \beta_{i(l)} \\
d)\ \log P(Y_{ijkl} = 1) &= \lambda_{ij} + \theta_k + \theta_l + \alpha_{i(k)} + \alpha_{j(l)} \\
e)\ \log P(Y_{ijkl} = 1) &= \lambda_{ij} + \theta_k + \theta_l + \beta_{j(k)} + \beta_{i(l)} \\
f)\ \log P(Y_{ijkl} = 1) &= \lambda_{ij} + \theta_k + \theta_l + (\alpha\beta)_{kl} \\
g)\ \log P(Y_{ijkl} = 1) &= \lambda_{ij} + \theta_k + \theta_l
\end{aligned}
\tag{15.7}
$$

In Table 15.6 we list these models, (15.3) and (15.7a) — (15.7g), along with the list of margins that specify each model. Recall from the definition of p_1 that if the relation under study is dichotomous, these parameters

Table 15.6. p_1 *parameters, models, and associated margins*

Model	Parameters included in the model	Margins
15.3	$\{\lambda_{ij}\}$, $\{\theta_k\}$, $\{\alpha_{i(k)}\}$, $\{\beta_{j(l)}\}$, $\{(\alpha\beta)_{kl}\}$	[12][13][24][23][14][34]
15.7a	$\{\lambda_{ij}\}$, $\{\theta_k\}$, $\{\beta_{j(l)}\}$, $\{(\alpha\beta)_{kl}\}$	[12][23][14][34]
15.7b	$\{\lambda_{ij}\}$, $\{\theta_k\}$, $\{\alpha_{i(k)}\}$, $\{(\alpha\beta)_{kl}\}$	[12][13][24][34]
15.7c	$\{\lambda_{ij}\}$, $\{\theta_k\}$, $\{\alpha_{i(k)}\}$, $\{\beta_{j(l)}\}$	[12][13][24][23][14]
15.7d	$\{\lambda_{ij}\}$, $\{\theta_k\}$, $\{\alpha_{i(k)}\}$	[12][13][24]
15.7e	$\{\lambda_{ij}\}$, $\{\theta_k\}$, $\{\beta_{j(l)}\}$	[12][23][14]
15.7f	$\{\lambda_{ij}\}$, $\{\theta_k\}$, $\{(\alpha\beta)_{kl}\}$	[12][34]
15.7g	$\{\lambda_{ij}\}$, $\{\theta_k\}$	[12][3][4]

appear in the models only when choices are made (that is, for example, $\alpha_i(0) \equiv 0$ and $\alpha_i(1) \equiv \alpha_i$).

Consider one of these models in more detail. In model (15.7b), there are no β's. This model assumes that all β's equal 0; thus, there are no differential popularity effects among the actors. By definition, we would expect this model to fit single relational social network data reasonably well only when the popularity of the actors is constant. If it were true that all β's were 0, we would expect (15.7b) to "fit" the observed dyadic interactions just as well as the full model (15.3). To test the null hypothesis,

$$H_0 : \beta_{j(l)} = 0 \text{ for all } j \text{ and } l,$$

we compare the goodness-of-fit statistics for the two models (15.7b) and (15.3).

Similarly, a comparison of the fit statistics for model (15.7a) or (15.7c) to (15.3) would test the null hypotheses

$$H_0 : \alpha_{i(k)} = 0 \text{ for all } i \text{ and } k,$$

or

$$H_0 : (\alpha\beta)_{kl} = 0 \text{ for all } k \text{ and } l, \text{ respectively.}$$

Model (15.7b) is hierarchically nested in model (15.3), so that the first model is a special case of the second. Thus, the fit statistic for (15.7b) will be equal to or larger than the fit statistic for (15.3). The comparison of G^2 statistics indicates whether the parameters are statistically different from zero. The difference between the two G^2's is a *conditional likelihood-ratio test statistic*, testing a null hypothesis that the parameters are indeed equal to 0. We statistically condition on the more complicated model and test to see whether we can simplify it by "dropping" terms.

In practice, to test these conditional hypotheses regarding sets of parameters, we take the G^2 for model (15.3), and subtract it from the G^2 for the model that does *not* contain the parameters being tested. For example, to test whether the β's are 0, we calculate two G^2's, one for the full model, and one for (15.7b). We get a difference score (G^2 for (15.7b) minus the G^2 for model (15.3)), a ΔG^2 that quantifies whether the additional parameters are significantly different from 0. This new statistic, ΔG^2, is approximately asymptotically distributed as a χ^2 random variable, with a certain number of degrees of freedom. Just as the statistic ΔG^2 is equal to the difference in G^2 for the two models, the degrees of freedom, Δdf, is equal to the difference in degrees of freedom for the two models. The model that contains more parameters is the alternative hypothesis model (H_A), and the model with fewer terms is the null hypothesis model (H_0). The Δdf is equal to the number of independent parameters being tested.

For example, when evaluating the null hypothesis, $H_0 : (\alpha\beta)_{kl} = 0$ (for all k, l), we reject H_0 if ΔG^2 is greater than the upper percentage point of the χ^2 distribution with $C(C-1)/2$ degrees of freedom. If ΔG^2 is statistically large compared to the χ^2 distribution on $C(C-1)/2$ degrees of freedom, we would conclude that the $(\alpha\beta)_{kl}$ parameters are statistically large and should be included in any model truly descriptive of the given network.

We should note that one reason the "asymptotic" distributions of G^2 or ΔG^2 are only approximations to χ^2 is due to the difficulty in achieving the "asymptotic" property itself. As the number of actors in a set of actors, g, increases, so do the number of $\alpha_{i(k)}$ and $\beta_{j(l)}$ parameters to be estimated $((g-1)(C-1))$, so even at the asymptote (g tending toward infinity), the number of parameters in p_1 and model (15.3) also gets infinitely large. We comment on these problems a bit later in this chapter.

The tests that can be conducted for parameters that model a single relation are listed in Table 15.7. The first test listed in Table 15.7 compares the fit of model (15.7a) with the fit of model (15.3). Model (15.7a) has no α's, so in conducting this comparison, we are testing the null hypothesis, $H_0 : \alpha_{i(k)} = 0$ for all i,k. The degrees of freedom for this test is $(g-1)(C-1)$. If ΔG^2 is not large, we cannot reject the null hypothesis, which means the actors are statistically equivalent with respect to their expansiveness (sensible perhaps in networks in which the number of ties is restricted by design to a constant value). The second test is the counterpart for testing the null hypothesis, $H_0 : \beta_{j(l)} = 0$ (for all partners j and all strengths l).

Table 15.7. *Tests of significance for parameters in model (15.3)*

Test	ΔG^2	Δdf	Null hypothesis
1	$15.7a - 15.3$	$(g-1)(C-1)$	$H_0 : \alpha_{i(k)} = 0$ for all i, k
2	$15.7b - 15.3$	$(g-1)(C-1)$	$H_0 : \beta_{j(k)} = 0$ for all j, k
3	$15.7c - 15.3$	$C(C-1)/2$	$H_0 : (\alpha\beta)_{kl} = 0$ for all k, l

The second test in Table 15.7 compares the fits of models (15.7b) and (15.3). It is a test of the null hypothesis, H_0 : all $\beta_{j(l)} = 0$. If ΔG^2 is large, we would conclude that the actors exhibit differential popularity, thus, the $\{\beta_{j(l)}\}$ parameters need to be included in any model that would adequately represent the data. If the statistic is not large, we would conclude the data may be described adequately without including effects for popularity.

The alpha, beta, and reciprocity parameters are independent sets of parameters in the sense that for any particular set of actors with measurements on a single relation, any of the three effects may be statistically large. Knowing the characteristics of the $\hat{\alpha}$'s for some network data set, for example, does not inform us about the characteristics of the $\hat{\beta}$'s, or the reciprocation parameter(s) present in that same network.

Examples. We have fit model (15.3) and its relatives, models (15.7a), (15.7b), and (15.7c), to a variety of data sets. We first demonstrate the model fits for the fabricated network of second-grade children, and then discuss the analysis of Krackhardt's friendship and advice relations at length. The second-graders and Krackhardt's network both consist of dichotomous relations, so we fit p_1 directly. Freeman's *EIES* communications network, which we also would like to model, has valued relations; thus, we must fit the more general model to it.

Fabricated Network of Second-Graders. Table 15.8 gives the goodness-of-fit statistics for each of the four models applied to the dichotomous friendship relation for the second-graders.

The information in this table indicates which parameters are statistically important for these fabricated data. We see that the expansiveness parameters are not very important (ΔG^2 is quite small). Knowing this, we would not bother to study the individual actor α_i parameter estimates in an attempt to distinguish among the children. On the other hand, the popularity parameters (the β's) are of interest in this network because

Table 15.8. *Goodness-of-fit statistics for the fabricated network*
Second-graders — friendship at the beginning of the year

Model	Null hypothesis	G^2	ΔG^2	Δdf
15.3		20.630		
15.7a	$H_0 : \alpha_{i(k)} = 0$ for all i and k	23.072	2.442	3
15.7b	$H_0 : \beta_{j(l)} = 0$ for all j and l	31.956	11.326	5
15.7c	$H_0 : (\alpha\beta) = 0$	22.564	1.934	1

Table 15.9. *Goodness-of-fit statistics for Krackhardt's network*
Krackhardt's high-tech managers — advice relation

Model	Null hypothesis	G^2	ΔG^2	Δdf
15.3		322.564		
15.7a	$H_0 : \alpha_{i(k)} = 0$ for all i and k	506.778	184.214	20
15.7b	$H_0 : \beta_{j(l)} = 0$ for all j and l	440.471	117.907	20
15.7c	$H_0 : (\alpha\beta) = 0$	339.632	17.068	1

Krackhardt's high-tech managers — friendship relation

Model	Null hypothesis	G^2	ΔG^2	Δdf
15.3		288.303		
15.7a	$H_0 : \alpha_{i(k)} = 0$ for all i and k	421.965	133.662	20
15.7b	$H_0 : \beta_{j(l)} = 0$ for all j and l	337.068	48.765	20
15.7c	$H_0 : (\alpha\beta) = 0$	312.455	24.152	1

$\Delta G^2 = 31.956 - 20.630 = 11.326$, which is large. We reported and discussed these parameter estimates earlier in the chapter (Table 15.4). Also noteworthy here is the fact that reciprocity does not seem to be a strong force for this friendship relation.

Krackhardt's Network. Now look at the analyses of Krackhardt's data, shown in Table 15.9. We analyzed both the advice relation and the friendship relation (separately). All three sets of parameters appear to be large when modeling either of the relations.

The α and β estimates are listed in Table 15.10. The expansiveness parameters indicate that, for the advice relation, actors 3, 5, and 18 are likely to give advice, while actors 2, 6, and 12 are unlikely to. Note also that actor 15 gives advice to all other actors. The popularity parameters for this relation indicate that actor 2 is very likely to receive advice, while actors 9 and 15 are very unlikely to receive advice. For friendship, the

Table 15.10. *Parameter estimates for Krackhardt's high-tech managers*

Actor	Advice $\hat{\alpha}_i$	$\hat{\beta}_i$	Friendship $\hat{\alpha}_i$	$\hat{\beta}_i$
n_1	−0.98	1.75	−0.37	1.40
n_2	−2.64	4.54	−1.46	2.36
n_3	2.63	−2.09	−1.36	0.66
n_4	1.40	−0.63	0.41	0.03
n_5	2.63	−2.09	0.60	0.34
n_6	−3.75	1.10	0.86	−1.84
n_7	−0.28	1.56	$-\infty$	0.04
n_8	−0.01	0.42	−2.22	0.83
n_9	2.02	−2.44	$-\infty$	1.39
n_{10}	1.95	−0.44	1.29	−3.17
n_{11}	−2.20	1.25	2.39	−0.41
n_{12}	−2.47	−0.08	−0.76	1.53
n_{13}	−0.13	−1.79	−0.58	−2.30
n_{14}	−1.58	0.79	−1.36	0.66
n_{15}	$+\infty$	−2.91	1.16	−0.74
n_{16}	−1.38	0.07	−1.18	0.19
n_{17}	−1.03	0.33	4.59	−0.96
n_{18}	2.55	1.48	−2.04	0.38
n_{19}	1.42	−2.27	1.33	−0.36
n_{20}	1.40	−0.63	−0.99	0.38
n_{21}	0.46	2.07	−0.33	0.33

expansiveness parameters indicate that actor 17 has many other actors as friends, while actors 7 and 9 (who make no choices) do not. Actor 2 is a relatively popular friend, while actor 10 is not. Note the dual role played by actor 2. This actor gives very little advice, but is a friend to many other actors.

The reciprocity parameters for the advice $((\hat{\alpha\beta})=2.233)$ and friendship $((\hat{\alpha\beta})=2.937)$ relations are both positive and large (relative to the actor-level parameters), indicating substantial tendencies toward mutuality.

The α and β estimates for the advice relation can also be studied by using attribute information on the tenure of each actor (the number of years of service in the organization). One way to use such information is to correlate the parameter estimates with this attribute variable.

The $\hat{\alpha}_i$'s are negatively correlated with tenure while the $\hat{\beta}_j$'s are positively correlated, indicating that more experienced workers seek advice less frequently than others and are the source of advice more frequently than others. Tenure has a very small correlation with the $\hat{\alpha}_i$'s and the $\hat{\beta}_j$'s for the friendship relation.

We note that there are other ways to incorporate attribute variables directly into our statistical models. We discuss another approach in the next section.

Other Analyses. In Table 15.8, we presented test statistics for the second-graders that told us (in general) whether the α, β, and $(\alpha\beta)$ parameters were statistically large. We could stop our statistical analyses at this point. For example, for the second-graders, we would summarize by saying that the network structure indicates strong differential popularity effects among the actors and that there is a small tendency for reciprocated friendship ties. Alternatively, we might proceed to study these results in more detail, by conducting other analyses to learn, for example, exactly which actors are significantly more or less popular than which others. To do so, we can use the methods reported in Wasserman and Weaver (1985), based on statistical theory for log-linear models for categorical data (see Bishop, Fienberg, and Holland 1975). These methods involve contrasts, as in the analysis of variance.

For example, the magnitude of each individual $\beta_{j(l)}$ parameter may be studied in turn, by calculating

$$t = (\hat{\beta}_{j(l)} - \beta^*)/S.E.(\hat{\beta}_{j(l)}),$$

where β^* is an a priori constant, specified in the null hypothesis (often $\beta^* = 0$), and $S.E.(\hat{\beta}_{j(l)})$ is the standard error of the parameter estimate, a value obtained as a function of information reported by statistical computing packages.

15.1.4 $\otimes$*Is p_1 a Random Directed Graph Distribution?*

Given our discussion of random directed graph distributions in Chapter 13, one important question is how p_1 compares to these distributions. Specifically, is p_1 a conditional uniform distribution for random graphs?

The answer to this question is yes, with a bit of explanation needed. First, note that p_1 is an exponential family of distributions, with minimal sufficient statistics consisting of the indegrees, outdegrees, and the number of mutual dyads. Thus, any two random digraphs with equal values of these statistics have identical fitted values from p_1. Thus, if we condition on specific values of $\{X_{i+}\}$, $\{X_{+j}\}$, and M, all random digraphs with these values have exactly the same probability of occurring. Thus, p_1 is identical to the random digraph distribution $U|\{X_{i+}\}, \{X_{+j}\}, M$, as discussed by Snijders (1991b).

But, p_1 is also a Bernoulli digraph distribution (see Karoński 1982; Palmer 1985; Bollobás 1985; Frank 1985, 1989; and, of course, Chapter 13). Such distributions focus on a set of p_{ij} probabilities, specifiying the probability that i chooses j, for all pairs of actors i and j. Since digraphs are representations of dichotomous relations, one can define θ_{ij} as the logit for p_{ij}:

$$\theta_{ij} = \log \left(\frac{p_{ij}}{1 - p_{ij}} \right).$$

If we assume that all ties are statistically independent (as with a general Bernoulli distribution), then the likelihood function can be written down.

Further, one can postulate an additive model for the logits, quite similar to p_1. The main difference between such a logit model and p_1 is that the off-diagonal elements of the sociomatrix, x_{ij} and x_{ji}, are not assumed by p_1 to be statistically independent. Indeed, the basic modeling unit of p_1 is the dyad, not the individual tie or arc. Thus, one can view p_1 as a Bernoulli dyad distribution, rather than a Bernoulli arc distribution, where all dyads, not ties or arcs, are assumed to be independent.

15.1.5 Summary

We have presented a class of models designed to study how ties from a single relation vary across actors. The class is comprehensive, and allows one to posit substantively meaningful parameters, all of which can be estimated and studied via significance tests.

But, there are a number of statistical problems with this class. These problems are caused by the lack of an asymptotic statistical theory — the number of parameters does not remain constant as the number of actors in the set increases. Even so, we note two facts. First, as g increases, the number of $(\alpha\beta)_{kl}$ parameters to be estimated ($C(C-1)/2$) remains constant. Thus, the test of reciprocity is not affected by the main statistical problem, and we can be confident that the asymptotic properties hold for this test. Secondly, we note that these problems are non-existent when incorporating attributes of actors into the models (which we describe in detail shortly). For now we note that subsets of actors can be formed on the basis of their attributes, such as gender (male and female). Then as g increases, the number of subsets remains fixed. Thus, if parameters depend on subset memberships, rather than the individual actors themselves, we can be confident that asymptotic distributions hold. We note that these uncertainties regarding the asymptotic distribution of G^2 force us to evaluate hypothesis tests more tentatively. For example, we do not attach p-values to these comparisons in general, but can do so when the modeling includes attribute variables.

Fortunately, one does not need an asymptotic statistical theory for the significance tests described here. There is an alternative approach. One can use permutation tests to compare matrices of fitted values, as discussed by Hubert and Baker (1978). Specifically, one can determine how close an observed data matrix is to a predicted, fitted matrix, by looking at a large number of permutations of the original data matrix, and comparing each to the "target." Details on such tests, as applied to social network data, can be found in Baker and Hubert (1981) and Krackhardt (1987b). We apply such technology to blockmodels in Chapter 16.

As a brief aside, we mention some researchers who have investigated models more complicated than (15.3), such as stochastic blockmodels (Wasserman and Anderson 1987; Wang and Wong 1987). Fienberg and Wasserman (1981a) also extended p_1 to allow for "differential reciprocity"; the $\{(\alpha\beta)_{kl}\}$ parameters are replaced with $\{(\alpha\beta)_{i(kl)}\}$ parameters, allowing the rates of reciprocation to depend on the sending or receiving actors. (The model that adds these parameters includes the margins: [12][134][234].) Further generalizations of this idea can be found in Wasserman and Galaskiewicz (1984).

15.2 Attribute Variables

We now wish to analyze data on the attributes for the g actors contained in $\mathcal{N}$ in conjunction with the relation measured between actors. We thus build models that use both network composition and network structure. We first discuss why information about the characteristics of the individual actors is helpful in modeling the relational information. We then modify our **Y**-array into a new contingency table (the **W**-array) that incorporates such attribute information. Once again, we use the small fabricated network of second-graders to illustrate. We will then modify the statistical model (15.3) designed for a single relational variable to allow for the simultaneous analysis of one or more actor attribute variables. Lastly, we offer more examples.

15.2.1 Introduction

Studying **Y** using statistical models for dyadic interactions is one way to summarize the information contained in a single relational variable measured on the $\binom{g}{2}$ pairs of actors from the set $\mathcal{N}$. In some applications, we might be interested in studying the patterns of dyadic interactions within and between subsets of persons who share similar characteristics. For example, we might be interested in understanding how a classroom of thirty children interacts. We would create **Y** based on a relation among the thirty actors. However, even simple theories might predict that boys and girls differ in the way they interact with others. For example, we might at least suspect that in a classroom of kindergarteners, children would be most likely to nominate as friends children of their same gender. We might be less interested in modeling individual differences in the interactions of thirty children than in understanding how gender affects the childrens' interactions. Thus, we might be led by theoretical concerns to model subset differences — the interactions of these thirty children in conjunction with the attribute of gender. We would form two subsets, boys and girls, and study the between- and within-subset interactions.

Attribute variables can be of interest in many different social networks. For example, network researchers might use variables such as gender, age, and socioeconomic status. Researchers studying dyadic interactions in married couples might suspect that communication patterns depend on attributes such as gender of the speaker, or whether the couple was in marital distress (Gottman 1979a). Researchers interested in modeling interorganizational behavior might wish to include the size of the organization or its industry as predictive attribute variables (Galaskiewicz 1979; Galaskiewicz and Marsden 1978; Wasserman and Galaskiewicz 1984).

Before we proceed with the methodology, it is important to note that the attribute variables, and hence the categorization of actors into subsets, must be chosen independently of the relation under study. Subsets must not be formed using the relational information; otherwise, the error rates of the tests discussed here will be affected. The use of attribute variables described here is a priori; a posteriori analyses will be described in Chapter 16.

For the small network of second-graders nominating friends, we use the attribute of age to distinguish between the 7- and 8-year-olds. We might hypothesize that children prefer to play with others of the same age, so 7-year-olds would choose other 7-year-olds as friends, 8-year-olds would choose 8-year-olds, but few 7-year-olds would have 8-year-olds as friends. Perhaps a competing hypothesis would be that children gravitate toward older children, so that the 7-year-olds nominate other 7-year-old children as well as 8-year-old children, whereas the 8-year-old children only nominate each other.

In our analysis of our other examples, we use the following attribute information: for Krackhardt's management network, there are two attribute variables of interest to us: age of actors, and seniority or tenure of actors in the organization. We categorized the employees into four subsets on the basis of their age and tenure with the organization:

(i) Those with 10 or fewer years of tenure and younger than 40 years of age

(ii) Those with 11+ years of tenure and younger than 40

(iii) Those with 10 or fewer years of tenure and older than 40 years of age

(iv) Those with 11+ years of tenure and older than 40

15.2.2 *The* W-*array*

Attribute variables were first introduced into models based on Holland and Leinhardt's p_1 by Fienberg and Wasserman (1981a). Individuals are placed into subsets using relevant actor characteristics, and actors within a subset are assumed to behave similarly (at least with regard to the measured relations being modeled). Specifically, p_1 (or model (15.3)) is postulated, and it is assumed that all actors within a subset have equal parameters; for example, if we partition actors based on gender, then every male actor shares a common expansiveness parameter α and a common popularity parameter β (as would the females). We give a formal mathematical definition of this assumption below.

Stochastic Equivalence. This assumption of comparable behavior of actors within subsets (with respect to some statistical model) has been viewed as a generalization of structural equivalence. Wasserman and Weaver (1985) termed this assumption *stochastic equivalence*, and Wasserman and Anderson (1987) developed this idea in more detail. Holland, Laskey, and Leinhardt (1983) and Wang and Wong (1987) proposed alternative versions of stochastic actor equivalence, all using generalizations of p_1 for their statistical models. We will discuss them in more detail in Chapter 16, along with the idea of a *stochastic blockmodel,* which follows naturally from the notion of stochastic equivalence.

Based on the assumption of equal parameters within subsets, our basic model can be greatly simplified. Rather than postulating and estimating separate expansiveness and popularity parameters for each individual actor, a single expansiveness parameter and a single popularity parameter is assumed for each subset. This simplification, enabled by the assumption of stochastic equivalence, allows us to estimate far fewer parameters.

Definition. A set of attribute variables is used to classify each of the g actors into one of S subsets. The size of S depends on how many attribute variables are used, and how many levels the individual attributes take on. With just a single, dichotomous attribute (such as gender) we need only $S = 2$ subsets. In other social network data sets, we may have more attribute variables with considerably more levels. For example, gender ("males" and "females") crossed with race ("Whites," "Blacks," and "Asians") would result in $S = 6$ subsets. We denote the subset to which the sending actor (i) belongs by $s(i)$, and the subset in which the receiving actor (j) belongs by $s(j)$. Thus, we have a mapping function $s(\bullet)$, where this function is defined a priori (based on attribute variables) and not on the basis of relational information.

We use subscripts for parameters which index the actors, and superscripts for subsets of actors. Thus, we will replace $\alpha_{i(k)}$ and $\beta_{j(l)}$ in model (15.3) by $\alpha_k^{[s(i)]}$ and $\beta_l^{[s(j)]}$, respectively, where the superscript indexes the subset modeled by that parameter.

The assumption of stochastic equivalence may be stated more precisely with this new notation. We assume that:

$$\alpha_{i(k)} = \alpha_k^{[s(i)]}$$

for all $n_i \in$ subset $s(i)$, and

$$\beta_{j(l)} = \beta_l^{[s(j)]}$$

for all $n_j \in$ subset $s(j)$.

We modify **Y** so that all actors with similar characteristics are aggregated into a single subset. To accomplish this, we aggregate over the elements in **Y**, collapsing over actors with identical attributes. In doing so, we obtain **W**, with elements $\{W_{s(i)s(j)kl}\}$, defined formally as

$$W_{s(i)s(j)kl} = \sum_{i \in s(i)} \sum_{j \in s(j)} Y_{ijkl}. \tag{15.8}$$

That is, we simply sum the relational data, coded as the elements of **Y**, over pairs (n_i, n_j) where actor i is a member of subset $s(i)$ and actor j is a member of subset $s(j)$.

The **Y**-array is of size $g \times g \times C \times C$, but the **W**-array can be much smaller. In general, the **W**-array (the aggregated **Y**-array), is of size $S \times S \times C \times C$, where S, the number of subsets, is usually much smaller than g. For example, in Krackhardt's network, twenty-one managers' friendship ($g=21$), aggregating on the basis of age (categorized into those younger than 40, and those older than 40) would give us only two subsets ($S = 2$). Thus, **W** for this example is $2 \times 2 \times C \times C$. The number of levels of the relational variable, C (the different strengths the relation can take on), remains the same for both **Y** and **W**.

An Example W-array. The **W**-array is symmetric in the same way that **Y** is symmetric, $W_{s(i)s(j)kl} = W_{s(j)s(i)lk}$. Unlike **Y**, however, the entries in **W** are usually not simply 0's and 1's, since they are sums of the 0's and 1's contained in the elements of **Y**. The entries in **W** are counts of the frequencies of the different dyadic states. In Table 15.11, we present the **w**-array obtained by collapsing over the **y**-array for the six second-graders, using the attribute of age. The children in the first subset are 7 years old (Eliot, Keith, and Sarah), and the children in the second subset are 8 years old (Allison, Drew, and Ross). This partitioning gives us two subsets of actors: $\{n_3, n_4, n_6\}$ and $\{n_1, n_2, n_5\}$. Note how the array is symmetric, and that entries in the table are integer counts, some of which are greater than 1. For example, consider the two values of "5" in this array. The lower-left entry of 5, cell (2,1,0,0), indicates there were five dyads with the following characteristics: The actor (i) was 8 years old and thus belonged in the second subset ($s(i) = 2$), the chosen partner (j) was 7 years old, and so belonged in the first subset ($s(j) = 1$), and neither actor chose the other — a null dyad. Due to the symmetry, these five null dyads also appear in cell (1,2,0,0), where the actor is a 7-year-old ($s(i) = 1$) and the partner is an 8 year-old ($s(j) = 2$).

Table 15.12 contains some of the **w**-arrays for Krackhardt's network, for both of the relations, using one or two attribute variables (tenure in the organization and age of actor). The first tenure subset consists of the managers with ten or fewer years of service, and the second subset consists of the managers with more than ten years of service. We also dichotomize age into two subsets: those actors forty years and younger, and those actors older than forty years. We will model these data sets shortly, but for now simply note that these **w**-arrays are of

Table 15.11. *The **W**-array for the second-graders using friendship and age (the first subset consists of the 7-year-old children, Eliot, Keith, and Sarah, and the second subset consists of the 8-year-old children, Allison, Drew, and Ross.)*

| | | $s(j) = 1$: 7-year-olds | | $s(j) = 2$: 8-year-olds | |
		$l: x_{ji} = 0$	$x_{ji} = 1$	$x_{ji} = 0$	$x_{ji} = 1$
$s(i) = 1$	$k: x_{ij} = 0$	6	0	5	1
	$x_{ij} = 1$	0	0	1	2
$s(i) = 2$	$x_{ij} = 0$	5	1	2	2
	$x_{ij} = 1$	1	2	2	0

more manageable sizes ($2 \times 2 \times 2 \times 2$ if we use one attribute variable or $4 \times 4 \times 2 \times 2$ if we use two attribute variables) than their corresponding y-arrays ($21 \times 21 \times 2 \times 2$ for both of the relations).

15.2.3 The Basic Model with Attribute Variables

The model we fit to this new contingency table (the **W**-array defined in equation (15.8)) is a special case of the basic model (15.3), subject to the constraints placed on the parameters (defined above), which arise through the use of the actor attribute variables and the assumption of stochastic equivalence. This version of model (15.3) follows:

$$\log P(Y_{ijkl} = 1) = \lambda_{ij} + \theta_k + \theta_l + \alpha_k^{[s(i)]} + \alpha_l^{[s(j)]}$$
$$+ \beta_k^{[s(j)]} + \beta_l^{[s(i)]} + (\alpha\beta)_{kl}, \qquad (15.9)$$

where n_i is a member of subset $s(i)$ and n_j is a member of subset $s(j)$ (for $s(i)$ and $s(j)$ between 1 and S). Note that the model is still postulated for dyads, so that the basic modeling unit remains unchanged. The use of attribute variables is taken into account in the parameter structure on the right-hand side of the equation above, where the α_i's are replaced with $\alpha^{[s(i)]}$'s, and so on. If each actor belonged to a unique subset of size 1, we would have $g = S$, and this model would be equivalent to model (15.3).

The parameter structure in (15.9) is simpler than in the basic model (15.3). There are fewer parameters to estimate. When fitting the model (15.3) to **Y**, we must estimate:

- $(g - 1)(C - 1)$ α's
- $(g - 1)(C - 1)$ β's
- $C(C - 1)/2$ $(\alpha\beta)$'s

Table 15.12. *The **W**-arrays for Krackhardt's high-tech managers, using tenure, and age and tenure*

Advice		$s(j) = 1$		$s(j) = 2$	
		$l: x_{ji} = 0$	$x_{ji} = 1$	$x_{ji} = 0$	$x_{ji} = 1$
$s(i) = 1$	$k: x_{ij} = 0$	32	20	39	9
(Less tenure)	$x_{ij} = 1$	20	38	48	14
$s(i) = 2$	$x_{ij} = 0$	39	48	20	23
(More tenure)	$x_{ij} = 1$	9	14	23	24

Friendship		$s(j) = 1$		$s(j) = 2$	
		$l: x_{ji} = 0$	$x_{ji} = 1$	$x_{ji} = 0$	$x_{ji} = 1$
$s(i) = 1$	$k: x_{ij} = 0$	74	12	68	15
(Less tenure)	$x_{ij} = 1$	12	12	14	13
$s(i) = 2$	$x_{ij} = 0$	68	14	52	15
(More tenure)	$x_{ij} = 1$	15	13	15	8

Advice	$s(j) = 1$		$s(j) = 2$		$s(j) = 3$		$s(j) = 4$	
$s(i) = 1$	18	11	7	5	12	7	18	1
(Less tenure, Younger)	11	32	3	3	15	11	23	3
$s(i) = 2$	7	3	0	1	6	1	3	0
(Less tenure, Older)	5	3	1	0	3	0	7	0
$s(i) = 3$	12	15	6	3	2	5	6	0
(More tenure, Younger)	7	11	1	0	5	8	14	5
$s(i) = 4$	18	23	3	7	6	14	6	4
(More tenure, Older)	1	1	0	0	0	5	4	6

Friendship	$s(j) = 1$		$s(j) = 2$		$s(j) = 3$		$s(j) = 4$	
$s(i) = 1$	44	8	14	1	25	7	27	5
(Less tenure, Younger)	8	12	3	0	7	6	7	6
$s(i) = 2$	14	3	2	0	9	1	7	2
(Less tenure, Older)	1	0	0	0	0	0	0	1
$s(i) = 3$	25	7	9	0	12	3	14	3
(More tenure, Younger)	7	6	1	0	3	2	5	3
$s(i) = 4$	27	7	7	0	14	5	12	4
(More tenure, Older)	5	6	2	1	3	3	4	0

When using attribute variables, and postulating S subsets of actors, we fit model (15.9) to $\mathbf{W}$ and estimate only $(S - 1)(C - 1)$ each of α's and β's, but still $C(C - 1)/2$ $(\alpha\beta)$'s, for all the combinations of a pair of relational tie levels. In network data sets where the number of actors (g) is large, this simplification can mean the estimation of many fewer parameters. For example, in Krackhardt's network with twenty-one actors and a simple dichotomous relation, when we model individual differences among actors, we would have $(21 - 1)(2 - 1) = 20$ α's, 20 β's, 1 θ, and 1 $(\alpha\beta)$, for a total of 42 independent parameters. If we aggregate the actors into four age and tenure subsets $(S = 4)$, and model the resulting $\mathbf{W}$-array, we estimate only $(4 - 1)(2 - 1) = 3$ α's and 3 β's, 1 $(\alpha\beta)$, and 1 θ, for a total of just 8 parameters.

This simplification is due to our stochastic equivalence assumption. All actors in a subset relate to all other actors statistically similarly and are also related to by all others statistically similarly. Statistical similarity implies that the probabilities of such interactions are constant. This similarity in the behavior of social interactions is assumed on theoretical grounds, using the attribute variables at hand.

The importance of this special case of our basic model to social network analysis is that it allows researchers to go beyond using only relational variables to understand network structure. With these models, information about the actors themselves, such as their age, gender, size, status, and so on, can also be used to help understand the network structure. One can study and test the association between the attribute variables and the relational variables by comparing model (15.3) fit to $\mathbf{y}$ with model (15.9) fit to $\mathbf{w}$, as we will discuss and demonstrate shortly.

Parameter Estimation and Testing. Parameter estimation and testing proceeds just as in fitting model (15.3) to $\mathbf{y}$. The correspondence between the margins and the parameters discussed earlier still applies. So, for example, to include the $\alpha_{i(k)}$'s in a model for $\mathbf{y}$, we fit the margins [13] and [24]. To include the $\alpha_k^{[s(i)]}$'s in a model for $\mathbf{w}$, we still fit the margins [13] and [24]. The difference is simply that in the first, the margins [13] and [24] are fit to the $\hat{\mathbf{y}}$-array (and are $g \times C$ in size) and in the second, the margins [13] and [24] are fit to the $\hat{\mathbf{w}}$-array (and are $S \times C$ in size). The margins themselves are quite different, since the sums are over different arrays. In Table 15.13, we list some special cases of model (15.9), alternatively dropping the α, β, and $(\alpha\beta)$ parameters, and give the rules for testing hypotheses regarding the various model parameters.

Table 15.13. *Parameters, models, and associated margins for models for attribute variables*

Model	Parameters included in the model		Margins
15.9a	$\{\lambda_{ij}\}, \{\theta_k\},$	$\{\alpha_k^{[s(i)]}\}, \{\beta_l^{[s(j)]}\}, \{(\alpha\beta)_{kl}\}$	[12][13][24][23][14][34]
15.9b	$\{\lambda_{ij}\}, \{\theta_k\},$	$\{\beta_l^{[s(j)]}\}, \{(\alpha\beta)_{kl}\}$	[12][23][14][34]
15.9c	$\{\lambda_{ij}\}, \{\theta_k\},$	$\{\alpha_k^{[s(i)]}\}, \{(\alpha\beta)_{kl}\}$	[12][13][24][34]
15.9d	$\{\lambda_{ij}\}, \{\theta_k\},$	$\{\alpha_k^{[s(i)]}\}, \{\beta_l^{[s(j)]}\}$	[12][13][24][23][14]

Test	ΔG^2	Δdf	Null hypothesis
1	15.9b − 15.9a	$(S-1)(C-1)$	$H_0 : \alpha_k^{[s(i)]} = 0$ for all i,k
2	15.9c − 15.9a	$(S-1)(C-1)$	$H_0 : \beta_k^{[s(j)]} = 0$ for all j,k
3	15.9d − 15.9a	$C(C-1)/2$	$H_0 : (\alpha\beta)_{kl} = 0$ for all k,l

The model fitting strategy for (15.9) is parallel to that for model (15.3), from the general logic to the specific margins fit and tests made. The arrays being modeled are usually quite a bit smaller, so the computations are easier to handle.

There is one important computational difference which concerns the likelihood-ratio statistics. When fitting models to a $\hat{\mathbf{y}}$-array using statistical packages designed for standard data, rather than just for social network data, one needs to divide the likelihood-ratio statistic G^2 obtained as output from the statistical package by 2 (to adjust for the fact that these arrays count each dyad twice). However, when fitting the models given in Table 15.13 to a $\hat{\mathbf{w}}$-array, the G^2's on the printouts must be adjusted in a slightly more complicated way. The reason for this adjustment is that while the "subset" models are fit to the aggregated array (defined in (15.8)), the model itself uses the dyad as its basic unit (in (15.9)). The adjustment that is needed takes the parameter estimates for a model with attribute variables (which are based on $S(S-1)/2$ pairs of subsets), and calculates fitted values for all $g(g-1)/2$ pairs of actors, then compares these fitted values to the relational data contained in the original sociomatrix.

The *FORTRAN* program *GSQUARE* (Iacobucci and Wasserman 1990) takes as input the fitted values for **w** as calculated by the standard log-linear model statistical packages, and the observed **y**-array. The program then calculates the correct, adjusted G^2.

Other than the adjustments that must be made to get the correct test statistics, the models fit to **y** and to **w** are analogous. The important distinction revolves around what is most interesting to the researcher. That is, a researcher wishing to model dyadic interactions at the individual actor level would analyze **y**. The researcher who has attribute variables, and is less interested in individual differences than in subset differences, would analyze **w**.

Testing the Statistical Importance of Attributes. Suppose that two (or more) attribute variables are available, along with the single, relational variable. We now discuss how one can use the above methodology to test directly that each attribute variable is statistically important.

If an attribute variable is statistically important, then actors within subsets defined by the categories of the attribute variable really do have equal parameter values. Thus, the partitioning of the actors based on the attribute variable has not only theoretical meaning but also statistical importance. With respect to model fits, the subset model will fit as well as an equivalent model not based on subsets.

To test the statistical importance of an attribute variable, one must fit two models: one that uses the attribute variable under study, and one that does not. These two models must otherwise be identical. Due to the hierarchical nature of the models described here, the model with the attribute variable includes the model without the attribute variable as a special case. Because these models are nested within each other (the model with the attribute variable being a null hypothesis, and the model without, an alternative hypothesis), standard likelihood-ratio tests can be used. One must fit these models to different **w**-arrays, and obtain the G^2's, whose difference becomes the likelihood-ratio statistic for the test of the importance of the attribute.

The details of this strategy are as follows. Use all the attribute variables to categorize the actors in S subsets. For example, if the network data set measured for $g = 30$ actors contains two attributes (gender — Males and Females — and race — White, Black, Asian, Other), then there are eight subsets that can be formed from the cross-classification of these two: White Males, White Females, Black Males, ... , Other Females. Thus, $S = 8$, and the $30 \times 30 \times C \times C$ **y**-array can be compressed through aggregation (summing over all actors in the eight subsets) into a $8 \times 8 \times C \times C$ **w**-array. Such aggregation assumes stochastic equivalence, so that actors differ only at the level of subsets.

One now fits models to this **w**-array, and finds the one that fits best. We will call this **w**-array the "big **w**," since one next forms another **w**, of smaller size. The best-fitting model found here is the alternative hypothesis model for the test of the importance of the attribute variable. The G^2 for this model should be recorded.

One now has to fit a model which does not use the attribute variable in question. One should form a second, smaller w-array, using all the *other* attribute variables (that is, exclude the one under study). For the above example, this means there will be a new **w**: a w-array based just on race (of size $4 \times 4 \times C \times C$). One then fits the "best-fitting" model found for the big **w** matrix to the smaller **w**, and obtains the G^2.

Then, to test that the attribute variable under study has no effect on the relational variable, we assume that the parameters from the model using all the attributes do not depend on this first attribute variable. If so, then the difference between the G^2 for the big **w** and the G^2 for the smaller **w**, which does not use the attribute variable, is a conditional likelihood-ratio statistic for the test of this hypothesis. We will illustrate this methodology shortly, using Krackhardt's high-tech managers, on which we have measurements on two attribute variables (age and tenure).

Some Difficulties Solved by Fitting Subset Models. We should mention some technical difficulties that can arise when fitting models to y-arrays. The first problem is practical and centers on the size of **y**. The second problem is theoretical, concerning the likelihood-ratio test statistics discussed in this chapter.

The practical issue is that the y-arrays, which have $g^2 C^2$ cells, can get quite large and become difficult to work with computationally. For Krackhardt's data set, the y-array is of size $21 \times 21 \times 2 \times 2$, with 1724 cells. Consider one of the attribute variables, age, categorized into just 2 categories (young and old). The **w**-array for these data is smaller, of size $2 \times 2 \times 2 \times 2$, or just 16 cells. It is wise to keep the data matrices small, since some computer packages for fitting log-linear models rely on the inversion of matrices, which can tax moderately sized computers.

The theoretical problem in fitting models to **y** is also related to the size of the array. This problem also arose in this chapter when we discussed the asymptotic distributions of G^2 and ΔG^2, which are very approximately χ^2. For the standard asymptotic statistical theory to apply here, g must increase. However, as g increases, the dimensions of the y-array grow. For example, adding one actor turns a $g \times g \times C \times C$ array into a table of size $(g+1) \times (g+1) \times C \times C$. This implies that the number of parameters and the size of the table both grow as g does, which violates one of the basic assumptions of standard asymptotic statistical theory for the tests in conjunction with model (15.3).

Tests made on typical categorical data analyzed with log-linear models are appropriate for large numbers of observations classified into the cells of a contingency table which is fixed in size. Larger numbers of observations in a network data set can only be obtained by increasing g. Unfortunately, doing so enlarges the **Y**-array. As we add actors to $\mathcal{N}$, and rows and columns to **Y**, we must also estimate more parameters. This problem was recognized by Holland and Leinhardt (1981), Fienberg and Wasserman (1981a, 1981b), Haberman (1981), and Reitz (1982).

Fortunately, this problem does not arise when modeling **W**. The size of this contingency table depends not on g, but on S (a function of the attribute variables) and C (a function of the relational variable), and hence is fixed. Adding actors to the network increases the counts in the cells of this array, but not the size of the table or the number of parameters. Of course, the choice of attributes and the magnitude of S should be made independently of the number of actors.

For this reason, researchers have cautioned networkers about the assumption that G^2 is asymptotically distributed as a χ^2 random variable when evaluating the fit of models to **Y**-arrays (see Fienberg and Wasserman 1981a; Haberman 1981; Wong and Yu 1989). In addition, these contingency tables are usually quite large and sparse (that is, they contain many 0's). We suggest that conclusions about model fit based on G^2 statistics for **Y**-arrays be stated cautiously. Statistical evaluations of model comparisons, based on ΔG^2, conditional likelihood-ratio statistics, are more sound because such statistics compare the fits of different models applied to the same data.

We emphasize that these problems (both the computational and statistical ones) do not arise when evaluating the fit of models applied to **W** (via G^2 statistics), or the comparison of fits to evaluate the statistical significance of parameters from models fit to **W** (via ΔG^2 statistics). Consequently, we recommend the use of actor attribute variables whenever possible.

15.2.4 Examples: Using Attribute Variables

Just as we fit model (15.3) and its variants to test for the statistical significance of the sets of $\{\alpha\}$'s, $\{\beta\}$'s, and $\{(\alpha\beta)\}$'s to the y-arrays under study, we have also fit model (15.9) and its variants to the corresponding w-arrays. In Table 15.14, we list the goodness-of-fit statistics for the fabricated network of second-graders, and indicate which sets of parameters are statistically important.

Table 15.14. *Goodness-of-fit statistics for the fabricated network, using attribute variables*

Second-graders — friendship at the beginning of the school year and age

Model	Null hypothesis	G^2	ΔG^2	Δdf	p-value
15.9		32.024			
15.9b	$H_0 : \alpha_k^{[s(i)]} = 0$ for all i and k	32.639	0.615	1	Not small
15.9c	$H_0 : \beta_k^{[s(j)]} = 0$ for all j and k	32.639	0.615	1	Not small
15.9d	$H_0 : (\alpha\beta)_{kl} = 0$ for all k and l	33.044	1.020	1	Not small

For the fabricated network of second-graders, we have aggregated over the ages of the children (two categories), so that $S = 2$. We can see from the table that none of the parameters ($\{\alpha\}, \{\beta\}, \{(\alpha\beta)\}$) are statistically large. Note that there is just one parameter in each set, because there are just two levels for the relational variable and just two subsets (thus, $S = C = 2$, so $(S - 1)(C - 1) = 1$ and $C(C - 1)/2 = 1$). Prior to aggregating over age, the popularity parameters were statistically important (see Table 15.8). Based on these analyses, we would choose a model that has just a θ parameter. There appears to be no difference between the two age groups with respect to expansiveness, popularity, or reciprocity.

We can study the hypothesis of no age effect further by comparing the G^2 obtained by fitting p_1 to **y** ($G^2 = 20.630$) to the G^2 obtained by fitting the analogous model to **w** ($G^2 = 32.024$). The first test statistic can be found in Table 15.8, and the second, in Table 15.14. The conditional likelihood-ratio statistic $\Delta G^2 = 11.39$ for this test, with $\Delta df = 8$, is not large. For this test, the null hypothesis is that (15.9) fits **w** as well as (15.3) fits **y**. Given the relatively small ΔG^2, we cannot reject this hypothesis; the simpler model described the data as well as the model with more parameters. This result means that the assumption of stochastic equivalence is reasonable — all 7-year-olds share common propensities for sending and receiving, as do all 8-year-olds. Rather than describe each individual child's behavior, we can describe the average behavior of a 7-year-old child and that of an 8-year-old without losing descriptive power.

Note that we can use the same logic to test the importance of multiple actor attribute variables. For example, if this included the attribute variable gender, we could test for the impact of gender and age (and

Table 15.15. *Parameter estimates for children's friendship and age*

Subset	$\hat{\alpha}$	$\hat{\beta}$
1 (7-year-olds)	−0.353	−0.353
2 (8-year-olds)	0.353	0.353

logically, their interaction) by comparing conditional likelihood-ratio statistics (ΔG^2's) as we have described in the previous section.

Because none of the α, β, or ($\alpha\beta$) parameters are statistically important here, we would not usually report and interpret the estimates. However, to illustrate how much simpler the parameter structure is (compared to modeling all actors via **y**), we list the parameter estimates in Table 15.15. The alpha and beta estimates suggest the 8-year-old children ($s(i) = 2$) are both more likely to nominate others ($\alpha_{k=1}^{[s(i)=2]}$ is positive) and to be nominated by others ($\beta_{k=1}^{[s(j)=2]}$ is positive) than are the 7-year-old children ($s(i) = 1$). The reciprocity parameter is positive, indicating some tendency for mutual ties. In conclusion, we note that this small network displays differential popularity tendencies, implying that the actors are chosen with differing rates. Aggregating the actors based on their age is important here — the children are not distinguishable once we put all the 7-year-olds and all the 8-year-olds together.

We now look at an analysis of Krackhardt's network of high-tech managers (shown in Tables 15.16 and 15.17). Here, we look at both the advice and friendship relations, but use the tenure and age attribute variables. We do three sets of models: one set using tenure, one using age, and one using both tenure *and* age.

First, we look at advice. Table 15.16 gives the goodness-of-fit statistics for four models for each of the three attribute variable collections, all fit to the advice relation. Actors differ substantially on advice seeking and receiving when classified by tenure, and when classified by age and tenure. However, actors differ only on advice *seeking* when classified by age; that is, younger actors are just as likely to receive advice as older actors. From these models, there also appears little tendency for the advice to be reciprocated. So, age and tenure interact with the advice relation, but in rather different ways.

Next, we look at friendship. Table 15.17 gives the goodness-of-fit statistics for four models for each of the three attribute variable collections, all fit to the friendship relation. The friendship relation is quite different (when studied with these models) from advice. From Table 15.17, one

Table 15.16. *Goodness-of-fit statistics for Krackhardt's managers and the advice relation, with attribute variables*

Krackhardt's high-tech managers, the advice relation and tenure

Model	Null hypothesis	G^2	ΔG^2	Δdf	p-value
15.9		547.121			
15.9*b*	$H_0 : \alpha_k^{[s(i)]} = 0$ for all i and k	564.804	17.683	1	$p < 0.001$
15.9*c*	$H_0 : \beta_k^{[s(j)]} = 0$ for all j and k	561.792	14.671	1	$p < 0.001$
15.9*d*	$H_0 : (\alpha\beta)_{kl} = 0$ for all k and l	549.809	2.688	1	$p = 0.101$

Krackhardt's high-tech managers, the advice relation and age

Model	Null hypothesis	G^2	ΔG^2	Δdf	p-value
15.9		547.265			
15.9*b*	$H_0 : \alpha_k^{[s(i)]} = 0$ for all i and k	576.188	28.92	1	$p < 0.001$
15.9*c*	$H_0 : \beta_k^{[s(j)]} = 0$ for all j and k	549.436	2.171	1	$p = 0.141$
15.9*d*	$H_0 : (\alpha\beta)_{kl} = 0$ for all k and l	548.465	1.200	1	Not small

Krackhardt's high-tech managers, the advice relation, and age and tenure

Model	Null hypothesis	G^2	ΔG^2	Δdf	p-value
15.9		508.541			
15.9*b*	$H_0 : \alpha_k^{[s(i)]} = 0$ for all i and k	553.820	45.279	3	$p < 0.001$
15.9*c*	$H_0 : \beta_k^{[s(j)]} = 0$ for all j and k	537.624	29.083	3	$p < 0.001$
15.9*d*	$H_0 : (\alpha\beta)_{kl} = 0$ for all k and l	513.838	5.297	1	$p = 0.0214$

can see that regardless of the attribute variable(s) used to classify the actors, the receipt of friendship ties is constant from subset to subset. But there is a difference in friendship nominations between the age groups. The younger and older actors have different numbers of friends. Their friendship expansiveness differs, as can be seen from the parameter estimates from model (15.9), fit to the friendship relation, using just age as the actor attribute variable. One finds that: $\hat{\alpha}^{[younger]} = 0.134$ and $\hat{\alpha}^{[older]} = -0.376$. Thus, younger actors are more likely to nominate others as friends, while older actors are considerably less likely to do so. Friendship nominations seem quite age-specific. Further, unlike the advice relation, there are large tendencies for these friendship ties to be reciprocated (in fact, $(\hat{\alpha\beta}) = 1.360$).

15.3 Related Models for Further Aggregated Data

We now describe several related models. The first class of models is similar to the models just described for dyadic data with subset-level

Table 15.17. *Goodness-of-fit statistics for Krackhardt's managers and the friendship relation, with attribute variables*

Krackhardt's high-tech managers, the friendship relation and tenure

Model	Null hypothesis	G^2	ΔG^2	Δdf	p-value
15.9		450.691			
15.9b	$H_0 : \alpha_k^{[s(i)]} = 0$ for all i and k	450.936	0.245	1	Not small
15.9c	$H_0 : \beta_k^{[s(j)]} = 0$ for all j and k	450.734	0.043	1	Not small
15.9d	$H_0 : (\alpha\beta)_{kl} = 0$ for all k and l	465.224	14.533	1	$p < 0.001$

Krackhardt's high-tech managers, the friendship relation and age

Model	Null hypothesis	G^2	ΔG^2	Δdf	p-value
15.9		447.096			
15.9b	$H_0 : \alpha_k^{[s(i)]} = 0$ for all i and k	450.985	3.889	1	$p = 0.0486$
15.9c	$H_0 : \beta_k^{[s(j)]} = 0$ for all j and k	447.139	0.043	1	Not small
15.9d	$H_0 : (\alpha\beta)_{kl} = 0$ for all k and l	461.688	14.592	1	$p < 0.001$

Krackhardt's high-tech managers, the friendship relation, and age and tenure

Model	Null hypothesis	G^2	ΔG^2	Δdf	p-value
15.9		438.390			
15.9b	$H_0 : \alpha_k^{[s(i)]} = 0$ for all i and k	449.738	11.348	3	$p = 0.010$
15.9c	$H_0 : \beta_k^{[s(j)]} = 0$ for all j and k	438.768	0.378	3	Not small
15.9d	$H_0 : (\alpha\beta)_{kl} = 0$ for all k and l	451.885	13.495	1	$p < 0.001$

parameters. It differs in that one now assumes that all actors belong to one and only one subset. In other words, we assume that all alphas are equal for all actors (or subsets), as are all betas.

The relevant array, which we call **V**, is a contingency table like **Y** or **W**, but aggregates over all actors or over all subsets of actors. In a sense, we have just a single subgroup, so that $S = 1$. The models we fit to such tables inform us about the network structure as given by the ties, without regard to the identities of the particular actors or their attributes. The models in the class contain parameters which do not depend on the actors or on their subsets; thus, these models focus strictly on the relations, not on the actors or their attributes.

The second class of models described here takes the models for **Y** and **W** and modifies them by allowing for attribute information and/or relational data that are ordinal (for example, "big," "medium," and "small" corporations, or "high," "medium," and "low" frequencies of communications). With these models, one can handle valued relational variables as well as valued attribute variables, such as size or socio-economic status.

15.3.1 Strict Relational Analysis — The V-array

In the same way that we aggregated individuals into a **W**-array so that we could fit models with subset-level parameters, and hence study stochastic equivalence, we can further aggregate **W**. We now want to consider models with neither actor-level nor subset-level parameters.

The models that we have presented in this chapter allow researchers to study patterns of ties for a single relational variable among individual actors (as coded by the entries of **Y**), or among subsets (as coded by the entries of **W**). We might wish to ignore the actors and their subsets altogether. Models postulated for such data focus on the relations alone, without consideration of who sent or received the ties, or of any attributes of these actors. Substantively, these models assume that all expansiveness (or popularity) parameters are constant across all actors or all subsets of actors. In other words, these parameters no longer depend on the actors. Thus, the α's (or β's), measuring differential actor expansiveness (or popularity) are 0; that is, there are no such differential tendencies.

We first define a new array, the **V**-array, with entries $\{v_{kl}\}$, which we can obtain by aggregating the entries in either **Y** or **W**:

$$
\begin{aligned}
V_{kl} &= \sum_{i=1}^{g} \sum_{j=1}^{g} Y_{ijkl} \\
&= \sum_{s(i)=1}^{S} \sum_{s(j)=1}^{S} W_{s(i)s(j)kl}.
\end{aligned}
\tag{15.10}
$$

This array is of size $C \times C$, and its entries give counts of the various types of dyads. For a dichotomous relation, the **V**-array is 2×2. For such a dichotomous relation, the count in the $(0,1)$ and $(1,0)$ cell, for example, equals the number of asymmetric dyads. In general, the off-diagonal cells of **V**, such as the (k,l)th cell $(k \neq l)$ give the counts of the number of dyads for which actors send ties at level k and receive ties at level l, distinct from k. The diagonal cells, because of "double counting" when summing over dyads, give twice the number of dyads for which actors send at level k and also receive at level k.

Most social network data sets are probably better modeled using parameters that allow for individual or subset differences, but there may be

Table 15.18. *The V-array constructed from the Y-array for the second-graders and friendship*

	$l: \quad x_{ji} = 0$	$x_{ji} = 1$
$k: x_{ij} = 0$	18	4
$x_{ij} = 1$	4	4

circumstances in which modeling a V-array might be appropriate. Frequently, the decision of whether to model individuals (using Y) or subsets (using W) or to aggregate over both (V) is primarily driven by theoretical issues. A V-array can be viewed as appropriate for statistical models with only one subset of actors. If stochastic equivalence is appropriate, then we can go from the Y- to the W-array. When considering whether to go from the W- to the V-array, we are simply further assuming all subsets, or all actors, are homogeneous with respect to the dyadic interactions on the relational variable under study. In other words, all alphas are equal, as are all betas, and are all equal to 0 (as we will see from the formal model given below). If this is a tenable substantive hypothesis, then such modeling is proper. And we can certainly study such hypotheses, by first fitting p_1 and then fitting special cases of it without the α's and without the β's.

The v-array for the fabricated network of second-graders is given in Table 15.18. The entries in this table do not depend on actors i and j, or on subsets $s(i)$ and $s(j)$. Instead, the $g(g-1) = 30$ ordered pairs of actors (each of the fifteen dyads is viewed from both perspectives) are classified only according to the strengths of the relational variable between the actors. The elements in this small array are the counts from the dyad census: there are 9 (18/2) null dyads, 2 (4/2) mutual dyads, and the off-diagonal entry (4) gives the number of asymmetric dyads. Note the table is symmetric. And also note, as mentioned above, that because the summation here is over all ordered pairs of actors, rather than over all unordered pairs of actors, dyads are counted twice; hence, the diagonal entries in the array are doubled dyad counts.

A statistical model for dyadic interactions that have been organized into a V-array follows:

$$\log P(Y_{ijkl} = 1) = \lambda_{ij} + \theta_k + \theta_l + (\alpha\beta)_{kl}. \tag{15.11}$$

Here, k and l take all possible integer values between 0 and $C - 1$. As noted, the α and β parameters of model (15.3) are set equal to 0. And we usually assume that the θ's and $(\alpha\beta)$'s sum to 0 across their respective subscripts; further, these latter parameters are symmetric: $(\alpha\beta)_{kl} = (\alpha\beta)_{lk}$.

As is proper, we give the statistical model in terms of the dyadic variables (Y_{ijkl}). Since the model is postulated at the level of the individual actors in a dyad, but the table has been aggregated over individuals, the goodness-of-fit statistics given as output of common statistical programs must be adjusted (as was necessary for fitting models to **W**).

Note the simplicity of this model — there are only two interesting parameters. The more substantively interesting parameters are the reciprocation parameters, the $\{(\alpha\beta)_{kl}\}$. The thetas are indicators of volume of ties sent and received at each relational strength. No parameters appear in the model that depend on the actors, i or j, or the subsets, $s(i)$ or $s(j)$, because we have aggregated over all these possibilities, and formed a table that cross-classifies only the levels of the relational variables.

To illustrate, let us look at the fabricated second-grade network. Recall that we have already demonstrated (see Table 15.8) that the children do differ with respect to their popularity effects; that is, the β's are statistically different from each other. Thus, strictly speaking, these parameters should not be all equated to each other. Nevertheless, we use this example for illustrative purposes. To fit model 15.11, we simply fit the saturated model [12] to the 2×2 **v** of Table 15.18.

The model clearly fits "perfectly"; that is, a 2×2 table has a total of 3 degrees of freedom (only the grand total of the table is fixed), and we have a model with three parameters, as follows: one for θ, one for $(\alpha\beta)$, and one for λ. The parameter estimates are: $\theta = 0.385$ and $(\alpha\beta) = 0.02$ (we have no interest in λ, since it appears in the model simply to insure that the probabilities sum to unity). Clearly, there is very little tendency for ties to be sent, but when ties are sent, there is some tendency for these ties to be reciprocated.

We have found these relational v-arrays most useful when modeling multirelational network data sets. In fact, the first use of such arrays was by Davis (1968a), who proposed methods for the analysis of two relations, and Galaskiewicz and Marsden (1978), who analyzed a social network data set containing three relations. In Chapter 16, we discuss statistical models for multiple relational social network data sets which incorporate associations or interactions for the relational variables under study. Such models can also be applied to the multirelational versions of the **Y**-, **W**-, or **V**-arrays.

15.3.2 Ordinal Relational Data

We now consider models for relations that not only are valued, but have ordered categories. For example, the strength of a relation might be measured with $C = 3$ levels, coded as 0, 1, or 2, indicating "no," "sometimes," and "often" frequency of phone calls between actors, or "strangers," "acquaintances," "friends," and "best friends," which might be coded as 0, 1, 2, and 3. Thus, we assume that the levels of the relational variable are ordered, with smaller values indicating weaker ties, and larger values representing stronger ties.

Log-linear models for discrete data have been extended to categorical variables whose categories are ordered (for example, Agresti 1984, 1990; Goodman 1979). For social network data, relational variables and attribute variables can be ordinal. Here, we modify the models of this chapter to incorporate the possibly ordinal measurement properties inherent in the data. The models discussed in this section are described in detail in Wasserman and Iacobucci (1986).

The statistical models (15.3) and (15.9) can be generalized to incorporate not only ordinal relational variables, but also ordinal attribute variables. For example, we might classify actors into five ordered subsets based on their university rank: lecturer, instructor, assistant professor, associate professor, and professor.

We begin by assuming that scores can be assigned to the ordered strengths of the relational variable. We label these scores $u_k : 0, 1, 2, \ldots$, $(C - 1)$, and center them to have a mean of zero. That is, we calculate the average score, $\bar{u} = \sum_{k=0}^{C-1} u_k / C$, and then subtract it from each of the u_k's. For example, with $C = 3$ strengths, we might assign the u_k scores of $u_1 = 0$, $u_2 = 1$, $u_3 = 2$, and center them to -1, 0, and 1, so that the centered scores have a mean of 0. If we had $C = 4$ strengths, we might assign the scores $u_1 = 1$, $u_2 = 2$, $u_3 = 4$, $u_4 = 8$, and center them to obtain $-2.75, -1.75, 0.25, 4.25$.

We use these scores to estimate a set of regression-like slope parameters. In model (15.3) there are $(g - 1)(C - 1)$ expansiveness parameters. We change these parameters by using the ordinal information. Specifically:

$$\alpha_{i(k)} = \alpha_i(u_k - \bar{u}).$$

The $(u_k - \bar{u})$'s are the assigned, centered scores. Because the u_k's are known, there are fewer parameters to estimate (assuming that C exceeds two categories). The α_i parameters are the "slope" parameters mentioned above. There are g alphas, one for each actor. The $\{\alpha_i\}$ effects sum to

0. Thus, instead of estimating $(g-1)(C-1)$ independent quantities, we estimate only $(g-1)$ parameters. The general expansiveness parameters $\{\alpha_{i(k)}\}$ are assumed to be linearly related to the scores assigned to the relational strengths.

Consider an example. Suppose the relation is frequency of interactions among children, which we have coded as "low," "medium," and "high." In model (15.3), we would estimate $(g-1)(3-1) = 2(g-1)\,\alpha_{i(k)}$ parameters. With the ordinal version of the model discussed here, we have only $(g-1)$ α_i's. These new α_i's do not depend on k.

Let us focus on the regression-nature of these parameters. The difference between the low category $(k = 0)$ and the medium category $(k = 1)$ is (for the ith actor) equal to $\alpha_i(u_1 - u_0)$. The difference between the medium category and the high category $(k = 2)$ is $\alpha_i(u_2 - u_1)$. If the two differences $(u_1 - u_0)$ and $(u_2 - u_1)$ are equal, which would be the case if the categories are equally spaced on the score variable, then $\alpha_{i(1)} - \alpha_{i(0)} = \alpha_{i(2)} - \alpha_{i(1)}$. Thus, the effect of "going from" the medium category $(k = 1)$ to the high category $(k = 2)$ is the same as the effect of going from the low category to the medium category. This constancy is identical to the change in a response variable in a regression, with a linear regression slope.

Similarly, the popularity parameters are simplified by taking the set of $\{\beta_{j(l)}\}$ effects, for a nominal relation, and replacing it with the set of $\{\beta_j\}$ effects for an ordinal relation. Specifically,

$$\beta_{j(l)} = \beta_j(u_l - \bar{u}).$$

In general, any parameters in models (15.3) and (15.9) can be revised to ordinal relational versions by replacing parameters that depend on the index k, with a simpler parametric structure using the known scores $\{u_k\}$. In addition to the alphas and betas, $\{\theta_k\}$ and $\{(\alpha\beta)_{kl}\}$ can be modified, giving rise to the following model:

$$\begin{aligned}
\log P(Y_{ijkl} = 1) \quad = \quad & \lambda_{ij} + \theta(u_k - \bar{u}) + \theta(u_l - \bar{u}) + \alpha_i(u_k - \bar{u}) \\
& + \alpha_j(u_l - \bar{u}) + \beta_j(u_k - \bar{u}) + \beta_i(u_l - \bar{u}) \\
& + (\alpha\beta)(u_k - \bar{u})(u_l - \bar{u}), \qquad (15.12)
\end{aligned}$$

where, as usual, k and l take on integer values between 0 and $C-1$. Note that there is only a single $(\alpha\beta)$ parameter in this model. Its interpretation is analogous to a measure of association between sending strengths and receiving strengths, much like in model (15.3) for dichotomous data.

If we use attribute variables to categorize the actors into $S < g$ subsets, then we can simplify model (15.12) even further:

$$
\begin{aligned}
\log P(Y_{ijkl} = 1) \quad = \quad & \lambda^{[s(i)s(j)]} + \theta(u_k - \bar{u}) + \theta(u_l - \bar{u}) \\
& + \alpha^{[s(i)]}(u_k - \bar{u}) + \alpha^{[s(j)]}(u_l - \bar{u}) \\
& + \beta^{[s(j)]}(u_k - \bar{u}) + \beta^{[s(i)]}(u_l - \bar{u}) \\
& + (\alpha\beta)(u_k - \bar{u})(u_l - \bar{u}).
\end{aligned}
\tag{15.13}
$$

Finally, the attribute variable(s) might also be ordered, so that we could assign scores to subset categories. For example, distinguishing actors by gender or race would result in dichotomous and discrete attribute variables. But such attribute variables are not ordinal. However, if we have measurements on some measure of socioeconomic status, we could form subsets on some categorization of this variable (for example, lower, middle, and upper class). More details and examples illustrating the application of these models for ordinal relational and attribute variables can be found in Wasserman and Iacobucci (1986).

15.4 ○Nondirectional Relations

Consider now a single, nondirectional relation. We now show how model (15.3) can be modified for such a relation. As an example, we examine Padgett's Florentine families.

There are (at least) two main differences between directional and nondirectional relations. First, the indegrees and outdegrees are equal for a nondirectional relation. Thus, there can be no difference between expansiveness and popularity parameters in a model. Second, because the states of the dyads for a nondirectional relation are either "on" or "off," there is no reciprocity. We cannot study the tendency for i to send a tie to j and not for j to send a tie to i since there are no asymmetric dyads. Thus, the models for nondirectional relations cannot contain reciprocity parameters.

15.4.1 A Model

We now present a model designed to reflect individual actor differences. Thus, it should be fit to a **Y**-array. Models for actors in subsets, which should be fit to a **W**-array, are similar: actors i and j would simply be replaced by subsets $[s(i)]$ and $[s(j)]$. We first must define the correct

Y-array, designed to reflect the dyadic states that are possible with a nondirectional relation:

$$Y_{ijk} = 1 \text{ if } X_{ij} = k$$
$$= 0 \text{ otherwise.} \quad (15.14)$$

The Y-array is a three-dimensional array, since the X matrix is symmetric by definition. Our model is

$$\log P(Y_{ijk} = 1) = \lambda_{ij} + \theta_k + \gamma_{i(k)} + \gamma_{j(k)}. \quad (15.15)$$

In this model, there are no α's and no β's. Rather, they are replaced by γ's. Each actor has a single set of γ parameters, indexed by the choosing strength (k). Note that there is no $(\alpha\beta)$ term.

This model is equivalent to [12][13][23], the no three-factor interaction model, fit to the Y-array. Log-linear model computer packages can be used to obtain fitted values. Various special cases of model (15.15) can be fit by dropping parameters. In these cases, corresponding margins of Y are added or deleted from the fitted log-linear model.

15.4.2 An Example

We fit several models to Padgett's Florentine network. The basic model (15.15) has goodness-of-fit statistics equal to 51.83 (for the business relation) and 87.97 (for the marriage relation). To study whether the families differ with respect to business or marriage, we fit the special case of the basic model without the γ parameters. Comparing the basic model to the model without these actor-level parameters, we found that the γ effects are large for both marital ties ($\Delta G^2 = 108.13 - 87.97 = 20.16$) and business ties ($\Delta G^2 = 90.42 - 51.83 = 38.59$). Degrees of freedom are 14 for marriage and 10 for business (since several of the families have infinite parameters). The conditional likelihood ratio statistic for the marriage relation is small, while that for business is not. Hence, we can conclude that the families are indeed different with respect to the volume and patterns of their marital and business ties to others. The $\hat{\gamma}_i$'s for the business and marital relations are given in Table 15.19. We focus just on the business relation, since these $\hat{\gamma}$'s appear to be more statistically important than those for the marital relation.

The largest negative $\hat{\gamma}$'s for business are for the families Pazzi, Salvati, and Tornabuoni. The families with the largest positive $\hat{\gamma}$'s are Medici, Barbadori, and Lamberteschi. As can be seen, five families have no business ties with the others, and hence have $-\infty$ parameter estimates.

Table 15.19. *Parameter estimates for Padgett's Florentine families*

Family	Actor	Business $\hat{\gamma}_i$	Marriage $\hat{\gamma}_i$
Acciaiuoli	n_1	$-\infty$	-1.106
Albizzi	n_2	$-\infty$	0.310
Barbadori	n_3	0.904	-0.265
Bischeri	n_4	0.290	0.310
Castellani	n_5	0.290	0.310
Ginori	n_6	-0.399	-1.106
Guadagni	n_7	-0.399	0.779
Lamberteschi	n_8	0.904	-1.106
Medici	n_9	1.444	1.539
Pazzi	n_{10}	-1.313	-1.106
Peruzzi	n_{11}	0.904	0.310
Pucci	n_{12}	$-\infty$	$-\infty$
Ridolfi	n_{13}	$-\infty$	0.310
Salvati	n_{14}	-1.313	-0.265
Strozzi	n_{15}	$-\infty$	0.779
Tornabuoni	n_{16}	-1.313	0.310

We also modeled these relations using wealth as an attribute of each actor. Families with wealth less than or equal to 40,000 lira formed one group, and families with more formed another. Half of the families fall into the wealthier group.

Aggregating families into these two wealth categories has a very large effect on the analysis. After aggregation, we fit models to $2 \times 2 \times 2$ three-dimensional **y**-arrays. For the analyses of the **w**'s, the $\hat{\gamma}$'s for marriage are not large ($\Delta G^2 = 1.21$ with $\Delta df = 1$) but they are for business ($\Delta G^2 = 7.59$ again with $\Delta df = 1$). These results suggest that wealth is quite important in distinguishing families who have business ties, but not for marital arrangements. That is, wealthy families enter into business relationships at different rates than less wealthy families, but wealth is not an important influence on marital ties.

15.5 ⊗Recent Generalizations of p_1

In this section, we briefly introduce some interesting developments and recent research on other generalizations of the p_1 model. These include Bayesian estimation of p_1 parameters as described in Wong (1987), and the pseudo-likelihood estimation described in Strauss and Ikeda (1988) designed for the Markov random graphs of Frank and Strauss (1986).

The Bayesian ideas offered by Wong (1987) allow a priori information about the α's and β's to be used in an effort to improve their estimation. The Bayesian approach assumes that the α's and β's are no longer fixed constants, but are random, possibly associated, variables. Wong assumes that these p_1 parameters are multivariate normal random variables, with some structured covariance matrix.

A Bayesian approach can help "smooth" estimation of parameters when fitting models to large, sparse contingency tables. On the down side, the algorithm developed by Wong is slow and has problems if the α's and β's are highly correlated (indicating that parameter redundancy and singular matrices can arise in the computation process). He focuses his attention on the α and β parameters, but presumably his approach could incorporate prior information on $(\alpha\beta)$ also.

Wong compares α and β estimates from the Bayesian approach to α and β estimates using maximum likelihood (ML) estimation, as we have described here. Wong states that the sets of estimates (Bayesian and ML) are usually different, and that even the relative ordering among the estimated α's and among the estimated β's may differ. (In particular, he notes that Bayesian methods cause estimates to "shrink" toward 0, compared to the ML estimates, and that more shrinkage occurs for the more extreme values of α or β.) Nevertheless, the correlations between the ML and Bayesian estimates for the example he analyzed were quite high. The correlation between the two sets of estimated α's was 0.891, and the correlation for the estimated β's was 0.966. Even so, prior information might change or even improve parameter estimates in other network data sets.

Another development to note is the work reported in Strauss and Ikeda (1990). They investigate a *pseudo-likelihood* estimation procedure, a generalization of maximum likelihood, that uses an approximate likelihood function which does not assume dyadic independence (see comments in Iacobucci and Wasserman 1990). The theoretical foundation of Strauss and Ikeda's work is found in Frank and Strauss (1986). Strauss and Ikeda derive a pseudo-likelihood as a function of each data point (x_{ij}), conditional on the rest of the data. Any interdependencies in the data can be directly modeled by this statistical conditioning, so no assumptions need to be made that the data points are all independent.

Strauss and Ikeda compared the performance of standard maximum likelihood estimates to their maximum pseudo-likelihood (MP) estimates both in a simulation study, and by analyzing the "like" relation measured on the monks in the monastery studied by Sampson (1967). In the simulations, they looked at the performance of the estimates in five replicated networks containing fifteen, twenty, or thirty actors. They found that MP and ML estimates performed equally well, as evaluated by a root mean squared error measure. The estimates had greater standard errors for the networks with fewer actors, but this would be true of any procedure — better precision usually occurs with larger data sets.

Under all the conditions for which both ML and MP estimates could be estimated, the two performed similarly. The main advantage in the use of MP estimation is that there are conditions under which MP estimates exist, but ML estimates do not. The MP approach further expands the applicability of p_1 because it can be used to fit models that do not assume dyadic independence, such as those described by Frank and Strauss (1986).

Strauss and Ikeda's comparisons also address the issue of how well the maximum likelihood estimation of p_1 parameters performs even under conditions where the assumption of dyadic independence is known to be violated. The fact that the ML estimates are as good as MP estimates is good news. We can proceed to use the relatively simple methods described here without much concern that violation of the assumption of dyadic independence will greatly affect the results. In addition, the ML and MP $\hat{\alpha}$'s were highly correlated (in fact, almost equal) in the reported analysis of the Sampson data, as were the ML and MP $\hat{\beta}$'s.

Another approach to dyadic independence models comes from the multilevel models common in medical and educational studies. Rosner's (1989) statistical work was motivated not by social network concerns, but by concerns in modeling ophthalmological data. The left and right eye of a person could be viewed as analogous to an actor and a partner in a dyad. Measures on the left or right eye (or actor or partner) clearly cannot be treated as independent; consequently, Rosner develops a logistic regression model for multilevel data, essentially a categorical data version of a linear model incorporating an intraclass correlation coefficient (see also Kraemer and Jacklin 1979).

Still other methods have been pursued by Frank and his colleagues (Frank, Hallinan, and Nowicki 1985; Frank, Komanska, and Widaman 1985; Frank, Lundquist, Wellman, and Wilson 1986; Wellman, Frank, Espinoza, Lundquist, and Wilson 1991). This research uses stochastic equivalence (or, as stated by these authors, "certain homogeneity assumptions") in conjunction with models for dyads and triads. All possible states of a dyad (X_{ij}, X_{ji}) become categories of a discrete random variable. All possible cross-classifications of actor attribute information become another variable. For example, using race and gender as attribute variables, one variable would have categories consisting of all pairs of the following subsets: white males, black males, white females, and black females.

The elements in each cell of the cross-classification of these two variables are the frequencies with which a specific type of actor (such as black females) interacts with other types of actors (such as white females) at the various dyadic states. Each row, then, describes a distribution of dyadic states for each pair of subsets of actors. The information in such a cross-classification is identical to that in a **W**-array. The similarities between all possible pairs of subsets are summarized by χ^2 statistics, and then the subsequent matrix of similarities is cluster analyzed (see Frank, Komanska, and Widaman 1985). The cluster analysis yields subsets that are distinct, and possibly separable, and subsets that are similar, and possibly aggregable.

Stochastic equivalence and comparisons of within-subset to between-subset relations are also examined by Marsden (1981, 1986, 1987, and 1989). A two-way table is created in which both the rows and columns represent the subsets (white males, black males, and so on). The elements of the matrix are densities of ties, for which several models can be developed. Such density matrices are like **w**-arrays, in that the rows and columns are indexed by the $[s(i)]$'s and $[s(j)]$'s. However, the density matrix essentially collapses over sending and receiving strengths k and l, so that the directions and reciprocation of the ties are lost.

Ties within and between subsets are also analyzed by Yamaguchi (1990). "Homophily" or "inbreeding" describe the expected tendencies for actors to have friends of the same attribute category as themselves. For example, this structural hypothesis would lead us to expect that white males would be more likely to chose each other as friends, than to choose men of other races or women. Yamaguchi also examines the links among the friends chosen by any given actor. Thus, the paper looks at both the ties between n_i and n_j's (in conjunction with the attribute information), and also the ties among the chosen n_j's.

Finally, Strauss and Freeman (1989) translate several classic substantive theories or hypotheses into statistical models that use network descriptors as parameters. For example, one model created is based on "small world" studies. Strauss and Freeman create a three-dimensional sociomatrix with elements x_{ijt}, equaling 1 if n_i passes the message to n_j at step t (and otherwise equaling 0). Elements of matrices such as this one can be studied using Markov models. A very similar model, focusing not on the "step" at which a message is sent but on its strength, was discussed by Elsas (1990) and commented upon by Iacobucci and Hopkins (1991). It is based on the social interaction theory and model of Scheiblechner (1971, 1972), and is derived from the common Rasch model in psychometrics (Scheiblechner 1977).

Another model discussed by Strauss and Freeman is the random and biased net paradigm of Rapoport (1953, 1957, 1963, 1979) and Rapoport and Horvath (1961), which began as a model of animal sociology (Rapoport 1949a, 1949b, 1950). This paradigm has been the subject of recent theory by Fararo and Skvoretz (1987). A variety of structural theories, such as Blau's (1977) social differentiation theory and Granovetter's (1973) strength-of-weak-ties principle, have been studied using the paradigm. Fararo (1981, 1983), Fararo and Skvoretz (1984), and Skvoretz (1983, 1985, 1990) have done extensive work on the mathematical aspects of this model, particularly approximations and simulations.

15.6 ⊗Single Relations and Two Sets of Actors

We now turn our attention to statistical models for two-mode social networks. We assume that we have two sets of actors, and a relation that is directed from actors in one set to actors in the other. Details of these models can be found in Iacobucci and Wasserman (1990), Wasserman and Iacobucci (1990), and Iacobucci and Hopkins (1992). The models and results presented here for one-mode networks are easily modified for this generalization. Because of this commonality, we will just briefly present these modifications.

15.6.1 Introduction

Define two actor sets: $\mathcal{N} = \{n_1, n_2, \ldots, n_g\}$, $\mathcal{M} = \{m_1, m_2, \ldots, m_h\}$. A tie originates at n_i and is directed toward the receiver m_j. The relational data recorded on the ordered pair (n_i, m_j) is denoted by x_{ij}.

We can study the tendency for actors in $\mathcal{N}$ to initiate ties and actors in $\mathcal{M}$ to receive ties. But since it is not possible for the tie $m_j \rightarrow n_i$ to occur, we cannot study tendencies for actors in $\mathcal{M}$ to initiate and tendencies for actors in $\mathcal{N}$ to receive. Thus, for this two-mode relation, we cannot study reciprocity.

With g actors in $\mathcal{N}$, and h actors in $\mathcal{M}$, there are gh dyads to consider, or gh relational variables to be modeled. We create a **Y**-array and fit various log-linear models. In this new situation, we create not a four-dimensional array, but a three-dimensional contingency table of size $g \times h \times C$, defined as follows:

$$
\begin{aligned}
Y_{ijk} &= 1 \text{ if the ordered pair } <n_i, m_j> \text{ takes on} \\
&\quad \text{the value } x_{ij} = k \\
&= 0 \text{ otherwise.} \quad\quad (15.16)
\end{aligned}
$$

The **Y**-array is thus defined by three variables: the actors in $\mathcal{N}$, the actors in $\mathcal{M}$, and the value of the tie between the two.

15.6.2 The Basic Model

Model (15.3) is a version of p_1 generalized to discrete-valued relations. It can be extended in a straightforward theoretical manner to two-mode networks. To begin, we note that only actors in $\mathcal{N}$ can send ties, while only actors in $\mathcal{M}$ can receive. Thus, a specific actor will have only one parameter: expansiveness parameters are estimated for the actors in $\mathcal{N}$, while popularity parameters are estimated for the actors in $\mathcal{M}$.

The basic model for two-mode networks simplifies further because reciprocity cannot occur; thus, we do not include the $\{(\alpha\beta)_{kl}\}$ parameters in our models. There can be only one tie within each dyad.

The basic model is:

$$
\log P(Y_{ijk} = 1) = \lambda_{ij} + \theta_k + \alpha_{i(k)} + \beta_{j(k)}. \quad\quad (15.17)
$$

We assume that the parameters in this model sum to 0 across k for each i or j.

The details of obtaining maximum likelihood estimates of the parameters of (15.3), such as the log likelihood function and the formula for the goodness-of-fit statistic G^2, are straightforward generalizations of the results for p_1. We refer the interested reader to Iacobucci and Wasserman (1990) and Wasserman and Iacobucci (1990).

We can simplify model (15.17) in only three ways. We can drop the α's, the β's, or both, from the basic model. These alternative models are listed below.

$$
\begin{aligned}
a)\, &\log P(Y_{ijk} = 1) = \lambda_{ij} + \theta_k + \beta_{j(k)} \\
b)\, &\log P(Y_{ijk} = 1) = \lambda_{ij} + \theta_k + \alpha_{i(k)} \quad\quad (15.18)\\
c)\, &\log P(Y_{ijk} = 1) = \lambda_{ij} + \theta_k
\end{aligned}
$$

When we compare the goodness-of-fit statistics for models (15.17) and

(15.18a), we have the conditional likelihood-ratio test statistic for the null hypothesis,

$$H_0 : \alpha_{i(k)} = 0 \text{ for all } i, k;$$

that is, there are no differences among the actors in $\mathcal{N}$ with respect to their expansiveness. The alternative hypothesis is (as usual) that some of these parameters are not 0. When comparing models (15.17) and (15.18b), we obtain the conditional likelihood-ratio test statistic for the null hypothesis

$$H_0 : \beta_{j(k)} = 0 \text{ for all } j, k.$$

If we were not able to reject either of these hypotheses, we would conclude that model (15.18c) is the best-fitting model. Such a null model is rather uninteresting because it states the actors in $\mathcal{N}$ have no differential expansiveness and actors in $\mathcal{M}$ have no differential popularity effects. Thus, ties are just functions of the strength at which those ties are made, not of the actors involved.

15.6.3 *Aggregating Dyads for Two-mode Networks*

We can use actor attribute variables, now for both sets of actors, to create a **W**-array, and equate parameters for all actors belonging to a subset.

For example, focusing on Galaskiewicz's CEOs and clubs network, we might classify the CEOs by the size of their firm (based perhaps on after-tax income for a recent year). We could also classify the clubs by some measure of their prestige: high; very high; and very, very high.

Using the notation first introduced in Chapter 3, we assume that we have Q_1 attribute variables for the actors in $\mathcal{N}$, and Q_2 attribute variables for the actors in $\mathcal{M}$. From these, we categorize the actors appropriately, to obtain S subsets for the actors in $\mathcal{N}$, and T subsets for the actors in $\mathcal{M}$. We need two mapping functions: $s(i)$, which maps the g actors $\{n_i\}$ in $\mathcal{N}$ to their subsets, and another function $t(j)$ to map the h actors $\{m_j\}$ in the second set $\mathcal{M}$ to their respective subsets. Thus, the subset memberships of the actors in $\mathcal{N}$ can be denoted by $s(n_1), s(n_2), \ldots, s(n_g)$, and the subsets to which the actors in $\mathcal{M}$ belong can be denoted by $t(m_1), t(m_2), \ldots, t(m_h)$.

To obtain a **W**-array we aggregate over actors in a subset, just as we did in the one-mode case:

$$W_{s(n_i)t(m_j)k} = \sum_{n_i \in s(n_i)} \sum_{m_j \in t(m_j)} Y_{ijk}. \tag{15.19}$$

Because the two sets of actors differ, we might use attribute variables for one set of actors, but not the other. Aggregating over actors in $\mathcal{N}$ yields:

$$W_{s(n_i)jk} = \sum_{n_i \in s(n_i)} Y_{ijk}. \tag{15.20}$$

Aggregating over actors in $\mathcal{M}$ yields:

$$W_{it(m_j)k} = \sum_{m_j \in t(m_j)} Y_{ijk}. \tag{15.21}$$

Thus, the **W**-array can be of size $S \times T \times C$, if we use attribute variables for both sets of actors, or $S \times h \times C$, or $g \times T \times C$, if we use attributes for just one of the sets of actors.

We can also aggregate completely over actors, and postulate models that do not contain any actor- or subset-level parameters. Aggregating over all actors gives a very simple one-dimensional **V**-array:

$$V_k = \sum_i \sum_j Y_{ijk} \tag{15.22}$$

describing only the relational data, not distinguishing among the sending or receiving actors. Models fit to this array would contain only λ and θ parameters. These latter parameters measure tendencies toward choices at the various strengths, but are independent of the natures of the sending and receiving actors.

We note that the goodness-of-fit statistics for models fit to either the **W**- or **V**-arrays require special computations just as in the one-mode situation. Standard output from statistical packages is not correct for G^2 statistics, even though the fitted probabilities are correct.

We can also consider ordinal relational variables, just as we did in the one-mode situation. We would model the relational data as follows:

$$\log P(Y_{ijk} = 1) = \lambda_{ij} + \theta(u_k - \bar{u}) + \alpha_i(u_k - \bar{u})$$
$$+ \beta_j(u_k - \bar{u}), \tag{15.23}$$

where the u's are the assigned, known scores. All theoretical and practical details of modeling and testing hypotheses about two-mode networks carries over from the procedures described in detail for one-mode networks.

15.7 Computing for Log-linear Models

Following are the computing steps necessary to fit the models described in this chapter and the next. Commands are listed and explained for each of the following statistical packages: *GLIM* (Baker and Nelder 1978), *SPSS^X* (Norusis 1985), *BMDP* (Dixon 1983), and *SYSTAT* (Wilkinson 1987). We highly recommend the use of the program *GLIM* or *SPSS^X*. Other statistical packages will work similarly to these two. For example, *BMDP* and *SYSTAT* are very similar to *SPSS^X*. (*SAS* is a very powerful and flexible package, but its *CATMOD* procedure is rather peculiar and has difficulties with contingency tables that have many 0's, which characterize **y**-arrays. Parameter estimates can disappear and become confounded as functions of each other, and it is up to the researcher to disentangle them.) The **Y**- and **W**-arrays used to illustrate each package are those data from the fabricated second-grader network.

15.7.1 Computing Packages

After the commands for these packages are presented, we describe how one obtains the model parameter estimates from the *u*-terms that are given on the computer printouts. Some of the packages use different constraints than others, and we note the differences here.

GLIM Commands.

```
$C TO FIT MODELS TO THE Y-ARRAY:
$ECHO
$OUTPUT 3
$UNITS 144
$FACTOR I 6 J 6 K 2 L 2
$CALC I=%GL(6,24): J=%GL(6,4): K=%GL(2,2): L=%GL(2,1)
$DATA Y
$READ
0 0 0 0  0 0 1 0  1 0 0 0  1 0 0 0  0 0 1 0  1 0 0 0
0 1 0 0  0 0 0 0  0 0 0 1  1 0 0 0  1 0 0 0  0 0 0 1
1 0 0 0  0 0 0 1  0 0 0 0  1 0 0 0  1 0 0 0  1 0 0 0
1 0 0 0  1 0 0 0  1 0 0 0  0 0 0 0  0 0 1 0  1 0 0 0
0 1 0 0  1 0 0 0  1 0 0 0  0 1 0 0  0 0 0 0  0 0 1 0
1 0 0 0  0 0 0 1  1 0 0 0  1 0 0 0  0 1 0 0  0 0 0 0
$C END DATA
$YVAR Y $LINK L $ERROR P
$FIT I*J + I*K + J*L + J*K + I*L + K*L $DISPLAY MDAR
$FIT I*J +         J*K + I*L + K*L $DISPLAY MDAR
$FIT I*J + I*K + J*L +     K*L $DISPLAY MDAR
```

```
$FIT I*J + I*K + J*L + J*K + I*L        $DISPLAY MDAR
$STOP

$C TO FIT MODELS TO THE W-ARRAY:
$ECHO
$OUTPUT 3
$UNITS 16
$FACTOR R 2 S 2 K 2 L 2
$CALC R=%GL(2,8): S=%GL(2,4): K=%GL(2,2): L=%GL(2,1)
$DATA W
$READ
 6 0 0 0  5 1 1 2  5 1 1 2  2 2 2 0
$C END DATA
$YVAR W $ERROR P $LINK L
$FIT R*S + R*K + S*L + S*K + R*L + K*L $DISPLAY MDAR
$FIT R*S +         S*K + R*L + K*L $DISPLAY MDAR
$FIT R*S + R*K + S*L +     K*L $DISPLAY MDAR
$FIT R*S + R*K + S*L + S*K + R*L        $DISPLAY MDAR
$STOP
```

An explanation of the commands follows. "ECHO" gets the commands entered onto the log of the computational session for review later. "OUTPUT 3" tells *GLIM* to write all results to a file called *TAPE3* (input and output instructions will vary with computer site). "UNITS x" tells *GLIM* the contingency table has x cells. "FACTOR" gives the variable name for each dimension of the table as well as the number of levels the discrete variable takes. "CALC" forms the factors needed for modeling and tells *GLIM* which data point goes in which cell of the table. The commands:

```
CALC I=%GL(G,G*C*C): J=%GL(G,C*C): K=%GL(C,C): L=%GL(C,1)
```

are used when reading in the **y**- or **w**-array with the last subscript changing fastest. (Compare the **y**-arrays and the **w**-arrays shown earlier.)

"DATA z" tells *GLIM* you are about to enter some data and you want that variable named z. "READ" then initiates the procedure and the data follow. There must be x numbers — the same number as in the units statement. "C" always denotes a comment ignored by *GLIM*. "YVAR q" tells *GLIM* the frequencies to be modeled are stored in the variable called q. "ERROR P" and "LINK L" are the commands signifying that *GLIM* should fit log-linear models. (Other error distributions and link functions give *GLIM* great flexibility.) "FIT" specifies the model. The first of the four models gives the full p_1 model and the remaining three models will provide significance tests for alpha, beta, and reciprocity parameters, respectively. "STOP" ends the *GLIM* session.

SPSS^X **Commands.** The data file is called "MY DATA A" and it contains the relations as follows:

```
                              0000000001111...
Column of Data File:   1234567890123...

Variable:       i j r s k l

                1 2 2 2 1 0
                2 1 2 2 0 1
                1 3 2 1 0 0
                3 1 1 2 0 0
                1 4 2 1 0 0
                4 1 1 2 0 0
                1 5 2 2 1 0
                5 1 2 2 0 1
                1 6 2 1 0 0
                6 1 1 2 0 0
                2 3 2 1 1 1
                3 2 1 2 1 1
                2 4 2 1 0 0
                4 2 1 2 0 0
                2 5 2 2 0 0
                5 2 2 2 0 0
                2 6 2 1 1 1
                6 2 1 2 1 1
                3 4 1 1 0 0
                4 3 1 1 0 0
                3 5 1 2 0 0
                5 3 2 1 0 0
                3 6 1 1 0 0
                6 3 1 1 0 0
                4 5 1 2 1 0
                5 4 2 1 0 1
                4 6 1 1 0 0
```

```
6 4 1 1 0 0
5 6 2 1 1 0
6 5 1 2 0 1
```

To fit models to a **y**-array, use the following program file (called "RUN-JOB SPSSX A"):

```
TITLE 'MY ANALYSIS'
FILE HANDLE A1 / NAME= 'MY DATA A'
DATA LIST FILE=A1
/I 1 J 3 R 5 S 7 K 9 L 11
HILOGLINEAR I J (1,6) K L (0,1)
/PRINT = ALL ASSOCIATION
/DESIGN I*J I*K J*L J*K I*L K*L
/DESIGN I*J      J*K I*L K*L
/DESIGN I*J I*K J*L      K*L
/DESIGN I*J I*K J*L J*K I*L
LOGLINEAR I J (1,6) K L (0,1)
/PRINT = ESTIM
/DESIGN I J K L  I BY J  I BY K  J BY L  J BY K
 I BY L  K BY L
```

To fit models to a **w**-array, use these commands:

```
TITLE 'MY W ANALYSIS'
FILE HANDLE A2 / NAME = 'MY DATA A'
DATA LIST FILE=A2
/I 1 J 3 R 5 S 7 K 9 L 11
HILOGLINEAR R S (1,2) K L (0,1)
/PRINT = ALL ASSOCIATION
/DESIGN R*S R*K S*L S*K R*L K*L
/DESIGN R*S      S*K R*L K*L
/DESIGN R*S R*K S*L      K*L
/DESIGN R*S R*K S*L S*K R*L
LOGLINEAR R S (1,2) K L (0,1)
/PRINT = ESTIM
/DESIGN R S K L  R BY S  R BY K  S BY L  S BY K
 R BY L  K BY L
```

The commands "TITLE," "FILE HANDLE," and "DATA LIST" initiate $SPSS^X$ and read in the data file. "HILOGLINEAR" generates hierarchical log-linear models and the fitting procedures. It is a fast procedure, both for typing in compact model statements, and in terms of computational running time. However, it does not give estimated u-terms. "LOGLINEAR" is a slower and more cumbersome procedure, but it will calculate estimated u-terms for small networks.

   BMDP **Commands.** To fit models to a **y**-array (contained in a data file, like that needed for $SPSS^X$):

```
/PROBLEM    TITLE IS 'MY ANALYSIS'.
/INPUT      VARIABLES ARE 6.
            CASES ARE 30.
            FORMAT IS '(I1,5I2)'.
            TABLE IS 6,6,2,2.
/VARIABLE   NAMES ARE I,J,R,S,K,L.
/TABLE      INDICES ARE L,K,J,I.
/FIT        MODEL IS IJ,IK,JL,JK,IL,KL.
            MODEL IS IJ,      JK,IL,KL.
            MODEL IS IJ,IK,JL,   KL.
            MODEL IS IJ,IK,JL,JK,IL.
/PRINT      EXPECTED. LAMBDA.
/END
```

To fit models to a **w**-array, replace i's and j's with r's and s's in the statements "TABLE" and "FIT," and replace the 6's with 2's on the fifth line.

   BMDP outputs its fitted values in a somewhat awkward form. Rather than listing the fitted values as a column vector with the subscripts $ijkl$ changing in the "last is fast" standard manner, *BMDP* creates L columns and then strings the subscripts kji in column vector format where the first subscript changes fastest.

   SYSTAT **Commands.** To fit models to a **y**-array, enter data in a file called "MY.DAT" which resembles the input to $SPSS^X$ given above. Then, commands entered on a personal computer follow:

```
SYSTAT
TABLES
USE MY.DAT
TABULATE I*J*K*L
MODEL I*J + I*K + J*L + J*K + I*L + K*L /FITTED, RESIDUALS
MODEL I*J + J*K + I*L + K*L /FITTED, RESIDUALS
MODEL I*J + I*K + J*L +      K*L /FITTED, RESIDUALS
```

```
MODEL I*J + I*K + J*L + J*K + I*L /FITTED, RESIDUALS
QUIT
QUIT
```

To fit models to a **w**-array, replace i's and j's with r's and s's. Unfortunately *SYSTAT* does not calculate estimates of u-terms.

15.7.2 From Printouts to Parameters

The values found in the printouts can be translated in simple ways to obtain estimates of the parameters of the models. We demonstrate here for α and $(\alpha\beta)$ of p_1, and note that the translation for β is analogous to that for α.

The table that follows contains some of the u-terms that $SPSS^X$ produces from fitting p_1 to the fabricated network of second-graders.

```
      K:     0       1
I=1  *-0.707*   0.707
I=2  *-0.408*   0.408
I=3  * 0.237*  -0.237
I=4  *-0.098*   0.098
I=5  * 0.488*  -0.488
I=6    0.488   -0.488
```

Having named the actors variable "I" and the relation sent variable "K," the u-terms corresponding to the IK interaction are used to derive the $\alpha_{i(k)}$. The key is to look at the subscripts. Because the IK margin is identical to the JL margin, the JL u-terms are also identical to the IK u-terms. (Similarly, just as the IL margin is equal to the JK margin, so are the JK and IL u-terms equal.)

We have notated several of the values in the table above with asterisks to indicate those values that $SPSS^X$ actually prints. We filled in the remainder of the table by subtracting the estimates in a given row from 0, since u-terms have the property that they sum to 0 across all indices (or in all directions).

The IK u-terms are translated to $\alpha_{i(k)}$'s by two simple steps. First, make all entries in the first column 0. Second, for dichotomous relations, multiply all the entries in the second column by 2 (Wasserman and Weaver 1985). These simple steps will result in the alpha estimates we reported earlier.

When C, the number of levels of the relational variable, is greater than two, the translation is as follows. First, for each row, subtract the value in the first column from every column (this will result in the first column equaling 0 for all rows, upon completion, and the remaining columns will also have been altered). Second, center Columns 2 through C.

For the reciprocity parameter, $SPSS^X$ calculated the estimated value as 0.769. The u-terms for this KL interaction can be written in a 2×2 table, as follows:

	L=0	L=1
K=0	0.769	-0.769
K=1	-0.769	0.769

To obtain the estimate of the model parameter $(\alpha\beta)$, place 0's in the first row and column, and then multiply the value 0.769 in the $(2,2)$ cell by 4. This translation yields the parameter estimate for the reciprocity parameter reported earlier.

For valued relations $(C > 2)$, take the following steps. First, for all cells (k,l) where k or l exceeds 2, subtract the value in the first column in row k, and subtract the value in the first row in column l, and add back the value in the $(1,1)$ (upper leftmost) cell. After all cells for which k or l exceed 2 have been modified, simply change all the values in the first row and column to 0.

The translation is slightly different for users of *GLIM*. The estimated u-terms that are produced for the IK interaction are those in the following table:

	K=0	K=1
I=1	0	0
I=2	0	-0.597
I=3	0	-1.888
I=4	0	-1.217
I=5	0	-2.391
I=6	0	-2.391

Notice that *GLIM* uses a constraint that the first row and the first column of any set of u-terms is defined to be 0. We maintain the first column of 0's, in accordance with standard model constraints, and we simply adjust the remaining columns. Thus, the second column in the table above needs to be "recentered." We compute the mean: $((0)+(-0.597)+(-1.888)+(-1.217)+(-2.391)+(-2.391))/6 = -1.414$, and subtract this value (-1.414) from each element in the second column, to obtain the following estimates (which are the estimated α's reported earlier):

```
        K=0              K=1
I=1     0     (    0  -  1.414)  =   1.414
I=2     0     (-0.597  -  1.414)  =   0.817
I=3     0     (-1.888  -  1.414)  =  -0.474
I=4     0     (-1.217  -  1.414)  =   0.197
I=5     0     (-2.391  -  1.414)  =  -0.977
I=6     0     (-2.391  -  1.414)  =  -0.977
```

When the relational variable is valued, the translation to obtain β's is the same as that to obtain α's. The first column remains 0, and all the remaining columns are recentered.

Finally, we note that the constraints *GLIM* uses are exactly those we use for the $(\alpha\beta)$ parameters, whether the relation is dichotomous or valued. That is, *GLIM* will print the following estimated u-terms for the KL interaction:

```
        L=0    L=1
K=0     0      0
K=1     0      3.077
```

Clearly, no further adjustment is required.

The standard errors of the model parameter estimates are also derived from slight adjustments of the standard errors of the u-terms. Drawing from Wasserman and Weaver (1985), the standard errors of the model parameter estimates for dichotomous relations are computed as follows:

$$SE[\hat{\alpha}_{i(1)}] = 2SE[\hat{u}_{13(i1)}]$$

$$SE[\hat{\beta}_{j(1)}] = 2SE[\hat{u}_{23(j1)}]$$

$$SE[\widehat{(\alpha\beta)}_{11}] = 4SE[\hat{u}_{34(11)}]$$

15.8 Summary

In this chapter, we began by presenting a model for one-mode network data that included effects for the expansiveness of sending actors, the popularity of receiving actors, and the reciprocity of the actors. We discussed models for dichotomous relations, and extended the models to include general discrete, and ordinal data. We discussed how to model individual actors, and then showed how to model subsets of actors. Thus, we can focus on the dyadic interactions in a network, or we can model both the ties and the actor attributes. We also showed how we might model the patterns in the relational data without considering the actors at all. We briefly described some of the current research on extending these modeling procedures. We demonstrated most of these methods on several examples to give the reader a better understanding of the practice and interpretation of the models and methods. We also described analogous models and methods for two-mode networks.

In the next chapter, we extend these models to multiple relations measured on a network. These multivariate models will allow testing somewhat different hypotheses about network structure. For example, many researchers have been interested in the problem of how one measures the similarity between network representations (Hubert and Arabie 1985; Hubert and Baker 1978; Katz and Powell 1953; Schultz and Hubert 1976; Wasserman 1987). The conformity between two sociomatrices can be measured using a "symmetric" index (like a measure of association), which would answer questions such as, "How similar are these two social networks?" For example, we would expect the relations such as "like" and "dislike" to be negatively associated, but relations such as "like" and "respect" to be positively associated. Alternatively, conformity can be measured in an "asymmetric" way, such as with regression models, to address such questions as, "How well can we predict the structure in one network knowing the structure in another?"

16

Stochastic Blockmodels and
Goodness-of-Fit Indices

As we noted in Chapter 10, the standard mathematical representation of a positional analysis frequently uses blockmodels to describe and study the equivalence classes (or positions) determined by a set of measured relations. Recall that a blockmodel consists of a partition of the actors in $\mathcal{N}$ into positions and a statement of how the positions relate to each other. The adequacy of this construct can be studied with the methods presented in this chapter. We have also noted that these representations of equivalences can also be found by using hierarchical clustering and multidimensional scaling.

A researcher must determine how well a blockmodel, or another mathematical representation of the positions among the actors, "fits" a given network data set. Such tasks are usually called *goodness-of-fit* problems in statistics, and we will present several goodness-of-fit indices here, all of which are designed to measure the fit of a blockmodel to a given network data set.

There have been two main approaches to this goodness-of-fit task in the literature. The first uses a standard data analytic technique of comparing the observed data set (in this case, the R sociomatrices $\mathbf{X}_1, \mathbf{X}_2, \ldots, \mathbf{X}_R$) to the predicted data set, which is based on the blockmodel to be evaluated. A number of measures for this comparison have been presented in the literature; here, we discuss several of them. Unfortunately, there is little consensus or agreement on such statistics. The second approach is more statistical and model-based. One can first assume that one of the dyadic interaction models, described in the preceding chapter, is operating, and then postulate a *stochastic blockmodel*. This strategy then allows one to conduct likelihood-based, statistical tests for goodness-of-fit. Here, we will discuss these two approaches.

The primary difference between these two approaches lies at the center of positional analyses. The definitions of equivalence and the algorithms commonly used to find a blockmodel make no use of statistical theory. Positional analyses are not statistical methods. This limitation prevents standard, parametric (that is, based on a specific parameterized family of probability distributions) statistical tests and measures from being used to determine directly how well a blockmodel fits a data set. (Some researchers commonly use blockmodel representations of network data to summarize statistically other aspects of a network data set; however, unless the blockmodel representation is independent of these other aspects, any statistical tests will not have accurate error rates. Specifically, it is not proper to use relational data to find a blockmodel representation, and then test this same representation on that data set.) If statistical tests are desired in a network analysis, we recommend the use of statistical methods from the beginning of the analysis. Such methods, as described in this chapter, can be used to find partitions of actors, and lead to proper statistical tests and measures of goodness-of-fit.

Yet another approach centers on the evaluation of a particular positional analysis technique using standard data sets. Such evaluative strategies are recommended by Everett and Borgatti (1990), who suggest several such examples. The idea here is to choose methods based on how they perform in practice. We, too, advocate such an approach, but until such data sets become standardized and their use routinized, a more quantitative evaluative approach is needed.

There is a compromise between parametric statistical models and the positional analyses described in earlier chapters. Nonparametric tests can be used to test specific hypotheses. Some methodologists, such as Hubert and Schultz (1976), Hubert and Baker (1978), Arabie, Boorman, and Leavitt (1978), Baker and Hubert (1981), Panning (1982a), and Noma and Smith (1985a), propose the use of the common nonparametric randomization test in which all possible ways of placing g objects (or actors) into B cells (or blockmodel positions) are considered. For each "way" or permutation of the data, an index can be computed, comparing the particular permutation to the blockmodel "prediction." An index is then computed, measuring how close each permutation of the data is to the prediction (or in general, a "hypothesis" matrix), thus generating an entire distribution of indices (called the permutation distribution). One of these permutations is the observed blockmodel or partition, actually derived from the relational data.

A permutation test of how well the predicted blockmodel or hypothesis fits the data is conducted simply by determining the fraction of the permutations that fit worse than the one actually observed (that is, the fraction of permutations that have indices indicating fits that are worse). The p-value for the test is this fraction, which is easily read from the permutation distribution as the tail probability beyond the index calculated for the observed blockmodel. We will illustrate this common type of nonparametric test in this chapter. This approach to data analysis, sometimes referred to as *combinatorial data analysis* (see Hubert and Schultz 1976; Hubert 1983, 1985, 1987; and Hubert and Arabie 1989), is quite similar to the approach to "testing" or evaluating blockmodels advocated by White, Boorman, and Breiger (1976) and White (1977), which is implemented by the *BLOCKER* algorithm of Heil and White (1976) (as mentioned in Chapter 9). Further, since permutation tests are nonparametric (that is, they make no assumptions about underlying distributions for the data), they can be used in a very wide range of network data analysis situations. Network researchers such as Laumann, Verbrugge, and Pappi (1974), Laumann, Marsden, and Galaskiewicz (1977), and Krackhardt (1987b, 1988) have questioned the use of standard significance tests for the comparison of networks (see also Faust and Romney 1985b). Permutation tests are a nice response to these concerns. We comment on, and illustrate this approach in this chapter.

The second approach, as mentioned, is based on statistical theory for social network data. This idea uses a statistical or *stochastic blockmodel* to represent mathematically the equivalence classes defined on the actors. A stochastic blockmodel is a direct generalization of the p_1 class of probability models for social networks described in detail in the previous chapter. This approach was introduced by Holland, Laskey, and Leinhardt (1983) and Wasserman and Anderson (1987), and generalized by Breiger (1981b), Frank, Hallinan, and Nowicki (1985), Frank, Komanska, and Widaman (1985), and Wang and Wong (1987).

Stochastic blockmodels use a different definition of equivalence. Specifically, they are based on *stochastic equivalence*. In brief, one first assumes a random directed graph distribution, such as p_1, and then focuses on the actor parameters. Two actors are stochastically equivalent, if we can interchange their parameters, without changing any of the probabilities of the distribution. Clearly, this approach is useful if a researcher is willing to assume that his or her data have been generated by a stochastic process; further, the task is simplified if he or she is willing to adopt

p_1 for this stochastic mechanism. As we have mentioned, it is relatively easy to assess how well a stochastic blockmodel "fits" a data set, since goodness-of-fit statistics are a natural by-product of the statistical modeling process. We discuss this approach in a later section of this chapter.

We begin with a very brief review of structural equivalence and blockmodels, and then introduce several goodness-of-fit indices for the fit of a blockmodel to a network data set. These goodness-of-fit indices are not based on p_1 but, rather, simply compare the fit of data to a postulated positional representation. After this, we will introduce stochastic equivalence and stochastic blockmodels, and describe a class of statistical tests (and associated test or goodness-of-fit statistics) for null hypotheses concerning the partitioning of actors into stochastic equivalence classes. This methodology will be illustrated on the countries trade network.

16.1 Evaluating Blockmodels

We now consider how to evaluate blockmodel representations without using any statistical models; this restriction will be relaxed later in this chapter. We assume that we have a collection of R dichotomous relations. This restriction to dichotomous data will be relaxed later in this section. We are not interested here in compounding any of these simple relations. We define any two actors i and j to be structurally equivalent by first considering all other actors k, not equal to i or j, within the set of actors. If i and j have the same ties to and from all the other actors, for all R relations, then actors i and j are said to be *structurally equivalent*. Mathematically,

Definition 16.1 *Actors i and j are* structurally equivalent *if $i \overset{x_r}{\to} k$ if and only if $j \overset{x_r}{\to} k$, and $k \overset{x_r}{\to} i$ if and only if $k \overset{x_r}{\to} j$, for all actors, $k = 1, 2, \ldots, g$, distinct from i and j, and relations, $r = 1, 2, \ldots, R$.*

This definition of equivalence generates a collection of equivalence classes among the g actors in the network. We can partition the actors into classes exhaustively and mutually exclusively; that is, there is one and only one class for each actor, and all actors are classified. We have labeled these classes $\mathscr{B}_1, \mathscr{B}_2, \ldots, \mathscr{B}_B$. It is customary in the blockmodeling literature to refer to these classes as *positions*.

Researchers usually assume some form of approximate structural equivalence in order to partition actors into positions or classes of similar actors. Thus, actors within a specific position are usually approximately structurally equivalent, such that they relate to and are related to by many, but not all, of the other actors outside the position in the same ways.

We can consider the pattern of these relations by using a reduced graph, with just B "nodal positions," representing the positions, rather than the actors. This reduced graph is then used as a solution for the representation of relations among approximately structurally equivalent actors within the positions. With perfect structural equivalence, if all actors in $\mathcal{B}_k$ relate to all actors in $\mathcal{B}_l$, then there is a line in the reduced graph from nodal position $\mathcal{B}_k$ to nodal position $\mathcal{B}_l$. The reduced graph generates a single sociomatrix, defined on B nodal positions, for each of the measured R relations. The sociomatrix for a specific relation is referred to as an *image matrix*, and is of size $B \times B$. We call the entire set of image matrices (one per relation), along with a description (or a mapping function) of which actors are assigned to which position, a *blockmodel*. A blockmodel is one way of representing the structural equivalences of actors and ties among and between structurally equivalent positions or classes (see Boorman and Levitt 1983a, 1983b). It is important to remember that a blockmodel is an ideal, since the actors rarely are exactly structurally equivalent.

When approximate definitions or relaxations of structural equivalence are used to identify positions, a rule for deciding whether a tie exists between positions must be used. With such rules, it is still possible to find image matrices and blockmodels. The approximate nature of many positional analyses is the source of the problem tackled in this chapter. If structural equivalence was always perfect, blockmodels would fit perfectly, and there would be no need for measures of fit.

16.1.1 Goodness-of-Fit Statistics for Blockmodels

Consider a specific blockmodel, consisting of a collection of R image matrices. The collection of image matrices is a $B \times B \times R$ matrix, labeled **B**, whose entries (sometimes called *blocks* or *bonds*, and denoted by $\{b_{klr}\}$) tell how actors in one position tend to relate to actors in other positions on the various relations. This blockmodel **B** presents all the ties among positions of approximately equivalent actors. The quantity b_{klr} equals 0 if there is not (or 1 if there is) a linkage (in the reduced graph, representing the blockmodel) from position $\mathcal{B}_k$ to position $\mathcal{B}_l$ on relation $\mathcal{X}_r$. A blockmodel also contains a mapping function defined on the actors (which we call $\phi(\bullet)$) which tells which position each actor belongs to. We will use this mapping function, as well as **B**, in this section.

As we have mentioned, one can view this blockmodel as an idealization, or an optimal model, in which actors in a specific position are predicted to be perfectly structurally equivalent. The truth, in practice, is that actors in a position are only approximately structurally equivalent. Actual data rarely enable us to find exact structural equivalences. Nonetheless, we usually like to see how close to the ideal the actors actually are; in other words, how approximate are our approximate structural equivalences. If the optimal model holds, then all actors in a position are exactly structurally equivalent actors and will behave in exactly the same way. The purpose of this chapter is to present methods for such studies.

Suppose we permute the original sociomatrices, so that the order of the actors matches the assignment of actors to positions, and then consider the submatrices that arise due to the partitioning of the g actors into B positions. All of the actors with the same value of the mapping function ϕ will be placed into the same actor subset (that is, assigned to the same position). The first g_1 rows and columns of the permuted matrix will contain all the actors with $\phi(i) = 1$, the next g_2 rows and columns will contain all the actors with $\phi(i) = 2$, and so forth. Each submatrix, which, in general, will be of dimension $g_k \times g_l$, will have a density measured on a scale between 0 and 1, which equals the proportion of ties that actually are present between actors. If all actors are perfectly structurally equivalent, this density will be either 0 or 1, as specified (or predicted) by the blockmodel (which always has an image matrix full of only 0's and 1's). The entire set of densities can then be compared to the blocks, or entries in the image matrices, which are only 0's or 1's, to determine how well a blockmodel fits (that is, how close to optimal the blockmodel really is).

If all the densities are 0's and 1's, the blockmodel fits perfectly, since the actors within the positions are exactly structurally equivalent. In this instance, all blockmodel criteria (including fat fits, lean fits, and α-blockmodels) yield exactly the same **B**. But rarely is this the case. To evaluate the fit of a blockmodel, we need methods and measures to compare the image matrices with the matrices of densities.

Alternatively, one can compare the original sociomatrices, which generate the image matrices, to their "predictions" under the blockmodel. Let us assume that actor i is in position $\mathscr{B}_k$ and actor j is in position $\mathscr{B}_l$. The predicted value for the tie (on $\mathscr{X}_r$) from actor i to actor j is equal to the link in the reduced graph from position $\mathscr{B}_k$ to position $\mathscr{B}_l$. If this link is present, the predicted value is unity, then all the structurally equivalent actors in $\mathscr{B}_k$ are predicted to interact with all the structurally equivalent actors in position $\mathscr{B}_l$; otherwise, if the arc is not present, the predicted value is 0. In this section, we discuss how to do these comparisons in order to evaluate how well a blockmodel fits a specific network data set.

Comparing Observed Densities to a Target Blockmodel. The elements in the observed sociomatrices are usually aggregated across positions to yield the densities of ties within each of the blocks. The density of ties within block b_{klr} (for $k \neq l$) is defined as

$$\Delta_{klr} = \frac{\sum_{i \in \mathscr{B}_k} \sum_{j \in \mathscr{B}_l} x_{ijr}}{g_k g_l} \tag{16.1}$$

for $k = 1, 2, \ldots, B$, $l = 1, 2, \ldots, B$, and $r = 1, 2, \ldots, R$. If $k = l$, so that we are considering the densities of ties from a position to itself, we calculate

$$\Delta_{kkr} = \frac{\sum_{i \in \mathscr{B}_k} \sum_{j \in \mathscr{B}_k} x_{ijr}}{g_k(g_k - 1)}, \tag{16.2}$$

since an actor is not allowed to choose itself (this is true in general; but see Chapter 10 for extensions). The most basic goodness-of-fit index for a blockmodel simply compares these densities, which can be viewed as elements of a $B \times B \times R$ matrix, $\mathbf{\Delta}$, to the blocks, or elements of the blockmodel $\mathbf{B}$. The matrix $\mathbf{\Delta}$ is the density table discussed in Chapters 9 and 10. Clearly the comparison of these two matrices, $\mathbf{B}$ and $\mathbf{\Delta}$, ignores which actors are in which blocks; indeed, all that matters here is how well the image matrix (without the mapping function) models the overall behavior of the approximately structurally equivalent actors in the B positions (as reflected by the densities). Only when all the densities are 0 or 1, can a blockmodel fit perfectly.

Thus, one measure of how well a blockmodel fits a data set can be based on the differences between the elements of $\mathbf{\Delta}$, and the elements of $\mathbf{B}$. If the blockmodel is constructed using the lean fit criterion, then a $b_{klr} = 0$ only when the corresponding density $\Delta_{klr} = 0$. Thus, any submatrices with 1's become oneblocks. Lean fits are sometimes called "zeroblock" fits, since only zeroblocks are fit perfectly. A "oneblock" fit is the opposite of a lean fit: $b_{klr} = 1$ only when the corresponding density $\Delta_{klr} = 1$. If the blockmodel is a fat fit, then the fit is a combination of a zeroblock and a oneblock fit: a $b_{klr} = 0$ only when the corresponding density $\Delta_{klr} = 0$, *and* a $b_{klr} = 1$ only when the corresponding density $\Delta_{klr} = 1$. Clearly, fat fits are perfect structural equivalence fits. They fit exactly only when all actors are exactly structurally equivalent. We note that for a lean fit, $b_{klr} = 1$ does not imply that the corresponding density Δ_{klr} is actually 1; in fact, the density only needs to be greater than 0. And for a oneblock fit, $b_{klr} = 0$ does not imply that the corresponding density $\Delta_{klr} = 0$; the density just needs to be less than unity. These very strict definitions usually force most researchers to construct blockmodels using the more realistic α-fit criterion. Regardless of the criterion chosen, it is rare for densities to be only 0's and 1's, so that the b's, which, by definition, can only be 0's and 1's, will rarely equal the Δ's.

A very simple goodness-of-fit index is the sum of the absolute differences between the elements of Δ and the elements of $\mathbf{B}$. Specifically, we calculate

$$\delta_{b1} = \sum_{r=1}^{R} \sum_{k=1}^{B} \sum_{l=1}^{B} |b_{klr} - \Delta_{klr}|. \tag{16.3}$$

This index, which varies from 0 to $B \times B \times R = RB^2$ (the number of entries in $\mathbf{B}$), attaining the maximum if the fitted blockmodel is completely reversed (0's instead of 1's and 1's instead of 0's) from the observed densities, is a crude indicator of fit. The smaller it is, the better the fit.

Another measure originated with Carrington, Heil, and Berkowitz (1979), and Carrington and Heil (1981). Their index is constructed using a maximum chi-squared argument, and by considering the worst possible fitting blockmodel for a particular data set. Such a fit would have 1's where 0's belong, and vice versa. Such a fit arises when the blockmodel is constructed from a "reverse" α-fit criterion. The worst possible α-fit arises when the observed density for a given block is exactly equal to α, since a slight change in the density necessitates that the "fitted" block value be changed from a 0 to a 1, or vice versa. The "goodness-of-fit" for a particular block then depends simply on how close Δ_{klr} is to α. A comparison of the densities to this "worst possible fit" will generate the largest possible goodness-of-fit index.

We first derive the Carrington-Heil-Berkowitz index for a single relation. Define g_k as the number of actors partitioned/assigned to position $\mathcal{B}_k$, and g_{kl} as the number of possible choices that can be made by actors in $\mathcal{B}_k$ of actors in $\mathcal{B}_l$. We have

$$g_{kl} = \begin{cases} g_k g_l & \text{if } k \neq l \\ g_k(g_k - 1) & \text{if } k = l. \end{cases} \tag{16.4}$$

We must also define a quantity, which varies from block to block, and depends on whether the block is a zeroblock (that is, if the density of the block is less than the prespecified α). This quantity, t_{kl}, is used in the formula for the goodness-of-fit measure, and is defined as:

$$
t_{kl} = \begin{cases} 1 & \text{if } \Delta_{kl} < \alpha \\ \frac{1-\alpha}{\alpha} & \text{otherwise.} \end{cases} \tag{16.5}
$$

Summing across blocks, and using the Carrington-Heil-Berkowitz maximum chi-squared statistic reasoning, yields their index

$$
\delta_{b2} = \sum_{k=1}^{B} \sum_{l=1}^{B} \left\{ \frac{[(\Delta_{kl} - \alpha)^2 g_{kl}]}{[(\alpha t_{kl})^2 g(g-1)]} \right\}. \tag{16.6}
$$

This index is a bit difficult to interpret; a simpler version appears below. Note, however, that t_{kl} is multiplied by α, so that the product of the two equals α when the density of a block is less than or equal to α, and $(1 - \alpha)$, when the density exceeds α. These two values are those that lead to the "worst-possible" fit, as mentioned above, and are the weights one needs to apply to the numerator quantity, $\Delta_{kl} - \alpha$, in order to calculate how well a blockmodel fits a data set. Carrington, Heil, and Berkowitz (1979) label this index b. We call it δ, our generic label for goodness-of-fit indices.

The index can be modified if the diagonal of the sociomatrix is not undefined, or if other entries in the sociomatrix are undefined, or structurally zero. The index δ_{b2} can be interpreted as a weighted sum of squared deviations from the worst possible fit, normalized using the largest possible deviations (the weights are, as mentioned, αt_{kl}). The index also distinguishes between the two possible types of blocks in an image matrix in its calculation.

Fortunately, there is a considerably easier formula for δ_{b2}. If we define

$$
o_{kl} = g_{kl} \Delta_{kl} = \text{number of 1's in the } (k,l)\text{th block}
$$
$$
o_{kl}^* = g_{kl} \alpha = \text{expected number of 1's in the } (k,l)\text{th block}
$$

then

$$
\delta_{b2} = \frac{1}{[g(g-1)\alpha]} \sum_{k=1}^{B} \sum_{l=1}^{B} \left\{ \frac{[(o_{kl} - o_{kl}^*)^2]}{[o_{kl}^*(t_{kl})^2]} \right\}, \tag{16.7}
$$

which compares the observed to the expected number of 1's across all blocks. This formula looks very much like a chi-squared statistic for testing goodness-of-fit of the observed counts in the cells to the expected counts.

It is easy to extend this index to multiple relations. We subscript o and t, with a third subscript, r, which takes on values indicating which relation is being considered. If a single α is used for all image matrices across all relations, then we define t_{klr} as

$$t_{klr} = \begin{cases} 1 & \text{if } \Delta_{klr} < \alpha \\ \frac{1-\alpha}{\alpha} & \text{otherwise} \end{cases} \qquad (16.8)$$

so that

$$\delta_{b2} = \frac{1}{[Rg(g-1)\alpha]} \sum_{r=1}^{R} \sum_{k=1}^{B} \sum_{l=1}^{B} \left\{ \frac{[(o_{klr} - o_{kl}^{*})^{2}]}{[o_{kl}^{*}(t_{klr})^{2}]} \right\}. \qquad (16.9)$$

One could, however, use a different α for each relation, such as the densities for the sociomatrices associated with each relation. This generates a blockmodel termed a μ-fit blockmodel by Carrington, Heil, and Berkowitz (1979). In this instance, we have $\alpha_1, \alpha_2, \ldots, \alpha_R$, and we define

$$t_{klr} = \begin{cases} 1 & \text{if } \Delta_{klr} < \alpha_r \\ \frac{1-\alpha_r}{\alpha_r} & \text{otherwise} \end{cases} \qquad (16.10)$$

and $o_{klr}^{*} = g_{kl}\alpha_r$ as the expected number of 1's in the (k, l)th block for the rth relation. Then, the multiple relation generalization of equation (16.7) allowing for unequal α's is

$$\delta_{b2} = \frac{1}{R} \sum_{r=1}^{R} \frac{1}{[g(g-1)\alpha_r]} \sum_{k=1}^{B} \sum_{l=1}^{B} \left\{ \frac{[(o_{klr} - o_{klr}^{*})^{2}]}{[o_{klr}^{*}(t_{klr})^{2}]} \right\}. \qquad (16.11)$$

Evaluating δ_{b1} and δ_{b2} is difficult. There is no statistical theory or distribution for the indices. One could use a permutation test, permuting the actors to arrive at a different assignment of actors to positions, and hence, an entire collection of Δ matrices. There will be one Δ, and hence one δ_{b1} and δ_{b2}, for every possible permutation of actors to positions. We have found that permutation tests are quite useful. Some of these tests are implemented in *UCINET*. However, the indices routinely calculated by *UCINET* are based not on the Δ's, but on the original sociomatrix entries. This package does not directly calculate many of the measures discussed in this chapter.

The methodology just discussed examines blocks, and the properties of blocks, and ignores the ties between the actors. As mentioned, it is also not statistical in nature. We now turn to the second approach to blockmodel goodness-of-fit, comparing the actual observed data to the ties between the individual actors, as predicted by a blockmodel. This second approach is quite amenable to permutation tests.

Comparing Observed Relational Linkages to a Target Block-model. Take the observed sociomatrices, with entries x_{ijr}, and use the mapping function for the blockmodel under consideration to arrive at the target, or "predicted," collection of ties for each pair of actors on each relation. The blockmodel classifies actor i into position $\mathcal{B}_{\phi(i)}$, and actor j into position $\mathcal{B}_{\phi(j)}$, and the image matrix tells whether ties are present among and between positions. So, the "target" matrix is a hypothesized sociomatrix in which all actors in a position have indentical ties to and from actors in other positions. Thus, the predicted value for x_{ijr} is

$$x_{ijr}^{(t)} = b_{\phi(i)\phi(j)r},$$ (16.12)

indicating whether the actors in the same position as i ($\mathcal{B}_{\phi(i)}$) are predicted by the blockmodel to have ties to the actors in the same position as j ($\mathcal{B}_{\phi(j)}$). We can view the $x^{(t)}$'s as elements of a target array, to which we compare the x's, the actual sociomatrix entries. The superscript (t) indicates that the matrix (or its entries) is the "target" matrix, calculated from the blockmodel. This target matrix is actually a hypothesis matrix, which is to be compared to the observed sociomatrix, and subsequently evaluated. We should note that this methodology is quite flexible, and can be used to compare $\mathbf{X}$ to any "hypothesis" matrix, even if the target or hypothesis matrix $\mathbf{X}^{(t)}$ is not generated from any particular blockmodel.

A number of goodness-of-fit indices exist for quantifying how close the observed $\mathbf{x}$ is to the target $\mathbf{x}^{(t)}$. Each index measures the similarity (or dissimilarity) of the target and the actual relational data. The index of choice depends on the advantages and disadvantages of each. We should note that there is no parametric statistical theory for any of them, but all can be evaluated using a nonparametric, randomization test approach.

For example, we can calculate the sum of the absolute differences between the entries of the observed and target matrices:

$$\delta_{x1} = \sum_{r=1}^{R}\sum_{i=1}^{g}\sum_{j=1}^{g}|x_{ijr} - x_{ijr}^{(t)}|.$$ (16.13)

The value of δ_{x1} is the number of entries in the observed sociomatrix $\mathbf{x}$ that are not indentical to their predicted values in the target sociomatrix $\mathbf{x}^{(t)}$. It is thus a measure of dissimilarity between the two matrices. This measure δ_{x1}, comparing a sociomatrix to a target matrix, is a simple function of the measure δ_{b1}:

$$\delta_{x1} = R \times g \times (g-1)\delta_{b1}.$$

A second index for comparing a sociomatrix to a target matrix is the *match coefficient,* used in *UCINET IV.* This quantity, which we will denote by δ_{x2}, is closely related to δ_{x1}. The match coefficient is the proportion of ties in $\mathbf{x}$ that are identical to $\mathbf{x}^{(t)}$. Specifically,

$$\delta_{x2} = 1 - \frac{\sum_{r=1}^{R} \sum_{i=1}^{g} \sum_{j=1}^{g} |x_{ijr} - x_{ijr}^{(t)}|}{R \times g \times (g-1)}. \tag{16.14}$$

This index is a similarity measure, so that large values indicate a closer fit between the observed data and the predicted target.

Yet another index is the *matrix correlation,* calculated using all the elements in $\mathbf{x}$ and all the elements in $\mathbf{x}^{(t)}$ (excluding diagonal elements if necessary):

$$\delta_{x3} = \frac{\sum_{r=1}^{R} \sum_{i=1}^{g} \sum_{j=1}^{g} x_{ijr}^{*} x_{ijr}^{(t)*}}{\sqrt{\sum_{r=1}^{R} \sum_{i=1}^{g} \sum_{j=1}^{g} x_{ijr}^{*2}} \sqrt{\sum_{r=1}^{R} \sum_{i=1}^{g} \sum_{j=1}^{g} x_{ijr}^{(t)*2}}}, \tag{16.15}$$

where the x^{*}'s and the $x^{(t)*}$'s are mean deviations; that is, they equal the differences of the x's from their overall mean, and the $x^{(t)}$'s from their overall mean, respectively. We note that all of these δ's can include diagonal entries in their sums, if such entries are defined.

This matrix correlation index δ_{x3}, since all the data values are dichotomous, can be calculated more simply, as demonstrated by Hubert and Baker (1978) for $R=1$. Specifically, we define

$$\begin{aligned}
o_{xx^{(t)}} &= \text{number of entries that equal 1 in both } \mathbf{x} \text{ and } \mathbf{x}^{(t)} \\
o_x &= \text{number of entries in } \mathbf{x} \text{ that equal 1} \\
o_{x^{(t)}} &= \text{number of entries in } \mathbf{x}^{(t)} \text{ that equal 1} \\
z_x &= \text{number of entries in } \mathbf{x} \text{ that equal 0} \\
z_{x^{(t)}} &= \text{number of entries in } \mathbf{x}^{(t)} \text{ that equal 0.}
\end{aligned}$$

Then, one can calculate

$$\delta_{x3} = \frac{g(g-1)o_{xx^{(t)}} - o_x o_{x^{(t)}}}{\sqrt{o_x o_{x^{(t)}} z_x z_{x^{(t)}}}}. \tag{16.16}$$

The index, δ_{x3}, used by many researchers over the years (see Arabie, Boorman, and Levitt 1978) was labeled $\Gamma(\mathbf{X}, \mathbf{X}^{(t)})$ by Hubert and Baker. As noted above, one can calculate δ_{x3} for any target or hypothesis matrix, and use it to evaluate the "hypothesis" that generated that particular $\mathbf{x}^{(t)}$.

Panning (1982a) and Noma and Smith (1985a) recommend the use of the squared multiple correlation coefficient R^2 for comparisons of $\mathbf{x}$ and $\mathbf{x}^{(t)}$. These authors argue for the use of R^2 as a goodness-of-fit measure to evaluate the fit of a blockmodel to data, and show how to use the statistic to find a "best-fitting" blockmodel. They note that the predicted value for a specific submatrix from the original sociomatrices is either a 0 or a 1, and that the sum of squares of deviations of the entries in the submatrix from this predicted value can be used as a measure of fit. From the sums of squares for all submatrices or blocks, one can calculate both a within-block sum of squares and a sum of squares deviation from the grand mean (analogous to within-subjects and total sums of squares in a one-way analysis of variance). The index R^2 is simply the ratio of these two sums of squares, subtracted from unity. The within-block or numerator sum of squares is the "total unexplained sum of squares," and the measure increases as this quantity becomes small, relative to the total (or denominator) sum of squares. Illustrations of the use of this index can be found in Panning (1982a, 1982b), and Noma and Smith (1985a). Calculations are detailed by Panning (1982a).

The utility of this index rests on an argument that blockmodeling is actually a form of an analysis of variance, in which the "independent" variables are the block densities, and the "dependent" variables are the observed entries within the sociomatrices. Hence, an "optimal" blocking should maximize the percent of explained variance, and lead a researcher to focus on R^2, the statistic that has this property. Panning (1982a) gives a strategy for finding blockmodels that have maximal R^2's. We note that one can generate a permutation distribution for this index (see Noma and Smith 1985a) simply by considering all possible permutations of the actors to positions, and calculating R^2 for each permutation. This leads to a valid, nonparametric statistical test for the goodness of an observed fit. The index is also easily used for multiple relation network data sets.

However, as several authors have noted, neither δ_{x3} and R^2 is well-suited for dichotomous data, and thus, not recommended. Carrington, Heil, and Berkowitz (1979) comment on the suitability of the use of correlation coefficients to compare two binary matrices. Faust and Romney (1985a) also comment on the use of correlation coefficients used to compare ties. The main problem with δ_{x3} and R^2 is that correlation coefficients are "designed" for continuous variables, where they measure the linear association between a pair of variables. This certainly is not the situation here.

Hubert and Baker (1978) show that for $R = 1$, the expected value of δ_{x3} is 0, where the distribution is taken over all possible permutation assignments of the actors into the prespecified number of positions, B, and compute the variance of this index. These two results lead nicely to a permutation test which yields the significance level (or p-value) of the observed δ_{x3}. A good illustration of this approach is given by Baker and Hubert (1981). The advantages of this approach are discussed by Arabie, Boorman, and Levitt (1978).

One (large) disadvantage of this index is that these results of Hubert and Baker have not been extended to multiple relations, $R > 1$. Further, as noted by Arabie, Boorman, and Levitt (1978), lean fits and their filled-in oneblocks are usually a "poor assumption" about underlying social structure. Thus, indices built around them may not be very accurate.

Other measures of association, comparing $\mathbf{x}$ to $\mathbf{x}^{(t)}$, can be found in Katz and Powell (1953), Hubert and Baker (1978), Zegers and ten Berge (1985), and Wasserman (1987). Some of them are implemented in *UCINET*. Carrington, Heil, and Berkowitz's (1979) measure, δ_{b2}, also falls into this category, since it can be written as a function of the observed data, rather than the observed densities (compare equations (16.6) and (16.7)). For $R = 1$, one can view this problem as a birelational network analysis, where the two relations are the observed and the target. In this setting, multivariate statistical models are appropriate; Wasserman (1987) shows how to compare an observed to a target sociomatrix using dyadic interaction statistical models.

Zegers and ten Berge (1985) suggest a *coefficient of identity*, defined as

$$\delta_{x4} = \frac{2\sum_{r=1}^{R}\sum_{i=1}^{g}\sum_{j=1}^{g} x_{ijr}x_{ijr}^{(t)}}{\sum_{r=1}^{R}\sum_{i=1}^{g}\sum_{j=1}^{g}[x_{ijr}^2 + x_{ijr}^{(t)2}]}, \tag{16.17}$$

where the x's and the $x^{(t)}$'s are not mean deviations (unlike the calculation for matrix correlation, equation (16.15)). This index is designed for variables measured on absolute scales (see Suppes and Zinnes 1963; Krantz, Luce, Suppes, and Tversky 1971). Data measured on an absolute scale do not remain invariant under any type of transformation, which is certainly true for dichotomous relational data. The δ_{x4} index measures how identical the two matrices are. Once again, there is no parametric statistical theory for this index.

16.1.2 Structurally Based Blockmodels and Permutation Tests

It should not be surprising to find that ties predicted by a blockmodel are extremely similar to the observed ties. After all, blockmodels are constructed from the ties in the first place. In an exploratory study, the researcher often seeks the "best" blockmodel of a given data set.

In such a case, if a permutation test shows that there are one or more assignments of actors to positions that yield a better match between the observed data and the target blockmodel, then the researcher might be interested in studying these better assignments of actors to positions. This strategy of assigning actors to positions in order to optimize an objective function (such as maximizing δ_{x2} or δ_{x3}), is a promising way to construct blockmodels. This direct construction of blockmodels has received considerable attention recently (Arabie, Hubert, and Schleutermann 1990; Batagelj, Ferligoj, and Doreian 1992; Batagelj, Doreian, and Ferligoj 1992).

Permutation tests can also be used to compare ties to entries of target matrices postulated by some theoretical structures. There are a variety of blockmodel image matrices for some theoretically important structures, such as cohesive subgroups, transitivity, and center-periphery. We illustrate a test of such theoretical structures shortly.

16.1.3 An Example

Turn now to the countries trades data set, and consider the evaluation of the blockmodels for these data first presented in Chapter 9. We used three of the relations (manufactured goods, raw or crude materials excluding fuel, and diplomatic exchange) to construct a blockmodel. The blockmodel had $B = 6$ positions, and the density tables (one for each relation) are given in Table 10.4. We note that this blockmodel is based on structural equivalence and correlation coefficients, using both rows and columns of the three sociomatrices. The densities of the three sociomatrices are 0.562, 0.556, and 0.668, respectively. The blockmodels are α-blockmodels, with these unique densities for each relation. The image matrices are given in Figure 10.5.

Comparing Densities to Blockmodels. For the countries trade network, we calculated the indices designed to compare observed density tables to blockmodels. The values of these indices are given in Table 16.1. As can be seen, the blockmodels fit the observed density matrices moderately well, and about the same overall. The fits are not spectacular, however.

Comparing Ties to Target Sociomatrices. We also calculated the indices designed to compare the actual ties to the target sociomatrices based on blockmodels. The values of the three δ_x indices designed for

Table 16.1. *Comparison of density matrices to target blockmodels –*
countries trade example

Relation	Index δ_{b1}	δ_{b2}
Manufactured goods	5.055	0.575
Crude materials	6.986	0.433
Diplomatic ties	6.766	0.490
All three relations	18.807	0.499

this purpose are given in Table 16.2. All of these goodness-of-fit indices
indicate that the sociomatrices are rather close to their target model
matrices.

We evaluated the match coefficient δ_{x2} (equation (16.14)) and the
matrix correlation index δ_{x3} (equation (16.15)) using permutation tests
to compare the actual ties coded in the sociomatrices $\mathbf{x}$ to the target
sociomatrices $\mathbf{x}^{(t)}$. Calculations were done using *UCINET*. We tested two
null hypotheses for each of the three relations studied:

$$H_{01} : \delta_{x2} = 0$$

and

$$H_{02} : \delta_{x3} = 0$$

versus alternative hypotheses that these indices are not zero. For these
tests, we obtained 1000 permutations of the rows (and simultaneously,
the columns) of the sociomatrix. Table 16.2 reports the calculated values
of the match coefficient and the matrix correlation for the example. We
also report the fraction of permutations out of 1000 in which the value
of δ_{x2} or δ_{x3} was greater than the actual, observed value of the index.
These fractions, given in parentheses below the values of the indices, are
nonparametric *p*-values for their respective null hypotheses.

These permutation tests indicate that the ties predicted by the blockmodel image matrices (including the assignment of actors to positions,
and the statements specifying the presence or absence of ties between
positions) are closer to the observed values of the relation than to any
other assignment of actors to positions. So, for the countries trade example, the blockmodel image matrices are good representations of the ties

Table 16.2. *Comparison of ties to target sociomatrices – countries trade example*

Relation	Index			
	δ_{x1}	δ_{x2}	δ_{x3}	δ_{x4}
Manufactured goods	86	0.844 (0.000)	0.687 (0.000)	0.858
Crude materials	111	0.799 (0.000)	0.593 (0.000)	0.819
Diplomatic ties	112	0.797 (0.000)	0.581 (0.000)	0.838

among countries. Clearly, the indices are not 0, and there are no "null" associations between data and model fits.

Other Analyses and Tests. One can evaluate how well a specific theoretical structure represents a given set of network data by constructing a target sociomatrix, $\mathbf{x}^{(t)}$, from the hypothesized theoretical structure.

Constructing the target sociomatrix, $\mathbf{x}^{(t)}$, requires several steps. The first step is to partition actors into positions. This partition could be the result of a positional analysis in which approximately equivalent actors are assigned to the same position (for example, using hierarchical clustering or *CONCOR*). The second step is to specify, for each pair of positions, whether a tie is present or absent. For some structures, such as cohesive subgroups, this decision is straightforward, since in a cohesive subgroup structure, ties are hypothesized only within, and not between, positions. However, for other structures, such as a hierarchy, or a center-periphery structure, the hypothesized presence or absence of a tie between positions depends on where the positions are "located" in the structure. For example, in a hierarchy, ties are directed from "lower" positions to "higher" positions. Thus, the order of positions in the blockmodel is important. One way to arrive at an ordering is to consider theoretically important attributes of actors in the positions. For example, one could hypothesize that ties of advice in a blockmodel of an organization form a transitive system in which ties are directed from each position to all positions whose members have, on average, longer tenure in the organization. Thus, the positions would be ordered by the average tenure of members. Finally, the target sociomatrix is constructed, as usual, using equation (16.12).

Let us now turn to our example to illustrate the evaluation of theoretical structures. Numerous authors have hypothesized that the world political and economic system is a center-periphery structure, in which more developed nations occupy central positions, and less-developed nations occupy peripheral positions. In the countries trade network, we have already ordered the positions from most central, $\mathcal{B}_1$, to least central, $\mathcal{B}_6$, based on the three image matrices presented in Figure 10.5. This ordering also appears to correspond well to the attributes of the positions, presented in Table 10.2.

A permutation test can be used to compare the target sociomatrix based on a center-periphery structure with the observed ties for the three studied relations in the countries trade example. The theoretical blockmodel image for a center-periphery structure was constructed with $B = 6$ positions, with oneblocks in the upper left triangle of the image matrix. The target sociomatrix for this image matrix was then compared to each of the three relations. For the manufactured goods relation, the matrix correlation $\delta_{x3} = 0.536$, and the match coefficient $\delta_{x2} = 0.772$; these values are the largest out of 1000 permutations. For the crude materials relation, $\delta_3 = 0.513$, and $\delta_2 = 0.759$; both are largest out of 1000 permutations. Finally, for the diplomatic ties relation, $\delta_3 = 0.532$, and $\delta_2 = 0.792$; both are the largest out of 1000 permutations. So, this assignment of countries to positions, and this ordering of positions, matches a center-periphery structure quite well.

The countries trade example seems to be consistent with a center-periphery structure, as confirmed by the permutation tests. The ordering of poountries. Core positions (for example $\mathcal{B}_1$, $\mathcal{B}_2$, and $\mathcal{B}_3$) have lower rates of population growth, higher secondary school enrollment, and higher energy consumption per capita, whereas peripheral positions (for example, $\mathcal{B}_4$, $\mathcal{B}_5$, and $\mathcal{B}_6$) have higher rates of population growth, lower rates of secondary school enrollment, and lower energy consumption per capita.

16.2 Stochastic Blockmodels

We now turn to a discussion of goodness-of-fit indices which are based on specific, parametric statistical models. This is a rather different approach to assessing the fit of a network data set to a particular partition of actors to positions. This statistical approach, based on the statistical models described in Chapter 15, has associated with it a natural goodness-of-fit index that follows directly from the models under consideration. As should be clear from the first section of this chapter, there is little unanimity on the choice of goodness-of-fit statistics for blockmodels, primarily because the statistics in use are not fit statistics for particular models. In fact, the statistics we have described could be applied in a wide variety of situations, not just blockmodeling social network data. The statistic discussed here has the advantage that it is appropriate for social network data, being modeled with p_1 and its relatives. It is also the obvious statistic to use in this situation, unlike those described in the previous section, whose choice is somewhat arbitrary. Thus, it has statistical properties (such as an asymptotic distribution), and is optimal (in the sense that it describes the fit of the models to the data better than any other statistic). This approach to evaluation was introduced by Fienberg and Wasserman (1981a), and developed by Holland, Laskey, and Leinhardt (1983), and Wasserman and Anderson (1987), primarily to provide a solution to the problem of which goodness-of-fit statistic to use. Breiger (1981b) comments on the use of stochastic blockmodels, and Wang and Wong (1987) offer a generalization of the p_1 class of models that includes blocking parameters (see also Frank, Hallinan, and Nowicki 1985, and Frank, Komanska, and Widaman 1985).

As pointed out by Holland, Laskey, and Leinhardt (1983), relational/positional analyses and blockmodels suffer from both the lack of an explicit model for data variability and formal goodness-of-fit tests. The stochastic models described in the previous chapters, while lacking methodology for incorporating roles and positions into an analysis, are clearly based on explicit formulations and have standard tests of fit.

In this section, we will describe a stochastic blockmodel, a model for social network data obtained by assuming a stochastic model for the relational data and then allowing the actors to be partitioned into subsets or blocks. We first assume that the partition is known a priori; that is, unlike with the blockmodels of Chapter 10, we do not use the relational data to partition the actors. Rather, the partitioning is accomplished using attribute information on the actors. Attribute variables can greatly reduce the number of parameters in a model (thereby providing more parsimony) through the modeling of a **W**-, rather than a **Y**-array. These stochastic blockmodels will be discussed for valued and multirelational data sets, and will be illustrated (as was done with the measures in the first part of this chapter) by using the countries trade network.

Wasserman and Anderson (1987) also describe stochastic a posteriori blockmodels, which are not based on exogenous actor attribute information. These posterior partitions are more difficult to find and evaluate statistically, but are highly desirable because of their similarity to relational analysis, which is also based on posterior partitions (found from the relations, rather than the attribute variables). These a posteriori stochastic blockmodels are very similar to the positional analyses of Chapters 9 and 10, since they use the relational data to obtain the positions; unfortunately, this "data dredging" does not allow for proper, significance tests of the fit of actors to the derived positions. Contrasting the a posteriori models to the a priori models described here, one can see that the use of a priori positions, independent of the relational data, leads to legitimate *p*-values for the desired significance tests.

The goal of such blockmodels centers on finding a good mapping of actors to positions, using the available relational data. Of the several methods for finding stochastic a posteriori blockmodels discussed by Wasserman and Anderson, correspondence analysis (see Wasserman, Faust, and Galaskiewicz 1990; Wasserman and Faust 1989; as well as Noma and Smith 1985b, and Barnett 1990) seems most useful. We use this and other techniques in this chapter to obtain a posteriori mapping functions, and hence stochastic goodness-of-fit indices for the countries trade data.

We begin with a formal definition of a stochastic blockmodel, and then, following Wasserman and Anderson (1987), show how this concept gives us stochastic equivalence of actors. A very special case of these definitions arises when we couple a stochastic blockmodel with an assumption that p_1 is operating. As we will show, this stochastic blockmodel can be viewed as a special case of p_1. We will also describe Wang and Wong's (1987) formulation, which gives a more general p_1 blockmodel. Such definitions and assumptions will then give us a natural goodness-of-fit index for stochastic blockmodels.

16.2.1 Definition of a Stochastic Blockmodel

We start with X_1, X_2, ... , X_R, as a collection of random variables consisting of measurements on R relational variables for a set of g actors. We put all of these R random matrices into a giant super-sociomatrix X (which is sometimes called the adjacency matrix for a *multigraph*), and define the probability distribution for X as $p(X) = \Pr(X=x)$. This distribution simply gives the probabilities that the various relational linkages between actors across all relations are equal to the specified values given as entries in the sociomatrices comprising x. We must also define X_{ij} as the vector of random variables associated with the R relation ties from actor i to actor j: $X_{ij} = (X_{ij1}, X_{ij2}, \ldots, X_{ijR})$. We use the dyad as the basic modeling unit. So, we pair X_{ij} with X_{ji} to form the collection of random dyads $D_{ij} : \mathbf{D}_{ij} = (X_{ij}, X_{ji})$, $i < j$.

A *stochastic blockmodel* is based on the probability distribution for X, as well as the mapping function which assigns the g actors to the positions $\mathcal{B}_1, \mathcal{B}_2, \ldots, \mathcal{B}_B$. The difference between a stochastic blockmodel and a blockmodel is the assumption of a probability distribution for all the ties. Specifically,

Definition 16.2 *Let $p(x)$ be the probability function for a stochastic multigraph (which is represented by the super-sociomatrix X). Further, we suppose that $\mathcal{B} = \{\mathcal{B}_1, \mathcal{B}_2, \ldots, \mathcal{B}_B\}$ is a mutually exclusive and exhaustive partition of the g actors into B positions, as specified by the mapping function ϕ. Then, with respect to $\mathcal{B}$, $p(x)$ is a stochastic blockmodel if the following two conditions are satisfied:*

(i) *The random dyadic variables $\mathbf{D}_{ij}$ are all statistically independent of each other.*

(ii) *For any actors $i \neq j$ and $i' \neq j$, if i and i' belong to the same position, then the random dyadic variables $\mathbf{D}_{ij}$ and $\mathbf{D}_{i'j}$ have the same probability distribution.*

This definition states that a stochastic blockmodel consists of a probability distribution (an illustration of which will be given shortly), and a mapping of the actors to blocks. If the blockmodel is stochastic, the ties, which are assumed to be random variables, must meet several probabilistic conditions. First of all, sticking with one of the basic assumptions of the stochastic models described in this part of the book, the dyads are independent of each other. Secondly, if two actors are in the same position, then ties that they send and/or receive are governed by the same probability distribution. This latter assumption implies that if we calculate any probability using $p(x)$, the probability is unchanged when we substitute actors belonging to a specific position for one another. As we point out shortly, this fact leads us to a definition of "stochastic equivalence," which generalizes the important concept of structural equivalence.

Holland, Laskey, and Leinhardt (1983) refer to stochastic blockmodels defined above as *pair-dependent stochastic blockmodels*, because of their focus on the dyad, rather than on individual ties X_{ij}. Without this focus, there is a major problem. One cannot model tendencies toward reciprocity, which can be a driving force in social structures. Without using the dyad as a modeling unit, one cannot model structural tendencies that occur at the level of the dyad. If we assume that the entire collection of random variables $\{X_{ij}\}$ is statistically independent (rather than the dyadic random variables), there is no way to determine whether reciprocity is an important property for a specific set of actors. Reciprocity can only be studied by looking at individual dyads, and a stochastic blockmodel that assumes that the ties in a dyad are statistically independent is not of much use.

We do note that this focus on ties rather than dyads makes stochastic blockmodels analogous to standard blockmodels, which implicitly assumes independence at the level of individual actors, rather than at the level of dyads. Stochastic equivalence and pair-dependent stochastic blockmodels fortunately assume dependence at the dyadic level, which thus allows a researcher to look at dyadic effects such as reciprocity.

16.2.2 Definition of Stochastic Equivalence

The definition of a stochastic blockmodel implies that actors within a specific position are "exchangeable" or "substitutable" with respect to the probability distribution $p(x)$. We formally define this exchangeability as *stochastic equivalence*:

Definition 16.3 *Given a stochastic "multigraph," represented by the collection of random matrices X, actors i and i' are* stochastically equivalent *if and only if the probability of any event concerning X is unchanged by an interchanging of actors i and i'.*

Stochastic equivalence is an important concept for stochastic social network models, and we have already used it in Chapter 15. The definition given here is stated quite formally, and in generality, so that it applies to any distribution $p(x)$, rather than just p_1 (which is a special case that we discuss below).

It should be clear that if we assume that X is stochastic (as is required for a *stochastic* blockmodel), then structurally equivalent actors are stochastically equivalent, but (as pointed out by Wasserman and Anderson 1987) not vice versa. Stochastic equivalence is more general than the structural version; and, in a probabilistic sense, it is considerably weaker. If actors i and i' are structurally equivalent, and $i \overset{\mathcal{X}_r}{\rightarrow} j$, then by definition, $i' \overset{\mathcal{X}_r}{\rightarrow} j$, for all r; however, if actors i and i' are just stochastically equivalent, then all that is required is that i and i' have the same *probability* of relating to j on the rth relation. This means that empirically, the relational linkages need not be identical for two actors to be stochastically equivalent. As we have mentioned throughout, structural equivalence is rare; one usually must adopt some approximation to it. And, stochastic equivalence appears to be a natural, substantively based alternative, which (unlike structural equivalence) is likely to hold exactly for a set of actors.

A blockmodel, based on structural equivalence, is deterministic, since it requires that relational linkages be either present (if actors in one position *relate* to actors in another) or absent (if actors in one position *do not relate* to actors in another). Viewed in this way, a blockmodel is a very special case of a stochastic blockmodel, in which all probabilities (specified by $p(x)$) are forced to be either 0 or 1. The flexibility of stochastic blockmodels (these probabilities can be anywhere between 0 and 1!) makes them especially attractive.

We note, as we will discuss later in this chapter, that one can obtain a measure of how stochastically equivalent two actors actually are. For some $p(x)$'s, stochastic equivalence is manifested as functions of the parameters. And if the actor-level parameters for two actors are statistically identical, the two actors are stochastically equivalent. It remains a task simply to evaluate the statistical equality of these actor-level parameters.

The easiest way to understand the implications of a stochastic blockmodel and stochastic equivalence is to consider particular $p(x)$ probability functions. This is our next topic.

16.2.3 Application to Special Probability Functions

We now describe two particular stochastic blockmodel probability distributions. Both assume that either p_1 is operating if $R = 1$, or one of the multirelational versions of p_1, if $R > 1$. The first model does not contain actor parameters and, as described by Fienberg and Wasserman (1981a) and Wasserman and Anderson (1987), equates actor parameters across all actors within a position. Thus, there are no individual actor parameters (only position parameters) in this model. The second model takes p_1 and then adds special blockmodel parameters, as postulated by Wang and Wong (1987), and keeps individual actor parameters. We discuss each of these stochastic blockmodels in detail.

A very important issue here is how to find the function which maps actors to positions. There are (at least) two approaches. The first is to assume that the function is known in advance, and depends on exogenous actor characteristics, such as age, gender, size, location, and so on. The second approach is a posteriori, and tries to find the mapping function using relational data. We comment on both of these.

Stochastic Blockmodels Based on p_1 without Actor Parameters. First assume that we have $R = 1$ relations, and that this relation is dichotomous. Referring to the basic model of Chapter 15, p_1, choose the following probability distribution for $p(x)$:

$$
\begin{aligned}
\Pr((X_{ij}, X_{ji}) = (m, n)) \quad = \quad & \exp\{\lambda_{ij} + m\alpha_i + m\beta_j \\
& + n\alpha_j + n\beta_i \\
& + (m + n)\theta + mn(\alpha\beta)\}.
\end{aligned}
\tag{16.18}
$$

This model, which is simply an equivalent statement of p_1 (see equation (15.2)), assumes that the dyads are statistically independent, so that the full $p(x)$ is found by multiplying equations (16.18) over all $\binom{g}{2}$ dyads. A stochastic blockmodel based on (16.18) will come equipped with a function mapping the actors into the B positions of $\mathcal{B}$.

The two conditions for a stochastic blockmodel are that the dyads be statistically independent (which, as we have noted, holds here) and that actors be "exchangeable" or stochastically equivalent if they belong to the same position (that is, the probability distribution remains unchanged if we exchange actors). Let us focus on this second condition. Notice that there are two sets of parameters in (16.18) that depend on the g actors: $\{\alpha_i\}$ for expansiveness, and $\{\beta_j\}$ for popularity. Clearly, if all α's are constant for actors within a particular position, as well as all β's, then the exchangeability condition is fulfilled. Hence, if we assume $p(x)$ $= p_1$, and require that, for all actors i and i' within position $\mathcal{B}_k$,

$$
\begin{aligned}
\alpha_i &= \alpha_{i'} \\
\beta_i &= \beta_{i'},
\end{aligned}
$$

then we get a stochastic blockmodel. Wasserman and Anderson (1987) refer to actors which have equal p_1 model parameters as *stochastic actor-equivalent*. If this equality holds, and we assume p_1, then clearly, actors within a particular position are stochastically equivalent.

Note that with equality of model parameters for all actors within a position, each position has its own α and its own β. No longer are there any individual actor parameters (but see below for a stochastic blockmodel that allows for both position and actor parameters). The number of α's (as well as the number of β's) is reduced from g to B. That is,

$$\alpha_i = \alpha_{i'} = \alpha^{[k]}$$
$$\beta_i = \beta_{i'} = \beta^{[k]},$$

if actors i and i' belong to position $\mathcal{B}_k$, for $k = 1, 2, \ldots, B$. Parameters are now associated with positions, rather than individual actors. Of substantive interest is how likely it is that an actor in one position relates to actors and is related to by actors in the same and other positions. Also of interest here is whether a partition into positions, based on one or more actor attribute variables, actually describes the relational data. In other words, are parameters really constant within a position? We will be able to answer this question with the models discussed below.

The big question is how to find such mapping functions that place actors into positions. Frequently, the functions arise from actor attribute variables, as we have demonstrated in Chapter 15. For example, the six second-grade children have been categorized into $B = 2$ positions based on their age, and stochastic blockmodels fit to these positions were discussed in the previous chapter. For other examples from the literature, Wasserman and Iacobucci (1986) analyzed the frequency of toy-offerings among a set of ninety children who were partitioned into positions based on their gender, and Galaskiewicz, Wasserman, Rauschenbach, Bielefeld, and Mullaney (1985) studied patterns of corporate board interlocking by partitioning firms into positions based on attributes of the firms such as size, number of employees, and information on the chief executive officers (such as club memberships).

We note that sometimes these functions can be found directly from the relational data. Such a posteriori stochastic blockmodels will be discussed in a later section.

To fit stochastic blockmodels, one works with a **w**-array, which is calculated by aggregating the **y**-array over all actors within positions. Details and examples are given in Chapter 15, including the statistical justification for this aggregation.

Extensions of stochastic blockmodels to more than one relation and to valued relations are straightforward. One must have equality of all parameters for all actors within a specific position. For example, if we have a set of α's for each relation, then the R expansiveness parameters for actor i would have to equal the R expansiveness parameters for actor i', for all pairs of actors i and i' within the same position. One first postulates an appropriate statistical dyadic interaction model and then adopts a mapping function for the actors to the positions.

○**Stochastic Blockmodels Based on p_1 with Actor Parameters.** Another approach to the development of a stochastic blockmodel based on p_1 comes from Wasserman and Galaskiewicz (1984) and Wang and Wong (1987). These authors note that p_1 completely ignores possible + a priori partitioning of actors into positions. As we have noted, the densities of the blocks (arising from the positions) may differ quite a bit. p_1 has a tendency to underestimate the probabilities of relational linkages in blocks with large densities, and overestimate the probabilities of relational linkages in blocks with small densities. Wang and Wong argue that one should add "blocking" parameters to p_1, thus adjusting fitted probabilities for possible position effects. Breiger's (1981b) statements that blocks are *internally homogeneous* (which is synonymous with stating that actors within positions are stochastically equivalent) can also be used theoretically to justify the addition of blocking parameters to p_1 (see Breiger 1981c, Goodman 1981, Marsden 1985, and Fienberg, Meyer, and Wasserman 1985). This approach has the advantage that the models have both individual actor parameters as well as blocking parameters, but the disadvantage that more parameters are estimated, and consequently, less parsimonious fits are required.

The Wang and Wong (1987) stochastic blockmodel takes p_1 and adds blocking parameters. These parameters reflect the tendencies for actors in position $\mathcal{B}_k$ to choose actors in position $\mathcal{B}_l$. We work with a single, dichotomous relation. Specifically, we define the indicator quantity

$$d_{ijkl} = \begin{array}{l} 1 \text{ if actor } i \in \mathcal{B}_k \text{ and if actor } j \in \mathcal{B}_l \\ 0 \text{ otherwise.} \end{array} \qquad (16.19)$$

There will be $B \times B$ of these indicator variables for each pair of actors, but all but one of them will be zero. The one that is unity indicates which submatrix of $\mathbf{X}$ contains the tie from i to j. We now take equation

(16.18), and add a set of blocking parameters $\{\zeta_{kl}\}$:

$$
\begin{aligned}
\Pr((X_{ij}, X_{ji}) = (m, n)) \quad = \quad & \exp\{\lambda_{ij} + m\alpha_i + m\beta_j \\
& +n\alpha_j + n\beta_i \\
& +(m+n)\theta + mn(\alpha\beta) \\
& +d_{ijkl}\zeta_{kl}\}.
\end{aligned}
\qquad (16.20)
$$

One will have a single ζ parameter in the probability model for each dyad.

There are B^2 ζ's, and to estimate them all, we require these parameters to have 0 row and column sums:

$$
\sum_{k=1}^{B} \zeta_{kl} \quad = \quad 0 \text{ for all } l
$$

$$
\sum_{l=1}^{B} \zeta_{kl} \quad = \quad 0 \text{ for all } k.
$$

Thus, there are $(B-1)^2$ independent blocking parameters (or degrees of freedom for this effect). The equation (16.20), coupled with the constraints given above, and the usual assumption of dyadic independence, give us a second $p(x)$ based on p_1. This $p(x)$, unlike the first, contains both actor *and* blocking parameters. We note that the ζ's can be either positive (indicating increases in tendencies for ties to form, as is the case with oneblocks) or negative (indicating decreases in tendencies for ties to form, implying that ties are more likely to disappear, as is the case with zeroblocks). Thus, there is no need to incorporate directly into the stochastic blockmodel information about which blocks are predominately 1's, and which blocks are mostly 0's.

Wang and Wong (1987) fit such a model to a classroom of $g = 27$ students and a friendship relation (see Hansell 1984). The fit of p_1 does not take into account a very strong gender effect apparent in this data set. Wang and Wong recommend that actors be partitioned into $B = 2$ positions based on gender (boys tended to choose boys, and girls to choose girls), and then modeled with a stochastic blockmodel based on p_1 containing both actor and a single blocking parameter. There is just one blocking parameter here, since there is only a single degree of freedom for the effect. That is, Wang and Wong had a single ζ_{bb}, indicating the tendency for boys to choose boys. By constraint, $\zeta_{bg} = 1 - \zeta_{bb}$, and $\zeta_{gb} = 1 - \zeta_{bb}$, so that the tendency for boys to choose girls was equal to the tendency for girls to choose boys. Lastly, again by constraint, $\zeta_{gg} = \zeta_{bb}$, so that one should interpret the single ζ parameter, ζ_{bb}, as reflecting the tendency for within-gender choices, and $1 - \zeta_{bb}$ as the tendency for between-gender choices.

As mentioned, one problem with this stochastic blockmodel is the large number of blocking parameters that appear in model (16.20) if B is at all large. One can fit as many as $(B - 1)^2$ blocking parameters, which may be too many. There are a variety of ways to reduce this number. As noted by Wang and Wong (1987), special cases can be obtained by a priori equating various ζ's. One possibility is to estimate just a single blocking effect, letting $\zeta_{kl} = \zeta$, for all k and l. Or, one can just fit B parameters, one for each diagonal block: $\zeta_{kl} = 0$, for all $k \neq l$, and ζ_{kk} unconstrained, for all k. This constraint implies that there are tendencies for actors to have ties to the actors within their respective positions, but no "additional" tendencies for actors to have ties to actors in other positions. Clearly, many other possibilities exist. Many of these fits will improve upon p_1. The important task is to choose the structure of the blocking parameters before looking at the data; otherwise, the error rates for the associated hypothesis tests will not be accurate.

To fit these stochastic blockmodels to data requires a special algorithm. Standard computing packages cannot be used. The maximum likelihood equations for the parameters in equation (16.20) can be easily written down (see Wang and Wong 1987, page 12), and can be solved using generalized iterative proportional scaling, as described by Darroch and Ratcliff (1972). The generalized iterative scaling algorithm is described in the appendix to Wang and Wong (1987), and proceeds in cycles of five steps (one step for each set of parameters). Special cases, obtained by setting sets of parameters to 0, can be fitted simply by omitting the associated step in the algorithm. Thus, one can test, for example, whether all the β's are 0, by fitting the full model and then comparing its fit to a model without these β's. Such a model comparison determines whether actors are equal in their popularity. Wang and Wong give various submodels, all special cases of their basic stochastic blockmodel, differing by the assumptions made about the block structure parameters. Of primary interest to us are the likelihood-ratio statistics, which, as we discuss shortly, can be used to evaluate the goodness-of-fit of a stochastic blockmodel.

16.2.4 Goodness-of-Fit Indices for Stochastic Blockmodels

As discussed earlier in this chapter, there is a large literature on indices designed to measure how well a blockmodel fits a given network data set. But most of these measures are lacking because they are not based on statistical models, and they do not have convenient and well-known distributions. One solution to this problem, discussed by Wasserman and Anderson (1987), begins with the assumption that one has a stochastic blockmodel, consisting of a $p(x)$ and a mapping of actors to B positions. The measure that arises naturally from this assumption is a statistically based goodness-of-fit index. The statistic is not costly to compute, nor ad hoc, nor designed for other contexts.

The proposal here is to use the likelihood-ratio statistic G^2 for the fit of the assumed stochastic blockmodel $p(x)$ as a goodness-of-fit index for the stochastic blockmodel. We note that this theory should be applied only to a priori stochastic blockmodels, because the "data mucking" that must be done to fit their a posteriori counterparts invalidates the use of statistical theory. Nonetheless, evaluating a posteriori stochastic blockmodels can be done using this index, but no statistical interpretation should be attached to it.

To calculate the index, we let $X^B = \{\hat{x}_{ijr}^B\}$ be the predicted values for the ties linking actor i to actor j on the rth relation contained in X, the observed stochastic multigraph, based on the fit of some assumed $p(x)$. Details on how to calculate such fitted arrays are given in Chapter 15, and involve the use of w-arrays (see also Fienberg, Meyer, and Wasserman 1985, and Iacobucci and Wasserman 1987) or the generalized iterative scaling algorithm, as discussed by Fienberg, Meyer, and Wasserman (1985) and Wang and Wong (1987).

Remember that this $p(x)$ is coupled with a mapping of actors to positions, usually done a priori, so that the fit depends crucially on how stochastically equivalent the actors within the positions actually are. Thus, the magnitude of the likelihood-ratio statistic reflects how well the mapping function actually describes the possible equivalences among the actors. The statistic is computed as follows:

$$G_B^2 = 2 \sum_{r=1}^{R} \sum_{i=1}^{g} \sum_{j=1}^{g} x_{ijr} \log \left(x_{ijr} / \hat{x}_{ijr} \right). \tag{16.21}$$

The subscript B indicates that the statistic is calculated for a specific stochastic blockmodel. The associated degrees of freedom equals the difference between the number of independent cells in X, and the number of independent estimated parameters of $p(x)$.

We will let G_g^2 be the likelihood-ratio statistic calculated using fitted values derived from p_1; that is, the subscript g indicates that the statistic is calculated assuming that each actor is mapped to a unique position: $B = g$. In this case, the asymptotic distribution of G_g^2 is not known; however, it should be close to a chi-squared distribution. Fortunately, when judging the fit of a stochastic blockmodel, G_B^2 depends only on B, the number of positions, and not on g; thus, it indeed does have an asymptotic χ^2 distribution.

We note that one does not have to evaluate G^2 using its theoretical distribution; that is, it is a nice statistic for studying goodness-of-fit, even if its asymptotic distribution is unknown. In such cases, permutation tests can be used to generate p-values for particular hypotheses.

An important question is how large G^2 will be if actors are perfectly stochastically equivalent. A glance at equation (16.21) indicates that the index equals 0 when all the x_{ijr}'s equal their fitted values; that is, when the stochastic blockmodel fits perfectly. Such perfect fits arise when actors are perfectly stochastically equivalent, as defined earlier.

There are many advantages to the use of $G^2{}_B$. First, as just mentioned, its asymptotic distribution should be close to the chi-squared distribution, although the determination of the exact degrees of freedom is not simple (see Fienberg and Wasserman 1981a, Haberman 1981, Wong and Yu 1989, Iacobucci and Wasserman 1990, as well as comments in Chapter 15). This distribution theory can be used to test the importance of the actor attribute variables used to obtain the mapping of the actors into the positions, as discussed and illustrated in Chapter 15.

Secondly, it is easy to compute, given the fitted values arising from the $p(x)$ in question. When statistical packages such as *SPSS, BMDP,* or *SYSTAT* are used to fit p_1 to individual actors (that is, to a y-array), $G_B^2 = G_g^2 = G^2/2$, where G^2 is the likelihood-ratio statistic given in the output. This adjustment is needed because each dyad is included in G^2 twice, rather than just once as in equation (16.21) (see Fienberg and Wasserman 1981a). When a stochastic blockmodel is fit to partitioned actors (that is, to a w-array), the correction to the value given as output from these programs is more complex, but the goodness-of-fit index (16.21) is easy to compute given the data and fitted values.

It is also computationally easy to determine if a special case of $p(x)$ fits the data better; that is, is there a $p(x)$, obtained by setting some of the parameters in the original stochastic blockmodel to 0, that is a more parsimonious fit? One can simply subtract the $G^2{}_B$ statistics for the two predictions. The difference in the statistics is a conditional likelihood-ratio statistic and is indeed asymptotically distributed as a chi-squared random variable, with degrees of freedom equal to the difference in degrees of freedom for the two $G^2{}_B$'s (see Fienberg 1980). Specifically, differences between likelihood-ratio statistics, say $\Delta G^2 = G^2_{B_1} - G^2_{B_2}$, where stochastic blockmodel $\mathscr{B}_1$ is a special case of stochastic blockmodel $\mathscr{B}_2$, are conditional likelihood-ratio statistics, and are asymptotically distributed as chi-squared random variables.

These limiting distributions are a much better approximation when this difference in degrees of freedom is not a function of g, the number of actors. This is true for hypotheses comparing two stochastic blockmodels that have a fixed number of positions, since differences will depend on the numbers of positions, rather than on g.

The lack-of-fit of a stochastic blockmodel as measured by G^2_B is decomposable into two parts; namely,

$$
\begin{aligned}
G^2_B &= 2\sum_{i<j}\sum_k\sum_l y_{ijkl}\log(\hat{y}^g_{ijkl}/\hat{y}^{\mathscr{B}}_{ijkl}) \\
&\quad + 2\sum_{i<j}\sum_k\sum_l y_{ijkl}\log(y_{ijkl}/\hat{y}^g_{ijkl}) \\
&= G^2_{(B,g)} + G^2_g,
\end{aligned}
\tag{16.22}
$$

where $\hat{y}^g_{ijkl}$ are the fitted values from p_1. The quantity G^2_g reflects the lack of fit of p_1 to the observed ties among individual actors, and the quantity $G^2_{(B,g)}$ reflects the lack-of-fit due to the assignment of actors to positions. The latter quantity is particularly useful for assessing how closely actors adhere to the definition of stochastic equivalence.

If one is interested in studying whether two specific actors are stochastically equivalent, rather than how closely the entire set of actors adheres to the definition of stochastic equivalence, one need only compare the fitted actor-level parameters. These estimated parameters should be equal for any two actors who are stochastically equivalent.

In addition to these advantages, the G^2 statistic has all the desirable characteristics mentioned by Carrington, Heil, and Berkowitz (1979). Specifically, the index uses all of the information imposed by a given blocking without sacrificing parsimony, it is sensitive to the nature of the data, and has a high degree of known precision (due to its asymptotic distribution). Comparisons of stochastic blockmodels with the same number of positions can be based on the statistic. If one desires to compare two stochastic blockmodels with differing number of positions (and one of the $p(x)$'s is not a special case of the other), then one can compare G^2's normalized by their degrees of freedom: G^2/df. This normalization is commonly used in categorical data analysis, and its evaluation is equivalent to that of a statistic divided by its mean. It equals the number of means from the mean that the statistic is. Clearly, G^2 is the logical measure to examine when working with categorical data, and much is known about its properties. We will now demonstrate its use on the examples discussed in this chapter.

16.2.5 ○*Stochastic a posteriori Blockmodels*

A major component of a stochastic blockmodel is the function ϕ that assigns actors to positions. A number of strategies exists for generating partitions of actors. Recall that actors assigned to the same position should be stochastically equivalent. There are two main strategies: a priori, as we have described earlier in this chapter, and a posteriori, using the actual relational data.

Consider now specific strategies for generating potential mapping functions and evaluation of these functions. The conditional likelihood-ratio statistic $G^2_{(B,g)}$ is proposed as an index that measures how closely actors adhere to the definition of stochastic equivalence for a given partition.

We first consider how to generate partitions. The assignment of actors to positions can be based on exogenous attribute information about the actors or on relational data. Examples of exogenous characteristics are age, gender, and income. This approach is straightforward and has been used by many, as discussed earlier in this chapter.

As an alternative to a priori classifications, Wasserman and Anderson (1987) explored ways of discovering a posteriori partitions based on relational data, a characteristic of "deterministic" blockmodeling procedures. The discovery of partitions based on relational data is a more difficult task than generating partitions based on attribute data. Techniques for identifying partitions a posteriori are reviewed here.

One possible strategy is to examine all possible partitions. Even with increases in computing power, such an approach is not practical, and certainly not efficient. For fixed B, the number of possible partitions for even moderately sized sets of actors is extremely large. Furthermore, researchers will typically want to examine partitions for different values of B.

Spatial Approaches: Parameter Plots. Another approach is to seek a spatial representation of the actors that reflects the ties between them. In such a representation, actors who are (approximately) stochastically equivalent should be close to each other, and those who are not equivalent should be far apart. When $p(x) = p_1$, actors who are stochastically equivalent have the same α's and β's, and the task of finding equivalent actors reduces to that of finding subsets of actors with (approximately) equivalent parameters. For the simple case of one binary relation, Wasserman and Anderson (1987) found that plots of $\hat{\beta}_i$ versus $\hat{\alpha}_i$ from fitting p_1 to the **y**-array were extremely useful. A set of potential partitions for different numbers of positions can be suggested by visually examining such plots.

Other possible graphical approaches are explored by Wasserman and Anderson (1987), and discussed by Wasserman, Faust, and Galaskiewicz (1990) and Wasserman and Faust (1989). These researchers plotted row versus column scores from the correspondence analysis of a sociomatrix. Correspondence analysis is a technique that seeks to scale simultaneously the rows and columns of a table such that rows that are similar have similar scores, and columns that are similar have similar scores (Greenacre 1984). Other possible graphical approaches are biplots (Gabriel 1982; Gabriel and Zamir 1979) and the *RC*-association model (Goodman 1985, 1986), both of which are related to correspondence analysis and also yield row and column scores (see Faust and Wasserman 1993). All of these methods can be applied to sociomatrices. The application, potential usefulness, and limitations of these methods are interesting, but will not be explored further here.

Cluster Analysis. Another approach, which is complementary to graphical methods for discovering equivalent actors, is cluster analysis. We used cluster analysis to find blockmodels. Since stochastic equivalence is operationally defined as equality of p_1 parameters, estimated parameters can be used in cluster analytic methods to find "optimal" partitions of actors. While cluster analysis can be used in addition to the parameter plots mentioned above, clustering techniques can also be used in more complex cases where the examination of parameter plots is difficult. For example, if there are more than two sets of parameters corresponding to individuals, as might be the case with multiple relations, the dimensionality of the parameter space equals the number of different sets of parameters. At most, three sets of parameters can be visually examined at any one time. Cluster analysis is not so limited. We discuss the advantages and the complementary nature of cluster analysis and the visual inspection of parameter plots later in this chapter.

Numerous cluster analytic methods exist that are potentially useful, but only two are mentioned here for use with a posteriori stochastic blockmodels. A promising method is Hartigan's (1975) *K-means* technique, which seeks to split objects into a fixed number of sets by maximizing the variation between sets relative to the variation within sets. This method requires an "objects by variables" matrix, which for our purposes corresponds to the "actors by estimated parameters" matrix. The parameters do not need to be rescaled or standardized. For different numbers of positions, the *K-means* technique will not necessarily yield nested sets of partitions.

If a nested set of partitions is desired, then a hierarchical cluster analysis method could be used. These methods successively join together objects and subsets until there is only one large cluster. The various methods differ with respect to the criterion used to join individuals/subsets at each stage. These methods operate on square symmetric matrices of (dis)similarities, so for our purposes, (dis)similarities between actors in the parameter space need to be computed. A logical choice for dissimilarities is the Euclidean distance between actors i and j, as given by p_1:

$$\text{Distance}(i, j) = \sqrt{(\hat{\alpha}_i - \hat{\alpha}_j)^2 + (\hat{\beta}_i - \hat{\beta}_j)^2},$$

which corresponds to the distances that are examined in parameter plots. Hierarchical methods may not be as useful as *K-means* cluster analysis, because the goal of a *K-means* analysis more closely resembles that of finding subsets of actors with equivalent parameters.

16.2.6 *Measures of Stochastic Equivalence*

Regardless of whether a mapping function is based on exogenous characteristics of the actors or on relational data, an index that measures the degree to which actors adhere to the definition of stochastic equivalence is needed. When partitions are based on exogenous information, an assessment of whether actors within positions are actually (or approximately) stochastically equivalent is desirable. When partitions are based on relational data, a means of identifying "optimal" or "good" mappings is essential. "Optimal" and "good" are defined in terms of stochastic equivalence.

As mentioned earlier in this chapter, the conditional likelihood ratio statistic $G^2_{(B,g)}$ is a natural index to evaluate the degree to which actors within positions adhere to the definition of stochastic equivalence. As was seen from the decomposition in equation (16.22), $G^2_{(B,g)}$ reflects the lack-of-fit due to the assignment of actors to positions. If the partition is based on exogenous information, then statistical tests are possible. Since $G^2_{(B,g)}$ is a difference between likelihood-ratio statistics, it is an asymptotic chi-squared random variable and can be used to test statistically whether actors assigned to positions by a particular mapping function are consistent with the definition of stochastic equivalence. If actors can be assigned to blocks without "significantly" reducing the fit of the model, then actors and the relations(s) are consistent with the definition of stochastic equivalence.

Even when a partition is not based on exogenous information, the statistic $G^2_{(B,g)}$ can be used to assess which of a number of different mapping functions for various numbers of blocks is the best in terms of producing partitions of actors which more closely adhere to the definition of stochastic equivalence. Remember that $G^2_{(B,g)}$ reflects lack-of-fit. For fixed B, the mapping function that yields the smallest $G^2_{(B,g)}$ is the "best" one. For fixed B, the difference between the $G^2_{(B,g)}$'s from two different partitions is hard to evaluate, because one model is not a special case of the other. However, the difference does indicate which partition is better and reflects the degree to which the actors within positions in one model are "more" stochastically equivalent than those in the other model.

For different magnitudes of B, the number of positions, mapping functions can be compared by computing and then studying the differences between $G^2_{(B,g)}$'s. When one partition is nested within the other, these differences are more meaningful, and have degrees of freedom equal to the difference in the number of estimated stochastic blockmodel parameters. We will let $G^2_{(B-1,B)} = G^2_{(B-1,g)} - G^2_{(B,g)}$, a quantity that will always be nonzero, where the stochastic blockmodel with $B - 1$ positions is a special case of the one with B positions, obtained by aggregating two of the positions into one. But remember it is still not proper to use these statistics for parametric hypothesis tests.

16.2.7 Stochastic Blockmodel Representations

Given a probability distribution $p(x)$ and a mapping function $\phi(\bullet)$ for a stochastic blockmodel, the positions and ties between positions need to be represented. These representations are used to interpret the model substantively, which is an important but relatively neglected aspect of blockmodeling (as mentioned in Chapter 10). In positional analyses using blockmodels, density tables, image matrices, and reduced graphs are three common ways in which the relations between positions are represented. Density tables and reduced graphs are useful in stochastic blockmodel analyses, but as we discuss below, image matrices are not necessary.

Of substantive interest are the empirical probabilities or relative frequencies that actors relate to and are related to by other actors. A density table (or matrix) contains these observed relative frequencies. Each row and column of the table corresponds to a position. The observed probabilities are

$$\Delta_{kl} = \begin{cases} (w_{kl10} + w_{kl11})/(g_k g_l) & \text{if } k \neq l \\ (w_{kk10} + w_{kk11})/[g_k(g_k - 1)] & \text{if } k = l, \end{cases} \tag{16.23}$$

where $\phi(i) = k$ and $\phi(j) = l$. The counts g_k and g_l are the number of actors in positions $\mathcal{B}_k$ and $\mathcal{B}_l$, respectively. The w's are the counts that are contained in the $\mathbf{w}$ matrix: w_{kl10} is the frequency of actors in position $\mathcal{B}_k$ who relate to but are not related to by the actors in position $\mathcal{B}_l$, and w_{kl11} is the frequency of actors in $\mathcal{B}_k$ who relate to and are related to by those in $\mathcal{B}_l$. Note that even though the diagonal entries of the sociomatrix $X_{ii} = 0$, this is not the case for data aggregated over positions. When $\phi(i) = \phi(j) = k$, Δ_{kk} is the relative frequency of actors in $\mathcal{B}_k$ who relate to each other.

Rather than an observed density matrix, a matrix of expected or predicted probabilities can be computed based on the stochastic blockmodel. The predicted probabilities are computed by replacing the observed frequencies in equation (16.23) by the predicted frequencies from the stochastic blockmodel. The predicted frequencies, $\hat{w}_{kl10}$ and $\hat{w}_{kl11}$, are the fitted values computed from fitting the appropriate log-linear model to the $\mathbf{w}$-array. Since the predicted probabilities for actors in the same position are equal, these predictions can also be computed as follows

$$\Pr(x_{ij} = 1) = \Pr(y_{ij10} = 1) + \Pr(y_{ij11} = 1),$$

where $i \neq j$; actors i and j are in positions $\mathcal{B}_k$ and $\mathcal{B}_l$, respectively; further,

$$\Pr(y_{ij10} = 1) = \hat{w}_{kl10}/(g_k g_l)$$

and

$$\Pr(y_{ij11} = 1) = \hat{w}_{kl11}/(g_k g_l)$$

for $k \neq l$. In addition,

$$\Pr(y_{ij10} = 1) = \hat{w}_{kk10}/(g_k(g_k - 1))$$

and

$$\Pr(y_{ij11} = 1) = \hat{w}_{kk11}/(g_k(g_k - 1))$$

for $k = l$. Remember that the **y**-array is the matrix, constructed from the sociomatrix, to which p_1 is actually fit.

Alternatively, $\Pr(y_{ijmn} = 1)$ can be computed from equation (16.18); that is,

$$\Pr(y_{ijmn} = 1) = \exp\{\hat{\lambda}_{ij} + m\hat{\alpha}^{[k]} + n\hat{\alpha}^{[l]} + m\hat{\beta}^{[l]} + n\hat{\beta}^{[k]}$$
$$+ (m + n)\hat{\theta} + mn\hat{\rho}\}.$$

While the predicted and observed density matrices can be compared to see how closely the model reproduces the observed probabilities, the predicted probabilities should be used in substantive interpretations of the model. The predicted density table contains the stochastic blockmodel-based probabilities of ties between actors in the same and different positions.

In "standard" blockmodels, image matrices are often used to represent the ties between positions. Similar to density tables, image matrices have rows and columns that correspond to positions and the entries carry information regarding ties between positions. The entries in image matrices are 1's and 0's and indicate whether or not a tie exists. In a stochastic blockmodel, ties between actors exist with certain probabilities, which can be anywhere in the range of 0 to 1; therefore, an image matrix is not needed for representing the ties between positions in a stochastic blockmodel analysis.

A third way of representing ties between the positions of a blockmodel is a reduced graph. Reduced graphs consist of nodes that correspond to positions, and arcs, representing positional relationships. In a blockmodel, arrows represent the existence of a tie. Reduced graphs for such blockmodels are pictorial representations of image matrices.

In a stochastic blockmodel, a reduced graph is based on the predicted density table. In this case, arcs are only drawn for the ties with large predicted probabilities, and the predicted probabilities are written on or next to the arrows to convey the probabilistic information. Reduced graphs based on predicted density tables are pictorial summaries of most of the information in the corresponding density tables. The tables contain more information, but the reduced graphs provide a visual summary of the information in the tables.

Table 16.3. *Fit statistics for p_1 and special cases*

	Model	Margins fit	G^2	ΔG^2	Δdf
(i)	$\theta, \{\alpha_i\}, \{\beta_j\}, \rho$	[12][13][14][23][24][34]	245.18		
(ii)	$\theta, \{\alpha_i\}, \{\beta_j\}$	[12][13][14][23][24]	252.56	7.38	1
(iii)	$\theta, \{\alpha_i\}, \rho$	[12][13][24][34]	298.35	53.17	18
(iv)	$\theta, \{\beta_j\}, \rho$	[12][14][23][34]	667.20	422.02	23

16.2.8 The Example Continued

Consider now the countries trade data, and the ties defined by trade of basic manufactured goods.

We fit p_1, as shown in equation (16.18), to this relation from the countries trade network. The models and fit statistics are reported in Table 16.3. The first column lists the parameters included in the model, and the second column lists the margins (that is, the log-linear model) of the y-array that were fit for each of the models. The first model, model (i), is the "full" p_1 model, and models (ii)–(iv) are special cases of it. The special cases were fit to see if a simpler model could be used to represent the ties.

As we have noted, the G^2's associated with models (i)–(iv) are not asymptotic chi-squared random variables, so we cannot attach p-values to the hypotheses they quantify. Since the ΔG^2's for models (ii)–(iv) are all large relative to their degrees of freedom, the reciprocity parameter ρ (deleted in model (ii)), the set of "popularity" parameters $\{\beta_j\}$ (deleted in model (iii)), and the set of "expansiveness" parameters $\{\alpha_i\}$ (deleted in model (iv)) should all be included in the model. Therefore, the "best-fitting" model must contain all parameters. All of the stochastic blockmodels fit will assume $p(x) =$ model (i) $= p_1$. Thus, the G^2 for model (i) will become G_g^2. This statistic will be the lower bound for the fit of all of the stochastic blockmodels (that is, all blockmodels will have $G_B^2 \geq G_g^2 = 245.18$).

Consider now whether the countries are stochastically equivalent. We will look for stochastic equivalence of the countries based on p_1 and its parameters. The next step in constructing a stochastic blockmodel is to choose or find a mapping function. We consider an a posteriori approach, and obtain estimates of the model parameters. From these, we should be able to generate mapping functions. The maximum likelihood estimates of the parameters of p_1 were computed from the fitted values $\hat{y}_{ijmn}$.

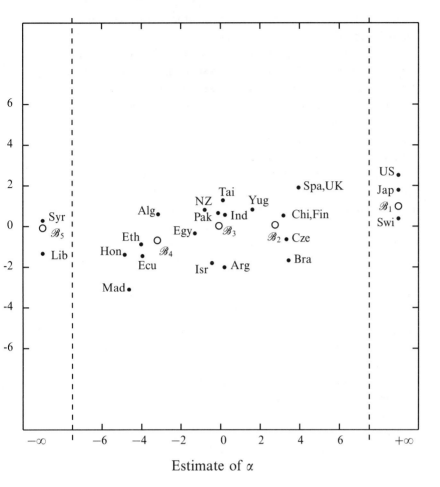

Fig. 16.1. Plot of $\hat{\alpha}_i$ versus $\hat{\beta}_i$

The estimated θ equals -0.668 and the estimated reciprocity parameter $\hat{\rho}$ equals 2.03. The latter indicates that trade between countries tends to be reciprocated. We will not only find a mapping function using a parameters plot, but will also consider cluster analysis as a tool.

Rather than giving the estimated α's and β's, we have plotted them in a parameter plot, shown in Figure 16.1. The points represent countries. Since Syria and Liberia did not export manufactured goods to any other country in the network, and since the United States, Japan, and

Switzerland exported goods to all of the other countries, the $\hat{\alpha}_i$'s for these countries equal $-\infty$ and $+\infty$, respectively.

Thus, we lose 5 degrees of freedom here, because we can estimate only 19 rather than 24 α's. To represent the countries with $\hat{\alpha}_i = \pm\infty$, these countries were placed at the extreme ends of the horizontal axis. Overall, the countries show more variation with respect to their exporting behavior ($\hat{\alpha}$) than they do with respect to their importing behavior ($\hat{\beta}$), even when disregarding the five countries with $\hat{\alpha}_i = \pm\infty$.

Figure 16.1 greatly facilitates the search for equivalent countries and allows us to find plausible mapping functions. Countries that have similar import and export patterns have similar $\hat{\alpha}$'s and $\hat{\beta}$'s. For example, Spain and the United Kingdom (as well as China and Finland) have nearly identical rows and columns in the sociomatrix, and their estimated parameters are approximately equal. The points corresponding to Spain and the UK, as well as those for China and Finland, are indistinguishable, which indicates that these countries are stochastically equivalent. The close proximity of Ethiopia, Ecuador, and Honduras suggests that these countries can be placed in the same position without significantly decreasing the goodness-of-fit of the stochastic blockmodel. Various possible mapping of countries to blocks for different values of B were generated by visually examining Figure 16.1. Some of these mappings are reported in the top half of Table 16.4.

Other mappings for $B = 2$ to $B = 10$ positions were generated by performing *K-means* cluster analyses of the countries using the distances obtained from the $\hat{\alpha}$ and $\hat{\beta}$. (A large value, 9, was substituted for ∞.) The clusters, which are listed in the lower half of Table 16.4, are nested (which is a fortunate coincidence). The cluster analyses confirmed many of the aspects seen in Figure 16.1. The partitions for $B = 5, 6,$ and 8 from the cluster analyses were also identified as possible partitions from the visual examination of Figure 16.1. The duplicate partitions are reported only once in Table 16.4, under the *K-means* section. The major differences between the partitions generated from the figure and those from the cluster analyses involve Yugoslavia. Based on Figure 16.1, Yugoslavia was generally assigned to the same position as Spain and the UK, but in the cluster analyses, it was assigned to the cluster containing Indonesia, New Zealand, Pakistan, and Thailand.

Table 16.4. *Fit statistics for p_1 stochastic blockmodels*

	B	$G^2_{(B,24)}$	$df_{(B,24)}$	$G^2_{(B,B-1)}$
Partitions from visual inspection				
{Jap,Swi,US} {Bra,Cze} {Chi,Fin,Yug} {Spa,UK} {Arg,Isr} {Alg} {Egy,Ind,NZ,Pak,Tai} {Ecu,Eth,Hon} {Mad} {Lib,Syr}	10	19.02	28	
{Jap,Swi,US} {Bra,Cze} {Chi,Fin,Yug} {Spa,UK} {Arg,Isr} {Alg} {Egy,Ind,NZ,Pak,Tai} {Ecu,Eth,Hon,Mad} {Lib,Syr}	9	23.45	30	4.43
{Jap,Swi,US} {Bra,Cze} {Chi,Fin,Yug} {Spa,UK} {Arg,Isr} {Alg,Egy,Ind,NZ,Pak,Tai} {Ecu,Eth,Hon,Mad} {Lib,Syr}	8	39.89	32	16.44
{Jap,Swi,US} {Bra,Cze} {Chi,Fin,Spa,UK} {Arg,Isr} {Alg,Egy,Ind,NZ,Pak,Tai,Yug} {Ecu,Eth,Hon,Mad} {Lib,Syr}	7	52.48	34	
{Jap,Swi,US} {Bra,Chi,Cze,Fin,Spa,UK} {Arg,Egy,Isr} {Alg,Ind,NZ,Pak,Tai,Yug} {Ecu,Eth,Hon,Mad} {Lib,Syr}	6	62.02	36	
Partitions from *K-means* cluster analysis				
{Jap,Swi,US} {Bra,Cze} {Chi,Fin,Spa,UK} {Arg,Isr} {Alg} {Egy,Ind,NZ,Pak,Tai} {Yug} {Ecu,Eth,Hon} {Mad} {Lib,Syr}	10	19.16	28	
{Jap,Swi,US} {Bra,Cze} {Chi,Fin,Spa,UK} {Arg,Isr} {Alg} {Egy,Ind,NZ,Pak,Tai} {Yug} {Ecu,Eth,Hon,Mad} {Lib,Syr}	9	23.68	30	4.52
{Jap,Swi,US} {Bra,Cze} {Chi,Fin,Spa,UK} {Arg,Isr} {Alg} {Egy,Ind,NZ,Pak,Tai,Yug} {Ecu,Eth,Hon,Mad} {Lib,Syr}	8	32.39	32	8.71
{Jap,Swi,US} {Bra,Cze} {Chi,Fin,Spa,UK} {Alg} {Lib,Syr} {Arg,Isr,Egy,Ind,NZ,Pak,Tai,Yug} {Ecu,Eth,Hon,Mad}	7	44.65	34	12.26
{Jap,Swi,US} {Bra,Cze} {Chi,Fin,Spa,UK} {Lib,Syr} {Arg,Isr,Egy,Ind,NZ,Pak,Tai,Yug} {Alg,Ecu,Eth,Hon,Mad}	6	53.68	36	8.03
{Jap,Swi,US} {Bra,Cze,Chi,Fin,Spa,UK} {Lib,Syr} {Arg,Isr,Egy,Ind,NZ,Pak,Tai,Yug} {Alg,Ecu,Eth,Hon,Mad}	5	64.09	38	10.41
{Jap,Swi,US} {Alg,Ecu,Eth,Hon,Mad} {Lib,Syr} {Bra,Cze,Chi,Fin,Spa,UK,Arg,Isr,Egy,Ind,NZ,Pak,Tai,Yug}	4	135.68	40	71.59
{Jap,Swi,US} {Alg,Ecu,Eth,Hon,Mad,Lib,Syr} {Bra,Cze,Chi,Fin,Spa,UK,Arg,Isr,Egy,Ind,NZ,Pak,Tai,Yug}	3	143.88	42	8.20
{Bra,Cze,Chi,Fin,Spa,UK,Arg,Isr,Egy,Ind,NZ,Pak,Tai,Yug,Jap,Swi,US} {Alg,Ecu,Eth,Hon,Mad,Lib,Syr}	2	191.35	44	47.47

Fit statistics for the various stochastic blockmodels are also given in Table 16.4. The first column shows the actual mapping of actors onto positions and the second indicates the number of positions. The third and fourth columns contain the conditional likelihood-ratio statistics $G^2_{(B,24)}$ and their degrees of freedom $df_{(B,24)}$, respectively. The last column contains the conditional likelihood-ratio statistics $G^2_{(B,B-1)}$ for nested models in which the more restrictive model has one less position. There are 2 degrees of freedom associated with each $G^2_{(B,B-1)}$, since two parameters are eliminated when we go from B positions down to $B-1$.

When the number of positions is fixed at $8, 9,$ or 10, the models in the upper and lower halves of Table 16.4 have approximately the same fit statistics; however, when $B = 6$ or 7, the models in the lower half fit noticeably better than those in the upper half. The *K-means* cluster analyses produced partitions at least as good as those generated from the parameter plot in Figure 16.1. Since the partitions in the lower half of Table 16.4 tend to have better fit statistics, are all nested, and cover a larger range of models for different numbers of blocks, the models in the top half were eliminated from further consideration. When the statistics $G^2_{(B,24)}$ for different numbers of positions are compared to the appropriate chi-squared distributions, the statistics for $B \geq 7$ are not statistically "important" (p-values $> .10$). The statistic $G^2_{(6,24)}$ is marginally important (p-value $= 0.029$), and the statistic $G^2_{(5,24)}$ is statistically "important" (p-value $= 0.005$). These fit statistics suggest that the 7- and possibly the 6-position blockmodels are the simplest ones that provide an adequate fit. Since the applicability of asymptotic theory in this example is questionable, other criteria must also be considered.

The fit statistics $G^2_{(B,B-1)}$ indicate the decrease in fit from reducing the number of positions from B to $(B-1)$ where two positions from the more general model are combined into one position in the more restrictive model. For models with 5 to 9 positions, the values for these statistics are relatively constant and range from 4.52 to 12.26. A large decrease in the fit occurs at $B = 4$ where $G^2_{(4,5)} = 71.59$. Given this fact, models with $B \leq 4$ were eliminated from further consideration. Since the 7 position model contains a position with just one country (that is, Algeria) and the 6 position model provides a reasonably good fit to the data, the 7-position model was also eliminated. The 5- and 6-position stochastic blockmodels differ in that Brazil and Czechoslovakia form a separate position in the 6-position model, but they are included in the cluster with China, Finland, Spain, and the United Kingdom in the 5-position blockmodel. The representation of each of these models

Table 16.5. *Predicted density matrix*

	$\mathscr{B}_1$	$\mathscr{B}_2$	$\mathscr{B}_3$	$\mathscr{B}_4$	$\mathscr{B}_5$
$\mathscr{B}_1$	1.000	1.000	1.000	1.000	1.000
$\mathscr{B}_2$	0.994	0.983	0.956	0.804	0.868
$\mathscr{B}_3$	0.904	0.770	0.576	0.192	0.276
$\mathscr{B}_4$	0.295	0.119	0.041	0.010	0.017
$\mathscr{B}_5$	0.000	0.000	0.000	0.000	0.000

was examined. The 5-position model was chosen, because the basic substantive interpretation is the same as the 6-position model, except for one minor difference, noted later. Based on a balance of parsimony and goodness-of-fit, our favorite solution is the 5-position blockmodel from the *K-means* cluster analysis. A substantive interpretation of this model follows.

The countries were mapped onto positions for this $B = 5$ position stochastic blockmodel as follows:

- $\mathscr{B}_1$: Japan, Switzerland, United States
- $\mathscr{B}_2$: Brazil, China, Czechoslovakia, Finland, Spain, United Kingdom
- $\mathscr{B}_3$: Argentina, Egypt, Indonesia, Israel, New Zealand, Pakistan, Thailand, Yugoslavia
- $\mathscr{B}_4$: Algeria, Ecuador, Ethiopia, Honduras, Madagascar
- $\mathscr{B}_5$: Liberia, Syria

The estimated values for the overall choice effect and the reciprocity parameter are -0.803 and 2.133, respectively, which are similar to those from p_1. The estimated values for $\alpha^{[k]}$ and $\beta^{[k]}$ correspond to the open circles labeled $\mathscr{B}_1 - \mathscr{B}_5$ in Figure 16.1. The positions differ mostly with respect to exports ($\hat{\alpha}^{[k]}$), but show some slight differences with respect to imports ($\hat{\beta}^{[k]}$). To represent explictly and to substantively interpret the ties between the positions, the predicted density matrix was computed and a reduced graph based on this matrix was drawn.

The predicted probabilities are given in Table 16.5. The countries in $\mathscr{B}_1$ exported goods to all of the other countries (that is, the entries in the first row of Table 16.5 all equal 1.00), and the countries in $\mathscr{B}_5$ did not export any goods to any of the other countries (that is, the entries in the last row all equal 0.0). The ties exhibit a "center-periphery" pattern; that is, the larger probabilities are in the upper left triangle, while the smaller

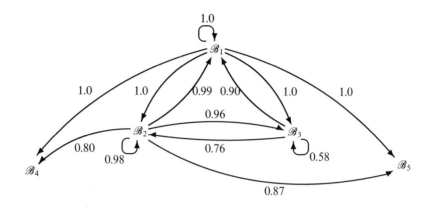

Fig. 16.2. Reduced graph based on predicted probabilities > 0.30

probabilities are in the lower right triangle. Countries in the positions $\mathscr{B}_1$, $\mathscr{B}_2$, $\mathscr{B}_3$ have large probabilities of exporting and importing goods from each other. The countries in positions $\mathscr{B}_1$ and $\mathscr{B}_2$ export goods to countries in $\mathscr{B}_4$ and $\mathscr{B}_5$ with large probabilities, but the countries in $\mathscr{B}_3$ export to $\mathscr{B}_4$ and $\mathscr{B}_5$ with small probabilities. Thus it appears that while $\mathscr{B}_1$ and $\mathscr{B}_2$ are similar, they are different from $\mathscr{B}_3$.

As noted earler, the predicted density matrices for both the 5 and 6 position blockmodels were examined. The basic difference between the 5 and 6 position blockmodels was that in the $B = 6$ model, the predicted probability that countries in the cluster {China, Finland, Spain, United Kingdom} imported goods from $\mathscr{B}_3$ was 0.88, while the same probability for the countries in the cluster {Brazil, Czechoslovakia} was only 0.51. In the 5 position model, the corresponding predicted probability for the combined positions is 0.77, which is intermediate between these two values.

Figure 16.2 is the reduced graph based on Table 16.5. It is a pictorial representation of the probabilities that basic manufactured goods are exported/imported between countries in the five positions. The nodes (positions) are labeled $\mathscr{B}_1 - \mathscr{B}_5$, and arcs are draw from one position to another position for probabilities greater than 0.30. The central-periphery pattern is well-illustrated in this figure. The positions $\mathscr{B}_1$ and $\mathscr{B}_2$ export to countries in all of the other positions, but differ with respect to probabilities. Countries in $\mathscr{B}_4$ and $\mathscr{B}_5$ appear quite similar with respect to importing, but referring to Table 16.5, we see that countries in $\mathscr{B}_4$

export goods to countries in other positions with small probabilities, while those in $\mathscr{B}_5$ do not export to any of the other countries.

16.3 Summary: Generalizations and Extensions

To summarize this chapter and this part of the book, we want to mention some ways to extend the models presented here to other types of network data. Perhaps the most important of these extensions are those that allow one to analyze multiple relational networks and networks that are measured over time. We very briefly discuss these extensions here.

16.3.1 Statistical Analysis of Multiple Relational Networks

There is a wide variety of models for network data consisting of measurements on two or more relations. These models are quite general, and are capable of describing the associations among the relations, the dependence of the relations on the actors themselves, and (if measured) the associations among attribute variables and the relations. Most of the models can be fit using standard categorical data analysis techniques, especially those found in the computer package *GLIM* (Baker and Nelder 1978; Payne 1985; and the appendix to Wasserman and Iacobucci 1986). These techniques are identical to those illustrated in the last chapter on simpler network data sets involving just one relation (although individual software, such as Weaver and Wasserman 1986, exists for some of these models). Other, more complicated models, need generalized iterative proportional fitting algorithms (Darroch and Ratcliff 1972) to find parameter estimates. Examples of the use of such models and many details about model fitting can be found in Wasserman and Galaskiewicz (1984), Wasserman and Weaver (1985), and Galaskiewicz, Wasserman, Rauschenbach, Bielefeld, and Mullaney (1985).

The first extensive models of multiple relations can be found in the work of Davis (1968a), and Galaskiewicz and Marsden (1978), who studied resource flows between organizations in a midwestern community. Galaskiewicz (1979) describes these data (see Andrews and Herzberg 1985, for the data) at length.

Another famous (actually, very famous) example is a multirelational data set based on Sampson's (1968) network of monks living in a cloister in upstate New York. These data have been analyzed by many network methodologists; in fact, an entire issue of *Social Networks* has been devoted to alternative methods applied primarily to these data (Faust

1988; Reitz 1988; Krackhardt 1988; and especially, Pattison 1988; also see the references in these papers).

Other important multiple relational analyses were proposed by Katz and Powell (1953) and Hubert and Baker (1978). Basic approaches to multiple relational analyses are given by Gottman (1979a, 1979b), Gottman and Ringland (1981), Budescu (1984), Wampold (1984), and Iacobucci and Wasserman (1988). The first extension of these dyadic interaction models to multiple relations came in Fienberg and Wasserman (1980) and Fienberg, Meyer, and Wasserman (1981). Their models extend Holland and Leinhardt's p_1 by focusing on the associations among the relations rather than on the similarities and differences among individual actor attributes. The most important work on statistical models for multiple relations can be found in Fienberg, Meyer, and Wasserman (1985) (see Fienberg 1985). Fienberg, Meyer, and Wasserman (1985) presented models that could include both actor and subset parameters, as well as interactions that measure the interrelatedness of the different relations. Novel applications of these models can be found in Wasserman (1987), Iacobucci and Wasserman (1987, 1988), and Wasserman and Iacobucci (1988, 1989).

Good multiple relational models must be designed to answer substantive questions such as

- How similar are the relations? How well do they "conform" or resemble each other?
- Which relation exhibits the strongest "reciprocity"?
- Are there any "multiplex" patterns (flows of different relations in the same direction)?
- Are there any patterns of "exchange" in which a flow in one direction for one relation is reciprocated by a flow in the opposite direction for a different relation?
- Are there any higher-order interactions, involving three or more flows for two or more relations?

Sometimes, one also seeks answers to questions concerning whether relational tendencies vary in strength or direction from actor to actor (or subset to subset). The primary concern of these studies is the individual actor. Examples of substantive questions that multiple relational models can also answer include

- Which actors have the most prestige or popularity?
- Which actors are involved in many relations, and which in few?

- Do actors enter into mutual interactions at different rates?
- Do any of the relational associations vary in strength across the actors or actor subsets?

The models mentioned here are designed to answer such questions.

16.3.2 Statistical Analysis of Longitudinal Relations

We now mention models for statistical analysis of relations that are measured *longitudinally*, or over time. That is, we assume that one is interested in a small number of simple relations, defined for a constant set (or sets) of actors, that are observed at more than one point in time.

There are many models that are designed for the analysis of such data. Some of these models make stochastic assumptions about the "sending" behaviors of the actors over time, while others assume that these behaviors are deterministic; that is, governed by a set of equations that do not incorporate any probabilistic assumptions. In deterministic models, the effect of any change in the system can be predicted with certainty (subject to a known starting point for the system). Differential equations are frequently the "driving forces" of such deterministic models. In the social and behavioral sciences, and to a lesser extent in the natural sciences, the effect of changes in a system usually cannot be forecast with certainty, primarily because of the unpredictable nature of the objects (often people) being modeled, or design limitations on the measurements. This uncertainty is more effectively modeled through the use of probability distributions on random variables (as we have described throughout this part of the book) instead of the "controlling" mathematical variables of a system of differential equations.

There are (at least) two approaches to stochastic models of longitudinal networks. The first allows a researcher to study the associations among the relational time measurements, and even permits one to determine which aspects of previous social structure best predict the present structure of a set of actors. Much of this research comes from Wasserman and Iacobucci (1988) and Iacobucci (1989). Some of these models can be fit using logistic regression (Haberman 1978, 1979; Agresti 1984, 1990; Cox and Snell 1989; Hosmer and Lemeshow 1989; and see Wellman, Mosher, Rottenberg, and Espinosa 1987; Hallinan and Williams 1989; and Galaskiewicz and Wasserman 1989, 1990, for illustrative applications of these models).

The second approach is older, and posits a variety of models designed for the study of networks as *stochastic processes*, evolving either in discrete or continuous time. These models, some of which are described by Holland and Leinhardt (1977b, 1977c), Hallinan (1978), Wasserman (1978, 1979, 1980), Runger and Wasserman (1979), Galaskiewicz and Wasserman (1981), and Mayer (1984), can be used to study how simple network characteristics, such as the dyad census and the indegrees, change over time. Most of them are Markov in nature, in either discrete or continuous time. The details of modeling social and behavioral science processes longitudinally with Markov models when only discrete observations on the process are available (as is usually the case with network data) have been spelled out in detail by Singer and Spilerman (1974, 1976, 1977, 1978).

The study of longitudinal social network data is not new; many researchers gathered such data, but adequate models for their analysis were not available until the late 1950's. The earliest models, which assumed that changes in network structure occurred at discrete time points (as opposed to a continuously changing process), appeared about the same time as the classic (and revolutionary) work of Bush and Mosteller (1955), Blumen, Kogan, and McCarthy (1955), and Kemeny and Snell (1960, 1962) on the use of discrete-time stochastic processes in the social and behavioral sciences (see also Coleman 1964, 1981). Early models were presented by Katz and Proctor (1959), Rainio (1966), Sørensen and Hallinan (1976), and especially Holland and Leinhardt (1977b, 1977c). Many of these models were reviewed by Wasserman (1978), and the framework presented by Holland and Leinhardt generalized by Wasserman (1979, 1980). Applications are numerous; in particular, extensive longitudinal analyses of the friendship data of Taba (1955), the fraternity data of Nordlie (1958) and Newcomb (1961), and the monastery data of Sampson (1968) can be found in the literature.

Other researchers have studied social networks evolving or disintegrating over time, but have not employed sophisticated statistical models. For example, Tutzauer (1985) uses graph theoretic notions to study how a network changes over time, specifically degenerating into a number of disconnected components. de Sola Pool and Kochen (1978) give a wide-ranging overview of network analysis, including a detailed study of the number of acquaintances that arise over time in a large network. They also propose mathematical models for this number, using the binomial distribution and Monte Carlo simulations of this acquaintance process. Such studies are common when studying the small world problem (see

Hunter and Shotland 1974; Lundberg 1975; and especially Milgram 1967, and Travers and Milgram 1969).

Doreian (1979a) examines the Davis, Gardner, and Gardner (1941) data set, which gives the social events attended by $g=18$ women in the Southern United States. The 14 events are arranged as rows of an actors × events attendance matrix (see Breiger 1974) chronologically, so that one could analyze this matrix using first the first column, then the first two, then the first three columns, and so forth, in order to give these data a longitudinal perspective. Doreian's analysis is the first longitudinal analysis of these data, and gives a dynamic perspective to these data not present in the analyses of Homans (1950), Breiger, Boorman, and Arabie (1975), White, Boorman, and Breiger (1976), Bonacich (1978), and Doreian (1979b). Doreian (see also Doreian 1988a) uses the graph theoretic method of q-connectivity (Atkin 1974, 1976, 1977) to analyze the sociomatrices that can be generated from these data.

An entirely different approach to longitudinal network analysis can be found in the work of Delany (1988). Delany models the allocation of scarce resources, especially jobs among individual actors, using computer simulations.

Research on the diffusion of innovations among the actors in a small, closed set has frequently utilized stochastic models to study how such innovations percolate through network structures. Rogers (1979) gives a thorough overview of such models and studies. Rapoport (1953) and Coleman, Katz, and Menzel (1957) have made important contributions to such modeling, and we refer the interested reader to reviews of this research in Kemeny and Snell (1962), Bartholomew (1967), and Coleman (1964).

Part VII
Epilogue

17

Future Directions

We conclude this book by speculating a bit about the future of social network methodology. The following comments include observations about gaps in current network methods and "hot" trends that we think are likely to continue. We also include some wishful thinking about the directions in which we would like to see network methodology develop.

17.1 Statistical Models

We believe that statistical models will be a major focus for continued development and expansion of network methods. Clearly scientific understanding is advanced when we can test propositions about network properties rather than simply relying on descriptive statements. Great steps have been made in statistical models for dyads (including p_1 and its relatives for valued relations, multiple relations, and for networks including actor attributes). We expect that further development of Markov graph models, logistic regressions, and so on will make statistical models more useful. Such models avoid the assumptions of dyadic independence, and thus promise to be more "realistic" than models of social networks that assume dyadic independence.

These future developments make use of very important research by Frank and Strauss (1986) and Strauss and Ikeda (1990) on Markov random graphs. Specifically, one can postulate statistical models for social networks which do not assume dyads are independent; in fact, the dependence structure of these models can be quite complicated. However, fitting them exactly is quite tedious computationally, unless one relies on the approximations described by Strauss and Ikeda, which allow one to calculate approximate maximum likelihood estimates of model parameters using logistic regression. These models, because of their generality and realism, have tremendous potential, which has yet to be realized.

We also expect that many of the currently descriptive methods (centralities, cohesive subgroups, positions, and relational algebras) will develop statistical counterparts. For example, current centrality analyses result in the assignment of a centrality score to each actor (for example, actor degree, closeness, or betweenness centrality) but provide no assessment of whether the value is statistically large (Faust and Wasserman 1992). Thus, one cannot answer such questions as, "Is actor i more central than actor j?" with a specifiable degree of certainty. Similarly, graph centralization methods calculate indices of how centralized a network is, but do not answer the question of whether or not a network is more centralized than one would expect given the density, distribution of actor indegrees and outdegrees, or the diameter of the graph.

In the same vein, a cohesive subgroup analysis results in a list of subsets of actors who meet a particular subgroup definition (for example a clique, n-clique, or k-plex) but provide no assessment of whether the subgroup is statistically more cohesive than would be expected by chance. An exception to the above statement is Alba's (1973) model for evaluating whether or not a given cohesive subgroup is more cohesive than expected given the number of nodes and lines in a graph. However, this model is (probably) not appropriate for assessing cohesive subgroups based on other definitions (for example, whether or not n-clique members are relatively closer to each other in a graph theoretic sense than they are to non-members).

Positional analysis ideas and techniques (such as structural equivalence, regular equivalence, and so on) result in the assignment of each actor to an equivalence class based on a particular equivalence definition, but there is no assessment of the appropriateness of the assignments. Goodness-of-fit statistics for structural equivalence blockmodels allow one to assess, a posteriori, whether a hypothesized model provides an adequate representation of the data (Arabie, Boorman, and Levitt 1978; Carrington, Heil, and Berkowitz 1979/80; Hubert and Baker 1978). Stochastic a priori blockmodels allow one to evaluate a partition of actors into classes specified ahead of time (Anderson, Wasserman, and Faust 1992; Fienberg and Wasserman 1981a; Holland, Laskey, and Leinhardt 1983; Wasserman and Anderson 1987). However, similar stochastic models do not exist for other equivalences, such as regular equivalences and ego algebra equivalence.

Algebraic models are primarily descriptive, but statistical versions of relational algebras and of local role algebras are beginning to be developed (Pattison and Wasserman 1993). Statistical versions of algebraic models should allow one to assess the fit of a given algebra, and to study statistically the associations among primitive and compound relations. The equivalences and inclusions among a set of relations measured on a specific network is one of the most important issues in multirelational studies, and a statistical approach to this problem should be quite welcome.

Such statistical approaches should be developed, and should become an integral part of any social network analysis.

17.2 Generalizing to New Kinds of Data

Another direction for future development is the extension of current methods to a wider range of network data. For the most part, social network methods have been developed to study one-mode networks with a single, usually dichotomous and nondirectional relation. Methods designed for these limited data can then (sometimes) be generalized to directional, valued, or multirelational networks, and less frequently to two-mode networks. By and large, it is rare for methods to be developed initially and explicitly for valued relations, two-mode networks, and especially multiple and longitudinal relations and ego-centered networks.

Centrality and prestige measures are well understood for dichotomous, nondirectional relations and for dichotomous, directional relations. Recently, centrality measures have been proposed for valued relations (Freeman, Borgatti, and White 1991). However, centrality and centralization measures for multiple relations have not been developed, nor have measures of centrality and centralization for two-mode networks.

There are some cohesive subgroup models for valued relations (Doreian 1969; Peay 1974; Freeman 1992b; Sailer and Gaulin 1984) and for directional relations (Peay 1975b). Some models can potentially be expanded to study cohesive subgroups in two-mode networks. For example, Alba and Kadushin's (1976) research on intersecting social circles, Freeman and White's (1993) description of Galois lattices, and Bonacich's (1972a) work on overlapping subgroups can be extended to two-mode networks. However, cohesive subgroup ideas have not been developed for multiple relations.

The definitions of equivalences (including structural, automorphic, regular, ego algebra, and so on) are well-understood for dichotomous, directional and nondirectional relations and for multirelational networks. It is not always obvious how to both define and measure equivalences for valued relations. Borgatti and Everett (1992b) discuss how to extend regular equivalence to two-mode networks.

These examples suggest that considerable work still must be done to extend current network methods to a wider range of kinds of network data. However, we do not expect that the most fruitful developments in descriptive techniques will be the continued addition of yet another centrality measure or yet another subgroup definition or yet another definition of equivalence. Rather, we expect that careful assessment of the usefulness of current methods in substantive and theoretical applications will be helpful in determining when, and under what conditions, each method is useful (perhaps in conjunction with statistical assumptions). Considerable work also needs to be done on measurement properties (such as sampling variability) of the current measures.

17.2.1 Multiple Relations

One area where there is clear need for continued work is developing methods to study multiple relations. Many standard network analysis procedures do not (currently) extend well to multiple relations (for example, centralities and cohesive subgroups). Some methods have been developed specifically for multiple relations. For example, relational algebras are defined for multiple relations (Boorman and White 1976; Boyd 1990; Pattison 1993) as are some statistical models (Fienberg, Meyer, and Wasserman 1985; Wasserman 1987; Wasserman, Faust, and Galaskiewicz 1990). However, good measures of the association between relations, or of multirelational properties (such as multiplexity and exchange), have yet to be developed. Developments in the merger of relational algebras with statistical methods promise to make major advances in this area.

17.2.2 Dynamic and Longitudinal Network Models

Network analysis and network models have often been criticized for being static. Although much work has been done on longitudinal models, applications of this methodology are sorely lacking. Models are quite complicated, and often require continuous records of network changes, which are often hard to collect. Wasserman (1978) reviews some older approaches, while newer methods are discussed by Wasserman and Iacobucci (1988), Iacobucci (1989, 1990), and Holland and Leinhardt

(1981). Good, easy-to-use methods for longitudinal network data would be an important addition to the literature.

17.2.3 Ego-centered Networks

An active area of current research in social network methodology is development of methods for measuring and analyzing properties of local or ego-centered networks. Although ego-centered networks are limited, this approach is likely to remain popular because of the relative ease of collecting ego-centered as compared to collecting full network data. In addition, the standardization of questionnaire formats for collecting ego-centered networks (as used in the General Social Survey, Burt, Marsden, and Rossi 1985) will make this form of data collection more widespread.

The applications of ego-centered networks are huge — from transmission of disease (Morris 1989, 1990, 1993) to studies of social support (Wellman 1979, 1988b, 1992b, 1993) to discussion networks (Marsden 1987, 1988) and many others. Due to the popularity of this paradigm, we expect such networks to become increasingly important.

When theoretical propositions are stated at the level of the individual, ego-centered networks might be appropriate for estimating network properties, without the cost of collecting full network data. Yet work needs to be done on how to measure important properties of the structure of ego-centered networks (Walker 1991), as well as on global models for entire populations (Pattison and Wasserman 1993).

17.3 Data Collection

The quality of generalizations about social networks is limited in part by the quality of the data on which the generalizations are based. Although some work has been done on the measurement error of network data (Holland and Leinhardt 1973) and the "accuracy" of network data collected through verbal reports (Bernard, Killworth, Kronenfeld, and Sailer 1985; Freeman and Romney 1987; Freeman, Romney, and Freeman 1987; Romney and Faust 1982) considerably less is known about the reliability and validity of network data (Marsden 1990b). We need a better understanding of the properties of different questions that are used to elicit network members from respondents, and of the influence of different question response formats (for example ratings versus full rank orders). More work needs to be done on developing procedures for collecting observational network data.

17.4 Sampling

Collecting network data on entire networks, where information is gathered on all actors, and ties are measured for all pairs of actors, requires a great deal of time and effort, especially when networks are large. It is thus important to be able to estimate network properties (such as network size, density, actor centralities, network centralization, tendencies for reciprocity or transitivity, and presence of subgroups) from samples. First steps have been taken by Erickson (Erickson and Nosanchuk 1983; Erickson, Nosanchuk, and Lee 1981), Granovetter (1977a), and the important work of Frank (1971, 1978b, 1981, 1988).

Considerable work remains in developing good techniques for network sampling and good measures of sampling variability for network concepts, especially for ego-centered and very large networks.

We also expect that techniques designed to sample networks will become quite useful for estimating "non-network" phenomena. For example, Bernard, Johnsen, and Killworth (1989), Klovdahl (1985, 1989), and recent unpublished research by Frank and Snijders have used network sampling methods to estimate the size of small populations (such as the number of fatalities in the Mexico City earthquake, the number of HIV-positives in a community, or the number of heroin users in a city).

17.5 General Propositions about Structure

One area of network analysis that needs more work is development of general propositions about the structure of social networks based on replication across a large number of networks. One can think of any number of such propositions that cannot be adequately tested without a large sample of networks. For example: Are relations of authority more (or less) likely to be transitive than relations of affection? Are communities better characterized as collections of non-overlapping subgroups or as center-periphery structures? Are more centralized organizations more efficient? Such propositions are stated at the level of the network, and cannot be tested by simply studying single communities or networks as "case studies," or using samples of ego-centered networks.

The now classic series of studies by Davis, Holland, and Leinhardt investigated hypothesized properties of networks, such as balance, clusterability, and transitivity to see whether or not these properties tended to hold in a sample of 384 sociomatrices (Davis 1979; Davis and Leinhardt 1972; Holland and Leinhardt 1979). More recent examples of studies incorporating replication across a number of independent networks include Bernard, Killworth and Sailer's research on informant accuracy (reviewed in Bernard, Killworth, Kronenfeld, and Sailer 1985) and Freeman's work of appropriate models of the notion of social group (Freeman 1992a). These studies test general propositions about networks using the network as the unit of analysis. Ideally, we should have a well-documented bank of network data sets, akin to the sample of sociomatrices compiled by Davis, Holland, and Leinhardt, on which to test hypotheses about networks.

17.6 Computer Technology

Major expansion in the *use* of network methods will likely result from continued advances in computer technology and software. In the last decade several fairly general purpose, widely available network analysis programs have been developed (*STRUCTURE, GRADAP, UCINET,* for example). This is quite an advance over the numerous special-purpose routines of earlier years! Greater availability of software for fitting a range of statistical models (including p_1 and its relatives, correspondence analysis, social influence models, and Bernoulli graphs), and models for local role algebras and Galois lattices, for example, will lead to greater use of this sophisticated methodology.

It is quite unfortunate that adequate statistical models are not included in any of the major social network analysis computer packages. Such inadequacies weaken the available packages.

In addition, more sophisticated graphics capabilities should make exploratory studies using visual displays of networks more fruitful. One should be able to display actor attributes and nodal or subgroup properties (such as expansiveness, centrality, or clique membership) along with the graph.

17.7 Networks and Standard Social and Behavioral Science

One area where a great deal of work remains is integrating network concepts and measures into more general social and behavioral science research. Although *network* is a catch phrase in many disciplines (from "networking" to "network corporations") the precise (and correct) use of network measures has not fully diffused to these areas. In part the usual institutional and intellectual barriers between disciplines inhibit diffusion. In addition, the (mis)perception of the technical sophistication required to use network ideas may dissuade potential users. Again, we expect the greater availability of network analysis software, and greater ease of interface with standard statistical analysis software (such as *SAS*, *SPSS*, and *SYSTAT*) will make network ideas more easily exportable to the wider community.

In addition, if and when greater consensus develops among network researchers about key network properties and measures, it should be easier to communicate appropriate use of network methods to non-network specialists. We hope that this book will help in this regard.

In conclusion, we are excited about the future prospects for social network methods, and look forward to incorporating these advances into the second edition of this book.

Appendix A
Computer Programs

This appendix lists and briefly describes the major computer programs that are available for social network analysis. We include a brief description of each program's capabilities and the address of the program's distributor. Programs are continuously being revised and updated, so the reader should consult the sources listed for the most current information. Also, new programs are constantly being developed.

Connections (the newsletter of the International Network for Social Network Analysis — *INSNA*) and *Social Networks* are good sources of information about new software for social network analysis. For information about membership in *INSNA*, contact

Stephen Borgatti
Department of Sociology
University of South Carolina
Columbia, SC 29208
USA

A.1 *GRADAP*

GRADAP: Graph Definition and Analysis Package (Sprenger and Stokman 1989) was developed through collaboration of researchers from the Universities of Amsterdam, Groningen, Nijmegen, and Twente (Sprenger and Stokman 1989). *GRADAP* explicitly analyzes network data represented as graphs, and includes a wide range of cohesive subgroup and centrality methods, and models for the distribution of in- and outdegrees. *GRADAP* runs on any *DOS* machine and is available from:

iec ProGAMMA
Kraneweg 8
9718 JP Groningen
THE NETHERLANDS

A.2 *KrackPlot*

KrackPlot (Krackhardt, Lundberg, and O'Rourke 1993) draws and prints sociograms, with options for including node labels and specifying coordinates for points. *KrackPlot* runs on any *DOS* machine and is distributed by:

Stephen Borgatti
Analytic Technologies
306 S. Walker St.
Columbia, SC 29205
USA

A.3 *NEGOPY* and *FATCAT*

NEGOPY Network Analysis Program (Richards 1989a) analyzes subgroups and individual roles in communication networks. *FATCAT* (Richards 1989b) allows one to analyze actor attributes along with network data. Although many early versions of *NEGOPY* were available for mainframe computers, the current version is available for the *DOS* machines. *FATCAT* is also available for *DOS* machines. Both *NEGOPY* and *FATCAT* are available from:

William D. Richards
Department of Communication
Simon Fraser University
Burnaby, BC V5K 1E1
CANADA

A.4 *SNAPS*

SNAPS (Social Network Analysis Procedures) for *GAUSS* (Friedkin 1989) is a collection of network analysis subroutines for use with the *DOS* software package *GAUSS*. *SNAPS* includes subroutines for calculating many graph theoretic properties of graphs and nodes, and for fitting social influence models. *SNAPS* runs on *DOS* machines equipped with math coprocessors and is distributed by:

APTECH Systems Inc.
26250 196th Place S.E.
Kent, WA 98042
USA

A.5 *STRUCTURE*

STRUCTURE (Burt 1989, 1991) contains programs for structural equivalence, cohesive subgroups, centrality, and models of contagion and autonomy. The basic edition of *STRUCTURE* runs on *DOS* machines. A virtual memory version runs on 80386-87 or higher *DOS* computers. For information about *STRUCTURE* contact:

Ronald Burt
Department of Sociology
University of Chicago
Chicago, IL 60637
USA

A.6 *UCINET*

UCINET (Borgatti, Everett, and Freeman 1991) contains network analysis programs for centrality, cohesive subgroup, and position and role methods, along with a basic p_1 model and programs for multidimensional scaling and hierarchical clustering. *UCINET* runs on *DOS* machines and is available from:

Stephen Borgatti
Analytic Technologies
306 S. Walker St.
Columbia, SC 29205
USA

Appendix B
Data

Following are the data sets analyzed in the book. Descriptions of these data sets can be found in Chapter 2.

B.1 Krackhardt's High-tech Managers

The three relations measured for Krackhardt's high-tech managers are advice (Table B.1), friendship (Table B.2), and reports to (Table B.3).

Table B.4 lists four actor attribute variables for the 21 high-tech managers. The attributes are age (in years), tenure (length of time employed by the company, in years), level in the corporate hierarchy (coded 1,2,3), and department of the company (coded 1,2,3,4).

B.2 Padgett's Florentine Families

The two relations measured for Padgett's Florentine Families are business (Table B.5) and marriage (Table B.6).

Table B.7 gives attribute variables for the families. Wealth is net wealth, measured in 1427, and is coded in thousands of lira. Number of Priorates is the number of seats on the Civic Council held between 1282 and 1344. And Number of Ties is the number of business or marriage ties in the total network data set containing 116 families.

B.3 Freeman's *EIES* Network

The three relations measured for Freeman's *EIES* network are acquaintanceship at time 1, January 1978, the start of the study (Table B.8); acquaintanceship at time 2, September 1978, the end of the study (Table B.9); and number of messages sent (Table B.10). The acquaintanceship relations are valued with the scale: 4 = close personal friend; 3 = friend; 2 = person I've met; 1 = person I've heard of, but not met; and 0

= unknown name or no reply. The set of 32 researchers included here are those that completed the study. The researchers analyzed here are numbered as follows in S. Freeman and L. Freeman (1979): 01, 02, 03, 06, 08, 10, 11, 13, 14, 18, 19, 20, 21, 22, 23, 24, 25, 26, 27, 32, 33, 35, 36, 37, 38, 39, 40, 41, 42, 43, 44, 45.

Table B.11 gives attribute variables for the researchers. The attributes are numbers of citations in 1978, discipline (coded as 1,2,3), and the discipline itself.

B.4 Countries Trade Data

The five relations measured for the countries trade network are trade of basic manufactured goods from the row country to the column country (Table B.12); food and live animals (Table B.13); crude materials, excluding food (Table B.14); minerals, fuels, and other petroleum products (Table B.15); and exchange of diplomats (Table B.16). The country codes can be found in Table B.12.

There are four attribute variables for the countries trade network, as shown in Table B.17. The attributes are average annual population growth between 1970 and 1981, average GNP growth rate per capita between 1970 and 1981, secondary school enrollment ratio in 1980, and energy consumption per capita in 1980 (measured in kilo coal equivalents).

B.5 Galaskiewicz's CEO and Clubs Network

Table B.18 gives the affiliation network of the chief executive officers of 26 corporations and their memberships/affiliations with 15 clubs, cultural boards, and corporate boards of directors. The set of 26 corporations were chosen from the complete set of 98 CEOs, and the set of 15 clubs were chosen from the complete set of 34 clubs. The corporations analyzed here are numbered as follows in Galaskiewicz (1985): 6, 7, 13, 14, 17, 18, 20, 21, 25, 26, 27, 28, 29, 32, 33, 35, 36, 42, 44, 46, 47, 48, 51, 52, 54, 55. The clubs are numbered as follows: 1, 2, 3, 4, 5, 7, 14, 15, 16, 17, 20, 28, 29, 30, 31. Clubs 1 and 2 are country clubs; clubs 3, 4, and 5, are metropolitan clubs; clubs 7, 14, 15, 16, 17, and 20 are boards of *FORTUNE* 50/50 firms; and clubs 28, 29, 30, and 31 are boards of cultural and religious organizations.

The co-membership matrix for CEOs and the event overlap matrix for clubs can be found in Chapter 8.

Table B.1. *Advice relation between managers of Krackhardt's high-tech company*

Manager	
1	0 1 0 1 0 0 0 1 0 0 0 0 0 0 0 1 0 1 0 0 1
2	0 0 0 0 0 1 1 0 0 0 0 0 0 0 0 0 0 0 0 0 1
3	1 1 0 1 0 1 1 1 1 1 1 0 1 0 0 1 1 0 1 1
4	1 1 0 0 0 1 0 1 0 1 1 1 0 0 0 1 1 1 0 1 1
5	1 1 0 0 0 1 1 1 0 1 1 0 1 1 0 1 1 1 1 1 1
6	0 0 0 0 0 0 0 0 0 0 0 0 0 0 0 0 0 0 0 0 1
7	0 1 0 0 0 1 0 0 0 0 1 1 0 1 0 0 1 1 0 0 1
8	0 1 0 1 0 1 1 0 0 1 1 0 0 0 0 0 0 1 0 0 1
9	1 1 0 0 0 1 1 1 0 1 1 1 0 1 0 1 1 1 0 0 1
10	1 1 1 1 1 0 0 1 0 0 1 0 1 0 1 1 1 1 1 1 0
11	1 1 0 0 0 0 1 0 0 0 0 0 0 0 0 0 0 0 0 0 0
12	0 0 0 0 0 1 0 0 0 0 0 0 0 0 0 0 0 0 0 0 1
13	1 1 0 0 1 0 0 0 1 0 0 0 0 1 0 0 0 1 0 0 0
14	0 1 0 0 0 0 1 0 0 0 0 0 0 0 0 0 0 1 0 0 1
15	1 1 1 1 1 1 1 1 1 1 1 1 1 1 0 1 1 1 1 1 1
16	1 1 0 0 0 0 0 0 0 1 0 0 0 0 0 0 0 1 0 0 0
17	1 1 0 1 0 0 1 0 0 0 0 0 0 0 0 0 0 0 0 0 1
18	1 1 1 1 1 0 1 1 1 1 1 0 1 1 1 1 0 0 1 1 1
19	1 1 1 0 1 0 1 0 0 1 1 0 0 1 1 0 0 1 0 1 0
20	1 1 0 0 0 1 0 1 0 0 1 1 0 1 1 1 1 1 0 0 1
21	0 1 1 1 0 1 1 1 0 0 0 1 0 1 0 0 1 1 0 1 0

Table B.2. *Friendship relation between managers of Krackhardt's high-tech company*

Manager																					
1	0 1 0 1 0 0 0 1 0 0 0 1 0 0 0 1 0 0 0 0 0
2	1 0 0 0 0 0 0 0 0 0 0 0 0 0 0 0 0 1 0 0 1
3	0 0 0 0 0 0 0 0 0 0 0 0 0 1 0 0 0 0 1 0 0
4	1 1 0 0 0 0 0 1 0 0 0 1 0 0 0 1 1 0 0 0 0
5	0 1 0 0 0 0 0 0 1 0 1 0 0 1 0 0 1 0 1 0 1
6	0 1 0 0 0 0 1 0 1 0 0 1 0 0 0 0 1 0 0 0 1
7	0 0 0 0 0 0 0 0 0 0 0 0 0 0 0 0 0 0 0 0 0
8	0 0 0 1 0 0 0 0 0 0 0 0 0 0 0 0 0 0 0 0 0
9	0 0 0 0 0 0 0 0 0 0 0 0 0 0 0 0 0 0 0 0 0
10	0 0 1 0 1 0 0 1 1 0 0 1 0 0 0 1 0 0 0 1 0
11	1 1 1 1 1 0 0 1 1 0 0 1 1 0 1 0 1 1 1 0 0
12	1 0 0 1 0 0 0 0 0 0 0 0 0 0 0 0 1 0 0 0 1
13	0 0 0 0 1 0 0 0 0 0 1 0 0 0 0 0 0 0 0 0 0
14	0 0 0 0 0 0 1 0 0 0 0 0 0 0 1 0 0 0 0 0 0
15	1 0 1 0 1 1 0 0 1 0 1 0 0 1 0 0 0 0 1 0 0
16	1 1 0 0 0 0 0 0 0 0 0 0 0 0 0 0 0 0 0 0 0
17	1 1 1 1 1 1 1 1 1 1 1 1 0 1 1 1 0 0 1 1 1
18	0 1 0 0 0 0 0 0 0 0 0 0 0 0 0 0 0 0 0 0 0
19	1 1 1 0 1 0 0 0 0 0 1 1 0 1 1 0 0 0 0 1 0
20	0 0 0 0 0 0 0 0 0 1 0 0 0 0 0 0 1 0 0 0 0
21	0 1 0 0 0 0 0 0 0 0 0 1 0 0 0 0 1 1 0 0 0

Table B.3. *"Reports to" relation between managers of Krackhardt's high-tech company*

Manager																					
1	0 1 0 0 0 0 0 0 0 0 0 0 0 0 0 0 0 0 0 0 0
2	0 0 0 0 0 0 1 0 0 0 0 0 0 0 0 0 0 0 0 0 0
3	0 0 0 0 0 0 0 0 0 0 0 0 0 1 0 0 0 0 0 0 0
4	0 1 0 0 0 0 0 0 0 0 0 0 0 0 0 0 0 0 0 0 0
5	0 0 0 0 0 0 0 0 0 0 0 0 0 1 0 0 0 0 0 0 0
6	0 0 0 0 0 0 0 0 0 0 0 0 0 0 0 0 0 0 0 0 1
7	0 0 0 0 0 0 0 0 0 0 0 0 0 0 0 0 0 0 0 0 0
8	0 0 0 0 0 0 0 0 0 0 0 0 0 0 0 0 0 0 0 0 1
9	0 0 0 0 0 0 0 0 0 0 0 0 0 1 0 0 0 0 0 0 0
10	0 0 0 0 0 0 0 0 0 0 0 0 0 0 0 0 0 1 0 0 0
11	0 0 0 0 0 0 0 0 0 0 0 0 0 0 0 0 0 1 0 0 0
12	0 0 0 0 0 0 0 0 0 0 0 0 0 0 0 0 0 0 0 0 1
13	0 0 0 0 0 0 0 0 0 0 0 0 0 1 0 0 0 0 0 0 0
14	0 0 0 0 0 0 1 0 0 0 0 0 0 0 0 0 0 0 0 0 0
15	0 0 0 0 0 0 0 0 0 0 0 0 0 1 0 0 0 0 0 0 0
16	0 1 0 0 0 0 0 0 0 0 0 0 0 0 0 0 0 0 0 0 0
17	0 0 0 0 0 0 0 0 0 0 0 0 0 0 0 0 0 0 0 0 1
18	0 0 0 0 0 0 1 0 0 0 0 0 0 0 0 0 0 0 0 0 0
19	0 0 0 0 0 0 0 0 0 0 0 0 0 1 0 0 0 0 0 0 0
20	0 0 0 0 0 0 0 0 0 0 0 0 0 1 0 0 0 0 0 0 0
21	0 0 0 0 0 0 1 0 0 0 0 0 0 0 0 0 0 0 0 0 0

Table B.4. *Attributes for Krackhardt's high-tech managers*

Manager	Age	Tenure	Level	Dept.
1	33	9.333	3	4
2	42	19.583	2	4
3	40	12.750	3	2
4	33	7.500	3	4
5	32	3.333	3	2
6	59	28.000	3	1
7	55	30.000	1	0
8	34	11.333	3	1
9	62	5.417	3	2
10	37	9.250	3	3
11	46	27.000	3	3
12	34	8.917	3	1
13	48	0.250	3	2
14	43	10.417	2	2
15	40	8.417	3	2
16	27	4.667	3	4
17	30	12.417	3	1
18	33	9.083	2	3
19	32	4.833	3	2
20	38	11.667	3	2
21	36	12.500	2	1

Table B.5. *Business relation between Florentine families*

Family																
Acciaiuoli	0	0	0	0	0	0	0	0	0	0	0	0	0	0	0	0
Albizzi	0	0	0	0	0	0	0	0	0	0	0	0	0	0	0	0
Barbadori	0	0	0	0	1	1	0	0	1	0	1	0	0	0	0	0
Bischeri	0	0	0	0	0	0	1	1	0	0	1	0	0	0	0	0
Castellani	0	0	1	0	0	0	0	1	0	0	1	0	0	0	0	0
Ginori	0	0	1	0	0	0	0	1	0	0	0	0	0	0	0	0
Guadagni	0	0	0	1	0	0	0	1	0	0	0	0	0	0	0	0
Lamberteschi	0	0	0	1	1	0	1	0	0	0	1	0	0	0	0	0
Medici	0	0	1	0	0	1	0	0	0	1	0	0	0	1	0	1
Pazzi	0	0	0	0	0	0	0	0	1	0	0	0	0	0	0	0
Peruzzi	0	0	1	1	1	0	0	1	0	0	0	0	0	0	0	0
Pucci	0	0	0	0	0	0	0	0	0	0	0	0	0	0	0	0
Ridolfi	0	0	0	0	0	0	0	0	0	0	0	0	0	0	0	0
Salviati	0	0	0	0	0	0	0	1	0	0	0	0	0	0	0	0
Strozzi	0	0	0	0	0	0	0	0	0	0	0	0	0	0	0	0
Tornabuoni	0	0	0	0	0	0	0	1	0	0	0	0	0	0	0	0

Table B.6. *Marital relation between Florentine families*

Family	
Acciaiuoli	0 0 0 0 0 0 0 0 1 0 0 0 0 0 0 0
Albizzi	0 0 0 0 0 1 1 0 1 0 0 0 0 0 0 0
Barbadori	0 0 0 0 1 0 0 0 1 0 0 0 0 0 0 0
Bischeri	0 0 0 0 0 0 1 0 0 0 1 0 0 0 1 0
Castellani	0 0 1 0 0 0 0 0 0 1 0 0 0 0 1 0
Ginori	0 1 0 0 0 0 0 0 0 0 0 0 0 0 0 0
Guadagni	0 1 0 1 0 0 0 1 0 0 0 0 0 0 0 1
Lamberteschi	0 0 0 0 0 0 1 0 0 0 0 0 0 0 0 0
Medici	1 1 1 0 0 0 0 0 0 0 0 0 1 1 0 1
Pazzi	0 0 0 0 0 0 0 0 0 0 0 0 0 1 0 0
Peruzzi	0 0 0 1 1 0 0 0 0 0 0 0 0 0 1 0
Pucci	0 0 0 0 0 0 0 0 0 0 0 0 0 0 0 0
Ridolfi	0 0 0 0 0 0 0 0 1 0 0 0 0 0 1 1
Salviati	0 0 0 0 0 0 0 0 1 1 0 0 0 0 0 0
Strozzi	0 0 0 1 1 0 0 0 0 0 1 0 1 0 0 0
Tornabuoni	0 0 0 0 0 0 1 0 1 0 0 0 1 0 0 0

Table B.7. *Attributes for Padgett's Florentine families*

Family	Wealth	Number of priorates	Number of ties
Acciaiuoli	10	53	2
Albizzi	36	65	3
Barbadori	55	.	14
Bischeri	44	12	9
Castellani	20	22	18
Ginori	32	.	9
Guadagni	8	21	14
Lamberteschi	42	0	14
Medici	103	53	54
Pazzi	48	.	7
Peruzzi	49	42	32
Pucci	3	0	1
Ridolfi	27	38	4
Salviati	10	35	5
Strozzi	146	74	29
Tornabuoni	48	.	7

Table B.8. *Acquaintanceship at time 1 between Freeman's EIES researchers*

Researcher	
1	0 4 2 2 2 2 2 2 2 2 2 2 2 2 2 2 2 3 2 2 2 2 2 2 2 3 2 2 2 2 4 2
2	4 0 2 0 1 0 3 3 4 1 3 0 2 2 2 3 2 0 1 2 3 2 0 2 0 0 2 1 2 3 4 4
3	3 1 0 4 1 0 0 2 0 2 4 4 0 4 1 2 2 2 1 2 2 2 4 2 0 2 0 1 1 1 0 0
4	2 0 2 0 2 0 0 2 2 2 2 2 2 2 2 1 0 0 4 2 2 2 2 2 2 0 2 2 2 0 2 0
5	3 0 0 2 0 0 0 2 3 2 2 1 0 2 1 2 2 0 1 2 2 2 0 2 1 0 1 2 2 0 2 2
6	3 0 0 0 0 0 0 2 0 0 0 0 0 2 0 1 0 0 2 0 1 0 0 0 0 0 2 0 2 0 2 0
7	3 2 1 0 0 0 0 2 2 0 1 0 3 0 0 0 0 0 0 0 0 0 0 0 0 0 0 2 0 0 0 0
8	2 2 2 2 2 0 0 0 1 0 2 0 2 2 2 2 2 0 1 2 2 1 1 2 2 0 2 0 2 2 0 0
9	3 4 0 0 2 0 0 2 0 0 1 0 2 1 0 0 0 0 0 0 1 3 0 0 0 0 3 0 0 0 0 4
10	2 1 3 3 2 0 1 2 2 0 2 3 0 1 2 2 2 0 2 3 2 2 4 2 2 0 0 2 2 2 0 0
11	1 3 2 1 1 0 0 3 1 1 0 0 0 2 1 2 2 0 1 2 2 2 1 2 2 0 2 1 1 0 1 0
12	1 0 1 2 0 0 0 1 0 3 0 0 0 2 0 1 0 0 2 2 2 2 0 0 2 0 0 0 2 2 0 0
13	3 3 1 2 1 0 3 3 2 1 1 0 0 1 1 1 0 0 2 1 1 1 1 0 0 2 4 2 2 2 3 3
14	3 2 4 2 3 0 0 3 2 1 2 3 1 0 3 4 3 2 3 3 3 4 3 3 3 2 1 2 4 3 2 0
15	3 2 2 3 1 0 1 2 2 2 2 1 0 3 0 2 2 0 2 1 2 1 2 2 2 0 0 0 3 0 2 0
16	2 2 2 1 3 0 0 3 1 0 2 0 0 3 2 0 3 0 1 2 4 3 0 3 2 0 0 0 2 0 0 0
17	3 2 3 0 2 0 0 3 2 1 2 0 0 3 2 2 0 0 1 3 3 3 0 2 0 0 0 1 1 0 2 0
18	4 1 2 0 0 0 0 0 0 0 2 0 0 2 1 0 0 0 1 0 0 0 0 1 0 2 2 1 2 2 4 0
19	2 0 2 4 1 0 0 2 0 2 0 2 0 2 2 1 0 0 0 1 2 3 2 2 2 0 2 2 1 2 0 0
20	2 2 2 2 2 0 0 2 0 3 2 2 0 3 1 2 2 0 2 0 3 4 2 3 3 0 0 2 3 1 0 0
21	3 3 2 2 2 0 0 3 1 2 3 2 0 2 3 4 3 0 2 2 0 3 2 2 3 0 1 2 2 1 0 1
22	2 2 2 3 0 0 0 2 3 2 2 0 0 3 0 3 2 0 3 3 3 0 0 4 2 0 0 2 4 0 0 0
23	2 0 4 3 0 0 0 0 0 4 0 1 0 2 1 1 0 0 2 2 2 1 0 1 2 0 0 1 2 0 0 0
24	2 2 2 2 2 0 0 3 2 2 2 2 0 3 2 3 2 0 3 3 3 4 2 0 3 0 2 2 4 0 0 0
25	2 2 2 2 1 0 0 2 0 3 2 2 0 3 2 3 0 0 2 4 3 3 3 4 0 0 0 1 0 0 0 0
26	4 1 2 1 1 0 1 1 0 1 1 1 2 2 1 1 0 3 2 1 1 2 1 2 1 0 0 2 2 0 3 0
27	2 2 1 2 1 0 0 2 2 1 1 0 4 1 1 1 1 0 1 1 1 0 0 0 0 0 0 0 0 2 0 0
28	3 2 0 3 0 0 0 0 0 1 1 0 1 2 2 2 0 0 3 2 2 3 0 2 1 2 1 0 2 0 2 0
29	2 2 2 2 2 0 0 2 0 2 0 2 0 3 2 2 0 2 2 2 2 4 2 3 0 2 2 2 0 2 2 0
30	3 4 1 0 0 0 0 4 0 2 0 0 2 2 0 2 2 2 2 2 2 2 0 0 0 0 2 1 2 0 0 2
31	4 4 2 2 2 2 1 2 2 0 2 0 2 2 2 1 2 3 2 0 1 2 2 2 0 2 2 2 2 2 0 0
32	3 3 0 1 2 0 0 3 4 0 1 0 2 1 0 1 0 0 1 1 1 0 0 0 0 0 2 0 0 3 3 0

Table B.9. *Acquaintanceship at time 2 between Freeman's EIES researchers*

Researcher	
1	0 4 2 2 2 2 2 3 3 2 3 2 3 2 2 2 2 3 2 2 2 2 2 2 2 3 2 2 3 2 4 3
2	4 0 2 2 1 2 2 3 4 2 3 0 2 2 2 2 2 2 2 2 2 2 2 2 2 2 2 2 2 3 4 4
3	3 1 0 4 1 0 0 2 0 2 4 4 0 4 1 2 2 2 1 2 2 2 4 2 0 2 0 1 1 1 0 0
4	2 2 2 0 2 2 0 2 2 3 2 2 1 2 2 2 0 2 4 2 2 2 2 2 2 2 2 2 2 2 2 0
5	3 0 0 2 0 0 0 2 3 2 2 1 0 2 1 2 2 0 1 2 2 2 0 2 1 0 1 2 2 0 2 2
6	4 2 0 0 0 0 0 3 0 2 2 0 0 2 2 2 0 0 2 0 2 0 0 3 0 2 2 2 3 0 4 2
7	3 2 1 0 0 0 0 2 2 0 1 0 3 0 0 0 0 0 0 0 0 0 0 0 0 0 2 0 0 0 0 0
8	3 2 2 2 2 2 1 0 1 2 4 1 2 2 2 2 2 2 2 2 2 2 2 2 2 0 2 1 2 2 2 4
9	3 4 0 0 2 0 0 2 0 0 2 0 2 1 0 1 2 0 0 0 2 2 0 0 0 0 3 0 1 0 2 4
10	3 0 2 3 2 0 1 2 1 0 2 3 2 1 2 2 2 2 2 4 2 2 4 2 2 0 2 2 3 2 2 1
11	3 2 2 2 2 2 0 4 2 2 0 0 2 2 2 2 2 2 2 2 2 2 1 2 2 0 2 2 2 0 3 3
12	2 0 1 2 0 0 1 1 0 3 0 0 0 2 1 1 0 0 2 3 2 1 1 1 2 0 0 1 0 1 2 2
13	3 3 1 2 1 0 3 3 2 1 2 0 0 1 1 2 0 2 2 1 2 2 1 0 0 2 4 2 2 2 3 3
14	3 2 4 3 3 0 0 3 0 2 2 3 2 0 3 4 4 2 3 3 3 4 3 3 3 2 2 3 4 3 3 2
15	3 2 2 3 1 0 0 2 2 2 2 2 0 3 0 2 2 0 2 1 2 2 2 2 2 0 1 0 3 0 3 1
16	2 2 2 2 3 2 0 3 1 2 2 0 0 3 2 0 2 0 2 2 4 3 0 2 2 2 1 1 2 0 2 2
17	3 2 3 1 2 0 0 3 2 1 3 1 1 3 2 3 0 1 1 3 3 3 0 2 0 1 2 1 2 2 2 2
18	4 2 2 0 0 0 1 2 0 0 2 0 1 2 0 0 0 0 0 0 0 0 0 0 0 2 2 0 2 2 4 1
19	2 0 2 4 1 0 0 2 0 2 0 2 0 2 2 1 0 0 0 2 2 3 2 2 2 2 0 2 2 1 2 0
20	2 2 2 2 2 0 0 2 0 3 2 2 0 3 1 2 2 0 2 0 3 4 2 3 3 0 0 2 3 1 0 0
21	3 3 2 2 2 0 0 3 1 2 3 2 0 2 3 4 3 0 2 2 0 3 2 2 3 0 1 2 2 1 0 1
22	2 2 2 3 0 0 0 2 3 2 2 0 0 3 2 3 2 0 3 3 3 0 0 4 2 0 0 2 4 0 0 2
23	3 2 4 3 0 0 0 2 0 4 0 1 0 3 1 1 0 0 3 2 1 1 0 2 2 0 0 2 3 2 2 0
24	3 2 2 2 3 2 0 3 2 2 3 2 2 3 2 3 2 2 2 3 3 4 2 0 3 0 2 3 3 2 2 2
25	2 2 2 3 1 0 0 3 0 3 2 2 0 3 2 3 0 0 2 3 3 3 3 3 0 0 0 1 2 0 0 0
26	4 1 2 1 1 0 1 1 0 1 1 1 2 2 1 1 0 3 2 1 1 2 1 2 1 0 0 2 2 0 3 0
27	3 2 2 2 2 2 0 3 3 2 2 0 4 1 2 2 2 2 2 1 2 2 1 2 0 0 0 0 2 2 2 2
28	3 2 0 3 0 0 0 2 0 1 1 0 2 2 2 2 0 0 3 2 2 3 0 2 1 2 1 0 2 0 2 2
29	3 2 2 3 2 2 0 3 0 3 2 3 2 4 3 2 2 2 2 3 2 4 2 4 0 2 2 2 0 2 3 2
30	3 3 1 2 0 2 0 3 0 2 2 0 2 2 0 2 2 2 2 2 2 2 0 2 2 0 3 2 3 0 3 3
31	4 4 2 2 2 3 2 2 2 2 3 2 3 2 3 2 2 3 2 2 2 2 2 2 2 2 2 2 3 2 0 4
32	4 4 0 2 2 2 0 4 4 2 3 0 2 1 0 3 2 0 0 1 2 3 1 1 0 2 2 1 3 2 4 0

Table B.10. *Messages sent between Freeman's EIES researchers*

Researcher	1	2	3	4	5	6	7	8	9	10	11	12	13	14	15	16	17	18	19	20	21	22	23	24	25	26	27	28	29	30	31	32
1	24	488	28	65	20	65	45	346	82	52	177	28	24	49	81	77	77	73	33	31	22	46	31	128	38	89	95	25	388	71	212	185
2	364	6	17	0	15	17	30	20	35	20	22	15	15	15	15	50	25	8	0	15	15	15	15	0	15	15	10	24	89	23	163	39
3	4	5	0	4	4	0	0	5	0	0	9	0	0	0	0	0	0	0	0	0	0	0	0	0	0	0	0	0	20	0	0	0
4	52	30	4	4	2	0	8	32	21	34	9	0	0	4	4	4	4	5	0	0	0	8	0	12	0	12	12	0	20	4	19	33
5	26	4	4	4	4	34	0	4	16	0	15	0	0	0	8	4	6	4	0	0	0	0	4	14	4	4	4	3	34	7	4	0
6	72	23	0	0	0	0	0	16	0	7	0	0	0	4	0	7	7	0	0	0	0	0	0	14	0	0	7	3	34	3	22	0
7	14	0	0	0	0	0	0	0	0	0	0	0	0	0	0	0	0	0	0	0	0	0	0	0	0	0	0	0	0	0	6	0
8	239	82	5	37	3	34	5	10	12	18	164	18	10	0	0	30	53	27	20	4	0	5	4	55	0	9	34	0	146	216	88	288
9	24	25	0	2	0	0	0	8	16	0	15	0	0	0	0	9	5	0	0	0	0	0	0	0	0	4	15	0	10	6	30	44
10	43	15	0	32	0	12	0	14	39	5	25	2	4	0	0	10	10	24	20	15	8	5	15	29	10	11	10	0	47	6	22	19
11	178	36	0	11	0	10	10	172	0	28	29	3	0	0	0	7	23	24	5	0	0	0	0	29	29	22	22	0	46	119	34	0
12	0	5	0	0	0	0	0	5	0	0	0	0	0	0	0	0	0	0	0	0	0	0	0	0	0	0	0	0	53	5	5	9
13	5	0	0	0	0	0	0	0	0	0	5	0	0	0	0	0	0	0	0	0	0	0	0	0	0	0	0	0	0	5	8	0
14	12	0	9	0	0	0	0	0	0	0	0	0	0	2	12	0	12	0	0	0	0	0	0	0	0	0	0	0	35	0	32	0
15	120	0	0	10	4	0	0	20	0	5	10	5	0	0	78	15	15	0	0	0	0	0	0	5	0	0	8	0	58	32	10	0
16	58	25	10	7	0	6	0	36	0	5	9	5	0	5	0	10	10	0	0	0	0	0	0	0	0	0	15	0	35	10	10	9
17	63	18	9	4	0	0	0	4	0	5	18	0	0	5	0	10	0	4	5	0	0	0	5	5	0	0	15	9	10	9	15	0
18	58	8	5	25	0	0	0	10	0	5	0	0	0	5	0	0	4	0	0	0	0	0	0	0	0	0	20	10	8	10	48	9
19	5	5	0	0	0	0	0	0	0	0	0	0	0	0	0	0	0	0	0	0	0	0	0	0	0	0	0	0	0	10	10	0
20	0	0	0	0	0	0	0	0	0	0	0	0	0	0	0	0	0	0	0	0	0	0	0	0	0	0	0	0	4	0	0	0
21	9	0	0	0	0	0	0	0	0	3	0	0	0	0	0	0	0	0	0	0	0	0	0	0	0	0	0	0	5	0	0	0
22	10	0	5	0	0	0	0	0	0	0	0	0	0	0	0	0	5	0	0	0	0	0	0	0	0	0	0	0	15	5	0	5
23	5	5	0	0	0	0	0	0	19	0	0	4	0	0	0	0	5	0	0	0	0	0	0	40	0	0	0	0	14	0	5	0
24	89	17	4	14	18	14	8	41	4	19	31	4	0	9	4	14	14	9	0	0	4	58	4	0	18	14	9	4	156	56	10	10
25	32	5	0	0	0	0	0	0	0	19	0	0	33	15	0	0	0	0	0	0	0	10	0	5	0	0	0	9	0	15	15	0
26	35	5	0	13	0	0	0	19	5	5	8	0	0	0	4	0	0	0	0	0	0	0	0	23	0	0	0	0	10	13	13	33
27	50	28	0	13	0	0	0	19	29	0	0	0	33	0	4	10	10	15	0	0	0	0	0	10	0	0	3	3	32	0	0	0
28	9	6	0	0	0	0	0	0	0	0	8	0	0	0	0	0	0	0	0	0	0	0	0	0	0	0	0	3	0	0	0	6
29	559	132	5	24	3	29	0	155	15	98	69	89	37	76	80	63	15	4	9	18	43	108	29	218	0	15	66	0	6	14	91	126
30	39	21	0	6	0	0	0	140	7	0	0	2	0	0	9	5	9	5	0	0	5	0	5	0	0	2	2	8	18	20	2	8
31	82	125	22	10	15	18	0	70	35	23	114	20	16	15	30	22	28	9	5	5	5	15	8	53	25	8	21	8	65	28	0	67
32	239	99	27	3	0	0	0	268	101	18	35	4	0	0	0	0	7	0	0	0	0	14	0	5	0	50	6	7	71	107	219	0

Table B.11. *Attributes for Freeman's EIES researchers*

Researcher	Original ID	Citations	Discipline code	Discipline
1	1	19	1	Sociology
2	2	3	2	Anthropology
3	3	170	4	Communication
4	6	23	1	Sociology
5	8	16	4	Psychology
6	10	6	4	Psychology
7	11	1	4	Psychology
8	13	9	2	Anthropology
9	14	6	2	Anthropology
10	18	40	1	Sociology
11	19	15	1	Sociology
12	20	54	1	Sociology
13	21	4	2	Anthropology
14	22	46	1	Sociology
15	23	17	1	Sociology
16	24	32	3	Statistics
17	25	23	4	Psychology
18	26	1	1	Sociology
19	27	34	1	Sociology
20	32	64	1	Sociology
21	33	11	3	Statistics
22	35	11	1	Sociology
23	36	31	1	Sociology
24	37	18	1	Sociology
25	38	4	1	Sociology
26	39	0	1	Sociology
27	40	4	3	Mathematics
28	41	56	1	Sociology
29	42	12	1	Sociology
30	43	2	2	Anthropology
31	44	0	4	Psychology
32	45	1	2	Anthropology

Table B.12. *Trade of basic manufactured goods between countries*

```
                                  1 1 1 1 1 1 1 1 1 1 2 2 2 2 2
                      Nation  1 2 3 4 5 6 7 8 9 0 1 2 3 4 5 6 7 8 9 0 1 2 3 4
 1  Alg           Algeria  0 0 0 1 1 0 0 0 0 0 0 0 1 0 0 0 0 0 0 0 0 0 0 1
 2  Arg         Argentina  1 0 1 1 0 1 0 0 1 0 1 1 1 0 0 0 1 1 1 0 1 0 1 0
 3  Bra            Brazil  1 1 0 1 1 1 1 0 1 1 1 1 1 1 0 1 1 1 1 1 1 1 1 1
 4  Chi             China  1 1 1 0 1 0 1 1 1 1 0 1 1 1 1 1 1 1 1 1 1 1 1 1
 5  Cze    Czechoslovakia  1 1 1 1 0 1 1 1 1 1 1 0 1 1 0 1 1 1 1 1 1 1 1 1
 6  Ecu           Ecuador  0 0 1 0 0 0 0 0 0 0 0 0 0 0 0 0 0 0 0 0 0 0 1 0
 7  Egy             Egypt  0 0 0 0 1 0 0 1 1 0 0 0 1 0 0 0 0 1 1 0 0 1 1 1
 8  Eth          Ethiopia  0 0 0 0 0 0 0 0 0 0 0 0 0 0 0 0 0 1 0 0 0 1 0 0
 9  Fin           Finland  1 1 1 1 1 1 1 1 0 1 1 1 1 0 0 1 1 1 1 1 1 1 1 1
10  Hon          Honduras  0 0 0 0 0 0 0 0 0 0 0 0 0 0 0 0 0 0 0 0 0 0 1 0
11  Ind         Indonesia  1 0 0 1 1 0 1 0 1 0 0 0 1 0 0 1 1 1 1 0 1 1 1 1
12  Isr            Israel  0 1 0 0 0 0 0 1 1 0 0 0 1 0 0 1 0 1 1 0 1 1 1 1
13  Jap             Japan  1 1 1 1 1 1 1 1 1 1 1 1 0 1 1 1 1 1 1 1 1 1 1 1
14  Lib           Liberia  0 0 0 0 0 0 0 0 0 0 0 0 0 0 0 0 0 0 0 0 0 0 0 0
15  Mad        Madagascar  0 0 0 0 0 0 0 0 0 0 0 0 0 0 0 0 0 0 0 0 0 0 1 0
16  NZ        New Zealand  1 0 0 1 0 0 1 0 0 0 1 0 1 0 0 0 1 1 0 0 1 1 1 1
17  Pak          Pakistan  0 0 0 1 1 0 0 0 1 0 1 0 1 1 0 1 0 1 1 1 1 1 1 0
18  Spa             Spain  1 1 1 1 1 1 1 0 1 1 1 1 1 1 1 1 1 0 1 1 1 1 1 1
19  Swi       Switzerland  1 1 1 1 1 1 1 1 1 1 1 1 1 1 1 1 1 1 0 1 1 1 1 1
20  Syr             Syria  0 0 0 0 0 0 0 0 0 0 0 0 0 0 0 0 0 0 0 0 0 0 0 0
21  Tai          Thailand  0 0 1 1 0 0 0 0 1 0 1 1 1 0 0 1 1 1 1 0 0 1 1 1
22  UK     United Kingdom  1 0 1 1 1 1 1 1 1 1 1 1 1 1 1 1 1 1 1 1 1 0 1 1
23  US      United States  1 1 1 1 1 1 1 1 1 1 1 1 1 1 1 1 1 1 1 1 1 1 0 1
24  Yug        Yugoslavia  1 1 0 1 1 0 1 1 1 0 1 1 1 0 0 1 1 1 1 1 1 1 1 0
```

Table B.13. *Trade of food and live animals between countries*

Nation	
Algeria	0 0 0 0 0 0 0 0 0 0 0 0 0 0 0 0 0 1 0 0 0 0 0 0
Argentina	1 0 1 0 1 1 1 0 1 0 1 1 1 0 0 1 1 1 1 1 1 0 1 1
Brazil	1 1 0 1 1 0 1 0 1 0 1 1 1 1 0 1 1 1 1 1 1 1 1 1
China	1 0 0 0 1 0 1 0 1 0 1 0 1 1 0 1 1 1 1 1 1 1 1 0
Czechoslovakia	0 0 1 0 0 0 1 0 1 0 0 0 1 0 0 0 0 1 1 1 1 1 1 1
Ecuador	0 1 1 0 1 0 0 0 1 0 0 0 1 0 0 1 0 1 1 0 0 1 1 1
Egypt	1 0 0 0 1 0 0 0 1 0 1 1 0 0 0 0 0 0 1 0 0 1 1 0
Ethiopia	0 0 0 0 1 0 0 0 1 0 0 1 1 0 0 0 0 1 1 0 0 1 1 0
Finland	1 0 0 0 1 0 1 0 0 0 0 1 1 1 0 0 0 0 1 1 1 1 1 1
Honduras	0 0 0 0 1 0 1 0 1 0 0 1 1 0 0 0 0 1 1 1 0 1 1 1
Indonesia	1 0 0 1 1 0 1 0 1 0 0 0 1 0 0 1 1 1 1 0 1 1 1 1
Israel	0 1 1 0 0 0 1 0 1 0 0 0 1 0 0 1 0 1 1 0 1 1 1 1
Japan	0 0 0 1 1 0 1 0 1 1 1 1 0 1 1 1 1 1 1 1 1 1 1 0
Liberia	0 0 0 0 0 0 0 0 0 0 0 0 0 0 0 0 0 1 1 0 0 0 0 1 0
Madagascar	0 0 0 0 0 0 0 0 1 0 0 0 1 0 0 0 0 1 1 0 0 0 1 0
New Zealand	1 0 0 1 0 1 1 0 1 1 1 0 1 0 0 0 1 1 1 1 1 1 1 0
Pakistan	1 0 0 0 1 0 0 0 1 0 1 0 1 0 0 1 0 0 1 0 0 1 1 0
Spain	1 1 1 1 1 1 1 0 1 1 1 1 1 0 1 0 0 1 1 1 1 1 1
Switzerland	1 1 1 1 1 0 1 1 1 0 1 1 1 1 1 1 1 0 1 1 1 1 1
Syria	1 0 0 0 0 0 1 0 0 0 0 0 0 0 0 0 1 0 0 0 0 0 0 0
Thailand	1 0 0 1 1 1 1 0 1 0 1 1 1 0 1 1 1 1 1 1 0 1 1 0
United Kingdom	1 0 1 1 1 0 1 1 1 1 1 1 1 1 1 1 1 1 1 1 1 0 1 1
United States	1 1 1 1 1 1 1 1 1 1 1 1 1 1 1 1 1 1 1 1 1 1 0 1
Yugoslavia	1 0 1 1 1 0 1 0 1 0 0 1 1 0 0 0 0 1 1 1 0 1 1 0

Table B.14. *Trade of crude materials, excluding food*

Nation	
Algeria	0 0 0 1 1 0 0 0 1 0 1 0 0 0 0 0 0 1 0 0 0 0 0 1
Argentina	1 0 1 1 1 1 0 0 1 0 1 1 1 0 0 0 0 1 1 0 1 0 1 1
Brazil	1 1 0 1 1 1 1 0 1 0 1 1 1 0 1 1 1 1 1 0 1 1 1 1
China	0 1 0 0 1 0 1 1 1 0 1 0 1 0 0 1 1 1 1 0 1 1 1 1
Czechoslovakia	0 0 0 0 0 0 1 0 1 0 0 0 0 0 0 0 0 1 1 1 0 1 0 1
Ecuador	0 0 0 0 0 0 0 0 1 0 0 0 0 0 0 0 0 0 0 0 0 1 1 0
Egypt	1 0 0 1 1 0 0 0 1 0 1 1 1 0 0 0 1 1 1 0 1 1 1 1
Ethiopia	1 0 0 0 1 0 1 0 0 0 0 1 1 0 0 0 0 1 1 1 0 1 1 0
Finland	1 1 0 1 1 1 1 0 0 0 1 1 1 0 0 1 1 1 1 0 1 1 1 1
Honduras	0 0 0 0 1 0 0 0 0 0 0 0 1 0 0 0 0 1 1 0 0 1 1 1
Indonesia	0 0 0 1 1 0 0 0 1 0 0 0 1 0 0 1 1 1 1 0 1 1 1 1
Israel	0 1 0 0 0 1 0 0 1 0 0 0 0 0 0 0 0 1 1 0 0 1 1 1
Japan	1 1 1 1 1 1 1 1 1 0 1 1 0 0 0 1 1 1 1 1 1 1 1 1
Liberia	0 0 0 0 0 0 1 0 0 0 0 1 1 0 0 0 1 1 1 1 0 1 1 1
Madagascar	0 0 0 0 0 0 0 0 0 0 0 0 1 0 0 0 0 1 0 0 0 1 1 0
New Zealand	1 1 0 1 1 0 1 0 1 0 1 1 1 0 0 0 1 1 1 1 1 1 1 1
Pakistan	0 0 0 1 1 0 0 0 0 0 1 0 1 0 0 0 0 1 1 0 1 1 1 0
Spain	1 1 1 1 0 1 1 0 1 1 1 1 1 0 0 1 1 0 1 1 1 1 1 1
Switzerland	1 1 1 1 1 1 1 0 1 0 1 1 1 0 0 1 1 1 0 1 1 1 1 1
Syria	1 0 0 0 1 0 0 0 0 0 0 0 1 0 0 0 0 1 0 0 0 1 0 1
Thailand	0 0 0 1 1 0 1 0 1 0 1 1 1 0 0 1 1 1 1 0 0 1 1 1
United Kingdom	1 0 1 1 1 1 1 1 1 0 1 1 1 1 0 1 1 1 1 1 1 0 1 1
United States	1 1 1 1 1 1 1 1 1 1 1 1 1 1 1 1 1 1 1 1 1 1 0 1
Yugoslavia	1 0 0 1 1 0 1 1 0 0 0 1 1 0 0 0 1 1 1 1 1 1 1 0

Table B.15. *Trade of minerals, fuels, and other petroleum products between countries*

Nation	
Algeria	0 0 1 0 0 0 1 0 0 0 0 0 1 0 0 0 0 1 1 1 0 1 1 1
Argentina	0 0 1 0 0 0 0 0 0 0 0 0 0 0 0 0 1 0 0 0 0 0 1 0
Brazil	1 1 0 0 0 1 0 0 0 0 0 0 0 1 0 0 0 0 0 0 0 1 1 0
China	0 0 1 0 0 0 1 0 1 0 1 0 1 0 1 1 1 1 0 0 1 0 1 0
Czechoslovakia	0 0 0 0 0 0 0 0 0 0 0 0 0 0 0 0 0 0 1 0 0 0 0 1
Ecuador	0 0 0 0 0 0 0 0 0 0 0 0 0 0 0 0 0 0 0 0 0 0 1 0
Egypt	0 0 0 0 0 0 0 0 0 0 0 1 0 0 0 0 1 0 0 0 1 1 1
Ethiopia	0 0 0 0 0 0 0 0 0 0 0 0 0 0 0 0 0 0 0 0 0 0 0 0
Finland	0 0 0 0 0 0 0 0 0 0 1 0 0 0 0 0 1 0 0 0 1 1 0
Honduras	0 0 0 0 0 0 0 0 0 0 0 0 0 0 0 0 0 0 0 0 0 0 0 0
Indonesia	0 0 0 0 0 0 0 0 0 0 0 1 0 0 1 0 1 0 0 1 1 1 0
Israel	0 0 0 0 0 0 1 0 0 0 0 0 0 0 0 0 0 0 0 0 0 0 0 0
Japan	1 1 1 1 0 1 1 0 0 1 1 0 0 0 0 1 1 1 0 0 1 1 1 0
Liberia	0 0 0 0 0 0 1 0 0 0 0 0 0 0 0 0 0 0 0 0 0 0 0 1
Madagascar	0 0 0 0 0 0 0 0 0 0 0 0 0 0 0 0 0 0 0 0 0 0 0 0
New Zealand	0 0 0 0 0 0 0 0 0 0 0 0 1 0 0 0 0 0 0 0 0 0 0 0
Pakistan	0 0 0 0 0 0 0 0 0 0 0 0 0 0 0 0 0 0 0 1 0 0 0
Spain	1 1 0 0 0 0 1 0 1 0 0 0 0 1 1 0 1 0 0 1 0 1 1 1
Switzerland	0 0 0 0 1 0 0 0 0 0 1 1 0 1 0 0 0 0 0 0 1 0 1
Syria	0 0 0 0 0 0 0 0 0 0 0 0 0 0 0 0 1 0 0 0 1 0 0
Thailand	0 0 0 0 0 0 0 0 0 0 0 0 0 1 0 0 0 0 0 0 0 1 0
United Kingdom	1 0 1 1 1 1 1 1 0 1 1 0 1 0 1 1 1 1 1 1 0 1 1
United States	1 1 1 1 0 1 1 1 1 1 1 1 1 1 1 1 1 1 1 1 1 1 0 1
Yugoslavia	1 0 0 0 1 0 0 0 0 0 0 1 0 0 0 0 0 1 1 1 0 0 1 0

Table B.16. *Exchange of diplomats between countries*

Nation	
Algeria	0 1 1 1 1 0 0 0 1 0 1 0 1 0 1 0 1 1 1 1 0 1 1 1
Argentina	1 0 1 1 1 0 1 0 1 1 1 1 1 0 0 0 1 1 1 1 1 0 1 1
Brazil	1 1 0 1 1 1 1 0 1 1 1 1 1 0 0 0 1 1 1 1 1 1 1 1
China	1 1 1 0 1 1 1 1 1 0 0 0 1 1 1 1 1 1 1 1 1 1 1 1
Czechoslovakia	1 1 1 1 0 1 1 0 1 0 1 0 1 0 0 0 0 1 1 1 0 1 1 1
Ecuador	0 1 1 1 1 0 1 0 0 1 0 1 1 0 0 0 0 1 1 0 0 1 1 1
Egypt	0 1 1 1 1 1 0 1 1 0 1 1 1 1 1 0 0 1 1 1 0 1 1 1
Ethiopia	1 1 0 1 1 0 1 0 1 0 1 0 1 1 0 0 0 1 1 0 0 1 1 1
Finland	0 1 1 1 1 0 1 0 0 0 1 1 1 0 0 0 0 1 1 0 0 1 1 1
Honduras	0 1 1 1 0 1 0 0 0 0 0 1 1 0 0 0 0 1 0 0 0 1 1 0
Indonesia	1 1 1 0 1 0 1 0 1 0 0 0 1 0 0 1 1 1 1 1 1 1 1 1
Israel	0 1 1 0 0 1 0 0 1 0 0 0 1 0 0 0 0 0 1 0 0 1 1 0
Japan	1 1 1 1 1 1 1 1 1 1 1 1 0 1 1 1 1 1 1 1 1 1 1 1
Liberia	1 0 0 1 0 0 1 1 0 0 0 1 1 0 0 0 0 1 1 0 0 1 1 0
Madagascar	1 0 0 1 0 0 1 0 0 0 1 0 1 0 0 0 0 0 1 0 0 1 1 0
New Zealand	0 0 0 1 1 0 1 0 0 0 1 1 1 0 0 0 0 0 1 0 1 1 1 1
Pakistan	1 1 1 1 1 0 1 0 0 0 1 0 1 0 0 0 0 1 1 1 1 1 1 1
Spain	1 1 1 1 1 1 1 0 1 1 1 0 1 0 0 0 1 0 1 1 1 1 1 1
Switzerland	1 1 1 1 1 1 1 0 1 0 1 1 1 0 0 0 1 1 0 0 1 1 1 1
Syria	1 1 1 1 1 0 0 0 0 0 1 0 1 0 0 0 1 1 1 0 0 1 1 1
Thailand	0 1 1 1 0 0 1 0 1 0 1 1 0 0 1 1 0 0 1 1 1 0 0 1
United Kingdom	1 0 1 1 1 1 1 1 1 1 1 1 1 1 0 1 1 1 1 1 1 0 1 1
United States	1 1 1 1 1 1 1 1 1 1 1 1 1 1 1 1 1 1 1 1 1 1 0 1
Yugoslavia	1 1 1 1 1 1 1 1 1 0 1 0 1 0 0 0 1 1 1 1 1 1 1 0

Table B.17. *Attributes for countries trade network*

Country	Pop. growth	GNP	Schools	Energy
Algeria	3.3	3.0	33	814
Argentina	1.6	0.3	56	2161
Brazil	2.1	5.3	32	1101
China	1.5	.	43	618
Czechoslovakia	0.7	.	44	6847
Ecuador	3.4	4.7	40	692
Egypt	2.5	5.6	52	595
Ethiopia	2.0	0.6	1	24
Finland	0.4	2.6	90	6351
Honduras	3.4	0.7	30	292
Indonesia	2.3	5.9	28	266
Israel	2.6	1.2	72	2813
Japan	1.1	3.4	91	4649
Liberia	3.5	-0.4	20	502
Madagascar	2.6	-1.9	12	74
New Zealand	1.5	0.3	81	4816
Pakistan	3.0	2.1	15	224
Spain	1.1	2.3	87	2944
Switzerland	0.1	0.7	55	5223
Syria	3.7	5.5	46	964
Thailand	2.5	4.2	29	370
United Kingdom	0.1	1.6	82	5363
United States	1.0	2.0	97	11626
Yugoslavia	0.9	4.7	83	2402

Table B.18. *CEOs and clubs affiliation network matrix*

CEO	1	2	3	4	5	6	7	8	9	10	11	12	13	14	15
1	0	0	1	1	0	0	0	0	1	0	0	0	0	0	0
2	0	0	1	0	1	0	1	0	0	0	0	0	0	0	0
3	0	0	1	0	0	0	0	0	0	0	0	1	0	0	0
4	0	1	1	0	0	0	0	0	0	0	0	0	0	0	1
5	0	0	1	0	0	0	0	0	0	0	0	0	1	1	0
6	0	1	1	0	0	0	0	0	0	0	0	0	0	1	0
7	0	0	1	1	0	0	0	0	0	1	1	0	0	0	0
8	0	0	0	1	0	0	1	0	0	1	0	0	0	0	0
9	1	0	0	1	0	0	0	1	0	1	0	0	0	0	0
10	0	0	1	0	0	0	0	0	1	0	0	0	0	0	0
11	0	1	1	0	0	0	0	0	1	0	0	0	0	0	0
12	0	0	0	1	0	0	1	0	0	0	0	0	0	0	0
13	0	0	1	1	1	0	0	0	1	0	0	0	0	0	0
14	0	1	1	1	0	0	0	0	0	0	1	1	1	0	1
15	0	1	1	0	0	1	0	0	0	0	0	0	1	0	1
16	0	1	1	0	0	1	0	1	0	0	0	0	0	1	0
17	0	1	1	0	1	0	0	0	0	0	1	1	0	0	1
18	0	0	0	1	0	0	0	0	1	0	0	1	1	0	1
19	1	0	1	1	0	0	1	0	1	0	0	0	0	0	0
20	0	1	1	1	0	0	0	0	0	0	1	0	0	0	1
21	0	0	1	1	0	0	0	1	0	0	0	0	0	0	0
22	0	0	1	0	0	0	0	1	0	0	0	0	0	0	1
23	0	1	1	0	0	1	0	0	0	0	0	0	0	0	1
24	1	0	1	1	0	1	0	0	0	0	0	0	0	0	1
25	0	1	1	0	0	0	0	0	0	0	0	0	1	0	0
26	0	1	1	0	0	0	0	0	0	0	0	1	0	0	0

References

Abell, P. (1970). The structural balance of the kinship system of some primitive peoples. In Lane, M. (ed.), *Structuralism*. New York: Basic Books.

Abelson, R.P., Aronson, E., McGuire, W.J., Newcomb, T.M., Rosenberg, M.J., and Tannenbaum, O.H. (eds.) (1968). *Theories of Cognitive Consistency*. Chicago: Rand McNally.

Abelson, R.P., and Rosenberg, M.J. (1958). Symbolic pseudo–logic: A model of attitudinal cognition. *Behavioral Science. 3*, 1–13.

Achuthan, S.B., Rao, S.B., and Rao, A.R. (1982). The number of symmetric edges in a digraph with prescribed out–degrees. In Vijayan, K.S., and Singhi, N.M., eds., *Proceedings of the Seminar on Combinatorics and Applications in honour of Professor S.S. Shrikhande on his 65th Birthday*, pages 8–20. Calcutta: Indian Statistical Institute.

Agresti, A. (1984). *Analysis of Ordinal Categorical Data*. New York: John Wiley and Sons.

Agresti, A. (1990). *Categorical Data Analysis*. New York: John Wiley and Sons.

Aitken, M., Anderson, D., Francis, B., and Hinde, J. (1989). *Statistical Modelling in GLIM*. Oxford: Clarendon Press.

Aitken, R.H. (1972). From cohomology in physics to q-connectivity in social science. *International Journal of Man-Machine Studies. 4*, 139–167.

Alba, R.D. (1973). A graph–theoretic definition of a sociometric clique. *Journal of Mathematical Sociology. 3*, 113–126.

Alba, R.D. (1981). Taking stock of network analysis: A decade's result. In Bacharach, S.B. (ed.), *Perspectives in Organization Research*, pages 39–74. Greenwich, CT: JAI Press.

Alba, R.D., and Kadushin, C. (1976). The intersection of social circles: A new measure of social proximity in networks. *Sociological Methods and Research. 5*, 77–102.

Alba, R.D., and Moore, G. (1978). Elite social circles. *Sociological Methods and Research. 7*, 167–188.

Aldenderfer, M.S., and Blashfield, R.K. (1984). *Cluster Analysis*. Newbury Park, CA: Sage.

Alexander, C.N. (1963). A method for processing sociometric data. *Sociometry. 26*, 268–269.

Allen, M.P. (1982). The identification of interlock groups in large corporate networks: Convergent validation using divergent techniques. *Social Networks. 4*, 349–366.

Allison, P.D. (1978). Measures of inequality. *American Sociological Review. 43*, 865–880.

Anderson, C.J., Wasserman, S., and Faust, K. (1992). Building stochastic blockmodels. *Social Networks. 14*, 137–161.

Anderson, J.G., and Jay, S.J. (1985). The diffusion of medical technology: Social network analysis and policy research. *The Sociological Quarterly. 26*, 49–64.

Anderson, N.H. (1971). Integration theory and attitude change. *Psychological Review. 78*, 171–206.

Anderson, N.H. (1977). Some problems in using analysis of variance in balance theory. *Journal of Personality and Social Psychology. 35*, 140–158.

Andrews, D.F., and Herzberg, A.M. (1985). *Data: A Collection of Problems from Many Fields for the Student and Research Worker*. New York: Springer–Verlag.

Anthonisse, J.M. (1971). *The Rush in a Graph*. Amsterdam: Mathematische Centrum.

Arabie, P. (1977). Clustering representations of group overlap. *Journal of Mathematical Sociology. 5*, 113–128.

Arabie, P. (1984). Validation of sociometric structure by data on individuals' attributes. *Social Networks. 6*, 373–403.

Arabie, P., and Boorman, S.A. (1979). Algebraic approaches to the comparison of concrete social structures represented as networks: Reply to Bonacich. *American Journal of Sociology. 86*, 166–174.

Arabie, P., and Boorman, S.A. (1982). Blockmodels: Developments and prospects. In Hudson, H.C. (ed.), *Classifying Social Data*. San Francisco: Jossey-Bass.

Arabie, P., Boorman, S.A., and Levitt, P.R. (1978). Constructing blockmodels: How and why. *Journal of Mathematical Psychology. 17*, 21–63.

Arabie, P., and Carroll, J. D. (1989). Conceptions of overlap in social structure. In Freeman, L.C., White, D.R., and Romney, A.K. (eds.), *Research Methods in Social Network Analysis*, pages 367–392. Fairfax, VA: George Mason University Press.

Arabie, P., Carroll, J.D., and DeSarbo, W.S. (1987). *Three–way Scaling and Clustering*. Newbury Park, CA: Sage.

Arabie, P., and Hubert, L.J. (1992). Combinatorial data analysis. *Annual Review of Psychology. 43*, 169–203.

Arabie, P., Hubert, L.J., and Schleutermann, S. (1990). Blockmodels from the bond energy approach. *Social Networks. 12*, 99–126.

Arney, W.R. (1973). A refined status index for sociometric data. *Sociological Methods and Research. 1*, 329–346.

Atkin, R.H. (1974). An algebra for patterns on a complex, I. *International Journal of Man–Machine Studies. 6*, 285–307.

Atkin, R.H. (1976). An algebra for patterns on a complex, II. *International Journal of Man–Machine Studies. 8*, 483–488.

Atkin, R.H. (1977). *Combinatorial Connectivities in Social Systems*. Basel: Birkhauser.

Auerbach, D.M., Darrow, W.W., Jaffe, H.W., and Curran, J.W. (1984). Cluster of cases of the acquired immune deficiency syndrome. *The American Journal of Medicine. 76*, 487–492.

Baker, F.B., and Hubert, L.J. (1981). The analysis of social interaction data. *Sociological Methods & Research. 9*, 339–361.

758   *References*

Baker, R.J., and Nelder, J.A. (1978). *The GLIM System,* Release 3, *Generalized Linear Interactive Modelling.* Oxford: The Numerical Algorithms Group.
Baker, W.E. (1986). Three–dimensional blockmodels. *Journal of Mathematical Sociology. 12,* 191–223.
Barnes, J.A. (1954). Class and committees in a Norwegian island parish. *Human Relations. 7,* 39–58.
Barnes, J.A. (1969a). Networks and political processes. In Mitchell, J.C. (ed.), *Social Networks in Urban Situations,* pages 51–76. Manchester, England: Manchester University Press.
Barnes, J.A. (1969b). Graph theory and social networks: A technical comment on connectedness and connectivity. *Sociology. 3,* 215–232.
Barnes, J.A. (1972). Social Networks. *Addison-Wesley Module in Anthropology. 26,* 1–29.
Barnes, J.A., and Harary, F. (1983). Graph theory in network analysis. *Social Networks. 5,* 235–244.
Barnett, G. (1990). Correspondence analysis: A method for the description of communication networks. Unpublished manuscript.
Barrera, M., Sandler, I.N., and Ramsay, T.B. (1981). Preliminary development of a scale of social support: Studies on college students. *American Journal of Community Psychology. 11,* 133–143.
Bartholomew, D.J. (1967). *Stochastic Models for Social Processes.* New York: John Wiley and Sons.
Batagelj, V., Doreian, P., and Ferligoj, A. (1992). An optimizational approach to regular equivalence. *Social Networks. 14,* 121–135.
Batagelj, V., Ferligoj, A., and Doreian, P. (1992). Direct and indirect methods for structural equivalence. *Social Networks. 14,* 63–90.
Bavelas, A. (1948). A mathematical model for group structure. *Human Organizations. 7,* 16–30.
Bavelas, A. (1950). Communication patterns in task-oriented groups. *Journal of the Acoustical Society of America. 22,* 271–282.
Bavelas, A., and Barrett, D. (1951). An experimental approach to organizational communication. *Personnel. 27,* 366–371.
Bearden, J., and Mintz, B. (1987). The structure of class cohesion: The corporate network and its dual. In Mizruchi, M.S., and Schwartz, M. (eds.), *Intercorporate Relations: The Structural Analysis of Business,* pages 187–207. Cambridge, England: Cambridge University Press.
Beauchamp, M.A. (1965). An improved index of centrality. *Behavioral Science. 10,* 161–163.
Bekessy, A., Bekessy, P., and Komlos, J. (1972). Asymptotic enumeration of regular matrices. *Studia Scientiarum Matematicarum Hungarica. 7,* 343.
Bellmore, M., and Nemhauser, G.L. (1968). The traveling salesman problem: A survey. *Operations Research, 16,* 538–558.
Berelson, B.R., Lazarsfeld, P.F., and McPhee, W.N. (1954). *Voting: A Study of Opinion Formation in a Presidential Campaign.* Chicago: University of Chicago Press.
Berge, C. (1973). *Graphs and Hypergraphs.* Amsterdam: North-Holland.
Berge, C. (1989). *Hypergraphs: Combinatorics of Finite Sets.* Amsterdam: North-Holland.
Berkowitz, S.D. (1982). *An Introduction to Structural Analysis: The Network Approach to Social Research.* Toronto: Butterworths.
Berkowitz, S.D. (1988). Markets and market-areas: Some preliminary

formulations. In Wellman, B. and Berkowitz, S.D. (eds.), *Social Structures: A Network Approach*, pages 261–303. Cambridge, England: Cambridge University Press.

Bernard, H.R., Johnsen, E.C., Killworth, P.D., McCarty, C., Shelley, G.A., and Robinson, S. (1990). Comparing four different methods for measuring personal social networks. *Social Networks. 12*, 179–216.

Bernard, H.R., Johnsen, E.C., Killworth, P.D., and Robinson, S. (1989). Estimating the size of an average personal network and of an event subpopulation. In Kochen, M. (ed.), *The Small World*, pages 159–175. Norwood, NJ: Ablex.

Bernard, H.R., and Killworth, P.D. (1977). Informant accuracy in social network data II. *Human Communications Research. 4*, 3–18.

Bernard, H.R., and Killworth, P.D. (1979). Deterministic models of social networks. In Holland, P.W., and Leinhardt, S. (eds.), *Perspectives on Social Network Research*, pages 165–186. New York: Academic Press.

Bernard, H.R., Killworth, P.D., Kronenfeld, D., and Sailer, L. (1985). On the validity of retrospective data: The problem of informant accuracy. *Annual Review of Anthropology. 13*, pages 495–517. Palo Alto: Stanford University Press.

Bernard, H.R., Killworth, P.D., and Sailer, L. (1980). Informant accuracy in social network data IV: A comparison of clique-level structure in behavioral and cognitive network data. *Social Networks. 2*, 191–218.

Bernard, H.R., Killworth, P.D., and Sailer, L. (1982). Informant accuracy in social network data V: An experimental attempt to predict actual communication from recall data. *Social Science Research. 11*, 30–66.

Beum, C.O., and Brundage, E.G. (1950). A method for analyzing the sociomatrix. *Sociometry. 13*, 141–145.

Beum, C.O., and Criswell, J.H. (1947). Application of machine tabulation methods to sociometric data. *Sociometry. 10*, 227–232.

Beyer, W.U. (1968). *CRC Handbook of Tables for Probability and Statistics,* Second Edition. Boca Raton, FL: The CRC Press.

Biggs, N.L., Lloyd, E.K., and Wilson, R.T. (1976). *Graph Theory 1736–1936.* Oxford, England: Clarendon Press.

Birkhoff, G. (1940). *Lattice Theory.* Providence, RI: American Mathematical Society.

Bishop, Y.M.M., Fienberg, S.E., and Holland, P.W. (1975). *Discrete Multivariate Analysis: Theory and Practice.* Cambridge, MA: The MIT Press.

Blau, P.M. (1977). *Inequality and Heterogeneity.* New York: Free Press.

Bloemena, A.R. (1964). *Sampling from a Graph.* Amsterdam: Mathematische Centrum.

Blumen, I., Kogan, M., and McCarthy, P.J. (1955). *The Industrial Mobility of Labor as a Probability Process.* Ithaca, NY: Cornell University Press.

Bock, R.D., and Husain, S.Z. (1950). An adaptation of Holzinger's *B*-coefficients for the analysis of sociometric data. *Sociometry. 13*, 146–153.

Bock, R.D., and Husain, S.Z. (1952). Factors of the tele: A preliminary report. *Sociometry. 15*, 206–219.

Boissevain, J. (1968). The place of non-groups in the social sciences. *Man. 3*, 542–556.

Boissevain, J. (1973). An exploration of two first-order zones. In Boissevain, J., and Mitchell, J.C. (eds.), *Network Analysis: Studies in Human Interaction.* The Hague: Mouton.

Boissevain, J., and Mitchell, J.C. (eds.) (1973). *Network Analysis Studies in Human Interaction.* The Hague: Mouton.

Bolland, J.M. (1985). Perceived leadership stability and the structure of urban agenda-setting networks. *Social Networks. 7*, 153–172.

Bolland, J.M. (1988). Sorting out centrality: An analysis of the performance of four centrality models in real and simulated networks. *Social Networks. 10*, 233–253.

Bollobás, B. (1985). *Random Graphs.* London: Academic Press.

Bonacich, P. (1972a). Technique for analyzing overlapping memberships. In Costner, H. (ed.), *Sociological Methodology, 1972*, pages 176–185. San Francisco: Jossey-Bass.

Bonacich, P. (1972b). Factoring and weighting approaches to status scores and clique indentification. *Journal of Mathematical Sociology. 2*, 113–120.

Bonacich, P. (1978). Using Boolean algebra to analyze overlapping memberships. In Schuessler, K.F. (ed.), *Sociological Methodology, 1978.* San Francisco: Jossey-Bass.

Bonacich, P. (1979). The 'common structure semigroup,' a replacement for the Boorman and White 'joint reduction.' *American Journal of Sociology. 86*, 159–166.

Bonacich, P. (1987). Power and centrality: A family of measures. *American Journal of Sociology. 92*, 1170–1182.

Bonacich, P. (1989). What is a homomorphism? In Freeman, L.C., White, D.R., and Romney, A.K. (eds.), *Research Methods in Social Network Analysis.* Fairfax, VA: George Mason University Press.

Bonacich, P., and McConaghy, M.J. (1979). The algebra of blockmodelling. In Schuessler, K.F. (ed.), *Sociological Methodology 1980*, pages 489–532. San Francisco: Jossey-Bass.

Bondy, J.A., and Murty, U.S.R. (1976). *Graph Theory with Applications.* New York: North-Holland.

Boorman, S.A., and Levitt, P.R. (1983a). Big brother and blockmodelling. *The New York Times*, November 20, 1983, page F3.

Boorman, S.A., and Levitt, P.R. (1983b). Blockmodels and self-defense. *The New York Times*, November 27, 1983, page F3.

Boorman, S.A., and Oliver, D.C. (1973). Metrics on spaces of finite trees. *Journal of Mathematical Psychology. 10*, 26–59.

Boorman, S.A., and White, H.C. (1976). Social structure from multiple networks II. Role structures. *American Journal of Sociology. 81*, 1384–1446.

Borgatti, S.P. (1988). A comment on Doreian's regular equivalence in symmetric structures. *Social Networks. 10*, 265–271.

Borgatti, S.P. (1989). *Regular Equivalence in Graphs, Hypergraphs, and Matrices.* Unpublished doctoral dissertation, University of California, Irvine.

Borgatti, S.P, Boyd, J.P. and Everett, M. (1989). Iterated roles: Mathematics and application. *Social Networks. 11*, 159–172.

Borgatti, S.P., and Everett, M.G. (1989). The class of regular equivalences: Algebraic structure and computation. *Social Networks. 11*, 65–88.

Borgatti, S.P., and Everett, M.G. (1992a). The notion of position in social network analysis. In Marsden, P. (ed.), *Sociological Methodology, 1992.* London: Basil Blackwell.

Borgatti, S.P., and Everett, M.G. (1992b). Regular blockmodels of mulitway, multimode matrices. *Social Networks. 14*, 91–120.

Borgatti, S.P., and Everett, M.G., and Freeman, L.C. (1991). *UCINET, Version IV.* Columbia, SC: Analytic Technology.

Borgatti, S.P., Everett, M.G., and Shirey, P.R. (1990). *LS* sets, lambda sets, and other cohesive subsets. *Social Networks. 12*, 337–358.

Bott, E. (1957). *Family and Social Network.* London: Tavistock.

Box, G.E.P., Hunter, W.G., and Hunter, J.S. (1978). *Statistics for Experimenters.* New York: John Wiley and Sons.

Boyd, J.P. (1969). The algebra of group kinship. *Journal of Mathematical Psychology. 6*, 139–167.

Boyd, J.P. (1983). Structural similarity, semigroups and idempotents. *Social Networks. 5*, 157–172.

Boyd, J.P. (1990). *Social Semigroups: A Unified Theory of Scaling and Blockmodelling as Applied to Social Networks.* Fairfax, VA: George Mason University Press.

Boyd, J.P., and Everett, M.G. (1988). Block structures of automorphism groups of social relations. *Social Networks. 10*, 137–155.

Bradley, R.A., and Terry, M.E. (1952). Rank analysis of incomplete block designs, I. The method of paired comparisons. *Biometrika. 39*, 324–345.

Breedlove, W.L., and Nolan, P.D. (1988). International stratification and inequality, 1960–1980. *International Journal of Contemporary Sociology. 25*, 105–123.

Breiger, R.L. (1974). The duality of persons and groups. *Social Forces. 53*, 181–190.

Breiger, R.L. (1976). Career attributes and network structure: A blockmodel study of a biomedical research specialty. *American Sociological Review. 41*, 117–135.

Breiger, R.L. (1979). Toward an operational theory of community elite structures. *Quality and Quantity. 13*, 21–57.

Breiger, R.L. (1981a). Structures of economic interdependence among nations. In Blau, P.M., and Merton, R.K. (eds.), *Continuities in Structural Inquiry,* pages 353–380. Newbury Park, CA: Sage.

Breiger, R.L. (1981b). Comment on Holland and Leinhardt, 'An exponential family of probability distributions for directed graphs.' *Journal of the American Statistical Association. 76*, 51–53.

Breiger, R.L. (1981c). The social class structure of occupational mobility. *American Journal of Sociology. 87*, 578–611.

Breiger, R.L. (1986). How to use *ROLE.* Unpublished manuscript.

Breiger, R.L. (ed.) (1990a). *Social Mobility and Social Structure.* Cambridge, England: Cambridge University Press.

Breiger, R.L. (1990b). Social control and social networks: A model from Georg Simmel. In Calhoun, C., Meyer, M.W. and Scott, W.R. (eds.), *Structures of Power and Constraint: Papers in Honor of Peter M. Blau,* pages 453–476. Cambridge, England: Cambridge University Press.

Breiger, R.L. (1991). *Explorations in Structural Analysis: Dual and Multiple Networks of Social Structure.* New York: Garland Press.

Breiger, R.L., Boorman, S.A., and Arabie, P. (1975). An algorithm for clustering relational data with applications to social network analysis and comparison with multidimensional scaling. *Journal of Mathematical Psychology. 12*, 328–383.

Breiger, R.L., and Ennis, J.G. (1979). Personae and social roles: The network structure of personality types in small groups. *Social Psychology Quarterly.*

42, 262–270.

Breiger, R.L., and Pattison, P.E. (1978). The joint role structure of two communities' elites. *Sociological Methods and Research. 7*, 213–226.

Breiger, R.L., and Pattison, P.E. (1986). Cumulated social roles: The duality of persons and their algebras. *Social Networks. 8*, 215–256.

Bronfenbrenner, U. (1943). A constant frame of reference for sociometric research. *Sociometry. 6*, 363–397.

Bronfenbrenner, U. (1944). A constant frame of reference for sociometric research: Part II. Experiment and inference. *Sociometry. 7*, 40–75.

Bronfenbrenner, U. (1945). The Measurement of Sociometric Status, Structure, and Development. *Sociometric Monographs*, No. 6. Beacon House, NY.

Brown, D.J.J. (1979). The structuring of Polopa feasting and warfare. *Man. 14*, 712–733.

Budescu, D.V. (1984). Tests of lagged dominance in sequential dyadic interaction. *Psychological Bulletin. 96*, 402–414.

Burgess, R.L. (1968). Communication networks in research and training. *Human Relations. 22*, 137–159.

Burt, R.S. (1975). Corporate society: A time series analysis of network structure. *Social Science Research. 4*, 271–328.

Burt, R.S. (1976). Positions in networks. *Social Forces. 55*, 93–122.

Burt, R.S. (1978a). Cohesion versus structural equivalence as a basis for network subgroups. *Sociological Methods and Research. 7*, 189–212.

Burt, R.S. (1978b). Applied network analysis: An overview. *Sociological Methods & Research. 7*, 123–212.

Burt, R.S. (1978/79a). Stratification and prestige among elite experts in methodological and mathematical sociology circa 1975. *Social Networks. 1*, 105–158.

Burt, R.S. (1978/79b). A structural theory of interlocking corporate directorates. *Social Networks. 1*, 415–435.

Burt, R.S. (1980). Models of network structure. *Annual Review of Sociology. 6*, pages 79–141. [Also Chapter 2 in Burt, R.S. (1982). *Toward a Structural Theory of Action*. New York: Academic Press.]

Burt, R.S. (1982). *Towards a Structural Theory of Action: Network Models of Social Structure, Perceptions, and Action*. New York: Academic Press.

Burt, R.S. (1983). Network data from archival records. In Burt, R.S., and Minor, M.J. (eds.), *Applied Network Analysis*, pages 158–174. Beverly Hills: Sage.

Burt, R.S. (1984). Network items and the general social survey. *Social Networks. 6*, 293–340.

Burt, R.S. (1985). General social survey network items. *Connections. 8*, 119–122.

Burt, R.S. (1986). A cautionary note. *Social Networks. 8*, 205–211.

Burt, R.S. (1987). Social contagion and innovation: Cohesion versus structural equivalence. *American Journal of Sociology. 92*, 1287–1335.

Burt, R.S. (1988a). Some properties of structural equivalence measures derived from sociometric choice data. *Social Networks. 10*, 1–28.

Burt, R.S. (1988b). The stability of American markets. *American Journal of Sociology. 94*, 356–395.

Burt, R.S. (1989). *STRUCTURE, Version 4.0*. Research Program in Structural Analysis, Center for the Social Sciences, Columbia University.

Burt, R.S. (1990). Detecting role equivalence. *Social Networks. 12*, 83–97.

Burt, R.S. (1991). *STRUCTURE, Version 4.2*. Center for the Social Sciences, Columbia University.

Burt, R.S., and Bittner, W.M. (1981). A note on inferences regarding network subgroups. *Social Networks. 3*, 71–88.

Burt, R.S., and Lin, N. (1977). Network time series from archival records. In Heise, D.R. (ed.), *Sociological Methodology, 1977*, pages 224–254. San Francisco: Jossey-Bass.

Burt, R.S., Marsden, P.V., and Rossi, P.H. (1985). A Research Agenda for Survey Network Data. Columbia University Workshop on Survey Network Data. Unpublished manuscript.

Burt, R.S., and Minor, M. (1983). *Applied Network Analysis, A Methodological Introduction.* Newbury Park, CA: Sage.

Bush, R.R., and Mosteller, F. (1955). *Stochastic Models for Learning.* New York: John Wiley and Sons.

Caldeira, G.A. (1988). Legal precedent: Structures of communication between state supreme courts. *Social Networks. 10*, 29–55.

Campbell, K.E., Marsden, P.V., and Hurlbert, J. (1986). Social resources and socioeconomic status. *Social Networks. 8*, 97–117.

Caplow, T.A. (1956). A theory of coalitions in the triad. *American Sociological Review. 21*, 489–493.

Capobianco, M. (1970). Statistical inference in finite populations having structure. *Transactions of the New York Academy of Science. 32*, 401–413.

Capobianco, M., and Frank, O. (1982). Comparison of statistical graph-size estimators. *Journal of Statistical Planning and Inference. 6*, 87–97.

Cappell, C.L., and Guterbock, T.M. (1992) The social and conceptual structure of sociology specialties. *American Sociological Review. 57*, 266–273.

Carley, K. (1986). An approach for relating social structure to cognitive structure. *Journal of Mathematical Sociology. 12*, 137–189.

Carley, K., and Hummon, N. (1993). Scientific influence among social networkers. *Social Networks. 15*, 71–108.

Carley, K., and Wendt, K. (1988). Electronic mail and the diffusion of scientific information. The study of *SOAR* and its dominant users. Unpublished manuscript.

Carrington, P.J., and Heil, G.H. (1981). *COBLOC*: A hierarchical method for blocking network data. *Journal of Mathematical Sociology. 8*, 103–131.

Carrington, P.J., Heil, G.H., and Berkowitz, S.D. (1979/80). A goodness-of-fit index for blockmodels. *Social Networks. 2*, 219–234.

Carroll, J.D., and Arabie, P. (1980). Multidimensional Scaling. In Rosenzweig, M.R., and Porter, L.W. (eds.), *Annual Review of Psychology.* Palo Alto, CA: Annual Reviews.

Carroll, J.D., Green, P.E., and Schaffer, C.M. (1986). Interpoint distance comparisons in correspondence analysis. *Journal of Marketing Research. 23*, 271–280.

Cartwright, D. (ed.) (1959). *Studies in Social Power.* Ann Arbor, MI: Institute for Social Research.

Cartwright, D., and Gleason, T.C. (1966). The number of paths and cycles in a digraph. *Psychometrika. 31*, 179–199.

Cartwright, D., and Harary, F. (1956). Structural balance: A generalization of Heider's theory. *Psychological Review. 63*, 277–292.

Cartwright, D., and Harary, F. (1968). On the coloring of signed graphs. *Elemente der Mathematik. 23*, 85–89.

Cartwright, D., and Harary, F. (1970). Ambivalence and indifference in generalizations of structural balance. *Behavioral Science. 15*, 497–513.

Cartwright, D., and Harary, F. (1977). A graph-theoretic approach to the investigation of system-environment relationships. *Journal of Mathematical Sociology. 5*, 87–111.

Cartwright, D., and Harary, F. (1979). Balance and clusterability: An overview. In Holland, P.W., and Leinhardt, S. (eds.), *Perspectives on Social Network Research*, pages 25–50. New York: Academic Press.

Chabot, J. (1950). A simplified example of the use of matrix multiplication for the analysis of sociometric data. *Sociometry. 13*, 131–140.

Chase, I.D. (1982). Behavioral sequences during dominance hierarchy formation in chickens. *Science. 216*, 439–440.

Clark, J.A., and McQuitty, L.L. (1970). Some problems and elaborations of iterative, intercolumnar correlational analysis. *Educational and Psychological Measurement. 30*, 773–784.

Cochran, W.G., and Cox, G.M. (1957). *Experimental Design*. Second Edition. New York: John Wiley and Sons.

Cohen, S., Mermelstein, R., Kamarck, T., and Hoberman, H. (1985). Measuring the functional components of social support. In Sarason, I.G., and Sarason, B.G. (eds.), *Social Support: Theory, Research, and Applications*. Dordrecht, The Netherlands: Martinus Nijhoff Publishers.

Cohen, S., and Syme, S.L. (1985). *Social Support and Health*. Orlando, FL: Academic Press.

Cohn, B.S., and Marriott, M. (1958). Networks and centres of integration in Indian civilization. *Journal of Social Research. 1*, 1–9.

Coleman, J.S. (1957). *Community Conflict*. Glencoe, IL: Free Press.

Coleman, J.S. (1964). *Introduction to Mathematical Sociology*. New York: Free Press.

Coleman, J.S. (1973). *The Mathematics of Collective Action*. Chicago: Aldine.

Coleman, J.S. (1981). *Longitudinal Data Analysis*. New York: Basic Books.

Coleman, J.S., Katz, E., and Menzel, H. (1957). The diffusion of an innovation among physicians. *Sociometry. 20*, 253–270.

Coleman, J.S., Katz, E., and Menzel, H. (1966). *Medical Innovation: A Diffusion Study*. Indianapolis: Bobbs-Merrill.

Coleman, J.S., and MacRae, D. (1960). Electronic processing of sociometric data for groups up to 1000 in size. *American Sociological Review. 25*, 722–727.

Collins, R. (1988). *Theoretical Sociology*. New York: Harcourt Brace Jovanovich.

Conrath, D.W., Higgins, C.A., and McClean, R.J. (1983). A comparison of the reliability of questionnaire versus diary data. *Social Networks. 5*, 315–322.

Cook, K.S. (ed.) (1987) *Social Exchange Theory*. Newbury Park, CA: Sage.

Cook, K.S., and Emerson, R.M. (1978). Power, equity, and commitment in exchange networks. *American Sociological Review. 43*, 721–739.

Cook, K.S., Emerson, R.M., Gillmore, M.R., and Yamagishi, T. (1983). The distribution of power in exchange networks: Theory and experimental results. *American Journal of Sociology. 89*, 275–305.

Coombs, C.H. (1951). Mathematical models in psychological scaling. *Journal of the American Statistical Association. 46*, 480–489.

Cox, D.R., and Snell, E.J. (1989). *Analysis of Binary Data*, Second Edition. London: Chapman-Hall.

Coxon, A.P.M. (1982). *The User's Guide to Multidimensional Scaling*. Exeter, NH: Heinemann.

Crane, D. (1972). *Invisible Colleges: Diffusion of Knowledge in Scientific Communities*. Chicago: University of Chicago Press.

Crano, W.D., and Cooper, R.E. (1973). Examination of Newcomb's extension of structural balance theory. *Journal of Personality and Social Psychology. 27*, 344–353.

Criswell, J.H. (1939). A sociometric study of race cleavage in the classroom. *Archives of Psychology. 33*, 1–82.

Criswell, J.H. (1943). Sociometric methods of measuring group preferences. *Sociometry. 6*, 398–408.

Criswell, J.H. (1946a). Foundations of sociometric measurement. *Sociometry. 9*, 7–13.

Criswell, J.H. (1946b). Measurement of reciprocation under multiple criteria of choice. *Sociometry. 9*, 126–127.

Criswell, J.H. (1947). Measurement of group integration. *Sociometry. 10*, 259–267.

Criswell, J.H. (1950). Notes on the constant frame of reference problem. *Sociometry. 13*, 93–107.

Cronbach, L.J., and Gleser, G.C. (1953). Assessing similarity between porfiles. *Psychological Bulletin. 50*, 456–473.

Cubbitt, T. (1973). Network density among urban families. In Boissevain, J., and Mitchell, J.C. (eds.), *Network Analysis: Studies in Human Interaction*. The Hague: Mouton Press.

Cuthbert, K.R. (1989). Social relations in Luzon, Philippines, using the reverse small world problem. In Kochen, M. (ed.), *The Small World*, pages 211–226. Norwood, NJ: Ablex.

Czepiel, J.A. (1974). Word of mouth processes in the diffusion of a major technological innovation. *Journal of Marketing Research. 11*, 172–180.

Darroch, J.N., and Ratcliff, D. (1972). Generalized iterative scaling of loglinear models. *Annals of Mathematical Statistics. 43*, 1470–1480.

David, H. A. (1988). *The Method of Paired Comparisons*. Second Edition. Oxford and New York: Oxford University Press.

Davis, A., Gardner, B., and Gardner, M.R. (1941). *Deep South*. Chicago: University of Chicago Press.

Davis, J.A. (1959). A formal interpretation of the theory of relative deprivation. *Sociometry. 22*, 280–296.

Davis, J.A. (1963). Structural balance, mechanical solidarity, and interpersonal relations. *American Journal of Sociology. 68*, 444–462.

Davis, J.A. (1967). Clustering and structural balance in graphs. *Human Relations. 20*, 181–187.

Davis, J.A. (1968a). Statistical analysis of pair relationships: Symmetry, subjective consistency, and reciprocity. *Sociometry. 31*, 102–119.

Davis, J.A. (1968b). Social structures and cognitive structures. In Abelson, R.P., Aronson, E., McGuire, W.J., Newcomb, T.M., Rosenberg, M.J., and Tannenbaum, O.H. (eds.), *Theories of Cognitive Consistency*. Chicago: Rand McNally.

Davis, J.A. (1970). Clustering and hierarchy in interpersonal relations: Testing two theoretical models on 742 sociograms. *American Sociological Review. 35*, 843–852.

Davis, J.A. (1977). Sociometric triads as multi-variate systems. *Journal of Mathematical Sociology. 5*, 41–60.

Davis, J.A. (1979). The Davis/Holland/Leinhardt studies: An overview. In Holland, P.W., and Leinhardt, S. (eds.), *Perspectives on Social Network Research*, pages 51–62. New York: Academic Press.

Davis, J.A., Holland, P.W., and Leinhardt, S. (1971). Comments on Professor Mazur's hypothesis about interpersonal sentiments. *American Sociological Review. 36*, 309–311.

Davis, J.A., and Leinhardt, S. (1968). The structure of positive interpersonal relations in small groups. Paper presented at the 1968 Annual Meeting of the American Sociological Association, Boston, Massachusetts, August 1968.

Davis, J.A., and Leinhardt, S. (1972). The structure of positive interpersonal relations in small groups. In Berger, J. (ed.), *Sociological Theories in Progress. Volume 2*, pages 218–251. Boston: Houghton Mifflin.

Davis, J.H. (1973). Group decision and social interaction: A theory of social decision schemes. *Psychological Review. 80*, 97–125.

Davis, R.L. (1953). The number of structures of finite relations. *Proceedings of the American Mathematical Society. 4*, 486–495.

Davis, R.L. (1954). Structures of dominance relations. *Bulletin of Mathematical Biophysics. 16*, 131–140.

Delany, J. (1978). Network dynamics for the weak–tie problem. Unpublished manuscript.

Delany, J. (1980). The efficiency of sparse personal contact networks for donative transfer of resources: The case of job vacancy information. Unpublished manuscript.

Delany, J. (1988). Social networks and efficient resource allocation: Computer models of job vacancy allocation through contacts. In Wellman, B., and Berkowitz, S.D. (eds.), *Social Structures: A Network Approach*, pages 430–451. Cambridge, England: Cambridge University Press.

de Sola Pool, I., and Kochen, M. (1978). Contacts and influence. *Social Networks. 1*, 5–51.

Dixon, W.J. (ed.) (1983). *BMDP Statistical Software*. Berkeley: University of California Press.

Dodd, S.C. (1940). The interrelation matrix. *Sociometry. 3*, 91–101.

Domhoff, G.W. (1975). A network study of ruling-class cohesiveness. *The Insurgent Sociologist. 5*, 173–184.

Donninger, C. (1986). The distribution of centrality in social networks. *Social Networks. 8*, 191–203.

Doreian, P. (1969). A note on the detection of cliques in valued graphs. *Sociometry. 32*, 237–242.

Doreian, P. (1974). On the connectivity of social networks. *Journal of Mathematical Sociology. 3*, 245–258.

Doreian, P. (1979a). On the evolution of group and network structure. *Social Networks. 2*, 235–252.

Doreian, P. (1979b). Structural control models of group structure. In Holland, P.W., and Leinhardt, S. (eds.), *Perspectives on Social Network Research*. New York: Academic Press.

Doreian, P. (1980). On the evolution of group and network structure. *Social Networks. 2*, 235–252.

Doreian, P. (1981). Estimating linear models with spatially distributed data. In Leinhardt, S. (ed.), *Sociological Methodology 1981*, pages 359–388. San Francisco: Jossey-Bass.

Doreian, P. (1986). Measuring relative strength in small groups and bounded networks. *Social Psychological Quarterly. 49*, 247–259.

Doreian, P. (1987). Measuring regular equivalence in symmetric structures. *Social Networks. 9*, 89–107.

Doreian, P. (1988a). Equivalence in a social network. *Journal of Mathematical Sociology. 13*, 243–282.

Doreian, P. (1988b). Borgatti toppings on Doreian splits: Reflections on regular equivalence. *Social Networks. 10*, 273–285.

Doreian, P. (1988c). Using multiple network analytic tools for a single social network. *Social Networks. 10*, 287–312.

Doreian, P. (1990). Mapping networks through time. In Weesie, J., and Flap, H. (eds.), *Social Networks Through Time*, pages 245–264. Utrecht, The Netherlands: ISOR-University of Utrecht Press.

Doreian, P., and Albert, L.H. (1989). Partitioning political actor networks: Some quantitative tools for analyzing qualitative networks. *Journal of Quantitative Anthropology. 1*, 279–291.

Doreian, P., and Fararo, T.J. (1985). Structural equivalence in a journal network. *Journal of the American Society for Information Science. 36*, 28–37.

Doreian, P., and Woodard, K.L. (1990). Interorganizational tie formalization as a dynamic process. Unpublished manuscript.

Dunbar, R., and Dunbar, P. (1975). *Social Dynamics of Gelada Baboons. Contributions to Primatology, Volume 6*. Basel, Switzerland: S. Karger.

Duquenne, V. (1991). On the core of finite lattices. *Discrete Mathematics. 88*, 133–147.

Durkheim, E. (1947). *The Division of Labor in Society*. Translated by George Simpson. Glencoe, IL: Free Press.

Eder, T., and Hallinan, M.T. (1978). Sex differences in children's friendships. *American Sociological Review. 43*, 237–250.

Edmonds, J., and Johnson, E. L. (1973). Matching, Euler tours, and the Chinese postman. *Mathematical Programming. 5*, 88–124.

Edwards, D.S. (1948). The constant frame of reference problem in sociometry. *Sociometry. 11*, 372–379.

Elsas, D.A. (1990). The Scheiblechner model: A loglinear analysis of social interaction data. *Social Networks. 12*, 57–82.

Emotions mapped by new geography. (1933, April 3). *The New York Times*, page 17.

Ennis, J.G. (1982). Blockmodels and spatial representations of group structure: Some comparisons. In Hudson, H.C. (ed.), *Classifying Social Data*, pages 199–214. San Francisco: Jossey-Bass.

Ennis, J.G. (1992). Modeling the intersection of sociological specialties. *American Sociological Review. 57*, 259–265.

Erbring, L., and Young, A.A. (1979). Individuals and social structure: Contextual effects as endogenous feedback. *Sociological Methods & Research. 7*, 396–430.

Erdös, P., and Renyi, A. (1960). On the evolution of random graphs. *Publications of the Mathematical Institute of the Hungarian Academy of Sciences. 5*, 17–61.

Erickson, B. (1978). Some problems of inference from chain data. In Schuessler, K.F. (ed.), *Sociological Methodology, 1979*, pages 276–302. San Francisco: Jossey-Bass.

Erickson, B. (1988). The relational basis of attitudes. In Wellman, B., and Berkowitz, S.D. (eds.), *Social Structures: A Network Approach*, pages 99–121. Cambridge, England: Cambridge University Press.

Erickson, B., and Kringas, P.R. (1975). The small world of politics. *Canadian Journal of Sociology and Anthropology. 12*, 585–593.

Erickson, B., and Nosanchuk, T.A. (1983). Applied network sampling. *Social Networks. 5*, 367–382.

Erickson, B., Nosanchuk, T.A., and Lee, E. (1981). Network sampling in practice: Some second steps. *Social Networks. 3*, 127–136.

Europa Publications (1984). *Europa Year Book.* London: Europa Publications.

Evans-Pritchard, E.E. (1929). The study of kinship in primitive societies. *Man. 29*, 190–194.

Everett, M.G. (1982). A graph theoretic blocking procedure for social networks. *Social Networks. 4*, 147–167.

Everett, M.G. (1985). Role similarity and complexity in social networks. *Social Networks. 7*, 353–359.

Everett, M.G., and Borgatti, S.P. (1988). Calculating role similarities: An algorithm that helps determine the orbits of a graph. *Social Networks. 10*, 77–91.

Everett, M.G., and Borgatti, S.P. (1990). A testing example for positional analysis techniques. *Social Networks. 12*, 253–260.

Everett, M.G., Boyd, J.P., and Borgatti, S.P. (1990). Ego-centered and local roles: A graph theoretic approach. *Journal of Mathematical Sociology. 15*, 163–172.

Fararo, T.J. (1973). *Mathematical Sociology.* New York: Wiley Interscience.

Fararo, T.J. (1981). Biased networks and social structure theorems. Part I. *Social Networks. 3*, 137–159.

Fararo, T.J. (1983). Biased networks and the strength of weak ties. *Social Networks. 5*, 1–11.

Fararo, T.J., and Doreian, P. (1984). Tripartite structural analysis: Generalizing the Breiger-Wilson formalism. *Social Networks. 6*, 141–176.

Fararo, T.J., and Skvoretz, J. (1984). Biased networks and social structure theorems. Part II. *Social Networks. 6*, 223–258.

Fararo, T.J., and Skvoretz, J. (1987). Unification research programs: Integrating two structural theories. *American Journal of Sociology. 92*, 1183–1209.

Fararo, T.J., and Sunshine, M.H. (1964). *A Study of a Biased Friendship Net.* Syracuse, NY: Youth Development Center.

Faucheux, C., and Moscovici, S. (1960). Etudes sur la créativité des groups tâches, structures des communications, et réussite. *Bulletin du C.E.R.P. 9*, 11–22.

Faust, K. (1985). *A Comparative Evaluation of Methods for Positional Analysis of Social Networks.* Unpublished Ph.D. dissertation. School of Social Sciences, University of California, Irvine.

Faust, K. (1988). Comparison of methods for positional analysis: Structural and general equivalences. *Social Networks. 10*, 313–341.

Faust, K., and Romney, A.K. (1985a). Does *STRUCTURE* find structure?: A critique of Burt's use of distance as a measure of structural equivalence. *Social Networks. 7*, 77–103.

Faust, K., and Romney, A.K. (1985b). The effect of skewed distributions on matrix permutation tests. *British Journal of Mathematical and Statistical Psychology. 38*, 152–160.

Faust, K., and Romney, A.K. (1986). Comment on 'A cautionary note.' *Social Networks. 8*, 213.

Faust, K., and Wasserman, S. (1992). Centrality and prestige: A review and synthesis. *Journal of Quantitative Anthropology. 4*, 23–78.

Faust, K., and Wasserman, S. (1993). Correlation and association models for studying measurements on ordinal relations. In Marsden, P.V. (ed.), *Sociological Methodology, 1993*, pages 177–216. Cambridge, MA: Basil Blackwell.

Feger, H., and Bien, W. (1982). Network unfolding. *Social Networks. 4*, 257–283.

Feger, H., Hummell, H.J., Pappi, F., Sodeur, W., and Ziegler, R. (1978). *Bibliographie zum Projeckt Analyse Sozialer Netwerke.* Wuppertal, West Germany: Gesamthochschule Wuppertale.

Feld, S.L. (1981). The focused organization of social ties. *American Journal of Sociology. 86*, 1015–1035.

Feld, S.L., and Elmore, R. (1982a). Patterns of sociometric choices: Transitivity reconsidered. *Social Psychology Quarterly. 45*, 77–85.

Feld, S.L., and Elmore, R. (1982b). Processes underlying patterns of sociometric choice: Response to Hallinan. *Social Psychology Quarterly. 45*, 90–92.

Fennema, M., and Schijf, H. (1978/79). Analysing interlocking directorates: Theory and methods. *Social Networks. 1*, 297–332.

Fershtman, M. (1985). Transitivity and the path census in sociometry. *Journal of Mathematical Sociology, 11*, 159–189.

Festinger, L. (1949). The analysis of sociograms using matrix algebra. *Human Relations. 2*, 153–158.

Festinger, L. (1954). A theory of social comparison processes. *Human Relations. 7*, 117–140.

Festinger, L. (1957). *A Theory of Cognitive Dissonance.* Evanston, IL: Row, Peterson & Co.

Fiedler, F.E. (1958). *Attitudes and Group Effectiveness.* Urbana: University of Illinois Press.

Fienberg, S.E. (1980). *The Analysis of Cross-Classified, Categorical Data.* Second Edition. Cambridge, MA: The MIT Press.

Fienberg, S.E. (1985). Multivariate directed graphs in statistics. In Kotz, S.L., Johnson, N.L., and Read, C.B. (eds.), *Encyclopedia of Statistical Sciences*, Volume 6, pages 40–43. New York: John Wiley and Sons.

Fienberg, S.E., Meyer, M.M., and Wasserman, S. (1981). Analyzing data from multivariate directed graphs: An application to social networks. In Barnett, V. (ed.), *Interpreting Multivariate Data*, pages 289–306. London: John Wiley and Sons.

Fienberg, S.E., Meyer, M.M., and Wasserman, S. (1985). Statistical analysis of multiple sociometric relations. *Journal of the American Statistical Association. 80*, 51–67.

Fienberg, S.E., and Wasserman, S. (1980). Methods for the analysis of data from multivariate directed graphs. In *Proceedings of the Conference on Recent Developments in Statistical Methods and Applications*, pages 137–161. Taipei, Taiwan: Institute of Mathematics, Academica Sinica.

Fienberg, S.E., and Wasserman, S. (1981a). Categorical data analysis of single sociometric relations. In Leinhardt, S. (ed.), *Sociological Methodology 1981*, pages 156–192. San Francisco: Jossey-Bass.

Fienberg, S.E., and Wasserman, S. (1981b). Comment on Holland and Leinhardt, 'An exponential family of probability distributions for directed graphs.' *Journal of the American Statistical Association. 76*, 54–57.

Fischer, C.S. (1982). *To Dwell Among Friends: Personal Networks in Town and*

City. Chicago: University of Chicago Press.

Flament, C. (1963). *Applications of Graph Theory to Group Structure.* Englewood Cliffs, NJ: Prentice-Hall.

Ford, L.R., and Fulkerson, D.R. (1962). *Flows in Networks.* Princeton, NJ: Princeton University Press.

Forsyth, E., and Katz, L. (1946). A matrix approach to the analysis of sociometric data: Preliminary report. *Sociometry. 9,* 340–347.

Foster, B.L. (1978/79). Formal network studies and the anthropological perspective. *Social Networks. 1,* 241–255.

Foster, B.L., and Seidman, S.B. (1982). Urban structures derived from collections of overlapping subsets. *Urban Anthropology. 11,* 177–192.

Foster, B.L., and Seidman, S.B. (1983). A strategy for the dissection and analysis of social structures. *Journal of Social and Biological Structures. 6,* 49–64.

Foster, B.L., and Seidman, S.B. (1984). Overlap structure of ceremonial events in two Thai villages. *Thai Journal of Development Administration. 24,* 143–157.

Fox, J. (1982). Selective aspects of measuring resemblance for taxonomy. In Hudson, H.C. (ed.), *Classifying Social Data.* San Francisco: Jossey-Bass.

Frank, O. (1971). *Statistical Inference in Graphs.* Stockholm: FOA Repro.

Frank, O. (1977a). Survey sampling in graphs. *Journal of Statistical Planning and Inference. 1,* 235–264.

Frank, O. (1977b). A note on Bernoulli sampling in graphs and Horvitz-Thompson estimation. *Scandinavian Journal of Statistics. 4,* 178–180.

Frank, O. (1977c). Estimation of graph totals. *Scandinavian Journal of Statistics. 4,* 81–89.

Frank, O. (1978a). Inferences concerning cluster structure. In Corsten, L.C.A., and Hermans, J. (eds.), *Proceedings in Computational Statistics.* Vienna: Physica-Verlag.

Frank, O. (1978b). Sampling and estimation in large social networks. *Social Networks. 1,* 91–101.

Frank, O. (1979a). Estimating a graph from triad counts. *Journal of Statistical Computation and Simulation. 9,* 31–46.

Frank, O. (1979b). Estimation of population totals by use of snowball samples. In Holland, P.W., and Leinhardt, S. (eds.), *Perspectives on Social Network Research,* pages 319–348. New York: Academic Press.

Frank, O. (1980). Sampling and inference in a population graph. *International Statistical Review. 48,* 33–41.

Frank, O. (1981). A survey of statistical methods for graph analysis. In Leinhardt, S. (ed.), *Sociological Methodology, 1981,* pages 110–155. San Francisco: Jossey-Bass.

Frank, O. (1985). Random sets and random graphs. In Lanke, J., and Lindgren, G. (eds.), *Contributions in Probability and Statistics in Honour of Bunnar Blom,* pages 113–120. Lund, Sweden: University of Lund Press.

Frank, O. (1988). Random sampling and social networks: A survey of various approaches. *Mathematiques, Informatique, et Sciences Humaines, 26,* 19–33.

Frank, O. (1989). Random graph mixtures. *Annals of the New York Academy of Sciences. 576, Graph Theory and Its Applications: East and West,* 192–199.

Frank, O., Hallinan, M., and Nowicki, K. (1985). Clustering of dyad distributions as a tool in network modeling. *Journal of Mathematical Sociology. 11,* 47–64.

Frank, O., and Harary, F. (1979). Maximum triad counts in graphs and digraphs. *Journal of Combinatorics Information and System Sciences. 4,* 286–294.

Frank, O., and Harary, F. (1980). Balance in stochastic signed graphs. *Social Networks. 2,* 155–163.

Frank, O., and Harary, F. (1982). Cluster inference by using transitivity indices in empirical graphs. *Journal of the American Statistical Association. 77,* 835–840.

Frank, O., Komanska, H., and Widaman, K.F. (1985). Cluster analysis of dyad distributions in networks. *Journal of Classification. 2,* 219–238.

Frank, O., Lundquist, S., Wellman, B., and Wilson, C. (1986). Analysis of composition and structure of social networks. Unpublished manuscript.

Frank, O., and Strauss, D. (1986). Markov graphs. *Journal of the American Statistical Association. 81,* 832–842.

Freeman, L.C. (1976). *Bibliography on Social Networks.* Monticello, IL: Council of Planning Librarians.

Freeman, L.C. (1977). A set of measures of centrality based on betweeness. *Sociometry. 40,* 35–41.

Freeman, L.C. (1979). Centrality in social networks: I. Conceptual clarification. *Social Networks. 1,* 215–239.

Freeman, L.C. (1980a). The gatekeeper, pair-dependency, and structural centrality. *Quality and Quantity. 14,* 585–592.

Freeman, L.C. (1980b). Q-analysis and the structure of friendship networks. *International Journal of Man-Machine Studies. 12,* 367–378.

Freeman, L.C. (1984). Turning a profit from mathematics: The case of social networks. *Journal of Mathematical Sociology. 10,* 343–360.

Freeman, L.C. (1986). The impact of computer based communication on the social structure of an emerging scientific speciality. *Social Networks. 6,* 201–221.

Freeman, L.C. (1988). Alliances: A new formalism for primary groups and its relationships to cliques and to structural equivalences. Unpublished manuscript.

Freeman, L.C. (1989). Social networks and the structure experiment. In Freeman, L.C., White, D.R., and Romney, A.K. (eds.), *Research Methods in Social Network Analysis,* pages 11–40. Fairfax, VA: George Mason University Press.

Freeman, L.C. (1992a). The sociological concept of "group": An empirical test of two models. *American Journal of Sociology. 98,* 152–166.

Freeman, L.C. (1992b). La resurrection des cliques: Application du trellis de Galois. *Bulletin de Métodologie Sociologique. 37,* 3–24.

Freeman, L.C., Borgatti, S.P., and White D.R. (1991). Centrality in valued graphs: A measure of betweenness based on network flow. *Social Networks. 13:*141–154.

Freeman, L.C., and Freeman, S.C. (1980). A semi-visible college: Structural effects of seven months of EIES participation by a social networks community. In Henderson, M.M., and MacNaughton, M.J. (eds.), *Electronic Communication: Technology and Impacts,* pages 77–85. AAAS Symposium 52. Washington, DC: American Association for the Advancement of Science.

Freeman, L.C., Freeman, S.C., and Michaelson, A.G. (1988). On human social intelligence. *Journal of Social and Biological Structures. 11,* 415–425.

Freeman, L.C., Freeman, S.C., and Michaelson, A.G. (1989). How humans see social groups: A test of the Sailer-Gaulin models. *Journal of Quantitative Anthropology*. *1*, 229–238.

Freeman, L.C., Roeder, D., and Mulholland, R.R. (1980). Centrality in social networks: II. Experimental results. *Social Networks*. *2*, 119–141.

Freeman, L.C., and Romney, A.K. (1987). Words, deeds and social structure: A preliminary study of the reliability of informants. *Human Organization*. *46*, 330–334.

Freeman, L.C., Romney, A.K., and Freeman, S.C. (1987). Cognitive structure and informant accuracy. *American Anthropologist*. *89*, 310–325.

Freeman, L.C., and Thompson, C.R. (1989). Estimating acquaintanceship volume. In Kochen, M. (ed.), *The Small World*, pages 147–158. Norwood, NJ: Ablex.

Freeman, L.C., and White, D.R. (1993). Using Galois lattices to represent network data. In Marsden, P.V. (ed.), *Sociological Methodology 1993*, pages 127–146. Cambridge, MA: Basil Blackwell.

Freeman, L.C., White, D.R., and Romney, A.K. (eds.) (1989). *Research Methods in Social Network Analysis*. Fairfax, VA: George Mason University Press.

Freeman, S.C., and Freeman, L.C. (1979). The networkers network: A study of the impact of a new communications medium on sociometric structure. Social Science Research Reports No. 46. Irvine, CA: University of California.

Frey, S.L. (1989). *Network Analysis as Applied to a Group of AIDS Patients Linked by Sexual Contact*. Unpublished Undergraduate Honors Thesis. Department of Psychology, University of Illinois, Urbana.

Friedell, M.F. (1967). Organizations as semilattices. *American Sociological Review*. *32*, 46–54.

Friedkin, N.E. (1981). The development of structure in random networks: An analysis of the effects of increasing network density on five measures of structure. *Social Networks*. *3*, 41–52.

Friedkin, N.E. (1984). Structural cohesion and equivalence explanations of social homogeneity. *Sociological Methods and Research*. *12*, 235–261.

Friedkin, N.E. (1986). A formal theory of social power. *Journal of Mathematical Sociology*. *12*, 103–126.

Friedkin, N.E. (1989). *SNAPS (Social Network Analysis Procedures) for GAUSS*. Unpublished manuscript, University of California, Santa Barbara.

Friedkin, N.E. (1990). A Guttman scale for the strength of an interpersonal tie. *Social Networks*. *12*, 239–252.

Friedkin, N.E. (1991). Theoretical foundations for centrality measures. *American Journal of Sociology*. *96*, 1478–1504.

Friedkin, N.E., and Cook, K.S. (1990). Peer group influence. *Sociological Methods & Research*. *19*, 122–143.

Friedkin, N.E., and Johnsen, E.C. (1990). Social influence and opinions. *Journal of Mathematical Sociology*. *15*, 193–206.

Friedmann, H. (1988). Form and substance in the analysis of the world economy. In Wellman, B., and Berkowitz, S. (eds.), *Social Structures: A Network Approach*, pages 304–325. New York: Cambridge University Press.

Fulkerson, D.R. (1960). Zero-one matrices with zero trace. *Pacific Journal of Mathematics*. *10*, 831–836.

Gabriel, K.R. (1982). Biplot. In Kotz, S., Johnson, N.L., and Reed, C.B. (eds.), *Encyclopedia of Statistical Sciences, Volume 1*, pages 263–271. New York: John Wiley and Sons.

Gabriel, K.R., and Zamir, S. (1979). Lower rank approximation of matrices by least squares with any choice of weight. *Technometrics. 21*, 489–498.

Galaskiewicz, J. (1979). *Exchange Networks and Community Politics.* Newbury Park, CA: Sage.

Galaskiewicz, J. (1985). *Social Organization of an Urban Grants Economy.* New York: Academic Press.

Galaskiewicz. J., and Krohn, K.R. (1984). Positions, roles, and dependencies in a community interorganizational system. *The Sociological Quarterly. 25*, 527–550.

Galaskiewicz, J., and Marsden, P.V. (1978). Interorganizational resource networks: Formal patterns of overlap. *Social Science Research. 7*, 89–107.

Galaskiewicz, J., and Wasserman, S. (1981). A dynamic study of change in a regional corporate network. *American Sociological Review. 46*, 475–484.

Galaskiewicz, J., and Wasserman, S. (1989). Mimetic and normative processes within an interorganizational field: An empirical test. *Administrative Science Quarterly. 34*, 454–480.

Galaskiewicz, J., and Wasserman, S. (1990). Social action models for the study of change in organizational fields. In Weesie, J., and Flap, H. (eds.), *Social Networks Through Time*, pages 1–30. Utrecht, The Netherlands: ISOR-University of Utrecht Press.

Galaskiewicz, J., Wasserman, S., Rauschenbach, B., Bielefeld, W., and Mullaney, P. (1985). The influence of corporate power, social status, and market position on corporate interlocks in a regional network. *Social Forces. 64*, 403–431.

Gale, D. (1957). A theorem on flows in networks. *Pacific Journal of Mathematics. 7*, 1073–1082.

Gamson, W.A. (1964). Experimental studies of coalition formation. In Berkowitz, L. (ed.), *Advances in Experimental Social Psychology*, Volume I, pages 81–110. New York: Academic Press.

Garrison, W.L. (1960). Connectivity of the interstate highway system. *Papers and Proceedings of the Regional Science Association. 6*, 121–137.

GAUSS (1988). *The GAUSS System Version 2.0.* Kent, WA: Aptech Systems.

Gerard, H.B., and Fleischer, L. (1967). Recall and pleasantness of balanced and unbalanced cognitive structures. *Journal of Personality and Social Psychology. 7*, 332–337.

Glanzer, M., and Glaser, R. (1959). Techniques for the study of group structure and behavior: I. Analysis of structure. *Psychological Bulletin. 56*, 317–331.

Glazer, A. (1981). A solution to the constant frame of reference problem. *Social Networks. 3*, 117–126.

Gokhale, D.V., and Kullback, S. (1978). *The Information in Contingency Tables.* New York: Marcel Dekker.

Goodenough, W.H. (1969). Rethinking "status" and "role": Toward a general model of the cultural organization of social relationships. In Tyler, S.A. (ed.), *Cognitive Anthropology*, pages 311–330. New York: Holt, Rinehart, and Winston.

Goodman, L.A. (1949). On the estimation of the number of classes in a population. *Annals of Mathematical Statistics. 20*, 572–579.

Goodman, L.A. (1961). Snowball sampling. *Annals of Mathematical Statistics. 32*, 148–170.

Goodman, L.A. (1978). *Analyzing Qualitative/Categorical Data.* Cambridge, MA: Abt Books.

Goodman, L. A. (1979). Simple models for the analysis of association in cross-classifications having ordered categories. *Journal of the American Statistical Association. 74*, 537–552.

Goodman, L.A. (1981). Criteria for determining whether certain categories in a cross-classification table should be combined, with special reference to occupational categories in an occupational mobility table. *American Journal of Sociology. 87*, 612–652.

Goodman, L.A. (1985). The analysis of cross-classified data having ordered categories: Association models, correlation models, and asymmetry models for contingency tables with or without missing entries. *Annals of Statistics. 13*, 10–69.

Goodman, L.A. (1986). Some useful extensions of the usual correspondence analysis approach and the usual log-linear models approach in the analysis of contingency tables. *International Statistical Review. 54*, 243–309.

Gottlieb, B.H. (1981). Preventive interventions involving social networks and social support. In Gottlieb, B.H. (ed.), *Social Networks and Social Support*, pages 201–232. Newbury Park, CA: Sage.

Gottman, J.M. (1979a). *Marital Interaction: Experimental Investigations*. New York: Academic Press.

Gottman, J.M. (1979b). Detecting cyclicity in social interaction. *Psychological Bulletin. 86*, 338–348.

Gottman, J.M., and Ringland, J.T. (1981). The analysis of dominance and bi-directionality in social development. *Child Development. 52*, 393–412.

Gould, P., and Gatrell, A. (1979). A structural analysis of a game: The Liverpool v. Manchester United Cup final of 1977. *Social Networks. 2*, 253–273.

Gould, R.V. (1987). Measures of betweeness in non-symmetric networks. *Social Networks. 9*, 277–282.

Granovetter, M. (1973). The strength of weak ties. *American Journal of Sociology. 81*, 1287–1303.

Granovetter, M. (1974). *Getting a Job: A Study of Contacts and Careers*. Cambridge, MA: Harvard University Press.

Granovetter, M. (1977a). Network sampling. Some first steps. *American Journal of Sociology. 81*, 1287–1303.

Granovetter, M. (1977b). Reply to Morgan and Rytina. *American Journal of Sociology. 83*, 727–729.

Granovetter, M. (1979). The theory-gap in social network analysis. In Holland, P.W., and Leinhardt, S. (eds.), *Perspectives on Social Network Research*, pages 501–518. New York: Academic Press.

Granovetter, M. (1982). The strength of weak ties: A network theory revisited. In Marsden, P.V., and Lin, N. (eds.), *Social Structure and Network Analysis*, page 105–130. Beverly Hills, CA: Sage.

Greenacre, M.J. (1984). *Theory and Application of Correspondence Analysis*. New York: Academic Press.

Greenacre, M.J. (1986). *SIMCA*: A program to perform simple correspondence analysis. *Psychometrika. 51*:172–173.

Gupta, M. (1985). Interpersonal tension: A two-factor approach to the *POX* situation. *Small Group Behavior. 16*, 303–323.

Gurevich, M. (1961). *The Social Structure of Acquaintanceship Networks*. Cambridge, MA: MIT Press.

Guttman, L. (1977). A definition of dimensionality and distance for graphs. In Lingoes, J.C. (ed.), *Geometric Representation of Relational Data*. Ann

Arbor, MI: Mathesis.

Haberman, S.J. (1978). *The Analysis of Qualitative Data*. Volume 1. New York: Academic Press.

Haberman, S.J. (1979). *The Analysis of Qualitative Data*. Volume 2. New York: Academic Press.

Haberman, S.J. (1981). Comment on Holland and Leinhardt, 'An exponential family of probability distributions for directed graphs'. *Journal of the American Statistical Association. 76*, 60–62.

Hage, P. (1973). A graph theoretic approach to the analysis of alliance structure and local grouping in Highland New Guinea. *Anthropological Forum. 3*, 280–294.

Hage, P. (1976a). Structural balance and clustering in Bushmen kinship relations. *Behavioral Science. 21*, 36–37.

Hage, P. (1976b). The atom of kinship as a directed graph. *Man* (n.s.). *11*, 558–568.

Hage, P. (1979). Graph theory as a structural model in cultural anthropology. *Annual Review of Anthropology. 8*, 115–136.

Hage, P., and Harary, F. (1983). *Structural Models in Anthropology*. Cambridge: Cambridge University Press.

Hage, P., and Harary, F. (1991). *Exchange in Oceania: A Graph Theoretic Analysis*. Oxford: Clarendon Press.

Hakimi, S.L. (1965). Optimum locations of switching centers and the absolute centers and medians of a graph. *Operations Research. 12*, 450–459.

Hall, A., and Wellman, B. (1985). Social networks and social support. In Cohen, S., and Syme, S.L. (eds.), *Social Support and Health*. New York: Academic Press.

Hallinan, M.T. (1972). Comment on Holland and Leinhardt. *American Journal of Sociology. 77*, 1201–1205.

Hallinan, M.T. (1974a). *The Structure of Positive Sentiment*. New York: Elsevier.

Hallinan, M.T. (1974b). A structural model of sentiment relations. *American Journal of Sociology. 80*, 364–378.

Hallinan, M.T. (1978). The process of friendship formation. *Social Networks. 1*, 193–210.

Hallinan, M.T. (1982). Cognitive balance and differential popularity in social networks. *Social Psychology Quarterly. 45*, 86–90.

Hallinan, M.T., and Hutchins, E.E. (1980). Structural effects on dyadic change. *Social Forces. 59*, 229–245.

Hallinan, M.T., and Kubitschek, W.N. (1988). The effects of individual and structural characteristics on intransitivity in social networks. *Social Psychology Quarterly. 51*, 81–92.

Hallinan, M.T., and Kubitschek, W.N. (1990). Sex and race effects on the response to intransitive sentiment relations. *Social Psychology Quarterly. 53*, 252–263.

Hallinan, M.T., and McFarland, D.D. (1975). Higher order stability conditions in mathematical models of sociometric or cognitive structure. *Journal of Mathematical Sociology. 4*, 131–148.

Hallinan, M.T., and Smith, S.S. (1985). The effects of classroom racial composition on students' interracial friendliness. *Social Psychological Quarterly. 48*, 3–16.

Hallinan, M.T., and Williams, R.A. (1987). The stability of students' interracial friendships. *American Sociological Review. 52*, 653–664.

Hallinan, M.T., and Williams, R.A. (1989). Interracial friendship choices in secondary schools. *American Sociological Review. 54*, 67–78.

Hammer, M. (1980). Reply to Killworth and Bernard. *Connections. 3*, 14–15.

Hammer, M. (1983). 'Core' and 'extended' social networks in relation to health and illness. *Social Science and Medicine. 7*, 405–411.

Hammer, M. (1985). Implications of behavioral and cognitive reciprocity in social network data. *Social Networks. 7*, 189–201.

Hammer, M., Polgar, S., and Salzinger, K. (1969). Speech predictability and social contact patterns in an informal group. *Human Organization. 28*, 235–242.

Hansell, S. (1984). Cooperative groups, weak ties, and the integration of peer friendships. *Social Psychology Quarterly. 47*, 316–328.

Harary, F. (1953). On the notion of balance of a signed graph. *Michigan Mathematical Journal. 2*, 143–146.

Harary, F. (1955a). The number of linear, directed, rooted, and connected graphs. *Transactions of the American Mathematical Society. 78*, 445–463.

Harary, F. (1955b). On local balance and *N*–balance in signed graphs. *Michigan Mathematical Journal. 3*, 37–41.

Harary, F. (1957). Structural duality. *Behavioral Science. 2*, 255–265.

Harary, F. (1959a). On the measurement of structural balance. *Behavioral Science. 4*, 316–323.

Harary, F. (1959b). Graph theoretic methods in the management sciences. *Management Science. 5*, 387–403.

Harary, F. (1959c). Status and contrastatus. *Sociometry. 22*, 23–43.

Harary, F. (1960). A matrix criterion for structural balance. *Naval Research Logistics Quarterly. 7*, 195–199.

Harary, F. (1969). *Graph Theory.* Reading, MA: Addison-Wesley.

Harary, F., and Norman, R.Z. (1953). *Graph Theory as a Mathematical Model in Social Science.* Ann Arbor: University of Michigan Press.

Harary, F., Norman, R.Z., and Cartwright, D. (1965). *Structural Models: An Introduction to the Theory of Directed Graphs.* New York: John Wiley and Sons.

Harary, F., and Palmer, E. (1966). Enumeration of locally restricted digraphs. *Canadian Journal of Mathematics. 18*, 853–860.

Harary, F., and Ross, I.C. (1957). A procedure for clique detection using the group matrix. *Sociometry. 20*, 205–215.

Hartigan, J.A. (1975). *Clustering Algorithms.* New York: John Wiley and Sons.

Hastie, R., Penrod, S., and Pennington, N. (1983). *Inside the Jury.* Cambridge, MA: Harvard University Press.

Hayashi, C. (1958). Note on sampling from a sociometric pattern. *Annals of the Institute of Statistical Mathematics. 9*, 49–52.

Heider, F. (1944). Social perception and phenomenal organization. *Psychological Review. 51*, 358–374.

Heider, F. (1946). Attitudes and cognitive organization. *Journal of Psychology. 21*, 107–112.

Heider, F. (1958). *The Psychology of Interpersonal Relations.* New York: John Wiley and Sons.

Heider, F. (1979). On balance and attribution. In Holland, P.W., and Leinhardt, S. (eds.), *Perspectives on Social Network Research*, pages 11–23. New York: Academic Press.

Heil, G.H., and White, H.C. (1976). An algorithm for finding simultaneous homomorphic correspondences between graphs and their image graphs. *Behavioral Science. 21,* 26–35.

Held, M., and Karp, R. M. (1970). The traveling salesman problem and minimum spanning trees. *Operations Research, 18,* 1138–1162.

Hempel, C.G. (1952). *Fundamentals of Concept Formation in Empirical Science.* In *Encyclopedia of Unified Science,* Volume 2, Number 7. Chicago: University of Chicago Press.

Henley, N.M., Horsfall, R.B., and De Soto, C.B. (1969). Goodness of figure and social structure. *Psychological Review. 76,* 194–204.

Higgins, C.A., McClean, R.J., and Conrath, D.W. (1985). The accuracy and biases of diary communication data. *Social Networks. 7,* 173–187.

Hill, M.O. (1974). Correspondence analysis: A neglected multivariate method. *Applied Statistics. 23,* 340–345.

Hill, M.O. (1982). Correspondence analysis. In Kotz, S., and Johnson, N.L. (eds.), *Encyclopedia of Statistical Sciences,* pages 204–210. New York: John Wiley and Sons.

Hiramatsu, H. (ed.) (1990). *Shakai Nettowaku.* Tokyo: Fukumura.

Hoaglin, D.C., Mosteller, F., and Tukey, J.W. (eds.) (1985). *Exploring Data Tables, Trends, and Shapes.* New York: John Wiley and Sons.

Høivik, T., and Gleditsch, N.P. (1975). Structural parameters of graphs: A theoretical investigation. In Blalock, H.M., et al. (eds.), *Quantitative Sociology,* pages 203–223. New York: Academic Press.

Holland, P.W., Laskey, K.B., and Leinhardt, S. (1983). Stochastic blockmodels: Some first steps. *Social Networks. 5,* 109–137.

Holland, P.W., and Leinhardt, S. (1970). A method for detecting structure in sociometric data. *American Journal of Sociology. 70,* 492–513.

Holland, P.W., and Leinhardt, S. (1971). Transitivity in structural models of small groups. *Comparative Group Studies. 2,* 107–124.

Holland, P.W., and Leinhardt, S. (1972). Some evidence on the transitivity of positive interpersonal sentiment. *American Journal of Sociology. 72,* 1205–1209.

Holland, P.W., and Leinhardt, S. (1973). The structural implications of measurement error in sociometry. *Journal of Mathematical Sociology. 3,* 85–111.

Holland, P.W., and Leinhardt, S. (1975). The statistical analysis of local structure in social networks. In Heise, D.R. (ed.), *Sociological Methodology, 1976,* pages 1–45. San Francisco: Jossey-Bass.

Holland, P.W., and Leinhardt, S. (1976). Conditions for eliminating intransitivities in binary digraphs. *Journal of Mathematical Sociology. 4,* 314–318.

Holland, P.W., and Leinhardt, S. (1977a). Notes on the statistical analysis of social network data. Unpublished manuscript.

Holland, P.W., and Leinhardt, S. (1977b). A dynamic model for social networks. *Journal of Mathematical Sociology. 5,* 5–20.

Holland, P.W., and Leinhardt, S. (1977c). Social structure as a network process. *Zeitschrift für Soziologie. 6,* 386–402.

Holland, P.W., and Leinhardt, S. (1978). An omnibus test for social structure using triads. *Sociological Methods and Research. 7,* 227–256.

Holland, P.W., and Leinhardt, S. (1979). Structural sociometry. In Holland, P.W., and Leinhardt, S. (eds.), *Perspectives on Social Network Research,* pages

63–83. New York: Academic Press.

Holland, P.W., and Leinhardt, S. (1981). An exponential family of probability distributions for directed graphs. *Journal of the American Statistical Association. 76*, 33–65 (with discussion).

Homans, G.C. (1950). *The Human Group.* New York: Harcourt Brace.

Homans, G.C. (1961). *Social Behavior: Its Elementary Forms.* New York: Harcourt, Brace & World.

Horsfall, R.B., and Henley, N.M. (1969). Mixed social structures: Strain and probability ratings. *Psychonomic Science. 15*, 186–187.

Hosmer, D.W., and Lemeshow, S. (1989). *Applied Logistic Regression.* New York: John Wiley and Sons.

Huang, G., and Tausig, M. (1990). Network range in personal networks. *Social Networks. 12*, 261–268.

Hubbell, C.H. (1965). An input-output approach to clique detection. *Sociometry. 28*, 277–299.

Hubert, L.J. (1974). Some applications of graph theory to clustering. *Psychometrika. 39*, 283–309.

Hubert, L.J. (1983). Inference procedures for the evaluation and comparison of proximity matrices. In Felsenstein, J. (ed.), *Numerical Taxonomy.* New York: Springer-Verlag.

Hubert, L.J. (1985). Combinatorial data analysis: Association and partial association. *Psychometrika. 50*, 449–467.

Hubert, L.J. (1987). *Assignment Methods in Combinatorial Data Analysis.* New York: Marcel Dekker.

Hubert, L.J., and Arabie, P. (1985). Comparing partitions. *Journal of Classification. 2*, 193–218.

Hubert, L.J., and Arabie, P. (1989). Combinatorial data analysis: Confirmatory comparisons between sets of matrices. *Applied Stochastic Models and Data Analysis. 5*, 273–325.

Hubert, L.J., and Baker, F.B. (1978). Evaluating the conformity of sociometric measurements. *Psychometrika. 43*, 31–41.

Hubert, L.J., and Schultz, L. (1976). Quadratic assignment as a general data analysis strategy. *British Journal of Mathematical and Statistical Psychology. 29*, 190–241.

Hummell, H., and Sodeur, W. (1987). Sturkturbeschrebung von positionen in sozialen beziehungsnetzen. In Pappi, F.U. (ed.), *Methoden der Netzwerkanalzyse.* Munich: Oldenbourg.

Hunter, J., and Shotland, R.L. (1974). Treating data collected by the small world method as a Markov process. *Social Forces. 52*, 321–332.

Iacobucci, D. (1989). Modeling multivariate sequential dyadic interactions. *Social Networks. 11*, 315–362.

Iacobucci, D. (1990). Derivation of subgroups from dyadic interactions. *Psychological Bulletin. 107*, 114–132.

Iacobucci, D., and Hopkins, N. (1991). The relationship between the Scheiblechner model and the Holland-Leinhardt "p_1" model. *Social Networks. 13*, 187–201.

Iacobucci, D., and Hopkins, N. (1992). Modeling dyadic interactions and networks in marketing. *Journal of Marketing Research. 29*, 5–17.

Iacobucci, D., and Wasserman, S. (1987). Dyadic social interactions. *Psychological Bulletin. 102*, 293–306.

Iacobucci, D., and Wasserman, S. (1988). A general framework for the statistical analysis of sequential dyadic interaction data. *Psychological Bulletin. 103*, 379–390.

Iacobucci, D., and Wasserman, S. (1990). Social networks with two sets of actors. *Psychometrika. 55*, 707–720.

IMSL (1987). *IMSL User's Manual: Stat Library*. Houston: IMSL, Inc.

Jacklin, C.N., and Maccoby, E.E. (1978). Social behavior at 33 months in same-sex and mixed-sex dyads. *Child Development. 49*, 557–569.

Johnsen, E.C. (1985). Network macrostructure models for the Davis-Leinhardt set of empirical sociomatrices. *Social Networks. 7*, 203–224.

Johnsen, E.C. (1986). Structure and process: Agreement models for friendship formation. *Social Networks. 8*, 257–306.

Johnsen, T.B. (1970). Balance tendencies in sociometric group structures. *Scandinavian Journal of Psychology. 11*, 80–88.

Johnson, A.D. (1939). An attempt at change in interpersonal relationships. *Sociometry. 2*, 43–48.

Johnson, J.C. (1986). Social networks and innovation adoption: A look at Burt's use of structural equivalence. *Social Networks 8*, 343–364.

Johnson, J.C. (1990). *Selecting Ethnographic Informants*. Newbury Park, CA: Sage.

Johnson, J.C., Boster, J.S., and Holbert, D. (1989). Estimating relational attributes from snowball samples through simulation. *Social Networks. 11*, 135–158.

Johnson, S. (1967). Hierarchical clustering schemes. *Psychometrika. 38*, 241–254.

Jordan, C. (1869). Sur les assemblages de lignes. *Journal für die reine und angewandte Mathematik. 70*, 185–190.

Kadushin, C. (1966). The friends and supporters of psychotherapy: On social circles in urban life. *American Sociological Review. 31*, 786–802.

Kadushin, C. (1982). Social density and mental health. In Marsden, P.V., and Lin, N. (eds.), *Social Structure and Network Analysis*, pages 147–158. Newbury Park, CA: Sage.

Kajitani, Y., and Maruyama, T. (1976). Functional expression of centrality in a graph – an application to the assessment of communication networks. *Electronics and Communication in Japan. 59–A*, 9–17.

Kapferer, B. (1969). Norms and the manipulation of relationships in a work context. In Mitchell, J.C. (ed.), *Social Networks in Urban Settings*, pages 181–244. Manchester, England: Manchester University Press.

Kapferer, B. (1973). Social network and conjugal role in urban Zambia: Towards a reformulation of the Bott hypothesis. In Boissevain, J., and Mitchell, J.C. (eds.), *Network Analysis: Studies in Human Interaction*, pages 83–110. Paris: Mouton.

Kaplan, K.J. (1972). On the ambivalence-indifference problem in attitude theory and measurement: A suggested modification in the semantic differential technique. *Psychological Bulletin. 77*, 361–372.

Karoński, M. (1982). A review of random graphs. *Journal of Graph Theory. 6*, 349–389.

Katz, E., and Lazarsfeld, P.F. (1955). *Personal Influence: The Part Played by People in the Flow of Mass Communications*. Glencoe, IL: Free Press.

Katz, L. (1947). On the matric analysis of sociometric data. *Sociometry. 10*, 233–241.

Katz, L. (1950). Punched card technique for the analysis of multiple level sociometric data. *Sociometry. 13*, 108–122.

Katz, L. (1952). The distribution of the number of isolates in a social group. *The Annals of Mathematical Statistics. 23*, 271–448.

Katz, L. (1953). A new status index derived from sociometric analysis. *Psychometrika. 18*, 39–43.

Katz, L., and Powell, J.H. (1953). A proposed index of the conformity of one sociometric measurement to another. *Psychometrika. 18*, 249–256.

Katz, L., and Powell, J.H. (1954). The number of locally restricted directed graphs. *Proceedings of the American Mathematical Society. 5*, 621–626.

Katz, L., and Powell, J.H. (1955). Measurement of the tendency toward reciprocation of choice. *Sociometry. 18*, 659–665.

Katz, L., and Powell, J.H. (1957). Probability distributions of random variables associated with a structure of the sample space of sociometric investigations. *Annals of Mathematical Statistics. 28*, 442–448.

Katz, L., and Proctor, C.H. (1959). The concept of configuration of interpersonal relations in a group as a time-dependent stochastic process. *Psychometrika. 24*, 317–327.

Katz, L., Tagiuri, R., and Wilson, T.R. (1958). A note on estimating the statistical significance of mutuality. *The Journal of General Psychology. 58*, 97–103.

Katz, L., and Wilson, T.R. (1956). The variance of the number of mutual choices in sociometry. *Psychometrika. 21*, 299–304.

Kauffman, S.A. (1969). Metabolic stability and epigenesis in randomly constructed genetic nets. *Journal of Theoretical Biology. 22*, 437–467.

Kelley, H.H., and Arrowood, A.J. (1960). Coalitions in the triad: Critique and experiment. *Sociometry. 23*, 231–244.

Kemeny, J.G., and Snell, J.L. (1960). *Finite Markov Chains.* Princeton, NJ: Van Nostrand.

Kemeny, J.G., and Snell, J.L. (1962). *Mathematical Models in the Social Sciences.* Waltham, MA: Blaisdell.

Kendall, M.G., and Smith, B.B. (1939). On the method of paired comparisons. *Biometrika. 31*, 324–345.

Kennedy, J.J. (1983). *Analyzing Qualitative Data: Introduction to Log Linear Analysis for Behavior Research.* New York: Praeger.

Kenny, D.A. (1981). Interpersonal perception: A multivariate round robin analysis. In Brewer, M.B., and Collins, B.E. (eds.), *Knowing and Validating in the Social Sciences: A Tribute to Donald T. Campbell.* San Francisco: Jossey-Bass.

Kenny, D.A., and LaVoie, L. (1984). The social relations model. In Berkowitz, L. (ed.), *Advances in Experimental Social Psychology,* Vol. 18. New York: Academic Press.

Kent, D. (1978). *The Rise of the Medici: Faction in Florence, 1426–1434.* Oxford: Oxford University Press.

Kephart, W.M. (1950). A quantitative analysis of intragroup relationships. *American Journal of Sociology. 55*, 544–549.

Khinchin, A.I. (1957). *Mathematical Foundations of Information Theory.* New York: Dover.

Kick, E.L. (n.d.) World-system structure, national development, and the prospects for a socialist world order. Unpublished manuscript.

Killworth, P.D. (1974). Intransitivity in the structure of small closed groups. *Social Science Research. 3*, 1–23.

Killworth, P.D., and Bernard, H.R. (1976). Informant accuracy in social network data. *Human Organization. 35*, 269–286.

Killworth, P.D., and Bernard, H.R. (1978). Reverse small world experiment. *Social Networks. 1*, 159–192.

Killworth, P.D., and Bernard, H.R. (1979). Informant accuracy in social network data III: A comparison of triadic structure in behavioral and cognitive data. *Social Networks. 2*, 10–46.

Killworth, P.D., Johnsen, E.C., Bernard, H.R., Shelley, G.A., and McCarty, C. (1990). Estimating the size of personal networks. *Social Networks. 12*, 289–312.

Kim, K.H., and Roush, F.W. (1984). Group relationships and homomorphisms of Boolean matrix semigroups. *Journal of Mathematical Psychology. 28*, 448–452.

Klovdahl, A.S. (1979). *Social Networks: Selected References for Course Design and Research Planning*. Monticello, IL: Vance Bilbiographies.

Klovdahl, A.S. (1985). Social networks and the spread of infectious diseases: The AIDS example. *Social Science & Medicine. 21*, 1203–1216.

Klovdahl, A.S. (1986). *VIEW-NET*: A new tool for network analysis. *Social Networks. 8*, 313–342.

Klovdahl, A.S. (1989). Urban social networks: Some methodological problems and possibilities. In Kochen, M. (ed.), *The Small World*. Norwood, NJ: Ablex.

Knoke, D. (1983). Organization sponsorship and influence reputation of social influence associations. *Social Forces. 61*, 1065–1087.

Knoke, D. (1990). *Political Networks: The Structural Perspective*. Cambridge, England: Cambridge University Press.

Knoke, D., and Burt, R.S. (1983). Prominence. In Burt, R.S., and Minor, M.J. (eds.), *Applied Network Analysis*, pages 195–222. Newbury Park, CA: Sage.

Knoke, D., and Kuklinski, J.H. (1982). *Network Analysis*. Newbury Park: Sage.

Knoke, D., and Rogers, D.L. (1979). A blockmodel analysis of interorganizational networks. *Sociology and Social Research. 64*, 28–52.

Knoke, D., and Wood, J.R. (1981). *Organized for Action: Commitment in Voluntary Organizations*. New Brunswick, NJ: Rutgers University Press.

Kochen, M. (ed.) (1989). *The Small World*. Norwood, NJ: Ablex Press.

Koehler, K., and Larntz, K. (1980). An empirical investigation of goodness-of-fit statistics for sparse multinomials. *Journal of the American Statistical Association. 75*, 336–344.

Korte, C., and Milgram, S. (1970). Acquaintance networks between racial groups: Application of the small world method. *Journal of Personality and Social Psychology. 15*, 101–108.

Krackhardt, D. (1987a). Cognitive social structures. *Social Networks. 9*, 109–134.

Krackhardt, D. (1987b). *QAP* partialling as a test of spuriousness. *Social Networks. 9*, 171–186.

Krackhardt, D. (1988). Predicting with networks: Nonparametric multiple regression analyses of dyadic data. *Social Networks. 10*, 359–382.

Krackhardt, D., and Kilduff, M. (n.d.). Diversity is strength: A social network approach to the constructs of organizational culture. Unpublished manuscript.

Krackhardt, D., Lundberg, M., and O'Rourke, L. (1993). *KrackPlot*: A picture's worth a thousand words. *Connections. 16*, 37–47.

Krackhardt, D., and Porter, L.W. (1985). When friends leave: A structural analysis of the relationship between turnover and stayers' attitudes. *Administrative Science Quarterly. 30*, 242–261.

Krackhardt, D., and Porter, L.W. (1986). The snowball effect: Turnover embedded in communication networks. *Journal of Applied Psychology. 71*, 50–55.

Krackhardt, D., and Stern, R.N. (1988). Informal networks and organizational crises: An experimental simulation. *Social Psychology Quarterly. 51*, 123–140.

Kraemer, H.C., and Jacklin, C.N. (1979). Statistical analysis of dyadic social behavior. *Psychological Bulletin. 86*, 217–224.

Krantz, D.H., Luce, R.D., Suppes, P., and Tversky, A. (1971). *Foundations of Measurement.* Volume I. New York: Academic Press.

Kroonenberg, P.M. (1983). *Three-mode Principal Component Analysis.* Leiden, The Netherlands: DSWO Press.

Kruskal, J.B., and Wish, M. (1978). *Multidimensional Scaling.* Newbury Park, CA: Sage.

Kullback, S. (1959). *Information Theory and Statistics.* New York: John Wiley and Son.

Kumbasar, E., Romney, A.K., and Batchelder, W.H. (n.d.). Systemic biases in social perceptions. Unpublished manuscript.

Lance, G.N., and Williams, W.T. (1967). A general theory of classificatory sorting strategies. *Computer Journal. 9*, 373–380.

Landau, H.G. (1951a). On dominance relations and the structure of animal societies. I. Effect of inherent characteristics. *Bulletin of Mathematical Biophysics. 13*, 1–19.

Landau, H.G. (1951b). On dominance relations and the structure of animal societies. II. Some effects of possible social factors. *Bulletin of Mathematical Biophysics. 13*, 245–262.

Landau, H.G. (1953). On dominance relations and the structure of animal societies. III. The condition for a score structure. *Bulletin of Mathematical Biophysics. 15*, 143–148.

Laumann, E.O. (1969). Friends of urban men: An assessment of accuracy in reporting their socioeconomic attributes, mutual choice, and attitude agreement. *Sociometry. 32*, 54–69.

Laumann, E.O., Gagnon, J.H., Michaels, S., Michael, R.T., and Coleman, J.S. (1989). Monitoring the AIDS epidemic in the United States: A network approach. *Science. 244*, 1186–1189.

Laumann, E.O., Galaskiewicz, J., and Marsden, P.V. (1978). Community structure as interorganizational linkages. *Annual Review of Sociology. 4*, 455–484.

Laumann, E.O., and Guttman, L. (1966). The relative associational contiguity of occupations in an urban setting. *American Sociological Review. 31*, 169.

Laumann, E.O., and Knoke, D. (1987). *The Organizational State: Social Choice in National Policy Domains.* Madison, WI: University of Wisconsin Press.

Laumann, E.O., and Marsden, P.V. (1979). The analysis of oppositional structures in political elites: Identifying collective actors. *American Sociological Review. 44*, 713–732.

Laumann, E.O., Marsden, P.V., and Galaskiewicz, J. (1977). Community–elite influence structures: Extension of a network approach. *American Journal of Sociology. 83*, 594–631.

Laumann, E.O., Marsden, P.V., and Prensky, D. (1989). The boundary specification problem in network analysis. In Freeman, L.C., White, D.R., and Romney, A.K. (eds.), *Research Methods in Social Network Analysis*, pages 61–87. Fairfax, VA: George Mason University Press.

Laumann, E.O., and Pappi, F. (1973). New directions in the study of elites. *American Sociological Review. 38*, 212–230.

Laumann, E.O., and Pappi, F. (1976). *Networks of Collective Action: A Perspective on Community Influence Systems*. New York: Academic Press.

Laumann, E.O., Verbrugge, L.M., Pappi, F.V. (1974). A causal modelling approach to the study of a community elite's influence structure. *American Sociological Review. 39*, 164–178.

Lawler, E.L. (1973). Cutsets and partitions of hypergraphs. *Networks. 3*, 275–285.

Lawler, E.L. (1976). *Combinatorial Optimization: Networks and Matroids*. New York: Holt, Rinehart, and Winston.

Lazarsfeld, P.F., and Merton, R.K. (1954). Friendship as a social process: A substantive and methodological analysis. In Berger, M., Abel, T., and Page, C.H. (eds.), *Freedom and Control in Modern Society*, pages 18–66. Princeton, NJ: Van Nostrand.

Leavitt, H.J. (1949). *Some Effects of Certain Communication Patterns on Group Performance*. Unpublished Ph.D. Dissertation. Massachusetts Institute of Technology, Cambridge, MA.

Leavitt, H.J. (1951). Some effects of communication patterns on group performance. *Journal of Abnormal and Social Psychology. 46*, 38–50.

Leifer, E.M., and White, H.C. (1987). A structural approach to markets. In Mizruchi, M.S., and Schwartz, M. (eds.), *Intercorporate Relations: The Structural Analysis of Business*, pages 85–108. Cambridge, England: Cambridge University Press.

Leik, R.K., and Meeker, B.F. (1975). *Mathematical Sociology*. Englewood Cliffs, NJ: Prentice–Hall.

Leinhardt, S. (1968). *The Development of Structure in the Interpersonal Relations of Children*. Unpublished Ph.D. Thesis, Department of Sociology, University of Chicago.

Leinhardt, S. (1971). *SOCPAC I: A FORTRAN IV* program for structural analysis of sociometric data. *Behavioral Science. 16*, 515–516.

Leinhardt, S. (1972). Developmental change in the sentiment structure of children's groups. *American Sociological Review. 37*, 202–212.

Leinhardt, S. (1973). The development of transitive structure in children's interpersonal relations. *Behavioral Science. 12*, 260–271.

Leinhardt, S. (ed.) (1977). *Social Networks: A Developing Paradigm*. New York: Academic Press.

Lenski, G., and Nolan, P.D. (1984). Trajectories of development: A test of ecological-evolutionary theory. *Social Forces 63*, 1–23.

Levine, J.H. (1972). The sphere of influence. *American Sociological Review. 37*, 14–27.

Lévi-Strauss, C. (1949). *Les Structures élémentaires de la parenté*. Paris: Presses Universitaires de France.

Light, J.M., and Mullins, N.C. (1979). A primer on blockmodeling procedure. In Holland, P.W., and Leinhardt, S. (eds.), *Perspectives on Social Network Research*, pages 85–118. New York: Academic Press.

Lin, N. (1975). Analysis of communication relations. In Hanneman, G.J., and McElwen, W.J. (eds.), *Communication and Behavior*. Reading, MA:

Addison-Wesley.

Lin, N. (1976). *Foundations of Social Research*. New York: McGraw-Hill.

Lin, N. (1989). The smallworld technique as a theory-construction tool. In Kochen, M. (ed.), *The Small World*, pages 231–238. Norwood, NJ: Ablex.

Lin, N., and Dumin, M. (1986). Access to occupations through social ties. *Social Networks. 8*, 365–385.

Lin, N., Ensel, W.M., and Vaughn, J.C. (1981). Social resources and strength of ties: Structural factors in occupational status attainment. *American Sociological Review. 46*, 393–405.

Lin, N., Vaughn, J.C., and Ensel, W.M. (1981). Social resources and occupational status attainment. *Social Forces. 59*, 1163–1181.

Lin, N., Woelfel, M., and Light, S.C. (1986). Buffering the impact of the most important life event. In Lin, N., Dean, A., and Ensel, W.M. (eds.), *Social Support, Life Events, and Depression*, pages 307–332. New York: Academic Press.

Lindzey, G., and Borgatta, E.F. (1954). Sociometric measurement. In Lindzey, G. (ed.), *Handbook of Social Psychology*. Volume 1, pages 405–448. Cambridge, MA: Addison-Wesley.

Lindzey, G., and Byrne, D. (1968). Measurement of social choice and interpersonal attractiveness. In Lindzey, G., and Aronson, E. (eds.), *Handbook of Social Psychology*. Volume 4, pages 452–525. Reading, MA: Addison-Wesley.

Linton, R. (1936). *The Study of Man*. New York: D. Appleton-Century.

Lipset, S.M., Trow, M.A., and Coleman, J.S. (1956). *Union Democracy: The Internal Politics of the International Typographical Union*. Glencoe, IL: Free Press.

Loomis, C.P., and Pepinsky. H.B. (1948). Sociometry, 1937–1947: Theory and methods. *Sociometry. 11*, 262–286.

Lord, F.M., and Novick, M.R. (1968). *Statistical Theories of Mental Test Scores*. Reading, MA: Addison-Wesley.

Lorrain, F., and White, H.C. (1971). Structural equivalence of individuals in social networks. *Journal of Mathematical Sociology. 1*, 49–80.

Luccio, F., and Sami, M. (1969). On the decomposition of networks into minimally interconnected networks. *Transactions on Circuit Theory CT. 16*, 184–188.

Luce, R.D. (1950). Connectivity and generalized cliques in sociometric group structure. *Psychometrika. 15*, 159–190.

Luce, R.D., Macy, J., and Tagiuri, R. (1955). A statistical model for relational analysis. *Psychometrika. 20*, 319–327.

Luce, R.D., and Perry, A.D. (1949). A method of matrix analysis of group structure. *Psychometrika. 14*, 95–116.

Lundberg, C. (1975). Patterns of acquaintanceship in society and complex organization: A comparative study of the small world problem. *Pacific Sociological Review. 18*, 206–222.

MacEvoy, B., and Freeman, L. (n.d.). *UCINET, Version 3.0*: A Microcomputer Package for Network Analysis. Mathematical Social Science Group, School of Social Sciences, University of California, Irvine.

Mackenzie, K.D. (1964). *A Mathematical Theory of Organizational Structure*. Unpublished Ph.D. Dissertation. University of California, Berkeley, CA.

Mackenzie, K.D. (1966a). Structural centrality in communication networks. *Psychometrika. 31*, 17–25.

Mackenzie, K.D. (1966b). The information theoretic entropy function as a total expected participation index for communication network experiments. *Psychometrika. 31*, 249–254.

MacRae, D. (1960). Direct factor analysis of sociometric data. *Sociometry. 23*, 360–370.

Majcher, Z. (1985). Matrices representable by directed graphs. *Archivum Mathematicum (BRNO). 21*, 205–218.

Mandel, M.J. (1983). Local roles and social networks. *American Sociological Review. 48*, 376–386.

Mariolis, P. (1975). Interlocking directorates and control of corporations: The theory of bank control. *Social Science Quarterly. 56*, 425–439.

Markovsky, B., Willer, D., and Patton, T. (1988). Power relations in exchange networks. *American Sociological Review. 53*, 220–236.

Marsden, P.V. (1981). Models and methods for characterizing the structural parameters of groups. *Social Networks. 3*, 1–27.

Marsden, P.V. (1985). Latent structure models for relationally defined social classes. *American Journal of Sociology. 90*, 1002–1021.

Marsden, P.V. (1986). Heterogeneity and tie strength: An analysis of second-order association. Unpublished manuscript.

Marsden, P.V. (1987). Core discussion networks of Americans. *American Sociological Review. 52*, 122–131.

Marsden, P.V. (1988). Homogeneity in confiding relations. *Social Networks. 10*, 57–76.

Marsden, P.V. (1989). Methods for the characterization of role structures in network analysis. In Freeman, L.C., White, D.R., and Romney, A.K. (eds.), *Research Methods in Social Network Analysis*, pages 489–530. Fairfax, VA: George Mason University Press.

Marsden, P.V. (1990a). Network sampling and network effects model. Unpublished manuscript.

Marsden, P.V. (1990b). Network Data and Measurement. *Annual Review of Sociology. 16*, 435–463.

Marsden, P.V., and Laumann, E.O. (1978). The social structure of religious groups: A replication and methodological critique. In Shye, S. (ed.), *Theory Construction and Data Analysis in the Behavioral Sciences*, pages 81–111. San Francisco: Jossey-Bass.

Marsden, P.V., and Laumann, E.O. (1984). Mathematical ideas in social structural analysis. *Journal of Mathematical Sociology. 10*, 271–294.

Marsden, P.V., and Lin, N. (eds.) (1982). *Social Structure and Network Analysis*. Newbury Park, CA: Sage.

Maucorps, P.H. (1949). A sociometric inquiry in the French army. *Sociometry. 12*, 46–80.

Mayer, T.F. (1984). Parties and networks: Stochastic models for relationship networks. *Journal of Mathematical Sociology. 10*, 51–103.

Mayhew, B.H., and Gray, L.N. (1972). Growth and decay of structure in interaction. *Comparative Group Studies. 3*, 131–160.

Mazur, A. (1971). Comments on Davis' graph model. *American Sociological Review. 36*, 308–311.

McCann, H.G. (1978). *Chemistry Transformed: The Paradigmatic Shift from Phlogiston to Oxygen*. Norwood, NJ: Ablex.

McConaghy, M.J. (1981a). The common role structure. *Sociological Methods and Research. 9*, 267–285.

McConaghy, M.J. (1981b). Negation of the equation. *Sociological Methods and Research. 9*, 303–312.

McKinney, J.C. (1947). *Educational Application of the Social Psychology of Mead.* Unpublished Master of Arts Thesis. College of Education, Colorado State University.

McKinney, J.C. (1948). An educational application of a two-dimensional sociometric test. *Sociometry. 11*, 356–367.

McPherson, J.M. (1982). Hypernetwork sampling: Duality and differentiation among voluntary organizations. *Social Networks. 3*, 225–249.

McPherson, J.M., and Smith-Lovin, L. (1982). Women and weak ties: Differences by sex in the size of voluntary organizations. *American Journal of Sociology. 87*, 883–904.

McQuitty, L.L. (1968). Multiple clusters, types, and dimensions from iterative intercolumnar correlational analysis. *Multivariate Behavioral Research. 3*, 465–477.

McQuitty, L.L., and Clark, J.A. (1968). Clusters from iterative intercolumnar correlational analysis. *Educational and Psychological Measurement. 28*, 211–238.

Merton, R.K. (1957) *Social Theory and Social Structure.* New York: Free Press.

Merton, R.K., and Kitt, A.S. (1950). Contributions to the theory of reference group behavior. In Merton, R.K., and Lazarsfeld, P.F. (eds.), *Continuities in Social Research: Studies in the Scope and Method of "The American Soldier."* Glencoe, IL: Free Press.

Messick, S. (1989). Validity. In Linn, R.L. (ed.), *Educational Measurement.* Third Edition, pages 13–103. New York: Macmillan.

Meyer, M.M. (1982). Transforming contingency tables. *Annals of Statistics. 10*, 1172–1181.

Michaelson, A.G. (1990). *Network Mechanisms Underlying Diffusion Processes: Interaction and Friendship in a Scientific Community.* Unpublished doctoral dissertation. University of California, Irvine.

Michaelson, A.G. (1991). Social relations and diffusion: Modified adoptions in a scientific community. Unpublished manuscript.

Milgram, S. (1967). The small world problem. *Psychology Today. 22*, 61–67.

Miller, H., and Geller, D. (1972). Structural balance in dyads. *Journal of Personality and Social Psychology. 21*, 135–138.

Mintz, B., and Schwartz, M. (1981a). Interlocking directorates and interest group formation. *American Sociological Review. 46*, 851–868.

Mintz, B., and Schwartz, M. (1981b). The structure of intercorporate unity in American business. *Social Problems. 28*, 87–103.

Mitchell, J.C. (ed.) (1969). *Social Networks in Urban Settings.* Manchester, England: Manchester University Press.

Mitchell, J.C. (1974). Social networks. *Annual Review of Anthropology. 3*, 279–299.

Mitchell, J.C. (ed.) (1980). *Numerical Techniques in Social Anthropology.* Philadelphia: Institute for the Study of Human Issues.

Mitchell, J.C. (1989). Algorithms and network analysis: A test of some analytical procedures on Kapferer's tailor shop material. In Freeman, L.C., White, D.R., and Romney, A.K. (eds.), *Research Methods in Social Network Analysis*, pages 391–365. Fairfax, VA: George Mason University Press.

Mizruchi, M.S. (1984). Interlock groups, cliques, or interest groups? Comment on Allen. *Social Networks. 6*, 193–199.

Mizruchi, M.S., and Bunting, D. (1981). Influence in corporate networks: An examination of four measures. *Administrative Science Quarterly. 26,* 475–489.

Mizruchi, M.S., Mariolis, P., Schwartz, M., and Mintz, B. (1986). Techniques for disaggregating centrality scores in social networks. In Tuma, N.B. (ed.), *Sociological Methodology, 1986,* pages 26–48. San Francisco: Jossey-Bass.

Mizruchi, M.S., and Schwartz, M. (1987). *Intercorporate Relations: The Structural Analysis of Business.* Cambridge, England: Cambridge University Press.

Mohazab, F., and Feger, H. (1985). An extension of Heiderian balance theory for quantified data. *European Journal of Social Psychology. 15,* 147–165.

Mokken, R.J. (1979). Cliques, clubs and clans. *Quality and Quantity. 13,* 161–173.

Mokken, R.J., and Stokman, F.N. (1978/79). Corporate-governmental networks in the Netherlands. *Social Networks. 1,* 333–358.

Moon, J.W. (1968). *Topics on Tournaments.* New York: Holt, Rinehart, and Winston.

Moore, G. (1979). The structure of a national elite network. *American Sociological Review. 44,* 673–692.

Moore, M. (1978). An international application of Heider's balance theory. *European Journal of Social Psychology. 8,* 401–405.

Moos, R.H., and Moos, B.S. (1981). *Family Environmental Scale Manual.* Palo Alto, CA: Consulting Psychologists Press.

Moreno, J.L. (1934). *Who Shall Survive?: Foundations of Sociometry, Group Psychotherapy, and Sociodrama.* Washington, D.C.: Nervous and Mental Disease Publishing Co. Reprinted in 1953 (Second Edition) and in 1978 (Third Edition) by Beacon House, Inc., Beacon, NY.

Moreno, J.L. (1946). Sociogram and sociomatrix: A note to the paper by Forsyth and Katz. *Sociometry. 9,* 348–349.

Moreno, J.L., and Jennings, H.H. (1938). Statistics of social configurations. *Sociometry. 1,* 342–374.

Moreno, J.L., and Jennings, H.H. (1945). Sociometric measurement of social configurations, based on deviations from chance. *Sociometric Monographs,* No. 3. Beacon House, NY.

Morgan, D.L., and Rytina, S. (1977). Comment on "Network sampling: Some first steps," by M. Granovetter. *American Journal of Sociology. 83,* 722–727.

Morris, M. (1989). *Networks and Diffusion: An Application of Loglinear Models to the Population Dynamics of Disease.* Unpublished Ph.D. Dissertation, Department of Sociology. University of Chicago.

Morris, M. (1990). Networks and diffusion: Modelling the effects of selective mixing on the spread of disease. Unpublished manuscript.

Morris, M. (1993). Epidemiology and social networks: Modeling structure diffusion. *Sociological Methods & Research. 22,* 99–126.

Morrissette, J.O. (1958). An experimental study of the theory of structural balance. *Human Relations. 11,* 239–254.

Mosteller, F. (1951). Remarks on the method of paired comparisons. I. The least squares solution assuming equal standard deviations and equal correlations. *Psychometrika. 16,* 3–11.

Mosteller, F., Fienberg, S.E., and Rourke, R.E.K. (1983). *Beginning Statistics with Data Analysis.* Reading, MA: Addison-Wesley.

Mouton, J.S., Blake, R.R., and Fruchter, B. (1955a). The reliability of sociometric measures. *Sociometry. 18,* 1–48.

Mouton, J.S., Blake, R.R., and Fruchter, B. (1955b). The validity of sociometric responses. *Sociometry. 18*, 181–206.

Moxley, R.L., and Moxley, N.F. (1974). Determining point-centrality in uncontrived social networks. *Sociometry. 37*, 122–130.

Mullins, N.C. (1973). *Theories and Theory Groups in Contemporary American Sociology*. New York: Harper & Row.

Mullins, N.C., Hargens, L.L., Hecht, P.K., and Kick, E.L. (1977). The group structure of cocitation clusters: A comparative study. *American Sociological Review. 42*, 552–562.

Nadel, S.F. (1957). *The Theory of Social Structure*. New York: Free Press.

Nahinsky, I.D. (1969). A group interaction stochastic model based on balance theoretical considerations. *Behavioral Science. 14*, 289–302.

Nehnevajsa, J. (1955a). Chance expectancy and intergroup choice. *Sociometry. 18*, 153–163.

Nehnevajsa, J. (1955b). Probability in sociometric analysis. *Sociometry. 18*, 678–688.

Nelder, J.A., and Wedderburn, R.W. (1972). Generalized linear models. *Journal of the Royal Statistical Society, Series A. 135*, 370–384.

Nemeth, R.J., and Smith, D.A. (1985). International trade and world-system structure, A multiple network analysis. *Review. 8*, 517–560.

Newcomb, T.M. (1953). An approach to the study of communicative acts. *Psychological Review. 60*, 393–404.

Newcomb, T.M. (1961). *The Acquaintance Process*. New York: Holt, Rinehart, and Winston.

Newcomb, T.M. (1965). Role Relationships. In Newcomb, T.M., Turner, R.H., and Converse, P.E. (eds.), *Social Psychology*. New York: Holt, Rinehart, and Winston.

Newcomb, T.M. (1968). Interpersonal balance. In Abelson, R.P., Aronson, E., McGuire, W.J., Newcomb, T.M., Rosenberg, M.J., and Tannenbaum, O.H. (eds.), *Theories of Cognitive Consistency*. Chicago: Rand McNally.

Newcomb, T.M. (1981). Heiderian balance as a group phenomenon. *Journal of Personality and Social Psychology. 40*, 862–867.

Nieminen, J. (1973). On the centrality in a directed graph. *Social Science Research. 2*, 371–378.

Nieminen, J. (1974). On centrality in a graph. *Scandinavian Journal of Psychology. 15*, 322–336.

Niesmoller, K., and Schijf, B. (1980). Applied network analysis. *Quality and Quantity. 14*, 101–116.

Nishisato, S. (1980). *Analysis of Categorical Data: Dual Scaling and Its Applications*. Toronto: University of Toronto Press.

Nolan, P.D. (1983). Status in the world economy and national structure and development. *International Journal of Comparative Sociology. 24*, 109–120.

Nolan, P.D. (1987). World system status, income inequality, and economic growth: A criticism of recent criticism. *International Journal of Comparative Sociology. 28*, 69–76.

Nolan, P.D. (1988). World system status, techno-economic heritage, and fertility. *Sociological Focus. 21*, 9–33.

Noma, E. (1982a). Untangling citation networks. *Information Processing & Management. 18*, 43–53.

Noma, E. (1982b). The simultaneous scaling of cited and citing articles in a common space. *Scientometrics. 4*, 205–231.

Noma, E., and Smith, D.R. (1978). *SHED*: A *FORTRAN IV* program for the analysis of small group sociometric structure. *Behavioral Research Methods and Instrumentation. 10*, 60–62.

Noma, E., and Smith, D.R. (1985a). Benchmark for the blocking of sociometric data. *Psychological Bulletin. 97*, 583–591.

Noma, E., and Smith, D.R. (1985b). Scaling sociomatrices by optimizing an explicit function: Correspondence analysis of binary single response sociomatrices. *Multivariate Behavioral Research. 20*, 179–197.

Nordlie, P. (1958). *A longitudinal study of interpersonal attraction in a natural group setting.* Unpublished Ph.D. dissertation, Department of Psychology, University of Michigan.

Norman, R.Z., and Roberts, F.S. (1972a). A derivation of a measure of relative balance for social structures and a characterization of extensive ratio systems. *Journal of Mathematical Psychology. 9*, 66–91.

Norman, R.Z., and Roberts, F.S. (1972b). A measure of relative balance for social structures. In Berger, J., Zelditch, M., and Anderson, B. (eds.), *Sociological Theories in Progress, II*, pages 358–391. New York: Houghton Mifflin.

Northway, M.L. (1940). A method for depicting social relationships obtained by sociometric testing. *Sociometry. 3*, 144–150.

Northway, M.L. (1951). A note on the use of target sociograms. *Sociometry. 14*, 235–236.

Northway, M.L. (1952). *A Primer of Sociometry.* Toronto: The University of Toronto Press.

Norusis, M.J. (1985). *SPSS^X: Advanced Statistics Guide.* Chicago, IL: SPSS.

Nosanchuk, T.A. (1963). A comparison of several sociometric partitioning techniques. *Sociometry. 26*, 112–124.

Osgood, C.E., and Tannenbaum, P.H. (1955). The principle of congruity in the prediction of attitude change. *Psychological Review. 62*, 42–55.

Padgett, J.F. (1987). Social mobility in hieratic control systems. Unpublished manuscript.

Padgett, J.F. (1990). Mobility as control: Congressmen through committees. In Breiger, R.L. (ed.), *Social Mobility and Social Structure.* New York: Cambridge University Press.

Padgett, J.F., and Ansell, C.K. (1989). From faction to party in Renaissance Florence: The emergence of the Medici patronage party. Unpublished manuscript.

Padgett, J.F., and Ansell, C.K. (1993). Robust action and the rise of the Medici, 1400–1434. *American Journal of Sociology. 98*, 1259–1319.

Pagel, M.D., Erdly, W.W., and Becker, J. (1987). Social networks: We get by with (and in spite of) a little help from our friends. *Journal of Personality and Social Psychology. 53*, 793–804.

Palmer. E. (1985). *Graphical Evolution.* New York: Wiley.

Panning, W.H. (1982a). Fitting blockmodels to data. *Social Networks. 4*, 81–101.

Panning, W.H. (1982b). Blockmodels: From relations to configurations. *American Journal of Political Science. 26*, 585–608.

Parker, G.R., and Parker, S.L. (1979). Factions in committees: The U.S. House of Representatives. *The American Political Science Review. 73*, 85–102.

Pattison, P.E. (1981). A reply to McConaghy. *Sociological Methods and Research. 9*, 286–302.

Pattison, P.E. (1982). The analysis of semigroups of multirelational systems. *Journal of Mathematical Psychology 25*, 87–118.

Pattison, P.E. (n.d.). Analysing local roles. Unpublished manuscript, Department of Psychology, University of Melbourne.

Pattison, P.E. (1988). Network models: Some comments on papers in this special issue. *Social Networks. 10*, 383–411.

Pattison, P.E. (1993). *Algebraic Models for Social Netwoks*. Cambridge, England: Cambridge University Press.

Pattison, P.E., and Bartlett, W.K. (1982). A factorization procedure for finite algebras. *Journal of Mathematical Psychology. 25*, 51–81.

Pattison, P.E., and Wasserman, S. (1993). Algebraic models for local social networks based on statistical methods. Unpublished manuscript.

Payne, C.D. (1985). *The GLIM System Release 3.77: Generalized Linear Interactive Modelling Manual*. Oxford: The Numerical Algorithms Group.

Peay, E.R. (1974). Hierarchical clique structures. *Sociometry. 37*, 54–65.

Peay, E.R. (1975a). Nonmetric grouping: clusters and cliques. *Psychometrika. 40*, 297–313.

Peay, E.R. (1975b). Grouping by cliques for directed relationships. *Psychometrika. 40*, 573–574.

Peay, E.R. (1980). Connectedness in a general model for valued networks. *Social Networks. 2*, 385–410.

Phillips, D.P., and Conviser, R.H. (1972). Measuring the structure and boundary properties of groups: Some uses of information theory. *Sociometry. 35*, 235–254.

Pitts, F.R. (1965). A graph theoretic approach to historical geography. *The Professional Geographer. 17*, 15–20.

Pitts, F.R. (1979). The medieval river trade network of Russia revisited. *Social Networks. 1*, 285–292.

Popping, R., Snijders, T.A.B., and Stokman, F.N. (1988). Triad counts. In Stokman, F.N., and Van Veen, F.J. (eds.), *GRADAP User's Manual, Volume III*. Amsterdam: The University of Amsterdam.

Price, K.O., Harburg, E., and Newcomb, T.M. (1966). Psychological balance in situations of negative interpersonal attitudes. *Journal of Personality and Social Psychology. 3*, 255–270.

Proctor, C.H. (1967). The variance of an estimate of linkage density from a simple random sample of graph nodes. *Proceedings of the Social Statistics Section, American Statistical Association, 1967*, pages 342–343.

Proctor, C.H. (1969). Analyzing prior data and point data on social relationships, attitudes, and background characteristics of Costa Rican Census Bureau employees. *Proceedings of the Social Statistics Section, American Statistical Association, 1969*, pages 457–465.

Proctor, C.H. (1979). Graph sampling compared to conventional sampling. In Holland, P.W., and Leinhardt, S. (eds.), *Perspectives on Social Network Research*, pages 301–318. New York: Academic Press.

Proctor, C.H., and Loomis, C.P. (1951). Analysis of sociometric data. In Jahoda, M., Deutsch, M., and Cook, S.W. (eds.), *Research Methods in Social Relations*, pages 561–586. New York: Dryden Press.

Radcliffe-Brown, A.R. (1940). On social structure. *Journal of the Royal Anthropological Society of Great Britain and Ireland. 70*, 1–12.

Rainio, K. (1966). A study on sociometric group structure: An application of a stochastic theory of social interaction. In Berger, J., Zelditch, M., and

Anderson, B. (eds.), *Sociological Theories in Progress*, Volume 1. Boston: Houghton Mifflin.

Rao, A.R., and Bandyopadhyay, S. (1987). Measures of reciprocity in a social network. *Sankhyā, Series A. 49*, 141–188.

Rao, A.R., and Rao, S.B. (1988). Measuring reciprocity in weighted social networks. Unpublished manuscript.

Rapoport, A. (1949a). Outline of a probabilistic approach to animal sociology. I. *Bulletin of Mathematical Biophysics. 11*, 183–196.

Rapoport, A. (1949b). Outline of a probabilistic approach to animal sociology. II. *Bulletin of Mathematical Biophysics. 11*, 273–281.

Rapoport, A. (1950). Outline of a probabilistic approach to animal sociology. III. *Bulletin of Mathematical Biophysics. 12*, 7–17.

Rapoport, A. (1953). Spread of information through a population with sociostructural bias: I. Assumption of transitivity. *Bulletin of Mathematical Biophysics. 15*, 523–533.

Rapoport, A. (1957). A contribution to the theory of random and biased nets. *Bulletin of Mathematical Biophysics. 19*, 257–271.

Rapoport, A. (1963). Mathematical models of social interaction. In Luce, R.D., Bush, R.R., and Galanter, E. (eds.), *Handbook of Mathematical Psychology*, Volume I, pages 493–579. New York: John Wiley and Sons.

Rapoport, A. (1979). A probabilistic approach to networks. *Social Networks. 2*, 1–18.

Rapoport, A., and Horvath, W.J. (1961). A study of a large sociogram. *Behavioral Science. 6*, 279–291.

Reis, H.T., Wheeler, L., Kernix, M.H., Spiegel, N., and Nezlek, J. (1985). On specificity in the impact of social participation on physical and psychological health. *Journal of Personality and Social Psychology. 48*, 456–471.

Reitz, K.P. (1982). Using log linear analysis with network data: Another look at Sampson's monastery. *Social Networks. 4*, 243–256.

Reitz, K.P. (1988). Social groups in a monastery. *Social Networks. 10*, 343–358.

Reitz, K.P., and Dow, M. (1989). Network interdependence of sample units in contingency tables. *Journal of Mathematical Sociology. 14*, 85–96.

Rice, R.E., and Richards, W.D. (1985). An overview of network analysis methods and programs. In Dervin, B., and Voigt, M.J. (eds.), *Progress in Communication Sciences*, Volume 6, pages 105–165. Norwood, NJ: Ablex Publishing Co.

Richards, W.D. (1989a). *The NEGOPY Analysis Program*. Unpublished manuscript, Department of Communication, Simon Fraser University.

Richards, W.D. (1989b). *FATCAT — for Thick Data*. Unpublished manuscript, Department of Communication, Simon Fraser University.

Roberts, F.S. (1976). *Discrete Mathematical Models*. Englewood Cliffs, NJ: Prentice-Hall.

Roberts, F.S. (1978). *Graph Theory and Its Applications to Problems of Society*. Philadelphia: Society for Industrial and Applied Mathematics.

Rodrigues, A. (1967). Effects of balance, positivity, and agreement in triadic social relations. *Journal of Personality and Social Psychology. 5*, 472–475.

Rodrigues, A. (1981). Conditions favoring the effects of balance, agreement, and attraction in $P - O - X$ triads. *Interdisciplinaria. 2*, 59–68.

Rodrigues, A., and Dela Coleta, J.A. (1983). The prediction of preferences for triadic interpersonal relations. *The Journal of Social Psychology. 121*, 73–80.

Rodrigues, A., and Ziviani, C.R. (1974). A theoretical explanation for the intermediate level of tension found in nonbalanced $P - O - X$ triads. *Journal of Psychology. 88*, 47–56.

Roethlisberger, F.J., and Dickson, W.J. (1961). *Management and the Worker.* Cambridge, MA: Harvard University Press.

Rogers, D.L. (1974). Sociometric analysis of interorganizational relations: Application of theory and measurement. *Rural Sociology. 39*, 487–503.

Rogers, E.M. (1979). Network analysis of the diffusion of innovations. In Holland, P.W., and Leinhardt, S. (eds.), *Perspectives on Social Network Research*, pages 137–164. New York: Academic Press.

Rogers, E.M., and Agarwala-Rogers, R. (1976). Communication networks in organizations. *Communication in Organizations,* pages 108–148. New York: Free Press.

Rogers, E.M., and Kincaid, D.L. (1981). *Communication Networks: Toward a New Paradigm for Research.* New York: Macmillan.

Rohlf, F.J., and Sokal, R.R. (1965). Coefficients of correlation and distance in numerical taxonomy. *The University of Kansas Science Bulletin. 45*, 3–27.

Roistacher, R.C. (1974). A review of mathematical methods in sociometry. *Sociological Methods and Research. 3*, 123–171.

Romney, A.K. (1993). Visualizing Social Networks. Keynote address. 13th Annual International Sunbelt Social Network Conference. Tampa, Florida.

Romney, A.K., and Faust, K. (1982). Predicting the structure of a communications network from recalled data. *Social Networks 4*, 285–304.

Romney, A.K., and Weller, S.C. (1984). Predicting informant accuracy from patterns of recall among individuals. *Social Networks 4*, 59–77.

Rosenberg, M.J., and Abelson, R.P. (1960). An analysis of cognitive balancing. In Rosenberg, M.J., et al. (eds.), *Attitude Organization and Change.* New Haven, CT: Yale University Press.

Rosenthal, N., Fingrutd, M., Ethier, M., Karant, R., and McDonald, D. (1985). Social movements and network analysis: A case study of nineteenth-century women's reform in New York state. *American Journal of Sociology. 90*, 1022–1054.

Rosner, B. (1989). Multivariate methods for clustered binary data with more than one level of nesting. *Journal of the American Statistical Association. 84*, 373–380.

Runger, G., and Wasserman, S. (1979). Longitudinal analysis of friendship networks. *Social Networks. 2*, 143–154.

Ryser, H.J. (1957). Combinatorial properties of matrices of zeros and ones. *Canadian Journal of Mathematics. 9*, 371–377.

Sabidussi, G. (1966). The centrality index of a graph. *Psychometrika. 31*, 581–603.

Sade, D.S. (1965). Some aspects of parent-offspring and sibling relations in a group of rhesus monkeys, with a discussion of grooming. *American Journal of Physical Anthropology. 23*, 1–18.

Sailer, L.D. (1978). Structural equivalence: Meaning and definition, computation and application. *Social Networks. 1*, 73–90.

Sailer, L.D., and Gaulin, S.J.C. (1984). Proximity, sociality, and observation: The definition of social groups. *American Anthropologist. 86*, 91–98.

St. John, R.C., and Draper, N.R. (1975). *D*-optimality for regression designs: A review. *Technometrics. 17*, 15–24.

Sampson, S.F. (1968). *A Novitiate in a Period of Change: An Experimental and*

Case Study of Relationships. Unpublished Ph.D. dissertation, Department of Sociology, Cornell University.

Sarason, B.R., Shearin, E.N., Pierce, G.R., and Sarason, I.G. (1987). Interrelations of social support measures: Theoretical and practical implications. *Journal of Personality and Social Psychology*. 52, 813–832.

Sarason, I.G., Levine, H.M., Basham, R.B., and Sarason, B.R. (1983). Assessing social support: The social support questionnaire. *Journal of Personality and Social Psychology*. 48, 1162–1172.

Scheiblechner, H. (1971). The separation of individual- and system-influences on behavior in social contexts. *Acta Psychologica*. 35, 442–460.

Scheiblechner, H. (1972). Personality and system influences on behavior in groups: Frequency models. *Acta Psychologica*. 36, 322–336.

Scheiblechner, H. (1977). The social structure of large groups. In Kempf, W.F., and Rep, B.H. (eds.), *Mathematical Models for Social Psychology*, pages 170–182. Chichester: John Wiley and Sons.

Schendel, U. (1989). *Sparse Matrices: Numerical Aspects with Applications for Scientists and Engineers*. London: Ellis-Horwood.

Schiffman, S.S., Reynolds, M.L., and Young, F.W. (1981). *Introduction to Multidimensional Scaling: Theory, Methods, and Applications*. New York: Academic Press.

Schott, T. (1986). Models of dyadic and individual components of a social relation: Applications to international trade. *Journal of Mathematical Sociology*. 12, 225–249.

Schott, T. (1988). International influence in science: Beyond center and periphery. *Social Science Research*. 17, 219–238.

Schultz, J.V., and Hubert, L.J. (1976). A nonparametric test for the correspondence between two proximities matrices. *Journal of Educational Statistics*. 1, 59–67.

Schwartz, J.E. (1977). An examination of *CONCOR* and related methods for blocking sociometric data. In Heise, D.R. (ed.), *Sociological Methodology 1977*, pages 255–282. San Francisco, Jossey-Bass.

Schweizer, T. (1991). The power struggle in a Chinese community, 1950–1980: A social network analysis of the duality of actors and events. *Journal of Quantitative Anthropology*. 3, 19–44.

Scott, J. (1988). Trend report: Social network analysis. *Sociology*. 22, 109–127.

Scott, J. (1992). *Social Network Analysis*. Newbury Park, CA: Sage.

Seed, P. (1990). *Introducing Network Analysis in Social Work*. London: Jessica Kingsley Publisher.

Seeley, J.R. (1949). The net of reciprocal influence: A problem in treating sociometric data. *Canadian Journal of Psychology*. 3, 234–240.

Seeman, M. (1946). A situational approach to intra-group Negro attitudes. *Sociometry*. 9, 199–206.

Seidman, S.B. (1981a). Structures induced by collections of subsets: A hypergraph approach. *Mathematical Social Sciences*. 1, 381–396.

Seidman, S.B. (1981b). *LS* sets as cohesive subsets of graphs and hypergraphs. Paper presented at the SIAM Conference on the Applications of Discrete Mathematics. Troy, NY, 1981.

Seidman, S.B. (1983a). Internal Cohesion of *LS* Sets in Graphs. *Social Networks*. 5, 97–107.

Seidman, S.B. (1983b). Network structure and minimum degree. *Social Networks*. 5, 269–287.

Seidman, S.B., and Foster, B.L. (1978a). A graph-theoretic generalization of the clique concept. *Journal of Mathematical Sociology. 6*, 139–154.

Seidman, S.B., and Foster, B.L. (1978b). A note on the potential for genuine cross-fertilization between anthropology and mathematics. *Social Networks. 1*, 65–72.

Seidman, S.B., and Foster, B.L. (1978c). *SONET–I* : Social network analysis and modeling system. *Social Networks. 2*, 85–90.

Shannon, C.E., and Weaver, W.W. (1949). *The Mathematical Theory of Communication.* Champaign: The University of Illinois Press.

Shaw, M.E. (1954). Group structure and the behavior of individuals in small groups. *Journal of Psychology. 38*, 139–149.

Sheardon, A.W. (1970). *Sampling Directed Graphs.* Department of Statistics, North Carolina State University. Unpublished doctoral dissertation.

Shimbel, A. (1953). Structural parameters of communication networks. *Bulletin of Mathematical Biophysics. 15*, 501–507.

Shotland, R.L. (1976). *University Communication Networks: The Small World Method.* New York: John Wiley and Sons.

Silvey, S.D. (1981). *Optimal Design.* London: Chapman-Hall.

Sim, F.M., and Schwartz, M.R. (1979). Does *CONCOR* find positions? Unpublished manuscript.

Simmel, G. (1950). *The Sociology of Georg Simmel*, ed. by Wolff, K.H. Glencoe, IL: Free Press.

Simmel, G. (1955). *Conflict and the Web of Group Affiliations.* Glencoe, IL: Free Press.

Singer, B., and Spilerman, S. (1974). Social mobility models for heterogeneous populations. In Costner, H. (ed.), *Sociological Methodology, 1973–1974*, pages 356–401. San Francisco: Jossey-Bass.

Singer, B., and Spilerman, S. (1976). The representation of social processes by Markov models. *American Journal of Sociology. 82*, 1–54.

Singer, B., and Spilerman, S. (1977). Trace inequalities for Markov chains. *Advances in Applied Probability. 9*, 747–764.

Singer, B., and Spilerman, S. (1978). Clustering on the main diagonal in mobility matrices. In Schuessler, K. (ed.), *Sociological Methodology, 1979*, pages 172–208. San Francisco: Jossey-Bass.

Skvoretz, J. (1983). Salience, heterogeneity, and consolidation of parameters: Civilizing Blau's primitive theory. *American Sociological Review. 48*, 360–375.

Skvoretz, J. (1985). Random and biased networks: Simulations and approximations. *Social Networks. 7*, 255–261.

Skvoretz, J. (1990). Biased net theory: Approximations, simulations, and observations. *Social Networks. 12*, 217–238.

Smith, D., and White, D. (1988). Structure and dynamics of the global economy: Network analysis of international trade 1965–1980. Unpublished manuscript.

Smith, S.L. (1950). *Communication Pattern and the Adaptability of Task-oriented Groups: An Experimental Study.* Cambridge, MA: Group Networks Laboratory, Research Laboratory of Electronics, Massachusetts Institute of Technology.

Sneath, P.H.A., and Sokal, R.R. (1973). *Numerical Taxonomy: The Principles and Practice of Numerical Classification.* San Francisco: Freeman.

Snijders, T.A.B. (1981a). The degree variance: An index of graph heterogeneity. *Social Networks. 3*, 163–174.

Snijders, T.A.B. (1981b). Maximum value and null moments of the degree variance. TW-report 229. Department of Mathematics, University of Groningen.

Snijders, T.A.B. (1987). Means and (co-)variances of triad counts in network analysis of subgroups. Unpublished paper # HB-87-848-EX in Heymans Bulletin, Psychological Institute, University of Groningen, The Netherlands.

Snijders, T.A.B. (1991a). Enumeration and simulation methods for 0-1 matrices with given marginals. *Psychometrika. 56*, 397–417.

Snijders, T.A.B. (1991b). Recent research on the $U|M, \{X_{i+}\}, \{X_{i+}\}$ distribution. Unpublished manuscript.

Snijders, T.A.B., and Stokman, F.N. (1987). Extensions of triad counts to networks with different subsets of points and testing underlying random graph distributions. *Social Networks. 9*, 249–275.

Snyder, D., and Kick, E. (1979). Structural position in the world system and economic growth 1955-70: A multiple network analysis of transnational interactions. *American Journal of Sociology. 84*, 1096–1126.

Sokal, R.R., and Sneath, P.H.A. (1963). *Principles of Numerical Taxonomy*. San Francisco: Freeman.

Sonquist, J., and Koenig, T. (1975). Interlocking directorates in the top U.S. corporations: A graph theory approach. *Insurgent Sociologist. 5*, 196–229.

Sørensen, A.B., and Hallinan, M.T. (1976). A stochastic model for change in social structure. *Social Science Research. 5*, 43–61.

Sprenger, C.J.A., and Stokman, F.N. (1989). *GRADAP: Graph Definition and Analysis Package*. Groningen, The Netherlands: iec ProGAMMA.

Stephenson, K. (1989). Social centrality: A study of group dynamics using gelada baboons. Unpublished manuscript.

Stephenson, K., and Zelen, M. (1989). Rethinking centrality: Methods and applications. *Social Networks. 11*, 1–37.

Stogdill, R.M. (1951). The organization of working relationships: Twenty sociometric indices. *Sociometry. 14*, 366–374.

Stouffer, S.E., Suchman, E.A., DeVinney, L.C., Star, S.A., and Williams, R.M. (1949). *The American Soldier: Adjustment During Army Life*. Princeton, NJ: Princeton University Press.

Strauss, D., and Freeman, L.C. (1989). Stochastic modeling and the analysis of structural data. In Freeman, L.C., White, D.R., and Romney, A.K. (eds.), *Research Methods in Social Network Analysis*, pages 135–183. Fairfax, VA: George Mason University Press.

Strauss, D., and Ikeda, M. (1990). Pseudolikelihood estimation for social networks. *Journal of the American Statistical Association. 85*, 204–212.

Sukhatme, P.V. (1938). On bipartitional functions. *Philosophical Transactions. 237A*, 375–409.

Suppes, P., and Zinnes, J.L. (1963). Basic measurement theory. In Luce, R.D., Bush, R.R., and Galanter, E. (eds.), *Handbook of Mathematical Psychology*, Volume II. New York: John Wiley and Sons.

Sylvester, J.J. (1882). On the geometrical forms called trees. *Johns Hopkins University Circle. 1*, 202–203.

Taba, H. (1955). *With Perspective on Human Relations: A Study of Peer Group Dynamics in an Eighth Grade*. Washington, DC: American Council of Education.

Tagiuri, R. (1952). Relational analysis: An extension of sociometric method with emphasis upon social perception. *Sociometry. 15*, 91–104.

Tagiuri, R., Blake, R.R., and Bruner, J.S. (1953). Some determinants of the perception of positive and negative feelings in others. *Journal of Abnormal and Social Psychology. 48*, 585–592.

Tagiuri, R., Bruner, J.S., and Kogan, N. (1955). Estimating the chance expectancies of positive and negative feelings in others. *Psychological Bulletin. 52*, 122–131.

Tam, T. (1989). Demarcating the boundaries between self and the social: The anatomy of centrality in social networks. *Social Networks. 11*, 387–401.

Tashakkori, A., and Insko, C.A. (1979). Interpersonal attraction and the polarity of similar attitudes: A test of three balance models. *Journal of Personality and Social Psychology. 37*, 2262–2277.

Taylor, H.F. (1970). *Balance in Small Groups*. New York: Van Nostrand Reinhold.

Taylor, M. (1969). Influence structures. *Sociometry. 32*, 490–502.

Theil, H. (1967). *Economics and Information Theory*. Chicago: Rand McNally.

Thibaut, J.W., and Kelley, H.H. (1959). *The Social Psychology of Groups*. New York: John Wiley and Sons.

Thurman, B. (1980). In the office: Networks and coalitions. *Social Networks. 2*, 47–63.

Thurstone, L.L. (1927). A law of comparative judgement. *Psychological Review. 34*, 273–286.

Tracy, E.M., Catalano, R.F., Whittaker, J.K., and Fine, D. (1990). Reliability of social network data. *Social Work Research and Abstracts. 26*, 33–35.

Travers, J., and Milgram, S. (1969). An experimental study of the small world problem. *Sociometry. 32*, 425–443.

Tucker, L.R. (1963). Implications of factor analysis of three-way matrices for measurement of change. In Harris, C.W. (ed.), *Problems in Measuring Change*, pages 122–137. Madison, WI: University of Wisconsin Press.

Tucker, L.R. (1964). The extension of factor analysis to three-dimensional matrices. In Gullikson, H., and Frederiksen, N. (eds.), *Contributions to Mathematical Psychology*, pages 110–119. New York: Holt, Rinehart, and Winston.

Tucker, L.R. (1966). Some mathematical notes on three-mode factor analysis. *Psychometrika. 31*, 279–311.

Tukey, J.W. (1977). *Exploratory Data Analysis*. Reading, MA: Addison-Wesley.

Tuma, N.B., and Hallinan, M.T. (1979). The effects of sex, race, and achievement on schoolchildren's friendships. *Social Forces. 58*, 126–146.

Tutte, W.T. (1971). *Introduction to Matroid Theory*. New York: Elsevier.

Tutzauer, F. (1985). Toward a theory of disintegration in communication networks. *Social Networks. 7*, 263–285.

Uhlenbeck, G.E., and Ford, G.W. (1962). *Theory of Linear Graphs*. Amsterdam: North-Holland.

United Nations (1984). *Statistical Papers: Commodity Trade Statistics. Series D. 34*, Numbers 1–1 through 1–24.

Useem, M. (1973). *Conscription, Protest, and Social Conflict*. New York: John Wiley and Sons.

Vaux, A. (1988). Measurement of social support. In Vaux, A. (ed.), *Social Support: Theory, Research, and Intervention*. New York: Praeger.

Velleman, P.F., and Hoaglin, D.C. (1981). *Applications, Basics, and Computing of Exploratory Data Analysis*. Boston: Duxbury Press.

Verbeek, A., and Kroonenberg, P.M. (1985). A survey of algorithms for exact distributions of test statistics in *r* by *c* contingency tables with fixed margins. *Computational Statistics and Data Analysis. 3*, 159–185.

Verbrugge, L. (1977). The structure of adult friendship choices. *Social Forces. 56*, 576–597.

Vinacke, W.E., and Arkoff, A. (1957). An experimental study of coalitions in the triad. *American Sociological Review. 22*, 406–414.

Vogt, F., and Bliegener, J. (1990). *DIAGRAM*. Technische Hochschule, Darmstadt. Fachhochschule Darmstadt.

Walker, M.E. (1991). Statistical models for social support networks. Unpublished manuscript.

Walker, M.E., and Wasserman, S. (1987). *TRIADS: A Computer Program for Triadic Analyses*. Urbana, IL: University of Illinois.

Wampold, B.E. (1984). Tests of dominance in sequential categorical data. *Psychological Bulletin. 96*, 424–429.

Wang, Y.J., and Wong, G.Y. (1987). Stochastic blockmodels for directed graphs. *Journal of the American Statistical Association. 82*, 8–19.

Wasserman, S. (1977). Random directed graph distributions and the triad census in social networks. *Journal of Mathematical Sociology. 5*, 61–86.

Wasserman, S. (1978). Models for binary directed graphs and their applications. *Advances in Applied Probability. 10*, 803–818.

Wasserman, S. (1979). A stochastic model for directed graphs with transition rates determined by reciprocity. In Schuessler, K.F. (ed.), *Sociological Methodology 1980*, pages 392–412. San Francisco: Jossey-Bass.

Wasserman, S. (1980). Analyzing social networks as stochastic processes. *Journal of the American Statistical Association. 75*, 280–294.

Wasserman, S. (1987). Conformity of two sociometric relations. *Psychometrika. 52*, 3–18.

Wasserman, S., and Anderson, C. (1987). Stochastic *a posteriori* blockmodels: Construction and assessment. *Social Networks. 9*, 1–36.

Wasserman, S., and Faust, K. (1989). Canonical analysis of the composition and structure of social networks. In Clogg, C.C. (ed.), *Sociological Methodology, 1989*, pages 1–42. Cambridge, MA: Basil Blackwell.

Wasserman, S., Faust, K., and Galaskiewicz, J. (1990). Correspondence and canonical analysis of relational data. *Journal of Mathematical Sociology. 15*, 11–64.

Wasserman, S., and Galaskiewicz, J. (1984). Some generalizations of p_1: External constraints, interactions, and non–binary relations. *Social Networks. 6*, 177–192.

Wasserman, S., and Galaskiewicz, J. (eds.) (1994). *Advances in Social Network Analysis: Research from the Social and Behavioral Sciences*. Newbury Park, CA: Sage.

Wasserman, S., and Iacobucci, D. (1986). Statistical analysis of discrete relational data. *British Journal of Mathematical and Statistical Psychology. 39*, 41–64.

Wasserman, S., and Iacobucci, D. (1988). Sequential social network data. *Psychometrika. 53*, 261–282.

Wasserman, S., and Iacobucci, D. (1989). *GSQUARE: A FORTRAN* program for computing G^2. Unpublished manuscript.

Wasserman, S., and Iacobucci, D. (1990). Statistical modeling of one-mode and two-mode networks: Simultaneous analysis of graphs and bipartite graphs. *British Journal of Mathematical and Statistical Psychology. 44*, 13–44.

Wasserman, S., and Weaver, S.O. (1985). Statistical analysis of binary relational data: Parameter estimation. *Journal of Mathematical Psychology. 29*, 406–427.

Weaver, S.O., and Wasserman, S. (1986). *RELTWO*–Interactive loglinear model fitting for pairs of sociometric relations. *Communications: Bulletin of the International Network for Social Network Analysis. 9*, 38–46.

Weesie, J., and Flap, H. (eds.) (1990). *Social Networks Through Time*. Utrecht, The Netherlands: ISOR/University of Utrecht.

Weick, K.E., and Penner, D.D. (1966). Triads: A laboratory analogue. *Organizational Behavior and Human Performance. 1*, 191–211.

Weinberg, S., and Goldberg, K. (1990). *Statistics for the Behavioral Sciences*. Cambridge, England: Cambridge University Press.

Wellens, A.R., and Thistlethwaite, D.L. (1971a). An analysis of two quantitative theories of cognitive balance. *Psychological Review. 78*, 141–150.

Wellens, A.R., and Thistlethwaite, D.L. (1971b). An analysis of three quantitative theories of cognitive balance. *Journal of Personality and Social Psychology. 20*, 82–92.

Weller, S.C., and Romney, A.K. (1990). *Metric Scaling: Correspondence Analysis*. Newbury Park, CA: Sage.

Wellman, B. (1979). The community question: The intimate networks of East Yorkers. *American Journal of Sociology. 84*, 1201–1231.

Wellman, B. (1983). Network analysis: Some basic principles. In Collins, R. (ed.), *Sociological Theory, 1983*, pages 155–199. San Francisco: Jossey-Bass.

Wellman, B. (1988a). Structural analysis: From method and metaphor to theory and substance. In Wellman, B., and Berkowitz, S.D. (eds.), *Social Structures: A Network Approach*, pages 19–61. Cambridge, England: Cambridge University Press.

Wellman, B. (1988b). The community question re-evaluated. In Smith, M.P. (ed.), *Power, Community, and the City*, pages 81–107. New Brunswick, NJ: Transaction Books.

Wellman, B. (1992a). Men in networks: Private communications, domestic friendships. In Nardi, P. (ed.), *Men's Friendships*, pages 74–114. Newbury Park, CA: Sage.

Wellman, B. (1992b). Which types of ties and networks give what kinds of social support? In Lawler, E., Markovsky, B., Ridgeway, C., and Walker, H. (eds.), *Advances in Group Processes, Volume 9*, pages 207–235. Greenwich, CT: JAI Press.

Wellman, B. (1993). An egocentric network tale. *Social Networks. 15*, 423–436.

Wellman, B., and Berkowitz, S.D. (1988). Introduction: Studying social structures. In Wellman, B., and Berkowitz, S.D. (eds.), *Social Structures: A Network Approach*, pages 1–14. Cambridge, England: Cambridge University Press.

Wellman, B., Carrington, P.J., and Hall, A. (1988). Networks as personal communities. In Wellman, B., and Berkowitz, S.D. (eds.), *Social Structures: A Network Approach*, pages 130–184. Cambridge, England: Cambridge University Press.

Wellman, B., Frank, O., Espinoza, V., Lundquist, S., and Wilson, C. (1991). Integrating individual, relational, and structural analysis. *Social Networks.*

13, 223–249.

Wellman, B., Mosher, C., Rottenberg, C., and Espinoza, V. (1987). The sum of the ties does not equal a network: The case of social support. Unpublished manuscript.

Wellman, B., and Wortley, S. (1990). Different strokes from different folks: Community ties and social support. *American Journal of Sociology. 96*, 558–588.

Wertheimer, M. (1923). Untersuchungen zur lehre von der gestalt, II. *Psychologische Forschung. 4*, 301–350.

White, C.J. Mower (1977). A limitation of balance theory: The effects of indentification with a member of the triad. *European Journal of Social Psychology. 7*, 111–116.

White, C.J. Mower (1979). Factors affecting balance, agreement, and positivity biases in *POQ* and *POX* triads. *European Journal of Social Psychology. 9*, 129–148.

White, D.R., and McCann, H.G. (1988). Cites and fights: Material entailment analysis of the eighteenth-century chemical revolution. In Wellman, B., and Berkowitz, S.D. (eds.), *Social Structures: A Network Approach*, pages 380–400. Cambridge, England: Cambridge University Press.

White, D.R., and Reitz, K.P. (1983). Graph and semigroup homomorphisms on networks of relations. *Social Networks. 5*, 193–234.

White, D.R., and Reitz, K.P. (1985). Measuring role distance: Structural, regular and relational equivalence. Unpublished manuscript, University of California, Irvine.

White, D.R., and Reitz, K.P. (1989). Re-thinking the role concept: Homomorphisms on social networks. In Freeman, L.C., White, D.R., and Romney, A.K. (eds.), *Research Methods in Social Network Analysis*, pages 429–488. Fairfax, VA: George Mason University Press.

White, H.C. (1961). Management conflict and sociometric structure. *American Journal of Sociology. 67*, 185–187.

White, H.C. (1963). *An Anatomy of Kinship*. Englewood Cliffs, NJ: Prentice-Hall.

White, H.C. (1970). Search parameters for the small world problem. *Social Forces. 49*, 259–264.

White, H.C. (1977). Probabilities of homomorphic mappings from multiple graphs. *Journal of Mathematical Psychology. 16*, 121–134.

White, H.C. (1981). Where do markets come from? *American Journal of Sociology. 87*, 517–47.

White, H.C. (1988). Varieties of markets. In Wellman, B. and Berkowitz, S.D. (eds.), *Social Structures: A Network Approach*, pages 226–260. Cambridge, England: Cambridge University Press.

White, H.C., Boorman, S.A., and Breiger, R.L. (1976). Social structure from multiple networks. I. Blockmodels of roles and positions. *American Journal of Sociology. 81*, 730–779.

White, H.C., and Breiger, R.L. (1975). Pattern across networks. *Society. 12*, 68–73.

Whiting, P.D., and Hillier, J.A. (1960). A method for finding the shortest route through a road network. *Operations Research Quarterly. 11*, 37–40.

Whitney, R.E. (1971). Agreement and positivity in pleasantness ratings of balanced and unbalanced social situations. *Journal of Personality and Social Psychology. 17*, 11–14.

Whitten, N.E., and Wolfe, A.W. (1973). Network analysis. In Honigmann, J.

(ed.), *Handbook of Social and Cultural Anthropology*, pages 717–746. Chicago: Rand McNally.

Wickens, T.D. (1989). *Multiway Contingency Tables Analysis for the Social Sciences*. Hillsdale, NJ: Lawrence Erlbaum Associates.

Wilkinson, L. (1987). *SYSTAT: The System for Statistics*. Evanston, IL: SYSTAT.

Wille, R. (1984). Line diagrams of hierarchical concept systems. *International Classification. 11*, 77–86.

Wille, R. (1990). Concept Lattices and Conceptual Knowledge Systems. Unpublished manuscript. Fachbereich Mathematik, Technische Hochschule Darmstadt.

Willis, R.H., and Burgess, T.D.G. (1974). Cognitive and affective balance in sociometric dyads. *Journal of Personality and Social Psychology. 29*, 145–152.

Wilson, T.P. (1982). Relational networks. An extension of sociometric concepts. *Social Networks. 4*, 105–116.

Winship, C. (1974). Thoughts about roles and relations. Part I: Theoretical considerations. Unpublished manuscript, Harvard University.

Winship, C. (1977). A distance model for sociometric structure. *Journal of Mathematical Sociology. 5*, 21–39.

Winship, C. (1988). Thoughts about roles and relations: An old document revisited. *Social Networks. 10*, 209–231.

Winship, C., and Mandel, M. (1983). Roles and positions: A critique and extension of the blockmodeling approach. In Leinhardt, S. (ed.), *Sociological Methodology 1983–1984*, pages 314–344. San Francisco: Jossey-Bass.

Woelfel, J., Fink, E.L., Serota, G.A., Barnett, G.A., Holmes, R., Cody, M., Saltiel, J., Marlier, M., and Gillham, J.R. (1977). *GALILEO: A Program for Metric Multidimensional Scaling*. Honolulu: East-West Communication Institute.

Wolfe, A.W. (1978). The rise of network thinking in anthropology. *Social Networks. 1*, 53–64.

Wolman, S. (1937). Sociometric planning of a new community. *Sociometry. 1*, 220–254.

Wong, G.Y. (1982). Round robin analysis of variance via maximum likelihood. *Journal of the American Statistical Association. 77*, 714–724.

Wong, G.Y. (1987). Bayesian models for directed graphs. *Journal of the American Statistical Association. 82*, 140–148.

Wong, G.Y., and Yu, Q.-Q. (1989). Computation and asymptotic normality of maximum likelihood estimates of exponential parameters of the p_1 model. Unpublished manuscript.

Woodard, K.L., and Doreian, P. (1990). Centralization: From action sets to structured interorganizational networks. Unpublished manuscript.

World Bank (1983). *World Bank World Tables*. Volumes I and II. Baltimore: The Johns Hopkins University Press.

Wright, B., and Evitts, M.S. (1961). Direct factor analysis in sociometry. *Sociometry. 24*, 82–98.

Wu, L. (1983). Local blockmodel algebras for analyzing social networks. In Tuma, N.B. (ed.), *Sociological Methodology 1983–84*, pages 272–313. San Francisco: Jossey-Bass.

Yamagishi, T. (1987). An exchange theoretical approach to defining positions in network structures. In Cook, K. (ed.), *Social Exchange Theory*, pages

149–169. Newbury Park, CA: Sage.

Yamaguchi, K. (1990). Homophily and social distance in the choice of multiple friends. *Journal of the American Statistical Association.* 85, 204–212.

Young, M.W. (1971). *Fighting with Food.* Cambridge: Cambridge University Press.

Zachary, W.W. (1977). An information flow model for conflict and fission in small groups. *Journal of Anthropological Research.* 13, 452–473.

Zachary, W.W. (1984). Modeling social network processes using constrained flow representations. *Social Networks* 6, 259–292.

Zajonc, R. (1960). Balance, congruity, and dissonance. *Public Opinion Quarterly.* 24, 280–296.

Zajonc, R. (1968). Cognitive theories in social psychology. In Lindzey, G., and Aronson, E. (eds.), *Handbook of Social Psychology.* Volume 4, pages 319–411. Reading, MA: Addison-Wesley.

Zegers, F., and ten Berge, J. (1985). A family of association coefficients for metric scales. *Psychometrika.* 50, 17–24.

Zeleny, L.D. (1940a). Measurement of social status. *American Journal of Sociology.* 45, 576–582.

Zeleny, L.D. (1940b). Status: Its measurement and control in education. *Sociometry.* 4, 193–204.

Zeleny, L.D. (1941). Measurement of sociation. *American Sociological Review.* 6, 173–188.

Zeleny, L.D. (1960). Status: Its measurement and control in education. In Moreno, J.L. (ed.), *The Sociometry Reader*, pages 261–265. Glencoe, IL: Free Press.

Name Index

Subject Index

List of Notation

A Single Relation:

$\mathcal{N} = \{n_1, n_2, \ldots, n_g\}$	the set of actors in a network or the set of nodes in a graph
$\mathcal{X}$	a single relation
g	the number of actors or nodes in $\mathcal{N}$
$\mathbf{X}$	the sociomatrix for relation $\mathcal{X}$
x_{ij}	elements of the sociomatrix $\mathbf{X}$; value of the tie from actor i to actor j
$i \rightarrow j$	a tie from actor i to actor j
$\mathbf{I}$	an incidence matrix
$\mathbf{X}^p$	the pth power of a sociomatrix

Multiple Relations:

R	the number of relations
$\mathcal{X}_r$	the rth relation, $r = 1, 2, \ldots, R$
$\mathcal{L}_r$	the set of lines for the rth relation
L_r	the number of lines in $\mathcal{L}_r$
$\mathbf{X}_r$	the sociomatrix for relation $\mathcal{X}_r$
x_{ijr}	elements of the sociomatrix $\mathbf{X}_r$

Graph Properties:

$\mathcal{L} = \{l_1, l_2, \ldots, l_L\}$	the set of lines
$l_k = (n_i, n_j)$	the line between nodes i and j
L	the number of lines in $\mathcal{L}$
$\mathcal{G}(\mathcal{N}, \mathcal{L})$	a graph consisting of node set $\mathcal{N}$ and line set $\mathcal{L}$
$d(n_i)$	the degree of node i; $d(n_i) = x_{+i} = x_{i+}$
Δ	the density of a graph

$d(i, j)$ · the geodesic distance between node i and node j

Directed Graph Properties:

$\mathcal{G}_d(\mathcal{N}, \mathcal{L})$ · a directed graph with nodes $\mathcal{N}$ and arcs $\mathcal{L}$

$l_k = < n_i, n_j >$ · the arc from node i to node j

$d_I(n_i)$ · the indegree of node i; equals x_{+i}

$d_O(n_i)$ · the outdegree of node i; equals x_{i+}

Signed and Valued Graphs:

$\mathcal{G}_\pm(\mathcal{N}, \mathcal{L}, \mathcal{V})$ or $\mathcal{G}_\pm$ · a signed graph with nodes $\mathcal{N}$, lines $\mathcal{L}$, and signs or values for the lines, $\mathcal{V}$

$\mathcal{G}_{d\pm}(\mathcal{N}, \mathcal{L}, \mathcal{V})$ or $\mathcal{G}_{d\pm}$ · a signed directed graph

$\mathcal{G}_V(\mathcal{N}, \mathcal{L}, \mathcal{V})$ or $\mathcal{G}_V$ · a valued graph with nodes $\mathcal{N}$, lines $\mathcal{L}$, and values, $\mathcal{V}$

v_k · the value or sign for line l_k

Two Mode Networks:

$\mathcal{N} = \{n_1, n_2, \ldots, n_g\}$ · the first set of actors

$\mathcal{M} = \{m_1, m_2, \ldots, m_h\}$ · the second set of actors

h · the number of actors in $\mathcal{M}$

$\mathscr{X}^{\mathcal{N}\mathcal{M}}$ · a relation from actors in $\mathcal{N}$ to actors in $\mathcal{M}$

$\mathscr{X}^{\mathcal{M}\mathcal{N}}$ · a relation from actors in $\mathcal{M}$ to actors in $\mathcal{N}$

$\mathbf{X}^{\mathcal{N}\mathcal{M}}$ · the sociomatrix for a relation from actors in $\mathcal{N}$ to actors in $\mathcal{M}$

$\mathbf{X}^{\mathcal{M}\mathcal{N}}$ · the sociomatrix for a relation from actors in $\mathcal{M}$ to actors in $\mathcal{N}$

Centrality and Prestige:

$C_A(n_i)$ · actor centrality index of type A for actor i

$P_A(n_i)$ · actor prestige index of type A for actor i

$C'_A(n_i)$ · standardized actor-level centrality index of type A for actor i

$P'_A(n_i)$ · standardized actor-level prestige index of type A for actor i

$C_A(n^*)$ · largest value of the particular actor centrality index for all g actors in $\mathcal{N}$

$C_D(n_i)$ · actor-level degree centrality index

$C_C(n_i)$ · actor-level closeness centrality index

$C_B(n_i)$ · actor-level betweeness centrality index

$C_I(n_i)$ · actor-level information centrality index

$C_D(n_i)$ · actor-level degree centrality index

C_A	group-level centralization index of type A; $A = D, C, B, I$
S_D^2	variance of the standardized degrees; index of centralization
S_C^2	variance of the standardized closeness centralities; index of centralization
S_I^2	variance of the standardized information centralities; index of centralization
$P_D(n_i)$	actor-level degree prestige index
$P_P(n_i)$	actor-level proximity prestige index
$P_R(n_i)$	actor-level rank prestige index

Cohesive Subgroups:

$\mathcal{G}_s$	a subgraph
$\mathcal{N}_s$	the set of nodes in subgraph $\mathcal{G}_s$
g_s	the number of nodes in subgraph $\mathcal{G}_s$
$\mathcal{L}_s$	the set of lines in subgraph $\mathcal{G}_s$
$d_s(i)$	the degree of node i in subgraph $\mathcal{G}_s$
$\lambda(i, j)$	the line connectivity of nodes i and j

Affiliations and Overlapping Subgroups:

$\mathcal{H} = (\mathcal{A}, \mathcal{B})$	a hypergraph with point set $\mathcal{A} = \{a_1, a_2, \ldots, a_g\}$, and edge set $\mathcal{B} = \{B_1, B_2, \ldots, B_h\}$
$\mathbf{A} = \{a_{ij}\}$	the sociomatrix for an affiliation network
$\mathbf{X}^{\mathcal{N}} = \{x_{ij}^{\mathcal{N}}\}$	sociomatrx of co-membership frequencies for actors in $\mathcal{N}$
$\mathbf{X}^{\mathcal{M}} = \{x_{kl}^{\mathcal{M}}\}$	sociomatrix of event overlap frequencies for events in $\mathcal{M}$

Structural Equivalence and Blockmodels:

$\mathcal{B}_k$	an equivalence class or position
g_k	the number of actors in equivalence class k
$\mathbf{B} = \{b_{klr}\}$	an image matrix for relation $\mathcal{X}_r$
B	the number of positions (equivalence classes)
Δ_{klr}	the density of block b_{klr}
d_{ij}	the Euclidean distance between sociomatrix entries for actors i and j
r_{ij}	the correlation between sociomatrix entries for actors i and j

Relational Algebras:

$U, T, V, \ldots$	capital letters refer to relations
iUj	a tie from actor i to actor j on relation U
$\circ$	the operation of composition
$T \circ U$	the composition of relations T and U
$i(TU)j$	a tie from actor i to actor j on the compound relation TU
$\mathscr{S}$	a set of distinct primitive and compound relations
$\mathscr{S}_{\mathscr{N}}$	the role structure for a network with actor set $\mathscr{N}$
R_S	the number of relations in $\mathscr{S}$
$\mathscr{Q}$	a partition (or reduction) of $\mathscr{S}$
R_Q	the number of elements in $\mathscr{Q}$
$\mathscr{Q}^{\text{JNT}}_{\mathscr{N}\mathscr{M}}$	the joint homomorphic reduction of $\mathscr{S}_{\mathscr{N}}$ and $\mathscr{S}_{\mathscr{M}}$
$R^{\text{JNT}}_{\mathscr{N}\mathscr{M}}$	the number of classes in $\mathscr{Q}^{\text{JNT}}_{\mathscr{N}\mathscr{M}}$
$\mathscr{Q}^{\text{CSS}}_{\mathscr{N}\mathscr{M}}$	the common structure semigroup for $\mathscr{S}_{\mathscr{N}}$ and $\mathscr{S}_{\mathscr{M}}$
$R^{\text{CSS}}_{\mathscr{N}\mathscr{M}}$	the number of classes in $\mathscr{Q}^{\text{CSS}}_{\mathscr{N}\mathscr{M}}$
$\delta_{\mathscr{S}_{\mathscr{N}}\mathscr{S}_{\mathscr{M}}}$	a measure of dissimilarity of role structures $\mathscr{S}_{\mathscr{N}}$ and $\mathscr{S}_{\mathscr{M}}$ based on the joint homomorphic reduction
$r_{\mathscr{S}_{\mathscr{N}}\mathscr{S}_{\mathscr{M}}}$	a measure of similarity of role structures $\mathscr{S}_{\mathscr{N}}$ and $\mathscr{S}_{\mathscr{M}}$ based on both the joint homomorphic reduction and the common structure semigroup

Positions and Roles:

$\phi_{\bullet}(i) = \mathscr{B}_{(\bullet)k}$	assignment of actor i to equivalence class $\mathscr{B}_{(\bullet)k}$ based on the equivalence definition "$\bullet$"
$\mathscr{B}_{(SE)k}$	an equivalence class based on structural equivalence
$\mathscr{B}_{(AE)k}$	an equivalence class based on automorphic equivalence
$\mathscr{B}_{(RE)k}$	an equivalence class based on regular equivalence
$\mathscr{B}_{(LRE)k}$	an equivalence class based on local role equivalence
$\mathscr{B}_{(EA)k}$	an equivalence class based on ego algebra equivalence

M_{ij}	a similarity measure of regular equivalence
$D(\mathscr{S}_i^*, \mathscr{S}_j^*)$	a dissimilarity measure of role equivalence
δ_{ij}	a dissimilarity measure of ego algebra equivalence

Dyads and Reciprocity:

$D_{ij} = (X_{ij}, X_{ji})$	the dyad, or 2-subgraph, consisting of actors i and j, for $i \neq j$
$\{D_{ij}\}$	collection of dyads
$< M, A, N >$	the dyad census; numbers of mutual, asymmetric, and null dyads
ρ_{KP}; ρ_B	indices of mutuality

Triads and Transitivity:

P-O-X	two actors and an "object," about which opinions are expressed
P-O-Q	a triple of three actors; P and O have opinions about Q
$+$; $-$	positive and negative signs for a line
PC; TC	the numbers of positive and total (semi)cycles in a (di)graph
T_{ijk}	the triad, or 3-subgraph, involving n_i, n_j, and n_k, $i < j < k$
$\mathscr{T}$	the set of all triads
$\mathbf{T} = \{T_u; u = 1, 2, \ldots, 16\}$	the sixteen count triad census
$\mathbf{l} = (l_u; u = 1, 2, \ldots, 16)$	a linear combination vector of the triad census
$\boldsymbol{\mu}_T$	the mean of the triad census; the vector of expected values of the T_u
$\boldsymbol{\Sigma}_T$	the 16×16 covariance matrix of the triad census
$\tau(\mathbf{l})$	a test statistic to test specific configurations derived from the triad census
τ_i; τ_t	test statistics for intransitivity and transitivity

Distributions:

$P(\bullet)$	the probability that the event "$\bullet$" occurs
S	the sample space of a random variable
$G_d(\mathcal{N})$	the set of all possible directed graphs with g nodes
U	the uniform random digraph distribution
$P_{ij} = P(X_{ij} = 1)$	the probability that a specific arc is present in

	a digraph; can be assumed constant over all arcs, and equal to P
B	the Bernoulli random digraph distribution
$\hat{\bullet}$	the maximum likelihood estimate of the unknown parameter "$\bullet$"
$U\|L = x_{++}$	the conditional uniform distribution which gives equal probability to all digraphs with L arcs and zero probability to all digraphs without x_{++} arcs
$U\|\{X_{i+}\}$	the conditional uniform distribution for random directed graphs that conditions on a fixed set of outdegrees: $X_{1+} = x_{1+}$, $X_{2+} = x_{2+}$, ..., $X_{g+} = x_{g+}$
$U\|MAN$	the conditional uniform distribution that conditions on a fixed dyad census: $M = m, A = a$, and $N = n$ dyads
$U\|M, \{X_{i+}\}, \{X_{i+}\}$	the conditional uniform distribution that conditions on the indegrees, the outdegrees, and the number of mutual dyads

p_1 and Relatives:

p_1	Holland & Leinhardt's model for a single, directional relation; contains parameters λ, θ, α, β, and $(\alpha\beta)$
$\mathbf{Y}$	a four dimensional array (of size $g \times g \times 2 \times 2$) derived from $\mathbf{X}$
$\mathbf{y} = \{y_{ijkl}\}$	a sample realization of $\mathbf{Y}$
$\mathbf{x}$	a sample realization of the random sociomatrix $\mathbf{X}$
$\mathbf{W}$	a $\mathbf{Y}$ array aggregated over subgroupings defined by actor attribute variables
$\mathbf{w}$	a sample realization of the random $\mathbf{W}$ array

Goodness-of-fit:

G^2	likelihood-ratio test statistic
ΔG^2	conditional likelihood-ratio test statistic
df; Δdf	degrees-of-freedom
δ_{b1}	simple goodness-of-fit index
δ_{b2}	Carrington-Heil-Berkowitz goodness-of-fit index

$x_{ijr}^{(t)} = b_{\phi(i)\phi(j)r}$	blockmodel predicted value
δ_{x1}	goodness-of-fit index comparing data to predicted values
δ_{x2}	goodness-of-fit index; match coefficient
δ_{x3}	goodness-of-fit index; matrix correlation

Stochastic Blockmodels:

| $X = \{x_{ijr}\}$ | super-sociomatrix of size $g \times g \times r$ |
| $p(x)$ | the probability distribution for the super-sociomatrix; also, a stochastic blockmodel |

Miscellaneous:

| $\bigcirc$ | a "tangential" section of the book |
| $\otimes$ | a "difficult" section of the book |